A

GENEALOGICAL DICTIONARY

OF

THE FIRST SETTLERS OF NEW ENGLAND,

SHOWING

THREE GENERATIONS

OF

THOSE WHO CAME BEFORE MAY, 1692,

ON THE

BASIS OF FARMER'S REGISTER.

BY

JAMES SAVAGE,

FORMER PRESIDENT OF THE MASSACHUSETTS HISTORICAL SOCIETY AND EDITOR OF WINTHROP'S
HISTORY OF NEW ENGLAND.

WITH TWO SUPPLEMENTS

IN FOUR VOLUMES.

VOL. I.

Originally Published
Boston, 1860-1862

Reprinted with
"Genealogical Notes and Errata,"
excerpted from
*The New England Historical
and Genealogical Register,*
Vol. XXVII, No. 2, April, 1873,
pp. 135-139

And

*A Genealogical Cross Index
of the Four Volumes
of the Genealogical Dictionary
of James Savage,*
by O. P. Dexter, 1884.

Genealogical Publishing Co., Inc.
Baltimore, 1965, 1969, 1977, 1981, 1986, 1990, 1994, 1998

Library of Congress Catalogue Card Number 65-18541
International Standard Book Number: 0-8063-0309-3
Set Number: 0-8063-0759-5

PREFACE.

Some explanatory introduction to so copious a work, as the following, will naturally be required; but it may be short.

In 1829 was published, by John Farmer, a Genealogical Register of the first settlers of New England. Beside the five classes of persons prominent, as Governors, Deputy-Governors, Assistants, ministers in all the Colonies, and representatives in that of Massachusetts, down to 1692, it embraced graduates of Harvard College to 1662, members of the Ancient and Honorable Artillery Company, as also freemen admitted in Massachusetts, alone, to this latter date, with many early inhabitants of other parts of New England and Long Island from 1620 to 1675. Extensive as was the plan of that volume, the author had in contemplation, as explained in his preface, calling it "an introduction to a biographical and genealogical dictionary," a more ambitious work, that should comprehend sketches of individuals known in the annals of New England, and "a continuation of eminent persons to the present time." Much too vast a project that appeared to me; and the fixing of an absolute limit, like 1692 (the era of arrival of the new charter), for admission of any family stocks, seemed more judicious. I suppose nineteen twentieths of the people of these New England colonies in 1775 were descendants of those found here in 1692, and probably seven eighths of them were offspring of the settlers before 1642.

My scope is wider than that of Farmer, of course, as it includes *every* settler, without regard to his rank, or wealth, since we often find, in the second or third generation, descendants of the most humble (thank God we are all equal before the

A *

law) filling honorable stations and performing important services. But far more narrow is my plan than his projected
dictionary, because, in a grandson of the first settler, it excludes
every other incident after his birth. Space for another than is
here given, would have demanded six volumes, while ten
volumes would have been needed for a fifth generation; and
since we now count eight, nine, or even ten generations of off-
spring from not a few of the earlier planters on our shores, fifty
volumes, each as ponderous as the present, might be filled with
details, whereof one tenth would seem ridiculous, one quarter
worthless, and one half wholly uninteresting.

That New England was first occupied by a civilized people
in so short a period before the great civil war broke out in our
mother country, though half a century and more after its ele-
mentary principles began to ferment, especially in Parliament,
and almost in every parish of the kingdom, was a very fortunate
event, if it may not be thought a providential arrangement for
the happiness of mankind. Even if our views be restricted to
the lineal origin of those people here, when the long protracted
impolicy of Great Britain drove our fathers into open hostility
and forced them to become a nation in 1776, in that century
and a half from its colonization, a purer Anglo Saxon race
would be seen on this side of the ocean than on the other.
Within forty years a vast influx of Irish, with not a few thousand Scotch and Germans has spread over this new country,
but certainly more than four fifths of our people still count their
progenitors among the ante-revolutionary colonists. From long
and careful research I have judged the proportion of the whole
number living here in 1775, that deduce their origin from the
kingdom of England, i. e. the Southern part of Great Britain,
excluding also the principality of Wales, to exceed ninety-eight
in a hundred. Every county, from Northumberland to Cornwall, Kent to Cumberland, sent its contribution of emigrants,
and the sparse population of the narrow shire of Rutland had
more than one offshoot in New England. But, during that
interval, great was the diversity of circumstances between the
old and the new country so far as the increase of their respective
numbers by incoming of strangers was affected. In 1660 the
restoration of Charles II. — in 1685 the expulsion of the two

hundred thousand Protestants from France, the desired invasion of William and Mary in 1689, and the settlement of the House of Hanover in 1714, each brought from the continent an infusion upon the original stock, the aggregate of which may not have been less than five or six per cent. of that into which it was ingrafted. Yet hardly more than three in a thousand, for instance, of Scottish ancestry, almost wholly the migration of the heroic defenders of Londonderry, that came, as one hundred and twenty families, in 1718 and 19, could be found in 1775 among dwellers on our soil; a smaller number of the glorious Huguenot exiles above thirty years longer had been resident here, and may have been happy enough by natural increase (though I doubt it) to equal the later band. If these be also counted three in a thousand, much fewer, though earlier still, must be the Dutch that crept in from New York, chiefly to Connecticut, so that none can believe they reach two in a thousand, while something less must be the ratio of Irish. Germany, Italy, Sweden, Spain, Africa, and all the rest of the world, together, did not outnumber the Scotch, or the French singly. A more homogeneous stock cannot be seen, I think, in any so extensive a region, at any time, since that when the ark of Noah discharged its passengers on Mount Ararat, except in the few centuries elapsing before the confusion of Babel. What honorable ancestry the body of New England population may assert, has often been proclaimed in glowing language; but the words of William Stoughton, in his Election sermon, 1668, express the sentiment with no less happiness than brevity: " GOD SIFTED A WHOLE NATION THAT HE MIGHT SEND CHOICE GRAIN INTO THE WILDERNESS."

By an instinct of our nature, we all love to learn the places of our birth, and the chief circumstances in the lives of our progenitors. More liberal than that is the sentiment by which our curious spirit desires knowledge of the same concomitants in the case of great benefactors of mankind; and the hope of ascertaining to a reasonable extent the early history of John Harvard was certainly one of the chief inducements of my visit to England early in 1842. I would have gladly given five hundred dollars to get five lines about him in any relation, private or public. Favored as I was, in this wish, by the counte-

nance and aid of His Excellency, E. Everett, then our minister
at London, no trace could be found, except in his signature to
the rules on taking his degrees at the University, when he is titled
of Middlesex.   Perhaps out of such research sprang my resolu-
tion to prosecute the genealogical pursuits of John Farmer.

In fulfilment of this great undertaking more than fifteen years
are already bestowed, and near two years longer may be necessary.   Yet the rule imposed, of admitting upon these pages
only the dates of birth and marriage, and names of children, of
a child born on our side of the ocean to a settler whose tent
was pitched here before May 1692, is severely adhered to, with
the exception only of so distinguished a man as Cotton Mather;
and even this variety may seem forced upon me by Farmer,
who had received him to the copious honors of marriage and
family.   Yet, in many cases, will be named great grandchildren
of first comers, and even in a very few, another generation,
making a fifth.   Explanation of this apparent deviation from
my own law is easy.   When Gov. Bradford and Gov. Winthrop
came here, each brought a son, or sons, and the same is seen of
Gov. Dudley and numberless others.   Now each child must be
rated as an emigrant no less than its father, so that John Bradford, John and Adam Winthrop, and Samuel Dudley are
equally entitled as their parents to have their grandchildren
entered in these pages; but William and Joseph Bradford, and
Joseph Dudley, sons of the Govs. born on our side of the
water, shall not have grandchildren in their respective lines.

My apparatus for this work will sometimes be found incomplete, yet to a great extent, the public records of Colonies,
Counties, and towns, where accessible, have been examined by
myself or friends.   Of the first ten folio volumes of our Suffolk
registry of deeds I had an abstract always lying near me, and
these embraced near one third of all the names of New England and more than half those in Massachusetts Colony; indeed for very many years, after the emigration from Europe
ceased, only two other counties, Essex and Middlesex had been
constituted.   It will be recollected, that large parts of Plymouth, New Hampshire, and Maine were occupied by those
who removed from Massachusetts, as was almost the whole of
Rhode Island, Connecticut, and New Haven colonies.   But

modern labors of distinguished antiquaries furnish us almost in full their early records; and more than nine tenths of the names in these separate communities, I think, must have been acquired for this work. But even in my native city of Boston three or four in a thousand may have escaped me, yet probably in the second or third ages from its foundation.

For the time of births, marriages, or deaths in each family I have labored assiduously to be correct, in hundreds of cases finding wrong dates given, and commonly without hesitation supplying the true. Where baptism is fixed, by a decent record, weeks, and even months before the date of birth, no fear of injuring the town clerk's credit can restrain belief in his mistake. But the copious source of vexation is the variety growing out of the Old and New Styles. In many thousand instances, I have turned to the perpetual almanac, to be sure that the day of baptism was truly, or not, recorded for Sunday, since the rite could, in the first century of New England, be performed only on that day. By this many printed errors may be corrected. As children are often seen to be baptized in January or February of the *same* year, by the ancient legal reckoning, that gives the parents' marriage in April or May, several weeks before, in our modern reckoning of the months, instead of so many months after, it is easy enough to put that right by calling those winter months not the eleventh and twelfth of the old year, as the statute absurdity required. Uniformly my chronology begins the year with 1 January; but to produce harmony between dates for the month of March is sometimes very difficult. A few town officers began to change the numerals for the year with the opening of the month, daring to ask, why the first month of 1679 should allow 24 of its 31 days to be drilled under old 1678, while the perverse will of the rulers in fatherland postponed the new-year's day until the 25th; and some records may be found, where the year ended in December; but this monstrous innovation did not begin before 1700, and the startling truth made irregular progress up to 1752, when Lord Macclesfield enlightened the legislature, and Chesterfield charmed it into consistency.

No apology would be necessary for filling room with enumeration of contributions from many friends other than such as are

open to all in printed volumes; but much of what is now
within every one's reach had been furnished in MS. to me, and
still more is from the same hands, in many cases, given first to
the light on my pages. Our town histories are crowding forward, and sometimes in less compact space than might be
wished. Windsor, though its History is large, has not equalled
ancient Woodbury in bulk, yet seems to contain all, with three-
fold of the interest, that might have contented us in the other.
The point of research may occupy long time, and be expressed
at last in brief phrase, so that no comparison can be made
between the result in different parts of the same field of battle
from taking only the numbers engaged in each. One initial
letter in this dictionary required a year and a quarter for its
complete preparation, more than three months were given to
each of several names, like Hall or Williams, and the progress
of a page has often demanded a week. It seemed my duty to
expose every error in our genealogy that has got imbedded in
any reputable book; and the suspicion of any such may lead
to a long train of inquiries before the refutation can be reached.
If my success has been less than my ambition, it has not been
owing to lack of industry, or to hurried operation. Printing of
the first volume began in Dec. 1858, and was prosecuted without interruption of a day to this time; while for the next
volume the careful amanuensis has ready for the compositor
two hundred pages, a part of which will be given to the press
to-morrow. For the access of new information that reaches us
almost every month, a constant watch is kept; and life and
health being continued, my contract with the community may
be decently discharged in the autumn of 1861.

A very extensive catalogue of gentlemen, that might be
graced by one of more than half a dozen ladies, could here be
supplied, were it useful to mention the smaller as well as the
greater contributors to these sheets. To Goodwin, Bond, Harris,
father and son, Kingsley, Abbot, Day, Shattuck, Lunt, and
Kilbourne, of the respectable file who have passed out of
active service, it would not be easy to state the respective proportions of indebtedness; nor could I specify the ratio of
benefit derived in my pages from benevolence of the living
Babson, Boltwood, Brayton, Budington, Clapp, Day, Edwards,

Felt, Field, Herrick, Hoadley, Jackson, Judd, Kelly, King, Kellogg, Lincoln, Locke, Otis, Paige, Patterson, Riker, Sargent, Sewall, Shurtleff, R. D. Smith of Guilford, Staples, Vinton, Wentworth, Whitmore, Willard, Wyman, and twice as many more. Not one of the living or dead could complain of my declaration, that from the distinguished antiquary of Northampton the acquisition exceeds that of any other ten contributors. Early in 1846 I had solicited the benefit of uniting his name with mine in producing these volumes; but while he shrank from the responsibility of such unbroken labor, I can offer several hundred pages of letters to vouch for his sympathy, and encourage my perseverance.

19 APRIL, 1860.

ABBREVIATIONS.

By the number of more or less imperfect words, that can be not much less than three hundred thousand in these volumes, very great saving of space was expected. Caution was given me, in the Genealog. Reg. XII. 362, against the woful disfiguring that would follow, if the specimen, offered by the publishers to attract subscribers, were to be taken for a sample. As most of these curtailments were common however in similar works, I dared to adhere to the plan, which has not, perhaps, repelled a dozen patrons; and even enlarged my list by addition of one that would occur about two thousand times. The word freeman, or freemen, may be seen, in its new shape, freem. without offence, I hope, to the taste of any subscriber. Familiar to all readers must be the short form given to our names of the months, nine in twelve, only May, June, and July having their whole beauty; and yet of these nine words the recurrence would probably show the mutilations on my pages to be fifteen or twenty thousand. Titles are always permitted even in other books to appear in brief, as Gov. or Esq. and when rep. may stand for representative, most who turn over a dictionary of this sort will approve the economy. It may happen that, by the accident of the printer's type, or my own carelessness, some word may be abbreviated that had better been printed in full, yet I submit, that the page will be seldom disfigured by such liberty, and probably the reader would not change more than once in five hundred examples. Confusion will not be caused so often as that, I hope; but if a pause be necessary, we all feel the same thing in turning to an English dictionary for definition of words only. Nobody reads continuously from page to page, even in the affluent vocabulary of Johnson; and when a sincere desire to verify a genealogy, or ascertain a special relationship, is felt, the time will not be grudgingly reckoned, if a sentence be not printed out in every word, but with one third or more of those words curtailed. In the following list every word thus abbrev. may not be found, because the shortening may by a judicious reader be referred to a class comprising many, as the adverbial terminations, *ly*, *bly*, wanting after *easi*. and *honora.*; or the perfect tense or participles of verbs, *ed;* or in substantives, *er* and *ent.*; or in either part of speech, ensu. mak. preced. and tak. without *ing* or *en.* For many having different meanings, as ch. for child, or children, or church; d. for death, died, or daughter; gr. for grand, great, grant, or graduate; mo. for mother or month, the one intended may be trusted to the student's sagacity.

But occasions of error in *names* of men or women I have scrupulously avoided, so that only one surname can be seen in my pages to be abbrev. and but a single name of bapt. Eliz. can hardly be mistaken, nor will the lamentation be loud, when a man's name so distinguished as that of the first Gov. of Mass. is spelled Winth. Geographical designations are forever meeting our eyes in briefer form than the legal one; and he has poor supply of current letters that requires to be told what shires in Eng. are meant by Bucks, Herts, or Notts.

THE LIST.

a.	for about.	easi.	for easily.
abbrev.	" abbrevia*tion* or ted.	educ.	" educa*tion* or ted.
acc.	" according to.	Eng.	" England.
acco.	" account.	eno.	" enough.
accu.	" accurate.	ens.	" ensign.
adj.	" adjoining.	ensu.	" ensuing.
adm.	" admission or admitted.	est.	" estate.
admin.	" administra*tion* or tor.	establ.	" establishment.
aft.	" after.	exc.	" except.
alleg.	" allegiance.	f.	" father.
ano.	" another.	fam.	" family.
approx.	" approximately.	fidel.	" fidelity.
ar. co.	" artillery company.	foll.	" follow*ing* or ed.
ascert.	" ascer*tain* or ained.	freem.	" free*man* or en.
b.	" born or birth.	giv.	" given or giving.
bapt.	" baptiz*ed* or sm.	gr.	" grand, great, grant or gradu-
bec.	" because or became.		ate.
bef.	" before.	gr.f.	" grandfather.
bot.	" bought or bottom.	gr.mo.	" grandmother.
br.	" brother.	gr.s.	" grandson.
bur.	" buried.	hers.	" herself.
capt.	" captain, cap*tured,* or ivity.	H. C.	" Harvard College.
catal.	" catalogue.	hims.	" himself.
ch.	for child, children, or church.	Hist.	" History.
clk.	" clerk.	hist.	" historian.
Co.	" County.	hon.	" honorable.
Col.	" Colony or Colonel.	honor.	" honorary.
Coll.	" College or Collections.	honora.	" honorably.
comp.	" company.	ign.	" ignorant.
confer.	" conferred.	Ind.	" Indians.
conject.	" conjecture.	inf.	" infant or informed.
cont.	" continued.	inhab.	" inhabitant.
contr.	" contract.	inq.	" inquiry.
corp.	" corporal.	ins.	" insert.
couns.	" counsellor.	inv.	" inventory.
cous.	" cousin.	judic.	" judicial or judicious.
coven.	" covenant.	k.	" killed or king.
ct.	" court.	kn.	" known.
d.	" died, death, or daughter.	ld.	" land.
Dart.	" Dartmouth College.	lieut.	" lieutenant.
deac.	" deacon.	liv.	" lived or ing.
decis.	" decision.	m.	" marri*ed* or age.
degr.	" degree.	maj.	" major.
devis.	" devised.	mak.	" making.
discip.	" discipline.	ment.	" mentioned.
div.	" division or divided.	milit.	" military.
docum.	" document.	min.	" minister.
ds.	" deaths or daughters.	mo.	" mother or month.

nam.	for named.	scatt.	for scatter*ing* or ed.
N. E.	" New England.	sec.	" second.
not.	" noted.	serg.	" sergeant.
o.	" oath.	sett.	" settlers or settler.
O. E.	" Old England.	serv.	" service or servant.
offic.	" official.	sev.	" several.
oft.	" often.	sh.	" share or ship.
ord.	" ordained.	sis.	" sister.
orig.	" origin.	spell.	" spell*ing* or ed.
peo.	" people.	surg.	" surgeon.
petitn.	" petition.	sw.	" swear or swore.
preced.	" preceding.	syl.	" syllable.
pro.	" probate or proved.	tak.	" taken.
prob.	" probab*le* or ly.	tho.	" though.
prop.	" property.	thot.	" thought.
propound.	" propounded.	thro.	" through.
propr.	" proprietors or proprietor.	transcr.	" transcribed.
provis.	" provision.	unit.	" unit*ing* or ed.
pub.	" public.	unm.	" unmarried.
rat.	" rated.	var.	" various or variation.
rec.	" record.	w.	" wife.
rep.	" report or representative.	wh.	" who or which.
repud.	" repudiated.	wks.	" weeks.
respectiv.	" respectively.	wid.	" widow.
s.	" son or sons.	yr.	" year.

with a few dozen others, that need not to be particularly mentioned, as the reader, without a compliment, may be presumed to supply meaning for himself to marks of frequent use, like points of the compass.

§ shows, that the man was Governor or President.

† " that he was Deputy Governor.

‡ " that he was an Assistant, or Counsellor.

• " that he was a Representative.

‖ " that he belonged to the Ancient and Honorable Artillery Company of Massachusetts.

GENEALOGICAL DICTIONARY

FIRST SETTLERS OF NEW ENGLAND.

ABBEE. See Abby.

ABBOT, ARTHUR, Marblehead, perhaps rem. to Ipswich, join. Winth. 1634, in the settlem. of that town, was liv. in 1671, and prob. d. bef. 1679. We kn. of issue, only Philip, whose descend. have tradit. that he came from Totness in Co. Devon, where he left good est. of wh. for sev. yrs. after migrat. the income was enjoy. by him. ARTHUR, Ipswich, perhaps s. of the preced. in 1671 made freem. then call. jr. and, in 1674, 35 yrs. old; by w. Eliz. wh. d. 17 Feb. 1738, aged 90, had Eliz. b. 6 June 1686, and prob. other ch. of wh. only Moses (f. of Rev. Hull of Charlestown), and Arthur of Ipswich, and Susanna, are nam. with prob. evidence. He d. bef. his w. BENJAMIN, Andover, s. of the first George of the same, m. 22 Apr. 1685, Sarah, eldest d. of Ralph Farnum of the same, had Benjamin, b. 11 July 1686; Jonathan, Sept. 1687; David, 29 Jan. 1689; and Samuel, 19 May 1694; and d. 30 Mar. 1703. DANIEL, Cambridge, came, prob. in the fleet with Winth. 1630, req. adm. as freem. 19 Oct. of that yr. and was rec. 18 May foll. at the same Ct. was fin. 5 sh. for refus. to watch &c. rem. a. 1639 to Providence, there d. a. 1650. DANIEL, Providence, perhaps s. of the preced. took o. of alleg. 1668 to the k. did not rem. during Philip's war, and may have been the town clk. there 1680. DANIEL, Branford, s. of Robert of the same, had Joseph, and prob. Stephen, and Hannah. EBENEZER, Andover, youngest s. of the first Thomas of the same, m. Eliz. Tucker, had Sarah, b. 7 June 1717; Eliz. 6 May 1719; Ebenezer, 6 Sept. 1721;

VOL. I.   1

John, 28 Feb. 1723; Philip, 11 Sept. 1725; Thomas, 28 May 1728, d. young; Sarah, again, 15 July 1730; Thomas, again, 22 Feb. 1733; Samuel, 16 June 1736; and Benjamin, 26 Jan. 1738. His w. d. Apr. 1743, and he m. Mary Ingalls. EDWARD, Taunton, 1643. Baylies, II. 267. GEORGE, Rowley, brot. from Eng. s. George, Nehemiah, and Thomas, and d. 1647. GEORGE, Windsor 1640, fin. for sell. to an Ind. a pistol, and powder; prob. was after at Norwalk among early sett. 1655, had there two ws. of wh. the latter was Joanna, and he outliv. her 8 yrs. but the ch. ment. in his will of 2 May 1689, pro. 11 Mar. foll. were by the former. They were Dorothy, w. of a Root; Priscilla, w. of a Clason; George, b. a. 1669; Daniel, a. 1672, liv. 1709, yet not kn. to have issue; Mary, m. after d. of her f. a Jackson; John; and Jonathan. GEORGE, Andover, 1643, had been some yrs. at Roxbury, m. 12 Dec. 1646, a maiden said, in reasonab. tradit. to have come in the same sh. with him, Hannah (call. Mary on town rec. of R.), d. of William Chandler of R. had John, b. 2 Mar. 1648; Joseph, 11 Mar. 1649, d. next yr. 24 June, the first d. on rec. of A. (where he is call. s. of Henry by mist.); Hannah, 9 June 1650; Joseph, again, 30 Mar. 1652, wh. was k. by the Ind. 8 Apr. 1676, the earliest victim of the war in that town; George, 7 June 1655; William, 18 Nov. 1657; Sarah, 14 Nov. 1659; Benjamin, 20 Dec. 1661; Timothy, 17 Nov. 1663; Thomas, 6 May 1666; Edward, d. young; Nathaniel, 4 July 1671; and Eliz. 9 Feb. 1673. He d. 24 Dec. 1681; and his wid. m. Rev. Francis Dane, as his third w. outliv. him, and d. 11 June 1711, aged 82. Hannah, m. 20 Dec. 1676, John Chandler; Sarah, m. 11 Oct. 1680, Ephraim Stevens; and Eliz. m. 24 Nov. 1692, Nathan Stevens. His s. Benjamin was afflict. by Eliz. Johnson, a witch, as she confess. in 1692; and she implicat. goody Currier in the diabolic. work. Yet the nature or degree of the afflict. is nowhere shown. Currier was execut. on acco. of other charges. The confess. of the nonsense, wh. prob. was the cause of Johnson's impun. is seen in 3 Mass. Hist. Coll. I. 124. Of this 'first George of Andover, said to have come from Yorksh. descend. are very num. of wh. forty-four with the fam. name, beside forty-nine others thro. fem. Abbots, had been gr. at some coll. in 1844. Seven s. and three ds. m. and resid. at A. while of 73 gr.ch. five sett. at Concord, N. H. four went to Conn. and two liv. at Billerica. Of seven farms, on wh. his s. liv. four were occup. by descend. in our day. GEORGE, Andover, s. of George of Rowley, b. in Eng. m. 26 Apr. 1658, Sarah Farnum, perhaps sis. of Ralph of A. had George, b. 28 Jan. foll. Sarah, 6 Sept. 1660; John, 26 Aug. 1662; Mary, 29 Mar. 1664; Nehemiah, 20 July 1667; Hannah, 20 Sept. 1668; Mehitable, 17 Feb. 1671, d. young; Lydia, 29 Sept. 1675; Samuel, 30 May 1678; and Mehitable, again, 4 Apr. 1680.

He d. 22 Mar. 1689 ; and his wid. m. 1 Aug. foll. Henry Ingalls, outliv. him, and d. 1728, aged 90. Sarah m. 19 Oct. 1682, John Faulkner ; Mary m. 13 May 1687, Stephen Barker ; Hannah m. 16 Apr. 1695, James Ingalls ; and Lydia, m. 28 Nov. 1695, Henry Chandler. GEORGE, Andover, s. of George the first of the same, m. 17 Apr. 1668, Dorcas, eldest d. of Mark Graves of the same, had Sarah, b. 1679, d. soon ; Joseph, 7 Oct. 1680, d. young ; ano. ch. Nathan, or Martha, 12 Feb. 1683, d. young ; Hannah, 26 Feb. 1685 ; Daniel, 10 Jan. 1688 ; Eliz. 25 July 1690 ; George, 22 Dec. 1692 ; Henry, 12 June 1696 ; and Isaac, 4 Apr. 1699. GEORGE, Andover, eldest s. of George the sec. of the same, and gr.s. of George of Rowley, m. 1689, Eliz. Ballard, had George, b. 17 July 1691 ; Uriah, 26 Nov. 1692 ; Jacob, 19 Mar. 1694 ; Eliz. 6 Nov. 1695 ; Sarah ; and Hannah. His w. d. May 1706 ; and he had sec. w. Hannah Easty. GEORGE, Norwalk, s. of George of the same, by w. Hannah, it is said, had George, Samuel, Ebenezer, Benjamin, Israel, Hannah, and Eliz. Success did not attend the diligent inq. of Hall in find. dates for the ch. or whether the f. had not rem. from N. JOHN, Hadley 1668, rem. early in the next yr. but no more is kn. JOHN, Andover, eldest s. of George the first of the same, m. 17 Nov. 1673, Sarah, eldest d. of Richard Barker of the same, had John, b. 2 Nov. 1674 ; Joseph, 29 Dec. 1676 ; Stephen, 16 Mar. 1678 ; Sarah, 7 Dec. 1680 ; Ephraim, 15 Aug. 1682 ; Joshua, 16 June 1685 ; Mary, 2 Jan. 1687 ; Ebenezer, 27 Sept. 1689 ; and Priscilla, 7 July 1691 ; was selectman, deac. and d. 19 Mar. 1721. His wid. d. 10 Feb. 1729. JOHN, aged 16, and Mary, 16, came in the Hopewell, Capt. Bundocke, from London, 1635 ; but whose ch. they were, is unkn. and prob. not of any resid. in our country. JOHN, Saco, adm. an inhab. of that town 12 June 1680, and ens. then chos. town clk. bef. wh. time the planta. had been so much disturb. by Ind. war, that Folsom, in his valu. Hist. 177, says, the rec. are lost. JOHN, Norwalk 1687, wheelwright, s. of George of the same, by w. Ruth, it is said, had John, Esther, and Mary. JOHN, Sudbury, s. of George the sec. of Andover, by w. Jemima had Jemima, b. 10 Oct. 1699 ; John, 3 Oct. 1701 ; Sarah, 10 Sept. 1704 ; Mary ; and Hannah ; rem. to Watertown, there was a millwright, and d. 24 Mar. 1718. His wid. m. John Beeks. JOHN, Andover, s. of the first Thomas of the same, m. Apr. 1710, Hannah Chubb, perhaps d. of Pascoe of the same, had Hannah ; Sarah, b. Mar. 1712, d. young ; Mary, 1716, d. young ; John, Feb. 1718 ; Sarah, 16 Aug. 1722 ; Mary, again, 23 Nov. 1727 ; and his w. d. 3 June 1733. He m. 1734, sec. w. Hepzibah Frye. JONATHAN, Norwalk, s. of George of the same, m. 5 June 1696, Sarah, d. of John Olmstead, had Jonathan, b. 6 Apr. 1697 ; Sarah, 16 June 1699 ; Eunice, 23 Jan. 1702 ; Mary, 8 July 1704 ; Debo-

rah, 3 Dec. 1707 ; Keziah, 17 Apr. 1711 ; Lemuel, 21 Mar. 1714 ;
Jane, 5 Oct. 1716 ; and Mindwell, 21 Dec. 1718. JOSEPH, New Haven
1683, s. prob. of Robert. JOSEPH, Marblehead, s. of the first Thomas
of Andover, by w. Sarah had Susanna, bapt. Aug. 1701 ; Joseph ; Sarah ; Ann ; and Hannah. NATHANIEL, Andover, youngest s. of George
the first of the same, m. 22 Oct. 1695, Dorcas Hibbert, prob. d. of Robert of Beverly, had Nathaniel, b. 1696 ; Mary, 8 Feb. 1698 ; a s. b. 20
June 1700, d. same day ; Joseph, 2 Feb. 1705 ; Tabitha, a. 1707 ; Jeremiah, 4 Nov. 1709 ; Joshua, 1711 ; Sarah ; Hannah ; Eliz. and Rebecca,
1717. His w. d. 7 Feb. 1743, and he d. 1 Dec. 1749. NATHANIEL,
perhaps of Ashford, s. of the first Thomas of Andover, m. 1710 Mercy
Hutchinson of Ashford, had Nathaniel, b. 1714 ; and no more is told of
him. NEHEMIAH, Ipswich, s. of George of Rowley, was brot. by his
f. from Eng. freem. in Mass. 1669, deac. at Topsfield 1686, d. Mar.
1707, leav. only s. Nehemiah. NEHEMIAH, Topsfield, s. of the preced.
m. 21 Jan. 1690, Remember, d. of John Fiske of Wenham, had John, b.
9 Apr. 1691 ; Nehemiah, 19 Oct. 1692 ; Sarah ; Mary ; and Mehitable,
17 Oct. 1700. His w. d. 12 July 1703, and he d. 1736. *NEHEMIAH,
Andover, s. of George the sec. of the same, m. 1691 Abigail Lovejoy,
prob. youngest d. of John the first of the same, had Nehemiah, b. 19 Jan.
1692 ; Abiel, 10 Aug. 1693 ; Zebadiah, 6 Apr. 1695 ; John, 31 Oct.
1697 ; Abigail, 30 Sept. 1699 ; Mary, 24 Mar. 1701 ; and Joseph, wh.
alone of the seven d. young. PETER, Fairfield, s. of Robert, k. his w.
Eliz. d. of John Evarts, and attempt. to k. Hannah, his only ch. for
wh. 16 Oct. 1667 he was execut. tho. it may hardly be doubt. that
he was insane, as he had been sev. yrs. bef. as at Branford, in 1658,
whither he went to help his f. and was taken the first day with insan.
See New Haven Col. Rec. II. 300. PHILIP, Ipswich, s. of Arthur
of the same, by w. Mary had Arthur, b. 3 Feb. 1694 ; Frances, 18
May 1696 ; Susanna ; and Mary, 26 July 1701. His wid. d. 11 Jan.
1730, but the date of his d. is not seen.• RICHARD, Kittery 1663,
was keep. of the prison in New Hampsh. 1684, as in Farmer's Ed.
of Belkn. I. 485, appears. ROBERT, Watertown, freem. 3 Sept. 1634,
when Col. Rec. gives the name Abbitt, was of Wethersfield 1640, and
New Haven 1642, where John, his s. b. many mos. bef. was bapt. 7 Oct.
1649 ; Abigail, b. 2 Oct. 1649, and Robert, brot. from Branford, where
the f. liv. bapt. 1 June 1651 ; Joseph, b. 20 Apr. 1652 ; Benjamin, 10
Jan. 1654, d. soon ; Daniel, 12 Feb. 1655, and Mary, 13 May 1657 ;
beside other ch. bef. 1649, as Peter, bef. ment. Sarah, wh. m. Matthew
Rowe ; and Deborah. He d. Sept. 1658 ; and his wid. Mary m. 4 Nov.
1659, John Robins ; and Deborah m. 1661, Nathan Andrews. His land
was in that part, call. E. Haven ; and a. 1649 he rem. to Branford.

His est. was distrib. 1660, in small portions to ch. Peter, Deborah, John, Daniel, Abigail, and Mary. His s. Robert had d. 30 Sept. 1658, it is said; but Joseph was alive, and perhaps provid. for otherwise, as by sev· yrs. of liv. with his mo. Matthew Rowe had the part of his w. tho. this fact may not certain. show that his w. was d. An Eliz. A. wh. m. at Guilford 3 Mar. 1654, Gabriel Harris of New London is, by the author of the Hist. of that city, in her p. 86, thot. to have been ano. of the ds. But the suggest. is embarrass. with obstinate difficult. and contradict. whelm the tradit. in self-destruct. SAMUEL, Sudbury, youngest s. of George the sec. of Andover, gr.s. of George of Rowley, by w. Joyce had Joyce, b. 18 Aug. 1706; Martha, 10 Mar. 1712; Samuel, 21 Aug. 1716; and George. THOMAS, Rowley, presum. to be youngest s. of George of the same, b. in Eng. is said to have m. but d. without issue 7 Sept. 1659. THOMAS, Andover, whose f. is not kn. may have come later from Eng. than others of the name, or been b. here, m. 15 Dec. 1664, Sarah Steward, whose f. is not nam. had Joseph, b. 16 Mar. 1666, d. next yr. Thomas, 1668; Sarah, 8 Jan. 1671; Joseph, again, 16 Aug. 1674; Dorothy, 2 Jan. 1676, d. at 2 yrs.; Nathaniel, 9 Jan. 1678; John, Oct. 1681; Dorothy, again; Mary, 22 July 1686; and Ebenezer, 23 Nov. 1690. He was a capt. and d. 6 May 1695; and his wid. d. Feb. 1716. Sarah m. 26 Nov. 1691, Joseph Chandler; and Dorothy m. 1710, one with so strange a name, as Braviter Gray. THOMAS, Kittery, perhaps s. of Richard of the same, was ens. 1688. THOMAS, Andover, s. of George the first of the same, m. 7 Dec. 1697, Hannah Gray, prob. not d. of Robert of the same, had Hannah, b. 10 Sept. 1700; Edward, 9 June 1702; Deborah, 1 Dec. 1704; George, 7 Nov. 1706; Zebadiah, 25 Jan. 1709; Benjamin, and Catharine, tw. 31 Mar. 1711; Aaron, 8 Aug. 1714; and Isaac, 24 Feb. 1717; and d. 28 Apr. 1728. His wid. d. 1763, aged 89. THOMAS, Andover, s. of Thomas the first of the same, m. Jan. 1707, Eliz. French, had only Thomas, wh. d. 9 Mar. 1729; and of the f. no more is told. TIMOTHY, Andover, s. of George the first of the same, taken by the Ind. when 12 yrs. old, and held sev. mos. 1676, m. 27 Dec. 1689, Hannah, d. of Mark Graves of A. had Timothy, b. 1 July 1693; Hannah, 19 Oct. 1695; and Dorcas, 6 May 1698. His w. d. 5 Nov. 1726, and he d. 9 Sept. 1730. WALTER, Exeter 1640, a vintner, d. Jan. 1667, leav. w. Sarah, wh. m. Henry Sherburne, and ch. Peter, William, Walter, John, Eliz. and ano. d. wh. m. a Wills, and gr.ch. Thomas, Joseph, and Sarah Wills. Possib. John of Saco, the ens. 1680, and Thomas of Kittery, the ens. 1680, were s. and gr.s. of this man. WILLIAM, Andover, s. of George the first of A. m. 19 June 1682, Eliz. d. of Nathaniel Geary of Roxbury, had Eliz. b. 29 Apr. 1683; William, 17 Mar. 1685; George, 19 Mar. 1687, d. at

1*

2 yrs. Ezra, 7 July 1689 ; George, again, 22 Dec. 1691, d. soon ; Nathan, 10 Dec. 1692 ; James, 12 Feb. 1695 ; Paul, 28 Mar. 1697 ;
Philip, 3 Apr. 1699 ; Hannah, 5 Apr. 1701 ; Caleb, 1704; and Zebadiah, 1706. His. w. d. Dec. 1712, and he d. 24 Oct. foll. From the
Abbots' Geneal. Reg. pub. 1847, great assist. has been obt. and in it very
few errors been detect.

ABBY, ABBEY, or ABBEE, JOHN, Salem 1637, when gr. of ld. was
made to him, of Reading later, and freem. 1685, then call. sen. so that
perhaps he had s. of the same name, and very prob. is it, that he had
others. JOHN, Wenham, an early sett. d. late in life, 1700, leav. wid.
Hannah, and ch. Richard, b. 9 Feb. 1683 ; prob. others. OBADIAH,
Enfield, 1682, m. Sarah, wid. of Joseph Warriner, to wh. she was sec. w.
had no ch. to be nam. in his will, 1752, the yr. he d. SAMUEL, Wenham, perhaps br. of John of the same, d. 1698. leav. wid. Mary, and ch.
Mary, aged 25 ; Samuel, 23 ; Thomas, 20 ; Eleazer, 18 ; Ebenezer, 16 ;
Mercy, 14 ; Sarah, 13 ; Hepzibah, 10 ; Abigail, 8 ; John, 7 ; Benjamin,
6 ; and Jonathan, 2. His wid. m. Abraham Mitchell. He was of Salem
vill. now Danvers, when adm. freem. 1690. Only the youngest ch. was
b. at W. and some discrepance from the pro. rec. as to the ages of most
of the ch. is furnish. me (by Mr. Felt) in the rec. of b. as that Ebenezer
was b. 31 July 1683 ; Mary, 1 Mar. 1685 ; Sarah, 6 July 1686 ; Hepzibah, 14 Feb. 1689 ; Abigail, 19 Nov. 1690 ; John, 4 June 1692 ; and
Benjamin, 4 June 1694. THOMAS, Enfield, perhaps br. of Obadiah, had
Sarah, b. 31 Mar. 1684 ; Thomas, 1686 ; Mary, 3 Feb. 1689, wh. d. bef.
her f. and John 1692 ; beside Tabitha. He d. 1728, leav. w. Sarah, and
in his will of Dec. 1720, she and the two s. are nam. as also two ds.
call. Sarah Geer and Abigail Warner. His s. Thomas had s. Obadiah,
and Thomas ; and John had John, Thomas, Daniel, and Richard ; but
prob. no gr.ch. ought here to be ins.

ABDY, MATTHEW, Boston, came in the Abigail, 1635, from London,
was a fisherman ; by w. Tabitha, d. of Robert Reynolds of B. wh. d.
1661, had Mary, b. 24 May 1648 ; and Tabitha, 24 Nov. 1652 ; beside
Matthew, nam. in the will of his gr.f. R. He next m. 24 May 1662,
Alice Cox, perhaps d. of Moses of Hampton. His s. foll. the same trade,
was so poor, that the petty bequests in his will are hardly to be thot. un-
fairly caricatur. in the humorous poem by Rev. John Seccombe, with the
title of Father Abby's will, of wh. in the admirab. Cyclopædia of Amer.
Literature, by Duyckincks, Vol. I. 126, is extract.

ABELL, BENJAMIN, Norwich, 1670. CALEB, Dedham, 1665, may
have been s. of the preced. rem. 1668, to Norwich, there m. July 1669,
Margaret, prob. d. of John Post of Saybrook, had a d. b. 1671, d. soon ;
Samuel, Oct. 1672 ; Experience, Dec. 1674 ; Caleb, Apr. 1677 ; John,

Dec. 1678 ; Theophilus, Nov. 1680 ; Joanna, Nov. 1683 ; Abigail, Mar. 1689 ; and Hannah, Oct. 1692. His w. d. Nov. 1700, and he m. 1701, Mary, wid. of Stephen Loomer of New London, wh. surv. him. He d. 17 Aug. 1731. Joshua, Norwich, perhaps br. of the preced. m. 1 Nov. 1677, Experience, d. of Nehemiah Smith of New London, and perhaps had sec. w. d. of John Gager. Preserved, Rehoboth, 1668, had Dorothy, b. 16 Nov. 1677 ; Joanna, 11 Jan. 1682 ; was lieut. of the comp. under Samuel Gallop in the romantic expedit. of Sir William Phips, 1690, against Quebec. Robert, Weymouth, came, prob. in the fleet with Winthrop, desir. adm. 19 Oct. 1630, and was made freem. 18 May foll. had Abraham, bur. 14 Nov. 1639 ; Mary, b. 11 Apr. 1642 ; rem. next yr. to Rehoboth, there d. Aug. 1663, leav. wid. and four more ch. beside Mary.

Abernethy, William, Wallingford, m. 1673 or 4, Sarah, d. of William Doolittle, had William, and Samuel, and d. 1718, when his two s. admin. on his est. Early this name was writ. Ebenetha, or Abbenatha, acc. Hinman ; but in mod. days the descend. use the spell. here giv.

Abington, William, Maine, 1642. Coffin.

Aborne. See Eborne.

Ackerly, Accorley, or Acrely, Henry, New Haven 1640, Stamford 1641 to 53, Greenwich 1656, d. at S. 17 June 1658, wh. is the date of his will. His wid. Ann, was 75 yrs. old in 1662. Haz. II. 246. Robert, Brookhaven, L. I. 1655, adm. freem. of Conn. jurisdict. 1664. See Trumbull, Col. Rec. I. 341, 428. Samuel, Brookhaven, 1655, perhaps br. of the preced.

Ackley, or Acly, James, Haddam, s. of Nicholas, by w. Eliz. had James, b. 17 July 1707 ; Nicholas, 16 Dec. 1708 ; and Nathaniel, 7 Nov. 1712. Nicholas, Hartford, 1655, rem. to Haddam, as early sett. and d. 29 Apr. 1695, leav. wid. and ch. John ; Thomas ; Nathaniel, wh. d. 27 Feb. 1710 ; James ; Hannah; Eliz. Mary ; Sarah, wh. m. William Spencer ; and Lydia. Field, 64, Hinman, 182. Samuel, Haddam, perhaps s. of the preced. by w. Bethia had Samuel, b. 8 Dec. 1703 ; Jerusha, 29 Mar. 1707 ; and Deborah, 11 July 1709. Thomas, Haddam, s. of Nicholas, d. 16 Jan. 1704, leav. wid. Hannah, and ch. Hannah, b. 24 Oct. 1696 ; Ann, 17 Sept. 1698 ; Thomas, 28 Jan. 1701 ; and Job, 14 Mar. 1703.

Acreman, or Akerman, Stephen, Newbury, m. 17 Dec. 1684, Sarah, prob. wid. of Amos Stickney.

Acres, often Ackers, Henry, Newbury, m. 13 Mar. 1674, Hannah, d. of Thomas Silver, had Catharine, b. 17 Mar. 1675 ; John, 2 Oct. 1678 ; Mary, 8 Oct. 1680 ; and John, again, 20 Jan. 1694 ; perhaps others. John, Boston 1656, liv. at that part call. Muddy riv. now Brookline, m. prob. bef. 1664, Desiretruth, d. of William Thorne of Boston, had bapt. at Roxbury, where his w. join. the ch. 8 July 1666, Eliz. and Desiretruth, perhaps not tw. on 15 July 1666, of wh. one, at least, d. soon; Eliz. 22 Nov. 1668; Deborah, 26 Feb. 1671; John, 10 Aug. 1673; William, 29 June 1679; and Mary, 20 May 1683; but this last was b. after he had rem. to Dunstable, so that she may have been older, when bapt. than the others.   At D. he had also Joanna.

ACTON, JOHN, North Yarmouth, a. 1685.   Sullivan, 185.

ACY, or ACIE, JOHN, Rowley 1663–77, was perhaps s. of William. THOMAS, Hadley 1678, rem. soon.   WILLIAM, Rowley 1643, after at Boston, where he had Joseph, bapt. at first ch. 28 June 1657, went again to R. there was liv. 1677.

ADAMS, ABRAHAM, Boston, cooper, perhaps s. of Nathaniel of Weymouth, had liv. at Falmouth, where bef. 1667 he m. Sarah, d. of Arthur Macworth, and from his wid. had gift of an isl. in Casco Bay.   Willis, I. 75.   Later in life he was an innholder, and one of that band of volunteers wh. took, Oct. 1689, a piratic. vessel, in the Vineyard Sound, after some resist. and brot. her into B.   His w. was Abigail, d. of Nicholas Wilmot, wh. in his will of 27 Sept. 1684, provides for her sh. of his est. From the will of Adams, made 6, pro. 18 Apr. 1700, we learn, that he had by a former w. i. e. Macworth's d. two ds. Sarah Grant and Jane Snelling, and by w. Abigail, made extrix. had Zechariah, Samuel, Abraham, Mary, Abigail, and Eliz.   ABRAHAM, Newbury, eldest s. of Robert, m. 16 Nov. 1670, Mary, d. of Richard Pettingell of the same, had Mary, b. 16 Jan. 1672; Robert, 12 May 1674; Abraham, 6 May 1676; Isaac, 26 Feb. 1679; Sarah, 13 Apr. 1681; John, 7 Mar. 1684; Matthew, 25 May 1686; Israel, 25 Dec. 1688; Dorothy, 25 Oct. 1691; and Richard, 22 Nov. 1693.   His w. d. 19 Sept. 1705; and he d. 12 Dec. 1714.   ‖ ALEXANDER, Boston, a shipwright, freem. 1648, ar. co. 1652, m. as is said, Mary Coffin, sis. of Tristram the first, had Mary, b. 19, bapt. 25 Jan. 1646; rem. to Dorchester, there had Susanna, 14 May 1648; John, 26 Feb. 1653; and Samuel, 7 May 1656.   ANDREW, Hartford 1643, then employ. as Hinman, 12, tells, in place of sch.master. CHARLES, Dover 1648, liv. in 1669 in that part, call. Oyster riv. was of the gr. jury 1688; had w. Temperance, s. Charles, and perhaps John; and was k. by the Ind. 1694.   Evidence is rec. 1712, to prove, that he possess. lds. there "above sixty yrs."   CHARLES, Dover, s. of the preced. had Charles, b. 1668; Sarah, 1671.   CHRISTOPHER, Braintree, a petition. with many others, in 1645, for a planta. on the land of Pumham.   He rem. E. and had fine est. at Kittery, where in his will in Suff. Reg. X. 105 of 13 June 1686, pro. 21 Sept. 1687, more than eight mos. after his d. by Gov. Andros, he names w. Margaret, and four ch. John,

Mark, Ann, and Mary, beside cous. Isaac Goodwright, to wh. are giv. two cows. DANIEL, Simsbury, 1683, m. prob. in 1687, Mary, d. of Samuel Pinney of the same, had Mary, bapt. 16 Jan. 1698 ; Thankful, 10 Apr. foll. and other ch. perhaps bef. and after, certain. Ephraim, 25 May 1701. EDWARD, New Haven 1640, Milford 1646, and Fairfield 1650, by his will of 7 Aug. 1671, gave est. to w. Margaret, ch. Samuel ; Abraham ; Mary Merwin, wh. was b. a. 1647 ; Nathaniel ; John ; and Nathan. John and Nathaniel d. without issue. *EDWARD, Medfield, s. of Henry the first, b. in Eng. freem. 1654, by w. Lydia had Lydia, b. 12 July 1653 ; Jonathan, 4 Apr. 1655 ; John, 18 Feb. 1657 ; Eliashib, 18 Feb. 1659 ; Sarah, 29 May 1660 ; James, 4 Jan. 1662 ; Henry, 29 Oct. 1663 ; Mehitable, 20 Mar. 1665 ; Elisha, 25 Aug. 1666, d. next mo. ; Edward, 28 June 1668 ; Bethia, 12 Apr. 1671, d. in few ds. ; Bethia, again, 18 Aug. 1672, d. in few ds. ; Abigail, 25 Jan. 1675 ; and Miriam 26 Feb. 1676 ; both d. soon. He was much employ. in public duties, ens. selectman for many yrs. rep. in the two first Gen. Cts. 1689, after overthrow of Andros, and d. 12 Nov. 1716. His w. had d. 3 Mar. 1676 ; but he had sec. w. whose name is not seen. His will of 19 May 1715, pro. 3 Dec. 1716, in our reg. XIX. 225, taking notice that his w. was provid. for bef. their m. and that his s. Jonathan, and John were, formerly, supplied by him with lds. and Edward with movab. and money, directs now, that his prop. be div. in nine equal parts, whereof the childr. of his s. Eliashib dec. to have two, James, and Henry, ea. two, and his ds. Lydia Daniel, Sarah Turner, and Mehitable Faxon, ea. one. EDWARD, Windsor, m. 25 May 1660, Eliz. d. of Thomas Buckland, and d. 15 Aug. 1683, leav. only ch. Mary, b. 28 Aug. 1671. ELEAZER, Medfield, eldest s. of the first Henry of the same, by w. Eliz. had Eliz. b. 1672 ; and Eleazer, 1673. FERDINANDO, Dedham, 1637, a shoemaker from London, freem. 13 May 1640, by w. Ann had Abigail, b. 15 Sept. 1638 ; Bethia, 10 June 1640 ; and Nathaniel, 16 Mar. 1643. In Aug. 1641 he had leave to go home on business ; but if he went, he came back next yr. Worthington, 103. GEORGE, Branford, m. 5 Sept. 1657, the wid. of Lesley Bradfield, I presume, as sec. w. and d. prob. 1675. His will of 1670 names w. and s. John only, but this s. was by former w. it may be suppos. for he made his will 10 Oct. 1677, and d. that yr. giv. his prop. to Noah Rogers and others, hav. no near relat. GEORGE, Watertown, by w. Frances had John, b. 6 Aug. 1645 ; George, 1647 ; Daniel ; Joseph, 6 Mar. 1657 ; and Mary ; rem. to Cambridge farms, now Lexington, and d. 10 Oct. 1696. GEORGE, Cambridge, that part now Lexington, s. of the preced. m. 20 Jan. 1684, Martha, d. of John Fiske of Watertown, had George, b. 28 Apr. 1685 ; Martha, 10 Jan. 1687 ; John, 2 Sept. 1688 ; of wh. three the Watertown ch. rec. at various times, show the bapt. Nathaniel; Sarah; both bapt. 12 June 1698 at W.; Benjamin, b. 20 Dec. 1701; and Bond thinks there may have, also, been Abigail, and Ann. HENRY, Braintree, came early to our country, and tradit. says from Braintree, in Co. Essex in 1632, but widely diverse is the origin by ano. tradit. had gr. in Feb. 1641, of 40 acres by vote of Boston, of wh. Braintree was part, i. e. the proportion for ten heads. Perhaps he was the first clk. of the town, after separat. from Boston, tho. more likely is it that his s. of the same name had the honor; and he d. or was bur. 8 Oct. 1646, leav. by tradit. eight s. yet only five are nam. in his will, 1646, pro. 8 June 1647, where appear Peter, John, Joseph, Edward, Samuel, and d. Ursula. Of this d. as tradit. took no notice, it may be that the number eight applied to s. means in truth ch. seven s. and one d. but names eno. for the s. may be seen, and certainly one is good, if not two beyond the devisees in the will, as Henry, Thomas, Jonathan, in some reports call. William. The inscript. on the monu. erect. by his descend. John Adams, sec. Presid. of the U. S. exhibits the popular story with characterist. strength: "In mem. of Henry Adams, wh. took his flight from the Dragon persecution, in Devonsh. Eng. and alighted with eight s. near Mt. Wollaston. One of the s. ret. to Eng. and, after tak. some time to explore the country, four rem. to Medfield, and the neighb. towns, two to Chelmsford. One only, Joseph, wh. lies here at his left hand, remain. here; wh. was an orig. propr. in the townsh. of Braintree incorpo. 1639." * ‖ HENRY, Braintree, s. of the preced. b. in Eng. a. 1604, as is thot. may, rather than his f. be regard. as the town clk. of 1640, m. 17 Nov. 1643, Eliz. d. of Moses Paine, had Eleazer, b. 5 Aug. 1644; Jasper, 23 June 1647; rem. to that part of Dedham, wh. bec. Medfield, of wh. also he was first town clk. there had Eliz. 11 Nov. 1649; John, and Henry, tw. 14 July 1652; Moses, 26 Oct. 1654; Henry, again, 19 Nov. 1657; and Samuel, 10 Dec. 1661, wh. d. young. He was of ar. co. 1652, rep. 1659, 65, 74 and 5, the lieut. k. by the Ind. 21 Feb. 1676, at his own door, as ment. by Increase Mather in hist. of Philip's war. His w. was mort. wound. the same night, at the ho. of Rev. Mr. Wilson, tho. she liv. a week. HENRY, Boston, m. 10 May 1660, Mary, d. of William Pitty of Weymouth. HENRY, Medfield, prob. s. of Edward of the same, m. 10 Dec. 1691, Patience Ellis, d. of Thomas. *JACOB, Newbury, s. of Robert of the same, m. 7 Apr. 1677, Ann Allen, or Ellen, had Dorothy, b. 26 June 1679; Rebecca, 26 Aug. 1680; rem. to Suffield, there had sev. ch. in his will, beside the two, b. at N. nam. Jacob; Daniel; Abraham, 10 Nov. 1687; John; Ann; Eliz. 16 Aug. 1692; and Sarah. Some of them, however, had perhaps been b. in a neighb. town. He was rep. for S. 1711, 14, and 17, in Nov. of wh. last he d. at the Ct. in Boston.

JAMES, Plymouth, s. of John of the same, wh. was of the first comers, went, 1643, to Marshfield, soon after to Scituate, there m. 16 July 1646, Frances, d. of William Vassall, had William, b. 16 May 1647 ; Ann, 18 Apr. 1649 ; Richard, 19 Apr. 1651, d. soon ; Mary, 27 Jan. 1653 ; and Margaret, 1654 ; all bapt. at the sec. ch. of S. Deane says, beside Martha, wh. m. 1678, Benjamin Pierce. On board the James of Plymouth one James, not prob. this man, d. 19 Jan. 1653, of wh. Kenelm Winslow was made admr. JAMES, Concord, 1672. JEREMY, Braintree, perhaps 1632, rem. soon to Cambridge, then call. Newtown, freem. 6 May 1635, rem. next yr. to Hartford, had three ws. of wh. the first is unkn. by name, by her he had Samuel, b. it is said 1643, bapt. certain. 23 Nov. 1645 ; and perhaps more. His sec. w. Rebecca, wid. of Samuel Greenhill, d. 1678, and by her he had other ch. prob. Ann, wh. m. Robert Sanford; Elinor, wh. m. Nathaniel Willet; and John, unless one or two were by former w. Rebecca, wid. of the sec. Andrew Warner, and d. of John Fletcher, was his third w. He long kept the ordinary, and d. 11 Aug. 1683, in his will, made seven days bef. he div. his est. half to childr. of s. John, and half to those of d. Willet. His wid. was 77 yrs. old at her d. 25 June 1715, and, no doubt, had provis. from the est. JOHN, Plymouth, one of the first comers, arr. in the Fortune, 9 Nov. 1621, m. Ellen or Elinor Newton, as the sagacity of Judge Davis presum. for she came in the Ann, 1623, and was prob. the only fem. N. of Chesapeak Bay with such bapt. name. He d. 1633, leav. w. and ch. James, John, and Susanna ; and the rec. 24 Oct. of that yr. shows decent est. for that day. The wid. m. June foll. Kenelm Winslow. JOHN, Cambridge, brot. from Eng. w. Ann, and d. Rebecca, bapt. bef. says Mitchell's Reg. when he adds five of the other ch. bapt. in his ch. in right of the mo. for the f. did not join bef. 13 May 1666, viz. Mary, b. 25 Oct. 1652 ; John, 1 May 1655 ; and Joseph ; but the "matchless" registrar does not ment. the day or days of bapt. tho. our thanks are hearty for his care to name Hannah, b. 8 Aug. 1657, bapt. 17 June 1660 ; and Daniel, 14 Sept. 1662. But Hannah d. early in 1661, 25 Jan. acc. Mitchell, 25 Feb. by Harris Epit. 169 ; and Daniel, d. 14 May 1685. Ano. Daniel had preced. him, but liv. not, I presume, long eno. to be bapt. He was a millwright, and Dr. Bond conject. that he was s. of George of Watertown, and when that was seen to be impossib. he suppos. he was br. So numberless are the shoots of this name, that I dare not foll. even so judicious a leader in this expedit. That he was s. of Henry the first, as amiable credulity would assume, is highly improb. since he came twenty yrs. or little less after that great N. E. progenitor, and so long outliv. him dying betw. June and Oct. 1706, and his w. still liv. Rebecca m. 24 Nov. 1669, Nathaniel Patten, and d. 18 Dec. 1677 ; Mary m. John Eames of Watertown, and d. 1681.

Inconsistencies appear in the fam. geneal. as to b. of her and her br. John.
JOHN, Chelmsford 1654, had been of Concord 1650, has been sometimes
thot. s. of the first Henry ; but the conject. is uncert. JOHN, Marshfield,
s. perhaps, of John of Plymouth, m. 27 Dec. 1654, Jane James, and
had Joseph, Martha, and perhaps other ch. JOHN, Hartford, s. prob.
eldest, of Jeremy of the same, had Rebecca, b. Aug. 1658 ; Abigail, Feb.
1660 ; Sarah, Mar. 1662 ; Jeremy, Aug. 1664 ; John, Sept. 1666 ; Jonathan, 6 Nov. 1668 ; and d. 1670, leav. wid. in expecta. of ano. ch. Of
the s. Jeremy went to Huntington ; and John to Great Egg harb. both
on L. I. JOHN, Dover, 1662, was, perhaps, s. of Charles the first of the
same. JOHN, Branford, s. of George of the same, by first w. d. 1677.
JOHN, Windsor, m. 1677, Abigail, d. of Humphrey Pinney, had Mary ;
Abigail, b. 1681 ; and John, early in 1683 ; all nam. in the will of their
gr.mo. Pinney, wh. d. 18 Aug. 1684, as if the mo. were d. He was,
prob. br. of Daniel, and rem. to Simsbury. JOHN, Salem, by w. Sarah
had Eliz. b. 20 Oct. 1682 ; Sarah, 13 Oct. 1684 ; Mary, 15 Feb. 1688 ;
John, 16 Mar. 1690 ; Margaret, 11 Feb. 1693, d. next yr. ; and Margaret, again, 8 Mar. 1696. JOHN, Sudbury, m. Hannah, d. of John Bent
the sec. had John, b. 12 Mar. 1684 ; Daniel, 1685 ; and Hannah, 1688.
JOHN, Medfield, s. of Henry the sec. had Samuel, b. 1684 ; Mary, 1687 ;
Patience, 1690 ; Ruth, 1691 ; Josiah, 1693 ; John, 1695 ; Isaac, 1697 ;
Richard, 1699 ; Joshua, 1701 ; Abigail, 1702 ; Bethia, 1705 ; and Michael, 1707. JOHN, Medfield, s. of Edward of the same, by first w. Deb-
orah had Edward, b. 1682 ; John, 1684 ; Daniel, 1686 ; Eleazer, 1687 ;
beside Obadiah, and Jonathan, whose dates are not giv. and by sec. w.
Susanna had Thomas, 1695 ; Susanna, 1697 ; Jeremiah, 1699 ; Abra-
ham, 1701 ; Bethia, 1702 ; Phineas, 1705 ; Hannah, 1707 ; and Esther.
JOHN, Boston, merch. third s. of Joseph the first, by w. Hannah, d. of
Christopher Webb, had Hannah, b. 24 Jan. 1685 ; John, 27 Sept. 1687 ;
both at Braintree ; Samuel, 6 May 1689 (wh. by w. Mary was f. of
Samuel, b. 16 Sept. 1722, H. C. 1740, one of the chief promoters of the
Amer. Revo. 1765–85, and Gov. of Mass. wh. d. 2 Oct. 1802) ; and by
sec. w. Hannah, d. of Anthony Checkley, Esq. m. 19 Oct. 1694, had Joseph, and Mary, tw. 20 Dec. 1695 ; Thomas, 29 Mar. 1701 ; and Abijah, 11 May 1702. He d. bef. 20 Jan. 1712. JONATHAN, Medfield,
call. sen. when his inv. of 15 Feb. 1692, was produc. at Prob. Ct. had
been thot. s. of the first Henry, tho. no other circumstance is to be discern. in support of such assumpt. than that Edward of M. wh. was a s.
of Henry gave to his eldest s. this name of Jonathan. Scrutiny has been
applied, and Vinton, 296, could find two ws. Eliz. and Mary, but ment.
no ch. JONATHAN, Boston, blockmaker, of wh. I learn from his will,
made 1 Apr. 1707, pro. 8 May next, that his w. was Rebecca, and that

he had Samuel, eldest s. beside Jonathan, Nathaniel, and James, and
four ds. Rebecca, Dorcas, Mary, and Lydia. His w. was d. of James
Andrews of Falmouth, driv. up by the war. JONATHAN, Medfield,
eldest s. of Edward of the same, m. 20 Mar. 1678, Mary Ellis, d. prob.
of Thomas of the same; but my acquisit. reach no further. JOSEPH,
Braintree, perhaps youngest s. of the first Henry, b. in Eng. a. 1626, was
a maltster, freem. 1653 or 5, his name appearing on both years, as the
wonderful carelessness of Secr. Rawson admits thirty, if not thirty-one
(if we include Dwight), out of thirty-two of the earlier yr. to be rein-
sert. two yrs. later with the sole addit. of one name at the top and one
at the foot of the list, m. 26 or 29 Nov. 1650, Abigail (not Mary, as
Alden has it), d. of Gregory Baxter (not, as is giv. by Thayer, of John,
wh. was her br.), had Hannah, b. 13 Nov. 1652 ; Joseph, 24 Dec. 1654 ;
John, 13 Jan. 1657, or 11 Feb. it being uncert. wh. date is prefer. on the
rec. (but as he d. in few ds. the earlier may denote b. and the latter, d.)
Abigail, 27 Feb. 1659 ; John, and Bethia, tw. 3 Dec. 1661 ; Mary,
9 Oct. 1663, d. soon; Samuel, 6 Sept. 1665 ; Mary, again, 25 Feb.
1668; Peter, 7 Feb. 1670 ; Jonathan, 31 Jan. 1672 ; and Mehitable,
bapt. 24 Nov. 1678, not as sometimes read 23 Nov. wh. was Saturday.
His w. d. 27 Aug. 1692 ; and he d. 6 Dec. 1694. Thayer's Fam. Memo.
in eleven pages furnish. large enumera. of descend. His eldest d. m.
10 Apr. 1672, Samuel Savil; Abigail m. John Bass jun.; Bethia m.
1680, John Webb; Mary m. 16 Dec. 1686, Samuel Webb ; and Mehitable m. 21 July 1697, Thomas White. His will, of 18 July 1694, gives
no ment. of s. Samuel or Jonathan, but provides for the others and the
five ds. using the name of hs. for all but the last. JOSEPH, Braintree,
eldest s. of the preced. m. 20 Feb. 1682, Mary Chapin, perhaps d. of
Josiah, had Mary, b. 6 Feb. foll. and Abigail, 17 Feb. 1684. This w. d.
14 June 1687, and he next m. Hannah, d. of John Bass, by wh. he had
Joseph, 1 Jan. 1690, H. C. 1710, min. of Newington from 16 Nov.
1715 to his d. 26 May 1783 ; John, 8 Feb. 1692, the deac. wh. d. 25
May 1761, and was (by Susanna, d. of Peter Boylston) f. of John, sec.
Presid. of the U. S. b. 19 Oct. 1735, wh. d. 4 July 1826, and was f. of
John Quincy, sixth Presid. of the U. S. ; Samuel, 28 Jan. 1694 ; Josiah,
8 Feb. 1696 ; Hannah, 21 Feb. 1698 ; Ruth, 21 Mar. 1700 ; Bethia,
13 June, 1702 ; and Ebenezer, 30 Dec. 1704. This w. d. 24 Oct. 1705,
and he d. at the mature age of 81, on 12 Feb. 1736 ; and his wid. Eliz.
(by wh. he had Caleb, 26 May 1710, that d. in few days ;) d. 14 Feb.
1739, aged 71. JOSEPH, Cambridge, s. of John of the same, m. 21 Feb.
1688, Margaret, d. of Thomas Eames, of Sudbury, had Joseph, b. 1689,
wh. liv. to the age of 85 ; Daniel, 1690 ; Cherry, if such be a possib.
name in that day, bapt. 31 Jan. 1697 ; John, 18 Apr. 1697 ; and Abi-

gail. MOSES, Sherborn, s. of Henry the sec. m. 15 Apr. 1681, Lydia, d. of Jonathan Whitney of the same, had Benoni, b. 3 Nov. foll. ; Lydia, 2 Feb. 1684 ; Eliz. 18 Sept. 1686, d. young ; Hannah, 8 Feb. 1688 ; Eliz. again, 25 Oct. 1689 ; Moses, 26 Nov. 1691 ; James, 7 July 1693 ; Isaac, 4 Mar. 1695 ; and Abigail, 7 Sept. 1697 ; was selectman 1701, and d. 1724. NATHANIEL, Newport 1639, may be that one of Weymouth 1642, wh. had Abraham, b. 16 Jan. 1643. NATHANIEL, Boston, turner, m. 24 Nov. 1652, Eliz. d. of Philemon Portmort, but whether she d. soon, and he had ano. w. Sarah is wholly uncert. for one Nathaniel of B. d. Oct. 1675, and his w. Sarah d. May 1685. Ano. NATHANIEL, Boston, blockmaker, if the modern copy of supposed rec. contempo. may be confided in, as in about nine tenths of its contents it may be, by w. Mary alone had Nathaniel, b. 10 Sept. 1653 ; Mary, 20 May 1655 ; Sarah, 9 Aug. 1657 ; David, 30 June 1659 ; Joseph, 19 June 1661 ; Eliz. 2 Mar. 1662, d. soon ; Benjamin, 10 Dec. 1665 ; Eliz. again, 2 Oct. 1667 ; Benjamin, again, 27 May 1671 ; Isaac, 7 Nov. 1673, and Mary, again, 23 Sept. 1677. No small part of this may have confirmat. in his will of 22 Mar. 1690, pro. 8 May next, in wh. his w. Mary, and s. Joseph and Isaac are well provid. for, as also d. Mary, wid. of Joseph Hipdich ; Sarah, w. of Richard Hunnewell, and Eliz. w. of Ebenezer Chaffin, but all subject to the discret. of their mo. and he takes notice that his s. Nathaniel had not only rec. his share of prop. and more, but owed him or money lent, and refus. to acknowl. the debt, so that out of his fatherly regard he can give him but one shil. See rec. in Vol. XI. 136. He d. 30 Mar. Perhaps his eldest s. NATHANIEL was a soldier in Philip's war, of Turner's comp. tho. rather is it more prob. that he was s. of N. of Weymouth, and liv. at Charlestown, m. Hannah, d. of Nicholas Wilmot, wh. remembers her in his will of 27 Sept. 1684. Of ano. NATHANIEL of Charlestown, blacksmith, possib. but not prob. s. of Samuel the first, who m. Ann d. of Nathaniel Coolidge of Watertown, I see so little reason to believe his claim to adm. on my page with his ch. that he must be left in his position with Bond. PETER, Medfield, s. of Henry the first, b. in Eng. freem. 1650, by w. Rachel had Peter, b. 20 July 1653, wh. was a physician at Medway, of wh. I kn. no more ; Hannah, 1658 ; Mary ; Jonathan, 1663, d. soon ; Jonathan, again, 15 May 1664 ; Ruth ; and prob. three others. A Peter d. in New Hampsh. 1671. PETER, Braintree, s. of Joseph the first, m. 12 Feb. 1695, Mary, d. of Christopher Webb, had Mary, b. 27 Jan. foll. ; Abigail, 13 Aug. 1698 ; Peter, 13 Aug. 1700 ; Hannah, 12 Oct. 1702 ; Esther, 11 Aug. 1707 ; Mehitable, 25 Nov. 1708 ; Jedediah, 21 Jan. 1711, H. C. 1733, min. of Stoughton ; and Bethia, 3 July 1713, wh. d. young. PHILIP, York, was of the gr. ury 1666, freem. 1680. *RICHARD, Weymouth, freem. 2 Sept. 1635, rep. in Nov. 1637, and Mar. 1638, had Samuel, b. 6 June 1639 ; beside ds. Sarah, 3 July 1637 ; and Ruth, 3 June 1642. RICHARD, Salem, came in the Abigail 1635, aged 29, was a bricklayer from Northampton, with Susan, 26, prob. his wife. Perhaps he liv. at Charlestown 1674, and may be the same wh. d. 6 Oct. of that yr. at Malden, whose w. Eliz. d. Nov. 1656. His will ment. w. prob. not mo. of any of the ds. Mary Clough, Sarah, w. of Edward Counts, both of Charlestown, Ruth Glover, and Hannah, b. Jan. 1663, unm. and made Excor. Lazarus Glover, perhaps h. of Ruth. RICHARD, Sudbury, had been a soldier in Moseley's comp. wound. in the gr. swamp fight, 19 Dec. 1675 ; by w. Rebecca had Richard, b. 11 Apr. 1680 ; Rebecca, 1682 ; Sarah, 1683 ; and John, 26 Oct. 1686. ROBERT, Salem 1638, a tailor, by one tradit. brot. from Devonsh. by ano. prob. of equal value, from the far distant Holderness in Co. York, had first liv. two or three yrs. at Ipswich, says Coffin, and had bef. com. over two ch. John and Joanna, and at Salem had Abraham, b. 1639, rem. to Newbury 1640, and had Isaac, a. 1648 ; Jacob, 23 Apr. 1649, wh. d. soon; and Hannah, 25 June 1650 ; Jacob, again, 13 Sept. 1651 ; beside, Eliz. Mary, and youngest Archelaus, of wh. some were b. bef. 1648. His w. Elinor d. 12 June 1677 ; and he m. 6 Feb. 1678, Sarah, wid. of Henry Short, wh. surv. to 24 Oct. 1697, he d. 12 Oct. 1682, aged 80. Joanna m. 4 Jan. 1654, Launcelot Granger ; Eliz. m. Edward Phelps, of Andover ; Mary m. 15 Nov. 1660, Jeremiah Goodrich ; and Hannah m. 10 Feb. 1682, William Warham. His will of 7 Mar. 1681, with confirmat. of 27 June 1682, pro. 28 Nov. next, calls John eldest, but declares Abraham Excor. and names other ch. Isaac, Jacob, Hannah, Joanna, Eliz. and Mary, the three last being m. beside the gr.ch. viz. three s. of Abraham, and his d. Mary. He left good est. See Geneal. Reg. IX. 126. ROGER, Roxbury, by. w. Mary, d. of Thomas Baker, wh. d. 28 June 1710, had Thomas, b. 19 Oct. 1675, d. soon ; Joseph, 13 Oct. 1676 ; Maria, 22 May 1678 ; Sarah, 15 Mar. 1680 ; Roger, 3 July 1681 ; Abigail, 10 Apr. 1683 ; Daniel, 6 Nov. 1684 ; and Hannah, 7 Apr. 1688, d. young. Copy of his will, of 14 Dec. 1713, is seen in Vol. XVIII. 129, as pro. 10 Mar. foll. It provides for eldest s. Joseph ; d. Mary, her ch. and childr. d. Sarah Smith, and her childr. d. Abigail, s. Daniel, and s. in law, John Robbins. But wh. was f. of this Roger is not found. SAMUEL, Charlestown, s. of Henry the first, b. in Eng. freem. 10 May 1643, m. Rebecca, d. of Thomas Graves, had Samuel, b. 3 July 1647 ; Rebecca ; Thomas, a. 1652 ; John ; and Catharine, 29 Oct. 1657 ; both d. young ; Catharine, again, 4 Jan. 1659 ; rem. to Chelmsford, there was town clk. 1679. His w. d. 8 Oct. 1664, and he m. 7 May 1668, Esther Sparhawk, d. of Nathaniel the first of Cambridge, and had four more ch. of wh. Nathaniel, Joseph, and Esther are kn. from will of their elder br. Thomas. He was a Capt. and d. 24 Jan. 1689, aged 72. His d. Rebecca m. John Waldo. SAMUEL, Fairfield, s. of Edward of the same, d. a. 1690, leav. w. and ch. * || THOMAS, Braintree, s. of Henry the first, freem. 10 May 1643, ar. co. 1644, by w. Mary had Mary, b. 24 July 1643, d. soon; rem. to Concord, there had Jonathan, and Pelatiah, tw. 6 Mar. 1646; Timothy, 2 Apr. 1648; George, 29 May 1650; Samuel; and Thomas; rem. to Chelmsford, there had Rebecca, 18 Sept. 1657; Eliz. 21 Oct. 1659; and Mary, again, 29 Oct. 1664; was town clk. selectman, rep. at sec. sess. 1673, and d. 20 July 1688, aged 76. His eldest four s. liv. at Ch. 1692. THOMAS, Charlestown, m. 2 Dec. 1654, Alice Roper, d. of John the sec. of Dedham, had Edith, b. 21 Feb. 1656; Susanna, bapt. 3 Feb. 1661; Sarah, b. 12 Mar. 1667; Samuel, Apr. 1669; and Abigail, 12 Sept. 1671; and he d. 14 Oct. 1697. THOMAS, New Haven, took o. of fidel. 7 Apr. 1657, m. 27 Nov. 1667, Rebecca, d. of William Potter, had only ch. Abigail, b. 29 Sept. foll. A ridicul. story of his being mistak. for King Charles II. at N. H. in 1652 may be read on p. 60 of the sec. Vol. of the rec. of that col. recently pub. and some slight connex. may be found in the affidavit of Capt. Bredan, made in 1661, showing that the governm. of N. E. "apprehended a gent. not many yrs. ago (suppos. him to be the K.) resolv. to send him for Eng. had not Sir Henry Moody and others better kn. His Ma.tie." We may read in Hutch. I. 215 that Capt. B. gave informat. of having seen the regicides at Boston. Sir H. Moody was of L. I. See N. Y. Col. Docum. Vol. III. 39. To the benevolence of C. J. Hoadley of Hartford I am indebt. for this curious, but unimport. matter. Charles II. knew well, that any place on the Europ. contin. would be better refuge for him. THOMAS, York, freem. 1680. THOMAS, Charlestown, s. of Samuel of the same, was a mariner, i. e. shipmaster, d. at Barbados. By his will of 28 Feb. 1684, made at age of 32, at C. pro. 3 June 1686, by Presdt. Dudley, he gave w. Mary his dwel. ho. and other est. names no ch. but fully indicat. his relations, father Samuel of Chelmsford, to wh. he gives £20, in ready money, a negro girl to his mo. Esther for life, and next to Rebecca Waldo, and at her decease to Susanna W., but with condition " she shall not serve above 20 yrs. from this time;" speaks of his uncle Thomas Graves, and calls Nathaniel, Joseph, and Benjamin A. his brothers, and Esther his sis. wh. should have resid. of his prop. after his w's d. It may be seen in Vol. XI. 2. WALTER, Charlestown, m. 15 Dec. 1657, Hannah, d. of Robert Moulton, the sec. of Salem, had John, b. 11 Oct. 1664; William, 1669; Jacob, 24 Dec. 1670; Hannah, 22 Aug. 1673; and perhaps others, earlier, or later, or both; in 1678, liv. on Malden side. WILLIAM, Cambridge 1635, or earlier, freem. 22 May 1639, rem. prob. bef. 1642,

to Ipswich, but at C. had William, Nathaniel, and Samuel, prob. b. in
Eng. and he d. 1661. WILLIAM, Ipswich, prob. s. of the preced. and
perhaps that passeng. in the Elizabeth and Ann from London, 1635,
aged 15, had John ; and William, b. 27 May 1650, H. C. 1671 ; and d.
Jan. 1659. WILLIAM, Dedham, s. of the preced. the earliest gr. of this
copious name, bec. the sec. min. at D. ord. 3 Dec. 1673, m. 21 Oct.
1674, Mary, d. of William Manning of Cambridge, had Mary, b. 12 Nov.
1675, d. soon; Eliphalet, 26 Mar. 1677, H. C. 1694, a disting. man,
min. of New London; William, 17 Jan. 1679. His w. d. 24 June 1679,
and he m. 29 Mar. foll. Alice, d. of William Bradford the sec. had Eliz.
b. 23 Feb. 1681 ; Alice, 3 Apr. 1682 ; William, 17 Dec. 1683 ; and
posthum. d. Abiel, 15 Dec. 1685. He had preach. at Boston the Gen.
Elect. sermon 27 May preced. and d. 17 Aug. next. Judge Sewall
informs us, that he attend. the funeral, and that prayers were public.
offer. then for the first time in N. E. on such an occasion. His wid. bec.
sec. w. of Major James Fitch of Norwich, and had eight more ch. Of
the m. of his ds. and later details of the fam. eno. may be seen in Worthington's Hist. of Dedham, Lamson's Centen. Disc., Allen in Geneal.
Reg. IX. 127, and in the large Mem. of Eliphalet, by Miss Caulkins,
4 Mass. Hist. Coll. I. 1. WILLIAM, Hartford 1650, perhaps bot. land
1653 at Farmington, and there d. 18 July 1655. His wid. Eliz. d. 3
Aug. foll. WILLIAM, Sudbury, by w. Eliz. had James, b. 31 Mar. 1674;
John, 8 Mar. 1676 ; and Richard, 22 Aug. 1678. In the Defence from
London, 1635, came one Dorothy A. aged 24, but whose w. or d. she
was, is unkn. to me. Farmer remarks, in 1836, that of this name fifty-
two had been gr. at Harv. twenty-three at Yale, and at all the other
N. E. coll. forty-two ; of wh. vast number, were min. eighteen of Harv.
six of Yale, and four of the other coll.

ADDINGTON, || ISAAC, Boston, 1640, freem. 1650, by w. Ann d. of Elder
Thomas Leverett, wh. outliv. him, had Isaac, b. 22, bapt. 26 Jan. 1645 ;
Ann, 10, bapt. 14 Mar. 1647 ; Rebecca, bapt. 11 Mar. 1649, as "four
days old ; " Sarah, 12, bapt. 20 Apr. 1651, d. 2 Aug. of next yr. and
Sarah, again, 11, bapt. 13 Feb. 1653 ; was chos. 1652 into the art. co.
when Whitman erron. calls him Israel; and he d. next yr. Ann m. Capt.
Samuel Maudesley; Rebecca m. Eleazer Davenport; and Sarah m.
Penn Townsend. ‡ * ISAAC, Boston, only s. of the preced. m. 1669, Eliz.
d. of Griffith Bowen of London, but formerly of Boston, had Eliz. b. 21
Sept. 1671, wh. d. bef. her f. He was bred for a surgeon, but was
almost wholly unkn. in later yrs. for that skill, bec. a rep. 1685, and
was forthwith chos. speaker, and next yr. Assist. By the new chart.
the k. under dictat. of Increase Mather, made him of the counc. and the
Secretary, in wh. offices he many yrs. was contin. unlike sev. of Math-

er's nominees ; and was appoint. after Judge of the highest ct. 1702, and its chief, next yr. His w. d. 2 Mar. 1713, and he m. 19 Nov. foll. Eliz. wid. of Hon. John Wainwright, and d. 19 Mar. 1715, leav. no ch. Sewall says his funer. was attend. on 23d by 20 counsellors. His wid. d. 22 Nov. 1742, aged 87.

ADDIS, WILLIAM, Gloucester 1642, one of the chief inhab. perhaps went home for a short time, but in 1658–62 liv. at New London, as a brewer. He had two ds. Milicent, wh. m. 28 Nov. 1642, William South-mayd, next William Ash, and, last, Thomas Beebe, wh. were all of New London ; and Ann, wh. m. 24 June 1653, at Boston, Ambrose Dart.

ADEY, WILLIAM, Plymouth, of wh. I learn only, that he was fin. in 1636, for work on Sunday.

ADGATE, THOMAS, Saybrook, had Eliz. b. 10 Oct. 1651; and Han-nah, 6 Oct. 1653 ; and by sec. w. Mary, wid. of Richard Bushnell, d. of Matthew Marvin, with wh. a. 1660, he rem. to Norwich, had Abigail, Aug. 1661 ; Sarah, Jan. 1663 ; Rebecca, June 1666 ; and Thomas, Mar. 1670. He was after at Saybrook, deac. and d. 1707. All the ds. were m. Eliz. to Richard Bushnell, 7 Dec. 1672; Hannah, to Samuel Loth-rop, but perhaps as sec. w. ; Abigail, to Daniel Tracy, 1682 ; Sarah, to Christopher Huntington the sec. and Rebecca, to Joseph Huntington. THOMAS, Norwich, s. of the preced. m. 15 June 1692, Ruth, d. of Ben-jamin Brewster of the same, had Thomas, and Matthew, was deac. and reach. to very old age.

ADGER, THOMAS, at Pemaquid, took o. of fidel. July 1674.

ADKINS, BENJAMIN, Middletown, s. of Josiah of the same, m. 8 June 1709, Jane Stevens of New Haven, had Sarah, b. 27 Mar. foll. ; Han-nah, 12 Oct. 1712; and his w. d. 16 Nov. next. He m. 9 May 1716, Eliz. Barnes, and had Eliz. b. 1717 ; Benjamin, 2 Nov. 1718; Daniel, 25 Mar. 1721 ; Rachel, 1723 ; Joel, 24 Apr. 1725 ; Ruth, 1728 ; Jemi-ma, 9 Nov. 1731 ; David, 20 June 1734, d. in few wks. ; David, again, 16 July 1736; and Elisha, 12 Aug. 1738, d. young; and this w. d. 20 May 1752. EPHRAIM, Middletown, youngest s. of Josiah of the same, m. 16 June 1709, Eliz. Whitmore, or Wetmore, perhaps d. of Thomas of the same, had Thomas, b. 5 Apr. foll. ; Ephraim, 18 July 1712, d. next yr.; Eliz. 6 Dec. 1714; Ephraim, again, 22 Mar. 1717, d. at 18 yrs.; Naomi, 6 June 1719 ; Ebenezer, 1 Oct. 1721 ; James, 9 Apr. 1724; and George, 26 Dec. 1726; and his w. d. 20 May 1752, says indefatigab. Hinman, in his new Edit. of 1852. But as he gives the same day for d. of the w. of Benjamin, the elder br. and the bapt. name of ea. was the same, without daring to guess wh. of the two is correct, I venture to doubt, that he fell into a very natural error, not observ. the repetit. Ephraim d. he says 26 Dec. 1760 ; and note is not found as to Benjamin.

Josiah, Middletown, d. 12 Sept. 1690, leav. seven ch. minors, Sarah, aged 16; Abigail, 14; Solomon, 12; Josiah, 10; Benjamin, 8; Ephraim, 6; and Eliz. 3; but by a former w. thot. to be an Andrews, others had rec· their portions, nam. Thomas, Samuel, and Eliz. Gilman, wh. perhaps was dec. bef. the m. 8 Oct. 1673, with Eliz. Whitmore, mo. of the young ones, for wh. and her ch. he made provis. in his will a few days bef. his d. Josiah, Middletown, s. of the preced. m. 16 Dec. 1708, Mary Wheeler, perhaps d. of John of Stratford, had Joseph, b. Sept. 1709; Mary, 14 Oct. 1710; Eliz. Feb. 1712; Abigail, 14 Nov. 1713; Josiah, 11 Oct. 1715; John, 14 Oct. 1717; and d. 1 Nov. 1724. Solomon, Middletown, eldest br. of the preced. m. 18 May 1709, Phebe Edwards of Northampton, had Abigail, b. 11 Apr. 1711; Samuel, 21 Sept. 1713; Hannah, 26 May 1715; Solomon, 10 Feb. 1717, d. next yr.; Phebe, 30 May 1719, d. soon; Solomon, again, 11 Aug. 1720; Phebe, again, and Esther, tw. 4 Aug. 1725; Jabez, 23 Apr. 1728, d. next yr.; Abigail, again, 6 Apr. 1729; Rebecca, 21 Nov. 1730; Jabez, again, 21 Nov. 1731, d. at 20 yrs. was a deac. and d. 1748, aged 70. Thomas, Hartford, perhaps br. of the first Josiah, d. 23 Oct. 1694, leav. ch. Mary, aged 22; Thomas, 21; William, 19; Jane, 16; Sarah, 12; Josiah, 9; and Benoni, 4. Hinman says, he request. his br. Gabriel, of wh. we kn. no more, to bring up the youngest boy; and that, in 1709, admin. on est. of the sec. Thomas was giv. to his br. Josiah. But he tells no more of the fam. Most of the descend. of the fams. of this name, not all of them, have chang. the spel. to Atkins.

Adverd, or Adford, Henry, Scituate 1640, m. 6 Oct. 1643, Thomasine Manson, had s. Experience; ds. Mary, Eliz. and Sarah; and d. at Rehoboth 1653. Mary m. 13 Mar. 1671, Abraham Jaquith of Woburn.

Ager, Agar, Auger, Eger, or Eager, William, adm. freem. 18 May 1631. I dare not attempt to indicate how close is the reality of relationship with those who spell Auger and Hagar.

Aglin, William, Boston 1676, is not heard of more.

Agnew, Ninian, Kittery 1676, was held in esteem suffic. to be made apprais. with Capt. John Wincoll, on estates of Roger Plaisted as well as of Richard Tozer, that yr.

Ainsworth, Anchor, Boston, had short resid. if any, for, under power of alienat. of 8 Sept. 1645, his lot of ld. was sold 30 Mar. 1647 by his attorn. Daniel, Roxbury 1648, was later of Dedham, d. 13 Nov. 1680; and Alice, his wid. d. 9 Jan. 1685. Edward, Roxbury, perhaps s. of the preced. m. 11 Jan. 1688, Joanna Hemenway, prob. d. of Joshua of the same, had Joshua, b. 22 Jan. 1689, d. next day; Hannah, 21 Jan. 1690; Edward, 18 Aug. 1693; Eliz. 18 Nov. 1695; Daniel, 7 Oct. 1697; Joanna, 31 Dec. 1699, or by other rep. 5 Oct. 1700, both dates

appear. on the rec. and Judah, 25 Jan. 1703.   Possib. the name has de-
generat. to Ensworth.

AKERS, THOMAS, Charlestown, had Thomas, Sarah, and Rachel, d.
prob. 1651, leav. wid. Priscilla, wh. m. "old William Knapp," and outliv. him.   Thomas, the s. had been gone many yrs. to the wars in Ireland, as his sis. Rachel testif. 22 Aug. 1659, and had not been heard of
for more than ten yrs.

ALBEE, or ALBY, BENJAMIN, Braintree 1641, freem. 18 May 1642,
had, unless the rec. be wrong, Hannah, b. 16 Aug. 1641 ; Lydia, 14 Apr.
1642 ; rem. to Medfield 1649, there had Benjamin 1653 ; and may have
been of Mendon or Swanzey 1669 ; most prob. the former.   See Col.
Rec. Vol. IV. pt. II. 434.   Hannah m. 25 Mar. 1663, Samuel Wight of
M.   In his hist. disc. a. Braintree, Whitney prints this name Alber.
JOHN, Salem 1637, freem. 10 May 1643, d. 1690. He may have the sec.
let. of his name pervert. and possib. was f. of Samuel Abby, or Abbee.
JOHN, Braintree, lost a serv. Francis Brown by d. 1640, and may have
been the freem. of 1670, if Paige's reading of the last name in the MS.
of Vol. IV. 651 be more correct than the governm. print. copy of that
Vol. pt. II. p. 584.   JOHN, Rehoboth, had Hannah, b. 10 Oct. 1673.

ALBESON, or ALLBERSON, JOHN, Yarmouth, perhaps s. of Nicholas,
m. 16 Mar. 1697, Eliz. Folland, had Jeconia, b. 2 Jan. 1698, d. next
mo. and David, 1 Nov. 1699.   NICHOLAS, Scituate 1636, disting. as
"the Swede," had ch. as tradit. goes, wh. he hims. bapt. but Deane found
on rec. nothing relat. to the man, exc. that, in Philip's war, the Ind.
burned his house, 20 May 1676, and the town voted a contrib. towards
rebuild. it.

ALBOROW, ALBOROUGH, ALBRO, ALDBURY, ALBROE, or ALSBER-
RIE, ‡JOHN, Portsmouth, R. I. 1655, was an Assist. 1671, and one of the
counc. appoint. by K. James II. for his Gov. Andros, 1687, as Hutch. I.
354 gives the list.   Gladly would we learn more of so promin. a man,
ancest. of the Rev. John A. Albro, D. D. of Cambridge, and speak with
confid. if rec. would permit.   Very reasona. may be the conject. that he
came, as a youth of 14 yrs. under charge of William Freeborne, in the
Francis from Ipswich, 1634, to Boston.   Freeborne was, we kn. of Boston, until the sad dissens. a. Mrs. Hutchinson, 1637, when he withdrew
in comp. of so many others with Gov. Coddington to purchase R. I.
What presumption may be drawn, from the mural tablet to Alborough in
the ch. of Stratford on Avon, whither the admir. of Shakespear annual.
resort, that this R. I. fam. came from Warwicksh. will be various. determin. by differ. jurors.   Alborow's d. Susanna m. 3 Jan. 1694, John Anthony of Portsmouth, as his sec. w.   His w. Dorothy, wh. was a wid.
Potter, and may therefore be thot. a sec. w. d. 19 Feb. 1696 in her 79th

yr. and the rec. show. me, that he d. 14 Dec. 1712, aged 95 yrs. wh. is a closer agreem. with custom ho. rec. so many yrs. bef. than is often found.

ALCOCK, FRANCIS, Newbury, came in the Bevis 1638, aged 26, in the employm. of Richard Dummer, as the Eng. custom ho. rec. tells; but that is the sole authority for call. him of Newbury, nor is any more kn. of him. * GEORGE, Roxbury, came in the fleet with Gov. Winth. 1630, with his w. a sis. of Rev. Thomas Hooker, but leav. only s. at home, desir. adm. as freem. 19 Oct. of that yr. and was rec. 18 May foll. Bef. the gather. of ch. at R. he was deac. at Dorchester, and his w. d. the first seas. He was a physician, rep. at the first ct. 14 May 1·634, and after, as well as deac. for Roxbury ch. He went home to bring his s. John, and at the same or foll. visit got sec. w. Eliz. by wh. he had Samuel, b. 16 Apr. 1637, H. C. 1659; and at his d. a. 30 Dec. 1640, the ch. rec. says he "left a good savor behind him, the poor of the ch. much bewailing his loss." Of his will, made ten days bef. an abstr. may be read in Geneal. Reg. II. 104. His wid. in Apr. foll. m. Henry Dingham, or Dengham, or Dengayne, a surgeon of Watertown. ‡ JOB, York 1666, s. of John of the same, made a lieut. 1677, and a magistr. under authority of Mass. 1678, and capt. 1681; by creation of William and Mary, in the new Chart. under adv. of Increase Mather, 1691 made a counsellor, but was next yr. left out, on the popul. revulsion against his patron. Hutch. II. 15, says only, that he was of Maine, yet strange is it, that both he, and Douglas, I. 486 should falsely spell his name, Alcot, and stranger still, that Mather should have put that error into his charter, prob. for the sake of euphony. JOHN, Kittery, adm. freem. of Mass. 1652, prob. rem. to York, had to div. his est. 1675, two s. Joseph, and Job, five ds. viz. Mary Twisden, w. of Samuel, perhaps, or of John the sec. Eliz. Banks w. prob. of Richard; Hannah Snell, w. perhaps, of George; Sarah Gittings, whose h. is a stranger to me; and Lydia Dummer, perhaps a maiden, sole ch. of ano. d. Yet conject. may be wearied in finding the connect. Joseph, adm. at the same time, was prob. his s. but Samuel may not have been. JOHN, Roxbury, s. of George of the same, b. in Eng. early in 1627, H. C. 1646, was a physician, but after leav. coll. went to Hartford, prob. on call of his uncle Hooker, to teach a sch. some time. He m. Sarah, d. of Richard Palsgrave of Charlestown, had Joanna, wh. d. soon after b. 5 Aug. or Sept. 1649; Ann, and Sarah, tw. bapt. 26 May 1650; Mary, 15 Aug. 1652; George, 25 Mar. 1655, H. C. 1673; John, b. 5, bapt. 15 Mar. 1657; prob. d. 5 May 1690, unm.; Eliz. bapt. 27 Mar. 1659; Joanna, again, 6 May 1660; and Palsgrave, 20 July 1662, wh. d. 24 Nov. 1710. His w. d. 29 Nov. 1665, aged 44; and he d. 27, was bur. 29 Mar. 1667. His will, of 10 May preced. names the eight ch. Sev. of the later ones were b. in Boston, where his profession fix. him, but they were car. to R. for bapt. He own. est. on Block isl. distrib. to heirs in 1677, but how acquir. I see not. Of his ch. Ann m. 1670, John Williams of Boston; Sarah m. 1670, Rev. Zechariah Whitman; Mary m. Joshua Lamb of Roxbury; and George, the scholar, mean. prob. to follow his f's profess. d. in London, where he made his will 27 Feb. 1677, pro. 9 Mar. after at Doctors Commons, the Prerog. Ct. of the archbp. of Canterbury. In it he divides to the five sis. the est. that came to him from f. and mo. after provid. a liberal mem. for the Roxbury sch. JOHN, Boston, s. of Thomas of the same, but b. at Dedham, m. Constance, d. of Humphrey Mylam, had Mary, b. 3 May 1678; Mylam, 8 Aug. 1680; Hannah, 5 Nov. 1682; Sarah, 18 Jan. 1685; Rebecca, 14 Aug. 1687; Eliz. 3 Apr. 1694; Constant, 17 Jan. 1697; and Sarah, again, 11 Jan. 1699. JOSEPH, York, eldest s. of John of that place, was adm. freem. of Mass. 1652, but d. bef. July 1678, when John Twisden was his admor. and he left a wid. PALSGRAVE, Roxbury, youngest s. of John of the same, had w. Esther, but no ch. as from his will, of 24 Nov. 1710, pro. 14 Dec. foll. in wh. he gave all his prop. to w. for life, is reasonab. conject. PHILIP, New Haven, perhaps s. of Thomas, m. 5 Dec. 1672, Eliz. d. of the w. of Thomas Mitchell, had John, b. 14 July 1675; Thomas, 1677; Eliz. 6 Feb. 1679; Philip, 19 Nov. 1681; and perhaps more; had come thither from Wethersfield, it is said, was a propr. 1685, and m. sec. w. 4 Apr. 1699, Sarah, wid. of Nathaniel Butler, and d. 1715. SAMUEL, Kittery 1652, then made freem. of Mass. was of York 1659. SAMUEL, Boston, youngest s. of George of Roxbury, was a physician, m. 24 Mar. 1668, Sarah, d. of John Stedman, and wid. of John Brackett of Cambridge, had four ch. ea. of wh. d. at few weeks old, and lie bur. near him. He was freem. 1676, and d. 1677, on 16 Mar. as says the gr. stone, or 17, by Hammond's Diary; but the rec. has 18. His wid. had third h. Dr. Thomas Graves of Charlestown, and fourth Hon. John Phillips of the same, and outliv. him. THOMAS, Boston, br. of George, came, no doubt, in the fleet with Winth. for his number in the list of ch. mem. is 46, by w. Margery had Mary, bapt. 3 Nov. 1635, d. young; Eliz. 10 Dec. 1637, d. soon; rem. to Dedham, there had Eliz. again, b. 4 Oct. 1638; Sarah, 28 Dec. 1639; Hannah, 25 May 1642; Mary, again, 4 Oct. 1644; Rebecca, 1646; and ret. to Boston had John, 2, bapt. 6 July 1651; perhaps Philip, intermed. He was freem. 6 May 1635, and d. 14 Sept. 1657. His wid. m. 16 Nov. 1660, acc. the rec. wh. I think should be 1659, John Benham; and of the ds. Eliz. m. 6 May 1656 Joseph Soper, and Mary m. 27 Sept. 1664, James Robinson of Dorchester. THOMAS, Hartford. — See Olcott.

ALDBURG, JOHN, a youth of 14, came in the Francis, 1634, under William Freeborne. — See Alborow.

ALDEN, *DAVID, Duxbury, s. of John of the Mayflower, was rep. 1689 and 90, after the overthrow of Andros; but Farmer was, I doubt, under mistake in making him Assist. 1690; and Winsor follow. him. His w. was Mary, d. of Constant Southworth, by wh. he had Benjamin, Samuel, and Alice. ‡*JOHN, Plymouth, passeng. in the first ship 1620, had not been assoc. at Leyden with the pilgrims, but was hired at Southampton as a cooper, with right of staying on this side or return. m. 1623, Priscilla, d. of William Mullins, wh. as well as his w. d. the first Feb. after land. We kn. only eight ch. by their names, John, b. perhaps 1623; Joseph, David, Jonathan, Eliz., Sarah, Ruth, and Mary; but in Bradford we find h. and w. liv. in 1650, "and have eleven ch. and their eldest d. hath five ch." Of these in May 1627, at the div. of cattle, only John and Eliz. are named, so that the other nine were b. later, but their dates of b. are not heard. He liv. most of his days at Duxbury, was rep. 1641, yet had been chos. an Assist. for the Col. 1633, to Gov. Winslow, and serv. 42 yrs. in that office, to every Gov. after Carver. Idly would tradit. attempt to magnify his merit, as the first to jump upon the rock at Plymouth land. when he was not of the party in the shallop that discov. the harbor, but contin. on board ship at Cape Cod. He was the last male surv. of the signers of the compact in that harbor, Nov. 1620, and d. 12 Sept. 1687, aged 84, or, by other acco. 88. Of the ds. Eliz. m. 18 Dec. 1644, William Peabody and d. 3 May 1717, aged 94, says her gr. stone; Sarah m. Alexander Standish; Ruth m. 12 May (Winsor has it 3 Feb.) 1657, John Bass of Braintree; and Mary m. Thomas Delano. JOHN, Duxbury, eldest s. of the preced. rem. to Boston, where the rec. says, perhaps erroneous. by w. Eliz. he had Mary, b. 17 Dec. 1659, for that date may be of d. of his w. since 1 Apr. foll. he m. (I suppose as sec. w.) Eliz. d. of William Phillips, and wid. of Abiel Everill, had John, b. 20 Nov. foll. d. soon; Eliz. 9 May 1662, d. at 2 mos.; John, again, 12 Mar. 1663; William, 16 Mar. 1664, d. soon; Eliz. again, 9 Mar. 1665; William, again, 5 Mar. 1666, d. soon; Zechariah, 8 Mar. 1667, d. soon; William, again, 10 Sept. 1669; Nathaniel, 1670; Zechariah, again, 18 Feb. 1673, H. C. 1692; Nathan, 17 Oct. 1677; and Sarah, 27 Sept. 1681. In the witchcraft madness of 1692, he suffer. many weeks imprisonm. as Calef and Hutch. II. 48, relate, yet recover. from the popul. persecut. and d. 14 Mar. 1702. His d. Eliz. m. John Walley, possib. gr.s. of Rev. Thomas; and next 30 Apr. 1702, Simon Willard, but this union is not clear to me. As his s. John had w. Eliz. it is diffic. from the Boston rec. to tell wh. John and Eliz. had the latest b. It might as easily be infer. that the witchcraft belong. to the

s. as the f., and indeed Thayer in his Geneal. makes the younger the suffer. in wh. he is foll. by Winsor, contrary to the general import of Calef and Hutchinson. With them I concur, for the s. was only 29 yrs. old, and more venerable age is usually found liable to assaults by the great adversary for such cases. JONATHAN, Duxbury, br. of the preced. m. 10 Dec. 1672, Abigail, d. of Andrew Hallet, had Andrew, Jonathan, John and Benjamin; but no dates are found for either. The two former, it is said, went to Lebanon. He was bur. 17 Feb. 1698, aged 70, says fam. tradit. and his wid. d. 17 Aug. 1725, aged 81. JOSEPH, Duxbury, br. prob. elder, of the preced. m. Mary, d. of Moses Simmons, rem. early to Bridgewater, had Isaac; Joseph, b. 1668; John, and, perhaps Eliz. and Mary; and d. 8 Feb. 1697. The ds. were m. one bef. and one after. From the passeng. in the Mayflower are fill. with details of descend. 28 pages of Thayer's Geneal. and in Collect. of Epitaphs, by Rev. Timothy Alden, compris. in 5 vols. is seen large proof of filial gratitude. Of this name eight had been gr. at Harv. in 1834, and two at Yale.

ALDERMAN, JOHN, Dorchester 1634, Salem 1636, when Jane, prob. his w. was mem. of the ch. had gr. of ld. at S. 1637, freem. 22 May 1639, d. 1657. See Winth. I. 144; and Felt, Ann. I. 171. WILLIAM, Windsor, 1672, soon after at Simsbury, m. 1679, Mary, d. of John Case of S. had Mary, b. 22 Sept. 1680; Thomas, 11 Jan. 1683; William, 20 Oct. 1686; Sarah, 1692; John, 1695; and Joseph, 1697; and d. at Farmington, 1697. His wid. m. 30 Mar. 1699, James Hillyer.

ALDIS, DANIEL, Dedham, s. of deac. John of the same, m. 23 Nov. 1685, Sarah Paine, perhaps d. of the sec. Moses of Braintree, had Sarah, b. 16 Oct. 1686; Daniel, 2 Dec. 1687, d. at 3 mos.; Ann, 21 Aug. 1692; Sarah, 27 Aug. 1695. His w. d. 17 Apr. 1711; and he d. 21 Jan. 1717; and this marks the last appear. of the fam. name on the town rec. His will made two days bef. names w. Sarah, s. in law William Bacon, d. Ann w. of Jonathan Onion, and gr.s. William Bacon; and may be seen in Vol. XX. 166. JOHN, Dedham, s. of Nathan, b. in Eng. m. 27 Sept. 1650, Sarah, d. of Philip Eliot of Roxbury, were both adm. of the ch. 29 Dec. foll. had Sarah, b. 9 June 1652, yet not bapt. bef. 12 June 1653; John, 12, bapt. 18 Feb. 1655; Mary, 29 Nov. 1657; Nathaniel, 1 Aug. 1659, d. at 2 yrs.; Daniel, 3 Aug. 1661; Nathaniel, again, 6 Mar. 1664, d. at 19 yrs. and Hannah, 4 July 1666. He was deac. and his w. d. 12 Nov. 1686; and he d. 21 Dec. 1700. Sarah m. 26 Apr. 1675, Gershom Hubbard; and Mary m. 21 Feb. 1679, Nathaniel Richards. JOHN, Dedham, s. of the preced. by w. Mary had Ruth, b. 14 Aug. 1695; and no more is heard of h. w. or ch. in D. but he had liv. at Wrentham, m. 23 May 1682, Mary Winchester, had Sarah, b. 26 Feb. foll.; Ethan, 11 May 1685; and Hannah, 19 Feb. 1688. NATHAN, Dedham, with w.

join. the ch. early in 1640 and 1641, respectiv. They had brot. from Eng. certain. Mary, wh. m. 15 Mar. 1643, Joshua Fisher, and perhaps other ch. beside John, bef. ment. He was made freem. 13 May 1640, was chos. one of the first two deac. and d. 15 Mar. 1676. The wid. named Mary, d. 1 Jan. foll. but she and s. John had admin.

ALDRIDGE, or ALDRICH, GEORGE, Dorchester, freem. 7 Dec. 1636, by w. Catharine had, beside Miriam, bur. 27 Jan. 1640; and Experience, wh. d. 2 Feb. 1642; and at Braintree, John, b. 2 Apr. 1644; Sarah, 16 Jan. 1646; Peter, 14 Apr. 1648; Mercy, 17 June 1650; Miriam, again, wh. d. 1 Dec. 1651, or 10 Mar. 1652, as the rec. reads; Jacob, 28 Feb. 1653; and Mattithiah, 10 July 1656. He was one of the first sett. at Mendon, 1663. GEORGE, Swanzey, 1669. HENRY, Dedham, had Mary, b. 19 Mar. 1643, d. soon; Samuel, 10 Mar. 1645; and perhaps bef. sett. at D. Thomas; was freem. 1645, and d. 23 Feb. 1646. His w. Mary, perhaps mo. of all these ch. m. Samuel Judson, wh. 7 June 1657 provid. by his will for her two s. and she next m. John Hayward, and outliv. him. JOHN, Braintree, s. of George, m. 31 Oct. 1678, Sarah, d. of Giles Leach of Bridgewater, if there be no error of date, for by w. Sarah he had Joseph, b. 25 Sept. 1676; and Jacob, 27 Dec. 1677; but that w. d. 25 Feb. foll. as is said. Perhaps there were two ws. JOSEPH, Braintree, perhaps br. of the preced. m. 26 Feb. 1662, Patience Osborne of Weymouth, perhaps d. of John, had Joseph, b. 14 July 1663; and Sarah, 27 Oct. 1677. ROBERT, Braintree, perhaps m. 25 Dec. 1656. THOMAS, Dedham, s. perhaps of Henry, m. 4 May 1675, Eliz. d. of the brave Capt. Thomas Prentice, wh. d. 5 Feb. foll. and he m. 16 Jan. 1678, Hannah, d. of Nathaniel Colburn, had Hannah, 17 Dec. 1679; John, 8 May 1681; Mary, 5 Aug. 1683; and Thomas, 17 Apr. 1685; was freem. 1677, and d. 23 Oct. 1694. With spell. of Aldrich four had been in 1829, gr. at Brown Univ. and none at Harv. or Yale. Perhaps this name bec. Eldridge sometimes.

ALEWORTH, FRANCIS, Dorchester, freem. 18 May 1631, went home the foll. yr. tho. he had been by the Court of Assist. in July, chos. lieut. of the comp. Ano. man with this surname, at the Court in Mar. 1631, was order. to go, "as unmeet. to inhab. here."

ALEXANDER, DANIEL, Windsor, s. of George, wound. in Philip's war, liv. after at Northampton, and d. unm. 1686, at Suffield. DAVID, Northampton, br. of Robert, bec. 3d h. of Eliz. wid. of Samuel Langton, d. of wid. Eliz. Copley. GEORGE, Windsor, m. 18 Mar. 1644, Susanna Sage, as by Parsons, in Geneal. Reg. V. 63, the surname is giv. (whose correctness is doubt. by scrupul. readers of the orig. rec. when the bapt. name is Susanna alone, not as print. "Su Sage;" and beside the date of the m. is not clear on that rec.) had (he says) John, b. 25 July 1645; (yet high

authority advises me, that the oldest ch. was prob. Abigail) ; a ch. wh. d.
1647, prob. very young; Mary, 20 Oct. 1648; Daniel, 12 Jan. 1651;
Nathaniel, 29 Dec. 1652 ; and Sarah, 8 Dec. 1654; rem. to Northampton, and d. 5 May 1703. Abigail, m. 16 June 1663, Thomas Webster;
Mary, m. 23 Sept. 1670, Micah Mudge; and Sarah, m. 6 July 1678,
Samuel Curtis. JAMES, Boston, serv. of Theodore Atkinson, d. 19 Aug.
1644. JOHN, Northampton, s. of George, m. 28 Nov. 1671, Sarah Gaylord, perhaps d. of Samuel of the same, had John, b. 24 Jan. 1673 ;
Nathaniel, Mar. 1676; Samuel, 6 Nov. 1678; Joseph, 16 Oct. 1681 ;
Ebenezer, 17 Oct. 1684; Sarah, 7 Feb. 1688; Thankful, 29 Mar. 1691 ;
and Eliz. His w. d. 3 Nov. 1732, and he d. 31 Dec. 1733. One of the
s. Ebenezer, a deac. of Northfield, was gr.f. of Caleb, Y. C. 1777, min.
of Mendon, translat. of Virgil, formerly well kn. to idle school boys.
JOHN, Newton, by w. Beatrice had Martha, b. 16 July 1668; Deliverance, 7 Jan. 1672 ; and Eliz. 16 Sept. 1674 ; was active in promot. separat. of the new town from old Cambridge, 1678, and d. 1696. JOHN,
New Hampsh. 1686, may have liv. at Groton, 1691. NATHANIEL,
Northampton, s. of George, m. 20 Jan. 1680, Hannah, d. of Samuel Allen,
had Hannah, d. 27 Oct. foll. few days old; Hannah, again, 26 Sept. 1681;
Ruth, 22 Feb. 1691; Thankful, 9 Jan. 1694; Thomas, 9 Apr. 1696, wh.
was drown. unm. ; Daniel, 14 Jan. 1699, d. young; beside Mindwell,
Sarah, and Abigail, whose dates are not ascert. perhaps b. after Hannah,
and bef. Ruth, but not rec. He d. 29 Oct. 1742, at Hadley, whither he
rem. late in life to live with a d. having no s. liv. ROBERT, Deerfield,
d. 1689, leav. "aged parents," unkn. to us, and giv. his prop. to brs. and
sis. John, David, Dorothy, w. of John Stebbins, Mary, w. of Benjamin
Barret, Martha, Deliverance, and Eliz. ROBERT, Boston, 1684, a Scotchman, may be the same as the preced. but not prob. and certain. is not
seen among the taxab. inhabs. of 1695. THOMAS, one of the comp. of
Capt. Lathrop, call. "the flower of Essex," k. in the fight at "Bloody
brook," 18 Sept. 1675. Of this name, in 1828, Farmer notes the gr. at
Yale were two, none at other N. E. coll. but eleven at N. J. and Union
Coll. Yet he might have found one at Dart.

ALFORD, ‖ BENJAMIN, Boston, merch. prob. s. of William, ar. co. 1671,
by w. Mary, d. of James Richards, Esquire, of Hartford, had Mary, b.
15 Sept. bapt. 14 Oct. 1683 ; John, bapt. (at third, or O. S. ch.) 5 July
1685 ; Benjamin, b. 5, bapt. 10 Oct. 1686; Judith, bapt. 16 Sept. 1688 ;
James, 19, bapt. 26 July 1691 ; Sarah, 17, bapt. 18 Mar. 1694 ; and
Thomas, whose date is not found. He had been a prisoner in Barbary,
and after ret. was a man of importance in B. His will of 19 Feb. 1697,
pro. thirteen yrs. after, provid. for all the ch. and w. wh. with his br. in
law, Benjamin Davis, he made Excors. The eldest s. John, wh. had good

est. was of Charlestown, m. 12 Nov. 1713, Margaret, d. of Col. Thomas Savage, third of that name, and d. 30 Sept. 1761, disting. as founder of the Alford Prof. of Nat. Theol. &c. at Harv. and for giv. large sum to the Soc. for Prop. Gosp. among the Ind. &c. in N. A. His w. outliv. him; but he had no issue. JOHN, Salem, 1668. REMAIN, New London, wh. d. 12 Aug. 1709, aged 63, by Miss Caulkins is styled Col. yet of unkn. desc. WILLIAM, Salem, 1635, came the yr. bef. from London, a mem. of the Skinners' comp. there, a merch. here; and his w. Mary in 1636 join. to the ch. had Nathaniel, bapt. 19 Mar. 1637; Samuel, 17 Feb. 1639; Bethia, 26 June 1642; beside Elisha, Mary, and Eliz. See a valu. letter of 13 Apr. 1634 brot. by him from Francis Kirbey to his fr. John Winthrop, s. of the Gov. print. in 3 Mass. Hist. Coll. IX. 267. He had favor. the party of Wheelwright, and under the name of Mr. Alfoot on the rec. in 1637, was disarm. by the Gen. Ct. and thereupon rem. for a season to New Haven, and there had, prob. two or more of his ch. b. bef. 1654. See Haz. II. 247. Yet he came back to Mass. but liv. at Boston; and by ano. w. Ann had John, b. 29 Nov. 1658, wh. d. at 2 mos. He d. Jan. 1677, was bur. 13th of that mo. being Saturday. The will of 13 Apr. with codic 9 July 1676, names no s. as then liv. but he gives £50 to ch. of his s. Nathaniel, if now alive, and £10 to wid. of s. Elisha, and made Extrix. his d. Mary, that had been w. of Peter Butler, and next of Hezekiah Usher, and had four ch. and ment. ds. Bethia, and Eliz. wh. had m. 1 Dec. 1659, Nathaniel Hudson. The whole of the debt of Hudson Leverett, and half of those of other poor debtors are remit. by it; and the codic was made, because his d. Mary had bec. w. of Hezekiah Usher, wh. was then d. She took third h. Samuel Nowell, outliv. him, and d. 14 Aug. 1693.

ALGER, ANDREW, Scarborough, 1651, had w. Agnes, and ch. John; Andrew; and Matthew; Eliz. wh. m. John Palmer; Joanna, wh. m. Elias Oakman, and, next, John Mills, both of Boston; beside a third d. wh. m. John Ashton, or Austin. He had call. his planta. Dunster, from the town near Minehead, in the N. W. part of Co. Somerset, where he was b. was constable 1661, and lieut. k. by the Ind. with his br. Arthur, Oct. 1675. The fam. fled to Boston, his will was pro. in Essex 24 June foll. and his wid. m. Samuel Walker. See Folsom, 156; and Willis, I. 139, wh. obs. that, in our days, the est. of the Southgate fam. includes part of the Alger domain. ANDREW, Falmouth, s. of the preced. was k. by the Ind. when they destroy. the town 1690, leav. only ch. the wife, it is said, of Matthew Collins. *ARTHUR, Scarborough, br. of the first Andrew, perhaps elder, perhaps was f. of that Arthur, jr. wh. own. alleg. to Mass. 1658; was constable 1658, rep. to Boston, 1671, when the Secretary makes his name Angurs, and 1672, when he cuts off the final

letter, was k. by the Ind. 1675, with his br. leav. wid. Ann, and childr.
but their names are not told. See Hubbard's Hist. of N. E. 600, and
Willis, as above. ISRAEL, Bridgewater, s. of Thomas, m. Patience, d. of
Nathaniel Hayward of the same, had Israel, b. 1689; Joseph, 1691;
Thomas, 1697; Nathaniel, 1700; and John, 1704. JOHN, Scarborough,
s. of Andrew the first, had sev. ds. of wh. Eliz. m. John Millikin. Willis.
MATTHEW, Scarborough, br. of the preced. and the last male of the fam.
d. 1690 of fever from the service in the sad expedit. of 1690 by Sir William Phips against Quebec, in wh. he command. a vessel, and got safe
back. Ib. SAMPSON, York, 1649, then of the gr. jury, freem. 1652,
constable, 1655. He may have been relat. of the foregoing fam. but the
name is variously writ. the sec. letter often being *u*, agreeing with the
sound, and when it is *n*, looking doubtful, whether Anger, or Angier, as
by the scrupulous Paige in Geneal. Reg. III. 193, or Angur, as by the
same hand on the next page, or Augur, as the same MS. is read by the
Editor of Mass. Col. Rec. IV, pt. I. page 358. THOMAS, Taunton, 1665,
m. 14 Nov. of that yr. Eliz. d. of Samuel Packard, had Israel, and Deliverance, perhaps others, bef. or after rem. to Bridgewater. Mitchell
shows, in his Hist. that most of this name in that vicin. call him their
anc. TRISTRAM, Scarborough.

ALISET, or ALLISET, JOHN, Boston 1689, chos. an overseer of cord
wood, as also in 1691, yet not found among taxab. inhab. of 1695.

ALLARD, HUGH, New Hampsh. 1674. One Eliz. A. m. 10 Dec.
1634, Robert Seaver at Roxbury; and this may well be thot. mistake
for Ballard, as the ch. rec. has it; yet no Ballard is kn. in R. so early by
many yrs. and a Mrs. Allard d. there 11 Aug. 1717, but she may have
been a Huguenot of later importa.

ALLARE, LOUIS, Boston, a Huguenot, adm. inhab. 1 Feb. 1692, but
in 1695 not seen.

ALLEN, ABRAHAM, Marblehead 1674. ALEXANDER, Windsor 1689,
a Scotchman, m. 1693, Mary Grant, had Alexander, b. 1695; John,
1697; and Mary, 1702; and by sec. w. Eliz. m. 1704, d. of John Allyn,
the famous Secr. of the Col. had Fitz John. He d. 19 Aug. 1708, by
his will made three days bef. dispos. of large prop. to ch. something to
brs. William and Robert at home, and £5. to the Scot's box in Boston.
His wid. m. John Gardiner, Esqr. of Gardiner's isl. ANDREW, Lynn
1642, m. Faith, d. of Edmund Ingalls, rem. to Andover, there d. 24
Oct. 1690. He left Andrew and John, both d. the next mo. after. AN-
DREW, Andover, s. of the preced. m. 1 Jan. 1682, Eliz. Richardson, had
Thomas, wh. d. 18 Dec. 1690, of smallpox, as had the f. 26 Nov. preced.
ARNOLD, Casco 1645, had w. Mary. BENJAMIN, Groton 1674, may have
been a soldier next yr. in Moseley's comp. for the Dec. campaign. BEN-

JAMIN, Salisbury, s. of William the first of same, m. 3 Sept. 1686, Rachel, wid. of Henry Wheeler, had Eliz. b. 6 Sept. 1687 ; Benjamin, 20 May 1689 ; Squire (so reads the rec.), 26 Mar. 1691 ; Jeremiah, 25 Mar. 1693 ; and no more is told. * ‖ BOZOAN, BOZOUN, or BEZOONE, Hingham 1638, came from Lynn, Co. Norfolk, arr. with w. and two serv. in the Diligent from Ipswich, was freeman 2 June 1641, rep. 1643, and 7 yrs. more, but not in seq. last in 1652 ; of ar. co. 1650, rem. to Boston, made his will 9 Sept. 1652, and d. 5 days after. In the Hist. of Winth. II. 221–236 his political promin. appears. His wid. Ann bore him, posthum. Bozoan, 13 Feb. 1653 ; and m. 13 May foll. Joseph Jewett of Rowley, and d. 4 Feb. 1661. His d. Martha m. Ebenezer Savage of Boston. *BOZOAN, Boston, s. of the preced. b. after his d. m. 1673, Rachel, d. of Jeremiah Houchin, wh. he succeed. in his gr. business, as a tanner, had ano. w. Lydia in 1679, was constable 1680, freeman 1682, one of the selectmen 1692, and rep. 1700. CALEB, Sandwich, eldest s. of George the sec. m. 8 Apr. 1670, Eliz. Sisson, had Richard, b. 8 Oct. 1673 ; Mary, 29 Feb. 1676 ; George, 19 May 1678 ; Hannah, 5 Nov. 1680 ; Caleb, 20 Mar. 1683 ; Eliz. 3 Dec. 1685 ; and James, 17 June 1689. *DANIEL, Boston, physician, by w. Mariana had John, b. 19 June 1680 ; Mary, 30 June 1681 ; Catharine, 15 Dec. 1682 ; Daniel, 6 Dec. 1683, d. young ; Benjamin, 26 Apr. 1687 ; and Daniel, again, 27 July 1688 ; was chos. rep. Sept. 1693, and d. 7 Nov. foll. His will of 17 Nov. preced. with codic. of 22d of the same, provides for w. and ch. as they attain full age. DANIEL, Charlestown, s. of Walter of the same, perhaps b. in Eng. but not prob. by w. Mary, d. of Rev. John Sherman by his first w. had David, b. 1 July 1659 ; Rebecca, 15 Jan. 1661, d. in 10 days ; rem. to Watertown, and had Mary, 1662 ; rem. to Lancaster, there had Samuel, 17 Apr. 1664 ; and Elnathan, 11 Feb. 1666 ; again rem. to W. and had Abigail ; Thomas, 1670, wh. d. next yr. ; Ebenezer, 26 Dec. 1674 ; Eliz. and Lydia. He may be that gent. nam. in an order of President Dudley's Counc. 8 Dec. 1686, relat. to Secretary's rec. See 3 Mass. Hist. Coll. VII. 162. He d. 7 Mar. 1694, and his neighb. Lawrence Hammond, highly extols his charact. in the Diary. Bond, wh. must be in error, as to his d. at Sudbury 1706, says, his s. David serv. in the expedit. to Canada, and d. 17 Oct. 1711 ; that Abigail m. Moses Palmer of Stonington ; and Eliz. m. Joseph Fletcher. One David, not his s. d. at Portsmouth, R. I. 10 Feb. 1685, aged 17. DANIEL, Swanzey, by w. Mary had Eliz. b. 28 Sept. 1673 ; and Christian, 26 Jan. 1675. DANIEL, Sandwich, sixth s. of George of the same, m. Bashua, d. of Ludowic Haxie, had Gideon, b. 17 May 1686 ; Hannah, 7 June 1688 ; Cornelius ; Daniel ; and Lydia. EDWARD, Ipswich, acc. a very doubtful tradit. came from Scotland, 1636, m. a Kimball, and had, as runs

the same story, fifteen s. and three ds. That acco. was giv. by Hon.
Samuel C. Allen to Farmer. In the Hist. of Hubbard, wh. was his
neighb. the burn. of his barn, 1670, is ment. With w. Sarah, wh. d. 12
June 1696, he rem. to Suffield, having had nine ch. and there had one, b.
1683; and ano. 1685. Of seven s. the names are told, but without dates,
exc. John, wh. is said to have been b. a. 1660, and was k. by the Ind.
11 May 1704 at Deerfield, where he had liv. from 1685; Edward, wh.
also liv. at D. there d. 1740, leav. a fam. William, wh. d. at Suffield,
1702; Benjamin, the anc. of Hon. Samuel C. had Joseph, wh. sett. at
Deerfield; David, and Samuel, both, it is said, went to N. J. and Caleb,
b. 31 Mar. 1685, prob. the youngest. Four ds. too are nam. Sarah, wh.
m. 21 Apr. 1685, Edward Smith; Martha, wh. m. Samuel Kent, jr.;
Abigail, m. Timothy Palmer; and Mary, of wh. nothing is told. ED-
WARD, Dedham, perhaps nephew of Edward Alleyn of the same, may
have been that Edward of Boston, a tailor, wh. m. 7 May 1652, Martha
Way, had Sarah, b. 22 Aug. 1653; and John, 8 June 1657. EDWARD,
Dover 1675, was s. of Hope of Boston, as such, sold 13 Nov. 1678, large
est. at Falmouth, now Portland, devis. to him from his f. After dilig.
inquiry I can learn no more of him. ELEAZER, emb. 27 May 1679 in
the Prudence and Mary, to come to Boston from Eng. but his visit may
have been only a trans. one, or he may have gone beyond the bounds of
N. E. at least we never again find his name. FRANCIS, Sandwich 1643,
m. 20 July 1662, Mary Barlow had Rachel, b. 3 July 1663; Abigail, 2
Aug. 1665; Abia, 10 Dec. 1666; Rebecca, 2 Aug. 1668; and Hannah,
25 Aug. 1672. * GEORGE, Lynn 1636, rem. next yr. to Sandwich, was
rep. 1641 and 2 at Plymouth. He was bur. 2 May 1648; and his will,
witness. by Rev. William Leveridge, and others, ment. s. Matthew, Henry, Samuel, and William, beside " five least ch." not nam. and made w.
Catharine Extrix. His ho. built, 1646, it is said, is in good repair, and
still occup. GEORGE, Sandwich 1643, perhaps s. of the preced. b. in
Eng. then in the list of those able to bear arms; may have been of Newport 1639, and at S. had (by w. Hannah) Caleb, b. 24 June 1646, or by
ano. acco. 1648; Judah, 14 or by ano. rec. 30 Jan. 1651; Ephraim, 14
Jan. 1653; Eliz. 20 Jan. 1655; James, and John, tw. 5 Aug. 1657, or
1658; Lydia, May 1660; Daniel, 23 May 1663; Hannah, 15 May
1666; and George, 20 June 1672. GEORGE, Weymouth 1641, rem. to
Boston, and by w. Susanna had Hannah, b. 10 Mar. 1645; Naomi, 26
Dec. 1646; Rachel, or Ruth, 3 Oct. 1648; Susanna, 11 May 1652; and
Elnathan, 26 Dec. 1653; but of his identity some doubt may be felt, for
in the list of freem. 1645 is a George, who prob. was not of Boston.
GIDEON, Swanzey 1669, rem. to Boston during Philip's war, and after it
to Milford, there was a promin. man, and d. early in 1693. At Swan-

zey, by w. Sarah he had John, b. 24 Oct. 1673, wh. d. bef. his f. He left wid. and five ch. Gideon; Sarah, and George, tw. 18 yrs. old; Hannah, 7, and Abigail, 4. His sec. w. was Ann, d. of Nathaniel Burr of Fairfield. * HENRY, Boston, a joiner, was of the ch. May 1644, freem. 1648, was prob. the deac. wh. by w. Judith had Judith, b. 26 Nov. 1673; Samuel, 12 Jan. 1675; Ebenezer, 30 Jan. 1676; Ephraim, 4 Jan. 1677; Joseph, 15 Sept. 1678; Henry, 8 July 1680; Benjamin, 4 Apr. 1682; and John, 17 Sept. 1683. He was rep. for Rowley 1674, and d. 6 Jan. 1696, leav. good est. but no will. HENRY, Milford 1660, by w. Sarah had Mary, b. 1663; Sarah, 1666; Miriam, 1669; Mercy, 1671; Henry, 1674; Frances, 1676; and George, 1678. His w. d. 1680; and he d. at Stratford, 1690. Both the s. were proprs. at M. 1713. By Lambert he is placed at M. 1645, and call. anc. of Col. Ethan Allen; but in ea. statem. he is erron. HOPE, Boston 1651, a currier, by w. Rachel had Jacob, b. 22 Feb. 1654; Joseph, 4 Oct. 1655; Leah, 16 May 1657, d. in few mos. Mary; and Benjamin; the last two, with the first two, and ano. Leah, yet call. Rachel, were bapt. 16 Sept. 1666. An elder s. Edward liv. at Dover, to wh. we learn from Willis invalua. Hist. of Portland I. 73, 159 he had devis. large part of an est. by him purchas. of George Cleves, wh. is the most beautif. quarter of the present city. When he d. is not kn. but it must have been bef. Nov. 1678, when George Bramhall purch. of the devisee. He left wid. Hannah, wh. m. Richard Knight bef. 1683. ISAAC, Rehoboth, m. 30 May 1673, Mary Bowen, perhaps d. of Henry, had Isaac, b. 3 Jan. 1675; Catharine, 18 Jan. of uncert. yr. the rec. being partially worn away. JAMES, Dedham 1639, freem. 1647, in Medfield 1652, by w. Ann had John, b. 4 Dec. 1639; Mary and Martha, tw. 11 Dec. 1641; Sarah, 4 May 1644; Joseph, 24 June 1652; besides James, Nathaniel, William, and Benjamin, prob. bef. and after the last ment. He d. 27 Sept. 1673. Some reason is perceiv. for holding this man to be br. of Rev. John Allin of Dedham. JAMES, Boston, one of the eject. min. was s. of a min. in Hampsh. and b. 24 June 1632, as is told, ent. of Magdalen Hall, 16 Mar. 1649, and of New Coll. Oxford, proceed. A. M. and was one of the fellows; arr. at Boston, 10 June 1662, m. 18 Aug. 1663, Hannah, d. of Richard Dummer, wh. d. 26 Feb. 1668, aged 21, prob. without ch. Soon he m. sec. w. Eliz. wid. of the sec. John Endicott, d. of Jeremiah Houchin, had Hannah, b. 22 July 1669; James, 24 Aug. 1670, H. C. 1689; John, 29 Feb. 1672; and Jeremiah, 27 Mar. 1673, wh. in 1715 was Treasr. of the Prov. His w. d. 5 Apr. after, and he m. 11 Sept. 1673, third w. Sarah, wid. of Robert Breck, d. of Capt. Thomas Hawkins (the names of both her f. and of her former h. being strangely pervert. in Drake's Hist. of Boston, 339), had Thomas, 20 May 1675, d. in few wks.

and Sarah, 11 Sept. 1679, wh. d. at 3 yrs. After some yrs. preach. there,
he was sett. in the midst of gr. disquiet, at the first ch. on the same day,
with Davenport (9 Dec. 1668), in vindicat. of whose charact. he was long
a strenuous oppon. of the third, or O. S. ch. that sprang out of the unhappy
circumst. by wh. he was brot. from New Haven. His last w. d. 25 Nov.
1705, and he d. 22 Sept. 1710. Dunton says, his s. James was a min. in
Eng. and d. at Northampton, but perhaps he is wrong, for he was young,
and our Coll. Catal. never gave him the Italics, tho. it marks him as Socius.
See 2 Mass. Hist. Coll. II. 101 and 3 M. H. C. VIII. 250. Both of the
Biogr. Dict. Eliot, briefly, and Allen, more at large, explain the difficult.
of his course. JAMES, Sandwich, perhaps s. of George the first, had
Amey, b. 22 Dec. 1665; and Abigail, 28 Sept. 1667, and prob. sev. others, yet it may be that some were b. after rem. to Tisbury, had w. Eliz.
and d. 25 July 1714, aged 77, leav. many descend. JEDEDIAH, Sandwich, m. Experience, d. of James Swift, had Experience, b. 30 Aug.
1670, d. soon; Experience, again, 30 Dec. 1671 ; Eliashib, 17 Oct. 1672 ;
Judah, 17 Oct. 1675 ; and Esther, 26 Mar. 1677. JEREMIAH, Salisbury,
s. of William the first of the same, took o. of alleg. 2 Dec. 1677, m.
1686, Ann, prob. d. of Thomas Bradbury. JOHN, Plymouth 1633, was
perhaps of Scituate, 1646, there d. 1662, prob. Sept. as his inv. bears
date 25 of that mo. leav. wid. Ann and s. John; but his nuncup. will,
made two days bef. his d. in wh. one ho. is giv. to Josiah Litchfield (then
a youth) in wh. the testator liv. and ano. to his w. was not pro. until 2
June of next yr. and that would now-a-days seem a dangerous delay.
See Geneal. Reg. VI. 94. JOHN, Dorchester 1632, kept an inn, and
was punish. for drunkenness of those to wh. that yr. he sold. * ‖ JOHN,
Charlestown, came, perhaps, in the Abigail, 1635, aged 30, with w. Ann,
30, from some part of Kent, join. the ch. 22 May 1641, and was adm.
freem. 2 June next; by w. Sarah had John, b. 16 Oct. 1640, bapt. 30
May foll.; Sarah, b. 11 Aug. 1642, d. at 4 mos.; Mary, 6 Feb. 1644 ;
and perhaps others, certain. Rebecca bef. Samuel, 29 Nov. 1656; and
Sarah, again, 11 May 1659, d. at 2 mos. He was of ar. co. 1639, and,
in 1657, the richest man in the town, a capt. and rep. 1668, and d. 27
Mar. 1675. His d. Mary m. Jonathan Rainsford, and next Joshua Hobart. See Budington, 249. By Sewall he is call. br. of Rev. Thomas,
if such be the mean. of the interleav. Almanac, giv. in Geneal. Reg.
VII. 206. JOHN, Springfield 1639, then tax. there, rem. soon, perhaps
to Rehoboth 1643, and to Newport 1651, thence to Swanzey 1669. Certain. one John at Newport m. 10, or 14 Oct. 1650, Eliz. Bacon, perhaps
sis. of Nathaniel of Barnstable, there had Eliz. b. July 1651 ; Mary, 4
Feb. 1653 ; John, Nov. 1654; Mercy, Dec. 1656 ; Priscilla, Dec. 1659 ;
and Samuel, Apr. 1661. JOHN, Newbury, had John, b. 28 Aug. 1656;

Samuel, 8 Apr. 1658; Joseph, 18 Mar. 1660; and Benjamin, 30 Jan. 1662. JOHN, New Haven, youngest s. of the first Samuel of the same, had Eliz. b. 11 Sept. 1653; Lydia, 26 Dec. 1656; both bapt. 23 May 1658; Hannah, 26 July, bapt. 27 Nov. 1659; Mary, 25 Feb. 1662, bapt. 30 Mar. foll.; John, 13 Dec. 1663, bapt. 13 Feb. foll.; and Sarah, 19 Nov. 1666, tho. the rec. of her b. is 25 Nov. unless in Geneal. Reg. IX. 357, a mark is transpos. as much I suspect, or the ch. rec. is careless, as very frequent. we kn. it is. But the true name is Alling (not Allen), in the first generat. as in later ones. See Alling. JOHN, Northampton, m. 8 Dec. 1669, Mary, d. of William Hannum, rem. to Deerfield, there was k. by the Ind. 18 Sept. 1675, the day of Bloody brook, leav. three ch. John, b. 1 Oct. 1670; Samuel, 1673; and Hannah, 1675. JOHN, Medfield, in his will of 2 July 1696, calls hims. aged and sickly, and gave all his prop. to br. Nathaniel, and his heirs. JOHN, Hartford. See Allyn. JOHN, Barnstable, m. Mary Howland, had John, b. 2 Apr. 1674; Mary, 5 Aug. 1675, d. at 2 yrs.; Matthew, 6 Aug. 1677, d. at 3 yrs. and Isaac, 8 Nov. 1679. JOHN, Malden, d. Nov. 1678, aged a. 30, and his wid. Mary d. Jan. next. JOHN, Salisbury, eldest s. of the first William of the same, m. 24 Aug. 1674, Mary, wid. of Jedediah Andros, had Hopestill, b. 11 Nov. foll. if the rec. be true, wh. d. young; Sarah, 9 Feb. 1677; Hopestill, again, 1 Jan. 1681, d. at 3 mos.; Mary, 27 Dec. 1681; Hannah, 22 Oct. 1686; and Ann, 4 Nov. 1689, d. soon; was a lieut. and his w. d. 28 Apr. 1695. He d. 27 Feb. 1697. In the sec. syllab. this name has *i*, instead of *e*, by town rec. JOHN, Marblehead 1668, may have been of Salem twenty yrs. later. JOHN, Sudbury 1681, s. of Walter. JOHN, Suffield, m. 22 Feb. 1682, Eliz. Prichard, had John, b. 21 Dec. foll. d. soon; John, again, 19 Jan. 1684; Richard, 19 Sept. 1685, d. young; rem. to Deerfield, there had Eliz. 1686; Sarah, 1688; Joseph, 1691; Benjamin, 1693; and Ebenezer, 1696. He and his w. were k. by the Ind. 11 May 1704. JONAH, Taunton, had Mary, b. 12 May 1663; Sarah, 4 Nov. 1665; Jonah, 17 Aug. 1667. His w. Constant d. 10 days after, I suppose, tho. by rec. it seems 27 Apr. He m. 14 Dec. foll. Frances Hill of Milton; but I fear the name should be Austin. Ano. Jonah of Taunton, on Col. rec. call. junr. had Esther, b. 3 Jan. 1663, unless there be confus. of names or dates. JOSEPH, Medfield 1649. JOSEPH, Newport, by w. Sarah, m. July 1662, had Abigail, b. 1 Apr. 1663; Rose, 1 Oct. 1665; Joseph, 4 Mar. 1668; John, 15 July 1669; Philip, 3 July 1671; William, 10 Aug. 1673; and perhaps he had own. ld. at Salem 1661. JOSEPH, Gloucester 1674, blacksmith, had Joseph, and d. 1724. JOSEPH, Watertown, s. of Walter, m. 11 Oct. 1667, Ann Brazier, whose f. is not nam. by Bond, but may have been Edward, had Abigail, b. Dec. 1668, d. soon; Rebecca, 8 Apr. 1670, d.

at 4 yrs.; Ann, 22 Aug. 1674, d. at 23 yrs.; Joseph, 16 June 1677;
Sarah; Deborah; Rachel; Nathaniel, 8 Dec. 1687; and Patience. His
w. d. Dec. 1720, and he d. 9 Sept. foll. His will of 15 Jan. 1713, names
w. Ann, two. s. and three youngest ds. and appoints Nathaniel Excor.
*Joseph, Braintree, youngest s. of the first Samuel, m. 30 Jan. 1671,
Ruth Leeds, had Joseph, b. 3 Jan. 1672; where the erron. rec. calls his
mo. Rebecca; Abigail, 28 Feb. 1674; Samuel, 5 Feb. 1676; and Benjamin, 31 Oct. 1679. By sec. w. Rebecca, wh. d. 23 Apr. 1702, he had
Rebecca, 9 Dec. 1681; John, 8 July 1686; and Mary, Mar. 1688. He
m. 27 Jan. 1705, Lydia Holbrook, wid. of Samuel; was town Treasr.,
Selectman, deac. and at last rep. 1715, and d. 20 Mar. 1727. His wid.
made her will 2 Apr. 1745, pro. 11 June foll. Joseph, Rehoboth, m.
10 Nov. 1673, Hannah Sabin. Joseph, Gloucester, s. of Joseph of the
same, m. 29 July 1680, Rachel Griggs, had Joseph, b. 2 June foll. Josiah, Boston, merch. k. by casual dischge. of a gun, 5 Apr. 1678.
Joshua, Yarmouth, had John, b. 20 Sept. 1672; but no more is kn. of
the f. Lewis, Watertown, m. 1664, Sarah, d. of Miles Ives, wh. d. 15
July 1703, had one ch. b. Nov. 1665, d. soon; Lewis, Dec. 1666, d.
soon; Sarah, 3 Jan. 1668; Abel, 15 Sept. 1669; Mary, 14 Apr. 1670;
and Ebenezer. For sec. w. he took a sis. of the first, and d. 24 Jan. 1708.
Matthew, Cambridge. See Allyn. Matthew, Sandwich 1643, s. of
George the first of the same, liv. later at Dartmouth, there (as I learn
from the Quaker rec.) by w. Sarah (whose surname was Kerly), m.
June 1657, had Dorothy, b. 8 Apr. 1659; Miriam, June 1661; Deborah,
May 1663; Samuel, Feb. 1666; Mary, Nov. 1668; Ahazadiah, not s.
27 Apr. 1671; and Matthew, 10 June 1677. Nathaniel, Dedham
1646. Nehemiah, Swanzey 1669, was bur. 24 June 1675, I suppose, a
victim of the first day of Philip's war. Nehemiah, Northampton, s. of
Samuel of Windsor, m. 21 Sept. 1664, Sarah, d. of Thomas Woodford,
had Samuel, b. 3 Jan. 1666; Nehemiah, 18 Oct. 1667, d. soon; Nehemiah, again, 6 Nov. 1669; Sarah, 22 Aug. 1672; Thomas, 17 Jan.
1675, d. next yr.; Hannah, bapt. 6 May 1677; Ruth, perhaps, 5 Jan.
tho. I think it must have been 4th, 1680; a ch. without name, 12 Aug.
1683, d. soon; and Silence, Aug. 1684. His wid. m. 1 Sept. 1687, Richard Burke; and the eldest s. had six ch. b. at Northampton, rem. to
Deerfield and had three more, of wh. Joseph, b. 1708, was f. of Ethan,
wh. gain. celebr. Nicholas, Dorchester, m. 3 July 1663, Mary, wid. of
the sec. Robert Pond, whose fam. name was Ball, and tradit. says, that
she was of Bury St. Edmunds. By her he had one or two ch. and after
his d. she m. Daniel Henshaw, and bore the third h. one ch. In some
rec. this man's name is giv. Ellen. Peter, Roxbury, by w. Mary had
James, b. 6 June 1692; Eliz. 20 Dec. 1694, d. at 14 yrs.; Mary, 17

Aug. 1697 ; and Sarah, 22 Apr. 1701, wh. d. at 8 yrs. PHILIP, perhaps of Rehoboth or that vicin. was a soldier of Gallop's co. 1690, in the ill-starred expedit. against Quebec. RALPH, Newport 1639, Rehoboth 1643, perhaps s. of George the first, and coming this last yr. from Sandwich, had Josiah, b. 3 Jan. 1647 ; Experience, 14 Mar. 1652 ; Ephraim, 20 Mar. 1657 ; beside Mary, bur. 18 Apr. 1675. He was one of the many Quakers imprison. 1659, at Boston, liberat. by order of Charles II. so much to the regret of John Hull and the larger part of our people. RICHARD, Salisbury, had Richard, wh. d. 8 June 1678. ROBERT, Sheepscot 1641, went home in 1658, and gave evidence 21 Feb. 1659, at Bristol, Eng. that he had kn. 17 yrs. in N. E. John Brown, a mason, wh. he left there (perhaps at New Haven, where was his home 1 July 1644), in June preced. in good health. He had resid. 1643, at New Haven, and next yr. took the o. of fidel. ROGER, New Haven. See Alling. SAMUEL, Braintree, perhaps as early as 1632, freem. 6 May 1635, by w. Ann, wh. d. 29 Sept. 1641, had Samuel, b. a. 1633 ; Mary ; Sarah, 30 Mar. 1639 ; and, by w. Margaret, whose f. is unkn. but wh. had been wid. of Edward Lamb, had James ; Abigail ; Joseph, 15 May 1650 ; and perhaps one or two preced. His will of 2 Aug. 1669 was pro. 16 Sept. foll. Mary, m. 24 Jan. 1656, Nathaniel Greenwood ; Sarah, m. Josiah Standish of Duxbury, as his sec. w. and Abigail, m. 1670, the sec. John Cary of the same. SAMUEL, Newport 1639. SAMUEL, Windsor 1636, was not, prob. br. of that Matthew, wh. wrote his name Allyn, as sometimes suppos. tho. he spell. the same way, had Samuel, Nehemiah, John, and Rebecca, beside two others. He was bur. 28 Apr. 1648, and his wid. m. William Hulbert, and with her ch. rem. to Northampton. SAMUEL, Northampton 1657, s. of the preced. m. 29 Nov. 1659, Hannah, d. of Thomas Woodford, had Hannah, b. 4 Feb. 1661 ; Thankful, 15 July 1663 ; Sarah, 28 July 1668 ; Joseph, 20 Nov. 1672 ; Samuel, 6 July 1675 ; Ebenezer, 21 July 1678 ; Thomas, Feb. 1681 ; and Mindwell, 4 Feb. 1683, beside two of unkn. names ; was freem. 1683, and d. 18 Oct. 1719, more than 80 yrs. old. His s. deac. Samuel, wh. m. 1699, Sarah Rust, was gr.f. of Rev. Thomas, H. C. 1762, one of whose s. is Rev. Dr. William, of Northampton, H. C. 1802, late Presid. of Bowdoin Coll. and a laborious author of the Amer. Biograph. Dict. Ed. 3, publ. 1857. * SAMUEL, Bridgewater, s. of Samuel the first, m. a. 1658, Sarah, d. of George Partridge, had Samuel, b. 1660 ; Asahel, perhaps meant by the strange rec. Essiel, 1663 ; Mehitable, 1665 ; Sarah, 1667 ; Bethia, 1669 ; Nathaniel, 1672 ; Ebenezer, 1674 ; Josiah, 1677 ; Elisha, 1679 ; and Nehemiah, 1681 ; and d. 1703, when his age is made 71. He was careful town clk. prais. by Mitchell, and rep. 1693. Descend. are very many. SAMUEL, Manchester, had, prob. s. of the same name, for in the petition from that town, as the head of a Comtee. in Geneal. Reg. X. 322, appears Samuel with suffix of senr. SAMUEL, Barnstable. See Allyn. SAMUEL, Sudbury, m. Eliz. d. of John Grout, had five ch. provid. for in the will of their gr.f. as f. had d. and his wid. m. lieut. John Livermore, by that will call. s. in law. § SAMUEL, Portsmouth, the royal Gov. of N. H. was a merch. of London, late in coming to our country, may for his progeny claim no place in this work. However he had w. Eliz. s. Thomas, and d. Eliz. wh. m. lieut. Gov. John Usher, and three other ds. d. 5 May 1705, only two days after the rep. of N. H. had offer. him proposals that necessarily implied the spuriousness of the gr. Indian deed to Wheelwright of 1629. See Farmer's Ed. of Belkn. I. 162, 3. *THOMAS*, Charlestown, s. of John, b. at Norwich, Co. Norfolk, 1608, bred at Gonville and Caius Coll. in the Univ. of Cambridge, where he took his degr. A. B. 1627–8 and A. M. 1631, came in 1638, and join the ch. of Boston 27 Jan. 1639, then call. "a studyent." was invit. June foll. to Charlestown, there some time bef. had m. Ann, d. of the Rev. Mr. Sadler of Patcham in Co. Sussex, presum. by me to have been wid. of blessed John Harvard, his predecess. as collea. with Rev. Zechariah Symmes. In his Ecclesiast. Ann. I. 379, Mr. Felt makes her accomp. Allen, as his w. but this seems highly improb. as the w. would naturally have unit. with our ch. soon after her h. if not at the same time, whereas no fem. mem. of the name of Allen was rec. into the Boston ch. for a long time after he had been sett. at C. exc. a maiden Eliz. 24 Mar. 1639 wh. two yrs. after m. Rev. Samuel Stone of Hartford. Bef. the coming of Allen, we kn. from the Hist. of the first ch. at Charlestown, by Budington, p. 247, where begins the invalu. catalogue, that "John Harvard and Ann Harvard his w." join. that ch. 6 Nov. 1637. From the Hist. of Harv. Coll. it is kn. that Allen was admor. on est. of Harvard, and paid the moneys bequeath. so that it can hardly be doubt. that the judgment of Felt was at fault, especially as, a few pages earlier, the diligent author had noted, that Harvard's wid. was "supposed to have m. Rev. Thomas Allen." His ch. were Mary, b. 31 Jan. bapt. 13 Feb. 1640; Sarah, 8 Aug. 1641, d. in Apr. foll.; Eliz. 17 Sept. 1643, d. in few days; and Mercy, 13 Aug. 1646, d. in few days. The rec. of bapt. for many yrs. after 1640, is lost. In 1651 he went home, and serv. at the same altar of St. Edmunds, in his native city, where he had officiat. bef. com. hither, when worried out of his diocese, 1636, by Bp. Wren; and again he suffer. in the gen. ejectm. of 1662; yet was with much affection sustain. by the worshipp. at a dissent. chapel, as long as such was tolerat. For a sec. w. he had Joanna, wid. of maj.-gen. Robert Sedgwick, wh. had been drawn to Eng. by partiality of Oliver Cromwell for men from this quarter. She had been of his flock at Charlestown, and prob. bore him no ch. and we hear of no s. but Thomas, wh. was of Lincoln's Inn some time, but resid. at Norwich 1692. The f. d. 21 Sept. 1673. See Frothingham, Budington, 3 Mass. Hist. Coll. VIII. 317, and Berry's Geneal. sub voce Sadler. THOMAS, Middletown. See Allyn. THOMAS, Scituate 1643. THOMAS, Barnstable. See Allyn. TIMOTHY, Marblehead 1648, may have liv. 1670, at Norwich. WALTER, Newbury 1640, there had Abigail, b. 1 Oct. 1641 ; and Benjamin, 15 Apr. 1647 ; and no more is to be seen in Coffin. Certain. he rem. to Watertown, and by w. Rebecca had others, as John, and Daniel (prob. s. of the first w.), wh. liv. at Sudbury, beside Joseph, perhaps all bef. 1657 ; and after d. of his w. he went to Charlestown, there m. 29 Nov. 1678, Abigail Rogers, and d. 8 July 1681. WILLIAM, Salem 1626, comp. of Conant, req. adm. 19 Oct. 1630, and was made freem. 18 May foll. had Samuel, b. 8 Jan. 1632 ; Deborah, bapt. 23 Apr. 1637 ; Bethia, 19 Jan. 1640; Onesiphorus, b. 6 June 1642 ; William, bapt. 31 May 1646; and Jonathan, 29 July 1649 ; but of these only the first came by the first w. as she d. Mar. 1632 ; and tho. the name of Eliz. is giv. by Felt among the earliest ch. mem. he could not mark, whether she were w. of William, much less, whether first or sec. By a depon. he gave 1664, it is judg. that he was b. a. 1602. WILLIAM, Newbury, nam. by Coffin as of Salem 1638, but no support can be found for any other, so early, than him who had then occup. there for twelve yrs. and prob. he is more correct in placing him at Salisbury from 1639 to 50 ;˙m. Ann, d. of Richard Goodale, had Ann, b. 4 Jan. 1640 ; Hannah, 17 June 1642 ; Mary, 29 July 1644 ; Martha, 1646; John, 9 Oct. 1648 ; William, 2 Oct. 1650 ; Benjamin, 1652 ; Joseph, 13 Oct. 1653 ; Richard, 8 Nov. 1655 ; Ruth, 19 Feb. 1658 ; and Jeremiah, 17 Feb. 1659. In Salisbury he is commonly nam. with prefix of respect, as Mr. and he d. 18 June 1686. His will, of 16 Sept. 1674, with codic. 7 Nov. 1676, names w. Ann, wh. d. end of May 1678, s. John, William, Benjamin, Richard, and Jeremiah ; ds. Abigail Wheeler, Hannah Ayer, Mary Hewes, and Martha Hubbard. His wid. Alice d. 1 Apr. 1687. Hannah m. 8 Oct. 1659, Peter Ayer. ˙ WILLIAM, Concord, d. Oct. 1659. WILLIAM, Sandwich, s. prob. of George the first, m. 21 Mar. 1650, Priscilla Browne. WILLIAM, Boston, made his will, ˙15 Dec. 1674, and d. soon. In it he gives all his prop. in hands of Jonathan Tyng, or elsewhere, to Lydia, w. of John Benjamin of Watertown, from wh. Bond seems to be justly authoriz. to infer, that Lydia was his d. but it may be doubted, for on 26 of next mo. John Benjamin renounc. the benefit of the will. She may have been his sis. for the will does not call her d. nor can I find any ch. on Boston rec. of b. but sis. or d. prob. the value of his goods was very small. WILLIAM, Salisbury, s. of William of the same, m. 5 July 1674, Mary, d. of John Harris of Rowley, had William, b. 30 June

1675, d. young; Stitson, 29 Jan. 1677; Ann, 3 May 1678; William, again, 14 June 1680; Abigail, 2 July 1683; Judith, 17 Jan. 1687, d. at 16 yrs.; Dorothy, 12 Aug. 1688; and Mary, 1 Dec. 1692, d. at 10 yrs. He d. 10 May 1700. How often the names of Allin, Allyn, Alling, or Alleyne, with sev. variat. may be found with the same letters as the foregoing, is beyond enumerat. With this spell. are found 27 gr. at Harv., 10 at Yale, and 8 at Dartm., beside 37 at other coll. of N. E. as Farmer saw.

ALLERTON, ISAAC, one of the pilgr. in the Mayflower, at Plymouth, 1620, at one time the richest of the Co. was an Assist. 1621, the sole officer for three yrs. under the Gov. He brot. w. Mary, three ch. Bartholomew, Remember, and Mary. His w. d. 25 Feb. after land. and he m. 1626, Fear, d. of Elder William Brewster, by wh. he had Isaac, H. C. 1650; and prob. no more. This w. d. 1633, and when he liv. at New Haven, 1646, he had third w. Joanna, wh. is honor. after d. of her h. as having giv. shelter to the regicides, Goffe and Whalley, tho. with the usual felicity of tradit. the merit was ascrib. to her gr.d. (then a small ch.) and liv. to 1684. As agent for the Co. he went to Eng. three or four times, but gave not satisfact. in the latter visit; and on his private business was oblig. to go, more than once, of all wh. large statem. is seen in the Hist. of Bradford. In 1643, the Dutch, with wh. he had passed some yrs. having lost the confid. of his early friends bef. 1631, would employ him, with Underhill, to raise from the Eng. a force for their protect. against the Ind. but soon after he was sett. at New Haven, and there d. 1659, insolv. Largely he had speculat. at the Eastward and soon after dismiss. from the Plymouth agency, had a trading-house at Machias, destroy. 1633 by the French, met various disasters by shipwrecks of his fishing vessels, in prosecution of wh. business he sometime was engaged at Marblehead, and join. Salem ch. 1647; but seems almost always unlucky. His eldest s. Bartholomew m. and liv. in Eng. as Bradford first taught us; Remember m. Moses Maverick of Salem; and Mary m. Elder Thomas Cushman, and d. 1699, the last surv. of the blessed band of the first ship, for wh. we may feel suffic. esteem without accept. the report of her being "over 90 yrs. old." Sarah was the name often ascrib. to Maverick's w. and Young's Chronicles of the Pilgrims, Russell's Guide to Plymouth, the accos. of Judge Davis, in his Ed. of Morton's Memor. of Dr. Bacon in 3 Mass. Hist. Coll. VII. 243, and of Cushman in Geneal. Reg. VIII. 265–70, are all subject to no little correction since the contempo. Hist. of Bradford has been brot. to light. ISAAC, New Haven, s. of the preced. and the only ch. nam. in the will of his f. tho. as the testator had not a shilling to give, the omiss. of other ch. need not be regret. For his f's wid. Isaac purchas. the portion of the domicil that the law would not give, and bestow. it on her for life, remaind. to his eldest d. Eliz. b. 27 Sept. 1653. His only other ch. was Isaac, b. 11 June 1655, wh. d. prob. bef. his f. and without issue. The f. is thot. to have rem. shortly after 1660, and Hutch. in his Hist. II. 461 speaks, as if there were male off-spring in Maryland, at his day. The w's name is not heard of, but the d. m. 23 Dec. 1675, Benjamin Starr, and next 22 July 1679, Simon Eyre the third. JOHN, Plymouth 1620, a sailor of the Mayflower, had made up his mind to partake the lot of the pilgr. as he sign. the compact in Cape Cod harb. but he d. bef. the ship sail. on her home voyage.

ALLEY, GILES, Lynn, of wh. we kn. no more but that, in Sept. 1668, he was call. 42 yrs. of age. HUGH, Lynn, wh. may have been elder br. of the preced. came in the Abigail, 1635, from London, aged 27, had Mary, b. 6 Jan. 1642; John, 30 Nov. 1646; Martha, 31 July 1649; Sarah, 15 Apr. 1651; Hugh, 15 Oct. 1653; Solomon, 2 Aug. 1656, one of the k. at Bloody brook, 18 Sept. 1675, in the comp. of Lothrop, call. "the flower of Essex;" Hannah, 1 June 1661; and Jacob, 5 Sept. 1663; d. 25 Jan. 1674. Mary m. 6 June 1667, John Lindsay; Sarah m. Aug. 1668, Eleazer Lindsay; and Martha m. 1 Apr. 1671, James Mills. HUGH, Lynn, s. of the preced. m. 9 Dec. 1681, Rebecca Hood, had Solomon, b. 11 Oct. 1682; Jacob, 28 Jan. 1684; Eleazer, 1 Nov. 1686; Hannah, 16 Aug. 1689; Richard, 31 July 1691; Joseph, 22 June 1693; and Benjamin, 24 Feb. 1696. JOHN, Lynn, eldest br. of the preced. m. 15 Aug. 1670, Joanna Furnell, had Sarah, b. 15 Apr. 1671; Mary, 25 Apr. 1673; John, Jan. 1676; Hannah, 22 Jan. 1680; Rebecca, 28 May 1683; Hugh, 15 Feb. 1686; and William, 14 July 1688; beside two ds. more, wh. prob. d. young. PHILIP, Boston, d. 1655 perhaps, for 7 Dec. of that yr. his wid. Susanna, wh. took admin. the next week, had m. William Pitts. See Ally. Strangely is this name convert. to Aealy by that vol. usual. suppos. to be a rec. in our City Register's office, correct. transcr. for Geneal. Reg. XI. 201, the first two letters being a diphthong. What sanctity should be attrib. to the official exemplar may easily be kn. by the flagr. case of falsehood on the very next page of the same Vol. XI. where it is also correct copy, assert. that a m. was solemniz. by John Winth. Gov. 5 Nov. 1657, when that magistr. had been near nine yrs. entomb.

ALLEYNE, *EDWARD, Dedham 1636, one of the founders of the ch. 8 Nov. 1638, freem. 13 Mar. foll. with prefix of respect, at the same time with his pastor, Rev. John Allin, spelt with e in the last syl. to wh. he may have had near relation. He was rep. four yrs. 1639–42, and on 8 Sept. of this last yr. d. at Boston on attend. in the Gen. Ct. so sudden. that his will was nuncup. Prob. he had no w. or ch. for his est. was giv. by him to kinsmen John Newton, and Edward Allen. EDWARD, Boston

1677, of wh. I am not able to say, whether he was the devisee in the will of the preced.

ALLIN, *JOHN*, Dedham, the first min. (formerly by me thot. erron. to be s. of Robert of Horley in Co. Oxford, matric. at Magdalen Coll. 27 June 1623, in his 18th yr. whereas it seems much more likely that he was of Cambridge Univ.) came over in 1637, was freem. 13 Mar. 1639, ord. 24 Apr. foll. From the date of his b. 1596, and of the entrance of Bp. Wren upon his diocese 1635, Brook, in Lives of the Pur. III. 456, concludes, that he had been a preach. at Ipswich in Suff. and some reason for conject. that he was of Surlingham in Norf. is found by Dr. Lamson, his successor at D. in our day. His actual serv. however, had been at Wrentham, Co. Suff. a. 30 miles N. E. from Ipswich. When I exam. the Reg. of the Univ. of Oxford, it did not occur to me, that the age giv. him at matric. must have been too small by 10 yrs. and it is very clear that the Oxford schol. was not our John, but of a differ. fam. and fate also. Margaret, his w. d. Apr. 1653; and by her we kn. of no ch. exc. John, b. at Wrentham 13 Oct. 1623, H. C. 1643, of course he was not, as Farmer surmis. "sent hither from Eng. to obt. an educat." but brot. by his f. For sec. w. he took 8 Nov. 1653, Catharine, wid. of Gov. Thomas Dudley, dec. 31 July preced. and she had first been wid. of Samuel Hackburne, had Daniel, b. 5 Aug. 1656, H. C. 1675; Benjamin; and Eleazer. He was of high esteem for learn. and d. 26 Aug. 1671, in his will, made three days bef. pro. five days after, ment. his s. John, as "educat. in learn." and "now of Eng." Of the youngest two s. nothing is heard; and not much of Daniel, wh. was librarian short time in 1677, took his A. M. 1678, liv. at Charlestown, mortgag. his Dedham est. to John Richards, and d. 1692. See Worthington, 47–9; and Lamson's Centu. Discourses. JOHN, Dedham, s. of the preced. b. in Eng. went home, was vicar of Rye in Co. Sussex, whence being eject. 1662, for nonconform. he went to London, there practis. med. with much success during the great plague of 1665, and was suppos. by William Winthrop in his MS. catal. to have d. but we have plenary evid. in his own letters to friends at Rye, (in one of wh. is ment. of the d. of his f. in N. E.) coming down to Mar. 1674, that he contin. in the serv. of humanity at London. LEWIS, Billerica. See Allen. WILLIAM, adm. freem. 18 May 1642, is of no certain resid. and the name spell. with single *l* and final *e*.

ALLING, FRANCIS, Roxbury, d. 1 Dec. 1692, of wh. no more is kn. to me, but that the town rec. of his bur. on the same day, spells Allen. *JAMES*, Salisbury, s. of Roger, was the third min. there, coming as success. to Wheelwright, m. 1688, Eliz. d. of Rev. Seaborn Cotton of Hampton, had Joanna, b. 5 Mar. 1690; Mary, 10 Apr. 1692; and Eliz. 2 Sept. 1694; and he d. 3 Mar. 1695. His wid. m. 14 Mar. 1699, Rev.

Caleb Cushing, his success. in the same pulpit. JOHN, New Haven, m.
14 Oct. 1652, Ellen Bradley, had, beside the six ch. giv. him under the
name of Allen (bec. his proof of tak. o. of fidel. in Apr. 1654 follows
that spell. wh. in the earlier list of July 1644 made no distinct. between
Allen and Alling, using only the first name), Samuel, b. 24 Mar. 1670;
and Martha, June 1623, wh. d. young; and he d. 1691, early, as the inv.
is of 26 Mar. His will of 6 May 1689, names the two s. John, and
Samuel, and ds. Eliz. wh. had m. John Hopson of Guilford, as his third
w., Lydia, wh. had m. a Wilcocks, and was d. so that her ch. his gr.ch.
Hannah Scranton, and Mary Guttridge should have her sh. and Sarah,
then unm. but wh. m. 1691, Samuel Atwater. He is call. sen. in the list
of proprs. 1685. JOHN, New Haven, not s. of the preced. tho. call. jun. but
s. of Roger of the same, m. Susanna, d. of Robert Coe of Stratford, had
Abigail, b. 23 Nov. 1673; Susanna, 16 Mar. 1676, d. young; Hannah,
23 May 1678; Mary, 14 Sept. 1680; Jonathan, 13 Oct. 1683; and
others, as is said. ROGER, New Haven, at the very begin. of the settlem.
1639, sign. the compact. m. Mary, d. prob. eldest ch. of Thomas Nash of
the same, had Mary, bapt. 26 Nov. 1643; Samuel, perhaps b. not bapt.
(as the Nash fam. p. 19, has it) 4 Nov. 1645; John (not bapt. as the
little vol. tells, but perhaps b.), 2 Oct. 1647; Sarah, perhaps bapt. 11
(certainly not 12, wh. was Monday, as giv. in the book); Eliz. and Susanna, said to be not rec. (perhaps both d. soon), leav. us to suppose that
those preced. had rec. evidence of bapt. to wh. wrong dates are append.
and James said to be b. 24 June 1657, and this may be correct. H. C.
1679; was serg. and deac. and treas. of the Col. 1661 and some yrs. after,
d. 27 Sept. 1674. In his will, wh. was nuncup. he names only five ch.
and directs, that James be brot. up to learning. His wid. Mary, wh. in
her will names the same five ch. d. 16 Aug. 1683. At New Haven the
fam. long remain. SAMUEL, New Haven, often spelt Allen, wh. see.
SAMUEL, New Haven, s. of Roger, m. 24 Oct. 1667, Eliz. d. of John
Winston, had Samuel, b. 16 Oct. 1668; John, 27 Mar. 1671; James, 29
July 1673; Roger, 9 Dec. 1675, d. young; Roger, again, July 1677;
Theophilus, 17 Feb. 1680; and Daniel; and his w. d. 8 Dec. 1682. By
sec. w. Sarah, d. of John Chedsey, m. 26 Oct. 1683, had Caleb, Sarah,
Eliz. and Esther. He was a propr. 1685, d. 28 Aug. 1707; and the ten
ch. were liv. 1709.

ALLIS, JOHN, Hatfield, s. of William, m. 14 Dec. 1669, Mary, wid. of
Nathaniel Clark, d. of Thomas Meakins, had Joseph, b. 1670; Abigail,
25 Feb. 1672; Hannah, 9 Oct. 1673; Ichabod, 10 July 1675; Eleazer,
23 July 1677; Eliz. 4 Apr. 1679; Lydia, 15 Aug. 1680, d. 1691; John,
10 May 1682; Rebecca, 16 Apr. 1683; William, 16 May 1684; Mary,
25 Aug. 1687, d. within 8 mos. and Nathaniel; but the oldest and the

4 *

youngest are not on rec. Ten of these were liv. 1705. He was a capt. and carpenter, employ. in build. many chhs. d. Jan. 1691. His wid. m. Samuel Belden, sen. JOSEPH, Hadley, signer of the petitn. against imposts 1668, was not s. of William. RICHARD, 22 June 1632, took o. of alleg. in London bef. embarc. in the Lion, wh. arr. at Boston 16 Sept. foll. but where he ever liv. in our country is unkn. Perhaps he went first to Roxbury, as did sev. of his fell. passeng. and if the discovery be ever made, I shall feel no surprise at find. that he is the same as R. Ellis of Dedham. SAMUEL, Hadley 1668, s. of William, by w. Alice, had Mehitable, b. 2 July 1677; Samuel, 20 Feb. 1679; William, 19 Oct. 1680; Mary, 6 July 1682; Thomas, 1684; Rebecca, 1687; and Sarah; and he d. 1691. All the seven ch. were liv. 1704. Their mo. the wid. of A. m. John Hawks, and was (with most of her h's fam.) k. at the destruct. by the French and Ind. of Deerfield, 29 Feb. 1704. WILLIAM, Braintree, had gr. from Boston of twelve acres for three heads, was freem. 13 May 1640, by w. Mary had John, b. 5 Mar. 1642; Samuel, 24 Feb. 1647; Josiah, wh. d. 15 Oct. 1651; Josiah, again, 20 Oct. 1651; William, 10 Jan. 1653, wh. d. at 9 mos.; William, again, 10 Jan. 1656; beside two ds. Hannah, wh. m. 1670, William Scott; and Mary, wh. d. unm. 1690; rem. to Hadley 1661, on the W. side of the riv. now Hatfield; was selectman 1662, lieut. of the cavalry, a deac. and his w. d. 1677. He m. 25 June 1678, wid. Mary Graves, made his will 2 Sept. at Hartford, 4 days bef. his d. 1678. His wid. Mary, d. of John Brownson, whose sec. h. John Graves, was k. so shortly bef. as 19 Sept. 1677, had in 1668 been wid. of John Wyatt, and was happy to gain for fourth h. Samuel Gaylord, m. 1682. His s. William was k. in the Falls fight, 19 May 1676. Sometimes his name appears Allice.

ALLISET, or ALLESET, JOHN, Boston, by w. Grace had Eliz. b. 19 Jan. 1684; Grace, 24 May 1686; Eliz. again, 5 July 1688; and Deliverance, 12 Oct. 1695.

ALLISON, JAMES, Boston 1644, by w. Christian had James, b. 20 Oct. 1650; and John, wh. d. 2 Apr. 1653. RALPH, Scarborough 1673, was a gr. landholder. RICHARD, Braintree. See Ellison, wh. may be a distortion of this; but in New Hampsh. contin. the name Allison.

ALLOTT, ADAM, Newbury, a tailor, came in the Bevis, 1638, from Southampton, aged 19 in the serv. of Richard Dummer; but no more is told of him.

ALLT, or AULT, JOHN, Portsmouth, 1631, sent out by John Mason, the Patentee of N. Hampsh. liv. at Dover most of his days after 1640, in 1679 was 73 yrs. old. His w. was Remembrance; ch. John; Remembrance, wh. m. John Rand; and a d. wh. m. Thomas Edgerly. Sometimes the name is Olt.

ALLY, THOMAS, Newbury, m. 9 Feb. 1672, Sarah, d. of Thomas Silver; was tax. at Rowley 1691. Tho. no connex. is seen, the name may
be of the same fam. as Alley, wh. see.

ALLYN, ‡JOHN, Hartford, s. of Matthew, b. in Eng. m. 19 Nov. 1651,
Ann, d. of Henry Smith of Springfield, gr.d. of William Pynchon, had
Ann, b. 18 Aug. 1654; Mary, 3 Apr. 1657; Margaret, 29 July 1660;
Rebecca, 2 Mar. 1665, d. young; Martha, 27 July 1667; and Eliz. 1
Dec. 1669. By sec. w. Hannah, d. of George Lamberton, wid. of Sam-
uel Welles of Wethersfield, I suppose, he had no ch. He was many
yrs. Secr. of the Col. after 1657, when he was lieut. rose to be col. an
Assist. in 1662, and many yrs. foll. and of the Counc. under Sir Edmund
Andros in 1687, and d. 6 Nov. 1696, leav. large est. to the five ds. Ann
m. 1676, as his sec. w. Joseph Whiting of Hartford; Mary m. 6 Oct.
1686, Col. William Whiting; Margaret m. a. 1684, William Southmayd
of Middletown, as his sec. w. Martha m. Aaron Cooke the third; and
Eliz. m. 21 Dec. 1704, as his sec. w. Alexander Allen of Windsor; and
next John Gardiner of Gardiner's isl. Increase Mather includes, in his
Relat. of Ind. Wars, the Account of the troubles preced. and during that
with the Pequots, writ. by Allyn, filling 19 of his pages. JOHN, New
London, only s. of Robert, m. 24 Dec. 1668, Eliz. d. of John Gager, had
Eliz. b. 24 Dec. 1669; and Robert, a. mid. of Sept. 1671. He had
helped in the settlem. of Norwich, but after d. of his f. went to N. L.
there d. 1709. JOHN, Barnstable, s. of Thomas, m. Mary Howland, had
John, b. 3 Apr. 1671; Mary, 5 Aug. 1675, d. young; Matthew, 6 Aug.
1677, d. young; Isaac, 8 Nov. 1679; and he rem. with his fam. ‡*MAT-
THEW, Cambridge 1632, was perhaps s. of Samuel of Chelmsford, Co.
Essex, freem. 4 Mar. 1635, rep. at March Gen. Ct. 1636, rem. prob. next
yr. to Hartford, thence in few yrs. to Windsor, for wh. he was rep. 1648
to 57, Assist. 1658 to 67, and chos. Commissr. for Unit. Col. 1660 and 4,
d. 1671. His ch. were all prob. b. in Eng. John, Thomas, and Mary,
wh. m. 11 June 1646, Benjamin Newberry, and his will of 30 Jan. 1671
names these and the gr.ch. Mary, d. of Newberry. Common. in his
autogr. the name has y, but high authority assures me, that it is not
always so; and in the rec. and print. books, it is nearly as often seen with
e as without. OBADIAH, Middletown, propound. for freem. Oct. 1672,
adm. next yr. m. 28 Oct. 1669, Eliz. d. of Thomas Sanford of Milford,
had Obadiah, b. 20 Sept. 1670; Thomas, 20 Sept. 1672, d. in few wks.
Thomas, again, 27 Sept. 1673; Mary, 15 Sept. 1675; Ann, 12 Sept.
1677; Thankful, 8 Sept. 1679; Samuel, 15 Mar. 1684; and John, 27
Sept. 1686; was deac. and d. 7 Apr. 1712. Prob. he was neph. of the
first Thomas, and the descend. have generally chang. the spell. to Allen.
ROBERT, Salem, 1637, adm. of the ch. 15 May 1642, had John, and

Sarah there bapt. Sunday foll. and Mary, 19 Nov. 1648; in 1651 rem.
to New London, and to the then adjoin. town of Norwich at its first settlem. 1659; but; high as is her authority on such a point, I hesitate to
adopt Miss Caulkins's opin. that, intermed. betw. Salem and New London,
he was of Saybrook. Tho. honor with the office of constable at Norwich
1669, he went back to N. L. and there d. 1683, where part of his farm
preserves in the harbor the name of Allyn's point. Other ch. beside
those at Salem he had, as Hannah and Deborah, both prob. at N. L.
Sarah m. 17 Feb. 1659, George Geer; Hannah m. Thomas Rose; and
Deborah was unm. at d. of f. *SAMUEL, Barnstable, s. of Thomas of
the same, m. 10 May 1664, Hannah, d. of Rev. Thomas Walley, had
Thomas, b. 22 Mar. 1665; Samuel, 19 Jan. 1667; Joseph, 7 Apr. 1671;
Hannah, 4 Mar. 1673; and Eliz. 26 Nov. 1681, wh. d. at 17 yrs. was
rep. three yrs. 1682-4. His w. d. 23 Oct. 1711, and he d. 25 Nov. 1726.
* THOMAS, Wethersfield 1636, not migrat. from Watertown, for Bond
has not nam. him, was br. of Matthew, with wh. he had extraord. con-
trovers. in the law, as is fairly infer. from Trumbull's Col. Rec. I. 211,
was made freem. 1652, rep. 1656; and soon after d. as might be conclud. from not seeing his name as rep. in any yr. subseq. nor in the list
of freem. for that town 1669; yet he may have rem. to Middletown, as
no list of that sort is found from that place in Trumbull, and one of the
name there was deac. wh. d. 16 Oct. 1688, having had no ch. but leav.
wid. Martha, perhaps, wh. had been wid. of Roger Jepson, and d. 1690.
She calls, in her will, Obadiah A. of M. cousin. *Y*. not *e* is seen in his
last syl. tho. in his bapt. rec. Apr. 1604 (if he were s. of Samuel of
Chelmsford Co. Essex), the spell. is the other way. THOMAS, Barnstable, had Samuel, b. 10, bapt. 18 Feb. 1644; John, bapt. 27 Sept. 1646;
and Mehitable, bapt. 26 Nov. 1648; and he d. Nov. 1680, at gr. age.
Mehitable m. 1 June 1667, Samuel Annable of the same. His first w. was
nam. Winifred; the sec. was a wid. but surnames are not found. THOMAS,
Windsor, s. of Matthew of the same, perhaps b. in Eng. m. Oct. 1658, Abigail, d. of Rev. John Warham, had John, b. 17 Aug. 1659, wh. d. young;
Matthew, 5 Jan. 1661; Thomas, 11 Mar. 1663; John, again, 1665;
Samuel, 3 Nov. 1667; Jane, 22 July 1670; Abigail, 17 Oct. 1672; Sarah, 13 July 1674; Esther, 29 Jan. 1676; and Benjamin, 1680. He was
made freem. 1659, and esteem. in the milit. serv. in wh. he rose to be
capt. and d. 14 Feb. 1696. THOMAS, Windsor, s. of the preced. m. 1686,
Martha, sec. d. of Simon Wolcott, wh. d. 7 Sept. of next yr. and in any
other particul. nothing is kn. WILLIAM, Stonington, had John, George,
Jane, and Eliz. to wh. on his d. 7 Sept. 1671, he left his prop. speak. of his
w. as if she liv. near Barnstaple in Devonsh. For the deficiencies of
this article, and the difficulty of determin. betw. Allyn, and Allen, and

Allyne, or Alleyne, I must confess, that, after long research, satisfact. is unattain. in sev. cases, so many individ. have, perhaps capricious. at various times, writ. their fam. names in differ. ways.

ALMY, or ALMOND, ‡CHRISTOPHER, Portsmouth, R. I. s. of William, b. in Eng. was an Assist. 1690. JOB, Portsmouth, R. I. br. of the preced. by w. Mary, d. of Christopher Unthank of Warwick, had William and Christopher, tw. Susanna, Audrey, Deborah, Catharine, and Mary, all perhaps minors, when he d. 1684. JOHN, Plymouth 1643, perhaps br. of the preced. m. Mary, d. of James Cole, rem. to Portsmouth, R. I. was a capt. in Philip's war, 1675, as named in Church's Mem. 53, and d. 1676. WILLIAM, Lynn, perhaps as early as 1631, went home, and came again, 1635, in the Abigail, aged 34, with w. Audrey, 32, and ch. Annis, 8 ; and Christopher, 3 ; rem. 1637, prob. to Sandwich, and certainly was freem. of Portsmouth, R. I. 1655. His will names ch. Christopher, John, Job, Ann, w. of John Green, and Catharine, w. of a West, whose bapt. name is not seen.

ALSOP, or ALSUP, DANIEL, New Haven, youngest s. of Joseph the first d. 11 Jan. 1689, prob. unm. GEORGE, Milford 1667, d. a. 1680 ; but was not constant resid. there, and notice of w. or ch. is not found, so that prob. he never m. Perhaps Eliz. A. mem. of the ch. at M. in Feb. 1643, was his sis. for Sylvanus Baldwin, her s. b. some yrs. after her m. that yr. with Richard B. calls him. "near kinsman" of George A. JOSEPH, New Haven, had come, at the age of 14, to Boston in the Elizabeth and Ann, 1635, from London, went to New Haven early, took o. of fidel. in 1644, bef. 1647 m. Eliz. the eldest d. of William Preston, had Joseph ; Eliz. b. 22 June 1650 ; Sarah, 8 Sept. 1652, but by ch. rec. worthy of very little regard, 15 Sept. 1651 ; Mary, 3 Oct. 1654 ; Abigail, 4 Sept. not as ch. rec. says 4 Nov. 1656 ; all bapt. 26 Apr. 1657 ; Hannah, b. 2 Dec. 1659 ; John, 3 Jan. 1662 ; Lydia, 26 July 1665 ; Daniel, 13 Aug. 1667 ; and Jemima, 10 Feb. 1670. He d. 8 Nov. 1698 ; and of the ch. this report is giv. Sarah, d. prob. unm. 24 Jan. 1699 ; Mary m. 2 Nov. 1680, as his sec. w. John Miles ; Abigail m. 14 July 1680, John Rowe ; Lydia m. 8 Nov. 1688, James Trowbridge ; one m. Thomas Talmadge ; and one, perhaps the same, m. John Paine. Hannah was a busy money making maiden, wh. was Adm'x of est. of her br. Daniel, and yrs. after bot. up the shares of her sis. in the est. of her f. manag. by her with much discret. Haz. II. 247. JOSEPH, New Haven, eldest s. of the preced. m. 25 Nov. 1672, Abigail, d. of John Thompson the first of the same, and d. 12 Jan. 1691. His will, of 1687, pro. 16 Feb. 1691, gave to his w. (wh. prob. had no ch.) and his brs. John and Daniel, all his est. a. £490. KEY, Boston 1668, merch. had w. Mary, who soon after his d. m. Capt. William Turner, whose victory at the Falls fight, 1676, gave his name to the spot. RICHARD, Newtown, L. I. 1686, by w. Hannah had Thomas, b. 7 Sept. 1687; Richard; John; Hannah; Deborah; Amy; and Eliz. d. Oct. 1718, aged 58; but his wid. wh. d. 23 Aug. 1757, was 90. He is suppos. to have been brot. in youth by his uncle Thomas Wardell of Newtown, wh. had no ch. and gave A. large est. See Riker's Ann. of Newtown, 335. THOMAS, Stratford, wh. came in the Elizabeth and Ann from London, 1635, aged 20, I think must have been br. of Joseph of New Haven, as they came together, and the younger, in 1651, inform. the Court, that his br. without nam. him, had d. at S. leav. some prop. and no more is kn. It may be, that the f. of these youths was that John, rated for a subsidy in 1598, to the same parish and at the same time with William Shakespear, nor would it be very extrav. to presume, that he, too, went up to London from Stratford on Avon. See my notes on Edward Jackson. TIMOTHY, New Haven 1646, mariner.

ALSOB, THOMAS, Salem vill. was a soldier, k. by the Ind. 16 July (unless 16 May be nearer the day of fight, and the other only date of rec.) 1690, with others at Casco. See Felt Ann. II. 509. Yet Willis I. 205, refer. to the same rec. spells the sufferer's name, as seems, at least, equal. likely to be correct, Alsop. But I would gladly see his origin.

ALVORD, ALEXANDER, Windsor, m. 29 Oct. 1646, Mary, d. of Richard Vore, or Voar, had Abigail, b. 6 Oct. 1647; John, 12 Aug. 1649; Mary, 6 July, 1651; Thomas, 27 Oct. 1653; Eliz. 12 Nov. 1655; Benjamin, 11 Feb. 1658; and Sarah, 24 June, 1660; rem. next yr. to Northampton, there had Jeremiah, 9 May 1663; Ebenezer, 23 Dec. 1665; and Jonathan, 6 Apr. 1669. His w. d. bef. 1683, and he d. 3 Oct. 1687. His sis. Joan m. 6 May 1646, Ambrose Fowler. Of his ds. Abigail m. 1666, Thomas Root; Mary m. 24 Mar. 1670, John Weller; Eliz. m. 1684, Henry Burt; and Sarah m. 10 July 1689, as his sec. w. James Warriner. BENEDICT, Windsor 1637, br. prob. elder, of the preced. was a soldier in the Pequot war that yr. m. 26 Nov. 1640, Joan Newton, had Jonathan, b. 1 June 1645; Benjamin, 11 July 1647; Josias, 6 July 1649; Eliz. 21 Sept. 1651; and Jeremy, 24 Dec. 1655; and d. 23 Apr. 1683. His only d. m. 20 Mar. 1672, Job Drake, and is nam. with only three brs. in the will of her f. one of the s. having d. bef. him. BENJAMIN, New London, s. of the preced. d. 12 Aug. 1709, as in Geneal. Reg. XI. 27, Miss Caulkins gives the inscript. on his gr. stone; but, she adds, no descend. are found, and he is not nam. in her copious Hist. BENJAMIN, Northampton, s. of Alexander, m. a. 1690, Deborah, d. of John Stebbins of the same, had Abigail, b. 1691; Eliz. Sept. 1693; Benjamin, 1695; Deborah, May 1698; Experience, 5 Oct. 1700; Jonah, 13 Apr. 1704; Sarah, 28 May 1707; and he d. 1715. His wid. m. 4 Apr. 1716, Henry Burt of Springfield. EBENEZER, Northampton, br. of the preced. m. a. 1692,

Ruth, d. of Joseph Baker, had Ebenezer, b. 24 Aug. 1693, d. young; Joseph, 1697; Mary, 24 June 1699; and Noah, 27 June 1701. His w. d. 4 Mar. 1706, and he m. Eliz. wh. perhaps was a wid. Bird, and had Ruth, 24 Aug. 1710; James, 22 July 1712, d. soon; Eliz. 7 Sept. 1713, Rebecca, 25 Oct. 1716, d. soon; Rebecca, again, 10 Feb. 1718; Ebenezer, again, 17 Dec. 1720; Sarah, 1723, d. soon; and Thomas, a. 1725; and d. 29 Nov. 1738. JEREMIAH, Windsor, youngest s. of Benedict, had Benedict, b. 1688; Newton, 1690; Jeremiah, 1692; Jonathan, 1696, d. young; Jane, 1699; Joanna, 1702; and Eliz. 1703, d. next yr. and perhaps more. JEREMIAH, Hatfield, s. of Alexander, m. at Deerfield, where he first rem. from his native town, 1691, Mehitable, wid. of Hezekiah Root, d. of Sampson Frary of D. had Jeremiah, b. 17 Feb. 1692, d. in few days; Jeremiah, again, 31 Mar. 1694, wh. was drown. at 24 yrs. and Mary, 20 Aug. 1696. His w. d. 7 Nov. foll. and in few yrs. he rem. to H. there m. Mary, d. of William Gull, had Eliz. 1703, d. young; Eliz. again, 1705; Hannah, 1707; and Ebenezer, 1710, wh. d. unm. JOHN, Northampton 1668, eldest s. of Alexander, m. Abigail, d. of Nathaniel Phelps, had no ch. and the date of his d. is not giv. But his w. b. 5 Apr. 1655, d. 26 Aug. 1756, reckon. by the vulgar on the rec. with the common fondness for exagger. in her 103d yr. She was the oldest person that ever d. in N. but exact truth, after the correct. of old style, makes her age 101 yrs. 4 mos. and 11 days. JONATHAN, Westfield, eldest s. of Benedict, m. 1681, Hannah Brown, had no ch. JONATHAN, Northampton, youngest s. of Alexander, m. 12 Jan. 1693, Thankful Miller, had Jonathan, b. 9 Apr. 1694, d. at 9 yrs.; John, 28 June 1696; Patience, 22 June 1701; Zebediah, 30 Oct. 1705, d. young; Mary, 21 July 1707; Thankful, 10 Aug. 1709; and Jonathan, again, 16 Nov. 1711; and d. 1729. JOSIAH, Windsor, s. of Benedict, rem. to Simsbury, there had w. and fam. but partic. are unk. THOMAS, Northampton 1678, s. of Alexander, m. 22 Mar. 1681, Joanna, d. of John Taylor of the same, had John, b. 10 Aug. 1682, d. in few days; Thomas, 28 Aug. 1683; John, again, 19 Oct. 1685; and Josiah, 7 Feb. 1688, d. young; and the f. d. 22 July 1688. His wid. m. 1690, Samuel King; and, next, 1702, Deliverance Bridgeman. Farmer notes gr. of this name two at Yale, one at Dart. and three at other N. E. coll. none at Harv. in 1828.

AMADOWN, ROGER, Salem 1637, Weymouth 1640, where by w. Sarah he had Sarah, b. 10 Aug. of that yr. and, at Boston, Lydia, 27 Apr. 1643; rem. 1648 to Rehoboth, prob. had sev. s. and d. 13 Nov. 1673.

AMAZEEN, JOHN, New Hampsh. 1683, call. John the Greek. Belkn. I. 479. There are descend.

AMBECK, AMBEEK, or AMBEECK, JOSEPHUS, Hartford, m. Mary, d. of Caspar Varleet, had Judith, b. 5 Dec. 1654, and liv. not many yrs. for the wid. m. 30 Dec. 1658, Paulus Schrick. All the parties were Dutch, and prob. confin. in the very narrow space to wh. the Eng. limit. the earliest sett. their predecess.

AMBLER, *ABRAHAM, Stamford, s. of Richard, m. 25 Dec. 1662, Mary, d. of Robert Bates, had Mary, b. 1 Jan. 1664; Abraham, 5 Jan. 1666; John, 18 Feb. 1668; Joshua, 8 Sept. 1670; Sarah, 1672; and others; but in his will, of 1699, ment. only s. John, d. Mehitable, and three ch. of his dec. d. Brown with his sec. w. Hannah; requir. John to provide for his gr.f. dur. life. He was freem., a propr. not only at S. but at Bedford a planta. to the N. now within the state of N. Y. and in 1686 was chief town officer there, rep. for S. in 1674. RICHARD, Watertown 1637, Weymouth (perhaps for short time) 1640, and Boston 1643, by w. Sarah had Sarah, b. 4 Dec. 1639; Abraham, 27 Sept. 1641, d. very soon; and Abraham, again, 22 Sept. 1642, all by Bond, giv. as at W. bef. 1650 rem. to Stamford, there was freem. 1669, and liv. at gr. age 1699.

AMBROSE, HENRY, Hampton 1641, or earlier, had Samuel, bapt. 25 July 1641; Ebenezer, 1643; Henry, b. June 1649; was adm. freem. 18 May 1642, liv. at Boston 1654, Charlestown 1656, had Abigail, b. 28 Dec. 1654, was a carpenter, and prob. work. at his trade in sev. places, certain. in 1650, at Salisbury, there not allow. as a commoner, yet d. there 1658, and his prop. was considera. His wid. bec. sec. w. of John Severance. Abigail m. Oct. 1672 William Osgood. HENRY, Salisbury, s. of the preced. m. Oct. 1672, Susanna, wid. of Timothy Worcester, had Dorothy, b. 21 Sept. 1673; Nathaniel, 26 Mar. 1675; d. soon; and Nathaniel, again, 26 Feb. 1677. JOSHUA, of wh. we gladly would kn. the f. and date of b. was gr. at H. C. 1653, went home, and was sett. as min. at Darley in Co. Lancaster, where he conform. to the ch. of Eng. at the time of ejectm. had the honor of A. M. at Oxford, and is not mark. in Mather's Catal. 1697, as d. See Calamy, II. 419. NATHANIEL, of unkn. parentage, like the preced. to wh. perhaps he was br. being gr. of H. C. 1653, was sometime connect. with the coll. prob. as tutor, went home and was sett. as min. at Kirkby in Co. Lancaster, whence in 1662, as non-conform. he was eject. Calamy, II. 417. SAMUEL, Salisbury, prob. eldest s. of the first Henry, by w. Hope had Abigail, b. 1 Apr. 1665; and Margaret, 12 Aug. 1668; but no more is heard of him.

AMBRY, or AMBERY, ROBERT, New Haven 1643, where often it appears EMRY, or EMERY, took o. of fidel. 1 July 1644, by w. Mary had Joseph, b. 14 Mar. 1650; and Mary, and John, prob. earlier; rem. to Stamford, there had Moses, b. 1652; and d. 21 July 1656. The wid. next yr. m. George Baldwin, or Boldin of Westchester.

AMEREDITH, MERRYDAY, or MEREDITH, JOHN, Kittery 1670, m. Joanna, d. of James Treworgye, but what little is told of him may be seen in Geneal. Reg. V. 345–8. He was constable 1671, liv. 1685, and she, prob. wid. July 1688.

AMES, HUGH, Boston 1667. JOHN, Duxbury, s. of Richard of Bruton, Co. Somerset, where, acc. fam. doc. he was b. 10 Dec. 1610, m. 20 Oct. 1645, Eliz. Hayward, rem. to Bridgewater 1656, d. 1698, leav. no issue, but gave the yr. preced. large est. to his neph. John, and his ch. See Mitchell's Hist. of B. JOHN, Bridgewater, only s. of William of Braintree (not, as was once thot. of the famous Franequer Profess. William), m. Sarah, d. of John Willis, had John, b. 14 Apr. 1672; William, 6 Nov. 1673; Nathaniel, 9 Oct. 1677; Eliz. 6 Sept. 1680; Thomas, 21 Feb. 1682; Sarah, 12 Oct. 1685; David, 30 Aug. 1688; and Hannah. Of the s. the oldest and the youngest, perhaps sett. at New London, and Miss Caulkins in her Hist. 264, lends countenance to the tradit. tho. of John only does she speak of perman. resid. 374; while of Nathaniel we kn. that he d. 1736, and was f. of that Nathaniel, celebr. for success of his Almanacs many yrs. and more for the super. eloq. of his s. Fisher, H. C. 1774, the first rep. from Boston in the Fed. Congr. 1789. WILLIAM, Braintree, br. of John the first, elder by fam. tradit. b. 6 Oct. 1605, came a. 1638, by w. Hannah had Hannah, b. 12 May 1641; Rebecca, Oct. 1642; Lydia, 2 June 1645; John, 24 May 1647; Sarah, 1 Mar. 1651; and Deliverance, 6 Feb. 1654; and he d. one mo. and 5 days after. Hannah m. 1660, John Hayden; and Sarah m. Thomas Hayward of Bridgewater. *WILLIAM*, Cambridge, came in the Mary Ann of Great Yarmouth 1637, with his mo. Joane, wid. of Rev. William, D. D. (wh. had proceed. A. B. 1607, at Christ's Coll. Cambridge, and widely disting. as Profess. in theolo. in Holland, where he d. 1633, in his 57th yr.) br. John, and sis. Ruth, wh. is call. 18 yrs. old. See 4 Mass. Hist. Coll. I. 100. They liv. first at Salem, but the mo. d. at Cambridge, whither she rem. to encourage her s. at his studies in the coll. and there she was bur. 23 Dec. 1644. He was gr. in the foll. yr. made freem. 1647, soon after went home, and in 1648 was sett. as collea. at Wrentham in Co. Suff. with his uncle, John Phillips, wh. had m. a sis. of his f. and was then a mem. of the Westminster Assemb. near the close of their anxious labors of more than five and a half years. Bef. the Mayor and Aldermen of London, 5 Nov. 1651, he preach. the annivers. sermon on the gunpowder plot, at St. Pauls, and was eject. 1662, d. 21 July 1689, in his 66th yr. By his first w. Susanna, he had only Eliz. wh. m. Robert Smith, a min. in the same ch. wh. d. in Aug. 1705; and that w. was bur. 6 Jan. 1652. For sec. w. he took, 26 Jan. 1653, Eliz. Wales, had Ruth, and Philip, both d. young; and this w. d. 19 Feb. 1683. These details are gather. from a Hist. of the Congregat. ch. at Wrentham in Old Eng. by John Brown, 1854; and from Hunter in 3 Mass. Hist. Coll. X. 169. Prob.

his br. John, wh. if we judge by order of names in the rec. of Wrentham, was the younger, went home with our scholar. Of this name nine had, in 1834, been gr. at Harv. none at Yale, one at Dart. and three at other N. E. coll. as Farmer found.

AMEY, or AMEE, JOHN, Woburn 1649, by w. Martha, d. of Edward Johnson, the historian, had Mary, b. 27 Feb. 1650; rem. to Boston 1653, had John, 4 or 12 Mar. 1654; Martha, 10 Nov. 1655; and William, 24 Mar. 1657. He was a ship carpenter. WILLIAM, Lynn, in 1637, with others, had liberty to rem. to begin settlem. of Sandwich.

AMORY, SIMON, Boston, freeman 1672, had w. Mary, and d. early in 1677. WILLIAM, said to have found a miner. hill above Deerfield, 1685. Felt.

AMOS, HUGH, Boston, freem. 1666, was of the 2d ch. had John, bapt. there that yr. perhaps rem. to Norwich, where he had Mary, b. Jan. 1671; and Samuel, Jan. 1673. These three ch. with ano. d. Ann div. his est. in 1707. He liv. on the E. side of the riv. now Preston, and his name designates one of the beautif. ponds of that town.

AMSBURY. See Armsbee.

AMSDEN, ISAAC, Cambridge, m. 8 June 1654, Frances Perriman, whose f. is unkn. had Isaac, b. 1656; and Jacob, 17 Nov. 1657; both bapt. 3 Nov. 1661, the mo. being adm. of the ch. few days bef. and he d. 7 Apr. 1659, if we take Harris's Epit. 169, for conclusive; but we might judge from Pro. rec. where ment. of admin. giv. 25 June 1661, to his wid. that he had d. only 19 days bef. The wid. m. 14 Feb. 1663, Richard Cutter. ISAAC, Cambridge, s. of the preced. m. 17 May 1677, Jane Rutter, perhaps d. of John of Sudbury, had Eliz. b. 3 Feb. foll. and I kn. no more. JACOB, Cambridge, s. of Isaac the first, d. 11 June 1701, as we learn from Harris, 29, and any thing else is learn. from nobody. JOHN, Hatfield, perhaps s. of the first Isaac by a w. bef. Frances, or even bef. he sett. at Cambridge, or came from Eng. there this man liv. ten yrs. but at H. d. 1696, leav. John and Isaac, of wh. the latter d. young, and the former resid. at Deerfield, where he was drown. 1742, and two of his s. were k. by the Ind. 1746. Descend. may be found there. Matchless Mitchell spells the name Embsden.

ANCHOR, THOMAS, Boston 1646.

ANDERSON, ARCHIBALD, Lynn, employ. at the iron works, came from Scotland, and d. 13 Aug. 1661. DAVID, New Haven 1639, whip. for drunk. and not much better in 1641, as in Col. Rec. I. 28 and 59 appears. DAVID, Charlestown 1675, prob. s. of John of Boston, by w. Catharine had John, wh. d. that yr. at 3 mos. David, bapt. 23 Sept. 1677, perhaps a posthum. ch. for his f. d. in May preced. on his way, as master of the ship Blessing, home from London. GAWEN, Roxbury, freem. 13 May

1640, of wh. no more is heard. JOHN, Boston 1647, shipwright, permit.
in 1652 to build a wharf, m. 3 Jan. 1655, I suppose for sec. w. Mary
Hodges of Charlestown (a former w. Jane hav. d. 4 May preced. and his
s. Samuel, prob. inf. d. 10 July foll.), by her had Joanna, b. 25 Dec. foll.
and Ann, 5 May 1657; and he d. 28 Sept. 1677. We learn from his
will of 3 days preced. pro. 31 Oct. foll. that he had elder ch. as Emma,
wh. m. 17 July 1655, John Brackenbury, afterwards m. Joseph Lynde,
and d. 2 Sept. 1703; Catharine, wh. m. 19 July 1655, John Phillips, and
d. 24 Feb. 1699; Mary, wh. as wid. Lynde, m. 27 July 1682, Rev.
Thomas Shepard, and, next, Hon. Samuel Hayman, and was bur. 20 Aug.
1717; and Joanna Newman; but much uncertain. hangs over these two
last ds. i. e. what Lynde was h. of the former, what Newman of the latter,
tho. much inquiry has been bestow. He had also Henry, who d. in Eng.
and left his prop. to the f. JOHN, Ipswich 1665, whose inv. was render.
3 May 1701, had been a soldier in the Province serv. Possib. but not
prob. he may have been one of the unhappy prisoners of the battle at
Worcester, 3 Sept. 1651 (that "crowning mercy" to Oliver Cromwell),
of wh. 272 were ship. in Nov. after, in the John and Sarah, from London,
to be sold here, arr. in May foll. at Boston. Beside this John, Alister,
David, and William A. were victims of the same cruel policy in the same
ship. Part of the prisoners of Dunbar, import. in the former yr. had been
well receiv. as Cotton wrote to Cromwell, and sold for 6, 7, or 8 yrs. ser-
vitude. Most of these unfortunate young men d. of scurvy, or of broken
hearts; and some of the exiles ran away, perhaps with good-will of their
purchasers, so that not one in fifty of these soldiers that foll. Charles II.
in the fatal fields of Dunbar and Worcester, and were sold in Boston, prob.
five hundred in num. liv. to have fams. in our country. JOHN, Salem
1673, a shipmaster, had been, perhaps, of Boston, 1655, and adm. with
w. Mary, of the sec. ch. 1672. RICHARD, New Haven, took o. of fidel.
7 Apr. 1657. ROBERT, in Mass. 6 June 1637 fin. for contempt £50,
wh. was soon remit. may have been only a transient visitor. See Col.
Rec. I. 198, 245. WILLIAM, New Haven, took o. of fidel. 7 Apr. 1657,
but neither of him, nor of Richard, who may have been his br. is any more
seen. WILLIAM, Watertown, of wh. Dr. Bond found only, that he sat on
a coroner's jury 26 July 1669. Gr. of this name up to 1828 Farmer
found two at Harv. two at Dart. one at Yale, and eleven at the other coll.
in N. E. and N. J. chiefly, I presume from the latter.

ANDREW, JOHN, Wickford 1674. NICHOLAS, Marblehead 1683,
freem. that yr. SAMUEL, Cambridge, s. of William of the same, b. prob.
in Eng. m. 27 Sept. 1652 (when prefix of respect is giv. on the rec.),
Eliz. White, whose f. is not kn. and wh. d. 24 Jan. 1687, aged 57, had
Samuel, b. 29 Jan. 1656, H. C. 1675; William, June 1658; both bapt.

bef. Mitchell's Reg. begins; John, 2, bapt. 10 Mar. 1661, wh. d. at 32
yrs.; Eliz. bapt. 12 Apr. 1663; Thomas, 21 May 1665, d. soon; Mary,
6 Jan. 1667, d. July foll. Thomas, again, 29 Mar. 1668; beside Jonathan,
wh. d. 8 May 1700, aged a. 30; and Mary, again, wh. d. 29 Feb. 1672.
He was often clk. treasr. and selectman, and d. 21 June 1701, aged a. 80.
See the invalu. "Cambridge Ch. gathering," by Newell with appx. of
Mitchell, and Harris's Epit. A person, "well skill. in mathemat." of this
name, as is ment. in Haz. I. 591, and Belkn. I. 57, is suppos. to be this
Cambridge man. See Col. Rec. III. 329 and 361. SAMUEL, eldest s. of
the preced. was min. of Milford, ord. 15 Nov. 1685, m. Abigail, d. of Gov.
Robert Treat, had Samuel, and prob. others, and d. 24 Jan. 1738. The
name has a final *s*. in the Conn. rec. but the Rev. owner reject. the addit.;
the ch. and town rec. of Cambridge admit the letter, tho. the indisput.
authority of the Coll. catal. deny, and discrimin. yet in his Hecatompolis
(ch. 7 of the Magn. I.) Mather sanctifies the intrusion. WILLIAM, Cambridge, mariner, the freem. of 4 Mar. 1634, by w. Mary, wh. d. 19 Jan.
1640, had Samuel and perhaps other ch. and d. bef. 1655. WILLIAM,
Ipswich, was sch.master there, and in sev. other towns, may not have been
br. of Rev. Samuel, and d. 19 July 1683. But in Geneal. Reg. VIII. 19,
the extr. from the interleav. Almanac of Sewall, noticing this event is
remark. diverse in the name from the careful writer on the Ipswich gr.
sch. in G. R. VI. 69, wh. makes Thomas Andrews succeed famous Cheever in the sch. 1 Aug. 1660, and teach. 23 yrs. and d. 10 July 1683.
Vehemently do I suspect, that one or the other is mistaken, that only one
man is intend. and the date of d. 10 or 19, easily reconcil. Of this name,
without *s*. in 1834, as Farmer mark. three had been gr. at Harv. three
at Yale, and one at some other N. E. coll.

ANDREWS, ANDROWS (or ANDROS, sometimes), ABRAHAM, Farmington, s. perhaps of Francis, rem. to Waterbury, had eight ch. Rebecca, b.
1672; Mary, 1674; Hannah, 1678; Abraham, 1680; Sarah, bapt. 9
Mar. 1684; Rachel, 1686; John, 1688; and Thomas, 1699. ABRAHAM,
Waterbury, s. of John of Farmington, m. Sarah, d. of Robert Porter of
Farmington, had John, bapt. 9 Mar. 1684; Abraham, 17, certain. not,
as said somewhere, 27 July 1687; at Farmington ch. both; beside
Mary, Benjamin, and Robert. He d. 3 May 1693, leav. as appears
by Pro. rec. these five ch. and a wid. Between that Pro. rec. at
Hartford, and the town rec. of F. as well as of W. disagreem. may
be found; at least it was hard to guess, with confidence, after large inquiry, which Abraham was s. of Francis, wh. of John; and Hinman, wh.
rather darkens the confus. saves hims. from anxiety by acknowledg. only
one Abraham, while he informs us, that sometimes the name is giv. Andros, or Andrus. His report of Francis gives him no Abraham, and tho.

he allows one to John, the report is incomplete. BENJAMIN, Farmington, s. of John, by w. Mary, had Benjamin, b. 1683; John, 1685; both,
with their mo. bapt. 10 Jan. 1687, prob. d. young; Mary, 26 Aug. 1688;
Benjamin, and John, again, tw. 19 May 1689; and Thomas, 1690; beside Daniel, bapt. 10 Sept. 1693; Samuel, 24 Nov. 1695; perhaps more.
*DANIEL, Salem, sch.master, in 1672, was, Dr. Bond thinks, s. of Thomas
of Watertown, liv. in the pt. call. the vill. now Danvers, for wh. in the
June Sess. 1689, the first yr. of liberty recov. from Andros, he was rep.
and in 1692 was charg. with the preposter. crime of witchcraft, perhaps
bec. he kn. more than some of his neighb. but was releas. early in the yr.
foll. when reason prevail. over the influence of Cotton Mather. DANIEL,
Farmington, s. of John, had Daniel, b. 9 Mar. bapt. 20 July 1673; Mary,
9, bapt. 13 Dec. 1674; Joseph, b. 10 Aug. 1676; Thomas, 1678; John,
10 June 1680; Martha, 17, bapt. 23 July 1682; Hannah, bapt. 18 Jan.
1685; Paul, 3 Jan. 1687; Stephen, 1 Dec. 1689, prob. d. soon; and
Stephen, again, 28 Sept. 1690. EDWARD, Newport 1639, perhaps
rem. to Saco, at least one of the name was freem. there 1653, acc.
Folsom, 123, of the planta. I suppose he means, for he does not appear in
the Col. list, d. 1668. EDWARD, Hartford 1655, sw. freem. 1657, had
Edward, wh. d. unm. and Solomon; beside ds. Mary, and Sarah, of wh.
the last m. Henry Treat of H. and next David Forbes. EDWARD, Warwick, among freem. there 1655, but no w. or ch. is heard of; may possib.
be he who was early of Newport. FRANCIS, Hartford 1639, had John,
bapt. 27 Sept. 1646; and Thomas, 2 Jan. 1648; rem. to Fairfield, there
d. 1662, or 3, his will being of 6 June of the former. pro. 5 Mar. of the
latter yr. In it he provides for four s. and five ds. viz. in addit. to the
two bef. ment. were Jeremiah, and Abraham, ds. Eliz. Mary; Esther;
Rebecca, wh. bec. sec. w. 7 July 1678, of Samuel Benedict of Norwalk;
and Ruth; beside Hannah, wh. had m. John Crampton, after of Norwalk.
Quite uncert. is it, whether his s. Abraham were the man, wh. d. 1693, or
he wh. had ch. 1699. *HENRY, Taunton, an orig. purchas. rep. 1639
and four next yrs. d. 1652, is chiefly kn. from his will of 13 Mar. in that
yr. pro. 10 Feb. foll. in wh. are nam. his w. Mary; and ch. Henry; Mary,
w. of William Hodges; Sarah; Abigail; and gr.s. John Hodges. The
wid. in her will of 14 Feb. 1654, calls hers. 43 yrs. old, and speaks of Sarah as little. Baylies, II. 282. In Emery, I. 48 he is shown to have
built the first meeting-ho. but this author inadvert. finds him permis. to
erect a saw-mill in 1659, wh. must be refer. to his s. HENRY, Taunton,
wh. was k. by the Ind. in Philip's war; and tho. descend. are said to be
num. I regret that no acco. of m. or name of w. or ch. is kn. JAMES,
Saco, s. of Samuel of the same, rem. with his mo. on her sec. m. to Falmouth, m. Sarah, d. of Michael Mitton, had Elisha, wh. was a lieut. so

early as 1689, under Church in his campaign against the E. Ind. and prob. James and Joshua that both d. bef. the f. He abandon. Falmouth in the war, and d. at Boston 1704, leav. wid. Margaret, whose surname is not seen, the s. Elisha, and three ds. Rebecca, w. of Jonathan Adams, of Boston ; Dorcas, w. of Ebenezer Davenport, of Dorchester; and Jane, w. of Robert Davis, but perhaps she had former h. JEDEDIAH, Dover 1657, rem. to Salisbury, there had Joseph, b. 10 Mar. 1670 ; and in 1674 ad- min. on his est. was commit. to his wid. Mary, wh. m. 24 Aug. in that yr. John Allen, as under his name may be seen. JEREMIAH, Bedford 1697, was s. prob. of Francis of Fairfield. JOHN, Kittery or Saco 1640. JOHN, Lynn 1650, may be he wh. was a baker, and d. at Ipswich 13 Mar. 1662, and his w. Sarah d. 29 Apr. 1666. JOHN, Farmington, one of the first sett. freem. 1658, by w. Mary had Mary, b. 1643; John, 1645 ; Han- nah, 1647, all bapt. 16 May 1658 ; Abraham, 1648; Daniel, 1650 ; Jo- seph, 1652 ; these three bapt. 2 Apr. 1654 ; Rachel, bapt. 9 Apr. 1654 ; but why all were not bapt. at once, may be left to plausible conject. Ste- phen, b. 1656 ; and Benjamin, 1659 ; and d. 1682. Of the ch. my knowl. is less complete ; John, eldest s. was prob. of Hartford, and had John, Joseph, Stephen, and others, yet m. or b. dates are blank ; Mary m. a Barnes ; Hannah m. Richards, prob. Obadiah ; and Rachel m. a Buck. JOHN, Ipswich 1642, had w. Jane, was oppress. imprison. by An- dros' admin. liv. in 1701. He was then 80 yrs. old, and his w. if alive, was one yr. younger. JOHN, Boston, a cooper, by w. Lucy, wh. d. 1 Sept. 1653, had no ch. kn. to me, but by w. Hannah had John, b. 21 Nov. 1656, prob. d. young ; Hannah, Mary, and Martha, these three, bapt. 2 June 1661 ; James, 1, bapt. 4 Dec. 1664 ; and James, again, bapt. 24 Mar. 1667. JOHN, Kittery, wh. d. 1671, left s. John, and a wid. Joan, wh. prob. bec. w. of Benjamin Atwell. JOHN, Hartford, s. of William of the same, had, by w. Mary, at the time of his d. 8 June 1690, only two liv. ch. Samuel, 20 yrs. old ; and Mary, 8. JOHN, Fairfield 1670, s. of Francis of the same, d. 1683, leav. two ch. JOHN, Ipswich, by w. Judith had Eliz. b. 7 Mar. 1685, was 36 yrs. old in 1684. JOHN, Hingham, wh. m. Patience Nichols in Sept. 1685, as in Geneal. Reg. II. 253, correct. by Errata in the introduct. is there call. s. of Capt. Thomas, but when it is said, that he was b. 1658, I fear it is only drawing a bow at a venture, for if b. that yr. it might seem as if he should be count. br. not s. of the Capt. since the other count. makes him gr.-gr.s. of the first Thomas of the same. *JOSEPH, Hingham 1635, s. of Thomas the first, b. in Eng. freem. 3 Mar. 1636, was the first town clk. constable, rep. 1636–8, had rem. to Duxbury soon after, but Joseph, Ephraim, and Thomas may have been b. bef. such rem. as only ch. at D. nam. is Abigail, 1647, wh. m. July 1667, John Wadsworth ; at D. he was a town officer 1654, and constable 1664,

d. 1 Jan. 1680, aged 83. Lincoln's Hist. of H. 42, 163. JOSEPH, Wethersfield, s. of John of Farmington, d. 1706, leav. six or more ch. of wh. I kn. neither the mos. nor their dates. NATHAN, New Haven, youngest s. of William the first of the same, took o. of fidel. 1 May 1660, m. Oct. 1661, Deborah, d. of Robert Abbot, wh. d. 1672, had Nathan, b. 18 Oct. 1662; Abigail, 20 Mar. 1667; and Daniel, 13 May 1669; and for sec. w. m. 6 Jan. 1676, Phebe Gibbard, d. of William, wh. d. 19 Dec. 1720, had Sarah, 27 Oct. 1676; Jedediah, 14 May 1678; Gideon, 9 Mar. 1680; and perhaps others. He was a man of large prop. at Wallingford 1670, and New Haven 1685. NICHOLAS, Marblehead, m. Eliz. d. of Edmund Nicholson of the same, bef. 1672. RALPH, Gloucester 1681, m. 12 Dec. 1682, Abigail, d. of Thomas Very. ROBERT, Ipswich, freem. 6 May 1635, kept an inn, and in Col. Rec. I. the name is spell. Andros as well as Andrews; had w. Eliz. nam. in his will, pro. 26 Mar. 1644, in wh. also eldest s. John and younger Thomas are ment. but not d. Rebecca, w. of Daniel Hovey, tho. her s. Daniel is; and d. Alice is, wh. m. William Franklin of Boston, as also her d. Eliz. Ano. ROBERT was of Topsfield 1661, and in 1675, a soldier of brave Capt. Gardner's comp. k. in the storming, 19 Dec. of the Narraganset fort. SAMUEL, Saco, came in the Increase, from London, 1635, aged 37, with w. Jane, 30; and ch. Jane, 3; Eliz. 2; and a serv. sent by a goldsmith of London; had here James, bef. ment. and d. bef. 1638. His wid. m. Arthur Mackworth of Falmouth, and bore him sev. ch. Folsom, 33, 123. Willis, I. 33. 3 Mass. Hist. Coll. VIII. 259. SAMUEL, Charlestown, d. prob. Oct. 1659, his inv. being of the last day of that mo. SAMUEL, Marlborough 1667, made the survey of that town, but was, perhaps, that Cambridge man, whose name is common. giv. without s final. SAMUEL, New Haven, elder br. of Nathan, b. in Eng. took o. of fidel. 1654, m. in 1661, Eliz. only d. of deac. William Peck of the same, had Samuel, b. 1 Feb. 1662, d. in one mo. Samuel, again, 30 Aug. 1663; William, 9 Feb. 1665; John, 4 July 1667, d. young; Nathaniel, 2 Aug. 1670; rem. to Wallingford 1672, had tw. 30 May 1673, wh. d. the same day; Eliz. 17 July 1674; Mary, 27 Mar. 1677; Joseph, 1679; Margery, 15 Jan. 1681; and Dinah, 25 July 1684. He d. 6 Oct. 1704, aged 69, in his will nam. w. Eliz. four s. and four ds. The date of wid. d. is not seen. SAMUEL, Hartford, s. of William of the same, freem. 1669, m. Eliz. d. of Thwait Strickland, d. Jan. 1712, his will being made 1, and his inv. dat. 29 of the same. He names in it s. Thomas, Nathaniel, John, and Samuel, ds. Abigail Stedman, and Eliz. A. wh. m. Joseph Day. Samuel, his s. was k. by the Ind. the same yr. above Deerfield. SOLOMON, Hartford, s. of Edward of the same, d. 1712, leav. only Mary. THOMAS, Dorchester 1635, had Thomas, bapt. 16 June 1639; and Susanna, wh. m. William Hopkins; and d. 20 Aug. 1667. His will of two wks. bef. ment. w. Ann, wh. d. 13 Jan. 1684; the s. and d. Susanna, with her childr. THOMAS, Hingham, brot. fam. or was brot. by his s. and d. 21 Aug. 1643, at gr. age. THOMAS, Cambridge, was first of Watertown, as Dr. Bond remarks, there hav. by w. Rebecca, Thomas, b. 15 Oct. 1641; Daniel; Rebecca, 18 Apr. 1646; and d. bef. 1649. His wid. m. 1648, Nicholas Wyeth, and d. Rebecca m. John Frost. THOMAS, Hartford, freem. 1667, was perhaps s. of Francis of the same. THOMAS, Ipswich, perhaps s. of Robert of the same, was that sch.master, wh. succeed. famous Ezekiel Cheever, 1 Aug. 1660, and cont. in that office to his d. 10 July 1683, never m. but his nephs. John A. of Salem, and Daniel Hovey jr. of I. had admin. on his est. THOMAS, Dorchester, prob. s. of Thomas of the same, m. 31 Dec. 1667, Phebe, d. of Richard Goard, had Thomas, b. 31 Dec. 1668; Joseph, 25 Dec. 1675; Thankful, 1 May 1680; and John, July 1686; and d. 6 Aug. 1704. THOMAS, Milford, s. of Francis, liv. there 1675–1700, m. Eliz. d. of Robert Porter of Farmington, had Hannah, and Mary, bapt. 31 May 1685; and a fam. perhaps, of other ch. THOMAS, Middletown, s. of William of Hartford, m. Hannah, d. of John Kirby of M. d. early in 1691, leav. seven ch. Thomas, John, Samuel, Hannah, Eliz. Sarah, and Abigail. His wid. m. Alexander Rollo. Early at Rowley, or Boxford, was one Thomas, and one at Dorchester 1641, unless this be rather thot. the veteran of Hingham. THOMAS, Hingham, s. of Joseph of the same, was a capt. in the extravag. expedit. of Sir William Phips, 1690, against Quebec, in wh. he perish. by smallpox, late in Nov. 1690, hav. made his will 26 of that mo. had Jedediah, b. 7 July 1674, H. C. 1695, wh. bec. a min. at Philadelphia. Lincoln, 116. Perhaps he had others. WILLIAM, Lynn 1634, may be one of the early freem. of this name, 4 Mar. 1634, or 4 Mar. 1635, or 13 May 1640; of wh. the last William's surname is giv. with o, instead of e in the last syl. but he of 1635 hav. the prefix of respect may seem rather to belong to Charlestown or Cambridge by proximity of other names in that day's list. From Lewis in Hist. of L. no light is deriv. here. WILLIAM, New Haven, a promin. man, sign. the compact 1639, prob. accomp. Gov. Eaton, and no doubt was first at Boston or Charlestown; at N. H. was active in milit. serv. and kept the ordinary, one of the founders of the ch. and hard. could get leave to give up his ordinary, had William, and Samuel, perhaps b. in Eng. but Nathan, bapt. at N. H. 17 Nov. 1639; and d. 3 Jan. 1664. WILLIAM, Hartford, one of the early sett. came to H. from Cambridge, first sch.master, and soon town clk. had w. Mary wh. d. at C. 19 Jan. 1640, and sec. w. Abigail, wh. m. Nathaniel Barding; and he d. betw. 1655 and 1663, leav. ch. John; Eliz. wh. m. 3 May 1655, Edward Grannis; Thomas; and Samuel, the youngest, one acco. says b. 20, but ano. acco. makes him bapt. 19 Oct. 1645. WIL-

LIAM, New Haven, s. of William of the same, b. in Eng. m. 31 Jan. 1640, Mary Chandler, had ch. b. 1651 and 1653, wh. d. soon. He desert. his w. went to Kinsale, and there, as was said, m. ano. In Oct. 1661, after his abs. of eight yrs. his w. obtain. divorce. But that may be story of ano. man, for this William m. Ann, wid. of William Gibbard, d. of William Tapp, and d. 4 Mar. 1676, as by the highest authority I am instruct. His fam. was early extinct. WILLIAM, Ipswich, had William, b. 23 Oct. 1674; John, 2 Feb. 1676; Ezekiel, June 1680; Eliz. 15 Jan. 1685, d. under 1 yr. His w. was Margaret, at this time, but she may not have been mo. of the former childr. Ano. WILLIAM of Ipswich had Solomon, b. 8 Aug. 1699. Perhaps one of these many Williams was a carpenter, wh. came in the James from Southampton, 1635. Confusion very easily arises between names of so common occur. with so slight variations of residence, and other circumst. Of this name, 1834, Farmer found fifteen gr. at Harv. eight at Yale, and six at other N. E. coll.

ANDROS, EDMUND, Boston, appoint. by James II. gen. Gov. of N. E. arr. at Boston, 20 Dec. 1686, had been a dozen or more yrs. Gov. of N. Y. bef. his promot. Here he exercis. rule without law above two yrs. His w. d. at B. Feb. 1688. On the first report of the land. in Eng. of William of Orange, the gr. body of the people, eager to throw off the yoke, seized on the Gov. and his adherents and imprison. them, 18 Apr. 1689. Five mos. he was held close prisoner, tho. once he escap. to R. I. but was arrest. there and sent back; and the k. gave order 30 July for his being brought to Eng. Hutch. II. 208, says, he d. in London, Feb. 1714, at advanc. age, having tasted once more the sweets of power, as Gov. of Virg. soon after his going home. JEDEDIAH, Salisbury, by w. Mary, had Joseph, b. 10 Mar. 1670. His wid. m. 24 Aug. 1674, lieut. John Allen.

ANGELL, JAMES, Providence, s. of Thomas, m. Abigail, only d. of Gregory Dexter. JOHN, Providence, br. of the preced. m. 7 Jan. 1670, Ruth Field, but of neither h. nor w. has any acco. reach. me. THOMAS, Providence, one of the earliest sett. with Roger Williams, one of the freem. 1655, and constable, had James and John, wh. there dwelt 1676, and did not rem. in Philip's war, beside ds. Amphyllis, Mary, Deborah, Alice, and Margery, whose descend. are num. He d. 1694, as is thot. for his will was pro. 18 Sept. of that yr. He came from London, as serv. or apprent. of Roger Williams, as one tradit. has it, but ano. tradit. says, of Richard Waterman. John took o. of alleg. June 1668, and so may have been elder, for James is thus mark. May 1682. Alice m. 26 Jan. 1670, Eleazer Whipple of P. and Mary m. Richard Arnold.

ANGIER, EDMUND, Cambridge 1636, youngest s. of John of Dedham, Co. Essex, where he was b. a. 1612, and br. of John, min. of some distinct. at Denton, near Manchester, had liv. with John Cotton at Boston in Lincolnsh. and intend. to embark with him for N. E. in 1633, but was for that time prevent. freem. 13 May 1640, m. Ruth, d. of famous William Ames, the profess. at Franequer, had John, b. 21 Aug. 1645, wh. was bur. 2 Jan. 1648; Ruth, 28 Sept. 1647; John, again, 22 Apr. 1649, d. young; Ephraim, aged 27 at his d. 16 Jan. 1679; Samuel, 17 Mar. 1655, H. C. 1673; and John, again, 21 June 1656, d. young. His w. d. 3 July 1656, and he m. 12 June 1657, Ann, d. of Christopher Batt (but in Mitchell's Bridgewater, 105, the name is erron. giv. Pratt), had Edmund, 20 Sept. 1659; Hannah, 1660; Mary, 1663; John, May 1664, d. at 2 mos. Nathaniel, May 1665; and Eliz. 1667; beside Sarah, not seen on rec. Ruth m. 28 June 1671, Rev. Samuel Cheever, of Marblehead; Eliz. m. 29 Oct. 1691, Rev. Jonathan Pierpont, of Reading; Sarah m. 13 Dec. 1698, Rev. Christopher Tappan of Newbury; Edmund, and Nathaniel d. very early. His sec. w. d. 3 Oct. 1688, aged 58, and he d. 4 Mar. 1693. JOHN, Boston, m. 1651, Hannah, d. of William Aspinwall, had John, b. 16 Sept. 1652, wh. is call. by John Cotton's will cous. JOHN, Mass. of wh. we kn. only (strange as it appears), that he was gr. of Harv. 1653, and d. 1657. JONATHAN, Salem, 1668. JOSEPH, Medford 1684, rem. to Dorchester, by w. Eliz. had Eliz. b. 8 Dec. 1694; Margaret, 21 Mar. 1697; Joseph, 20 June 1702; Benjamin, 22 June 1704; rem. to Framingham, there had Mary, 31 Aug. 1709; and he d. of cancer, 30 Nov. 1718. His wid. d. 24 Jan. 1732. SAMUEL, Rehoboth, s. of Edmund of Cambridge, ord. at R. 15 Oct. 1679, m. 2 Sept. 1680, Hannah, only d. of Presid. Oakes (wh. d. 5 Dec. 1714, aged 54), had Ames, b. 29 June 1681, H. C. 1701; Hannah, 10 Aug. 1682, d. unm. at 32 yrs.; Ruth, 1684, wh. did not, as Mitchell supposed, m. Rev. John Shaw of Bridgewater; Samuel, Sept. 1687; Oakes; Ephraim; Uriah; Eunice; and John, 1701, H. C. 1720, the min. of Bridgewater, wh. d. 14 Apr. 1787. He rem. to the W. pt. of Watertown, now Waltham, and was install. 25 May 1697, d. 24 Jan. 1719. SAMPSON, York 1653, then allow. to sw. alleg. to Mass. See Col. Rec. IV. pt. i. 129. Of this name Farmer found twelve had, in 1834, been gr. at Harv. and four at all other N. E. coll.

ANNABLE, ANNIBLE, or ANNIBALL, *ANTHONY, Plymouth, came in the Ann 1623, with w. Jane, and ds. Sarah, and Hannah, was one of the first sett. at Scituate 1630, and found. of the ch. there, 8 Jan. 1635, had a ch. without name, bur. 8 Apr. of that yr. Deborah, there bapt. 7 May 1637; rep. 1639; rem. with his min. Rev. John Lothrop to Barnstable, of wh. he was rep. 1646, and often after. There he had, perhaps, Susanna, and his first w. d. Dec. 1643; and he m. 3 Mar. 1645, Ann Clark, or, in Geneal. Reg. IX. 315, Ann Alcock, by wh. he had Samuel, b. 2

Jan. bapt. 8 Feb. 1646 ; and Ezekiel, bapt. 29 Apr. 1649. The sec. w. was bur. 16 May 1651, and he m. soon third w. Ann Barker, by wh. he had Desire, 16 Oct. 1653, and the w. was bur. a. 16 Mar. 1658. Deane, 213, to reconcile these ms. with his notions of propriety, suppos. an Anthony jr. but it is clearly to be seen by the rec. that such invention is unnecess. Of the ds. Sarah m. 23 Nov. 1638, Henry Ewell; Hannah m. 3 Mar. 1645 (wh. is the same time with her f. taking sec. w.), Thomas Boreman; Susanna m. 13 May 1652, William Hatch; and Desire m. 18 Jan. 1677, John Barker. JOHN, Ipswich 1642, d. 8 Oct. 1664, of wh. we can see nothing more, but that he is call. a tailor in 1651, in Coffin's gatherings, where also I find MATTHEW call. 18 yrs. old in 1672. SAMUEL, Barnstable, s. prob. eldest, of Anthony, m. 1 June 1667, Mehitable, d. of Thomas Allyn of the same, had Samuel, b. 14 July 1669 ; Hannah, 16 Mar. 1672, d. in Aug. foll.; John, 19 July 1673; and Ann, 4 Mar. 1675.

ANNIS, ABRAHAM, Newbury, prob. s. of Charles, by w. Hannah had Charles, b. 10 Feb. 1694 ; Hannah, 19 Nov. 1698 ; John, 1 May 1700 ; Stephen, 1 Feb. 1702 ; and Sarah, 9 Sept. 1705. CHARLES, in Geneal. Reg. VII. 349 print. Carmac, Newbury, b. 1638, at Enniskillen, Ireland, m. 15 May 1666, Sarah, d. of Aquila Chase, had Charles; Priscilla, b. 8 Nov. 1677 ; Hannah, 15 Nov. 1679 ; Ann, 28 Dec. 1681 ; and prob. more, wh. are not in rec. JOSEPH, Newbury, prob. s. of Charles, by w. Dorothy had Dorothy, b. 1 Nov. 1692 ; Sarah, 14 Mar. 1694; Aquila, 14 June 1695 ; Seaborn, 1 Jan. 1697 ; Hannah, 19 Nov. 1698 ; Abigail, 25 Sept. 1700 ; and Joseph, 14 Jan. 1703 ; but the Hannah may belong to Abraham.

ANTHONY, ABRAHAM, Portsmouth, R. I. s. prob. of first John of the same, m. 26 Dec. 1671, Alice, d. of William Waddell, had John, b. 17 Nov. 1672 ; Susanna, and Mary, tw. 29 Aug. 1674, both d. soon ; William, 31 Oct. 1675 ; Susanna, again, 14 Oct. 1677 ; Mary, again, 2 Jan. 1680 ; Abraham, 21 Apr. 1682 ; Thomas, 30 June 1684, d. at 21 yrs.; Alice, and James, tw. 22 Jan. 1686, of wh. the latter d. at 18 yrs.; Ammi, 30 June 1688 ; Isaac, 10 Apr. 1690 ; and Jacob, 15 Nov. 1693 ; and his w. d. at the age of 84 in the ho. of s. William, 1734. JOHN, Portsmouth, R. I. one of the freem. 1655, and may have rem. to Providence ; but tho. to denote the earliest resid. at first I built on conject. too slight to be ment. yet for his coming we have perfect kn. that he took o. of alleg. and suprem. 24 Mar. 1634, with intent to emb. in the Mary and John, but was delay. for passage in the Hercules a few days after. He had liv. in the beautif. village of Hempstead, near London, and d. 28 July 1675, aged 68. In his will, made 5 days bef. he names his ch. John, Joseph, Abraham, Susanna, w. of John Tripp, and Eliz. w. of James Greene. His wid. Frances d. 12 Oct. 1692. JOHN, Portsmouth, R. I. s. prob. eldest,

of the preced. m. 23 Nov. 1669, Frances, youngest d. of William Waddell, had John, b. 28 June 1671; Joseph, 28 Oct. 1673; William, 18
July 1676; Susanna, 1 Jan. 1679, d. at 19 yrs.; Mary, 16 June 1681, d.
young; Sarah, 1 Oct. 1683, d. next yr.; Eliz. 14 Sept. 1686; Alice, 26
Apr. 1689; and Samuel, 8 Oct. 1691. As he took sec. w. 3 Jan. 1694,
Susanna, d. of John Alborow, it may be that his former w. was misrepr.
as wid. of his f. By this w. he had Albro, 25 Sept. 1694; Sarah, 1 Aug.
1697; and John 16 Feb. 1699; and d. 20 Oct. 1715. JOSEPH, Portsmouth, R. I. br. of the preced. m. 5 Apr. 1676, Mary, d. of Thomas Wait,
had John, b. 10 Sept. 1678; Joseph, 19 May 1682; Susanna, 24 Oct.
1684; and Thomas, wh. d. young.

ANTRAM, OBADIAH, Salem, s. of Thomas of the same, left good est. to
w. Martha, of wh. no ch. is ment. when he was lost at sea on voyage to
Nevis or other W. I. isl. THOMAS, Salem, came in the James from
Southampton, 1635, arr. at Boston, 3 June, is called a weaver of Salisbury, Co. Wilts, in the ship's clearance; had gr. of ld. 1637, was of the
ch. 1639, freem. 18 May 1642, d. 1663; had bapt. Obadiah, 7 June 1640;
Mary, 16 July 1643; and John, 29 Mar. 1646.

APPLEBY, THOMAS, Rye, 1662–72, perhaps d. 1690 at Woodbury.

APPLEGATE, JOHN, Gravesend, L. I. 1650, with Eliz. perhaps his mo.
it may be wid. of Thomas, and prob. his s. John, was of Oyster bay 1685.
He bot. ho. and ld. 1662, at Fairfield, and there was liv. in 1670, as the
Conn. jurisdict. could not be preserv. at L. I. One of the name was at
F. 1697; and a John A. made his will 1704 nam. no ch. but giv. est.
to his w. Avis, and br. Thomas A. and his ch. A John was complain.
of at Milford for sell. liquor, and Bartholomew A. at the same time.
THOMAS, Weymouth 1635, was licens. to keep ferry to Braintree, but
next yr. turned out; had w. Eliz. whose tongue was sentenc. by the ct.
to be confin. by cleft stick.

APPLETON, ISAAC, Ipswich, s. of the sec. Samuel of the same (by his
sec. w.), m. Priscilla, d. of Thomas Baker of Topsfield, and gr.d. of dep.
gov. Symonds, had Priscilla, b. 1697; Mary, 1701; Isaac, 1704; Eliz.
Martha; Rebecca, and Joanna; and he d. 1747. Of this only s. Isaac,
wh. had many s. descend. the venerable Jesse, Dart. Coll. 1792, Presid.
of Bowdoin, and he was gr.f. of the brs. Samuel, Nathan, and Ebenezer,
as also of their cous. William, all disting. merch. of Boston, wh. are of the
thirteenth generat. from John of Great Waldingfield in Co. Suffolk, wh.
d. 1414, the remotest kn. ancest. of the fam. *JOHN, Ipswich, eldest s. of
Samuel, the progenit. was b. 1622 at Little Waldingfield in Co. Suff. and
brot. at the age of thirteen yrs. by his f. m. Oct. 1651, Priscilla, d. of the
Rev. Jose Glover, wh. d. 1638, on his passage to our country to estab. the
first print. press, had John, b. 17 Oct. 1652; Samuel; Priscilla, 1657,

wh. m. Rev. Joseph Capen of Topsfield ; Jose, 1660, wh. was a merch. of Boston, and d. unm. 18 Nov. 1721; Eliz. wh. m. 12 Nov. 1673, the sec. Richard Dummer; Sarah, wh. m. Daniel Rogers, not Samuel, as the beautif. Memorial of the fam. has it; and Mary, 1673, wh. m. Nathaniel Thomas of Marshfield. He was lieut. capt. and major, rep. 1656 many yrs. up to 1679, yet not freem. bef. 1682, if we follow the official lists ; but as a strenuous asserter of liberty against the governm. after the nullificat. of the old chart. one of the most disting. he had the honor of being imprison. at Boston, fin. £50, and bound in £1000 for a yr. on acco. of resistance to the arbitra. taxation. See Revo. in N. E. justif. His will of 16 Feb. 1698, was pro. 27 Mar. 1700, but he d. 4 Nov. 1699. ‡* JOHN, Ipswich, eldest s. of the preced. m. 23 Nov. 1681, Eliz. eldest d. of Presid. Rogers, had Eliz. Nathaniel, b. 9 Dec. 1693, H. C. 1712, the min. of Cambridge; Margaret; Daniel, b. 1695; and Priscilla, 1697. He was freem. 1682, largely employ. in pub. offices, town clk. 1687, rep. 1697, and next yr. a council. in wh. place he serv. many yrs. beside being judge of pro. d. 11 Sept. 1739. JOHN, Ipswich, s. of Samuel the sec. eldest by his sec. w. rem. perhaps to Salem, m. there 1689, Rebecca, d. of John Ruck, had John, b. 1695; and Benjamin. He had for sec. w. m. 1700, a wid. Dutch, but wh. was her bapt. name, or wh. was her former h. or f. or when she d. are all untold; but he d. 1724. OLIVER, Ipswich, youngest br. of Isaac of the same, by w. Sarah had Joseph; John, b. 1707; Oliver, 1712 ; Samuel, 1713; Daniel; Nathaniel, 1721 ; beside Joanna, and two more ds. but I regret to mark the deficiency of dates, and sometimes of names. He was well provid. for in the will of his f. and d. 1759. * SAMUEL, Ipswich, s. of Thomas of Little Waldingfield Co. Suffk. b. 1586, came 1635, with fam. hav. project. earlier settlem. as is well infer. from the expressn. in a letter of his neighb. our first Gov. Winth. 14 Aug. 1630, soon after arr. here, to his s. John in Eng. that Mr. A. can have no cows, because more than half of their stock d. on the passage. He was sw. freem. 25 May 1636, and chos. rep. next yr. He serv. in that capacity no other yr. and d. at Rowley 1670. The w. brot. by him from Eng. was Mary Everard, and their five ch. all b. bef. his coming over, were John, bef. ment. b. 1622; Samuel, 1624; Sarah, 1627, wh. m. prob. 1652 or 3, Rev. Samuel Phillips of Rowley, in whose ho. the f. d.; Judith, wh. m. 12 Dec. 1657, Samuel Rogers of I. and d. 1659 ; and Martha, wh. m. Richard Jacob of I. ‡* SAMUEL, Ipswich, s. of the preced. bapt. 1624 at Little Wallingfield, brot. in 1635 by his f. m. Hannah, d. of William Paine of I. had Hannah, wh. m. William Downes of Boston ; Judith, wh. m. 1678, Samuel Wolcott of Wethersfield ; and Samuel, b. 1654; and by sec. w. m. 8 Dec. 1656, Mary, d. of John Oliver of Newbury, had John, b. 1660 ; Isaac, 1664 ; Joanna, wh. m. Nathaniel Whipple ; and Oliver,

1676.   He was a man of the highest repute in civ. and milit. serv. rep.
1668 and often after to 1681, when he was made Assist. and by ann.
elect. cont. in that rank to the time of overthrow of the chart. governm.
1686.   In 1675 he had com. of all the Mass. forces on Conn. riv. and late
in the season, when succeed. by Major Savage in that quarter, was transfer. to the expedit. against Narraganset for the bloody and decisive action
of 19 Dec.   Resolute in support of the liberty of the people against the
unlawf. taxation in 1687, he was imprison. by Andros, and hardly releas.
See Hutch. I. 365.   In the new Chart. of William and Mary, 1691, he
was made one of the council, tho. by the pop. vote left out at the foll.
elect. d. 15 May 1696; and his will of 17 Apr. 1695 was pro. 25 May
of next yr.   SAMUEL, Ipswich, s. of John the first, d. 1693, leav. wid. and
four ch. Jose, Samuel, Thomas, and John; but the fam. Memo. supplies
no larger acco.   ‡ SAMUEL, Ipswich, eldest s. of Samuel the sec. m. Eliz.
d. of William Whittingham, had Samuel, Whittingham, Hannah, Martha,
and Eliz.   He was much in pub. serv. of the counc. 1703, was head of
one of the regim. 1707 against Port Royal, and d. 30 Oct. 1725.   His
wid. m. 1726 Rev. Edward Payson of Rowley.   Of this name, in 1834,
gr. were twelve at Harv. three at Dart. and seven at other N. E. coll.
of wh. none at Yale.

APPLIN, JOHN, Watertown, m. 23 Nov. 1671, Bethshua, d. of Thomas
Bartlett, had John, b. 15 Oct. 1672, d. at 18 yrs.; Bethshua, 1 May 1673;
acc. Bond 9; Mary, 11 Oct. 1677; Hannah, 25 Mar. 1680; Thomas, and
Edward, tw. 15 Mar. 1682; of wh. the latter d. in a few days; Abiel, 12
May 1684; Mehitable, 7 Apr. 1688; and John, again, 3 May 1692.   His
w. d. 8 Oct. 1692; Bethshua m. 3 Jan. 1698, John Stratton; Mary m.
30 July 1716, John Anderson, as his sec. w.; Hannah m. 11 May 1703,
John Farr; and Mehitable m. 27 Sept. 1711, Benjamin Headley.   He
was ask. in Apr. 1703, to keep a sch. at Groton, and was short time at Lit-
tleton; may have been not b. in N. E. and was liv. 1725.

ARBUCKLE, WILLIAM, Boston 1684.

ARCHER, or ARCHARD, BENJAMIN, York 1680, was perhaps s. of John
of Salem.   HENRY, Roxbury, m. 4 Dec. 1639, Eliz. d. of John Stow of
the same, had Rachel, John, Isaac, and Theophilus, nam. in the will of
Rachell Bigg of Dorchester, made 17 Nov. 1646, and perhaps others, after
rem. to Ipswich or bef. as there is reason for conject. that all were b. at I.
He was freem. 2 June 1641; and his w. d. there 11 Apr. 1669.   JOHN,
Portsmouth, R. I. freem. 1655, was prob. the man ment. in Hubbard's
Ind. Wars, whose s. was k. 25 June 1675, the first day of hostil.   JOHN,
Stamford 1660.   JOHN, Salem 1668, cooper, had gr. of ld. 1676, and ad-
min. on his est. was giv. 26 Feb. 1694, to his s. Benjamin, and Thomas.
SAMUEL, Salem, 1630, req. adm. as a freem. 19 Oct. of that yr. but I see

not, that he was ever sw. in, yet marshal in 1650, and 1, call. 50 yrs. old in 1665, had w. Susanna, s. Samuel, prob. others ; was a carpenter, and d. Dec. 1667. The wid. Susanna m. Richard Hutchinson. SAMUEL, Andover, freem. 1668, had m. 21 May 1660, Hannah, d. of John Osgood ; but was perhaps of Salem, and s. of the preced.

ARDELL, WILLIAM, Boston 1687, merch. rem. to Portsmouth, and was made, 1699, Sheriff of the Prov. of N. H. Belkn. I. 155.

AREY, RICHARD, Edgartown 1652, d. 19 Nov. 1669, leav. John, wh. d. 12 Oct. 1675.

ARIN, WILLIAM, Dover, was k. says Mr. Quint, in Geneal. Reg. V. 449, by the Ind. 28 June 1689.

ARMITAGE, or ARMATAGE, ELEAZER, Lynn, m. 18 Oct. 1669, Hannah Needham, perhaps d. of Edmund. GODFREY, Lynn 1630, a tailor, rem. to Boston, freem. 14 Mar. 1639, by w. Sarah, perhaps d. of William Webb, had Samuel, b. 7, bapt. 12 Oct. 1645, prob. d. young ; Rebecca ; and Samuel, again, b. 14 Apr. 1651. This last has mo. in the rec. nam. Mary. By the will of Rebecca Webb, wid. of William, all her est. was giv. to her gr.ch. Rebecca A. HENRY, Boston, came in the ship Society from Barbadoes, where he emb. 11 Mar. 1679, may have been only a transient visit. return. home, and taking this Col. in his way ; at least no more is kn. of him. JOSEPH, Lynn 1630, perhaps br. of Godfrey, freem. 9 Mar. 1637, by w. Jane, wh. d. 3 Mar. 1677, had John, and Rebecca, wh. m. 14 Nov. 1665, Samuel Tarbox, kept the first inn of that town, tho. he was a tailor, and d. 27 June 1680, aged 80, says Lewis. MANASSEH, a s. of H. C. 1660, wh. glad. would I find some, the minutest, story of, as date of b. or wh. was his f. or any thing else more than in the Magnalia, IV. 137, where he is mark. by a star, as evid. that he was d. 1698. SAMUEL, Boston, perhaps s. of Godfrey, a serj. had £10 a yr. in 1674 and 5, for carry. the halbert. THOMAS, Lynn, came in the James from Bristol, 1635, with Rev. Richard Mather and others, rem. 1637, to Sandwich. Lewis. He had gr. of ld. 1641 at Stamford, where he may have been on a visit ; at least, he did not settle there. TIMOTHY, Boston 1677, mariner, m. a d. of Richard Richardson.

ARMS, WILLIAM, Hatfield, a soldier in Philip's war, 1676, serv. under Capt. William Turner, m. 1677, Joanna Hawks, had eight ch. there, rem. to Sunderland, thence to Deerfield, where he d. 1731 ; and there liv. his s. John, Daniel, and William ; and six of the name had, in 1828, been gr. at N. E. coll.

ARSMBEE, or ARMESBEY, sometimes, as in Baylies, AMSBURY, THOMAS, Taunton 1668, had Thomas, b. 23 Feb. 1669 ; Mary, 3 Oct. 1671 ; Rebecca, 26 May 1672, (if we believe the rec.) ; and Judith 8 Jan. 1674.

ARMSTRONG, BENJAMIN, Norwich, by w. Rachel had Benjamin, b. 20

Nov. 1674; John, 5 Dec. 1678; Joseph, 10 Dec. 1684; and Stephen, 31 Mar. 1686; made his will 5 Nov. 1717, and d. 10 Jan. foll. In that doc. Stephen is not ment. and prob. was d. Benjamin jr. sett. at Windham. GREGORY, Plymouth, d. 5 Nov. 1650. See 2 Mass. Hist. Coll. III. 184. JONATHAN, Westerly, or Pawcatuck, in that debatab. part of the Narraganset territ. call. in the native speech, Misquamicuck,.by the Eng. Squamicuck, claim. by Conn. jurisdict. as belong. to their planta. of Stonington, 1670, rem. to Norwich 1678, perhaps, for then ld. was gr. to him. He prob. rem. after to Roxbury, where his d. Mercy d. 2. Oct. 1694, and Martha d. 15 Dec. 1709. MATTHEW, Boston 1664, mariner, perhaps had come from Maryland, for I find his wid. in 1672, sold est. in Somerset Co. of that Prov.

ARNOLD, §‡ BENEDICT, Providence 1636, eldest s. of William the first, b. in Eng. 21 Dec. 1615, perhaps in Co. Nottingham, m. Damaries, d. of Stukely Wescott, had Godsgift; Josiah; Benedict, b. as tradit. tells, in 1641; Freelove; Oliver; and Caleb; beside other ds. Damaris, Priscilla, and perhaps Penelope; was the richest man in the Col. and by thoro. acquaint. with the manners as well as lang. of the aborig. bec. the most effect. auxil. in all negotiat. with them. In 1653 he rem. to Newport, was chos. Assist. next yr. and in 1663 made by the royal chart. Presid. and by ann. elect. so cont. for eight yrs. and d. 1678. His will of 24 Dec. 1677, with codic. of 10 June foll. was pro. 1 July. Both Godsgift, and Freelove, are by differ. auth. made to m. Edward Pelham, and, possib. he had the two; Penelope is said to have m. Roger Goulding; and Damaris m. John Bliss. See R. I. Hist. Coll. II. 51, and III. 294; Callender; Winth. and Knowles. ‡ * BENEDICT, Newport, s. of the preced. had been an Assist. 1690 to 95, and was rep. 1699; m. 9 Mar. 1671, Mary, perhaps nam. Turner, had Godsgift, b. 19 May 1672; Sion, 12 Sept. 1674; Mary, 1678; Content, 26 Feb. 1681; Benedict, 28 Aug. 1683; and Caleb. By sec. w. Sarah Mumford, whose f. I do not kn. he had Comfort, 21 May 1695; Ann, 14 July 1696; and Sarah, 3 Nov. 1698; and he d. 4 July 1727 in his 86th yr. His wid. d. 14 Oct. 1746, aged 78. CALEB, Portsmouth, R. I. s. perhaps youngest, of Benedict the first, by w. unkn. to me, but by Potter thot. d. of Capt. Samuel Wilbor, had William, Samuel, Oliver, Josiah, Sarah, and Penelope, and d. 1719. DANIEL, Hartford. s. of John of the same, often spell. ARNALL, or ARNOLL, had w. and childr. whose names are unkn. was freem. 1665, and d. 10 May 1691. EDWARD, Boston 1640, by w. Martha had Barachiah, b. 22 Feb. 1654; Mary, 16 Sept. 1655; and Eliz. 7 May 1657; and d. 8 Aug. 1657. ELEAZER, Providence, s. of the first Thomas, sw. alleg. May 1671, and d. 29 Aug. 1722. ELISHA, Providence, s. of Stephen the first, took o. of alleg. May 1682, m. the same yr. Susanna Carpenter,

ARNOLD. 65

d. of William sec. of the same, had Ephraim, Elisha, and a d. of whose
name rec. is not found, nor of date of b. of either of the ch. His will
was pro. 2 Apr. 1711. EPHRAIM, Braintree, s. of Joseph, by w. Mary
had Samuel, b. 1 Jan. 1689; Mary, 1 Oct. 1690; and Ephraim, 21 July
1695. HENRY, Hartford 1683 to 90, and after, yet no more is kn. tho.
he had w. and childr. ISRAEL, Providence, eldest s. of Stephen the first
of the same, sw. alleg. May 1671; m. 16 Apr. 1677, wid. Mary Smith,
d. of James Barber, had Israel, b. 18 June 1678; and nine more ch. of
not one of wh. is rec. of b. kn. nor other means of find. even their names,
exc. in the will that gives all the ten. They were William, Elisha, Stephen, James, Joseph, Josiah, Mary, Sarah, and Barbara. He d. 1717.
JASPER, came in the Abigail, 1635, aged 40, from London, with Ann,
perhaps his w. 39, but no more is heard of either. JOHN, Cambridge,
freem. 6 May 1635, went as an orig. propr. to Hartford, there d. 1664,
very aged, leav. Josiah, Joseph, and Daniel, ment. in his will of 20 Aug.
pro. Dec. foll. in that yr. as also gr.ch. Mary Buck, but wh. was her f. or
mo. is not discern. His w. was Susanna. ‖ JOHN, Boston 1642, a plasterer,
freem. 10 May 1643, ar. co. 1644, prob. a single man, at least was so on
join. the ch. 22 Apr. 1643. His admor. Samuel A. of Marshfield, enter.
claim. 29 Oct. 1661, to certain lds. in Boston, as the right of his intest.
JOHN, Weymouth, s. of Joseph of Braintree, a soldier on Conn. riv. 1675,
may be that one of Moseley's comp. Dec. 1675, whose name in Geneal.
Reg. VIII. 242 is made Arvell; by w. Mary had William, b. 22 Nov.
1678; Mary, 12 Sept. 1681; Margaret, 14 Oct. 1683; and James.
JOHN, Providence, s. of Thomas the first of the same, took o. of alleg.
May 1671, and d. 5 Jan. 1722. JOHN, Norwich 1680, rem. to Boston
in few yrs. and may indeed have first liv. there, was that prison-keeper,
wh. had custody of many of the respectab. inhab. of Salem, charg. with
witchcraft, especial. of one woman of whose safety he was the happy
means, under a forged order for discharge, as the curious myth is told in
a letter that Hutch. had partly copied, II. 61; and the letter writer assures us, that he saw the return of the officer on the docum. and was told
by the jailer, that for that discharge he was turned out of his office. In
1700 he went to New London, there was an anchorsmith, m. 6 Dec. 1703,
Mercy, wid. of Samuel Fosdick, had Ruhamah, b. 7 Sept. 1704; and Lucretia, 26 Aug. 1706; and d. 26 Aug. 1725, says the gr.stone, "aged a.
73 yrs." JOSEPH, Braintree, m. 8 June 1648, Rebecca Curtis, wh. d. 14
Aug. 1693, had William, b. 16 Mar. 1649; John, 2 Apr. 1650; Joseph,
18 Oct. 1652; Samuel, 7 Aug. 1658; and Ephraim, 4 Jan. 1664; many
of whose descend. may be seen in Thayer's Geneal. JOSEPH, Haddam,
s. of John of Hartford, was one of the first sett. and d. 22 Oct. 1691, leav.
John, aged 29; Joseph, 26; Samuel, 23; Josiah, 21; Susanna, 16;
6 *

Jonathan, 12 ; and Eliz. 9.   He was adm. freem. at Hartford 1658.
Hinman, 111, of the first Ed. slightly erron. as in his Ed. 2d p. 58, was corrected.   JOSIAH, Hartford, br. of the preced. freem. 1657, was liv. 1683.
JOSIAH, Providence, s. of Benedict the first, was a capt. m. Mary, eldest
d. of Thomas Ward of Newport, had Josiah, Edward, and William, wh.
all d. bef. he made his will, pro. 1724, as did also ano. w. Sarah, as prob.
sev. ds. besides Abigail, Mary, Content, Catharine, Comfort, without hs.
But six others, call. eldest ds. Eliz. Odlin, Ann Tibbal, Frances Allen,
Sarah Sanford, Penelope, and Freelove are ment.   In addit. to this num.
flock, Benedict, his eldest s. and Josiah, the youngest, with gr.s. Jonathan
Law, are ment.   He calls hims. of Jamestown, wh. is the isle of Conanicut, on wh. he had good est.   OLIVER, Jamestown, br. of the preced. in
his will pro. 1697 names w. Phebe and five ch.   By her he had Damaris,
b. 1680 ; Phebe, 1682, d. young ; Patience, 1684 ; Mary, 1687 ; Sarah,
1689 ; and Oliver, 1694.   ‡ RICHARD, s. of Thomas the first of Providence by sec. w. sw. alleg. 1670, was an Assist. 1681, and nam. in the
royal commiss. of counc. to Sir Edmund Andros, 1687.   He m. Mary, d.
of Thomas Angel, had Mary, Richard, Thomas, and John, and d. 22 Apr.
1710.   RICHARD, Providence, call. jun. when he took o. of alleg. 1682,
was s. of the preced.   * SAMUEL, Sandwich 1643, br. of John of Boston,
liv. after at Yarmouth, of wh. he was rep. 1654 and 6, and there by w.
Eliz. m. at Yarmouth, had Samuel, b. 9 May 1649 ; Seth ; and Eliz. wh.
m. Abraham Holmes of Rochester.   He was third min. of Marshfield, at
wh. place he was ord. 1658, and d. 1 Sept. 1693, aged 71.   SAMUEL,
Rochester, first min. of that town, ord. 1684, was s. of the preced. and d.
bef. 1717.   2 Mass. Hist. Coll. IV. 259–62.   SETH, Duxbury, br. of the
preced. had Edward, b. 24 Mar. 1680 ; Penelope, 21 Apr. 1682 ; Desire ;
Benjamin ; James ; and perhaps Eliz. wh. m. a Winsor.   ‡ STEPHEN,
Providence 1636, br. of Gov. Benedict, b. in Eng. m. 24 Nov. 1646, Sarah, d. of Edward Smith of Rehoboth, had Esther, b. 22 Sept. 1647 ;
Israel, 30 Oct. 1649 ; Stephen, 27 Nov. 1654 ; Eliz. 2 Nov. 1659 ; Elisha,
18 Feb. 1662 ; Sarah, 26 June 1665 ; and Phebe, 9 Nov. 1676 ; was an
Assist. 1667.   In his will he ment. all these, and gr.ch. James Dexter,
and Esther Hawkins.   When he d. is not kn. but his wid. Sarah d. 15
Apr. 1713.   THOMAS, Watertown, arr. from Virginia, whither he came
from London, May 1635, in the Plain Joan, bring. ch. perhaps Thomas,
said to have been b. 2 May 1625 ; Nicholas ; and Susanna (of wh. the
former two d. young), was made freem. of Mass. 13 May 1640, m. I suppose for sec. w. Phebe, d. of the first George Parkhurst, had Ichabod, b.
1 Mar. 1641 ; Richard, 22 Mar. 1643 ; John, 19 Feb. 1648 ; Ebenezer,
17 June 1651 ; after being fined once for neglect. the law of bapt. and
twice for neglect of pub. worship, with increas. weight, and his d. Susanna

hav. m. 7 Apr. 1654 John Farnum of Boston, wh. favor. the Bapt. views
of ordinances, he was driv. to Providence, liv. in that pt. now Smithfield,
sw. alleg. 1666, and d. Sept. 1674. He had been bapt. 18 Apr. 1599.
THOMAS, Providence, call. jun. when he took o. of alleg. June 1668, was
s. of the preced. by sec. w. and d. 3 Dec. 1726. Confus. in parts of the
rec. of this fam. in R. I. is found, but it may be avoid. by caution, as the
fam. tradit. makes sec. w. of the first Thomas to be Park, instead of Parkhurst, and where it tells, that a d. m. a Vernon, it may be easy blunder
for Farnum. WILLIAM, Hingham 1635, br. of the first Thomas, b. as is
said, 1589, had Benedict, Thomas, Stephen, beside one d. Joanna, wh. m.
Zechary Rhodes, and ano. Eliz. wh. m. Thomas Hopkins, all b. as is thot.
in Eng. rem. 1636, with Roger Williams to Providence, and was one of
the found. of the first Bapt. ch. on our side of the ocean, had gr. of ld. at
Newport 1638, but I presume resid. at P. was among freem. 1655.
Backus notes, that he was anc. of the infamously unhappy Benedict of
West Point. Of the ch. of one Arnold of Reading recov. from sickness near
to d. we may read the story in Mather's Life of Brock, Magn. IV. 142,
that is lamenta. extravag. and seems more ridicul. than extravag. Arnold is
the name of a parish in Eng. a. 6 miles N. from the borough of Nottingham. Three of this name had in 1834 been gr. at Yale, two at Dart. and
five at other N. E. coll. of wh. none at Harv.

ARROWSMITH, EDMUND, Pemaquid 1655. Sullivan, 287.

ARTHUR, JOHN, perhaps of Salem, had m. Priscilla, d. of John Gardner of the same, and had childr. but after his d. she with the ch. went to
her f. then liv. at Nantucket, yet it is not my happiness to find any other
of this surname on our side of the ocean.

ARTSEL, JOHN, Springfield, sw. fidel. 31 Dec. 1678, or the next day,
as the name is giv. by Boltwood, but other spell. may have sometimes
been used.

ASH, GEORGE, Hartford 1682. JOHN, Dover 1659, m. at Salisbury,
14 Aug. 1667, Mary, perhaps Bartlett. WILLIAM, Gloucester 1647, m.
Milicent, d. of William Addis, wid. of William Southmayd, was a mariner, rem. a. 1650 to New London, where his wid. for third h. m. Thomas
Beebe.

ASHBURN, or ASHBORN, JOSEPH, Milford 1675–1713.

ASHBY, ANTHONY, Salem 1665, m. Abigail, d. of Richard Hutchinson,
had Gershom, and Abigail, both bapt. 12 June 1670; and perhaps Benjamin, and Eliz. June 1684; had license to sell beer and cider, 1670,
Felt, I. 418. 2 Mass. Hist. Coll. VIII. 106. The name is there kept up,
and Edward Ashber, Beverly, freem. 1683, may be descend. ANTHONY,
New London 1688, prob. s. of the preced. tho. Caulkins, 351, considers
him the same, had Anthony, and two ds. Mary, and Hannah, old eno. to

join the ch. Feb. 1694. There, too, descend. were seen. BENJAMIN, Salem 1674, s. perhaps of Anthony the first, by w. Hannah had John, bapt. June 1693; Jonathan, 23 Sept. 1694; and prob. others. He was a shipbuild. EDWARD, Beverly, freem. 1683, perhaps s. of the first Anthony. Felt. THOMAS, New Haven, whose goods were order. to be apprais. 3 Apr. 1640, as he was lately drown. in co. with Thomas Johnson. Sometimes, perhaps, the first Anthony may be print. Ashley.

ASHCRAFT, JOHN, Stonington 1662, m. 12 Sept. 1670, Hannah Osborne, had John, b. 1671; Hannah, 1675; Ephraim, 1677; and Mary, 1680. Prob. descend. are there; and one Thomas A. mariner from Boston, d. Sept. 1724, at Bay of Honduras, leav. will made here 13 Jan. 1723.

ASHDOWN, JOHN, Weymouth, a soldier in Philip's war, at the Falls fight. No descend. were kn. 1736, when ld. was gr. to rep. of all in that stout band.

ASHFIELD, WILLIAM, Malden, by w. Jane had Mary, b. 20 Dec. 1691.

ASHLEY, sometimes ASHLY, DAVID, Springfield, eldest s. of Robert of the same m. 24 Nov. 1663, Hannah, d. of Henry Glover of New Haven, had Samuel, b. 26 Oct. 1664; David, 10 Mar. 1667; John, 27 June 1669; Joseph, 31 July 1671; Sarah, 19 Sept. 1673; rem. bef. Philip's war to Westfield, there had Mary, and Hannah, tw. 14 Dec. 1675, of wh. Mary d. soon; Jonathan, 21 June 1678; Abigail, 27 Apr. 1681; Mary, again 3 Mar. 1683; and Rebecca, 30 May 1685. Some of these ch. are on rec. in both towns. He d. 8 Dec. 1718. See Davis, Hist. of W. Jonathan, the min. of Deerfield, wh. used to pray for k. George, after the war of our revo. began, and Joseph, min. of Winchester, and after of Sunderland, both Y. C. 1730, and cousins, were his gr.s. One of the lines to seventh generat. is shown by Davis in Geneal. Reg. II. 394. EDMUND, Boston 1670, had liv. at Ipswich. EDWARD, Maine 1630, was prob. from Bristol, Eng. and may be he, who had a lot, a. 1650, at Gloucester, but it is not prob. EDWARD, Boston, freem. 1677, by w. Mary had William, b. 24 June 1674; Mary, 28 Apr. 1676; and Dorothy, 11 July 1687. The name in Prince's Ann. Winth. I. 29. Folsom, 46, and Baylies, I. 153 hardly can be refer. to the mem. of the first ch. at B. JONATHAN, Springfield, s. of Robert, m. 10 Nov. 1669, Sarah, d. of William Wadsworth of Hartford, whither he rem. 1682, and d. there 1705, leav. Jonathan, Joseph, Samuel, Sarah, and Rebecca. JOSEPH, Springfield, br. of the preced. m. 1685, Mary, d. of Joseph Parsons of Northampton, had Joseph, Ebenezer, Mary, Abigail, and Benjamin, rem. to Wethersfield, and d. 18 May 1698. His wid. m. 2 Mar. foll. Joseph Williston. ROBERT, Springfield 1639, perhaps had been of Roxbury a short time, as most of the early S. people were drawn from R. by

Pynchon, had David, b. 8 June 1642 ; Mary, 6 Apr. 1644 ; Jonathan, 25 Feb. 1646 ; Sarah, 23 Aug 1648 ; Joseph, 6 July 1652 ; and perhaps more. He d. 29 Nov. 1682, and his w. Mary, d. 19 Sept. foll. Mary, his d. m. 18 Oct. 1664, the sec. John Root of Farmington, after of West-field. THOMAS, Maine 1654, may have rem. to Boston 1658, where w. Joanna d. 27 Dec. 1661, and he m. the last of next mo. wid. Hannah Broome. THOMAS, Boston, by w. Mary had Mary; b. 1 Sept. 1681; Thomas, 3 Dec. 1682; and Ann, 17 Sept. 1684. WILLIAM, Wells, ap-point. constable there 4 July 1659. Eight of this name had in 1767 been gr. at Yale, and since that date one at Harv. and one at Dart.

ASHTON, HENRY, Boston 1673, from Co. Lancaster, Eng. was, I sup-pose, of Providence 1676, one of the men entitled, for staying out the war, to rec. an Ind. for a slave. JAMES, Providence 1639, freem. 1655, sw. alleg. to Charles II. May 1666, and perhaps rem. to New Jersey. JOHN, Scarborough, m. for his sec. w. Susanna, d. of Richard Foxwell of the same, but the date is uncert. yet prob. betw. 1670 and 80, and ·in the great Ind. war 1675–6, was of Marblehead. Southgate, p. 82 makes him have for first w. a d. of Andrew Alger, but after rem. says, he m. Mary, d. of Nicholas Edgcomb, wid. of George Page. Yet the same w. is ascrib. to John Austin, and all that we can be sure of, is that nothing is sure a. the matter. THOMAS, Providence 1639, perhaps br. of James. Both are call. proprs. and that no more can be told of either, is rather remarka.

ASHWOOD, JAMES, Boston. See Astwood.

ASLETT, or ARSLEBY, JOHN, Newbury, m. 8 Oct. 1648, Rebecca Ayer of Haverhill, rem. to Andover, there had Hannah, wh. m. a Brown ; Re-becca, b. 6 May 1652, m. 15 Dec. 1674, Timothy Johnson ; Mary, 24 Apr. 1654, m. 20 Nov. 1671, Samuel Frye; John, 16 Feb. 1657; Sarah, 14 Jan. 1659, d. soon; Ruth, 8 Aug. 1660 ; Sarah, again, 14 Aug. 1662, m. a Cole ; Eliz. d. 15 Mar. 1667 ; Samuel, d. 20 Dec. 1669 ; both, prob. inf.; and d. 6 June 1671. JOHN, Andover, s. of the preced. m. 8 July 1680, Mary Osgood, d. of Capt. John, d. 1728. Sometimes the name is Aslebe. See Abbot, Hist. 13, 26, and 201.

ASPINWALL, or ASPENALL, ELEAZER, Meriden, s. of Peter, had per-haps been sent by his f. to sett. at Woodstock, or New Roxbury, as it was first call. took charge, 1720, of a great farm belong. to Gov. Belcher, lying betw. Hartford and New Haven, had w. Mary, and ch. Aaron, Mary, Ann, and sev. others ; and Hinman says, he d. 1742, the inv. of good est. being of 2 July. JOSEPH, Cambridge, tw. br. of the preced. in early life was a mariner, trad. to very diverse regions, France, Jamaica, South America, at New York was a lieut. m. a niece of Lord Bellomont, and for sec. w. had the wid. of Samuel Smith, and died near his birthplace a. 1743. The fam. of this name at New York are deriv. from him. NATHANIEL, Woodstock, br. of the preced. had gone with his younger br. Thomas under their neighb. Capt. Andrew Gardner, in that disastrous expedit. of Sir William Phips, 1690, against Canada, in wh. young Aspinwall and his commander perish. After ret. m. a Bowen, as fam. tradit. tells, had Nathaniel, and Peter; but no more is kn. exc. from his will of 15 Feb. 1712, at W. pro. at Boston (as W. was call. of Co. Suffk.) 4 June 1713, in wh. the name of his w. Abigail is seen, but neither names nor number of ch. PETER, Dorchester, came from Tox-teth Park, adj. Liverpool, Co. Lancaster, but was early of Boston, in that part call. Muddy riv. now Brookline, where he purch. with Robert Sharp the large gr. of William Colbron, tho. he join. with the ch. of D. Fam. tradit. makes his first w. a Merrill, and in sixteen yrs. she d. with-out ch. but more exact is my inform. of his m. with Alice Sharp, "one of our br. Mr. William Tyng's maid serv." as the rec. of Cotton's ch. has notice of her adm. 9 Oct. 1642, because the same rec. tells of her hav. "now the w. of one Peter Aspinwall of D." letters of recommend. 30 Mar. 1645. I suppose she was sis. of Robert, but brot. no ch. to her h. On 12 Feb. 1662 he m. Remember, d. of Peter Palfrey of Reading, and had by her ten ch. Samuel, b. Nov. 4 or by Boston rec. 10, bapt. 16 foll.; Peter, 4 or by Boston rec. 14 June 1664; Nathaniel, 5 June 1666; Thomas, 21 Jan. 1668; Mehitable, bapt. 19 Dec. 1669, who d. unm. long past mid. life; Eliz. b. 24, bapt. 26 Nov. 1671; Eleazer and Joseph tw. b. 9 Nov. 1673; Mary, 4 Aug. 1677; and Timothy, 1682, d. at Bos-ton, dur. apprent. of smallpox; but of the time of his d. or his wife's I have no acco. Eliz. m. first a Stevens of Salem, next Daniel Draper of Dedham; and Mary m. a Baker of Northampton. His will of 29 Nov. 1687 pro. 28 Jan. 1692, in Vol. VIII. 67, names w. and the half score of ch. all alive. PETER, Woodstock, s. of the preced. one of the early sett. sent by his f. to help on the plant. of New Roxbury, as it was first call. m. a wid. Leavens, prob. from Roxbury, had one d. only kn. without name. SAMUEL, Brookline, eldest s. of Peter the first, m. Sarah Stevens of Roxbury, had Thomas; Samuel, H. C. 1714; Mehitable; Eliz. and Sarah; was a lieut. at the capt. of Port Royal 1690, and capt. at the time of his d. wh. occurr. by drown. in Charles riv. 6 Sept. 1727. His s. Thomas was f. of William, H. C. 1764, a disting. physician of the early part of this cent. and f. of lieut. Col. Thomas, H. C. 1804, late con-sul of the U. S. at London, so well kn. for his studies in our early hist. wh. still enjoys a valu. part of the orig. homestead of Peter the first. * ‖ WILLIAM, Charlestown 1630, prob. came in the fleet with Winthrop, serv. on the first jury of inquest in the Col. 28 Sept. of that yr. was one of the first mem. of the ch. being No. 10, and chos. one of the two deac.

at organiz. of ch. soon rem. to Boston, freem. 3 Apr. 1632, rep. chos. in place of Henry Vane, wh. went home Aug. 1637; but as a supporter of Wheelwright, and follow. of the teach. of Mrs. Hutchinson, was dismiss. disarm. disfranch. and banish. First he went to R. I. with so many other of his fellow saints, and was Secr. of that Col. but short time he liv. at New Haven 1641 and 2, yet came again, by favor of Court, to Boston, was clk. of the writs, or recorder, and ar. co. 1643; certain. a propr. at Watertown, tho. never resid. there, went home, and in 1653 publish. a queer book as prognostic of the millennium to open in 20 yrs. No mortificat. was felt prob. by him for non-arriv. of this fifth monarchy, as I suppose he did not even live to see the success of the rival dynasty. Cromwell alone was powerful eno. to retard such event, and the whole body of the people of Eng. with unanim. that was never bef. or since equal. in that kingd. by calls for the restor. of the ho. of Stuart postpon. the success of such enthusiasm. Of his fam. my report will be less exact than should be expect. yet that is not for failure of diligent inquiry. By w. Eliz. (somehow sis. of Christopher Stanley, more prob. of his w. Susanna, wh. bec. w. of Lieut. William Phillips) he had Edward, b. 26 Sept. 1630, d. soon; Hannah, 25 Dec. 1631; and of neither is the rec. of bapt. preserv. Eliz. of whose b. the town rec. is defic. was bapt. 22 Sept. 1633; Samuel, equal. unkn. by town rec. was bapt. 20th Sept. 1635; Ethlannah, b. 1, bapt. 12 Mar. 1637; and Dorcas, b. in his banishm. 14 Feb. 1640, and perhaps Mary. Hannah m. 1651, John Angier.

ASTWOOD, JAMES, Roxbury, came (with w. Sarah and a ch. wh. soon d.) in May 1638, had James, b. 29 Nov. 1638; John, 20 Sept. 1640, d. at 6 mos. John, again, whose b. is wrong on rec. of town, as he was bapt. 6 Mar. 1642; Joseph, 19 Nov. 1643, d. soon; Joseph, again, 10 Nov. 1644; both these dates being giv. as rec. of b. that may well be doubt. as both were the days of bapt. Sarah, bapt. 14 June 1646; and Mary, 26 Dec. 1647; of whose dates of b. it may be slightly lament. that we are ign. He was freem. 22 May 1639, rem. to Boston to bec. one of the found. of the sec. ch. where the name is writ. prob. as sound. Ashwood. The d. Mary, d. 21 Jan. 1652; and he d. the yr. after. His will of Sept. 1653, pro. 13 Oct. foll. is abbrev. in Geneal. Reg. VII. 337; and his wid. refus. execut. of that instrum. by wh. the est. was div. into seven parts, excus. hers. as going to Eng. In Vol. VIII. 62 of the same periodic. where the name appears Astod, as if the alphabet were short, as p. 275 proves were the assets, not above $\frac{1}{6}$ in the £, we see adequate apology. ‡ * JOHN, Roxbury, came by the Hopewell, Capt. Bundocke, in the spring of 1635, aged 26, a husbandman from Stanstead Abbey, Co. Herts, at R. had a w. Martha, wh. may have come in the same ship, was freem. 3 Mar. 1636, rem. to Milford 1639, there m. next yr. Sarah, wid.

of Sylvester Baldwin, was chos. rep. 1643 and 4, afterwards an Assist. of the Col. and a Commissionr. of the Unit. Cols. in 1653, went home, as agent, the next yr. and d. at London soon. His wid. d. Nov. 1669.

ATCHINSON, or ATCHISON, JOHN, Hatfield 1672, k. by the Ind. 19 Sept. 1677, leav. Eliz. Mary, John, and Benoni, of wh. the last d. 1704 at Springfield, and John d. 1738 at Brimfield.

ATHEARN, * SIMON, Martha's Vineyard, had come from New Hampsh. it is said, and m. Mary Butler, was rep. 1692, first under the new chart. by wh. that isl. was tak. from New York, and giv. to Mass. d. 26 Feb. 1714, aged 71. His ch. Solomon, Jethro, and Zerviah were bapt. at Barnstable, 14 July 1700, in right of his w. Descend. are num. at the Vineyard.

ATHERSTON, JOHN, Boston, came from London, 1634, in the Susan and Ellen, aged 24; but we see not any acco. of his resid. ret. or d.

ATHERTON, CONSIDER, Dorchester, s. of Humphrey of the same, m. 19 Dec. 1661 Ann Annable, as Mr. Clapp, the histor. of D. assures me, and I wish he could say, whose d. she was, had Humphrey, whose pious duty in repair. the sepulchre of his gr.f. the town reward. by gr. of 9 acres of meadow. *HOPE*, Hatfield, s. of Humphrey, after leav. coll. taught for some time the gr. sch. at Dorchester, began in 1669 to preach, was ord. 1671, freem. 1672, m. 1674, Sarah, d. of John Hollister of Wethersfield, had Hope, and Joseph, tw. b. 7 Jan. 1675, of wh. Hope prob. d. soon; and Sarah, 26 Oct. 1676. He serv. as chaplain, in Philip's war, to those forces employ. in the neighb. and at the battle of the Falls in Montague was present, 18 May 1676, under Capt. Turner, whose name has been since giv. to the cataract. During the retreat he was thrown from his horse, and lost in the woods; and tradit. tells (Hoyt's Antiq. Research. 133, 4), that the Ind. to wh. he in his destitut. offer. to surrender, so reverenc. or fear. his madness or sanctity, as to refuse to rec. him. He reach. home uninjur. exc. in the mind, hav. strange hallucinat. prob. from exhaust. or sleeplessn. or hunger, and d. 8 June 1677. The wid. m. Timothy Baker. ‡ * ‖ HUMPHREY, Dorchester 1636, came, perhaps, from Preston in Lancash. where the name contin. so late as 1780; was freem. 2 May 1638, ar. co. the same yr. and its capt. 1650, often selectman, and rep. nine yrs. fr. 1638, but not in success. yrs. and an Assist. chos. ann. 1654 to his d. and in 1656, succeed. Sedgwick, as Major-Gen. He d. 16 Sept. 1661, says the inscript. print. in Alden's Epit. and as that was Monday, and prob. refers to the cause of his d. thrown from his horse, on return from milit. rev. on Boston common by rid. over a cow, I prefer to say 17 Sept. (a. one o'clock, A. M. acc. the MS. of John Hull's Diary). Capt. Johnson, in Wonderwork. Provid. of Zion's Saviour, gives him good character; and Hubbard excites our fears, that everybody did not value him so highly, when he remarks, that by some "the manner of his d. was noted as a judgmt." Of what sin this *judgmt.* was thus *noted*, we may hardly venture to guess, tho. when mortals direct the bolts of eternal justice, their aim is commonly unanimous. Strange, it seems to me, is the indefiniteness of our knowl. of so promin. a man; for even the name of his w. is not seen. Yet ten or eleven ch. are kn. at least by name, and one or more there may have been of unkn. names; one or more b. in Eng. one or more of unkn. sex, if we are compel. to guess by their names; and one or more d. bef. the f. Of s. the oldest was Jonathan; of ds. Catharine (sometimes call. Eliz.), but wh. of the two, both b. in Eng. was elder, is uncert. Other ch. were Rest, bapt. 26 May 1639; Increase, 2 Jan. 1642; Thankful, 28 Apr. 1644; Hope, 30 Aug. 1646, H. C. 1665, bef. ment.; Mary, wh. must not be the same as Margaret, whose dates of b. or bapt. are equally undiscov.; Watching, bapt. 24 Aug. 1651; Patience, 2 Apr. 1654; and Consider. Great persev. was need. to learn, that Catharine m. 1650, Timothy Mather; Margaret m. 30 Dec. 1659, James Trowbridge, and d. 17 June 1672; Rest m. 15 Mar. 1661, Obadiah Swift; Thankful m. 2 Apr. 1665, Thomas Bird jr.; Mary m. 9 Apr. 1667, Joseph Weeks; and Patience m. Isaac Humphrey. JAMES, Dorchester, perhaps br. of the preced. rem. to Lancaster, where he had James, b. 13 May 1654; and Joshua, 13 May 1656; and soon after ret. to D. and liv. 1678 at Milton, but at last rem. to Sherburn, and d. 1707, aged 86, unless deduct. be made for a common dispos. to exagger. If conject. be indulg. that he was s. of Humphrey (wh. seems to me improb.) very large subtract. will be need. JONATHAN, Dorchester, eldest s. of Humphrey, a mariner, had admin. of est. of the f. and trouble eno. with the interest by his f. with Gookin, Hudson, and others taken in the Narraganset lds. and there he had to plant, I believe, a s. Increase, unless this were his br. But wh. was his w. or what fam. he had, is unkn. JOSHUA, Lancaster, s. of James, m. Mary Gulliver of Milton, had sev. ch. of wh. I kn. only, that the sixth and youngest s. Peter was f. of Joshua, H. C. 1762, wh. was f. of Hon. Charles H. of Amherst, N. H. gr. at H. C. 1794. WATCHING, Dorchester, s. of Humphrey, m. 23 Jan. 1678, Eliz. d. of Samuel Rigby, had two ch. whose names are not told. WILLIAM, Boston, came from Barbados, in the ship Nathaniel, emb. 4 Oct. 1671. Of this name, in 1834, five had been gr. at Harv. and two at Dart.

ATKINS, ‖ABRAHAM, may have been of Boston, or some neighb. town, as he is of ar. co. 1642. HENRY, Yarmouth 1641, rem. to Plymouth, by w. Eliz. m. 9 July 1647, had Mary, b. 13 Mar. 1649, wh. d. at 2 yrs. Samuel, 24 Feb. 1652, wh. d. young; Isaac, 15 June 1654, d. young; rem. to Eastham, there had Isaac, again, 14 June 1657; and his w. d. 14 Mar. 1662. He m. 25 Mar. 1664, Bethia Linnell, had Desire, 7 May

1665; John, 15 Dec. 1666, d. young; Nathaniel, 25 Dec. 1667; Joseph, 4 Mar. 1669; Thomas, 19 June 1671; John, again, 6 Aug. 1674; Mercy, 24 Nov. 1676; and Samuel, again, 25 June 1679. JAMES, Roxbury, had been of Braintree, was a soldier in the Narraganset bloody campaign, of Dec. 1675, by w. Margaret had James, b. Feb. 1683, d. at 1 yr.; James, again, 31 Mar. 1684; and no more is heard of him. JOSEPH, Eastham, s. of Henry, by w. Martha had Joseph, b. 9 Dec. 1701; Martha, 9 Nov. 1711; Ann, 12 Dec. 1713; Paul, 11 Aug. 1716; James, 25 Dec. 1718; John, 18 Jan. 1721; Uriah, 7 Sept. 1722; and Hannah, 4 Apr. 1725. MATTHEW, Boston, freem. 1673, in Col. Rec. call. of sec. ch. at the date of Oct. tho. the ch. list gives him not until Dec. NATHANIEL, Eastham, s. of Henry, had Nathaniel, b. 21 Nov. 1694; Henry, 2 Aug. 1696; Bethia, 4 May 1698; Joshua, Apr. 1702; Isaiah, 24 Feb. 1704; and Eliz. 4 Jan. 1709. THOMAS, Boston, carpenter, by w. Mary had Eliz. b. 30 Dec. 1672; Thomas, 26 Feb. 1674; and by w. Abigail had Abigail, 3 June 1688; and Richard, 12 Oct. 1689. In 1676 he was made capt. of the first fire engine introd. into the town. THOMAS, Hartford. See Adkins. TOBIAS, Boston, by w. Ann had Ann, b. 2 July 1684; and Eliphal, 4 Dec. 1688. By m. of a d. Catharine, of Gov. Joseph Dudley with Joseph Atkins, the name of Dudley A. has long been perpet. as at Harv. Coll. 1748, 1784, and 1816, the sec. in the list, wh. took in addit. the name of Tyng from an earlier ancest. was a disting. gentleman at Newburyport and Boston. See 3 Mass. Hist. Coll. II. 280.

ATKINSON, ADKINSON, or ATKESON, JOHN, Newbury, s. of the first Theodore, was a hatter, m. 27 Apr. 1664, Sarah Mirick, had Sarah, b. 27 Nov. 1665; John; Thomas, 27 Dec. 1669, wh. may be well rec. as H. C. 1691, whose d. is not mark. in the catal. but Coffin foll. Mather, makes it bef. 1699; Theodore, 23 Jan. 1672, drown. at 13 yrs.; Abigail, 8 Nov. 1673; Samuel, 16 Jan. 1676; Nathaniel, 29 Nov. 1677; Eliz. 20 June 1680; and Joseph, 1 May 1682. JOSEPH, Exeter, in Geneal. Reg. VIII. 77, said to have been adm. freem. 14 July 1657, at that place; upon wh. arises the quest. by what authority was he adm. and no more can, I think, be told. LUKE, New Haven, of the earliest sett. sign. the compact 1639, bef. 1643 is count. with fam. of four, m. 1 May 1651, prob. as sec. w. Mary, d. of Richard Platt of Milford, had Mary, b. 1652; Hannah, 1653; and Sarah, 1655; rem. next yr. whither is unkn. perhaps to Middletown, for there his wid. m. 3 Jan. 1667, Thomas Whitmore, or Wetmore, and bore him two ch. nam. in his will by their gr.f. Platt in 1683. MARMADUKE, Scituate, m. 1670, Mary, d. of Edward Jenkins, and in 1674 she obt. divorce for his desert. Deane. THEODORE, Boston, 1634, feltmaker, came, in the employm. of John Newgate, from Bury in Co. Lancaster, join. the ch. 11 Jan. 1635, freem. 18 May 1642, by first w. Abigail had John, bef. ment. whose day of b. or bapt. is not found (but we may doubt, that Geneal. Reg. VII. 349 mak. him 44 yrs. old in 1678 is too liberal by seven or eight yrs.); Theodore, b. 19, bapt. 28 Apr. 1644; Nathaniel, 28, bapt. 30 Nov. 1645, H. C. 1667, d. by Mather's Catal.; Abigail, 24 Aug. 1647, d. young; Thomas, 1654; Abigail, again, 9 Dec. 1657; and by sec. w. m. Oct. 1667, Mary, d. of Rev. John Wheelwright, wid. of Edward Lyde, had John, again, 13 June 1672; and d. Aug. 1701, aged 89. Abigail, m. Abraham Spencer. THEODORE, Boston, s. of the preced. m. Eliz. d. of Edward Mitchelson, had Eliz. b. 25 June 1668; Theodore, 3 Oct. 1669; Edward, 8 Sept. 1671; and Abigail, 13 Dec. 1672. He was k. by the Ind. in the gr. fight of 19 Dec. 1675, serv. as serj. in Davenport's comp. at Narraganset; and his wid. m. 15 Nov. foll. Henry Deering. Theodore the third was a counsel. of New Hampsh. 1716, and d. 1719, leav. Theodore, b. at Newcastle 20 Dec. 1697, H. C. 1718, wh. bec. secr. counsel and ch. judge of that Prov. and d. 22 Sept. 1729; the fifth Theodore, his s. H. C. 1757, hav. d. without issue, in the same rank of counsel. 28 Oct. 1769. THOMAS, Concord, freem. 7 Dec. 1636, by w. Susanna had Susanna, b. 28 Apr. 1641; and Hannah, 5 Mar. 1644; and he d. Nov. 1646. Both of the ds. m. Caleb Brooks, the elder on 10 Apr. 1660, and d. 19 Jan. 1669. THOMAS, Plymouth 1638. Eight of this name had been gr. in 1838, at Harv. and two at Dart.

ATWATER, DAVID, New Haven 1638, came from London, sign. the planta. coven. 4 June 1639, had Mercy, b. 29 Feb. bapt. 5 Mar. 1648; Damaris, b. 2 Nov. but the ch. rec. has bapt. 21 Oct. 1649, and usually the town rec. is far more to be relied on than that of the ch. at New Haven, tho. the contrary is true in most towns, yet here the day assign. for bapt. in Geneal. Reg. IX. 357 may be true, tho. in a wonderful proportion, almost one half of the instances, it can be prov. to be wrong; David, 13 July, bapt. I judge, 3 Aug. tho. Mr. White gives it 13 Aug. 1651, wh. we kn. is mistake; Joshua, 11 Jan. bapt. prob. 6 Feb. 1653, ch. rec. as Mr. White gives it, being 11, wh. was Friday, when John Davenport would rather have anathematiz. than bapt. any ch.; John, 1 Nov. 1654, bapt. I presume, 5 of the same, tho. ch. rec. has 1, wh. was Wednesday; Jonathan, b. 12 July 1656; Abigail, 3 Mar. 1660, bapt. 1 Apr. foll.; Mary, 31 Mar. 1662, bapt. 20 Apr. foll. as I judge, tho. the ch. rec. as Mr. White prints it, be 22; Samuel, b. 17 Sept. 1664; and Ebenezer, 13 Jan. 1667; all of wh. are nam. as liv. May 1676, by the will of his br. Joshua. He d. 1692, and in his will the yr. bef. names all the s. exc. Joshua, wh. had liv. at Wallingford, had a w. but no ch. prob. and there d. 1681. Of the ds. I kn. the m. of four, Mercy to John Austin, and Damaris to John Punderson, both on 5 Nov. 1667; Abigail to Nathaniel Jones,

7 Oct. 1684; and Mary to Ichabod Stow of Middletown, 1688. JOHN, Salem, s. of Joshua, had rem. with his mo. from Boston on her m. with Higginson, by w. Mehitable, d. of Francis Wainwright of Ipswich, had John b. 20 Dec. 1687; Francis, 2 Oct. 1690; and perhaps Rebecca; but certain. his w. d. soon, and he m. Mary, youngest d. of Seaborn Cotton, and hims. d. bef. mid. age, drown. as I have heard, 2 Feb. 1692. His young wid. m. 1695, Samuel Partridge of Hatfield. JONATHAN, New Haven, s. prob. of David of the same, m. 1 June 1681, Ruth, eldest d. of Rev. Jeremiah Peck, first min. of Greenwich, had Joshua, b. 21 Feb. 1682; David, 5 Aug. 1683; Jeremiah, 31 Jan. 1685; Mary, 31 Dec. 1686; Ruth, 31 Dec. 1688; Jonathan, 1 Nov. 1690; Lydia, 18 Apr. 1693; Joseph, 9 Dec. 1694; Stephen, 4 Dec. 1696; and Damaris, 9 Oct. 1698. ‡*JOSHUA, New Haven 1638, br. of David, a merch. from London, sign. the coven. 1639, m. 6 May 1651, Mary, d. of Rev. Adam Blackman of Stratford, had Ann; Samuel, b. 20 June 1654, prob. d. young; Joshua, 10 Apr. bapt. 21 Nov. 1658; and Mary, 1659; was rep. 1652, rem. 1655 to Milford, there had the last named two ch. was Assist. and Treasr. of the Col. but rem. in 1659 to Boston, there had Mary, b. 15 Jan. 1660; John, 14 Aug. 1662, bef. ment.; Abigail, 23 Jan. 1664; Jane, with an alias Grace, on our rec. 9 Sept. 1666; Elinor, 23 Apr. 1669; and Benjamin, 16 May 1673; was a busy trader, d. 16, bur. 18 May 1676, leav. wid. wh. in few mos. m. Rev. John Higginson of Salem, and d. 9 Mar. 1709. Ann m. 1672, Jeremiah Dummer, the goldsmith of Boston, and was mo. of the famous Jeremy; and Mary m. John Clark, wh. d. in Barbary of smallpox, and she next m. 8 Nov. 1694 John Coney, outliv. him, and d. 12 Apr. 1726. Both these ds. and Rebecca, a gr.d. but no s. are nam. in the will of Higginson's wid. JOSHUA, Boston, s. of the preced. by w. Rebecca had Rebecca, b. 25 Feb. 1687; and by w. Mary, as the rec. (perhaps untrustworthy in this name) says, had Samuel, b. 3 Mar. 1688. Easy eno. may be the conject. as to error, that the writer in the clerk's office took Mary as w. of Joshua, bec. he saw such connex. of parents with ch. few yrs. bef. but equal. easy is the other suppos. that Rebecca was not the true name of the w. but carelessly giv. bec. the ch. had that name. To this latter suggest. is perhaps to be add. that it is somewhere writ. that Joshua m. Mary, wid. of Samuel Smith, and d. of Samuel Maverick. After long research, I am not enlight. eno. to speak with decis. SAMUEL, New Haven, prob. br. of Jonathan of the same, m. 1691, Sarah, d. of the first John Alling. In the New Haven fam. the name is perpet. and gr. at Yale in 1834 were count. fifteen, two at other N. E. coll. none at Harv.

ATWELL, BENJAMIN, New London, by w. Mary had Thomas, b. 1670; Mary, 1672; William, 1674; John, 1675; Joseph, 1678; Richard, 1679;

Samuel, 1681; and Benjamin, 1683. BENJAMIN, Scarborough 1663, s. of a wid. b. bef. Sept. 1640, when his mo. was a wid. but bec. w. of Richard Martin, was after of Falmouth, there k. by the Ind. 11 Aug. 1676, leav. Joseph only 5 yrs. old. Willis, I. 37, 134, 140 and 3. One Joan A. wh. testif. 1688, that she was 60 yrs. old, had been, I think, wid. of John Andrews, and was then wid. of Benjamin Atwell. JOHN, Lynn 1650. JOSEPH, Kittery, s. of Benjamin, was, it is said, brot. up by William Scriven, but no more is heard.

ATWOOD, ALEXANDER, Northampton, freem. 1684. ELDAD, Eastham, prob. s. of Stephen, m. 14 Feb. 1684, Ann Snow, perhaps d. of Mark, had Mary, b. Nov. 1684; John, 10 Aug. 1686; Ann, Jan. 1688; Deborah, Mar. 1690; Sarah, Apr. 1692; Eldad, 9 July 1695; Ebenezer, Mar. 1698; and Benjamin, June 1701. ‖ HERMAN, Boston 1642, s. of John, came from Sanderstead, Co. Surrey, a. 15 miles from London, in employm. of Thomas Buttolph, adm. of the ch. 24 Feb. 1644, ar. co. 1644, freem. 1645, m. 11 Aug. 1646, Ann, d. of William Cop, had John, b. 5 Oct. 1647; and Sarah, bapt. 26 May 1650; and he d. 1651. His wid. m. 10 Mar. 1652, Thomas Saxton, and d. 23 June 1661. ‡ JOHN, Plymouth 1636, came from London, was an Assist. 1638, treasr. of the Col. 1641 to his d. 1644, had good est. leav. wid. Ann, but no issue, unless that Mary Wood, very often used for Atwood, wh. m. 11 Dec. 1661, John Holmes, wh. bec. min. of Duxbury, were his d. wh. is very unlikely, for in his will of 20 Oct. 1643, as Winsor, 180, tells, he names no ch. but gives most of his prop. to w. wh. d. 1 June 1654, and in her will, of 27 Apr. 1650, she divides her est. betw. br. and sis. Robert and Mary Lee, and her neph. William Crowe. Her he had nam. br. Lee and his w. and their ch. Ann and Mary, beside his little kinsman, William Crowe. ‖ JOHN, Boston, s. of Herman, ar. co. 1673, was its lieut. 1695, and deac. of the sec. ch. by first w. Sarah had John, b. 23 May 1671, d. young; James, 3 June 1673; Samuel, 18 May 1687; and Sarah, 11 Nov. 1688; and by sec. w. Mary, d. of Francis Smith, m. 27 Oct. 1690, had Mary, bapt. 6 Sept. 1691; John, again, b. 16, bapt. 18 Feb. 1694; Samuel, bapt. 29 Mar. 1696; Ann, b. 19, bapt. 20 June 1697; Eliz. bapt. 21 Aug. 1698; Abigail, 19 Nov. 1699; and Joshua, b. 10, bapt. 13 Apr. 1701. He d. 26 Aug. 1714, and his wid. d. 18 Mar. 1729. JONATHAN, Woodbury, s. of Thomas of Wethersfield, m. 5 Nov. 1701, Sarah, d. of Roger Terrill, had Nathan, b. 6 Sept. 1702; Mary, 22 Oct. 1703, d. soon; Mary, again, 20 Apr. 1705; Jonathan, 9 Sept. 1710; and Oliver, 11 Mar. 1717; was a physician, and d. 1 Jan. 1733, as Cothren, 490, says, but 11 Feb. of that yr. acc. Hinman. JOSEPH, Taunton, m. 1 Jan. 1680, Esther, d. of James Walker, had Joseph, b. 4 Aug. 1681; John, 28 Feb. 1683; Ephraim; and perhaps Joanna. His w. d. 8 Apr. 1696, aged 46, and he

d. 12 Feb. foll. aged 47. JOSIAH, Wethersfield, br. of Jonathan, m. 16 Feb. 1710, Bathsheba, d. of Bezaleel Lattimore, had Abigail, b. 6 Dec. foll.; Oliver, 1 Mar. 1716; Jedediah, 28 June 1719; Josiah, and Hezekiah, tw. 13 Apr. 1727; and Asher, 27 Dec. 1729. MEDAD, Eastham, s. of Stephen, by w. Esther had Mercy, b. 26 June 1686; Abigail, 15 June 1689; David, 20 Oct. 1691; Samuel, 20 Mar. 1695; Esther, 15 Mar. 1699; Phebe, 9 June 1702; and Nathan, 27 June 1705. OLIVER, Malden, youngest s. of Philip the first m. in 1700 Ann Betts. PHILIP, Malden 1653, came from London in the Susan and Ellen, 1635, aged 13, or in the Planter, aged 12, for, I suppose, by the doub. entry only one boy is meant, had Rachel, b. Aug. 1653; Mary, Jan. 1656; Philip, Sept. 1658; Abigail, Dec. 1662; Eliz. Aug. 1669; and Oliver, Apr. 1671; all prob. by w. Rachel, d. I judge, of William Bachiler of Charlestown, wh. d. 5 Feb. or 7 Nov. 1674, the same rec. in Geneal. Reg. X. 241, coming from a most scrupulous hand, giv. both dates. He m. 7 Apr. 1675, Eliz. Grover, wid. of Thomas, and she d. 3 Apr. 1688. His d. Eliz. m. 26 Nov. foll. Philip Fowle. Perhaps he liv. some yrs. at Bradford. PHILIP, Lynn, s. prob. of the preced. m. at Bradford, 23 July 1684, Sarah Tenny of B. had at Malden, Susanna, b. 1 Feb. 1687; Sarah, 13 Apr. 1689; Rachel, 15 Nov. 1691; but perhaps others bef. or after rem. STEPHEN, Eastham, m. 6 Nov. 1644, Abigail, d. of John Dunham, had John, d. soon; Hannah, b. 14 Oct. 1669; prob. Eldad; and Medad, 16 Jan. 1659; and d. Feb. 1694. THOMAS, Hartford 1664, by idle tradit. call. a capt. under Cromwell, was really a physician, and, 1668, of Wethersfield, by w. Abigail had Abigail, b. 30 Sept. of that yr.; Andrew, 1 Sept. 1671; Jonathan, 8 June 1675; and Josiah, 4 Oct. 1678; all liv. at his d. 1682. THOMAS, Ipswich, d. 3 Apr. 1694; and his wid. Eliz. by wh. I kn. not that he had issue, m. 9 Sept. 1697, John West of the same, and d. 20 Aug. 1720. WILLIAM, Charlestown, freem. 1652. Of this name four have been gr. at Yale, all descend. of Herman, of wh. John M. of the class of 1814, and Charles, 1821, are brs. of Harriet Newell, the celebr. missionary in the E. Ind.

AUBREY, ‖WILLIAM, Boston, merch. came in virtue of a contr. made 1650, from London, factor for the iron works at Lynn, and was adm. 1652 of ar. co. m. 18 Jan. 1653, Rachel, d. of Secr. Edward Rawson.

AUDLEY, EDMUND, Lynn, 1641. Lewis. JOHN, Boston 1632, thus spell. on the ch. rec. where his name stands No. 139; but common. it is Odlin or Odlyn, wh. see.

AUGER, AGAR, or AUGUR, ANDREW, Saco, or Scarborough, perhaps better entit. See Alger. BENJAMIN, Salem, s. of William of the same, a shipwright, m. Ann, d. of Thomas Cromwell, had Benjamin, and Thomas, perhaps others, and d. Nov. 1671. His wid. m. 26 June 1672, David

Phippen. JOHN, Boston, by w. Hannah had John, b. 16 Sept. 1652.
JONATHAN, Salem, br. of Benjamin, had perhaps Jonathan, wh. d. young;
and Mary, ment. in a deed of 1709; but we. kn. not his w. nor of him
any thing more, exc. that in testif. 19 Oct. 1716, he call. hims. 77 yrs. old.
NICHOLAS, New Haven 1643, a physician and trader, sw. alleg. 5 Aug.
1644, had brs. John and Robert (unless the latter were neph.) to wh. with
sis. Esther Coster he gave most of his est. that was a good one, by will of
20 Sept. 1669, being "bound on a voyage to Boston." Yet he got back
safe, and liv. sev. yrs. He was the sufferer, I judge, in 1676 and 7, on
the voyage from Boston to N. H. cast away on a desolate isl. in the little
vessel with Ephraim How, near Cape Sable, relation of wh. in Mather's
best manner, may be read in Magn. VI. appropr. call. Thaumaturgus, c. 1.
Of his inv. of £1638 the date is 26 Feb. 1678. The larger part his sis.
had, to br. John (prob. then in Eng.) the beq. was only £20, and John's
s. Nicholas had £100, and ano. s. had £40, and Robert, £150. After
Mrs. Coster d. 5 Apr. 1691, Robert, the next of kin, resist. pro. of her
will, cont. some beq. for "support of religion and learning;" but he met
with no success. ROBERT, New Haven, prob. neph. tho. Dodd calls him
br. of the preced. m. 20 Nov. 1673, Mary, d. of dep. gov. Matthew Gilbert, had Esther, b. 19 Oct. 1677; John, 26 Nov. 1678, d. young; Ann,
14 Nov. 1682; Mary, again, 1683, d. soon; and John, again, 16 Nov.
1686; but the last was by sec. w. THOMAS, Watertown 1663, of wh.
Bond, writing his name Agar, found not w. or ch. but prob. he rem. to
Taunton, for the rec. of that town tells, that he m. Nov. 1665, Eliz. Packer.
But I think she may have been d. of Samuel Packard of Bridgewater,
and her h. liv. in that town, perhaps, but they had then no magistr. authoriz. to solemn. m. WILLIAM, Salem 1636, perhaps earlier, for he was
adm. freem. of Mass. 18 May 1631, when the Secr. gave the name Agar;
by w. Alice had Benjamin, bapt. 12 Feb. 1637; and Jonathan, 10 Nov.
1639; beside elder ch. Joseph, and Abigail, wh. bec. w. of Joseph Kib-
ben, or Kibby; and he d. 1654. His will of 31 May, pro. Nov. in that
yr. names the w. and four ch. but notes, that Joseph was abroad. WIL-
LIAM, Malden, m. 7 Dec. 1659, Ruth, d. of Abraham Hill, had William, b.
20 Apr. 1661, d. soon; William, again, 30 Nov. 1662; ano. perhaps John,
Oct. 1667.

AUGUSTINE, JOHN, Reading 1677, had come from the Isle of Jersey,
and had serv. in the comp. of Turner in the latter part of Philip's war,
and in that yr. by deed on our rec. sold to John Brock of the same place
all the goods and chat. ho. and lds. left to him by f. and mo. He m. 10
Jan. 1678, Eliz. d. of John Brown of Watertown, as Bond, 145, tells; and
in 1680 took a gr. of ld. at Falmouth from Presid. Danforth, and bot.
more; but on destr. by the Ind. and French, 1690, he rem. to Lynn, but

went back to F. 1719. He left wid. Eliz. and ch. Samuel, John, Ebenezer, Thomas, David, Sarah, and Abigail, of wh. descend. are found in the
vicin. to this day.   Gradual change occurs in his name to Gustan, or
Gustin, and is justif. by his own writ. but the wild perversity of a scrivener had pleasure in turning him into Augustine John.   See Suff. Deeds,
X. 131, and Willis, I. 161, 210.

AULT, sometime writ. OLT, JOHN, Portsmouth 1631, sent out by Mason,
the royal propr. liv. at Dover 1648 to 1657, in wh. yr. he was 73 yrs. old,
and was liv. 1679. By w. Remembrance he had John; Remembrance,
wh. m. John Rand; and ano. d. wh. m. Thomas Edgerly.

AUSTIN, ANTHONY, Rowley, freem. 1669, had Richard, b. 1666; An-
thony, 1668; John, 1672; rem. to Suffield, there had Nathaniel, 1678;
Eliz. 1681, d. young; Eliz. again; 1684; Esther, 1686; and d. 1708, his
w. hav. d. ten yrs. bef.   Descend. are num.   DAVID, New Haven, s.
of John, by w. Abigail had Abigail, b. 5 Apr. 1699 ; David, 25 Oct. 1703;
Stephen, 1 Jan. 1705; Jonathan, 27 Apr. 1708; Mercy, 1710; and Lydia.
EBENEZER, Charlestown, s. of the sec. Richard, m. 8 July 1685, wid.
Thankful Benjamin, had Sarah, b. 24 Oct. foll. if no error be in the rec.
Eliz. 26 Apr. 1687; and his w. d. 4 Mar. 1691.   He m. 27 Jan. 1692,
Rebecca, d. of Samuel Sprague of Malden, had Benjamin, 24 Feb. 1697;
Rebecca, 8 Feb. 1700; both prob. d. young; Ebenezer, 21 Jan. 1704;
John, 15 May 1706 ; Nathaniel, 3 Feb. 1708; Timothy, 16 Dec. 1710,
prob. d. young; Rebecca, again, 21 Aug. 1715; Benjamin, again, 9 Mar.
1717 ; Timothy, again; and Samuel, 6 May 1721 ; and d. 16 Jan. 1723.
From this last Benjamin, wh. m. 9 Dec. 1742 Eliz. Waldo, came Hon.
Jonathan L. b. 22 Dec. 1747, H. C. 1766, wh. was f. of Hon. James T.
late Atty. Gen. of Mass. H. C. 1702 ; and Hon. Benjamin, b. 18 Nov.
1752, long a promin. politician.   FRANCIS, Dedham, whence he rem. to
Hampton 1640, there had, by w. Isabella, both Jemima, and Sophia, bapt.
24 Jan. 1641 ; but I kn. no more.   JOHN, New London 1647, rem. after
1651, to Greenwich, next in few yrs. to Stamford, there d. 25 Aug. 1657,
leav. wid. Catharine, s. Samuel wh. d. soon after his f. d. Eliz. wh. m. a.
1670, Joseph Finch; and perhaps John, wh. was a landholder 1687–1701
both in G. and S.   JOHN, New Haven, m. 5 Nov. 1667, Mercy, d. of the
first Joshua Atwater, had John, b. 23 Apr. 1669, d. at six yrs.; David,
23 Feb. 1671, bef. ment.; Joshua, 3 Sept. 1673; Mary; John, and Hannah, tw. 14 Oct. 1677 ; Mercy, 17 Apr. 1680, d. young; a s. 5 Apr. 1683,
d. soon; and his w. d. nine days after.   He m. 21 Jan. 1685, Eliz. Brackett, and had Sarah, 23 Jan. 1686; and Eliz. 1687.   In 1675, a wid.
Joan Jones, perhaps near relat. gave him very good est. and he d. 1690 ;
and his wid. was d. 1695.   JOHN, Scarborough, wh. m. a d. of Andrew
Alger, is more common. call. Ashton, wh. see, also Southgate, 82.   A

JOHN of Hartford m. Mary, wid. of Nathaniel Hooker, may be one generat. later than the s. of him of New Haven. JONAH, Hingham 1635,
came in the Hercules, with w. Constance, from Sandwich, Co. Kent. He
was of Tenterden ; and the mayor of that borough, John Austin, perhaps his f. or near relat. certif. a. tak. the o. in 3 Mass. Hist. Coll. VIII.
274. Perhaps he first sat down at Cambridge, then call. Newtowñ, and
was not many yrs. at H. being found at Taunton 1643, and he d. there
30 July 1683. JONAH, Taunton, prob. s. of the preced. m. perhaps
Frances, d. of John Hill of Dorchester, tho. Col. Rec. makes her h. to be
Jonah Allen senr. He d. 10 May 1676, some yrs. bef. his f. and of ch. I
hear only of John, b. 1 July 1671. See Baylies II. 270. JOSEPH,
Hampton 1642, Dover 1648, was of the gr. jury 1651, and d. 1663. His
will of 6 June 1662, directs equal div. of his prop. betw. all his ch. but the
name only of Thomas has reach. us. In 1659 he took sec. w. Sarah,
wid. of William Story, d. of Elder Edward Starbuck; and she had third
h. Humphrey Varney. JOSEPH, Charlestown, s. of Richard the sec. m.
10 Nov. 1692, Eliz. Pitts; and I kn. no more. LEONARD, New Haven,
br. of John, a weaver, d. 1678 unm. MATTHEW, York 1659, was k. by
the Ind. a. 1704. RICHARD, Charlestown, came in the Bevis, from
Southampton, 1638, with w. and two ch. He was then aged 40, and had
been a tailor at Bishopstoke in Co. Hants. RICHARD, Charlestown, prob.
s. of the preced. brot. by him from Eng. m. 11 Nov. 1659, Abigail, d.
of William Batchelder, had Samuel, b. 1660 ; Ebenezer, 27 Aug. 1662;
Abigail, 24 Apr. 1664; Richard, 30 Nov. 1665; Joseph, 24 Feb. 1667;
Benjamin, 24 Jan. 1669; William, 6 Aug. 1671; Eliz. 6 May 1673;
Rachel, 7 May 1676; James, 17 June 1679; and John, 10 Dec. 1681.
His w. d. 1 Feb. 1694, aged 56; and he d. 15 Aug. 1703, aged 71. Abigail m. 11 Sept. 1688, John Kettle jr. Eliz. m. Jonathan Loring of Boston ; and of sev. of the ch. no acco. is seen, so that, perhaps, some d. young.
RICHARD, Charlestown, s. of the preced. m. 27 Nov. 1691, Mehitable, d.
of William Welsteed, and d. 6 Sept. 1694. *SAMUEL, Dover 1649, was
of Wells, and constable 1655, and rep. 1682. SAMUEL, Charlestown, s.
of Richard the sec. by w. Sarah had Abigail, Sarah, Mary, Mehitable,
Ann, and Samuel, and d. 23 June 1716. THOMAS, Greenwich 1675,
perhaps s. of John the first, rem. to the adj. town of Bedford, there liv.
1686–97. THOMAS, Dover, s. of Joseph of the same, by w. Ann had
Rose, b. 1678 ; Sarah, 1682; Nathaniel, 1687 ; Thomas, 1689; Joseph,
1692 ; Nicholas, and Ann, tw. 1695; Samuel, 1698; and Benjamin, 1704.
WILLIAM, Charlestown, s. of Richard the sec. m. 30 June 1696, Hannah
Trarice, d. prob. of John of the same ; but I find no more of him. One
of this surname, whose bapt. name is not seen, would have gone home in
1638, from New Haven, with large prop. but was taken by the Turks,

and sold at Algiers with w. and fam. as is relat. in Winth. Hist. II.
12, 13; so that prob. no descend. remain. Gr. in 1838 at Harv. were
ten, Yale eight, and Dart. one.

AVERILL, WILLIAM, Ipswich 1638, d. 1653, leav. w. Abigail, and seven
ch. not nam. but in his will describ. It was made 3 June 1652, and pro.
29 Mar. foll. WILLIAM, Topsfield 1664, was prob. s. of the preced.
Easily this name in old MS. is mistak. for Avery, sometimes for Averitt,
and may even be used for Everitt, wh. see.

AVERY, CHRISTOPHER, Gloucester, a weaver, came, I conject. from
Salisbury in Co. Hants, as one of the same name liv. in the age preced.
at that city; was selectman 1646, and sev. yrs. more, in 1653 his w. was
in Eng. in 1658 he rem. to Boston, and in 1666 to New London. He
had brot. from Eng. s. James, perhaps other ch. and was old eno. in 1667
to claim release from watch. and train. prob. d. in few yrs. Descend.
have been num. and respectab. * JAMES, Gloucester, s. of the preced. b.
in Eng. a. 1620, m. 10 Nov. 1643, Jane Greenslade of Boston, had Hannah, b. 12 Oct. 1644; James 16 Dec. 1646; and Mary, 19 Feb. 1648;
rem. that yr. to New London, there had Thomas, 6 May 1651; John, 10
Feb. 1654; Rebecca, 6 Oct. 1656; Jonathan, 5 Jan. 1659; Christopher,
30 Apr. 1661; both d. young; Samuel, 14 Aug. 1664; and Joanna, 1669.
He was held in high esteem, lieut. capt. rep. 1659, often after to 1669,
serv. in Philip's war, when he command. the Pequot allied force, and was
liv. in Feb. 1694. JAMES, New London, s. of the preced. m. Deborah,
d. prob. eldest of Edward Stallion, and well perpet. the fam. name. tho.
in Caulkins I see not names and dates of ch. JOHN, Dorchester 1642,
rem. to Boston, d. 31 July 1654. JOHN, of New Hampsh. was one of
those wh. solicit. the protect. of Mass. in 1689. JONATHAN, Dedham, s.
of William, m. 22 July 1679, Sybil, d. of the sec. Nathaniel Sparhawk of
Cambridge, had Margaret, b. 9 Nov. 1681, d. young; Sybil, 11 Aug.
1683; Margaret, again, 20 Aug. 1686; and Dorothy, 4 July 1688; and
he d. 16 Sept. 1694. His wid. m. Rev. Michael Wigglesworth. JOSEPH,
(not John, as Mather, in his ambitious cap. 2 of Magn. III. 77, mislead
all succeed. writers, until the recent publicat. of our contemp. Col. Rec.
I. 154); would have been call. of Marblehead, as he was going to that
settlem. from Ipswich, when he was lost 15 Aug. 1635, by shipwreck of
the little bark in wh. with his fam. of eleven, as his cous. and fellow passeng. Thomas Thacher tells in his Narrative. By that, one of the most
affecting and effective stories of disasters of this sort, Dr. Young enrich.
his Chronicles of Mass. From Winth. I. 165, we hear of the w. and six
small ch. that perish with him, but the resid. no doubt, were serv. He
had been a min. in his native Co. prob. of Wiltsh. and I judge had come
in the James from Southampton that brot. his kinsman Thacher, but

nobody informs us, at wh. of the Univ. he was bred, or of wh. parish he had taught. Hubbard, 200, may not be taken for authority as to his coming in the Angel Gabriel (if so he meant to be understood), for he was arr. at Boston the day bef. the Angel Gabriel weighed her anchor below Bristol. Thacher, as in the rec. bef. cited, was by our Gen. Ct. made admor. and in his inv. as well as the appoint. the dec. is named Joseph. One wh. reads with appreciative skill the authentic Narrative will disregard the acco. in the Magnalia, nor wonder, why the most heedless of authors call. him John. ROBERT, Dedham, perhaps s. of William of the same, was the freem. of 1690, I think, spelt Awry in the invalua. list of Mr. Paige, Geneal. Reg. III. m. 13 Apr. 1676, Eliz. d. of Job Lane, had Eliz. b. 21 Dec. 1677; Rachel, 1 Sept. 1679; Robert, 28 Nov. 1681; John, 26 Feb. 1685 or 4 Feb. 1686; H. C. 1706; Jonathan, 20 Jan. 1695; and Abigail, 8 May 1699; and he d. 4 Oct. 1722. SAMUEL, New London, youngest s. of James the first, liv. on that side made Groton, of wh. town he was first officer, 1705. THOMAS, Salem, came in the John and Mary, was a blacksmith, and freem. 28 Dec. 1643. THOMAS, New London, s. of James the first, m. Ann, d. of Benjamin Shapley. * ‖ WILLIAM, Dedham, a physician, or apothecary, prob. both, ar. co. 1654, had William, b. a. 1646; Mary; Robert, a. 1649; Jonathan, 26 May 1653; Rachel; Hannah, 27 Sept. 1660; and Ebenezer, 24 Nov. 1663, wh. prob. d. young, as he is not nam. in the will of his f. 15 Oct. 1683. He was a lieut. 1673, of the town's comp. and freem. 1677; possib. the bookseller, ment. by Thomas, in his Hist. II. 411, certain. the rep. for Springfield 1669, and he d. at Boston 18 Mar. 1687, aged a. 65. His w. Margaret had d. 28 Sept. 1678. Of the ds. Mary m. 5 Nov. 1666, James Tisdale; Rachel m. 22 May 1676, William Sumner; and Hannah m. the same day, Benjamin Dyer. WILLIAM, Dedham, s. of the preced. had, by w. Mary, d. of Job Lane of Malden, Mary, b. 21 Aug. 1674; Sarah, 9 Oct. 1675; William, 21 Mar. 1678; and Hannah, 7 Jan. 1680; and his w. d. 11 Oct. 1681, aged 29. He m. 29 Aug. 1682, Eliz. White, had Samuel, 15 May 1683; Eliz. 16 May 1684; John, 26 Dec. 1685; Joseph, 9 Apr. 1687, H. C. 1706; and Deborah, 5 May 1689. This w. d. 3 Oct. 1690, and he m. 25 Aug. 1698, wid. Mehitable Worden, relict of Samuel, a d. of Gov. Thomas Hinckley, and d. 15 Dec. 1708. In the Coll. Catal. it may be seen, that the first two of this name are not rank. by seniority, or by date of ordin. (both being min. John of Truro, the first there, ord. Nov. 1711, and Joseph, also the first of Norton, ord. 26 Oct. 1714), or by alphabet. priority, wh. may, no doubt, be explain. by regard to the rules that of old regulat. the assignment of places.

AVIS, JOHN, Boston 1679, banish. from the Col. that yr. with sev. others, on suspicion of hav. set the terrible fire of that yr. He had serv. perhaps on Conn. riv. in Philip's war. WILLIAM, Boston, perhaps br. of the preced. had John, b. 1664.

AVISTON, or AVESSON, JOHN, Reading, freem. 1685.

AWARDS, RICHARD, Newport 1638, had been of Boston.

AWKLEY, MILES, Boston, by w. Mary had Eliz. b. 1635 ; and Miles, 1 Apr. 1638.

AXEY, * JAMES, Lynn 1630, rep. 1654, d. 7 June 1667 ; and his wid. Frances, d. 13 Oct. 1670.

AXTELL, HENRY, Sudbury, perhaps s. of Thomas, rem. 1660 to Marlborough, there m. 14 June 1665, Hannah, whose fam. name I do not see; was k. by the Ind. Apr. 1676 ; and the wid. m. 16 July 1677, William Taylor, perhaps of Concord. NATHANIEL, New Haven 1639, intend. to go home, made his will 27 Jan. 1640, and d. in few wks. bef. embark. at Boston. THOMAS, Sudbury, wh. was bur. 8 Mar. 1646, had w. Mary and sev. ch. the youngest perhaps, Mary, b. June 1644 ; the inv. sw. to 6 May 1646. The wid. m. 19 Sept. 1656, John Goodenough.

AYERS, or AYER, HENRY, whose name is spel. Eares often, was among freem. 1655, at Portsmouth, R. I. JAMES, Dover 1658. JOHN, Salisbury 1640, had Hannah, b. 21 Dec. 1644, rem. to Ipswich 1646, Haverhill 1647, there d. 31 Mar. 1657. His will of 12 Mar. pro. 6 Oct. foll. names w. Hannah, ch. John ; Nathaniel ; Hannah, wh. m. 24 Mar. 1663, Stephen Webster ; Rebecca ; Mary ; Obadiah ; Robert ; Thomas ; and Peter. JOHN, Haverhill, s. of the preced. b. in Eng. m. 5 May 1646, Sarah, d. of John Williams of the same, and next, after 1659, Susanna, d. of Mark Symonds of Ipswich, and rem. to Brookfield as one of its first sett. there k. by the Ind. when they destroy. the town, 3 Aug. 1675. He kept the inn, and his ch. were (beside Sarah) Samuel, John, Thomas, Joseph, Mark, Nathaniel, and Edward ; of wh. some liv. at B. after its renova. Ano. JOHN, perhaps s. perhaps neph. of the preced. was of Ipswich, lately from Haverhill, in 1679, and had w. Mary. OBADIAH, Newbury, by w. Hannah had John, b. 2 Mar. 1663. * PETER, Haverhill 1646, youngest s. prob. of the first John, m. 8 Oct. 1659, Hannah, d. of the first William Allen, was freem. 1666, rep. 1683, 5, 9, and 90, d. at Boston 3 Jan. 1699, aged a. 66, by his gr. st. ROBERT, Haverhill, br. of the preced. freem. 1666, m. 1659, Eliz. d. of Henry Palmer of the same, had Samuel. SAMUEL, perhaps of Lynn, perhaps of Ipswich, a youth, serv. to John Baker, as in docum. in the Rec. Commrs. hands of London, copied for me, came from Norwich in May 1637, in the Mary Ann of Yarmouth, aged 15, as he call. hims. tho. his master, embark. a mo. earlier and design. to take this appr. yet had reason to direct him to have passage in a later ship, made him 14 ; yet tho. liv. in 1668, whether he had fam. is unkn. to me. SAMUEL, Haverhill, s. of Robert, freem. 1683, m. Eliz. d. of Simon Tuttle the first, had Obadiah, H. C. 1710; John; and James; was the chief selectman, and k. by the French and Ind. when they surpris. the town 29 Aug. 1708. SAMUEL, Newbury, by w. Abigail had Stephen, b. 23 Mar. 1689; by w. Sarah had Jabez, 27 Dec. 1690; but Coffin seems to intend two h's as well as two ws. in wh. he may be correct, tho. it appears strange, that no other ch. is nam. no date of m. of either ment. nor d. of either h. or w. THOMAS, Haverhill 1646, prob. s. of John the first, may have rem. to Newbury, there had John, b. 12 May 1657, and was freem. 1666. THOMAS, Newbury, by w. Hannah had Abraham, b. 18 June 1688; Sarah, 29 Aug. 1690; and Mehitable, 5 Apr. 1693. WILLIAM, Hartford 1651-9, whose name is often giv. Ayres or Eyres, is, in all other respects, unkn. ZECHARIAH, Andover, m. 27 June 1678, Eliz. d. of the first Aquila Chase of Newbury.

AYLET, JOHN, Boston, merch. m. 21 Nov. 1654, Mary, d. of Capt. Thomas Hawkins, had Mary, b. 8 Oct. 1655, and he sold, the same yr. to William Hudson that est. wh. had been prop. of his f.-in-law, call. "by the name or sign of Noah's ark." His w. prob. d. early, and he, I think, must have gone home.

AYRAULT, or AYROULD, NICHOLAS, Wethersfield, a physician, driv. by the revocat. of the edict of Nantz to fly his native ld. wh. prob. was Rochelle, a. 1686, or earlier, m. at Providence Marian Breton, had Peter, Nicholas, and other ch. and d. 1706. Of Nicholas jr. and Peter, see acco. in Hinman. SAMUEL, R. I. a physician, by Hinman, Ed. 2, p. 90, presum. to be br. or f. of the preced. but nothing definite as to fam. of these Huguenots is easily accessib. No doubt he came betw. 1685 and 9; but it would not surprise me to have it ascertain. that Hinman's Samuel was the same as STEPHEN, Newport 1685, one of the blessed army of French protestant exiles. His s. Daniel m. 9 May 1703, Mary Robineau of New York.

AYRES, EDWARD, Kittery 1685. MARK, and NATHANIEL, N. H. 1689 req. protect. of Mass.

AZELL, HUMPHREY, Kittery 1682, was one of the found. of Bapt. ch. there.

BAALAM, CHARLES, is the name of a passeng. last on the list, coming to Boston from London 1656, aged 18, in the Speedwell, the same voyage on wh. came the earliest Quakers; and tho. it is not charg. against him, that he was of that sect, yet is it almost certain that he soon left this ld.

BABB, JONATHAN, Springfield, took o. of alleg. with Samuel, perhaps his br. 31 Dec. 1678, or the next day, but no more is kn. of either. PHILIP, Kittery 1652, and next yr. was assoc. under commiss. from Mass. with Maj. Bryan Pendleton, Nicholas Shapleigh, and others, in the governm. of Isle of Shoals, and a few yrs. later liv. there, in 1666 was empow. to take depons. The name is perpet. in N. H.

BABBAGE, BABBIDGE, sometimes BABRIDGE, CHRISTOPHER, Salem,

freem. 1665, by w. Agnes had Ruth, b. 20 Mar. bapt. 8 May 1664; and
John, 15 Apr. 1666; and his w. d. 17 Nov. 1667.   He m. 5 Oct. 1674,
wid. Hannah Carlton, perhaps relict of John of Haverhill, had Hannah,
15 July 1675, and Mary, 7 Mar. 1677.

BABBIT.   See Bobbit.

BABCOCK, DAVID, Dorchester 1640.   GEORGE, Boston, wh. d. 2 Sept.
1695, perhaps was he that Gov. Eaton brot. over 1638 to New Haven,
conditio. to serve six yrs. call. Badcock.   JAMES, Westerly 1661, whither
he rem. from Newport, had by first w. (whose name is not heard) James,
b. a. 1641; John, 1644; Job; and Mary.   By tradit. it is said, that he
came from Co. Essex, and on giv. evid. with his two elder s. 1670, call.
them 29 and 26 yrs. respectiv. he sw. that he was 58, and spells with d.
at the end of his first syllab.   From the idle and discord. tradit. that he
brot. from Eng. childr. b. from 1612 to 1620 (when the f. would have
been betw. 1 and 8 yrs. old), this testim. relieves the geneal.   A sec. w.
Eliz. and three ch. by her, one nam. Joseph, the oldest only 9 yrs. old,
are provid. for in his nuncup. will, 12 June 1679, of wh. s. John and Job
were witness. as also to Job were giv. his smith's tools, beside gifts to Mary
Champlin, his d. thot. to be w. of William, and to s. Joseph, when he comes
to 21 yrs.   JAMES, Westerly, eldest s. of the preced. d. 1685, leav. wid.
Mary, and eldest s. James, as the rec. of W. it is said, proves; but names
of other ch. are not giv.   They were Sarah, Jane, Mary, Hannah, Eliz.
William, and Job.   Part of the acco. of this James may be easily confus.
with that of his br. John.   JOB, Westerly, a miller, prob. br. of the preced. d. a. 1718, and in his will calls eldest s. Job, other ch. John, Benjamin, Jane Braman, Sarah Hall, Mary Tanner, Eliz. Brand, Hannah, and
Mary.   JOHN, Stonington 1670, s. of the first James, wh. had prob. own.
ld. on both sides of the riv. within disput. bounds of Conn. and R. I.   He
had. w. Mary, ch. James, Ann, Mary, John, Job, George, Elihu, Robert,
Joseph, and Oliver.   Fam. tradit. makes his w. to be a Lawton, perhaps
sis. of George the first; and it may be nearer the truth, when it tells of
his runaway match with the d. of his master, their kind recept. by the Ind.
in the wilderness, discov. of his d. and her h. some four yrs. after by the
bride's f. and forgiveness, liberality &c. than as it relates his d. 19 July
1719, "aged over one hundred yrs."   For ano. John, perhaps his s. that
protraction of days, tho. unlikely, might be correct, yet the f. d. from
twenty to forty yrs. too early, and his wid. m. bef. 1700 Erasmus Babbit.
Indeed his d. is marked 1685, and his wid. nam. Mary, and eldest s. James,
but these three items concur. with those of his br. James, lead us to ap-
prehend that the geneal. may be confus. between them.   RETURN, Dartmouth bef. 1686, and liv. to be nam. Nov. 1694 in deed of confirmat. of
the town.   Strange is the combinat. of errors, in Hinman, 111, a. one

James B. wh. went to Leyden in Holland 1620, join. the friends of Robinson, and came in the Ann, 1623, to Plymouth, the narrat. enlarg. a. the
resid. of the fam. there. Now we kn. that no passeng. of this name came
in that ship; and I have very strong reason, after much inquiry, to doubt
that any such man liv. in the Col. for its earliest forty yrs. Of this name,
in 1834, both forms of spell. inclus. seven had been gr. at Yale, and five
at Harv. as Farmer found.

BABER, WILLIAM, Boston 1648, had John.

BABSON, EBENEZER, Gloucester, youngest s. of James, wonderf. be-
wilder. by diabol. agency, as told by Rev. John Emerson, his spiritu.
guide, to C. Mather, and in its appropr. place, Magn. VII. 82–84, may be
read. Niles, in his tale, 3 Mass. Hist. Coll. VI. 231, seems more cautious,
or less inclin. to honor Satan. JAMES, Gloucester, came, no doubt in
comp. with his mo. Isabel (a wid. wh. had lds. there, 1644, and after
until her d. 6 or 8 Apr. 1661, aged 81, or more, as also gr. in 1637 at
Salem), m. 16 Nov. 1647, Elinor Hill, sis. of Zebulon, had James, b. 29
Sept. 1648; Elinor, 15 June 1651; Philip, 15 Oct. 1654; Sarah, 15
Feb. 1657, d. at 20 yrs; Thomas, 21 May 1658; John, 27 Nov. 1660;
Richard, 1 June 1663; Eliz. 8 Oct. 1665; and Ebenezer, 8 Feb. 1668,
the bef. ment. playmate with the devil. He was freem. 1666, and d.
1683. His s. Thomas serv. long in Philip's war.

BACHILER, BACHELOR, BACHELLER, BACHELDER, BATCHELOR, or
BATCHELDER, ALEXANDER, Portsmouth 1652, of wh. I kn. no more, but
that he was the ferryman. DAVID, Reading, s. of John the first, of the
same, is no otherwise kn. to me. HENRY, Ipswich, a brewer, from Dover,
Co. Kent, came in 1636, with w. Martha, and four serv. as set forth in
3 Mass. Hist. Coll. VIII. 276, bec. the founder of a num. line, as was
thot. in former days from so many spring. at Ipswich; prob. ch. of two
brs. of Henry; but any kn. of his childr. is not gain. and we kn. only that
he d. 2 Feb. 1679, and his wid. d. 4 Apr. 1686. Yet inv. of his est. was
not ret. bef. many yrs. Its date is 15 May 1696. Of his br. John are
nam. three ch. John, Josiah, and Hannah; and of his br. Joshua are nam.
three, John, Eliz. and Hannah Warner, w. I presume of John Warner,
unless her d. Hannah be meant, if these names are found in order of distrib. of the est. as is most prob. HENRY, Reading, prob. s. of Rev. Stephen, may be he, wh. was persecut. 1660, as a Quaker. JOHN, Dedham,
had been of Watertown, freem. 6 May 1635, not, as Bond states, 13 May
1640, that being the day of ano. hav. the same name, was selectman of W.
1636, and at D. had Samuel, b. 8 (Bond says 11) Jan. 1640; Jonathan,
and David, b. 14, bapt. 24 Dec. 1643, describ. in the homely phrase of
ch. rec. "being the childr. of one burthen to our br. J. B. and his w. our
sis." when it would have been agreeable to see her name. He rem. Mr.

Haven, 13, says, to Hampton. JOHN, Salem 1638, perhaps earlier, had
gr. of ld. 1639, was the freem. of 13 May 1640, is by tradit. said to be
from Dorsetsh. but more prob. was that tailor from Canterbury, Co. Kent,
wh. came in 1636, perhaps br. of Henry, bef. ment. by w. Mary had at
S. John, bapt. Jan. 1639, d. at 7 yrs.; Mary, Sept. 1640; Abigail, 12
Feb. 1643; Hannah, 23 June 1644, d. soon; Hannah, again, 25 May
1645; John, again, 23 June 1650; and Joseph, 8 May 1653; and d. 13
Nov. 1675, his w. Eliz. hav. d. three days bef. unless some confus. of
name exist in the report. JOHN, Reading, freem. 1666, had Jonathan,
wh. d. 4 Dec. 1653; David; and John, but the order of b. is not seen,
beside Samuel, wh. d. 25 Mar. 1662, the mo. Rebecca hav. d. sixteen
days bef. and he d. May 1676. Of ano. JOHN, freem. 1670, it is not kn.
where he liv. but it may well seem, that he was s. of the preced. bec. he
d. at Reading, 1705. JOHN, Salem, prob. s. of the first John, m. 14 Aug.
1673, Mary Herrick, perhaps d. of Zechary, had John b. 26 Apr. 1675;
and Jonathan, 29 Mar. 1678; was one of the jurors in the sad witchcraft
trials, and recant. magnanimous. from their damnable verdicts. John P.
late Presid. of the Berksh. Med. Inst. and other descend. of this stock give
uniform. spell. of their name Batchelder. *JOSEPH, Salem, a tailor, perhaps
elder br. of John the first, came, 1636, from Canterbury, Co. Kent, with
w. Eliz. one ch. and three serv. acc. the certif. of the Mayor of Sandwich, where they emb. was freem. Mar. 1638; rem. to Wenham, of wh.
he was rep. 1644. What was the name of the ch. he brot. or whether he
had more on our side of the water, or when he d. are unkn. JOSHUA,
Ipswich, br. of Henry, of the same, came from Kent, but no more can be
heard of him, exc. that he had at least three ch. John, Eliz. and Hannah
Warner, w. of Daniel of the same, entit. to sh. in the est. of his br. Henry.
MARK, Wenham, freem. 1663, may have been s. of the preced. or not,
was a soldier in the comp. of Gardner, and in the great battle of 19 Dec.
1675 was k. with his capt. NATHANIEL, Hampton, eldest s. of the Rev.
Stephen, b. a. 1611, m. 1656 Deborah, d. of John Smith, and had, it is
said, seventeen childr. (only nine by her), many of whose names it might
be not easy to find, but one was Nathaniel. At Woburn he took sec. w.
31 Oct. 1676, Mary Wyman, wid. of John, and d. of Rev. Thomas Carter, had eight ch. and from Coffin's gatherings in Geneal. Reg. VI. 207
we learn that he had third w. Eliz. STEPHEN, Lynn, the first min. there,
b. a. 1561, came to Boston in the William and Francis, 5 June 1632,
from London, preach. at L. next yr. was freem. 6 May 1635, and next yr.
was at Ipswich, perhaps at Yarmouth 1637, but in 1638 went to Newbury,
in 1639 to Hampton, whence in 1641 he was dism. and some time after
may be heard of at Saco. Willis, I. 37. Finally in 1653 or 4 he went
home, leav. third w. Mary here, wh. pray. for div. in 1656, bec. he was

gone to Eng. and had tak. new w. Her suit may hardly have prosper.
for, in his Hist. of Lynn, Lewis copies from York rec. sentence against
her, in 1651, for adultery, and that she and her paramour were whip. for
it. Prob. he had good reason for leav. her, and in few yrs. after, he d.
1660, at Hackney, near London. Some acco. tho. imperf. we have of four
s. and three ds. One had m. in Eng. John Sanborn, wh. was d. bef. the
fam. cross. the ocean; ano. call. Theodata, had, in Eng. prob. m. Christopher Hussey, after of Lynn, rem. to Hampton, and she d. 1649 ; and Deborah m. John Wing of L. wh. rem. to Sandwich. Names of s. were
Henry, Nathaniel, bef. ment. Francis, and Stephen, wh. both were of
London, and the last is said to have been liv. 1685, but the dates of b.
are all unkn. Descend. are very num. ee Winth. I. and II. in many
places ; Prince's Ann. sub. 1632 ; and Lewis, most copiously, Ed. 2d pp.
78, and 92–97. WILLIAM, Charlestown 1634, freem. 1644, by w. Jane
had Seaborn, bapt. 11 Jan. 1635, prob. d. young; Abigail, 2 July 1637 ;
and by w. Rachel had Joseph, b. 20 Aug. 1644 ; and he d. says the gr.
st. 20 Feb. 1670, aged a. 72. His will made nine days bef. gives us
knowl. of other ch. beside Joseph and Abigail, wh. are nam. in it. She
had m. 11 Nov. 1659, Richard Austin. The w. Rachel was made Ex'trix,
and provis. in the will follows for her d. of the same name, w. of Philip
Atwood, as I judge ; for Susanna, his gr.ch. d. of Susanna his d. wh. had
m. 2 Nov. 1664, John Lawrence, and was d. and for sev. other gr.ch.
named Cromwell, of whose f. or mo. I have inq. assidu. but in vain.
Correct spell. of various fam. with name of so nearly sim. sound, must be
unattain. and after trying differ. heads, I felt compel. to use only one.
Under its many shapes, in 1829, Farmer found eleven had been gr. at N.
E. coll.

BACKUS, FRANCIS, Saco, one of the selectmen 1688. STEPHEN, Norwich 1660, s. of William, by w. Sarah, d. of Lyon Gardiner, had Sarah,
b. Apr. 1668 ; Stephen, Oct. 1670; Mary, Nov. 1672; Ruth, 19 Dec.
1674; Lydia, Nov. 1677 ; and Timothy, 7 Oct. 1682. WILLIAM, Saybrook 1638, had there William and Stephen, rem. to Norwich a. 1660, was
freem. 1663, and d. June 1664, leav. sec. w. Ann, wh. d. May 1670.
WILLIAM, Norwich, s. of the preced. m. Eliz. (prob. the eldest d. of William Pratt of Saybrook), wh. d. 1730, aged 87, had William, b. 1660 ;
John, 1661 ; perhaps Sarah, 1663 ; Samuel, 1665 ; Joseph, 6 Sept. 1667;
and Nathaniel, 1669 ; and d. a. 1720. Of this name twelve had, in 1828,
been gr. at Yale and Dart. Coll. Rev. Isaac, disting. min. of Middleborough, d. 1806, aged 82.

BACON, *ANDREW, Hartford 1639, one of the orig. proprs. b. prob. in
Rutlandsh. Eng. had perhaps been of Cambridge, was rep. 1642 to 56,
soon after rem. to Hadley, and d. 1669. His w. was Eliz. wh. had been

wid. of Timothy Standley, brot. from Eng. as his w. but he had no ch.
DANIEL, Charlestown, s. prob. of one Michael, br. of ano. brot. from Ireland as tradit. goes, freem. 26 May 1647 was an orig. project. of settlem.
at Woburn 1640, there had Thomas, b. 13 Apr. 1645; John, 8 Sept.
1647; Isaac, 4 Apr. 1650; Rachel, 4 June 1652; Jacob, 2 June 1654;
Lydia, 6 Mar. 1656; Daniel; and John; rem. a. 1669 to Cambridge vill.
now Newton, says Jackson, wh. tells of his w. Mary Read of Bridgewater,
and that he d. 7 Sept. 1691. His wid. d. within 4 wks. DANIEL, Boston
1660, s. of the preced. rem. perhaps to Salem, there m. 1 Aug. 1664, Susanna, d. of Michael Spencer, had Daniel, b. 1665; Daniel, again, 1669;
both d. early; Susanna, and Mary, tw. 1670; and Daniel, again, 1673.
DANIEL, Dedham, s. of John of the same, m. 21 Apr. 1685, Eliz. Martin,
perhaps d. of Richard, had Daniel, Isaac, and Timothy. FRANCIS, Boston, of wh. I see no more, exc. that he was freem. 1665. GEORGE,
Hingham, a mason, came in the Increase, from London 1635, aged 43,
with ch. Samuel, 12; Susan, 10; and John, 8; and d. 1642. Lincoln's
Hist. 43. ISAAC, Newton, s. of Daniel of the same, d. 1684, leav. w.
Abigail, wh. d. 10 July 1715, but no ch. JACOB, Newton, br. of the preced. by w. Eliz. had Eliz. b. 26 Mar. 1677, d. next yr.; Jacob, 9 Mar.
1680; John, 27 Feb. 1683; Eliz. again, 12 May 1684, d. young; Ruhami, 8 Apr. 1686, d. young; Mary, 1689; Eliz. again, 6 May 1692;
and Isaac, 28 June 1698; and by sec. w. Dorothy, d. of Ralph Bradhurst
of Roxbury, had Ruhami, again, 18 Dec. 1700; Abigail, 16 Feb. 1702;
John, and Dorothy, tw. b. at Roxbury, 30 July 1704; and Ralph, Nov.
1706. JAMES, Roxbury 1673, freem. 1674. JEREMIAH, Barnstable, s. of
Nathaniel the first, m. 10 Dec. 1686, Eliz. Howes, perhaps d. of Joseph of
Yarmouth, had Sarah, b. 16 Oct. 1687; Ann, 16 Nov. 1688; Mercy, 30
Jan. 1690; Samuel, 15, bapt. 17 Apr. 1692; Joseph, 15, bapt. 23 June
1695; Ebenezer, 11 Mar. bapt. 19 June 1698; Eliz. bapt. 17 Sept. 1699,
d. soon; Nathaniel, 11, bapt. 15 Sept. 1700; Job. b. 23 Mar. 1703; and
Eliz. again, 6 Aug. 1705. JOHN, Dedham, s. of Michael the first, of the
same, b. in Ireland, as tradit. gives it, freem. 1647, (the name spell. with k)
by w. Rebecca had John, b. 17 July 1656; Rebecca, 1658, wh. m. 13
Feb. 1679, John Gay; Daniel, 10 Mar. 1661, bef. ment.; Samuel, 8 Oct.
1665; and Thomas, 23 Aug. 1667; beside Mary, wh. m. Nathaniel
Kingsbury; and Susanna, wh. m. Jonathan Dewing; and he d. 17 June
1683. His wid. d. 27 Oct. 1694. Of this first John descend. still enjoy
part of their ancestral prop. and from this stock is the Rev. Leonard of
New Haven, the perspicacious stud. of early N. E. manners. JOHN,
Charlestown, perhaps s. of Daniel the first, for all the knowl. of wh. we
are indebt. to Hammond's Diary, relat. that his ch. (as if he had but one)
d. 18 Mar. his w. on 20th, and hims. on 7 Apr. 1678, all of smallpox.

John, Dedham, eldest s. of the first John of the same, m. 15 Dec. 1683, Lydia Dewing, perhaps d. of Andrew of the same, had Lydia, Rebecca, John, and Michael, perhaps others, and d. 27 Oct. 1732. JOHN, Barnstable, s. of Nathaniel the first, m. 17 June 1686, Mary Howes, perhaps d. of Joseph of Yarmouth, had Hannah, b. 7 June 1687; Desire, 15 Mar. 1689; Nathaniel, 16 Jan. 1692; Patience, 15 June 1694; John, 24 Mar. 1697; all bapt. 2 Oct. 1698; Isaac, b. 29 Mar. 1699; Solomon, 3 Apr. 1701; and Jude, 9 Dec. 1703. JOHN, Watertown, and Newton, perhaps youngest br. of Jacob, freem. 1690, by w. Abigail, wh. d. 10 July 1715, had Mary, bapt. I suppose, at W. as Bond furnishes the fact, 25 Dec. 1687; and John, b. 28 Mar. 1689. JOSEPH, Farmington 1686, had w. wh. join. the ch. Jan. 1687. MICHAEL, or MIGHILL, Dedham 1640, brot. it is said, from Ireland, w. and four ch. Michael, Daniel, John and Sarah, nam. in his will, of 14 Apr. 1648, pro. in the foll. spring. His w. had d. 1647. MICHAEL, Woburn, eldest s. of the preced. prob. liv. some time at Charlestown, but at W. by w. Mary had prob. Michael, unless he were b. at C.; Eliz. b. 4 Jan. 1642; and Sarah, 24 Aug. 1644, perhaps others. His w. d. 26 Aug. 1655, and he m. 26 Oct. foll. Mary Noyes, wh. d. 19 May 1670; rem. to Billerica a. 1678, had no more ch. and d. 4 July 1688. MICHAEL, Woburn, eldest s. of the preced. m. 22 Mar. 1660, Sarah, d. of Thomas Richardson of the same, had Mary, b. 1 Mar. 1661; Sarah, 24 Aug. 1663; Abigail, 5 Mar. 1666; and he d. I think, bef. his f. ‡ * NATHANIEL, Barnstable, m. 4 Dec. 1642, Hannah, d. of Rev. John Mayo, had Hannah, b. 4 Sept. 1643, bapt. 8 Dec. 1644; Nathaniel, b. 5, bapt. 15 Feb. 1646; Mary, 12, bapt. 20 Aug. 1648; Samuel, 25 Feb. bapt. 9 Mar. 1651; Eliz. b. 28 Jan. 1654; Jeremiah, 8 May 1657; Mercy, 8 Feb. 1660; and John. He was propos. as freem. 1645, chos. rep. 1655, and made an Assist. of Plymouth Col. 1667. Mercy, m. 18 July 1683, John Otis, third of that name. NATHANIEL, Middletown 1653, is call. s. of William of the parish of Stretton, Co. Rutland, by w. Ann, d. of Thomas Miller of the same, had Nathaniel, wh. d. 8 Apr. 1655; Hannah, b. 14 Apr. 1655; Andrew, 4 Feb. 1657, d. at 5 yrs.; Nathaniel, 20 July 1659, whose name was chang. for Thomas; John, 14 Mar. 1661; Mary, 7 Apr. 1664; Andrew, again, 10 June 1666; Abigail, 13 July 1670; Lydia, 18 Feb. 1673; perhaps ano. Nathaniel, whose date may be lost. His w. d. 6 July 1680, and he m. 17 Apr. 1682, Eliz. Pierpont, prob. wid. of one whose name is not seen, had Beriah, 17 Aug. of the same yr. unless we suppose an error in the rec. of m. or of b. He was neph. of Andrew, had part of his uncle's est. and d. 27 Jan. 1706, hav. made his will 1698, pro. twelve days after his d. in wh. are nam. s. Thomas, John, Andrew, Nathaniel, and Beriah, with ds. Hannah, Mary, Abigail, and Lydia. Evidence, giv. in 1661, by deac. John Fletcher of Milford (wh. d. the foll. yr.) relative to the ancestry of this Nathaniel, at wh. was present a party advers. interest. might, without violence, be constr. to refer equally to the Barnstable fam. tho. it is less prob. NATHANIEL, Barnstable, s. of the first Nathaniel, m. 27 Mar. 1673, Sarah, d. of Gov. Hinckley, had Nathaniel, b. 9 Sept. 1674; Mary, 9 Oct. 1677; Eliz. 11 Apr. 1680; and Samuel, 20 Jan. 1682. His w. d. 16 Feb. 1687; and he d. Dec. 1691. RICHARD, may be that passeng. in 1635 on board the James from Bristol, call. Becon by Richard Mather, when he relates the loss of his right hand in the gr. Aug. storm, for wh. see Young's Chron. of Mass. 475. Certain. no more is kn. of him. SAMUEL, Barnstable, m. 9 May 1659, Martha Foxwell, had Samuel, b. 9 Mar. 1660; and Martha, 6 Jan. 1662. SAMUEL, Barnstable, s. of Nathaniel the first, m. 17 Dec. 1675, Mary, d. of John Jacob of Hingham, whither he rem. had Hannah, b. 12 Oct. 1676, d. at 2 mos.; Hannah, again, 10 Feb. 1678; and Mary, 7 Feb. 1680; and he d. 18 Feb. 1681. THOMAS, Roxbury 1665, had Joseph, b. 1 Jan. 1666; and George, 12 Sept. 1671, wh. d. at 2 yrs. and the f. d. 25 Oct. 1701. WILLIAM, Salem 1640, had Isaac, bapt. 12 Sept. 1641; and d. 1653, leav. wid. Rebecca, d. it is said, of Thomas Potter of Coventry, wh. had been mayor of that borough. They had liv. in Dublin, and, on the outbreak of the Irish rebellion, she was sent over here, says tradit. and her h. foll. soon; but her br. Humphrey P. and other relat. perish. in the massacre. Some community of origin may be, perhaps, traced to this tradit. and to that of Michael; yet the flight from the rebellion would seem more natural in that early day to be direct. to Eng. Felt says, William was freem. after 1643; but the evidence is not seen. In 1834 Farmer found the gr. of this name to be seven at Yale, four at Harv. and four at other N. E. coll. the earliest of wh. Jacob, H. C. 1731, min. of Plymouth, was gr.gr.s. of the first Michael.

BADCOCK, EBENEZER, Sherburn, s. of Robert, by w. Hannah had Abigail, b. 5 Mar. 1687; Hannah, 28 Sept. 1690, prob. d. young; Hannah, again, 25 Mar. 1694; and Ebenezer, 4 Sept. 1697; was selectman 1711, and d. 15 Dec. 1717. GEORGE, New Haven 1640, serv. of Gov. Eaton, under indent. for six yrs. may have rem. to Dorchester, liv. in that pt. now Milton, perhaps br. of Robert of the same, had George, b. 26 Feb. 1658; possib. other ch. GEORGE, Milton, s. perhaps of the preced. or of Robert, had, as Morse supposes, Dorothy, wh. m. Ebenezer Wood, and, it may be, more; yet this seems very loose, without dates. JAMES, Portsmouth, R. I. among freem. in 1655, rem. to the other side of Narraganset Bay. See Babcock, and observe, that the strange delusion of Hinman a. the glorious comp. of Leyden pilgr. by the Ann, 1623, is adopt. by Morse, as if such a brat were better rear. than stifled. ROBERT, Dorchester 1648, next of Milton, had Nathaniel, b. 14 Mar. 1658; Ebenezer, bapt. at D. 5

July 1663; Eliz. 24 Oct. 1666; beside other ch. of wh. one I think, was George. Harv. Coll. Catal. has the spell. unchang.

BADGER, GILES, Newbury 1635, m. Eliz. d. of Edmund Greenleaf, had John, b. 30 June 1643; and d. 10 July 1647. His will, of 29 June, was pro. in Sept. and his wid. m. 16 Feb. foll. Richard Brown. JOHN, Newbury, s. of the preced. by w. Eliz. wh. d. 8 Apr. 1669, had John, b. 4 Apr. 1664, d. soon; John, again, 26 Apr. 1665; Sarah, 25 Jan. 1667; and James, 19 Mar. 1669. For sec. w. he. m. 23 Feb. 1671, Hannah, d. of Stephen Swett, had Stephen, 13 Dec. foll.; Hannah, 3 Dec. 1673; Nathaniel, 16 Jan. 1676; Mary, 2 May 1678; Eliz. 30 Apr. 1680; Ruth, 10 Feb. 1683; a s. 9 Mar. 1685, d. soon; Abigail, 29 June 1687; and Lydia, 30 Apr. 1690. He d. 31 Mar. 1691, and his w. at near the same date, both of smallpox. NATHANIEL, Newbury 1635, br. of Giles, perhaps elder, had w. Hannah, but I can hear no more of him, nor of ano. br. RICHARD. THOMAS, New Haven 1639, of wh. no good is told. In 1834 four gr. of this name had come from Yale, two from Harv. and two from other N. E. coll.

BADLAM, WILLIAM, Boston, by w. Joan had John, b. 8 Feb. 1687; may be the same man that had, at Weymouth, by w. Mary, William, 20 Dec. 1693; and Mary, 14 July 1699.

BADMAN, JOHN, Boston, by w. Sarah had Lydia, b. 26 Apr. 1656. No more is kn.

BAGG, JOHN, Springfield, m. 1659, Hannah, d. of Henry Burt of the same, had ten ch. of wh. few are report. as Daniel at Westfield; John, at Springfield, d. 5 Sept. 1683; and Hannah, wh. m. 3 Feb. 1681, Nathaniel Sikes, and liv. to 13 May 1740.

BAGLEY, JOHN, wh. had, I suppose, been one of Lyon Gardiner's men at Saybrook in 1637, should be found at Watertown 1643, but Bond in his all embracing vol. has not appoint. him a place there. ORLANDO, Salisbury, m. 6 Mar. 1654, Sarah, d. of Anthony Colby, had prob. Orlando, and perhaps other ch. ORLANDO, Amesbury, s. prob. of the preced. took o. of fidel. 20 Dec. 1677, freem. 1690, m. 22 Dec. 1681, Sarah Sargent, perhaps d. of William of the same, had Sarah, b. 27 Feb. 1683; John, 21 Jan. 1685; Jacob, 13 Dec. 1687, and Orlando, next day; and Judith, 13 Nov. 1690. SAMUEL, Weymouth, by w. Mary had Samuel, b. 7 Sept. 1658; and perhaps more. SAMUEL, Weymouth, s. of the preced. m. Mary, d. of Shadrach Thayer, of Braintree, had James, bapt. 8 July 1688; Sarah, 17 May 1696; Abigail, 1 Oct. 1699; and Mary, 5 July 1702.

BAGNALL, WALTER, Scarborough 1628, at Richmond's Isle, had gr. deal. with the Ind. of the neighb. wh. for some imprud. or perhaps worse treat. after some yrs. k. him. See Winth. I. 62; Willis, I. 15 and 21, and Southgate 10.

Bailey, Elias, Newtown, L. I. 1656. Henry, Falmouth, liv. bef. 1690, in that pt. now Cape Elizabeth. Willis, I. 216. Hilkiah, Scarborough 1645. James, Rowley 1663, then aged 51. James, Newbury, s. of John the sec. of the same, m. 17 Sept. 1672, Mary, d. of George Carr, of Salisbury, had Mary, b. 6 July 1673 ; Isaac, 22 Oct. 1681, H. C. 1701; and perhaps more. Commonly the first syl. of his name is with *y* instead of *i*, and his f. and brs. may better appear under the later place. John, Hartford, was constable in 1656, but prob. bef. 1669 rem. to Haddam. *John*, Watertown, a min. b. at Blackburn, in Lancash. 24 Feb. 1644, came in 1683, preach. some time as assist. to Rev. Samuel Willard, at third, or O. S. ch. in Boston, but was sett. as success. to famous John Sherman, at W. 6 Oct. 1686. His w. Lydia, by wh. he had no ch. d. 12 Apr. 1690; and in 1692 he rem. to Boston again, bec. assist. min. at first ch. 17 July 1693, and d. 12 Dec. 1697. John Dunton highly commends his serm. and Mather has giv. one of the best ch. of the Magn. to his honor. He left wid. Susanna, wh. m. Rev. Peter Thacher. To a br. Henry, of Manchester in Eng. he wrote in 1688, of his love to mo. and sis. Lydia in his native ld. of his own infirm health here, and in a querulous temper. The Magnalia, III. 232 finds, in his early serv. in Ireland the wounds to his constitut. " wh. could never be recover." All that need be kn. of him is well told by Francis, in Hist. of W. 52, 8, and 141. John, Scituate, m. 25 Jan. 1673, Sarah White, had John, b. 5 Nov. 1673 ; Sarah, Oct. 1675 ; Mary, Dec. 1677 ; Joseph, Oct. 1679 ; Benjamin, Apr. 1682 ; William, Feb. 1685 ; Hannah, Jan. 1688; and Samuel, Aug. 1690. For sec. w. 9 Dec. 1699 he took Ruth Clothier, if the name be right, and d. 1718. I presume he was b. on this side of the water, but wh. was his f. is not seen. The two elder s. perpet. the line at S. Mary, m. 1 Jan. 1701, James Perry, and Hannah m. 24 Dec. 1716, James Briggs. John, Marshfield, m. 9 May 1677, Ann Bourne, prob. d. of John. Joseph, Bradford, s. of Richard, of Salem, by w. Abigail had Abigail ; Richard, b. 30 Sept. 1675 ; and perhaps others, was a deac. Palmer, a miller, came in the Planter, 1635, aged 21, from Kingston, near London, but no more is heard of him. Richard, Lynn, came in the Bevis from Southampton, 1638, in the serv. of Richard Dummer, aged, prob. 15 yrs. br. of James of Rowley, m. Edna Lambert, prob. d. of Francis of Rowley, had Joseph, but no other ch. is ment. in his will of 1648. His wid. m. Ezekiel Northend of R. bef. 15 Nov. 1649. Richard, Newport, 1670, was an import. man, clk. of the Council of the Col. and nam. in the will of John Clark to be one of the Trust. of his charity. Samuel, New Haven 1643. Samuel, Weymouth, by w. Mary had Mary, b. 30 Apr. 1661; James, 21 Feb. 1664; John, 12 Dec. 1668; and Joseph, 18 Dec. 1672. Theophilus, Lynn 1645, m. perhaps Ruth, d. of Thomas Ivory the first, and d. 1694. THOMAS, Weymouth, freem. 13 May 1640, by w. Ruth had Christian, b. 26 Feb. 1662; Samuel, 21 Feb. 1666; Mary, 10 Feb. 1670; and Sarah, 29 Sept. 1674. THOMAS, Milford, was a propr. 1646, says Lambert. *THOMAS*, Watertown, a min., younger br. of Rev. John, by w. Rebecca had Thomas, bapt. 19 Aug. 1688; but he had bef. his b. made a will 26 Nov. 1686, in wh. Bond says, he names s. John, his w. brs. John and Henry; and he d. 21 Jan. 1689, aged only 35. His wid. m. 26 Apr. 1694, William Brown the sec. of Salem. Of this name, includ. Bayley, that is perpet. interfer. with this, as does this with that, the gr. in 1834 at Harv. are eleven, at Dart. five, Yale two, and the other N. E. coll. count nine, beside seven, spelled Baylies, of wh. four are at Harv.

BAKER, ALEXANDER, Boston, ropemaker, came in the Elizabeth and Ann, 1635, aged 28, from London, with w. Eliz. 23; and ch. Eliz. 3; and Christian, 1; had Alexander, b. 15 Jan. 1636; Samuel, 16 Jan. 1638; John, 20 June 1640; Joshua, 30 Apr. 1642; Hannah, 29 Sept. 1644; all bapt. 5 Oct. 1645, as he and his w. were adm. of the ch. the preced. day, was freem. 1646; had, also, William, 15 May 1647; Benjamin, 16 Mar. 1653; Josiah, 26 Feb. 1655; and Josiah, again, 26 Feb. 1658, if we accept the rec. Not one of the four last were bapt. in first ch. wh. may provoke inq. for the reason. At Gloucester he had sat down on first coming; and in the gr. to Rev. Richard Blinman, 1642, the same ld. is giv. that had bef. been offer. to Alexander B. His d. Christina m. 18 July 1654 Simon Roberts. CORNELIUS, Salem, m. 26 Apr. 1658, Hannah, d. of John Woodbury, had Hannah, b. 14 Oct. 1660, d. at 2 yrs. Hannah, again, 28 Nov. 1662; liv. on Beverly side 1671–86. DANIEL, Yarmouth, s. of Francis, m. 27 May 1674, Eliz. d. of William Chase the sec. had Daniel, b. 1675; Samuel, 1676; Eliz. Hannah, 1696; Thankful, 1698; and Tabitha, 1700. EBENEZER, Salem, a soldier in Gardner's comp. wound. 19 Dec. 1675, in the gr. Narraganset battle. EDWARD, Lynn 1630, freem. 14 Mar. 1638, had w. Jane, certain. five s. perhaps other ch. beside d. Mary, wh. m. 7 Nov. 1662, George Sumner of Dorchester, hav. foll. her to Northampton where B. liv. many yrs. Leav. s. Joseph and Timothy at N. whose names are misprint. Batter in Geneal. Reg. IX. 88; he went back to L. there d. Mar. 1687, giv. est. to s. John of Dedham, Edward, and Thomas, of Lynn. EDWARD, Lynn, s. of the preced. m. 7 Apr. 1685, Mary, d. of Capt. John Marshall, was ens. of the milit. and freem. 1691. FRANCIS, Boston, came in the Planter, 1635, aged 24, m. 1641, Isabel Twining, perhaps d. of William, had Nathaniel, b. 27 Mar. 1642; rem. to Yarmouth, and there had John; Samuel, 1 May 1648; Daniel, 2 Sept. 1650; William; Thomas; Eliz. wh. m. John Chase; and Hannah, wh. m. a Pierce, and he d. 1696, in 85th yr. In his will of 4 Mar. 1693, as all these ch. but Samuel are nam. it may be thot. that he was d. His wid. d. 16 May 1706. JAMES, Dorchester, kn. to us solely by the gr.stone, wh. tells, that he d. 30 Mar. 1721, aged 69 ; but we may guess, that he was f. of that James, whose gr.stone says, that he " d. 24 Aug. 1734, aged 60 yrs. 20 days." JEFFREY, Windsor, m. 25 Nov. 1642, Joan, d. of William Rockwell, had Samuel, b. 30 Mar. 1644 ; Hepzibah, 10 May 1646 ; Mary, 15 July 1649 ; Abiel, a d. 23 Dec. 1652, d. young; and Joseph, 18 June 1655 ; in wh. yr. the f. d. His wid. m. 1668, Richard Ingram. JOHN, Ipswich, 1634, freem. 14 May of that yr. perhaps, is in later yrs. ment. in the town rec. with prefix of respect ; yet so frequent is the con-cur. of this name of bapt. with the surname, as to justify doubt, whether that day's freem. were not JOHN, ment. by Frothingham, 80, as com. to Charlestown 1630, and rem. 1637, or that JOHN, of wh. Winth. II. 29, tells, how he rem. from Boston to Newbury, grew rich too fast, went thence to York, and back with contrition to B. Assignm. of resid. be-comes especial. diffic. in such cases, as in the freem. of 2 June 1641, where twice John Baker is count. and after minute comparis. of the incid. belong. to the names above and below each John, a confid. conject. may be offer. that one was of Ipswich, perhaps he wh. was b. at Norwich, Co. Norf. a grocer, that came 1637, aged 39, to Boston, in the Rose of Yarmouth, with Eliz. his w. 31, three ch. Eliz. John, and Thomas, four serv. Mercy, and Ann Alexarson, aged 24, and 20, respectiv. Bridget Bull, 32 ; and Samuel Ayres or Acres, 14, as certif. copy of rec. from her Majesty's Remembrancer Office instr. me. For the other, Charlestown is entitl. unless better claim. appear, for he had, by w. Rebecca, there bapt. Sarah 13 Sept. 1640, may be the *JOHN, wh. rem. 1642 to Dover, and was rep. 1650. JOHN, Boston, that early mem. of the ch. wh. by w. Charity had Charity, bapt. 12 Apr. 1635, may be the freem. of 18 May 1642. JOHN of Wells, wh. may be the man, that had ho. in 1675 on w. side of Kenne-beck riv. near Arowsick isl. when the war broke out, was, we kn. sw. freem. 1653; but tolerab. sure am I, that JOHN of Woburn was not, since he was sentenc. to be whip. and to m. Susanna Martin (the inflict. of the latter pt. of the punish. being on 28 May 1654) ; by her he had John, b. 25 Mar. preced. Mary, 22 Feb. 1656 ; Joseph, 15 June 1657, d. soon ; Joseph, again, 1 Feb. 1660 ; Susanna, 15 Mar. 1652, d. soon ; Susanna, again, 12 Apr. 1663 ; a s. whose name is not seen on the rec. 8 Mar. 1664, d. next week ; Samuel, 21 Apr. 1665 ; Benjamin, 24 May 1667 ; James, 10 June 1670 ; Jonathan, 2 Apr. 1674 ; and William, 18 Aug. 1679. ‖ JOHN, Boston, blacksmith, ar. co. 1644, had m. Joan, eldest d. of Thomas Swift, of Dorchester, sev. yrs. (prob. ten) bef. 5 Nov. 1657, wh. date from the MS. vol. in the Boston office of reg. usual. accept. as a rec. while it is only a copy, is *truly* print. from the *false* certif. of Gov. John Winth. wh. d. 26 Mar. 1649, as the error may be read in Geneal. Reg. XI. 202. By her he had John, wh. d. young, 25 June 1654; Thomas, b. 12 Feb. 1654; Samuel, 16 Apr. 1655, d. in 3 mos.; Nathaniel, 4 Apr. 1656, d. soon; of wh. four ch. the false certif. on rec. would make all b. bef. the m. Also he had John, again, 17 July 1658, d. in few mos. and Eliz. 26 June 1660; and d. I think in July 1666, leav. good est. but in his will of 26 Mar. preced. names only the s. Thomas, and d. Eliz. JOHN, Dorchester, s. perhaps of Richard, freem. 1673, m. 11 July 1667, Preserved, d. of Thomas Trott, had Sarah, b. 12 July 1668; Mary, 10 Nov. 1670, d. at 2 mos. John, 25 Nov. 1671; James, 4 Aug. 1674; Mary, again, 24 Aug. 1676; Thankful, 13 Apr. 1679; Hannah, 22 July 1682, d. at 1 yr.; Eliz. 18 July 1684; Hannah, again, 11 July, 1687 d. at 3 yrs. and Abijah, posthum. 25 Feb. 1691. He d. 26 Aug. 1690, and his wid. d. 25 Nov. 1711. JOHN, Roxbury, had only Thomas, b. there 20 May 1676. JOHN, Boston, m. 8 Jan. 1664, Thankful, eldest d. of sec. Hopestill Foster, had John, b. 26 Feb. 1665; Silence, wh. d. 28 July 1666. His w. d. 27 Jan. 1698, and he d. 7 Nov. 1732, aged 87. JOHN, Ipswich, m. 13 May 1667, Catharine, d. of Rev. William Perkins, had Eliz. b. 1670; John; and perhaps others. JOHN, Yarmouth, s. of Francis, by w. Alice had John, b. May 1672; Bethia, Nov. 1673; Sarah, Sept. 1677; Jonathan; Isaac; Mary; and Eliz. JOHN, Hull, freem. 1677. JOHN, Hartford, was there as early as 1665, m. Lydia, d. of John Baysey, had John, Baysey, and Joseph, all s. and perhaps other ch. JOHN, Dorchester, freem. 1677. JOHN, New London 1678, perhaps s. of William. JOHN, Dedham, s. of Edward, was liv. there 1678, may have been f. of that Daniel, b. 18 Apr. 1686, H. C. 1706, wh. was min. of Sherborn, ord. 1713. JOHN, Woburn, perhaps s. of John of the same, m. 18 Oct. 1682, Hannah, d. of George Polley, had Hannah, b. 5 Dec. 1683, d. soon; Hannah, again, 3 Aug. 1685; and John, 27 June 1687, perhaps more. JOSEPH, Northampton, s. of Edward, m. 5 Feb. 1663, Ruth, d. of William Holton, was k. by the Ind. 29 Oct. 1675, with his s. Joseph, b. 20 Jan. 1665; leav. Ruth, b. 6 May 1668; Mary, 5 Sept. 1670; and Samuel, 11 Sept. 1672. Joseph was the name giv. to his posthum. s. b. 25, bapt. 30 Jan. foll. JOSEPH, Boston 1675, a tailor. JOSEPH, Windsor, s. of Jeffrey of the same, m. 30 Jan. 1677, Hannah, wid. of Thomas Buckland the younger, d. of Nathaniel Cook, had Joseph, b. 13 Apr. 1678; Lydia, 5 July 1681; and Samuel, wh. d. 16 Oct. 1685. The f. d. 11 Dec. 1691; and his wid. m. John Loomis. JOSEPH, Woburn, prob. s. of John the first, of the same, m. 4 Oct. 1686, Hannah Bauk, if rightly this name be writ JOSHUA, New London, s. of Alexander, m. 13 Sept. 1674, Hannah, wid.

of Tristram Minter, had Eliz. b. 9 May 1676; Alexander, 16 Dec.
1677; Joshua, 5 Jan. 1679; John, 24 Dec. 1681; Hannah, and Sarah,
tw. 18 Jan. 1684; Mercy; Benjamin; and Patience; and he d. 27 Dec.
1717, his w. surv. His d. Eliz. m. Richard Atwell. LANCELOT, Boston,
by w. Judith had Eliz. b. 13 Dec. 1644; rem. to New Haven, and had
John, 1651. MARK, Hampton 1678. NATHANIEL, Hingham 1635, by
w. (wh. is ment. but not nam. in the will of her f. William Lane of
Dorchester), had Mary, wh. m. 16 Dec. 1657, John Loring, perhaps
his only ch. and d. 3 June 1682. In his will of 11 May preced. after
provis. for his wid. and two Ind. slaves, he gave most of his prop. to gr.-
childr. yet with a reasona. mem. to six ch. of his late br. Nicholas, of
Scituate. See Lincoln, Cent. Addr. 39. Farmer mistook him for s. of
Nicholas. NATHANIEL, Yarmouth, eldest s. of Francis, had three s.
Samuel, b. 29 Oct. 1670; Nathaniel, 27 Jan. 1672; and prob. the other
was nam. Silas, says Mr. Otis. Both he and his w. d. Dec. 1691, as Mr.
O. assures me. *NICHOLAS, Hingham 1635, br. of the first Nathaniel,
freem. 3 Mar. 1636, rep. 1636 and 8, rem. to Scituate, there was ord.
1660, third min. of the first ch. and was of such good temper as to reconcile the two chhs. wh. had quarrel. for thirty yrs. Mather, with his
habitual carelessness, says, in the Magn. III. 219, " he had but a private
educat." taking occasion to utter one of his brilliant clauses; yet I found
at St. John's Coll. Cambr. that he had his A. B. 1631–2, and A. M. 1635.
A short time he stopped at Roxbury. His w. that prob. was mo. of all
his ch. d. 1661, and he next yr. took ano. of wh. the bapt. name Grace
only is kn. and d. 22 Aug. 1678, aged 67. Her he made Extrix. of his
will, in wh. he names six ch. Samuel, Nicholas, Eliz. Sarah, Deborah,
and Mary. All the ds. were m. Mary, 26 Feb. 1662, to Stephen Vinal;
Eliz. m. 1664 to John Vinal; Sarah m. 1671, Josiah Litchfield; and
Deborah m. 1678, Israel Chittenden. Deane, 181–3. NICHOLAS, Marblehead, wh. Willis, I. 135, says m. Eliz. d. of George Bartlett of Scarborough, may have been s. of the preced. but we want the illumin. of
a date. Of one Nicholas, late of Boston, mariner, wh. may have been a
gr.s. of Rev. Nicholas, admin. was gr. 8 Oct. 1695, to his mo. in law,
Jane Colyer of Hull. ‖RICHARD, Dorchester, 1639, freem. 18 May
1642, ar. co. 1658, by w. Faith, d. of Henry Withington, wh. d. 3 Feb.
1689, had Mary, b. 27 Apr. 1643, beside five other ds. perhaps, and
certain. two s. only one having date, and one even without a giv. name,
as by his will of 7 Oct. 1689 is shown, viz. John; James; Thankful, w.
of William Griggs; Eliz. w. of a Pratt; Hannah, b. 9 Jan. 1663, wh.
had m. 5 May 1685, John Wiswall; Sarah, then dec. wh. had been w. of
James; and one, the w. of Samuel Robinson. He had been selectman
1653, constable, 1663, and d. 25 Oct. 1689, as Geneal. Reg. V. 395

teaches. ROBERT, Salem, wh. had gr. of ld. 1637, was k. by casualty
1640. See Winth. II. 24. ROBERT, Roxbury, by w. Mary had
Robert, b. 29 Oct. 1673, wh. d. at 11 yrs.; Mary, 11 Oct. 1675; Sarah,
24 Dec. 1676; Matthew, 5 Sept. 1678, wh. d. at 17 yrs.; Joseph, 4 Nov.
1680; Benjamin, 15 Aug. 1682; and Ann, 8 June 1685; and he d. 25
Oct. 1720. Ment. on the rec. of d. is seen of two ch. viz. Eliz. 11 Sept.
and Jonathan, 24 Sept. 1694, of neither of wh. can the b. be found.
SAMUEL, Lynn, came in the Elizabeth and Ann 1635, aged 30, from
London; but he was of Co. Kent, says tradit. and d. 16 Dec. 1666.
SAMUEL, Marshfield, not s. of Nicholas, as was once thot. m. 29 Dec.
1656, Elinor, d. of Kenelm Winslow, had Kenelm, b. 23 Mar. 1658;
Lydia, 18 Feb. 1660; Eliz. 18 Mar. 1662; Alice, 19 May 1663; and
Elinor, 1665; beside others in 1667, 9, and 71, of whose names, in the
mutilat. state of the rec. no certainty can be attain. His w. d. or was
bur. 27 Aug. 1676, and he m. 21 Feb. foll. Patience, wid. perhaps of the
first Moses Simmons of Duxbury, had Samuel. SAMUEL, Windsor
1669, m. 30 June 1670, Sarah, eldest d. of Nathaniel Cooke of the same.
SAMUEL, Hull, s. of Rev. Nicholas, freem. 1677, m. Fear, d. of Isaac
Robinson, rem. to Barnstable, there had adm. with his w. 1687, to that
ch. on dism. from H. ‡ THOMAS, Milford 1639, Easthampton, L. I.
1650, was, perhaps, that Assist. of Conn. from 1658 to 63. THOMAS,
Roxbury, s. of John the first of Ipswich, freem. 1649, by w. Eliz. had
Eliz. b. 2 Oct. 1641; John; Joseph, 24, bapt. 27 Feb. 1648; Sarah, 24,
bapt. 28 Apr. 1650; Mary, bapt. 6 June 1652, d. in 5 weeks; Mary,
again, 11 Sept. 1653; and for sec. w. took 27 Mar. or May 1663, Mary,
d. of Robert Gamlin, had Thomas, b. 7 Jan. 1664; and Mary, 27 July
1667; and he d. 28 Jan. 1684, "old, blind, godly," in the express. rec.
of ch. His s. Thomas was k. by the Ind. at Sudbury fight, Apr. 1676,
surely a very young soldier, under Wadsworth, but he had serv. in the
Narraganset campaign as one of Johnson's comp. in Dec. bef. i. e. less
than twelve yrs. old. No incid. of those days more striking. gives proof
of the extens. reach of the perils. Sarah m. 19 Apr. 1671, Sebas Jackson; and Mary m. Roger Adams. THOMAS, Lynn, s. of the first Edward of the same, m. 10 July 1689, Mary Lewis, perhaps d. of John.
In June 1730, he testif. that he was 77 yrs. old, and that Andrew Townsend of L. wh. he had well kn. 55 yrs. was wound. in the gr. Narraganset
fight, 19 Dec. 1675, under Capt. Gardner. * THOMAS, Topsfield, freem.
1665, m. a. 1673, Priscilla, d. of Dept. Gov. Samuel Symonds, had Priscilla, and prob. more ch. was a milit. officer, and rep. 1686, 9, and 90.
THOMAS, a min. 1678 at Newport, I hear nothing more of. THOMAS,
New London 1686, may have been s. of William, and certain. left ch.
but names and dates of them are unkn. One THOMAS, of Boston, was

head of a fam. 1691; and ano. THOMAS at Lynn was freem. 1691.
THOMAS, Yarmouth, youngest s. of Francis, by w. Bathsheba had Mary,
b. 7 Apr. 1701; and Thomas, 4 Mar. 1703. TIMOTHY, Northampton,
s. of Edward, freem. 1676, m. 16 Jan. 1672, Grace, d. of John Marsh of
Hadley, had Grace, b. 1673, d. soon; Timothy, 1675; and his w. d. 31
May 1676. For sec. w. he took Sarah, wid. of Rev. Hope Atherton, d.
of John Hollister, and had John, b. 3 Feb. 1680; Thomas, 14 May 1682;
Edward, 12 Nov. 1685; Prudence, 14 May 1687; and Deliverance, 13
Nov. 1689. His w. d. 8 Dec. 1691; and he d. 30 Aug. 1729. His
third s. was the youth, wh. m. Christina, d. of Richard Otis, that was
taken by the Ind. at 3 mos. old, from Dover, with her mo. when they k.
her f. 1689, and car. to Canada, there after a priestly educat. made a
Catholic by bapt. and m. a Frenchman, wh. had by her two ch. bef. his
d. Baker had been made a pris. by the Ind. prob. tak. to Canada in
1704, and in differ. capacity in 1714, accomp. Col. Stoddard to bring
home the prisoners from Quebec. Many descend. in N. E. and remote
parts spring from this m. among others Hon. John Wentworth, late M.
C. from Chicago, and present mayor of that prosper. city. WALTER,
Scituate, was suspect. in 1651, of murder of John Winter; but no support was found for that surmise. WILLIAM, Charlestown 1633, freem.
3 Sept. 1634, hav. join. the ch. in Aug. 1633, was one of the petitnrs.
in favor of Wheelwright, but seasona. chang. his mind, and contin. in
good stand.; by w. Joan had Sarah, bapt. 20 May 1638; Stephen, 20
Feb. 1642; and Martha, 21 Apr. 1644; was a selectman 1646, and d. 8
Nov. 1658. His wid. d. 26 Sept. 1669. Frothingham, 82, 5. WILLIAM,
Plymouth 1643, may, I think, have been first of R. I. as early as 1638,
and prob. went thither again, being count. among the freem. 1655, at
Portsmouth. WILLIAM, Boston, pump-maker, m. 23 Sept. 1651, Mary,
d. of Edmund Eddington, had Mary, b. 16 May 1652, d. at 3 mos.;
John, 14 Dec. 1653; and William, 19 Oct. 1655. His w. d. 12 Dec.
foll. and he m. 22 Apr. next, Pilgrim, eldest d. of John Eddy of Water-
town. But gr. uncert. or confus. appears after this, for Bond, 203, and
755, makes a doubt, whether she were w. of P. Stedman bef. or after
Baker. Yet she was young, when B. m. her, and he rem. prob. to
Concord, and there he or ano. William d. leav. wid. Mary and s. William.
His inv. is of 17 June 1679. WILLIAM, New London 1652–60, was per-
haps f. of Thomas. WILLIAM, Yarmouth, s. of Francis, by w. Mercy had
Mercy, b. 6 Jan. 1692; William, 8 Jan. 1694; Dorcas, 15 Nov. 1696;
Experience, 8 Jan. 1698; Judah, 2 Mar. 1701; Eliz. 11 Feb. 1703;
Josiah, 16 Dec. 1704; Joanna, 8 Feb. 1707; and Patience, 27 Feb.
1709; and d. 1727. His wid. d. 1753. Of this name, 1834, Farmer
counts nine gr. at Harv. seven at Yale, four at Dart. and seven at the

other coll. in N. E.   Prob. as the name is so very common, some fams. are omit.

BALCH, BENJAMIN, Beverly, eldest s. of the first John of the same, m. Sarah, d. of the first Thomas Gardner, had Samuel, b. 1651; John, 1654; Joseph, a soldier of "the flower of Essex" under Capt. Lathrop, k. by the Ind. 18 Sept. 1675, at Bloody brook; and Freeborn, 9 Aug. 1660; and he d. a. 1706, many yrs. after his w. as we infer from her not being ment. in his will of 18 Jan. 1689.   Being call. 77 yrs. old, it has been hastily assum. that he was the first b. of Mass. as the late Dr. Bentley stoutly assert. the same honor for John Massey, and brot. forward, as his best evid. the cradle, in wh. he was rocked.   But Felt seems to prove, that Roger, s. of Roger Conant, was b. at Salem bef. Massey or Balch.   FREEBORN; Salem, youngest s. of the first John, disappears a. 1658, prob. going for Eng. that yr. and not heard of after.   JOHN, Salem, one of the earliest sett. of Mass. from the vicin. of Bridgewater, Co. Somerset. came, it is said with suffic. probabil. in 1623, with Robert Gorges, to make establishm. at Cape Ann, or Nantasket, and on encouragem. from White the min. of Dorchester, a most earnest promoter of the colony, rem. with Roger Conant to plant at Salem, on Beverly side, then call. Bass riv. He req. adm. as freem. 19 Oct. 1630, and took the o. 18 May foll.   By his w. Margaret, one of the earliest mem. of the ch. of Higginson, was b. Benjamin, a. 1629, John, and Freeborn; but he had sec. w. Agnes, or Annis, nam. with those s. in his will of 15 May, pro. 28 June 1648. JOHN, Beverly, s. of the preced. m. Mary, d. of Roger Conant, had Mary, wh. d. young; and it is not seen, that he had other issue.   He was drown. 16 June 1662, and his wid. m. William Dodge.   Good memoir of this fam. is print. in Geneal. Reg. IX. 233.   Farmer notes, that in 1829 five of this name had been gr. at Harv. and one at Dart.

BALCOM, or BOLKCOM, ALEXANDER, Providence, call. junr. when he sw. alleg. May 1682, tho. of an earlier Alexander there, perhaps his f. I find nothing.   He rem. to that pt. of Rehoboth, since call. Attleborough, m. Sarah, d. of John Woodcock, had William, b. 3 Sept. 1692; Catharine, 7 Feb. 1694; Alexander, 4 Apr. 1696; John, 29 Apr. 1699; Baruch, 12 June 1702; Sarah, 8 Feb. 1704; and Joseph, 23 Feb. 1706; and d. 31 Jan. 1728.   See the valua. Hist. of Attleborough, by Daggett. HENRY, Charlestown 1674, m. Eliz. d. of John Haines.

BALDWIN, BENJAMIN, Milford, sec. s. of Joseph the first of the same, long bef. the will of his f. rem. prob. with the gr. migrat. to N. J. a. 1668; or at least no more of him is kn.   DANIEL, Milford, s. of Nathaniel of the same, m. 27 June 1667, Eliz. d. of Henry Botsford, had Daniel, b. 1668; Eliz. 1670; both d. young; Samuel, 29 Dec. 1673; Daniel, again, 1678; John, 1679; and Eliz. again, 1680.   DANIEL, Woburn, s. of Henry the first,

m. 6 Jan. 1685, Hannah, d. prob. of Joseph Richardson of the same, had Hannah, b. 21 Aug. 1686 ; Phebe, 13 May 1690; Henry, and Joseph, tw. 15 Mar. 1693; Susanna, 31 Mar. 1694; Daniel, 16 Dec. 1695 ; Dorcas, 18 Oct. 1697 ; Joseph, again, 17 Mar. 1699 ; Dorcas, again, 11 Aug. 1701 ; John, 28 Aug. 1703 ; Rebecca, 19 Dec. 1705 ; Benjamin, 30 Mar. 1707 ; and Phebe, again, 28 Dec. 1708. DAVID, Milford, youngest br. of Benjamin, m. 11 Nov. 1674, Mary, d. of John Stream of the same, had three s. whose names are not kn. to me, and d. 1689. GEORGE, Boston, by w. Ann had John, b. 25 Oct. 1639, wh. d. under 4 yrs. perhaps rem. to Warwick, there was among the freem. in 1655. In 1672 one of this name was at Huntington, L. I. but we may not infer, that he was the same, as this fam. name was very abund. especial. in Conn. whose peop. spread much upon L. I. HENRY, Portsmouth 1631, sent by Mason, the patentee. See Adams, Ann. 18. HENRY, Woburn, freem. 1652, was, as is said, from Devonsh. m. 1 Nov. 1649, Phebe, eldest d. of Ezekiel Richardson, of the same, had Susanna, b. 30 Aug. 1650, d. soon; Susanna, again, 25 July 1652 ; Phebe, 7 Sept. 1654; John, 28 Oct. 1656 ; Daniel, 15 Mar. 1659 ; Timothy, 27 May 1661; Mary, 19 July 1663, d. within 6 mos.; Henry, 15 Nov. 1664; Abigail, 20 Aug. 1667 ; Ruth, 21 July 1670; and Benjamin, 20 Feb. 1673; was deac. and d. 14 Feb. 1698. HENRY, Woburn, s. of the preced. m. 4 May 1692, Abigail, d. of David Fiske the sec. had Henry, b. 12 Jan. 1693 ; David, 9 Apr. 1696; Isaac, 20 Feb. 1700; Abigail, 13 Feb. 1702, d. soon; James, 11 July 1705, d. at 4 yrs.; Abigail, again, 19 Nov. 1707 ; James, again, 19 Oct. 1710; and Samuel, 31 Aug. 1717. David, his s. was f. of William, H. C. 1748 ; and of Samuel, H. C. 1752 ; and James, his s. was f. of Loammi, A.A.S. the friend and corresp. of Count Rumford, and project. the Middlesex canal, the earliest undertak. of that kind in N. E. Loammi, H. C. 1800, a gr. civil engineer, was s. of that Loammi. JOHN, Dedham, one of the first sett. by w. Joanna had John, b. 24 June 1635, perhaps more. JOHN, Milford 1639 (s. of that Sylvester, wh. coming from Eng. in the Martin, 1638, to Boston, with this s. d. on the voyage, leav. good est.), by first w. Mary had John, b. 1640 (wh. d. unm. a. 1677, on a voyage); Josiah, 1642 ; Samuel, 1645 ; Nathaniel, 1648 ; Eliz. 1649 ; and Joseph, 1651 ; and he m. 1653, Mary, d. of Obadiah Bruen, had Mary, b. 7 Sept. 1654; Sarah, 25 Dec. 1655 ; Abigail, Nov. 1658, bapt. at New Haven, 27 Mar. foll.; Obadiah, Oct. 1660; George, 1662 ; Hannah, 1664; and Richard, 1666; rem. a yr. or two after to Newark, N. J. but came back to M. He made his will 24 May 1681, and d. bef. 5 July next; in that instr. he names all the ch. exc. Samuel, Mary, and Sarah, wh. as well as his w. were prob. d. and we learn from it, that Eliz. had m. a Porter; that Abigail had m. a Baldwin ; and Hannah m. 17

Jan. of next yr. Dr. John Fiske. JOHN, Guilford, m. 12 Apr. 1653,
Hannah Birchard, prob. d. of Thomas, had John, b. 5 Dec. 1654; Hannah, 6 Oct. 1656; and Thomas, 1662; but he had rem. 1662 to Norwich.
JOHN, Stonington 1671, rem. to New London, there m. 24 July 1672, sec.
w. Rebecca, wid. of Elisha Cheesebrough, had Rebecca, b. 20 May 1673;
Mary, 24 Feb. 1675; Sylvester, 4 Mar. 1677; Sarah, 1680; and Jane,
bapt. Oct. 1681; and d. 19 Aug. 1683. From giv. a ch. the name Sylvester, Miss Caulkins infers, that the f. was s. of the s. of him of the same
name wh. d. 1638 on his voyage to our shore. JOHN, the passeng. in the
Speedwell to Boston from London, 1656, aged 21, with Mary, 20 (perhaps his sis. more prob. his w.), may not be certain. determin. among so
many of this name. JOHN, Salem, m. Sept. 1664, Arabella, d. of John
Norman, had Hannah, b. 15 Oct. 1667; and John, 26 Nov. 1668. JOHN,
Billerica, may have been petitnr. in 1653 for gr. of Chelmsford, m. 15
May 1655, Mary Richardson, prob. eldest d. of Thomas of Woburn, had
sev. ch. of wh. the first, Mary, b. 28 July 1659, d. four days after, was
freem. 1670, and d. 25 Dec. 1687, leav. s. John, Jonathan, and Thomas;
ds. Susanna, Phebe, and Mary, whose descend. are very num. in all that
region. JOHN, Hadley 1671. JOHN, Milford, eldest s. of Nathaniel of
the same, m. 19 Nov. 1663, Hannah, d. of Richard Osborn, had one s. b.
1665, and perhaps soon rem. to Newark. JOHN, Milford, eldest s. of
John the first, of the same, m. 30 Oct. 1663, Hannah, d. of Obadiah
Bruen, sis. of the sec. w. of his f. had one s. b. 1665; ano. nam. Richard,
1666; rem. to Newark, where, it is said, are descend. JOHN, Guilford,
s. of John of the same, m. 1680, Experience Abell, rem. to Lebanon,
there d. 1705, leav. wid. one s. John, and four ds. JONATHAN, Northampton 1668, prob. s. of Joseph, was of Milford 1674. JOSEPH, Milford
1639, by w. Hannah had Joseph, b. 1640; Benjamin, 1642; Hannah,
1644; Mary, 1645; all bapt. at once; Eliz. 1646; Martha, 1647; Jonathan, 1649; David, 1651; and Sarah, 1653; rem. a. 1663, to Hadley,
there was freem. 1666; m. for sec. w. Isabel Northam, wid. of James,
wh. had come with her s. John, as wid. Catlin, from Newark, N. J. For
third w. he took Eliz. wid. of William Warriner of Springfield, and d. 2
Nov. 1684. His wid. d. 25 Apr. 1696; by a will in 1680 he dispos. of
est. judiciously, thus, ld. in Hadley to childr. of his eldest s. Joseph, then
d. ld. in Milford to Benjamin, Jonathan, and David; personal prop. to his
eldest d. Hannah, w. of Jeremiah Hull of New Haven, to Mary, w. of John
Catlin of Arthur Kill, N. J. to Eliz. w. of James Warriner of Springfield,
to John, and Hannah Hawkes, ch. of John of Hatfield, in right of their
mo. Martha, dec. and to Sarah, w. of Samuel Bartlett of Northampton,
wh. was ano. ch. perhaps youngest, of the testator. JOSEPH, Hadley, s.
of the preced. made freem. 1670, had first w. Eliz. and next m. Sarah,

d. of Benjamin Cooley, and d. in mid. life, 21 Nov. 1681, leav. Joseph,
James, Samuel, Mary, and Hannah ; but whether these ch. were all by the
sec. w. or whether she m. sec. h. is not told to me. Of the s. Joseph soon
rem. to Malden ; James to Milford ; and in short time this name had van-
ish. from H. JOSIAH, Milford, s. of John the first, m. 25 June 1667,
Mary Camp, d. prob. of Edward of New Haven, and d. 1683, leav. young
w. and seven ch. whose names I see not. NATHANIEL, Milford 1639,
had John, bef. ment. b. bef. 1640 ; Daniel, 1644 ; Nathaniel, 1645 ; Abigail, 1648, all by w. Abigail, wh. d. 22 Mar. 1648. He next m. Joanna
Westcoat, wid. it is said, of Richard of Fairfield (but of him I kn. nothing),
liv. at F. 1654, had Sarah, Deborah, and Samuel ; d. 1658, and his wid.
m. Thomas Skidmore. His ch. went back to M. NATHANIEL, Milford,
not s. of the preced. was k. in the gr. swamp fight, 19 Dec. 1675. Other
Nathaniels there were at M. nearly at the same time, as in 1677 one is
nam. senr. and ano. junr. in a div. of town lds. but ten yrs. later one call.
weaver, the other, cooper. NATHANIEL, Milford, s. of Nathaniel the first,
m. 1671, Henry Botsford's d. Hannah, had Eliz. b. 1672 ; Hannah, 1674 ;
Nathaniel, 1676 ; possib. Esther, 1683 ; and Samuel, 1684. One Nathaniel d. at M. 1692 ; and that Nathaniel, wh. fell in Philip's war may
have been a stranger to this blood. That s. of the first John wh. bore
this name would have been among the later inhab. of M. PETER, Salem,
m. 27 May 1672, wid. Rachel Dell. Felt. RICHARD, Braintree 1637,
had d. Jane, and from Winth. II. 348 is seen all that is kn. *RICHARD,
Milford 1640, came not with f. and mo. prob. (of wh. he was eldest s.) in
the Martin to Boston 1638, but foll. soon ; m. 1642, Eliz. Alsop, sis. of
Joseph Alsop the first, of New Haven, had Mary, bapt. 1643 ; Eliz.
1644 ; Sylvanus, b. 1646 ; Sarah, bapt. 1649 ; Temperance, 1651 ; Mary,
again, 1653 ; John ; Theophilus, bapt. at New Haven, 19 Sept. 1658 ;
Zechariah, b. 22 Sept. 1660 ; Martha, 1 Apr. 1663 ; and Barnabas,
posthum. bapt. 1666. In some rec. will be seen Theophilus, b. 26 Apr.
1659 ; but perhaps it is an error of the yr. He was town clk. 1648, and
rep. 1660 to his d. 23 July 1665. Perhaps he was one of the first sett.
at Derby, as ment. by Trumbull, Col. Rec. I. 274, 322. He left good
est. to his ch. and wid. wh. m. William Fowler. Of the ch. a suffic. story
is obtain. Eliz. m. 1663, Zechariah Burwell ; Sarah m. 1667, Samuel
Riggs ; Temperance m. 14 Jan. 1674, Nathan Burwell ; Mary m. but I
find not her h. ; Martha m. 1681, Samuel Nettleton ; Zechariah, and
Barnabas liv. at M. in 1713 ; and the rest are herein account. for exc.
John, wh. had gone to Eng. as in 1702 was said, twenty-five yrs. bef. and
was thot. to be d. SAMUEL, Milford 1664, s. of John the first, was drown.
1674, leav. wid. Rebecca, wh. m. it is said, a Prince of Boston, wh. is
unkn. to me. SYLVANUS, Milford, eldest s. of Richard of the same, m.

20 Sept. 1670, Mildred, d. of Rev. Peter Prudden of the same, of wh. I regret to be able to tell only that he was liv. 1713. SYLVESTER, the passeng. wh. d. 1638, on the voyage of the Martin from Eng. to Boston, was s. of Richard of St. Leonards in the parish of Aston Clinton, near Wendover in Co. Bucks, where his f. by will of 18 Feb. 1632, had given him a cottage and close, wh. his wid. (wh. had m. John Astwood, and was then his wid.) gave 1 Oct. 1666 to Edward Baldwin of Guilford, Co. Surrey, call. him "kinsman." He brot. w. Sarah, and perhaps all his ch. (exc. Richard), ds. Sarah, Mary, Martha, Ruth, and s. John. "On the main ocean, bound for N. E." his nuncup. will was made 21 June, and pro. 13 July of that yr. bef. Dept. Gov. Dudley by oaths of Chad Brown, Francis Bolt, James Weedon, and John Baldwin, presumed to be his s. The est. was good, and provision liberal for the six ch. as well as the wid. to wh. with s. Richard our Gen. Ct. 4 Sept. foll. commit. the admin. After some time liv. at New Haven, and Milford, she m. 1640, Capt. John Astwood of M. when her prop. was valu. at £800, beside sev. parcels of ld. She long outliv. him, and in her will of 9, pro. 20 Nov. 1669, she provides for s. John, and John his s. for Sylvanus, s. of her s. Richard, dec. and three of her ds. (one prob. hav. d.) of wh. two were m. Sarah, first w. of Benjamin Fenn, and Mary, wid. of Robert Plum, beside six gr.ds. THEOPHILUS, Milford, s. of Richard of the same, m. 8 Feb. 1683, Eliz. Campfield, perhaps d. of Thomas, and d. 1698, leav. four ch. THOMAS, Norwich, s. of John of Guilford, m. 1684, Sarah, d. of John Caulkins, wh. d. next yr. and he m. 1692, Abigail Lay, prob. d. of John of Lyme, by her had four s. and four ds. Of this Norwich stock descend. it is thot. the late Rev. Dr. B. of Boston, Hon. Simeon, and Gov. Roger S. Baldwin, gent. of high repute in Conn. TIMOTHY, Milford 1639, had right in New Haven 1640 to lot of ld. had first w. Mary, wh. d. 21 July 1647, and he m. 1649, wid. Mary Mepham, relict of John, of Guilford; by the first he had Mary, bapt. 1643, wh. m. 21 Oct. 1660, Benjamin Smith; Hannah, 1644, wh. m. 12 Dec. 1667, as his sec. w. Elnathan Botsford; Sarah, 1645, wh. m. 14 Dec. 1663, Samuel Buckingham. He had by the sec. w. Abigail, b. 1650, d. at 10 yrs.; Ann, 1655, d. soon; and Timothy, 1658; and d. 17 Jan. 1665. His wid. took third h. Thomas Tapping. The only s. liv. at M. TIMOTHY, Woburn, s. of Henry the first of the same, by w. Eliz. had Eliz. b. 29 May 1688; Timothy, 20 Nov. 1689; Ralph, 28 June 1691; Hannah, wh. d. 6 Sept. 1692; and he rem. to Stoneham, there was liv. 1726. Of this name Yale counts her gr. up to 1834, thirty-four, while at Harv. and Dart. only three ea. and seven only at all the other N. E. coll. if Farmer be correct, as usual.

BALL, ALLEN, ALLIN, or ALLING, New Haven 1643, by w. Dorothy had John, b. 15 Apr. 1649; Eliphalet, 11 Feb. 1651; and Alling, 27 June 1656; beside Mary, or Mercy, wh. m. 10 Feb. 1676 George Pardee sec. of the same, and perhaps others bef. or after, or both. He was a capt. and his w. d. 22 Feb. 1690. ALLING, New Haven, s. of the preced. m. 24 Nov. 1678, Sarah, d. of John Thompson the first of the same, had Sarah, b. 26 Aug. 1679; Lydia, 30 Jan. 1681; Alling, wh. d. young; Mercy; Mabel; and Alling, again. He was a capt. and d. 1710. ED- WARD, Branford 1667, rem. that yr. to Newark N. J. had Caleb, Abigail, Joseph, Lydia, Moses, and Thomas; of wh. the last was progenit. of a great multitude. ELIPHALET, New Haven, s. of Alling the first, m. 13 Feb. 1673, Hannah Nash, d. of John of the same, and d. 11 July foll. His wid. m. 2 Apr. 1689 Thomas Trowbridge sen. FRANCIS, Dorches- ter, rem. to Springfield, there m. 1644, Abigail, d. of Henry Burt, had Jonathan, b. 1645; and Samuel; was drown. in the riv. Oct. 1648. His wid. m. next yr. Benjamin Mun, and next, 14 Dec. 1676, lieut. Thomas Stebbins. FRANCIS, Dorchester, m. 27 Jan. 1664, Abigail Salter, had John, b. 15 Apr. 1665, d. next yr.; Abigail, 14 Aug. 1667; Francis, 21 Feb. 1670; and Benjamin, 30 Aug. 1675. JOHN, Isle of Shoals 1649, of wh. I learn, only from our Suff'k Prob. rec. that he was one of the debtors to est. of Isaac Grosse, of Boston, wh. prob. suppl. him with outfits for his fishing. JOHN, Concord, freem. 1650, had brot. from Wiltsh. as is said, s. Nathaniel, and John, was bur. 1 Oct. 1655. JOHN, Watertown, s. of the preced. b. in Eng. m. Eliz. d. of John Pierce of the same, had John, b. 1644; Mary; Esther; Sarah, 1655; and Abigail, 20 Apr. 1658, wh. d. soon; was much troubled by insan. of his w. wh. made separat. needful. After her d. he m. 3 Oct. 1665, Eliz. d. prob. of Thomas Fox, had Joseph, b. 12 Mar. 1670; rem. to Lancaster, where he had short resid. 1643, there was k. by the Ind. 10 Sept. 1675. JOHN, Watertown, s. of the preced. m. 17 Oct. 1665, Sarah, d. of George Bullard of the same, had Sarah, b. 11 July 1666; John, 29 June 1668; James, 7 Mar. 1670; Joseph, 1 May 1674; Jonathan, 29 Mar. 1680; Daniel, 2 Aug. 1683; and Abigail, 5 Oct. 1686; and he d. 8 May 1722. JOHN, New Haven, s. of Alling the first, m. 1678, Sarah, d. of Henry Glover, had Eliphalet, b. 29 May 1680; John, 30 Sept. 1685; Sarah, 26 Sept. 1687; Hannah, 12 Jan. 1690; Mercy, Apr. 1692; Mary, 21 Oct. 1694; and Caleb, 6 June 1697. He and Hannah, wid. of his br. Eliphalet were among proprs. 1685. JONATHAN, Springfield, eldest s. of Francis of the same, m. a. 1685, Susanna, wid. of Nicholas Worthington (wh. had been his sec. w. and bore him two ch.), and had twelve ch. of wh. half d. young, and the others were Samuel, Sarah, Francis, Benjamin, Jonathan, and Joseph, whose respective dates are not kn. He was a capt. and liv. to 95 yrs. d.

21 May 1741; but his w. d. 9 Mar. 1727. MATTHEW, Dorchester 1652, was liv. in 1664 to sign a petn. to the Gen. Ct. but no more can be heard of him. NATHANIEL, Concord, s. perhaps elder, of the first John, in the will of Ralph Mousall call. cousin, i. e. neph. by w. Mary had John, wh. d. 27 July 1649; Nathaniel, b. 28 Sept. 1649, d. at 2 mos.; Ebenezer; Eleazer; John, again, 15 Aug. 1660; and perhaps others; liv. in that pt. of C. which is now Bedford. RICHARD, Salisbury 1651, rem. to Dover 1668, yet perhaps only for short time. SAMUEL, Northampton, s. of Francis of Springfield, was freem. 1681, and d. 1689, leav. Francis, Mary, Eliz. and Abigail. His wid. Mary m. 11 Apr. 1690, Benjamin Stebbins. WILLIAM, New Haven 1643, d. Apr. 1648. Of this name in 1834 Farmer found gr. at Harv. Yale and Dart. two at each, and five at the other N. E. coll.

BALLANTINE, ‖ JOHN, Boston, s. of William of the same, was a capt. twice of ar. co. into wh. he was chos. 1682, col. of regim. by w. Lydia, d. prob. of William Barrett of Cambridge, had John, b. 15 Mar. bapt. 4 Apr. 1675, H. C. 1694; Lydia, b. 2 June 1676, d. young; William, 23 Aug. 1679; and Lydia, again, 24 Oct. 1682. He had sec. w. Mary Saxton, wid. of unkn. h. whose maiden name was Woodward, whose f. by no research has been ascert. and d. 27 Apr. 1734, in his 81st yr. and she d. 10 Nov. 1740 in her 86th. *‖JOHN, Boston, s. of the preced. m. 9 Mar. 1703, Mary, d. of Hon. Adam Winthrop, had John, H. C. 1735, (that min. of Westfield, wh. d. 12 Feb. 1776); beside Mary, and William; was of ar. co. 1694, was in high esteem, and perhaps the rep. of 1726, tho. in Geneal. Reg. VI. 371 this honor is ascrib. to his f. wh. was then rather advanc. in life, and whose d. was only short time bef. that of this s. 2 Jan. foll. WILLIAM, Boston, cooper, m. 23 July 1652, Hannah, d. of Angel Hollard (not Holland, as too often giv.) had John, b. 29 Sept. 1653, bef. ment.; William, 22 Sept. 1655; David, 24 Aug. 1656; the two latter d. young; William, again, 20 Dec. 1657, d. young; David, again, 5 Feb. 1659; Eliz. 8 Mar. 1660; Benjamin, 22 July 1661; Hannah, 15 Nov. 1662; Sarah, 18 Sept. 1664; William, again, 26 Nov. 1665; Susanna, 2 Feb. 1667; and Jonathan, 19 Sept. 1669. His will of 6 Dec. 1669, but few days bef. he d. names w. Hannah and only seven ch. so that it may be conclud. that Benjamin and Sarah, not ment. had d. young. Of the inv. of any cooper in the early yrs. I have common. found a good result, and such was his; yet more import. are the questions of his b. and of his coming. Differing in opin. from a disting. descend. (Hinman in Geneal. Reg. VII. 376,) because he calls him " a Scotch gent. from Ayr. as early as 1653," I ought to offer reasons. H. contrary to the common error, that is of assum. too early a yr. for the arr. of an ancest. on our shore, takes a date that would afford currency

to a suspicion of his being one of the melancholy exiles from the triumph
of the civ. war. Surely he was here pretty early in 1651, prob. a yr.
or two bef. as otherwise he would hardly have gain. Hollard's d. so early.
A Scot we may easily believe he was, one of the founders, we kn. of the
Charit. Soc. of that nation, wh. with the ever active spirit of nationality
begun in Boston 1657, then compos. of twenty-seven mem. of whose names
his is tenth. No sufferer in the cause of Charles Stuart can be supposed
so early to have acquir. social position and property to contribute to " the
box." See Drake's Boston, 455. A cooper was more likely, two hundred
yrs. ago, to have been bred at Glasgow than its neighboring little vill. of
Ayr; and one of those tradesmen, whose motto was " let Glasgow flourish,"
would hardly be call. gent. of A. Often the name appears Bellantine,
sometimes Ballentyre.

BALLARD, JARVIS, Boston 1670, merchant, perhaps not perman.
resid. JOHN, Lynn, s. of William the sec. of the same, b. prob. in
Eng. had William, b. 1 Oct. 1667 ; Sarah, early in July 1669 ; Rebecca,
1 Apr. 1671 ; Jane, 1 Dec. 1674 ; John ; Priscilla, 20 Dec. 1680 ; rem.
to Andover, there m. sec. w. 16 Nov. 1681, Rebecca Hooper, perhaps d.
of William of Reading, had William, 8 Nov. 1683, d. soon ; and Dorothy,
30 Jan. 1685. He d. 1715, aged 62, but this, tho. the rec. says it, seems
to me twenty yrs. short of the truth. JOSEPH, Andover, br. of the
preced. m. 28 Feb. 1666, Eliz. Phelps, d. perhaps of Edward the first,
had Joseph, and two ds. of wh. one, Tabitha, d. 30 Mar. 1687 ; and the
other d. 24 Feb. 1691. His w. d. 27 July 1692, and he m. 15 Nov. foll.
wid. Rebecca Horne, but of wh. she was relict I see not, and d. 1722.
NATHANIEL, Lynn, wh. may have been br. of the preced. m. 16 Dec.
1662, Rebecca Hudson, perhaps d. of Thomas, had Mary, b. 13 June
1666 ; Nathaniel, 4 Dec. 1670, d. at less than 2 yrs. ; Susanna, 12 June,
1673 ; Eliz. 2 Nov. 1675 ; Esther, 14 Feb. 1678 ; Sarah, 13 May 1681 ;
Jemima, 20 Jan. 1684 ; and William 23 Apr. 1686. He d. 12 Jan.
1722 ; and his wid. d. 16 May 1724. Mary m. Moses Haven of
Framingham. ROBERT, Portsmouth R. I. is among the freem. of 1655.
SAMUEL, Charlestown, freem. 1680, by w. Lydia had Lydia, b. 27 Oct.
1670 ; John, wh. d. at 30 yrs. ; and Eliz. 24 Feb. 1673 ; and his w. d. 1
May 1678. On 1 Sept. foll. he m. Hannah Belcher, perhaps eldest d.
of Andrew the first ; was a lieut. and d. 12 Nov. 1708, aged 70. WIL-
LIAM, Lynn 1630, as claim. for him, tho. of that date I feel less confident
than of that of 1634, when he came in the Mary and John, Capt. Sayres,
from London, tak. the oath to qualify him for embarc. 26 Mar. had w.
and childr. and d. in few yrs. mak. a day or two bef. his nuncup. will, as
may be seen in Geneal. Reg. II. 183, giv. one half to w. one half to be
div. among ch. ‖WILLIAM, Lynn, perhaps s. of the preced. came in the

James from London, 1635, aged 32, with w. Eliz. 26; and ch. Esther, 2; and John, 1; freem. 2 May 1638, ar. co. 1638, liv. I think, at Newbury, for short time, but fix. at Andover, there may have had sev. ch. and d. 10 July 1689. One of his ch. Sarah m. 24 Feb. 1670, Henry Holt; and his wid. Grace d. 27 Apr. 1694. WILLIAM, Andover, perhaps s. of the preced. m. 20 Apr. 1682, Hannah Hooper, prob. d. of William of Reading, perhaps as sec. w. for by former one must have been b. Rebecca, 2 Oct. 1668; unless some confus. can be refer. to rec. Barry labor. much on this fam. in his Hist. of Framingham, 172, yet not to his thorough satisfact. Where he saw evid. of William's tak. o. of freem. 18 May 1631, that no other eyes discern, must be noted as one of the few errors in that valua. vol.

BALLOU, MATURIN, Providence 1639, ought to have his descend. noted, were it in my power. One of the same name, Bapt. min. of Richmond, N. H. 1770, was f. of a race of preach. of distinct.

BALSTONE, or BAULSTON, JAMES, Boston, m. Sarah, d. of Ralph Root of the same, had Sarah, b. 26 Aug. 1653; John, 3 Dec. 1654; and James, 22 June 1657. JOHN, Boston, had w. Lydia, wh. join. the first ch. 22 Aug. 1647. Whether he were br. of Jonathan, or William, does not appear; yet it seems likely eno. that he was of one or both. JOHN, Boston, came from London, where he, with others, had made a contr. 31 May 1687, with Judith, wid. of Stephen Winthrop, they being then a. to emb. for N. E. He d. here 6 June 1706, aged 86, so that possib. he is the same as the preced. tho. not very prob. JONATHAN, Boston, by w. Mary had John, b. Oct. 1645; Mary; Jonathan, 2 Mar. 1652; Prudence, 28 May 1655; Lydia, 9 Oct. 1656, d. at 3 mos.; James, 1657, yet I fear this may be repetit. of the s. of James; Robert, 1662; and Benjamin, 1663. Mary m. a. 1668, Isaac Vergoose. ‡WILLIAM, Boston, came, no doubt, with Winthrop's fleet, desir. adm. as freem. of the comp. 19 Oct. 1630, and took the o. 18 May foll. by w. Eliz. wh. d. early, had d. Pity, bapt. Oct. 1630, being the third ch. so favor. in rec. of our first ch. Other ch. here bapt. were William, 14 Apr. 1633; Mary, 14 Sept. 1634; Mehitable, 24 Jan. 1636; and Meribah, 9 Apr. 1637; I presume, all by sec. w. Eliz. and all these d. bef. him; beside ano. d. Eliz. after his banishm. He was in steady employm. for town affairs, trusted among the worthiest, chos. a selectman 1637, yet in the latter part of the same yr. was disarm. with the majority of his fellow worship. as being under the fascinat. of Mrs. Hutchinson, and sev. favorers of Wheelwright, went, 1638, to Portsmouth R. I. wh. his assoc. purch. that season, was held there in high regard, made an Assist. 1639, 41, and 56, named in the royal chart. 1663, and d. 14 Mar. 1679, aged 78. His wid. d. 14 Apr. 1683, aged 86. See Haz. II. 612; 2 Mass. Hist. Coll. VII. 98 and any of the Histories of

Winthrop, Hutchinson, Barry, or Arnold. His d. Eliz. m. the sec. John Coggeshall, a. 1647, bore him two s. and one or more ds. but by mut. consent they separat. after wh. he having gain. liberty from the governm. to m. again in June 1655, she next mo. obtain. the same license, and thereupon m. Thomas Gould of Wickford.

BAMBRIDGE, BANBRIDGE, BAINBRIDGE, or BAINBRICK, GUY, Cambridge 1634, freem. 4 Mar. 1635, was bur. 10 Apr. 1645; and his wid. Justice long surv.

BAMPSTER, EDWARD, New Haven. See Banister.

BANCROFT, EPHRAIM, Windsor, s. of John of the same, m. 1 May 1681, Sarah, d. of John Stiles sec. had Ephraim, b. 8 Feb. 1683; John, 1685, d. soon; Sarah, 1687; John, 1690; Benjamin, 1694, d. young; Nathaniel, 1698; Daniel, July 1701; and Thomas, 1703, d. young. JOHN, Lynn, perhaps with w. Jane, came in the James, from London, Apr. 1632, arr. 12 June in 8 wks. passage, d. a. 1637, leav. wid. and s. John and Thomas. The name is spell. with r instead of n in the official vol. at Westminster, that tells how John and his w. were qualif. to pass to N. E. and in Eng. both forms are common eno. But in our country we had not for one century, if not two, such a surname as Barcroft; tho. in our print. Col. Rec. I. 108, we read that John Barcrofte ent. into recognis. in £40, with Samuel Maverick surety in £20, conditio. that Jane, w. of said John should be of good behavior, yet in the Index the n is giv. for r. JOHN, Lynn, s. perhaps of the preced. unless it be more likely, that he was gr.s. to wh. the judgm. inclines, when we see, that he m. 24 Sept. 1678, Eliz. Eaton, prob. d. of the first John of Reading, then few days more than sixteen yrs. old. JOHN, Windsor, m. 3 Dec. 1650, Hannah Dupper (if such be the true spell.), had John, b. Dec. 1651; Nathaniel, 19 Nov. 1653; Ephraim, 15 June 1656; Hannah, 6 Apr. 1659; and Sarah, 26 Dec. 1661. He d. 1662, and his wid. m. John Lunden. NATHANIEL, Westfield, m. 1675, Hannah Gardner, prob. d. of Samuel of Hadley, and d. 10 Feb. 1724. Ch. were John; Nathaniel; Benjamin, b. 6 June 1684, d. in few days; Eliz. 31 Oct. 1685; Edward, 30 May 1688, d. at 19 yrs. of a wound by Ind. a few weeks bef. in July 1707; and their wid. mo. d. 15 Mar. 1728. NATHANIEL, Windsor, s. of John of the same, m. 26 Dec. 1677, Hannah, d. of John Williams of the same, had John, b. 28 Jan. 1679; and Nathaniel, 25 Sept. 1680. ROGER, Cambridge 1636, freem. 18 May 1642, d. 28 Nov. 1653. His will of two days preced. gave all to w. Eliz. exc. small sums to Rev. Mr. Mitchell and Elder Frost. His wid. m. 23 May 1654, Martin Saunders, of Boston, and next. deac. John Bridge of C. and thot. hers. bound to take fourth h. Edward Taylor. THOMAS, Reading, s. of John the first, b. in Eng. m. at Dedham, 15 Sept. 1648, Eliz. d. of Michael Metcalf, had Thomas, bapt. 28 Dec. 1651, d.

soon; Eliz. b. 7 Dec. 1653; Thomas, again; Sarah, 14 Mar. 1658, d.
young; Ralph, 20 Aug. 1660, d. within 12 mos.; Ruhama, 27 June 1662;
John; Ebenezer (or Eleazer, as in ano. rec. he is call.), 26 Apr. 1667; and
Mary, 16 May 1670; was freem. 1678, and d. 12 Mar. 1705. His wid.
d. 1 May 1711; and d. Eliz. m. 26 May 1674, Joseph Brown. Of THOMAS,
s. of the preced. wh. m. Sarah, d. prob. of Jonathan Poole, was deac. and
d. 12 June 1718, is relat. in the Magn. IV. ch. 1, to establ. a favorite
theory of the writer's f. the wonderful story of restoration from the smallpox. With his usual reverence for that f. Mather, in Life of Brock,
unites his own opin. In 1828 Farmer found of this name four gr. at
Harv. one at Dart. one at Brown, none at any other N. E. coll. Rev.
Aaron, D. D. a min. of highest charact. ord. at Worcester 1 Feb. 1786,
there d. 1839, was s. of Samuel from the Reading stock, and f. of Hon.
George, H. C. 1817, the eloquent historian of the U. S.

BAND, ROBERT, Southampton, L. I. 1644, wh. is all I hear of him.

BANFIELD, THOMAS, Charlestown, d. 21 June 1676.

BANGS, *EDWARD, Plymouth, b. perhaps 1592, at Chichester, Co.
Sussex, came in the Ann, 1623, and m. after 1627, as is presum. Lydia,
d. of Robert Hicks, had Rebecca; John; Sarah; Jonathan, b. 1640;
Lydia; Hannah; Joshua; Bethia, 28 May 1650; Mercy, and Apphia,
tw. 15 Oct. 1651. He had rem. with Gov. Prence, 1644, to Eastham,
was a shipwright, and direct. the labor, says a reasona. tradit. on the first
vessel built in the Col. tho. earlier ones had been launch. in Mass. was
rep. 1647, and sev. other yrs. d. 1677, in his will of that yr. 19 Oct. pro.
5 Mar. 1678, furnish. evid. to us, that all his ch. were then liv. exc. Rebecca, wh. had m. 26 Oct. 1654 Jonathan Sparrow, and left childr. Sarah m. 1656, Thomas Howes; Lydia m. 24 Dec. 1661, Benjamin Hig-
gins; Hannah m. 30 Apr. 1662, John Doane; Bethia m. Gershom Hall
of Harwich; Mercy m. 28 Dec. 1670, Stephen Herrick; and Apphia m.
the same day, prob. John Knowles, and next Joseph Atwood. No certainty is attaina. as to order of births of most of these ch. JOHN, Eastham, s. prob. eldest of the preced. m. 23 Jan. 1661, Hannah, d. of John
Smalley; was a lieut. perhaps; but very loose is the tradit. as to him,
prob. confus. his youngest br. with him. *JONATHAN, br. of the preced.
m. at Eastham, 16 July 1664, Mary, d. of Samuel Mayo of Barnstable,
had Edward, b. 30 Sept. 1665; Rebecca, 1 Feb. 1668; Jonathan, 30
Apr. 1670, d. in few days; Mary, 14 Apr. 1671; Jonathan, again, 4 May
1673; Hannah, 14 Mar. 1676; Tamosin, May 1678; Samuel, 12 July
1680; Mercy, 7 Jan. 1682; Eliz. 15 May 1685; Sarah, Aug. 1687;
and Lydia, 2 Oct. 1689. He was a capt. rep. to Plymouth 1674, and
five other yrs. in 1692 to Boston under the new chart. had sec. w. Sarah,
wh. d. 11 June 1719, aged 78; and next yr. he propos. to m. Ruth, prob.

wid. of John Young the sec. and d. of Daniel Cole, wh. led him to Harwich, and there he d. 9 Nov. 1728. Of his eldest s. Edward, wh. d. 22 May 1746, by w. Ruth, wh. d. 22 June 1738, was b. Edward, whose s. Benjamin was f. of Hon. Edward, H. C. 1779, wh. was f. of the late Edward D., the dilig. and faithful Secr. of Mass. JOSHUA, Eastham, youngest s. of Edward the first, m. 1 Dec. 1669, Hannah, d. of John Scudder, had Joshua, wh. d. young; was lieut. and d. 14 Jan. 1710. In his will of 13 Feb. 1707, nam. not nor refer. to any issue, he ment. w. Hannah, wh. next m. Moses Hatch.

BANKS, GEORGE, New Haven 1646. *JOHN, Windsor, one of the first sett. m. a d. of Charles Taintor of Wethersfield, as tradit. tells, had one ch. b. there, where he was town clk. 1643, rem. soon after to Fairfield, of wh. he was rep. sev. yrs. betw. 1651 and 66, rem. to Rye, and was rep. from that town 1670–3; had good est. made his will 12 Dec. 1684, and d. next mo. He ment. in it w. Mary (not, prob. his first), s. John, Samuel, Obadiah, and Benjamin; ds. Susanna Sturges, Hannah, w. of Daniel Burr, and Mary Taylor. His s. Joseph had d. Oct. 1682, perhaps unm. as he gave est. to four brs. and sis. Mary Taylor; of Samuel nothing is kn. but Obadiah d. we are told, in Fairfield Feb. 1691, and Benjamin next yr. and both at F. and Greenwich, adjac. to Rye, the name contin. 1713. JOHN, Greenwich, s. of the preced. had w. Abigail, and d. 14 July 1699. JOSEPH, wh. embark. 12 Mar. 1679 for N. E. by the William and Susan, was only trans. visit. as is presum. from never being heard of on this side of the water. RICHARD, Kittery, 1649, was liv. at York 1673, had m. Eliz. d. of John Alcock, for she had sh. of his est. He took o. of alleg. to the k. 22 Mar. 1681. RICHARD, Boston, one of the found. of the first society for Episcop. worship 1686. Four of this name by Farmer are found gr. at Yale 1834.

BANISTER, or BANNISTER, CHRISTOPHER, Marlborough 1657, m. Jane, d. of Thomas Goodenow, had Mary, b. 1672; and he d. 30 Mar. 1678. EDWARD, New Haven 1639, had w. Ellen, and a d. made his will 8 May 1649. See N. H. Col. Rec. I. 479. JOHN, Marlborough, m. 1695, Ruth Eager, whose deriv. I kn. not, having not met the name so early in N. E. had John, b. 1696; Ruth, 1699, d. soon; Mary, 1700; Ruth, again, 1702; Jane, 1705; Huldah, 1707; Martha, 1710; and Sarah, 1713; was a lieut. and d. 19 July 1730, aged 59. THOMAS, Boston 1685, by w. Sarah had Samuel, b. 11 July 1686; Hannah, 30 Sept. 1688, d. soon; Mary, 10 July 1690; and Hannah, again, 19 Mar. 1692; and d. 1709. He had come to B. with fam. and good sh. of prop. as from his will of 25 Jan. with codic. of 13 July, pro. 20 Aug. foll. in that yr. is appar. It provides for w. Sarah, d. Mary, s. Thomas, H. C. 1700, Samuel, and John, and gives to his gr.ch. Thomas, eldest s. of his s. Thomas, £500, besides annuity for his mo. and equal sums to his br. John, sis. Ann Carter, and Mary Alline, wh. all were of Banbury in Oxfordsh.

BANSHOTT, THOMAS, embark. at Southampton, 1638, aged 14, in the Bevis for Boston; but where he dispos. of hims. after arr. at Boston, is beyond my kn.

BANT, GILBERT, Boston, by w. Mercy had Mary, b. 28 Apr. 1689; Gilbert, 30 Oct. 1694; William, 4 Feb. 1698; and Eliz. 11 July 1701, was a capt.

BARBER, EDWARD, Dedham, d. July 1644. EDWARD, Dorchester, perhaps s. perhaps f. of the preced. d. 9 June 1677, in his 80th yr. * ‖ GEORGE, Dedham 1643, ar. co. 1646, freem. 1647, m. 24 Nov. 1642, Eliz. Clark, had Mary, b. 27 Aug. 1643, d. in 3 mos.; Mary, again, 31 Jan. 1645, d. soon; Samuel, 6 Jan. 1647; John, 13 Mar. 1649; and Eliz. 11 Apr. 1651; rem. to Medfield, there had Hannah, 16 Apr. 1654; Zechariah, 29 Sept. 1656; and Abigail, 29 Oct. 1659; was rep. 1668 and 9, and the chief milit. officer. JAMES, Dorchester, a tailor, m. 1683, had Eliz. bapt. 18 May 1684; James, 29 May 1687; Patience, 20 Oct. 1689; and Ebenezer, 1 Nov. 1702 (but he may have been b. some yrs.); and d. 13 Oct. 1732, aged a. 80. His wid. Eliz. d. 4 Dec. 1739, aged 81. JOHN, Salem 1637, carpenter, adm. of the ch. 3 Apr. 1642. JOHN, Dover 1659. JOHN, Windsor, s. of Thomas of the same, m. Sept. 1663, Bathsheba Coggin, or Cogens, had Joanna, b. 8 Apr. 1667; John, 14 July 1669; rem. to Springfield, there had Return, 1672, d. soon; and Mary, 1678; was deac. and d. 27 Jan. 1712. Ano. JOHN of Springfield there was, not s. of the preced. as ea. on 31 Dec. 1678 or the foll. day sw. alleg. but wh. was senior, it may not be easy to prove. *JOHN, Medfield, s. of George, freem. 1671, was rep. 1677; by w. Abigail had John, b. 24 Apr. 1676; Abigail, 26 Apr. 1679; Eliz. 28 Nov. 1681; George, 5 Dec. 1684; and Abiah, 12 Sept. 1689. JOSIAH, Simsbury, m. 22 Nov. 1677, Abigail, d. of Nathaniel Loomis, had Abigail, b. 12 Mar. 1679. RICHARD, Dedham, freem. 13 May 1640; d. 18 June 1644, leav. prob. neither w. nor ch. for by his will the est. wh. was small, was giv. to the poor. SAMUEL, Medfield 1678, eldest s. of George, by w. Mary had Mary, b. 20 Feb. 1675; Samuel, 7 Jan. 1677; James, 25 Dec. 1680; Hannah, 25 Sept. 1683; Thomas, 4 July 1686; and Mary, again, 28 May 1693. SAMUEL, Windsor, s. of Thomas, by first w. Mary had Thomas, b. 7 Oct. 1671; Samuel, 26 Jan. 1674; and by sec. w. a d. of John Drake, prob. Hannah, had John, 25 Jan. 1677; and Hannah, 4 Oct. 1681. THOMAS, Windsor, came in the Christian, 1635, aged 21, resid. prob. at Dorchester first, was engag. in the Pequot war, I suppose, under Stoughton, m. 7 Oct. 1640, Joan, had John, bapt. 24 July 1642; Thomas, 14 July 1644; Sarah, 19 July 1646; Samuel, 1 Oct. 1648; Mary, 12 Oct. 1651; and Jo-

siah, 5 Feb. 1654; and d. 1662, as did his w.   His d. Mary m. 8 July
1669 John Gillett.   Josiah had fam. in W. but I have not particul. acco.
THOMAS, Windsor, s. of the preced. m. Dec. 1665, Mary, d. of the first
William Phelps, had Mary, b. 11 Jan. 1666; Sarah, 2 July 1667 ; rem.
to Simsbury.   THOMAS, Gloucester 1662, rem. perhaps 1669 to Newbury,
m. 27 Apr. 1671, Ann, d. of Aquila Chase, had Thomas, b. 16 Feb. 1672 ;
and prob. Eliz. bef. he rem. to Suffield, there had Joseph, and Benjamin,
tw. b. 1677 ; Aquila, 1679 ; Ann, 1681 ; John, 1684; and Moses, 1687 ;
and d. 25 July 1689.   WILLIAM, Salem 1639, of Marblehead 1648, may
be the man wh. had gr. of ld. in Dorchester 1638.   WILLIAM, Salem,
perhaps s. of the preced. m. 4 Mar. 1673, Eliz. Reick, or (if Lewis did
not mistake, as I fear), Kirk, had Eliz. b. 1 Nov. 1673, d. at 3 mos. and
William 8 Jan. 1675.   Perhaps he was of Lynn.   WILLIAM, Killingworth 1667.   ZECHARIAH, Medfield, youngest s. of George of the same,
m. 30 Aug. 1683, Abial Ellis, had Benoni, b. 9 Sept. 1684; Zechariah,
19 Oct. 1685 ; Joseph, 4 Oct. 1687 ; Abiel, 4 Oct. 1691; John, 12 Oct.
1693; Ruth, 5 Mar. 1695; Thomas, 2 May 1698 ; Eliz. 6 July 1700 ;
and Mary, 26 May 1703.

BARCROFT.   See Bancroft.

BARD, JOHN, Lynn, had John, b. 29 Jan. 1678.   Sometimes this spell.
is substit. for Beard, and perhaps opposite mistake may even the balance.

BARDEN, THOMAS, R. I. an inhab. of that Col. 1675.   WILLIAM, Marshfield 1643, rem. to Barnstable, m. Feb. 1661, Deborah Barker, d. of John
of M. had Mercy, b. 1 Nov. 1662; Deborah, 28 June, 1665; John, 17
Mar. 1668 ; Stephen, 15 Apr. 1669 ; Abraham, 14 May 1674; Joseph,
Sept. 1675; and Ann, 26 Aug. 1677.

BARDING, NATHANIEL, Hartford 1636, yet not an orig. propr. had
only ch. Sarah, by first w. and by sec. w. Abigail, wid. of William An-
drews, the sch.master had none, and d. 1674.   His d. m. 11 Sept. 1645,
Thomas Spencer, wh. call. a s. Nathaniel Barding to perpet. the name.
His will speaks of these ch. of William Andrews, viz. Samuel, John, and
Thomas, and of Samuel's w. Eliz.

BARDWELL, ROBERT, Hatfield, a soldier in Philip's war, 1676, a partak. in the Falls fight under Capt. Turner; m. 29 Nov. 1676, Mary, d.
of William Gull, had Ebenezer, Samuel, John, Thomas, Mary, Sarah,
Esther, Thankful, and Abigail, and d. 1726.   Samuel and Thomas went
to Deerfield, but of them I kn. no more.

BAREFOOTE, † ‡ WALTER, of Great Island (Newcastle) N. H. 1660,
was a counsel. of the Col. 1682, and Dept. Gov. 1685, d. a. 1688, and his
will may be read in our Suffk. Reg.   His conduct in office is much
spoken against, and something prejudicial to his charact. is seen in a
depon. of William Davis, of Mar. 1677, as to facts more than fourteen yrs.

bef. for wh. see Geneal. Reg. V. 358. Chalmers, in Pol. Ann. 509, gives a letter of his, 29 Mar. 1683, wherein he remarks, that his experience of more than 25 yrs. in the country enables him to speak, as very shrewdly he does, of the clerical influence prevalent here.

BARGE, * GILES, Scarborough, m. Eleanor, wid. of Jonas Bayley of the same, was selectman 1669, and rep. in 1682 ; and Southgate says, he rem. to Dorchester.

BARGER, PHILIP, Boston, a Huguenot exile a. 1685, came first to Casco, with Pierre Baudouin, as in Willis is told I. 185. He d. 1703, leav. wid. Margaret, and prob. s. Philip, wh. d. 1720. The b. of Mary is found on our town rec. but it is not clear whether ch. of the elder or the younger Philip.

BARKER, BARZILLAI, Rowley, eldest s. of James the first, of wh. I can tell no more. BENJAMIN, Andover, s. prob. youngest, of Richard first of the same, m. 2 Jan. 1689, Hannah Marston, d. perhaps of John, and d. 1750, aged 83. EBENEZER, Andover, br. of the preced. m. 25 May 1686, Abigail Wheeler, perhaps d. of David, d. 1747, aged 95. EDWARD, Boston 1650, by w. Jane had Eliz. b. 17 July of that yr. ; Mary, 15 Feb. 1653 ; John, 15 Jan. 1654 ; Sarah, 9 Mar. 1655 ; and Thomas, 1657. He may, or may not, be the same as EDWARD of Branford 1667, wh. was a man of distinct. there. FRANCIS, Concord, d. 1655. FRANCIS, Duxbury, s. of Robert the first, m. 5 Jan. 1675, Mary, d. of Thomas Lincoln the husbandman, of Hingham, had Joshua, b. 16 Nov. 1676 ; Eliz. 31 Oct. 1677 ; Josiah, 21 Sept. 1679 ; Francis, 18 Oct. 1681 ; and Ruth, 31 Jan. 1683. ISAAC, Duxbury, br. of the preced. m. 28 Dec. 1665, Judith, d. of Gov. Thomas Prence, had Rebecca, Lydia, Judith, Martha, and ano. d. without a name ; beside Francis ; Samuel, b. 1693 ; Isaac ; Jabez ; and Robert. JAMES, Rowley, freem. 7 Oct. 1640, d. 1678, leav. w. Mary, and ch. Barzillai, James, Nathaniel, Eunice, w. of John Watson, and Grace. He was not, like most of the Rowley early sett. from Yorksh. but came from Ragwell in Co. Suffolk. † ‡ JAMES, Newport 1651, a friend of John Clark, nam. in the royal chart. 1663, when he was an Assist. was chos. Dept. Gov. in 1678. His w. was Sarah, d. of William Jeffrey; but I think his first w. was a d. of Hon. Jeremiah Clark. See Haz. II. 612, Knowles, 312. Perhaps he had s. JAMES, wh. m. a d. of Amos Wescott. JAMES, Dover 1653. JAMES, Suffield 1679, Springfield 1686, had childr. at both, as I hear, but kn. no more than that he d. 1723. JOHN, Duxbury, m. 1632, Ann, d. of John Williams of Scituate, rem. to Marshfield 1638, and was drown. 1652. He had d. Deborah, wh. m. William Barden ; and s. John b. a. 1650. His wid. m. Abraham Blish, or Blush. JOHN, Scituate, s. of the preced. a promin. man, m. 18 Jan. 1677, Desire, youngest d. of Anthony Annable, had John, b. 4 May 1678 ; Desire, 22 Sept. 1680 ; Ann, 26 Aug.

1682, d. soon; Ann, again, 1 Nov. 1683. His w. d. 24 July 1706; and he m. the same yr. Hannah, wid. of Rev. Jeremiah Cushing, wh. d. 30 May 1710; and he d. 1 Dec. 1729 leav. wid. Sarah, wh. d. 7 Sept. 1730, aged 70. JOHN, Andover, s. of Richard, perhaps eldest, m. 6 July 1670, Mary Stevens, had Ephraim, wh. d. 21 Feb. 1695; was a lieut. and d. 1722. JOHN, Lyme 1676, or few yrs. later. JOSEPH, Weymouth, had bef. June 1652, m. Ruth, by Dorothy King, in her will of that date, call. d. and he was by her made Excor. Yet evid. it is, that the Excor's w. was b. to a former h. of the testator, not nam. King. NATHANIEL, Rowley, freem. 1677, was s. of James, and gladly would I find more of him. NICHOLAS, Boston 1655, carpenter, had d. Esther, wh. m. 10 Feb. 1652, Ambrose Dew, but as no more can be found of him, I must conclude, that her f. had brought her from Eng. RICHARD, Andover 1645, was one of the found. of the ch. there, by w. Joanna had John, William, Richard, Ebenezer, Stephen, and Benjamin, wh. all sett. in A. beside ds. Sarah, wh. m. 17 Nov. 1673, John Abbot; Esther, wh. m. 10 Aug. 1676, John Stevens; and Hannah, wh. m. 27 May 1680, Christopher Osgood; and he d. 18 Mar. 1693. RICHARD, Andover, s. of the preced. m. 21 Apr. 1682, Hannah Kimball, had Richard, wh. d. 22 Dec. 1698; and nothing more is kn. to me. ROBERT, Duxbury 1648, br. of the first John, had Robert; and from his will of 18 Feb. 1689, we kn. that other ch. were Francis, Isaac, Rebecca, w. of William Snow, and Abigail Rogers, but wh. was h. of this last is not seen. ROBERT, Duxbury, s. perhaps eldest, of the preced. had two ws. Alice, and Hannah, and ch. Abigail, b. 24 Aug. 1682; James, 1 Jan. 1684; Caleb, 24 May 1685; Deborah, 7 Dec. 1686; Susanna, 20 Dec. 1689; Robert, 5 July 1693; Alice, 3 June 1695; Lydia, 5 Sept. 1697; all these by Alice; and by the next w. Isaac, 15 Mar. 1699; Mary, 13 May 1701; and Margaret, 18 Apr. 1704. STEPHEN, Andover, s. of the first Richard, m. 13 May 1687, Mary, d. of George Abbot the sec. of the same, but I hear nothing of issue. ‖ THOMAS, Rowley, perhaps br. of James of the same, freem. 13 May 1640, ar. co. 1641, d. 1650. His wid. Mary, m. 16 July 1651, Rev. Ezekiel Rogers, as his third w. but whether she bore ch. to either h. is not kn. THOMAS, Boston, by w. Jane had Thomas, b. 23 Aug. 1657; was freem. 1678. WILLIAM, Andover, s. of the first Richard, m. 20 Feb. 1677, Mary Dix, but whose d. she was, is undiscov. had John, wh. d. 13 Apr. 1689, and no more is in my power to tell, save that the f. d. 1718, aged 71. WILLIAM, Salem, freem. 1678, may be the same as the preced.

BARLOW, *AARON, Rochester, by w. Beulah had Eliz. b. 22 Aug. 1684; Mary, 30 Mar. 1688; Shubael, 13 May 1691; and Nathan, 1 July 1697. He was rep. 1690, says Samuel Davis in 2 Mass. Hist. Coll. IV. 260. BARTHOLOMEW, Boston, cooper 1648–57, in wh. last yr. he d.

26 Sept. by nuncup. will giv. to his s. Thomas what little he had, refusing any thing to serv. EDWARD, Malden, m. Mary, d. of James Pemberton, bef. 1660, as in her f.'s will is read, and had childr. as the same docum. proves, but no names can be heard. GEORGE, Exeter 1639, Saco 1652, was a preach. at both, and elsewhere, but, in 1653, was forbid. by the Gen. Ct. to preach or prophesy on penalty of £10 for every offence. He had been that very yr. sworn freem. of Mass. 5 July at Wells, but rem. to Plymouth a. 1660, and there essay. to be a lawyer. Greenleaf in Eccl. Sk. 52; Bishop's N. E. Judged, 389; and Sewell's Hist. I. 571. GEORGE, Milford, had bef. 1690, m. a d. of Vincent Stetson, as in the will of S. appears. JAMES, Suffield 1680, m. 10 Jan. 1688, Sarah, d. of Thomas Huxley of the same, d. 16 Mar. 1690, leav. James, b. 27 Jan. 1689. JOHN, Fairfield 1668, d. 1674, in his will of 28 Mar. of that yr. ment. w. Ann, s. John, and ds. Eliz. Frost, Martha, w. of James Beers, Deborah, w. of John Sturges, Ruth, w. of Israel Bradlee, and Isabella Clapham. JOHN, Fairfield, perhaps s. of the preced. m. Abigail, d. of Robert Lockwood. MOSES, Rochester, perhaps br. of Aaron of the same, had rem. thither from Sandwich bef. 1684. THOMAS, Fairfield 1653, had been a juror in 1645, by w. Rose acc. Hinman, in Ed. sec. p. 131, had Phebe, Deborah, and Mary, and made his will 8 Sept. 1658. THOMAS, Boston, by w. Eliz. (whose ch. by two later h.'s in choos. their guardian, Joseph Royall, call him uncle) had Eliz. b. 13 Nov. 1657; and Sarah, 18 July 1659; and d. 23 Oct. 1661. His wid. m. 24 Feb. next John Coombs of Boston, and in 1669, m. John Warren. Barlow's prop. had been so much reduc. by C. that after his d. the Court gave most of his resid. to B.'s only ch. Sarah. Sometimes this name appears in early rec. Barley. Joel, kn. as the author of the Columbiad, an heroic poem, and of Hasty Pudding, an agreeable one, was by Hinman, in his first Ed. p. 14, call. a descend. of that Thomas of Fairfield, tho. on later inq. he found him s. of Samuel, b. at Reading, Conn. 24 Mar. 1754, Y. C. 1778. He transfer. his alleg. from the muses to worldly politics, and d. 24 Dec. 1812, min. plenipo. of the U. S. represent. their honor and independ. foll. in the train of Napoleon the first (like the vassal kings, wh. felt none of this American's audacious enthusiasm), in the madman's march to Moscow, at a wretched ho. on the desolate plains of Poland.

Hide, blushing glory, hide Pultova's day.

BARNABY, JAMES, Plymouth, m. 8 June 1647, Lydia, d. of Robert Bartlett, had, perhaps, James, and Stephen. His wid. m. John Nelson of Middleborough. JAMES, Plymouth, s. prob. of the preced. by w. Joanna had James, b. 1698, and Ambrose, 1706. STEPHEN, Plymouth, perhaps br. of the preced. m. 1696, Ruth Morton (whose f. is not kn. to me), had Lydia, Ruth, Eliz. Timothy, and Hannah; and by sec. w. Judith, wid. of Joseph Church, had Joseph, b. 1712.

BARNARD, BARTHOLOMEW, Boston 1651, carpenter, had perhaps been and a doz. yrs. bef. at York, and brought from Eng. a fam. Matthew, perhaps others, of wh. I see no rec. BARTHOLOMEW, Hartford, perhaps s. of the preced. m. Oct. 1647, Sarah, d. of Thomas Birchard, d. 1698, leav. John, Joseph, and four ds. Eliz. Wadsworth, Sarah Steele, wh. was b. 3 Dec. 1648; Mary Bemis, and Hannah, unm. at the date of his will, 1692. BENJAMIN, Watertown, youngest s. of John first of the same, by w. Sarah had Sarah, b. 1692; and Benjamin, 24 Aug. 1693; and d. 12 Sept. 1694. His wid. m. 12 Jan. 1699, Samuel Winch of Framingham. CHARLES, Hartford 1681. FRANCIS, Hartford 1644, rem. 1659, or soon after, to Hadley, freem. 1666; in 1683, petitn. the governm. to pay him their debt, and d. 3 Feb. 1698, aged 81. He had m. 15 Aug. 1644, Hannah, sis. of Matthew and Renold Marvin, had Thomas, H. C. 1679; Samuel; Joseph; Hannah; John; and Sarah, wh. d. 1676. Hannah m. 1667, Dr. John Westcar of Hadley, and next, 1680, Simon Beaman of Hadley and Deerfield. He is ancest. of all the divines of this name from Harv. exc. John, H. C. 1700, and Jeremiah, H. C. 1773. By sec. w. Frances, wid. of John Dickinson, d. of Nathaniel Foote (per contr. 21 Aug. 1677), he had no ch. See the admirab. Foote genealogy of Goodwin. JAMES, Sudbury, s. of John of Watertown, m. 8 Oct. 1666, Abigail, youngest d. of Rev. George Phillips, perhaps youngest ch. wh. d. Sept. 1672, had no ch. and he d. 1720, leav. wid. Sarah. JAMES, Watertown, youngest s. of John the sec. of the same, m. 16 Dec. 1692, Judith, eldest d. of Samuel Jennison of the same, had James, b. 3 Aug. 1696; Samuel, 19 July 1699; Isaac, 13 Mar. 1702; and Hannah, 1 June 1705; and d. 23 Jan. 1726; and his wid. m. in May foll. John Bemis. JOHN, Cambridge, came, prob. in the Francis from Ipswich, 1634, aged 36, with w. Mary, 38, was perhaps the freem. of 4 Mar. 1635, rem. 1636, to Hartford, thence to Hadley 1659, or soon after, and d. 1664, leav. no ch. He left good est. made his kinsman Francis B. Excor. giv. much to Morgan and Thomas Bedient, ch. of his sis. Mary, then liv. in O. E. wh. came over to enjoy it. His wid. Mary d. next yr. and she gave much of her est. to Daniel and William Stacy, of Barnham, near Malden in Co. Essex, her brs. and £10, to bring up Thomas, s. of Francis Bedient to sch. This legacy was well bestow. for the f. was poor, and the s. worthy. JOHN, Watertown, came 1634, aged 30, with w. Phebe, 27, s. John, 2, and Samuel, 1, in the Elizabeth, from Ipswich; perhaps was freem. 3 Sept. 1634; had here Hannah; James, bef. ment.; Mary, b. 7 Nov. 1639; Joseph, 12 Nov. 1642; Benjamin, bef. ment. and Eliz. was a selectman 1644, and was bur. 4 June 1646. His wid. d. 1 Aug. 1685. Hannah

m. 25 June 1655, Samuel Goffe; Mary m. 16 June 1662, William Barrett, both of Cambridge; and Eliz. m. 7 Jan. 1671, John Dix of W. JOHN, Watertown, s. of the preced. b. in Eng. m. 15 Nov. 1654, Sarah, d. of John Fleming of the same, had John, b. 24 Aug. 1656, d. soon; John, again, 30 Oct. 1657; Sarah, 19 Sept. 1659, d. at 4 mos.; Samuel, 25 Mar. 1664; Sarah, again, Feb. 1666, d. next mo.; James, 14 Jan. 1667; Ann, Sept. 1670; Phebe, 8 Aug. 1673; and Jane, 17 May 1678. He was freem. 1671; and his d. Ann m. 16 Dec. 1692, Nathaniel Bowman, and Jane m. 15 Jan. 1713, John Smith, and liv. over 85 yrs. JOHN, Nantucket, only s. of Robert of the same, m. 25 Feb. 1669, Bethia, d. of Peter Folger, and they were drown. 6 June foll. JOHN, Hadley, s. of Francis, with wh. he rem. from Hartford, d. without issue, perhaps unm. being k. at Bloody brook, with Capt. Lathrop, 18 Sept. 1675. ‖ JOHN, Boston, s. of Matthew of the same, ar. co. 1677, freem. 1678, by w. Esther, wh. d. 1689, had John, b. 6 Nov. 1681, H. C. 1700 (a min. of much distinct. ord. 18 July 1716, d. 24 Jan. 1770, for whose very interest. autobiogr. the curious reader will turn to 3 Mass. Hist. Coll. V. 178); and by sec. w. had William, 30 Aug. 1691; Jonathan, 15 Jan. 1693; and Matthew, 17 June 1694; and d. Dec. 1732. His wid. liv. to 94th yr. 31 Jan. 1758. JOHN, Watertown, s. of the sec. John of the same, m. 5 Mar. 1683, Sarah, d. of Richard Cutting, had only Eliz. b. 29 Oct. 1684, by her; and he m. 17 Nov. 1692, Eliz. d. of John Stone of the same, had Sarah, b. 25 Jan. 1694; and this w. d. 6 May foll. and 23 July next he m. Mary, d. of Joseph Morse the sec. of the same, had John, 27 June 1695; Mary, 1 Apr. 1697; Fleming, 19 Apr. 1699; Joseph, 21 May 1700; Jonathan, 20 May 1703; Lydia, 2 May 1705; and Grace, 31 Mar. 1707. His will of 12 Aug. 1727, was pro. 27 Mar. 1732, as Bond tells. JOSEPH, Northampton, s. of Francis, m. 13 July 1675, unless more prob. date be 19 Dec. or 13 Jan. after (as ea. of the three is giv.), Sarah, d. of Elder John Strong, rem. to Deerfield, had John, Joseph, Thomas, Samuel, Ebenezer, Sarah, Rebecca, Hannah, Abigail, and Thankful, but no dates are kn. of their b. He was mort. wound. by the Ind. 18 Aug. and d. 6 Sept. 1695. JOSEPH, Springfield, s. of Richard of the same, a shopkeep. d. 3 Dec. 1728 leav. ch. Eliz. Mary, Sarah, and Joseph. MASSACHIEL, Weymouth, had Mary, b. 27 Sept. 1637; and Sarah, 5 Apr. 1639; but of him I hear no more. ‖ MATTHEW, Boston, carpenter, s. of Bartholomew, b. in Eng. ar. co. 1660, freem. 1673, was a lieut. and d. 9 May 1679, aged 54; by first w. Sarah, wh. d. 31 Aug. 1659, had John, b. 29 Sept. 1654; Thomas, 14 Apr. 1657; and by sec. w. Alice, wh. d. 1663, had Benjamin 6 Jan. 1663. Ano. w. he had, prob. nam. Martha, by Nicholas Davis of York call. cousin, in his will of 27 Apr. 1667. NATHANIEL, Boston, m. 11 Feb. 1659, Mary, d. of John Lugg, perhaps rem. to Nantucket, there

had Mary, b. 24 Feb. 1667 ; Hannah, 19 July 1669 ; John, 24 Feb. 1671;
Nathaniel, 24 Nov. 1672 ; Stephen, 16 Feb. 1675 ; Sarah, 23 Mar. 1677;
and Elinor, 18 June 1679.   But high Nantucket authority claims that
the f. of those seven ch. came in 1650, with his uncle, Robert Barnard,
from Eng. whose d. he m. and there d. 3 May 1718, as also that his w.
d. 17 Mar. preced.   Of the right Nathaniel, I suppose, Thomas of Salisbury was the f. and he (whether h. of the d. of Lugg or not) is call. progenit. of all the inhabs. of the isl. of this name.   RICHARD, Springfield,
d. 19 Nov. 1683, had six ch. of wh. Joseph alone, bef. ment. is kn. to me.
Sometimes he is call. Barnet.   ‖ RICHARD, Boston, br. of Matthew, m. 2
Mar. 1659, Eliz. d. of Benjamin Negus, was of ar. co. 1662, and d. Dec.
1706.   ROBERT, Salisbury, had only s. John, b. 2 Mar. 1642, and a.
1663 rem. to Nantucket, there d. 1682 ; and his wid. Joanna d. 31 Mar.
1705.   ROBERT, Andover, one of the found. of the ch. 1645, had Stephen, John, and Hannah, wh. m. 13 June 1662, John Stevens.   Of this
stock was Jeremiah, H. C. 1773, min. of Amherst, N. H.   SAMUEL,
Watertown, s. of John the first, and brot. by him from Eng. took o. of
alleg. 1652, but prob. d. unm.   SAMUEL, Boston 1671.   SAMUEL, Hadley, s. of Francis, d. 1728, leav. Samuel, and two ds.   SAMUEL, Watertown, s. of John the sec. of the same, housewright, m. 4 Apr. 1700, Mercy,
youngest d. of Rev. John Sherman, had Esther, b. (if Bond's rec. be right)
9 Sept. 1700 ; Eliz. bapt. 18 Jan. 1702 ; Grace, b. 14, bapt. by name of
Mercy 20 Aug. 1704 ; and Samuel, bapt. 14 Apr. 1706, as Bond tells ;
but he adds, that he soon after rem. prob. to Cambridge ; and there he
may have had more ch.   STEPHEN, Andover, s. of Robert, m. 1 May
1671, Rebecca How, but of him I hear no more.   THOMAS, Salisbury, by
w. Helen had Thomas, b. 10 May 1641 ; Nathaniel, 15 Jan. 1643; Martha, and Mary, tw. 22 Sept. 1645 ; Sarah, 28 Sept. 1647 ; Hannah, 24
Nov. 1649 ; Ruth, 16 Oct. 1651 ; John, 12 Jan. 1655 ; and a d. 20 Jan.
1657 ; and he was k. by the Ind.   Sarah m. 31 Jan. 1667, William
Hacket ; and Hannah m. 28 Oct. 1673, Benjamin Stevens.   THOMAS,
Salisbury, eldest s. of the preced. by w. Sarah had Thomas, b. 22 Jan.
1664 ; took o. of alleg. Dec. 1677.   THOMAS, Boston 1678, a carpenter,
was, prob. s. of Matthew, but no more is found of him.   *THOMAS*, Andover, s. of Francis, ord. as collea. with Dane 1682, d. 13 Oct. 1718, in 61st
yr.   He had m. 14 Dec. 1686, Eliz. d. of Theodore Price, wh. d. 10 Oct.
1693 ; and next m. 28 Apr. 1696 Abigail Bull, wh. d. 1702 ; and next
m. 1704 Lydia Goff.   Of his ch. the dates are not all giv. nor is any d.
nam. the s. were Thomas, b. 1688, wh. d. without issue, bef. his f.
John, 26 Feb. 1690, H. C. 1709, wh. succeed. his f. in the pulpit at A.
ord. 8 Apr. 1719, and d. 14 June 1758, leav. Thomas, H. C. 1732, min.
at Newbury and Salem, and Edward, H. C. 1736, min. of Haverhill.

TOBIAS, of the first class at H. C. 1642, went soon to Eng. as Johnson, in Wonderwork. Provid. 165, tells; but of him no more is heard. In his enum. of gr. 1834, Farmer would have count. at Harv. 13 up to 1774, and 2 more since, and Yale 3. Prince I. 151, nam. one of this name at Weymouth as a min. yield. I fear, too much to tradit. as letters from the oldest people there give no confirmat. Perhaps for the early yrs. of the planta. a lay br. officiat. in part of the serv.

BARNES, BENJAMIN, Farmington, s. of Thomas of Hartford, rem. to Waterbury, had w. Sarah, and ch. Joseph; Thomas, bapt. 8 June 1690, at F.; Ebenezer; and perhaps others. CHARLES, Easthampton, L. I. 1663, a sch.master, was s. of William of East Winch, near Lynn, Co. Norfk. Esqr. as is told. DANIEL, New Haven 1644, perhaps was propr. 1685. JAMES, Boston, had w. Hopestill, wh. d. 19 Aug. 1676; and he was freem. 1681. JOHN, Plymouth 1632, prob. of Yarmouth 1639, m. Mary Plummer (whose f. is not kn.), had John b. that yr. wh. d. 25 Dec. 1648; Jonathan, 3 June 1643; Lydia, 24 Apr. 1647; beside Hannah, and an elder d. Mary, wh. m. 1659, at Plymouth, Robert Marshall. His w. d. 2 June 1651, and he had sec. w. Jane, at P. whither soon after d. of his first w. he rem. and there d. 1671 by violence of one of his cattle. See Haz. I. 326. JOHN, Concord 1661, m. 1664, Eliz. d. of William Hunt, was prob. f. of deac. John of Marlborough, (wh. d. in 86th yr. 5 Apr. 1752); and was k. by the Ind. at Sudbury fight, Apr. 1676. JOHN, Boston 1669, s. of Thomas of Hingham, a cooper, m. Eliz. Heaton, d. of Nathaniel; but I kn. nothing more of him. JOHN, New Haven, prob. s. of Thomas of the same, was a propr. 1685. JONATHAN, Plymouth, s. of John, m. 4 Jan. 1666, Eliz. d. of William Hedge of Yarmouth, had Mary, b. 14 Aug. 1667; John, 5 Mar. 1669; William, 14 Feb. 1670; Hannah, 11 Nov. 1672; Lydia, 4 July 1674; Eliz. 16 Aug. 1677; Sarah, 28 Feb. 1680; Esther, 18 Feb. 1682; and Jonathan, 27 Aug. 1684; beside two more ds. of names unkn. JOSEPH, Farmington, s. of Thomas of the same, had Jacob, b. 18 Sept. 1687, bapt. soon after; Abigail, bapt. 23 Feb. 1690; Eliz. 9 Oct. 1692; Mary, 17 Feb. 1695. JOSHUA, Yarmouth, came in 1632, and was bound for 5 yrs. from land. to Mr. Paine, in 1642 was fin. for scoff. at relig. or disturb. worship; perhaps was of Easthampton, L. I. in 1650. MATTHEW, Braintree 1640, a miller, had Sarah, b. 29 Aug. 1641, rem. to Boston 1652, there by w. Rebecca had Alice, 22 Dec. 1652; and Hannah, 14 Mar. 1655. His w. d. 19 Sept. 1657, and he m. 4 Nov. foll. Eliz. wid. of Thomas Hunt of Boston, and d. perhaps, at Malden, June 1667. His d. Sarah m. 26 Dec. 1660, John Tomline. Of ano. MATTHEW of Boston, I find, that by w. Sarah he had John, b. 29 Sept. 1654. MAYBEE, Middletown, s. of Thomas, of New Haven, m. 1691, Eliz. d. of Rev. Samuel Stow of M. but I hear of him no

more. NATHANIEL, Boston 1675, a merch. of wh. I hear no more, but
that in 1679 he was chos. clk. of the writs, i. e. town clk. OBADIAH,
New Haven 1640. PETER, Hingham, youngest s. of Thomas the first,
m. July 1679, Ann Canterbury, d. of Cornelius, had Cornelius, b. 24
Aug. 1684, d. young; and John, 10 Dec. 1685. RICHARD, Marlborough, had come in the Jonathan, 1639, with his mo. Agnes (wh. was
then w. of Thomas Blanchard), and her mo. Agnes Bent, and the gr.mo.
the mo. and a younger ch. d. on the voyage, so that he was some yrs.
under care of his uncle John Bent, and was put apprent. to said Blanchard, when Barnes was only ten yrs. old, wh. also bec. his guardian. After d. of Blanchard, May 1654, John Grout of Sudbury was made
guardian; and for part of this early hist. see Geneal. Reg. IX. 371. He
m. 16 Dec. 1667, perhaps as sec. w. wid. Deborah Dix, but all inq.
wh. was her first h. is baffled, neither the diligence of Bond, nor the skill
of Dr. Harris being adequate to solve it. Yet the list of ch. accepted,
from Barry by Bond, seems hardly to consist with the prior list of ch. she
had b. Leonard, John, and William. See Bond, 753. However some
may be adm. as Sarah, b. 1669; Richard, 1673; and Abigail, 1683, wh.
m. 1705, Peter Bent. He d. 22 Jan. 1708. RICHARD, Marlborough, s.
prob. of the preced. m. Ann, youngest d. of the first Jonathan Hide of
Cambridge, but I learn no more. THOMAS, Hingham 1637, freem. 1645,
came with w. Ann from Hingham, O. E. had Thomas, and John, both
bapt. 21 May 1643, of wh. the first d. young; Eliz. 8 Dec. 1644; Ann;
Hannah, June 1647, d. young; James, 8 Apr. 1649; and Peter, 6 June
1652. Ann m. a Brimsden of Boston. THOMAS, Salem, by w. Mary
had Benjamin, b. 1 Oct. 1655; Thomas, 1657, d. soon; Mary, 12 Oct.
1658, d. at 2 yrs.; and Mary, again, 19 Mar. 1662; and was drown. Dec.
1663. THOMAS, Hartford 1639, rem. to Farmington, had Benjamin,
bapt. 24 July 1653; Joseph, 1655, and prob. Thomas, wh. m. Mary, d. of
Richard Jones. THOMAS, New Haven 1643, br. of Daniel of the same,
rem. to Middletown, and d. 1693. He had serv. in the Pequot war, 1637,
and left s. John; Thomas, b. 26 Aug. 1653; Daniel, 29 Aug. 1659, bapt.
1661, on the same day with Abigail, his sis. b. 16 Mar. 1657, but the day
on the rec. of ch. is a false one, 27 June, which was a Thursday; and
Maybee, b. 25 June 1663, as the careful town rec. tells, bapt. not, as the
careless ch. rec. tells, 20 July of that yr. wh. was on Monday; beside three
other ds. of wh. Eliz. perhaps eldest, was b. 28 May 1650. His w. Mary
d. 1676. THOMAS, Swanzey 1669, was a promin. man in the Bapt. ch.
there, had Eliz. b. 14 Feb. 1675, and prob. others. THOMAS, Marlborough, the freem. 1673, wh. pray. for a gr. of Ind. ld. bec. his ho. and goods
had been burn. by the enemy in Philip's war, may be he wh. came from
London 1656, aged 20, in the Speedwell. THOMAS, New Haven, s. of

Thomas of the same, had Mary, b. 1682; Thomas, 24 July 1684, d. young; Thomas, again, 26 July 1687; Sarah, 1689; Rebecca, 12 Mar. 1691; Abigail, 10 June 1693; Eliz. 10 Nov. 1695; Deborah, 1 Feb. 1698; Hannah, 31 May 1702; Samuel, 11 Apr. 1705; Nathaniel, 11 Jan. 1707; and Abraham, 1711. THOMAS, Farmington, prob. s. of Thomas of the same, had Ruth, bapt. 23 Oct. 1692; and Eliz. 21 July 1695. One THOMAS, of N. Hampsh. 1690, was of those wh. pray. for protect. of Mass. jurisdict. WILLIAM, Salisbury 1640, freem. 2 June 1641, by w. Rachel had Mary, wh. m. 23 June 1659, sec. John Hoyt; William, wh. d. 11 June 1648; Hannah, b. 25 Jan. 1644; Deborah, 1 Apr. 1646; Jonathan, 1 Apr. 1648; Rachel, 30 Apr. 1649, wh. m. 2 Mar. 1668 or 9 (both dates being giv.), Thomas Sargent; Sarah, wh. m. 8 Sept. 1670, Thomas Rowell, and next, 26 Oct. 1676, John, or more prob. Thomas Harvey, as the Amesbury rec. gives the name; and Rebecca, wh. m. Moses Morrill. Deborah m. 19 Dec. 1663, Samuel Davis. He was one of the first sett. of Amesbury a. 1654. It has been thot. that he is the man in the list of passengers by the Globe from London for Virginia, 1635, and the names of William Brown, and Richard Wells in the same list are seen, both, also, found at Salisbury. But those surnames are so frequent on both sides of the ocean, that the argument must not be pressed too far. Some persons might, at that time, think it easy to go from one part of America to another; but most of those for Virginia were not puritans, and all wh. would come to New Eng. especially from London, easily gained direct, instead of circuitous passage. Of this name, includ. those spelt without e, Farmer, in 1834, count. seven gr. at Yale, five at Harv. and five at other N. E. coll.

BARNETT, BARTHOLOMEW, MATTHEW, ROBERT, and others, may seem to be only perverse spell. for Barnard, wh. see. But *THOMAS*, New London, wh. preach. there 1686 and 7, must be print. with this form of the name, out of regard to that Eccl. Hist. of N. E. call. the Magnalia, III. 4, where this man is insert. in the third classis, tho. with studied carelessness, Mather omits his bapt. name. Caulkins could find no more than this useful designat. for this side of the water; while in vain I search Palmer's Non. Conf. Mem. III. 150 and 1 for ment. of any but Andrew of Trin. Col. Cambr. and Joshua, s. of Humphrey of Shropsh. wh. were respectable among the cler. confessors.

BARNEY, *JACOB, Salem, freem. 14 May 1634, had John, bapt. 15 Dec. 1639, was rep. 1635, 8, 47, 53, and d. 1673, aged 72. JACOB, Salem, s. of the preced. perhaps b. in Eng. m. 18 Aug. 1657, Hannah Johnson, wh. d. 5 June 1659; and next he m. 26 May 1660, Ann Witt, d. of Jonathan of Lynn or Salem, had Hannah, b. 2 Mar. 1661, prob. d. young; Sarah, 12 Sept. 1662; Abijah, 31 Oct. 1663; John, 1 Aug. 1665;

Jacob, 21 May 1667; Ruth, 27 Sept. 1669; Dorcas, 22 Apr. 1671; Joseph, 9 Mar. 1673; Israel, 17 June 1675; Jonathan, 29 Mar. 1677; Samuel, 10 Feb. 1679; and Hannah, again, 6 Feb. 1681, wh. m. John Cromwell. JACOB, Boston 1668, was one of the found. of the first Bapt. soc. in the town; yet no more is told of him, even in the valu. Hist. of Boston by Mr. Drake.

BARNUM, or BARNAM, RICHARD, may perhaps be thot. of Boston, as he was a corpo. in Moseley's comp. k. in the bloody assault, on Sunday, 19 Dec. 1675, upon the Narraganset fort. THOMAS, Norwalk 1662, was bef. that at Fairfield, and after at Danbury, had Thomas, b. 9 July 1663; John, 24 Feb. 1678; Hannah, 14 Oct. 1680; and Ebenezer, 19 May 1682; but six more ch. he had, two s. four ds. yet at N. are no more rec. nor can I find the names of these six, or either of them, or of either of two ws. one of wh. outliv. him, wh. d. 1695.

BARRELL, GEORGE, Boston 1638, a cooper, freem. 10 May 1643, d. 2 Sept. foll. In Geneal. Reg. II. 383 is an abstr. of his will, made 28 May, pro. 30 Oct. of that yr. giv. ho. and lds. to w. Ann for life, provid. for ch. John, James, and Ann, and two gr.ch. when they shall be 21 yrs. old; but the names of these two seem strangely spelt. "The tools of his trade" lead the diligent compiler, in a note, to explain, that he seems "to have been a mason;" but I follow the ch. rec. at his adm. into that body, 5 Sept. 1641, as prob. the correct designat. and Mr. Drake from town rec. shows it. His d. Ann had m. William Semond. JAMES, Boston, s. of the preced. prob. b. in Eng. was liv. in 1677; but the rec. has no acco. of a fam. ‖JOHN, Boston, cooper, br. of the preced. b. in Eng. ar. co. 1643, and 1656 was ens. of that disting. co. by w. Mary, d. of Elder William Colbron, had John b. 6 Aug. says the town rec. but the more trustworthy ch. rec. says, bapt. 3 Aug. 1645, d. young; Mary, b. 16 Mar. 1647; Hannah, 23 Apr. 1651; John, again, 15 Mar. 1653, d. young; William, 28 July 1654; and John, again, 1656; and d. 29 Aug. 1658. His. wid. m. Daniel Turell. But in the will of gr.f. Colbron, ano. s. James, is rememb. JOHN, Watertown, by w. Eliz. had Abigail, b. 20 Apr. 1658; but the wide-seeing eye of Dr. Bond did not discern this inhab. and therefore I am compel. to trust the Middlesex rec. of b. JOHN, Boston, s. prob. of John of the same, by w. Eliz. had Eliz. b. 4 Apr. 1677. THOMAS, the Mass. freem. of 1645, was of Braintree; but of him I can see no more, and can feel no doubt that what appears Barrill in print, should be Barrett. WILLIAM, Boston, br. of George of the same, d. 20 Aug. 1639. WILLIAM, Scituate, perhaps s. of John of Boston, tho. Deane calls him s. of William, m. 1680, Lydia, d. of John Turner, wid. of John James, had William, b. 1683; Lydia, 1684; Mary, 1686; and James, 1687.

BARRETT, BENJAMIN, Hatfield, a soldier under Capt. Turner, 1676, wh. may have been s. of Humphrey, but more prob. of John of Malden, m. 1677, Sarah Graves, perhaps d. of John of Hadley, and sec. w. Mary, sis. of Robert Alexander, rem. to Deerfield, and d. 1690, leav. ch. Benjamin, John, Jonathan, Sarah, and Rebecca. CHARLES, Newport, by w. Catharine, wh. he took at Barbados, had Rosamond, b. May 1665, as the Friends' rec. proves to me, but it certif. no more. HUMPHREY, Concord 1640, freem. 1657, wh. d. Nov. 1662, aged 70, had Thomas, wh. was drown. in the riv. 1660; Humphrey; and John, by Shattuck said to have sett. at Marlborough. His wid. Mary, in her will, of 15 June, pro. 20 Oct. 1663, names s. John and Humphrey, and gr.ch. Mary B. as also her br. Oliver, wh. d. Sept. 1671. *HUMPHREY, Concord, s. of the preced. freem. 1682, had, I suppose, m. a d. of Robert Hawes of Roxbury, wh. in his will calls him s. had Joseph, and Benjamin, was rep. Oct. 1691. JAMES, Charlestown, m. Hannah, d. of Stephen Fosdick, had James, b. 6 Apr. 1644; Hannah, 21 Mar. 1648; Mary; Sarah; John, 6 May 1655; and Stephen, special. nam. in the will of gr.f. Fosdick. He d. 16 Aug. 1672; and his wid. d. 1681. Hannah m. John Scolley. JAMES, Malden, s. of the preced. m. 11 Jan. 1672, Dorcas, d. of Thomas Green of the same (that Thomas, wh. d. 1682), had James, b. 1672; John, 1675; and Jonathan, 1678; and d. 1694. JOHN, Taunton 1643. *JOHN, Malden 1653, had Benjamin, b. 18 Dec. of that yr. rem. to Wells, there was made constable 1657, ens. 1660, rep. 1681. Perhaps he was br. of James; and his w. Mary was d. of Edmund Littlefield of W. wh. in his will of Dec. 1661, pro. 17 Apr. foll. names her and s. John, prob. mean. the h. JOHN, Marlborough, s. of Humphrey the first, m. 19 Sept. 1656, Mary Pond of Sudbury, and d. July 1711, leav. s. John. JOHN, Chelmsford, by w. Sarah had Lydia, b. 22 Sept. 1659; and (unless we suppose error in the rec.) Samuel, 16 June 1660. JOHN, Charlestown, m. 6 June 1664, Eliz. Cousins, rem. to Chelmsford, there in 1679, call. sen. so that ano. of the same name was liv. there. JOHN, Stratford 1671. JOHN, Charlestown, s. of James of the same, was prob. never m. but of slender health, made his will, 1678, in wh. he opens with say. he was 23 yrs. old, not likely to live long, and directs, that mo. brs. and sis. should have his prop. It was pro. 1682. JOSEPH, Chelmsford, freem. 1676, was perhaps s. of the sec. Humphrey. ROBERT, Charlestown 1674, d. 1675, and his wid. Hannah d. 5 Jan. 1691. STEPHEN, wh. serv. as commissary for Conn. in Philip's war, 1675. I have been unable to discov. any thing more a. his resid. or fam. STEPHEN, Charlestown, s. of James the first, m. 14 May 1680, Eliz. (of an undecyph. or hieroglif. name, whereof the initial is M.) and he d. 1689. THOMAS, Braintree, may prob. be he, wh. came at 16 yrs. in the Increase, 1635, was made freem. 1645, tho. the print. list has Barrill, and was of the number of petitnrs. for gr. of ld. at Warwick that our Gen. Ct. had confiscat. and to part of wh. they gave 10,000 acres forfeit. by the misbeliev. friends of Gorton; m. 14 Sept. 1655, Frances Woolderson, had Martha, b. 17 Sept. 1656; Mary, 17 Apr. 1658; and perhaps others, and d. at Chelmsford 1668, in his will of 1 July 1662, pro. 6 Aug. foll. names w. Margaret, eldest s. John; Thomas; and Joseph, the youngest. THOMAS, Cambridge, had w. Lydia, and rem. to Marlborough, there d. Jan. 1673, in his will of 16 Jan. pro. 1 Apr. foll. provid. for w. and three ch. WILLIAM, Cambridge, br. of the preced. by w. Sarah, d. of Richard Champney of the same, m. 19 Aug. 1656, had Lydia, b. 17 Sept. 1657; and John, 1660. His w. d. 21 Aug. 1661, and he m. 16 June 1662, Mary, d. of John Barnard, had William, b. 3 May 1665; Edward, 8 Jan. 1667; Samuel, 7 Feb. 1669; and Bartholomew, 1 Apr. 1672, wh. d. next mo. She d. 28 Mar. 1673, and he took for third w. 8 Oct. foll. Mary Sparhawk, d. of Nathaniel of the same, and d. 16 Mar. 1689, aged a. 60. By John Pool of Reading, in his will, Barrett is call. s. in law, wh. seems to prove, that P. had m. the mo. of B.'s first w. Of this name the gr. at Harv. in 1832 were 7, at Dart. 3, and at other N. E. coll. 4.

BARRON, DANIEL, Woburn 1653, was perhaps s. of Ellis the first. ELLIS, or ELLIZ, Watertown, freem. 2 June 1641, brot. from Eng. prob. three or four ch. for Bond names the issue in this order, Ellis; Mary, wh. m. 10 Dec. 1650, Daniel Warren; Susanna, wh. m. 14 Dec. 1653, Stephen Randall; Hannah, wh. m. a. 1659, Simon Coolidge; John; Sarah, b. 4 July 1640; Moses, 1 Mar. 1643; and Peter, a soldier in Moseley's comp. k. by the Ind. Sept. 1675. He had two ws. Grace (thot. to be mo. of all those ch.), and Hannah, wid. of Timothy Hawkins, m. 4 Dec. 1653; was constable 1658, selectman 1668, and d. 30 Oct. 1676. His will made four days bef. pro. 19 Dec. foll. provides for w. for the seven ch. remain. after loss of Peter, and for gr.ch. Eliz. Barron. ELLIS, Watertown, s. of the preced. m. Hannah, d. of Timothy Hawkins, and Bond gives the date wh. I have taken for m. of her mo. with the f. of this h. tho. he may be right, and possib. mo. and d. f. and s. were m. on one day, yet it seems less prob. He had Ellis, b. 22 Apr. 1655; Hannah, 6 Mar. 1658; Eliz. 14 Apr. 1660, d. soon; Sarah, 4 Nov. 1662; and perhaps Eliz. again; rem. to Groton, there had Grace, 29 July 1665; Mehitable, 22 June 1668; Timothy, 18 Apr. 1673; Dorothy, 6 Mar. 1675, perhaps d. young; and Abigail, 14 Nov. 1676. At Lancaster he made his will 31 Dec. 1711, pro. 7 Oct. foll. wh. teaches us the names of hs. for six of his ds. Abigail Houghton, Mehitable Parker, Hannah Cady, w. of James, Eliz. Philbrick, w. of Ephraim, Sarah Taylor, and Grace Stevens. He had prefer. L. to G. after the equal destruction of both. From Groton he was driv. in Philip's war, and reappears at W. with w. Lydia. ELLIS, Lancaster, s. of the preced. m. 27 May 1679, Mary, d. of Rev. John Sherman, and how venerable rec. may distort a name is shown here, where the clk. must certif. that Eliz. Barron jr. m. Mary Sherman; and he had sec. w. Lydia, unless Bond have confus. him with his f. as he suspect. JOHN, Groton, s. of Ellis the first, had John, b. 4 Apr. 1665; Moses, 26 Mar. 1669; Ellis, 4 June 1672; and Eliz. 28 Sept. 1677; but the name of his w. or date of his d. is not seen. MOSES, br. of the preced. may have liv. at Woburn, at least he m. Mary, eldest d. of Isaac Learned of that place, but prob. d. early. TIMOTHY, Watertown, a weaver, s. of Ellis the sec. m. 10 Mar. 1698, Rachel, d. of Samuel Jennison of the same, had Joseph, bapt. 30 Oct. foll.; Timothy, 1 July 1700; Peter, b. 26 July 1702; Samuel, Oct. 1704, d. next mo.; and Hannah, 6 Aug. 1709; and his wid. Rachel m. John King. Of Oliver, H. C. 1788, it is said by William Winthrop, in his interleav. catal. that he d. 1809, a physician in the Isle of Man.

BARROWS, or BARROW, JAMES, Dover, was tax. 1670, says Mr. Quint, but he tells no more. JOHN, Plymouth, had w. Deborah, s. Robert, Benajah, Joshua, and Ebenezer, beside two ds. when he d. 12 Jan. 1692. ROBERT, Plymouth, perhaps br. of the preced. m. 28 Nov. 1666, Ruth, d. of George Bonum, had Eliezur, b. 15 Sept. 1669, wh. d. soon; and no more is kn. of the f. ROBERT, Plymouth, s. of John, m. Lydia Dunham, had Robert, b. 1689; Thankful, 1692; Elisha, 1695; Thomas, 1697; and Lydia, 1699.

BARRY, JOHN, New London 1659, may have been only transient, as he is seen only as a witness to deed of ld.

BARSHAM, JOHN, Portsmouth, or as Bond thinks, of Exeter, eldest s. of William, by w. Mehitable had Annabel, b. 31 May 1670; Mary, 26 Feb. 1672; Dorothy, 2 Feb. 1674; Sarah, 11 Aug. prob. 1675; and William, 25 Apr. 1678. JOSHUA, Watertown, br. of the preced. outliv. his f. but in Bond's opin. was never m. NATHANIEL, Watertown, br. of the preced. m. 13 Mar. 1679, Eliz. eldest d. of the first William Bond, was town clk. selectman sev. yrs. and a lieut. in the wretched expedit. of Phips against Quebec, 1690, after a capt. had no ch. and d. 2 Aug. 1716. His wid. d. 23 Dec. 1729. PHILIP, Deerfield, k. by the Ind. at Bloody brook, with Capt. Lathrop, 18 Sept. 1675, left w. and perhaps ch. WILLIAM, Watertown, came, it is thot. 1630, freem. 9 Mar. 1637, by w. Ammiel, or Annabel, had John, b. 8 Dec. 1635, H. C. 1658; Hannah, 7 Jan. 1638; William; Joshua, 15 Mar. 1641; Susanna, 28 Jan. 1642; Nathaniel, 1644; Sarah; Mary, 24 June 1648; Rebecca, 12 Dec. 1657; and Eliz. 29 July 1659. He d. 13 July 1684, in his will of 23 Aug. preced. with codic. of 15 Apr. foll. not nam. w. leads us to infer, that she was d. No doubt he was a man of good public spirit, selectman 1653,

and fill. other office of import.   Hannah m. 19 Dec. 1656, John Spring
jr.; Susanna, and Sarah m. and had ch. but their hs. are not mark.;
Mary m. 7 May 1675, deac. John Bright, and next, 12 Dec. 1700,
Hananiah Parker of Reading; Rebecca m. 14 May 1683, Edward Winship of Cambridge; and Eliz. m. 5 July 1694, Adam Eve of Boston;
yet to so odd a name Bond puts a quere for place, while my suspicion
attaches more to the person's spell.

BARSTOW, BAIRSTO, or BERESTO, ‖ GEORGE, Boston, came from London, in the Truelove, 1635, aged 21, was in 1636, favor. with gr. of ld.
at Dedham, but prob. went not thither bef. 1642, ar. co. 1644, no w. or
ch. at D. is ment. bef. he rem. to Scituate, there beside some childr. wh.
d. early, had Margaret, bapt. 24 Feb. 1650; and George, b. Mar. 1652,
bapt. 12 June 1653, after d. of his f. at Cambridge, on 18 Mar. of that yr.
His wid. Susanna, d. of Thomas Marrett, or Marryott, of Cambridge, d.
17 Apr. 1654.   GEORGE, Roxbury, prob. s. of the preced. by w. Mary had
Susanna, b. 2 Nov. 1684; and George, Aug. 1687.   Perhaps he rem. to
Rehoboth, there had Samuel, 1 May 1705; and d. 6 Apr. 1726.   JERE-
MIAH, Scituate, s. of John of Cambridge, by w. Lydia had John, and
Jeremiah; the last was tak. by the Ind. a few weeks after d. of his f. (wh.
fell in the Rehoboth fight 26 Mar. 1676), and soon k. by them.   His wid.
m. 1677, Richard Standlake.   JOHN, Cambridge, usually writ. Baistoe,
was youngest br. of George the first, by w. Hannah had Michael, b. 1653;
John; and Jeremiah; was drown. 13 Feb. 1658, aged 33, by fall. thro.
ice of Charles riv. travel. from Dedham in the night.   JOHN, Scituate,
br. of Jeremiah of the same, m. 1678 Lydia, d. of William Hatch sec. of
the same, had Job, b. 8 Mar. 1679; Jeremiah, 28 Aug. 1682; John, 15
Feb. 1684; Jerusha, 21 Nov. 1687, d. soon; Susanna, 5 May 1689;
Abigail, 8 Mar. 1692; and Lydia, 26 Mar. 1696.   JOSEPH, Scituate, s.
of William the first, m. 16 May 1666, Susanna, d. of Thomas Lincoln, the
husbandman, of Hingham (wh. d. very aged, 31 Jan. 1730), had Susanna,
b. 3 June 1667; Joseph, 22 Jan. 1675; Benjamin, 1 Mar. 1679; Deborah, 26 Dec. 1681; and Samuel, 1 Jan. 1683; and d. 17 Apr. 1712.
His ho. was a garrison 1675.   MICHAEL, or MILES, Charlestown, eldest
br. of George the first, with w. Marcia join. the ch. 5 Dec. 1635, and was
made freem. 3 Mar. foll. rem. bef. 1642 to Watertown.   He was from
Shelf, near Halifax, Co. York, W. Riding, s. of Matthew, says Bond, bapt.
17 Nov. 1600, m. 16 Feb. 1625 Grace Halstead, wh. Bond, 677, notes as
the same with Marcia.   He brot. prob. his w.'s sis. Susanna, wh. d. unm.
As he had no ch. his will of 23 June 1674 proves his est. good, as was
the spirit in which he div. it (see Geneal. Reg. VIII. 169); and his w.
hav. d. 20 July 1671, many relat. partook, beside the benefac. to his spirit.
guide, Rev. John Sherman, the farm of 100 acres.   He d. 1676, not, as

sometimes said, the day of date of his will. He wrote his name Bairstow.
MICHAEL, Watertown, eldest s. of John of Cambridge, freem. 1690, m.
12 Jan. 1677, Rebecca, d. of John Train of W. had only ch. Hannah, b.
20 Jan. 1679. WILLIAM, Dedham, next br. of Michael the first, came
with his younger br. George, in the Truelove, 1635, aged 23, from London, where their names at the custom ho. were writ. Beresto, by w. Ann
had Joseph, b. 6 June 1639, bapt. 25 Apr. 1641, his mo. join. the ch.
that mo. ; Mary, 28 Dec. 1641, bapt. next Sunday ; Patience, 3 Dec.
1643, bapt. 9 June foll. He rem. to Scituate, there had, prob. Sarah ;
and ano. d. whose name is not seen ; certain. Deborah, Aug. 1650 ; William, Sept. 1652 ; and Martha, 1655 ; and he d. 1 Jan. 1669. His wid.
m. John Prince of Hull. Patience m. Moses Simmons, 1662, as Bond,
678, tells ; Mary m. 14 May 1656, William Ingram of Boston ; Sarah
m. a. 1665, Nathaniel Church ; Deborah m. 9 Nov. 1670, Philip Shattuck ; and Martha m. 9 Dec. 1674, Samuel Prince, s. of the h. of her mo.
Worthington calls him Wilkin, wh. is more strange than his spell. Bear-
stowe. WILLIAM, Scituate, s. of the preced. by w. Sarah had Rebecca,
b. 12 Mar. 1676 ; Martha, 1678 ; a s. bapt. 7 Nov. 1680, says Barry,
prob. d. young, but his name is not told by B. ; Ann, 26 June 1681 ;
William, 23 Nov. 1684 ; Mary, 21 Feb. 1687 ; Benjamin, 22 July 1690 ;
and Susanna, 8 Mar. 1693. Descend. of two of the four brs. are much
distrib. in Fairhaven, Rochester, Hanover, and perhaps Salem ; and six
of the name, if one without *r* may be incl. are seen among Farmer's gr. at
N. E. coll. in 1834.

   BARTHOLOMEW, * HENRY, Salem 1635, said by tradit. to have arr. 7
Nov. of that yr. was freem. 17 May 1637, then aged 36, by w. Eliz. had
Eliz. bapt. there 3 Oct. 1641 ; Hannah, 12 Feb. 1643 ; John, 10 Nov.
1644 ; Abraham, 8 Nov. 1646 ; Eleazer, 29 July 1649 ; Abigail, 6 Oct.
1650 ; William, 3 Oct. 1652 ; Eliz. again, 2 July 1654 ; and Henry, 10
May 1657 ; was rep. 1645, and 17 yrs. more, but not as Felt makes him, in
his list for 1635, prob. then mistak. him for William, as he did also in citing
testimon. against Mrs. Hutchinson. A. 1679 he rem. to Boston, and his
w. d. 1 Sept. 1682 ; and he d. 22 Nov. 1692. His d. Abigail m. 2 Jan.
1672, Nehemiah Willoughby. HENRY, Salem, s. of the preced. had w.
Catharine, but no ch. and d. 1698, leav. in his will of 25 Sept. 1694, no
subj. of remark. JOSEPH, Boston 1667, mariner, may have been s. of
William. ‖ RICHARD, Salem, 1638, br. of Henry the first, freem. 2 June
1641, ar. co. 1643, d. 1646. * WILLIAM, Ipswich, came from London
1634, in the sh. with Rev. John Lothrop, Zechary Symmes, and Mrs.
Ann Hutchinson, arr. Sept. Against the scheme of that lady's revela-
tions he was a ready witness, as Hutch. in Hist. II. 510 exhibits him.
Made freem. 4 Mar. 1635 he was a rep. 1635, and 7 yrs. more ; rem. as

a merch. to Boston, a. 1660, perhaps at Marblehead 1674, and d. at Charlestown 18 Jan. 1681. His d. Mary m. 24 Dec. 1657, Matthew Whipple
of Ipswich. WILLIAM, Roxbury, perhaps s. of the preced. a carpenter, m.
17 Dec. 1663, Mary Johnson, prob. d. of Isaac of the same, had Isaac, b.
1 Nov. 1664; William, 16 Oct. 1666; Mary, 26 Oct. 1668; and Eliz.
15 Mar. 1674; rem. soon after, and may have been of Branford 1685.

BARTLETT, ABRAHAM, Middletown, youngest s. of George of Guilford,
m. 11 June 1693, Mary Warner, d. of the first Andrew of the same, had
Mary, b. 18 May 1694; Abraham, 4 Mar. 1697; Joseph, 24 Oct. 1699;
Timothy, 25 Mar. 1702; and Ebenezer, 6 Nov. 1705; and d. 20 Feb.
1731. His wid. d. 28 May 1738, aged 74. * BENJAMIN, Duxbury, s.
of Robert of Plymouth, m. 1656, Sarah, d. of Love Brewster, had Benjamin, Samuel, Ichabod, Ebenezer, and Rebecca, prob. all by that w. but
he had in 1678 a sec. w. Cicely. He was rep. 1685, as in Baylies, IV.
19. BENJAMIN, Windsor, s. of John of the same, m. July 1665, Deborah
Barnard, had Deborah, b. 3 Apr. 1666; Benjamin, 21 June 1668, d.
young; Isaiah, 9 Dec. 1670, d. soon; Isaiah, again, 26 July 1672;
Ephraim, 17 Jan. 1674; Jehoida, 2 Nov. 1675; and Benjamin, again, 5
Dec. 1677. CHRISTOPHER, Newbury 1635, m. 16 Apr. 1645, first w.
Mary; had Mary, b. 15 Oct. 1647, d. young; Ann, 28 Sept. 1650; Martha, Mar. 1653; Christopher, 11 June 1655; and Jonathan, 5 July 1657,
d. at 2 yrs.; and his w. d. 24 Dec. 1661. He m. 19 Dec. 1663, Mary
Hoyt, perhaps d. of John, had John, 13 Sept. 1665, wh. d. at 3 mos. and
the f. d. 15 Mar. 1670, aged 47. CHRISTOPHER, Newbury, s. of the preced. m. 29 Nov. 1677, Deborah Weed, d. of John of Salisbury, had
Christopher, b. 26 Feb. 1679; Deborah, 23 June 1680; Mary, 17 Apr.
1682; Ann, 29 Mar. 1684; Lydia, 19 Apr. 1688; Hannah, 2 Nov. 1689;
Sarah, 23 Oct. 1691; Abigail, 7 Nov. 1695; Samuel, 16 May 1698; and
Mehitable, 18 Oct. 1701; and he d. 14 Apr. 1711. DANIEL, Guilford,
br. of Abraham, m. 11 Jan. 1686, Sarah, d. of deac. John Meigs, wh. d.
8 Apr. 1688, leav. only ch. Daniel, b. 31 Mar. bef. Next he m. 11 Feb.
1691, Concurrence, d. of Henry Crane, of Killingworth, had John, 21
Jan. 1692; Nathaniel, 10 Feb. 1694, d. at 10 mos.; Deborah, 4 Nov.
1695; George, 7 Feb. 1698; Nathaniel, again, 1 July 1700; and Ebenezer, 12 Feb. 1702. His w. d. 9 Oct. 1703; and he next m. 8 Oct. 1707,
Susanna Lord of Saybrook, had Collins, 7 Mar. 1709, d. young; Lucy,
23 June 1713; Jared, 1 Mar. 1715, d. at 6 mos.; and Sarah, 22 July
1717. He d. 14 Nov. 1747, and his wid. d. 2 Feb. 1758. * GEORGE,
Guilford 1641, of Branford 1649, m. 14 Sept. 1650, Mary, d. of Abraham
Cruttenden, had Eliz. b. Mar. 1652; Mary, 1 Feb. 1654; John, 9 Nov.
1656, wh. d. under 3 yrs.; Hannah, 5 Nov. 1658; Daniel, 14 Dec. 1665;
Abraham, 19 Feb. 1667; and Deborah, 1668. He was lieut. rep. 1665,

deac. and d. 3 Aug. 1669; and his wid. d. next mo. Eliz. m. 29 Aug. 1677, Abraham Fowler; Mary m. 10 July 1673, Nathaniel Stone; and Deborah m. 16 Mar. 1687, John Spinning. GEORGE, Scarborough 1663, wh. d. 1674, had d. Eliz. wh. m. Nicholas Baker of Marblehead, as teaches Willis, I. 135. HENRY, Braintree, was one of the comp. of brave Capt. Johnson, in the gr. Narraganset fight. ISAIAH, Windsor, s. of John of the same, m. 3 Dec. 1663, Abia Gillet, had John, b. 12 Sept. 1664. JEHOIADA, Hartford, s. of John of Windsor, had Martha, b. 28 July 1674. JOHN, Newport 1639. JOHN, Newbury 1635, came, 1634, in the Mary and John from London, was of Co. Kent, freem. 17 May 1637, had John, but other ch. is not kn. and d. 13 Apr. 1678, and his wid. Joan d. 5 Feb. foll. JOHN, Windsor 1640, br. of George of Guilford, had Isaiah, b. 13 June 1641; Benjamin, bapt. 26 Mar. 1643; Hepzibah, b. 14 July 1646; Jehoiada, bapt. 23 Dec. 1649; and Mehitable, 11 May 1651; was liv. 1669. JOHN, Newbury, s. of John of the same, m. 5 Mar. 1660, Sarah, d. of John Knight, had Gideon, b. 18 Dec. foll.; and Mary; was freem. 1669. JOHN, Weymouth, by w. Sarah had John, b. 11 Feb. 1666. JOHN, Marblehead 1674. JOHN, Newbury, s. of Richard the sec. of the same, call. (to disting. him as one of four contempo. Johns there), the tanner, m. 29 Oct. 1680, Mary Rust, had Mary, b. 17 Oct. 1681, wh. d. at 5 mos.; John, 24 Jan. 1683; Mary, again, 27 Apr. 1684; Nathaniel, 18 Apr. 1685; Dorothy, 22 Aug. 1686; Sarah, 27 Nov. 1687; Hannah, 13 Mar. 1689; Nathan, 23 Dec. 1691; Abigail, 12 Aug. 1693; and Alice, 18 Mar. 1695; and d. 24 May 1736. JOSEPH, Plymouth, s. of Robert of the same, had Robert, Joseph, Benjamin, Elnathan, Mary, Hannah, and Lydia. JOSEPH, Cambridge vill. or Newton, m. 27 Oct. 1668, Mary Waite, had Mary, b. 17 Feb. 1672; Joseph, and Mary, tw. 5 Mar. 1673; Eliz. 5 Feb. 1677; John; and Sarah; and d. 26 Dec. 1702. His wid. d. 21 Dec. 1721. Eliz. m. 8 Mar. 1709, James Prentiss, says Jackson; but he makes him, in a later part of his Hist. m. that same day, Eliz. d. of Henry of Marlborough; and Sarah m. 1708, Jonathan Willard. JOSEPH, Newton, s. of the preced. by w. Hannah had Thomas, b. 25 July 1697; Benjamin, 24 May 1699; Eliz. 23 Sept. 1701, d. next yr.; Joseph, 8 Apr. 1703; and perhaps Ebenezer. His w. d. Dec. 1730, and he m. 1732, Mercy Hyde, wh. d. 2 yrs. after, and he d. June 1750. JOSEPH, Newbury, fifth s. of Richard the third of the same, was a soldier, taken at the assault on Haverhill, 29 Aug. 1708, when his capt. Wainwright was k. by the Ind. and held in captiv. four yrs. of wh. he left a narrat. and d. 1754. See the excel. Hist. of Coffin, 331. NATHANIEL, Newbury, whose f. is not heard of by me, had James, and Mary, Dec. 1679. Coffin. NICHOLAS, Kennebunk 1651, was liv. at Salem 1700, as Willis shows, I. 67. RICHARD, Newbury 1637, shoemaker, br. of the first

Christopher, had brot. two s. and one d. and others he had here, tho. we
are igno. of the dates of any but the youngest, and approx. the eldest.
Their names were Richard, b. 1621, prob. the first b. John, Christopher,
Joanna, and Samuel, wh. was b. 20 Feb. 1646; and the f. d. 25 May
1647. RICHARD, Newbury, s. prob. eldest of the preced. b. in Eng. by
w. Abigail had Richard, b. 21 Feb. 1649; Thomas, 7 Sept. 1650; Abi-
gail, Mar. 1653; John, 22 June 1655; Hannah, 18 Dec. 1657; and
Rebecca, 23 May 1661. His w. d. 1 Mar. 1687, and he d. 1698, aged
76. RICHARD, Newbury, eldest s. of the preced. m. 18 Nov. 1673,
Hannah, d. of John Emery, had Hannah, b. 8 Nov. 1674; Richard, 20
Oct. 1676; John, 23 Sept. 1678; Samuel, 8 July 1680, d. at 5 yrs.;
Daniel, 8 Aug. 1682; Joseph, 18 Nov. 1686; Samuel, again, 2 May
1689; Stephen, 21 Apr. 1691; Thomas, 14 July 1695; and Mary, 15
Nov. 1697. His eldest s. was gr.f. of Richard of Pembroke, N. H. whose
gr.s. Richard was late Secr. of the State; and Stephen, his seventh s. was
f. of Gov. Josiah, b. at Amesbury, Nov. 1729, one of the signers of the
declara. of Indep. ROBERT, Plymouth, came in the Ann, July 1623, m.
1628, Mary, d. of Richard Warren, had Benjamin; Joseph, b. 1638;
beside six ds.; Rebecca, m. 20 Dec. 1649 William Harlow; Mary, m.
10 Sept. 1651, Richard Foster, and next, 8 July 1659, Jonathan Morey;
Sarah, m. 23 Dec. 1656, Samuel Rider of Yarmouth; Eliz. m. 20 Dec.
1661, Anthony Sprague, of Hingham; Lydia, b. 8 June 1647, m. James
Barnaby, and next John Nelson, of Middleborough; and Mercy, b. 10
Mar. 1651, m. 25 Dec. 1668, John Ivey of Boston. He was of the first
purch. of Dartmouth, and d. 1676, aged 73; and his wid. m. 24 Oct.
1692, or 1699, Thomas Delano. Unhap. both yrs. are giv. in Winsor's
Hist. ROBERT, Hartford, an orig. propr. had been of Cambridge 1632,
if, as is prob. he came in the Lion, arr. 16 Sept. of that yr. had Samuel;
Nathaniel, wh. d. unm.; Abigail; and Deborah, bapt. 8 Mar. 1646;
rem. to Northampton, a. 1655, there was k. by the Ind. 14 Mar. 1676.
Abigail, m. 17 Dec. 1657, John Stebbins of N. as his sec. w. and Deborah
m. John Cowles jr. of Hatfield. ROBERT, New London 1658, br. of
William, and heir to his est. had w. Sarah, wh. d. first, and he d. 1673.
He had no ch. nor is any relationsh. ascertain. betw. these brs. and either
of the scores with the same patronym. By nuncup. will he gave to the
town all his prop. for support of a sch. in grateful remembr. of wh. is
nam. the N. L. Bartlett Gram. Sch. and as he was a merch. of mark,
Bartlett's reef in the sound preserves his mem. ROBERT, Marblehead
1674, may have been br. of John of the same, was freem. 1683, and m.
Mary, youngest ch. of Rev. William Walton of the same. SAMUEL,
Newbury, s. of Richard the first, freem. 1672, m. 23 May 1671, Eliz. d.
of William Titcomb, had Eliz. b. 13 May 1672; Abigail, 14 Apr. 1674;

Samuel, 28 May 1676; Sarah, 7 July 1678; Richard, 13 Feb. 1680; Thomas, 13 Aug. 1681; Tirzah, 20 Jan. 1684; and Lydia, 5 Nov. 1687. His w. d. 26 Aug. 1690, and he d. 15 May 1732. SAMUEL, Northampton, eldest s. of Robert of the same, m. 1672, Mary, d. of James Bridgeman, wh. d. 1674, in so unnatur. manner, that her h. f. and others less expos. to mak. wrong judgm. ascrib. this to witchcraft, and upon that capit. charge was Mary, w. of Joseph Parsons, sent down to Boston for trial. In May 1675, she was acquit. By sec. w. Sarah, d. of the first Joseph Baldwin, he had Samuel, b. 1677; Sarah, 1679; Mindwell, 1681; Joseph, 1683; Ebenezer, 1685; Eliz. 1687; Preserved, 1689; William, 1693; David, 1695; and Benjamin, 1696; all these liv. to m. and the f. d. 1712. THOMAS, Watertown 1631, came in the employm. of William Pelham, I think, the yr. bef. and is call. by Bond, an orig. propr. and freem. 4 Mar. 1635, not 6, as he had print. p. 18, was made ens. 1639, and by w. Hannah had Hannah, bur. 26 Aug. 1639; Mehitable, b. 15 July 1640; Hannah, again, 6 Aug. 1642; Bathshua, 17 Apr. 1647; and Abial, 28 May 1651; was often selectman, and d. 26 Apr. 1654, aged a. 60. In his will the w. and four ch. are provid. for, and she d. 11 July 1676. Mehitable m. 7 Jan. 1658, Henry Spring; Hannah m. 19 Jan. 1668, John Kendall; Bathshua m. 23 Nov. 1671, John Applin; and Abial m. 24 Oct. 1669, Jonathan Saunderson. THOMAS, Newbury, s. of Richard the sec. m. 1685, Tirzah Titcomb, and d. 6 Apr. 1689. His wid. m. James Ordway. WILLIAM, New London 1647, d. in a. ten yrs. leav. wid. Susanna, but no ch. Of this name Farmer found, in 1834, sixteen gr. at Harv. eight at Yale, and thirty-one at the sev. other coll. of N. E.

BARTOLL, JOHN, Marblehead, by w. Parnel had Mary, b. 1 Feb. 1643. His wid. sold, 1665, to John Hooper, parcel of ld. at M. next to Robert Hooper. WILLIAM, Lynn, m. Susanna Woodbury, d. prob. of Humphrey of Salem, as sec. w. had Susanna, b. 25 Jan. 1666, wh. I presume, d. young, for at Salem he brot. to be bapt. 25 July 1669, William, John, Robert, Thomas, Samuel, Mary, and Alice; beside Andrew, 22 Aug. 1680. Rev. Cyrus A. min. of Boston, Bowd. Coll. 1832, is of later stock than this work regards.

BARTON, ‡ BENJAMIN, Warwick, s. of Rufus of Providence, m. 8 June 1669, Susanna, d. of the celebr. Samuel Gorton, was freem. 25 Mar. in the same yr. chos. an Assist. 1674, and d. 1720. In his will of 22 Oct. of that yr. are nam. ch. Rufus, Andrew, Phebe, Naomi, and Susanna. Ano. d. wh. had m. 16 May 1697, Jabez Green of Providence, was then prob. dec. EDWARD, perhaps of Exeter 1657, was of Cape Porpus to d. June 1671, leav. a wid. to admin. on his prop. EDWARD, Pemaquid, perhaps s. of the preced. was adm. freem. of Mass. 1674. JAMES, Newton 1688, had been of Boston, where he had good est. and was a rope-maker, by w. Margaret had Margaret; John, b. 5 Sept. 1686; and others, for wh. the rec. of b. furnishes no light. He d. 1729, aged 86, leav. wid. wh. d. 1731, aged 87. Jackson, in his will of 1729, finds two ds. if not three, as Margaret Simpkins, and Ruth Cook, gr.s. Thomas Stanton, to-gether with gr.s. James, John, Samuel, and Michael, all rememb. The four last may be thot. s. of John. His d. Margaret had m. 23 Dec. 1699, Robert Calef. JOHN, Salem, s. prob. of the preced. a physician, m. 20 Apr. 1676, Lydia Roberts, perhaps d. of Thomas of Boston, had John, b. 2 Feb. 1677, d. in 5 days; John, again, 30 Jan. 1678, d. young; Thomas, 17 July 1680; Zaccheus, 1 Apr. 1683; Eliz. Oct. 1685; and Samuel, 30 Aug. 1688. He was a capt. went home more than once, and d. on a voyage to Bermuda. Thomas and Samuel were men of good repute in Salem, the former a physician, many yrs. town clk. col. of the reg. m. 10 May 1710, Mary, gr.d. of Dept. Gov. Willoughby, had John, H. C. 1730; and d. 28 Apr. 1751; the latter had two ws. Mary Butler, and Eliz. Marston, and d. 13 Mar. 1772. MARMADUKE, of some part of Mass. was in 1643, condemn. to slavery, and to be brand. but in the Col. Rec. II. 16, the offence is not set out. MATTHEW, Salem, by w. Sarah had Matthew, b. 1682. RUFUS, Providence, had fled from persecut. by the Dutch at Manhattan, and sat down 1640, at Portsmouth, R. I. In Winth. II. 323 is a let. from him to the Gov. in 1648, and a few mos. after he d. in such a manner, as caus. one to be charg. with his murder, but without convict. By the town council of P. as Judge Brayton assures me, a sort of distrib. as testamenta. of his est. was made 20 Mar. 1666 to the ch. Eliz. Benjamin, wh. was then under 21 yrs. of age and Phebe, with wid. Margaret, wh. m. Walter Todd. Phebe m. 23 May 1671, Richard Cod-ner of Swanzey. *STEPHEN, Bristol, perhaps s. of the preced. or of Thomas, was rep. 1690, at Plymouth, Ct. and under the new chart. 1692, at Boston. THOMAS, Mass. 1646, may have been br. of Rufus.

BARTRAM, JOHN, Stratford, had Hannah, b. 1668, perhaps other ch. and d. 1675. WILLIAM, Lynn, by w. Sarah had Rebecca, and Esther, tw. b. 3 Apr. 1658; and Ellen, 17 Oct. 1660; perhaps rem. to Swanzey 1669. Baylies, III. 241. Yet I doubt the Swanzey man may have been ano. Esther m. 18 June 1677, John Newhall of L.

BASCOM, THOMAS, Dorchester 1634, came perhaps in July 1633 with the comp. that sat down at D. then, tho. Dr. Harris wish. to number him as of 1630, rem. to Windsor, there had Abigail, b. 27 June 1640; Thomas, 20 Feb. 1642; Hepzibah, 14 Apr. 1644; rem. to Northampton, a. 1661, and there d. 9 May 1682.. An elder d. Hannah m. John Broughton, and, next, William Janes; Abigail m. 2 Dec. 1656, John Ingersol; and Hep-zibah m. 1662, Robert Lyman. His wid. Avis d. 1676. THOMAS,

Northampton, s. of the preced. m. 1667, Mary, d. of Thomas Newell of Farmington, had Thomas, b. 1668 ; John, 1672, wh. went to Lebanon ; and Mary, wh. d. young; and he d. 11 Sept. 1689. Of this f. and s. the names are misprint. BOSTOUN, in Geneal. Reg. IX. 89, as are sev. others in the same list various. distort. As the copy was procur. from the Mass. archives for that publicat. by a careful hand, we can be sure, that the orig. signatures were not very plain. Farmer, in 1836, count. gr. of this name in the N. E. coll. ten, of wh. two ea. for Harv. Yale, and Dart.

BASS, JOHN, Braintree, s. of Samuel the first, m. 3 or 13 by rec. Feb. 1658, or (as differ. reading of the same numerals for mos. and days would express), 12 May 1657, Ruth, third d. of John Alden, the Mayflower passeng. had John, b. 26 Nov. 1658 ; Samuel, 25 Mar. 1660 ; Ruth, 28 Jan. 1662 ; Joseph, 5 Dec. 1665 ; Hannah, 22 June 1667; Mary, 11 Feb. 1669, or 70; and Sarah, 29 May 1672. His w. d. 12 Oct. 1674; and he d. 12 Sept. 1716, aged 83. JOSEPH, Braintree, younger br. of the preced. had w. Mary, wh. d. without ch. 15 Mar. 1678 ; and he, by w. Deborah, had Deborah, bapt. 23 Dec. 1700 ; and d. a. 16 Jan. 1714. PETER, York 1680. *SAMUEL, Roxbury 1632, freem. 14 May 1634 ; rem. in 1640 to Braintree, was the first deac. there 50 yrs. rep. 1641, and oft. later ; by w. Ann had Samuel, Mary, and Hannah, b. prob. in Eng. and John, Thomas, Joseph, and Sarah, b. here. His w. d. 5 Sept. 1663, and he d. 30 Dec. 1694, aged 93, hav. seen 162 descend. His d. Mary m. 20 Sept. 1647, Elder John Capen of Dorchester, as his sec. w.; Hannah m. 15 Nov. 1651, Stephen Paine ; and Sarah m. deac. John Stone of Watertown, a. 1662, bore him ten ch. next m. 10 May 1693, Joseph Penniman, and was liv. Sept. 1739. SAMUEL, Braintree, s. of the preced. b. in Eng. freem. 1648, m. Mary, d. of Robert Howard, had Mary, b. 26 Apr. 1643 ; and he d. early in 1653. His wid. m. 7 Apr. 1659, Isaac Jones. Samuel, the soldier in Dec. 1675 of the brave Capt. Johnson's comp. must have been that s. of John, wh. was less than sixteen yrs. old in that terrible campaign. THOMAS, Braintree, s. of Samuel the first, m. at Medfield, 4 Oct. 1660, Sarah, d. of Nicholas Wood of M. had Abigail, b. 2 Jan. 1668 ; Samuel, 20 Dec. 1669 ; Mary, 20 Apr. 1672 ; John, 26 Mar. 1675 ; and Mehitable, 18 Sept. 1678, wh. d. in Jan. foll. as had the mo. in Dec. He m. 1680, Susanna, prob. the wid. of Nathaniel Blanchard of Weymouth. He was deac. at B. Very large acco. of this fam. in later times may be seen in Thayer's Geneal. but of gr. at N. E. coll. in 1834 Farmer could have seen few, if any, exc. seven at Harv. three first of wh. were min.

BASSAKER, BUSSAKER, or BUSICOT, PETER, Boston, whipt for drunken. Sept. 1636, rem. bef. 1643, to Hartford, was after at Warwick most of his days, had d. Mary, wh. m. 15 Dec. 1670, Peter Spicer of Norwich; Abigail, wh. m. Hugh Stone; and Peter, perhaps only s. wh. accident. shot. hims.

BASSETT, ELISHA, Lynn, s. of William of the same, had w. Eliz. but I kn. no more. HENRY, Newport, was freem. 1655. JOHN, New Haven 1647, d. Feb. 1653, leav. Robert, and perhaps other ch. JOHN, New Haven, prob. s. of William, m. as is thot. Mercy, d. of Christopher Todd, and was a propr. 1685. JOSEPH, Hingham, m. Oct. 1677, Martha Hobart. NATHANIEL, Yarmouth 1672, s. of William the first comer, m. a d. of John Joyce. PETER, Boston, perhaps in 1678, a physician, may be the same wh. took o. of alleg. at York 1680. ROBERT, New Haven 1643, s. of John the first, b. in Eng. was a shoemaker, and town drummer. SAMUEL, New Haven, perhaps s. of John the first of the same, m. Mary, d. of Abraham Dickerman, was a propr. 1685. THOMAS, Windsor 1641, had come in the Christian 1635, aged 37, and prob. first sat down at Dorchester, tho. not ment. there, and bef. 1653 rem. to Fairfield, d. 1668, leav. w. and ch. but their names are not heard. * WILLIAM, Plymouth, came in the Fortune 1621, with w. Eliz. had Sarah, William, and Eliz. count. in the div. of cattle 1627, but neither of the three is reckon. in the div. of ld. 1623, so that we may believe they were b. in the interval, liv. at Duxbury in 1637, and was rep. 1640, and four yrs. more; in 1652, with Gov. Bradford and others join. in purch. of Dartmouth, rem. to Bridgewater, and d. 1667. His d. Sarah m. 1648, Peregrine White; and Eliz. m. 8 Nov. of the same yr. Thomas Burgess. WILLIAM, Lynn 1640, a farmer, had William; John, b. Nov. 1653; Miriam, Sept. 1655; Mary, Mar. 1657; Hannah, 25 Feb. 1660; Samuel, 18 Mar. 1664; and Rachel, 13 Mar. 1666. WILLIAM, New Haven, s. perhaps of John the first, b. in Eng. m. 1648, the wid. of William Ives, had Hannah, b. 13, bapt. 15 Sept. 1650; John, b. 1652; Samuel, 1655; Abiah, bapt. 7 Feb. 1658; and perhaps more, and d. 1684. Hannah m. 8 Nov. 1670, John Parker. A good-wife B. was execut. for a witch, it is thot. at Stratford. Kingsley, 101. WILLIAM, Salem, s. perhaps of William of Lynn, m. 25 Oct. 1675, Sarah Hood, d. of Richard, had Sarah, b. 6 Dec. 1676; William, 2 Oct. 1678; Mary, 13 June 1680; and John, 8 Sept. 1682. Descend. are wide. dispers. Rev. Nathan, H. C. 1719 of Charleston, S. C. was of the stock of the first comer William.

BASSOM, or BASSUM, THOMAS, Windsor, had Abigail, b. 7 June 1640; Thomas, 20 Feb. 1642; and Hepzibah, 14 July 1644. WILLIAM, Watertown 1636, as Dr. Francis, 131, gives the name; but Bond is silent, and I conject. that it was abbrev. for Bassumthwaite, wh. d. early, and his wid. had share of lds. with other Watertown sett. at Sudbury 1639. See Barry, Hist. of Framingham, 134. Yet one William Bassom there was a propr. at Wethersfield, perhaps br. of Thomas of Windsor.

BASTARD, JOSEPH, Fairfield, m. 1685, Hannah, wid. of Esbon Wakeman, and d. 1697, leav. good est. If research should show, that he came from Boston, it might be presum. that he was s. of Joseph Barstow.

BASTARR, JOSEPH, Cambridge, a tailor, had w. Mary, and d. Mary, b. 13 May 1643; rem. to Boston 1647, had Joseph, 25 or 29 Sept. of that yr.; Benjamin, 4 Apr. 1652; Susanna, 1 Sept. 1654; and John, 25 Mar. 1657.

BATCHELOR, or BATCHELDER. See Bachiler.

BATEMAN, EDWARD, Maine, was one of the purch. from the Ind. Sachem, Robin Hood, of the region a. Woolwich, 1654. Drake's Book of the Ind. III. 97. ELEAZER, Woburn, m. 2 Nov. 1686, Eliz. d. of Joseph Wright, had Eliz. b. 11 July 1688; Mary, 16 June 1696; Joseph, 7 Sept. 1699; Martha, 16 Feb. 1702; Thomas, 20 May 1704; and Ruth, 25 July 1707, JOHN, Boston, by w. Hannah had John, b. Dec. 1644; Hannah, 10 Mar. 1646; Eliz. 30 Sept. 1647; all bapt. 14 May 1648; Sarah, bapt. 7 Oct. 1649, tho. town rec. makes her b. 6 May 1651; Rachel, b. 28 May, bapt. 1 June 1651; Mary, 16, bapt. 23 Jan. 1653, d. young; William, 8, bapt. 11 Mar. 1655; Joseph, b. 28 Aug. 1658; and Mary, again, bapt. 9 Sept. 1660. Perhaps he rem. to Woburn, for there Hannah m. 12 June 1667, Zechariah Green; and Sarah m. 3 July 1671, John Green, both of W. JOHN, Woburn, s. perhaps of the preced. m. 30 June 1680, Abigail Richardson, prob. d. of Theophilus, had Abigail, b. 18 Oct. 1682, d. soon; Abigail, again, 1 Jan. 1685; John, 13 Aug. 1687; William, 29 Sept. 1690, d. young; William, again, 3 May 1693; and Peter, 3 Nov. 1695. Perhaps he rem. JOSEPH, Boston, s. of John of the same, was of Turner's comp. in Philip's war, 1676. NATHANIEL, Watertown 1640, is not ment. by Bond. THOMAS, Concord, freem. 18 May 1642, d. 6 Feb. 1669, aged 54, leav. by w. Martha, s. Thomas, Peter, wh. d. at Woburn 13 Feb. 1676, John, and Ebenezer; beside ds. Martha, Eliz. wh. was b. 6 Mar. 1660, and Sarah. Eight days bef. he d. all these are nam. in his will. WILLIAM, Charlestown 1638, had long bef. been in the Col. as he was adm. freem. 18 May 1631, so that he prob. came in the fleet with Winth. perhaps rem. to Chelmsford, tho. as two of the name were in Mass. it is uncert. for WILLIAM of Concord, br. of Thomas, was prob. the freem. of 2 June 1641 (since his name in the list is next to that of William Hunt of C.), yet he rem. to Fairfield 1650, or earlier there d. 1658, in his will of 24 Mar. 1656, giv. £5 to gr.ch. Joseph Middlebrook, and one half of his est. to s. Thomas, "now of Concord," the other half to s.-in-law Henry Lyon.

BATES, BENJAMIN, Hingham, youngest s. of Clement that he brot. from Eng. was freem. 1672, and d. of smallpox 28 Nov. 1678. He was a lieut.

had w. Jane, nam. in his will, made two weeks bef. his d. giv. est. to her
and the ch. of his br. hav. as we are therefore led to infer, no ch. of his
own. BENJAMIN, Hingham, s. of James of the same, prob. rem. after d.
of his f. to Huntington, L. I., but many yrs. bef. was a soldier in Dec. 1675
of Johnson's comp. CLEMENT, Hingham, a tailor, said to be from Co.
Herts, but more prob. from Kent, came in the Elizabeth, 1635, aged 40,
with w. Ann, 40, and ch. James, 14; Clement, 12; Rachel, 8; Joseph,
5; Benjamin, 2; and two serv. and here had Samuel, and perhaps other
ch. was freem. 3 Mar. 1636, and d. 17 Sept. 1671. CLEMENT, Hingham,
s. of the preced. brot. from Eng. by his f. d. bef. 1669, leav. wid. Ruth,
wh. in a petitn. to the governm. of the Col. Apr. 1676, set forth, that she
had two s. Clement and Solomon, serv. with Capt. Lothrop when "the
flower of Essex" was slain, that Clement was k. by the Ind. soon after at
Westfield, wherefore she pray. that Solomon might be disch. EDWARD,
Boston 1633, came with Thomas Leverett, as his apprent. in the Griffin,
freem. 9 Mar. 1637, was disarm. as a favorer of Wheelwright, had John,
bapt. 23 Jan. 1642. * EDWARD, Weymouth, freem. 13 Mar. 1639, had
Prudence, b. 11 June that yr. and Increase, 28 Dec. 1641, was rep. 1639–41
and 60, as well as ch. Elder. EDWARD, Weymouth, perhaps s. of the preced. by w. Eliz. had Susanna, b. 6 Feb. 1680; Edward, 3 Feb. 1683; John,
16 Jan. 1686; and Mary, 11 Dec. 1697. FRANCIS, Topsfield 1661, m.
Ann Oldham, d. of Sarah O. and gr.d. of Richard North, had Ebenezer,
b. 20 Jan. 1662; but my dilig. inquir. has not learn. what Oldham m.
Richard North's d. GEORGE, Boston, a thatcher, freem. 25 May 1636,
liv. at Muddy riv. now Brookline, went to Exeter, but came back. Belkn.
I. 20. INCREASE, Weymouth, s. of Edward the first, by w. Mary had
Edward, b. 31 Jan. 1682; Ebenezer, 1 Mar. 1686; and Ann, 23 Aug.
1695. * JAMES, Dorchester, husbandman, came in the Elizabeth, 1635,
aged 53; with w. Alice, 52; and ch. Lydia, 20; Mary, 17; Margaret,
12; and James, 9; freem. 7 Dec. 1636, selectman next yr. and after;
rep. for Hingham, 1641. He was perhaps br. of Clement, and d. 1655.
His wid. d. 14 Aug. 1657. Lydia m. Roger Williams of D.; Mary m.
Hopestill Foster; and Margaret m. Christopher Gibson. He had a s.
Richard, wh. liv. at a hamlet, call. the town of Lid in Co. Kent, whence,
prob. the fam. came. JAMES, Hingham, eldest s. prob. of Clement of the
same, m. 19 Apr. 1642, or 3, Ruth Lyford, that may be conject. as d. of
Rev. John, left by him when he went to Virg. had John, b. 1649 at Scituate, where he liv. some yrs. but ret. to H. had Benjamin, bapt. 15 July
1655, perhaps others; and d. 5 July 1689. He petitn. the Gov. and
Assist. for relief on acco. of two s. prest into the serv. against the Ind.
His wid. d. 9 Mar. foll. Deane thot. him s. of James of Dorchester,
but so do not I. His d. Rachel m. 8 May 1684, Caleb Lincoln.

*JAMES, Haddam 1667, prob. s. of James of Dorchester, where he m. Ann, d. of the first Henry Withington, and soon after went home, and came again soon, perhaps went again to Eng. and came back soon, may have first been at Huntington, L. I. d. bef. 1692, when of his ch. at Haddam were Samuel, bapt. at Dorchester, 18 June 1648; James; John; Hannah; Margaret, bapt. at D. 19 June 1664; Mary, bapt 11 Mar. 1666; and Eliz. He was rep. for H. 1670, and often after. Mary m. 16 Aug. 1685, William Hough of Saybrook. The late Hon. Isaac C. Bates, U. S. senator, was prob. a descend. by one of these s. who rem. to Durham, whose s. rem. to Granville, Mass. JOHN, Weymouth, by w. Susan had Edward, b. 10 Dec. 1655; was perhaps of Chelmsford 1666, freem. 1682. See Allen, Hist. of C. 169. JOHN, Haddam, perhaps br. of James of the same, was of Stamford 1669, had John, b. 1678; and Solomon 1680. JOHN, New London 1677, had bapt. there John, 4 May 1679; Solomon, 1 Aug. 1680; and Sarah, 27 Aug. 1682; but, no more being ment. of him, I think he may be the same as the preced. easily rem. from town to town. JOSEPH, Hingham, s. of Clement, b. in Eng. m. Jan. 1659, Esther Hilliard, perhaps d. of Anthony of the same, had Joseph, Caleb, Hannah, Joshua, Bathsheba, Clement, Eleazer, and perhaps others. He was freem. 1672. JOSEPH, Hingham, s. of the preced. m. 3 Jan. 1684, Mary, d. of the first Samuel Lincoln. ROBERT, Wethersfield 1640, rem. to Stamford, there d. 11 June 1675, leav. s. John; d. Mary Ambler, w. of Abraham, and s.-in-law John Cross, ment. in his will of that date. He was one of the first purch. of S. 30 Oct. 1640. ROBERT, Lynn, had John, wh. d. 5 Mar. 1672; Rebecca, b. 29 Aug. 1673; and Sarah, 16 July 1676. SAMUEL, Hingham, youngest s. of Clement the first, m. 1666, Lydia, d. of Thomas Lapham of Scituate, was freem. 1672. SAMUEL, Saybrook, m. 2 May 1676, Mary, d. of Robert Chapman of the same, had Samuel, b. 15 Apr. foll. d. at 8 mos.; Ann, 19 Sept. 1678; Silence, 27 July 1680; Samuel, again, 8 Nov. 1682; James, 16 Dec. 1683; Robert, 22 Dec. 1686; Stephen, 1 June 1689; Ephraim, 29 May 1692; Daniel, 18 Aug. 1697; and d. 28 Dec. 1699.

BATSON, *JOHN, Kennebunk, perhaps s. of Stephen, m. 1660, Eliz. Saunders, perhaps d. of John of Wells, was rep. at the Gen. Assemb. at York 1682 and 4. ROBERT, Marshfield, m. 13 July 1676, Ann Winter, perhaps d. of Christopher. STEPHEN, Saco 1636, then had w. Mary, and d. Margery, rem. to Cape Porpus, or Kennebunk 1653, was made freem. that yr. Folsom, 33, 124. From his will of 8 Mar. 1674, it is learn. that he had s. John; and d. Eliz. Ashley, perhaps w. of William; d. Margery Young, perhaps w. of Rowland; and d. Mary Brookhouse, of whose h. I search in vain for indicat. beside gr.ch. John Trott, perhaps s. of Simon.

BATT, * CHRISTOPHER, Newbury, tanner, came from the city of Salisbury, Co. Wilts, in the Bevis, emb. at Southampton, 1638, aged 37, with w. Ann, 32; sis. Dorothy, 20; and five ch. under 10 yrs. freem. 13 Mar. 1639, rem. to Salisbury, of wh. he was rep. 1640, 1, 3, and 50, rem. to Boston, and there was casu. k. 10 Aug. 1661 by a s. firing at a mark in the orchard. His wid. made her will 14 Mar. 1679, call. hers. 76. We kn. not the names of those ch. he brot. from Eng. but one was prob. Thomas, for he carr. on the business of his f. at B. Eight or more were b. in this country, for Coffin ment. thirteen, yet gives dates of only three, John, b. at S. 4 Mar. 1641; Paul, and Barnabas, tw. 18 Feb. 1643. Others (part b. in Eng.) were Christopher, Ann, Samuel, Jane, Sarah, Abigail, Timothy, Ebenezer, and Eliz. This last d. 6 July 1652, perhaps young; Ann m. 12 June 1657, Edmund Angier; Jane m. 3 Apr. 1661, Dr. Peter Toppan, and may therefore be supposed to have been b. on our side of the water, while the other side must be thot. birthplace of Ann, as she was sec. w. of Angier. Christopher was of Dover in 1662; Paul was a glazier, and Timothy a tailor, both freem. 1673, at Boston, and both prob. certain one of them interest. in the tannery; and of Samuel it is said that he was a min. in Eng. and infer. that he never came back to this ld. if he was, as is prob. b. here. NICHOLAS, Newbury, perhaps br. of the preced. came in the James from Southampton, with w. Lucy, arr. at Boston 3 June 1635, is call. in the ship's clearance, "of the Devizes, linen weaver," had Sarah, b. 12 June 1640, and two more ds. He d. 6 Dec. 1677; and his wid. Lucy d. 26 Jan. 1679.

BATTELLE, or BATTLE, JOHN, Dedham, eldest s. of Thomas, m. 18 Nov. 1678, Hannah Holbrook, had Hannah, b. 26 July 1680; Mary, 12 Mar. 1684; John, 17 Apr. 1689; Ebenezer, 2 Jan. 1692; and d. 30 Sept. 1713. JONATHAN, Dedham, br. of the preced. m. 15 Apr. 1690, Mary Onion, perhaps d. of Robert, had Martha, b. 13 Mar. foll.; Jonathan, 3 Jan. 1693; Sarah, 20 Oct. 1698; and Abigail, 11 Dec. 1699. ROBERT, Boston, d. 23 Dec. 1658, perhaps was only trans. visit. and if not, I can tell no more, but that in Dearborn's book, call. Boston Notions, p. 44, he is call. freem. 1657, when no such name appears, nor even any bapt. name of Robert in that yr. THOMAS, Dedham 1642, m. 5 Sept. 1648, Mary, d. of Joshua Fisher, had Mary, b. 6 bapt. 12 May 1650; John, 1, bapt. 3 July 1653; Sarah, b. 1654; Jonathan, 24 July 1658; and Martha, 19 Aug. bapt. 9 Sept. 1660, d. at 14 yrs. He was freem. 1654, in 1664 liv. at Sudbury, but of D. again in 1674. His w. d. 7 Aug. 1691, and he d. 8 Feb. 1706, call. "the aged." In the will of their gr.f. Fisher, of wh. Battle was an overseer, most of the ch. are ment. Mary m. 20 Mar. 1677, John Bryant; and Sarah m. 23 Oct. 1679, Silas Titus. Very improb. seems to me the recent tradit. that he came to N. E. from France; and Cothren enlarges the extrav. of it by transfer of the circumst. imagin. to his s. John. In the will of John Luson, a neighb. of Battelle, John and Mary B. were kind. rememb. but he gave the larger part of his prop. (having no near relative this side of Eng.) to their f. spelt by the testator, Battely.

BATTEN, BENJAMIN, Boston, merch. m. Oct. 1671, Eliz. d. of John Cullick, Esqr. HUGH, Dorchester 1658, m. Ursula, d. of John Greenway, and d. 8 June 1689. JOHN, Lynn, had John, b. 1 Sept. 1671.

BATTER, * EDMUND, Salem, a maltster from Salisbury, Co. Wilts, came in the James from Southampton, Apr. 1635, arr. 3 June, with w. Sarah, freem. 3 Mar. foll. rep. 1637, and 16 yrs. more. His w. d. 20 Nov. 1669, and he m. 8 June foll. Mary, d. of maj.-gen. Daniel Gookin, had Edmund, b. 8 Jan. 1674; and d. 1685, aged 76. Other ch. were Daniel, Mary, and Eliz. but prob. most of these, if not all, were by former w. EDMUND, Salem, s. of the preced. m. Martha, d. of Benjamin Pickman the first. JOSEPH, and TIMOTHY of Northampton 1668, as print. in Geneal. Reg. IX. 88, are fictitious people, the real names being of s. of Edward Baker. NICHOLAS, Lynn, freem. 14 Dec. 1638, had gr. of 60 acres. Lewis, 103, tells no more of him.

BATTING, or BATTENS, William, Saco, a. 1659, Scarborough 1663.

BAXTER, DANIEL, Salem 1639, by w. Eliz. had Eliz. b. Sept. 1644; Susanna, Sept. 1646; Rebecca; and Priscilla, June 1652. Susanna m. 12 July 1665, Isaac Hyde. GEORGE, Providence, in 1650 was constitu. umpire betw. the Dutch Col. of New Netherlands and New Haven Col. for settl. the boundary. Hutch. I. 159; but in Appendix, 515, his signat. is erron. print. Theo. Baxter. See Haz. II. 169, 173. Bancroft, II. 306. Knowles, 319. He carr. the royal chart. 1663, from Boston to Newport. GREGORY, Roxbury 1630, came, prob. in the fleet with Winth. freem. 6 Mar. 1632, by w. Margaret Paddy, wh. d. 13 Feb. 1662, had Bethulia, or Bethia, b. June 1632; Abigail, Sept. 1634; and John, 1 Dec. 1639; rem. next yr. to Braintree, and d. 21 June 1659. His will of 2, with codic. of 19 of that mo. names the w. ch. Bethia, and Abigail, only, as ws. of their h's. and s. John. See Geneal. Reg. IX. 136. Bethia m. Samuel Deering; and Abigail m. 29 Nov. 1650, Joseph Adams. JAMES, Marblehead 1668. JOHN, Braintree, s. of Gregory, m. 24 June 1660, Hannah, d. of Thomas White of Weymouth, had (beside sev. other ch. of wh. Hannah, w. of Joseph Dyer of Weymouth was one) Joseph, b. 4 June 1676, H. C. 1693, min. of Medfield, ord. 21 Apr. 1697. He was a lieut. and d. 29 Apr. 1719. JOHN, Charlestown, m. 2 Mar. 1659, Hannah Trumbull, d. of John of the same, and d. 15 May 1687, aged a. 60; and his wid. d. 27 Apr. 1703. JOHN, Salem, m. 25 Nov. 1667, Abigail Whitney (but, of so common a surname, it is diffic. to find the f.) had John, b. 14 Dec. 1668; Abigail, 15 Dec. 1670; Eliz. 25 May 1673; and Mary,

26 Dec. 1674, wh. d. within 9 mos. NICHOLAS, Boston 1639, mariner, by w. Ann had Mary, b. Feb. 1640, bapt. 1 Sept. 1644, wh. m. 1658, John Bull. But the rec. says, also, that by the same maid. name she m. 1660, Thomas Buttolph; and this is true, and the other rec. no doubt a mistake. NICHOLAS, Boston, prob. s. of the preced. was gunner at the castle 1674–6, perhaps later, and d. 10 Jan. 1692. RICHARD, Hingham, came 1638, in the Diligent from old Hingham, employ. by Francis James, says Lincoln in Centen. Addr. 44. THOMAS, Fairfield 1654, had w. Bridget, wh. for his desertion of her, obt. divorce in 1662. See Haz. II. 285. WILLIAM, Marblehead 1674. Six of this name had, in 1815, been gr. at Harv.

BAY, or BAYES, MATTHEW, Ipswich 1659. THOMAS, Dedham, by w. Ann had Ruth, b. 2, bapt. 16 July 1643; and Thomas, 1, bapt. 22 Mar. 1646; rem. to Boston.

BAYLEY, BENJAMIN, Boston 1673. GUIDO, Salem, by w. Eliz. had Eliz. b. 27 July 1642; and Joseph, 6 Nov. 1644. HENRY, Salem 1638, liv. on Beverly side 1671. HENRY, Salisbury, s. perhaps of John the first, by w. Rebecca had Henry; and Rebecca, b. a. 1640. ISAAC, Newbury, s. of John the sec. of same, m. 13 June 1683, Sarah, d. of John Emery of the same, had Isaac, b. 30 Dec. 1683; Joshua, 30 Oct. 1685; David, 12 Dec. 1687; Judith, 11 Feb. 1690; and Sarah, 11 Feb. 1692. His w. d. 1 Apr. 1694; and he m. sec. w. 5 Sept. 1700, Rebecca Bartlett, but prob. had no more ch. at least Coffin names none. JAMES, Rowley 1641, by w. Lydia had John, b. 1642; James, 1650; Thomas, 1653; and Samuel, 1658; beside Damaris, w. of Thomas Leaver; and Lydia, w. of . . . . . . Platt, but whether of Abel, or James, or John, or Jonas, or Jonathan, or Samuel, my inquiries do not ascertain. JAMES, Salisbury, s. of John the sec. was freem. 1673, m. 17 Sept. 1672, Mary, d. of George Carr of the same, had Mary, b. 5 July 1673, and Isaac, 22 Oct. 1681; rem. to Salem vill. now Danvers, there was a preach. but neither Bentley's Hist. nor Felt's Ann. of Salem (the best places to seek for such informat.) tells us whether he was ever ord. yet it is safely infer. that he was not, for the latter writer instr. us, that in Apr. 1680, a commit. was chos. to obtain ano. preach. instead of him; see II. 589. We kn. also, that he was succeed. by the unfortun. George Burrows. By Sprague, Ann. of the Amer. Pulpit, I. 186, Bailey's d. is mark. for 1707, and Coffin, 351, more precise, 17 Jan. at Roxbury. I venture a conject. that he is the one ord. at Weymouth, 26 Sept. 1703, as told in 1 Mass. Hist. Coll. IX. 195; yet the rec. of d. at Roxbury of James Bailey calls him Esqr. JOHN, Salisbury, a weaver from Chippenham, Co. Wilts, came, in the Angel Gabriel, from Bristol, Apr. 1635, and was cast away at Pemaquid, in the great storm of 15 Aug. He rem. 1650 to Newbury (where prob.

he had been resid. bef. settlem. of S.), and d. 2 Nov. of next yr. His w. never came over the ocean, and he was afraid to go back for her and his other childr. Robert and two or more ds. But in his will he tried to tempt them hither by parts of his est. JOHN, Salisbury, s. of the preced. came with his f. m. Eleanor Emery, perhaps d. of John of Newbury, had ·Rebecca, b. 24 Nov. 1641; and John, 18 May 1643, d. at 20 yrs. rem. to Newbury, and there had Sarah, 17 Aug. 1644; Joshua, d. young; Joseph, 4 Apr. 1648; James, 12 Sept. 1650, H. C. 1669; Joshua, again, 17 Feb. 1653; Isaac, 22 July 1654; Rachel, 19 Oct. 1662; Judith, 3 Aug. 1665, d. at 3 yrs. He was freem. 1669, and d. Mar. 1691, aged 78. JOHN, Rowley, eldest s. of James of the same, freem. 1669, m. Mary, d. of Thomas Mighill of the same, had Nathaniel, b. 1675; Thomas, 1677; and James, 1680, beside two ds. JOHN, Weymouth, freem. 1673, and ano. JOHN of Weymouth, freem. 1681, prob. belong to fams. brief acco. of wh. appears under Bailey. JONAS, Scarborough 1650–63, sw. alleg. to Mass. 1658, m. Eliz. wid. of George Dearing, for a first w. and next Elinor, wid. of John Jackson, wh. surv. him, and he d. 1663. His will of 11 Nov. of that yr. pro. 9 Feb. foll. direct. his body to be bur. next his w. Eliz. in the orchard, gave most of his est. to w. Elinor, legacies to six s. of Robert Jordan, to Francis Neale sen. and his s. and two ds. to John Jackson, perhaps s. of his w. to his br. Nicholas Baley, as he spel. the name, to Eliz. and John Bryers and others, but he had no ch. JOSEPH, Huntington, L. I. was adm. as freem. of Conn. 1664. JOSEPH, Newbury, s. of John the sec. by w. Priscilla had Rebecca, b. 25 Oct. 1675; Priscilla, 31 Oct. 1676; John, 16 Sept. 1678; Joseph, 28 Jan. 1681; Hannah, 9 Sept. 1683; Daniel, 10 June 1686; Judith, 11 Feb. 1690; Lydia, 25 Nov. 1695; and Sarah, 14 Feb. 1698. He rem. to Kennebunk, there was k. by the Ind. Oct. 1723. NICHOLAS, Saco 1663, br. of Jonas, had perhaps been of New Haven 1644, and may have been br. of Samuel at New Haven in the same yr. See Bailey. ROBERT, came from London in the Hopewell, Capt. Babb, in the autumn of 1635, aged 23; and ano. ROBERT, came in the Confidence from Southampton, 1638, aged 23; but nothing more is to be heard of either of them. SAMUEL, Boston 1685. THOMAS, New London 1652, m. 10 Jan. 1656, Lydia, d. of William Redfyn, or Redfield, had Mary, b. 14 Feb. 1657; Thomas, 5 Mar. 1659; John, Apr. 1661; William, 17 Apr. 1664; James, 26 Sept. 1666; Joseph; and Lydia, bapt. 3 Aug. 1673, wh. m. Andrew Lester; was a soldier under Lothrop and fell at Bloody brook, 18 Sept. 1675. His wid. m. 1676, William Thorne; the s. Thomas, John, and William left descend.; Mary m. Andrew Davis.

BAYNLY, THOMAS, Concord, d. 18 May 1643, leav. prob. no w. nor ch. See his nuncup. will in Geneal. Reg. II. 185, and in Oct. preced. he was witness.

BAYSEY, JOHN, Hartford, weaver, an orig. propr. by w. Eliz. had
Lydia, wh. m. John Baker; Mary, wh. m. Samuel Burr; and Eliz. bapt.
24 Aug. 1645, wh. m. Paul Peck; and d. 1671.   His wid. d. 1673.   In
the will made the last yr. of his life, he gave ld. to d. Eliz. and her s.
Paul Peck.   A s. of Baker, and a gr.s. of Burr had ea. the name Baysey
giv. for perpetuat.

BAZICOTT, PETER, Warwick, one of the freem. 1655; and without kn.
whether this were a Dutch, French, or English name, we may be sure
it was variously spelt.   See Bassaker.

BEACH, or BEECH, BENJAMIN, Stratford 1659, was s. of Richard of
New Haven, I judge, and m. 1 Feb. 1678, Sarah, d. of John Welles of
the same, had Sarah, b. 4 May 1679; and Hannah, Sept. 1681; and he
d. 10 Apr. 1715.   His wid. m. Ambrose Thompson.   ISAAC, Newton
1678, then part of Cambridge, had w. Mary, wh. d. 1724, and he d. 1735,
aged 90, without ch.   In Hist. of N. it is said, that he gave his prop.
1727, to the first Isaac Jackson, to wh. he had taught the carpenter's trade.
JOHN, Stratford 1660, s. of Richard, of New Haven, if he were not br.
as seems prob. m. a d. of Thomas Staples, of Fairfield, was one of the
early sett. at Wallingford 1670.   RICHARD, Cambridge 1635, soon after
at Watertown, had (by w. Mary) John, b. 6 Aug. 1639; and Mary, 11
Dec. 1641; and by sec. w. Martha had Isaac, 5 July 1646; Martha, 10
Mar. 1650; Abigail, 4 June 1653; Joseph, 15 Dec. 1655; and Richard,
28 Oct. 1657; and d. 24 Oct. 1674.   Martha m. 24 Jan. foll. Joseph
Whitney.   RICHARD, New Haven 1639, one of the signers of the orig.
compact, m. a. 1640, the wid. of Andrew Hull, and had, in her right, there
bapt. in 1642, Mary, b. in June of that yr.; Benjamin, b. Oct. 1644;
Azariah, July 1646; and Mercy 1648; all three bapt. 21 May of that
yr. rem. to New London 1667.   THOMAS, Milford 1658, br. of Richard,
had liv. at New Haven, and there, by w. Sarah, d. of deac. Richard Platt of
M. had Sarah, b. 1 Mar. 1654; but at M. had John, 19 Oct. 1655; Mary,
1657; Samuel, 1660; and Zopher, 1662; and he d. in that yr.   His wid.
m. Miles Merwin, and d. 1670.   Thirteen of this name are seen in the
last list of gr. at Yale.

BEACHAM.   See Beauchamp.

BEACHEN, ROBERT, Fairfield 1669.

BEADLE, JOSEPH, Marshfield 1652, d. 1 Sept. 1672.   NATHANIEL,
Salem, m. 20 Apr. 1671, Mary Hicks, perhaps d. of Richard of Boston,
had Thomas, b. 21 Jan. 1672; Mary, 20 Nov. 1673; Nathaniel, 17 Dec.
1675; John, 29 Apr. 1678, d. soon; Eliz. 25 Oct. 1679; and John, again,
12 Aug. 1683.   SAMUEL, Charlestown 1658, rem. to Salem, by w. Susanna had Abigail, b. 24 Sept. 1661, d. next mo. and his w. d. 13 Feb.
foll. and he d. 10 Mar. 1664.   SAMUEL, Salem, perhaps s. of the preced.

m. 10 June 1668, Hannah Lemon, d. of Robert of the same, had Nathaniel, b. 29 Mar. 1669; Samuel, 11 Oct. 1672; Thomas, 28 Nov. 1673, d. under 3 yrs. and Susanna, 20 Apr. 1676. Bef. this date he was wound. in Philip's war, and as an invalid, in 1683, was permit. to keep an inn. THOMAS, Salem, mariner, perhaps br. of Nathaniel of the same, m. 18 Sept. 1679, Eliz. d. of Abraham Drake of Hampton, had Eliz. b. 9 July 1681; Mary, 5 Apr. 1683; Thomas, 16 Mar. 1685, d. young; Benjamin, 7 Sept. 1687; Thomas, again, 10 Feb. 1690; and John, 14 Feb. 1692. He was capt. 1686, trad. to Barbadoes, and d. 23 May 1700 at Gloucester.

BEAL, or BEALS, ABRAHAM, Charlestown, by w. Catharine had Abraham, wh. d. 16 Jan. 1657; Abraham, again, 17 Nov. foll. and Isaac, 10 Oct. 1662. ARTHUR, York 1680. BENJAMIN, Dorchester 1674, rem. to Boston 1676. CALEB, Hingham, s. of John, b. in Eng. m. 30 Dec. 1664, Eliz. Huet, perhaps d. of Thomas of the same, had a d. b. 30 Mar. 1666, d. soon; Caleb, 17 Mar. 1670; Joseph, 7 Jan. 1672; Solomon, bapt. June 1673, d. soon; Eliz. 18 Nov. 1674; Josiah, 31 May 1676, d. soon; Josiah, again, 24 Oct. 1677; Joshua, 6 Nov. 1678, d. soon; Joshua, again, 6 Sept. 1680; Ruth, 25 Mar. 1683; and Benjamin, 2 June 1687, d. soon; was freem. 1672, and d. 18 June 1716, aged 79. His wid. d. 31 Dec. 1721. Ruth m. 1703, Peter Lincoln. JACOB, Hingham, youngest s. of John, freem. 1672, d. unm. 7 Jan. 1718. *JEREMIAH, Hingham, br. of the preced. b. in Eng. m. 18 Nov. 1652, Sarah, d. of William Ripley of the same, had Jeremiah, bapt. 13 May 1655; Sarah, 3 July 1659, wh. m. 21 Jan. 1680, John Lane; Lazarus, b. 7 Sept. 1661; Phebe, 2 Mar. 1664, d. next yr. Mary, 6 May 1666; and Eliz. 16 May 1669, wh. m. 1708, Ephraim Lane; was freem. 1657, rep. 1692 and 1705, and d. 10 Aug. 1716, aged 85. * JOHN, Hingham, a shoemaker from old Hingham, Co. Norf. came with w. five s. three ds. and two serv. in the Diligent, 1638, from London, adm. freem. 13 Mar. 1639, had Jacob, bapt. 2 Oct. 1642, and no other ch. perhaps here, exc. Rebecca, wh. d. unm. after Oct. 1657. He was rep. 1649, and his w. Nazareth d. 23 Sept. 1658; but he took sec. w. 10 Mar. 1659, Mary, wid. of Nicholas Jacob, d. 1688 (as Sewall in his Diary, sub. 1 Apr. ment.), in his 100th yr. tho. perhaps the report may not have been exact. Of his ds. Martha m. 16 May 1640, it is said, William Falloway, of Plymouth, and next 29 June 1649, Samuel Dunham; Mary m. 30 Dec. 1647, James Whiton; and Sarah m. 22 Mar. 1649, Thomas Marsh, and next 1 Sept. 1662, Edmund Sheffield of Braintree. His will of 27 Sept. 1687, pro. 18 June foll. names the six s. and ds. Sarah, Mary, and Martha. JOHN, Hingham, s. of Edmund (wh. never came over), being a. to go home, made his will 26 Oct. 1657, pro. 28 July foll. as print. in Geneal. Reg. IX. 38, by wh. we are taught that the ch. of John the first were his cous. and infer, that he had no w. or ch. JOHN, Hingham, s. prob. eldest, of the first John of the same, freem. 1672, m. 6 Jan. 1659 the w. Eliz. wh. brot. him Eliz. b. 19 Nov. foll. and d. next yr. and he m. 14 Nov. 1660, Mary Gill, d. of Thomas, had Mary, 7 Sept. 1661, wh. m. 3 Sept. 1683, John Stowell ; John, 26 Mar. 1665, d. soon; John, again, 17 Sept. 1667, d. next yr.; John, again, 19 Dec. 1669 ; Thomas, 15 Mar. 1672; and Hannah, 13 Mar. 1676, wh. m. Nathaniel Hobart; and d. 12 Sept. 1694. JOSEPH, Portsmouth, sent over by Mason the patentee in 1631. Adams, 18. JOSHUA, Hingham, s. of John the first, by w. Eliz. wh. d. 12 Jan. 1689, had Eliz. b. May 1663, d. soon; a s. 25 Jan. 1665, wh. d. in few wks. Sarah, 7 Oct. 1667, prob. d. young; Abigail, 24 Apr. 1671, wh. m. Stephen French; and Josiah, 4 June 1676, d. in few days. He m. 10 Apr. 1689, Mary, wid. of Samuel Stowell, but prob. had no other ch. for in his will he ment. only his ch. Stephen and Abigail French, and gr.ch. Samuel, David, Jonathan, Daniel, Eliz. Mary and Hannah French, their ch. and he d. bef. 7 Apr. 1718. * NATHANIEL, Hingham, br. of the preced. b. in Eng. was perhaps at Marshfield 1643, but for short time, freem. 1650, rep. 1677, 83, 91 and 3, d. 20 Dec. 1708. His will pro. 29 Dec. foll. names s. Nathaniel, eldest s. bapt. Oct. 1648 ; Martha, bapt. Aug. 1646, wh. had m. 1668, John Chubbuck, w. of Samuel Stodder; d. Mary Lee of Boston; gr.d. Sarah (d. of Sarah Greenleaf, dec.), gr.s. Thomas Baker (s. of d. Christiana, wh. was perhaps bapt. 19 Nov. 1654, m. 1 Nov. 1674, Thomas B. and d. 20 Sept. 1677) ; gr.s. Solomon Beal (s. of Nathaniel) ; d. Hannah, wh. m. 15 Dec. 1676, John Fearing; and gr.s. Thomas Chubbuck ; but he had, also, not ment. in that docum. John, bapt. 25 Aug. 1650, d. at 5 yrs.; John, again, 8 Mar. 1657, d. soon; John, again, b. 7 Dec. 1659, d. under 9 yrs.; and Susanna, wh. m. 14 Dec. 1686, Benjamin Jones, wh. prob. d. bef. her f. NATHANIEL, Hingham, s. of the preced. serv. in brave Capt. Johnson's comp. Dec. 1675, d. bef. his f. as I judge, leav. s. Solomon. ROGER, Saco 1658, perhaps a Quaker, at least was charg. with disturb. pub. worship. SAMUEL, Charlestown, by w. Susanna had Dorothy, b. 8 Mar. 1659, and of him no more is kn. SAMUEL, Salem, m. 28 Mar. 1682, Sarah Lovell (but Lewis, 134, calls him of Lynn, and s. of Thomas, and names the w. Patience L.), had Samuel, b. 3 July 1685 ; and Ebenezer, 30 Jan. 1688; was prob. an early sett. at Dunstable. THOMAS, Cambridge 1634, freem. 8 Dec. 1636, d. 7 Sept. 1661. Matchless Mitchell, in the reg. of his ch. names his w. Sarah, but ment. no ch. nor does his will (wherein he calls hims. a. 63 yrs. old), made 24 Aug. preced. THOMAS, Lynn, had Samuel, and William, as Lewis says, and we wish he had said more. WILLIAM, Plymouth, came in the Fortune, 1621, has sh. in the div. of ld. early in 1624, but in 1627, at the div. of cattle is not ment. so must be count. d. or rem. WILLIAM, Marblehead 1679, then in his 49th yr. had m. in 1655, Martha, d. of Humphrey Bradstreet. WILLIAM, Dunstable 1684, br. of Samuel of the same, m. at Salem, 7 Apr. 1685 (tho. Lewis says, with higher prob. 5 Mar. 1684), Mary Hart, had William, b. 12 Mar. 1685 ; and Eliz. 16 Nov. 1686, if Fox is correct. He was, in 1692, one of the wretch. witness. against Philip English, charg. with witchcraft, as is well shown on p. 497, of Drake's Hist. of Boston.

BEAMAN, GAMALIEL, Dorchester, came in the Elizabeth and Ann, 1635, aged only 12 yrs. spel. at the London custom ho. Bement, by w. Sarah had Thomas, b. 1649 ; Joseph, 1651 ; Gamaliel, 1653; Mary, 1656; all bapt. 14 June 1657 ; Sarah, b. 19 Jan. 1658 ; rem. to Lancaster, there had Noah, 3 Apr. 1661 ; Thankful, 18 Apr. 1663; and perhaps John ; and d. 23 Mar. 1678. JOHN, Lancaster, perhaps s. of the preced. had Sarah, b. 25 Jan. 1681 ; rem. to Taunton, and had Gamaliel, 29 Feb. 1684; prob. rem. again to Lancaster, and d. at Sterling, 1745. See Worcester Mag. II. 39. THOMAS, Marlborough, perhaps eldest s. of Gamaliel, by w. Eliz. had Eliz. b. 1679 ; Eleazer, 1683 ; Sarah, 1685 ; and Abraham, 1692. WILLIAM, Salem 1637, spel. the first syllab. without a, and at the London custom ho. Beamond, when he emb. in the Elizabeth, 1635, aged 27, as in the next article.

BEAMOND, or BEAMON, DANIEL, Springfield, s. of Simon of the same, took o. of alleg. 31 Dec. 1678, or next day. JOHN, wh. came in the Elizabeth from London, 1635, aged 23, may have liv. at Salem 1640, and at Scituate 1643. SIMON, Springfield, m. 1655, Alice Young, had John, b. 1657 ; Daniel, 1659 ; Thomas, 1660 ; Josiah, 1663 ; Benjamin, 1671 ; beside three ds. and d. 1676. WILLIAM, Saybrook, perhaps br. of John, came in the same ship, at the same time, aged 27, m. 9 Dec. 1643, Lydia, d. of Nicholas Danforth, had Lydia, b. 9 Mar. 1645 ; Mary, 12 Nov. 1647; Eliz. 2 Mar. 1650; Deborah, 29 Nov. (prob.) 1652; Abigail, 20 Feb. 1655 ; Samuel, 28 Feb. 1657 ; and Rebecca, 7 Sept. 1659. Lydia, m. 3 Feb. 1668, Samuel Boyes, and next, 15 Apr. 1684, Alexander Pygan ; Mary m. 3 Jan. 1672, John Tully ; Eliz. m. 26 Mar. 1677, Capt. John Chapman ; and Deborah m. 27 Sept. 1681, Thomas Gilbert, and d. 17 June 1683. He was freem. of Conn. 1652, and his w. d. 16 May 1686 ; and he d. 4 Feb. 1699. His w. was the only fem. nam. among eight grantees of S. in the will of Joshua, s. of Uncas, the Ind. sachem.

BEAMSLEY, ‖ WILLIAM, Boston 1632, freem. 25 May 1636, ar. co. 1656, by w. Ann had Ann, b. 13 Feb. 1633 ; Grace, 10, bapt. 20 Sept. 1635 ; Mercy, 9, bapt. 10 Dec. 1637 ; Samuel, and Habakuk, tw. 24 Jan. bapt. 7 Feb. 1641, both d. Apr. foll. Hannah, bapt. 17 Dec. 1643, " a. 4 days old ; " beside Eliz. and Mary, both, perhaps, b. bef. com. from Eng. and by w. Martha, wh. had been, I presume, wid. Bushnell, had Abigail, b. 8 Feb. 1646, wh. prob. d. young. In his will, made 14 Sept. pro. 28 Oct. 1658, provis. is made for wid. and for Ann, w. of Ezekiel Woodward; Grace, w. of Samuel Graves of Ipswich; Mercy, wh. m. 17 Oct. 1656, Michael Wilborne, and next Andrew Peters, of Ipswich; Hannah, w. of Bushnell, wh. after m. 16 Oct. 1661, Abraham Perkins; Eliz. w. of Edward Page; Mary, w. of Robison, wh. after m. Thomas Dennis; and for Edward Bushnell, perhaps s. of his w. by her former h. The ch. made sale of the est. in Nov. 1668, when perhaps his wid. was dec.

BEAN, BEANE, or BEANES, JOHN, Exeter 1677. MICHAEL, Kittery 1653. PHILIP, Salem, had gr. of ld. 1637. WILLIAM, Salem 1668; but in Ed. 2 of his Ann. Mr. Felt makes the name Beere; and it has been read Beebe.

BEARD, AARON, Pemaquid, or neighb. 1674, sw. fidel. to Mass. JAMES, Milford 1642, came with his mo. Martha, tw. brs. and three sis. his f. dying on the voyage, as the fam. tradit. tells, wh. adds, that he was eldest ch. and that it adds no more should not discourage large inq. JEREMY, Milford, br. of the preced. is altogether barren of any informat. in fam. tradit. but of JOHN, Milford, the other br. of the preced. that source of intellig. is more bountif. He was a man of import., had two ws. but wh. was first may need investigat. One, perhaps the earlier, had been by name of Hannah Hawley m. to John Ufford, or Offit, and at her desire divorc. By her he had sev. ch. and by Abigail, d. of Richard Hollingworth, perhaps the sec. had prob. no ch. was capt. in one of the expedit. against the Ind. 1675. The list of proprs. 1713 at M. has sev. of this name wh. were descend. of him or his brs. JOSEPH, Dover, s. of William, suffer. loss of his garris. ho. 1694, and left a wid. Esther bef. 1705. THOMAS, Salem 1629, shoemaker, came that yr. in the Mayflower, was freem. 10 May 1643, bot. next yr. the ho. and ld. of Nicholas Shapleigh at Portsmouth, then call. Strawberry Bank, perhaps was f. of that THOMAS of Scarborough, perhaps of Dover, wh. d. 1679, that by w. Mary had William, b. 12 May 1664, d. at 2 weeks; and Hannah, 24 Oct. 1666. Yet it may be that this Thomas was s. of William. THOMAS, Ipswich, freem., perhaps, of Boston, 1675, a mariner. WILLIAM, Dover 1640, had Joseph, b. 1655, was "the good old man" k. by the Ind. at Durham 1675. See Hubbard's Ind. Wars, and Young's Chron. 186.

BEARDING. See Barding.

BEARDSLEY, sometimes BEADSLEY, THOMAS, Milford 1647. * WILLIAM, Stratford, a mason, came in the Planter 1635, aged 30, with w. Mary, 26; and ch. Mary, 4; John, 2; and Joseph, 6 mos. He was freem. of Mass. 7 Dec. 1636, yet in what ch. he was mem. is unkn. and resort. to conject. I find some reason in favor of Concord. He was in

Conn. rep. 1645, but in Hinman, 113, little is told of him. At Yale in 1828 seven gr. of this name are seen.

BEARSE, BEARCE, or BEIRCE, AUSTIN, or AUGUSTINE, Barnstable, came in the Confidence 1638, aged 20, from Southampton, and join. Lothrop's ch. in Apr. 1643, had Mary, b. 1640; Martha, 1642; both bapt. 7 May 1643; Priscilla, 10 Mar. 1644; Sarah, 29 Mar. 1646; Abigail, 19 Dec. 1647; Hannah, 18 Nov. 1649; Joseph, 25 Jan. 1652; Esther, 2 Oct. 1653; Lydia, late in Sept. 1655; Rebecca, 26 Sept. 1657; and James, late in July 1660. Of this sec. s. as no more is heard, it is suppos. that he d. young; but for the nine ds. we know only three that m., Sarah, in Aug. 1667 to John Hamlin; Abigail, 12 Apr. 1670 to Allen Nichols; and Rebecca, 17 Feb. 1671 to William Hunter. JOSEPH, Barnstable, s. of the preced. m. 3 Dec. 1675, Martha, d. of Richard Taylor, wh. d. 27 Jan. 1728, aged 76, had Mary, b. 16 Aug. 1677; Joseph, 21 Feb. 1680; Benjamin, 21 June 1682; Priscilla, 31 Dec. 1683, d. at 3 mos.; Ebenezer, 20 Jan. 1685; John, 8 May 1687; these four s. were bapt. 16 Dec. 1688; Josiah, 10 Mar. 1690, bapt. 10 Apr. 1691; and James, b. 3 Oct. 1692.

BEARSLEY, BEARDSLEY, BERDSLEY, or BERSLEY (possib. BIRDSEYE), DANIEL, Stratford 1675, s. of William of the same. JOHN, Stratford 1668, br. of the preced. JOSEPH, Stratford, br. of the preced. freem. 1669, had Joseph, b. 1666; John, 1 Nov. 1668; Hannah, 1671; and perhaps others. SAMUEL, Stratford, br. of the preced. freem. 1669, had Abigail, b. Aug. 1664; Samuel, 1 Sept. 1666; William, 2 Mar. 1669; Daniel, 3 Apr. 1671; John, 1673; Benjamin, Dec. 1677; and Mary, 1680. THOMAS, Fairfield, perhaps br. of William, d. 1656. THOMAS, Stratford, may have been s. of the preced. or of William, and d. 1676. *WILLIAM, Stratford 1644, was rep. 1645, and often after, and d. 1661. His will of 28 Sept. 1660, names w. and four s., Daniel, John, Joseph, and Samuel; gives to ds. m. £10 ea. and a large sum to be distrib. by the w. to other ch. prob. younger, and unm. of wh. were certain. William, and Thomas. Of the grs. at Yale, in 1828, were seven Beardsleys.

BEAUCHAMP, EDWARD, Salem 1637, join. with the ch. 29 Dec. 1639, and his w. Mary join. the foll. yr., was freem. 28 Feb. 1643, had Samuel, bapt. 31 Oct. 1641, wh. d. 20 Nov. 1662; Mary, 10 Sept. 1643, d. young; Mary, again, 27 June 1647, d. Mar. 1668; and Eliz. 23 July 1648. His w. had d. in the same week with her d. Mary; and he m. 8 Nov. 1670, wid. Eliz. Metcalf. JOHN, Boston, leather-dresser, a Huguenot, brot. prob. most of his ch. to N. E. but it is not kn. when or where he land. first. By w. Marguerite, we see in rec. of B. that he had here Catharine, b. 10 June 1687; and Peter, 17 Apr. 1702, perhaps youngest of

the stock, if not even the sole of N. E. b.   Had the rec. of that French
ch. been preserv. we should less often be driv. to conject.   In the print.
list of taxab. inhab. of B. 1695, publ. by Dearborn in his Boston Notions,
the French names are frequent. spel. strangely; yet among them may
our Huguenot leather-dress. be misrepresent. as John Bashoon.   He bot.
of Daillè, their first min. his ho. in what is now Washington str. and left
by his will £10 to the ch.   He rem. after 1711 to Hartford, there d. at
the age of 88, 14 Nov. 1740, leav. large est.   Two s. John, and Adam
had d. bef. him in S. Carolina; and ds. nam. in the will, were Mary,
Catharine, Mary Ann, Margaret, and Susanna.   Mary was w. of
Rauchon, and had d. Mary Sigourney; Catharine had m. Latoille, and
had s. Isaac; Mary Ann m. a Lawrence, and her s. John bec. Treasr. of
Conn.   Margaret m. a Chenevard, and her descend. were long at H.
and at the time of the d. of her f. Susanna was unm.   ROBERT, Ipswich,
writ. Beacham, as always pronounc. in Eng. in 1651 had w. Isabel, rem.
1654, prob. to Norwalk, and 1664 to Fairfield, there was liv. 1670, with
w. Eliz. wh. had perhaps got back to I. where wid. Eliz. B. was bur. 18
Jan. 1687.

BEAUMONT, or BEMENT, THOMAS, New Haven 1639, m. the wid. of
Eleazer Stent, mo. of Eleazer and Eliz. S. but had no ch. by her, and d.
1686.

BECK, ALEXANDER, Boston, freem. 3 Sept. 1634, by w. Mary, wh. d.
2 May 1639, had prob. no ch. but he soon m. Eliz. Hinds of Roxbury,
had Ephraim, and Deliverance, tw. b. 1, bapt. 7 June 1640; Strange,
bapt. 5 June 1642, a. 5 days old; tho. the unworthy copy of town rec.
of births has the monstrous assert. of these three, as b. at once; and
Manasseh, b. 8, bapt. 12 Oct. 1645.   HENRY, Dover, came in the Blessing, 1635, aged 18, emb. at London late in July, as I saw in the rec. of
London custom ho. for that yr. so far more prob. than the tradit. giv. by
Coffin in Geneal. Reg. XI. 256, of his com. the same yr. in the Angel
Gabriel, wreck. at Pemaquid the mid. of Aug.   The Blessing did not
reach Boston bef. Oct.   Part of the same story is, that he was from
Hertfordsh. wh. is so near to London, whence sixteen ships brought passeng. to Boston, that we can never believe he would have gone to the
other side of the kingdom, for the voyage of the Angel Gabriel, begin.
at Bristol, 22 June.   He m. Ann Frost, had Joshua; Thomas, b. a.
1657; Caleb; and Henry; beside d. Mary, wh. m. a White.   Coffin adds,
that he liv. to be 110; and how gr. this would appear to be exag. we
may better judge, when the time of his d. is ascertain.   MANASSEH,
Boston, s. of Alexander, was freem. 1672, and this is all I kn. of him.
THOMAS, Dover, prob. s. of Henry, in Coffin's rep., m. Mary Frost, had
eight ch. of wh. he names Thomas, Joshua, Abigail, Henry, Mary,

Samuel, and Hannah; and he d. 7 Nov. 1734, aged 77. His wid. Mary
d. 25 Feb. 1753, aged 94.

BECKET, JOHN, Salem, shipwright, ment. first in 1655, d. 26 Nov.
1683, aged a. 57, leav. wid. Margaret, then 56 yrs. old, ch. William,
Mary, Sarah, John, and Hannah the youngest. His wid. m. Philip
Cromwell, and d. at ninety yrs. Mary m. 20 July 1675, Daniel Webb.
JOHN, Salem, s. of the preced. m. 26 Sept. 1711, Susanna Mason, had
Mary, b. 25 July 1712. STEPHEN, Roxbury, came from Ipswich in the
Francis, 1634, aged 11 yrs. only, and under the charge of Richard Pep-
per, wh. after a few yrs. at R. rem. to Conn. prob. for that Col. was resid.
of his apprent. in 1649. See Beckwith. WILLIAM, Salem, s. of John
the first, by w. Hannah had John, b. 10 Aug. 1684; Hannah, 17 July
1685; and Margaret, 14 May 1688.

BECKFORD, or BICKFORD (more common in early days), GEORGE,
had, in 1666, w. Christian, and serv. Hugh Hancock, as Coffin tells in
Geneal. Reg. VI. 243; but of what settlem. he was, we must trust to
conject. for Dover. JOHN, Dover 1647, in 1669 was of that part call.
Oyster riv. now Durham, freem. of Mass. 1671, had s. John, and Joseph.
JOHN, Dover, s. of the preced. by w. Temperance, d. of William Furber
of the same, had Thomas, b. 1660; Hannah, 5 Nov. 1665; and Benjamin, 20 Oct. 1672. He or s. John m. Eliz. d. of Jeremy Tibbets of the
same, but confus. easily aris. betw. fam. connex. of sec. and third John.
SAMUEL, Salisbury, m. a d. of Edward Cottle, and rem. to Nantucket,
where he purchas. 12 Nov. 1678, a half sh., had Eliz. b. 16 Feb. 1672;
and Deborah, 5 Feb. 1674. THOMAS, Dover, or Durham, br. of the sec.
John, m. Bridget, d. of William Furber. He was in gr. danger at the
assault by the Ind. 18 July 1694, saved by skill and courage, as may be
read in the Magn. VII. appx. art. 20; or Farmer's Belkn. I. 140.

BECKLEY, RICHARD, New Haven 1639, rem. to Wethersfield bef.
1668, had prob. two ws. of wh. the latter was a d. of John Deming, ch.
Sarah, perhaps b. in Eng. m. 21 Oct. 1657, John Church of Hartford;
John, b. 6 Mar. 1642; Mary, bapt. 12 Sept. 1647; Benjamin, 27 Jan.
bapt. 10 Mar. 1650; Nathaniel, b. 13 Oct. 1652, bapt. 15 Oct. 1653;
and Hannah, 14 Oct. 1656; and d. 5 Aug. 1690 at W.

BECKWITH, JOSEPH, Lyme, s. of Matthew, by w. Susanna had Sarah,
b. 14 Apr. 1677; and Joseph, 15 Apr. 1679. MATTHEW, New London
1652, Hartford 1658, then a freem., and had first liv. there 1639, rem. to
Branford, there in 1668 was one of the founders of ch., thence to Lyme,
there d. 21 Oct. 1680, aged a. 70, by fall in a dark night down a ledge
of rocks. See Rev. Mr. Bradstreet's journal in Geneal. Reg. IX. 50.
He had two ds. beside s. Matthew, John, and Joseph. His wid. m. Samuel Buckland; and of the ds. one m. Benjamin Grant; the other, Robert

Gerard ; but the name of either is not seen. Matthew, Lyme, s. of the preced. by w. Eliz. had Matthew, John, and James, the last b. 1 June 1671, and all were bapt. 10 Sept. foll. Jonah, b. 27 Dec. 1673 ; Prudence, 22 Aug. 1676 ; Eliz. 4 Feb. 1679 ; Ruth, 14 Mar. 1681 ; and Sarah, 15 Dec. 1684. A sec. w. Eliz. wid. of Peter Pratt, wh. she m. after divorce from John Rogers, was d. of Matthew Griswold. Her he m. 1691, had a d. Griswold ; and he d. 4 June 1727, in his will nam. all the ch. exc. Sarah, perhaps dec. and his wid. d. next mo. Nathaniel, Lyme, s. perhaps of Matthew the first, there in 1675, had Nathaniel, b. 28 May 1679, and was liv. 1690. Of descend. some are still at New London, Miss Caulkins says, and often call. Becket ; while at Branford it appears Bickatt. Stephen, Norwalk 1654, rem. soon, but came back after 1671. Perhaps he was that passeng. in the Francis, ment. under Becket. Thomas, Roxbury 1650, rem. perhaps to Fairfield, and left his w. wh. obtain. divorce 1655.

Bedell, Bedle, or Beedle, Robert, New London 1648, had, perhaps, been at Wethersfield, where Hinman, 164, ranks him among first sett. there prob. had Robert, b. 1642 ; and he rem. 1650, to Newbury, I presume. Robert, Salisbury, s. prob. of the preced. by w. Martha had Mary, b. 31 July 1666 ; rem. to Newbury, and had Thomas, 30 Apr. 1668 ; Eliz. 22 Nov. 1669 ; Judith, 29 Mar. 1671, d. at 2 yrs. Robert, 5 Jan. 1675 ; Judith, again, 8 Mar. 1676, d. next yr.; and John, 23 Apr. 1678. Coffin, in his Hist. says Hannah, perhaps his w. d. 15 Nov. 1678.

Bedford, Nathan, Scarborough, was constable 1665, kept the inn 1675, and d. 1681 by drown. In Southgate's Hist. the strange wildness of a story, how he was murder. by the venerab. Joshua Scottow, may be read. He left wid. Ann.

Bedient, Morgan, Hadley, came with his mo. Mary from Staines, near London, to rec. the est. devis. by her br. John Barnard, and d. bef. reach. his majority. Thomas, Hadley, younger br. of the preced. b. 1654, a co-devisee, came with his mo., rem. to Fairfield, and d. a. 1698.

Bedurtha, Bedortha, or Bodurtha, John, Springfield, s. of Rice, was drown. 18 Mar. 1683, with his f. and Lydia, w. of his br. Joseph, and Mercy, d. of his br. Samuel. Joseph, Springfield, br. of the preced. had three ws. and eleven ch. but details are not kn. to me, tho. in Geneal. Reg. XII. 176, we almost discov. one of the ws. *Rice, Reice, Reise,* or Roise (as if the surname were not suffic. various in spel.), Springfield, m. 1646, Blanch Lewis, had Joseph, b. 1649 ; Samuel, 1651 ; John, 1654 ; beside two younger ch. and he was drown. with s. John. Samuel, Springfield, s. of the preced. had two ws. of wh. one was Mary, wid. of Abel Leonard, wh. he m. July 1691, and he had fourteen ch. but I kn. nothing of them, only that he d. 1728.

BEDWELL, SAMUEL, Boston, m. 2 Feb. 1654, Mary Hodgkinson, per-haps had that SAMUEL, of Middletown, wh. d. 5 Apr. 1715, or may be the same.

BEEBE, or BEEBY, JAMES, Hadley, m. 24 Oct. 1667, Mary, d. of Rob-ert Boltwood, had Mary, b. 18 Aug. 1668, d. young; James, 9 Dec. 1669, d. young; Rebecca, 8 Dec. 1670; Samuel, 26 June 1672; and Mary, again, 1675. Perhaps, as this fam. soon rem. it may, in some branches, be found Bibby. JAMES, Stratford, m. 19 Dec. 1679, Sarah, d. of the first Thomas Benedict, had Sarah, b. 13 Nov. 1680; and James; rem. to Norwalk, thence to Danbury, and may be the same as the fore-going. JOHN, New London 1651, m. Abigail, d. of James York of Stonington, had John, Benjamin, and Rebecca; was twenty yrs. serj. and in 1690 lieut., liv. to gr. age, d. a. 1708. His wid. d. 9 Mar. 1725, aged 86. Rebecca m. Richard Shaw of Easthampton, L. I. NA-THANIEL, New London, youngest br. of the preced. rem. 1670, or earlier, to Stonington, had prob. no ch. and d. 17 Dec. 1724, aged 93. SAMUEL, New London, br. of the preced. m. Agnes, d. of William Keeny, had also sec. w. Mary. His ch. were Samuel, William, Nathaniel, Thomas, Jonathan, Agnes, Ann, Susanna, and Mary; but I am unable to div. them betw. the ws. yet doubt not, that nearly all were by the first. He own. the chief part of Plumb Isl. and rem. to it, d. 1712, aged 91, leav. wid. Of the ds., Agnes m. John Daniels; Ann m. Thomas Crocker; Susanna m. Aaron Fountain; and Mary m. Richard Tozer. THOMAS, New London 1651, br. of the preced. m. Milicent, wid. first of William Southmayd, and next of William Ash, d. of William Addis, had only s. Thomas, and ds. Hannah, wh. m. 1697, John Hawke; Milicent, wh. m. Nicholas Darrow; and Rebecca, wh. m. Nathaniel Holt; and he d. 1699. His s. wh. never m. d. 1727.

BEECHER, or BEACHER, ISAAC, New Haven, had Isaac, b. 1650; Samuel, 1652; and Eleazer, 1655. Perhaps he had other ch. His mo. Hannah, a wid. in her will, 1657, ment. two ch., this Isaac, and William Potter, s. of her former h. in Eng. In 1685 Isaac sen. Isaac jun. and Eleazer were proprs. * THOMAS, Charlestown 1630, freem. 6 Nov. 1632, had been engag. as capt. of the Talbot, 1629, in bring. passeng. to our country, and next yr. with Winthrop's fleet, when his w. Christian, wh. had been w. of Thomas Copper of Wapping, near London (wh. left her a freehold est. at Harwich), came with him, and was of the first ten mem. of the ch. He was one of the earliest selectmen of the town, and at the first gen. ct. 14 May 1634, when repr. came, he was one (all former gen. cts. being inclus. of every freem. of the Col.), and serv. sev. foll. sessions, made capt. of the castle 1635, and d. 1637. His inv. 29 July of this yr. made by Ralph Sprague, Abram Palmer, and Thomas

Ewer, shows £405. 16s. His wid. became sec. w. of Nicholas Easton,
and d. 20 Feb. 1665. No ch. of B. is seen on any rec. tho. Frothingham, 80, thinks Dr. Lyman Beecher, Y. C. 1797, a descend. prob. on
recent suggest. But the progenit. of this disting. fam. was Isaac.

BEEDER, perhaps BEEDE, THOMAS, Newport 1639.

BEEFORD, RICHARD, Gloucester 1643, by w. Mary had John, b. 26
Oct. Mary, 26 June, Hannah, 25 Jan. but in either case the rec. gives
not yr. yet allows us to assume that they were all bapt. 1647, and the roll
goes on, Ruth, b. 23 Mar. 1648; Nathaniel, 30 Apr. 1650; and Richard,
the last week of Apr. 1653.

BEERS, or BEERE, ANTHONY, Watertown 1646, by w. Eliz. had
Samuel, b. 9 May 1647, d. soon; Ephraim, 5 July 1648; John, 20 Jan.
1652; Esther, 16 Oct. 1654; and Samuel, 2 May 1657, d. at four mos.
beside three earlier ds. as Bond thinks, Eliz. wh. m. 7 Apr. 1663, Henry
Gooddin; Bethia, wh. m. 25 or 27 Mar. 1664, David, or Daniel Mettup,
Medup, Medap, or Meddup, dates as well as names various in Bond;
and Mary, wh. m. 1, or 19 Apr. 1665, John Smith; and was freem.
1657; rem. to Roxbury, and had Barnabas, 6 Sept. bapt. 17 Oct. 1658;
rem. again to Fairfield, there was drown. bef. 1676. BARNABAS, Stratford, s. of Anthony, had a fam. but partic. are unkn. ELIEZUR, Watertown, s. (Bond thinks eldest) of Capt. Richard, m. late in life, 21 Apr.
1690, Susanna, d. of Robert Harrington, wid. of John Cutting, and d.
without issue, 5 Dec. 1701. His wid. m. 2, or 21 Jan. 1705 (Bond
gives both dates), Peter Cloyes. ELNATHAN, Watertown, br. of the
preced. m. a. 1681, Sarah, d. of Joseph Tainter, had Mary, b. Mar.
1682, d. soon; Richard, Feb. 1683, d. soon; Simon, 19 July 1684;
Mary, again, 11 Feb. 1688; and Richard, again, 17 Feb. 1691. HENRY,
Newport, perhaps br. of John of the same, m. 20 Sept. 1668, Patience,
d. of Richard Scott, had Henry, b. 7 Sept. 1673; Catharine, 22 Oct.
1675; John, 29 Dec. 1678; Catharine, again, 25 Feb. 1681; Charles, 4
Sept. 1683; and Mary, 15 Sept. 1684. JAMES, Fairfield 1659, was not,
in my opin. s. of Capt. Richard, as Cothren thinks (tho. he may have
been br.), had good est. and d. Nov. 1694, leav. by his will, w. Martha;
ds. Martha, w. of Joseph Bulkley; Deborah, w. of Samuel Hull; Eliz.
w. of John Darling; s. Joseph; and childr. of s. James, then dec. and
his wid. Martha d. Feb. 1698. JAMES, Fairfield, s. of the preced. d.
1691, leav. ch. James, David, Sarah, and Mary. JOHN, Newport,
was s. of Edward in Co. Dorset, m. 4 Sept. 1664, Patience, d. of
Thomas Clifton, had Mary, b. 6 Aug. 1666; Edward, 1 Aug. 1669;
and Patience, 6 Sept. 1671; and he d. that yr. at sea. JOHN, Gloucester, m. 20 Jan. 1673 Mary Fowler, had Joseph, b. 7 Dec. 1675.
JOHN, Stratford, s. of Anthony, a soldier, severe. wound. at the gr. battle

of Narragansett, 19 Dec. 1675, for wh. in 1677 he had gr. of relief; recov. so far as to have w. Mary, by her Samuel, b. 9 Nov. 1679, made his will 9 Feb. 1683, d. soon after. By that his prop. was giv. to w. and ch. but if Samuel d. young, part of it should go to br. Barnabas, he to pay portion to sis. Eliz. Peck, and to sis. Johnson of Salem. JOSEPH, Fairfield, s. of the elder James, by w. Abigail had Joseph, b. 13 Mar. 1688 ; and d. early in 1697, leav. good est. and other ch. Abigail and James. PHILIP, Salem 1637. RICHARD, Marshfield 1636, bore arms 1643, was liv. in 1661, witness of will of John Rogers. * RICHARD, Watertown, freem. 9 Mar. 1637, serv. in the Pequot war, was rep. 1663–75, had Sarah, bur. 10 Oct. 1639 ; Sarah, again, wh. m. 24 June 1660, Isaac Stearns, and next, 23 July 1677, Thomas Wheeler ; Mary, b. 10 Mar. 1643, wh. m. Joseph Rice of Sudbury, as Bond thinks; Eliezur, wh. was made admin. joint. with his mo. of the will of f. Judith, b. 26 Mar. 1646, wh. m. an Allen ; Elnathan, bef. ment. ; Jabez, 4 Aug. 1661 ; Eliz. wh. m. 25 May 1710, Samuel Ward, as his sec. w. Richard, 22 Oct. 1659 ; and Abigail, Apr. 1662, d. very soon. He was capt. and k. in Philip's war at Squakeag, now Northfield, 4 Sept. 1675, prob. hav. time only to make nuncup. will, after being wound. ROBERT, Rehoboth, m. 25 June 1673, Eliz. Bullock, perhaps d. of Richard, had Benjamin, b. 6 June foll. and was k. by the Ind. 29 Mar. 1676. See Bliss in his valua. Hist. of Rehoboth, 96. THOMAS, New Haven 1654. Sometimes the name is Beares.

BEETFIELD, or BITFIELD, SAMUEL, Boston, constable 1652, d. 1 Sept. 1660, left wid. Eliz.

BEHONEY, PETER, Watertown, by w. Sarah had Sarah, b. 12 Aug. 1688 ; and Peter, 13 Mar. 1690. Sarah m. 4 Aug. 1703 (bef. 15 yrs. old) George Robinson. PETER, Framingham, s. of the preced. m. 26 Jan. 1713, Bridget Beal, was liv. there 1747.

BEIGHTON, SAMUEL, Boston, cooper, by w. Ann had John, b. 19 Sept. 1684 ; Samuel, 6 Apr. 1686 ; Ann, 29 Jan. 1688 ; James, 28 Mar. 1690 ; and Ebenezer, 30 Sept. 1692, perhaps posthum. for admin. on est. of his f. was giv. to his mo. 21 Oct. foll.

BELCHER, ‖ ANDREW, Sudbury 1639, ar. co. 1642, m. 1 Oct. 1639, Eliz. d. of Nicholas Danforth of Cambridge, and B. rem. thither, was a taverner, had Eliz. b. 17 Aug. 1640 ; Jemima, 5 Apr. 1642 ; Martha, 26 July 1644 ; Mary ; Andrew, 1 Jan. 1647 ; and Ann, 1 Jan. 1649; and he d. 26 June 1680, his w. surv. Eliz. m. 31 Mar. 1668, Pyam Blowers ; Jemima m. 5 Dec. 1660, Capt. Joseph Sill ; Mary m. 23 June 1662, Joseph Russell ; and Martha m. 13 July 1664, Jonathan Remington, and d. 16 July 1711. But the m. of Samuel Ballard, 1 May 1678, with Hannah Belcher, as his sec. w. is found on rec. and who she was, unless the youngest d. is difficult to find. Ann and Hannah are often, confound. ‡ ANDREW, Cambridge, s. of the preced. had traffic at Hartford, there m. 1 July 1670, Sarah, d. of Jonathan Gilbert, had Andrew, b. 12 Mar. 1672, at H. but most of his other ch. as Deborah, wh. d. young, shortly bef. her mo. and ano. Deborah wh. d. few weeks after her mo. wh. d. 26 Jan. 1689 ; Mary, b. 7 Mar. 1680 ; Ann, 30 Mar. 1684; and Martha, 29 Mar. 1686, were all b. at Charlestown; but Eliz. 12 Jan. 1678 ; and Jonathan, 8 Jan. 1682, at Cambridge, H. C. 1699. He was freem. 1677, one of the import. Comtee. of Safety at the insurrect. against Andross, rem. to Boston a. 1702, when he was chos. a Counsel. to his d. 31 Oct. 1717. Ano. d. was Sarah Foye at Charlestown, and she outliv. her f. Mary m. George Vaughan of Portsmouth, and d. 3 Feb. 1700. He was a prosper. merch. and the ds. m. other great connex. Eliz. to Daniel Oliver ; Martha to Stoddard ; and Ann to Oliver Noyes. Jonathan, his s. was made the royal Gov. of his native prov. 1730 to 41, and d. in the chair of Gov. of N. J. 31 Aug. 1757, his wid. long surv. and his s. Andrew, H. C. 1724, and Jonathan, H. C. 1728, enjoy. reputa. old age. See Eliot's Biog. Dict. EDWARD, Boston 1630, came, prob. in the fleet with Winth. was made freem. with prefix of respect, 18 May 1631, and in his latter days prob. for sec. w. m. wid. Wormwood. His No. on the list of ch. mem. is 60, but there his name is in the old copy Edmund. EDWARD, Boston, s. of the preced. m. 8 Jan. 1656, Mary Wormwood, d.-in-law (says the rec.) of Mr. Edward B. sen. had Satisfaction, b. 23 Feb. 1657 ; and John, 1658. GREGORY, Braintree, came to Boston 1634, was freem. 13 May 1640, bef. wh. he had assist. in found. of the ch. at Br. had Samuel, b. 24 Aug. 1637 ; Mary, 8 July 1639 ; Joseph, 25 Dec. 1641 ; Gregory, and two other s. earlier or later, and d. 21 June 1659. His wid. Catharine, in her will of 1680, names three s. Josiah, Moses, John, and d. Eliz. Gilbert, whose h. I cannot guess, if she were m. nor her f. if not ; beside Mary Marsh, prob. w. of Alexander, m. 19 Dec. 1655. GREGORY, Braintree, mariner, s. of the preced. had Joseph. JEREMY, Ipswich, came in the Susan and Ellen, 1635, aged 22, freem. 13 Mar. 1639, by first w. had Samuel, H. C. 1659 ; Jeremy ; and John ; perhaps more, if she liv. to 1652. But on 30 Sept. of this yr. he made contr. of m. with Mary Lockwood, wh. perhaps was d. of Edmund, by her had Judith, b. 19 Aug. 1658 ; Mary, 12 July 1660 ; David, 1662 ; and Richard, 10 Sept. 1665 ; and d. Mar. 1693. A wid. B. prob. his, d. Oct. 1700. JEREMY, Boston, 1672, perhaps s. of the preced. d. 6 Jan. or Feb. 1722, aged 81 and ½ yrs. JOHN, Braintree, by w. Sarah had Sarah, b. 27 June 1656 ; and John, 11 Mar. 1659. Perhaps he was s. of Gregory the first. JOSEPH, Milton, prob. s. of the first Gregory, by w. Rebecca had

John, b. 1 Apr. 1667; Joseph, 14 May 1668, H. C. 1690, min. of Dedham, wh. d. 27 Apr. 1723; and perhaps eldest s. was deac. Gregory, wh.
d. at Braintree 4 Nov. 1727, aged 63. JOSIAH, Boston, s. of Gregory
the first, m. 3 Mar. 1655, Ranis, d. of Edward Rainsford, had Josiah,
b. 23 Dec. 1655; John, 9 Oct. 1657, d. soon; John, again, 23 Dec. 1659,
d. soon; John, again, 1 Sept. 1661; Eliz. 10 July 1663; Joseph, 14
Oct. 1665; Rebecca, 21 Dec. 1667; Edward, 14 Feb. 1670; Dorothy,
28 Oct. 1673; Abigail, 10 Mar. 1675; Ruth, 21 Dec. 1678; and Benjamin, 20 Mar. 1681. He was one of the found. of third, or O. S. ch.
and d. 3 Apr. 1683, aged 52. MOSES, Braintree, freem. 1671, was
prob. br. of the preced. RICHARD, Ipswich, youngest s. of the first
Jeremy, m. 20 Mar. 1689, Mary Simpson, prob. d. of Thomas of Salisbury, had Jane, b. 26 Mar. 1690; David, 19 Dec. 1691; Ruth, 22 Dec.
1693; and Thomas, 29 May 1696. SAMUEL, Braintree, eldest s. of
Gregory the first, m. at Dorchester, 15 Dec. 1663, Mary, d. of Roger
Billings, had Moses. SAMUEL, Newbury, s. of the first Jeremy, as is
thot. preach. some yrs. at Isle of Shoals, was ord. 10 Nov. 1698 at N.
but went to his native Ipswich, there d. 10 Mar. 1715 in 76th yr. and
his wid. d. 14 Nov. 1723. Readily is it confess. that of the two Samuels
much doubt has exist. wh. m. the d. of Billings, or wh. was the min.
Of this name seven had been gr. at Harv. in its first ninety yrs. and
only one in its last hundred and thirty.

BELCONGER, JOHN, Newbury, m. 12 Apr. 1666, Sarah Kelly, d. of
John, had Mary, b. 7 Dec. 1666.

BELDEN, or BELDING, DANIEL, Hatfield, s. of William, m. 10 Nov.
1670, Eliz. d. of the sec. Nathaniel Foote, had William, b. 1671; Richard, 1672; Eliz. 8 Oct. 1673; Nathaniel, 26 June 1675; Mary, 17 Nov.
1677; Daniel, 1 Sept. 1680; Sarah, 15 Mar. 1682; Esther, 29 Sept.
1683; Abigail, 1686, d. soon; Samuel, 10 Apr. 1687; rem. to Deerfield,
and had John, 24 June 1689, d. soon; Abigail, again, 18 Aug. 1690;
John, again, 28 Feb. 1693; and Thankful, 21 Dec. 1695. His w. with
s. Daniel, and the youngest two ch. were k. by the Ind. 16 Sept. 1696,
when Samuel, and Abigail, two others of the ch. were wound. and hims.
with two more, Eliz. and Esther, were taken off to Canada, whence he
came back 1698, and m. 17 Feb. 1699, Hepzibah, wid. of Thomas Welles,
of Hatfield, whose three ds. had been, 6 June 1693, knock. on the head by
the Ind. of wh. one recov. This w. d. of William Buell, at the onslaught
upon Deerfield, 29 Feb. 1704, was taken by the Ind. and carr. a short
distance on the way to Canada, when her strength fail. and she was k.
For third w. he took Sarah, wid. of Philip Mattoon, d. of John Hawkes of
Hadley, and d. 14 Aug. 1732. His wid. d. 17 Dec. 1751, near 75 yrs.
from her first m. and in her 95 yr. HENRY, Woburn 1641. JOHN,

Wethersfield 1657, s. of Richard, had John, b. 1658; Jonathan, 1661; Joseph, 1663; Samuel, 1666; Sarah, 1668; Daniel, 1670; rem. 1672 to Norwalk, there had Ebenezer 1673; Lydia, 1675; and Margaret, 1677; and he d. that yr. aged 46. RICHARD, Wethersfield 1640, had Samuel, and prob. John, both b. in Eng. SAMUEL, Wethersfield, s. of the preced. b. in Eng. by w. Mary had Mary, b. 1655; Samuel, 1657; Stephen, 1658; adm. freem. of Conn. 1657, rem. to Hatfield, and had Sarah, 1661; Ann, 1665; Ebenezer, 1667; and John, 1669. Perhaps he was of Norwalk 1672. His w. was k. by the Ind. 19 Sept. 1677; and he m. 25 June 1678, Mary, wid. of Thomas Wells of Hadley, wh. d. 1690. Next he m. 1691, Mary, wid. of John Allis; and for fourth w. in 1705, had Sarah, wid. of John Wells, and d. 1713. SAMUEL, Hatfield, s. of the preced. m. Mary, wid. of Dr. Thomas Hastings, for sec. or third w. WILLIAM, Wethersfield 1646, by w. Thomasine, had Samuel, b. 1647; Daniel, 20 Nov. 1648; John, 1650; Susanna, 1651; Mary, 1652; and Nathaniel, 1654. Gr. of this name were not seen by Farmer at any N. E. coll. in 1828, exc. Yale, where they count. sixteen.

BELKNAP, ABRAHAM, Lynn 1637, rem. to Salem, where Mr. Felt notes his d. 1643. It was early in Sept. of that yr. Lewis, 89, gives him s. Abraham, and Jeremy. But good reason may easily be found for giv. him other ch. certain. Joseph, and Samuel, besides, prob. Hannah, wh. m. the sec. Christopher Osgood. ABRAHAM, Haverhill, s. of the preced. took o. of alleg. 28 Nov. 1677; but no more is heard of him; nor any thing of his supposed br. Jeremy. ‖ JOSEPH, Salem, a youth, s. of Abraham the first, b. prob. in Eng. rem. to Boston, ar. co. 1658, freem. 1665, was one of the found. of the third or Old South ch. 1668, whence he took dism. to Hatfield, there liv. in good esteem from 1682 to 96, then came back to Boston, and d. 14 Nov. 1712, aged 82. By w. Ruth he had Joseph, b. 26 Jan. 1659; Mary, 25 Sept. 1660; Nathaniel, 13 Aug. 1663; Eliz. 1 July 1665; and by sec. w. had a d. wh. d. soon; and by third w. Hannah, d. of Thomas Meakins, of Hatfield, wh. d. 26 Dec. 1688, had Thomas, 29 June 1670; John, 1 June 1672; Hannah; Ruth; Abigail; and Abraham, 26 Apr. 1682. Mary m. a Grafton; Eliz. m. a Patterson, and liv. in Eng. and Ruth m. her cous. John Meakins. JOSEPH, Boston, eldest s. of the preced. leather breeches maker, m. Deborah, d. of Jeremiah Fitch of the same, wh. d. 20 Apr. 1687, had Mary, b. 24 Nov. 1684, d. soon; Joseph, 18 Nov. 1685; and Jeremy, 1 Jan. 1687. He next m. 1 Apr. 1690, Abigail, d. of Thomas Buttolph the sec. and had Thomas, 24 Jan. 1691, d. young; Abigail, 29 Feb. 1692; Mary, 15 Oct. 1694; Nicholas, 15 Oct. 1695; Buttolph, 29 Dec. 1697; Nathaniel, 18 Dec. 1699; Ruth, 2 Mar. 1702, d. soon; Eliz. 13 Apr. 1708; Lydia, 17 Jan. 1710; and Abraham; and d. 30 Mar.

1716. His wid. d. 9 June 1734. Jeremy, wh. foll. the trade of his f. had Joseph, whose s. Jeremy, b. 4 June 1744, H. C. 1762, was the amiab. and learn. histo. of New Hampsh. author of the Foresters, and of thehigh. valua. vols. of Amer. Biogr. SAMUEL, Salem, joiner, s. of Abraham the first, b. in Eng. by w. Sarah had Mary, b. 17 Aug. 1653, d. young; Mary, again, 14 Oct. 1656; Abraham, 4 June 1660; and Samuel, 1 May 1662; was of Malden 1671, but rem. to Haverhill, there took o. of fidel. 28 Nov. 1677, had Joseph, 25 Mar. 1672; and Patience, 17 Sept. 1675; and perhaps Ebenezer. His w. d. 18 Apr. 1689. THOMAS, Woburn, glover, s. of Joseph the first, m. 6 Mar. 1694, Jane Cheney, perhaps d. of Thomas of Roxbury, had Thomas; Jane, b. 4 Nov. 1699; Benjamin, 3 May 1702; Hannah, 18 May 1704; ano. d. 1709; and perhaps Joseph, beside Samuel, b. 24 May 1707; but dates of b. are not kn. for all. He d. 15 Oct. 1755. Perhaps Abraham B., Esqr. of Johnston, R. I. wh. d. 1820, in his 92d yr. was a descend. of the first of the name here.

BELL, ABRAHAM, New Haven 1639, rem. a. 1647 to Charlestown, d. early in 1663. Admin. of his est. £154. 1. 1. was giv. to his w. Catharine, wh. d. 29 Aug. 1692, aged 68. I see no ch. but Isaac, bapt. at C. 12 Oct. 1662. FRANCIS, Stamford, then call. Rippowams, 1641, had been early at Wethersfield, was a lieut. 1666, but not freem. of Conn. Col. bef. 1676, tho. he was adm. of that of N. H. 1641. His w. Rebecca d. 1684, and he d. 8 Jan. 1690. From his will of 24 May preced. we gain something as to his fam. Jonathan is the only s. nam. d. Mary Hoyt, and four s. of his d. Rebecca, w. of Jonathan Tuttle, the mo. hav. d. 2 May 1676. JAMES, New Haven, took o. of fidel. 1644; perhaps was br. of Abraham, and may have rem. to Taunton, where one of this name had Jane, b. 4 Apr. 1658; John, 15 Aug. 1660; James, 10 July 1663; Nathaniel, 7 Jan. 1665; Sarah, 15 Sept. 1666; Eliz. 15 Nov. 1668; Mary, 7 July 1669, if the rec. be trustworthy; Joseph, 27 June 1670; and Esther, 15 Aug. 1672. JOHN, Sandwich 1643, Yarmouth 1657, d. prob. bef. 1676, tho. his est. was not sett. until 27 Sept. 1700. He left Eliz. wh. m. Samuel Berry; and Mary, wh. m. a Nickerson. *JONATHAN, Stamford, only s. of Francis, m. Mary Crane, perhaps d. of Jasper, had Jonathan, b. 1663; Hannah, 1665; Rebecca, 1667; and his w. d. 26 Oct. 1671. Next yr. he m. Susanna, d. of Rev. Abraham Pierson of Newark, N. J. and had Abigail, 1673, d. young; Abraham, 1675; Mercy, 1678; John, 1681; a d. 1683, whose name is hard to be decyph. James, 1684; Susanna, 1686; and Mary, 1689. He was a rep. 1670, and d. 11 Mar. 1699, in his will of 24 Nov. preced. nam. the w. Susanna, and seven of his ch., omit. Rebecca, Abigail, the illegib. d. and James, prob. all dec. PHILIP, Boston 1668. ROBERT,

Hartford, a tailor, had John, 6 yrs. old; Robert, 4; and Mary, 1 and ¾ at his d. 29 July 1684. SHADRACH, Portsmouth, prob. or other New Hampsh. settl. by w. Rachel had Shadrach, b. 3 July 1685; Eliz. 19 Mar. 1687; Mesheck, 29 Jan. 1690; Benjamin, 5 Aug. 1695; and Thomas, 12 May 1699. THOMAS, Roxbury, freem. 25 May 1636, had Sarah, b. 4 Oct. 1640; John, bapt. 9 Apr. 1643, d. in few wks. and Mary, 28 Sept. 1645; went home bef. 1654 with his fam. and d. 1672. By his will of 29 Jan. in that yr. he gave good est. to the gr. sch. at R. and his name is held in high esteem for his benevo. ‖ THOMAS, Boston 1637, was of ar. co. 1643, by w. Ann had John, b. 24 Aug. 1638, d. soon; John, again, 4 Mar. 1640, d. soon; Tabitha, 24 Mar. bapt. 4 Apr. 1641, d. at 13 yrs.; Thomas, 3, bapt. 7 Aug. 1642; Hopestill, bapt. 21 July, but the careless copy of town rec. says b. 2 Aug. 1644; More-mercy, 14, bapt. 17 Jan. 1647; Deborah, 29 Nov. bapt. 1 Dec. 1650; and Joseph, bapt. 9 Oct. wh. town rec. says b. 1 Nov. 1653, d. soon; but the last two were in right of his w. Deborah. He was the pub. execu-tioner in 1649, and d. 7 June 1655. His wid. m. 7 May foll. William Mullins. THOMAS, Stonington 1667–79, perhaps earlier. One THOMAS B. in the 50th yr. of his age gave testimo. a. the Lynn iron works, in 1681. Of this name Dart. counts eight as her gr. of wh. the first, Samuel, of Chester, the gov. was gr.s. of John, early an inhab. of Lon-donderry, and so may well be thought of that noble col. of Scotch-Irish, wh. hardly more than half so many as the sad gleanings of the fields of Dunbar and Worcester, transplant. hither seventy years earlier, prob. outnumber by fifty-fold, if not a hundred, the political exiles' progeny.

BELLAMY, JOHN, New Haven 1644, merch. from London, had w. but no ch. here bef. his embarka. Jan. 1646, with Capt. Lamberton, on that sad voyage to London, from N. H. wherein so many of the flower of the Col. were lost. Against that tradit. nothing can be alleg. unless it be dis-credit. so far as B. is implicat. in it, by non-appear. of his name on any rec. at N. H. MATTHEW, New Haven, was sch.master at Stamford 1658, but Cothren thinks he was first at Fairfield, bot. and sold ld. at S. up to 1670, but m. at N. H. 1671, Bethia, d. of Timothy Ford, had Matthew, b. a. 1672; Bethia, 3 Aug. 1673, d. soon; Eliz. Nov. 1674, d. soon; and Mary, 1675, wh. m. 28 Jan. 1703, Elijah How; exercis. his skill at Guilford and Killingworth, and in 1675 had gr. of ld. at Saybrook, bot. ho. there next yr. wh. he sold in 1677. His w. d. in 1687, and per-haps he, too, was d. or absent in parts unkn. for he had not been ment. several yrs. bef. 1689 when his childr. were put under guardiansh. MATTHEW, Wallingford, s. prob. of the preced. tho. by tradit. declar. to be s. and posthum. of a suppositit. John, and had two ws. and ten or eleven ch. Part of this may be true, as that his first w. was Sarah, sis.

of Richard Wood of W. and her fifth ch. was Joseph, b. 20 Feb. 1719, of Y. C. 1735, a very disting. theolog. among the systemat. rulers of opin.

BELLEW, or BELLOU, WILLIAM, Dover 1644.

BELLFLOWER, BENJAMIN, Reading, a quaker, wh. after sent. of banish. for his opin. renounc. it, as in Hutch. I. 201, 2, is told. He had m. 3 Feb. 1659, w. Abigail, and d. 24 Feb. 1661, or as ano. rep. is, 1670, at Salem. HENRY, Reading, 1656, had Hannah, b. 17 Jan. 1657 ; and Deliverance, 2 May 1662.

BELLINGHAM, § † ‡ * RICHARD, Boston, had been recorder of old Boston from 1625 to 1633, when he partook largely of the desire to migr. and with w. and s. Samuel came, tho. in what ship is not found, in 1634, and was chos. a selectman in Aug. after join. the ch. with his w. on 3 of that mo. and bef. long a rep. made in 1635, dept. gov. and twelve times after, some yrs. was treasr. of the Col. and gov. in 1641, and sev. times after, in all ten yrs. of wh. from 1665 to 72 inclus. beside being always an Assist. maj. gen. in 1664, and d. 7 Dec. 1672, the last surv. of the patentees in the Chart. aged above 80 yrs. says the Cambridge Almanac of next yr. He rem. to Ipswich, and after to Rowley, hav. est. and near friends at each place ; but liv. not long at either. For sec. w. he m. 1641, Penelope, the young sis. of Herbert Pelham, Esq. wh. had embark. 15 May 1635, aged 16, in the Susan and Ellen. Beside the impropr. of this match, in point of age, it was unduly solemniz. as in Winth. Hist. is told. By her he had Hannah, bapt. 14 Aug. 1642 ; John, H. C. 1661, wh. next yr. was agent for his f. at Rowley in care of ld. that had been his uncle William's ; James, b. 3, bapt. 10 May 1646 ; and Grace, wh. d. 3 Sept. 1654 ; and these are all of wh. we find notice. His wid. liv. near 30 yrs. d. 28 May 1702. For her and s. Samuel he provid. in his will, that was however so perversely drawn, as to be set aside by the Gen. Ct. Of his weakness as ch. magistr. other strange instances are relat. by the early hist. of N. E. but the most to be regrett. was his enmity, at a later day, to the foundat. of the O. S. or 3d ch. of Boston, that ceas. only with his life. Gov. Coddington of R. I. wh. had been, in their day of small things, much assoc. with B. in both Bostons, almost exults at his completion of the measure of his iniquity in distraction, closing his " Demonstration of True Love " in this emphatic style : " The hand of the Lord cuts him off, not giving him repentance to life, that other sons of Belial of his persecuting spirit might be warned, not to put the evil day far from them." Without sympathy in the triumph of Gov. C. it is grateful to me to remark, that the unbrok. reign of dismal bigotry from 1649 to 1672 inclus. under Dudley, Endicot, and Bellingham, hard, harder, hardest, betw. the mild wisdom of Winth. and the tolerant dignity

of Leverett, came to its end with that last of the triumvirs of Mass.
SAMUEL, Boston, s. of the preced. was of the earliest class of H. C. 1642,
and at Rowley next yr. but soon went to Europe, stud. at Leyden, and
there took his degr. of M. D. liv. most of his days in or near London;
had only ch. Eliz. and her by first w. In Apr. 1695 he m. at L. wid.
Eliz. Savage, wh. is unkn. to me; and he sent her over to manage his
affairs in this country. In Boston she made her will, Nov. 1697 in wh.
she bestow. munificently to the coll. to ministers, and friends here, but
gave back chief est. to her h. She sail. for Eng. 8 Nov. and was lost by
shipwreck on the coast of Ireland 3 Feb. foll. The orig. indentures to
convey est. that he had sett. on his w. made at London Sept. 1698,
and others of July 1700, in wh. he and his d. unite to convey to Ch.
Just. Sewall, as purchaser, the beautiful Boston est. were long in my
possess. and were giv. to a better custodian. WILLIAM, Rowley, br. of
Richard, freem. 12 Oct. 1640, d. 1650, left prob. no fam. for his will,
pro. 24 Sept. in that yr. gave his est. to neph. Samuel.

BELLOWS, BENJAMIN, Lancaster, youngest ch. of John, b. prob. 1678
or 9 at Marlborough, after the ret. of the exiles from a safer residence at
Concord, m. 1704, Dorcas, wid. of Henry Willard of Lancaster, had
Mary, b. 1707; Judith, 1708; Joanna, 1710; and Benjamin, 26 May
1712. The name of his youngest s. is perpet. in the Bellows Falls
of Conn. riv. where he found. the beautif. town of Walpole. JOHN,
Concord 1645, had come in the Hopewell, Capt. Bundock, from London,
Apr. 1635, aged 12, m. 9 May 1655, Mary Wood of Marlborough, perhaps d. of his fellow-passeng. John W. had Mary, b. 22 Apr. 1656;
Samuel, 22 Jan. 1658, d. young; Abigail, 6 May 1661; Daniel; and
Benjamin. He rem. to M. Such was the statement in Farmer, as orig.
print. with slight addit. from rec. by me; and in F.'s interleav. copy no
correction or enlargement is found. Yet the variance of acco. in Ward
and Barry is so material, that tho. the two may be only one authority, it
must be giv. They say, the ch. were Isaac, b. 13 Sept. 1663, wh. d. a.
1746; John, 13 May 1666; Thomas, 7 Sept. 1668; Eliezur, 13 Apr.
1671; Daniel, 15 Mar. 1673, d. young; and Nathaniel, 3 Apr. 1676, b.
at Concord, no doubt caused by the exposure of M. in Philip's war.
The f. d. 10 Jan. 1684, as erron. is said, for his will was pro. bef. that
date, and Ward tells, that his wid. Mary d. 1707. Barry adds, that
Eliezur by w. Esther had Thomas, b. 30 Sept. 1693; and that the descend. of John have been num. in Marlborough and Southborough.
John's will, made 19 June 1683, pro. 2 Oct. foll. names w. five s. and
two ds. omit. the s. Benjamin, wh. had been adopt. by a rich man; so
that we may be sure the enumerat. of Farmer was defect. Abigail m.
19 Apr. 1682, Isaac Lawrence. MATURIN, Providence 1645. ROBERT,
Boston 1654.

BELVILLE, CHRISTIAN, Charlestown, a Frenchman, m. 9 June 1656, by Gov. Endicott, " to the Lady Frances Hopkins." Who this lady was, I would gladly kn. but the rec. tells no more. The h. in 1658 was taxab. for small est.

BEMIS, EPHRAIM, Watertown, s. of Joseph, by w. Eliz. had Eliz. and Sarah, by ch. rec. shown to be bapt. 1687; by town rec. Rebecca, b. 16 Jan. 1685; and Abigail, 10 Jan. 1687; but Bond thinks he may have had others, and possib. rem. to Windham; but was liv. Nov. 1712 to take share of est. of his f. JAMES, New London 1647, had gr. of ld. 1649 was constable 1664, and d. next yr. leav. wid. Sarah, and d. Rebecca. The wid. m. 1673, Edward Griswold of Killingworth. Rebecca m. 1 Apr. 1672, Tobias Minter of Newfoundland; and 17 June 1674 m. John Dymond of Fairfield; and 2 Aug. 1682 m. Benedict Satterlee of K. JOHN, Watertown, br. of Ephraim, m. Mary, d. of Robert Harrington, had Beriah, b. 23 June 1681; Susanna, 24 Dec. 1682; Joseph, 17 Nov. 1684; John, 6 Oct. 1686; Mary, 24 Sept. 1688; Samuel, 1690; Lydia; Hannah, 9 Oct. 1694; Isaac, 1696; Jonathan, 30 Apr. 1699, prob. d. soon; Jonathan, again, 17 Nov. 1701; Abraham, 26 Nov. 1703; Susanna, and Hannah, tw. 3 Dec. 1705; and his w. d. 8 Sept. 1716. He m. 1 Jan. foll. as Bond says in two places, tho. in later passages he twice says 27 Feb. Sarah, wid. of Jonathan Phillips, d. of Nathaniel Holland; and next m. 30 May 1726, Judith, wid. of James Barnard, eldest d. of Samuel Jennison, as the same indefatig. author instructs us; but by neither had ch. His resid. was in that part, wh. bec. Waltham. JOSEPH, Watertown 1640, by w. Sarah had Sarah, b. 15 Jan. 1643; Mary, 16 Sept. 1644; Joseph; Ephraim, 1647, both d. young; Martha, 24 Mar. 1649; Joseph, again, 12 Dec. 1651; Rebecca, 17 Apr. 1654; Ephraim, again, 25 Aug. 1656; and John, Aug. 1659. He was often selectman, and d. 7 Aug. 1684, wh. is the date of his will. His wid. liv. prob. to 1712. Sarah m. 2 Oct. 1694, John Bigelow, as his sec. w. but d. prob. bef. div. of her f.'s est. in 1712; Mary m. 16 Feb. 1684, Samuel Whitney; and Rebecca m. 11 Apr. 1684, John White, wh. was k. in few weeks by a bull, and she next m. 1 Apr. 1686, Thomas Harrington. Of this name six had in 1835 been gr. at Harv. and one at Dart. Rev. Stephen, wh. d. Nov. 1828 at Harvard, Mass.

BENDALL, ‖ EDWARD, Boston 1630, came prob. in the fleet with Winth. freem. 14 May 1634, ar. co. 1638, by w. Ann, wh. d. 25 Dec. 1637, had Freegrace, bapt. 5 July 1635; and by w. Mary, from Roxbury, had Reform, b. 18 Oct. bapt. 24 Nov. 1639; Hopedfor, 29, bapt. 31 Oct. 1641; Moremercy, bapt. 25 Sept. 1642, a. two days old; Mary, b. May 1644, prob. d. soon; and Restore, 13, bapt. 30 Dec. 1649. He was one of uncom. enterprise, project. and used a diving bell to rem.

from the chan. the wreck of a ship bef. the dock, call. Bendall's, being the chief place of trade. He d. 1682. ‖ Freegrace, Boston, eldest s. of the preced. ar. co. 1667, was clk. of the Sup. Ct. 1670, m. Mary, d. of Francis Lyell, and with her was drowned, 6 June 1676, returning from Noddle's Island to town, by the overset. of his boat in a sudden squall. I have not learn. the names of any of the eight ch. that he left, of wh. the town rec. says, five were "too small to shift for themselves."

BENDISH, ‖ THOMAS, Mass. perhaps only trans. visitor, yet of ar. co. 1671.

BENEDICT, DANIEL, Norwalk, s. perhaps youngest, of Thomas, was a soldier in Philip's war, m. Mary Marvin, perhaps d. of Matthew of the same, had Mary, Daniel, Mercy, and Hánnah; and he rem. a. 1690, to Danbury. JAMES, Norwalk, br. of the preced. m. 10 May 1676, Sarah, d. of the first John Gregory, had Sarah, b. 16 June 1677; Rebecca; Phebe; James; John; Thomas; and Eliz. He prob. rem. to Danbury. JOHN, Norwalk, br. of the preced. m. 11 Nov. 1670, Phebe, d. of the first John Gregory, had Sarah; Phebe, b. 21 Sept. 1673; John, 3 Mar. 1676; Jonathan; Benjamin; Joseph; James, 15 Jan. 1686; Mary, or Mercy; and Thomas. He succeed. his f. as deac. SAMUEL, Norwalk, br. of the preced. m. 7 July 1678, Rebecca, prob. d. of Francis Andrews of Fairfield, had Thomas, b. 27 Mar. 1679; and Abraham, 21 June 1681; but by former w. whose name is not seen, had Joanna, b. 22 Oct. 1673; and Samuel, 5 Mar. 1675; beside Rebecca, Esther, and Nathaniel, prob. all by the sec. w. With others he purch. a. 1685, that planta. wh. bec. Danbury. * THOMAS, Southold, L. I. bef. 1650, had come a. 1639 to Mass. at the age of 22, and soon after m. Mary Bridgham, a fellow-passeng. He was the only s. it is said, of William of Nottinghamsh. had Thomas, John, Samuel, James, Daniel, Betty, Mary, Sarah, and Rebecca, all b. at S. and after liv. short time at Huntington, and Jamaica, he rem. a. 1665 to Norwalk, there was deac. selectman, town clk. and rep. in 1670. Date of his d. is not seen in Hall. Betty m. John Slawson of Stamford; Mary m. 11 Nov. 1670, John Olmstead of N.; Sarah m. 19 Dec. 1679, James Beebe of Stratford; and Rebecca m. Dr. Samuel Wood. THOMAS, Norwalk, eldest s. of the preced. m. at Jamaica, L. I. Mary Messenger, had Mary, b. 4 Dec. 1666; Thomas, 5 Dec. 1670; Hannah, 8 Jan. 1676; Esther, 5 Oct. 1679; Abigail, 1682; and Eliz. whose date Hall does not tell. He was deac. and d. 1690. See Hazard, Hist. Coll. II. 151. Very extended lines of descend. have spread from Conn. Of this name the gr. at Yale in 1849 were fourteen.

BENGILLEY, JOHN, Ipswich, freem. 1678, if the spell. in Col. Rec. V. 539, as print. by the careful reading of Mr. Pulsifer, be not a mistake, as I think it is, for Pengilley, wh. see, as giv. by Paige, in Geneal. Reg. III. 245.

BENHAM, JOHN, Dorchester, prob. came in the Mary and John, 1630, freem. 18 May 1631, had req. that privilege 19 Oct. bef. by first w. had Joseph, and John; rem. 1640 to New Haven, and m. at Boston, as sec. w. 16 Nov. 1659, or, as the rec. says, 1660 (perhaps erron.), Margery, wid. of Thomas Alcock of Dedham, wh. d. in few weeks after reach. New Haven, and he d. 1661. JOHN, New Haven, s. prob. elder of the preced. b. perhaps in Eng. as he was adm. to take the o. of fidel. 1654, m. 1669, Mercy, d. of George Smith of the same, had John, perhaps, as both John, and John jr. were proprs. at New Haven 1685, yet the latter (unless s. of the sec. John by an earlier w.) may have been s. of his br. Joseph. JOSEPH, New Haven, prob. s. of the first John, sw. fidel. 1654, m. at Boston, 15 Jan. 1657, Winifred King, whose f. is not kn. was one of the first sett. at Wallingford 1670.

BENJAMIN, ABEL, Charlestown, youngest ch. of the first John, m. 6 Nov. 1671, Amity Myrick, perhaps d. of John, had John, Mary, and Abigail, this last b. 26 Aug. 1680. All these are ment. in his will of 5 July 1710, and gr.s. John; beside his br. Joshua. ABEL, Watertown, s. of the sec. John of the same, by w. Abigail had Abel, b. 1695, d. young; Jonathan, 18 Feb. 1697; Abigail, 7 Sept. 1699; Caleb, 28 Jan. 1702; Ann, 21 Jan. 1704; Abel, again, 31 Mar. 1706; Rebecca, 11 Jan. 1708; Eliz. Jan. 1711, d. soon; Eliz. again, 3 July 1712, and Mary, 8 Aug. 1714; and he d. 4 Mar. 1720. CALEB, Wethersfield or Hartford, br. of the first Abel, d. 8 May 1684; leav. Mary, Abraham, Sarah, John, Martha, Caleb, and ano. by one report, perhaps from the pro. office; but from earlier rec. we find, that his ch. were seven, Mary, b. 15 Sept. 1671; Abigail, 27 Apr. 1673; Sarah, 17 Feb. 1675; John, 5 Nov. 1677; Samuel, 14 Feb. 1680; Martha, 19 Jan. 1681; and Caleb, 1683. His w. to wh. admin. was giv. 4 Sept. 1684, was Mary, d. of Samuel Hale of Wethersfield, and she, I presume, was mo. of these ch. DANIEL, Watertown, s. of the sec. John of the same sw. fidel. Dec. 1677, m. 25 Mar. 1687, Eliz. d. of Jonathan Brown of W. had Daniel, b. 15 Jan. 1688, d. soon; Daniel, again, 27 Dec. foll.; John, bapt. 23 Nov. 1690, d. young; Jonathan; Samuel, 30 Jan. 1696; Eliz. 22 Mar. 1698; Lydia, 8 Sept. 1699; Patience, 17 Oct. 1701; Mary, 21 Sept. 1705; and John, again, 4 Aug. 1709; and d. 13 Sept. 1719. His wid. d. 8 Aug. 1740. JOHN, Watertown, came in the Lion, 16 Sept. 1632, to Boston, and was made freem. 6 Nov. foll. and 20 May next yr. was appoint. constable by the Gen. Ct. a propr. in Cambridge, rem. a. 1637, to W. and d. advanced in yrs. (or at least old eno. to be excus. from milit. train. eleven yrs. bef.) 14 June 1645, leav. wid. Abigail, and ch. of wh. most were b. in Eng. and the exact order may be uncert. but John was eldest s. b. a. 1620; Abigail, eldest d. while the next ch. Samuel was b.

1628; Mary, the next, d. 10 Apr. 1646, had made a will, certain. after m. of her sis. Abigail, prob. few days bef. her d. yet it was set aside, as of one under age; prob. b. on our side of the water were Joseph; Joshua, a. 1642; Caleb; and Abel. His will is abstr. in Geneal. Reg. III. 177, and the wid. d. 20 May 1687, aged 87. Abigail m. a. 1641, Joshua Stubbs of W. JOHN, Watertown, eldest s. of the preced. prob. came with his f. by w. Lydia, d. of William Allen, as Bond thinks, had John, b. 10 Sept. 1651; Lydia, 3 Apr. 1653; Abigail, 14 July 1655; Mary, 2 Aug. 1658; Daniel, 12 Sept. 1660; Ann, 4 Aug. 1662; Sarah, 1663; and Abel, 20 May 1668. He was freem. 1668, and d. 22 Dec. 1706, aged 86; and his wid. d. 1709. Lydia m. Thomas Batt of Boston; and Sarah m. 30 Mar. 1687, William Hagar. JOHN, Watertown, eldest s. of the preced. by w. Mehitable had John, b. 15 Apr. 1699; and, perhaps bef. him, Lydia, for she was bapt. 10 Sept. of that same yr. as Bond, p. 27, tells; but I see reason to think he was of Boston and had by the same w. John, b. 4 Sept. 1679; and Sarah, 8 May 1686; and prob. rem. to W. and he d. 18 Nov. 1708. JOSEPH, Barnstable, s. of the first John, m. 10 June 1661, Jemima, d. of Thomas Lambert, or Lombard, sold est. at Cambridge 30 Oct. 1686, that came to him, his deed says, from f. John dec. and by this means we kn. of his descent. He liv. some yrs. at Yarmouth, where from the imperfect rec. we find sev. ch. but not all, nor in all cases the dates of those nam. Abigail; Joseph; Hannah, Feb. 1668; Mary, Apr. 1670; Mercy, 12 Mar. 1674; and Eliz. 14 Jan. 1680. He rem. to New London, d. 1704, leav. wid. Sarah, and ch. Joseph, aged 30; John, 22; "Abigail, Jemima, Sarah, Kezia, Mary, and Mercy, all a. 20," says the admirab. accurate and precise pro. docum. JOSHUA, Charlestown, br. of the preced. d. 6 May 1684, aged 42, leav. wid. Thankful, but no issue. RICHARD, Watertown, perhaps br. of the first John, as he came so early as 1632, in the same ship, by w. Ann had Ann, b. 1 Sept. 1643, rem. to Southold, L. I. 1663, or earlier, and was adm. freem. of Conn. 1664. SAMUEL, Watertown, s. of the first John, b. in Eng. by w. Mary had Mary, b. 12 May 1660, beside Samuel, John, and Abigail, all earlier, but next yr. rem. to Hartford, made his will 18 Sept. 1669, "a little bef. he d." Some imperf. accos. of Samuel, and John, his s. are furnished by Hinman.

BENMORE, CHARLES, Boston, by w. Eliz. had Lydia, b. 27 Feb. 1677; Stephen, 25 May 1678; and Martha, 4 Aug. 1686. PHILIP, Dover, m. 28 Sept. 1669, Rebecca, wid. of Thomas Nock, to wh. in his will of 20 May 1676, pro. 27 June foll. he had giv. all his est.

BENNETT, AMBROSE, Boston, m. 15 Apr. 1653, Mary Simons, had John, b. 19 Feb. 1654; Ambrose, 21 Mar. 1656; and perhaps he rem. ANTHONY, Gloucester, rem. to Beverly, next to Rowley, by w. Abigail had Anthony, b. 12 Nov. 1679. ARTHUR, Dover 1665, m. a d. of John Goddard; but no more is heard. DAVID, Rowley 1678, a physician, by first w. Mary had David, and Sarah; by sec. w. Rebecca, wh. d. 26 Mar. 1712, d. of Capt. Roger Spencer, and sis. of Sir William Phips, had Spencer, b. 6 June, bapt. 9 Aug. 1685; and youngest s. William; and d. 4 Feb. 1719, it is said, in 103d yr. of his age, prob. very much exagger. This Spencer B. adopt. by his uncle (the famous adventurer, and wealthy Gov. of Mass.) took the name of Phips, the uncle hav. no ch. was gr. at Harv. 1703, rais. to be of the counc. lieut. gov. 1733, and d. at Cambridge, 4 Apr. 1757. He was f. of David, H. C. 1741, wh. at the revo. grateful. adher. to the crown, and d. in Eng. 7 July 1811, aged 87. ED-MUND, or EDWARD, Weymouth, freem. 25 May 1636, rem. to Rehoboth 1643, perhaps was that Edward of Providence 1676, wh. resid. there thro. Philip's war. ELISHA, Boston 1675, mariner, s. of Samuel. FRAN-CIS, Boston 1650, by w. Alice had Mary, b. 15 Sept. of that yr. wh. prob. d. young; James, 14 Feb. 1652; and Eliz. 20 Dec. 1654, d. in few weeks; and he was drown. at Noddle's isl. 4 Dec. of next yr. His wid. m. 8 Aug. 1656, Ralph Hutchinson, wh. took James and Eliz. with their mo. to Northampton. GEORGE, Boston, drown. 27 Mar. 1652, by w. Audry had one ch. in his lifetime, and prob. a posthum. one. GEORGE, Lancaster, was k. by the Ind. as Harrington tells, 22 Aug. 1675. HENRY, Salem, 1630, on the Marblehead side, was of Ipswich, 1665, as in 2 Mass. Hist. Coll. VIII. 107, appears. HENRY, Lyme, m. 27 Jan. 1673, Sarah Champion, eldest d. of Henry, had Caleb, b. 11 Oct. 1675; Rose, 15 Nov. 1677; John, 26 Dec. 1680; Love, 19 Mar. 1685; Dorothy, 19 May 1688; and Henry, 29 July 1691; and d. 1726. JAMES, Concord, freem. 13 Mar. 1639, by w. Hannah, eldest d. of the first Thomas Wheeler of C. had Hannah, b. 1 June 1640; Thomas, 16 Oct. 1642; rem. with his f.-in-law to Fairfield, 1644, there had two more ch. and perhaps others, for in 1670 were three fams. of this name in that town. JAMES, Northampton, s. of Francis, m. 1675, Mary Broughton, d. prob. of the first John, had Mary that yr. and the 19 May next he was k. by the Ind. in the Falls fight. His wid. m. the same yr. Benoni Stebbins; and Mary m. John Field, and d. 1697. JOHN, Marblehead or Salem 1633, may have been short time at Windsor, 1647, but seems perman. resid. at S. 1648, yet in 1660 at New London. JOHN, Charlestown, d. prob. May 1674, at least his inv. is of 23d of that mo. JOHN, Stoning-ton, had John, b. 24 Feb. 1659, d. in four yrs. William, 1660; John, again, 1666; Joseph, 1681; and others not kn. and d. 22 Sept. 1691. JOHN, Beverly, s. of Peter of Bristol, Eng. came hither from Virginia 1668, m. 1671, Deborah Grover, d. I think, youngest of Edmund, rem. to Middleborough 1692, was one of the found. of the first ch. there,

26 Dec. 1694, and its deac. He d. 21 Mar. 1718, in his 76th yr. and his w. d. the next day in her 70th yr. Of ch. no name is found, but of John, wh. it is said, left issue. JOHN, a soldier of that comp. under Lothrop, call. the flower of Essex, k. at Bloody Brook, 18 Sept. 1675, by the Ind. JOHN, Boston 1675, mariner, s. of Samuel, but when he was b. or d. or where his f. resid. is unkn. JOHN, Stonington, s. of John of the same, m. 1687, Eliz. Parke, had John, and Samuel. JOSEPH, Newport, by w. Margaret had Joseph, b. 1 Oct. 1674, and no more could I learn of him at N. Perhaps he was s. of Robert of the same. PETER, Boston, s. of Richard of the same, had w. Mary, d. of Edward Porter, had posthum. d. Susanna, wh. m. John Love; but both Peter and w. were d. while his f. was liv. RICHARD, Salem 1636, prob. rem. soon to Boston, where in Jan. 1642, he was rec. by w. Sybil, wh. d. 13 Sept. 1653, had Peter, b. 18 Jan. 1649; Susanna, 2 Feb. 1651, wh. m. Jonas Clark, and Richard, 3 Sept. 1653, wh. d. bef. six mos. was surveyor of roads that yr. was the same constable, 1665, beaten by Sir Robert Carr, one of the royal commissnrs. as pleasant. is told in Hutch. I. 254, and Snow's Hist. of Boston, 137, 147, with fuller details in Drake, 373–5. His will has codic. of 6 July 1677, and was pro. 8 Sept. foll. so we have near. the date of his d. His sec. w. Margery, m. 11 July 1655, as wid. Gurgefield, or Goochfield, either an unusual name. ROBERT, Newport, among the freem. in 1655, by w. Rebecca had Robert, b. Mar. 1650; and perhaps others. SAMUEL, Lynn, a carpenter, came in the James, from London, 1635, aged 24, ar. co. 1639, at Rumney marsh, now Chelsea, own. large farm, had, as Lewis, 63, tells, Samuel, Elisha, and John; and I almost venture to add a d. Lydia, wh. d. at L. 2 Sept. 1661. SAMUEL, Providence, bef. and after 1645, sw. alleg. to the k. May 1666. THOMAS, Fairfield 1664. WILLIAM, Plymouth 1631–3, was of Salem 1637, and d. 1683 in the 80th yr. of his age. WILLIAM, Stonington, s. of John, m. 1678, Susanna Bright, had William, and Henry. Of this name, including those with single *t*, Farmer makes the gr. in 1834, six at Yale, and three at Harv.

BENNING, RALPH, Boston, by w. Ann had Ralph, b. 24 June 1661; d. 14 Nov. 1663, and his wid. m. 8 June foll. Henry Dering.

BENSON, JOHN, Hingham, came from Southampton, 1638, in the Confidence, aged 30, with w. Mary, and ch. John, and Mary, under four yrs. old, had grant of ld. at H. that yr. says Lincoln, 47. He was of Caversham in Oxfordsh. but both the names of place and person were strangely misspelt in Geneal. Reg. II. 109. JOHN, Rochester, by w. Eliz. had Mary, b. 10 Mar. 1689; Sarah, 15 July 1690; Ebenezer, 16 Mar. 1693; John, 10 June 1696, d. soon; Joseph, and Benjamin, tw. 16 Mar. 1697; Bennett, 10 Sept. 1698; Martha, 5 Mar. 1703; Joshua, and Caleb, tw. 29 Jan. 1705; and Samuel, 22 Mar. 1707. JOSEPH, Hull, perhaps s. of the preced. freem. 1678, had, in Dec. 1675, been a soldier of Johnson's comp. for the bloody Narragansett fight.

BENT, JOHN, Sudbury, came in the Confidence, 1638, aged 35, from Southampton, a husbandman of Penton in the same co. with w. Martha, and ch. Robert, William, Peter, John, and Ann, all, by custom ho. rec. under 12 yrs. old; went home the same yr. to bring more of his fam. and came again next yr. in the Jonathan, had gr. of ld. 1639, was freem. 13 May 1640, had Joseph, b. 16 May 1641; Martha; and perhaps others. His mo. Agnes, sis. Agnes Blanchard, and her inf. ch. d. on the voyage in the Jonathan. He was one of the proprs. of Marlborough; but d. at S. 27 Sept. 1672. His wid. d. 15 May 1679. His d. Ann (I think call. Agnes at a later day) m. Edward Rice; and Martha m. 1663, Samuel Howe. His will, made a few days bef. he d. made w. Martha, and eldest s. Peter excors. and gives to other s. Joseph, and John, d. Agnes Rice, and her s. John, d. Martha, and her h. Samuel, his s. John Howe, beside two gr.ch. Peter, s. of Peter B. and Hannah, d. of John B. JOHN, Marlborough, s. of the preced. b. in Eng. m. 1 July 1658, Hannah, d. of John Stone, had Hannah, b. 6 May 1661; and prob. by sec. w. Martha, d. of Matthew Rice, had John, 29 Nov. 1689; and David; and d. Sept. 1717. His est. was in Framingham. JOSEPH, Marlborough, youngest br. of the preced. by w. Eliz. had Experience; Eliz. b. 1673; and Joseph, 1675; and was k. that yr. by accid. shot of pistol in the hd. of his eldest br. Peter. JOSIAH, Marshfield, m. 30 June 1666, Eliz. Bourne, perhaps d. of John of the same. PETER, Sudbury, eldest s. of the first John liv. at d. of his f. by w. Eliz. had Peter, b. 15 Oct. 1653; Eliz. Patience; Agnes, 1661; Martha; John, 1663; Hopestill, 1672; and Zaccheus; beside John, again, 1676, b. at Cambridge, whither the fam. prob. rem. for safety from the Ind. But Barry, 182, presumes this John to be s. of Peter's s. Peter. Cambridge rec. shows John, s. of Peter and Eliz. d. 20 Apr. 1676. The f. d. says Barry, prob. in Eng. a. 1678. ROBERT, Newbury, d. 30 Jan. 1648.

BENTLEY, JOHN, Charlestown, perhaps s. of William, d. 20 Nov. 1690. RICHARD, Charlestown, in 1690 had w. Margaret. WILLIAM, a passeng. to Boston, 1635, aged 47, in the Truelove, with John, 17, and Alice, 15, perhaps his ch. but where he pitch. his tent, is unkn. to me, as also is any thing a. Mary, a passeng. the same yr. in the Defence, aged 20. Bentley is a parish in the deanery of Doncaster, and s. part of Yorksh.

BENTON, ANDREW, Milford, 1639, rem. a. 1660 to Hartford, d. 1683, tho. Lambert says 1681, leav. by first w. these ch. Andrew, Samuel, Joseph, Mary, and Dorothy; and by sec. w. Ann, wh. d. 1686, these,

Ebenezer, Lydia, and Hannah, wh. m. Edward Scofield of Haddam. DANIEL, Guilford 1669. EDWARD, Guilford 1650, was of Hartford 1659, and again of G. 1669. EDWARD, Wethersfield a. 1660, perhaps s. of the preced. d. 19 Feb. 1698, aged 60, by w. Mary left Samuel, Edward, Rebecca, Mary, Ellen, and Dorothy, all of full age, exc. Edward; but his youngest ch. Daniel, b. Mar. 1682, d. at four mos. JOSEPH, Milford, s. of Andrew, m. 10 Feb. 1698, Sarah, d. of Bevil Waters of Hartford. This surname is found in New Hampsh.

BERESFORD, HENRY, is the name of a soldier under Capt. Turner, in Philip's war 1676.

BERKLEY, RICHARD, New Haven, 1651, may be easy mistake for Beckley.

BERNARD. See the copious name of Barnard.

BERNON, GABRIEL, Newport, a Huguenot, s. of André, b. at Rochelle, in France, 6 Apr. 1644, escap. soon after, or, as one rep. has it, shortly bef. the revocat. of the Edict of Nantes, tho. for his relig. he suffer. two yrs. imprisonm. if tradit. be correct, and came to Boston, resid. some yrs. here, and after 1691; but in 1718 was one of the chief support. of the Ch. of Eng. at Kingstown; and in his 92d yr. at Providence d. 1 Feb. 1736. By first w. Esther, d. of Francois Leroy of Rochelle, had ten ch. (of wh. he brot. eight), and by sec. w. wh. was Mary Harris, four more. See Knowles, 431. His only s. d. in early life; but the progeny of sev. ds. are kn. in our day; and one of them, Mary, m. Gabriel Tourtellot, a fellow-passeng. from France.

BERRY, AMBROSE, Saco 1636, d. and was bur. 3 May 1661, leav. wid. Ann; m. 1653, as Ann Bully. ANTHONY, Yarmouth 1643, was after of Gloucester, there, I think, m. Eliz. d. prob. of Henry Travers, for, in 1665, after d. of Richard Window, wh. had m. the wid. of Travers, she claim. as his d.-in-law. CHRISTOPHER, Salem 1640, and Felt knows no more of him. EDMUND, Sandwich 1643. EDWARD, Salem, a weaver, had Edward, b. in Eng. and m. a. 1668, Eliz. wid. of Roger Haskell, was of Marblehead 1679. EDWARD, Salem, s. of the preced. brot. by his f. whose trade he foll. from Devonsh. JOHN, Boston 1644, may have liv. at Portsmouth 1665. JOHN, Ipswich, m. 17 Jan. 1671, Hannah Hodges, perhaps d. of Andrew. She d. 29 May 1676, and he m. 24 Jan. foll. Mary Chapman, d. of Edward. JOHN, Yarmouth, s. of Richard, had Judah, Ebenezer, Eliz. Experience, and Mary. RICHARD, Barnstable, or Yarmouth, 1643, may have rem. to Boston, there in 1647, liv. with Thomas Hawkins, but went back to Y. and had John, b. 29 Mar. 1652; one, 11 July 1654; Eliz. 5 Mar. 1656; one, 12 May 1659; one, 23 Aug. 1662; one, 16 Oct. 1663; one, 5 Oct. 1668; one, 1 June 1670; one, 31 Oct. 1673; and one, 16 Dec. 1677. Of the eight, whose names are not seen, Joseph, wh. d. 7 Sept. 1681, and Nathaniel, wh. d. 7 Feb. 1694, were two, but their dates of b. are not ascertain. by the rec. Eliz. m. 28 Nov. 1677, Josiah Jones. SAMUEL, Yarmouth, br. of John, of the same, m. Eliz. d. of John Bell, had one d. b. 19 Jan. 1683; Eliz. 21 Dec. 1685, perhaps, as the last fig. is lost; Patience, 22 June 1687; John, 9 July 1689; Samuel, Nov. 1691; and Desire, 29 June 1694. THOMAS, Boston 1668–73, a mariner, by w. Grace, wh. d. 17 May 1695, aged a. 58 yrs. says her gr.stone, had Thomas, b. 1663. THOMAS, Boston, the gr. of H. C. 1685, wh. was d. bef. 1698 by Mather's catal. and in the succeeding one hundred and sixty yrs. remains with no nearer approx. to exact date, may have been s. of the preced. He had m. 28 Dec. 1686, Margaret, d. of John Rogers, Presid. of H. C. had rem. to Ipswich, there had Eliz. b. 20 Sept. 1693; and Thomas, 1695, H. C. 1712. His wid. m. 25 Nov. 1697, Presid. Leverett. WILLIAM, Portsmouth 1631, one of the peop. sent by Mason, for his planta. but in 1635 had rem. to Newbury, there was adm. freem. 18 May 1642, and d. 1654. His d. Eliz. m. a. 1652, John Locke, and his wid. Jane, m. Nathaniel Drake. WILLIAM, Newcastle, perhaps s. perhaps gr.s. of the preced. by w. Judah, had Eliz. b. 15 Oct. 1686; Nathaniel, 13 Feb. 1689; Stephen, 18 Jan. 1691; William, 18 Nov. 1693; Jeremiah, 8 Mar. 1695; Frederic, 15 Jan. 1699; Abigail, 15 Mar. 1700; and Jane, 26 Jan. 1702.

BESBEDGE, BESBITCH, or BEESBEECH, ELISHA, Scituate, by Deane presum. to be s. of Thomas, b. in Eng. came prob. with him, had Hopestill, b. 1645; John, 1647; Mary, 1648; Elisha, 1654; Hannah, 1656; all bapt. at sec. ch. in S. and Deane also gives him Martha, wh. m. 1677, Jonathan Turner. He rem. to Duxbury, and d. 12 Nov. 1695. Mary m. 15 Jan. 1678, Jacob Beals; and Hannah m. 1687, Thomas Brooks. His s. Elisha, acc. Winsor, d. 1715; but no more is told of him. HOPESTILL, Scituate, eldest s. of Elisha, had w. Sarah, wh. after his d. m. 27 Feb. 1696, Joseph Lincoln of Hingham; but whether he had ch. or no, I see not. JOHN, Duxbury, br. of Hopestill, m. 13 Sept. 1687, Joanna, d. of William Brooks, had Martha, b. 13 Oct. 1688; John, 15 Sept. 1690; Elijah, 29 Jan. 1692; Mary, 28 Mar. 1693; Moses, 20 Oct. 1695; and Elisha. *THOMAS, Scituate, came in the Hercules 1635, with six ch. and three serv. emb. at Sandwich, Co. Kent, was deac. of the first ch. of S. that he join. 30 Apr. 1637, but rem. to Duxbury, prob. for the relig. quarrels at S. was rep. for D. 1643. He was, by Deane, suppos. to d. early, but he had rem. again, and d. at Sudbury, 9 Mar. 1674. His will, of 25 Nov. 1672, pro. 7 Apr. 1674, is copious in geneal. inform. tho. begin. with order. for bur. his body at E. end of the ch. gives gr.s. Thomas, eldest s. of d. Mary, w. of William Brown of Sudbury, all the ho. and lds. in the parishes of Hedcorn, and Frittenden,

Co. Kent, in O. E. names gr.-gr.childr. Mary, Thankful, and Patience, ds. of said Thomas Brown, also other ch. of his d. Mary, seven in num. viz. William, Edmund, Hopestill, Susanna, Eliz. Sarah, beside the eldest Mary, w. of Benjamin Rice of S. and her s. Ebenezer, his gr.-gr.ch. also d. Alice, w. of John Bourne of Marshfield, m. 18 July 1645, and her s. Thomas, the oldest ch. and Sarah, the youngest, and the other sis. without more exact designat. also Experience, s. of Joseph and Eliz. Bent; made William and Edmund, s. of his d. Mary, excors. and Capt. Hopestill Foster of Dorchester, overseer. His d. Alice d. May 1686. In rec. of O. E. this name is very common. Besbeech, but in N. E. is become Bisby or Bisbee.

BESSEY, ANTHONY, Lynn, came in the James 1635, from London, aged 26, rem. 1637 to Sandwich, was many yrs. active in holy serv. to the Ind. See 3 Mass. Hist. Coll. IV. 184. His will of 10 Feb. 1657, names w. Jane, ch. Ann, Mary, Eliz. Nehemiah, and David; this last was b. 23 May 1649. The inv. of his est. was taken 21 May 1657.

BEST, JOHN, Salem, a tailor, came in the Hercules 1635, from Sandwich, was of the parish of St. George, city of Canterbury. JOHN, Salem, a currier, prob. s. of the preced. m. 10 Oct. 1670, Susanna Duren, had John, b. 5 Sept. 1671; and Susanna, 28 Jan. 1674. ROBERT, Sudbury, whose name is writ. Beast, by Barry, 184; in his will names not w. or ch. but only cous. William Hunt, and his five ch. Samuel, Nehemiah, Isaac, Eliz. and Hannah.

BESWICK, GEORGE, Wethersfield, d. 1672.

BETSCOMBE, or BETSHAM, RICHARD, Hingham 1635, freem. 9 Mar. 1637.

BETTS, JOHN, Cambridge 1640, prob. came 1634, aged 40, in the Francis from Ipswich, when the custom ho. officer spell. his name Beetes. See Boston News Letter of 1826, I. 266. In 1642 he had sh. in "the farms," now Lexington, and d. 21 Feb. 1663, leav. I presume, no ch. Of his est. only £67. 4. 8. by inv. the wid. Eliz. had admin. and she d. 2 Jan. 1664, in her will of 10 Dec. preced. giv. ho. to John Bridge, and legacies to more than 50. Bridge, wh. d. above a yr. later, in his will speaks of his sis. Betts. This man seems to me the same as he wh. made propos. to our Gov. and Comp. in London, July, 1629, of divers things for the good and advancement of the planta. and the benefit of the comp. See Col. Rec. I. 48, or Young's Chron. of Mass. 84. JOHN, Wethersfield, bef. 1648 had John, wh. d. at Huntington, L. I. 1697, a d. Abigail, and perhaps others, by w. Abigail, from wh. he obtain. a divorce in 1672. Prob. he was s. of a wid. Mary at Hartford 1640, and sev. yrs. after. JOHN, Charlestown 1678, had w. Mary, wh. d. 5 Feb. 1679; and sec. w. Eliz. and he d. 22 May 1684. His wid. m. John Fosdick.

RICHARD, Ipswich 1648, said to have come from Hemel Hempstead, Co. Herts, rem. to Newtown, L. I. 1656, there was in high esteem many yrs. and d. 18 Nov. 1713, at the age of 100, to render wh. great number of yrs. doubtful, the stupidity of tradit. adds, that he dug his own gr. By w. Joanna, Riker says, he had Richard; Thomas; Joanna, wh. m. John Scudder; Mary, wh. m. Joseph Swazey; Martha, wh. m. Philip Ketchum; Eliz. wh. was first w. of Joseph Sackett; and Sarah, wh. m. Edward Hunt. RICHARD, Newtown, L. I. s. of the preced. d. 4 Nov. 1711, leav. Richard, Robert, Thomas, Sarah, Eliz. Joanna, Abigail, and Mary, beside wid. Sarah, wh. may have been mo. of all these ch. ROBERT, Watertown 1636, but Bond can tell no more. ROGER, Milford, 1658, had then gr. of ld. but had been of New Haven 1644, where he took o. of fidel. and of Branford 1646, and d. 31 Aug. 1658. By w. Ann, he had Samuel, Peter, and Mercy all carr. from Branford to New Haven for bapt. 1 June 1651, of wh. Peter d. in tw. yrs. beside Hannah, prob. eldest of all; Roger, b. 20 Feb. 1652; and Mary. The wid. m. John Cabell of Fairfield, and d. 1683, giv. all her prop. to s. Samuel, with order to pay legacies to the other ch. without nam. them. ROGER, New Haven 1680, s. of the preced. SAMUEL, Branford, br. of the preced. was a propr. 1679. SAMUEL, Norwalk, s. of Thomas of the same, m. 16 Dec. 1692, Judith, d. of John Reynolds, had Mary, b. 10 Sept. 1693; Samuel, 28 Oct. 1695; Stephen, 1 Aug. 1698; Nathan, 5 Nov. 1700; Hepzibah, 29 Oct. 1703; and Judith, 25 Aug. 1714. THOMAS, Guilford 1650, Milford 1658, Norwalk 1664, in Hall's valua. Hist. of N. p. 62, is favor. with larger num. of ch. in 1672, than any other person, of wh. eight were b. bef. he rem. to N. viz. Thomas; John, b. 30 June 1650; Hannah, 12 Nov. 1652; Stephen, 10 May 1655, d. young; David, 4 Oct. 1657; these at G. Samuel, 4 Apr. 1660, at M. and James, Mary, and Sarah, b. at N. He d. 1688, aged 72, in his will of 10 May in that yr. nam. the five s. wh. in 1694 were all proprs. As no ment. of Hannah is seen, tho. she had m. 13 Nov. 1672, she may have d. Mary is call. w. of John Raymond; and Sarah was unm. THOMAS, Newtown, L. I. s. of Richard the first, m. a. 1683, Mercy, d. of Daniel Whitehead, d. 1709, and his wid. m. 1711 Joseph Sackett, as third w. He left Richard; Thomas, b. 14 Aug. 1689; Daniel; Mercy; Abigail; Joanna; Mary; Eliz. and Deborah. WILLIAM, Dorchester, turner, had, I think, been at Barnstable, but first at Scituate, there had join. the ch. of Lothrop, 25 Oct. 1635, and m. Feb. 1639, Alice, a maiden of the Bay, and rem. with his min. to B. there had Hannah, bapt. 26 Jan. 1640; Samuel, 12 Feb. 1643; and s. Hope, 16 Mar. 1645. In the list of those able to bear arms 1643, Geneal. Reg. IV. 258, it appears Beetes.

BETTY, JAMES, Salem, by w. Sarah had Mary, b. 9 Nov. 1661.

BEVANS, or BEVENS, ARTHUR, Glastonbury, d. 15 Dec. 1697, leav. wid. Mary, and twelve ch. b. 1676–1696, of wh. no particul. are designat. BENJAMIN, Farmington, had Benjamin, and John, there bapt. 1 Dec. 1689. ROWLAND, Boston, bef. 1660, sold his est. to Daniel Stone.

BEWETT, BUET, or BUITT, GEORGE, Sandwich 1643. HUGH, banish. from Mass. for heresy, 1640, under pain of d. and to be hanged, if he come back. See Col. Rec. I. 312, and Winth. II. 19. This was in Dec. and he went forthwith to Providence, where he fill. many yrs. offices of import. by frequent elections. Staples in his Ann. of P. is the evidence of all his good desert ; but the name disappears with him, and no w. or ch. is told of. See Arnold's Hist. of R. I. Vol. I.

BIBBLE, JOHN, Boston 1637, Malden 1644, d. July 1653. His wid. Sibell m. Jan. 1659, Miles Nutt, and next, 30 Oct. 1674, John Doolittle. Ann, prob. his d. was a favorer, 1651, of Matthews, and, I think, bec. w. of Robert Jones of Hull, where the f. d. See Geneal. Reg. IX. 306.

BICKNELL, * JOHN, Weymouth, by w. Mary had Naomi, b. 21 June 1657 ; Ruth, 26 Oct. 1660 ; Joanna, 2 Mar. 1663 ; Experience, 20 Oct. 1665 ; Zachary, 7 Feb. 1668 ; Thomas, 27 Aug. 1670 ; Eliz. 29 Apr. 1673 ; and Mary, 15 Mar. 1678 ; beside one, 10 Apr. 1682, whose name appears not on the rec. was rep. 1677. JOHN, Weymouth, perhaps s. of the preced. by w. Sarah had John, b. 24 Nov. 1688 ; Zechariah, 28 Oct. 1691 ; Benjamin, 8 June 1694 ; Joseph, 28 Feb. 1699 ; and prob. other ch. RICHARD, Pemaquid, freem. 1674, but in the list he is call. Bucknell. ZACHARY, Weymouth, prob. br. of the first John, unless it be likely that he was f. and d. bef. Mar. 1637, when William Read bot. his ho. ZECHARIAH, Weymouth, s. of John the first, by w. Hannah had Zechariah, b. 9 Jan. 1695.

BICKNOR, or BICKNER, JOHN, Charlestown, perhaps s. of William, d. 4 Jan. 1679, aged a. 30 yrs. JOSEPH, Charlestown, s. of Thomas, serv. in Capt. William Turner's comp. in Philip's war. SAMUEL, Charlestown 1678, perhaps br. of the preced. THOMAS, Charlestown, perhaps br. of William, had Joseph, b. 8 Dec. 1655. WILLIAM, Charlestown 1658, d. 16 Aug. 1659, leav. wid. Martha, by wh. he had Benjamin, b. 14 Sept. 1656 ; and Martha, 28 Dec. 1658. Often this name is seen Bicknell, or Bignall, or even, I think, Buckner.

BIDDLE, JOHN, Hartford 1639, d. 1687, leav. John, Joseph, Samuel, and Daniel, beside ds. Sarah House, Hannah Waddams, and Mary Meekins, prob. w. of John of H. JOHN, Hartford, s. of the preced. m. 7 Nov. 1678, Sarah, d. of Thomas Wells, perhaps sec. w. d. 3 July 1692, leav. John, b. 1 Sept. 1679 ; Hannah, 31 Aug. 1680 ; Sarah, 19 Aug. 1681 ; Thomas, 27 Dec. 1682 ; Jonathan, 5 Mar. 1684 ; David, 1687 ;

and James, 1691. JOSEPH, Marshfield, m. 28 Oct. 1636, wid. Rachel Deane (wh. had come over the yr. bef. in the Planter, aged 31), and d. 1672, leav. no ch. but giv. est. to his w. to her d. Martha (wh. m. 28 Dec. 1674, James Clement, and next James Powell), and to his serv. Jacob Bumpus, beside Rev. Mr. Arnold, as in his will of 17 Apr. 1671. SAMUEL, Hartford, s. of the first John, m. Eliz. d. of Thomas Stow, wh. d. early, and for sec. w. took, I think, Sarah, d. of Daniel Harris. This name, sometimes spel. Biddell, or Beadle, may be the same as Bedell, and easi. become Bidwell, so that Hon. Barnabas Bidwell, M. C. from Mass. s. of Rev. Adonijah, was thot. to be of this fam.

BIDFIELD, BEDFIELD, or BETFIELD, SAMUEL, Boston, cooper, freem. 2 June 1641, and my conject. is, since his name is not found in our list of ch. mem. that he was liv. then at Braintree, but was a constable of Boston 1652, had two ds. and d. 1660. By his will, of 12 May 1659, he provid. for w. Eliz. s. Samuel Plummer, wh. had, I suppose, m. his d. Mary, and John and Samuel Stevens, ch. of his d. Eliz. and William S. of Newbury dec. and at N. I suppose he d. His inv. of 13 Sept. 1660, shows good est. See Drake's Hist. of Boston, 250 and 331, with Geneal. Reg. X. 83.

BIDGOOD, or BETGOOD, Boston, merch. from Romsey in Hants, came in the Confidence from Southampton, 1638, was of Ipswich 1642.

BIGELOW, BAGULEY, or BIGLOW, DANIEL, Sudbury, of that pt. wh. bec. Framingham, s. of the first John, m. Abial, d. of Thomas Pratt of Watertown, had Abigail, b. 28 Oct. 1689; Daniel, 24 Nov. 1691; Abiel, 20 Jan. 1693; Susanna, 4 May 1696; Ephraim, 12 May 1698; and Lydia, 2 Jan. 1702. JAMES, Watertown, youngest br. of the preced. m. 25 Mar. 1687, Patience, d. of Jonathan Brown, had James, bapt. 6 May 1688. His w. d. soon; and he m. 3 July 1693, Eliz. Child, youngest d. of John of the same, had John, 15 Nov. 1694; Patience, 30 Sept. 1695; and Abraham, 12 Nov. 1699. This sec. w. d. 20 Apr. 1697, and he m. next 15 June 1708, Joanna Erickson of Boston, and d. 20 Jan. 1728. His wid. m. within a yr. Adam Smith. JOHN, Watertown 1636, blacksmith, found by Mr. Somerby to be s. of Randle of Wrentham in Co. Suffk. and bapt. 16 Feb. 1617, of course by the hand of Rev. John Philip, the rector, who came to our country two yrs. after B. and liv. some time at Dedham, but on the overthrow of the Bishops' domination in Eng. went back to his old living. He m. 30 Oct. 1642, Mary, d. of John Warren, wh., Bond says, was the earliest m. on town rec. had John, b. 27 Oct. foll.; Jonathan, 11 Dec. 1646; Mary, 14 or 18 Mar. 1649; Daniel, 1 Dec. 1650; Samuel, 28 Oct. 1653; Joshua, 5 Nov. 1655; Eliz. 15 or 18 June 1657; Sarah, 29 Sept. 1659; James; Martha, 1 Apr. 1662; Abigail, 4 Feb. 1664; Hannah, Mar. 1666, d. very soon, as

did, also, a s. without name in Dec. 1667.   His w. d. 19 Oct. 1691, and
he m. 2 Oct. 1694, Sarah, d. of Joseph Bemis of W. and d. 14 July
1703.   His will of 4 Jan. of that yr. was pro. 28 July foll.   His inv.
shows good est.   JOHN, Hartford 1668, s. of the preced. m. Rebecca, d.
as Bond says, of Jonathan Butler, but ano. friend had taught me, that it
was George Butler, and d. without issue, 1722 ; giv. his est. to Jonathan,
s. of Samuel Butler.   By one rept. his w. was Mary.   JONATHAN,
Hartford, br. of the preced. m. a. 1671, Rebecca, d. of serj. John Shepard, by her had Jonathan, b. 1673 ; Rebecca ; John ; Mary, wh. by
Goodwin was erron. call. d. of the sec. w. Sarah ; and Violet ; whose
dates are not kn. but all these liv. to m.   For sec. w. he took Mary, d.
of Samuel Olcott, and by her had Samuel, bapt. 13 Mar. 1687, d. soon ;
Abigail, 2 Nov. 1690; Daniel, 26 Mar. 1693 ; and Samuel, again, 31
Mar. 1695 ; beside an inf. bur. 5 Mar. 1697, two days bef. its mo.   He
m. third w. Mary Benton, but had no ch. by her, wh. after his d. m. 19
Mar. 1713, deac. John Shepard, and d. 23 Dec. 1752.   JOSHUA, Watertown, youngest s. of John the first, m. 20 Oct. 1676, Eliz. d. of Thomas
Flagg, had Joshua, b. 25 Nov. 1677 ; Jonathan, 22 Mar. 1680 ; John, 20
Dec. 1681 ; Benjamin, 20 Jan. 1684 ; Mercy, 1686 ; Eliz. 3 Aug. 1687 ;
David, 30 Apr. 1694; Joseph, 29 Dec. 1695 ; Daniel, bapt. 29 Aug.
1697 ; Ebenezer, b. 4 Sept. 1698 ; Gershom, Sept. 1701 ; and Eliezer,
14 Mar. 1705.   His w. d. 1729.   In Philip's war he was wound. but
liv. to be near 90, d. 21 Feb. 1745 at Westminster, whither, with his
youngest s. he rem. only three yrs. bef.   The late Hon. Timothy, H. C.
1786, was gr.s. of Daniel, s. of this Joshua, so that the error of Bond,
841, is plain, tho. not uncommon, in suppress. a generat.   SAMUEL,
Watertown, br. of the preced. m. 3 June 1674, Mary, d. of Thomas
Flagg (of wh. ch. two others m. other ch. of the first John Bigelow), had
John, b. 9 May 1675 ; Mary, 12 Sept. 1677; Samuel, 18 Sept. 1679 ;
Sarah, 1 Oct. 1681 ; Thomas, 24 Oct. 1683 ; Martha, 4 Apr. 1686 ;
Abigail, 7 May 1687 ; Isaac, 19 Mar. 1690 ; and Deliverance, 22 Sept.
1695.   He was adm. freem. 1690 ; his w. d. 1720; and he d. a. 1731.
The Rev. Jacob, H. C. 1766, was s. of Jacob, gr.s. of Thomas, and gr.-
gr.s. of this Samuel.   Many variat. in spell. of this fam. name will be
found in early rec. but the gr. at Harv. in 1834, either with two or three
syllab. amount to eighteen, two at Yale, one at Dart. and five at other
N. E. coll.

  BIGGS, or BIGG, || JOHN, Boston 1630, came prob. with Winth. and is
among the first hundred mem. of our ch. freem. 4 Mar. 1634; rem. next
yr. to Ipswich, yet came back soon, and was one of the favorers of
Wheelwright, disarm. Nov. 1637.   His first w. Mary d. 10 Jan. 1650.
Prob. he was some yrs. of Dorchester, next at Exeter, but was of ar. co.

1641. For sec. w. he had Mary, d. of John Dassett, wh. outliv. him, and ano. h. Capt. John Minot, wh. d. Aug. 1669, and she d. a. 1676. One Rachell B. a wid. came in the Elizabeth, 1635, from London, liv. at Dorchester, wh. in her will of 17 Nov. 1646, calls her s. aged, names Hopestill Foster her neph. and he, I judge, was a fellow passeng. and to him she gives her prop. In the rec. at the custom ho. a curious error may be seen, as print. by me in 3 Mass. Hist. Coll. VIII. 261, careful. tak. at her Majesty's Remembrancer Office, formerly in Westminster Hall, since rem. to Carlton Ride, giv. her age 6. THOMAS, Exeter 1652–7, may have been s. of the preced. TIMOTHY, Boston 1665. WILLIAM, Middletown, d. 1681, leav. six ch., William, aged 15 ; Mary, 14 ; Thomas, 9 ; Eliz. 8 ; Sarah, 6 ; and John, 4. He had been, on acco. of his age, in Oct. 1676, excus. from poll tax.

BILL, JAMES, Boston, came prob. with his mo. 1638, by w. Mehitable had James, b. 23 Nov. 1651 ; Jonathan ; Joseph ; and Joshua. He was freem. 1683. JOHN, Boston, came in the Hopewell, Capt. Bundocke, 1635, aged 13, emb. at London early in Apr. and may be the same wh. d. Dec. 1638. Among passeng. at London, the same week, by the Planter, in the custom ho. rec. is nam. Mary Bill, aged 11. JONATHAN, Boston, s. prob. of James, d. 1729, aged 77. JOSEPH, Boston, br. of the preced. was freem. 1690. PHILIP, New London, on Stonington side, came a. 1665, from Ipswich in Mass. bring., perhaps, Philip, Samuel, John, and Eliz. had there Jonathan, bapt. 5 Nov. 1671 ; and Joshua, 29 Dec. 1675 ; and d. 8 July 1689, leav. wid. Hannah, wh. m. Samuel Buckland. PHILIP, New London, s. of the preced. was constab. 1689, on Groton side, had Margaret, wh. d. the same day with her gr.f. This fam. is still in Conn. SAMUEL, New London, br., I presume, of the preced. m. bef. 1670 prob. Mercy, d. of Richard Haughton, and no more is kn. to me. SAMUEL, Boston, s. of Thomas of the same, had w. Eliz. and ch. Richard, and Samuel, wh. was old eno. to be m. 1702 to Sarah Shapley ; and he d. 18 Aug. 1705. ‖ THOMAS, Boston, ar. co. 1657, m. 14 Jan. 1653, wid. Eliz. Nichols, and d. of William Sargent, brot. by him from London to Malden, had Samuel ; Sargent, b. 26 Feb. 1658 ; and his w. d. next week. By sec. w. Abigail, d. of Michael Willis, he had Sarah, Sept. 1659 ; Mary, 15 Aug. 1661 ; Thomas, 24 Dec. 1664 ; Susanna, 18 Mar. 1666 ; Michael, 27 Dec. 1667 ; and James, 31 Oct. 1669 ; was freem. 1671, and d. 29 Oct. 1696. Some presumpt. that he was br. of James is encourag. bec. both were memb. of the sec. ch.

BILLINGS, or BILLING, EBENEZER, Dorchester, s. of Roger the first, m. Hannah, d. of John Wales, had Richard, b. 21 Sept. 1675, H. C. 1698, min. of Little Compton ; Ebenezer, 13 July 1677 ; Zipporah, 20

Mar. 1679; Jonathan, 24 Apr. 1681, bapt. 17 July foll. at Roxbury;
Eliz. 8 Mar. 1683; Hepzibah, 11 May 1685; Mary, 22 June 1687;
Benjamin, 31 May 1689; Samuel, 30 Apr. 1691; Beriah, and Bezaleel,
tw. 24 Dec. 1692; Hannah, 3 Jan. 1697; and Elkanah, 1698. He was
freem. 1690; and his wid. Hannah, d. 19 Oct. 1732. EBENEZER,
Stonington, s. prob. of the first William of the same, by w. Ann had
Ann, b. 7 Oct. 1681; Ebenezer, 1 Jan. 1684; William, 4 Apr. 1686;
James, 4 Oct. 1688; Zipporah, 16 May 1691; Margaret, 11 Sept. 1693;
Jemima, bapt. 26 May 1695; Increase, b. 15 May 1697; and Thankful,
5 July 1698. JOHN, Portsmouth 1640, was one of the ch. inhab. freem.
1660. Belkn. I. 28. JOHN, Concord, s. of Nathaniel, m. 11 Nov. 1661,
Eliz. Hastings, and d. 1704. JOSEPH, Braintree, gr.s. perhaps, of the
first Roger, as in his will appears, by w. Hannah had Eliz. b. 13 July
1691; Hannah, 23 Mar. 1693; and Joseph, 17 May 1695. NATHAN-
IEL, Concord, freem. 2 June 1641, had Nathaniel, and John, wrote his
name Billin, and d. 24 Aug. 1673. NATHANIEL, Concord, the freem. of
1673, was prob. s. of the preced. RICHARD, Hartford 1650, wh. as
Hinman, 115, says, was in the Col. bef. 1640, rem. 1661, to Hadley, the
W. side of the riv. that bec. Hatfield, there d. 13 Mar. 1679; and his w.
Margery, by wh. he had only ch. Samuel, d. 5 Dec. foll. ROGER, Dorchester 1640, freem. 10 May 1643, by w. Mary had only Mary, b. 10
July 1643, wh. d. in few mos. and the w. liv. not long. By sec. w.
Hannah, he had Mary, again; Hannah; Joseph; Ebenezer; Roger, 18
Nov. 1657; Eliz. 27 Oct. 1659; and Zipporah, 21 May 1662, d. at 14
yrs. This w. d. 25 May 1662; and by third w. Eliz. d. of John Pratt,
wh. outliv. him, had Jonathan, wh. d. young; and the f. d. 15 Nov. 1683,
by his will provid. for w. Joseph, s. of dec. s. Joseph; his own Ebenezer
and Roger; s.-in-law, John Penniman, wh. had m. 24 Feb. 1665, his d.
Hannah; and d. Mary with her s. Moses. She had m. 15 Dec. 1663,
Samuel Belcher of Braintree. Seven pages in Thayer's Genealog. Reg.
are fill. by his descend. ROGER, Dorchester, s. of the preced. m. 22
Jan. 1678, Sarah, d. of the first Stephen Paine of Braintree, had Hannah,
b. 21 Jan. 1679; Joseph, 27 May 1681; John, 10 Mar. 1683; Roger, 9
Jan. 1685; William, 27 July 1686; Sarah, 27 Feb. 1689; Stephen, 27
Aug. 1691; Moses, 20 Nov. 1696; Ann, 4 Aug. 1698; Abigail, 15
Feb. 1700; Eliz. 11 Jan. 1702; and Isaac, 9 July 1703. All these ch.
were liv. at the d. of their mo. 19 Sept. 1742. But the newspaper that
relates the dec. of the wid. does not inform us when the f. d. yet it
magnifies the wonder by mak. as many ds. as s. fourteen in all, and all
alive. SAMUEL, Newport, m. 5 Jan. 1658, Seaborn, d. of Richard Tew,
had Amie, b. 20 Oct. foll.; Mary, 5 Apr. 1662; and perhaps more on
Friends' rec. at R. I. SAMUEL, Hadley, s. of Richard of the same, m.

1661, Sarah, d. of Richard Fellows, had Sarah, wh. d. 15 July 1674; Samuel, b. 8 Jan. 1665; Ebenezer, 29 Oct. 1669; Richard, 7 Apr. 1672; John, 11 Oct. 1674; and Sarah, again, 1676; and he d. 1 Feb. 1678. His s. John was k. by the Ind. 15 July 1698. Descend. are very num. in that region. WILLIAM, Dorchester, or perhaps Braintree, a propr. 1654, of Lancaster, m. at D. 12 Feb. 1658, Mary, whose surname is not seen in the rec. Perhaps he rem. to New London, where Miss Caulkins shows a William, in 1667, fined for neglect of train. and very soon after to Stonington, there had William, Joseph, Mary, and Lydia, bapt. 1 Sept. 1672. Of these Mary d. young, and Joseph, prob. bef. his f. Ano. Mary he brot. to bapt. 14 Mar. 1675. He d. 16 Mar. 1713, in his will ment. as his ch. William, Ebenezer, and six ds. but their names are not read. Perhaps this last period may refer to WILLIAM, Stonington, s. prob. of the preced. wh. by w. Hannah had Abigail, and Dorothy, perhaps not tw. but bapt. 1 July 1677; Eliz. 28 Sept. 1679; Patience, 4 Mar. 1683; Joseph, and Mary, 29 May 1692; and Prudence, 9 Dec. 1694. Gr. in 1829, Farmer found eight at Yale, four at Harv. and three at other N. E. coll.

BILLINGTON, FRANCIS, Plymouth, younger s. of John, b. in Eng. m. 1634, Christian, wid. of Francis Eaton, rem. bef. 1648, to Yarmouth, and Gov. Bradford, in 1650, tells, that he had eight ch. Of them I can hardly name half, and the order is imperf. ascertain. One was, I presume, Rebecca, b. 8 June 1647; but older must have been Martha, wh. m. 10 Jan. 1661, Samuel Eaton; older than her, perhaps, was Isaac, one of the found. of the first ch. at Middleborough, wh. d. 11 Dec. 1709, aged 66; ano. whose name appears not on the rec. was b. 25 Feb. 1652; and Mary, wh. m. 27 June 1681, John Martin, perhaps as sec. w. JOHN, Plymouth 1620, came in the Mayflower with w. Helen, and two s. John, wh. d. bef. his f. but after the div. of cattle in 1627, and Francis, bef. ment. He was hang. for murder in 1630, of John Newcomen. See Bradford's Hist. 276, and Winth. I. 36. THOMAS, Exeter 1650, d. at Taunton, Apr. 1662.

BILLS, or BILLES, MATTHEW, Dover 1654. ROBERT, Charlestown, came 1635, in the Pied Cow, a husbandman, aged 32, and d. 15 Dec. of the same yr. Admin. of his est. was giv. 1638 to John Knowles, wh. had, prob. in Eng. m. his sis. wid. of Ephraim Davis. See Geneal. Reg. XII. 54. But of John Knowles's resid. we can be sure of no more, than that it was not Watertown. THOMAS, Barnstable, perhaps s. of William, m. 3 Oct. 1672, Ann, prob. d. of William Twining, had Ann, b. 28 June 1673; and Eliz. 23 Aug. 1675. His w. d. nine days after, and he m. 2 May 1676, Joanna Twining, d. of ano. William and niece of the former w. had Nathaniel, 25 June 1677; Mary, 14 Apr. 1679; Mehitable, 26 Mar. 1681; Thomas, 22 Mar. 1684; Gershom, 5 June

1686; and Joanna, 2 Dec. 1688. Most of these were b. at Eastham. WILLIAM, Barnstable 1640, one of the first sett.

BINGHAM, NATHANIEL, Windham, s. of Thomas the first, m. 25 July 1705, Sarah Lobdell, had Isaac, b. 1 July 1709; Mehitable, 21 Nov. 1713; and Jeremiah, 27 Jan. 1716; was deac. and d. 16 Dec. 1754. His wid. d. 28 June 1763. THOMAS, Norwich, m. 12 Dec. 1666, Mary Rudd, had Thomas, b. 11 Dec. 1667 ; Abel, 25 June 1669; Mary, July 1672 ; Jonathan, 15 Apr. 1674; Ann, Aug. 1677 ; Abigail, 4 Nov. 1679 ; Nathaniel, 3 Oct. 1681; Deborah, 18 Dec. 1683 ; Samuel, 28 Mar. 1685 ; Joseph, 15 Jan. 1688; and Stephen, Apr. 1690 ; rem. to Windham, there was deac. and d. 16 Jan. 1730, aged a. 88. His w. had d. 4 Aug. 1726, a. 78 yrs. old. THOMAS, Norwich, s. of the preced. m. 17 Feb. 1692, Hannah, d. of William Backus, and d. 1 Apr. 1710. Caulkins.

BINGLEY, THOMAS, Boston 1665, m. 1673, Abigail, d. of Thomas Buttolph, wid. of David Saywell. WILLIAM, Newbury 1659, m. 27 Feb. 1660, Eliz. Preston, had William, b. 24 Feb. 1662 ; and prob. Eliz. wh. m. John Chase.

BINNEY, JOHN, Hull 1679, may have come few yrs. bef. by w. Mercy had John, b. 31 May 1680; Samuel, 1681; Mercy, 15 Dec. 1682 ; Isaac, 25 June 1685 ; Thomas, 3 Feb. 1687 ; and Eliz. 3 Dec. 1690, wh. m. 12 Dec. 1710 George Vickers of H. He d. 10 Nov. 1698, and his wid. Mary d. 19 Jan. 1709. JOHN, Hull, s. of the preced. m. 3 May 1704, Hannah, d. prob. of the sec. Thomas Paine of the same, had John, b. 23 Apr. 1705 ; Joshua, 26 Jan. 1707 ; Mercy, 5 May 1709, d. at 17 yrs.; Amos, 5 Feb. 1711 ; Elkanah, 28 Dec. 1715; Hannah, 18 Oct. 1717 ; Dorcas, 20 June 1721; Barnabas, 22 Mar. 1723 ; and Phebe, 11 Nov. 1725 ; was deac. 1734, town clk. and treas. m. sec. w. Nov. 1757, Sarah Crosby, and d. 30 June 1759. Amos was progenit. of the Boston fam. and Barnabas was gr.f. of the disting. lawyer of Phila. Horace, H. C. 1797, LL. D. SAMUEL, Hull, br. of the preced. m. 11 Nov. 1701, Rebecca Vickers, and d. 12 Feb. 1724, had Eliz. b. 25 Dec. 1702 ; Samuel, 4 Dec. 1704; Isaac, 19 Dec. 1706; Rebecca; and Caleb. THOMAS, Boston, br. of the preced. by w. Margaret, wh. d. 16 Sept. 1743, had eleven ch. of wh. Jonathan was one, wh. went to Halifax, N. S. 1753, and was progenit. of the fams. in that prov. of this name.

BINKS, or BINCKS, sometimes BRINKS, BRYAN, Boston, with Peter Johnson, was agent of the husbandmen's comp. of adventurers, whose little vessel, the Plough, from London, with ten passeng. 1632, was disabl. on the voyage from Boston to the W. I. therefore put back, and was here brok. up. From Eng. she had come to Sagadahoc. He went to Virg. Winth. I. 58 and 60.

BINNS, JONAS, Dover 1648.

BINSON. See Benson.

BIRCH, JONATHAN, Dorchester 1667, was prob. s. of Thomas. SIMON, Mass. 1635. Felt. THOMAS, Dorchester, wh. d. 3 Oct. 1657, in his will of 4 June 1654, speaks of six ch. tho. Joseph (eldest s. perhaps eldest ch. hav. double portion), Jeremiah, and Mary only are nam. No dates of the b. of either being kn. I much incline to suppose, that some, if not all, were b. in Eng. THOMAS, Swanzey, m. 24 Jan. 1684, Bath-sheba Sanford.

BIRCHARD, BURCHARD, or BIRCHALL, JAMES, Norwich, s. of John of the same, m. 17 Mar. 1696, Eliz. d. prob. of sec. Matthew Beckwith, had, beside sev. ds. whose names are not seen, James, b. 1699; Matthew, 1702; John, 1704; and Daniel, 1718; was liv. 1745, then call. "old James B." JOHN, Boston 1655, s. of Thomas, b. in Eng. m. 22 July 1653, Christian Andrews, rem. to Norwich bef. 1660, had Thomas, b. Oct. 1654, d. at four yrs.; Catharine, 1656, d. soon; John, 1657, d. next yr.; John, again, 1659, d. young; Mary, 1661, d. young; Samuel, 15 July 1663; James, 16 July 1665; Abigail, Nov. 1667; Thomas, again, Jan. 1669; John, again, Feb. 1671; Joseph, Feb. 1673; Benjamin, 1675, d. same yr.; Mary, again, June 1677; and Daniel, Nov. 1680. He was a man of note and activ. clk. of the County Ct. in 1673, in 1692, was one of the purch. of Lebanon, with youngest three s. rem. to plant the town, and d. there 17 Nov. 1702, leav. wid. Jane, wh. may have been mo. of none of these ch. See Caulkins, Hist. of Norwich, 98. SAMUEL, New London, s. of John of Norwich, m. a. 1695, Ann, d. of David Caulkins of the same, had Samuel, bapt. 2 May 1697; and Ann, 26 Oct. 1701; and prob. he rem. * THOMAS, Roxbury, came in the Truelove from London 1635, aged 40, with w. Mary, 38, and prob. ch. Eliz. 13; Mary, 12; Sarah, 9; Susan, 8; John, 7; and Ann, 18 mos. was adm. freem. 17 May 1637; when the spell. is Bircher, yet in the custom ho. rec. at London was giv. Burchard, and he wrote it Birchwood; rem. to Hartford, where he had been an original propr. tho. not a first sett. again rem. to Saybrook, of wh. he was rep. 1650 and 1, and d. 1684. Plausib. conject. may be rais. that he went back to R. where it appears by the ch. rec. " goodw. Birchard was bur. 24 Mar. 1655," and as the town rec. is silent, it would be thot. that she was on a visit to her old friends, and it might be suggest. that they liv. within the edge of Dorchester, where the rec. gives dec. of one Thomas B. 3 Oct. 1657. Sarah m. 1647, at Hartford, Bartholomew Barnard. See Porter, 9, 23, and 43; and Hawes, 79. THOMAS, Norwich, s. of John of the same, m. 1708, Sarah Webb, had Thomas, b. next yr. but no more can be found of him.

BIRD, JAMES, Hartford 1657, s. of Thomas the first, was adm. freem.

21 May of that yr. with his br. Joseph, m. Lydia Steele, perhaps d. of John of Farmington, whither he rem. had James; Thomas; Hannah; Rebecca; Lydia; Mehitable, bapt. 12 Mar. 1682; and Eliz. 23 Nov. 1684. He d. 1708; but his wid. Lydia liv. to 1759, as is said; no doubt, however, without truth. JAMES, Dorchester, s. of Thomas of the same, was a tanner, had w. Mary, and ch. James, bapt. 16 Feb. 1673; Eunice, 23 July 1682; Ebenezer, 10 Feb. 1684; a d. Bebee, 22 Aug. 1686; Priscilla, 20 May 1688; and Henry, 23 Mar. 1690; was freem. 1690, d. 1 Sept. 1733. JATHNIEL, Ipswich, had gr. of ld. 1641, yet prob. Farmer mistook the Christian name; and there was at I. that yr. a wid. B. JOHN, adm. freem. of Mass. 1645, of wh. I can find no more. JOHN, Dorchester, s. of Thomas of the same, m. Eliz. d. of Richard Williams of Taunton, had John, bapt. 14 Apr. 1672; Abiel, 27 Apr. 1673; Damaris, b. 18, bapt. 19 Sept. 1675; Hannah, bapt. 23 Dec. 1677; a ch. wh. name is not seen, 16 May 1680; Eliz. 7 Jan. 1683; Deiton, a d. 23 Oct. 1687; and Silence, 2 Feb. 1690; was selectman 1694, 5 and 6, and d. 2 Aug. 1732. His w. had d. 20 Oct. 1724, aged 77. JOSEPH, Hartford, s. of the first Thomas, had Eliz., Samuel, Nathaniel, Thomas, James, Joseph, Mary, and Mindwell. In 1679 he liv. at Farmington, where the last nam. ch. was bapt. 27 Feb. 1681. SIMON, Boston, came 1635, aged 20, in the Susan and Ellen, from London, where he had learn. bad tricks, for in Oct. of that yr. he was sentenc. to be whip. tho. not the worst of a set of boys, that ran away from their master, stole a boat, etc. See Col. Rec. I. 162. He liv. at Winisemit, or Rumney marsh, now Chelsea, was freem. 1644, but excommun. in July 1646, restor. soon after, and sober eno. to be made constable 1655, rem. to Billerica, there d. 7 July 1666. His will, of 4 Jan. preced. names sev. cousins, but no ch. and made his w. Mary extrix. THOMAS, Hartford, d. bef. 1653, leav. beside James and Joseph, bef. ment. two ds. wh. all mov. to Farmington, and there all four had fams. THOMAS, Scituate 1627, or later, tho. in his Hist. 221, Deane ment. a tradit. in favor of 1623, wh. he did not stigmatize as he should. THOMAS, Dorchester, 1640, by w. Ann, wh. d. 20 Aug. 1673, had Thomas, b. 4 May 1640, bapt. 18 July 1641; John, 11 Mar. 1642, bapt. that yr.; Samuel, 1644, bapt. that yr.; James, 1647; Sarah, bapt. 12 Aug. 1649, wh. d. 2 Apr. 1669; and Joseph, wh. d. 26 Sept. 1665. He made his will, 12 July 1666, and d. 8 June foll. in his 64th yr. THOMAS, Dorchester, eldest s. of the preced. a tanner, m. 2 Apr. 1665, Thankful, d. of Humphrey Atherton, had Joseph, Thankful, Sarah, Thomas, Ann, Mary, Submit, and Mercy, all bapt. 24 June 1683, "the mo. very lately adm. to full commun."; Patience, 9 Dec. foll. and Benjamin, 6 June 1686, "then 2 or 3 mos. old." He was freem. 1690, and d. 30 Jan. 1710, and his wid.

d. 11 Apr. 1719, aged 77 yrs. Of this name, in 1829, Farmer found gr. four at Yale, two at Harv. and two at other coll. in N. E.

BIRDEN, JOHN, a gr. of Harv. Coll. 1647, went to Eng. to exercise his faculties, indicat. by *Italic* types, and that is all that is kn. of him.

BIRDLEY, GILES, Ipswich 1648, had w. Eliz. and ch. Andrew, b. 5 Sept. 1657; James, 10 Feb. 1660; Giles, 13 July 1662; and John; and d. 1668. His will of 18 July was pro. 20 Sept. in that yr. TYLER, Ipswich 1648, br. perhaps of the preced. if such be the true spell. of the surname, of which some doubt is felt. Mr. Hammatt, the judicious critic, of Ipswich annals, thot. it the same as Burley.

BIRDSALL. See Burdsall.

BIRDSEYE, JOHN, Milford 1639, rem. 1649 to Stratford, there was emin. for serv. in ch. and town. Trumbull, I. 109. In his will of 22 Aug. 1689 he names sec. w. Alice Tomlinson, and confirms their contr. of m. also ment. s. John, and d. Joanna, w. of Timothy Wilcockson, m. 28 Dec. 1664. JOHN, Stratford 1668, was s. of the preced. Rev. Nathan, Yale 1736, d. 1818 at S. in 103d yr. Variat. in spell. this name shows Birdsey and Burdsie.

BIRGE, DANIEL, Windsor, s. of Richard, m. 5 Nov. 1668, Deborah, d. of Thomas Holcomb, had Eliz. b. 25 Apr. 1670; d. young; Deborah 26 Nov. 1671; Eliz. again, 3 Feb. 1675; Mary, 25 Dec. 1677; Daniel, 16 Sept. 1680; and Abigail, June 1685. The w. d. 26 May foll. and by sec. w. he had John, 1689; Cornelius, July 1694; and Esther, 1697. He d. 26 Jan. 1698, when the eight ch. were liv. to partake est. with the wid. JOHN, Windsor, br. of the preced. m. 28 May 1679, Hannah, youngest d. of Robert Watson of the same, had John, b. 4 Feb. 1680; Hannah, 1681; Jeremiah, 1685; and Mary, 1687. His w. d. 24 July 1690; and he d. 2 Dec. 1697, leav. no other ch. JOSEPH, Windsor, youngest br. of the preced. had w. Mary, wh. d. 11 Apr. 1690. He d. Dec. 1705, and next mo. his s. Joseph chose a guardn. Other ch. he had elder, but their names are unkn. RICHARD, Windsor 1636, so that we may judge he had been of Dorchester, m. 5 Oct. 1641, Eliz. d. of William Gaylord, had Daniel, b. 24 Nov. 1644; Eliz. 28 July 1646, d. soon; Jeremy, 6 May 1648, wh. was k. 22 Oct. 1668, by fall of a tree; John, 14 Jan. 1650; and Joseph, 2 Nov. 1651, in wh. yr. the f. d. The wid. m. 22 Apr. 1653, Thomas Hoskins.

BISBEE, or BISBY. See Besbedge.

BISCOE. See Briscoe.

BISCON, ISAAC, Boston, no doubt a Huguenot from France, came 1690, with w. and was adm. a resid. 1 Feb. 1691. I kn. no more.

BISHOP, EDWARD, Salem 1639, had there bapt. Hannah, 12 Apr. 1646; Edward, 23 Apr. 1648; and Mary, 12 Oct. 1651; and was one

of the found. of the ch. 1667, at Beverly. With his w. Sarah he was
imprison. on charge of witchcraft, Apr. 1692, yet, happily, they were not
too old to escape by break. gaol, for wh. their prop. was seiz. and by s.
Samuel redeem. Felt calls the name Edmund once, but in three places
after gives it as here. One Bridget B. of the same town had been charg.
with the same damnable offence in 1680 ; when the great adversary was
foil. but he easily prevail. with the judges, in June 1692, when the poor
woman was so much more infirm, to consent to her being hanged.
HENRY, Newport 1639. HENRY, New Haven, took o. of fidel. 1644,
and was farmer for Rev. John Davenport. HENRY, Ipswich, perhaps
br. of Nathaniel, m. at Boston, 20 Feb. 1657, wid. Eliz. Wilbore, and d.
bef. 1664. †‡*JAMES, New Haven 1648, was secr. of the Col. 1651,
rep. 1665 in the first sess. after the union with Conn. Assist. 1668, and
Dep. Gov. 1683 until his d. 22 June 1691. He had b. at Branford,
Hannah, 29 May, bapt. at N. H. 1 June 1651 ; others b. at N. H.
Grace, 17 Jan. 1653, bapt. prob. 20 Feb. foll. certain. not 30, as print.
in Geneal. Reg. IX. 358 ; Sarah, 28, bapt. 29 July 1655 ; Eliz. 3 July
1657, not seen among the bapt. ; Abigail, 30 Oct. 1659, bapt. 22 Jan.
foll. ; John, 17 May 1662, not seen among the bapt. ; Ruth, 22 Nov.
1664, bapt. 12 Dec. foll. the w. having d. 26 Nov. He m. 12 Dec. 1665,
Eliz. d. of Micah Tompkins of Milford, and had Samuel 21, bapt. prob.
25 Nov. 1666 ; Mary, b. 14 Mar. 1669 ; James, 27 July 1671 ; and Rebecca, 10 Dec. 1673. Some of the days giv. for bapt. in Geneal. Reg.
we kn. are wrong, bec. they were not Sundays, and exc. on this day no
such cerem. could be perform. as by Davenport hims. we may be taught,
in 3 Mass. Hist. Coll. X. 61. In those cases the nearest first day of the
week is substitut. by me. See Trumbull, I. 336. Eliz. m. 12 Sept.
1677, Eleazer Giles. JAMES, Duxbury 1679, was liv. 1710, and Winsor, as his ch. counts Ebenezer, Abigail, John, and Hudson. JOB, Ipswich 1648, s. of Thomas of the same, m. Eliz. d. of Rev. George Phillips
one that he brot. from Eng. had prob. only Eliz. wh. d. 27 Feb. 1652 ;
but by sec. w. had Dinah, b. 19 June 1657 ; Sarah, 19 May 1659 ; and
Hannah, 24 Dec. 1662. JOHN, Newbury, a carpenter, m. Oct. 1647,
Rebecca, wid. of Samuel Scullard, wh. may have d. in Eng. and d. of
Richard Kent of N. had John, b. 19 Sept. 1648 ; Rebecca, 15 May
1650 ; Joanna, 24 Apr. 1652 ; Hannah, 10 Dec. 1653 ; Eliz. 31 Aug.
1655, d. next yr.; Jonathan, 11 Jan. 1657 ; Noah, 20 June 1658 ; and
David, 26 Aug. 1660 ; rem. first to Nantucket, thence, with other neighb.
1667, to found the town of Woodbridge, N. J. from wh. he was the first
rep. in the Assemb. 1668, under Gov. Carteret a counsel. 1672, and d.
1684. His s. John, of Rahway, was of Gov. Hamilton's counc. 1693.
See Whitehead's E. Jersey, 42, 52, 77, and 134. JOHN, Boston 1644,

was chos. min. at Stamford, whither he went on foot, had w. Rebecca, and ch. Stephen, Joseph, Ebenezer, Benjamin, beside one, perhaps nam. Whiting, that d. early, all ment. in his will. For sec. w. he had Joanna, d. of Capt. Thomas Willet, wid. of Rev. Peter Prudden of Milford. His will, made 16 Nov. 1694, pro. 12 Mar. foll. instructs us as to these ws. and his ch. wh. were all by the first. As early as 1640 he had been at Taunton. He preach. near 50 yrs. wrote a Latin epit. on Richard Mather (whence a presumpt. arises, that he was from Dorchester), wh. may be read in the Magnalia of the gr.s. cap. 20 of III. or p. 131. But the dignity of the subject, the value of the poetry, or even his serv. in the ch. was less operative, I suppose, in draw. this compliment to Bishop, than the pun on his name, for he is made, in that immortal work, to sign, J. Episcopius. JOHN, Guilford 1639, had w. Ann, s. John, and Stephen, and d. bef. 7 Jan. 1661, when his inv. was taken. They are nam. in the will of the wid. pro. June 1676 at Hartford; as also her s.-in-law, James Steele, wh. had m. 18 Oct. 1651, I suppose, her d. Bethia; gr.d. Eliz. Hubbard, perhaps d. of George. JOHN, Guilford 1648, s. of the preced. was b. in Eng. m. 13 Dec. 1650, Susanna, d. of Henry Goldham, had Mary, b. 28 Nov. 1652; John; Nathaniel; Susanna; Eliz.; Samuel, 28 Oct. 1670; Sarah, 22 Jan. 1674; and Abigail, 25 June 1680; and he d. Oct. 1683. His wid. d. 1 Nov. 1703, and the partition of her est. Jan. 1704, gives ano. s. Daniel, and shows how some of the ds. were m. Mary Field had bef. been w. of John Hodgkin, and of Isaac Johnson, as is said; Susanna Blatchley was w. of Moses; Eliz. Scranton was perhaps wid. of the sec. John of G. wh. had prob. m. her as wid. of Thomas Clark of the same; and the other two ds. were unm. as presum. from no surnames being giv. JOHN, Salem, k. by the Ind. 17 Apr. 1689. JOHN, New Haven 1689, m. Abigail, d. of Nathaniel Willet of Hartford, and I hear no more. NATHANIEL, Boston, currier, as early as 1634, own. a lot at Ipswich 1638, but seems to have prefer. B. freem. 1645, by w. Alice, d. of James Mattocks, had Sarah, b. 20 Mar. 1635; Ruth, 14 Apr. 1639; Joseph, 14 July 1642; Benjamin, 31 May, bapt. 2 June 1644; John, 29 bapt. 31 Jan. 1647; beside Samuel, whose d. by the more ancient copy of our rec. (for we have no orig. for very many yrs.) 7 Mar. 1647, is made the day of his b. by the absurdity of more recent copy; in his room was b. ano. Samuel, perhaps the same yr.; Hannah, bapt. 11 Feb. 1649, at 7 days old; and Rebecca, b. 8 Apr. 1652. When he d. is unkn. but his wid. m. 22 Nov. 1659, John Lewis. Sarah m. 18 Sept. 1654, Samuel Bucknell, and Ruth m. 15 Apr. 1656, John Pierce. RICHARD, Salem 1635, freem. 18 May 1642, d. 30 Dec. 1674. His first w. wh. brot. him Thomas, John, Nathaniel, beside a d. to m. John Dorland, perhaps ano.

16 *

w. of John Bly, was the wid. of Richard King (in whose right he had admin. on King's est. gr. 2 June 1635), and she d. 24 Aug. 1658; and he next m. 12 or 22 July 1660, Mary, wid. of William Gott. His s. Nathaniel and John went to Southampton on L. I. Mr. Felt says. RICHARD, Plymouth, was unhapp. m. 5 Dec. 1644, Alice wid. of George Clark, and she was hang. Oct. 1648 for murder of Martha Clark her ch. SAMUEL, Boston, s. of Nathaniel of the same, or perhaps of Thomas, was gr. H. C. 1665; and mark. as d. 1687 by the latest catal. yet in an earlier one, was said to d. 1703. SAMUEL, Bradford, s. of Thomas of Ipswich, by w. Esther had John, wh. was a physician at Medford; and d. Mar. 1681. STEPHEN, Guilford 1650, s. of John first of the same, b. in Eng. m. 4 May 1654, Tabitha Wilkinson, had Stephen, b. 20 Dec. 1655; Tabitha, 14 Sept. 1657; Caleb, 24 Jan. 1660; David, 8 Dec. 1663, d. young; Mehitable, 12 Sept. 1668; Hannah, 27 Mar. 1671, d. young; Josiah, 20 Mar. 1674, d. young; Ebenezer, 5 Aug. 1675; and James, 18 Aug. 1678. He d. 1 Aug. 1690, and his wid. d. 21 Dec. 1692, the six liv. ch. being all nam. in the wills of both f. and mo. Tabitha m. Nathaniel Foote; and Mehitable m. 1704, John Whitehead. *THOMAS, Ipswich 1636, was perhaps br. of Nathaniel, rep. 1666, d. 7 Feb. 1671, leav. wid. Margaret, wh. rem. to Boston, and ch. Samuel, John, Thomas, Job, and Nathaniel, with large est. THOMAS, Salem, s. of Richard of the same, had Richard, but Felt could give no date. THOMAS, Roxbury, by w. Prudence, wh. d. 8 Oct. 1680, by ch. rec. but 11 by town rec. had Thomas, b. 30 Sept. bapt. 3 Oct. preced. and ano. w. Eliz. was bur. 11 Dec. 1681; and he m. 7 June 1683, Ann, or Hannah Gary, wh. d. 16 Sept. 1691, and he d. 29 June 1727, aged 81 by the gr.stone. Perhaps he was s. of the first Thomas. *TOWNSEND, Salem, freem. 2 Sept. 1635, rep. 1636, 7 and 40, had Leah, bapt. 19 June 1637; and John, 31 July 1642; but was censur. in 1645, for slighting that ordin. Of this name, in 1833, had been gr. seven at Yale, and seven at other N. E. coll.

BISS, JAMES, Boston, by w. Jemima had Martha, b. 23 Feb. 1668.

BISSELL, BENJAMIN, Windsor, s. of Thomas of the same, d. 5 May 1698, leav. good est. with wid. Abigail, wh. is thot. to have been d. of Thomas Allyn, and to have m. as his sec. w. after d. of Bissell, Rev. John Williams of Deerfield. JACOB, Simsbury, s. of Samuel of Windsor, had w. Mary, and s. Jacob, b. 8 June 1694, wh. d. at 16 yrs. and the f. d. 1 Aug. 1694. His wid. m. 1698, Peter Buell. *JOHN, Windsor 1639, is said to have come from Eng. with Rev. Ephraim Hewett, was rep. 1648–57, and d. 3 Oct. 1677, aged 85, had John, Thomas, Samuel, Nathaniel, Mary, and Joice, of wh. Nathaniel, bapt. 27 Sept. 1640, was perhaps the only one b. on our side of the ocean. His w. d.

21 May foll. and his next w. d. 29 Nov. 1665 ; but of both the names
are unkn. Mary m. 12 Apr. 1649, Jacob Drake, and Joice m. 17 Nov.
1665, Samuel Pinney. JOHN, Windsor, s. of the preced. b. in Eng. m. 17
June 1658, Isabel, d. of Maj. John Mason, had Mary, b. 22 Feb. 1659 ;
John, 4 May 1661 ; Daniel, 29 Sept. 1663 ; Dorothy, 10 Aug. 1665 ;
Josiah, 10 Oct. 1670 ; Hezekiah, 30 Apr. 1673 ; Ann, 28 Apr. 1675 ; and
Jeremiah, 22 June 1677. He liv. long, rem. to Lebanon, thence to Coventry. JOHN, Windsor, s. of Samuel, m. 26 Aug. 1680, Abigail, d. of
William Filley, had Abigail, b. 3 Aug. 1681 ; and John, 1683; and d. early
in 1685, his inv. being of 27 Jan. JOSEPH, Windsor, s. of Thomas of the
same, had Joseph, b. early in 1688 ; Benoni, 1689 ; and d. that yr. at
Simsbury. NATHANIEL, Windsor, s. of John the first, m. 25 Sept. 1662
Mindwell, youngest d. of deac. John Moore, had Mindwell, b. 3 Oct.
1663 ; Nathaniel, 7 Jan. 1666; Jonathan, 3 July 1668, d. young ; Hannah, 12 Jan. 1671 ; Abigail, 14 Sept. 1673, d. young ; Jonathan, again,
14 Feb. 1675 ; Abigail, again, 9, bapt. 11 Mar. 1677 ; Eliz. 15 Mar.
1679 ; and David, 1682. His w. d. 24 Nov. 1682, and he m. Dorothy,
d. of Joseph Fitch, had a s. wh. d. without name, 14 Aug. 1684 ; and
Dorothy, 1686. This w. d. 28 June 1691, but the d. of h. is not kn.
SAMUEL, Windsor, br. of the preced. prob. b. in Eng. m. 11 June 1658,
Abigail, d. of Thomas Holcomb, had John, b. 5 Apr. 1659; Abigail, 6
July 1661 ; Jacob, 28 Mar. 1664 ; Mary, 15 Sept. 1666 ; Samuel, 11
Jan. 1669, d. at 29 yrs. leav. wid. Mary, and ch. unb. Mary ; Benajah,
30 June 1671, wh. d. bef. his f. Joshua ; Eliz. 4 Jan. 1678 ; Deborah,
29 Oct. 1679 ; and Hannah, 1682. His w. d. 17 Aug. 1688 ; and he
took sec. w. Mary, and d. 3 Dec. 1700. THOMAS, Windsor, br. of the
preced. b. in Eng. m. 11 Oct. 1655, Abigail, d. of deac. John Moore, had
Thomas, b. 12 Oct. 1656 ; Abigail, 23 Nov. 1658 ; John, 26 Jan. 1661 ;
Joseph, 18 Apr. 1663 ; Eliz. 9 June 1666 ; Benjamin, 9 Sept. 1669 ;
Sarah, 8 Jan. 1672 ; Ephraim, 11 Apr. 1676, d. in few days ; Esther, 2
Apr. 1677, d. at one yr. ; Ephraim, again, 4 Nov. 1680 ; Isaac, 22 Sept.
1682 ; and Ebenezer, wh. d. 22 Aug. 1689, prob. young. and the f. d. 31
July preced. Abigail m. 1678, Nathaniel Gaylord ; Eliz. m. 1682,
John Stoughton, and d. 1688. THOMAS, Windsor, s. of the preced. m.
at Northampton, 15 Oct. 1678, Esther, d. of Elder John Strong, had
Esther, b. 10 Sept. bapt. 5 Oct. 1679 ; Abigail, b. 20 Oct. 1681 ; Thomas,
1683, Eunice, 1686 ; Nathaniel, 1690, d. young; Nathaniel, again, 1694
and Jerijah, 1698. Eight of this name had, in 1834, been gr. at Yale,
and one at Dart.

BITNER, WILLIAM, Andover, m. 1648, Sarah, d. of Edmund Ingalls
of the same. No more of him is seen.

BITTLESTONE, BIDLESTON, or BIDDLESTONE, Thomas, Cambridge,

had w. Eliz. and only d. Eliz. perhaps only ch. and d. 23 Nov. 1640. His will, of 30 Oct. preced. leav. to Rev. Robert Fordham a fellow pas- seng. memo. of kindness, giv. in abstr. Geneal. Reg. II. 263, leads me to feel sure, that he had not long been in the country, and prob. that Wil- liam wh. d. 5 Oct. 1640, was his s.   More than ⅔ of his inv. of prop. £271. 2. 2. was in money.   His wid. d. 1 July 1672, and his d. had m. 13 Dec. 1650, John Briscoe of Watertown.

BITTS, JAMES, Boston, "the Scotchman," to wh. Capt. Keayne, in Dec. 1653, by codic. to his will, gave 20s.   Perhaps he was a prisoner, taken in the battle of Dunbar, 3 Sept. 1650, sent over the yr. after to be sold here (of whose recept. here Cotton wrote to the Ld. General Crom- well in that curious letter, preserv. in the invalu. vol. call. Hutch. Coll.), for of that cargo of human flesh we have no invoice; while his name is not seen in the doleful consignm. of 272 others by the John and Sarah, suppl. from the fatal field of Worcester, call. Cromwell's *crowning* mercy, in the foll. yr.

BIXBY, DANIEL, Andover, m. 2 Dec. 1674, Hannah, prob. d. of Thomas Chandler of the same, had Daniel, Thomas, David, and Joseph, and d. 1717.   JONATHAN, Newton 1691, s. of Joseph the sec. by w. Rachel, m. 1709, had Rachel, perhaps others, certain. Hannah, posthum. 30 Apr. 1715, he having d. 1714, prob. under mid. age.   In Hist. of N. Jackson could find little of him to tell.   JOSEPH, Salisbury, an early sett. m. 1647, Sarah, wid. of Luke Heard, wh. came from Assington, Co. Suff. and her maid. name was Wyatt, as Farmer tells; was of Ipswich 1649, and Rowley 1667, but I can tell no more.   JOSEPH, Boxford, perhaps s. of the preced. m. 1682, Sarah Gould, had Sarah, Joseph, Jonathan, George, Daniel, Benjamin, Mary, and Abigail, and d. a. 1704.   NA- THANIEL, Ipswich 1637, of wh. Mr. Felt can tell me no more.   THOMAS, Salem 1636; and equal. short is the tale for him.   Very freq. is the name in our early rec. Bigsbee, as it was pronounc. and not rarely is heard in our day.   A wid. Mary B. was receiv. into Boston ch. 20 June 1640; but of wh. she had been w. is not found.

BLACHLEY, AARON, Branford, m. 1686, Sarah, wid. of Robert Foot. MOSES and THOMAS, of the same town, engag. 1667, in form. ch. cove- nant, prob. were brs.

BLACK, DANIEL, Rowley 1680, in the pt. wh. bec. Boxford.   One of the prisoners, after the sad gleanings at Worcester fight, 3 Sept. 1651, sent over here for sale by the John and Sarah, bore this name, and may be the sufferer possib. but not prob. as near all of the poor fellows d. bef. his date, of homesickness or the scurvy.   GEORGE, Gloucester, by w. Dorothy, had Thomas, b. 9 June 1658, d. soon; and Ruth, 3 Sept. 1659.   HENRY, freem. of Mass. 1645, of wh. no more is heard by me.

See Blake. JOHN, Charlestown 1634, with w. Susanna, adm. of the ch. 4 Jan. foll. yet not being nam. by Frothingham causes a doubt as to resid. but he was adm. freem. 29 May 1644. At Salem, Felt finds a John, 1636, wh. he thinks the same and freem. 6 Mar. 1632, wh. seems inconsist., had Lydia, bapt. 25 Dec. 1636, d. soon; Lydia, again, 3 June, 1638; and ano. d. 27 Nov. 1640, not nam. on the rec. He d. at Beverly, 16 Mar. 1675, in 66th yr. and his wid. Freeborn d. 1681, aged 46. JOHN, Beverly, s. prob. of the preced. freem. 1670. MILES, Sandwich 1643. RICHARD, freem. of Mass. 1645. Not seldom this name is confus. with Blake.

BLACKBURNE, ‖ WALTER, Boston 1640, had, perhaps liv. at Roxbury, was of ar. co. 1638, freem. 22 May 1639, went home 1641, leav. w. Eliz. but whether the h. came back, or she foll. him, no means of telling are within reach.

BLACKFORD, NICHOLAS, Newport, among the freem. of 1655.

BLACKLEACH, BENJAMIN, Cambridge, m. Dorcas, d. of Nathaniel Bowman, had Nathaniel, and Benjamin, as from the will of the f. of their mo. is learn. The wid. m. a March. * JOHN, Salem 1634, freem. 6 May 1635, an active merch. rep. 1636, by w. Eliz. beside John, had Exercise, bapt. 24 Jan. 1637; Joshua, 23 Feb. 1639; Eliz. 12 Dec. 1641, d. soon; Benoni, May 1643; Eliz. again, 4 Aug. 1644; and Solomon; rem. to Boston, where his d. Exercise m. 24 Aug. 1660, Richard Rasor; thence rem. to Hartford, went home prob. in 1678 (unless it were his s. John, that went) but next yr. came again, and d. at Wethersfield, 23 Aug. 1683. His w. Eliz. d. a few weeks earlier. JOHN, Boston, s. of the preced. by w. Eliz. had John, b. 1660, rem. next yr. to Hartford, there bot. of his f. the est. that Elder Goodwin sold him, went to Eng. in 1678, but next yr. emb. for Boston, 8 Mar. in the Mayflower, with a ch. wh. may have been sent there for educat. and, after long resid. at Wethersfield, d. 9 Sept. 1703, aged 77, and the rec. is prob. aggrav. by 10 yrs. His wid. d. 1708, aged 74. His ds. then were Eliz. Harris, and Mary Olcott, w. of John, wh. had first been wid. of Thomas Welles, and after d. of O. was w. of Joseph Wadsworth the intrepid preserver of the Col. Chart. in the famous Charter Oak of Hartford. His s. John d. 1700, leaving only s. John. RICHARD, Stratford 1685, then call. hims. 30 yrs. old. WILLIAM, Boston, perhaps transient resid. for short period betw. 1641 and 9. Sometimes this name appears Blacklidge.

BLACKLEY, or BLAKESLEY, EDWARD. See Blakesley. JOHN, New Haven, eldest s. of Samuel, had John, b. 15 July 1676; Hannah, 6 Aug. 1681; Mary, 15 May 1683; and perhaps others. SAMUEL, New Haven, m. 3 Dec. 1650, Hannah Potter, liv. first at Guilford, there had

John, b. 22 Oct. 1651, but at N. H. others; Hannah, 22 Oct. 1657, wh. d. young; Mary, 2 Nov. 1659; Samuel, 8 Apr. 1662; Ebenezer, 17 July 1664; and Hannah, 22 May 1666; these four bapt. 16 Sept. of this last yr. in right of their mo. Jonathan, 3 Mar. 1669, d. soon; and ano. s. Apr. 1672, wh. d. soon; as had the sec. Hannah; and he d. 17 May 1672, leav. only four ch. of wh. three s. were proprs. in 1685 at N. H. His wid. m. Henry Brooks. THOMAS, wh. came in the Hopewell, Capt. Babb, from London, 1635, aged 20, is by Hinman, 116, found in some pt. of Conn. but, unluck. he tells not where. In many rec. the name is inextric. confus. with Blatchley.

BLACKMAN, BENJAMIN, Dorchester, youngest s. of John of the same, had Keziah, bapt. 18 June 1693; Eliz. 16 Dec. 1694; Susan, 28 Nov. 1697; George, 31 Mar. 1700; Jemima, 15 Mar. 1702; Hepzibah, 24 June 1704; Mary, 6 July 1707; Eliphalet, and Benjamin, both 4 May 1712; but the name of his w. is unkn. HENRY, Charlestown, of wh. I can hear nothing, but that he d. a. 1674, and that leave to sell his ho. in favor of his ch. (only one) was giv. May 1675, to John Trumbull of C. JOHN, Dorchester 1640, perhaps earlier, by w. Mary, d. of Robert Pond, had John, b. 10 Aug. 1656; Jonathan, 1 Jan. 1658; Sarah, bapt. 17 July 1659; Joseph, b. 27 June 1661; Mary, bapt. 18 Oct. 1663; and Benjamin, 31 Dec. 1665; was freem. 1665, and d. 28 Apr. 1675, leav. wid. Sarah, by wh., perhaps, he had Adam, 9 Dec. 1670; and Abraham, 8 Feb. 1675. JOHN, Dorchester, s. of the preced. m. 26 Mar. 1685, Jane, d. of William Weeks, had Thankful, bapt. 14 Feb. 1686; John, 14 Aug. 1687; Eliz. 31 Mar. 1689; Josiah, 8 Mar. 1691; Mary, 1 May 1692; Jane, 18 Feb. 1694; Joseph, 5 Feb. 1696; Hannah, 12 Mar. 1699; Ebenezer, 9 June 1700; and Renew, 27 Aug. 1704.

BLACKMORE, JAMES, Providence, m. Mary, d. of William Hawkins, but no date is kn. to me, exc. that he bot. ld. of Thomas James, Jan. 1690, and had JOHN, wh. when he sold that est. 15 Feb. 1717, call. hims. s. and heir of James. JOHN, Lynn, rem. 1637, to Sandwich, as Lewis says, without telling his bapt. name. As the surname is so very rare, it may be lawful to conject. that he was f. of Henry of Charlestown, whose w. Mary d. 26 Mar. 1671, in her 24th yr. and of that Providence John no more is in my power to tell. WILLIAM, Scituate 1665, Deane says, came that yr. from Eng. m. 1666, Eliz. Banks, had Peter, b. 1667; John, 1669; Phebe, 1672; and William, 1675; was k. by the Ind. 21 Apr. 1676, and next yr. his wid. m. Jacob Bumpus. Phebe m. Ebenezer Holmes; Peter d. 1692, leav. Joseph, and Jane; William d. 1698, without ch. and John was then liv.

BLACKWELL, JEREMY, came in the Truelove, 1635, aged 18, and that is all I have gain. a. him. JOHN, Sandwich, s. perhaps eldest, of Michael of the same, by w. Sarah had John, b. 26 Dec. 1675; Nathaniel, 16 Dec. 1676; Desire, 20 Dec. 1678; Alice, 8 May 1681; Jane, 3 Nov. 1682; Lettice; and Caleb. He d. 1688; and at the distrib. of the est. of their gr.f. wh. d. 1709, neither Desire, nor Caleb, nor Nathaniel, is nam. tho. both Caleb and Nathaniel are nam. in his will. JOHN, Boston, was one of the purchas. 1684, of a large tract from Mass. for hims. and others in London, and at the last elect. in 1686, bef. loss of our chart., was candid. to be chos. an Assist. See Hutch. Coll. 543. Douglass, I. 419. Belkn. I. 116, and Col. Rec. V. 467, 504. JOSHUA, Sandwich, br. of the preced. had Joshua, b. 12 Jan. 1683; Mary, 5 Oct. 1684; Samuel, 13 Apr. 1689, beside Michael, Sarah, Jane, and four other ds. not nam. at the distribut. of est. of the gr.f. MICHAEL, or MYLES, Sandwich, had Michael, b. 1 June 1648, wh. d. at 25 yrs. prob. unm.; John; Joshua; and Jane. Hardly can I doubt, that this man is he designat. in the Col. list of those able to bear arms 1643, as Miles Black, Geneal. Reg. IV. 257.

BLACKWOOD, *CHRISTOPHER*, Scituate, bot. 1641, the ho. of Rev. John Lothrop, and succeed. him as preach. but next yr. sold the est. to Chauncy, wh. bec. the sett. min. and B. went home. See Lechford, 41; and Deane, 172, 222.

BLAGDEN, SAMUEL, New Hampsh. with most others, in 1691, solicit protect. of Mass.

BLAGGE, HENRY, Braintree, brickburner, had Philip, b. 24 Mar. 1643, rem. prob. to Boston 1653, d. 1662, leav. wid. Eliz. and s. Nathaniel, a brickmaker, wh. is very near, I judge, to the same trade with his f. He left good est. of wh. 19 Aug. of that yr. admin. was giv. to the wid. for self and seven ch. Often the spell. is Blague, and, I think, sometimes Black.

BLAGUE, JOSEPH, Saybrook, m. 10 Feb. 1685, Martha Kirtland, d. prob. of Nathaniel of the same, had Eliz. b. 26 May 1687; Joseph, 17 Nov. 1689, d. at 2 yrs.; Mary, 27 Aug. 1692; Joseph, again, 7 Oct. 1694; and where he was b. the spell. may have differ.

BLAISDELL, or BLASDALE, HENRY, Salisbury, by w. Mary had Ebenezer, b. 17 Oct. 1657; Mary, 29 May 1660; and Henry, 28 May 1663; rem. to Amesbury, there was freem. 1690; may have been s. of Ralph. RALPH, Salisbury 1640, but part of that yr. was liv. at York, by w. Eliz. had Mary, b. 5 Mar. 1642; Ralph, 1643; beside, perhaps, Henry, b. in Eng. 1633; and certain. Sarah, wh. d. 17 Jan. 1647. I think some ground for conject. there is that the f. went away and d. For in Aug. 1667, a wid. B. was there and then d. when Mary, d. of her h. was w. of John or Joseph Stowers, as we may prefer to award the bapt. name, under the light of Geneal. Reg. VIII. 53 and 4. The name

is found in New Hampsh. and one of the M. C. of that State in 1809–10
was Daniel B.

BLAKE, CHRISTOPHER, Boston 1663, a tailor. EDWARD, Dorchester,
s. of William, b. in Eng. m. Patience, d. of John Pope, had Edward,
wh. d. 30 Sept. 1676 ; Jonathan; Solomon; Mary, wh. m. a Pitcher;
Sarah, wh. m. Richard Talley ; Jane m. a Kilton; Susanna m. Nathaniel
Wales ; and Abigail, wh. m. 31 Dec. 1695, Obadiah Swift the sec. but I
regret to add, that my acco. of this fam. is very indistinct. He was a
cooper in Boston, and from his prosper. business enabl. to rem. near to his
native fields 1678, then bec. Milton, where he d. 1692, in his will of 31
Aug. in that yr. nam. those seven ch. but giv. little more inform. GEORGE,
Gloucester 1640, was selectman 1644, by w. Dorothy had Rebecca, b.
1641 ; Deborah; Prudence, 15 Apr. 1647 ; Eliz. 31 May 1650; Mary,
14 Feb. 1652 ; Thomas, 9 June 1658 ; and Ruth, 5 Sept. 1659 ; rem.
to Andover, where Prudence m. 6 July 1666, Moses Tyler. He d. 17
Feb. 1699 ; and his wid. d. 12 Feb. 1702, at Boxford, wh. was formerly
part of A. HENRY, Boston, by w. Eliz. had Eliz. b. 28 Oct. 1652 ;
Martha, 2 Nov. 1655 ; and Rebecca, 5 July 1657. He d. 26 July 1662.
Farmer suppos. he might be the H. Black wh. was made freem. 1645 ;
but I see some reas. for differ. opin. * JAMES, Dorchester, s. of William
the first, b. in Eng. freem. 1652, rep. 1677, was deac. and rul. Elder, m.
a. 1651, Eliz. eldest of the ch. of deac. Edward Clap, had James, b. 15
Aug. 1652 ; John, 16 Mar. 1657 ; Eliz. 3 Oct. 1658; Nathaniel, 4 July
1659 ; Jonathan, 12 July 1660 ; Sarah, 28 Feb. 1665, d. next yr.; and
Joseph, 27 Aug. 1667. His w. d. 16 Jan. 1694, and he m. 17 Sept.
1695, at Rehoboth, Eliz. Hunt, and d. 28 June 1700, aged 77. His
will, made two days bef., is very abund. in giv. fam. connex. JAMES,
Dorchester, eldest s. of the preced. was deac. m. 6 Feb. 1682, Hannah
Macy, wh. d. 1 June foll. their only ch. Eliz. d. in Nov. preced. few days
after b. He next m. 8 July 1684, Ruth Batchelder, had Hannah, b. 16
Sept. 1685, d. at one yr.; James, 30 Apr. 1688 (the dilig. collect. of the
Annals of D. for wh. we are so much indebt.), wh. d. 4 Dec. 1750 ; and
Increase, 8 June 1699. His will of 8 Aug. 1721, provides for the two s.
and their mo. wh. d. in her 90th yr. 11 Jan. 1752 ; but he had d. 22 Oct.
1732. JASPER, Hampton, d. 11 Feb. 1673, had Dorothy, or Deborah,
b. 17 Sept. 1668, wh. m. 22 Jan. 1689, Nathaniel Locke of the same.
But in his will he names w. Deborah, and ch. Timothy, Israel, John,
Jasper, and Deborah, and cous. Samuel Dalton. JEREMIAH, New London 1680, of wh. Miss Caulkins tells that he bot. ld. 1681, and was there
1688. ‖ JOHN, Dorchester, s. of William the first, b. in Eng. ar. co.
1642, freem. 1644, m. 16 Aug. 1654, wid. Mary Shaw (says the Boston
rec.), but wh. had been her former h. or whose ch. she was, I see not.

Perhaps he liv. some yrs. in Boston, a. 1663; and d. there early in 1689, and from his will of 10 Jan. in that yr. that gives to w. and to his brs. and neph. and nieces, beside others, but no ch. may safely be infer. that he left none. Yet he had Hannah, b. 16 Jan. 1659, wh. prob. d. young, and the Geneal. Reg. IX. 176, erron. makes him f. of deac. John, wh. was his neph. JOHN, Dorchester, sec. s. of James the first, had w. Mary, wh. may have borne to him Mary, 26 Apr. 1687; John; and Samuel, 26 Sept. 1691; but of this last nothing is heard, nor of John, except that he d. 19 Apr. 1689, very young. By sec. w. Hannah he had Hannah, b. 8 Sept. 1693; Eliz. 21 Feb. 1696; John, again, 23 Apr. 1698; and Josiah, 11 Mar. 1700. No full report of the m. of either w. is within reach, nor can dates of b. of all of the ch. be found. Yet he was town clk., deac. and d. 2 Mar. 1718. JOHN, Middletown, m. 1673, Sarah, d. of Richard Hall of the same, had Mercy, b. 16 Nov. of that yr.; Sarah, a. 1675; Mary, 29 July 1677; Eliz. 16 Mar. 1679; Abigail, 25 Jan. 1681; John, 19 Mar. 1683; Jonathan, 27 July 1685; Stephen, 15 July 1691; and Richard, wh. d. at 11 mos. JOHN, Hampton, took o. of alleg. 26 Apr. 1678. JOHN, Boston, joiner, had w. Sarah, and s. Richard, as from his will, 8 Oct. 1692, is learn. I presume he had not many yrs. liv. here, for he speaks of prop. in Eng. as well as in N. E. wh. he gives wholly to w. and makes her extrix. so that the s. was prob. young. JOSEPH, Dorchester, youngest s. of James the first, by w. Mehitable had Hopestill, b. 11 Jan. 1691; Nathaniel, 6 Sept. 1692, d. in few weeks; Eliz. 5 Dec. 1693; Mehitable, 23 Mar. 1696; Joseph, 8 Mar. 1699; Zipporah, 8 Jan. 1701; Ruth, 10 Dec. 1702; Ann, 3 Mar. 1705; Jeremiah, 13 Mar. 1707; Sarah, 14 July 1709, and Ebenezer, 22 Oct. 1712; and the f. d. 1 Feb. 1739. NATHANIEL, Boston 1676. PHILIP, Boston 1676. RICHARD, Andover 1645, one of the found. of the ch. perhaps was passeng. in the Confidence 1638, from Southampton, aged 16. In 1644 he was at Dorchester, but this seems slight ground for the tradit. that he was br. of William the sec. He d. 1695, therefore he was, I think, too young to be omit. in numb. of s. of the f. tho. William had br. Richard, b. four yrs. it is said, later than hims. We may well think that Richard d. young. ‖ WILLIAM, Dorchester, wh. came 1630, in the Mary and John, was eldest s. of Giles of Little Baddow, Co. Essex, had brot. with him William, b. 1620; James, 1623; John; and Edward, bef. ment. and perhaps Ann, wh. m. Jacob Legare; in 1636 went to Springfield with Pynchon, yet contin. hardly more than a yr. He was a very useful citizen, freem. 14 Mar. 1639, ar. co. 1646, selectman, town clk. etc. and d. 25 Oct. 1663, aged 69. His wid. Agnes, prob. mo. of all his ch. d. 22 July 1678. To her his will, made 3 Sept. 1661, pro. 28 Jan. 1664, refers, and to five ch. of wh. four were s. but none are nam.

*WILLIAM, Dorchester, eldest s. of the preced. b. in Eng. had Samuel, b. 14 May 1650; Ann, 6 Mar. 1653; Mary, 20 Mar. 1655; and William, 22 Feb. prob. 1657; Nathaniel, 4 July 1659; Edward, 13 Apr. 1662; Experience, 17 June 1665 ; beside Susan, wh. d. 4 May 1676 ; and at Milton (lately set off from D.), of unkn. date, Mehitable. All these, exc. William, wh. had been press. 1675, for a soldier in Philip's war, and enroll. in Moseley's comp. and prob. d. of the hardships of the Narragansett serv. are nam. in his will of 23 June 1703. From this we learn all the surnames of h's of his ds. Ann, m. 18 Dec. 1676, Thomas Gilbert, the only one of wh. I learn the date or bapt. name ; however strange such ignorance may appear. The others are call. Mary Willis, Experience Carver, and Mehitable Briggs. He was rep. for M. sev. yrs. His wid. Hannah, wh. certain. was not mo. of the earliest ch. d. 4 Aug. 1729, aged 90. At the N. E. coll. in 1835, Farmer found thirteen gr. of this name, eleven of them at Harv.

BLAKEMAN, ADAM (as I saw that he wrote at the University, as he usual. did after, tho. some of his descend. would have it Blackman), b. in Staffordsh. was bred at Christ's Coll. Oxford, being matricul. 28 May 1617, in his 19th yr. preach. in the Cos. of Leicester and Derby bef. he came over, wh. was a. 1638, and was soon after at Guilford, but in 1640 bec. the first min. of Stratford. His ch. exc. Benjamin, were prob. all b. in Eng. and he d. 7 Sept. 1665 ; and the wid. Jane d. 1673. Lechford, 43, miscalls him Blackwell. In the Magn. III. 94, c. 7, Mather exults at his chance for a pun ; Trumbull tells something; and the ch. rec. of Roxbury, a little; but we rejoice in his will of 16 Mar. 1665, as copious in informat. One d. and five s. Mary, James, Samuel, Benjamin, John, and Deliverance are ment. in it; and from later report the last was a wild youth, wh. gave his mo. much disquiet. His Latin bks. he would give to Joshua Atwater, s. of his d. Mary, if he were educ. for the min. tho. first intend. for s. Benjamin, wh. first chose ano. way of life ; yet, in the end, the gr.s. refus. the legacy, and Benjamin took to learn.

* BENJAMIN, Malden, youngest s. of the preced. after gr. at coll. 1663, was preach. at M. and there ord. 1674; m. 1 Apr. 1675 (not Sarah, as strangely is seen in the rec. of M., but) Rebecca, d. of Joshua Scottow, wh. d. as her gr.stone tells, 21 Mar. 1715. He gave up his pulpit 1678, rem. next yr. to Saco, there was a magistr. but he for some short term preach. at Scarborough. During the great French and Ind. war being driv. to Boston, he serv. 1683, as rep. for S. but contin. to live at B. At 3d ch. were bapt. his ch. Benjamin, 13 Sept. 1685 ; and Rebecca, 14 Apr. 1689. See Belkn. I. 125 ; and Hutch. I. 364. DELIVERANCE, Stonington, s. of Rev. Adam, b. in Eng. d. 20 Apr. 1702, leav. Adam, b. 1687. EBENEZER, Stratford, s. of John the first, m. 4 Oct. 1681,

Patience, d. of John Wilcoxson, had Dorothy, b. 18 Mar. 1683 ; John, 4 Apr. 1685 ; Eliz. 18 Feb. 1688 ; and Ebenezer, 9 Aug. 1690. By sec. w. m. 3 Nov. 1692, Abigail, d. of wid. Hannah Curtis, had Jonathan 24 Apr. 1696 ; David, 6 Jan. 1698, d. at 5 yrs. ; Abigail, 20 Nov. 1700, d. at 3 yrs. ; Nathan, 29 Sept. 1702 ; and Sarah, 3 Apr. 1705 ; and he d. 1715. JAMES, Stratford, br. of Deliverance, b. in Eng. m. 1657, Miriam, d. of Moses Wheeler, had Sarah, b. 25 Apr. 1658 ; Mary, 24 Apr. 1661 ; Hannah, 21 Jan. 1665 ; Jane, 26 Oct. 1668 ; Miriam, 8 Feb. 1671 ; Zechariah, 26 May 1678 ; Adam, 1 Jan. 1683 ; and James, 4 Dec. 1686 ; and d. 1689 ; his will being pro. 7 Nov. of that yr. made 18 July bef. JOHN, Wethersfield, br. of the preced. b. in Eng. m. a. 1653, Dorothy, d. of Rev. Henry Smith, and rem. to Stratford, had John, Ebenezer, and Joseph ; and d. 1662. His will of 19 Jan. in that yr. was pro. 26 Nov. foll. and his wid. m. 31 Oct. 1665, Francis Hall of S. wh. d. 1689. Her third h. was Mark Sension of Norwalk, wh. d. 1693 ; and her fourth, a. 1694, was deac. Isaac Moore of Farmington, and she d. a. 1706. After the d. of her first, she was sought by John Thomas, but Rev. Adam had in his will giv. her £5, " if she m. not John Thomas," and take her friends' adv. or contin. a wid. JOHN, Fairfield, s. of the preced. m. Mary, d. of wid. Hannah Curtis of Stratford, whose h. was not discov. by the diligence of Goodwin, had Abraham, b. 25 Oct. 1694, nam. as only ch. in his will of 6 Sept. 1706. JOSEPH, Stratford, br. of the preced. m. 14 July 1674, Hannah, d. of Francis Hall, had Joseph, b. 30 Apr. 1675 ; John ; Samuel ; Abigail ; and Rebecca. For sec. w. he m. 29 Jan. 1705, Esther Wheeler. SAMUEL, Stratford, s. of Rev. Adam, b. prob. in Eng. m. Nov. 1660, Eliz. eldest d. of the first Moses Wheeler, had s. b. Jan. 1662, d. at two mos. ; Abigail, 11 Nov. 1663 ; Adam, 4 Dec. 1665 ; and Joanna, 4 Dec. 1667 ; and he d. 27 Nov. foll. His wid. m. 1670, Jacob Walker ; and Abigail m. 4 Dec. 1679, Hezekiah Dickinson, and was mo. of famous Jonathan, Presid. of N. J. Coll.

BLAKESLEY, EBENEZER, New Haven, was an early sett. and no more is told. Trumbull, Cent. Ser. 32. EDWARD, Roxbury, was bur. 3 Nov. 1637, had good est. as his inv. of 25 Dec. foll. proves, and his d. Sarah, wh. had admin. of it, d. in May after. See Blackley, and Blatchley.

BLANCHARD, GEORGE, Charlestown 1658, s. of Thomas, b. in Eng. d. 18 Mar. 1700, aged 82, leav. Nathaniel ; Hannah, wh. m. 7 Dec. 1682, Thomas Shepard of the same, but not the min. and Sarah, m. 22 Aug. 1687, Thomas Dean of Concord. JOHN, Charlestown, br. of the preced. b. in Eng. freem. 1649, by w. Eliz. had Hannah, b. 6 Jan. 1659, and other ch. as Benjamin, James, Sarah, Mary, Nathaniel, Joseph, and Thomas, perhaps more, some of wh. left large posterity, but he rem. to

Dunstable in its early day, was there one of the found. of the ch. 16 Dec. 1685, and a deac. yet dates and other details are not seen. JOHN, Newbury, d. of smallpox, 24 July 1678. JONATHAN, Dunstable, perhaps s. of Thomas, was, in 1681, one of the town officers. JONATHAN, Andover, s. of Samuel, m. 26 May 1685, Ann, d. prob. of John Lovejoy. JOSEPH, Boston, d. Dec. 1637, but whether ch. or adult, is not seen. JOSEPH, Charlestown, s. of George of the same, m. 13 Apr. 1681, Hannah, d. of Thomas Shepard of the same, had Eliz. b. 30 Sept. 1682, d. in few mos.; Hannah, 14 Feb. 1684, d. in few days; Joseph, 7 Mar. 1686; Thomas, 28 Jan. 1688; Moses, and Aaron, tw. 4 Mar. 1690, of wh. Moses d. in few hours; and prob. Stephen. JOSEPH, Dunstable, s. of deac. John, m. 25 May 1696, Abiah, d. of Joseph Hassell, wh. d. 8 Dec. 1746, had Eliz. b. 15 Apr. 1697; Esther, 24 July 1699; Hannah, 28 Oct. 1701; Joseph, 11 Feb. 1704; Rachel, 23 Mar. 1705, prob. d. soon; Susanna, 29 Mar. 1707; Jane, 19 Mar. 1709; Rachel, again, 23 Mar. 1712; and Eleazer, 1 Dec. 1715; and d. 1727. NATHANIEL, Charlestown, s. of Thomas, b. in Eng. m. 16 Dec. 1658, Susanna Bates, rem. to Weymouth, had John, b. 27 Mar. 1660; Mary, 1 Dec. 1662; Nathaniel, 25 Sept. 1665; Edward, 7 June 1668; perhaps Susanna, 12 Aug. 1671; and Mercy, 14 Apr. 1674. His wid. m. 1680, prob. Thomas Bass, as his sec. w. and Mary m. Thomas Faxon the third. PETER, New London 1662, liv. prob. on the R. I. bounds. SAMUEL, Charlestown, s. of Thomas, came in the Jonathan 1639, aged 10 yrs. as is said, m. 3 Jan. 1655, Mary, d. of Seth Sweetser, rem. after 1664, to Andover, and d. Apr. 1707. Some of his ch. were Jonathan; Joseph; Thomas, wh. m. 22 May 1699, Rose Holmes of Marshfield, and d. 1759, aged 85; John; perhaps Hannah, wh. m. 24 May 1699, Stephen Osgood. See Abbot, Hist. of Andover, 39. THOMAS, Braintree 1646, soon after rem. to Charlestown, came in the Jonathan from London in 1639, with sev. ch. of wh. Thomas was one, all prob. by a first w. His sec. w. wh. had been wid. Agnes Barnes, a sis. of John Bent, d. with her inf. also, on the voyage, and he d. 21 May 1654. In his will, of five days earlier, he ment. w. Mary, ch. Nathaniel, Samuel, and George, and George's s. Joseph. His wid. stood up for the orthodoxy of Marmaduke Matthews at Malden, to wh. town Thomas had rem. THOMAS, Charlestown, on Mistick or Malden side, s. of the preced. b. in Eng. by w. Ann, or Hannah, had Mary, and Sarah; and he d. early in Feb. 1651. His wid. m. 18 Oct. foll. Richard Gardner of Woburn. THOMAS, Dunstable, s. of deac. John, by first w. Tabitha had Tabitha, b. 27 Feb. 1689; Hannah, 29 Nov. 1690, both at Woburn; Abigail, 5 May 1694; and John, 20 May 1696. His w. d. 29 Nov. foll. and he m. 4 Oct. 1698, Ruth Adams of Chelmsford, had Thomas, 12 Aug. 1699; William, 1701; and Ruth, 1 Apr.

1703; and d. 9 Mar. 1727. WILLIAM, Salem 1637, freem. 2 June 1641; prob. had w. Ann, d. of James Everill, rem. to Boston, and here join. our ch. May 1647, had John, b. 18 Sept. 1652; and d. 1 Oct. of that yr. His will of four days bef. pro. 18 Nov. foll. names mo. Ann (wh. I find, had ld. 1638 at S.), w. Hannah; ch. John, and Henry; br. John; f.-in-law Everill, whose three ch. he also rememb. and childr. of sis. Gorlick. His wid. m. 13 May 1655, George Manning. Of this name, in 1834, the gr. at Harv. were five; at Yale, and Dart. two ea.

BLAND, JOHN, Edgartown 1646, d. a. 1667, leav. w. Joanna, by wh. he had ds. Annabel, and Isabel. The latter m. Thomas Lovett of Hampton.

BLANDFORD, JOHN, Sudbury 1641, an orig. propr. m. wid. Dorothy Wright, had Sarah, b. 27 Jan. 1643; Hannah, 7 Mar. 1644; John, 6 Mar. 1646; Stephen, 3 Dec. 1649; and perhaps more. He had come in the Confidence, 1638, from Southampton, aged 27, in employm. of Walter Haynes, prob. bring. w. Mary, wh. d. 4 Dec. 1641; and I presume belong. to Co. Wilts. His will of 21 Oct. 1687, pro. 23 Nov. foll. bef. Sir Edmund Andros, gave all his est. to w. Dorothy for her life, but names s. Stephen, d. Maynard; beside s.-in-law Jabesh Brown, and Edward Wright; the latter s. of his w. by former h. and the other, I doubt not, h. of his d. Hannah. Sarah m. 11 Sept. 1665, Elias Keyes. STEPHEN, Sudbury, s. of the preced. m. Susanna, d. of Robert Long, of Charlestown. THOMAS, Watertown, m. 18 Dec. 1673, Eliz. Eames (perhaps d. of Thomas of Dedham), the rec. then spell. his name Blaynford; and no more is kn. of him.

BLANDING. See Blanton.

BLANEY, JOHN, Lynn 1659, m. 11 July 1660, Hannah King, perhaps d. of Daniel the first, had John, b. 5 May 1661; Daniel, 3 Aug. 1664; Henry, 15 Aug. 1666; Hannah, 11 Nov. 1667; Joseph, 2 Oct. 1670; and Eliz. 17 Aug. 1673. For sec. w. he m. Nov. 1678, Eliz. wid. of old Thomas Purchas, or Purchis. Lewis's Hist. 134, says descend. of his s. Joseph are still at L. JOHN, Charlestown, m. perhaps in 1668 or 9, Sarah, wid. of John Powell of the same, had Susanna, b. 13 June 1673, and the mo. d. 18 Oct. 1694, aged 51.

BLANTON, BLANTAINE, or BLANDING, WILLIAM, Boston 1640, a carpenter from Upton in Co. Worcester, freem. 10 May 1643, by w. Phebe had William; Phebe, bapt. 21 Aug. 1642; and Mary, 3 Aug. 1645; and d. 15 June 1662. His will of 25 Apr. preced. names s. William, for not giv. to wh. more of his est. he ment. one reason, "because he will not hearken to my counsel;" and the two ds. to wh. he dispos. all his prop. after d. of his w. with provis. should they die, "then his elder br. Ralph, and, if he have no ch. then sec. br. John, both of Upton on Severn in Worcestersh. should have it." He own. ld. in that pt. of Bos-

17 *

ton call. Muddy riv., now Brookline, and was engag. in the iron works at Taunton. WILLIAM, Rehoboth, prob. s. of the preced. took w. 4 Sept. 1674, Bethia, whose surname is not heard, had Obadiah, b. 14 Apr. 1679; and Samuel, 11 Apr. 1680.

BLATCHFORD, * PETER, New London, had serv. 1637 (bef. that town was sett.), in the Pequot war, when very young, for wh. he had gr. of ld. was constable, and a valu. citizen, in 1669 rem. to Haddam, for wh. he was rep. that and the foll. yr. and d. 1671, leav. wid. Hannah, d. of Isaac Willey, and three ch. Joanna, 5 and ½ yrs. old; Peter, 4; and Mary, 1 and ½. His wid. m. Samuel Spencer.

BLATCHLEY, AARON, Guilford, s. of Thomas, m. 1665, Mary, d. of Daniel Dodd, had Mary; Thomas, wh. d. 1692; Ebenezer; Hannah, b. 1674, d. young; Daniel, 1676; Joseph; Benjamin; Sarah; and Susanna; but the order is very uncert. and prob. one or two of these may have been offspring of sec. w. He rem. to Newark, N. J. after m. a. 1686, Sarah, wid. of Robert Foote of Branford. MOSES, Guilford 1672, younger br. of the preced. m. Susanna, d. of John Bishop of the same, had Abigail, b. 10 Dec. 1676, d. young; Moses, 10 Jan. 1679; David, 1680, d. soon; Mehitable, 1681, d. next yr.; Mehitable, again, 1683; Abraham, 1684; Abigail, again, 1686; David, again, 1689; Bashua, 1692; and Abial, posthum. 1693, or 4. He d. 15 Oct. 1693; and his wid. d. Oct. 1729. SAMUEL, Guilford 1650. See Blackley. * THOMAS, Hartford 1640, rem. to New Haven 1643, took o. of fidel. next yr. but in two yrs. more was of Branford; encourag. the rem. of others to Newark, N. J. but did not go; in 1667 and three yrs. foll. was rep. By w. Susanna he had Aaron; Moses, b. 25 May 1650, both bapt. 1 June 1651 at New Haven; Miriam, I think, bapt. 2 May 1652; and Abigail. In his latter days he was of Guilford, and d. at Boston, a. 1674, prob. on a trading visit. His wid. m. Richard Bristow; d. Miriam m. 1670, Samuel Pond. Blachley and Blackley, sometimes represent this name, especially the latter, wh. see.

BLAXTON, JOHN, Cumberland, s. of William, sold the ld. deriv. from his f. and in 1692, rem. with his w. Catharine to Providence; where prob. in 1700, or shortly bef. was b. his s. John, perhaps, thence, the same yr. to Rehoboth, in that part set off as Attleborough, and from this town, as fearing he might bec. a pauper, was warn. to depart 1713. He had acquir. an unsocial temper, and liv. as a hermit; but that affection or affectation could be as well indulg. in the new resid. at Branford, wh. with high probabil. is thot. to have been his resort. His s. John there d. as the gr.stone rec. 3 Jan. 1785, unless ano. John of so unusual surname be assum. and that would be contrary to all reasona. inferences. WILLIAM, Boston 1625, or 6, was bred at Emanuel, often call. the Puritan, Coll. Cambridge, where he had his degr. 1617, and 1621, and was prob. ord. in Eng. but had no kn. cure, came in unkn. sh. at uncert. time, for undiscov. cause, and sat down, alone, on the peninsu. now the ch. part of Boston, where he contin. some four or five yrs. after the arr. of the Gov. and comp. and was adm. freem. 18 May 1631, having req. that benefit in Oct. preced. He rem. a. 1634, or 5 (and was the earliest perman. civiliz. resid. in the unborn Col.) to the neighb. of Providence (as it was soon after nam.), prob. from dissatisfact. with the puritan rigidity of Mass., built his ho. on meadow at Study hill, as he nam. the beautiful seclusion near the bank of a river, since call. Blackstone, as our Secr. prefer. to spell his name, wh. is restored now to the true form, in wh. I saw it writ. by hims. on the University books. His new resid. was at the place since call. Cumberland; but he came to Boston once more to m. 4 July 1659, Sarah, wid. of John Stephenson, had only s. John, and d. 26 May 1675, a few weeks only bef. the gr. Ind. war, in wh. his planta. was destroy. Right to admin. on his est. and give guardiansh. to his s. was assum. by Plymouth Col. wh. reckon. their bounds to include that spot, and the discretion of the governm. of R. I. prevent. controv. a. jurisdict. It is presum. that the fam. name is not extinct, tho. for many yrs. by many writers the supposit. was confident. entertain. Very respect. descend. have for five or six generat. enjoy. an est. at Branford, wh. was prob. acquir. by his gr.s. Diligent research by L. M. Sargent, Esq. ten yrs. since was crown. with satisfact. result, and his regard for the character of the emigrant was exhibit. in copious publicat. of the process of inq. See Holmes, Ann. I.; Winth. I. 44 and 5; 2 Mass. Hist. Coll. X. 170; and 3 Mass. Hist. Coll. VIII. 247; Bliss, Hist. of Rehoboth; Daggett's Hist. of Attleborough, 29.

BLAYDEN, WILLIAM, New Haven 1641, d. late in 1661, prob. unm. The inv. of 3 Jan. foll. shows petty est.

BLEASE, JOHN, Cambridge, bur. 23 Apr. 1646, may be misspelt, or is a strange name on rec.

BLIGH, JOHN, Salem. See Bly. THOMAS, Boston 1652, sailmaker, was perhaps that man nam. in Hutch. Coll. 267, and Haz. Hist. Coll. II. 359, serv. in the expedit. under Willard, 1654, for bring. Ninicraft to submit. He had Thomas, b. 1656, and prob. was expos. to maledict. as a Quaker 1658.

BLIN, PETER, Wethersfield, had four ch. b. 1675–81; but the names are not seen.

BLINMAN, RICHARD, Gloucester 1641, came from Chepstow, in Co. Monmouth, that is separat. from Gloucestersh. only by the riv. Wye. There he had preach. and with much effect, if it be true, as is said, that many wh. accomp. or follow. him from home, and had with him first set down at Marshfield, soon after reach. Plymouth in 1640, pursued his pleasure in cross. to the opposite side of the bay coming under ano. jurisdict. and chang. the name of their town from Cape Ann to Gloucester, the city, where sev. of them had been b. He had gr. of ld. in 1641, and was made freem. 7 Oct. of the same yr. By w. Mary he had Jeremiah, b. 20 July 1642; Ezekiel, 11 Nov. 1643; and Azrikam, 2 Jan. 1646; rem. Oct. 1650, to New London, and drew thither many of his Gloucester friends. Fewer, perhaps, follow. him to New Haven, whence after short resid. and sell. some of his library to the Col. in May 1659, he went home, carry. all his ch. exc. Jeremiah, wh. was at New London so late as 1663. His w. is thot. to have been sis. of deac. William Parke of Roxbury, but with slight grounds. He d. at Bristol, "in a good old age," says Calamy, II. 610.

BLISH, or BLUSH, ABRAHAM, Barnstable, by w. Ann, wh. d. 26 May 1651, had Sarah, b. 2, bapt. 5 Dec. 1641; Joseph, 5, bapt. 9 Apr. 1648; and by sec. w. Hannah, wid. of John Barker of Duxbury, had Abraham, 16 Oct. 1654. This w. d. 16 Mar. 1658, and he m. 4 Jan. foll. Alice Derby, and d. 7 Sept. 1683. ABRAHAM, Boston, one of the found. of the ch. in Brattle str. 1698, from the rarity of the union of such names, may well be suppos. s. of the preced. JOSEPH, Barnstable, s. of the first Abraham, m. 15 Sept. 1674, Hannah Hull, had Joseph, b. 13 Sept. 1675; John, 17 Feb. 1677, wh. d. young; Ann, Feb. 1679; Abraham, 27 Feb. 1681; Reuben, 14 Aug. 1683; Sarah, Aug. 1685, d. young; Thankful, Sept. 1687; John, again, 1 Jan. 1692; d. under 20 yrs.; Tristram, Apr. 1694; Mary, Apr. 1696; and Benjamin, Apr. 1699.

BLISS, GEORGE, Lynn, rem. 1637, to Sandwich, says Lewis, to wh. Mr. Felt adds, that he was of Newport 1649, then aged 58, and he is seen in the list of freem. 1655. JOHN, Newport, s. of the preced. freem. 1669, m. Damaris, d. of Benedict Arnold the first, had Freelove, b. 17 Nov. 1672. JOHN, Northampton, s. of the first Thomas, was prob. b. at Hartford, whence, after d. of his f. of wh. perhaps he was youngest ch. he was by his mo. car. to Springfield. There he m. 7 Oct. 1667, Patience, d. of Henry Burt, had John, b. 7 Sept. 1669; Nathaniel, 26 Jan. 1671; Thomas, 29 Oct. 1673, wh. liv. to 12 Aug. 1758; Joseph, 1676, wh. d. at gr. age, unm.; Hannah, 16 Nov. 1678; Henry, 15 Aug. 1681, d. young; and Ebenezer, 1683, wh. d. 4 Nov. 1761; and rem. to Springfield, where most of his life passed, and he d. 10 Sept. 1702. JONATHAN, Rehoboth 1655, s. prob. eldest of Thomas of the same, b. in Eng. by w. Miriam Harmon, sis. prob. of Nathaniel, had Ephraim, b. 1649; Rachel, 1651; Jonathan, 1653, d. young; Mary, 1655; Eliz. 1657; Samuel, 1660; Martha, 1663; Jonathan, again, 1666; and Dorothy, and Bethia, tw. 1668. JONATHAN, Rehoboth, s. of the preced. m. 23 June 1691, Miriam, d. of the sec. William Carpenter, had Jonathan, b. 5 June 1692; Jacob, 21 Mar. 1694; Ephraim, 28 Dec. 1695, d. young; Elisha, 4 Aug. 1697; Ephraim, again, 15 Aug. 1699; Daniel, 21 Jan. 1702; Noah, 18 May 1704; and Miriam, 19 Nov. 1705; and his w. d. 21 May foll. Next he m. Mary French, had Mary, 1711, wh. d. soon; Mary, again, 25 Nov. 1712; Hannah, 7 Jan. 1715; and Bethia, 10 May 1716; and he d. 16 Oct. 1719. LAW-RENCE, Springfield, s. of Thomas of the same, was prob. b. in Eng. m. 25 Oct. 1654, Lydia, d. of deac. Samuel Wright, had Lydia, b. 29 Nov. 1655; d. at four mos.; Sarah, 11 May 1657, d. in one mo.; Sarah, again, 4 Apr. 1658, d. next yr.; Samuel, 7 June 1660, d. in two wks.; Samuel, again, 16 Aug. 1662; Hannah, 26 May 1665; Sarah, again, 27 Nov. 1667; William, 28 Apr. 1670; and Pelatiah, 19 Aug. 1674. The last five liv. beyond mid. age; but the f. d. 1676. His wid. m. 1678 John Norton of S. NATHANIEL, Springfield 1645, br. of the preced. b. in Eng. rem. from Hartford soon after d. of his f. and m. 20 Nov. 1646, Catharine, d. of deac. Samuel Chapin, had Samuel, b. 7 Nov. 1647, wh. liv. to 19 June 1749; Margaret, 12 Nov. 1649, wh. m. 2 May 1672, Nathaniel Foote, and d. Apr. 1745; Mary, 23 Sept. 1651; and Nathaniel, 27 Mar. 1653, wh. d. 23 Dec. 1736. Notwith-stand. this tendency to long life in the ch. the f. was bur. 18 Nov. 1654. His wid. m. 31 July foll. Thomas Gilbert, by him had four ch. and m. 28 Dec. 1664, Samuel Marshfield, and had four more, so as to count one doz. ch. On 31 Dec. 1678, or the next day, Samuel, sen. Samuel, jr. and Samuel tert. took o. of alleg. being over 16 yrs. old, and enrol. in the milit. at S. They were a s. of Nathaniel, a s. of Lawrence, and their uncle. SAMUEL, Springfield, br. of the preced. was perhaps b. at Hart-ford, m. 10 Nov. 1665, Mary, d. of John Leonard of S. had Hannah, b. 20 Dec. 1666; Thomas, 8 Feb. 1668; Mary, 4 Aug. 1670; Jonathan, 5 Jan. 1672; Martha, 1 June 1674; Sarah, 10 Sept. 1677; Experience, 1 Apr. 1679, d. at 18 yrs.; Mercy, 18 July 1680; Ebenezer, 29 July 1683; Margaret, 11 Sept. 1684; and Esther, 2 Apr. 1688. He d. 23 Mar. 1720; and his wid. d. 21 Mar. 1724. SAMUEL, Norwich, s. of Thomas of the same, m. 8 Dec. 1681, Ann, d. of John Elderkin, had Thomas, b. Sept. 1682; Samuel, 13 Nov. 1684; Eliz. 28 Feb. 1687; John, 23 Oct. 1690; Pelatiah, 19 Nov. 1697; and Thankful, 7 Mar. 1700. He d. 30 Dec. 1729; and his wid. d. 17 May 1748. SAMUEL, Springfield, s. of Lawrence, m. Hannah, d. of John Stiles, the sec. of Windsor, had Hannah, b. 1 May 1689; Sarah, 6 Jan. 1692, wh. d. at 15 yrs.; Lydia, 24 Nov. 1695; and Samuel, 29 Mar. 1701; and his w. d. Dec. 1704. THOMAS, Hartford, was an early, but not orig. sett· of whose com. from Eng. nothing is kn. but his first resid. was in that pt.

of Boston call. the mount, afterwards Braintree, now Quincy. In 1639 or 40 he is first ment. in Conn. at the same time with Thomas, jr. wh. may be the freem. of 18 May 1642 in Mass., there left by his f. whose d. is early heard of, tho. exact date is not gain. His wid. Margaret was very resolute and capable, and after two or three yrs. rem. with all her ch. exc. Thomas, and Ann, to Springfield, there d. 28 Aug. 1684. She had nine ch. and it has been absurd. said, that all were brot. from Eng. Of most, this is true. Ann, wh. m. 29 Apr. 1642, Robert Chapman of Saybrook; Mary m. 20 Nov. 1646, Joseph Parsons; Thomas; Nathaniel; Lawrence; and perhaps Samuel; were b. in Eng. but our side of the water may claim, prob. Sarah, m. 20 July 1659, John Scott; Eliz. m. 15 Feb. 1670, as his sec. w. Miles Morgan; possib. Hannah, wh. d. 25 Jan. 1662, unm. and certain. John. THOMAS, Weymouth, was possib. the freem. of 18 May 1642, but next yr. certain. rem. to Rehoboth, there d. June 1649. His will, by careless statem. in Geneal. Reg. IV. 282, said to bear date of 8th of that mo. but also on same day to be brot. into Ct. gives valua. inform. a. his ch. Jonathan, to wh. he devis. his ho., his eldest d. whose bapt. name is not told, w. of Thomas Williams; Mary, w. of Nathaniel Harmon of Braintree; s.-in-law (perhaps mean. s. of his w.) Nicholas Ide, and his s. Nathaniel. From find. no ment. of him after 1649 at R. I suppose, confus. of him with Thomas of Norwich was easy. THOMAS, Norwich, 1660, s. of Thomas the first, had been of Hartford, and early after d. of his f. rem. to Saybrook, a. the end of Oct. 1644, took w. Eliz. had Eliz. b. 20 Nov. 1645; Sarah, 26 Aug. 1647; Mary, 7 Feb. 1649; Thomas, 3 Mar. 1652, wh. d. 29 Jan. 1682, prob. unm.; Deliverance, Aug. 1655; Samuel, 9 Dec. 1657; all bef. rem. from S. and at N. had Ann, Sept. 1660, the sec. Eng. ch. b. in that place; Rebecca, Mar. 1663; and he d. 15 Apr. 1688. By will, made two days bef. (req. by the insuffer. tyranny of Sir Edmund Andros to be brot. to Boston for proof and rec., support. his retainers by the fees of office), provis. for w. Eliz. six ds. and only s. Samuel, is seen. Of this name, in 1834, four had been gr. at Harv. four at Dart. seventeen at Yale, beside six at other N. E. coll. of wh. most disting. are Rev. Daniel of Concord, b. at Springfield, Jan. 1715, Y. C. 1732, d. 11 May 1764; his s. Daniel, b. 1740, H. C. 1760, d. in the Prov. of New Brunswick 1806; Jonathan, H. C. 1763, Ch. Just. of the Sup. Ct. of N. B. and George, Y. C. 1784, LL. D. wh. d. 8 May 1830, aged 65.

BLODGET, or BLOGGET, sometimes BLOGHEAD, DANIEL, Cambridge, s. of Thomas, b. in Eng. freem. 1652, rem. to Chelmsford, m. 15 Sept. 1653, Mary, d. prob. of Benjamin Butterfield, had Thomas, b. 25 June foll.; Ann, 2 Nov. 1655; and Daniel, 6 Jan. 1657, perhaps others, and d. 28 Jan. 1672, leav. beside those three, Benjamin, aged 14. JONA-

THAN, Salisbury, m. 7 Feb. 1689, Mary, d. perhaps of Rev. Joseph
Rowlandson, had Hannah, b. 15 Jan. foll. ; Daniel, 12 Sept. 1691, d. in
few days ; Mary, 11 Oct. 1692 ; and Joseph, 12 Aug. 1694, wh. d. at
2 yrs. * SAMUEL, Woburn 1654, br. of Daniel, b. in Eng. m. 13 Dec.
1655, Ruth, d. prob. of Stephen Iggleden of Boston, had Ruth, b. 28
Dec. 1656; Samuel, 10 Dec. 1658; Thomas, 26 Feb. 1661; Sarah, 17
Feb. 1668; and Martha and Mary, tw. 15 Sept. 1673; perhaps the last
two or three by sec. w. He was rep. 1693, and d. 3 July of that yr.
THOMAS, Cambridge, came in the Increase from London, 1635, aged 30,
with w. Susanna, 37, if custom ho. rec. be true; ch. Daniel, 4 ; and
Samuel, 1 and ½; was adm. freem. 3 Mar. 1636; had here Susanna, b.
June 1637 ; and Thomas, wh. d. 7 Aug. 1639. He made his will, as
giv. in Geneal. Reg. II. 185, 10 Aug. 1641, pro. 8 July foll. in wh. the
w. and three ch. are prov. for. His wid. m. 15 Feb. 1644, James Thompson of Woburn ; and his d. of the same name m. 28 Nov. 1655, Jonathan Thompson. THOMAS, Woburn, s. prob. of Samuel, m. 11 Nov.
1685, Rebecca Tidd, d. prob. of John, had Thomas, b. 5 Aug. 1686;
ano. ch. wh. d. 13 Apr. 1688 ; Rebecca, 5 June 1689; Ruth, 14 Oct.
1694; Joseph, 17 Sept. 1696; Abigail, 7 Nov. 1698; and Samuel,
17 June 1702. Three of this name, says Farmer, in MS. had been gr.
at Dart. and three at younger N. E. coll. in 1834.

BLOIS, or BLOYS, EDMUND, Watertown, was freem. 22 May 1639,
but Bond well presumes, that he had been here sev. yrs. as his w. Mary,
aged 40, with s. Richard, 11, came, to join him, in the Francis, from Ipswich, 1634, and this renders it prob. that he was of a Suffk. fam. His
w. d. 29 May 1675, and he m. 27 Sept. foll. Ruth, d. of Hugh Parsons,
and d. at gr. age, bef. April, 1681. It is said he was b. 1587. The
wid. liv. to Dec. 1711. FRANCIS, Cambridge, perhaps br. of the preced.
freem. 2 June 1641, was bur. 29 Sept. 1646. RICHARD, Watertown, s.
of Edmund, b. in Eng. m. 10 Feb. 1658, Michal, d. of Robert Jennison,
had Richard, b. 7 Dec. 1659 ; Mary, 11 Dec. 1661; and s. Michael, 3
Apr. 1664. He was a serj. and d. 7 Aug. 1665. His wid. m. 11 July
1667, John Warren. On Cambridge rec. the name is Blosse, and in
that of the Col., Bloyce. RICHARD, Watertown, s. of the preced. m.
26 Sept. 1688, Ann, d. of James Cutler of Cambridge Farms, now Lexington, had Richard, b. 25 Jan. 1701; James, 3 Nov. 1702; Samuel,
26 Jan. 1705 ; and Ann, 10 Aug. 1707. He was freem. 1690.

BLOMFIELD, or BLUMFIELD, HENRY, Salem 1638. JOHN, Mass. d.
a. 1640, leav. s. John, beside Thomas, wh. was made admor. THOMAS,
Newbury, an early sett. d. 1639, leav. a lame d. and s. Thomas; yet he
may be the same as the preced. THOMAS, Newbury, s. of the preced.
had Mary, b. 15 Jan. 1642; Sarah, 30 Dec. 1643; John, 15 Mar. 1646;

Thomas, 12 Dec. 1648 ; Nathaniel, 10 Apr. 1651 ; Ezekiel, 1 Nov.
1653 ; Rebecca, 1656 ; Ruth, 4 July 1659 ; and Timothy, 1 Apr. 1664.
He next yr. rem. to Woodbridge, N. J. where his s. Thomas was rep.
in 1675.   WILLIAM, Hartford 1639, had liv. in some part of Mass. perhaps Newbury, after arr. at Boston in the Elizabeth, 1634, from Ipswich, Co. Suff'k. aged 30, with w. Susan, 25, and ch. Sarah, 1 ; was adm.
freem. of Mass. 2 Sept. 1635, prob. had other ch. beside John, bapt. 24
Aug. 1645 ; and Samuel, 12 July 1647 ; bef. rem. 1650 to New London ;
thence in 1663 to Newtown, L. I.   Sarah m. Simon Sacket of Springfield, and to her only ch. Joseph with his mo. the gr.f. B. gave his New
London est. after she had m. Woodward.   Hardly is the report of this
gent. utter. with adequate distinctness by the Conn. historians.   Porter
makes his rem. "perhaps to N. J." mistak. him prob. for Thomas; and
Hinman, 117, says only, that he was gone from H. 1663, down the Conn.
riv.   This name, in the third generat. had bec. Bloomfield.   A gov. of
N. J. in our day, was Joseph, a descend. of Thomas.

BLOOD, JAMES, Concord 1639, freem. 2 June 1641, idly reput. by
some, solely from similar surname, to be br. of that Col. B. kn. in Eng.
hist. for gr. boldness in steal. from the Tower, 1671, the crown and
regalia of Charles II. and the greater impudence, by wh. he gain. not
only impun. but an est. from the jolly k.   See the curious let. from the
w. of the regicide Goffe to her h. in 3 Mass. Hist. Coll. I. 60.   He had
perhaps brot. from Eng. all or most of these four s. Robert, James, Richard, John, wh. d. unm. 30 Oct. 1692, had here Mary, b. 12 July 1648 ;
and he d. 17 Nov. 1683.   * JAMES, Concord, s. of the preced. m. 26 Oct.
1657, Hannah, d. of Oliver Purchis of Lynn, had only ch. Sarah, b. 5
Mar. 1660, wh. m. William Wilson ; was an early propr. of Groton,
deac. and rep. for Sudbury 1660, unless this honor belong. (as to me
seems prob.) rather to his f. and d. 26 Nov. 1692.   Shattuck.   One
JAMES, of Concord, possib. the same as preced. but more prob. his neph.
and still more likely to be s. of ano. stock, had w. Eliz. wh. d. at Lynn,
Dec. 1676 ; and he m. 19 Nov. 1679, Isabel, the young wid. of David
Wyman, d. of John Farmer of C.   JAMES, Groton, s. of Richard, m.
7 Sept. 1669, Eliz. Longley, d. of William the first of the same, had
Richard, b. 29 May 1670, d. soon ;   Mary, 1 Sept. 1672 ;   Hannah, wh.
d. acc. Butler, 6 Jan. 1676 ; and Eliz. 27 Apr. 1675.   By sec. w. Abigail
he had James, b. 12 Aug. 1687 ; John, 16 Mar. 1689 ; and Martha, 20
Oct. 1692.   On 13 Sept. preced. he was k. by the French and Ind.
JOSEPH, Groton, br. of the preced. by w. Hannah had sev. ch. and rem.
to Mendon, next to Dedham.   NATHANIEL, Groton, br. of the preced.
m. 13 June 1670, Hannah, d. of James Parker (wh. d. 14 Jan. 1728,
aged 81), had Ann, b. 1 Mar. 1671 ; Eliz. 7 Oct. 1673; Sarah, 2 Apr.

1675; Mary, 17 Apr. 1678; Nathaniel, 16 Jan. 1680; and Joseph, 3 Feb. 1682. RICHARD, Lynn, had Sarah, b. June 1648; Nathaniel, Apr. 1650; and Hannah. RICHARD, Groton, br. of James the first of Concord, by w. Isabel had Mary, wh. d. 19 Apr. 1662; James; Nathaniel; Eliz. and Joseph; was the chief of the orig. proprs. and d. 7 Dec. 1683. The date of b. of all is unkn. but Butler's Hist. has their ms. and ds. Eliz. m. 1 Dec. 1686, Thomas Tarbell, third of that name. ROBERT, Concord, br. of the preced. m. 8 Apr. 1653, Eliz. d. of maj. Simon Willard, had Mary, b. 4 Mar. 1655; Eliz. 14 June 1656; Sarah, 1 Aug. 1658; Robert, 2 Feb. 1660; Simon, 5 July 1662; Josiah, or Joshua, 6 Apr. 1664; John, 29 Oct. 1666; Ellen, 14 Apr. 1669; Samuel, 16 Oct. 1672; James, 1673; Ebenezer, 15 Feb. 1676; and Jonathan, as giv. by Shattuck, to wh. credible report adds Abigail. His w. d. 29 Aug. 1690; and one Sarah, perhaps his d. d. at Roxbury, 28 July 1690. He was one of the orig. petiturs. for incorp. of Groton, and d. 27 Oct. 1692. Descend. are very num.

BLOSSOM, PETER, Barnstable, perhaps s. of Thomas, m. 4 June 1663, Sarah Bodfish, had Mercy, b. 9 Apr. 1664, d. young; Thomas, 20 Dec. 1667; Samuel, 1669, d. young; Joseph, 10 Dec. 1673; Thankful, 1675; Mercy, again, Aug. 1678; and Jabez, 16 Feb. 1680. THOMAS, one of the Pilgrims, wh. came from Leyden to Plymouth, but being on board the Speedwell, was disappoint. of passage in the Mayflower from Eng. and soon went back to encourage emigra. of the residue. A s. wh. came and return. with him, d. bef. Dec. 1625, and two other ch. had been b. in the interval. See a good let. from him to Gov. Bradford in Young's Chron. of the Pilgr. 480. He came again, 1629, prob. in the Mayflower, if the belov. name would attract the few for Plymouth, when the larger part of the fellow-voyagers with Higginson were bound for Salem; was deac. and d. after short possessn. of the land of promise, in the summer of 1633. Prince, Annals, 437, of Ed. 1826. His wid. Ann m. 17 Oct. of that yr. Henry Rowley; and d. Eliz. m. 10 May 1637, Edward Fitzrandle. THOMAS, Plymouth, s. of the preced. had w. Sarah, m. 18 June 1645, d. of Thomas Ewer of Charlestown, and d. Sarah; liv. at Barnstable 1643, was drown. 22 Apr. 1650. Admin. was gr. to his wid. 4 June of that yr.

BLOTT, JOHN, Charlestown 1634, of wh. no more is kn. ROBERT, Charlestown 1634, had come in 1632, prob. to Roxbury, freem. 4 Mar. 1635; was at Boston 1644; had w. Susanna, wh. d. 20 Jan. 1660. He d. 1665, for his will of 27 May 1662, has a codic. 27 Mar. of latter yr. and was pro. 2 Feb. after, inv. being tak. 22 Aug. bef. In it he names eldest d. Mary, wh. (we kn. by Roxbury ch. rec.) came in 1632, and soon after had m. Thomas Woodford of Roxbury, many yrs. bef. rem. to

Hartford, and was prob. d. as he gives to her childr. ; Sarah, wh. had m. 6 Oct. 1652, Edward Ellis of Boston ; Joanna, wh. had m. Daniel Lovell of Braintree, and was, perhaps, d. as his gift is to her childr. and also to childr. of ano. d. wh. had been w. of Richard Tozer of Boston, and many yrs. d. and her eldest s. John Green ; besides one he calls s.-in-law Daniel Turin, or some such name. THOMAS, Charlestown 1635, perhaps br. or s. of the preced.

BLOWERS, JOHN, Barnstable 1643, Boston 1654, by w. Tabitha had Tabitha, b. 12 Feb. 1655; Mary, 25 Apr. 1657 ; John, 1659 ; and Thomas, 1665. PYAM, Cambridge, m. 31 Mar. 1668, Eliz. d. of Andrew Belcher, wh. d. 29 May 1709, aged 69, and he d. three days after, aged 71. For his services in discov. on the coast of Carolina, 1663, he had grant of five hundred acres there, but prob. he never claim. them. He had Thomas, b. 27 July, d. 14 Aug. 1669 ; Samuel, 14 Jan. d. 21 Feb. 1671; Jonathan, 8 Feb. 1673 ; Ann, or Hannah, 4 July 1674, d. 16 Jan. 1676; Eliz. 19 July 1675 ; Ann, again, 16 July 1676 ; Thomas, again, 1 Aug. 1677, H. C. 1695, not 1698, as print. in Geneal. Reg. VIII. 179 ; Pyam, 29 July, d. 14 Aug. 1679 ; John, 22 Oct. 1680; and Andrew, 27 Aug. d. 21 Oct. 1682. THOMAS, Beverly, s. of the preced. ord. 29 Oct. 1701, d. 1729, had John, wh. liv. at Boston, and was f. of Samson Salter, b. 10 Mar. 1742, H. C. 1763, the disting. lawyer and judge, wh. d. 25 Oct. 1842, the oldest gr. exc. Holyoke, of the Inst. (tho. since there have been two surpassing them), aged 100 yrs. 7 mos. 4 days after correct. of the style. Of Thomas, a passeng. in the Truelove from London, aged 50, emb. Sept. 1635, I have found nothing.

BLUNT, SAMUEL, Charlestown 1681, had w. Ann, wh. d. 8 Aug. 1715, aged 62. WILLIAM, Andover, a. 1668, by w. Eliz. wh. d. 11 July 1689, had William, wh. d. 1738, aged 67 ; Samuel, wh. d. 18 July 1684 ; and Hanborough. WILLIAM, s. of the preced. had David, b. 1699 ; Jonathan ; Ebenezer ; and John, H. C. 1727, ord. at Newcastle, N. H. 20 Dec. 1732, wh. was the ancest. of the fams. of B. at Newcastle and Portsmouth, and d. 7 Aug. 1748, aged 41.

BLUSH. See Blish.

BLY, JOHN, Salem, brickmaker, m. perhaps as sec. w. 11 Nov. 1663, Rebecca Golt, or Gott, perhaps d. of deac. Charles, had John, b. 27 Jan. 1665 ; Benjamin, 8 Oct. 1666; Mary, 25 May 1668 ; Rebecca, 20 July 1671; Edmund, 14 Sept. 1672 ; Hannah, 8 Oct. 1674; and William, 17 Sept. 1676 or 1678. Rebecca m. 22 May 1692, James Gillingham. SAMUEL, Lynn, m. 19 Dec. 1678, Lois, d. of Thomas Ivory, had Theophilus, wh. d. 12 June 1681.

BOADEN, or BODEN, AMBROSE, Scarborough 1658, prob. assoc. with Andrew Alger, may have come from the same part of Somersetsh. k. by the Ind. prob. Oct. 1675. His s. AMBROSE was an inhab. 1658. THOM-AS, Marblehead 1668.

BOARDMAN, SAMUEL, one of the first sett. at Wethersfield 1636. See Boreman. THOMAS, Yarmouth 1643, a carpenter, from London, first at Plymouth, 1634, at Sandwich, 1638, had m. first w. Lucy, wh. d. 8 Nov. 1676, had a s. b. in London and a d. Eliz. here, wh. d. 20 Dec. 1676. He m. next, Eliz. wid. of lieut. John Cole, d. of Samuel Rider. Other ch. prob. by first w. were Thomas, Susanna, and Thankful; and he d. Aug. 1689, very aged.

BOBBIT, EDWARD, Taunton 1643, m. 7 Sept. 1654, Sarah, d. of Miles Tarne of Boston, and was liv. at T. 1675. His ch. were Edward, b. 15 July 1655; Sarah, 20 Mar. 1658; Hannah, 9 Mar. 1660; Damaris, 15 Sept. 1663; Elkanah, 15 Dec. 1665; Dorcas, 20 Jan. 1667, d. at 7 yrs.; Esther, 15 Apr. 1669; Ruth, 7 Aug. 1671; Deliverance, 15 Dec. 1673, all ds. by the rec. Sarah m. 25 Mar. 1680, Samuel Pitts. Perhaps the name in recent times has bec. Babbit.

BOCKFORD, ELNATHAN, Milford, m. bef. 1679, a d. of John Fletcher.

BODE, BOOD, or BOADE, HENRY, Saco 1635, Wells 1641, [Willis, I. 49.] freem. of Mass. 1653, d. 1657. Folsom, 119. His wid. Ann m. Samuel Wensley of Salisbury.

BODERIT, JOHN, Boston, by w. Jane had Susanna, b. 27 Nov. 1686, and no more is heard of this strange name.

BODFISH. See Bootfish.

BODINGHAM, JOHN, a passeng. for N. E. in the Friendship, from Eng. 15 Aug. 1679, but where or when he reach. the ld. is unkn.

BODKIN, WILLIAM, Boston, by w. Mary had John, b. 25 Mar. 1680; and Eliz. 15 Aug. 1682.

BODMAN, JOHN, Boston, by w. Sarah had John, b. Aug. 1645, as the town rec. has it; but ch. rec. says Benjamin, bapt. 7 Sept. 1645; Manoah, 6 Mar. 1647; and Joseph, 17 Oct. 1653. What time he d. is not kn. but his wid. was one of the first mem. of the third or O. S. ch. JOSEPH, Westfield 1685, perhaps s. of the preced. after d. of first w. Hepzibah, 15 Jan. 1686, hav. b. Lydia, 10 days bef. wh. d. in two wks. He rem. to Hatfield, m. 1687, Naomi Church, had Manoah, William, Sarah, Mary, Lydia, and Samuel; d. 1711. Of his s. Samuel alone had ch. SAMUEL, Boston, by w. Mary had Sarah, b. 2 June 1682. WIL-LIAM, Watertown, by w. Frances had Rebecca, b. 1 Nov. 1643.

BODWELL, HENRY, Newbury, was in capt. Lathrop's comp. call. the flower of Essex, in the battle 18 Sept. 1675, at Bloody brook, and severely wound. See Coffin, 388. He m. 4 May 1681, Bethia, d. of John Emery, had Bethia, b. 2 June 1682; rem. to Andover, had Henry and Josiah, tw. wh. d. 29 and 31 Jan. 1685.

Boggust, John, Salem 1630, prob. came in the fleet that yr. and d. within few mos.

Bogle, Alexander, Boston 1672, was one of the soldiers in capt. Oliver's comp. wound. in the gr. fight 19 Dec. 1675.

Bohonion, or Bohannon, John, Boston, by w. Mary had John, b. 9 May 1658; Margaret, 8 Jan. 1660; John, again, 23 Aug. 1661; Patrick, 14 Feb. 1665; Abigail, 26 Sept. 1667; and James, 20 Oct. 1670.

Bolcom. See Balcom.

Bollard, Isaac, Boston, m. 3 Jan. 1655, Sarah, d. of Thomas Jones of Dorchester. Of this name some natural distrust may be felt.

Bolles, Thomas, New London 1667, his w. Zipporah, and eldest two ch. Mary, bapt. 27 July 1673, and Joseph, 25 Apr. 1675 were murder. 6 June 1678 by John Stodder, a young man, wh. on his confess. was execut. therefor. He d. 26 May 1727, aged 84, a valua. man. His youngest ch. John was sav. from the violence, and from him the num. race in that vicin. descend.

Bolt, Francis, Milford, came to Boston in the Martin, 1638, and with the Baldwins, his fellow-passeng. soon rem. thither, join. the ch. Jan. 1640; perhaps had w. Sarah, s. Philip, and d. Susanna, ment. in the rec. of M. and d. 1649.

Bolton, John, Bridgewater, s. prob. of Nicholas, tho. Mitchell cautious. calls him descend. of N. of Dorchester, and says that, he is report. to have come from Stonington, with w. Sarah, but gives him ch. John, b. 1686; Samuel, 1688; Sarah, 1690; Eliz. 1692; Nicholas, 1695; Mary, 1697; Elisha, 1700; Joseph, 1704; Nathaniel, 1706; and Abigail, 1709. It seems altogether an even chance and no more, that he was s. or gr.s. of Nicholas, Dorchester 1643. See Boulton. William, Newbury, m. 16 Jan. 1655, Jane Bartlett, wh. d. 6 Sept. 1659, had Mary, b. 25 Sept. 1655; m. 2d w. 22 Nov. 1659, Mary Dennison, had William, b. 27 May 1665; Ruth, 1 Aug. 1667; Eliz. 23 May 1672, d. at 2 yrs.; Eliz. again, 8 Nov. 1674; Sarah, 5 Apr. 1677; Hannah, 18 July 1679; and Joseph, 8 July 1682. William and Sarah, the ch. both d. 30 Mar. 1694; and the f. d. 27 Mar. 1697.

Boltwood, Robert, Hartford 1648, rem. 1659 to Hadley, freem. 26 Mar. 1661, d. 6 Apr. 1684, an enterpris. and brave man; by w. Mary, wh. d. 14 May 1687, had only s. Samuel, ment. below, and these ds. Sarah, wh. m. 31 May 1666, Isaac Warner of Hatfield, and next, in 1696, deac. John Loomis of Windsor; Lydia, wh. m. 2 Apr. 1674, John Warner of Springfield, and d. 26 Jan. 1683; Martha, wh. m. 1 Apr. 1674, Daniel Warner of Hatfield, and d. 1710; and Mary, wh. m. 24 Oct. 1667, James Beebee of Hadley, and d. 19 Aug. 1676. Samuel,

Hadley, s. of the preced. rem. to Farmington, m. Sarah, d. of capt. William Lewis, had five s. and five ds. rem. to Deerfield, and was k. 29 Feb. 1704 in the assault by Fr. and Ind. His wid. d. 10 Aug. 1722, aged 70. Of the ch. Samuel, b. 12 Oct. 1679, m. Hannah Alexander, and d. 1738; Sarah m. Nathaniel Kellogg; Eliz. m. Eleazer Mattoon; Robert, b. 19 Apr. 1683, was k. at the same time with his f.; Ebenezer was of Berwick; Rebecca, b. 1691, bec. sec. w. of Daniel Shattuck, 7 May 1724; Solomon, b. 2 July 1694, d. 20 Sept. 1762, was ancest. of Ebenezer, H. C. 1773, and of Lucius M. Will. Coll. 1814.

BOND, GRIMSTONE, Boston, by w. Eliz. had Eliz. b. 22 Aug. 1683; Joseph, 27 Apr. 1685; and Mary, 13 Aug. 1688; freem. 1690. I find it spell. sometimes Bowde. JOHN, Newbury, 1642, m. 5 Aug. 1649, Esther Blakely, had John, b. 10 June 1650; Thomas, 29 Mar. 1652, d. at 8 wks.; Joseph, 14 Apr. 1653; Esther, 3 Sept. 1655; Mary, 16 Dec. 1657; and Abigail, 6 Nov. 1660, rem. to Rowley, thence to Haverhill, d. 1675. His wid. m. 5 May 1675, the sec. John Williams of H. Esther m. Aquila Chase; and Abigail m. 2 Mar. 1676, Ezra Rolfe. JOHN, Plymouth, k. by a cartwheel, June 1661. JOHN, Watertown, sec. s. of William first of the same, m. 6 Aug. 1679, Hannah, d. of John Coolidge, and had John, b. 12 Apr. 1680; William, 11 Nov. 1681; Hannah, 1 July 1683, d. young; Eliz. 20 Mar. 1685; Abigail, 6 Nov. 1686; Sarah, 25 Aug. 1688; and Daniel, 21 June 1690; and he d. of smallpox, 1 Mar. 1691, hav. in his will provid. for w. and the six ch. JONAS, Watertown, br. of the preced. a very active man, serv. under Walley, in the 1690 exped. against Quebec, and d. 21 Apr. 1727; m. first, 29 Jan. 1689, Grace, d. of John Coolidge, wh. d. 11 Apr. 1699, had Sarah, b. 30 May 1690; Jonas, 10 Dec. 1691; Henry, a. 1694; and Josiah, 20 Jan. 1696; and sec. Eliz. wid. of John Prentice, d. of capt. Edward Jackson of Newton, without issue. JOSEPH, Haverhill, prob. s. of Newbury John, took o. of alleg. 28 Nov. 1677. NATHANIEL, Watertown, s. of William the first, m. 27 Feb. 1685, Bethia, youngest d. of John Fuller of Cambridge, and had Nathaniel, b. 3 Mar. 1686; Bethia; and John, bapt. 23 Nov. 1690; was a lieut. and d. a. 1 Apr. 1700. NICHOLAS, York, freem. 1652, perhaps rem. to Hampton, where Nicholas B. was k. by the Ind. 17 Aug. 1703, but far more prob. is it that this was s. of John of Plymouth; liv. at Salisbury first, there m. 5 Dec. 1684, or 7, Sarah, perhaps d. of Rev. Joseph Rowlandson, had Thomas, b. 10 Oct. 1688; William, 13 June 1696; and Joseph, 1 Apr. 1700. * ROBERT, Easthampton, L. I. was made a magistr. 1658, and rep. 1659, 60, and 1, rem. to New Jersey and was in 1668 of the counc. tak. by Gov. Carteret. Whitehead's N. J. 52 and 3 Mass. Hist. Coll. X. 84. SAMPSON, Boston, 1682, one of the eject. min. from Co. Cumberland, was employ. at first ch. as assist. to Rev. James Allen for some time, but was compell. to give up this place for preach. a sermon not compos. by him, rem. to Barbados, thence, perhaps, to Bermuda, and there d. Hutch. I. 427. Emerson, Hist. of first ch. 134. Calamy, II. 150. Thomas, a passeng. emb. in Eng. 29 May 1679 for Boston in the Elizabeth ; but it may be fear. that he never reach. his destin. or else, he soon d. or went home again. Thomas, Watertown, third s. of William of the same, m. 30 Sept. 1680, Sarah, d. of Thomas Woolson, and had Thomas, b. 29 May 1683 ; Sarah, 2 Dec. 1685 ; William, 1 Feb. 1688 ; Mary, bapt. 7 Dec. 1690 ; John, b. 14 July 1695 ; and Isaac, 22 June 1698 ; and d. 17 Dec. 1704. * William, Watertown 1649, third s. of Thomas of Bury St. Edmonds, in Co. Suff'k. bapt. there 3 Sept. 1625, at St. James ch. brot. prob. 1630, in the fleet with Winth. by his aunt Eliz. w. of Ephraim Child ; m. 7 Feb. 1650, Sarah, d. of Nathaniel Briscoe, wh. d. 16 Feb. 1693 ; bot. of Rev. John Knowles, after he went home, 5 Mar. 1655, the farm that K. purch. of capt. William Jennison ; was oft. rep. in the col. days, in the couns. of safety during the insurrect. against Andros, and first speaker of the ho. after the new chart. a man of great energy ; had 2d w. 1695, Eliz. wid. of John Nevinson, and d. 15 Dec. 1695. His wid. surv. a. 25 yrs. His ch. were William, b. 1 Dec. 1650 ; John, 2 Dec. 1652 ; Thomas, 23 Dec. 1654 ; Eliz. 30 Nov. 1656, wh. m. 13 Mar. 1679, Nathaniel Barsham ; Nathaniel, 19 Jan. 1659, d. soon ; Nathaniel, again, 9 Jan. 1660, unless confusion of style in the fam. geneal. has made two out of one ; Sarah, 27 July 1661, wh. m. 29 Jan. 1690, Palsgrave Wellington ; Jonas, 19 July 1664 ; and Mary, wh. m. 22 June 1693, Richard Coolidge. His descend. Henry of Philadelphia, bestow. many yrs. on the filial duty of publish. the Watertown geneal. to fill the admira. vol. of the Hist. of W. William, Watertown, s. of the pred. m. 2 June 1680, Hepzibah, only d. of Thomas Hastings, had Margaret, b. 1 Oct. 1680 ; three Williams, of wh. the last was b. 24 May 1695 ; Deliverance, 2 May 1686 ; Eliz. ; Mary ; Samuel ; and others, wh. d. young. Four of this name had been gr. at Harv. and four at the other N. E. coll. in 1834.

Bondet, *Daniel*, Oxford, min. of the Huguenots, or French Protestants, 1691. 3 Mass. Hist. Coll. II. 61.

Bondfield, or Bonfield, George, Marblehead 1676. Dana, 8.

Bonham, or Bonum, George, Plymouth, m. 20 Dec. 1644, as sec. w. Sarah, d. of George Morton, had, prob. Ruth, wh. m. 28 Nov. 1666, Robert Barron ; Patience, wh. m. 28 Dec. 1670, Richard Willis; Sarah, b. 4 Dec. 1649, d. early in 1650 ; and Sarah, again, 12 Jan. 1651, d. prob. soon ; Sarah, again, 10 Dec. 1653 ; d. 28 Apr. 1704, aged 86. Nicholas, Barnstable, perhaps br. of George, m. 1 Jan. 1659, Hannah,

d. of Samuel Fuller the sec. had Hannah, b. 8 Oct. 1659 ; Mary, 4 Oct. 1661 ; and Sarah, 16 Feb. 1664.

BONNER, JOHN, Boston 1678, by w. Mary had Jane or John, b. 10 Jan. 1686, d. in few mos.; Jonah, 8 July 1687, d. in few days; and Mary, 28 Jan. 1689, d. at 10 yrs. He rem. to Cambridge, there had Jane, 2 May 1691 ; John, 6 Dec. 1693 ; and Thomas, 6 Jan. 1696; and his w. d. 20 Apr. 1697. Soon after he went to Eng. with his ch. See Geneal. Reg. V. 174.

BONNEY, THOMAS, Charlestown, shoemaker, came in the Hercules, 1635, from Sandwich, in Kent, rem. early was one of the proprs. of Bridgewater 1645, but liv. at Duxbury, where he m. Dorcas, d. of Henry Sampson, had one or more s. prob. and Mary, wh. m. 14 Dec. 1675, John Mitchell.

BONYTHON, or BONIGHTON, JOHN, Saco 1636, s. of Richard, Casco 1658, had his ho. burn. by the Ind. 1675 [Willis, I. 44. 138]; and d. bef. 1684, leav. wid. s. John ; and hav. an ill epit. Folsom, 116. RICHARD, Saco 1631, was a capt. and magistr. and held court 25 Mar. 1636, and d. a. 1650, paid as large a rate for support of min. as any one in 1636. His d. Sarah m. Richard Foxwell, and ano. m. Richard Codman. Bonython is the name of a place in Cornwall.

BOOBYAR, JOSEPH, Marblehead 1668.

BOOMER, MATTHEW, Newport, a freem. there 1655, had fam. of wh. details are unkn.

BOOSY, * JAMES, Wethersfield 1635, by w. Alice had Joseph, b. perhaps bef. sett. at Wethersfield; Mary, b. 10 Sept. 1635; Hannah, 10 Feb. 1642 ; Sarah, 12 Nov. 1643 ; and James, 1 Feb. 1646 ; rep. from 1639 till his d. 22 June 1649. His wid. m. James Wakeley, and d. 1683. Of his ch. Mary m. the first Samuel Steele; Hannah m. as is believ. John Pratt; Sarah m. 2 June 1659, Nathaniel Stanley; and James d. under age. The will, of 21 June 1649, gives good portion to each of the five ch. JOSEPH, had w. Esther, but no ch. and d. at West Chester, but had liv. at Fairfield 1655, and his wid. m. Jehu Burr.

BOOTFISH, or BODFISH, JOSEPH, Barnstable, prob. s. of Robert, m. June 1674, Eliz. Bessey, had John, b. 6 Dec. 1675 ; Joseph, Oct. 1677 ; Mary, 1 Mar. 1680; Hannah, May 1681; Benjamin, 20 July 1683; Nathan, 27 Dec. 1685 ; Ebenezer, 10 Mar. 1688 ; Eliz. 27 Aug. 1690; Rebecca, 22 Feb. 1693 ; Meletiah, 7 Apr. 1695 ; Robert, 10 Oct. 1698 ; and Sarah, 20 Feb. bapt. 6 Apr. 1701. ROBERT, Lynn, freem. 6 May 1635, rem. 1637 to Sandwich, and d. there or at Barnstable, a. 1651; hav. had Joseph, b. 3 Apr. 1651, and prob. others earlier, one 27 Mar. 1648, whose name is not giv. Perhaps a s. Robert, and one or more ds. were b. in Eng. or at Lynn. At Barnstable, Bridget, prob. his wid. m. 15 Dec. 1657, Samuel Hinckley, f. of Gov. Thomas, as his 2d w.; Eliz.

m. Nov. 1659, John Crocker, perhaps his 2d w.; and Sarah m. 4 June 1663, Peter Blossom. These three are thot. to be, all, ds. of Robert.

BOOTH, EBENEZER, Stratford, s. of Richard, m. Eliz. d. of Richard Jones of Haddam, had three s. Benjamin, Edward, and Ebenezer, beside ds. Deborah, Eliz. and Abigail, all liv. at his d. and he gave to Nathaniel s. of his s. Ebenezer, and d. 1732. EPHRAIM, Stratford, eldest s. of Richard, in his will of Feb. 1683, short. bef. his d. names w. Mary, and minor ch. Richard, Mary, Joanna, Bethia, and cous. Samuel Hawley. GEORGE, Lynn, by w. Alice had Eliz. b. 15 Mar. 1674; rem. to Salem, there had Benjamin, 10 Mar. 1676; Alice, 6 July 1678; and Susanna, 21 Sept. 1680. HUMPHREY, Charlestown, merch. m. Rebecca, d. of Rev. Zechariah Symmes. JOHN, Scituate 1656, had Joseph, b. 1659; John, 1661; Benjamin, 1667; Abraham, 1671; beside Eliz. Mary, Grace, and Judith. JOHN, Southold, L. I. 1659, refus. o. to Conn. jurisdict. JOHN, Scituate, s. of John of the same, m. 1687, Mary, d. of Anthony Dodson; and had Anthony, b. 1689; and perhaps d. bef. mid. age. His wid. Mary m. 1697, Abraham Bardin, a Scotchman, as says Deane; but he tells no more. JOHN, Woodbury, s. of Richard, m. 14 June 1678, Dorothy, d. of Thomas Hawley of Roxbury, had Thomas, b. 13 Mar. 1679; and John; but Cothren names no more. JOSEPH, Stratford, youngest s. of Richard, in his will, of 14 Aug. 1703, pro. Jan. foll. names w. Eliz. d. Hannah, s. James, Joseph, Robert, David, and Nathan, but ano. s. Zechariah is omit. His est. was good. MICHAEL, Roxbury, had Martha, b. 29 Apr. 1688, by a young woman wh. had unit. with the ch. in 1681, own. her sin on 8 July after this ch. was b. and had it bapt. on the Sunday foll. Perhaps the f. ran away, for no m. is found. RICHARD, Stratford 1640, m. a sis. of the first Joseph Hawley, had Eliz. b. 12 Sept. 1641; Ann, 14 Feb. 1644; Ephraim, Aug. 1648; Ebenezer, 19 Nov. 1651; John, 6 Nov. 1653; Joseph, Feb. or 8 Mar. 1656; Bethia, 18 May 1658; and Joanna, 21 Mar. 1661; was a select-man 1669, and on freem.'s list the same yr. and after 1673, prob. liv. many yrs. He testif. that he was 80 yrs. old in 1687. His d. Eliz. m. 19 Oct. 1658, John Minor. * ROBERT, Exeter 1645, rem. to Saco 1653, or earlier, of wh. he was rep. 1659 to 1670, d. 1672, aged 68; was some yrs. the preach. Prob. of his will, without date, made four days bef. he d. was made 10 Mar. 1673, but the inv. was tak. 26 Oct. preced. By the will his wid. Deborah, ch. Simon, Robert, Mary Penewell, Elinor, Martha, and Rebecca are provid. for. His ch. were Mary, b. 30 Sept. 1627; Ellen, Feb. 1634; Simeon, 10 May 1641; Martha, 12 Apr. 1645; and Robert, 24 July 1655. Martha m. 2 Oct. 1663, John Laighton; Ellen m. July 1652, Nicholas Bully; and Mary m. 1647, Walter Penewell. SIMEON, Fairfield, or perhaps Hartford, m. 5 Jan. 1664, Rebecca, d. of

Daniel Frost, wh. d. 25 Dec. 1688, rem. to Enfield, an early sett. with William, b. a. 1664 ; Zechariah, a. 1666 ; and ds. Eliz. a. 1668 ; Mary, a. 1670 ; all b. bef. he went thither. He was, perhaps, s. of the preced. had sec. w. m. 8 Sept. 1693, wid. Eliz. Elmore, had Sarah, 11 Dec. 1695 ; and Phebe, 1697 ; and d. at Hartford 1703. Dr. Pease, in Hinman, 168, tells us, that William m. 30 Aug. 1693, Hannah, d. of John Burroughs, had Caleb, b. 1695 ; and Joshua, 1697 ; d. 1753, aged 89 ; that Zechariah, m. 15 July 1691, Mary Warriner, and a 2d w. 26 May 1696, Mary Harmon; had two s. John, b. 1697, and Joseph ; and d. 28 May 1741. Three of this name had been gr. in 1834 at Yale.

BOOTMAN, JEREMIAH, Salem, m. 8 Oct. 1659, Esther Lambert, had Mary, b. 4 July 1660 ; Jeremy, 4 Nov. 1662 ; and Mather, or, perhaps Martha, 11 Sept. 1665.

BORDEN, BRYANT, perhaps of Malden, m. Eliz. d. of John Lewis. JOHN, came from Kent, in the Elizabeth and Ann, 1635, aged 28, with w. Jane, 23 ; and ch. Matthew, 5 ; and Eliz. 3 ; but it is not kn. where he first sat down ; yet in 1650 one of the name is found at Stonington, whence he perhaps rem. 1660, to Lyme. JOHN, New London, may have been s. of the preced. m. 11 Feb. 1662, Hannah, eldest d. of William Hough, had John, Samuel, Hannah, William and Sarah, tw. and Joanna, wh. were all bapt. at New London, the last was b. 11 Jan. 1680. He liv. at Lyme, and d. 1684. JOHN, Newport, s. of Richard, by w. Mary had Richard, b. 25 Oct. 1671 ; Amy, 30 May 1678 ; Joseph, 3 Dec. 1680 ; Thomas, 13 Dec. 1682 ; and Hope, 3 Mar. 1685. JOSEPH, Newport, br. of the preced. by w. Hope had Sarah, b. 17 Apr. 1664 ; and William, 31 Dec. 1667 ; rem. to Barbados. MATTHEW, Portsmouth, eldest s. of Richard of the same, m. 4 Mar. 1674, Sarah Clayton, had Mary, b. 20 Sept. 1674 ; Matthew, 14 Aug. 1676 ; Joseph, 17 July 1678 ; Sarah, 29 Dec. 1680 ; and Ann, 5 Jan. 1683. RICHARD, Portsmouth R. I. by w. Joan had Matthew, b. May 1638, "the first Eng. ch. b. on R. I."; John, Sept. 1640 ; Joseph, 3 Jan. 1643 ; Sarah, May 1644 ; Samuel, July 1645 ; Benjamin, May 1649 ; and Amie, Feb. 1654. He was, perhaps, br. of first John. SAMUEL, Warwick, a freem. call. jr. 1655. THOMAS, Providence 1663, m. 20 Jan. 1664, Mary, d. of William Harris of the same, had Mary, b. Oct. 1664 ; Dinah, Oct. 1665 ; William, 10 Jan. 1668 ; Joseph, 25 Nov. 1669 ; Mercy, 3 Nov. 1672; Experience, 8 June 1675 ; and Meribah, 19 Dec. 1676. This name was Burden, in early days, often.

BORDMAN, AARON, Cambridge, s. of William, had Mary, b. 1674, d. soon ; Mary, again, 1679, d. soon; Mary, again, 1689 ; and perhaps other ch. was college cook, or steward, after his br. ANDREW, Cambridge, br. of the preced. freem. 1674, m. 15 Oct. 1669, Ruth Bull, had four ch. wh. all d. young, was steward of the coll. d. 15 July 1687, aged 42. DANIEL, Ipswich, m. 12 Apr. 1662, Hannah, d. of Richard Hutchinson. He was br. of Thomas call. Boreman. THOMAS, Lynn 1637, rem. to Sandwich. Lewis. He bec. one of the first purch. of Middleborough. WILLIAM, Cambridge, s. of Rebecca, w. of Stephen Day, wh. he accomp. from Eng. 1638, in the John of London, may have liv. two or three yrs. at New London, but went back, 1649, to Cambridge; freem. 1652; by w. Frances had Moses, wh. d. 16 Mar. 1662; hav. reach. manhood, and own. two houses; Rebecca; Andrew; Aaron; Frances; Martha; Mary, b. 9 Mar. 1656; William, 6 Dec. 1657; and Eliz. Aug. 1660; a major, was college cook, says Sewall, a long time, d. 25 Mar. 1685, aged 71. Martha m. 17 Apr. 1672, Daniel Epes of Salem. WILLIAM, Malden, perhaps s. of the preced. by w. Sarah had Lydia, b. 2 May 1687; was freem. 1690, d. 14 Mar. 1696. Nineteen of this name had been gr. at the N. E. coll. 1834. Often this is writ. Boardman, wh. see.

BOREL, SAMUEL, Boston, by w. Martha had Deborah, bapt. 1 Feb. 1691; Samuel, 23 Apr. 1693; Catharine, 14 Sept. 1695; Michael, 3 Oct. 1697; John, 22 Oct. 1699; Isabella, 7 Sept. 1701; Samuel, again, 23 Apr. 1704; and Nathaniel, 7 Jan. 1711.

BOREMAN, or BORDMAN sometimes, DANIEL, Wethersfield, s. of Samuel, m. 8 June 1683, Hannah Wright, had Richard, b. 1 Sept. 1684; Daniel, 12 July 1687, Y. C. 1709; Mabel, 30 May 1689; John, 18 Nov. 1691, d. at 21 yrs.; Hannah, 18 Dec. 1693; Martha, 10 Dec. 1695; Israel, 6 Oct. 1697; Timothy, 5 July 1699, d. soon; Timothy, again, 20 July 1700; Joshua, 18 Nov. 1702; Benjamin, 10 Mar. 1705; and Charles, 13 June 1707; and d. 20 Feb. 1724. The wid. d. 25 Feb. 1746, aged 83. ISAAC, Wethersfield, eldest br. of the preced. by w. Abiah had Isaac, b. 21 July 1666; Samuel, 7 July 1668; Thomas, 14 Nov. 1671; and Eunice, 29 June 1682; and he d. 12 May 1719. The wid. d. 6 Jan. 1723. JONATHAN, br. of the preced. may have not liv. at Wethersfield, certain. m. 22 Oct. 1685, Mercy, d. of John Hubbard of Hatfield, had Mercy, b. 4 July 1687; Joseph, 18 Apr. 1690, d. young; Jonathan, 16 May 1697; Abigail, 20 May 1700, d. at 18 yrs.; Hepzibah, 16 Feb. 1702; and he d. 21 Sept. 1712. NATHANIEL, Wethersfield, youngest br. of the preced. m. 30 Apr. 1707, Eliz. d. of Return Strong of Windsor, had only s. Nathaniel, b. 19 Feb. 1711; and d. 29 Nov. 1712, aged 49. * SAMUEL, Ipswich 1639, rem. prob. to Wethersfield with s. Isaac, b. 3 Feb. 1642; had there Mary, b. 14 Feb. 1644; Samuel, 8 Oct. 1648; Joseph, 12 Mar. 1651; John, Jan. 1653; Sarah, 8 Mar. 1656; Daniel, 4 Aug. 1658; Jonathan, 4 Feb. 1661; Nathaniel, 12 Apr. 1663; and Martha, 12 Aug. 1666, prob. d. young; rep. 1657–67. John and Joseph d. without ch. SAMUEL, Wethersfield, s. of the preced. m. 8 Feb. 1682, Sarah, d. of lieut. James Steele of Hartford, had

Mary, b. 13 Nov. 1683; Sarah, 13 Mar. 1686, d. in few days; Hannah, 27 June 1687, d. next yr.; David, 1 June 1692; and Joseph, 6 Apr. 1695; and d. 23 Dec. 1720. The name was turn. to Boardman and other forms. * THOMAS, Ipswich, freem. 4 Mar. 1635, rep. 1636, rem. prob. to Barnstable, there m. 3 Mar. (other rec. says 1 Mar.) 1645, Hannah, d. of Anthony Annable, had Hannah, b. May 1646; Thomas, Sept. 1648; Samuel, July 1651; Desire, May 1654; Mary, Mar. 1656; Mehitable, Sept. 1658; and Tristram, Aug. 1661; and d. 25 May 1679. The name is Burnam in Geneal. Reg. IX. 315. THOMAS, Ipswich, perhaps s. of the preced. freem. 1682. WILLIAM, perhaps of Wethersfield 1645, was of Guilford 1650.

BORLAND, FRANCIS, Boston 1684, but whether this be the yr. of his first com. is not kn. His d. Jane m. 4 Sept. 1750, John Still Winthrop, Y. C. 1737.

BOSTWICK, or BOSTICK, ARTHUR, came from Co. Chester, acc. tradit. with s. John, to Stratford, an early sett. bef. 1650, had then w. Ellen, and they agreed in 1674, that the unit. prop. be div. into halves, her sh. to feoffees. She was sec. w. and d. near the begin. of 1678. By former w. he had John, and other childr. whose names are unkn. tho. tradit. (wh. has no support), names them Arthur and Zechariah. JOHN, Stratford 1666 or earlier, s. of Arthur, b. in Eng. m. Mary, d. of John Brimsmead, had John, b. 4 May 1667; Zechariah, 24 or 28 July 1669; Joseph, 11 May 1672; Mary, 14 Feb. 1675; Eliz. 1 Oct. 1677; and Jane, 13 Apr. 1680. He d. 1689, leav. good est. JOHN, s. of the preced. by w. Abigail had John, b. 1689; Robert; Ebenezer; Joseph; Nathaniel, 1699; Lemuel, 1704; beside two ds. as tradit. tells, when he rem. 1707 to the young planta. of New Milford, there had Daniel, 1708; and Mary, 8 Feb. 1715. JOSEPH, Stratford, youngest br. of the preced. m. 14 June 1698, Ann Burr, had Abigail, b. 24 Sept. 1700; Abraham, 5 Sept. 1702; and Hannah, 3 Jan. 1705. ZECHARIAH, Stratford, br. of the preced. had Zechariah; Ephraim; Jonathan, b. 1 Apr. 1697; Susanna, 22 Nov. 1700; Parnel, 15 Apr. 1702; Eliz. 12 May 1704; Meredith; and Martha; but wh. was his w. is unkn.

BOSWAY, WILLIAM, is the name borne on the rolls of Turner's comp. 1676, of whose resid. I am less solicitous, because so many are incorrect. writ. that we can easily doubt the accuracy of this.

BOSWELL, JAMES, Wethersfield 1658, d. 24 Dec. 1660, prob. without fam. JOHN, Boston 1630, prob. came in the fleet with Winth. early mem. of the ch. d. soon. SAMUEL, Bradford, a. 1663, Rowley 1671, had Samuel. SAMUEL, Boston, possib. s. of the preced. by w. Mary had Richard, b. 9 June 1678. Sometimes this name is Buswell.

BOSWORTH, BENJAMIN, Hingham 1635, came, perhaps, in the Elizabeth Dorcas 1634 with Henry Sewall, and may have been s. of Edward, wh. prob. d. on the passage; at least, in the Col. Rec. I. 123, provis. for a wid. B. is made, and Ib. 152, he with Jonathan and Nathaniel B. is order. to pay unto S. several sums for money disburs. by him in the transport. of Edward and his fam. But I am confus. betw. the two Benjamins, the younger of wh. m. 7 Dec. 1670, Eliz. d. of Secr. Morton. BENJAMIN, Hull, prob. s. of the preced. m. 27 Nov. 1666, Hannah, d. of Secr. Morton, had Hannah, b. 21 Dec. 1669; for 2d w. m. 16 Nov. 1671, Beatrice, wid. of Abraham Josselyn, after some yrs. rem. to Marlborough and Stow, freem. 1680, and some yrs. later to Boston under the filial care of her d. Rebecca Stevens; d. Nov. 1700, and his wid. d. Jan. 1712, aged 88. She is one of the persons wh. was said to have been k. by the Ind. at the assault on Lancaster, 1676. HANANIEL, Ipswich 1648, rem. I suppose, to Haverhill, where is found, in 1674, Hannah, prob. his w. or d. JOHN, of Hull perhaps was the freem. 14 May 1634. One JOHN, of Hull, was a soldier, in Dec. 1675, of Johnson's comp. JONATHAN, Cambridge 1634, perhaps br. of Benjamin the first, rem. soon to Hingham, thence, 1669, to Swanzey, tho. Lincoln says Rehoboth, wh. was prob. a prior stage in 1661. JONATHAN, Swanzey, had Hannah, b. 5 Nov. 1673. JOSEPH, Hull, freem. 1680, perhaps youngest br. of first Benjamin, rem. to Rehoboth, there had Joseph, b. 27 Sept. 1679; and Eliz. 17 Nov. 1681. NATHANIEL, Hull 1661, freem. 1680, prob. br. of the sec. Benjamin, m. 7 Dec. 1670, Eliz. d. of Secr. Nathaniel Morton of Plymouth, wh. d. 6 Apr. 1673, and was bur. 8, says the rec. two hours bef. Gov. Prince. But in the Life of late John Howland, she is call. his d. had Nathaniel, b. 22 Mar. 1673; Eliz. 24 Nov. 1676; John, 7 June 1678; Samuel, 16 Feb. 1680; Mary, 2 June 1682; Ephraim, 24 Sept. 1684; Lemuel, 15 Oct. 1686; Joseph, 10 July 1689; Bridget, 2 June 1691; and Jeremiah, 21 June 1693; but of these, certain. the last nine were by sec. w. Mary. He is call. junr. So that ano. Nathaniel was, prob. there, wh. may been his f. or cous. The f. and his eldest four ch. all d. within 3 wks. Aug. 1693. SAMUEL, Boston, s. of Zaccheus, or Zechariah, as the ch. rec. at the first bapt. names him, by w. Mercy, d. of Thomas Bumstead, had Samuel, Zaccheus, Joseph, and Jeremiah. ‖ ZACCHEUS, in some rec. ZECHARIAH, Boston 1630, prob. came in the fleet with Winth. freem. 25 May 1636, was of importance eno. to be disarm. Nov. 1637, ar. co. 1650, d. 28 July 1655. His will, made five days bef. was pro. 5 Oct. foll. See Geneal. Reg. V. 443. By his w. Ann, wh. after his d. m. 17 Oct. 1656, Thomas Cooper of Rehoboth, he had d. Restored, bapt. 26 Aug. 1638; Eliz. 26 July 1640; and Samuel, b. 4, bapt. 12 Mar. 1643; beside Sarah, wh. d. July 1645, hav. been bapt. 27 of the same, at 3 days old; Eliz. m. John Morse.

BOTHAM, ROBERT, Ipswich 1652.

BOTSFORD, ELNATHAN, Milford, eldest ch. of Henry, m. first, 12 Dec. 1664, Eliz. d. of John Fletcher, had only Eliz. b. 1665 ; and m. sec. w. 12 Dec. 1667, Hannah, d. of Timothy Baldwin, had Esther, b. 1668 ; Samuel, 1670 ; Mary, 1672 ; and Joanna, 1674 ; beside Henry, Joseph, Timothy, John, Hannah, and Sarah, nam. in his will of 4 Aug. 1691 ; those others being also nam. exc. Joanna. HENRY, Milford 1639, had by w. Eliz. wh. join. the ch. 1640, Elnathan, bapt. 14 Aug. 1641 ; Eliz. and Mary, prob. tw. 21 May 1643 ; Hannah, Dec. 1645 ; Esther, 1647 ; and Ruth, 1649. His will of 1 Feb. 1686, is foll. by the inv. of 15th Apr. same yr. ment. w. Eliz. and the ds. of wh. Hannah was d. leav. the will says, four ch. Eliz. m. 27 June 1665, Daniel Baldwin ; Mary m. 8 Jan. 1668, Andrew Sandford ; Hannah m. 12 Mar. 1671, Nathaniel Baldwin ; Esther m. 27 June 1665, Nathaniel Wheeler of Newark ; and Ruth m. John Baldwin of Newark, both rem. from M. He d. says Lambert, in 1686. The name long contin. there.

BOUGHEY, ELIZ., Roxbury, m. 24 Jan. 1643, Robert Harris, and to that name I refer.

BOUGHTWHORE, or BOUGHTWHORET, ROBERT, freem. of Conn. 20 May 1658. Some reason may be found for suppos. this name writ. for Boltwood.

BOULTER, MATTHEW, Hampton 1649. NATHANIEL, Hampton 1644, perhaps br. of the preced. by w. Grace had, perhaps, Mary ; certain. Nathaniel ; Joshua, b. 1 May 1655, d. soon ; Joshua, again, 23 Jan. 1657, d. at 4 yrs. ; Rebecca, 12 Oct. 1659, d. at 2 yrs. ; Grace, 27 Dec. 1662, d. next mo. ; Hannah, 27 June 1665 ; Eliz. 23 Feb. 1669, wh. m. 6 May 1689, Joseph Fanning ; and John, 2 Dec. 1672. He calls hims. 60 yrs. old in 1685, d. 14 Mar. 1693. Adams, Annals, 397. NATHANIEL, Hampton, s. of the preced. took o. of alleg. 1678. RICHARD, Weymouth, freem. 1653, liv. 1662. STEPHEN, Newbury 1668, is not ment. in Coffin's copious Hist. and so may seem only transient. THOMAS, Weymouth 1661, by w. Experience had Hannah, b. 30 Nov. 1662 ; and by w. Hannah had Experience, 19 Jan. 1672 ; and Ebenezer, 23 Apr. 1688. He was one of the first project. of settlem. of Mendon, a. 1660.

BOULTON, NICHOLAS, Dorchester 1643, freem. 1644, by w. Eliz. had Thankful, bapt. 14 Oct. 1649 ; John ; and Eliz. wh. m. 25 Oct. 1676, Experience Willis. He d. 27 May 1683, three days after mak. nuncup. will, nam. w. Eliz. extrix. See Bolton.

BOUND, WILLIAM, Salem, freem. 17 May 1637, had by w. Ann, there bapt. James, 25 Aug. 1636 ; Andrew, 12 Aug. 1638 ; and Philip, 7 Dec. 1640 ; m. 2d w. 12 July 1669, Mary Haverlad. Felt.

BOURDEN, JOHN and WILLIAM were of Watertown 1657, and the former sw. fidel. 1652.

BOURLE, WILLIAM, Charlestown, a soldier in Moseley's comp. k. in the Narraganset fight, 19 Dec. 1675 ; but my suspicion of the spell. of the name is very great, tho. to offer a substitute is not easy.

BOURNE, ELISHA, Sandwich, s. of Richard, m. 26 Oct. 1675, Patience Skiff, d. perhaps, of James of the same, had Nathan, Elisha, Eliz. Abigail, Bathsheba, Hannah, and Mary, but as no date is giv. for any one, I fear we can hardly be sure of the order of success. He d. 1706. GARRETT, or JARRARD, or GERALD, or GERARD, or JARRETT, perhaps JARED, Boston, in the employm. of Elder William Colborne in June 1634, when adm. to the ch. possib. came with him, 1630, freem. 6 May 1635, had John, b. 30 July 1643, d. next mo. but the rec. of his bapt. at Roxbury, 6 Aug. calls him Gerard, as does the town rec. of b. at R. and on 30 May foll. his w. Mary, not Ann, as the modern *copy* of rec. has it, d. He resid. was at Muddy riv. now Brookline, in the early day appurten. to Boston, and there in 1654 he was appoint. a constable ; but in Boston he had Jarat (so writ.) bapt. 7 Mar. 1651, and in 1665 rem. to R. I. *HENRY, Plymouth, or Scituate, perhaps both 1634, rem. 1639 to Barnstable, of wh. he was rep. 1644, had there Dorcas, bapt. 26 Aug. 1649. JOB, Sandwich, s. of Richard, m. 1664, Ruhama Hallett, d. of Andrew, had Timothy, b. 1666 ; Eleazur, 1670 ; Hezekiah, 1675 ; John ; and others ; certain. Hannah, 1667. JOHN, Salem 1637, s. or more prob. br. of Thomas, rem. 1649, to Gloucester, there by w. Mary had Bethia, b. 11 Oct. 1651 ; rem. next yr. JOHN, Marshfield, s. of Thomas, perhaps b. in Eng. m. 18 July 1645, Alice, d. of Thomas Besbedge the sec. m. on town's book, being in his will of Nov. 1672 so describ. and her ch. nam. Thomas, b. 1647 ; and Sarah, 1663, with allusion to other sis. wh. were Eliz. b. 1646 ; Alice, 1649 ; Ann, 1651 ; Martha, 1653, and Mary, 1660 ; there was bur. 8 Dec. 1684 ; and his wid. was bur. 9 May 1686. NEHEMIAH, Charlestown 1638, shipbuilder, was also of Dorchester, tho. Dr. Harris has not giv. him a resid. rem. to Boston 1640, freem. 2 June 1641, went to Eng. in 1644, and serv. in the army of the Parl. as maj. of Rainsborough's reg. ; by w. Hannah had Nehemiah, b. 10 June 1640, and Hannah, b. 10, bapt. 14 Nov. 1641 ; but prob. at last carr. his fam. to Eng. and may be the man ment. in a let. of the w. of Goffe, the regicide, in 1672. See 3 Mass. Hist. Coll. I. 60 and IX. 268. Winth. II. 245. RICHARD, Lynn 1637, rem. to Sandwich, was the first instruct. of the Ind. at Mashpee, begin. in 1658, ord. 1670 by Eliot and Cotton ; m. July 1677, Ruth Winslow, wid. of Jonathan, d. of William Sargent, but it was by former w. whose name we find not, that his ch. were b. ; Job ; Elisha, b. 1641 ; and Shearjashub, 1643. He d. 1682.

Copious acco. is in Gookin's Hist. Coll.; Hubbard, 659, 60; and Davis's Ed. of Morton's Mem. 408. * SHEARJASHUB, Sandwich, s. of the preced. m. Bathshua Skiff, prob. d. of James of the same, had Melatiah; Ezra, b. 1667; Mary, 1678, d. young; Sarah, 1680; Mary, again, 1681; Remembrance, 1683; and Patience, 1686; was oft. a rep. of Plymouth Col. and the Prov. of Mass.; d. 7 Mar. 1719, aged 75. His youngest s. Ezra, a man of distinct. d. Sept. 1764, aged 88, of wh. three gr.s. were in the Congr. of U. S. 1794. Baylies, II. 283, 4. THOMAS, early at Marshfield, may prob. have come from Co. Kent, bring. fam. hav. been at Plymouth 1637, freem. of that col. 2 Jan. 1638, had w. Eliz. bur. 18 July 1660, aged 70, was a man of substance and repute, d. a. 1664, aged 83, leav. wid. Martha, ch. prob. all by w. Eliz. John, above ment.; Martha, wh. m. 1. John Bradford, s. of the Gov. 2. Thomas Tracy, d. at Norwich 1689; Eliz. m. 9 Dec. 1638, Robert Waterman; Ann m. 21 June 1640, Nehemiah Smith; Margaret m. Josiah Winslow, br. of Gov. Edward; and Lydia m. Nathaniel Tilden. His will of 2 May 1664, made s. John excor. names ea. d. and Lydia, d. of Lydia, beside John, Thomas, Joseph, and Robert Waterman, and Mr. Arnold, his min. THOMAS, Marshfield, prob. s. of John, m. 18 Apr. 1681, Eliz. d. of John Rouse, had Eliz. wh. d. 14 Apr. 1689. WILLIAM, Duxbury 1638, may rather, perhaps, be Burne. Eleven of this name had been gr. at H. C. 1834, and four at Brown and Bowd.

BOUTELL, BOUTWELL, BOUTELLE, or BOWTELL, HENRY, Cambridge, m. 24 or 25 June 1657, Eliz. Bowers, prob. wid. of George, and d. soon, prob. for he made his will six days after, in wh. he names his "belov. w." but gives his dwell.-ho. to his friend lieut. William Johnson of Woburn. But the same man, as it seems to me, had been resid. at New Haven, witness, in Aug. 1653, and took o. of fidel. there May foll. JAMES, Salem and Lynn 1635, freem. 14 Mar. 1639, d. 1651, in his will of 22 Aug. pro. 26 Nov. of that yr. names w. Alice, s. James, and John, and d. Sarah. JAMES, Reading, s. of the preced. m. 1665, Rebecca, d. of deac. Thomas Kendall, had James, b. 6 Apr. 1666; Thomas, 23 Mar. 1669; John, 19 Oct. 1671; Rebecca, 25 Dec. 1674; Sarah, 7 July 1677; Tabitha, 11 May 1679, d. in few days; Tabitha, again, 22 May 1680; Kendall, 15 Jan. 1682; Mary, 28 Oct. 1685; and Eliz. 9 Oct. 1687; his w. d. 30 Aug. 1713, aged 68; and he d. 5 Dec. 1716, aged 74. Thro. this branch is deriv. the late Timothy Boutelle, a learned lawyer. JOHN, Cambridge, by w. Margaret had Mary, b. 26 Oct. 1646; and John, wh. d. 10 Mar. 1674, aged 21; and the f. d. 30 Aug. 1676, aged a. 60. JOHN, Reading, s. of James the first, m. 10 May 1669, Hannah Davis, prob. eldest d. of George of the same, had John, b. 26 Feb. 1670; Hannah, 3 June 1672; Sarah, 3 Dec. 1674, d. under 2 yrs.; James, 6 Sept. 1677; Mary, 29 Jan. 1679; Eliz. 2 Mar. 1683;

Sarah, 20 Aug. 1686; Susannah, 26 Feb. 1689; and Thomas, 6 Feb. 1692. Of this branch is descend. George S. Boutwell, late Gov. of Mass. THOMAS, Reading, perhaps the same as T. Boutle, wh. was call. on an import. jury 1646, as appears in N. E. Jonas cast up, pr. in 2 Mass. Hist. Coll. IV. 110. This name is spell. only to vary the accent, with final *e*, of wh. form in 1834 four had been gr. in N. E. coll.

BOUTINEAU, STEPHEN, Boston, a Huguenot merch. came from La Rochelle to Casco, 1686, accomp. his friend Baudouin, 1690, to Boston, and m. 22 Aug. 1708, his d. Mary, had six s. four ds. it is said, of wh. in the rec. I find Anna, b. 24 Apr. 1709; James, 27 Jan. 1711; John, 1 Apr. 1713; Mary, 5 Aug. 1715; Eliz. 11 Feb. 1717; Mary, again, 18 Jan. 1719, Stephen, 22 May 1721; Peter, 11 Dec. 1722; Thomas, 11 Oct. 1724; and Isaac, 22 June 1726. He was Elder of the Fr. ch. and in 1748, unit. with the pastor and few remain. proprs. in alienat. their est. Willis, I. 185. Snow, 202.

BOUTON, * JOHN, Norwalk 1654, or earlier, m. 1 June 1657, Abigail, d. of Matthew Marvin, had John, b. 30 Sept. 1659; Matthew, 24 Dec. 1661; Rachel, 15 Dec. 1667; Abigail, 1 Apr. 1670; and Mary, 26 May 1671; but this was 2d w. for he had fam. bef. sett. at Norwalk, and his d. Bridget m. 1665, Daniel Kellogg. He was selectman, rep. 1671, and often after to 1685; and a fam. tradit. is, that he came in the Assurance, of London, 1635, aged 20, of course to Boston, went soon to Hartford. JOHN, Norwalk, s. of the preced. had Jachin, Joseph, and perhaps more. Rev. Nathaniel, of Concord, N. H. is a descend. b. at Norwalk, and in his Addr. on the two hundredth anniv. well sustain. the pristine charact. of his nat. town. RICHARD, Fairfield, br. of first John, d. 1665, leav. only ch. Ruth, by w. Ruth. The wid. d. next yr.

BOWD, JOSEPH, Boston, by w. Eliz. had Eliz. b. 20 Aug. 1657.

BOWDEN, BOUDEN, or BOADEN, AMBROSE. See Boaden. BENJAMIN, New Haven, a propr. 1685. JOHN, Boston 1668, a mason. RICHARD, Boston, by w. Martha had Eliz. b. 18 May 1661. WILLIAM, Maine 1642.

BOWDITCH, JOHN, Boston, m. a. 1682, Temperance, d. of John French the first of Braintree. She d. 12 Aug. 1720. He prob. had est. at that part of Boston call. Braintree. WILLIAM, Salem 1639, from Devonsh. no doubt, as the fam. name is there freq. had gr. of ld. 1643, by w. Sarah had Nathaniel, bapt. 12 Feb. 1643; but left only ch. William, prob. older, possib. b. in Eng. an officer of the customs, under the col. admin. whose d. 1681, was sudden, as well as untimely. See Col. Rec. V. 324, for the prudent act of the governm. His sole surv. ch. William, b. Sept. 1663, was emin. at Salem, for usefulness, m. 30 Aug. 1688, Mary, d. of Thomas Gardner, d. 28 May 1728. This third William had seven ch. but of the s. Ebenezer, b. 26 Apr. 1703, m. 15 Aug. 1728, Mary, d. of

Hon. John Turner, and d. 2 Feb. 1768, alone, left male issue. His s. Habakkuk was f. of Nathaniel, the great American astronomer, translat. of La Place.

BOWDOIN (so made from the sound of the old French BAUDOUIN), ‡ JAMES, Boston, s. of Pierre, b. at La Rochelle, in France, merch. brot. by his f. (escap. from the persecut. of Louis XIV.) to Casco, now Portland, thence soon to Boston, m. 18 July 1706, Sarah Campbell, perhaps d. of John, the postmaster, had James, b. 5 May foll. d. in few mos.; Mary, and Eliz. tw. 27 June 1708, of wh. Eliz. d. in two wks.; John, 22 Aug. 1709, d. at two yrs.; Peter, 19 May 1711, d. next'yr.; and William, 14 June 1713, H. C. 1735. His w. d. 21 Dec. 1713, and he m. 16 Sept. foll. Hannah, d. of George Pordage, had Samuel, b. 25 July foll. d. next yr.; Eliz. 25 Apr. 1717; Judith, whose date of b. 1719, is deriv. (like that of the preced. sis.) not from rec. of town, but fam. memor.; and James, 7 Aug. 1726, H. C. 1745. His sec. w. d. 2 Aug. 1726, and he m. 24 Apr. 1735, wid. Mehitable Lillie. He was one of the richest men in B. made one of his majesty's council under our free chart. and d. 8 Sept. 1747, aged 71, leav. five ch. above ment. Mary, m. 12 Feb. 1729, Belthazar Bayard; Eliz. m. 26 Oct. 1732, James Pitts; and Judith, m. 12 June 1744, Thomas Flucker. § ‡ JAMES, Boston, youngest s. of the preced. m. 15 Sept. 1748, Eliz. d. of John Erving, had James, b. 22 Sept. 1752, H. C. 1771, wh. was min. plenipo. of U. S. at Madrid; and Eliz. wh. m. Sir John Temple, the first British Consul Gen. to our country, one of whose ds. was w. of the late Thomas L. Winthrop, Lieut. Gov. of Mass. and mo. of Hon. Robert Charles W. He was a disting. patriot of the Revo. and bef. had serv. in the council of the Prov. 1757–69, when the royal Gov. put a negat. upon him, presid. of that convent. of 1780 for fram. the Constit. of Mass. and first presid. of the A. A. S. and Gov. of the Comwth. 1785 and 6, during the worst of the delusions that produc. Shay's rebell. and d. 6 Nov. 1790. With felicity that leaves nothing to be desir. his charact. was portra. by his gr. gr.s. R. C. Winthrop in an Address at Bowdoin Coll. wh. deriv. its name from the uncle of the orator, the most disting. benefact. MICHAEL, Lynn 1690. Lewis MS. PIERRE, was, I think, translat. into Eng. (at the same time with the fam. name) and became PETER, Boston, had been a physician at La Rochelle bef. the revocat. of the Edict of Nantz, on wh. he fled forthwith to Ireland 1685, as the most natural resort of persecut. Protestants, thence came next yr. to Casco with w. Eliz. wh. d. 19 Aug. 1720, aged 77, and two s. John, wh. went early to Virg. and sett. there in Northampton Co. where descend. remain; and James, bef. ment. and two ds. In little over two yrs. with sev. other Huguenots he rem. to Boston, there more than sixteen yrs. was a prosper. merch. d. Sept. 1706. By will of 16 June 1704, all his est. of wh. inv. was £1,344, a good prop. for that day, was giv. to w. for life. Of his ds. Mary m. 22 Aug. 1708, Stephen Boutineau ; but the other, Eliz. perhaps earlier had m. a Robins, as fam. tradit. tells neither date, nor bapt. name, nor resid. nor issue, I suppose he may have been a Huguenot, and liv. in ano. Col. The wid. in her will of 5 Sept. 1717, gives, I believe, no light on this point, and yet ment. her s. John as hav. d. leav. childr. A strange complicat. of errors, as to the time of his d. the condition of his worldly affairs, and the age of his eldest s. as if he were left a minor, beyond the usual blunders of happy tradit. had so overgrown the fam. hist. as greatly to mislead the Rev. William Jenks, in his Eulogy, deliv. 1813, after the dec. of the founder of Bowdoin Coll. Quite extensive was the spread of these misconcept. from the deserv. high esteem of the writer's exact information on all subjects his modesty suffers him to treat. WILLIAM, Boston, eldest s. of the first James, m. 1739, Phebe, d. of John Murdock of Plymouth, had three ds. of wh. the two elder d. young, and the third, Sarah, b. 17 Oct. 1761, m. her first cous. James, and he d. 24 Feb. 1773, at Roxbury.

BOWE, ALEXANDER, Charlestown 1658, rem. to Middletown, d. 6 Nov. 1678; by w. Sarah wh. d. 16 Apr. 1665, had Samuel, b. 28 Jan. 1660; Sarah, 20 June 1662; Mary, 18 Jan. 1665, d. at 2 mos.; and he m. 26 Nov. 1673, Rebecca, d. of Richard Hughes of Guilford, had Ann, 10 Sept. 1674 ; Mary, again, 5 Dec. 1676 ; and, posthum. Rebecca, 19 Apr. 1679. NICHOLAS, Cambridge, m. 26 June 1684, Sarah Hubbard, wh. d. 26 Jan. 1689 ; and for 2d w. m. 6 May 1690, Dorcas Champney. The name soon bec. Bowes.

BOWEN, GRIFFITH, Boston 1638, from Llangenydd, Glamorgansh. freem. 22 May 1639, by w. Margaret had Esther, bapt. 10 Feb. 1639, wh. d. 28 Mar. 1654; Abigail, 18 Apr. 1641 ; Peniel, b. 10 May 1644 ; and Eliz. wh. m. Isaac Addington. He was some yrs. at Roxbury, but went home and liv. at London 1670. HENRY, Boston, by w. Frances had Mary, b. 14 Aug. 1657. HENRY, Roxbury, perhaps s. of Griffith, m. 20 Dec. 1658, Eliz. Johnson, had Henry, b. 13 Oct. 1659, bapt. 12 Feb. foll. wh. was a soldier in Dec. 1675 of Johnson's comp. ; Eliz. 26, bapt. 27 Jan. 1661 ; John, 1, bapt. 7 Sept. 1662 ; Margaret, d. young ; Maria, b. 12 Sept. 1666 ; Margaret, again, 26 Jan. 1668 ; Penuel, 8 Mar. 1671 ; Esther, 8 Mar. 1675 ; and Isaac, 20 Apr. 1676. His wid. Eliz. d. 20 Apr. 1701. JOHN, Plymouth 1651. * OBADIAH, Swanzey, rep. 1681, had been of Rehoboth 1657, an active mem. of the Bapt. communion, had s. Obadiah, beside Isaac, b. 30 Sept. 1674. OBADIAH, Swanzey, s. of the preced. had Hezekiah, b. 19 Nov. 1682. RICHARD, Rehoboth 1643, d. 4 Feb. 1675, and his wid. d. the same yr. RICHARD, Rehoboth, call. jr. 1658, perhaps s. of the preced. m. Mary

Titus. THOMAS, Salem 1648, was of New London 1657–60, rem. to Rehoboth, d. 1663. His wid. Eliz. was, in 1669, w. of Samuel Fuller of Plymouth. His will, of 11 Apr. 1663, made her extrix. names his s. Richard, and br. Obadiah. THOMAS, Marblehead 1674, may have been s. of the preced. Sixteen of this name had been gr. at N. E. coll. 1834.

BOWERS, BENANUEL, Charlestown 1656, s. of George, m. 9 Dec. 1654, Eliz. Dunster, perhaps a niece of Presid. D. had George, b. 3 Feb. 1655; suff. much abuse, as a Quaker, by prison, whip. and fine, in 1677. Frothingham, 173. 4. Col. Rec. V. 153, 68. GEORGE, Plymouth 1639, rem. to Cambridge, where his w. Barbara d. 25 Mar. 1644; m. 15 Apr. 1649, Eliz. Worthington, had Jerathmeel, b. 2 May 1650, beside Benanuel, John, H. C. 1649; Patience; and Silence; some, if not all, by former w. and d. late in 1656, his will of 8 Nov. being pro. 30 Dec. of that yr. and his wid. I think, m. 25 June 1657, Henry Bowtell, or Boutwell. JERATHMEEL, Chelmsford, s. of the preced. JOHN, Medfield 1649. JOHN, Derby, s. of George, prob. b. in Eng. was a sch.master at Plymouth, perhaps the earliest, went in the same business 1653, to New Haven, on invit. of Gov. Eaton, there taught until 1660, and after in other towns; was preach. after Pierson left Branford, in 1667, to Feb. 1673; soon after was sett. at D. and there d. 14 June 1687. His will, rec. at D. bears date 8 Jan. 1685. His w. was Bridget, d. of Anthony Thompson of New Haven, wh. surv. him, and he had there bapt. Ruth, 20 Dec. 1657; and Samuel, 5 Nov. 1665; beside Mary, prob. b. after Ruth, and bef. Samuel, wh. m. 1682, Samuel Nichols; John, b. at Guilford, 3 Dec. 1667; and Ann, wh. m. 1703, Francis French. Ruth m. John Frisbie, and next, William Hoadly. JOHN, s. of the preced. was not of H. C. as Mather, mistak. him for f. asserts; but of quality to be a min. is by Trumbull fix. 1688 at Rye, and in Mather's Hecatompolis, Magn. I. c. 7, is insert. as min. of Rye 1696. He may have gone to Derby, where his d. is rec. 23 Sept. 1708; or the Rye min. may be ano. man, tho. it is not prob. JOHN, Greenwich, call. 43 yrs. old in 1681, m. after 1685, perhaps for sec. w. Hannah, wid. of Joshua Knapp, d. in 1694, leav. no ch. His wid. d. Jan. 1696. MATTHEW, Cambridge, prob. s. of George, d. 30 Jan. 1645. SAMUEL, Derby, s. of Rev. John, m. 1687, Ruth Wooster, and m. 1691, Lydia French of the same, had ch. b. 1692, 4, &c. was liv. in 1717. MORGAN, Norwich 1660, wh. was there in 1700, had come in from Saybrook. Six of this name had been gr. in 1834 at N. E. coll.

BOWING, THOMAS, Marblehead 1648, is the same as Bowen.

BOWKER, or BOUKER, ‖ EDMUND or EDWARD, Dorchester, ar. co. 1646, m. Mary Potter, rem. to Sudbury, d. Mar. 1666. JOHN, Marlborough, m. 8 Feb. 1678, Mary Howe, was, perhaps, s. of the preced. and freem. 1685.

BOWLAND, ELIZ. (if there be no mistake in this name), call. of Boston, m. 2 Aug. 1655, Mr. Samuel Lee of Virg.

BOWLES, ‖ JOHN, Roxbury 1639, freem. 13 May 1640, ar. co. 1645, rul. elder, d. 1680, bur. 24 Sept. was k. by a cartwheel running over him. On 22 Aug. his will was made, and pro. 5 Oct. foll. By it his s. John was made excor. names w. Sarah, d. Eliz. White, d. Mary Gardner, and ment. money paid to Daniel Smith by order of his w. His first w. Dorothy, wh. d. of smallpox, and was bur. the same day, 3 Nov. 1649, had no ch. it is thot. He m. 2 Apr. 1650, Eliz. d. of Isaac Heath, had Eliz. b. 3, bapt. 23 Feb. 1651; Isaac, bapt. 15 May, and d. 1652; John, bapt. 17 July 1653, H. C. 1671; and Mary, b. 20, bapt. 29 Apr. 1655. His w. d. 6 July foll. A third w. Sarah, wh. may have been wid. of Francis Chickering, as bef. m. him she had been of John Sibly, surv. to 2 Sept. 1686, but her will was of 21 June 1681. In it she gives equal portions to her br. Joseph How, s. Daniel Smith, Esq. Samuel Newman, Thomas Metcalf, William Symmes, doub. portion to s. Mr. John Bowles, and equal portions to d. Eliz. Gardner, s. Thomas Gardner, John White, and Timothy Dwight. Mary m. 17 Nov. 1673, Thomas Gardner; and Eliz. m. perhaps, John White. * JOHN, s. of the preced. freem. 1680, m. 16 Nov. 1681, Sarah, d. of Rev. John Eliot, jr. wh. d. 23 May 1687, had John, wh. d. early; John, again, b. 15 Mar. 1685, H. C. 1702, a promin. man; and Sarah, 15 Nov. 1686, d. at six mos.; rep. 1689 and 90, and speaker of the ho. d. 30 Mar. 1691; but in 1688 when he was chos. rul. elder, it was hoped he would preach, and be adjunct with apostle Eliot, if his health improv. JOSEPH, Wells 1640, wh. usually is writ. Bolles, went home, but came again from Eng. in the Speedwell, 1656, aged 47, of good charact. liv. 1680, when he took o. of alleg. His d. Mary m. a. 1676, Charles Frost, but could not be first w. of first Charles. RICHARD, Dover 1666.

BOWMAN, FRANCIS, Watertown, eldest s. of Nathaniel, sw. fidel. 1652, m. 26 Sept. 1661, Martha, d. of capt. John Sherman, had Francis, b. 14 Sept. 1662; John, 19 Feb. 1665; Martha, 2 Mar. 1667, d. at 9 mos.; Nathaniel, 9 Feb. 1669; Joseph, 18 May 1674; Ann, 19 Sept. 1676; Samuel, 14 Aug. 1679; Jonathan, d. 1682; and Martha, again, 4 Apr. 1685; and he d. 16 Dec. 1687. He rem. to Cambridge Farms, now Lexington. JOHN, Plymouth 1633. Haz. I. 327. NATHANIEL, Watertown, came, prob. in the fleet with Winth. 1630, req. to be adm. freem. 19 Oct. of that yr. by w. Ann had beside Francis bef. ment., Mary, wh. was bur. 10 Mar. 1638; Joanna, bur. 20 Nov. 1638; Nathaniel, b. 6 Mar. 1641, perhaps other ch. bef. and after; but the rec. must be follow. that Dorcas was b. 31 Jan. 1639, bur. 6 Feb. 1639; Joanna, again, 20 Nov. 1642; Dorcas, again, wh. m. Benjamin Blackleach of Cambridge, and had 2d h. a March. He d. 26 Jan. 1682, in his will of 21 Oct. 1679, nam. s. Francis, Nathaniel, d. Dorcas March, and her ch. Nathaniel, and Benjamin, and gr.d. Hannah Turner, prob. d. of 2d Joanna. NATHANIEL, Wethersfield 1668, prob. s. of the preced. an important man, in 1669 m. Rebecca, d. of Rev. Henry Smith, wh. had been divorc. from her h. lieut. Samuel Smith of New London for desert. d. Jan. 1707, without ch. Twelve of this name are in the Catal. of H. C. gr. Perhaps some Boreman has assum. it.

BOWSTREETE, WILLIAM, Concord, freem. 22 May 1639, d. or was bur. 31 Oct. 1642. His will, made 8 days bef. names his sis. Eliz. Newman, to her and ch. giv. all his est. It is abstr. in Geneal. Reg. II. 385.

BOYDEN, THOMAS, Watertown, came in the Francis from Ipswich, 1634, aged 21, next yr. was of Scituate, serv. of William Gilson, join. their ch. 17 May, freem. 1647, by w. Frances had Thomas, b. 26 Sept. 1639; Mary, 15 Oct. 1641; Rebecca, 1 Nov. 1643; and Nathaniel, 1650; rem. to Boston 1651, had Jonathan there, b. 20 Feb. 1652; and Sarah, 12 Oct. 1654. His w. Frances d. 17 Mar. 1658, and he m. 3 Nov. foll. wid. Hannah Morse, and rem. in few yrs. to Medfield. THOMAS, Groton, s. of the preced. m. Martha, d. of Richard Holden, had afterwards rem. to Woburn; but return. to G. and d. 15 Nov. 1719. But the rec. of Woburn has "by their mo.'s req. because of their rem. to and fro. in the Ind. war," Martha, 14 June 1667; Eliz. 24 May 1670; John, 29 Nov. 1672; Jonathan, 27 Sept. 1675; and Joseph, 24 Apr. 1678.

BOYEN, HENRY, Boston, m. 17 Oct. 1656, Frances, d. of Arthur Gill.

BOYES, BOYS, BOYCE, or BOIES, ANTIPAS, Boston 1659, merch. engag. in 1661 on great purch. of ld. at Dover, with Valentine Hill, whose d. Hannah he had m. 24 Jan. 1660, had Antipas, and d. July or Aug. 1669. His will, 3 July of that yr. was pro. 18 Aug. and after giv. est. to s. he says, if uncle Richard Rose wishes, he may bring him up and rec. the prop. The s. went, I think. to Eng. JOSEPH, Salem 1639, freem. 18 May 1642, had Esther, bapt. 21 Feb. 1641; Eliz. 6 Mar. 1642; Joseph, 31 Mar. 1644; and Benjamin, 16 May 1647. JOSEPH, Salem, prob. s. of the preced. m. 4 Feb. 1668, Sarah Meacham, perhaps d. of Jeremiah, had Sarah, b. 4 Dec. foll. * MATTHEW, Roxbury, freem. 22 May 1639, rem. to Rowley, was rep. 1641, 3, 5, and 50. He went home, as I find, by letters from Eng. Apr. 1657, he was then liv. near Leeds, in Yorksh. and still liv. in Feb. 1677, hav. tak. sec. w. in his old age, only two yrs. bef. He prob. had a fam. here, but after his ret. home, prob. his s. Joseph, a divine of some distinct. was b. at Leeds. See Geneal. Reg. XII. 65. RICHARD, New Hampsh. d. as early as 1677. SAMUEL, Saybrook, m. 3 Feb. 1668, Lydia, d. of Wil-

liam Beamond, went to liv. at Barbados, there had Joseph, wh. he brot.
to S. where he d. 22 Mar. 1683 ; at S. had Samuel, b. 6 Dec. 1673 ; and
Michael, 26 May 1683, wh. d. in less than a mo. and f. d. 4 Oct. of same
yr. aged 49. His wid. m. 15 Apr. 1684, Alexander Pygan. Four of
this name had been gr. at Wms. Coll. 1834.

BOYKETT, or BOYKIM, JARVIS or GERVASE, New Haven, a carpenter,
came first to Charlestown with one serv. in 1635 or 6 from Charington,
in Kent. 3 Mass. Hist. Coll. VIII. 276. He rem. 1639 to New Haven,
there had Nathaniel, b. Sept. 1641, bapt. 11 Dec. 1642 ; Bethia, bapt.
30 Apr. 1643 ; and Sarah, 18 Jan. 1646 ; and d. Jan. 1662, leav. wid.
Isabel, wh. d. 1673, and in her will ment. ch. Nathaniel, Sarah, and d.
Dennison. Sarah m. 1675, Samuel Edwards of Northampton. NA-
THANIEL, New Haven, s. of the preced. subscr. to the col. laws 1 May
1660 his assent, and d. 1705.

BOYLE, ALEXANDER, Boston, one of the first of the Scot's Charit.
Soc. 1684.

BOYLSTON, THOMAS, Watertown, s. of Thomas, perhaps of London,
wh. was s. of Henry of Litchfield, came in the Defence from London,
1635, aged 20, by w. Sarah had Eliz. b. 21 Sept. 1640 ; Sarah, 30 Sept.
1642 ; and Thomas, 26 Jan. 1645 ; d. 1653 ; his wid. Sarah m. 12
May 1655, John Chenery, and d. 14 Sept. 1704. Eliz. m. Apr. 1658,
John Fisher of Medfield ; and Sarah m. Thomas Smith. His f. was a
clothworker of London, as descr. in the deed of ho. and ground to his
agent, Sept. 1639 from Gregory Stone. Often the name is giv. Boyson.
THOMAS, Boston, perhaps s. of the preced. a farmer, liv. at Muddy riv.
whereby the best access to publ. worship for him and his fam. was Roxbury, m. 13 Dec. 1665, Mary, d. of Thomas Gardner, had Edward ;
and bapt. at R. Richard, 29 Jan. 1671 ; Abigail, 1674 ; Zabdiel, 9 Mar.
1679 ; Lucy, prob. 1682 ; Rebecca, b. 15, bapt. 20 Sept. 1685 ; Dudley, 19
Aug. 1688 ; besides Peter ; Sarah ; Mary ; Joanna ; and Thomas, first
town clk. of Brookline, wh. may have been bapt. elsewh. He serv. perhaps as surgeon, in Philip's war, and d. 1695 ; his wid. was Mary. A
monstrous tradit. in Thacher's Med. Biog. of Zabdiel, that his f. after
receiv. a degr. of M. D. at Oxford, came over and sett. at Brookline in
1635, shows how worthless are such foundations, even if support. by a
descend. This Zabdiel, the successful introducer of inocul. for smallpox
on our side of the ocean, was made F. R. S. and d. 1 Mar. 1766. His
s. Thomas, a physician, of Boston, d. 13 May 1750, without ch. Richard, of Charlestown, s. of sec. Thomas, d. 25 Apr. 1752, and his wid.
Mary d. 16 Apr. 1764, aged 86.

BOYNTON, or BOYINGTON, CALEB, Newbury, s. of William of Rowley,
m. 24 June 1672, Mary Moore, had William, b. 24 July 1673, liv. at

Rowley, freem. 1684. JOHN, Rowley 1643, m. Helen Pell of Boston, and d. 1670. JOHN, Northampton, freem. 1684. * JOSEPH, Rowley 1678, perhaps s. of John, rep. 1693, and sev. yrs. more; town clk. 1679; as was one of same name perhaps his s. in 1697, wh. had m. Sarah, d. of Richard Swan, a. 1678, and d. 16 Dec. 1730. JOSHUA, Newbury, br. prob. of Caleb, m. 9 Apr. 1678, Hannah Barnet, had William, b. 26 May 1690. Coffin, wh. gives ano. JOSHUA, also m. Apr. 1678, Sarah Browne, had Joshua, b. 4 May 1679, wh. liv. 91 yrs. 5 mos. 14 days; and John, 15 July 1683. SAMUEL, Rowley 1691, paid good tax that yr. but wh. was his f. is unkn. THOMAS, Salem, wh. in the rec. is writ. Bouenton, m. 30 Dec. 1671, Sarah Southwick, had Thomas, b. 1 Mar. 1672; Benjamin, 24 July 1675; and Abigail, 25 July 1695. Felt. WILLIAM, Rowley, freem. 13 May 1640, said to have been b. 1605, had w. Eliz. and s. Caleb, and Joshua; bot. 1657 at Newbury a farm of John Clark; and his wid. d. at Salisbury, a. 1687. But ano. WILLIAM, or the same, perhaps, by w. Mary had Mary, and liv. at Salisbury, where Mary, his d. m. 5 Nov. 1670, John Eastman. Three of this name had been, 1834, gr. of N. E. coll.

BRABROOK, or BRAYBROOK, JOHN, Watertown, by w. Eliz. had Eliz. b. 4 Nov. 1640; John, 12 Apr. 1642; and Thomas, 4 May 1643; first was at Hampton 1640, rem. to Newbury, where liv. his uncle, Henry Short, and d. 28 June 1662. Coffin has, perhaps, here made some confus. for I find the inv. of B. tak. Dec. 1654. Ann B. wh. d. at Roxbury 20 May 1648, may have been his mo. JOSEPH, perhaps of Malden, m. Sarah, d. of John Lewis, and may have liv. at Concord 1672. RICHARD, Ipswich, was b. it is said, in 1613. By w. Joanna wh. was his wid. liv. 1681, had Mehitable, wh. m. 2 Nov. 1669, John Downing. THOMAS, Concord, s. of John, m. 1669, Abigail Temple, and d. 1692. WILLIAM, Lynn, rem. says Lewis, 1637, to Sandwich.

BRACY, or BRACIE, JOHN, Wethersfield, came a. 1647, from New Haven (where first he, with prefix of respect, sat down in 1644, and had Susanna, and John, both bapt. 5 Sept. 1647), with his mo. Phebe Martin, whose f. William Bisby of London had bot. an est. at W. for her, and her ch. by former h.; d. 1709, aged 70. Other ch. of Bracey, by same Phebe, were Thomas, prob. a Stephen, Constant, wh. m. John Morray, and Phebe, wh. m. Joseph Dickinson. STEPHEN, Swanzey 1669, [Baylies, II. 241.] rem. to Hartford, d. 1692, leav. Stephen, John, Henry, beside ds. Elishaba, Phebe, Eliz. and Ann. He drop. the final y, yet perhaps did not change the sound, as of two syl. Descend. in Conn. have been disting. THOMAS, Ipswich 1635, may have been, Felt thinks, possib. the Mr. Bracy of Branford in Mather's first classis, in the carelessness of the Magn. III. 214, call Brucy, and not favor. with a Christian name. THOMAS, Wethersfield, br. of John, bef. 1678 rem. to Hatfield, d. there 1704.

BRACKENBURY, JOHN, Charlestown and Boston, m. 17 July 1655, Amie or Emma, d. of John Anderson, had JOHN, b. 9 Aug. 1657, wh. liv. at Charlestown, where his w. Dorcas d. 30 June 1682, aged 25. He had enlist. 1676 in the comp. of the brave capt. Turner, but was disch. bef. march. far. His wid. m. Joseph Lynde, and d. 1 Sept. 1703. RICHARD, Salem, came in the Abigail with Gov. Endicott, arr. 6 Sept. 1628, freem. 14 May 1634, had w. Ellen; a d. Hannah, bapt. 1 June 1651; one of the found. of ch. at Beverly, d. 1685, aged 83, leav. s. Miles. SAMUEL, Rowley, prob. s. of William, a physician, wh. preach. two yrs. but was not ord. yet rem. to Boston, and d. of small-pox, says Hull's Diary, 11, or by ano. rec. 16 Jan. 1678. SAMUEL, Boston 1677, had Samuel, bapt. 12 May 1700, was a physician, d. at Malden 26 Nov. 1702; but one Samuel, wh. may have been the preced. or not, by w. Mercy, in Boston, had Mary, b. 12 Mar. 1674; and the Malden rec. makes Samuel to have Samuel, there, Feb. 1673. WIL-LIAM, Charlestown, a baker, came in the fleet with Winth. it is thot. with w. Ann, req. to be freem. 19 Oct. 1630, but not appearing to support his claim in May foll. was postpon. by the rule after adopt. join. the ch. late in 1632, freem. 4 Mar. 1633, had Mary, bapt. 29 June 1634; was a selectman four yrs. d. at Malden, where he was of the chief inhab. Aug. 1668, aged 66, leav. by will of 24 July preced. est. to w. Alice, s. Samuel, H. C. 1664, ds. Ann, w. of William Foster, and Mary, w. of John Ridgway. Frothingham, 79. His wid. d. 28 Dec. 1670, as the gr.stone says; but other auth. makes it 24 Jan. after.

BRACKETT, ANTHONY, Portsmouth 1640, rem. to Exeter, there liv. 1657, but perhaps after at Casco. ANTHONY, Falmouth 1662, perhaps s. of the preced. m. Ann, d. of Michael Mitton, had Anthony; Seth, wh. was k. by the Ind. May 1690; Mary, wh. was liv. 1717, unm.; Elinor, wh. m. Richard Pulling of Boston; and Kezia, wh. m. Joseph Maylem; by 2d w. Susanna, d. of Abraham Drake of Hampton, wh. he m. Sept. 1679, had Zechariah and others. He was tak. by the Ind. with his w. and all his fam. exc. her br. Nathaniel Mitton, wh. was k. at the ho. 11 Aug. 1676; but by admirab. peril esc. some days after; was lieut. and capt. in the war, and finally was k. at his ho. 21 Sept. 1689. His s. Anthony was a serviceab. man, as lieut. and capt. in Ind. hostilit. For abund. informat. see Willis. JAMES, Boston, a cooper, s. of Rich-ard, freem. 1673, rem. to Braintree 1675, by w. Sarah had Joseph, Nathan, and sev. ds. d. 8 Apr. 1718, aged 72. JAMES, Beverly, freem. 1675. JOHN, Boston, s. prob. of Peter, merch. freem. 1666, m. 23 Aug. 1662, Sarah, d. of John Stedman of Cambridge, had Sarah, bapt. at C.

5 June 1664, d. 19 Sept. 1665; and John, bapt. at C. 21 Apr. 1667. He d. that yr. See Newell's Ch. Gath. 55. His wid. m. 24 Mar. 1668, Samuel Alcock. Her third h. was Thomas Graves; and fourth, John Phillips. JOHN, Billerica, s. of Richard, m. Hannah, d. of William French, and had ten ch. His w. d. 9 May 1674, and he m. 3 Mar. 1675, Ruth Ellis, and had four ch. and d. 18 Mar. 1686. JOSIAH, Billerica, br. of the preced. m. 4 Feb. 1673, Eliz. Waldo, prob. d. of Cornelius of Chelmsford, had one d. b. 1674, rem. to Braintree, and had ano. d. 1678. * ‖ PETER, Braintree, freem. 10 May 1643, ar. co. 1648, rep. 1644, and often after, for his own town, and for Scarborough in 1673 and 4, and he was deac. By first w. Priscilla, had Martha; Peter; John, b. 30 Nov. 1641; Joseph, 13 Oct. 1642; and prob. other ch. for the Boston gr. of ld. to him, 1640, was for twelve heads. Ano. ch. by the same w. was Hannah, b. 14 Aug. 1656, but she d. June foll. His last w. was Mary, wid. of Nathaniel Williams, wh. bec. one of the first of the third ch. mem. after d. of this h. In his latter days he liv. in Boston. In 1662 he purch. of the Ind. the tract on wh. Mendham was erect. Martha m. 23 Nov. 1655, Robert Twelves. PETER, Biller-ica, prob. s. of Richard, m. 7 Aug. 1661, Eliz. Bosworth, freem. 1680. His w. d. 30 Nov. 1686, and he m. 30 Mar. foll. wid. Sarah Foster of Cambridge. * ‖ RICHARD, Boston 1632, prob. br. of first Peter, freem. 25 May 1636, ar. co. 1639, dism. with w. Alice to Braintree ch. 5 Dec. 1641, deac. ord. 21 July 1642, town clk. many yrs. third capt. of the town, d. 5 Mar. 1691, aged 80 yrs. says the gr.stone. By his w. Alice, wh. d. 1690, aged 76, he had Hannah, bapt. 4 Jan. 1635; Peter, and John, perhaps tw. both bapt. 7 May 1637; Rachel, 3 Nov. 1639; Mary, b. 1 Feb. 1642; James; Josiah, 8 July 1652; and Sarah. Of the ds. Hannah m. Samuel Kingsley of Billerica; Rachel m. 15 July 1659, Simon Crosby; Mary m. 24 July 1662, Joseph Thompson; and Sarah m. 1675, Joseph Crosby of Braintree. THOMAS, Salem, punish. for attend. Quaker worship, 1658; had Thomas, bapt. 7 Dec. 1645, d. at 22 yrs.; Mary, 4 Feb. 1649; and Joseph, 15 June 1651, d. young, as also d. Lydia. THOMAS, Falmouth, br. of sec. Anthony, m. Mary, d. of Michael Mitton, and was k. by the Ind. 11 Aug. 1676, and his w. and ch. tak. into captiv. at the same time with his br. His w. d. in captiv. but three ch. surv. and liv. at Greenland. Willis. THOMAS, Wickford 1674. WILLIAM, Portsmouth 1624, one in the empl. of Mason, the patentee, spell. Bracken often. Adams, Ann. Six of this name had been, in 1834, gr. at Harv. Dart. and Wms. coll.

BRADBURY, * THOMAS, Salisbury, an orig. propr. but it is not kn. where he was sett. bef. going to that town, yet prob. at Ipswich, freem. 13 May 1640, rep. 1651 and six yrs. more, recorder for the Co. of Norfolk,

when New Hampsh. was part of Mass. was a capt. and d. 16 Mar. 1695.
His w. Mary, d. of John Perkins, after 56 yrs. of good cohabit. was
accus. of witchcraft in the dark hours of 1692, but her age was not
sufficient to condemn her; she was acq. and d. 20 Dec. 1700. The ch.
were Wymond, b. 1 Apr. 1637; Judith, 2 Oct. 1638; Thomas, 28 Jan.
1640; Mary, 17 Mar. 1642; Jane, 11 May 1645; Jacob, 17 June
1647, wh. d. at Barbados, 1669; William, 15 Sept. 1649; Eliz. 7 Nov.
1651; John, 20 Apr. 1654, wh. d. 24 Nov. 1678; Ann, 16 Apr. 1656,
d. young; and Jabez, 27 June 1658, wh. d. 28 Apr. 1677. Mary m. 17
Dec. 1663, John Stanian; Judith m. 9 Oct. 1665, Caleb Moody, as his
sec. w.; Jane m. 15 Mar. 1668, Henry True; and Eliz. m. 12 May
1673, John Buss. WILLIAM, Salisbury, s. of the preced. had Mary as
first w. and next, Rebecca, wid. of Samuel Maverick, d. of Rev. John
Wheelwright, m. 12 Jan. or more prob. Mar. 1672; d. 4 Dec. 1678,
and his w. d. 20 of the same mo. He left William, b. 16 Oct. 1672;
Thomas, 24 Dec. 1674; and Jacob, 1 Sept. 1677; the last two rememb.
in the will of their gr.f. Rev. John Wheelwright of S. WYMOND, Salisbury, eldest s. of Thomas, m. 7 May 1661, Sarah, d. of Robert Pike,
had Sarah, b. 26 Feb. 1662; Ann, 21 Nov. 1666; and Wymond, 13
May 1669; d. that yr. at Nevis; and his wid. m. 10 May 1671, John
Stockman of S.

BRADBUTH, ROBERT, Beverly, freem. 1678, is all that can be learn.
of a name that my reverence for records is not high eno. to compel the
accept. of, tho. I can hardly be so bold as to inq. if it may not mean
Bradbury.

BRADDOCK, ROBERT, New Hampsh. d. 1677. Kelly.

BRADE, JOSEPH, Marblehead 1668.

BRADFIELD, LESBY, Wethersfield 1643, or earlier, rem. to Branford.
His wid. m. 5 Sept. 1657, George Adams.

BRADFORD, ALEXANDER, Dorchester 1638, in his will, of wh. abstr.
is in Geneal. Reg. III. 81, made 17 Aug. 1644, pro. 2 Oct. 1645, names
w. Sarah, br. Walter Merry, but no ch. * JOHN, Plymouth 1643, Duxbury 1645, eldest s. of Gov. William, wh. did not come over the seas till
some yrs. after his f. rem. 1653 to Marshfield, was rep. of ea. town;
thence a. 1660 to Norwich, there d. 1678, without ch. His wid. Martha
d. of Thomas Bourne of Marshfield, m. bef. 20 Feb. 1680, lieut. Thomas
Tracy, and d. a. 1689. Caulkins, Hist. of Norwich, 100. JOSEPH,
Plymouth, youngest br. of the preced. m. 25 May 1664, Jael, d. of Rev.
Peter Hobart of Hingham, had Joseph, b. 18 Apr. 1665; and Elisha;
d. 10 July 1715; and his wid. d. 1730, aged 88. His s. Elisha nam.
one of his 13 ch. Carpenter, in honor of the boy's gr. gr.mo. ‖ MOSES,
Salisbury 1669, perhaps s. of Robert, rem. to Boston, ar. co. 1677, d. 23

Mar. 1692 by drown. MOSES, Boston, by w. Eliz. had John, b. 18
Sept. 1693; Thomas, 24 Dec. 1697; Robert, 30 Aug. 1699; Eliz. 20
Sept. 1701; Joseph, 14 May 1705; and James, 22 Sept. 1707. ROB-
ERT, Boston 1640, tailor, freem. 1642, by w. Martha had Moses, bapt.
10 Mar. but town rec. says, b. 2 Aug. 1644; and Martha, 9, bapt. 16
Nov. 1645. His will, 16 Nov. 1677, names w. Margaret, wh. d. 12
Mar. 1697, aged 92, and the same docum. calls Martha w. of Peter
Maverick. §‡ WILLIAM, Plymouth, came in the Mayflower, 1620, with
w. Dorothy (m. at Leyden, 30 Nov. 1613), surnam. May, wh. fail. to
reach the ld. of promise, being drown. at the anchorage in Cape Cod, 7
Dec.; was b. or bapt. Thursday, 19 Mar. 1590, at Austerfield, a village
tak. its name, perhaps, from lying in the extreme South of Yorksh. His
f. William was bur. 15 July 1591, and this his youngest ch. hav. gain.
some instruct. in letters from the noble spirits of William Brewster, and
John Robinson, left his native country, at the age of 18, to seek freedom
of worship in Holland. There he m. the first w. presum. to have been
a May, prob. a fugitive from Eng. for religion's sake, with her parents;
had John, above ment. He was chos. Gov. after d. of Carver, early in
1621, aged only 31, and until his d. 9 May 1657, the date of his nuncup. will, was by ann. elect. every yr. cont. exc. three, when Edward
Winslow, and two, when Thomas Prence partook the burden. On 14
Aug. 1623, he m. a lady with wh. he had been acquaint. many yrs. bef.
Alice, wid. of Edward Southworth, wh. came in the Ann a few days bef.
from Eng. whose maiden name was Carpenter, as has been infer. from
the phrase in Plymouth ch. rec. under 1667, mention of the d. of Mary
Carpenter, wh. d. 19 Mar. of that yr. in her 91st yr. of course b. 1577.
But she was so much older than this sec. w. of the Gov. that possib. she
may have been d. of one, wh. after m. a Reyner, and had Alice. For
tradit. at Plymouth made Alice, this w. of Bradford, to be sis. of Rev.
John Reyner. See Davis in Morton's Mem. 217, in notis, and Young's
Chron. of Pilgr. 353, in notis. Reyner was a name of distinct. in the
neighb. of Bradford's youth, and Carpenter was not. She surv. till 26
Mar. 1670, aged 79, and had William, b. 17 June 1624; Mercy, wh. m.
15 June or 21 Dec. 1648 (such is the diversity of rec. tho. the later date
is more prob.) Benjamin Vermayes; and Joseph, above ment. 1630.
Winsor mistakes in mak. this youngest ch. tw. with Mercy, for she is
nam. at the div. of cattle, 1627. Mather, Magn. II. c. 1; Shurtleff's Recol.
of the Pilgr. in Russell's Guide to Plymouth; Davis's Morton's Memo.;
Belkn. Amer. Biog.; Hutchinson's Hist. of Mass.; Young's Chron. of
the Pilgr.; and the last acquisit. to our minute details in Hunter's Founders of New Plymouth, London 1854; beside the noble confessor's own
Hist. Boston 1856, as Vol. III. in 4 Mass. Hist. Coll. † ‡ * WILLIAM,

Plymouth, s. of the preced. rep. 1657, assist. 1658, was wound. in the gr. Narraganset fight, 19 Dec. 1675, and carr. the ball in his body to the end of life; was dep.-gov. of the Col. from 1682 till arr. of new chart. exc. when one of Sir E. Andros's counc. 1687 and 8; d. 20 Feb. 1704; by first w. Alice, d. of Thomas Richards of Weymouth, wh. d. 12 Dec. 1671, had John, b. 20 Feb. 1653, wh. m. 5 Feb. 1674, Mercy, d. of Joseph Warren, and d. 8 Dec. 1736, his w. outliv. him 12 yrs.; William, 11, bapt. 25 Mar. 1655, wh. m. 1679, Rebecca, d. of Benjamin Bartlett, and d. 1687; Thomas, wh. was of Norwich, had part of est. of his uncle John, with wh. he had liv. perhaps m. Hannah, d. of Rev. James Fitch, and d. 1708; Alice, wh. m. first, 27 Mar. 1680, Rev. William Adams of Dedham, as his sec. w. and next, was sec. w. of Hon. James Fitch of Norwich; Hannah m. 28 Nov. 1682, Joshua Ripley of Hingham, wh. rem. to Windham, Conn. after hav. two ch.; Mercy, bapt. 2 Sept. 1660 at Boston ch. wh. m. 16 Sept. 1680, Samuel Steele of Hartford; Meletiah, wh. m. John Steele of Norwich; Samuel, b. 1668, m. Hannah Rogers, and d. 1714; Mary m. William Hunt; and Sarah m. Kenelm Baker. By sec. w. wid. Wiswall, he had only Joseph, wh. d. 17 Jan. 1747, at New London. By third w. Mary, wid. of Rev. John Holmes of Duxbury, d. of John Wood, or Atwood, of Plymouth, he had Israel, wh. m. Sarah, d. of Benjamin Bartlett, jr.; Ephraim, m. 13 Feb. 1710, Eliz. Bartlett; David, wh. m. 1714, Eliz. Finney, and d. 1730; and Hezekiah, wh. m. Mary Chandler; the last four liv. at Kingston. Shurtleff, ut sup. His s. Samuel, beside four ds. had three s. Gershom of Kingston; Perez, H. C. 1713, a counsel. of Mass.; and Gamaliel, also a counsel. whose s. Gamaliel, a col. in the army of the Revo. d. 1806, f. of the late Alden, H. C. 1786, Secr. of Mass. wh. d. 1843. Alden, Coll. of Epit. III. 246, 7. Fourteen of this name had been, in 1834, gr. at Harv. and seventeen at other coll. of N. E.

BRADHURST, RALPH, Roxbury, m. 13 June 1677, Hannah, d. of John Gore, had Rhoda, b. 17 May 1678; Dorothy, 1 Mar. 1680; Hannah, 14 Dec. 1682; and Abigail, 4 July 1685. His w. d. 10 July 1686, and he had sec. w. Martha, wh. d. 6 Aug. 1693. A third w. Hannah, d. 16 Apr. 1710; but no more of him appears in the rec. of Roxbury. Rhoda m. 13 Mar. 1704, John Colburn.

BRADING, JAMES, Newbury, rem. to Boston 1659, m. 11 Oct. of that yr. Hannah, d. of Joseph Rock, had Eliz.; James, b. 1662; and Joseph. His d. Eliz. was first w. of Edward Bromfield.

BRADISH, JAMES, Newtown, L. I. 1656–64. JOSEPH, Sudbury, eldest s. of Robert, by w. Mary had Mary, b. 10 Apr. 1665; Sarah, 6 May 1667; Hannah, 14 Jan. 1669; and Joseph, 28 Nov. 1672. ROBERT, Cambridge 1635, by w. Mary, wh. d. Sept. 1638, had Joseph, b. in May bef. By w. Vashti he had Samuel, b. 13 Feb. 1640, d. 6 July 1642 ; John, 3 Dec. 1645, wh. prob. d. at Boston 12 Oct. 1696; and Samuel, again, 28 Nov. 1648, d. next mo. The f. d. a. 1659, and in his will of 12 May 1657, we learn, that he had others by the first w. as it names Mary Gibbs, prob. w. of Matthew of Sudbury, James, and Hannah as his ch. speaks of s.-in-law Ezekiel Morrell, and br. Isaac M. See Geneal. Reg. IX. 225. I infer, that Joseph B. a pirate, sent to Eng. with the notorious capt. Kidd, 1699, from Boston, and execut. at London, was gr.s. of Robert, and prob. s. of Joseph. See let. of John Higginson in 3 Mass. Hist. Coll. VII. 210.

BRADLEY, or BRADLEE, ABRAHAM, New Haven, s. of William of the same, m. 25 Dec. 1673, Ann, d. of John Thompson, had John, b. 12 Oct. 1674; Hannah, 8 Nov. 1682; and perhaps others. BENJAMIN, New Haven, br. of the preced. m. 29 Oct. 1677, Eliz. d. of John Thompson, had Eliz. b. 11 Sept. 1678 ; Sarah, 7 June 1680; Hannah, 18 Apr. 1682 ; Susanna, 10 July 1684 ; and prob. others. DANIEL, New Haven, sw. fidel. 1657, had w. but no ch. d. Dec. 1658, and his est. went, after the wid.'s portion, to Joshua, Nathan, Stephen, and William Bradlee, and the w. of John Alling, wh. was Ellen Bradlee. William was call. br. and such prob. was the relat. of the other heirs. DANIEL, Haverhill, came in the Elizabeth from London, 1635, aged 20, k. by the Ind. 13 Aug. 1689. He m. 21 May 1662, prob. Mary, d. of John Williams of the same, had sev. ch. but we kn. not their names, births, or full partic. about his fam. DANIEL, Haverhill, prob. s. of Daniel of the same, with w. Hannah, and ch. Mary and Hannah were k. by the Ind. 15 Mar. 1697. FRANCIS, Fairfield, the freem. of 1664, was of Branford 1660, and rem. to F. m. Ruth, d. of John Barlow of the same, had ch. kn. only by his will of 4 Jan. 1689, to be John, Francis, Daniel, Joseph, Ruth, w. of Thomas Williams, and Abigail, unm. His w. was liv. when he d. late in that yr. ISAAC, Branford 1667, rem. to New Haven 1683, where his name was long cont. by a mult. of descend. He had Isaac ; William ; Samuel ; Daniel, b. 20 Dec. 1696; Sarah; and Eliz. JOHN, Salem, d. June 1642, at Dorchester, by nuncup. will, pro. 29 of next mo. ment. only w. and br.-in-law William Allen. JOHN, Dedham, by w. Catharine had Salathiel, b. 16 Mar. 1642, d. at six wks. JOHN, Dover 1667. JOSEPH, Haverhill, had a garrison at his ho. wh. was surpris. 8 Feb. 1704, when his w. for the sec. time was tak. by the Ind. and carr. away, her inf. ch. b. after her capt. dying of want. Abraham, his s. liv. to 1754, at Concord, N. H. His ch. Joseph, Martha, and Sarah had been k. 11 Mar. 1697 by the Ind. JOSEPH, New Haven, eldest s. of William of the same, m. 25 Oct. 1667, Silence, d. of John Brocket, had a d. b. and d. 1669; Abigail, 9 Sept. 1671 ; Mary, 6 Dec. 1674; Joseph,

15 Feb. 1678; Samuel, 3 Jan. 1681; Martha, Aug. 1683; and he d. in Jan. 1705, leav. w. and five ch. ment. in his will of 4 Dec. preced. JOSHUA, New Haven, br. of Daniel of the same, had only Joshua, b. 31 Dec. 1665, perhaps rem. JOSHUA, Rowley 1663. NATHAN, Guilford, by w. Esther had Ann, b. 16 Nov. 1669; Mary, and Abigail, tw. 13 Mar. 1672; Esther, 2 Nov. 1674, d. young; Esther, again, 14 Apr. 1677; Daniel, 9 June 1680, d. young; Nathan Noah as the rec. has, perhaps by mistake, giv. the name of the ch. 18 Sept. 1685; and Patience, 6 Apr. 1688. He next m. 1694, Hannah, wid. of Joseph Tuttle, d. of Thomas Munson, wh. d. next yr. and he m. 16 May 1698, Rachel, wid. of Thomas Strong; and he d. 1710. NATHANIEL, Dorchester, d. 26 July 1701, aged 70. PETER, New London 1654, mariner, by w. Eliz. wh. is believ. to have been d. of Jonathan Brewster, had Eliz. b. 1655; Peter, 1658; and Lucretia; and he d. 1662. His wid. m. Christopher Christophers; and d. Lucretia m. his s. Richard. Eliz. the d. m. 22 Sept. 1670, Thomas Dimond. PETER, New London, s. of the preced. m. 9 May 1678, Mary, d. of Christopher Christophers, had Christopher, b. 11 July 1679, wh. went to Southold, L. I. and the f. d. Aug. 1687. RICHARD, Boston, by w. Ann had Ann, b. 16 Dec. 1651; Deliverance, 3 Apr. 1655, and John, wh. d. at Liverpool, May 1676, leav. wid. Mary. STEPHEN, Guilford, at New Haven sw. fidel. 1660, m. 9 Nov. 1663, Hannah, d. of George Smith of New Haven, and had Hannah, b. 1 Sept. 1664; Sarah, 14 Feb. 1667, d. young; Stephen, 1 Oct. 1668; Daniel, 21 Oct. 1670; Eliz. 31 Dec. 1671; Abraham, 13 May 1674; and Sarah, again, 17 Oct. 1676. He m. Mary, wid. of the sec. William Leete; and d. 20 June 1702. WILLIAM, New Haven, m. 18 Feb. 1645, Alice Prichard, perhaps d. of Roger of Springfield, had Joseph, bapt. 4 Jan. 1646; Martha, Oct. 1648; Abraham, b. 24 Oct. 1650; Mary, 30 Apr. bapt. 1 May 1653; Benjamin, 8, bapt. 12 Apr. 1657; Esther, 29 Sept. bapt. 25 Nov. 1659; Nathaniel, b. 26 Feb. 1661; and Sarah, 21, bapt. 25 June 1665. He d. 1691, made his will 22 June 1683, in wh. he ment. all the s. d. Munson, w. of Samuel; Mary, w. of Samuel Todd; and d. Brackett; but whether this last was Esther or Sarah is uncert. WILLIAM, Dorchester 1664, of wh. no more is heard by me, than that he sign. the petn. that yr. WILLIAM, New Haven, s. of Isaac, m. 7 Jan. 1713, Eliz. Chedsey, had Caleb, b. 17 Oct. 1714; Ebenezer, 25 Mar. 1716; Joseph, 13 July 1718; Eliz.; Desire; and James, 15 June 1726. Twenty-two of this name had been gr. at the N. E. coll. in 1834.

BRADSHAW, ‖ HUMPHREY, Cambridge, ar. co. 1642, by w. Patience had Sarah, b. 3 May 1653; John, 24 June 1655; and Ruth, 3 Nov. 1657. He took sec. w. 24 Mar. 1665, Martha, wid. of William Russell, wh. after his d. had third h. 24 May 1683, Thomas Hall, and she d.

1694. JOHN, Medford, s. of the preced. by w. Mary had Mary, b. 8 May 1687; Sarah, 8 Sept. 1690, d. soon; Ruth, 29 Nov. 1692; John, 11 Feb. 1695; Jonathan, 18 Dec. 1696; Sarah, again, 19 Mar. 1699; Samuel, 29 Aug. 1700; Susanna, 23 Dec. 1702; Abigail, 1704; Hannah, 31 Jan. 1706; Stephen, 16 Sept. 1707; and Simon, 3 Oct. 1709; and d. 19 Mar. 1745. His wid. d. 18 Apr. 1758, aged 90.

BRADSTREET, ‡ * DUDLEY, Andover, third s. of Gov. Simon, freem. 1674, rep. 1677, 90 and 1, col. of the militia, nam. by James II. of the counc. to Gov. Joseph Dudley, yet patriot, and of the counc. of safety 1689, m. 12 Nov. 1673, Ann, wid. of Theodore Price, d. of . . . . . . Wood, had Margaret, b. 19 Feb. 1674; Dudley, 27 Apr. 1678, H. C. 1698, wh. m. 4 May 1704, Mary Wainwright, min. of Groton, ord. 17 Nov. 1706, dism. 1712, d. in Eng. 1714, of smallpox, after being ord. in Episc. form ; and Ann, 5 Nov. 1681, d. soon. In the ferocious prosecut. 1692, for witchcraft, he was so lenient, or judiciously incredul. of the crimes imput. to his neighb. as to be strongly suspect. of the same horrid or ludicrous offence. Abbot's Hist. 18, 19. * HUMPHREY, Ipswich, came in the Elizabeth from Ipswich, Eng. 1634, aged 40, with w. Bridget, 30 ; and ch. Hannah, 9; John, 3 ; Martha, 2 ; and Mary, 1 ; had b. here, Moses ; Sarah, 1638 ; and Rebecca; freem. 6 May 1635, rep. 1635, d. 1655. His will, made 21 July, was pro. 25 Sept. foll. Hannah m. Daniel Rolfe, and next, 12 June 1658, Nicholas Holt, and d. 20 June 1665; Martha m. William Beale ; and all the other ds. were m. one to Nicholas Wallis. HUMPHREY, Rowley, physician, s. of Moses, rem. to Newbury, there by w. Sarah had Dorothy, b. 19 Dec. 1692 ; Joshua, 24 Feb. 1695; Sarah, 14 Jan. 1697; Humphrey, 1700, d. young; Daniel, 13 Feb. 1702 ; Moses, 17 Feb. 1707; and Betty, 16 May 1713 ; and he d. 11 May 1717. His wid. m. 9 June 1719, Edward Sargent. JOHN, Rowley 1651, s. of Humphrey the first, brot. by his f. from Eng. was never m. it is thot. rem. 1657, to Marblehead, d. 1660. JOHN, Salem, youngest s. of Gov. Simon, m. 17 June 1679, as one report is, but by ano. 11 June 1677, Sarah, d. of Rev. William Perkins of Topsfield, had Simon, b. 14 Apr. 1682 ; John, 30 Jan. 1693 ; Margaret, 27 Nov. 1696; and Samuel, 4 Aug. 1699. Perhaps he had others, Mercy, and three other ds. for the removal from one town to ano. sometimes caus. omission in rec. of either. In 1681 he was of Salem, but prob. liv. most of his days at Topsfield, yet perhaps had some est. at Rowley, d. 11 Jan. 1719. MOSES, Ipswich, s. of the first Humphrey of the same, had four ch. of wh. we kn. with certainty only Humphrey, b. 6 Jan. 1670, bef. ment. * SAMUEL, Boston, eldest br. of the preced. freem. 1656, went to Eng. next yr. and spent four yrs. as his mo. tells, mak. verses on each event ; there prob. stud. for a profession ; was a physician, rep. for Andover

1670, m. 1662, Mercy, youngest d. of capt. William Tyng, wh. d. 6
Sept. 1670, had Eliz. b. 29 Jan. 1664, d. young; Ann, 17 Nov. 1665, d.
young; Mercy, 20 Nov. 1667; Simon, 15 Oct. 1669, d. soon; and Ann,
3 Sept. 1670; Mercy, m. Dr. James Oliver of Cambridge, d. a wid. 29
Mar. 1710. By sec. w. tak. in Jamaica, he had John, 1676; Simon,
again, a. 1680; and Ann, again; and d. prob. at Jamaica, in Aug. 1682.
§ † ‡ SIMON, Cambridge, Ipswich, Boston, was a few yrs. at Andover,
and spent his latest days at Salem, after Sept. 1695; b. in Mar. 1603,
at Horbling, in Lincolnsh. s. of Simon, a min. it is said, bred at Emanuel, Cambr. Univ. enter. there 1617, and matricul. 9 July 1618, as a
sizer, had his A. B. 1620, and A. M. 1624, came in the fleet with Winth.
1630, chos. an assist. 18 Mar. bef. and so cont. by ann. elect. 48 yrs.;
secr. 23 Aug. 1630 to 1636; dep.-gov. 1673–8; gov. 1679 to 1686, and
again after the rising against Sir E. Andros 1689-92; d. 27 Mar. 1697.
By his first w. Ann, d. of Gov. Thomas Dudley (a lady of some celebr.
for poetical talent, wh. d. 16 Sept. 1672, at Andover), m. as the fam.
hist. in Geneal. Reg. IX. 113, says, a. 1628, wh. to me seems a yr. or
two earlier than prob. tho. we kn. it was bef. the Apr. embark. in 1630,
had Samuel, H. C. 1653, bef. ment.; Dorothy, wh. m. 14 June 1654,
Rev. Seaborn Cotton; Sarah, wh. m. 1. Richard Hubbard of Ipswich,
and 2. capt. Samuel Ward; Simon, b. 28 Sept. 1640, H. C. 1660;
Hannah, wh. m. 3 June 1659, Andrew Wiggin of Exeter; Mercy, b.
1647, wh. m. 31 Oct. 1672, maj. Nathaniel Wade; Dudley, 1648, bef.
ment.; and John, 22 or 31 July 1652, bef. ment. His sec. w. Ann, wid.
of capt. Joseph Gardner, d. of Emanuel Downing, younger by more
than thirty yrs. wh. he m. 6 June 1676, d. 19 Apr. 1713, aged 79.
SIMON, New London, sec. s. of the preced. ord. 5 Oct. 1670, d. 1683;
m. 2 Oct. 1667, his first cous. Lucy, d. of Rev. John Woodbridge,
and she next m. capt. Daniel Epps. He had Simon, b. 2 Aug. 1669, d.
soon; Simon, again, 7, bapt. 12 Mar. 1671, H. C. 1693, min. of Charlestown, wh. was honor. in office, m. 7 May 1700, Mary Long, d. 31 Dec.
1741, leav. Simon, H. C. 1728, min. of Marblehead; Ann, b. 3 Dec.
1672, bapt. 5 Jan. foll.; John, 3, bapt. 5 Nov. 1676; and Lucy, 24,
bapt. 31 Oct. 1680. Ten of this name had been gr. in 1834, at Harv.
three others at Dart. and Yale.

BRAGDON, ARTHUR, York 1640, constable 1648, freem. 1652, was b.
as he test. a. 1597. In 1680, SAMUEL and THOMAS, prob. his s. liv.
there, and took o. of alleg. and 13 Oct. 1703, the w. and five ch. of
Arthur, prob. a gr.s. were k. by the Ind. Penhallow's Ind. Wars. Pike
says w. and two ch. were k. and the eldest d. carr. away. Niles gives
it Brandon.

BRAGG, EDMUND or EDWARD, Ipswich 1646, and there liv. in 1700.
Prob. his d. Mary m. 1 Jan. 1669, Joseph Eveleth, the centenarian.

BRAINARD, or BRAINERD, DANIEL, Hartford, rem. to Haddam, as early sett. there m. a. 1665, Hannah, d. of Jared Spencer, had Daniel, b. 1665 or 6; Hannah, 20 Nov. 1667; James, 1669; Joshua, 1671; William, 1673; Caleb, 1675; Hezekiah, 1682; and Elijah, 1686; was a deac. and d. 1 Apr. 1715, aged 74. Who was his f. or where he was b. is uncert. Hannah m. a. 1692, Thomas Gates. DANIEL, East Haddam, s. of the preced. by w. Susanna had Susanna, b. 9 Aug. 1689; Daniel, 28 Sept. 1690; Hannah, 12 June 1694; Noadiah, 4 Apr. 1697; Stephen, 27 Feb. 1699; Bezaleel, 17 Apr. 1701; Mary, 10 Sept. 1703; was deac. and d. 28 Jan. 1743. ‡ HEZEKIAH, Haddam, br. of the preced. m. 1 Oct. 1707, Dorothy, wid. of Daniel Mason of Lebanon, d. of Rev. Jeremiah Hobart, had nine ch. of wh. David, b. 20 Apr. 1718, the disting. missionary to the Ind. was one; an Assist. of the Col. d. at Hartford, 24 May 1727, aged, by his gr.stone, 45. The name appears Brainwood sometimes.

BRAITON. See Brayton.

BRAMAN, or BRAYMAN, JOSEPH, Rehoboth, had Experience, b. 10 Nov. 1682. THOMAS, Marlborough, freem. 1685.

BRAME, BRAM, or BREAM, BENJAMIN, Boston 1668, a cooper, had w. Ann, and s. Benjamin, wh. were jointly made Admors. 6 Oct. 1693, of his est. BENJAMIN, Boston, s. of the preced. by w. Eliz. had Ann, b. 23 July 1694, bapt. 28 July 1695; Eliz. 11 Apr. 1697; Sarah, 27 Aug. 1699; and Benjamin, 26 Jan. 1701.

BRAMHALL, GEORGE, Dover 1670, Casco 1678, k. by the Ind. 1689, left wid. Martha, ch. Joseph, George, Hannah, and Joshua, wh. all rem. to Plymouth. George was at Hingham 1733; Hannah m. Jonathan Hall of Harwich; and Joshua ret. to Falmouth 1729, there liv. some yrs. but went again to Plymouth. Willis. JOSEPH, a wine-cooper, long resid. at Falmouth, d. 1716, at Boston, leav. wid. Grace without ch. He was s. of George the first; and his will is of 22 Dec. 1715.

BRANCH, ARTHUR, Saybrook 1636, rem. soon after 1649. 3 Mass. Hist. Coll. III. 143. EXPERIENCE, Marshfield, perhaps s. of John of the same, had w. Lydia, wh. d. 5 Nov. 1697, and he d. nine days after. JOHN, Scituate, s. of Peter, b. in Eng. m. at Marshfield, 6 Dec. 1652, Mary Speed, had John, wh. was k. at Rehoboth fight, under capt. Michael Pierce, 26 Mar. 1676; Eliz. b. 1656; Peter, 1659; Thomas, wh. d. at Boston 1683; and Mercy, 1664; and d. 17 Aug. 1711. PETER, wh. would have been of Concord or Scituate, a carpenter, from Holden, near Tenterden in Kent, d. on board the sh. Castle, very soon after arr. as by his will, abstr. in Geneal. Reg. II. 183, is prov. It has no date of time or place, names s. John, wh. he binds to Thomas Wyborne for eleven yrs. from 16 June 1638, perhaps the day of mak. the will.

WILLIAM, Springfield 1644, freem. 1648, m. 11 Jan. 1644, Joan Farnum, wh. d. 12 Oct. 1675 ; had sec. w. Catharine, wid. of Arthur Williams, as bef. she was of Joshua Carter, m. 12 Feb. 1677, wh. d. 8 Aug. 1683, as did he on 16 Sept. foll. No ch. by either w. is kn.

BRAND, BENJAMIN, s. of John B. Esqr. of Edwardstone, next parish to Groton, and so near neighb. in his nat. ld. to Winth. with wh. he came in the Arbella, 1630, req. adm. as freem. 19 Oct. at first gen. court, but went home, perhaps with Wilson, Gov. Coddington, and Sir R. Saltonstall, Apr. foll. certain. was not made freem. He had two s. and two ds. in later life in Eng. Winth. I. 370. GEORGE, Roxbury, baker, m. 24 July 1643, Martha, d. of William Heath, had prob. no ch. freem. 1650, prob. d. away from home, but his wid. Martha d. at R. 1 Aug. 1686. THADDEUS, Lynn, by w. Sarah, wh. d. 13 Dec. 1675, had Mary, b. 12 Feb. 1671, d. 19 Oct. 1675 ; Eliz. 16 Aug. 1673, d. 26 Oct. 1675 ; and Mary, again, 27 Nov. 1675. THOMAS, Salem, cooper, came in the fleet with Higginson 1629. WILLIAM, a Quaker, came in the Speedwell, 1656, aged 40, from London. Hutch. I. 169, calls him Brend, but it is of no conseq. for he was sent away in the same ship.

BRANDISLY, JOHN, Watertown at first, perhaps, freem. 4 Mar. 1635, rem. early to Wethersfield, d. 1639, leav. wid. Rachel, wh. m. Anthony Wilson of Fairfield, one s. and four ds.

BRANDON, WILLIAM, Weymouth, had w. Mary, and ch. Thomas, Sarah, Mary, and Hannah, all minors, when he made his will 31 Aug. 1646 ; and he d. shortly after.

BRANE, THOMAS, a husbandman, aged 40, came in the Abigail to Boston, 1635.

BRANKER, JOHN, Dorchester, freem. 6 Nov. 1632, a sch.master, rem. after 1635 to Windsor, d. 1662. His wid. Abigail, wh. had brot. him no ch. m. Rev. John Warham a. Oct. in that yr. and outliv. him until 18 May 1684.

BRANSON, GEORGE, Dover 1648, rem. to York, freem. 1652, k. at the age of 47, by a bull, 25 July 1657. Coffin.

BRASIER, HENRY, New Haven 1639.

BRATCHER, AUSTIN, Charlestown, at Cradock's planta. d. 1630, by hand of Walter Palmer, and a jury was charg. to inq. of it, on whose inq. P. was disch.

BRATELER, or BRATELY, JOHN, Salem 1638. Felt. PETER, Salem 1686, mariner. Felt.

BRATTLE, EDWARD, Boston, s. of Thomas, by w. Mary had Thomas, b. 20 Sept. 1696. He was liv. in the early part of 1713, when his br. Thomas made his will. * ‖ THOMAS, Charlestown 1656, rem. next yr. to Boston, m. Eliz. d. of capt. William Tyng, had Thomas, wh. d. 5

Sept. 1657, a few hours old; Thomas, again, b. 20 June 1658, H. C. 1676; Eliz. 30 Nov. 1660; William, 22 Nov. 1662, H. C. 1680; Catharine, 26 Sept. 1664; Bethia, 13 Dec. 1666; Mary, 10 Aug. 1668; and Edward, 18 Dec. 1670; ar. co. 1672, was a capt. one of the found. of the third or O. S. ch. rep. 1671 and 2 for Lancaster, and 1678 and 9 for Concord. His w. d. 9 Nov. 1682, in a surpris. sudden way, as told by Judge Sewall, wh. was present, in her own ho. at a great wedding of his cous. Daniel Quincey with Ann Shepard, her niece. See the val. hist. by Budington, of first ch. of Charlestown, 219. He d. 22 July foll. leav. est. by inv. £7827, 16, 10, prob. the largest in N. E. Of the ds. Eliz. m. 3 Jan. 1677, Nathaniel Oliver; Catharine m. 20 May 1680, John Eyre, next m. 13 Nov. 1707, Wait Winthrop, surv. him, and d. 2 Aug. 1725; Bethia m. a. 1684, or 5, Joseph Parsons, d. 4 July 1690; and Mary m. 20 Aug. 1689, John Mico, surv. him, and d. 22 Dec. 1733. Thomas, Boston, s. of the preced. one of the found. of Brattle str. ch. and twenty yrs. Treasr. of Harv. coll. in its days of severest trial, d. 18 May 1713. He was never m. I suppose. His letter, 1692, giv. acco. of the witchcraft infat. pr. in 1 Mass. Hist. Coll. V. 61, is the most judicious explana. of the processes of the judicial blindness, and must be read by whoever wishes to understand that malignant epidemic. See also, Quincy's Hist. of Harv. Coll. William, Boston 1677, one of the ch. merch. prob. br. of first Thomas. William, Cambridge, s. of first Thomas, ord. 25 Nov. 1696, a learned man, and most val. min. F. R. S. d. 15 Feb. 1717. He m. 3 Nov. 1697, Eliz. d. of Nathaniel Hayman of Charlestown, had only ch. William, H. C. 1722, the Brigadier, f. of Thomas, H. C. 1760. She d. 28 July 1715. Holmes, Hist. of Cam. Quincy, I. 414.

Brawne, George, Dover, perhaps s. of Michael, by w. Mary had Michael, b. 1 June 1679. Mihill, or Michael, Dover 1655, had Michael, b. 1643; perhaps others; was liv. 1675.

Bray, John, Kittery 1660, shipwright, kept an inn 1674, rem. in the war to Gloucester, perhaps, there m. 10 Nov. 1679, Margaret Lambert, as sec. w. had Margery, wh. m. a. 1680, William, f. of Sir William Pepperell. Osmond, Weymouth, d. Feb. 1649, as might be judg. from his inv. 23 of that mo. but I testify that this name is a blunder of a booby clk. for Clement Briggs. See Briggs. Richard, Dover 1657, Casco 1658, was, prob. at the fort in Boston, 1687, a gunner's mate. A Richard B. of Exeter, d. at Lynn, 1665. Robert, Salem 1668, by w. Thomasin had Daniel, b. 29 Nov. 1673, perhaps others, and was lost at sea, a. 1692. Thomas, New Haven, had Hannah, wh. m. 25 Aug. 1659, Thomas Paine of Boston. Thomas, Gloucester, shipwright, m. 3 May 1646, Mary Wilson, had Mary, b. 16 Jan. 1647; Thomas, 31

Mar. 1649, d. in Aug. 1653; ano. Thomas, 16 May 1653, d. soon; John, 14 May 1654; Nathaniel, 21 June 1656; Thomas, again, 19 Jan. or Feb. 1659; Hannah, 21 Mar. 1662; and Esther, 13 Apr. 1664. He d. 30 Nov. 1691, and his wid. d. 27 Mar. 1707. Hannah m. 4 Feb. 1678, John Roberts. WILLIAM, York 1680.

BRAYTON, FRANCIS, Portsmouth, R. I. 1643, when he was adm. to dwell, by w. Mary had Francis, Stephen, and four ds. Martha Pierce, the eldest, Eliz. Bouren, and Sarah, w. of Thomas Gatchell, as by his will of 17 Oct. 1690, pro. 5 Sept. 1692, we gain their names, and that of his wid. Mary; we learn, also, that he had d. Mary, wh. d. bef. 1671. In a depon. made 30 Jan. 1674, he is said to be 62 yrs. old. FRANCIS, Portsmouth, R. I. s. of the preced. adm. freem. of the town, 3 Dec. 1670, m. 18 Mar. 1671, or 2, Mary, d. of Thomas Fish of the same, had Mary, b. 1 Jan. 1676; Thomas, 14 June 1681; Francis, 17 Feb. 1684; David, 23 Oct. 1686; Mehitable, 12 Jan. 1693; and Benjamin, 8 Sept. 1695. STEPHEN, Portsmouth, R. I. younger br. of the preced. m. 8 Mar. 1679, Ann, d. of Peter Tolman of Newport, had Mary, b. 12 Feb. 1680; Eliz. 8 Dec. 1681; Ann, 6 July 1683; Preserved, 8 Mar. 1685; and Stephen, 2 Aug. 1686.

BRAZEEL, PHILIP, is the strange name, perhaps misspelt, of one in Gallop's comp. of Phips's exped. against Quebec. See Geneal. Reg. IX. 354.

BRAZIER, EDWARD, Charlestown 1658, had prob. Thomas, bapt. 29 Apr. 1660; Abigail, 18 Dec. 1664; Rebecca, 24 Nov. 1667; and he d. 3 May 1689.

BREAD, THOMAS, embark. in Eng. 22 June 1679, in the Providence, for Boston, but no more is kn.

BRECK, EDWARD, Dorchester 1636, freem. 22 May 1639, came, prob. from Ashton, in Co. Devon, was an officer of the town 1642, 5, 6, and after, d. 2, or 6, Nov. 1662, leav. Robert, wh. he brot. from Eng.; John; Mary, bapt. 6 Aug. 1648; Eliz. and Susanna. The w. d. 11 Nov. 1653. His wid. Isabel, wh. was his sec. w. and had been bef. wid. of John Rigby of D. m. 14 Nov. 1663, Anthony Fisher; Mary m. 9 Jan. 1667, Samuel Paul; Eliz. m. 11 Mar. 1670, John Minot; and Susanna m. 20 Mar. 1674, or 5, John Harris. But he must have had ano. d. for his will of 30 Oct. 1662, only 3 days bef. his d. ment. d. Elinor. JOHN, Medfield, wh. d. 3 Jan. 1660, is by Morse regard. as br. of Edward, and he thinks it prob. that he had John, wh. d. at Medfield 20 Aug. 1690. JOHN, Dorchester, s. of Edward, a tanner, had by w. Susanna, wh. d. 8 Feb. 1712, aged a. 64 yrs. Edward, John, Nathaniel, besides five ds. and was, also, f. of Rev. Robert, b. 7, bapt. 10 Dec. 1682, H. C. 1700, wh. preach. short season at Newtown, L. I. and after was min. of Marlborough, ord. 25 Oct. 1704, a man of learning, d. 6 Jan. 1732. The f. was a capt. and oft. a selectman, freem. 1690, d. 17 Feb. 1691, aged 40 yrs. says his gr.stone. ROBERT, Dorchester, elder br. of the preced. b. in Eng. freem. 1649, m. 4 Jan. 1654, Sarah, d. of capt. Thomas Hawkins, rem. to Boston, was a merch. adm. inhab. of the town 28 Nov. foll. had Mary, b. 19 Apr. 1655; and Robert, 24 June 1658. I think he had former w. Margery, and by her had Robert, wh. d. 11 July 1655. His wid. bec. 11 Sept. 1673, third w. of Rev. James Allen of Boston. THOMAS, Dorchester, m. 12 Feb. 1657, Mary, d. of John Hill, had Mary, b. 17 Dec. 1657; rem. to Medfield, had there Susanna, 10 Sept. 1663, but d. Aug. foll.; Susanna, again, 10 May 1667; John, 4 Mar. 1671; Bethia, 20 Dec. 1673; Nathaniel, and Samuel, tw. 1 Mar. 1682; if Morse's Geneal. Reg. be correct. Four of this name had been gr. at Harv. and six at other N. E. coll. in 1834.

BREDANE, BRYAN, Malden 1671, had Samuel, b. June of that yr.

BREDCAKE, meaning Cakebread, THOMAS, a capt. prob. of Salem, had leave, 12 Nov. 1644, to take two guns from the fort there, and the next day a commission from our Gen. Ct. for a yr. to take any Turk. pirate. Col. Rec. I. 79 and 83.

BREED, ALLEN, Lynn 1630, as Lewis says, m. 28 Mar. 1656, Eliz. Knight, prob. sec. w. had ch. perhaps all by first w. Allen, Timothy, Joseph, and John; freem. 1681, yet b. 1601, d. 17 Mar. 1692. He is one of the grantees in the deed from the Ind. of South Hampton, L. I. 1640, but either did not rem. or soon came back. ALLEN, Lynn, s. of the preced. prob. b. in Eng. had Joseph, b. 12 Feb. 1658; Allen, 30 Aug. 1660; John, 18 Jan. 1663; Mary, 24 Aug. 1665; Eliz. 1 Nov. 1667; Samuel, 25 Sept. 1669; and his w. Mary d. 30 Nov. 1671. He was freem. 1684. JOHN, Lynn, br. of the preced. m. 28 Dec. 1663, Sarah Hathorne, had Sarah, b. 28 Dec. 1667; William, 18 May 1671; Ephraim, 16 Dec. 1672; Ebenezer, 15 Apr. 1676; and his w. Sarah d. 22 Nov. foll. He m. 4 Mar. 1678, Sarah Hart, but, prob. had no more ch. and d. 28 June of the same yr. Descend. are very num. JOHN, Stonington, s. of Allen the sec. m. 8 June 1690, Mercy, d. of Gershom Palmer, had num. offspr. and d. 1751, if we believe the gr.stone, a. 90 yrs. old, wh. seems very prob. but the same witness testif. to the m. state in a most religious manner a. 64 yrs. wh. is vulgar exagger. of 3 yrs. His wid. d. the yr. foll. JOSEPH, Lynn, prob. s. of first Allen, had Mary, b. 4 July 1684; was freem. 1691. TIMOTHY, s. of first Allen, I suppose, m. 3 Mar. 1680, Sarah Newhall, d. prob. of John the first, had Joseph, b. 18 Apr. 1681; was freem. 1691. Sometimes the rec. has Bread, or Braid. Four of the name had been, in 1834, gr. at Yale.

BREEDEN, BRADING, BRADON, or BREDING, JAMES, Boston, m. 9 Oct. 1657, Hannah, d. of Joseph Ruck or Rock. THOMAS, Boston

1656, a merch. of large prop. went home and came again, perhaps more than once ; was made Gov. of his Prov. of Nova Scotia by deputat. from Col. Thomas Temple, in Oliver's day, and again, after the restor. when Temple was a baronet. He lent large sums to Sir Thomas, and had mortg. of his estates on this side of the water, 1667. 2 Mass. Hist. Coll. VIII. 105, and 3 M. H. Coll. VII. 120. Haz. II. 462. Hutch. Coll. 339.

BREME, JOHN, Casco 1661, a fisherman.

BRENTON, * EBENEZER, Swanzey, s. of Gov. William, by w. Priscilla had Ebenezer, b. 1687, H. C. 1707 ; Martha, 1689 ; William, 1694; Sarah, 1697 ; beside Ann, wh. m. Martin Howard, and Eliz. wh. m. Edward Perkins. His w. d. 1705 ; but he long surv. till a. 1766, if Potter be correct, was rep. 1693 ; and a major in latter days. JAHLEEL, br. of the preced. collect. of the customs at Newport for the whole col.; d. 8 Nov. 1732, without ch. RICHARD, Boston, had Barnabas, bapt. 24 Jan. 1635. § * WILLIAM, Boston 1633, came, perhaps, in the Griffin with Cotton, as he join. the ch. a few days after the teacher ; said to have been b. at Hammersmith ; freem. 14 May 1634, rep. 1635, selectman 1634-7 ; went to Rhode Isl. was there in high office, 1638, and presid. 1659-63, but had come back to Boston betw. 1650 and 8 ; every yr. was a selectman in 1652-7, contrib. more than any other inhab. exc. Henry Webb, to subscript. for erect. of town house, yet tho. at Portsmouth, R. I. part of 1655, at B. is rec. a s. b. 14 Nov. 1655; was Gov. of R. I. 1666, 7, and 8 ; liv. at Taunton 1670-2, and d. at Newport, 1674. On Merrimack riv. a large tract long call. Brenton's farm, now the town of Litchfield, in New Hampsh. was gr. to him in 1658; and the S. point of R. I. by him nam. Hammersmith (from his birthpl. near London), where gr. fortificat. are erect. for secur. of Newport harb. is usually kn. as Brenton's. At Boston by w. Martha, d. of Thomas Burton, as is in fam. tradit. report. had Mehitable, b. 28 Nov. 1652, m. Joseph Brown of Charlestown, and d. 14 Sept. 1676; Jahleel, 14 Nov. 1655, bef. ment. and b. at other towns, Eliz. wh. m. 28 Mar. 1672, John Pool of Boston ; William ; Ebenezer, bef. ment. ; Sarah, m. Rev. Joseph Eliot of Guilford; and Abigail, m. Stephen Burton of Bristol. To these seven may be add. John, if the slight tradit. that he was oldest s. be credit. but certain. Martha, w. of John Card, as Brenton by deed of 16 Dec. 1667 gave him portion of est. that would have gone to his w. then dec. and Mary, w. of Peleg Sanford, as to him, in deed of 22 Dec. 1665, B. gives her portion. An absurd tradit. about him in a recent Eng. Biog. of his descend. the late Sir Jahleel B. needs neither notice nor refut. of other errors. WILLIAM, Bristol, s. of the preced. one of the early sett. was a mariner, Collector of Boston 1691, and by w. Hannah, had William, his eldest ch. also Samuel, and Jahleel, b. 15 Aug. 1691, wh. last by two ws. had 22 ch. of wh. the eighth, Jahleel, b. 22 Oct. 1729, d. Jan. 1802, was a Rear admiral in the Br. navy, and f. of the late Sir Jahleel, b. at Newport, 22 Aug. 1770. Of all the descend. of first William, it is believ. those wh. were liv. at the Revo. adher. to the royal gov.

BRESSEY, ... New Haven, possib. the min. of wh. Mather, in Magn. III. 214, writ. the name Brecy, says he knows nothing, but that he went home. He had, in a former page, 2 of same Book, assign. him to Branford ; but we presume he was never ord. See Bracey.

BRETT, ELIHU, Bridgewater, s. of William, by w. Ann had Mary, Margaret, and Elihu ; d. 1712. NATHANIEL, Bridgewater, br. of the preced. m. 1683, Sarah, d. of John Hayward, had Alice, b. 1686 ; Seth, 1688 ; Mehitable, 1692 ; Sarah, 1695 ; Hannah, 1699 ; William, 1702 ; and Nathaniel, 1704 ; was a deac. d. 1740. * WILLIAM, Duxbury 1640, rem. to Bridgewater, of wh. he was one of the first proprs. 1645, and rep. 1661, by w. Magaret had William, Elihu, Nathaniel, Alice, Lydia, and Hannah ; was a rul. elder, and often preach. when the Rev. Mr. Keith was unable, d. 17 Dec. 1681, aged 63. A very large measure of elegiac verse was inflict. on him by the pastor. His d. Alice m. Joseph Hayward, and Hannah m. Franklin Cary. WILLIAM, s. of the preced. m. Eliz. d. of John Cary, had only ch. Bethia, was deac. and d. 1713. Mitchell.

BRETTON, PHILIP LE, Falmouth, left out the French particle from his name, rem. to Boston, d. 1737. He was, perhaps, from Rochelle, certain. a Huguenot, a rigger ; in his will, 6 Aug. 1736, takes notice of his adv. age, and ment. ch. Peter, Daniel, Mary, Eliz. Rachel, Sarah, Jane, and Ann, and of s.-in-law Edward Dumaresque. Willis, I. 186.

BREWER, CHRISTOPHER, Lynn, wh. may be the same as the foll. had Abigail, b. 4 Dec. 1664. CRISPUS, Lynn, freem. 1684, had Rebecca, b. 28 Oct. 1667. DANIEL, Roxbury, came in the Lion, with w. arr. at Boston 16 Sept. 1632, freem. 14 May 1634, d. early in 1646, names, in his will of 12 Jan. that yr. w. Joanna, wh. d. 7 Feb. 1689, aged 87 ; s. Daniel, prob. b. in Eng. ; Nathaniel, b. 1 May 1635; and ds. Ann, Joanna, and Sarah. This last b. 8 Mar. 1638, m. 19 Nov. 1656, John May. Ann d. 13 Mar. 1659. ‖ DANIEL, Roxbury, s. of the preced. prob. b. in Eng. ar. co. 1666, m. 5 Nov. 1652, Hannah, d. of Isaac Morrill, had one ch. b. 9 Mar. 1660, d. at b.; Hannah, 5 July 1665 ; Daniel, 7 Feb. 1669 ; d. 9 Jan. 1708, aged 84. His wid. Hannah d. 6 Oct. 1717. His s. DANIEL, H. C. 1687, was min. of Springfield, ord. 16 May 1694, m. 23 Aug. 1699, Catharine, d. of Rev. Nathaniel Chauncy, had Catharine, Eunice, and prob. other ch. and d. 5 Nov. 1733. JOHN, Cambridge, by w. Ann, his first, had John, b. 10 Oct. 1642 ; and Hannah, 18 Jan. 1645;

rem. prob. to Sudbury, perhaps after m. 23 Oct. 1647, Mary, d. of the first John Whitmore, prob. and had Mary, b. 23 Sept. 1648 ; William, 6 Oct. 1653 ; and Sarah, 27 Mar. 1658. JOHN, Sudbury, prob. s. of the preced. d. 1 Jan. 1691; m. Eliz. d. of Henry Rice, had John, b. 1669; Eliz. 21 May 1671; Hannah; James, 10 Sept. 1675 ; Sarah, 14 Jan. 1678; Mary, 1680 ; Abigail, 5 Apr. 1682 ; Martha, 5 Mar. 1685; and Jonathan, 21 June 1689. NATHANIEL, Roxbury, s. of first Daniel, by w. Eliz. wh. d. 25 June 1661, had Eliz. b. 22 May bef.; m. sec. w. Eliz. d. of Robert Rand of Charlestown, had Joanna, b. 20 Jan. bapt. 12 Apr. 1663 ; and Nathaniel, b. 16 July 1667 ; was freem. 1674, and d. 26 Feb. 1694. THOMAS, Ipswich 1642, freem. 1652, when the Col. rec. calls him of Roxbury. His d. Mary m. 21 Aug. 1656, William Lane of Boston ; and his d. Sarah m. 29 Nov. 1657, Thomas Webster of Hampton, where the f. d. 23 Mar. 1690, as a writer of much research and unusual precision in Geneal. Reg. IX. 160, conject. THOMAS, Lynn, m. 4 Dec. 1682, Eliz. Graves, had Mary, b. 10 Nov. 1684; Rebecca; Crispus; Thomas ; and John. Five of this name had been gr. at Harv. in 1834, and six at Yale.

BREWSTER, BENJAMIN, New London 1654, s. of Jonathan, m. Feb. 1659, Ann Dart, sis. perhaps, of Richard of the same, had Mary, b. prob. at N. L. Dec. 1660 ; at Norwich, Ann, Sept. 1662; Jonathan, Nov. 1664; Daniel, Mar. 1667 ; William, Mar. 1669 ; Ruth, 16 Sept. 1671 ; Benjamin, 28 Nov. 1673; and Eliz. 23 June 1676. He d. 10 Sept. 1710. Caulkins, Hist. Norwich, 115. FRANCIS, New Haven 1640, was from London, prob. with w. Lucy and fam. in all count. nine heads ; and lost with Gregson, Lamberton, and others, going home in the ship built at New Haven, Jan. 1646. He may well seem to have been f. of Nathaniel, gr. in the first class at H. C. 1642, and of Joseph. His wid. m. Thomas Pell, and was d. Sept. 1669. Above ten pages of N. H. Col. Rec. are occup. with trifling details on a trial of her for slander, but this was bef. her m. to sec. h. and may have contribut. to produce it in order to obt. manly protection. His est. was good, amt. of inv. £555. JOHN, Portsmouth 1665. See Bruster. * JONATHAN, Plymouth, eldest s. of Elder William, b. at Scrooby, in Co. Notts, on the road to Doncaster in Yorksh. from wh. it is only 12 or 13 miles dist. in a manor belong. to the archbp. of York, under wh. his gr.f. was tenant on long lease, had been instruct. only by his glorious f. either in his native ld. or the doz. yrs. resid. in Holland, where he was left by the Elder to take care of two sis. with his own fam. Without the sis. he came in the Fortune 1621, in June 1636, was in command of the Plymouth trading ho. on Conn. riv. and gave notice to John Winthrop, gov. of the fort at Saybrook, in a letter in my possess. of 18 June, of the evil designs of the Pequots ;

rem. to Duxbury, of wh. he was rep. 1639, the earliest assemb. of deputies in that Col. thence to New London, bef. 1649, there was select-man, d. bef. Sept. 1659, hav. in Sept. 1656 project. to ret. to Eng. with his fam. By w. Lucretia, he had William, and Mary, both, prob. but the first, certain. b. in Holland; Jonathan; Benjamin, bef. ment.; also, Grace, Ruth, Hannah, and perhaps Eliz. some of these b. prob. at New London. Mary m. 12 Nov. 1645, John Turner of Scituate; Eliz. m. a. 1654, Peter Bradley; Grace m. 4 Aug. 1659, Daniel Wetherill; and Ruth m. John Picket, and next, Charles Hill, and d. 30 Apr. 1677. JONATHAN, Duxbury, s. of the preced. is seen among the freem. in 1643, with his br. William, but prob. they both went to New London with their f. JOSEPH, New Haven 1646, s. of Francis. LOVE, Plymouth, s. of Elder William, b. prob. in Holland, possib. in Eng. came, with his f. in the Mayflower, rem. to Duxbury, m. 15 May 1634, Sarah, d. of Wil-liam Collier, had Sarah, wh. m. 1656, Benjamin Bartlett; Nathaniel; William; and Wrestling. He d. not long after his will of 1 Oct. 1650, and his wid. m. Richard Park of Cambridge, and, after his d. 1665, went back to Duxbury. NATHANIEL, New Haven, one of the earliest gr. of Harv. prob. s. of Francis, brot. from London, went to Eng. sett. as min. at Alby, in Co. Norf. had the degr. of B. D. from Dublin Univ. came back after the restorat. and preach. some time from Oct. 1663, at the first ch. in Boston; at last was sett. at Brookhaven, L. I. 1665; m. Sarah, d. of Roger Ludlow, d. 1690, leav. s. John, Timothy, and Daniel, whose descend. are still found there. The extravag. tradit. a. his age giv. by a gr.s. as if he were 95, when only 48 yrs. from H. C. is in John Adams' Works, II. 441. It is not prob. that Francis was neph. of the disting. Elder, and any remoter relat. is uncert. Indeed that of Francis, and of Joseph, is found. on conject. only, but very prob. NATHANIEL, Dux-bury, s. of Love, liv. not long after reach. manhood, for I see nothing of his serv. exc. with his br. William on two coroner's inq. in Dec. 1673, and he d. bef. Nov. 1676, when by Plymouth Rec. it appears, that admin. on his est. was giv. to Robert Vixon of Eastham; but wh. was R. V. is not seen. Perhaps V. was a creditor, and Nathaniel may have gone to live at E. WILLIAM, Plymouth, the famous Elder, claim. of liberal Christians everlast. gratitude, as the earliest of disting. Puritan laymen in Eng. came in the Mayflower, 1620, with his w. two younger s. the w. of the eldest, and her s. William. He was b. 1563 (prob. but earlier by some computa.) at Scrooby, in Nottinghampsh. at the manor hall of wh. vill. belong. to the archbp. of York, he afterwards long resid. the same house at wh. Cardinal Wolsey had made his last stop, bef. reach. home in his final journey, on compulsory retirement from court, after banishm. by King Henry VIII. thirty yrs. earlier. His f.

21 *

prob. William, was tenant under liberal lease from archbp. Sandys, and
the s. was educ. some time at Cambridge Univ. and his f. bec. as sub-
tenant of Scrooby manor, the possessor of that very resid. of the
Cardinal, and the s. therein worship. God accord. to the simple forms of
the chief protestants of Protestantism. After very honora. serv. with
Davison, secr. of Queen Eliz. he partook in the fall of that statesman,
the conseq. of the Queen's heartless deception and treachery; and
abandon. 1587, political life. Devot. hims. for many yrs. to relig. he
was the first promin. layman wh. reject. conform. to the ceremon. of the
ch. of Eng. He was in the employm. of the crown, however, as postmaster bef. Apr. 1594, at Scrooby, above a doz. yrs. after leav. London;
there he m. the w. Mary. With his young friend, Bradford, after a doz.
yrs. to be made Gov. of New Plymouth, and others, he pass. a. 1607 or
8, into Holland for enjoym. of worship without the many idle forms, on
wh. King James had set his heart, and was rul. Elder of the ch. at
Leyden of wh. John Robinson was teach. as he had been prob. at
Scrooby. His ds. Patience and Fear, came in the Ann, 1623; and on
5 Aug. of next yr. Patience m. Thomas Prence, afterwards the gov. and
d. 1634; and Fear m. 1626, Isaac Allerton, as his sec. w. and d. 1633.
His w. d. bef. 1627; and Gov. Bradford says the s. Wrestling d. bef.
him, never m. He had early rem. to Duxbury, and there, under the
same roof with Love, d. 16 Apr. 1643, after one day's illness. His inv.
has proof in the titles of the books of honora. regard for letters. See
Geneal. Reg. IV. 174. Bradford's Memoir of him is in Young's Chron.
of the Pilgr. 461. See, also, Davis's Morton; Hunter's First Colonists
of N. E., of wh. the best impres. is in 4 Mass. Hist. Coll. I. 52; and
Shurtleff's Recollect. of the Pilgr. in Russell's Guide to Plymouth. It
may be useful to mark the error of so valua. an auth. as Baylies, in II.
6, where he gives to our most glorious of the Mayflower's passeng. three
ch. Lucretia, Mary, and William, and is even so rash as to say, two of
them were b. in America. Yet if b. on our side of the water, he ought
to have presum. they could not, from his age, be ch. of the Elder. The
first was w. others, ch. of Jonathan. WILLIAM, Duxbury, s. of Jonathan,
was prob. b. at Leyden, went in Aug. 1645, under serg. Nash, as
part of the forty men to be furnish. by this smallest Col. to repress the
peril from the Narragansets, and encourage the friendsh. of Uncas [see
Bradford's Hist. 431–6], and serv. in that exped. 17 days, was count.
among the freem. in 1643, and prob. went with his f. to New London.
*WILLIAM, Duxbury, s. of Love, m. 2 Jan. 1673, Lydia, d. of George
Partridge, and d. 3 Nov. 1723. Whether he had ch. is not kn. but he
was in good esteem, and was rep. 1675. WRESTLING, Plymouth,
youngest s. of the gr. Elder, b. prob. at Leyden, in Holland, came with

his f. in the Mayflower, d. " a young man unm." bef. his f. says Gov. Bradford, but Caulkins, in Hist. of Norwich, 115, refers to an idle tradit. that
makes him ancest. of Sir Christopher Brewster of our days.   Sir
Christopher perhaps may descend from a gr.s. of the Elder, and youngest
s. of Love, wh. rec. this name, prob. sev. yrs. after d. of his uncle.   In
a very agreea. Memoir of the " Life and Time of Elder Brewster," by
Rev. Ashbel Steele, Phila. 1857, the author too easi. assum. that this s.
of the great Elder was of Portsmouth 1629, and built up his case on
three piles of fictitious paper: The first, a forged deed of 6 Dec. 1629
(wh. fell on Sunday), of ld. in Portsmouth, that was not so call. bef.
May 1653, but always Strawberry Bank, with prob. false grantor and
witnesses, and writ. in language of one hundred and fifty yrs. later use;
next, a fabricat. fam. rec. whereby it is shown, that Wrestling B. was m.
1630 to E. S. had s. John, b. 20 Jan. 1631, and daur. 3 May 1636,
nam. Love Lucretia!!! and the w. d. in childbed, thirty-eight yrs. after
(perhaps the ch. had it liv. would have seem. to require double name,
and so been bapt. Mephistophiles Beelzebub) ; that E. S. the w. is call.
d. of Augustine Story, one of the illustrious grantees in the more
ambitious forgery of the Wheelwright deed of all New Hampsh. from
the Ind. made also on Sunday in an *earlier* mo. of the *same* yr. and little
more than eight yrs. after Wrestling came over the Atlantic, with his f. ;
and the third fountain of evidence is from many, near. all spurious, ac-
counts of business transactions, wh. by patient investigat. are found to
be almost wholly fanciful.   In his new Ed. Mr. Steele will, no doubt,
correct those childish fictions of the last century.   WRESTLING, Duxbury, br. of Nathaniel of the same, had, with his br. William, gr. of lds.
(in honor of the rever. serv. of their gr.f. dec.) at Swanzey, provid. they
went there to liv.; but I presume neither of them accept. the favor, as
they cont. at D.   By w. Mary he had sev. ch. and d. 1 Jan. 1697.   He
was constable in 1680, and serv. on jury in 1682 and 4.   Ten of this
name had been gr. at N. E. coll. in 1834.

BRIARD. See Bryer; and (such is the carelessn. of subordin. of-
ficials), the man may appear as Friard.

BRICE, THOMAS, Gloucester 1642, a ship-carpent. d. 1691.

BRICKET, NATHANIEL, Newbury, had Nathaniel, b. 20 Dec. 1673, d.
young; John, 3 May 1676; James, and Mary, tw. 11 Dec. 1679; and
Nathaniel, again, 23 Sept. 1683, drown. at 4 yrs. old.

BRICKNALL, EDWARD, Boston 1681, by w. Mary had Edward, b. 20
Dec. 1682; John, 11 Sept. 1684; and Mary, 15 Sept. 1689.   Often this
name is Bicknell.

BRIDGE, EDWARD, Roxbury, freem. 22 May 1639, had w. Mary, and
ch. Mary, b. 18 Nov. 1637 ; and Thomas, 31 Mar. or May 1639 ; and,

perhaps, other ch.; and d. 20 Dec. 1683, aged 82. Mary m. I think, 23 Nov. 1661, Samuel Gay. *JOHN, Cambridge 1632, perhaps br. of the preced. freem. 4 Mar. 1635, rep. 1637, was deac. and often select-man, d. Apr. 1665. He was f. of Matthew, and Thomas, brot. from Eng. beside a d. Sarah, b. 16 Feb. 1649, wh. prob. d. young. His sec. w. Eliz. was wid. of Martin Saunders of Boston, as she had first been of Roger Bancroft, and got a fourth h. Edward Taylor. His will ment. w. s. Matthew, Dorcas, d. of his s. Thomas, and sis. Betts. JOHN, Roxbury, s. prob. of Edward, by w. Prudence, d. of William Robinson of Dor-chester, had Mary, b. 21 Apr. 1661, bapt. 29 Mar. 1663; Prudence, b. 11 June 1664; Margaret, 18 July 1666, d. at 4 yrs.; Edward, 9 Sept. 1668; John, 11 Jan. 1671; and Margaret, again, 11 Mar. 1672 or 3; and he d. 20 Aug. 1674. Mary m. 23 Mar. 1681, Joseph Lyon; Pru-dence m. 2 June 1684, John May. JOHN, Boston 1671, d. Sept. 1672, own. a ho. there. JOHN, Wickford, R. I. 1674. ‖ MATTHEW, Cam-bridge, s. of first John, b. in Eng. by mischance k. John Abbot in May 1637, was of ar. co. 1643, m. Ann, d. of Nicholas Danforth, had John, b. 15 June 1645; Ann; Martha, 15 or 19 Jan. 1649, d. young; Matthew, 5 May 1650; Samuel, 14 Feb. 1653, says his gr.stone, but town rec. has 17 Feb. and County rec. 24, d. 25 Feb. 1673; Thomas, 1 June 1655, by gr.stone, but 1656 by town rec. d. 28 Mar. 1673; and Eliz. bapt. 18 Sept. 1659. He d. 28 Apr. 1700; and his wid. d. 2 Dec. 1704. Ann m. 4 June 1668, Samuel Livermore; and next, Oliver Wellington, and d. 28 Aug. 1727, aged 81, perhaps exagger. by ten yrs. MATTHEW, Cambridge, s. of the preced. by w. Abigail Russell, d. of Joseph of Cam-bridge, wh. d. 14 Dec. 1727, aged 56, had nine ch. and d. 29 May 1738. His will, made shortly bef. names s. Matthew, Joseph, John, and Samuel, beside ds. Abigail Whitney, Eliz. and Martha, ch. of his d. Ann, w. of Abraham Watson, and gr.s. William Russell. The ch. were Mary, b. 19 June 1688, mo. of William Russell; Ann, 12 Sept. 1691; Matthew, 1 Mar. 1694; Abigail, 1 Apr. 1696; Joseph, 8 July 1698; John, 1 Sept. 1700; Eliz. 30 Nov. 1703; Samuel, 2 May 1705; and Martha, 20 Sept. 1707. ‖ SAMUEL, Boston 1671, a carpenter, freem. 1672, ar. co. 1679. THOMAS, Cambridge, s. of first John, b. in Co. Essex, Eng. by w. Dorcas had Dorcas, b.˙ 16 Feb. 1649, wh. m. 3 Jan. 1666, Daniel Champney, and d. 7 Feb. 1684. Both he and his w. were d. 10 Mar. 1657, when their inv. was tak. THOMAS, Boston, merch. b. at Hackney, near London, 1657, came here and was bred at Harv. where he had his A. B. 1675; after preach. in Jamaica, New Providence, Ber-muda, and West Jersey, bec. min. of the first ch. ord. 10 May 1705, d. 26 Sept. 1715, of apoplexy. Eliot's Biogr. Dict. WILLIAM, Water-town 1636, Boston 1643, had Peter, b. Jan. 1644. WILLIAM, Charlestown, by w. Persis had Rebecca, b. 2 Feb. 1644, d. soon; Samuel, 25 Mar. 1647; was freem. 1647. Ten of this name, of wh. five were clerg. includ. Rev. Thomas, whose degr. was hon. are on H. C. catal. 1818.

BRIDGES, EDMUND, Lynn, came in the James from London, 1635, aged 23, freem. 7 Sept. 1639, had by first w. Alice, Edmund, b. a. 1637; John; and perhaps by sec. w. Eliz. at Rowley had Mehitable, 26 Mar. 1641; Bethia; Obadiah, a. 1646; Faith; Hackaliah, wh. was lost at sea, a. 1671; and Josiah; his w. d. Dec. 1664, at Ipswich; and by third w. m. 6 Apr. 1665, Mary Littlehale, prob. wid. of Richard, may have had Mary, and he d. 13 Jan. 1685, in his will nam. w. Mary, and ch. John, Josiah, Faith Black, Bethia, and Mary. Bethia m. 26 Oct. 1669, Joseph Peabody. Perhaps the London custom ho. gives Bridges, tho. on Col. rec. it is only a monosyl. EDMUND, Topsfield, s. of the preced. m. 11 Jan. 1660, Sarah, d. of William Towne, had Edmund, b. 4 Oct. foll.; Benjamin, 2 Jan. 1665; Mary, Apr. 1667; rem. to Salem, there had Hannah, 9 June 1669; and Caleb, 3 June 1677; and d. a. 1682. His wid. m. Peter Cloyes, and barely escap. with life in the witchcraft delus. JOHN, Andover, s. of Edmund the first, m. 5 Dec. 1666, Sarah, d. of James How of Ipswich, if the pedigree of Bridges, in Geneal. Reg. VIII. 252, be right. By this first w. wh. d. not at Andover, or at least is not on the rec. he had James, b. a. 1671; and Sarah; and by a sec. w. m. 1 Mar. 1678, but not at Andover, Mary Post, a wid. perhaps of John of Woburn, had Mary, b. 27 Jan. 1679; Samuel, 19 July 1681; Eliz. 5 June 1683; and Mehitable, 29 Apr. 1688. JOSIAH, Ipswich, br. of the preced. m. 13 Nov. 1676, Eliz. Norton, and a sec. w. m. 19 Sept. 1677, Ruth Greenslip, and left ch. whose childr. says the pedigree, are num. OBADIAH, Ipswich, br. of the preced. m. 25 Oct. 1671, Mary Smith, and had sec. w. Eliz. and d. a. 1677, leav. three s. not nam. in the pedigree, wh. however, tells that his wid. m. 7 Oct. 1680, Joseph Parker of Andover. ‡ * ‖ ROBERT, Lynn 1640, freem. 2 June 1641, ar. co. 1641, went home, but came back in 1643, was a capt. rep. 1644, speaker 1646, Assist. 1647 to 56, when he d. His house was burn. Apr. 1648. Winth. II. 237. From Lewis, Hist. of Lynn, we do not learn, whether he had w. or ch. WILLIAM, Mass. freem. 1647, is prob. the man of Watertown 1636, without final s.

BRIDGHAM, ‖ HENRY, Dorchester 1641, freem. 1643, rem. to Boston 1644, was a tanner, ar. co. 1644, constable 1653, was a capt. and d. Jan. 1671, leav. good est. By w. Eliz. wh. surv. he had Joseph, bapt. 14 Dec. 1645; Jonathan; John, b. Sept. 1645, H. C. 1669; Joseph, again, 17 Jan. 1652; Benjamin, 3, or 4 May 1654, ar. co. 1674; Hopestill, 29 July 1658, d. young; Samuel, 17 Jan. 1661; Nathaniel, 2 Apr. 1662, d. young; and James, 12 May 1664. JOHN, Ipswich, s. of the preced. a physician, d. 2 May 1721. JONATHAN, Boston, eldest s. of Henry, was a tanner, freem. 1675, of wh. I kn. only that he was liv. 1676. * ‖ JOSEPH, Boston, br. of the preced. ar. co. 1674, freem. 1678, rep. 1697, had been in 1690 for Northampton, deac. and rul. Elder of first ch. d. 5 Jan. 1709. His wid. Mercy, d. of John Wensley of B. m. 8 Dec. 1712, Hon. Thomas Cushing, and d. 3 Oct. 1740. SAMUEL, Marlborough 1675. Four of this name had been gr. in 1834, at Harv. and one at Brown Univ.

BRIDGMAN, JAMES, Hartford 1641, or earlier, Springfield 1645, had b. at H. Sarah, his eldest ch. wh. m. 3 May 1659, Timothy Tileston of Dorchester; John, b. 7 July 1645; Thomas, 14 Jan. 1647, d. soon; Martha, 20 Nov. 1649, wh. m. 1668, Samuel Dickinson of Hatfield; Mary, 5 July 1652, wh. m. 1672, Samuel Bartlett, and d. in 2 yrs. He rem. to Northampton 1654, had there James, b. 30 May 1655, d. soon; Patience, June 1656, d. in 7 mos.; and Hezekiah, June 1658, d. at 9 mos. His w. Martha d. 31 Aug. 1668, and he d. Mar. 1676. JOHN, Salem, 1637, by w. Eliz. had Mary, bapt. 8 Sept. 1650. Farmer says he d. a. 1655. JOHN, Northampton, only surv. s. of James, m. 11 Dec. 1670, Mary, eldest d. of Isaac Sheldon, d. 7 Apr. 1712, leav. ch. Mary, John, Deliverance, James, Isaac, Sarah, Ebenezer, Thomas, Martha, Hannah, and Orlando, and had three wh. d. young. The last nam. was builder of Bridgman's fort, S. of fort Dummer, and f. of Thomas, H. C. 1762, a lawyer, wh. d. 1771 in New Hampsh. Two more of this name had been gr. at Harv. in 1834, and three others at other N. E. coll.

BRIEN, or BRIAN, RICHARD, a soldier in Moseley's comp. Dec. 1675, whose resid. is unkn. THOMAS, Plymouth, whip. in 1633, for run. from his master, Samuel Eddy.

BRIERSLEY, or BRIERS, JOHN, Gloucester, by w. Eliz. had John, b. 29 May 1658; Benjamin, Jan. 1660, d. soon; and Mary, Jan. 1661, d. soon.

BRIGDEN, or BRIDGEN, THOMAS, Charlestown, was of Faversham, Kent, came in the Hercules, 1635, from Sandwich, with w. Thomasine and two ch. freem. 3 Mar. 1636, and d. 20 June 1668. He had Zechary, b. 2 Aug. 1639, H. C. 1657. His will, of 1 May 1665, makes w. extrix. names s. Thomas, and his ch. Thomas, Zachary, and John; d. Mary, w. of Henry Kimball, and her ch. Zachary, Mary, and Sarah; and d. Sarah. In a codic. of 16 June 1668, two other gr.ch. Henry K. and Michael B. are provid. for. The rec. of the town, in some confus. gives his adm. as inhab. 1634, but does not ins. his name in the gen. list of 1636, while the more careful ch. rec. has adm. of him and w. in Dec. 1635. THOMAS, Charlestown, s. of the preced. had w.

Mildred, only d. of Michael Carthrick of Ipswich, and by her, Sarah, b. 3 Jan. 1656; Zechariah, 8 Aug. 1658; and Thomas, all bapt. 5 Aug. 1660; John, 29 Sept. 1661; Michael, 5 June 1664; Nathaniel, 30 Dec. 1666; Timothy, 18 Dec. 1670; and Elias, 26 Jan. 1673. His w. surv. him and her gr.stone says d. July 1726, aged 96. Next yr. in Dec. Thomas, prob. gr.s. of first Thomas, unit. with the ch. Michael, prob. also gr.s. d. 12 June 1709, aged 45 ; and Michael, chos. a deac. 1752, d. 18 Aug. 1767, aged 70. ZECHARIAH, Charlestown, s. of the first Thomas, was a preach. at Stonington, d. 1663. Trumbull, I. 287.

BRIGGS, CLEMENT, Plymouth, came in the Fortune, 1621, prob. young; rem. to Dorchester, there m. 1630, or 1631, early, Joan Allen, for officiat. at wh. cerem. Thomas Stoughton, the constable, was fin. £5. at the Mar. Court, 1631; thence he rem. to Weymouth 1633, had s. Thomas, b. 14 June 1633; Jonathan, 14 June 1635; John; David, 23 Aug. 1640; and Clement, 1 Jan. 1643. Grievous is our feeling of regret at find. the Court, in June 1638, led to forbid the w. to come into the comp. of Arthur Warren, as we are compell. to fear the m. was imprud. Bef. he d. he had ano. w. Eliz. Of his will, the abstr. is giv. in Geneal. Reg. VII. 233 ; but the envelope of it is label. Mary Mouth, wh. the blundering clk. read for Weymouth, the resid. of the testator. His inv. of 23 Feb. 1649 not. in the same Vol. p. 228, was label. Osomunt Bray, full evid. of knowl. by the scrivener of the old writ. In Vol. IX. 347, the correct name is giv. His s. Thomas was of Taunton 1668, and num. descend. in that vicin. CORNELIUS, Scituate, s. of Walter, was ensign in Philip's war under eld. brs. James, the lieut. and John, capt.; m. 1677, the wid. of Samuel Russell, one of his fellow-soldiers, wh. had fallen the yr. preced. had Cornelius, b. 1678 ; Joseph, 1679; and James, 1683. EDMUND, Topsfield 1667. JAMES, Scituate, s. of Walter, lieut. in the gr. war, m. 1678, Rebecca, d. of deac. Joseph Tilden, had Joseph, b. 1678; Mary, 1682 ; James, 1687 ; Benjamin, 1695 ; and perhaps others. JOHN, Lynn, came, prob. in the Blessing, 1635, aged 20, rem. to Sandwich 1637, there d. 1641. His w. Catharine had admin. 1 June. JOHN, Newport 1638, or Portsmouth 1650, was freem. there 1655, had Thomas, and an elder s. viz. JOHN, Warwick, b. 1642, wh. m. Frances, d. of Edward Fisher of Portsmouth, R. I. had John, b. 25 Jan. 1668; James, 12 Feb. 1671; Frances, 26 Feb. 1673; and Richard, 1 Feb. 1675. He liv. at Kingstown in 1678, when his w. was nam. Hannah. JOHN, Boston 1673, s. of William, rem. that yr. to Lyme, there by w. Mary had William, b. 30 July 1672 or 3; and Peter, 5 Feb. 1680. JOHN, Scituate, s. of Walter, had Hannah, b. 1684; Deborah, 1685; and John, 1687. He was a capt. in the war. Deane, 225. JONATHAN, Taunton, perhaps s. of Clement, had Jonathan, b. 15 Mar.

1668; and David, 6 Dec. 1669. MATTHEW, Hingham, m. May 1648, Deborah, d. of Matthew Cushing, wh. d. bef. her f. Matthias is more common name of this man. RICHARD, Taunton, perhaps s. of Clement, m. 15 Aug. 1662, Rebecca Hoskins, had William, b. 21 Nov. 1663; Rebecca, 16 Aug. 1665; Richard, 7 Apr. 1668; John, 13 Feb. 1673; Joseph, 15 June 1674; Benjamin, 15 Sept. 1677. THOMAS, Portsmouth, R. I. younger s. of the first John of the same, had in 1678 w. Mary, and no more can I learn a. him. WALTER, Scituate 1643, had w. Frances, and d. a. 1684. His will, of that yr. names w. s. John, James, Cornelius, and d. Hannah Winslow. WILLIAM, Boston by w. Mary had Hannah, b. 28 Aug. 1642, wh. m. 10 Sept. 1657, John Harris. Perhaps he rem. to Lyme betw. 1670 and 1680; at least one of this name was inhab. there at that period. WILLIAM, Taunton, perhaps br. of Jonathan, m. 6 Nov. 1666, Sarah Macumber, perhaps d. of William of Marshfield, had William, b. 25 Jan. 1668; Thomas, 9 Sept. 1669; and Sarah, the next day; Eliz. 4 Nov. 1672; Mary, 14 Aug. 1674; Matthew, 5 Feb. 1677; John, 19 Mar. 1680; and his w. d. next day. This name seems common thro. many Cos. in Eng. but chief. Norfolk. Five had been gr. at Harv. and fourteen at other N. E. coll. in 1834.

BRIGHAM, * JOHN, Sudbury, s. of Thomas, rem. to Marlborough, of wh. he was rep. 1689 and 90, had Sarah, b. 27 Mar. 1674; Mary, 6 May 1678; Jotham, 6 June 1680; Hannah, 27 Mar. 1683; and Thomas, 6 May 1687. SAMUEL, Sudbury, youngest s. of Thomas, rem. to Marlborough, freem. 1690, by w. Eliz. d. of Abraham Howe of M. wh. d. 26 July 1739, aged 75, had Eliz. b. 24 Mar. 1685; Hepzibah, 25 Jan. 1687; Samuel, 25 Jan. 1689; Lydia, 5 Mar. 1691; Jedediah, 8 June 1693; Jotham, 23 Dec. 1695; Timothy, 10 Oct. 1698; Charles, 30 Dec. 1700; Persis, 10 July 1703; and Antipas, 16 Oct. 1706. He was a capt. and d. 24 July 1713. * SEBASTIAN, Cambridge 1636, rem. to Rowley, was capt. 1644, rep. 1650. Johnson's Hist. of N. E. 193, and Gage, in Hist. of Rowley, give this spel. of the name, wh. Farmer had under Bridgham. The bapt. name must be influential in prevent. mistake, and the local historian likely to be correct. THOMAS, Cambridge, came in the Susan and Ellen, 1635, aged 32, freem. 18 Apr. 1636, was not of Watertown, as Bond thot., did not rem. to Sudbury, as Farmer had said, by w. Mercy Hurd, m. prob. after com. from Eng. had Thomas, b. a. 1642; John, b. 9 Mar. 1645, above ment.; Mary, wh. prob. d. bef. her f.; Hannah, 9 Mar. 1650, or 1; and Samuel, 12 Jan. 1653, above ment.; all nam. in his will pro. early in 1654. He made his will 7 Oct. and d. 8 Dec. 1653. His wid. m. 1 Mar. 1655, Edmund Rice; and next, 1664, William Hunt. THOMAS, Sudbury, s. of the preced. rem. to Marlborough, m. 27 Dec. 1665, Mary, was freem. 1690, had

Thomas, b. 24 Feb. 1667, wh. d. bef. his f.; Nathan, 17 June 1671; David, 11 Aug. 1673, d. young; Jonathan, 22 Feb. 1675; David, again, 12 Apr. 1678; Gershom, 23 Feb. 1681 (the last two d. bef. their f.); Elnathan, 7 Mar. 1683; and Mary, 26 Oct. 1687. He made his will 21 Apr. 1716, wh. was pro. 2 June 1717. Six of this name had been gr. at Harv. in 1834, and an equal number in aggreg. at the other N. E. coll.

BRIGHT, *FRANCIS*, Charlestown, s. of Edward of London, bred at Oxford, matric. of New Coll. 18 Feb. 1625, aged 22, and by famous John Davenport instr. in divinity, in 1629 came from Rayleigh, in Essex, with w. and two ch. to Salem, in the Lion's Whelp, prob. sat down at Charlestown, took some discouragem. and went home 1630 in the Lion. HENRY, Charlestown 1630, prob. from Ipswich, in Suff.'k s. of Henry of Bury St. Edmunds, came in the fleet with Winth. was very early, No. 48, enrol. in the ch. but not long after rem. to Watertown, there m. 1634, Ann, d. of Henry Goldstone, had Ann, wh. at her bur. 28 Oct. 1639, was call. 4 yrs. old; Abigail, b. 12 Oct. 1637, wh. m. a. Aug. 1659, Elisha Odlin; Mary, 23 or 27 Apr. 1639, wh. m. 15 Oct. 1657, Nathaniel Coolidge; John, 14 May 1641; Ann, again, 17 Mar. 1644, m. 26 May 1670, Samuel Ruggles of Roxbury, as his sec. w. I presume; Eliz. m. as sec. w. 23 July 1674, or 5 July 1675 (as various acco. are giv.), deac. Walter Hastings of Cambridge; Nathaniel, 5 May 1647; and Beriah, 22 Sept. 1651, m. 30 Nov. 1671, Isaac Fowle of Charlestown. He was freem. 6 May 1635, held in high esteem, deac. and d. 9 Oct. 1686, aged 84. He had elder br. Thomas, of Ipswich, Eng. wh. in his will, of unkn. date, but pro. 1626, ment. this Henry, sis. Eliz. and other sis. as minors. That Eliz. wh. was in 1657, wid. Dell of Bow, near London, gave in her will to this br. £200, and to each of his 7 ch. £10. all wh. was paid here in 1658 and 9. Large pedigree from the time of Henry VII. prepar. by Somerby, is giv. by Dr. Bond. This Henry was for many yrs. call. jr. because HENRY, a poor man of the same name, liv. at W. was always spok. of as senior, as he might well be, without our giv. full credit to the rec. of his d. 14 Sept. 1674, aged one hundred yrs. and upwards, or ano. rec. says a. 109 yrs. But as the amt. of his inv. was only £2, 9, 6, any affinity is highly improb. JOHN, Watertown, s. of the wealthy Henry, m. 7 May 1675, Mary, d. of William Barsham, had no ch. freem. 1671, was deac. and d. 17 Aug. 1691. His wid. m. 12 Dec. 1700, as his sec. w. Hananiah Parker of Reading. NATHAN-IEL, Watertown, br. of the preced. m. 21 or 26 July 1681, Mary, d. of Simon Coolidge, had Mary, b. 7 Oct. 1682; Henry, 16 Aug. 1684; Nathaniel, 18 Dec. 1686; John, 5 Apr. 1689; Joseph, 11 July 1692; Hannah, 7 Aug. 1694; Abigail; Benjamin, 19 July 1698; and Mercy.

Four ds. and first nam. four s. surv. ; but from not being in the will, 22 Sept. 1725, Benjamin may well be presum. to have d. bef. his f. Of these ch. descend most of the name in our country. SAMUEL, Mass. freem. 1645, but where he dwelt is unkn. THOMAS, Watertown 1640, may have been neph. of the first ment. Henry.

BRIGHTON, SAMUEL, Boston, by w. Ann had James, bapt. 30 Mar. 1690 ; and Ebenezer, 2 Oct. 1692. The error of this name, wh. should be Samuel Beighton, was caus. by false index. See Beighton. THOM-AS, came from London to Boston in the Truelove 1635, aged 31.

BRIGNALL, WILLIAM, Dedham, m. Martha, d. of Michael Metcalf, had William, d. soon after, and his wid. m. 2 Aug. 1654, Christopher Smith. The s. was liv. when gr.f. made his will, in wh. he was rememb. ten yrs. later.

BRIMBLECOME, JOHN, Boston 1654, woolcomber, m. 14 Jan. 1656, Barbara, wid. of George Davis, liv. not long there, but perhaps rem. to Marblehead bef. 1674. PHILIP, Marblehead 1668, was, perhaps, br. of the preced.

BRIMSDEN, or BRIMSDELL, ROBERT, Lynn, m. 15 Apr. 1667, Bathsheba Richards, was of Boston 1672, merch. m. I think, Ann, d. of Thomas Barnes of Hingham, for sec. w.

BRIMSMEAD, BROWNSMAYD, BRINSMEID, BRINSMEAD, or BRINS-MADE, oft. BRINSLEY, DANIEL, Stratford, s. of John, by w. Sarah, d. of Caleb Nichols (but ano. acco. erron. makes her d. of the first Daniel Kellogg), d. Oct. 1702, without will, leav. good est. wid. wh. m. John Betts of Norwalk, and ch. Mary, aged 18; Daniel, 15; Abigail, 11; Samuel, 8 ; and Ruth, 2. * JOHN, Charlestown 1637, freem. 2 May 1638, by w. Mary had Mary, b. 24 July, bapt. 3 Aug. 1640 ; and John, b. 2 Mar. 1643 ; Daniel; and Zechary, wh. was drown. Aug. 1667 ; prob. rem. to Stratford bef. 1650, was rep. 1669, and 71, and d. 1673, leav. good est. to wid. Mary, and ch. John, Daniel, Paul, Samuel, Mary, w. of John Bostwick, and Eliz. WILLIAM, Dorchester, d. early in 1648, his will, 10 Dec. 1647, of wh. abstr. is in Geneal. Reg. III. 266, names s. William and Alexander, ds. Ebbet and Mary. This last m. 17 Sept. 1667, Benjamin Leeds. WILLIAM, Marlborough, s. of the preced. b. perhaps at Dorchester, was bred at H. C. and should have been gr. 1654 or 5, when, by a change in the durat. of studies for the first degr. from three yrs. to four, he and sixteen more, if Mather may be believ. Magn. IV. 135, felt so much aggriev. as to forego the advantage of longer resid. Something different is the version to be seen in the delightful Ann. of the Am. Pulpit, I. 256. He preach. a. 1660–65 at Plymouth, and went thence to the new town of M. where he was ord. 3 Oct. 1666, never m. and d. 3 July 1701. For the little that can be kn. of him, see 1 Mass. Hist. Coll. IV. 47, and IX. 179, and 3 M. H. C. VII. 297.

BRINKS, BRYAN, Saco. Sullivan, 304, et seq. Williamson, I. 238, 240. But it is doubt. whether he ever came to our country. No time is giv.

BRINLEY, ‡ FRANCIS, Newport 1652, s. of Thomas (an auditor of revenues of the Kings, Charles I. and II., as by the inscript. on his tomb in the mid. aisle of the ch. at Datchett, Co. Bucks, betw. Coln-brook and Windsor, is told, tho. it is not specif. whether the revenues were from tolls, or rents, or subsidies. The same voice from the tomb informs us that he was b. 1591, at the city of Exeter, m. Ann Wase of Pettiworth, in Co. Sussex, had five s. and seven ds. and d. 1661, so that he could have serv. his blessed maj. Charles II. only one yr. Addit. knowl. is gain. from the will, made 13 Sept. 1661, as that he had est. at Newcastle and in Yorksh. as well as at Datchett, and that his ch. were only five left to him, two ds. Mary, then wid. of Peter Sylvester, and Grizel, w. of Nathaniel Sylvester of Shelter Isl. on our side of the world, and three s. Francis, Thomas, and William). This eldest s. was b. 5 Nov. 1632, and had prob. escap. from the evils brot. on the fam. by the loyalty of his f. but went back to Eng. prob. in 1655, came again in the Speedwell to Boston 27 July of next yr. m. Hannah Carr, d. perhaps of Caleb, of Newport, had Thomas and William; was an Assist. of R. I. 1672, and d. 1719. 1 Mass. Hist. Coll. V. 252. William d. at Boston 1693, unm. ‖ THOMAS, Boston, s. of the preced. ar. co. 1681, one of the found. of King's Chapel 1686, went to Eng. there m. Mary Apthorp, had Eliz.; Francis, b. 1690, at London, bred at Eton; and William; and d. of smallpox, 1693, as did his youngest s. The wid. with her two ch. came to reside with their gr.f.; and after his d. she liv. at Roxbury with her s. wh. had five s. and two ds. as fam. tradit. relates.

BRINTNALL, THOMAS, Boston, by w. Esther had Samuel, b. 2 Dec. 1665; Thomas, 1 Nov. 1669; Nathaniel, 1671; John, 3 Mar. 1673; Joseph, 3 Mar. 1674; and Mehitable, 1685; liv. at Muddy riv. THOMAS, Sudbury, s. of the preced. m. 23 May 1693, Hannah, d. of maj. Simon Willard, had Thomas, prob. bef. going to S. and there Parnel, b. 27 Sept. 1696; William, Y. C. 1721; Paul, 20 Mar. 1701; Nathaniel, 1703; Jerusha, 15 Oct. 1704; Dorothy, 21 Dec. 1706; and Susanna, Apr. 1708 or 9; was capt. and he d. 2 Aug. 1733.

BRISANTON, THOMAS, appears on the roll of brave capt. Turner's comp. in Mar. 1676, left at Quaboag, and the true name may have been mistak.

BRISCOE, BENJAMIN, Boston, shoemaker, m. 1656, Sarah, d. of Philip Long, had Philip, wh. d. very soon; Hannah, b. 6 Feb. 1658; Sarah, 18 July 1660; William, 7 Apr. 1663; Ann, 31 Jan. 1664; Mary, 22 Dec. 1665; John, 20 Jan. 1667; Rebecca, 20 Feb. 1669; Benjamin, 2

May 1671; and Susanna, 9 Feb. 1674. Sarah was b. at Lynn. DAN-
IEL, Boston, s. of William, adm. of the ch. 17 Apr. and made freem. 18
May 1642, d. the same mo. says Boston rec. or 8 of the foll. mo. by
drown. See Winth. II. 66, wh. erron. calls him Nathaniel. EZEKIEL,
Boston, br. of the preced. mariner, by w. Rebecca had Ezekiel, b. 25
Feb. 1670; and Mary, 17 Dec. 1673; d. next yr. JAMES, Milford
1670, br. of Nathaniel of the same, was freem. 1671, m. 6 Nov. 1676,
Sarah Wheeler, d. of William, had Sarah, b. 25 Mar. 1678; James, 25
Aug. 1679; and Hannah; and he d. a. 1710. JOHN, Watertown, s. of
Nathaniel, b. in Eng. prob. 1622, m. 13 Dec. 1650, Eliz. d. of Thomas
Bittlestone of Cambridge, wh. d. 28 Aug. 1685, had John, b. 5 Oct.
1651, d. young; Eliz. 18 Dec. 1653, m. 20 Nov. 1679, Abraham Jackson; Thomas, 1 Apr. 1655; Mary, 22 Nov. 1658, m. Edward Goffe;
and Sarah, 14 Mar. 1661, d. young. He was selectman 1664, and many
subseq. yrs. and d. 18 Oct. 1690. JOSEPH, Boston, perhaps s. of William, b. in Eng. m. 30 Jan. 1652, Abigail, d. of John Compton; was
drown. 1 Jan. 1658, had only Joseph, b. 21 Aug. 1658, to wh. his gr.mo.
Compton left, Nov. 1664, all her little est. £16. 16. JOSEPH, Boston, s.
of the preced. by w. Rebecca had Rebecca, b. 16 Sept. 1679; Joseph, 4
Jan. 1681, d. soon; Joseph, again, 8 Jan. 1682; John, 30 Jan. 1684;
and Sarah, 1 Aug. 1686. NATHANIEL, Watertown, had w. Eliz. bur.
20 Nov. 1642, and ch. Nathaniel; Mary, wh. m. Thomas Broughton, and
d. early, prob. in 1644; John, bef. ment.; and Sarah, wh. m. 7 Feb.
1650, William Bond. He was a rich tanner, selectman 1648, and 50,
involv. in controversy, by wh. we may presume, he was led to go home,
where more freedom of opin. was allow. to be express. A characterist.
letter of 1652 to Broughton, wh. is in print, 3 Mass. Hist. Coll. I. 32,
was made a subject of investiga. See, also, Winth. I. 392, and II. 93.
NATHANIEL, Cambridge 1639, s. of the preced. b. no doubt in Eng.
usher of Eaton at Harvard, wh. cruelly beat him, and he prob. rem. to
Milford, was an early sett. without doubt bef. 1646; d. 1683, Lambert
says; yet he was not liv. in 1677 to partake a div. of lds.; but had s.
Nathaniel, bapt. 1646; and James, 1649. NATHANIEL, Milford, s. of
the preced. m. 29 Nov. 1672, Mary Camp, perhaps d. of Nicholas, had
James, b. 14 Aug. 1673; Mary, 15 Nov. 1675; Samuel, 4 Apr. 1678;
Sarah, a. 1681; Abigail, 1 Nov. 1684; John, a. 1687; and Dinah, a.
1690; and he d. next yr. THOMAS, Watertown, s. of John, m. 24
Dec. 1684, Hannah, d. of Samuel Stearns, had John, b. 22 Oct. 1685;
Eliz. bapt. 17 July 1687; and Thomas, May 1689. He d. bef. 15 Oct.
1690, the date of the will of his f. and his wid. m. 28 Sept. 1718, Samuel
Gookin. WILLIAM, Boston 1640, tailor, freem. 2 June 1641, had w.
Cicely, and d. betw. 1662 and 70. By some of the name the *r* was drop.

BRISENTON, THOMAS, Springfield 1678. See Brisanton.

BRISTOW, or BRISTOL, HENRY, New Haven 1647, had Rebecca, b. 4 Feb. bapt. 10 Mar. 1650; Samuel, 3, bapt. 7 Dec. 1651; Mary, b. 1653; and by sec. w. Lydia Brown, m. 1656, Lydia, 3 Jan. bapt. 7 Feb. 1658; John, 4 Sept. bapt. 27 Nov. 1659; Mary, 1 Sept. bapt. 9 Nov. 1661; Hannah, 10 Dec. 1663, bapt. 13 Feb. foll.; and Abigail, 19, bapt. 23 Apr. 1666. RICHARD, Guilford 1640–69, m. perhaps as sec. or third w. Susanna, wid. of Thomas Blatchley of the same. As the city of Bristol was formerly call. Bristow, this fam. name prob. has chang. in conformity.

BRITTEL, JOHN, Salem, had a gr. of ld. 1637, prob. rem. soon.

BRITTERIDGE, RICHARD, Plymouth, came in the Mayflower, 1620, d. ten days after land. being the first of the sad roll.

BRITTON, or BRITTAINE, JAMES, Weymouth, a favorer of Lenthall, for some aspersion of the min. at other places was in Mar. 1639, whip.; and 21 Mar. 1644 was hang. for adultery. Winth. I. 289, and II. 157–9. Lechford MS. as in 3 Mass. Hist. Coll. III. 403. JAMES, Woburn, d. 3 May 1655. He, or the preced. may have come from London, in the Increase, 1635, aged 27, if the custom ho. rec. of the embark. of James Bitton lost a single letter; wh. is not improb. for the official name seems very strange.

BROADRIDGE, RICHARD, Casco 1680.

BROADWAY, EDMUND, Gloucester 1653, sold his est. there that yr.

BROCK, HENRY, Dedham 1642, d. 1652, leav. w. Eliz. and ch. John, Eliz. and Ann, nam. in his will, made 22 Apr. 1646, but w. d. bef. the will was pro. 19 Oct. 1652. JOHN, Reading, b. 1620, says Mather's Magn. IV. 141, at Stradbrook in Suffk. came in 1637, may have been s. of the preced. and also freem. 18 May 1642, but both points are uncert. and the latter highly improb. H. C. 1646, soon after taught a sch. preach. at Isle of Shoals, Farmer thot. 12 yrs. long eno. to allow one or two marvels occur. there, as well as those at Reading about him to be relat. in his biogr. was ord. at R. 13 Nov. 1662, and m. the same day, Sarah, wid. of Samuel Hough, his predecess. in the pulpit, d. of Rev. Zechariah Symmes, wh. d. 27 Apr. 1681, and he d. 18 June 1688. 3 Mass. Hist. Coll. II. 312. RICHARD, Watertown, came in the Elizabeth and Ann, 1635, aged 31, from London, d. 24 Oct. 1673 or 4. WILLIAM, Salem 1639. W. Gibbs.

BROCKETT, BENJAMIN, New Haven, s. of John of the same, m. 24 Mar. 1669, Eliz. d. of Thomas Barnes, had a d. b. and d. 1671; John, 3 June 1672; Mary, 6 May 1675; Hannah, 19 Mar. 1678; and he d. 22 May 1679. His wid. prob. m. John Austin. JOHN, New Haven 1639, a signer of the first coven.; had John, bapt. 31 Jan. 1643; Be fruitful, and Benjamin, tw. 23 Feb. 1645; Mary, prob. 25 Sept. 1646; Silence,

4 June 1648; Abigail, b. 10, bapt. 24 Mar. 1650; Samuel, 14, bapt. 18 Jan. 1652; Jabez, 1654; was of the earliest sett. at Wallingford 1670, as was his s. Samuel; there the f. d. 12 Mar. 1690, aged 80. He made his will nine days bef. nam. four s. and ds. Mary Pennington, w. of Ephraim; Silence Bradley, w. of Joseph; and gives legacy to John Paine, presum. to be h. or s. of his d. Abigail. JOHN, New Haven, s. of the preced. had Mary, b. 18 Feb. 1675; John, 23 Oct. 1676; Eliz. 26 Nov. 1677; Moses, 23 Apr. 1680; Abigail, 31 Mar. 1683; and prob. others. In early days, as sometimes in our own, the name was Brackett.

BROCKLEBANK, JOHN, Rowley, had Samuel, b. 1655. SAMUEL, Rowley, came, says tradit. but it omits, as usual, to say when, with his br. the preced. and their mo. Jane, wh. d. 1668; was a deac. and capt. k. in Philip's war, Hubbard says 18, but prob. 21 Apr. 1676, in battle, at Sudbury, aged 48, leav. wid. Hannah, and ch. Samuel, b. 1653; Francis, 1655; Hannah; Mary; Eliz.; Sarah; and Joseph, b. 1674. His wid. m. Richard Dole of Newbury; her d. Hannah m. John Stickney, and ds. Mary, and Sarah, m. sever. William and Henry, s. of Richard Dole. SAMUEL, Rowley, s. of the preced. m. Eliz. Platts, had John, b. 1686; Francis, 1694; beside five ds. Descend. at Rowley are num. as well as in Maine, New Hampsh. and Vermt.

BROCKWAY, WOOLSTONE, Saybrook 1664, by w. Hannah, wh. d. 6 Feb. 1687, had Hannah, b. 14 Sept. 1664; William, 25 July 1666; Woolstone, 7 Feb. 1668; Mary, 16 Jan. 1670; Bridget, 9 Jan. 1672; Richard, 30 Sept. 1673; Eliz. 24 May 1676; Sarah, 23 Sept. 1679; and Deborah, 1 May 1682. Hannah m. Thomas Champion. This name, on the Lyme side of the riv. after, may now be Brockwell.

BRODBENT, JOSHUA, provost-marshal, and Shf. of New Hampsh. 1681, m. at Woburn, 6 Apr. 1685, Sarah Osborn, perhaps wid. of Thomas of Malden.

BROMFIELD, ‡ * ‖ EDWARD, Boston 1675, was third s. of Henry, wh. was s. of Arthur, and b. 10 Jan. 1649, at Haywood ho. in the New Forest, Hants; merch. ar. co. 1679, a gent. of high esteem, rep. 1693, one of the counc. 1708; m. 1678, Eliz. d. of James Brading, had only Eliz. wh. d. unm. 1717. His sec. w. m. 4 June 1683, Mary, d. of Rev. Samuel Danforth, had six ch. wh. d. young; and she d. 17 Oct. 1734, he hav. d. 2 June preced. leav. two ds. Mary, b. 2 June 1689; Sarah, 11 Oct. 1692; and Edward, 5 Nov. 1695. One d. Frances, b. 8 June 1694, had m. Rev. John Webb of Boston, and d. 14 Sept. 1721. * ED-WARD, Boston, s. of the preced. m. 21 Feb. 1722, Abigail Coney, had Edward, b. 30 Jan. 1723, H. C. 1742, a man of talents, untimely cut off, 18 Aug. 1745; Abigail, 9 Jan. 1725, wh. m. Hon. William Phillips; Henry, 12 Nov. 1727, liv. at Harvard until 23 Feb. 1820; John, 25

Apr. 1729 ; Mary, 15 Sept. 1730; both d. soon; Sarah, 20 Apr. 1732, m. Jeremiah Powell, Esqr. wh. in the war of the Revo. was, most of the time, head of the gov. of Mass. ; Thomas, 30 Oct. 1733, an emin. merch. in London ; Samuel, 7 Oct. 1736, tho. ano. rec. has ano. date; Mary, again, wh. m. William Powell, Esq. ; and John, 1743. He d. 10 Apr. 1756, after fill. many import. offices, rep. 4 yrs. from 1739, but especial. honor. as overseer of the poor thro. long period.

BROMLEY, LUKE, Stonington, m. Hannah, d. of Thomas Stafford, wh. names her in his will; and he next m. Thomasine Packer, had Thomasine, b. 1692 ; William, 1693 ; and Thomas, 1695 ; d. 1697.

BRONSDEN, ROBERT, Boston, merch. freem. 1690 ; had Eliz. wh. m. Samuel Greenwood.

BRONSON. See Brownson.

BROOKHAVEN, ‖ JOHN, Rhode Isl. 1669, a capt. call. 1671, citiz. of London, perhaps ar. co. 1681.

BROOKING, BRUCKEN, or BROOKEN, GODFREY, drown. 20 Dec. 1681, leav. w. and four young ch. of wh. one was William. JOHN, Boston 1658, by w. Eliz. had John, b. 11 May 1659, d. in three mos. ; Eliz. 26 May 1660; John, again, 17 Feb. 1662 ; Jane, 16 June, 1664 ; Christian, 22 July 1667 ; Mary, 20 Jan. 1670; Abigail, 8 Oct. 1671 ; Mercy, 15 Dec. 1676 ; Jonathan, 18 Oct. 1678; and William, 17 Sept. 1681. His will of 27 Oct. 1682 was pro. 25 Apr. foll. JOHN, Boston, prob. s. of the preced. by w. Abigail, had John, b. 23 Sept. 1687. WILLIAM, Portsmouth 1631, sent over by Mason to his planta. by w. Mary, d. perhaps of Thomas Walford, wh. rem. thither from Charlestown, had Rebecca, wh. m. bef. 1679, Thomas Pomeroy ; Mary, wh. m. a Lucy ; Sarah, wh. m. a. 1684, Jacob Brown ; Martha, wh. m. John Lewis ; and next, a Rendall ; ano. d. m. John Rous ; but the dilig. collector of these details in Geneal. Reg. IX. 220, suggests that there were only five ds. and that one of the last two hs. had m. Rebecca, wid. of Pomeroy. His wid. m. William Walker.

BROOKS, or BROOKES, sometimes BROOKE, CALEB, Concord, s. of capt. Thomas, prob. b. in Eng. freem. 1654, rem. to Medford 1672, and d. 29 July 1696 ; m. 10 Apr. 1660, Susanna, d. of Thomas Atkinson, wh. had five ds. (Susanna, b. 27 Dec. 1661 ; Mary, 18 Nov. 1663, d. next yr. ; Mary, again ; Rebecca ; and Sarah) ; and d. 19 Jan. 1669 ; by sec. w. Hannah, sis. of the former w. had Ebenezer, b. 24 Feb. 1671, ancest. of John, Gov. of Mass. ; and Samuel, 1 Sept. 1672, ancest. of late Hon. Peter C. Shattuck, Hist. of Concord. He d. at Medford 29 July 1696 ; leav. large est. Mary m. Nathaniel Ball ; Sarah d. unm. or, as one story is, m. 18 Oct. 1705, Philemon Russell. Rebecca d. unm. His wid. d. 10 Mar. 1709. DANIEL, Concord, s. of Joshua of the same, m.

9 Aug. 1692, Ann Meriam, had Daniel, b. 5 June 1693, d. soon; Samuel, 5 May 1694; Hannah, 21 Feb. 1696; Job, 16 Apr. 1698; Mary, 2 Mar. 1700; John, 1 Feb. 1702; David, 6 May 1709; Timothy, 30 Aug. 1711; Daniel, 19 Apr. 1720; Josiah, 21 May 1722; and Ann, 20 Mar. 1725, unless, as I much susp. some of Bond's dates, p. 722, are wrong. He made his will 6 Jan. 1729, and d. 18 Oct. 1733. EBENEZER, Woburn, by w. Martha had Eunice, b. 18 Mar. 1688, d. at 11 yrs.; John, 22 Mar. 1690; Ebenezer, 8 Aug. 1691; Eleazer, 13 July 1694; Martha, 24 Mar. 1697; Eunice, 14 Feb. 1700; and Priscilla, 17 Feb. 1702. EBENEZER, Medford, s. of Caleb of the same, m. a. 1693, Abigail, d. of Dr. Thomas Boylston, had Caleb, b. 8 July 1694; Ebenezer, 23 Mar. 1698; Abigail; Thomas, 8 Apr. 1705; Samuel, 1709; beside Mary, Hannah, and Rebecca, whose dates are unkn. and he d. 11 Feb. 1742; and his wid. d. 26 May 1756. GERSHOM, Concord, br. of Caleb, freem. 1672, m. 12 Mar. 1667, Hannah, d. of Richard Eccles, had Mary, b. 6 May 1667; Hannah, 29 Mar. 1668; Joseph, 16 Sept. 1671; Tabitha, 31 Mar. 1674; Daniel, 14 Mar. 1678; and Eliz. 18 June 1680. He d. 1686; and his wid. d. 2 June 1716. GILBERT, Scituate, came in the Blessing from London, 1635, aged 14, liv. with William Vassall; after at Marshfield, by w. Eliz. wh. Deane says, was d. of Gov. Edward Winslow (wh. by some is disput.), beside Gilbert and John, presum. by D. to have been b. at Marshfield, had Eliz. b. 1645; Sarah, 1646; Mary, 1649; Rachel, 1650; Bathsheba, 1655; Rebecca, 1657; and Hannah, 1659; all bapt. at S. was at Rehoboth 1679–83, there m. Sarah, wid. of Samuel Carpenter. HENRY, Concord, freem. 14 Mar. 1639; had Joseph, b. 12 Apr. 1641. HENRY, Wallingford, m. 21 Dec. 1676, Hannah Blackley, had Thomas, b. 27 Mar. 1679; and he contin. at W. to 1713. He came, says tradit. from Cheshire, Eng. and may have been s. of John of New Haven, or perhaps his br. HENRY, Woburn, perhaps the same as him of Concord, d. 12 Apr. 1683, his w. Susanna hav. d. 15 Sept. 1681, but I find not the m. nor age. He m. 12 July 1682, Annis Jaquith. His will was of 18 July 1682. In it he names this w. and the ch. John, Timothy, wh. was of Billerica, Isaac, and Sarah, w. of John Mousall, wh. were then liv. ISAAC, Woburn, perhaps s. of the preced. freem. 1672, m. 10 Jan. 1666, Miriam Daniels, had Sarah, b. 14 May 1667, d. soon; Miriam, 29 May 1668, d. soon; Isaac, 13 Aug. 1669; Henry, 4 Oct. 1671; Miriam, again, 16 Dec. 1673; but no more is there on rec. and he d. 8 Sept. 1686. JOHN, Woburn, perhaps br. of the preced. freem. 1651, m. 1 Nov. 1649, Eunice d. of John Mousall, had John, b. 23 Nov. 1650, d. at 3 yrs.; Sarah, 21 Nov. 1652; Eunice, 10 Oct. 1655; and Joanna, 22 Mar. 1659; beside, after, John, again, 1 Mar. 1664; Ebenezer, 9 Dec. 1666; Deborah, 20

Mar. 1669; and Jabez, 17 July 1673; his w. Eunice d. 1 Jan. 1684.
He m. 25 Feb. 1684, Mary Richardson, and d. 1691. JOHN, New
Haven 1649, had three ch. there bef. 1656; perhaps more, and may
have been, after, of Wallingford, and there had Hannah, b. 9 Feb. 1664;
Ruth, 7 Feb. 1666; Sophia; and Eliz. 6 Dec. 1668, but perhaps these
were tw.; Mary, wh. may have been his d. m. at Wallingford, 12 Jan.
or July 1674, Matthew Ford. John and Henry were proprs. of New
Haven 1685. JOHN, Windsor, m. 25 May 1652, Susanna Hanmore,
had John, b. 16 May 1660, d. young; Samuel, 6 Jan. 1663; Eliz. 27
June 1664; Mary, 21 May 1665, d. young; Joanna, 2 Feb. 1669;
Mary, again, 25 Nov. 1670; Lydia, 7 Aug. 1672; and Susanna, 22 Sept.
1675. His w. d. 7 Nov. 1676. He rem. to Simsbury, there d. 3 Sept.
1682, leav. Samuel and five ds. JOHN, Woburn, s. prob. of John of the
same, m. 30 Jan. 1685, Mary Cranston, had Mary, b. 4 Dec. 1685;
John and Ebenezer, tw. 30 Dec. 1686, both d. in few days; Mary, again,
1 Apr. 1688; Sarah, 14 Aug. 1692; John, 28 Nov. 1694; Abigail, 19
Aug. 1697; Timothy, 14 Feb. 1700; Isaac, 1703; and Nathan, 1 Nov.
1706. JOHN, Charlestown, s. of Robert, d. 25 Dec. 1687, aged 31.
JOSEPH, Concord, youngest s. of Joshua, m. 26 June 1704, Rebecca
Blodget, had Mary, b. 1705; Abigail, 1707; Rebecca, 28 Aug. 1708;
Joseph, 16 Oct. 1710; Nathan, 1 Mar. 1712; Hannah, 16 Apr. 1714;
Amos, 20 Dec. 1716; Jonas, 18 Oct. 1718; Isaac, 17 Mar. 1720; and
James, 6 Aug. 1723; all, exc. Abigail, wh. d. young, liv. to be nam. in
the will of May 1746. He d. 17 Sept. 1759; and his wid. d. 25 Jan.
1768. JOSHUA, Concord, eldest s. of capt. Thomas, b. in Eng. freem.
1652, m. 17 Oct. 1653, Hannah, d. of capt. Hugh Mason of Watertown,
had Hannah; Noah, b. 1655; John, 1657; Grace, 10 Mar. 1661;
Daniel, 15 Nov. 1663, gr. gr.f. of late Hon. Eleazar of Lincoln; Thom-
as, 9 Sept. 1666, d. young; Esther, 4 July 1668; Job, 26 July 1675;
Hugh, 1 Jan. 1677; and Joseph, 1681. Hannah m. 15 Jan. 1678,
Benjamin Peirce; Esther m. 17 Aug. 1692, Benjamin Whittemore;
Grace m. 1686, Judah Potter; and Eliz. m. 1705, Ebenezer Meriam.
Shattuck. NATHANIEL, Scituate, eldest s. of William, m. 1678, Eliz. d.
of Richard Curtis, had William, Gilbert, and Nathaniel, of ea. of wh.
descend. are num. at S. NOAH, Concord, s. of Joshua, m. Dorothy
Wright of Sudbury, had Dorothy, b. 18 Oct. 1686; Joshua, 14 Oct.
1688; Ebenezer, 14 Feb. 1690; Samuel, 14 May 1694; Benjamin, 22
Apr. 1698; Mary, 25 Jan. 1700; Thomas, 18 May 1701; and Eliz. 27
Feb. 1704. He d. 1 Feb. 1738, aged 82; and his wid. d. 15 Mar. 1750,
aged 90, by gr.stones. RICHARD, Lynn, came in the Susan and Ellen,
1635, aged 24, rem. to Easthampton, L. I. where he was of the first
sett. 1650. RICHARD, Boston 1674, gunsmith. ROBERT, New London,

perhaps was the mercer of Maidstone, Kent, wh. came, 1635, in the Hercules, from Sandwich, with w. Ann, and seven ch. for, in 1650, to one of this name, with *es* final, ld. was gr. in that town, and descend. of the grantee are there. ROBERT, Plymouth, m. Eliz. d. of Gov. Edward Winslow, had John, bef. ment. b. a. 1657; and d. bef. 22 Sept. 1669, when his wid. m. George Curwin of Salem. ROBERT, Boston, adm. an inhab. 28 Nov. 1654, says the Boston rec. Vol. I. 113, as plain as is print. (tho. with erron. date of 31 Oct. preced.) in Drake's Hist. p. 336. Yet am I perfectly satisf. on large investiga. that BRECK is the true name; for Brooks is not found either in births, m. or deaths. See Breck. SAMUEL, Medford, youngest s. of Caleb, m. Sarah, d. of Dr. Thomas Boylston, had Samuel, b. 3 Sept. 1700 ; and Sarah, 17 Apr. 1702. He d. 3 July 1733, leav. good est. in lds. *THOMAS, Concord, freem. 7 Dec. 1636, when he was inhab. of Watertown, own. est. at Medford, and Watertown, perhaps as early as 1634; was capt. and rep. 1642, and six yrs. more, by w. Grace had s. Caleb, b. 1632, prob. in Eng.; Gershom ; and Joshua, bef. ment. ; and Mary, wh. m. Timothy Wheeler; wh. four surv. to make partit. of his est. one mo. after his d., perhaps Hannah, wh. m. Thomas Fox, 13 Dec. 1647, and d. without ch. bef. her f. His w. d. 12 May 1664; and he d. 21 May 1667. THOMAS, Kittery 1640. THOMAS, Haddam, among the first sett. may have come in the Susan and Ellen, 1635, aged 18, and been br. of Richard of Lynn ; he had a ho. at New London 1659, but had gone in 1661, with w. Lucy ; had m. Alice, d. of Jared Spencer, next yr. and had at H. Sarah, b. Dec. 1662; Thomas, June 1664 ; Mary, June 1666 ; and Alice, Dec. 1668 ; and d. 18 Oct. of that yr. His wid. m. 1673, Thomas Shaler. THOMAS, Portsmouth, R. I. a freem. 1655, by w. Hannah had Hannah, b. 6 July 1672 ; and Mary, 28 Jan. 1674, as the Friends' rec. at Newport shows. THOMAS, Scituate, s. of William, m. 1687, Hannah Bisby, had Thomas, b. 1688 ; and Joanna, 1695. With his s. the male line of this br. bec. extinct. THOMAS, Wallingford, eldest s. of Henry of the same, m. 25 Mar. 1702, Martha Hotchkiss, had, as in Geneal. Reg. V. 355, Stephen, b. 28 May 1702 ; Mary, 14 May 1704 ; Thomas, 14 Feb. 1706; Enos, 15 Feb. 1708; Cornelius, 10 Sept. 1711; Martha, 21 Feb. 1714; Mehitable, 23 Feb. 1716; Benjamin, 23 Apr. 1720; Henry, 2 Mar. 1723 ; and Thankful, 19 Dec. 1725. TIMOTHY, Woburn, prob. s. of Henry of the same, m. 2 Dec. 1659, Mary, d. of John Russell, had Timothy, b. 10 Nov. 1660, d. soon ; Timothy, again, 9 Oct. 1661; John, 16 Oct. 1662 ; beside a d. wh. m. a Mason of Swanzey; and perhaps rem. to Swanzey a. 1679. TIMOTHY, s. of the preced. m. Mehitable, wid. of Eldad Kingsley, but whether he liv. at Rehoboth, or elsewhere, had former w. or not, or any ch. is unkn. to me. One

TIMOTHY, was of Billerica 1679. WILLIAM, Scituate, came in the Blessing, 1635, aged 20, perhaps br. of Gilbert, was of Marshfield 1643, m. wid. Susanna Dunham of Plymouth, had Hannah, b. 1645; Nathaniel, 1646, bef. ment.; Mary, 1647; Sarah, 1650, m. Joseph Studley; Miriam, 1652, m. John Curtis; Deborah, 1654, m. Robert Stetson, jr.; Thomas, 1657, bef. ment.; and Joanna, 1659, wh. m. 13 Sept. 1687, John Bisby of Duxbury. Deane. WILLIAM, Springfield, m. 1654, Mary, d. of Henry Burt, had 8 s. and 8 ds. 1655–79. The s. were William, John, Ebenezer, Nathaniel, Joseph, Benjamin, Deliverance, and Jonathan, of wh. the two first nam. were k. by the Ind. 27 Oct. 1675, at Westfield. He rem. to Deerfield, there d. 1688, and his wid. d. next yr. WILLIAM, Milford, among early sett. m. Sarah, wid. of William Wheeler, d. 1684. I have includ. herein all whose names are giv. as Brook, Brooks, Brooke, or Brookes, bec. it is impossib. to discrim. in the capricious spell. Thirteen in the form above used had, in 1834, at Harv. and six at the other N. E. coll. been gr.

BROOMAN, JOSEPH, Rehoboth, m. 29 Sept. 1681, Sarah, wid. of John Savage of R. says Col. Rec.

BROOME, GEORGE, Boston, d. Feb. 1662. A wid. Hannah Broome m. the last of Jan. 1662, Thomas Ashley. Perhaps there is error of a yr. in rec. ROGER, came in the Truelove, 1635, aged 17.

BROUGH, or BRUFF, EDWARD, Marshfield 1643. WILLIAM, Boston 1654.

BROUGHTON, ‖ GEORGE, Dover or Kittery 1680, perhaps s. of Thomas, was certain. in Mass. long bef. being of ar. co. 1667, and ten yrs. earlier at Berwick; m. prob. Abigail, d. of Rev. John Reyner; may have been the one ment. by Hubbard, in Ind. Wars, as of Salmon Falls riv. 1675, but kn. to be, in 1682, a capt. at K. His wid. m. 30 Mar. 1696, and d. 31 Dec. 1716. JOHN, Northampton, among the earliest sett. m. Hannah, eldest d. of Thomas Bascom, had John, wh. rem. to Conn.; Hannah, b. 1656; Sarah, 1658; and Thomas, 1661. He d. 16 Mar. 1662, and his wid. m. William Janes. JOHN, Northampton, s. of the preced. m. 1678, Eliz. d. of the first Matthew Woodruff, and rem. to Conn. THOMAS, Watertown, 1643, came from Gravesend, below London, 1635, to Virginia, in the America; by w. Mary, d. of Nathaniel Briscoe, had a ch. b. 3 Mar. 1644, d. in a wk.; Eliz. 15 Jan. 1646; rem. to Boston 1650, had Mary, 5 July 1651; Thomas, 26 May 1653, d. young; rem. to Boston 1650, had Mary, 5 July 1651; Thomas, 26 May 1653, d. young; Nathaniel, 5 Dec. 1654; Thomas, again, 23 Dec. 1656; Hannah, 28 Dec. 1658; Sarah, 9 June 1660; and Patience, 14 Apr. 1663; was a merch. of gr. business, own. the mills at Salmon Falls perhaps, and d. 12 Nov. 1700, aged 84. THOMAS, Boston, s. of the preced. perhaps m. Sarah, d. of Edward Rawson, and d. 4 Dec. 1702. Thomas, Northampton, s. of John, sett. at Deerfield, was k. by the Ind. with w. and three ch. in June 1693.

BROWN, ABRAHAM, Watertown, prob. s. of Thomas of Hawkedon, Co. Suff'k. near Bury St. Edmunds, freem. 6 Mar. 1632, by w. Lydia had Lydia, b. 22 Mar. 1633; Jonathan, 15 Oct. 1635; Hannah, 1 Mar. 1639, d. soon; and Abraham, 6 Mar. 1640; beside Sarah, and Mary, perhaps brot. from Eng.; was selectman many yrs. and surveyor. The time of his d. was 1650. His wid. m. 27 Nov. 1659, Andrew Hodges of Ipswich, but after his d. in Dec. 1665, she came again to Watertown, and d. 27 Sept. 1686. Sarah m. 16 Dec. 1643, George Parkhurst; Mary m. 10 Apr. 1650, John Lewis of Charlestown, as sec. w. and, next, a Cutler; and Lydia m. William Lakin. ABRAHAM, Boston, merch. arr. first time 20 June 1650, m. 19 Aug. 1653, Jane Skipper, had Mary, b. 19 Dec. 1654; went home 1654, next yr. was tak. by a Barbary pirate, but soon ransom. and the foll. yr. came again to B. had Jane, 9 Aug. 1657; freem. 1664, m. 1 May 1660, Rebecca, d. of Hezekiah Usher, had Hezekiah, b. 22 Aug. 1661; Rebecca, 26 Aug. 1663; and Eliz. 17 Nov. 1664, wh. m. Peter Butler, jr. ABRAHAM, Watertown, s. of Abraham of the same, m. 5 Feb. 1663, Mary, d. of Edward Dix, had Lydia, b. 11 Nov. 1663, wh. m. 30 Dec. 1688, George Woodward; and Abraham, 1665, d. at 13 yrs. He d. 1667, and his wid. m. next yr. Samuel Rice of Sudbury, and d. 18 June 1678. ABRAHAM, Salisbury, s. of the first Henry of the same, m. 15 June 1675, Eliz. Shepherd, had s. b. 10 Jan. 1676, d. in a wk.; Sarah, 25 Jan. 1677; Ann, 19 Nov. 1679; Eliz. 29 Mar. 1682; Bethia, July 1684; Hannah, 7 Nov. 1686; Abraham, 16 Mar. 1691; and Samuel, 16 Nov. 1694; and d. 26 Mar. 1733. ALEXANDER, Kennebeck 1674. ANDREW, Scarborough 1658, was constable in 1670, and had, in 1663, five s. of wh. Southgate gives names of four, Andrew, John, Joseph, and Charles. ARTHUR, Saco 1636. BENJAMIN, Hampton, s. of John of the same, m. Sarah, d. of William Brown of Salisbury, had William, b. 5 June 1680; Sarah, 11 Sept. 1681, d. young; Benjamin, 20 Dec. 1683; Eliz. 16 July 1686; John, 18 Mar. or May 1688; Jacob, 1 Mar. 1691; Stephen, 17 July 1693; Mary, 1696; Thomas, 21 May 1699; and Jeremiah, 20 Nov. 1701. His w. d. a. 1730; he, a. 1736, very old. ‡ * BENJAMIN, Salem, s. of first Hon. William, m. it is said, Mary, d. of Rev. John Hicks, a nonconform. min. in Eng. wh. d. 26 Aug. 1703, had only two ds. Sarah, and Mary. He was rep. of his nat. town 1693 and 9, of the Exec. counc. 1702–5, a liberal benefact. of Harv. Coll. d. 7 Dec. 1708. BENONI, Hartford, youngest s. of Nathaniel of the same, d. 1688, prob. unm. holding some office. BOAZ, Concord, s. of Thomas, m.

8 Nov. 1664, Mary Winship, had Boaz, b. 31 July 1665 ; Thomas, 12 May 1667 ; Mary, 31 Oct. 1670 ; Edward, 20 Mar. 1672 ; rem. to Stow, was freem. 1673. CHAD, Providence, came first to Boston, in July 1638, in the Martin, as bef. dep.-gov. Dudley, he swore, in support of a nuncup. will of a fellow-passeng. dying on the ocean ; was sett. at the Bapt. ch. 1642 after Roger Williams. It has been thot. by some, that he was earlier on our side of the water, and that imperfect rec. proves it, on p. 14 of the Vol. I. of Col. Rec. of R. I. as to his incorp. in town fellowsh. with others at Providence, wh. bears date 20 Aug. without a yr. Now the supplying of the numerals for the yr. can admit those wh. the transcriber used, 1637, by no means ; for that day was Sunday, when no civil compact could have been enter. into, and bef. that day in the former yr. the place was kn. as Moshasuck, prob. the *sec.* use of the designat. of the mod. city being in the foll. mo. at the bapt. of the s. of Roger Williams, Providence, late in Sept. 1638. Earlier than Aug. 1638 his name, I suppose, will not be found. He brot. w. Eliz. and s. John, aged a. 8 yrs. prob. other ch. for we kn. not the b. of any of his five s. The other four were James, Jeremiah, Judah, alias Chad, and Daniel. No connex. is trac. betw. Chad and Henry, of the oldest proprs. His gr.ch. James was min. of the same ch. This is the progenit. of the fam. so much disting. as the patrons of Brown Univ. at P. CHARLES, Rowley 1648. CORNELIUS, Reading, s. of Nicholas of the same, m. 6 Mar. 1665, Sarah Lamson, had Nicholas, b. 7 Apr. 1666, d. soon ; Cornelius, 3 June 1667 ; Sarah, 23 Dec. 1668 ; John, 8 Aug. 1671 ; Abigail, 5 Apr. 1674, d. soon ; Samuel, 13 Sept. 1675 ; Mary, 1 Jan. 1679 ; and Hannah, 28 Aug. 1680. CHRISTIAN, Salisbury, one of the first sett. 1640, a wid. brot. prob. three s. and d. 28 Dec. 1641. Her s. were Henry, George, and William. DANIEL, Providence 1646, m. 25 Dec. 1669, Alice He- renden, prob. d. of Benjamin, had Judah ; Sarah, b. 10 Oct. 1677 ; Jeremiah ; and perhaps more ; and d. bef. 10 Nov. 1710. EBENEZER, New Haven, s. of Francis, m. 28 Mar. 1667, Hannah, d. of John Vincent of the same, had Hannah, b. 1 Feb. 1668 ; s. without name, 4 Oct. 1669 ; Ebenezer, 12 Nov. 1670 ; Rebecca, 20 Apr. 1672 ; Mary, 6 Aug. 1674 ; Eliz. 13 May 1679 ; Eunice, 26 Oct. 1681 ; and James, 22 Feb. 1684 ; perhaps more. *EDMUND,* first min. of Sudbury, came over 1637, freem. 13 May 1640, ord. in Aug. foll. d. 22 June 1677, had w. wh. had been wid. of John Lovering, as Barry says, but no ch. EDMUND, Dorchester, s. of deac. William of Sudbury, freem. 1650, by w. Eliz. had John, bapt. 22 Aug. 1652 ; Eliz. b. 1658 ; and Samuel, 1661 ; rem. to Boston, and was a shopkeeper 1694, there, when his sec. or third w. was Eliz. wid. of Hopestill Foster, and d. soon after. He may be the man, wh. m. 14 Feb. 1654, Eliz. Okley, or Oakley, if we suppose the date of bapt. of

first ch. too early by 4 yrs. or this not to be the first w. She had Mary,
15 Dec. 1656; John, 9 Oct. 1660; and, perhaps, Elisha; for ED-
MUND, Boston, by w. Eliz. had Mary, 15 Dec. 1656. EDWARD, Boston,
a very early propr. perhaps came in the employm. of William Colbron,
tho. at his adm. of the ch. in June 1634 it is writ. Edmund, freem. 6
May 1635, may have gone to Newport 1639. EDWARD, Salem 1638,
d. a. 1659. EDWARD, Ipswich, freem. 2 June 1641, had w. Faith, and
s. Thomas, wh. d. bef. his f.; in his will of 9 Feb. 1660 ment. s. Joseph,
and John, and a d. not nam. ELEAZER, New Haven, s. of Francis, sw.
fidel. in 1657, m. Sarah, d. of Thomas Bulkley, had Eleazer, b. 6 Jan.
1663; Gershom, 9 Oct. 1665; and Daniel, 16 Jan. 1668. ELEAZER,
Chelmsford, freem. 1674, was, perhaps, s. of Thomas of Concord.
EPHRAIM, Salisbury, s. of William, by w. Sarah had Ephraim, b. 3 Sept.
1680; William, 25 Mar. 1684; Sarah, 5 Mar. 1687; Mary, 22 Jan.
1689; Abner, 28 Feb. 1691; and Jacob, 2 June 1693; and the f. d.
five days after. His wid. m. Apr. 1703, Samuel Carter; and next, 5
Oct. 1719, Benjamin Eastman. FRANCIS, New Haven 1639, d. 1668;
by w. Mary had John, bapt. 7 Apr. 1640; Eleazer, 16 Oct. 1642, bef.
ment.; Samuel, 7 Aug. 1645; Ebenezer, 21 June 1646; Ebenezer,
again, 4 July 1647; and Lydia. He d. 1668, and his will of 13 Apr.
in that yr. names w. Mary, four s. and d. Lydia. * FRANCIS, Stamford
1660, constable 1663, rep. 1665, 7, and 9. He had been a serv. of Henry
Wolcott of Windsor, and bot. out the residue of his term in 1649, and
was a small trader in 1651; in Farmington, bot. and sold lds. 1656; at
S. m. Martha, wid. of John Chapman, had s. Joseph, and nothing more
is kn. of him but that in 1683 he gave his s. ld. and does not appear
among proprs. of 1687. FRANCIS, Newbury, s. of Francis, b. in Eng.
perhaps neph. of Thomas, d. 1691, aged 59, hav. m. prob. sec. w. 31
Dec. 1679. Coffin, 296. FRANCIS, Newbury, s. of Thomas, b. in Eng.
m. 21 Nov. 1653, Mary Johnson had Eliz. b. 17 Oct. 1654; Mary, 15
Apr. 1657, m. 15 Dec. 1675, Nathan Parker; Hannah, 1659, d. soon;
Sarah, 10 May 1663; John, 13 May 1665; Thomas, 1 July 1667, d.
aged 22; Joseph, 28 Sept. 1670; Francis, 17 Mar. 1674; and his w. d.
4 Apr. 1679. He had by sec. w. Benjamin, 22 Apr. 1681. GEORGE,
Newbury 1635, a carpenter, br. of Richard, one of the first sett. had
come in the Mary and John 1634, freem. 13 May 1640, d. 1 Apr. 1642.
* GEORGE, Haverhill, prob. s. of Christian, m. 25 June 1645, Ann
Eaton, d. of John of Salisbury; rep. 1672, 5, 80, and 92. He made
his will 26 June 1699. His w. d. 16 Dec. 1683, and 17 Mar. foll.
he m. wid. Hannah Hazen; d. 31 Oct. 1699. He had no ch. but gave
est. to Richard H. s. of his w. GEORGE, Stonington 1680, may be the
same, whose will, of 14 Sept. 1736, names w. Charity, eldest s. George,

other s. Peter, John, and William, besides eldest d. Eliz. Stanton, d.
Sarah Champlin, w. of Joseph C. and d. Ruth B. HENRY, Boston,
an early propr. purchas. also, in 1648; prob. went home, was of London
1668. HENRY, Salisbury, b. 1615, came with his mo.; an orig. propr.
of course in 1639, was br. of George of Haverhill, by w. Abigail had
Nathaniel, b. 30 June 1642; Abigail, 23 Feb. 1644; Jonathan, 25 Nov.
1646, prob. d. young; Philip, Dec. 1648; Abraham, 1 Jan. 1650;
Sarah, 6 Dec. 1654; and Henry, 8 Feb. 1659. He was a shoemaker,
d. 6 Aug. 1701; and his wid. d. 23 Aug. 1702. Abigail m. 1 June
1664, Samuel French; and Sarah m. 12 June 1673, Andrew Greeley.
HENRY, Salisbury, youngest ch. of the preced. m. 17 May 1682, Hannah Putnam, had John, b. 15 Apr. 1683; Rebecca, 1 Oct. 1684; Abraham, 4 July 1686; Hannah, 20 Mar. 1689, d. young; Eliezer, 18 Feb.
1691; Henry, 17 June 1693; Benjamin, 25 June 1695; Mehitable, 20
Sept. 1698; Nathaniel, 21 Dec. 1700; Joseph, bapt. 18 Sept. 1703;
and Hannah, 9 June 1705; rem. to Salem, where some of the ch. were
b. and he d. 25 Apr. 1708. His wid. in will of 9 May 1730, speaks of
six s. then liv. and ds. Rebecca and Hannah. HENRY, Providence
1652, sw. alleg. in June 1668, had Richard, Joseph, and prob. Henry
and other ch. In his will of 27 Sept. 1690 ment. w. Hannah. HENRY,
Providence, call. jr. when he took o. of alleg. in May 1682, may have
been s. of the preced. HOPESTILL, Sudbury, s. of deac. William, m.
1686, Abigail Haynes, and for sec. w. had Dorothy, wid. of Rev. and
unhappy Samuel Paris, and d. 1729. HUGH, Salem 1628, com. with
Endicott, in opin. of Mr. Felt, sent to relief of the Ind. at Ipswich 1631,
perhaps rem. to Boston. HUGH, Boston (in opin. of Farmer, the same
as the preced. but, in mine, more prob. was his s.), by w. Sarah had Job,
b. 29 Mar. 1651; Hugh, wh. d. 16 July 1652; and Sarah, 16 Aug.
1653, wh. d. 2 Jan. foll. and the improb. rec. in Geneal. Reg. X. 218,
tells, that ano. Sarah d. 3 Apr. 1654. ICHABOD, Cambridge, s. of
Thomas of the same, by w. Martha had John, b. 1 Nov. 1696, H. C.
1714, the min. of Haverhill; Martha, 16 June 1699; Priscilla, 14 Dec.
1702; Sarah, 26 Sept. 1706; and his w. d. 1 Sept. 1708. He m. 13
June 1709, Margaret Odlin, perhaps youngest d. of Elisha of Boston,
had Abigail, b. 8 May 1710, and d. 1728, the five ch. and the mo. of the
youngest all surv. ISAAC, Newbury, s. of Thomas of the same, m. 22
Aug. 1661, Rebecca, perhaps d. of John Bayley, jr. had Ruth, b. 26
May 1662; Thomas, 15 Sept. 1664; Rebecca, 15 Mar. 1667; and he d.
13 May 1674. * JABEZ, Sudbury 1667, prob. s. of Thomas of Concord,
freem. 1680; by w. Hannah had Mary, b. 26 Nov. 1672; and Sarah,
20 May 1680; was of Stow, rep. under the new chart. 1692. JACOB,
Billerica, one of the proprs. 1659, m. 16 Oct. 1661, Mary Tapley.

JACOB, Hampton, s. of John of the same, m. Sarah, d. of William Brookin of Portsmouth, had John; Samuel, b. 4 Nov. 1686; Abraham, Jan. 1689; Joshua, 1 Apr. 1691; Sarah, 1693; Jacob, 22 Dec. 1695; Abigail, 3 Mar. 1698; Jonathan, 24 Feb. 1700; and Jeremiah, bapt. with the eight preced. 28 June 1702; and he d. 13 Feb. 1740, aged, it is said, 87. ‖ JAMES, Boston 1630, being No. 61 in the ch. list, freem. 4 Mar. 1634, by w. Grace had James, b. 30 Aug. bapt. 7 Sept. 1645, ar. co. 1643; d. 1651, his will of 9 May, pro. 7 Aug. is abstr. in Geneal. Reg. VII. 335. It gave ho. and ld. to the ch. if his s. d. bef. 21 yrs. of age, and provid. for w. wh. was extrix. JAMES, Charlestown 1633, adm. of the ch. 10 Mar. 1634, freem. 25 May 1636, had w. Eliz. and ch. John, bapt. 1 Mar. 1639; and Mary, 3 Mar. 1640. JAMES, Newbury, came with w. 1634, says Coffin, from Southampton, was one of the first sett. 1635; freem. 17 May 1637, a selectman 1638; preach. at Portsmouth, but came back to N. 1656, or earlier. Ano. ‖ JAMES, Charlestown, by w. Judith had John, b. 4 Jan. 1638; James, 20 Feb. 1643, wh. d. young; James, again, 19 Aug. 1647; and Nathaniel, 21 Nov. 1648, ar. co. 1639, may be the dangerous man, disarm. as a supporter of Wheelwright 1637. Frothingham, 82. JAMES, Newbury, s. of Joseph, a youth of 17, came in the James 1635, from Southampton, arr. at Boston 3 June 1635. But the difficulty of discrim. betw. the many of this name, even by aid of ws. and ch. is insurmount. He, by w. Sarah, d. of capt. John Cutting, had Samuel, b. 14 Jan. 1657; Hannah, bapt. 12 Sept. 1658; and Abraham, 14 Oct. 1660; had, also, Mary, b. 25 May 1663; Abigail, 24 Oct. 1665; and Martha, 22 Dec. 1667. He was a glazier, rem. to Salem, there d. 1676. His will of 29 Jan. 1674, names w. Sarah, and ch. John, James, Samuel, Abraham, Sarah, wh. was m.; Ann, or Hannah, Mary, Abigail, and Martha. JAMES, Taunton 1643, s. of John, the Assist. b. in Eng. we may be sure, went with his f. to Swanzey, chos. 1665 an Assist. may well be presum. the preacher, put by Mather, in his *third* classis, at S. unless more than usual confidence is felt in his authority, wh. it is believ. inquiry will not justify, for no durat. in office is ment. nor is any reason kn. for giv. him place in that rather than the sec. classis. He m. Lydia, d. of John Howland, and d. 29 Oct. 1710, aged 87, leav. James, wh. d. 1725, at Barrington; Jabez; and d. Dorothy Kent. Baylies, IV. 18. JAMES, Salem, s. of Elder John, m. 5 Sept. 1664, Hannah, d. of Henry Bartholomew, had James, b. 3 Feb. 1666, d. young; Bartholomew, 31 Mar. 1669; Eliz. 26 Jan. 1671; Hannah, 9 Mar. 1673; and James, again, 23 May 1675. On 12 Nov. of the last yr. he was found d. in Cecil Co. Maryland, where he was on a trad. voyage, k. by a negro. JAMES, Salem 1678, s. of James, the glazier, foll. the trade of his f. m. 16 Jan. 1670, Hannah Huse, at Charlestown, there had James, b. 3 Feb.

1671; Samuel, 3 Dec. 1672; and at Ipswich, Hannah, 13 Nov. 1676, d. young; and at S. Sarah, 10 Aug. 1678; and rem. to Newbury, there had Benjamin, 21 Mar. 1681; Abraham, 17 Mar. 1683, d. in few mos.; Joseph, 19 May 1685; and Hannah, 16 Nov. 1687. He d. 27 Feb. 1708, and his wid. d. 18 Nov. 1713. JAMES, Hatfield 1678, m. 7 Jan. 1674, Remembrance Brook, had Mary, b. 1677; Abigail, 8 Sept. 1678; and Thankful, 1 June 1682; rem. to Deerfield, and had Sarah, 1683; James, 1685; Mindwell, 1686; Hannah, 1688; Mercy, 1690; Eliz. 1693, d. at 5 yrs.; and John, 1695. He rem. after, to Colchester; and his d. Abigail, prob. was that capt. on the fatal day of 29 Feb. 1704, carr. to Canada, but ret. safe. JAMES, Branford 1679, a landholder, may have rem. and been of Norwalk 1687, had Isaac, b. 1 Mar. 1690; and either bef. or aft. James, wh. prob. is the man that m. 1714, Joanna Whitehead. JAMES, Rehoboth, s. of James of the same, by w. Margaret had Margaret, b. 28 June 1682; d. 15 Apr. 1718, in his 60th yr. His wid. d. 5 May 1741, aged 84. JOB, Boston 1672, suppos. to be d. when inv. was tak. by William Brown, 2 Jan. 1675, was, per- haps, s. of Hugh. JOHN, Pemaquid 1625. ‡ JOHN, Salem 1629, a lawyer from London, one of the purch. of the patent from Sir Henry Roswell, engag. (being one of the Assist. of the Mass. Co. and sw. a yr. and a half bef. Endicot took the requisite o.) in Mar. of that yr. to emb. with Samuel his br. in the fleet with Higginson; came in May, reach. S. in June, and soon after, they wish. to foll. the Episc. form of service, caus. such a schism, that Endicot sent them home in the returning sh. and in Sept. or Oct. they were again at London, and came not to our country any more. See the candid views of Eliot, Eccl. Hist. of Mass. in 1 Mass. Hist. Coll. IX. 3 and 4. That JOHN, whose d. 28 Feb. 1687, is ment. in early rec. of New Hampsh. "aged 98 yrs." may possib. have gain. *such* reputa. by his f. hav. done some brave act against the Spanish enemy even later than the Armada yr. to wh. wild tradit. refer. the b. of his s. JOHN, Watertown 1632, arr. 16 Sept. at Boston, from London, in the Lion; freem. 3 Sept. 1634, by w. Dorothy had Hannah, b. 10 Sept. 1634; and Mary, 24 Mar. 1637; and he was bur. 20 June of that yr. aged 36. By prob. geneal. he was s. of John of Hawkedon, Co. Suff'k. in that ch. bapt. 11 Oct. 1601, and so neph. of Abraham and Richard. ‡ JOHN, Plymouth, had acquaint. with the Pilgr. at Leyden bef. 1620, but his yr. of com. is unkn. liv. in 1636 at Duxbury; in 1643 at Taun- ton; Assist. for 17 yrs. from 1636, and serv. as Commissnr. of the Unit. Col. from 1644 for 12 yrs. had James, above ment.; and Mary, wh. m. 6 July 1636, Thomas Willet; perhaps more, certain. John, and d. at Swanzey, near Rehoboth, where he had large est. 10 Apr. 1662. His will, made three days bef. provides for the five ch. that his s. John left to his care, and names s. James, and w. Dorothy excors. also names d. Mary Willet, and gr.d. Martha, w. of John Saffin, d. of Willet. His wid. Dorothy d. at Swanzey, 27 Jan. 1674, aged 90. See Davis, in Morton's Mem. 295–7. JOHN, Salem 1637, freem. 2 May 1638, rul. elder of the ch. had John, bapt. Sept. 1638 ; and James, June 1640 ; d. 1685. JOHN, Hampton 1639, d. 28 Feb. 1687, a. 98 yrs. as is said. Much more prob. is the age set against his name, 40, on his embark. 17 Apr. 1635, at the London custom ho. especially if he be that baker, whose fellow-passeng. were two serv. James Walker, aged 15, and Sarah Walker, 17, the latter of wh. in 1640, bec. his w. as descend. suppose. By what I think the wrong statement, he was b. 1589, and this maiden was b. 1618. Beside the number and dates of his ch. disprove or make highly improb. the great age: Sarah ; John, b. 1644 ; Eliz. ; Benjamin ; Jacob, 1653 ; Mary, 13 Sept. 1655 ; Thomas, 14 July 1657 ; and Stephen, 1659, wh. was k. by the Ind. at Scarborough 29 June 1677. JOHN, Maine 1641, s. of Richard of Barton Regis. Co. Gloucester, m. Margaret, d. of Francis Hayward of the City of Bristol, as he told Robert Allen of Sheepscot, for R. A. so swore on 21 Feb. 1659 at Bristol, Eng. (as there rec.) that he kn. for 17 yrs. J. B. of Newharbor, a mason, and that he was in good health in N. E. June preced. JOHN, Rehoboth, or Swanzey, s. of John of the same, b. prob. in Eng. m. a d. of William Buckland, had John, the eldest, Joseph, Nathaniel, Lydia, and Hannah, all of wh. in his will of 31 Mar. 1662, of wh. he made John, his f. the excor. he gave to his care, and d. soon. Hannah m. 7 Jan. 1676, her cousin Hezekiah Willet. JOHN, Ipswich 1641, may have come in the Elizabeth, 1635, aged 40, from London, or have been the tailor from Badstow, in Essex, near Chelmsford, in the Defence, from London, 1635, aged 27. But whichever sh. he came in, he had w. Sarah, and by her the ch. Sarah ; John ; Benjamin ; and Eliz. ; prob. b. there ; and at Hampton had Jacob, b. 1653 ; Mary, 13 Sept. 1655 ; Thomas, 14 July 1657 ; and Stephen, 1659, k. by the Ind. 29 June 1677 at Scarborough. Sarah m. 13 Mar. 1661, John Poor ; and Eliz. m. 23 Dec. 1669, Isaac Marston. JOHN, Taunton 1643, s. of Hon. John, may be the John of Providence 1646, and after. JOHN, Milford 1648, had John ; Mary ; and Esther ; all bapt. 16 Dec. 1649 ; Joseph, 1652 ; Mary, 1653 ; John, again, b. 12 July 1655 ; Hannah, bapt. not 3, as the perpetual blunders of Davenport's ch. has it, but 2 May 1658 at New Haven ; and Phebe, 1660. His w. was Mary, and he prob. rem. to Newark, N. J. JOHN, New Haven, prob. s. of Francis of the same, m. 1 Jan. 1661, Mary, d. of John Walker of the same, had Mary, b. 2 May 1664 ; John, 9 Jan. 1667 ; Hannah, 7 Aug. 1669 ; and Grace, 9 Jan. 1673. She petitn. for divorce, and obt. it Oct. 1674. JOHN, Newport, a freem. 1655. JOHN, Cambridge, call. a Scotchman, m. 24 Apr. 1655, Esther, d. of Thomas Makepeace, and in

her f.'s will, eleven yrs. after, is call. of Marlborough. He had Joseph,
b. 8 Feb. 1656, k. casual. at 15 yrs.; Eliz. 26 Mar. 1657; Sarah, 18
July 1661; Mary, 19 Dec. 1662; all at C. and at M. had John, 27 Nov.
1664; Esther, 1667, d. soon; Thomas, 1669; Daniel, 1671; Deborah,
1673; Abigail, 9 Mar. 1675; and Joseph, 1677; next yr. he rem. to
Falmouth, and prob. at the sec. destruct. of that town was driv. away,
and came to Watertown, there dates his will 20 Nov. 1697, in wh. w.
Esther, s. John, Thomas, Daniel, and Joseph, d. Deborah, w. of Jeremiah Meacham, and s.-in-law John Gustin, wh. had m. 10 Jan. 1678,
Eliz.; John Adams, Thomas Darley, or Darby, and John Hartshorn, are
ment. JOHN, Providence, wh. sw. alleg. in May 1666, may be the same
as bef. ment. but ano. John of P. sw. alleg. in May 1682. JOHN, Salem,
s. of Elder John, m. 2 June 1658, Hannah, d. of Rev. Peter Hobart of
Hingham, had John, b. 4 Apr. 1659, d. next mo.; John, again, 21 Feb.
1662; Samuel, 14 Mar. 1663, d. at 9 mos.; Peter, 1 Mar. 1664, d.
soon; and Abiel, 21 Mar. 1673. * JOHN, Reading, m. 12 or 18 Oct.
1659, Eliz. d. of John Osgood of Andover, had Eliz. b. 5 Oct. 1660, d.
soon; Eliz. again, 22 Dec. 1661; Sarah, 3 Aug. 1664, d. young; Sarah,
again, 19 Nov. 1667, d. young; Mary, 30 May 1671, d. at 2 yrs.; and
his w. d. 31 July 1673. He was capt. freem. 1679, rep. 1679, 80, 2, and 3;
d. 1717, aged 81. JOHN, Newbury, m. 20 Feb. 1660, Mary Woodman,
had Judith, b. 5 Dec. 1660; and Mary, 8 Mar. 1662. He was s. of
James of Charlestown. JOHN, Reading, eldest s. of Nicholas, m. Ann,
d. of Rev. John Fiske, wh. d. 30 May 1681, had Ann, b. 1678; and he
m. 1682, sec. w. Eliz. wid. of Rev. Joseph Emerson of Mendon, and she
d. 4 Sept. 1693, aged 55. He m. third w. Rebecca, wid. of lieut. Samuel Sprague of Malden, wh. surv. him, and d. 8 July 1710, aged 76.
He, instead of that former John of R. may have been the rep. or capt.
or both. JOHN, Providence, s. of Chad, m. Mary, d. of Obadiah Holmes,
the sufferer by the Mass. persecut. had John, b. 18 Mar. 1662; James,
1666; Obadiah, Martha, and Deborah. JOHN, Hampton, s. of John the
first of the same, had a farm giv. 1666 by his f. at the Falls, and so may
be suppos. to have m. bef. the Ind. war of Philip, in wh. he serv. longer
time than any other man of his town; but no w. or ch. is kn. and he d.
29 Aug. 1683. * JOHN, Salem, m. 27 Jan. but by ano. acco. 30 June
1669, Hannah, d. of Francis Collins, had Priscilla, b. 1 June 1669;
Margaret, 23 Apr. 1671; Joseph, 11 Sept. 1673; William, 1 Dec.
1677; Hannah, 22 July 1678; and Mary, 4 Jan. 1680; but some
confus. evid. appears in rec. of dates of one or two. He was, perhaps, rep. for Marblehead, under the new chart. 1692, and for Salem
1707, 9, and 13; may have d. 14 Apr. 1719. JOHN, a passeng.
emb. in Eng. 16 May 1679 on the Prudence for Boston, may have
never arr. or soon went home, or sat down in some other town, or

(wh. is the least likely), he might have gone home to purchase goods in Eng. for trade here. JOHN, Duxbury, by w. Ann had Ann, b. 19 Sept. 1673; and John, 1675; was a capt. JOHN, Swanzey or Rehoboth, a capt. had John, b. 28 Apr. 1675. JOHN, Newbury, s. of *sec.* Newbury Francis, m. 20 Aug. 1683, Ruth, d. of Abel Huse, had John, b. 27 Oct. 1683; and Isaac, 4 Feb. 1685; and perhaps more. He was, I suppose, the man whose ho. was assail. by the Ind. on 7 Oct. 1695, and nine persons carr. into captiv. but all by fresh pursuit were retak. tho. some d. of wounds. See Coffin, 161, 2, and strange incidents of the case in Niles, 3 Mass. Hist. Coll. VI. 238. JOHN, York 1680. JOHN, Billerica, m. 22 Apr. 1682, Eliz. d. of George Polley, had John, b. 27 Mar. 1683, d. next day; John, again, 22 Jan. 1684; Eliz. 6 July 1685, d. soon; Eliz. again, 10 Feb. 1687; and Hannah, 27 Apr. 1689. JOHN, Middletown, prob. s. of Nathaniel of the same, m. 1 Apr. 1685, Ann Porter, had Thomas, b. 1686; Hannah, 1688; John, 1691; Mary, 1693; and Abigail, 1701. JOHN, Roxbury, by w. Eliz. had Edmund, b. 3 Jan. 1686, and Edmund, again, 16 Jan. 1687; is, perhaps, the one wh. d. at Dorchester, 14 May 1725. JOHN, Stonington, m. Oct. 1692, Eliz. d. of Ephraim Miner, had John, b. July 1693, d. next yr.; Jonathan, 15 Mar. 1695; Eliz. Mar. 1697; Hepzibah, Sept. 1699; John, again, Dec. 1701; Ichabod, 12 Mar. 1704; Prudence, 28 Apr. 1707; Jedediah, 28 Apr. 1709; Mehitable, Aug. 1712; and Mary, Aug. 1716. JONATHAN, Reading, a man of substance, whose d. Eliz. m. 30 Sept. 1663, Hananiah Parker. JONATHAN, Watertown, s. of the first Abraham, m. 11 Feb. 1662, Mary, d. of William Shattuck, had Mary, b. 6 Oct. foll.; Eliz. 19 Sept. 1664; Jonathan, 25 Oct. 1666, d. young; Patience, 6 Mar. 1669; Abraham, 26 Aug. 1671; Samuel, 21 Oct. 1674; Lydia, 31 Mar. 1677; Ebenezer, 10 Sept. 1679; Benjamin, 27 Feb. 1682; and William, 3 Sept. 1684; and d. 1691. His wid. d. 23 Oct. 1732, not quite so old as her gr.stone at Waltham says. JONATHAN, Salem, m. 28 June 1664, Abigail Burrill. JONATHAN, Windsor, s. of Peter of the same, m. 1696, Mindwell Loomis, had Mindwell, b. 1699. JOSEPH, Concord, made his will 26 Sept. 1671, wh. was witness. by Rev. Edward Bulkley, but all else is unkn. JOSEPH, Charlestown, s. of Hon. William of Salem, freem. 1673, was a preach. but not ord. tho. unanim. invit. to succeed Shepard 1678, a fellow of the Corp. involv. in the matter of Presid. Hoar; d. 9 May of that yr.; his w. Mehitable, d. of Gov. William Brenton, hav. d. 14 Sept. 1676. JOSEPH, Reading, s. of Nicholas of the same, m. 26 May 1674, Eliz. d. of Thomas Bancroft of the same, had Eliz. b. 15 Jan. 1676; Nicholas, 22 Sept. 1677; Joseph, 16 Nov. 1679; Thomas, 14 Apr. 1682; Ebenezer, 12 Jan. 1685, d. soon; Ebenezer, again, 16 June 1688, d. young; Hepzibah, 23 Feb. 1693; and a s. 20 Feb. 1695,

d. soon; and the f. d. 16 Oct. 1723. JOSEPH, Lynn, m. 22 Dec. 1680, Sarah Jones, had Joseph, b. 12 Apr. 1682, may have been of Ipswich, when made freem. 1683. JOSEPH, Stamford, s. of Francis of the same, propr. there in 1683–1701. JOSEPH, Rehoboth, youngest s. of sec. John of the same, m. 10 Nov. 1680, Hannah Fitch, had Joseph, b. 21 Nov. 1681; Hannah, 21 Nov. 1682 ; Jabez, 30 Dec. of unkn. yr. JOSEPH, Watertown, s. of John of Marlborough, m. 15 Nov. 1699, Ruhamah Wellington, had Ruhamah, b. 15 July 1701 ; Daniel, 21 Dec. 1703 ; John, 5 May 1706 ; Joseph, 2 Sept. 1708 ; rem. 1709 to Lexington, there had James, Josiah, Benjamin, and William, was deac. and d. 11 Jan. 1766, and his wid. d. 1 July 1772, aged 92. JOSHUA, Newbury, s. of first Newbury Richard, freem. 1673, m. 15 Jan. 1669, Sarah, d. of William Sawyer, had Joseph, b. 18 Oct. 1669 ; Joshua, 18 May 1671 ; Tristram, 21 Dec. 1672 ; Sarah, 5 Dec. 1676; Ruth, 29 Oct. 1678 ; and Samuel, 4 Sept. 1687, H. C. 1705, wh. was first min. of Abington. JOSIAH, Marblehead 1668, was prob. s. of Nicholas of Lynn, and m. 1666, as is said, Mary Fellows. NATHANIEL, Hartford 1647, m. 23 Dec. 1647, Eleanor Watts, d. of Richard, rem. to Middletown 1654, thence to Springfield, had Nathaniel, b. 9 June 1649 ; Thomas, 31 Oct. 1655, both d. young; was mort. wound. 5 Oct. 1675 ; left Hannah, the eldest, b. 15 Apr. 1651, wh. m. 5 Nov. 1669, Isaac Lane ; Nathaniel, again, 15 July 1654 ; John, 15 Apr. 1657, and Benoni, 15 Mar. 1659. NATHANIEL, Ipswich, m. 16 Dec. 1673, Judith Perkins, had James, b. 1 June 1685 ; freem. 1685 ; was, perhaps, of Rowley afterwards. *NATHANIEL, Salisbury, eldest s. of Henry, m. 16 Nov. 1666, Hannah, d. of Samuel Fellows ; had Hannah, b. 3 Apr. 1668 ; may have liv. few yrs. and perhaps had ch. at Hampton, but back at S. had Abigail, 1 Feb. 1676 ; perhaps Ephraim ; ds. Abra, 20 Nov. 1680 ; Ruth, 9 Aug. 1685 ; beside Nathaniel, 24 July 1689. He was a capt. freem. 1690, rep. 1691, k. by the Ind. at Andover, 22 Feb. 1698. NATHANIEL, Middletown, s. of Nathaniel of the same, m. 2 July 1677, Martha Hughes, d. of Richard of Guilford, had Mary, b. 2 Mar. 1678; Martha, 3 Feb. 1680, d. at 18 yrs.; Eleanor, 30 June 1681 ; Nathaniel, 18 Sept. 1683 ; and d. 9 May 1712. The wid. d. 30 May 1729. NICHOLAS, Exeter, or that region, d. early in 1648. *NICHOLAS, Lynn 1630, as Lewis conject. but I think 7 yrs. too early, s. of Edward, of Inkberrow, 8 ms. from Droitwich, Worcestersh. ; freem. 7 Sept. 1638, rep. 1641, rem. to Reading 1644, and d. 5 Apr. 1673. His eldest s. John went in 1660 to Eng. but came back, and was excor. of the will of 29 Mar. 1673, made by his f. pro. 17 June foll. in wh. w. Eliz. other ch. Josiah ; Edward, b. 15 Aug. 1640 ; Eliz. and Joseph, 10 Dec. 1647 ; possib. ano. Sarah, 26 June 1650, are ment. This fam. had e final. NICHOLAS, Portsmouth,

R. I. a freem. 1655. PETER, Plymouth, came in the Mayflower, 1620, m. two ws. and had two ch. by ea. says Gov. Bradford, after his com. here, and both of those by the first w. had been m. and one of them had two ch. when the Gov. wrote in 1650. For his first w. conject. assigns him the wid. Ford wh. had come in the Fortune 1621 ; but, of course, this must have been after the land div. in 1624 ; and he, at the div. of cattle, 1627, has assoc. with him Martha and Mary, perhaps w. and d. He is somewhere call. br. of John of P. and both liv. on Duxbury side. He d. 1633, and Standish and Brewster took his inv. 10 Oct. of that yr. PETER, New Haven 1639, had Mercy, bapt. 6 Apr. 1645 ; and Eliz. 1 Aug. 1647 ; rem. to Stamford, where his w. Eliz. d. 21 Sept. 1657 ; and he m. 27 July 1658, Unity, wid. of Clement Buxton, and d. 22 of the mo. foll. His s. Ebenezer had d. the day preced. but he may have also had Thomas, and Hackaliah, by the first w. both of wh. rem. to Rye. His wid. m. 9 Mar. foll. Nicholas Knapp. PETER, Plymouth, I suppose, s. of Peter of the same, b. after 1627, as his name does not appear in the div. of cattle that yr. He was with Gov. Bradford and thirty others among the first purch. of Dartmouth in 1652. PETER, Windsor, m. 15 July 1658, Mary, d. of Jonathan Gillett, had Mary, b. 2 May 1659 ; Hannah, 29 Sept. 1660; Abigail, 8 Aug. 1662 ; Hepzibah, 19 Nov. 1664; Peter, 2 Mar. 1667 ; John, 8 Jan. 1669 ; Jonathan, 30 Mar. 1670 ; Cornelius, 30 July 1672 ; Esther, 22 May 1673 ; Eliz. 9 June 1676 ; Deborah, 2 Feb. 1679 ; and Sarah, 20 Aug. 1681 ; the twelve were nam. at his d. 9 Mar. 1692, as all liv. Hannah was m. to one not kn. ; Abigail m. 1683, Samuel Fowler ; Esther m. 1700, · William Barber ; and Deborah m. 1696, John Hosford. PETER, Windsor, s. of the preced. m. 1696, Mary Barber, d. prob. of the sec. Thomas of the same. PHILIP, Salisbury, s. of Henry of the same, m. 24 June 1669, Mary, d. of the first Isaac Buswell, had Susanna, b. 8 Mar. 1670; Mary, 23 Feb. 1672, d. in few mos. ; a s. 1 Apr. 1673, d. in few days ; Abigail, 4 June 1675 ; Mary, 1676; Sarah, 18 Mar. 1678; George, 1 July 1680 ; Phebe, 2 Oct. 1681, wh. d. at 19 yrs. ; and Hannah, 5 Feb. 1683. His w. d. 27 Nov. foll. and he d. 21 July 1729. * RICHARD, Watertown 1630, prob. br. of first Abraham, came in the fleet with Winth. freem. 18 May 1631, hav. req. the privilege 19 Oct. preced. was rul. eld. as he had been in a London ch. rep. at the first gen. ct. of delegates 1634, and every time to 1639, and again 1647–55, exc. 1653 ; rem. to Charlestown, and d. betw. Aug. 1659 and Mar. 1661, the dates of mak. and prob. of his will. That instr. of wh. wid. Eliz. was extrix. nam. s. Thomas, and gr.s. Richard, and George ; but the est. was not adequate, it is thot. to tempt either over the ocean. Winth. I. 58. His wid. m. 12 May 1662, Richard Jackson of Cambridge. RICH-

ARD, Ipswich, bef. 1638 rem. to Newbury, was br. of George, and with him came in the Mary and John, 1634, freem. 6 May 1635, d. 26 Apr. 1661; by w. Edith, wh. d. Apr. 1647, had Joseph, wh. d. young; Joshua, b. 10 Apr. 1642; Caleb, 7 May 1645; and by sec. w. Eliz. wid. of Giles Badger, m. 16 Feb. 1648, had Eliz. 20 Mar. 1649; Richard, 18 Feb. 1651; Edmund, 17 July 1654; Sarah, 7 Sept. 1657; and Mary, 10 Apr. 1660. RICHARD, Hingham, m. Nov. 1648, at Weymouth, Eliz. Marsh. RICHARD, Charlestown, call. *old* in 1658, d. Oct. 1660. Highly prob. is it, that he is the same as the rul. Eld. of Watertown. His will, of 16 Aug. 1659, names w. Eliz. made extrix. s. Thomas; gr.s. Richard, and George; beside apprent. Jonathan Simpson. RICHARD, Southold, L. I. made freem. of Conn. 1662. RICHARD, Newbury, s. of Richard of the same, m. 7 May 1674, Mary Jaques, had only s. Richard, b. 12 Sept. 1675, H. C. 1697, min. of Reading, wh. m. 22 Apr. 1703, Martha Whipple, had sev. ch. (of wh. one was John, b. 2 Mar. 1706; and ano. was Martha, m. 12 Mar. 1730, Rev. Samuel Wigglesworth, as his sec. w.) and d. 20 or 29 Oct. 1732. RICHARD, Providence, s. of Henry of the same, by w. Mary had Malachi, b. 1 Feb. 1698; Mercy, 12 Dec. 1703; William, 3 June 1705; and Richard, 28 Feb. 1712. This last liv. over one hundred yrs. of wh. very many he serv. as proprs. clk. Judge Staples remembers him, as seat. in his doorway within two yrs. of the latest. Gathering at his ho. on the hundredth birthday, rumor went, that his friends made him dance; but, at least, what was then done "shortened his days." I hope not much. ROBERT, Cambridge, came in the Truelove, 1635, aged 24, m. 8 May 1649, Barbara Eden, freem. 1649, d. 23 Nov. 1690, aged only 70, acc. inscript. on gr.stone, as giv. in Cambridge Epit. by wh. his wid. wh. d. 1 June 1693, is said to be aged 80. We may therefore doubt, that here must be error in that very correct work, as we kn. there is, when it marks him freem. 1639. This custom ho. date is inconsist. with the gr.stone; and no Robert B. is among freem. for many yrs. bef. or after. Mitchell's Reg. in Cambr. ch. Gathering, gives him no ch. SAMUEL, Salem 1629, br. of first John, and one of the patentees, nam. (tho. not an Assist. as his br. was), of the counc. to Endicott, 30 Apr. but never qualif. by tak. the oath as requir. and both by him sent back the same summer of their com. SAMUEL, Wallingford, was liv. at New Haven 1670, s. of Francis of the same, m. 2 May 1667, Mercy, d. of William Tuttle of the same, had Abigail, b. 11 Mar. 1669; Sarah, 8 Aug. 1672; Rachel, 14 Apr. 1677; Francis, 7 Oct. 1679; after wh. he rem. to W. there had Samuel, wh. was k. by his mo. 20 June 1691, with an axe, and she was convict. 1 Oct. foll. of murder; but the court had sense eno. to set aside the verdict, as it was clearly a case of insanity.

The f. d. in that yr. but, after the trial, sent an effective petitn. to the Court. Only three ch. were then liv. Sarah, w. of Joseph Doolittle, Rachel, and Francis; the wid. still liv. in 1695. * SAMUEL, Salem, perhaps br. of Hon. William, may be he, wh. m. at Boston, 9 July 1661, Mary, d. of James Mattock; rep. 1675. SAMUEL, Eastham, m. 19 Feb. 1683, Martha Harding, had Bethia, b. 22 Jan. 1684, d. next yr.; Bethia again, 9 Sept. 1685; Martha, 24 June 1688, d. young; and Samuel, 7 Nov. 1690; d. 3 Dec. 1691, aged 31. STEPHEN, Newbury, in his will of 3 Aug. 1656, names w. Sarah, ch. Sarah, w. of Ordway; Abigail, w. of Rogers; Ann; Mary; John; and Stephen. THOMAS, Newbury, a weaver, of Malford, in Wilts, came from Southampton 1635, by the James, in employm. of Thomas Antram, reach. Boston 3 June, bring. w. Mary, wh. d. 2 June 1655; freem. 22 May 1639; had Mary, b. 1635, the first Eng. ch. of the town; Isaac; and Francis; may have been of Ipswich 1641; d. by a fall 8 Jan. 1687, aged 80. Malford is a parish in the hundr. of North Damenham, a. 6 ms. from Malmsbury, and 5 from Chippenham, in Co. Wilts, on the map of that sh. in Camden's Britannia, call. Christian Malford, perhaps too long a name for modern maps. In this geogr. detail I am more full, bec. (tho. print. by me, in 1843, 3 Hist. Coll. VIII. 319), a descend. sent lately to Eng. to explore the seat of his ancestors, and his agent's ansr. was "finds no such place in Eng. as Malford." In despair, the inquir. accept. Walford, in Wales for the derivat. of his anc. as if, in those early days, from that distant principality, a weaver would travel with his w. so far as Southampton to embark, when Bristol and other ports would have been so much nearer. Mary m. 13 May 1656, Peter Godfrey, and d. 16 Apr. 1716. THOMAS, Concord 1638, perhaps br. of Rev. Edmund, being among orig. proprs. of Sudbury 1637, freem. 14 Mar. 1639, by w. Bridget had Boaz, b. 14 Feb. 1642; perhaps Jabez, 1644; Mary, 26 Mar. 1646; Eleazer, July 1649; and Thomas, 1651. His w. d. 5 Jan. 1681, and he rem. prob. to Cambridge, d. 3 Nov. 1688. THOMAS, Cambridge, m. 7 Oct. 1656, Martha, wid. of Richard Oldham, had Mary, b. 28 Apr. 1658, d. young; Mehitable, 13 May 1661; Mary, again, 1 Nov. 1663, prob. d. young; Ebenezer, 15 June 1665; Ichabod, 5 Sept. 1666; and Martha, 19 Oct. 1668; and d. Dec. 1690. His will of 23 Nov. preced. ment. the w. and four ch. THOMAS, Lynn (not, prob. s. of Nicholas, as Lewis inf. Farmer), by w. Mary had Mary, b. 10 Feb. 1656, d. young; Sarah, 20 Sept. 1657, d. young; Joseph, 16 Jan. 1659; Sarah, again, b. 13 Oct. 1660, d. young; Jonathan, wh. d. 12 Sept. 1666; Mary, again, b. 28 Aug. 1666; Jonathan, again, 24 Jan. 1669; Eleazur, 4 Aug. 1670; Ebenezer, 16 Apr. 1672; Daniel, 29 Nov. 1673; Ann, and Grace, tw. 4 Jan. 1675, d. in few days; and Daniel, again, 1 Feb. 1677; d. 28 Aug.

1693. Mary m. 24 Aug. 1685, Thomas Norwood. Thomas, Sudbury, s. of William, m. 1667, Patience Foster, wh. d. Aug. 1706, aged 52. He m. Mary Phips of Cambridge, wid. of Solomon, jr. d. of dep.-gov. Thomas Danforth, and he d. 7 May 1709, was bur. at Boston. He was a maj. and his d. Mary m. 8 Jan. 1691, Jonathan Willard of Roxbury. Barry notes that he gave, by his will, prop. in Hedcom and Tenterden in Kent. Thomas, Lynn, call. junr. m. 8 Jan. 1678, Hannah Collins, had Samuel, b. 8 Dec. 1678 ; and Hannah, 5 Dec. 1680. Thomas, Stonington, by w. Hannah had Samuel, b. 8 Dec. 1678; Hannah, 5 Dec. 1680 ; Mary, 26 May 1683 ; Jerusha, Dec. 1687; Sarah, 11 July 1689; Thomas, 14 Feb. 1692; Eliz. 9 May 1694; Daniel, 9 Oct. 1696; Priscilla, 28 Jan. 1699; and Humphrey, 16 Sept. 1701. Thomas, Concord, s. of Thomas, was town clk. d. 4 Apr. 1718. Thomas, Hampton, s. of John of the same, m. Abial, d. of Joseph Shaw, had Thomas, b. 14 Dec. 1686; Joseph, 30 Jan. 1689 ; Sarah, 3 Apr. 1691 ; Eliz. 21 Apr. 1694 ; Ebenezer, 1696; and Josiah, 15 Feb. 1701. His w. d. 21 Dec. 1739, aged 77 ; and he d. 29 June 1744, almost 87 yrs. old. William, Boston 1633, in employm. of Gov. Winth. by w. Thomasine had Sarah, bapt. 11 May 1634. He may have had ano. d. Rebecca, wh. m. 3 Feb. 1653, James Hudson, as sec. w. and d. 14 Nov. foll. ‡ * William, Salem, s. of Francis of Brandon, in Co. Suffk. came, perhaps, in the Love, 1635, aged 26, from London, with w. Mary, of the same age, had been, it may be prob. a mem. of the Fishmongers Co. His w. it is said, was sis. of Rev. John Youngs, and d. the yr. after land. By sec. w. Sarah, d. as the fam. report says, of Rev. S. Smith of Great Yarmouth, Eng. but more prob. of Samuel Smith of our Wenham, wh. d. 10 Feb. 1668, he had William, b. 14 Apr. 1639; John, Oct. 1641, d. 1669 ; Samuel, 31 July 1644, drown. at 11 yrs. ; Joseph, H. C. 1666, bef. ment. ; Benjamin, 1648, bef. ment. ; Sarah, 23 Dec. 1649, wh. m. 1665, Thomas Deane; Mary, 16 Jan. 1656, m. Wait Winthrop, and d. 14 June 1690 ; and James, 28 Dec. 1658, d. soon. He was freem. 1649, rep. 1654, 9, and 66, Assist. 1680-3, and d. 20 Jan. 1688. His will, made 12 Mar. preced. with codic. of 19, names of ch. only William, Benjamin, and d. Winth. * William, Sudbury, an orig. propr. m. 15 Nov. 1641, Mary, d. of Thomas Besbeech or Bisby, had Mary, b. 18 May 1643, wh. m. a. 1662, Benjamin Rice; Thomas, 22 May 1644, bef. ment.; William; Edmund, 27 Nov. 1653, bef. ment. ; Hopestill, 8 July 1656, bef. ment. ; Susanna; and Eliz. 23 July 1659. He was a deac. perhaps br. of Rev. Edmund, freem. 2 June 1641, a capt. and rep. under the new chart. 1692. William, Gloucester, a selectman 1644, m. 15 July 1646, Mary, wid. of the first Abraham Robinson, had Mary, b. 28 July 1649 ; and he d. 3 May 1662. His will of 29 Apr. bef. names w. and d. Mary, beside

s.-in-law Abraham R. WILLIAM, Plymouth, m. 16 July 1649, Mary
Murcock, had Mary, b. 14 May 1650; George, 16 Jan. 1652; William,
1 Apr. 1654; and Samuel, early in Mar. 1656; beside John, James,
and Mercy; yet some of these, perhaps most, were b. at Eastham; and
d. a. 1694. WILLIAM, Salisbury 1641, br. of George of Haverhill,
m. 1645 or 6, Eliz. Munford, had Mary, b. 14 June 1647; William,
24 Feb. 1649, d. young; Ephraim, 24 June 1650; Martha, 5 July
1654; Eliz. 6 Aug. 1656, wh. m. 3 Aug. 1679, Samuel Clough;
and Sarah, 12 Apr. 1658, wh. m. Benjamin Brown of Hampton; and
he d. 24 Aug. 1706. WILLIAM, Boston, soapboiler, liv. prob. some yrs.
at Salem, had James, wh. d. 15 Nov. 1653; but perhaps others earlier,
possib. at S. and d. 1662, leav. wid. Hannah, and six ch. to ea. of wh.
by will of 1 July 1662, he gave one shil. WILLIAM, Boston, m. 24
Apr. 1655, Eliz. d. of George Ruggles of Braintree, had Mary, b. 16
Mar. foll.; and Sarah, 8 Jan. 1657. Ano. WILLIAM, Boston, prob. br.
of Job, had by w. Lydia, wh. d. 30 July 1680, aged 46, Mary, b. 23
Apr. 1657. Perhaps this is the man, m. by dep.-gov. Bellingham, 11
Apr. 1656 to some fem. in the Geneal. Reg. XI. 201, call. William
Parchment. Surely we may presume this to be wanton folly, or in-
excusab. carelessness. Was it design. for a sneer at the dep.-gov.?
‡ WILLIAM, Salem, s. of Hon. William, m. 29 Dec. 1664, Hannah, d. of
George Curwin; had William, b. 28 July 1666, d. soon; Hannah, 16
Mar. 1668, d. soon; Samuel, 8 Oct. 1669; William, again, 5 Sept. 1671,
d. very soon; John, 2 Nov. 1672; Sarah, 10 Dec. 1674, d. at 14; and
Mary, 22 Aug. 1679. His w. d. 21 Nov. 1692; and he m. 26 Apr.
1694, Rebecca Bayley, was freem. 1665, one of Andros's counc. 1687-9,
and of the counc. of safety, when the usurp. was put down, not nam. by
Increase Mather in the chart. of 1692, but chos. next yr. by a full vote
of the reps. of the people, and d. 23 Feb. 1716. The benefact. to Harv.
Coll. of this gent. of his f. br. and s. are honorab. commemo. by Quincy
in his great work. One of his s. Samuel was rep. couns. and judge, and
d. June 1731, f. of William, H. C. 1727, and of Samuel, H. C. 1727.
This last was f. of William, H. C. 1755, a judge of the Sup. Court 1775,
wh. adher. to the crown, and after some yrs. was Gov. of Bermuda, d.
1802. WILLIAM, Charlestown, m. 5 Jan. 1665, Eliz. Downs. WILLIAM,
Salem, liv. I presume, on Marblehead side in 1674, and earlier, by w.
Sarah had John, b. 10 Oct. 1669; Joseph, Aug. 1672; and Benjamin,
Aug. 1674. WILLIAM, Sudbury, s. of William, m. 11 Jan. 1676, Mar-
garet, d. of deac. John Stone of Cambridge, and d. 1705. WILLIAM,
Charlestown, m. 29 Feb. 1672, Mary Goodwin, wh. d. 28 July 1678,
aged 22; and by her had Job, bapt. 3 Oct. 1675. He had sec. w. Mary
Lothrop, m. 21 May 1679, wh. d. 23 Dec. 1713, aged 54. He d. 19 Oct.

1724, aged 78. Of this name (some with final *e*, more without it), it seems impossib. to unravel the whole line and lines. It will be seen, that I have giv. at least, a fair sample. Thirty-six of the name had, in 1834, been gr. at Harv. alone, and Mr. Farmer says fifty-nine others at the various coll. of N. E. N. J. and Union of N. York. Of these, eleven had been clerg. from H. C. and the same number from the others.

BROWNELL, GEORGE, Portsmouth, R. I. s. of Thomas of the same, m. 4 Dec. 1673, Susanna, d. of Richard Pierce, had Susanna, b. 25 Jan. 1676; Sarah, 14 June 1681; Mary, 8 Dec. 1683; Martha, 18 Feb. 1686; Thomas, 1 June 1688; Joseph, 5 Dec. 1690; Wait, 3 Oct. 1693; and Stephen, 3 Dec. 1695. THOMAS, Portsmouth, R. I. a freem. 1655.

BROWNING, HENRY, New Haven 1639, had, bapt. in right of Mary, his w. Hannah, 5 Jan. 1640; Zephaniah, 11 Oct. 1640; and Ebenezer, 10 May 1646; next yr. sold his est. to William Judson, and prob. went home, at least rem. JOSEPH, Boston 1683, printer and bookseller, a Dutchman, of wh. good charact. is giv. by John Dunton, in his Life and Errors, describ. his visit from Eng. to Mass. 1686, but he spells the name Brunning, as does, also, the Prob. rec. when admin. of his est. was giv. 25 Aug. 1691, to his wid. Mary. He d. 8 Apr. preced. See also Thomas, Hist. of Print. II. 413. MALACHI, Boston, had small est. at Watertown, but in B. d. 27 Nov. 1653; had not w. or ch. kn. to Bond, but he marks his d. five yrs. later. NATHANIEL, Portsmouth, R. I. a freem. 1655, m. Sarah, d. of William Freeborn, by him brot. from Eng. may have had Samuel. SAMUEL, Portsmouth, R. I. perhaps s. of Nathaniel of the same, is by Potter thot. to have m. Rebecca, youngest d. of capt. Samuel Wilbor. THOMAS, Salem, freem. 17 Apr. 1637, had Mary, bapt. 7 Jan. 1638; and Deborah, 31 Jan. 1647; was of Topsfield 1661, d. Feb. 1671, aged 83. Felt. He left no s. but four ds. by his will are nam. Mary, w. of Edmund Towne; Eliz. w. of James Symonds; Sarah, wh. had m. 20 Nov. 1661, Joseph Williams; and d. Meacham; Deborah, not nam. in it had m. John Perkins, and was d. THOMAS, Watertown 1658, serv. of John Fleming, or of Thomas Fanning, perhaps of both, at differ. times, when justice was invok. whip. for steal.

BROWNSMAYD, JOHN, Stratford 1650.

BROWNSON, BRUNSON, or recently BRONSON, ABRAHAM, Lyme, s. of John, m. 2 Sept. 1674, Ann, d. of Matthew Griswold, had Ann, b. 5 Oct. 1675; Abraham, 29 Mar. 1677; Mary, 21 Jan. 1679; Mercy, 21 Mar. 1681; Eliz. 12 Aug. 1682; Sarah; and Frances; at a milit. elec. 1678 had half of the votes of the co. to be lieut. CORNELIUS, Woodbury, s. of Richard of Farmington; tho. Cothren could not tell his w. yet he names the ch. there bapt. Richard, in May 1692; Cornelius, Dec. foll.; Eliz. Mar. 1694; Abraham, May 1697; Stephen, b. 12 May

1699 ; Timothy, 14 June 1701; John, bapt. Apr. 1704; and Amos, b. Oct. 1707, d. at 3 mos. ISAAC, Farmington, s. of the first John, unit. with the ch. there 25 May 1684, and had Isaac, John, Samuel, Joseph, and Mary, all bapt. 29 June foll. ; Thomas, 11 Apr. 1686; and Ebenezer, 7 Apr. 1689. JACOB, Farmington, br. of the preced. had w. 1679, s. Isaac, bapt. 28 Nov. 1686; and Hannah, 28 Oct. 1688. JOHN, Hartford 1639, rem. to Farmington, there was one of the found. of the ch. 13 Oct. 1652, d. 1680, leav. Jacob, b. 1640 ; John, 1643; Isaac, bapt. 7 Dec. 1645 ; Abraham, 28 Nov. 1647; had ds. Mary, Dorcas, and Sarah, bef. Jacob, John, and Isaac; sett. at Waterbury. Mary m. John Wyatt; Dorcas m. Stephen Hopkins; and Sarah m. John Kilbourn as sec. w. outliv. him, and d. 4 Dec. 1711. RICHARD, Farmington, br. of John, d. 1687, had, bapt. 29 May 1659, Abigail, then a. 15 yrs. old; John, 20 Feb. 1659, a. 13 yrs.; as had been Cornelius, a. 5 yrs.; Hannah, a. 3 yrs.; and Eliz. a. 1 yr. all bapt. 17 July 1653, I presume, tho. Goodwin in Geneal. Reg. XI. 323, prints it 19, wh. was on Tuesday, and so not to be thot. of; Eede, or Edith, 22 Apr. 1655 ; and Mary, 13 Feb. 1659 ; beside Samuel; all exc. one d. nam. or describ. in the will. For sec. w. he took Eliz. wid. of George Orvis, wh. had been wid. of David Carpenter of F. SAMUEL, Waterbury, s. of the preced. m. Lydia, d. of John Warner first of the same.

BRUCE, JAMES, Haverhill 1677. JOHN, Sudbury, by w. Eliz. had Hannah, b. 1672 ; Mary, 1680; Eunice, 1684 ; and Martha, 1685. Perhaps he had male ch. earlier. PETER, Haverhill 1677. ROGER, Marlborough, by w. Eliz. had Samuel, b. 24 Mar. 1691; Abijah, 27 Nov. 1693; rem. to Framingham, had Elisha, 14 Sept. 1695 ; Rebecca, 22 Feb. 1698; Sarah, 2 Mar. 1700; Daniel, 22 Feb. 1701; Thomas, 5 Jan. 1704 ; Hannah, 18 Feb. 1706; Deliverance, 9 Sept. 1709; and David, 9 June 1711; d. 16 Sept. 1733.

BRUEN, JOHN, New London, s. of Obadiah, by w. Esther had Eleazer, Joseph, and John, but prob. some, perhaps all, b. after his rem. to Newark; d. a. 1696, when the Lords proprs. made gr. of ld. to his wid. * OBADIAH, Gloucester, came, 1640, prob. with Rev. Richard Blinman, had first set them down at Marshfield, and ask. for adm. as freem. of Plymouth jurisdict. Mar. 1641, but speedily went to the opposite side of the Bay. He was freem. 19 May 1642; selectman in 1642, and sev. foll. yrs. and rep. 1647, 8, 9, and 51, in wh. last yr. with his spiritual guide he rem. again to New London, there was town clk. 15 yrs. often rep. and is nam. in the royal chart. 1662 ; but hav. purch. 11 June 1667, with assoc. the ld. in N. J. now the city of Newark, he rem. thither, where the fam. has always flour. He was youngest s. of John B. Esq. of Bruen Stapleford, Cheshire, bapt. 25 Dec. 1606, at Tarves, near

Chester, bec. a draper at Shrewsbury in the adjoin. Co. Salop, had w. Sarah and ch. Mary, bef. com. over, and here Rebecca; Hannah, b. 9 Jan. 1644; and John, 2 June 1646. The time of his d. is unkn. but he was alive 1680. In spel. the name slight variety occurs. A let. of 11 Oct. 1679 to his d. and her h. at New London, from Newark, to tell of the d. of their min. the first Pierson, is sign. Ob. Brewen, but by the w. Sarah Bruen. His d. Mary m. 1653, John Baldwin of Milford, as his sec. w.; Hannah m. 1663, John Baldwin of Milford, s. of the h. of her sis. but perhaps d. soon, as he is said to have d. on a voyage unm. but it may be that her h. was ano. of the frequent Johns; Rebecca m. 1663, Thomas Post of Norwich, as his sec. w. Rev. Matthias, b. at Newark, 11 Apr. 1793, Columb. Coll. 1812, d. 11 Nov. 1829, was a descend. of high reput.

BRUFF. See Brough.

BRUNDISH, JOHN, perhaps of Watertown at first, freem. 4 Mar. 1635, rem. early to Wethersfield, d. 1639, leav. wid. Rachel, wh. m. Anthony Wilson of Fairfield, one s. and four ds.

BRUNETT, HENRY, Boston, merch. d. early in 1687.

BRUNNING. See Browning.

BRUSH, GEORGE, Woburn, said to be a Scotchman, m. 20 Dec. 1659, Eliz. d. of William Clark, had William, b. 21 Nov. 1660, d. in few wks.; William, again, 20 Oct. 1661, d. in two wks.; Eliz. 26 Jan. 1663, d. young; Mary, 15 June 1665; William, again, 28 Apr. 1667; John, 18 June 1670; Eliz. again, 24 Aug. 1672; George, 18 Jan. 1674, d. same day; Joseph, 11 Jan. 1675, d. at one yr.; Joseph, again, 29 Dec. 1676; Samuel, 28 Mar. 1680; Margery, 24 Apr. 1684; and Lydia, 10 Apr. 1687; was freem. 1690, and d. 13 Aug. 1692. The name is made Brace. His d. Mary m. 4 June 1683, Walter Cranston. THOMAS, Southold, L. I. 1662, freem. of Conn. 1664. WILLIAM, Woburn, s. of George, m. 15 Mar. 1693, Eliz. Gould, had Mary, b. 6 Dec. 1693; William, 11 Mar. 1696; John, 9 Nov. 1698; Samuel, 11 Mar. 1701; Abigail, 29 Mar. 1702; Thomas, 20 Mar. 1705; James, 16 June 1708; Rebecca, 26 Sept. 1709; and Lydia, 24 Aug. 1712; was a lieut. after serv. in the Ind. war 1690.

BRUSTER, JOHN, Portsmouth 1665, had m. Mary, d. of Roger Knight, one of Mason's men, so long bef. Dec. 1656, that her f. at Dover, writ. to his s.-in-law in that mo. speaks of his w. "Mary and the dear childr." was freem. 1672, of gr. jury 1687. Descend. are num. but they spell for Brewster, the name on Col. rec. is Breuster.

BRYAN, ‡ ALEXANDER, Milford 1639, a man of influence in the Col. of New Haven, and after union with Conn. Assist. 1668–73. Ann, prob. his w. d. there 20 Feb. 1661, and he m. the wid. of Samuel Fitch, the

24 *

sch.master of Hartford, and d. betw. 20 July and 6 Nov. 1679, at gr. age. He had Richard, and other ch. we infer, for his will names, beside that s. only gr.ch. and gr. gr.ch. sprung, indeed, from him; yet he prob. had ds. Susanna, wh. d. at Middletown 1670, and Joanna, wh. m. 9 Apr. 1652, Owen Morgan, unless one or both were wid. of other s. wh. had d. bef. the testat. He names gr.ch. Alexander, and his s. Alexander; gr. gr.ch. John, and Mary Maltby; gr.ch. Samuel B.; gr.ch. Sarah, wh. bec. w. of Samuel Fitch, s. of his own w.; gr.ch. Hannah Harriman, and her three ch.; and neph. Thomas Oviatt. ALEXANDER, Milford, eldest s. of Richard, m. Sybil, d. of Rev. John Whiting of Hartford, had Ann, b. 8 Sept. 1674; Alexander, 15 June 1677, d. soon; John, 12 July 1680; Alexander, again, 24 Nov. 1683; Ebenezer, 2 Feb. 1690; and Augustine, 25 Apr. 1694; and d. 1701. His wid. m. 1705, Hugh Gray of Huntingdon, L. I. it is said, but after his d. was liv. at Milford in 1711. This name sometimes ends with *t*, and in Mather's list of the Conn. magistr. has a final *s*, but the barbarism of the London printer is prob. chargea. with it. Often in early rec. here it is Bryer. JOHN, Taunton 1637, d. 28 Apr. 1638, as two of his friends said, prov. his nuncup. will, giv. all his prop. to s. John, wh. was perhaps not then in the country, for he desir. John Gilbert to have charge of the prop. for him. Eliz. Poole, the found. of the sett. in that yr. preced. and Jane, prob. her younger sis. or niece, hav. aid in mak. the inv. (of wh. the sum was £43.) I infer that he had come in her comp. JOHN, Taunton 1639, s. prob. of the preced. one of the first purch. and long an inhab. RICHARD, Milford, s. of first Alexander, b. in Eng. by w. Mary had Alexander bef. ment. b. 1651; Mary, and Hannah, tw. 1654; Samuel, bapt. 1659; John, 1662, d. young; Abigail, 1664, d. unm. 1698; Richard, 1666; Frances, 1668; and Sarah, 1670. He m. 1678, Eliz. wid. of Richard Hollingworth, d. of Michael Powell of Boston, wh. d. 1698, had Eliz. b. 1679; and Joseph, 1684. He had large est. being, as had been his f. the richest man in town. It was partly in Eng. on L. I. at New Haven, Elizabethtown, N. J. Providence, and Milford. His wid. m. John Durand, and, fourth h. a Treat, and d. 1706. Mary m. John Maltby of New Haven, and, next, a Howell of L. I.; Hannah, m. Rev. John Harriman of New Haven; Frances m. Joseph Treat of Milford; Sarah m. Samuel Fitch, wh. d. early, leav. only ch. Sarah; and she m. next, a. 1696, Mungo Nisbett, and d. in two yrs. SAMUEL, Milford, s. of the preced. m. 25 Dec. 1683, Martha, d. of Rev. John Whiting, had Mary, b. 1685; Martha, 1689; Susanna, 1691; Abigail, 1693; Sybil, 9 June 1695; and Jerusha, 4 July 1697; and d. 1698, leav. wid. Martha. THADDEUS, Lynn 1675.

BRYANT, ABRAHAM, Reading, freem. 1673, m. Mary, d. of Thomas

Kendall, wh. d. 8 Mar. 1688, aged 40; and he m. Ruth, wid. of Samuel Frothingham, prob. for sec. or third w. *JOHN, Scituate 1639, m. 14 Nov. 1643, Mary, d. of George Lewis of Barnstable, had John, b. 17 Aug. 1644; Hannah, 25 Jan. 1646, m. 1665, John Stodder of Hingham; Joseph, 1646, d. young; Sarah, 29 Sept. 1648; Mary, 24 Feb. 1650, d. young; Martha, 26 Feb. 1652; and Samuel, 6 Feb. 1654. His w. d. 2 July 1655, and he m. 22 Dec. 1657, Eliz. d. of Rev. William Wetherell, wh. d. soon; and in 1664 he m. Mary, d. of Thomas Hiland, had Eliz. 1665; Benjamin, 1669; Joseph, again, 1671; Jabez, 1672; Ruth, 1673; Thomas, 1675; Deborah, 1677; Agatha, 1678; Ann, 1680; and Elisha, 1682. He was rep. 1677–8, and his will was dat. 1684. JOHN, Plymouth, m. 23 Nov. 1665, Abigail Bryant, perhaps d. of Stephen of the same. JOHN, Scituate, s. of John of the same, had John, b. 1677; Jonathan, 1679; Mary, 1682; David, 1684; Joshua, 1687; Samuel, 1689; and Martha, 1691. RICHARD, New Haven 1654, may have been s. of Alexander Bryan, and have no right to the final letter. ROBERT, a soldier in Turner's comp. in Philip's war, of whose resid. I am ign. SAMUEL, Scituate, s. of first John, d. in the strange expedit. of Sir William Phips against Quebec. STEPHEN, Duxbury 1643, rem. to Plymouth 1650, m. Abigail, d. of John Shaw, had John, b. 7 Apr. 1650; Mary, 29 May 1654; Stephen, 2 Feb. 1658; Sarah, 28 Nov. 1659; Lydia, 23 Oct. 1662; and Eliz. 17 Oct. 1665. THOMAS, Marblehead 1642. THOMAS, Scituate, s. of first John, a man of distinct. rep. 1725, 30, 3, and 4, was f. of Rev. Lemuel, H. C. 1739, a disting. man of Braintree. WILLIAM, Boston, taverner, by w. Hannah, wh. surv. him, had Hannah, b. 26 June 1683; Benjamin, 6 July 1686; William, 5 Oct. 1687; John, 25 Mar. 1689; and d. bef. 22 Nov. 1697 when adm. was gr. to his wid. Some make the name Briant.

BRYER, or BRIARD, ELISHA, New Hampsh. 1689, prob. liv. at Portsmouth, where he m. 4 Oct. 1689, Abigail Drew, perhaps d. of James, had Margaret, b. 30 Nov. 1693; Abigail, 11 Dec. 1695; Samuel, 18 Sept. 1697; Sarah, 2 Feb. 1700; and Mary, 21 Aug. 1702. RICHARD, Lynn, d. 8 Oct. 1665. RICHARD, Newbury, m. 21 Dec. 1665, Eleanor Wright, wh. d. 20 Aug. 1672, had Richard, b. 19 Aug. 1667; Eliz. 11 May 1669; and Ruth, 27 Dec. 1670.

BUCK, EMANUEL, or ENOCH, Wethersfield, by w. Sarah had Ezekiel, b. 1650; John, 1652; Jonathan, 1655; and by sec. w. Mary, d. of John Kirby of Middletown, had David, 1667; Sarah, 1667; Hannah, 1671; Eliz. 1676; Thomas, 1678; and Abigail, 1682. Here is a strange confus. of names, yet the W. rec. ment. the man by both prefixes, in diff. places; and the surname was varied into Book, or Bouk, as he wrote it. EPHRAIM, Woburn, m. 1 Jan. 1671, Sarah Brooks, had Sarah,

b. 11 Jan. 1674; Ephraim, 13 July 1676; John, 1 Jan. 1679, d. in few
days; John, again, 7 Feb. 1680; Samuel, 13 Nov. 1682; Eunice, 7 July
1685; Ebenezer, 20 May 1689; and Mary, 28 Oct. 1691. HENRY,
Wethersfield, m. 31 Oct. 1660, Eliz. d. of Josiah Churchill, had Samuel,
b. 1664; Martha, 1667; Eliz. 1670; Mary, 1673; Sarah, 1678; Ruth,
1681; Mehitable, 1684; and Henry. He d. 7 July 1712. * ISAAC,
Scituate 1647, town clk. rep. 1663, 4, and 5; bore arms 1643, and was
the lieut. 1676, wh. repuls. the Ind. assault on the town, d. 1695, leav.
wid. Frances, and ch. Thomas, Joseph, Jonathan, Benjamin, Eliz. wh.
was w. of Robert Whitcomb, Mehitable, w. of Stephen Chittenden,
Ruth, m. 17 Jan. 1677, Joseph Garrett, not Gannett, as print. in Geneal.
Reg. IX. 316, and Deborah, w. of Henry Merritt. JAMES, Hingham
1638, came in the Diligent, that yr. with one serv. John Morfield, from
old Hingham, freem. 22 May 1639. JOHN, Hingham, br. of the preced.
came, prob. in the same sh. rem. 1650, to Scituate, m. Eliz. d. of Samuel
Holbrook of Weymouth, had Eliz. b. 1653; Mary, 1655; Joseph, 1657;
John, 1659; Hannah, 1661; Susanna, 1664; Benjamin, 1665; Deborah, 1670; Robert, 1672; and Rachel, 1674. He m. 1693, the wid. of
sec. Edward Dotey, wh. was prob. Sarah, sis. of famous Elder Faunce,
and d. 1697, or, rather, his will bears that date. ROGER, Cambridge,
came in the Increase 1635, aged 18, perhaps s. of William, had Mary,
b. 1638, wh. d. 31 Aug. 1669; John, 3 Sept. 1644; Ephraim, 26 July
1646; Mary, 23 June 1648; Ruth, 6 Nov. 1653; and Eliz. 5 July 1657;
perhaps others. His w. Susanna d. 10 Sept. 1685. Prob. he had other
ch. for Harris's Epit. ment. d. of Nathaniel, 19 July 1672; of Ann, 13
Apr. 1675; and of Samuel, 21 Sept. 1690. WILLIAM, Cambridge,
ploughwright, came in the Increase 1635, aged 50, d. 24 Jan. 1658.
His s. Roger had admin. in Apr. foll. A Christian B. came in the
Blessing 1635, aged 26.

BUCKINGHAM, DANIEL, and SAMUEL, Milford 1669, were perhaps s.
of Thomas. Of the former we learn nothing more than that he m. 1661,
Hannah, d. of William Fowler the sec. of M. and of Samuel, only that
he was b. 1640, and m. 14 Dec. 1663, Sarah Baldwin, d. of Timothy, and
call. Anthony Hawkins his uncle. THOMAS, Milford 1639, one of the
chief men, had Thomas, bapt. 8 Nov. 1646; d. 1657, on a visit at Boston. *THOMAS*, Saybrook, s. of the preced. was min. 1669, d. 1 Apr.
1709, aged 63, wh. disproves a fond tradit. that he was b. on the passage of his parents, wh. came over with Prudden, and went to M. as one
of the first sett. 28 Nov. 1639. If he were then alive, his age should
have been call. 71. He had not a coll. educ. but was ord. 1670; and
enjoys the distinc. of being one of the found. of Yale Coll. By w.
Esther, d. of Thomas Hosmer of Hartford, m. 20 Sept. 1666, had Esther,

b. 10 June 1668 ; Thomas, 29 Sept. 1670, wh. m. 16 Dec. 1691, Margaret Griswold; Daniel, 2 Oct. 1672; Stephen, 4 Sept. 1675 ; Samuel, 26 May 1678, d. next mo.; Samuel, again, 24 July 1679, d. 5 Jan. 1685 ; Hezekiah, 21 June 1682; Temperance, 6 Jan. 1685 ; and Ann, 2 Aug. 1687. In Mather's Hecatompolis he and Thomas, H. C. 1690, min. of Hartford, wh. was from Milford, not s. (as often said), but perhaps neph. of Rev. Thomas of Saybrook, and Stephen, H. C. 1693, min. of Norwalk, s. of the Saybrook min. appear together. Stephen m. Sarah, d. of Rev. Samuel Hooker, and d. 13 Feb. 1746, aged 70, leav. no ch. ; and his f. m. 10 Aug. 1703, for sec. w. Mary, her mo. THOMAS, Hartford, not s. of the preced. m. 29 Nov. 1699, Ann, d. of Rev. Isaac Foster, his predecess. d. 19 Nov. 1731, aged 62, leav. only s. Joseph, Y. C. 1723.

BUCKLAND, sometimes BUCKLINE on rec. BENJAMIN, Braintree, m. Rachel, d. of John Wheatley, had Leah, perhaps rem. to Rehoboth, there had David, b. 22 Mar. 1675 ; and d. a. 1679, for his wid. m. 22 Sept. of that yr. John Loring of Hingham. Leah m. 1687, Thomas, s. of said John. JOSEPH, Rehoboth, perhaps s. of the preced. had Matthew, b. 16 Sept. 1674; beside Nehemiah, wh. was bur. May 1677 ; Nehemiah, again, 31 Mar. 1678; and Lydia, 5 Sept. 1680. NICHOLAS, Windsor, s. of first Thomas, m. 21 Oct. 1668, Martha, d. of John Wakefield of New Haven, had John, b. 13 Mar. 1673, d. soon; Hannah, 1 Sept. 1674; John, again, d. 20 Dec. 1675, very young; Martha, 1 Mar. 1678 ; and John, again, 17 July 1681. SAMUEL, New London 1674, m. first, the wid. of the first Matthew Beckwith, and, next, a. 1690, Hannah, wid. of Philip Bill, and d. in 1700. She d. 1709. THOMAS, freem. 6 May 1635, of Mass. prob. of Dorchester, for he rem. soon to Windsor, serv. in the Pequot war, 1637, m. Temperance, d. of Nicholas Denslow, had Timothy, b. 10 Mar. 1639 ; Eliz. 21 Feb. 1641 ; Temperance, 27 Nov. 1642 ; Mary, 2 Oct. 1644, d. young ; Nicholas, 21 Feb. 1647 ; Sarah 24 Mar. 1649 ; Thomas, 2 Feb. 1651, d. young ; and Hannah, 18 Sept. 1654; d. 28 May 1662, and his wid. d. 1681. Temperance m. John Ponder ; Sarah m. John Phelps; and Hannah m. 14 Aug. 1681, Joshua Welles. THOMAS, Windsor 1670, s. of the preced. m. Hannah, d. of Nathaniel Cooke of the same, had one ch. wh. liv. not long. He d. 28 May 1676, and his wid. m. 30 Jan. 1677, Joseph Baker. TIMOTHY, Windsor, s. of the preced. m. 27 Mar. 1662, Abigail, d. of Richard Vore, had Timothy, b. 20 Apr. 1664, d. soon ; Thomas, 23 June 1665 ; Abigail, 11 Nov. 1667 ; Mary, 7 Nov. 1670 ; Sarah, 10 Apr. 1673 ; Hannah, 28 June 1676 ; and Eliz. 26 Feb. 1679. WILLIAM, Hingham 1635, rem. to Rehoboth 1658, and was bur. 1 Sept. 1679. A d. of his m. John Brown, jr. of R. Baruch and Joseph, perhaps his s. were of R. 1690 ;

and it is found on rec. that John Bucklin, wh. may be a name of the same stock capricious. varied, d. 20 June 1677. WILLIAM, Hartford, d. 13 May 1691, leav. William, and Charles. He was not relat. of Thomas.

BUCKLEY, JOSEPH, Boston, merch. m. Joanna, d. of Richard Shute, wid. of Nathaniel Nichols, perhaps in 1688, and by his will of 24 Nov. 1700, pro. 19 Mar. 1702, provides for that w. during her life to have his dw. ho. wh. had been giv. him by f.-in-law, but to s. Joseph, the eldest, Richard, and Thomas, £300. ea. as he comes to 21 yrs. THOMAS, a soldier of Lothrop's comp. k. 18 Sept. 1675, at Bloody brook. In this form often appears the more disting. name of Bulkly.

BUCKLINE, JOHN, Rehoboth, bur. 20 June 1677, as was NEHEMIAH, 19 May preced. Perhaps they were ch. of Joseph Buckland.

BUCKMAN, JOHN, Boston, by w. Hannah had Hannah, b. 5 July 1653. One of this name was a soldier in Moseley's comp. Dec. 1675. See *under* Bucknam.

BUCKMINSTER, JAMES, Sudbury 1640, an orig. propr. Shattuck. JOSEPH, Boston, s. of Thomas, by w. Eliz. d. of Hugh Clark of Watertown, had Joseph, b. 31 July, bapt. 23 Sept. 1666 ; and the f. d. 20 Nov. 1668. His posthum. d. Eliz. was bapt. 10 Jan. foll. In his rec. Eliot calls him Buckmaster; the resid. being at Muddy riv. Roxbury rec. contain no m. b. or d. tho. convenience of worship took him and his fam. to the ch. there. The wid. Eliz. d. at Framingham, where her s. liv. from wh. by w. Martha, d. of John Sharp, m. 12 May 1686, descend the disting. stock of this name. THOMAS, Scituate, perhaps gr.s. of that Thomas, whose Almanac, comput. for 1599, in his 67th yr. is now bef. me, rem. to Boston, where on the ch. rec. of his adm. 4 Oct. 1645, " upon let. of dism. from the ch. of Scituate " (his w. Joan being rec. the same day), he is call. laborer ; but the spell. in both cases is as in our day. Yet it is strange that Deane omits the name. He liv. at what is now Brookline, prob. worship. at Roxbury, where Hannah, bapt. 28 June 1646, may have been his d. and have d. young. He was freem. 1646, and d. 28 Sept. 1656; in his will of 2 Sept. pro. 23 Nov. in that yr. ment. w. Joanna, s. Zechariah, ds. Eliz. w. of Thomas Spowell, Mary, w. of Henry (as Barry thinks was his name) Stevens, Dorcas, w. of Clement Corbin, or Corbett, s. Thomas, Joseph, and Jabez, d. Spowell's two ch., d. Stevens's two ch., d. Corbin's ch., Zechary's ch. and, last, d. Sarah. A s. Lawrence, prob. the eldest, had made his will, 27 Nov. 1645, bound to sea, perhaps d. bef. ret. as it was pro. 4 July after. He is presum. from it to have been unm. See Geneal. Reg. III. 178. Dorcas had m. 7 Mar. 1655, the same day with her br. Zechariah ; and Sarah m. 30 Sept. 1657, John Lawrence. Jabez was prob. m. and d. Sept. 1686. The wid. m. 1 Sept. 1661, Edward Garfield of Watertown. THOMAS, Boston, a carpenter, s. of the preced. d. Dec. 1659, leav. wid. Mary. Inv. of his est. amt. to £39. 16. ZECHARIAH, Boston, br. of the preced. m. 7 Mar. 1655, Sarah Webb, had prob. sev. ch. rem. among early sett. to Sherborn, there d. after 1691. His wid. Sarah d. at Roxbury 27 June 1704.

BUCKNAM, JOSES, Malden, s. of William, by w. Judith Worth, m. 1 May 1673, had Samuel, b. Apr. 1674; Judith, 7 Aug. 1676; Sarah, 1680; Mary; Susanna, 8 Aug. 1685; William, 22 Feb. 1688; Edward, 22 May 1692; and Lydia, posthum. 23 Mar. 1695; and d. 24 Aug. 1694. But by a former w. prob. d. of George Knower, he had Joses, b. Jan. 1667; Hannah, Aug. 1669; and Eliz.; and prob. John. His wid. m. John Lynde. WILLIAM, Charlestown 1647, on the Mistick side, wh. bec. Malden, had by first w. only ch. John; and by sec. w. Sarah had Joses, b. 1641; Eliz. 1644; Mercy, 14 Feb. 1648; Sarah, July 1650; William, Aug. 1652; Mehitable, Aug. 1654; Edward, Sept. 1657; Samuel, wh. d. 13 Sept. 1658, prob. a few hours old; and Samuel, again, Feb. 1660; and d. early in 1679. Eliz. m. Benjamin Whittemore, and d. 18 July 1726; Mercy m. 7 Dec. 1669, Benjamin Webb; Mehitable m. Samuel Waite; and Sarah m. 24 July 1676, Samuel Shattuck. WILLIAM, Malden, s. of the preced. m. 11 Oct. 1676, Hannah Waite, had no ch. and d. 17 Sept. 1693, giv. all his prop. to w. by his will. A John Buckman, perhaps the same name, was of Boston 1673, was prob. gr.ch. of Prudence Wilkinson, and of first William. Of him, I presume, it is, that Sewall, in his Diary, under 30 Oct. 1696, relates, that he had been perfectly dumb for eighteen yrs. and had his speech restor. It is almost certain that he was the first s. of the first William, wh. in his will, explain. why he gave him so small a portion was, bec. he had been infirm from early youth, and was tak. by his gr.mo.

BUCKNELL, SAMUEL, Boston, m. 18 Sept. 1654, Sarah, d. of Nathaniel Bishop, had Sarah, b. 17 May 1655, and she d. next yr.

BUCKNER, CHARLES, Dover, sch.master 1657, rem. in few yrs. to Boston, had w. Mary.

BUDD, EDWARD, Boston 1668, and sev. yrs. bef. a carver. * JOHN, New Haven 1639, liv. some yrs. at Southold, on L. I. as a freem. of Conn. a lieut. 1661, and rep. for Greenwich 1664, and for the Unit. Col. of Conn. 1666, and after. He was rep. for Milford in 1677, Trumbull, II. 318, then call. him Bird. JONATHAN, New Haven 1643, had fam. of six, and rem. but to what place is unkn.

BUDDINGTON, BODINGTON or BUDINGTON, WALTER, Stonington 1668, rem. to New London, and d. 1689, leav. no ch. but his nearest of kin was Walter, a neph. constable at N. L. 1695, on Groton side.

BUDLEY, ANDREW, Ipswich, prob. s. of Giles of the same, m. 14 Mar.

1682, Mary Conant, whose f. is not kn. but no doubt she was gr.d. of Roger the first, had Rebecca, b. 29 Mar. 1683; Andrew, 5 Apr. 1686, d. at 4 mos.; Martha, 3 Mar. 1692, d. next yr.; Andrew, again, 15 June 1694; Martha, again, 28 Apr. 1696; Sarah, 6 Oct. 1698; and Eliz. 25 Aug. 1700; but perhaps the mo. of this last was Rebecca. He d. 1 Feb. 1718, aged 60 yrs. Rebecca m. Robert Kinsman. GILES, Ipswich 1648, of wh. we learn from his will of 18 July 1668, pro. 29 Sept. foll. most of the little we kn. that he left w. Eliz. and ch. Andrew, b. 5 Sept. 1657; James, 10 Feb. 1660; and John, perhaps youngest, for he had 'Giles, 13 July 1662, wh. prob. d. bef. his f. JAMES, Ipswich, s. of the preced. m. 25 May 1685, Rebecca Stacey, perhaps d. of Thomas and she d. 21 Oct. 1686; but by w. Eliz. he had William, b. 27 Feb. 1693; Joseph, 6 Apr. 1695; and Thomas, 5 Apr. 1697. Some confus. of this name with Burley occurs on the rec. wh. is also giv. in the Coll. catal. and it is seen, also, Birdley; yet in mod. times it is, I suppose, writ. Burleigh.

BUDLONG, FRANCIS, Warwick, m. 19 Mar. 1669, Rebecca, wid. of Joseph Howard, d. prob. of John Lippit, had John, and other ch. bef. or after, or·both, was k. with his w. and all the fam. exc. John, by the Ind. Nov. 1675, wh. carr. John away, but soon restor. him. JOHN, Warwick, s. of the preced. had three s. John, Moses, and Daniel, wh. was less than 21 yrs. old; beside ds. Rebecca Pierce, Mary Pierce, and Isabel, under 18 yrs. as we learn from his will of 4 Oct. 1731. He liv. to 1744.

BUELL, PETER, Windsor, s. of William, rem. 1670 to Simsbury, d. 8 Jan. 1729, had Samuel, Ephraim, William, and Jonathan, beside seven ds. He had sec. w. Mary, wid. of Jacob Bissell, but wh. was the first w. is unkn. or how many of his ch. were by her is uncert. yet as this w. was not m. bef. 1698, it is highly prob. that she was not mo. of all his ch. The ds. were Abigail, Martha, Mary, Sarah, Hannah, Miriam, and Esther. These are all nam. as well as w. in his will of 28 June bef. his d. but some were not liv. SAMUEL, Windsor, eldest br. of the preced. m. 13 Nov. 1662, Deborah Griswold, d. of Edward, and rem. to Killing-worth, had, beside Samuel, b. 20 July 1663, at W. and at K. had Deborah, 18 Oct. 1665; Hannah, 6 Sept. 1667, d. young; Mary, 28 Nov. 1669; John, 17 Feb. 1672; Hannah, again, 4 May 1674; William, 18 Oct. 1676; David, 15 Feb. 1679; Josiah, 16 Mar. 1681; Mehitable, 22 Aug. 1682; Peter, 3 Dec. 1684; and Benjamin, 1686. His w. d. 7 Feb. 1719, and he d. 11 July 1720. WILLIAM, Windsor, one of the first sett. by w. Mary, m. 18 Nov. 1640, had Samuel, above ment. b. 2 Sept. 1641; Mary, 3 Sept. 1642; Peter, 19 Aug. 1644; Hannah, 8 Jan. 1647; Hepzibah, 11 Dec. 1649; Sarah, 21 Mar. 1653 or 4; and Abigail, 12 Feb. 1656; d. 16 Nov. 1681; and his wid. d. 2 Sept. 1684.

His will, of 26 July 1681, names the two s. and d. Mary, but refers to others; and the will of the wid. 29 Aug. 1684, names d. Mary Mills, m. 23 Feb. 1660; Sarah was d. unm. and Abigail is not nam. prob. d. young; Hannah m. 17 Sept. 1663, Timothy Palmer; Hepzibah m. 12 Jan. 1673, Thomas Welles of Hatfield. WILLIAM, Salisbury, but whether bef. or after Oct. 1650, I kn. not. He and his w. were at that time indict. in Plymouth col. as Bapt. Baylies, II. 211.

BUFFINGTON, BENJAMIN, Salem, s. of Thomas, had Benjamin, b. 4 May 1699, and two other s. JOHN, Salem 1676. THOMAS, Salem, spelt Bovanton, m. 30 Dec. 1671, Sarah Southwick, perhaps d. more prob. gr.d. of Lawrence of the same, had Thomas, b. 1 Mar. 1672; Benjamin, 24 July 1675; and Abigail, 25 July 1695. THOMAS, Salem, eldest s. of the preced. m. 28 Feb. 1699, Hannah Ross, had sev. ch. whose names are not seen.

BUFFUM, CALEB, Salem, s. prob. of the first Robert, m. 26 Mar. 1672, Hannah, d. of the first Joseph Pope, had Caleb, b. 14 May 1673; and Robert, 1 Dec. 1675. JOSEPH, Salem, perhaps br. of the preced. had Joseph. His w. was punish. 1658 for attend. a Quaker meeting, with her s. and perhaps she was again punish. 1662, with her d. w. of Robert Wilson, and her sis. Smith, perhaps w. of James or John. Felt. JOSHUA, Salem, perhaps br. of the preced. by w. Damaris, d. of Joseph Pope, had Joseph; was banish. 1659, on pain of d. Prob. the sentence could not be carr. into effect, but he went to Eng. and got security against such monstrous injust. ROBERT, Salem 1638, is said to have come from Yorksh. in 1634, but perhaps the yr. is too early, as Felt first saw ment. of him in 1638. Perhaps he was f. of all the preced. had w. Thomasin, and d. Mary, wh. m. Jeremiah Neal. His will was refus. pro. bec. the witnesses would not sw. but only affirm.

BUGBY, EDWARD, Roxbury, came in the Francis from Ipswich 1634, aged 40, with w. Rebecca, 32, and d. Sarah, 4; had Joseph, b. 6 June 1640; and a ch. b. and d. Aug. 1642, acc. town rec. He join. the ch. Aug. 1665, "an old man," says the rec. and when he d. 27 Jan. 1669, "aged, as is said, above 80," I suppose, no discredit of the report is intend. His will, of 26 Nov. preced. names only s. Joseph, and Sarah, w. of Richard Chamberlain, wh. is made excor. EDWARD, Roxbury, by w. Abigail, d. of Richard Hall, had Abigail, b. 1 Oct. 1694; John, 2 Oct. 1696, d. 29 Jan. 1703; and other ch. in his will, 23 Jan. 1703, pro. next mo. he refers to, but does not name, more than John. His f. is not kn. JOHN, Roxbury, had w. Joanna, wh. d. 11 July 1690; and he d. 16 Jan. 1704, in his will names ch. John, Thomas, Mary, and Joanna. Thomas, b. Apr. 1668, had fam. JOSEPH, Roxbury, s. of the first Edward, by w. Experience, d. of Andrew Pitcher, had Joseph, b. 17 Sept.

1664; Rebecca, 16 Sept. 1666; Edward, 31 Jan. 1669; Samuel, 31 Aug. 1673; Abigail, 16 Nov. 1676; Mehitable, 20 Aug. 1679; Jonathan, 23 May 1682; and Josiah, 2 Nov. 1684. RICHARD, Roxbury, came in the fleet with Winth. prob. and req. adm. as freem. 19 Oct. 1630, was sw. 18 May 1631, had w. Judith, both of the very early mem. of the ch. He d. bef. 1641, and his wid. m. Robert Parker, and had John, bapt. 27 Mar. 1642, yet the town rec. does not ment. his time of d.

BULGAR, RICHARD, Boston, came, prob. in the fleet with Winth. freem. 18 May 1631, had John, bapt. 20 Apr. 1634; was of the party of Mrs. Hutchinson, and of so much conseq. at Roxbury as to be disarm. went first to R. I. in 1638 with Coddington, but next yr. to Exeter. He was a bricklayer. Belkn. I. 20. I believe he went back to R. I. and there was 71 yrs. old in 1679.

BULFINCH, JOHN, Salem 1640, freem. 18 May 1642. Ann, adm. of the ch. 1641, perhaps was his w. He rem. from S. but whither is not kn. Of this name seven had been gr. at H. C. in 1822, but all of a later stock.

BULKLEY, *EDWARD*, Concord, eldest s. of Rev. Peter, b. in Eng. bapt. at Odell 17 June 1614, came to our country bef. his f. being adm. of Boston ch. 22 Mar. 1635, freem. 6 May foll. and adm. also in Plymouth jurisdict. 5 June 1644, was min. of Marshfield, ord. 1643, until 1658, and the next yr. succeed. his f.; preach. the elect. sermon, 1680; d. at Chelmsford 2 Jan. 1696, but was bur. at Concord. His w. is unkn. but he had ch. Sarah, b. 12 June 1640; Peter, at C. 3 Nov. 1641; Eliz. wh. m. 7 Dec. 1665, Rev. Joseph Emerson, next, capt. John Brown of Reading; and John, wh. d. young at M. beside Jane, wh. m. 20 Mar. 1684, Ephraim Flint. ELIEZER, Wethersfield, br. of the preced. liv. in 1659, when the will of his f. provides well for him, d. prob. in no long time after, as he is never ment. as freem. or otherwise. *GERSHOM*, New London, br. of the preced. m. at Concord 24 or 26 Oct. 1659, Sarah, d. of Presid. Chauncy, wh. d. 3 June 1699, had Peter, b. 7 Nov. 1660; after some yrs. preach. at N. L. rem. to Wethersfield, there install. and preach. 1666–77, when he was dism. at his own req. for feeble health, was rep. 1679 for W. and practis. as a surgeon, hav. in such capac. serv. in sev. exped. dur. Philip's war; was a great politician in support of Andros, and d. 2 Dec. 1713; hav. made his will 26 May 1712. Beside ds. Catharine, wh. m. Richard Treat, and d. bef. her f.; and Dorothy, wh. m. Thomas Treat, he had Edward, b. 1672; John, 1679, H. C. 1699, first min. of Colchester; and Charles, wh. in fam. memo. is call. first b. *JOHN*, br. of the preced. b. in Eng. bapt. at Odell, 19 Oct. 1619, came in the ship with his f. freem. 18 May 1642, went to his nat. ld. and had a living at Fordham, whence, being eject. 1662, he rem. to Wapping, near London, practis. physic with success, and d. a. 1689. Calamy's Acc. II. 311. He was of the first class of gr. at Harv. 1642, and ranks in the catal. next after Sir George Downing. JOHN, Fairfield 1669, s. of Thomas. JOSEPH, Fairfield, br. of the preced. m. Martha, d. of the elder James Beers, had lds. 1672 from his mo. and four s. Thomas; Daniel; Joseph, b. 9 May 1682; and Peter, 21 May 1684; are ment. on rec. PETER, Concord, the first min. there, s. of Edward, D. D. of Odell, in the hundr. of Willey, Bedfordsh. b. 31 Jan. 1583, was bred at St. John's Coll. Cambridge, where he proceed. A. M. 1608, and was chos. a fellow; had a consider. est. from his f. a moderate non-conform. wh. he succeed. in his nat. parish, and serv. at that altar twenty yrs. thro. favor of Lord Keeper Williams, then Bp. of Lincoln, his diocesan. [Brooks' Lives of the Puritans, III. 318.] He came in the Susan and Ellen, 1635, his age at the custom ho. call. 50, and (for more perfect decept. of the governm. spies), his w. Grace, 33, appears to be emb. in ano. ship; and s. John, 15, some wks. earlier, beside Benjamin, 11, and Daniel, 9 (wh. two tho. *not* names of his s. yet may stand for them), all three in the same ship with hims. but set down at intervals in the rec. both of time and space; and, of course, his cleric. charact. did not appear, or he would have been stop. He was first of Cambridge, but next yr. went to Concord, and was install. 6 Apr. 1637, d. 9 Mar. 1659. His wid. rem. to New London, and bot. a ho. 1663, there d. 21 Apr. 1669. By first w. Jane, d. of Thomas Allen of Goldington, he had Edward, above ment.; Mary, bapt. 24 Aug. 1615, d. in few mos.; Thomas, b. 11, bapt. 18 Apr. 1617; Nathaniel, 29 Nov. 1618, d. at 9 yrs.; John, 17 Feb. 1620, H. C. 1642; Mary, again, 1 Nov. 1621, d. at 3 yrs.; George, 17 May 1623; Daniel, 28 Aug. 1625; Jabez, 20 Dec. 1626, d. under 3 yrs.; prob. Joseph; and perhaps one or two more; and by sec. w. Grace, d. of Sir Richard Chitwood, or as ancient. spell. Chetwode, had Gershom, b. 6 Dec. 1636, or 2 Jan. as fam. memo. has it, of course at Concord (not, as is strangely said in Geneal. Reg. VII. 269, on the voyage), H. C. 1655; Eliezer, prob. 1638; Dorothy, 2 Aug. 1640; and Peter, 12 June or more prob. 12 Aug. 1643. His will, giv. at large in Gen. Reg. X. 167, of 14 Apr. 1658, in his 76th yr. with codic. of 13 Jan. and 26 Feb. foll. was pro. 20 June next. It names seven ch. tak. notice that Thomas was d. yet rememb. his wid.; calls Mr. Samuel Haugh, cous.; and gives his folio bible to Oliver St. John, Ch. Just. of the Com. Pleas; and makes his w. extrix. ‡ * PETER, Concord, eldest s. of the Rev. Edward, m. 16 Apr. 1667, Rebecca, d. of Joseph Wheeler, had Edward, b. 18 Mar. 1669; Joseph, 7 Oct. 1670; John, 10 July 1673; and Rebecca, 1681; was capt. and maj. rep. 1673–6, in wh. last yr. he was speaker, and sent to Eng. as agent to defend the col. against compl. of heirs of Gorges and Mason, faithful. and prudent. execut. the serv. and ret. Dec. 1679, Assist. 1677 for 8 yrs. d. 24 May 1688, at mid. age, "and," says Danforth, in Hutch. Coll. 566, "verily his sun did set in a cloud." His wid. Rebecca m. Jonathan Prescott; and d. Rebecca m. Jonathan Prescott, jr. PETER, Fairfield, youngest s. of the Rev. Peter, a physician, in his will of 25 Mar. 1691, in 49th yr. of his age, as he calls it, of course younger than his namesake neph. names two eldest ds. Grace and Margaret, and s. Peter, seven and a quarter yrs. old, but refers to other childr. without nam. Gershom, and Dorothy, for wh. we are compel. to turn to the will of his br. Gershom of Wethersfield, wh. was made excor. of this will, but declin. to act. His est. was small, and two neph. John and Joseph, wh. resid. at F. undertook admin. and soon gave it up. No small dexterity is need. to avoid confus. betw. the Peter of Edward, the Peter of Gershom, wh. I intentional. omit, and the Peter of Peter, wh. is entit. to a place here, as s. of one wh. came from Eng. THOMAS, Concord, s. of the first Peter, b. in Eng. freem. 13 Mar. 1639, m. Sarah d. of Rev. John Jones, had Sarah, b. 12 Aug. 1640, rem. with f.-in-law to Fairfield, there d. a. 1658. The wid. m. Anthony Wilson, and after his d. by her will of 26 Apr. 1677, gave lds. to two s. John and Joseph, beside books, and other prop. and to ds. Sarah, w. of Eleazer Brown, Rebecca, w. of Joseph Whelpley, and d. Hannah, perhaps unm. books and other prop. A Thomas B. was, it is said, of Rowley in 1643. THOMAS, Boston, by w. Esther had Elinor, b. 16 Sept. 1685; and Thomas, 1 Nov. 1686. Perhaps he rem. WILLIAM, Ipswich 1648, had William, wh. d. 1660; and he rem. to Salem; d. 2 June 1702, aged 80. His w. Sarah, wh. came 1643, was, in 1692, indict. for witchcraft, but acquit. Felt. Eleven of this name, oft. writ. Buckley, had been gr. at Yale in 1834, and only one at Harv. in the same yrs. yet four bef. the found. of Yale.

BULL, DAVID, Saybrook, s. of Thomas, m. 27 Dec. 1677, Hannah, d. of Robert Chapman, had Susanna, b. 4 July 1679; Hannah, 30 Apr. 1681; and Abigail, 16 Mar. 1683, d. at 3 mos. It is believ. the other ch. d. young. § HENRY, Roxbury, came in the James from London, 1635, aged 25, freem. 17 May 1637, rem. to Boston, by fam. tradit. is deriv. from South Wales; and less worthy tradit. makes him br. of Thomas of Conn.; the Roxbury ch. rec. says, "being weak and affectionate, was tak. and transport. with the opin. of familism, &c. as may be seen in that story," wh. the Roxbury min., Welde, hims. produc. He was among the Boston majority of heretics disarm. went to R. I. with Mrs. Hutchinson, was one of the purch. 1638, his being the 18th name of the signers of the compact or covenant for civ. governm. in that yr.;

Gov. of the col. 1685 and 9, d. Jan. 1694, in 95th yr. is the exagger. by ten yrs. of surv. By w. Eliz. wh. d. 1665, he had Jireh, b. Sept. 1638 at Portsmouth; Henry; Esther; and Mary; of wh. Esther d. young; and Mary, wh. m. James Coggeshall, liv. very long. For sec. w. he m. the wid. of Gov. Nicholas Easton. HENRY, came in the Elizabeth, 1635, aged 19. He belong. to London, and perhaps went home. HENRY, Narraganset, s. of the first Henry, prob. younger, m. Ann Cole, d. of John of the same, had Ephraim, b. 23 Jan. 1692, wh. d. young; Ann; and Henry, b. 1687; and the f. d. bef. mid. age; and his wid. d. 21 May 1704, aged 43. ISAAC, Boston, m. 22 June 1653, Sarah, d. of John Parker. JIRAH, or JERAH, s. of Gov. Henry, prob. elder, kept a garrison ho. at Narraganset, in Philip's war, Dec. 1675; had by first w. Godsgift Arnold, d. prob. of the first Benedict, Jirah, b. 1682; Benjamin, 1685; and Benedict; and his w. d. 23 Apr. 1691. He took sec. w. Sarah, wh. may have borne him some ch. as Henry, Ephraim, and Ezekiel. JOHN, Boston 1658, feltmaker, m. Mary, d. of Nicholas Baxter, wh. is undoubted. a wrong name of the f. of the bride, had John, b. 14 July 1663, d. young; James, 16 July 1665; Mary, 29 Oct. 1667; Mehitable, 1 Jan. 1670; John, again, 14 Mar. 1672; Henry, 12 Mar. 1674; Margaret, 19 May 1676; Martha, 7 Aug. 1678; Samuel, 19 Dec. 1680; and Jonathan, 24 Feb. 1683. His w. Mary d. 23 Aug. 1723, aged 83. JOHN, Hingham, a soldier in capt. Johnson's comp. wound. in the gr. Narraganset battle 19 Dec. 1675. But he had ch. bef. and after, had m. 21 Nov. 1672, Mary, d. of Edmund Pitts of H. and had Mary, b. 19 Dec. 1673, d. soon; ano. ch. 4 Apr. 1675; John, 7 Apr. 1677, d. soon, and Deborah, wh. d. next yr. His w. d. 18 Sept. 1696; and he m. 4 Mar. foll. Margaret Damon, perhaps d. of John of Scituate, had Mary, b. 7 Dec. 1697; Deborah, 16 Oct. 1699; John, 10 Dec. 1707, wh. d. at 3 yrs.; and Eliz. 8 Apr. 1712; and he d. 1 Dec. 1720. JONATHAN, Saybrook, s. of Thomas, a brave soldier, capt. 1690, when Schenectady was destr. by Ind. instig. by the Fr. m. 19 Mar. 1685, Sarah, d. of Rev. John Whiting, had Susanna, b. 26 Dec. foll.; Sarah, 25 Aug. 1687; Sybil, 13 Apr. 1690; Ruth, 21 Apr. 1692; Abigail, 24 July 1694; Jonathan, 14 July 1696; Moses, 18 May 1699; and Ebenezer, 27 Aug. 1701, and d. 17 Aug. 1702, aged 53. Perhaps Goodwin, 332, mistakes in mak. him gr.s. of the first Thomas. JOSEPH, Hartford, br. of the preced. m. 11 Apr. 1671, Sarah Manning of Cambridge, had Sarah, b. 11 July 1672; Joseph, 9 Aug. 1675; Daniel, 9 Nov. 1677; Caleb, 1 Feb. 1680, and may have been at Wickford, R. I. 1674. ROBERT, Saybrook 1649, m. Dec. of that yr. Phebe, whose name on the rec. if correct. giv. by Rev. Mr. Nash, is incredib. had Mary, b. 7 Dec. 1651; John, 10 Mar. 1653; Phebe, Aug. 1655; and Robert, 1 Mar. 1663.

Phebe m. 1676, Samuel Chalker. From a part of Saybrook rec. giv. in Geneal. Reg. V. 249, it may be infer. that his s. John went to Eng. sett. in Co. Gloucester, there had childr. and the conject. may be indulg. that from that shire the fam. orig. came. Thomas, Hartford, came in the Hopewell, capt. Babb, emb. at London, Sept. 1635, aged 25, was of Boston or Cambridge first, but accomp. Hooker next May, had w. Susanna, wh. d. 1680, aged 70; serv. well in the Pequot war, 1637, and in 1675 was in command at Saybrook, when Andros attempt. to gain the place for his master, the D. of York, and he steadily and successf. resist. him. [See Chalmers' Polit. Ann. 581, and Trumbull, Hist. I. 346.] He d. 1684, in his will nam. ch. Thomas; David of Saybrook, wh. was bapt. 9 Feb. 1651; Jonathan, bapt. 25 Mar. 1649; and Joseph of Hartford; Ruth, w. of Andrew Bordman of Cambridge; Abigail Buck; and a third d. Bunce. Thomas, Farmington, s. of the preced. m. Esther, d. of John Cowles, wh. d. 1691, aged 42, had John, b. 1671, wh. d. bef. his f. but left issue; Samuel, 1676; Susanna, 1679; Jonathan, bapt. 14 May 1682; Sarah, b. 1684; and Daniel, 1687. Cothren says, he m. sec. w. 1692, Hannah Lewis, wh. liv. to 1728. Descend. have been num. and respect. Ano. Thomas in Dec. 1675 was a soldier in Moseley's comp. set off for the bloody Narraganset exped. William, Cambridge 1644, had, by w. whose bapt. name was Blyth, Rebecca, b. 27 Aug. 1644; John, 9 Mar. 1647; Mary, 9 Mar. 1649; William, 10 Sept. 1652; Samuel, 17 Sept. 1654; and Elisha, 21 June 1657, wh. all liv. to be ment. in his will, made 21 May 1687, pro. 12 Oct. foll. tho. Harris, Epit. says he d. 13 Sept. 1688, aged 72. His wid. d. 23 Sept. 1690, aged 72. William, Cambridge, s. of the preced. m. 3 Jan. 1674, Abiah, d. of William Perry, had Abiah, b. 3 July 1675; William, 24 May 1678; and Andrew, 18 Jan. 1684. He liv. at Watertown, and had sec. w. 13 Nov. 1693, Eliz. Underwood, prob. a wid. Nine of this name had been gr. at Yale 1834.

Bullard, Benjamin, Watertown, a. 1642, as Bond, 147, gathers, but Morse finds him at div. of lds. in 1637, m. a d. of Henry Thorpe, rem. to Medfield, freem. 1668, perhaps had s. Benjamin by a former w. and he may have been, tho. prob. not, b. in Eng. Of this s. (by former or later w.) sis. are nam. Ann and Maudlin, yet the mo. has no name; and no approach to reasonab. conject. as to the time of his d. is offer. by Morse, while Bond has confus. f. and s. Benjamin, Dedham, s. of the preced. m. 1659, Martha Pidge, d. of Thomas, had Mary, b. 14 Sept. 1663, d. young; Samuel, 26 Dec. 1667; Benjamin, 1 Mar. 1670; Hannah, 6 Aug. 1672; and Eleazer, 27 June 1676. His w. d. 4 Jan. foll. and he m. 1677, sec. w. Eliz. had John, 7 Mar. 1678; Eliz. 31 Jan. 1682; Mary, 20 Feb. 1684; Malachi, 8 Mar. 1686; and Isaac, 25 July

1688. He liv. in that part of Dedham wh. was early made Medfield, and later cut into Sherborn. GEORGE, Watertown, freem. 2 June 1641, whose w. Margaret d. Feb. 1640 ; and he m. Beatrice Hall of Boston, had Mary, b. 12 Feb. 1640 ; Jacob, 6 Apr. 1642 ; and prob. Sarah ; Jonathan, 12 July 1647 ; and perhaps Joanna. He had ano. w. (I presume the third), 20 Apr. 1655, Mary Marplehead, says Dr. Bond, tho. Morse confines him to one w. ISAAC, Dedham, s. of the first William, b. in Eng. m. 11 Apr. 1655, Ann, wid. of John Wight, had Hannah, b. 24 Feb. 1656 ; Sarah, 7 Jan. 1658 ; Samuel, 22 Dec. 1659 ; Judith or Judah, 10 May 1662 ; Ephraim. 20 July 1664, d. in few days ; Ann, 17 Apr. 1666 ; John, 26 June 1668, d. in few days ; Mary, 29 May 1669 ; and William, 19 May 1673 ; and d. 1676. Ano. ISAAC is sometimes suppos. to have been at Watertown bef. 1636, one of the seven or eight mythical brs. but, if any thing more than shadow, he early d. or went home ; and of ano. ISAAC, presum. s. of John, the notice is too slight to found upon. JOHN, Dedham 1638, perhaps eldest s. of the first William, but Morse thinks him br. of William, freem. 13 May 1640, by w. Magdalen had Abigail, b. 8 Oct. 1641 ; Joseph, 26 Apr. 1643 ; and Hannah, 1 Oct. 1645, or, by ano. acco. 1 Feb. 1646. JONATHAN, Watertown, s. of Benjamin, m. 9 Dec. 1669, Esther, d. of Joseph Morse, had Esther, b. 13 Aug. 1671 ; Jonathan, 25 Dec. 1672 ; Hannah, 3 Feb. 1675 ; and perhaps Joseph. JOSEPH, Medfield 1678, s. of John, by w. Sarah had Joseph, b. 12 Sept. 1665, d. soon ; Sarah, 11 Nov. 1667 ; Joseph, again, 28 Mar. 1670 ; Samuel, 15 Sept. 1672 ; Rachel, 15 Nov. 1674 ; Solomon, 13 July 1679, d. soon ; Ebenezer ; and Hannah. NATHANIEL, Dedham, s. of William of the same, b. perhaps in Eng. m. 1658, Mary, d. of Edward Richards, had Mary, b. 24 Dec. 1659 ; Susanna, 19 Aug. 1661 ; Sarah, 31 July 1665 ; Judith, or Judah, 5 Aug. 1667 ; Martha, 6 Aug. 1670 ; and Nathaniel, the 3d wk. in Jan. 1680, wh. d. next yr. and the f. was freem. 1690, and d. 1705. ROBERT, Watertown, bur. 24 June 1639, was aged 40, and h. of Ann, but no more of him was discov. by Bond. But he suppos. him to be br. of Benjamin, George, Maudlin, and Ann. SAMUEL, Dedham, eldest s. of Isaac of the same, m. 1683, Hannah, perhaps d. of James Thorpe, and rem. to Dorchester. THOMAS, Northampton 1668. WILLIAM, Dedham 1636, freem. 13 May 1640, had Isaac, Nathaniel, Eliz. wh. m. Moses Collier of Woodbridge, N. J. and Mary, wh. m. 1650, John Farrington of D. Perhaps some of these were b. in Eng. and he may have had more. By sec. w. Mary, wid. of Francis Griswold of Charlestown, where he resid. 1658-77, he had none ; and he d. early in 1687, in D. at the ho. of his d. the wid. Farrington. In his will, of 5 July 1679, importing that he was then 85 yrs. old, he names the two ds. and two s tho. the elder s. was d. Prob. he was elder br. of Benjamin or George, or Robert, perhaps of all. WILLIAM, Dedham, s. of Isaac of the same, m. 1697, Eliz. eldest d. of Robert Avery of the same, had William, b. 1698; Eliz. 1699; Jemima, 1702; Ann, 1705; and Isaac, 1709; and d. 1746. Of this name, that sometimes in old rec. appears Bulward, five had been gr. in 1834 at Harv. two at Yale, one at Dart. and five at other N. E. coll.

BULLEN, ELISHA, Medfield and Sherborn, s. of Samuel, m. 31 May 1683, Hannah Metcalf, prob. d. of John of M. had Elisha, b. 14 Aug. 1684; Samuel, 24 Nov. 1687; Jonathan, 13 Jan. 1695, d. in few days; Hannah, 28 June 1697; and Miriam, 23 Aug. 1702. EPHRAIM, Sherborn, br. of the preced. had both been of Medfield 1678, by w. Grace had Mary, Ephraim, John, and Grace; but Morse, in his Geneal. p. 20, makes all the four b. after d. of his w. JOHN, Medfield 1649. JOHN, Medfield, s. of Samuel, m. 3 Jan. 1684, Judith Fisher, had Judith, b. 23 Oct. 1689; John, 31 Jan. 1692; David, 14 Jan. 1694; Michael, 2 Apr. 1696; Mary, 26 Feb. 1699; Silence, 21 May 1701, d. soon; and Samuel, 20 Aug. 1702. JOSEPH, Medfield, s. of Samuel, m. 15 Mar. 1675, Abigail Sabin, was freem. 1677, prob. d. without issue, for in his will of 28 Dec. 1703, he names none, but giv. est. to sev. nephs. and nieces, and makes w. Abigail extrix. SAMUEL, Dedham, freem. 2 June 1641, m. 10 Aug. 1641, Mary, d. of Samuel Morse, had Mary, b. 20 July 1642; Samuel, 19 Dec. 1644; Eliz. 3 Feb. 1647; Joseph, 6 Sept. 1651; Ephraim, 18 July 1653; Meletiah, 15 Sept. 1655; Elisha, 26 Dec. 1657; Eleazer, 26 Apr. 1662, d. in few days; Bethia, 1 Aug. 1664; and John, perhaps bef. the last two. He was deac. and d. 16 Jan. 1692; and his wid. d. 14 Feb. foll. In hist. of Framingham, Barry, giv. the distrib. of est. 1697, shows, that Mary m. a Clark; Eliz. m. a Wheelock, but was then d. leav. childr.; Meletiah, m. a Fisher, and was d. leav. childr.; and Bethia m. a Colburn; that Ephraim was d. leav. childr. and that Samuel, Joseph, Elisha, and John, as well as Mary and Bethia were liv.

BULLIER, JULIAN, Saybrook, m. 15 Jan. 1666, Eliz. Brooks. He d. 14 Jan. 1678, and his wid. m. 28 Apr. foll. James Fitzgerald.

BULLIS, PHILIP, Boston, mariner, m. 3 Dec. 1663, Judith, d. of John Hart, wid. of Robert Ratchell, had Eliz. b. 19 Nov. 1664; John, 8 Jan. 1669; Thomas, 3 Aug. 1671; and Rachel, 28 Sept. 1673; serv. in Gillam's comp. 1676, on Conn. riv. and next yr. was at B.

BULLIVANT, BENJAMIN, Boston 1685, a physician from London, made atty.-gen. as being of noble fam. acc. John Dunton, wh. kn. him in L., act. under Andros, and on the outburst, Apr. 1689, was for his office imprison. yet did not after rem. I suppose he had brot. w. from Eng.

and kn. that he had d. Hannah, bapt. 3 Jan. 1686, at O. S. ch. but there no other ment. of the name occurs, at least, neither he nor w. is in the print. list of mem. Easi. he assum. the Episcop. form of worship, and soon was one of the two first wardens of King's Chap.

BULLOCK, DAVID (not OVID, as Baylies, II. 217, in str. pervers. gives it), was of Rehoboth 1668. EDWARD, Dorchester, came in the Elizabeth 1635, aged 32, went home 1649, mak. his will 25 July of that yr. pro. 29 Jan. 1657, giv. his prop. to w. for her life, and after to his d.-in-law Hannah Johnson, and appoint. Humphrey Atherton, Augustine Clement, and George Weeks trustees for its purposes. But wh. the resid. legatee was, is not to be ascert. and the testator did not ret. ERASMUS, Newport 1638, had gr. of ho. lot in Boston that yr. but, tho. he had resid. five yrs. at B. the spirit of his party carr. him to the refuge of his antinom. friends. HENRY, Charlestown, came in the Abigail 1635, a husbandman from Co. Essex, aged 40, with w. Susan, 42, and ch. Henry, 8, wh. d. 1657; Mary, 6; and Thomas, 2; rem. after 1638, to Salem, there had gr. of ld. 1643, and 2 Dec. 1663; and d. 27 of same mo. JOHN, Providence, in May 1682 took o. of alleg. JOHN, Salem 1680, perhaps s. of Henry, was favor. bec. in the preced. Ind. war he had been crippled. RICHARD, Rehoboth 1643, rem. soon after 1644, and was freem. of May 1646, tho. it is not seen of what town he was inhab. again rem. to Newtown, L. I. a. 1656, but went soon back to R. and there d. 1667. SAMUEL, Rehoboth, m. 12 Nov. 1673, Mary Thurber, wh. d. 4 Oct. foll. when d. Mary was b. and he m. 26 May 1675, Thankful Rouse, had Thankful, b. 1681.

BULLY, NICHOLAS, Saco, constable 1664.

BUMPASS, more often BUMPAS, or BUMPUS, EDWARD, Plymouth, came in the Fortune 1621, liv. on Duxbury side bef. 1634, but most of his days at Marshfield, had Faith, b. 1631; Sarah; John, 1636; Edward, 1638; Joseph, 1639; Jacob, 1644; Hannah, 1646; and, perhaps, Thomas; was with the first purch. of Dartmouth 1652. Sarah m. Mar. 1659, Thomas Durham. As the rec. of M. tells, that " Hannah, wid. of old Edward B. d. 12 Feb. 1693," and that Edward B. d. nine days bef. I presume, that this was her s. not her h. JACOB, Scituate, s. of the preced. m. 1677, Eliz. wid. of William Blackmore, had Benjamin, b. 1678; and Jacob, 1680. JOHN, Middleborough, br. prob. eldest, of the preced. had Mary, b. 1671; John, 1673; Samuel, 1676; and James, 1678; may have rem. and had more ch. some bef. these foll. b. at Rochester, Sarah, 16 Sept. 1685; Edward, 16 Sept. 1688; and Jeremiah, 24 Aug. 1692. JOSEPH, Middleborough, s. of Edward, was first of Plymouth, there had Lydia, b. 2 Aug. 1669; Wybra, 15 May 1672; Joseph, 25 Aug. 1674; Rebecca, 17 Dec. 1677; James, 25 Dec. 1679; Penelope, 21 Dec.

1681; Mary, 12 Aug. 1684; and Mehitable, 21 Jan. 1692. THOMAS, Barnstable, br. perhaps, of the preced. m. Nov. 1679, Phebe, d. of John Lovell, had Hannah, b. 28 July 1680; Jane, Dec. 1681, bapt. 5 July 1696; Mary, Apr. 1683; Samuel, Jan. 1685; Thomas, May 1687; Sarah, Jan. 1689; Eliz. Jan. 1691; Abigail, Oct. 1693; the last six, with ano. ch. John, all bapt. 21 June 1696; and Benjamin, 27 Mar. 1703. The name is an easy pervers. from the French, Bon pas. Descend. are very num.

BUMSTEAD, EDWARD, Boston, freem. 13 May 1640, had Joseph, b. 1653. JEREMIAH, Boston, s. of Thomas, b. in Eng. d. 27 Feb. 1709, aged 72. ‖ THOMAS, Roxbury, as says the ch. rec. " came to this ld. July 1640, brot. two small ch. Thomas, and Jeremiah," and adds, " his d. Hannah, b. 25 Jan. 1641," tho. town rec. has it, 20 Jan. 1639. By w. Susanna he had Mary, bapt. at R. 24 Apr. 1642, and rem. to Boston, there had Joseph, bapt. 24 Nov. 1644, " a. 7 days old ; " Mercy, 20 Jan. 1650; and Joseph, again, 23 Oct. 1653 ; was of ar. co. 1647, and d. 22 June 1677. Winth. in his Hist. II. 203, ment. remark. preserv. of the life of one of his ch. His will of 25 May bef. his d. names ch. Jeremy ; Hannah, wh. m. 18 Apr. 1659, Thomas Shearer, or Sherwood ; Mary, w. of Ambrose Dawes ; and Mercy, w. of Samuel Bosworth.

BUNCE, THOMAS, Hartford 1636, serv. next yr. in the Pequot war, had, prob. by a d. of capt. Thomas Bull, under wh. he had act. in that war, ch. Thomas ; John ; Sarah, wh. m. John White of Hatfield, and, next, Nicholas Worthington ; Mary, b. 17 Sept. 1645, wh. m. Thomas Meakins of Hatfield, and, next, John Downing ; and Eliz. wh. m. Jacob White of Hartford, br. of John bef. nam.

BUNDY, JOHN, Plymouth 1643, rem. to Boston, by w. Martha had Martha, b. 2 Nov. 1649 ; and Mary, 5 Oct. 1653. He liv. after, prob. at Taunton, there his d. Patience d. 27 Mar. 1665 ; and he had James, 29 Dec. 1664 ; and Sarah, 4 Mar. 1669. His w. d. 1 May 1674 ; and Mary m. 5 Jan. preced. unless the better date be 1675. JOHN, Taunton, s. perhaps, of the preced. m. 9 Jan. 1677, Ruth Surney of Mendham (unless so strange a name be writ. for Turney), had John, b. 6 Oct. foll. ; Joseph, 1 Jan. 1680 ; and Edward, 13 Aug. 1681. SAMUEL, Taunton, perhaps br. of the preced. had Samuel, b. 4 Oct. 1670.

BUNKER, *BENJAMIN*, Malden, s. of George, ord. 9 Dec. 1663, d. 2 Feb. 1670. That he well fill. his post of duty, tho. never m. (as seems to be essential to the charact. of a N. E. min.) we may be confid. for the long and lamenta. verses of his senior collea. Michael Wigglesworth, reveal no tendency to fiction. GEORGE, Charlestown 1634, freem. 4 Mar. 1635, as a support. of Wheelwright, he was disarm. Nov. 1637, yet in May foll. the Gen. Court made him constable of C. and by the end of a yr. he had gr. from the same power of fifty acres, so we may not doubt, that he was convinc. of the errors in doctrine that had misled him. By w. Judith (wh. prob. he brot. from Eng. with his s. John) he had Benjamin, bapt. 20 Sept. 1635, H. C. 1658, bef. ment.; Jonathan, 8 Apr. 1638; and she d. 10 Oct. 1646. For sec. w. he took Margaret, wid. of deac. Edward Howe of Watertown, and he d. in 1664 or 5, for 4 Oct. of that latter yr. was pro. his will, made 12 May preced. In latter yrs. he rem. to Malden, but he own. bef. and after, the summit of that hill of glory bear. his name. His eldest s. John, with the other two s. ds. Mary, Martha, and Eliz. surv. Eliz. m. Edward Burt. GEORGE, Ipswich, s. of William, a Huguenot in Eng. liv. at Topsfield after m. with Jane Godfrey, and there was drown. 26 May 1658. His wid. gave inv. of £300. 20 June foll. At the date of his d. the ch. were Eliz. aged 12; William, 10; Mary, 6; Ann, 4; and Martha, 1 and ½. His wid. soon m. Richard Swain, went to Nantucket with those ch. and she d. 31 Oct. 1662, the earliest, in rec. of d. on that isl. Ann m. Joseph Coleman. JAMES, Dover 1653, had James, and perhaps Joseph, and John, and d. 1698. JOHN, Malden, eldest s. of George the first, b. in Eng. a. 1632, m. 16 Sept. 1655, Hannah Miller, had Hannah, b. Oct. 1656, d. young; Mary, 29 Dec. 1658; John, Jan. 1661, d. in few days; John, again, May 1662; Edward; and Joseph, Feb. 1666; and d. 10 Sept. 1672; in his will, made the same day, names eldest s. John, eldest d. Mary, s. Edward, and Joseph, and d. Hannah, wh. m. 2 May 1689, as his sec. w. Samuel Newman of Rehoboth. JOHN, Portsmouth or Dover, s. of James, was one of the many wh. in 1690, desir. Mass. jurisdict. to be stretch. over N. H. JONATHAN, Charlestown, s. of George of the same, m. 30 Jan. 1663, Mary Howard, and d. 2 June 1678, as tells the gr. stone, but rec. says 1677. He prob. had fam. yet not to be found on rec. WILLIAM, Topsfield, s. of George of the same, was nam. for his gr. f. in Eng. and after d. of his f. and m. of his mo. again, was carr. by her to Nantucket in 1658, m. 11 Apr. 1669, Mary, d. of Thomas Macy, founder of that settlem. had George, b. 22 Apr. 1671; John, 23 July 1673; Jonathan, 25 Feb. 1675; Peleg, 1 Dec. 1676; Jabez, 7 Nov. 1678; Thomas, 8 Apr. 1680; and Benjamin, 28 May 1683; and d. 1712.

BUNN, or BUNNE, EDWARD, Hull, had, prob. by first w. that d. Eliz. wh. m. Oct. 1673, Joseph Howe of Boston; but for sec. w. m. 20 Aug. 1657, Eliz. Mason; and d. soon after mak. his will of 14 Apr. 1673, in wh. he names only w. Eliz. cous. Sarah, James Mason, and Samuel Lee. He was one of the earliest sett. of Nantasket, his right being ackn. in 1642, bef. it got the name of Hull. MATTHEW, Hull, by w. Esther had Matthew, b. 9 June 1659; Nathaniel, 23 Mar. 1664; and Esther, 2 Nov. 1665. It has been sometimes thot. that this name was the same as

Binney ; but no evidence appears. The fam. of two syl. was early at the same town, and it may be, that some ambitious possessor of the shorter name may have stretch. it.

BUNNILL, BENJAMIN, New Haven, took o. of fidel. 7 Apr. 1657, was, perhaps, s. of William, and a propr. 1685. WILLIAM, New Haven, an early inhab. m. Ann, d. of Benjamin Wilmot, wh. in his will of 7 Aug. 1669, speaks of the four ch. of his d. as heirs of pt. of his small est. so that it may be inf. that both d. and h. were d.

BURBANK, CALEB, Rowley 1691, may have been s. of John. JOHN, Rowley, freem. 13 May 1640, in his will of 5 Apr. 1681 (as Coffin finds, Geneal. Reg. VI. 245), names w. Jemima, ch. John, Caleb, and Lydia. JOHN, Haverhill, perhaps s. of the preced. m. 15 Oct. 1663, Susanna, d. of Nathaniel Merrill, rem. a. 1680 with sev. ch. to Suffield, where his w. d. 1690 ; and tho. he had sec. and third w. yet no more ch. The name in that neighb. is com. JOSEPH, came, 1635, in the Abigail from London, aged 24, when at the custom ho. it was writ. Borebancke ; but where he sat down is unkn.

BURBEEN, JOHN, Woburn, a tailor, came from Scotland, it is said, m. 16 Apr. 1660, Sarah Gould, had Mary, b. 2 July 1661 ; John, 9 Aug. 1663; James, 15 May 1668 ; and perhaps no more, for his w. d. 14 May 1670. He d. 8 Jan. 1714. Joseph, and Paul, gr. at H. C. of the yrs. 1731 and 1743, liv. to advanc. age, yet prob. this name is extinct in N. E.

BURCH, GEORGE, Salem, by w. Eliz. had Mary, b. 30 Nov. 1659, d. young; Eliz. 4 June 1662 ; John, 28 May 1664; Mary, again, 26 Sept. 1667 ; Abigail, 16 Aug. 1669 ; and George, 27 Apr. 1671 ; and d. 1 Oct. 1672. JOSEPH, Dorchester 1671.

BURCHALL, NATHAN, New Haven 1643, serv. of Robert Newman, sw. to fidel. 5 Aug. 1644.

BURCHAM, EDWARD, Lynn 1636, freem. 14 Mar. 1639, was clk. of the writs 1645, went home 1656, and I kn. not whether he came back. His d. Frances m. 8 June 1660, Isaac Willy.

BURCHARD, or BURCHER, EDWARD, Plymouth, came in the Ann, 1623, perhaps had w. as two sh. in div. of ld. next spr. were giv. but he d. or rem. for in div. of cattle, 1627, he took no pt. THOMAS, see Birchard.

BURCHSTED, JOHN HENRY, Lynn, a German physician from Silesia, says Lewis, 134, m. 24 Apr. 1690, Mary, wid. of Nathaniel Kirtland, had Henry, b. 3 Oct. foll. and d. 20 Sept. 1721, aged 64. The s. foll. the same profess. but I kn. no more of him.

BURDEN, FRANCIS, Portsmouth, R. I. among freem. 1655. GEORGE, Boston, shoemaker, came in the Abigail 1635, aged 20, was adm. of the ch. 9 Jan. 1637, and freem. 17 May foll. next Nov. disarm. for heresy, yet not driv. away, by w. Ann had Thomas, b. 1 Apr. 1637, d. very soon; Elisha, bapt. 3 Feb. 1639; Ezekiel, b. 25 Mar. 1641; Joseph, and Benjamin, tw. b. 21 Apr. 1643, both d. soon, but Joseph was bapt. 30 of that mo.; Hannah, 4 May 1645, "a. 20 days old;" and prob. others. At Braintree he had lot, 1639, for five heads, so that he must have had two serv. or apprent. But he went home with w. and ch. after mak. his will 15 Oct. 1652, wh. was pro. here 30 Apr. 1657. ROBERT, Lynn, m. a. 1650, Hannah, d. of William Witter, if we obey the authority of Coffin in Geneal. Reg. VI. 245, but both names are wrong there, Witter means Winter, and Burden stands for Burditt, wh. see. Greater mistakes may be seen in other copies from early rec. by other collectors. WILLIAM, Duxbury, or Marshfield, is well seen in Barden.

BURDICK, or BURDICT, BENJAMIN, Westerly, s. of Robert of the same, in his will of 25 Apr. 1736, names w. Jane, and s. Peter, Benjamin, John, David, William, Elisha, ds. Mary Lewis, and Rachel Sisson. ROBERT, Newport, made freem. 22 May 1655; rem. to Westerly bef. 1661, m. Ruth, d. of Samuel Hubbard of N. had Robert, Hubbard, Thomas, Benjamin, and Samuel, beside Naomi, wh. m. Jonathan Rogers; Tacy, wh. m. Joseph Maxson; Ruth, wh. m. John Phillips; and Deborah, wh. m. Joseph Crandall; and d. 1692. THOMAS, Westerly 1680, s. of Robert. This name is oft. confound. with Burditt.

BURDITT, or BURDETT, GEORGE, Salem 1635, came from Yarmouth, Co. Norf'k. where by pop. elect. he had preach. two yrs. but leav. w. and childr. at home in distress, was in gr. esteem at S. freem. 2 Sept. 1635, had gr. of ld. and preach. there near two yrs. and in 1637 or 8, went to Dover, there had much quarrel, and thence to York, and was forced to go home at last. Winthrop is large in reprobat. of him, Hubbard is strong; and the crim. proceed. of Cts. under Gorges' governm. for adultery and other charges, make it plain that N. E. was not the right place for him. ROBERT, Malden, m. Nov. 1653, Hannah Winter, had Thomas, b. Sept. 1655; Hannah, Nov. 1656; Joseph; Mary; Sarah; and Ruth, in May 1666; and he d. 16 June of next yr. by will of the same day ment. the w. and ch. and provid. also for ano. unb. THOMAS, Malden, eldest s. of the preced. by w. Hannah had Thomas, b. 13 Jan. 1683; Eliz. 19 Aug. 1686, d. young; Eliz. again, 28 Aug. 1688; and by w. Eliz. had Mary, 25 Dec. 1690; and John, 8 May 1693. His w. d. 26 Jan. 1718, aged a. 65, and he d. 20 Jan. 1729, in 74th yr. by gr.stone.

BURDSALL, HENRY, Salem, freem. 2 May 1638.

BURDSIE, the same as Birdseye; and here I supply some deficiency in that article. The contr. of m. with Alice, wid. of Henry Tomlinson, to wh. in his will JOHN B. refers, was of 8 Oct. 1688. He d. a. 1694, aged 74. By his first w. Philippa he had John, b. at Stratford, Mar. 1641, and Joanna, Nov. 1642. So it is clear, that he rem. from Milford to S. earlier by some yrs. than Trumbull, in his Hist. suppos. Joanna m. 28 Dec. 1664, Timothy Wilcockson. JOHN, Stratford, s. of the preced. m. 11 Dec. 1669, d. prob. youngest, of William Wilcockson, had Hannah, b. Feb. 1671; Mary, Nov. 1675; Mary, May 1678, d. next yr.; Abel, Nov. 1679; Joseph, Feb. 1682; and Dinah, 1688. He d. 1697, and his wid. d. 20 Sept. 1743, aged 92. Joseph was f. of Rev. Nathan, wh. was b. 8 Aug. 1714, so that the venerable man was a little older than was said in my acco. of Birdseye.

BURFEE, EDMUND, Boston, had w. Mary, wh. d. 15 Aug. 1658.

BURGE, GILES, Dorchester 1682. JACOB, Sandwich, s. of Thomas the first, m. 1 June 1660, Mary Nye, d. prob. of Benjamin of the same, had Samuel, b. 8 Mar. 1671; Ebenezer, 2 Oct. 1673; and Jacob, 18 Oct. 1676. JOHN, Chelmsford, m. 9 June 1662, Mary, wid. of Isaac Larned, eldest d. of Isaac Stearns, as Allen, Hist. of C. 169, tells; and in June 1676, m. Jane, wid. of John Gornell, wh. d. 4 Apr. 1678; and he d. 22 Oct. foll. JOHN, Yarmouth, s. of the first Thomas, m. 8 Sept. 1657, Mary Worden, prob. d. of Peter the sec. of the same, had John, Thomas, Joseph, Samuel, Jacob, Martha, and four other ds. JOSEPH, Sandwich, br. prob. youngest, of the preced. had Rebecca, b. 17 Jan. 1667; Dorothy, 12 Nov. 1670, wh. d. prob. at 16 yrs.; Joseph, 18 Nov. 1673; and Benjamin, 5 May 1681. *THOMAS, Lynn, rem. 1637, to Sandwich, with fam. there may have add. to the ch. carr. with him only Joseph, and perhaps Jacob. He was of the chief men, rep. 1646 and after; d. 27 Feb. 1685, presum. to be 82 yrs. old. His d. Eliz. m. 12 Feb. 1652, Ezra Perry. THOMAS, Sandwich, s. prob. eldest, of the preced. perhaps b. in Eng. m. 8 Nov. 1648, Eliz. Basset, d. of William, one of the *first comers*, was divorc. 10 June 1661, and rem. to R. I. and at Newport was resid. 1671, hav. w. Lydia.

BURGESS, or BURGISS, sometimes BURGES, ABRAHAM, took pass. 11 Apr. 1679 in the William and John from London for N. E. but whether he ever reach. our shore, or what bec. of him, is unkn. FRANCIS, Boston, by w. Joyce had Benjamin, b. 11 Oct. 1654. One Francis, possib. his s. was of Moseley's comp. in the campaign of Dec. 1675. JAMES, Boston, came, prob. in the Hopewell, capt. Bundocke, from London 1635, aged 14, m. 19 Oct. 1652, Lydia Mead, d. of Gabriel, had John, b. 1654; Benjamin, 1655; John, again, 21 Feb. 1657; and d. 27 Nov. 1690. JOHN, Yarmouth 1678, is prob. mistak. for Burge. *JOSEPH, Rochester, possib. misspel. for Burge, was first rep. for that town in one of the last Gen. Cts. of Plymouth, i. e. 1689. RICHARD, Sandwich 1643, as Coffin thinks, rem. to York 1660. ROBERT, Lynn 1655, m. 12 Apr. 1671, Sarah Hall. ROGER, Boston, had w. Sarah, wid. of Wil-

liam King, d. of George Griggs, wh. d. 24 Nov. 1664. ROGER, Haverhill, old eno. 28 Nov. 1677, to take o. of alleg. on enrolm. in the milit.
* THOMAS, Duxbury 1637, next yr. rem. to Sandwich, was rep. 1646,
and one or two yrs. more, was f. of Thomas, &c. as under Burge is told.
THOMAS, Concord 1660. Of this name, in 1834, gr. at Brown and Yale
have been five, and none at Harv. or Dart. yet two at H. and one at D.
as monosyl. Burge, and no such at Yale. Hon. Tristram, Brown 1796,
may desc. from Joseph, at least, was b. at Rochester. Very num. are
the cases of modern turn. of one syl. to two.

BURKBY, THOMAS, Rowley 1643.

BURKE, JAMES, Hingham. See Buck. RICHARD, Concord, had gr.
of ld. 1686, at Stow, m. at Northampton, 1 Sept. 1687, perhaps as sec.
w. Sarah, wid. of Nehemiah Allen, d. of Thomas Woodford, had John,
b. 19 July 1689; but he had s. Richard and Jonathan long bef.

BURLEIGH, RICHARD, Ipswich, a. 1690. Felt. Possib. he was s. of
Giles Budley, wh. see.

BURLINGHAM, or BURLINGAME, JOHN, Kingstown, R. I. s. of Roger,
m. Mary, d. of Moses Lippit, and of him no more is kn. ROGER,
Stonington 1654, Warwick 1660, by w. Mary had John, b. 1 Aug. 1664;
and Thomas, 6 Feb. 1667, but nothing more is found of him, or w.
or ch. exc. that his d. Mary m. 19 Dec. 1689, Amos Stafford, liv. 72 yrs.
with him, had thirteen ch. as is said, was b. six days after him, and d.
at equal distance, aged 97, some part of wh. may be true, but the newspaper that ment. his (Stafford's) d. at 97, makes the wid. 92. Five
yrs. discrepancy in a tradit. is not of high import. See Geneal. Reg.
VIII. 368. THOMAS, Warwick, or Kingstown, s. of Roger, m. Martha,
d. of Moses Lippit, as from wills of her f. and h. is gain. but I profit no
more.

BURLISSON, EDWARD, Suffield 1677, had John, Fearnot, Return,
Mary, and Edward, and d. 1698.

BURMAN, THOMAS, Barnstable, in his will of 9 May 1663, makes his
w. Hannah extrix. names s. Thomas, Tristram, Samuel; ds. Hannah,
Desire, Mary, and Mehitable.

BURN, JOHN, Plymouth 1651. RICHARD, Lynn, rem. 1637 to Sandwich. THOMAS, Marshfield 1648. WILLIAM, Duxbury 1638.

BURNAP, ISAAC, Reading, s. of Robert, m. 8 Nov. 1658, Hannah
Antram, perhaps d. of Thomas; d. 18 Sept. 1667, in his will of two
days preced. names no w. or ch. but ment. f. Robert, brs. Robert, and
Thomas, sis. Ann, and Sarah, and cous. Thomas B. JOHN, Reading,
freem. 1691, as were JOSEPH, ROBERT, and THOMAS, all at the same
time, of the same town. ROBERT, Reading, had, I think, been of Roxbury, whither he brot. from Eng. Thomas, b. a. 1624, and Richard, 1627,

both, perhaps, liv. 1682. But the name in rec. of Roxbury, when he lost an inf. ch. 18 Nov. 1642, is Burnet, tho. it appears not again. The w. was there Margaret Davis; but by w. Ann at Reading he had Sarah, b. 5 Nov. 1653; Robert, 28 Feb. 1658; and Mary, 17 June 1661; and this w. d. eight days after, and he took ano. w. 28 May 1662, Sarah . .

BURNELL, JOHN, Salem 1665. ROBERT, Lynn 1690. SAMUEL, Boston 1676, s. of William of the same. TOBIAS, Portsmouth, came from Alphington, Co. Devon, went in Sept. 1673, to Barbados, and d. soon. WILLIAM, Boston, had John, Samuel, and Sarah, and the dispos. of his est. at Pulling Point, appears in his will of 16 Apr. 1660, abstr. in Geneal. Reg. IX. 230, and it is curious to collate this with an earlier will of 5 Mar. of the same yr. in Geneal. Reg. X. 270, brot. out by the exempl. dilig. of Mr. Trask. Both have refresh. evid. of his dread of Quakers. Yet a scruple is felt whether that will of Mar. were not a later draft; if the legal reckon. of the yr. be foll. it must be so thot. and it was incomplete for want of witness. Hard is it, often to disting. this name from Burnett.

BURNETT, or BURNIT, JOHN, Charlestown, m. 7 Apr. 1684, Mary Rice of Reading. ROBERT, Roxbury, may be Burnap, wh. see. THOMAS, Lynn, m. 3 Dec. 1663, Mary, d. of John Pearson, as Felt gives it in Geneal. Reg. V. 94.

BURNHAM, BURNAM, or BURNUM, JEREMIAH, Dover 1680, s. of Robert, desir. 1690, protect. of Mass. jurisdict. to be extend. to the Prov. of N. H. JOHN, Ipswich, was 22 yrs. of age there in 1638. RICHARD, Hartford, s. of Thomas, m. 11 June 1680, Sarah, d. of Michael Humfrey of Windsor, had Hannah, b. 1683; Rebecca, 1685; Mercy, bapt. 22 Apr. 1688; Mary, 18 May 1690; Richard, July 1692; Martha, 28 Oct. 1694; Esther, 28 Mar. 1697; Charles, 30 July 1699; Susanna; and Michael, 1705. ROBERT, Boston, by w. Francis had Robert, b. 25 Sept. 1647; Eliz. 27 Oct. 1651; and he rem. to Dover in 1657, or earlier, there had Robert, 21 Aug. 1664, the former s. Robert hav. d. 25 Feb. preced. In 1671 he was adm. freem. and in 1690 he desir. jurisdict. of Mass. again. His s. Samuel and Jeremiah are provid. for in his will of 12 June 1691, pro. 29 Sept. foll. of wh. w. Frances was extrix. A slight error is seen in the name of resid. of this man, and ano. in the list of freem. 1671, Geneal. Reg. III. 241, Mr. Paige, reading the orig. MS. as abridgm. for Dorchester, wh. real. is Dover. SAMUEL, Dover 1686, s. of the preced. THOMAS, Ipswich 1647, prob. br. of John, m. Mary, d. of John Tuttle, had Ruth, b. 1 July 1657, d. same mo.; Ruth, again, 23 Aug. 1658; Joseph, 26 Sept. 1660; Nathaniel, 4 Sept. 1662; Sarah, 28 June 1664; Esther, 19 Mar. 1666; beside Thomas, John, James, Mary, Joanna, and Abigail; and he d. 19 May 1694. He had serv. in the Pequot exped. but whether it were, 1636, under Endicot, or the more effective one, 1637, of Stoughton, is not told, tho. we may infer, it was the earlier. His d. Sarah m. a Clark, wh. d. soon, and she next m. 6 Aug. 1684, Mesheck Farley. THOMAS, Springfield 1651. THOMAS, Ipswich, perhaps s. of Thomas the first, m. 13 Feb. 1666, Lydia Pingree, d. perhaps, of Moses, had Thomas, b. 19 Jan. 1667; Phebe, 16 Mar. 1668; Moses, 24 Jan. 1670; Lydia, 6 Dec. 1674; Aaron, 12 Sept. 1676; Eleazer, 5 Sept. 1678; Abigail, 2 June 1680; Daniel, 4 Apr. 1682; and Mary, 1685. His w. d. 14 Mar. 1689, and he d. 21 Feb. 1728, aged 82. THOMAS, Hartford, rem. to Windsor, after mid. age prob. and d. 1688, leav. Thomas, John, Samuel, William, and Richard (wh. all had fams.) beside four ds. Descend. are very num. THOMAS, Windsor, s. of the preced. m. 4 Jan. 1677, Naomi, d. of Josiah Hull of the same, had Thomas, b. 16 Apr. 1678; John, 22 May 1681; and these bapt. at Hartford, Sarah, 7 Mar. 1686; Naomi, 3 June 1688; Abigail, 25 Mar. 1694; and Josiah, 6 Sept. 1696. THOMAS, Ipswich, perhaps neph. of Thomas the first, for hardly may he be thot. s. of Thomas the sec. of same, m. 16 Dec. 1685, Esther Bishop, and by sec. w. Susanna (wh. d. 27 May 1728), had Susanna, b. 29 Jan. 1693; Thomas, 12 Feb. 1695; and Benjamin, 21 Dec. 1696. WILLIAM, Malden, had Edward, b. Sept. 1657, but no more is kn. Of this name, in 1634, five had been gr. at Dart. three at Harv. and five at the other N. E. coll.

BURNS, EDWARD, Hingham, freem. 1666. LAWRENCE, Marblehead 166 .

BURNYEAT, JOHN, Newport 1672, trans. apostle with George Fox. THOMAS, Providence 1666, may have been br. of the preced. at least in doctr.

BURPH, possib. BURFEE, STEPHEN, Rehoboth, in Col. Rec. said to have m. 29 May 1674, Eliz. Perry, by me would be regard. so strange a name as almost to invite invasion of conject. upon those sacred premises where no error can be suppos. It may have been Burpee, tho. I had not bef. heard of the name so early in N. E.

BURR, BENJAMIN, Hartford, an early sett. had two s. Samuel, the elder (made freem. with his f. 1658), and Thomas, b. 26 Jan. 1646, and two ds. Mary, wh. m. 15 Jan. 1657, Christopher Crow, and, next, Josiah Clark, and Hannah, wh. m. Andrew Hillier, all liv. at the time of his d. 1681, and he may have had others. His wid. Ann d. 31 Aug. 1683. DANIEL, Fairfield, freem. 1668, s. of Jehu the first, had m. 11 Dec. 1678, Abigail, d. of Henry Glover of New Haven, and took sec. w. Elinor, wh. present. inv. of his prop. 1695, so that it can safely be infer. that he was then d. but whether he had ch. by either is not kn. DANIEL, Fairfield, s. of Jehu the sec. left wid. Eliz. and ten ch. to div. his est. (which

was quite large), acc. inv. of 14 July 1727. Of six s. we may judge
the order of success. in age to concur with the arrangem. at pro. office,
Jehu; Stephen; Peter; David; Moses, Y. C. 1734; and Aaron, Y. C.
1735; and more confid. can we presume, that sev. of the ds. Hannah,
Mary Wheeler, Eliz. Hull, and Jane Sherwood were b. bef. sev. of the s.
I wish the hs. of the m. ds. could be respectiv. assign. Moses and Aaron
were minors; and their brs. Stephen and Peter were several. made
guardns. Nine of these ch. had ea. £545. and double that sum was sh.
of the eldest s. The youngest s. Aaron, b. 4 Jan. 1717, was the disting.
good man, presid. of N. J. coll. f. of the more disting. (but not as a good
man), Aaron of N. Y. the great manager of the polit. change for our country
in 1800, wherein he was made third Vice-Presid. of the U. S. * JEHU,
Roxbury 1630, came, prob. in the fleet with Winth. req. adm. as freem.
19 Oct. of that yr. and was sw. 18 May foll. Of his w. the bapt. name
is not seen, tho. she was, at the same time with h. mem. of the ch. He
was a carpenter, appoint. in 1633, by the Col. governm. to see to "the
bridges betw. Boston and Roxbury," wh. suggests interest. queries in our
topogr. In 1636 he rem. with Pynchon to the foundat. of Springfield,
and for that town, not suppos. to belong to Mass. in 1638, was rep. at
Hartford; and soon after went to Fairfield, of wh. he was rep. 1641, 5,
and 6, prob. d. soon after. Four s. Jehu, John, Daniel, and Nathaniel,
are kn. and perhaps he had not other ch. How easy mistakes occur in
read. ancient MS. is well exhibit. in this man's case. Copy from entr. in
Col. rec. 1630 and 1631, of his name, print. in my list of freem. as
Appndx. to Winth. II. 361, giv. it John; and the well-practis. eyes of
Pulsifer, transcrib. for the Antiq. Soc. of Worcester, and the more
scrupulous Paige, in the Reg. of N. E. Hist. Genealog. Soc. III. 90 and
1, were equal. deceiv. and even Felt, wh. had giv. so many yrs. of his
life to those rec. fell under the same delusion; while, to immortalize the
wrong, it is assert. by Trumbull, in Conn. Col. Rec. I. 12. In read. the
sec. and fourth letters of this bapt. name, not one in a thousand experts
would be likely to differ from us, as John appears in the reverse proportion to Jehu. Yet from the unusual distinctness of the Roxbury ch.
rec. wh. I have examin. and the concur. later ones at Springfield and
elsewhere, all doubt is dispel. Trumbull, in his Index, correct. the error
of his text; and the 1853 Ed. of Winthrop's Hist. II. 441, has giv. the
true name. * JEHU, Fairfield, s. prob. eldest, of the preced. perhaps b.
in Eng. m. Mary, d. of Andrew Ward, had sev. ch. certain. Daniel and
Esther, in the will 1665 of their gr.mo. Ward. But other childr. he
had, prob. some by this w. and some by ano. w. Esther, wid. of
Joseph Boosy. He was a promin. man, rep. 1659, 60, and after
junct. of Conn. with N. H. sev. yrs. In Philip's war he was capt

trust. as one in a commissn. with gr. powers; and d. prob. in 1692, as
the inv. of his est. was made 31 Oct. of that yr. The will 'of 11 Jan.
1690 names ch. Daniel; Peter, H. C. 1690; Samuel; Esther; Eliz.;
Sarah; Joanna; and Abigail (of wh. some were minors); beside Mary,
wh. had m. Samuel Wakeman, and was d. leav. a d. * JOHN, Fairfield,
br. of the preced. perhaps b. after his f. came to Roxbury, was adm.
freem. of Conn. 1664, rep. 1666, and with his br. Jehu, 1670, and more
yrs. was major, and d. 1694. His w. was, it is said, Sarah Fitch, but
whose d. she was is not told, and for the ch. in partial default of rec. we
must accept his will, nam. John, b. 2 May 1673; David; Samuel, 2
Apr. 1679, H. C. 1697; Jonathan; Sarah, 25 July 1675; Mary, 19
Aug. 1683; and Deborah; the last two unm. Joseph, b. 21 June 1677,
and Ebenezer, 7 Feb. 1682, d. bef. their f. The wid. Sarah, in her will,
of 8 June 1696, names only the ds. Sarah Chauncy, wh. m. 29 June
1692, Rev. Charles of F., Mary, Deborah, and s. Samuel. JOHN,
Hingham, s. of Simon, m. 24 Dec. 1685, Mary, d. of John Warren of
Boston, and d. 8 Dec. 1716, aged a. 57, and his wid. d. 5 June 1742,
aged 78, as the gr.stones tell. *JONATHAN*, Dorchester, b. at Redgrave
in Co. Suff k. it is said, bred at Corpus Christi, in Cambridge Univ. where
he took his degr. 1623, and 1627, was rector of Rickingshall, in his
native ld. but was silenc. by his primate, Laud, and came with w. Frances,
and three young ch. to this asylum 1639. In the sec. foll. winter he was
call. to be collea. with Mather, but d. 9 Aug. 1641, aged 36, leav. Jonathan, H. C. 1651; John; and Simon, wh. were b. in Eng. and Mary, b.
a. 1640, at D. wh. m. Zechariah Long of Charlestown, and d. 2 Aug. 1681.
Of John, and Simon, as nothing is relat. it may be infer. that both d.
early; but the mo. m. a. 1643, Hon. Richard Dummer of Newbury,
outliv. him, and d. 19 Nov. 1682, aged 70. Winth. II. 22, and Magn.
III. 78. JONATHAN, Hingham, s. of the preced. was a physician, of wh.
we kn. only, that he accomp. the forces in the crusade of Sir William
Phips against Quebec, and d. of smallpox, 28 Nov. 1690. Nothing is
seen of w. or ch. NATHANIEL, Fairfield, s. of Jehu the first, freem.
1664, had m. Sarah, d. of Andrew Ward, as his wid.'s will, of 1665,
names this d. and her two ch. Sarah, and Nathaniel. Both these ch. d.
bef. the f. wh. had sec. w. Ann, and d. 26 Feb. 1712. His will of four
days bef. names seven ch. viz. the dec. Nathaniel, wh. had left four ch.
and John, Daniel, Esther, Ann Allen, Rebecca Sherwood, and Mary
Labarre. PETER, Fairfield, s. of sec. Jehu, after leav. coll. taught a sch.
two or three yrs. bec. a judge of the Sup. Ct. of Conn. and d. 1724, or 5.
Good est. is exhibit. in his inv. of 18 Feb. of the latter yr. SAMUEL,
Hartford, s. of Benjamin of the same, m. Mary, d. of John Baysey, wh.
d. bef. her h. and he d. 29 Sept. 1682, leav. ch. Samuel, then aged 19;

John, 12 ; Mary, 10; Eliz. 7 ; and Jonathan, 4. SIMON, Hingham,
perhaps br. certain. not s. of Rev. Jonathan, as Rev. Dr. Harris made
him (wh. was also mistak. in the desc. of Aaron), had ch. Esther, wh.
d. 20 Dec. 1645 ; Henry, d. 14 Feb. 1647 ; Rose, d. June 1647 ; and
Hannah, b. 7 Aug. 1646 ; and he d. bef. Mar. 1693, when Simon, and
John, the only surv. ch. div. the est. mak. provis. (acc. the expres. but
unwrit. will of their f.) for their niece, Hannah Hobart, d. of John, wh.
had m. Apr. 1674 their sis. of the same name. SIMON, Fairfield, s.
prob. of Jehu the first, unless there be error in his evid. giv. Feb. 1682,
call. him a. 48 yrs. old. THOMAS, Hartford, younger s. of Benjamin, by
w. Sarah had Thomas ; Samuel ; Benjamin ; Joseph, bapt. 31 July
1687 ; Jonathan, 19 June 1692 ; Ann, 11 Nov. 1694 ; Isaac, 4 July
1697, Y. C. 1717 ; Daniel, 12 May 1700 ; Caleb, 20 Feb. 1704, prob.
d. young ; and Sarah, 1708 ; beside Abigail, and Hannah ; and he d.
1731, in his will nam. seven s. and four ds. Of this name, Farmer
found, in 1829, seven gr. at Yale and four at Harv.

BURRAGE, BENJAMIN, Scarborough 1640, serv. of John Winter.
JOHN, Charlestown 1637, freem. 18 May 1642, by w. Mary had Mary,
bapt. 9 May 1641 ; Hannah, b. 14 Dec. 1643 ; Eliz. and Nathaniel, 28
Dec. 1655, d. next yr. and his w. d. bef. this s.   By sec. w. Joanna, wh.
d. 25 Dec. 1689, aged 65, he had William, b. 10 June 1657, and Sarah,
24 Jan. 1659 ; and he d. 1 Jan. 1678. Hannah m. 1662, John French
of Billerica, as his sec. w. and Eliz. m. 15 Sept. 1668, Thomas Dean,
wh. d. in few yrs. and she m. 12 Aug. 1680, John Poor. JOHN, Scarborough 1640, br. of Benjamin, was that yr. in serv. of John Winter,
was f. of William, and his wid. m. Thomas Hammatt. JOHN, Charlestown, perhaps s. of first John of the same, had Bethia, bapt. 26 May
1661 ; Ruth, 5 Mar. 1665 ; and he d. 18 Jan. 1681. THOMAS, Lynn,
by w. Eliz. m. 1687, had Eliz. John, Thomas, Mary, Bethia, and Ruth.
*WILLIAM, Scarborough, s. of John of the same, was town clk. select-
man, rep. 1684, and, almost by compuls. was a preach. four yrs. succeed.

BURRILL, EPHRAIM, Weymouth, s. of John, by w. Lydia had Lydia,
b. 23 Apr. 1689 ; Mary, 23 May 1690 ; Samuel, 7 Oct. 1691 ; Ephraim,
14 Feb. 1695 ; John, 12 Jan. 1698 ; and Sarah, 28 May 1699 ; perhaps
more. FRANCIS, Lynn, s. of George, b. prob. in Eng. by w. Eliz. had
(beside ch. b. bef. 18 Oct. 1653, when the will of its gr.f. refers to it),
Eliz. b. 1 Dec. 1655 ; James, 21 Dec. 1657 ; Joseph, 18 Dec. 1659 ;
Mary, 16 May 1661, d. young; Lydia, 13 June 1663 ; Hannah, 19
May 1665 ; Mary, again, 7 Feb. 1668, d. at 10 days ; Deborah, 23 July
1669, d. in few wks. ; Moses, 12 Apr. 1671 ; Esther, 15 Jan. 1674 ;
Sarah, 11 Apr. 1676, d. same yr. ; and Samuel ; and d. 10 Nov. 1704.
GEORGE, Lynn 1630, was one of the richest plant. brot. prob. from Eng.

w. Mary, s. George, and Francis, here had John, b. 1631; and both h. and w. d. 1653. Lewis. His will of 18 Oct. in that yr. pro. in June foll. ment. the three s. and ch. of Francis. GEORGE, Boston, s. of the preced. a cooper, m. Deborah, d. of Nicholas Simpkins, had George, b. 13 Feb. 1654; Samuel, 10 Jan. 1656; Sarah, wh. m. John Souther; wh. beside gr.ch. Abraham Gourden, are all nam. in his will of 4 Oct. 1693, pro. 14 July 1698, nine days after his d. JAMES, a soldier of Turner's comp. in Mar. 1676, I suppose, was s. of Francis of Lynn. Whether he surv. the campaign, or perish. with his capt. is unkn. JOHN, Roxbury 1632, or earlier, by w. Sarah had Sarah, b. July 1634, wh. m. Richard Davis, and, next, Samuel Chandler, and d. Aug. 1665. He was a shoemak. rem. to Boston 1648, or bef. and d. prob. in Feb. 1657. His will of 3 Aug. 1654 names only w. and d. *JOHN, Lynn, s. of George the first, m. 10 May 1656, Lois, d. of Thomas Ivory, had John, b. 15 Nov. 1658 (much disting. as town clk. 31 yrs. rep. 22 yrs. and speaker 10 yrs. of wh. Hutch. II. 234, says, the Ho. "was as fond as of their eyes," and couns. 1720, d. 10 Dec. 1721, leav. no ch.) was freem. 1686, unless this was the son's date (the latest in the list bef. the usurpat. of Andros), a capt. rep. 1691, 2, and 7, and d. 24 Apr. 1703. Other ch. were Sarah, 16 May 1661; Thomas, 7 Jan. 1664; Ann, 15 Sept. 1666; Theophilus, 15 July 1669; Lois, 27 Jan. 1672; Samuel, 20 Apr. 1674, d. in few days; Mary, 18 Feb. 1677; and Ebenezer, 13 July 1679, wh. was a valu. publ. serv. as rep. and couns. many yrs. and d. 6 Sept. 1761, hav. had, by w. Martha Farrington, ten ch. of wh. were Ebenezer and Samuel, often reps. of their native town, and this younger Ebenezer was gr.f. of James, b. 25 Apr. 1772, at Providence, that bec. Ch. Just. of the Sup. Ct. of R. I. one of the ablest men the State ever had, and her senat. of the U. S. JOHN, Weymouth, by w. Rebecca had Thomas, b. 2 Feb. 1659; perhaps others, bef. Ephraim, 19 July 1664. Of this name, whether f. or s. was one serv. in the comp. of Isaac Johnson, Dec. 1675, prob. enga. in the deadly assault, when his capt. was k. JOHN, Weymouth, perhaps s. of the preced. by w. Mercy had Eliz. b. 25 Sept. 1689; Thomas, 26 May 1692; John, 19 Feb. 1695; and perhaps more. WILLIAM, New Haven, had Mary, b. 1650; and Ebenezer, 1653. Of New Haven proprs. 1685, were John, and Samuel, unless the names on the rec. be read Burwell or Bunnill.

BURRINGTON, WILLIAM, Portsmouth, R. I. by w. Jane had Abigail, wh. d. 4 Dec. 1711; and his s. Robert d. 11 Aug. 1728.

BURRITT, JOHN, Stratford, s. of William, was propound. for freem. 1671, and liv. 1698, and prob. many yrs. more, for his inv. of good est. was brot. by his neph. Josiah, Feb. 1727. He was unm. STEPHEN, Stratford 1668, br. of the preced. m. 8 Jan. 1674, Sarah, d. of Isaac

Nichols, wh. outliv. him, had Eliz. b. 1675 ; William, 1677, d. young ;
Peleg, 1679 ; Josiah, 1681 ; Israel, 1687 ; Charles, 1690 ; and Ephraim,
1693 ; d. early, 1698, his inv. of good est. being of 4 Mar. in that
yr. the wid. and six. ch. to enjoy it. WILLIAM, Stratford, an early
sett. d. 1651, leav. wid. Eliz. wh. surv. thirty yrs. and in her will of
2 Sept. 1681 names s. Stephen, and John, and d. Mary Smith, as her ch.

BURROWS, or BURROUGHS, ‖ FRANCIS, Boston 1685, ar. co. 1686, a
merch. from London, much, commend. by John Dutton, for his kindness,
in his Life and Errors. He m. for sec. w. 29 Dec. 1709, wid. Eliz.
Heath, wh. had been w. of Thomas Gross ; and for her and four ds. of
G. by her he made good provis. in his will short. bef. his d. and by her it
is prob. he had no ch. as in it he ment. only ch. Sarah, wh. had m. capt.
John Brown of Salem.　GEORGE, Roxbury, bred at H. C. where he had
his A. B. 1670, the most promin. victim of the diabolic. fanaticism of
1692, was thot. by Farmer, at one time, s. of John of Salem, tho. he
after suppos. that Jeremiah of Scituate might be his f.　I can feel no
doubt, however, that he was s. of that " Mrs. Rebecca Burrows, wh. came
from Virg. that she might enjoy God in his ordinance in N. E." as
apostle Eliot's rec. ment. her unit. with the ch. 19 July 1657, when her
s. must have been quite young, and he was adm. to the same privilege
12 Apr. 1674.　Prob. his f. had d. in Virg. and we may hope, that the
mo. also had gone to ano. world bef. the sad proof of pervers. of God's
ordin. in her chos. refuge by the horrib. proceed. against her only ch.
By w. whose name is not seen, he had Rebecca, bapt. 12 Apr. 1674, the
same day of his join. the ch. and George, I think, 21 Nov. 1675, both at
R.　He preach. at Falmouth as early, in opin. of Willis, as 1674, but at
the latest, in the summer of 1676, where for his good serv. he had gr. of
200 acres, and when the Ind. destroy. that town, 11 Aug. of that yr.
with surv. inhab. he escap. to Bangs's isl. in the harb. whence he wrote
those details of the disast. sent by maj. Pendleton to the Gov. and
Counc. at Boston.　In Salisbury he had ano. ch. Hannah, b. by w. Hannah (perhaps not the first w.) 27 Apr. 1680, and was invit. Nov. foll. to
preach at Salem vill. now Danvers, and there had Eliz. bapt. 4 June
1682 ; but in a. two yrs. went E. to his former flock, certain. was at F.
1683 ; and it may be fear. that dissatisf. at his leav. Danvers was a
moving cause of his unhappy fate.　On the sec. sack. of Casco by the
Ind. 1690, he was again driv. to the W. and preach. at Wells, until a worse
enemy, the gr. adversary, assail. him.　He may have for short season
renew. his engagem. at Salem vill. but on 8 May 1692, he was sent to
Boston, charg. with offence of witchcr. kept nine wks. in prison, tried 3
Aug. at Salem, and by Ct. unduly organiz. condemn. in few days, and
hang. on 19 of that mo.　Cotton Mather publish. for the entertainm. of

the reader, as he terms it, an acco. of this tr. and execut. at wh. latter
he assist. In the Ann. of Salem, Felt relates, "after he was hung, C. M.
believ. him to have been justly dealt with, and perceiv. the impression
wh. his last words and appearance had made to the contra. endeav. to
convince the peop. that no wrong had been done." One mo. from that
day, Giles Cory suffer. punishm. on the same preposter. charge as B.
but by the monstr. old common law requirem. was press. to d. for stand.
mute under the indictm. This was the last, as well as the first, instance
of such barbar. inflict. Mather was not, I think, present to witness this
triumph over the devil in the enforc. silence of his victim by the
ministers of the law. Had the sheriff invit. his aid, perhaps he would
have declin. the advantage; and we can hardly doubt, that the fact of
the other sufferer being a min. and s. of the coll. in wh. the f. of M. then
sat as Presid. exclud. all undue feel. of tenderness in many of the
spectators, especial. in him wh. Calef tells us, rode on a horse to instr.
the witnesses at the solemn scene. Tardy vindicat. in small degr. of this
innoc. was made by the governm. on petitn. of his elder s. Charles,
provis. in 1711, for his heirs. So late as 1774, his ld. at Falmouth,
against wh. the formalit. of forfeit. had not been applied, was sold by
George and Thomas B. of Newburyport, his descend. Of the ch. beside
the four bef. ment. we hear of Mary, wh. m. and liv. at Attleborough, and
Jeremiah, wh. was insane, possib. in conseq. of the treatm. of his f. but
whether the last w. (a d. of Thomas Ruck), wh. surv. him, were sec. or
third, is not told; Rebecca liv. at Boston, w. of a Tolman, it is said;
George liv. at Ipswich; Hannah, from tradit. was w. of a Mr. Fox, wh.
liv. in Boston, near Barton's point; and Eliz. m. Peter Thomas of Boston, progenit. of the late Isaiah of Worcester, LL. D. found. of the
Amer. Antiquar. Soc. See Farmer, in Mem. of Gr. of H. C. Geneal.
Reg. I. 37, with copious refer. Hutch. Upham, and Willis. JAMES,
Boston 1674, a tailor. JEREMIAH, Scituate 1647, m. May 1651, a
Huet, perhaps d. of Thomas of Hingham, had Jeremiah, b. 1652; John,
1653; Eliz. 1655; and Mary, 1657; and d. 1660. JEREMIAH, Scituate, eldest s. of the preced. had Jeremiah, but wh. was the w. or date of
m. or b. of s. or d. of either h. or w. is not seen. JOHN, Salem 1637,
was from Yarmouth, a cooper, com. that yr. in the Mary Ann, aged 28,
with w. Ann, 40, unless the Westminster rec. from custom ho. of Y. be
wrong. JOHN, New Haven 1644, may be the same as him of Newtown,
L. I. 1656. JOHN, New London, s. of Robert, m. 14 Dec. 1670, Mary,
d. of John Culver, had John, b. 2 Sept. 1671; Mary, 14 Dec. 1672;
Hannah, 9 Oct. 1674; Margaret, 5 Oct. 1677; Samuel, 5 Oct. 1679;
Robert, 9 Sept. 1681; and Abigail, 10 Aug. 1682. JOHN, Enfield 1684,
d. a. 1693, leav. wid. and ch. John, Hannah, and Sarah. ROBERT,

Wethersfield, m. 1645, Mary, wid. of Samuel Ireland, rem. to New London 1650, had John, and perhaps others, for descend. still liv. there; and his w. d. Dec. 1672, and he in Aug. 1682. His success. spell. Burroughs, and most of the foregoing have, at times, done the same. WILLIAM, Providence 1641, came, perhaps, in the Susan and Ellen, 1635, aged 19, was among freem. 1655, and liv. 1663, but w. or ch. are unkn.

BURSELL, or BURSTALL, JAMES, Yarmouth 1643, d. Oct. 1676, leav. three ds. JOHN, Yarmouth 1643, perhaps b. of the preced. of wh. no more is kn. It may seem a strange name, and certain. is not now found.

BURSLEY, BURSLEM, or BURSLIN, * JOHN, an early sett. at Weymouth reckon. some 3 or 4 yrs. among "old planters," and was soon after at Dorchester, req. adm. as freem. 19 Oct. 1630, and was sw. 18 May foll. When first nam. he is call. Mr. and was rep. 1636, m. at Sandwich, 28 Nov. 1639, Joanna, d. of Rev. Joseph Hull of Barnstable, had fix. at Barnstable, and there was his d. Mary bapt. 30 July 1643; John, 22 Sept. 1644, d. in few wks.; Joanna, 1 Mar. 1646; Eliz. 25 Mar. 1649; and John, again, 11 Apr. 1652; beside the first ch. wh. d. sudden. 25 Jan. 1641, very young; prob. Temperance, wh. m. Dec. 1677, Joseph Crocker of B.; and Jemima, wh. m. Shubael Dimmock, as sec. w. He was at Exeter 1643 and 5, short time at Hampton, but of Kittery 1647–53, went back to the neighb. of Barnstable, there d. prob. 1660. His wid. bec. sec. or third w. of the first Dolor Davis. Mary m. 25 Apr. 1663, John Crocker; and Eliz. m. Nov. 1666, Nathaniel Goodspeed, and, next, Oct. 1675, Increase Clap. JOHN, Barnstable, s. of the preced. m. Dec. 1673, Eliz. d. of sec. John Howland of the same, had Eliz. b. Oct. 1674, wh. d. next yr.; Mary, Oct. 1675, d. in few mos.; John, 1 Mar. 1678; Mary, again, 23 May 1679; Jabez, 21 Aug. 1681; Joanna, 29 Nov. 1684; Joseph, 29 Jan. 1687; Abigail, 27 Aug. 1690; Eliz. again, 5 Aug. 1692; and Temperance, 3 Jan. 1695. Descend. of his youngest s. enjoy to this day the est. of the first ancest. In Eng. a parish is nam. Burslem.

BURT, BENJAMIN, Deerfield, s. of David, m. 19 Oct. 1702, Sarah, d. of Daniel Belden, had Jonathan, and perhaps other s. DAVID, Northampton, s. of Henry, b. in Eng. one of the first sett. at N. m. 18 Nov. 1655, Mary, d. of deac. William Holton, had David, b. 14 July 1656, k. by a cart 30 Aug. 1660; Jonathan, 1 May 1658, d. at 4 yrs.; Henry, 20 Aug. 1660; Mary, 18 Mar. 1663, d. at 3 yrs.; Sarah, 2 May 1665; Hannah, 2 Sept. 1667, d. young; David, again, 25 Aug. 1669, a soldier, tak. by the French and Ind. 9 Feb. 1690, from Schenectady to Canada, whence he never ret.; Jonathan, 5 Sept. 1671; Joseph, 26 Sept. 1673; Mary, again, 3 May 1676; Ruth, Apr. 1677, says the

rec. prob. 1678 was meant; Benjamin, 17 Nov. 1680 ; and John, 29
Apr. 1682, k. by the Ind. up the riv. May 1709. He d. 1690, and his
wid. m. Joseph Root, and d. 1718. Sarah m. 1688, Robert Porter, and
d. next yr. ; Mary m. 14 Feb. 1706, as sec. w. Dr. Thomas Hastings of
Hadley, and, next, m. Samuel Belden the younger; and Ruth m. 1710,
Nehemiah Allen. EDWARD, Charlestown 1651, s. of George, by w.
Eliz. d. of George Bunker, had Mary, b. 28 Sept. 1657 ; and got a
patent to make salt, grant. 1652, for ten yrs. by our Gen. Ct. GEORGE,
Lynn 1635, d. 2 Nov. 1661, leav. George, wh. went to Sandwich ;
Hugh; and Edward, bef. ment. Lewis. HENRY, Roxbury, had his ho.
burn. for wh. loss the Gen. Ct. made a gr. to the town of £8. in Nov.
1639 ; rem. to Springfield next yr. was there clk. of the writs (tho. rec. of
the b. of his own ch. is not found), and d. 30 Apr. 1662. His wid. Ulalia
d. 29 Aug. 1690, and of his ch. we kn. names for Jonathan ; David;
Nathaniel; Sarah, wh. m. first, 1643, Judah Gregory, and, next, Henry
Wakley; Abigail, wh. m. first, 1644, Francis Ball; next, 1649, Benjamin Mun, and bore him five ch. and next m. lieut. Thomas Stebbins,
whose s. m. her d. Abigail; Mary, wh. m. 1654, William Brooks, and
bore him eight s. and eight ds.; Eliz. wh. m. 24 Nov. 1653, Samuel
Wright, jr. ; Patience, wh. m. 7 Oct. 1667, John Bliss; Mercy, wh. m.
17 Jan. 1667, Judah Wright; Hannah, wh. m. 1659, John Bagg, and
had ten ch. ; and Dorcas, wh. m. 28 Oct. 1658, John Stiles. The four
last nam. of these eight ds. of course, were b. after his rem. to S. and in
neither rec. of town nor ch. at R. is his name to be seen. A tradit. is
preserv. that the mo. of these ch. " was laid out for d. in Eng. put into
the coffin, but signs of life appear. at her funer. she recov. came to N. E.
sett. at S. and here had nineteen ch." What degr. of credit may be
yield. to this acco. quot. from Dr. Stiles, wh. was very benign. in hear.
such chronicles, may well be ask. but the answer will prob. depend on
the spirit. educat. and habits of the respond. HENRY, Northampton, s.
of David, m. 1684, Eliz. d. of Alexander Alvord, had only Joseph, b. 1
Dec. 1685 ; and Eliz. 2 May 1687, both mo. and ch. d. in few days. He
m. 9 Dec. foll. Hannah, d. of Henry Denslow of Windsor, had Samuel,
b. 8 Sept. 1688, wh. with the mo. d. next yr. and by third w. Mary had
David, 17 July 1691 ; Ebenezer, 2 Feb. 1693; Mary, 24 Aug. 1694, d.
soon; Mary, again, 9 Oct. 1695 ; Thomas, 26 Dec. 1697 ; Hannah, 1
Aug. 1700; Eliz. 31 Mar. 1702, d. young; and Noah, 17 Aug. 1707,
wh. d. at 18 yrs. and the f. d. 26 Sept. 1735. HENRY, Springfield, s. of
the first Jonathan, had for sec. w. 4 Apr. 1716 (the first being unkn.
to me, as, also, is the point, whether she had issue) Deborah, wid. of
Benjamin Alvord, d. of John Stebbins. HUGH, Lynn, br. of George,
came, prob. in the Abigail 1635, aged 35, with w. Ann, 32, and Hugh,

15 ; and Edward, 8, perhaps his nephs. His will, of Dec. 1650, pro. 21 of same, leaves some uncert. what HUGH he was, that was call. 70 yrs. old, or thereabouts, on giv. evidence Mar. 1661 ; for one, call. of Lynn, jr. prob. s. of George, had Mary, b. 21 July 1647. JAMES, Newport, 1639. JAMES, Taunton, prob. s. of Richard, had w. Ann, wh. d. 17 Aug. 1665. Ano. JAMES of Taunton d. 10 June 1743, says the gr.stone, " aged a. 84 yrs." and the same evid. commemo. ano. James, perhaps his s. as d. 29 Mar. 1774, in 88th yr. This name is well perpet. JOHN, Springfield 1639, rem. soon. JONATHAN, Springfield, eldest s. of Henry, b. in Eng. m. at Boston, 1651, Eliz. Lobdell, had Eliz. b. 29 Dec. 1652, wh. m. 29 Jan. 1673, Vicary Sikes; Jonathan, 12 Sept. 1654 ; Sarah, 4 Sept. 1656, wh. m. 1675, Benjamin Dorchester, and, next, 1677, Luke Hitchcock; John, 23 Aug. 1658; Mercy, 7 Aug. 1661, wh. d. at 22 yrs. and Henry, 11 Dec. 1663 ; was a man of note, and deac. His w. d. 11 Nov. 1684, and he m. 14 Dec. 1686, Deliverance, wid. of Thomas Hanchet, and d. 19 Oct. 1715. NATHANIEL, Springfield, younger br. of the preced. m. 15 Jan. 1663, Rebecca, perhaps d. of Richard Sikes, had Nathaniel, b. 18 Jan. 1664; Rebecca, 20 Dec. 1665; David, 20 May 1668; John, 23 Aug. 1670 ; Sarah, 17 July 1673, d. soon ; Sarah, again, Apr. 1675; Experience, 23 Jan. 1678, and Dorcas, 20 Feb. 1681. His w. d. 28 Jan. 1712, and he d. 29 Sept. 1720. His resid. was in that pt. now Longmeadow. RICHARD, Taunton, one of the purch. 1639, was d. bef. 1675, had Richard and prob. James. Charity, w. or wid. of the younger, or elder Richard, d. 3 June 1711. Baylies, I. 286, and II. 270 and 8. ROGER, Cambridge, by w. Susan had Samuel, b. 6 Feb. 1643. THOMAS, Salem, m. 18 Nov. 1672, Mary Southwick, but whose d. or wid. she was, is unkn. WILLIAM, Charlestown, one of capt. Moseley's comp. k. 19 Dec. 1675, in the gr. Narraganset fight. From the diverse spell. of this man's name, in Geneal. Reg. VIII. 242, and Drake's Hist. of Boston, 414, where it is giv. Bourle, some puzzle is rais. but whichever be correct, we kn. that Charlestown had but a single William on the roster for that campaign, and either form is not great pervers. Of this name, Farmer counts at N. E. and Union, and N. J. coll. fifteen gr. in 1834.

BURTON, BONIFACE, Lynn 1630, freem. 6 May 1635, d. 13 June 1669, "being a hundred and fifteen yrs. old," says John Hull's Diary, print. in the Transact. of the Amer. Antiq. Soc. III. 229, yet liable to a false construct. of the date. Of course, we doubt, some exaggera. is here ; and in one of Sewall's interleav. Almanacs, that for 1673, two yrs. are deduct. as in Hutch. I. 269. Nearer to contempo. evid. must be the Diary, yet his s.-in-law overcame his usual reverence for "father Hull," and he would not (with his habitual fondness for finding cases of

longev.) have subtract. a week without appar. authority. Had he boldly
struck off a dozen more yrs. skeptics would agree or would rejoice with
him. Yet B. was the oldest man, says Lewis, fondly, wh. ever liv. in
Lynn. This kindly affect. writer, in a generat. nearer to his own, enjoy.
the finding of a black woman of equal age in the same happy town.
Well stricken in yrs. at his com. over, must Burton seem, and prob. he
brot. some fam. or at least had little progeny here ; and careful scrutiny
proves, in many such instances, that peop. past mid. life, after reach.
our shores, grew old very fast. BONIFACE, Boston, perhaps s. perhaps
gr.s. of the preced. d. 1667, from whose will, nam. only w. Frances, we
infer, that he left no ch. and *kn.* that he gave nothing to the centenary,
but that his largest bequest was ten shillings to Increase Mather. It is
possib. that the testator was that very aged Lynn man, and the only one
of so uncom. name. EDWARD, Charlestown 1633, rem. prob. to Hingham, there had gr. of ld. 1647, and d. bef. 1675, when convey. of it was
giv. by his ch. of wh. I see no more. JOHN, Salem, a tanner, from
1637 to 1684, when he d. hav. been worried for a Quaker, 1659, 60,
and 1. See Felt. RICHARD, Charlestown, was exempt. in Oct. 1675,
as one of the ferrymen, from milit. impressm. STEPHEN, Swanzey
1683, m. 4 Sept. 1684, Eliz. only d. of Gov. Josiah Winslow, and
strange is it, that we kn. so little of him. Prob. he was s. of Thomas,
had for first w. Abigail, d. of Gov. William Brenton of R. I. and
in 1680 he join. with John Walley, Nathaniel Byfield, and Nathaniel
Oliver, men of large est. and distinct. in purch. the Mount Hope est. seat
of the gr. Sachem, Philip, from the Col. of Plymouth, assum. as fruit of
their conq. and sett. Bristol. Next yr. he was made constable at Boston, with Paul Dudley, Adam Winthrop, Edward Raynsford, and Giles
Dyer. THOMAS, Hingham 1640, m. Margaret, d. of John Otis, had
Hannah, bapt. 30 May 1641 ; Phebe, 12 May 1644 ; Ruth, Aug. 1646,
d. next yr. and Sarah, 13 May 1649 ; but it is said, that his d. Martha
m. William Brenton, and if so, then she was by a former w. prob. b. in
Eng. He was one of the gr. disturbers of our political state, as in
Winth. Hist. II. 262, 302, may be read. Very curious manifesto of our
Gen. Ct. contain. in the glorious Coll. of Hutch. 212, alludes to him as
" an old grocer of London," and his perversity is imput. to " his age and
some other infirmities." This hardly consists with the dignity of a legislature ; and had the docum. been prepar. by the Assist. they might have
ascrib. his heretical pravity in so factious desire of religious liberty to
long resid. at Newport after 1639. WILLIAM, Warwick, m. Ann, or
Hannah, d. of John Wicks, had Susanna, wh. m. 11 Dec. 1684, sec.
Samuel Gorton. Elder, and perhaps younger ch. he had, as Eliz. wh.
m. 30 Oct. 1674, Thomas Hedger ; Hannah, m. a Carpenter ; John, b. 2

May 1667; Elkanah, of wh. all that is told is his m. of a Clark; and
Rose, wh. m. a Fowler. Yet a sec. w. Isabel (d. of John Potter), long
surv. him, and may have been mo. of one or more. His will was pro.
25 June 1714.

BURWELL, JOHN, Milford 1639, had Samuel, bapt. 11 Oct. 1640;
Ephraim, 19 May 1644; Nathan, 1646; and Eliz. 1647; but he had, bef.
com. to M. s. John, and Zechariah, perhaps both b. in Eng. and d. 17 Aug.
1649. He was from Co. Herts, left wid. Alice, wh. m. next yr. Joseph Peck
from New Haven, a single man, and she d. 19 Dec. 1666. JOHN, Milford,
s. of the preced. had John, and two other ch. without name, and d. 1665.
NATHAN, Milford, br. of the preced. m. 14 Jan. 1674, Temperance, d.
of Richard Baldwin, had Alice, b. Dec. foll. and Temperance, bapt. 1676.
SAMUEL, br. of the preced. m. perhaps, Sarah, d. of the first Benjamin
Fenn, had Sarah, bapt. 1663; Samuel, 1665, d. soon; Samuel, again,
1667; Joseph, 1676; and John, 1678; tho. possib. this last may have
been s. of Nathan. He was among proprs. of New Haven 1685, as
print. in Geneal. Reg. I. 157, but ano. copy of that list gives the name
Bunnill, and I fear it has not seldom bec. Burrill in print. ZECHARIAH,
Milford, s. of the first John, m. 1663, Eliz. Baldwin, but from the gr.
host of that name, I am unable to select a f. for her. He soon rem. to
Newark, N. J.

BUSBY, ‖ ABRAHAM, Boston, linen-weaver, s. of Nicholas, freem.
1650, ar. co. 1647, m. 23 Sept. 1659, perhaps as sec. w. Abigail, wid. of
Joseph Briscoe, and d. 20 Mar. 1687. NICHOLAS, Watertown, weaver,
came from old Norwich to Boston 20 June 1637, then aged 50, with w.
Bridget 53, and four ch. Nicholas, John, Abraham, and Sarah, was
freem. Mar. 1638, selectman 1640, and 41, rem. to Boston 1646, constable there 1649, and d. 28 Aug. 1657. His will of 25 July preced.
giv. "all his books of physic" to eldest s. John, adds that he was then in
Eng. all his books of divinity to Abraham, also ment. eldest d. Ann, w.
of William Nickerson of Boston, weaver; d. Catharine Savory; youngest
d. Sarah, w. of John Grout of Sudbury, wh. had been w. of Thomas
Cakebread; and his gr.s. Joseph, s. of Nicholas, wh. was d. His w.
Bridget surv. him 3 or 4 yrs. NICHOLAS, Boston, s. of the preced. b.
in Eng. m. 1652, Martha, d. of John Cheney, the young wid. of Anthony
Sadler, had Joseph, and d. bef. his f.

BUSH, EDWARD, Salem, m. 17 Oct. 1665, Mary Hyde (spell. on the
rec. Hidz, in most scrupul. conform. with sound), had Edward, b. 2 Sept.
1667, d. in few mos. Again he m. 1 Aug. 1678, young wid. Eliz. Pitman, wh. long surv. had Eliz. b. 30 Apr. foll.; Edward, again, 1 Mar.
1682, d. soon; Ann, 25 Feb. 1683; Benjamin, 7 May 1685; Edward,
again, 2 Aug. 1687; Estwick, 22 Mar. 1689, d. young; and Estwick,

again, 14 May 1693. JOHN, Cambridge, took o. of fidel. 1652, by w.
Eliz. had Joseph, b. 16 Aug. 1654; Eliz. 14 Aug. 1657; Daniel, 4
Apr. 1659; Abiah, 2 Mar. 1661; and Mary, 17 Nov. 1662; and d. 1
Jan. 1663. JOHN, Wells, constable 1654, allow. to preach in 1662.
JONATHAN, Springfield 1678, Enfield 1685, had ch. b. in both towns.
JOSEPH, Newton, prob. s. of John, by w. Hannah had Lydia, b. 14 Sept.
1692; and Zechariah, 26 Sept. 1696; perhaps Joseph; and d. 1723.
His wid. d. 1736. RENOLD, RANDALL, or RANDOLPH, Cambridge
1641, liv. on S. side of the riv. now Brighton, may have had w. and ch.
but no certainty is attain. SAMUEL, Suffield 1679, Springfield 1686, at
Westfield, by w. Mary, wh. d. 2 Aug. 1687, had Ebenezer, b. 9 days
preced. and by sec. w. had Abigail, 12 June 1705; and he d. 7 May
1733. Of this name, in 1834, three had been gr. at Yale, and three at
Dart. none at Harv. as Farmer saw.

BUSHELL, EDWARD, Boston, was a merch. 1676. A Ruth B. wh.
came, at the age of 23, in the Abigail 1635, m. next yr. Edward
Mitchelson of Cambridge.

BUSHNELL, FRANCIS, Guilford 1639, d. 1646, had brot. from Eng. s.
Francis, and d. Rebecca, that m. John Lord of Hartford, and d. very
soon after her f. FRANCIS, Saybrook, s. of the preced. b. in Eng. had
Samuel, and five ds. as is said; but I presume that Eliz. wh. m. 2 July
1651, William Johnson, and Martha, wh. m. 1 Jan. 1664, Jonathan
Smith of Wethersfield, are all that are kn. He was deac. and had favor
of the Ind. (as in the will of Joshua, s. of Uncas, 1677, giv. him and
others large tract of ld. is pro.) d. 4 Dec. 1681, aged 81. FRANCIS,
Salem 1639, may be that carpenter, com. in the Planter, 1635, aged 26,
with w. Mary, 26, and d. Martha, 1; but if he were, he rem. soon to
pts. unkn. unless he be found at Norwalk, 1672. JOHN, Salem, a glazier,
came in the Hopewell, capt. Bundocke, 1635, aged 21, had gr. of ld.
1637, but prefer. to live at Boston, where, by w. Jane, he had Dorothy,
b. 19 Feb. 1652; Sarah, 24 Mar. 1655; Eliz. 30 Aug. 1657, and perhaps others, certain. William; and possib. at S. may have had Mary, wh.
m. 3 Oct. 1657, George Robinson. JOHN, Saybrook, s. of John (but
resid. of f. is not told, perhaps it was Eng.) m. 15 May 1665, Sarah, d.
of John Scranton of Guilford, had John, b. 5 Mar. 1666; Sarah, 17
Sept. 1668; Hannah, 10 Nov. 1670; Mary, 20 Feb. 1673; and Eliz. 23
Dec. 1674. He was one of the devisees in the will of the s. of Uncas.
JOSEPH, Norwich, eldest s. of Richard, m. 28 Nov. 1673, Mary, d. of
Thomas Leffingwell, had Mary, b. 10 Mar. 1675; Joseph, 27 June 1677;
Jonathan, 7 Oct. 1679; Daniel, 1681, d. soon; Deborah, 21 Sept. 1682;
Hannah, 8 Sept. 1684; Nathaniel, 12 Feb. 1686; Rebecca, 7 Mar.
1688; Abigail, 21 July 1690; Rachel, 27 Oct. 1692; and Jerusha,

17 Nov. 1695. He d. 23 Dec. 1746, not, as in the careful Hist. of N. by error of the press, is giv. 1748. His w. d. 31 Mar. 1745. RICH-ARD, Saybrook, m. 11 Oct. 1648, Mary, d. of Matthew Marvyn, had Joseph, b. May 1651; Richard, Sept. 1652; Mary, Jan. 1655; and Maria, Mar. 1657. He d. early, and his wid. m. Thomas Adgate. Mary m. Sept. 1674, Thomas Leffingwell, jr. RICHARD, Norwich, s. of the preced. m. 7 Dec. 1672, Eliz. d. of Thomas Adgate, had Ann, b. 4 Dec. 1674; Caleb, 26 May 1679; Benajah, 4 May 1681; and Eliz. 31 Jan. 1685; was a capt. and d. 27 Feb. 1727. SAMUEL, Saybrook, s. of William the first, m. 7 Oct. 1675, Patience, d. of Jonathan Rudd, had Abigail, b. 27 July 1677; Judith, 14 Sept. 1679; Samuel, 21 Aug. 1682; Jonathan, 10 Apr. 1685; Daniel, 20 Feb. 1688; Nathaniel, 18 Feb. 1691; Hepzibah, and Ebenezer, tw. 19 Aug. 1701. SAMUEL, Saybrook, s. of Francis, m. 17 Apr. 1684, Ruth, d. of Zechary Sanford. WILLIAM, Saybrook, s. of John of Boston, or more prob. his br. if the custom ho. rec. at London be right in the age of John, had, by rec. of S. Joshua, b. 6 May 1644; Samuel, Sept. 1645; Rebecca, 5 Oct. 1646; William, 15 Feb. 1648; Francis, 6 Jan. 1650; Stephen; and Thomas, 4 Jan. 1654; Judith, Jan. 1656; and Abigail, Feb. 1660; and d. 31 Aug. 1684. WILLIAM, Saybrook, perhaps s. of the preced. or of John of Boston, had William; Abigail, wh. m. 25 June 1679, John Seward; Judith, 5 Feb. 1681, wh. m. Joseph Seward; and Lydia, wh. m. 14 July 1686, Caleb Seward, all s. of William S. wh. all had plentif. issue, and liv. to good age. He was nam. one of the devisees in the will of the Ind. Sachem Joshua, was a lieut. and d. 12 Nov. 1683. One Bushnell, of whose bapt. name no clue is found, d. at Boston, 28 Mar. 1636, in the employm. of John Winth. the younger. His wid. Martha had, perhaps, borne him a s. Edward, in Eng. and here, a few wks. after d. of her h. had Mary. She join. with ch. of Boston 3 Feb. 1639, and on 17 of same mo. brot. that d. to be bapt. and, I think, bec. w. of William Beamsley, and perhaps it was this d. Mary wh. m. 3 July 1657, George Robinson. Of this name, the gr. in 1829, Farmer count. two at Williams Coll. five at Yale, of wh. in 1775, was David, an ingen. mechanic.

BUSHROD, PETER, Northampton, a soldier in capt. William Turner's comp. there stat. in Apr. 1676, and 19 May was in the Falls fight. After the war, he m. Eliz. d. of William Hannum, had John, b. and d. 1680; Eliz. 1681; John, again, b. and d. 1683; Samuel, 1684; Hannah; and Abigail, 1689. His w. d. 5 May 1690; and he d. 21 Oct. foll. Only two of the ch. were then liv. Abigail, alone of the six reach. mature age and m. 1716, Samuel Classon. THOMAS, Mass. 1639. Felt.

BUSKET, JAMES, came to Boston, in the Christian, 1635, aged 28, but no more is kn.

BUSS, BUSSE, or BUSSEY, *JOHN*, Durham, a physician and preach. b. a. 1640, m. 12 May 1673, Eliz. d. of Thomas Bradbury of Salisbury, freem. 1674, when he was of Concord, began to preach 1678, and serv. at D. near forty yrs. but was not ord. lost his library in destruct. of his ho. by the Ind. 1694, and d. 1730, aged 96. Belkn. I. 139. JOSEPH, Concord, s. of William, m. 23 Dec. 1674, Eliz. d. of John Jones, and d. 1681. He had Ann, b. 1675; William, 1677, wh. d. at 14 yrs.; Dorcas; and Joseph, 23 Aug. 1680. NATHANIEL, Concord, br. of the preced. m. 1668, Mary Haven, and d. 17 Dec. 1717. WILLIAM, Concord, freem. 14 Mar. 1639, was a lieut. and d. 30 June 1698, but ano. acco. is 31 Jan. 1698. By w. Ann he had Richard, b. 6 July 1640; Ann, 8 Feb. 1642; Nathaniel, 15 Mar. 1647; and Joseph, 4 May 1649; and he had sec. w. Dorcas, wid. of John Jones, wh. d. 22 Nov. 1709. Joseph, and William, wh. were k. by the Ind. 27 June 1689, at maj. Waldron's garris. ho. may have been s. of him or of John. Ann m. 20 Oct. 1659, William Wheeler of C.

BUSSAKER. See Bassaker.

BUSWELL, BUZZELL, BUSSELL, or BUZWELL, ISAAC, Salisbury, freem. 9 Oct. 1640, perhaps brot. s. Samuel, and William from Eng. and here m. 1641, Mary Eastow, prob. d. of William, wh. d. 29 Sept. of the same yr. and by sec. or third w. had Mary, b. 29 Aug. 1645; and Isaac, 29 July 1650; and d. Mary m. 24 June 1669, Philip Brown. ISAAC, Salisbury, s. of the preced. m. 12 or 19 May 1673, Susanna, d. of the first Isaac Perkins, had Sarah, b. 29 Nov. 1676; and Mary, 23 Dec. 1678; and he prob. d. soon after, for his wid. m. 22 June 1680, William Fuller, jr. of Hampton. JOHN, Salisbury, perhaps br. of the first Isaac, had w. Margaret, wh. d. 29 Sept. 1642. Phebe, prob. his d. m. 2 May 1645, John Gill of the same. JOHN, Woburn, had Samuel, wh. d. 1 Dec. 1667. ROBERT, Andover, s. of Samuel, m. 9 Dec. 1697, Hannah Tyler. SAMUEL, Salisbury, perhaps s. of Isaac the first, b. in Eng. m. 8 July 1656, Sarah Keyes, perhaps d. of Robert, had Isaac, b. 5 Aug. 1657; John, 7 Oct. 1659; Samuel, 25 May 1662; William, 5 Aug. 1664; Robert, 8 Feb. 1667; and James, 20 Mar. 1669. He may have liv. short time, in 1668, at Marblehead. * WILLIAM, Salisbury 1650, perhaps br. perhaps s. of the first Isaac, was a capt. and rep. 1679, d. 21 June 1699. WILLIAM, Portsmouth, m. 5 Sept. 1687, Ruth, d. of Hon. Elias Stileman, and descend. are not few, I believe, in N. H.

BUTCHER, JOHN, Boston, m. 30 Jan. 1662, Mary Deane. JOHN, Roxbury, by w. Sarah had Sarah, b. 10 Oct. 1695; Eliz. 17 Feb. 1699; and he d. 10 Nov. foll. ‖ ROBERT, Boston, ar. co. 1676, was freem. 1677, and that is all I hear of him.

BUTLAND, WILLIAM, Boston, of wh. I kn. only that, in Nov. 1655, he demand. as admor. from capt. Clark, the wages due to his s. Thomas, a mariner, lately dec. prob. on a voyage.

BUTLER, DANIEL, Wickford 1674. DANIEL, Hartford, perhaps youngest s. of Richard of the same, had, by w. Mabel (wh. bec. sec. w. of sec. Michael Taintor), only d. Eliz. GILES, wh. came in the James from Southampton 1635, to Boston, arr. 3 June, was call. in the custom ho. of Marlborough, in Co. Wilts, but all else is unkn. *HENRY*, Dorchester, came a. 1642, it is said, from some pt. of Kent, m. Ann, d. of John Holman, by his first w. and had John, bapt. 6 July 1651, in this yr. was adm. freem. Very curious is the coincid. that one H. B. took that yr. his A. B. at Harv. in the catal. being not in *Italic*, tho. he preach. some yrs. at Milton, went home, and by Calamy, Vol. II. 611, is made min. at Yeovil, in Somersetsh. and to d. 24 Apr. 1696, aged a. 72. In Aug. 1673, he, then in Eng. made deed in considerat. of £160. pd. by Thomas Holman, the younger br. of his w. of his rights in ld. both in Dorchester and Milton, tho. perhaps the phrase is varied only by the ignorance of the grantor, whether the div. of the town of D. since his rem. left his acres in the old, or transfer. them to the new. Certain. he early taught the sch. at D. and tradit. (that sometimes delights in improb.) made him to be bred at Cambridge Univ. instead of Harv. JAMES, Woburn 1676, had John, b. 22 July 1677, progenit. of a very num. line, rem. I suppose, to Billerica. JAMES, Boston, s. of Stephen, by w. Grace had Mary, b. 21 Feb. 1684; Grace, 2 May 1685; Eliz. 23 Dec. 1686; and James, 21 Aug. 1688. See Geneal. Reg. I. 167. ‖ JOHN, Boston, ar. co. 1644, perhaps the freem. 1649, said to have been a physician, was prob. of Hartford 1666, certain. freem. there 1669; rem. to Branford, there d. 1680; by two ws. had four ds. and s. John, Richard, Jonathan, and Jonas. He may be a differ. man; but prob. is that physician, whose creditor, John Winchcombe, of Boston, claim. 5 Oct. 1682, admin. on est. and gave inv. 5 Feb. foll. of £11. 3 only. JOHN, New London, m. prob. Catharine, d. of Richard Haughton of the same, had John, wh. m. a. 1700, beside a d. wh. d. 1689, perhaps young; but full details Miss Caulkins was unable to give. JOHN, Boston 1676, a haberdasher, may easi. be mistak. for the first John. JOHN, Woburn, s. of James, by w. Eliz. had Eliz. b. 4 Sept. 1704; John, 22 June 1706; Samuel, 3 May 1708; Sarah, 10 Jan. 1710; Joseph, 1 Dec. 1713; Phebe, 25 Jan. 1715; Mary, 27 Dec. 1716; Jacob, 10 Nov. 1718; Abigail, 5 Nov. 1720; Sarah, again, 9 Nov. 1724; and he rem. to New Hampsh. and d. 1759. Nine of his ch. liv. to m. and descend. are num. of wh. one was the dilig. hist. of Groton, that amply illustr. the geneal. JOSEPH, Wethersfield, s. prob. of Richard of Hartford, m. a. 1667, Mary, d. of William Goodrich, had Richard, b. 1667; Benjamin, a. 1673; Joseph,

a. 1675; Mary, a. 1677; Gershom, a. 1683; and Charles, a. 1686; all nam. in his will. He d. 10 Dec. 1732, aged 84; and his wid. d. 1 June 1735. NATHANIEL, Wethersfield, br. of Joseph, of wh. no more is told. NICHOLAS, Dorchester, came from Eastwell, in Co. Kent, it is said, with w. Joyce, three ch. of wh. one was John (possib. bapt. 22 Sept. 1645), and five serv. 1636, as by rec. of custom ho. at Sandwich, Eng. is pro. freem. 14 Mar. 1639; rem. 1651 to Martha's Vineyard, where descend. are yet. His d. Lydia m. 19 May 1647, John Minot of D. PETER, Boston, m. Mary, d. of William Alford, by whose will we learn, that he had Peter, Hannah, Samuel, and Mary, wh. was b. 21 Jan. 1655; but dates of his m. of b. of each of the other ch. and of his own d. are not seen. His wid. m. Hezekiah Usher, as third w. and brot. her ch. Samuel, Hannah, and Mary B. to be bapt. at O. S. ch. 14 Mar. 1675. This renders it prob. that her s. Peter had been bapt. in the lifetime of his f. or was too big a youth to be then offer. A third h. Samuel Nowell, she outliv. and d. 1693. PETER, Boston, s. of the preced. was a capt. m. Eliz. d. of Abraham Brown, freem. 1690, and d. 19 Aug. 1699, leav. Peter; John; Eliz.; Mary, b. 21 Feb. 1694; Hezekiah, 10 June 1695; and Alford, 3 Feb. 1699. Rec. is found of earlier ch. Mary, 26 Sept. 1686; and Samuel, 26 Mar. 1690; but they prob. d. young. The wid. m. 8 Jan. 1713, Ephraim Savage, as fourth w. * RICHARD, Cambridge 1632, freem. 14 May 1634, rem. to Hartford bef. 1643, was rep. 1656-60, a deac. and d. 6 Aug. 1684. By first w. he had Thomas, Samuel, and Nathaniel; by sec. w. Eliz. had Joseph; Daniel; Mary, wh. m. 29 Sept. 1659, Samuel Wright; Eliz. wh. m. an Olmstead; and Hannah, wh. m. a Green. His wid. d. 11 Sept. 1691. RICHARD, Stratford 1650 to 85, had two ds. Mary, wh. m. 7 June 1655, John Washburn, and, next, Thomas Hicks of Hempstead, L. I. and Phebe, wh. m. Benjamin Peak, wh. sometimes wrote his name Peat. SAMUEL, Wethersfield, s. of Richard, was deac. and of him I can tell no more, but that his d. Mary m. 21 Jan. 1692, Ebenezer Hopkins of Hartford. STEPHEN, Boston 1652, by w. Jane had Benjamin, b. 2 Aug. 1653, d. young; Benjamin, again, 10 Feb. 1659; Isaac, 9 Oct. 1661, d. soon; Isaac, again, 29 May 1664, d. young; James, 2 Aug. 1665; Isaac, again, 10 Aug. 1667; and by sec. w. Mary had William, 10 Oct. 1671. THOMAS, Lynn, rem. 1637, to Sandwich, but had stop. some time at Duxbury, had at S. Patience, b. 28 Sept. 1648; Dorothy, 23 Jan. 1651; perhaps more, but was, again, of Duxbury 1657. THOMAS, Hartford, s. of Richard, m. Sarah, d. of Rev. Samuel Stone, had, beside eight or nine ds. s. Thomas, Samuel, Joseph, and John. THOMAS, New London, d. 20 Dec. 1701, aged 59. Miss Caulkins thot. him anc. of Cols. Walter and John, disting. for service on the royal side in the Mohawk campaigns dur. our Revo. WALTER, Greenwich, 1672. WILLIAM, Cambridge 1634, br. of Richard the first, freem. 6 May 1635, rem. to Hartford bef. 1641, m. Eunice, sis. of Tristram Coffin, wh. came to N. E. 1642 ; but he d. 1648, without w. or ch. leav. by will of 11 May in that yr. good est. to br. Richard chief. as in Trumbull, Coll. Rec. I. 482. WILLIAM, Ipswich, m. 1675, then aged 22, the w. Sarah, whose surname has not been heard, had William, b. 1 June 1677 ; Thomas, and Ralph, tw. 15 Sept. 1682, of wh. Ralph d. May 1684 ; was freem. 1682, and liv. 1708, as was his s. William.

BUTT, or BUTTS, NATHANIEL, Dorchester, s. prob. eldest, of Richard, m. 16 Sept. 1698, Eliz. d. of capt. John Breck, and d. 10 Dec. 1721, of smallpox ; but, whether he had issue, is not kn. His wid. d. 20 Oct. 1743, aged 67. RICHARD, Dorchester, by w. Deliverance, wh. d. 22 July 1699, aged 74, had Jerebiah, or Sherebiah, b. 18 Sept. 1675 ; but, as this is the first appear. of the surname in D. he may have had other ch. in ano. town bef. rem. thither, where were bapt. Barachiah, and Hannah, tw. 11 Jan. 1680; Mary, 2 July 1682 ; and Joseph, 18 May 1684. From the gr.stone of this last, we find that he d. 29 Mar. 1713. Older ch. than Sherebiah were Nathaniel and Samuel, yet neither is nam. in the will of the f. made 30 July 1690, bec. " going forth a soldier in the present exped. against the French," i. e. the abortive crusade to Quebec. It was not pro. until 8 Feb. 1694, for it made Deliverance, the w. extrix. and gave her all his prop. but to the ch. at her discret. Admin. de bonis non was giv. 1699 to Sherebiah. His mo. I presume, had been wid. Woodward (tho. name and resid. of h. are unkn.) for the rec. at the ch. is " 26 May 1678, was the w. of R. B. bapt. being lately adm. a mem. At the same time her childr. bapt. whose names are Smith Woodward, Nathaniel, Samuel, Sherebiah, and Eliz." the last four, prob. being Butts.

BUTTELS, LEONARD, Boston 1643, had w. Judith. Prob. the same as Buttolph.

BUTTER, or BUTTERS, ISAAC, Medfield, freem. 1666. WILLIAM, Woburn, by w. Rebecca had William, b. 18 Sept. 1689, d. very soon ; William, again, 24 Mar. 1691, d. young ; Rebecca, 10 Oct. 1693, d. young ; Lydia, 11 June 1695 ; Rebecca, again, 30 Aug. 1698 ; and perhaps he rem.

BUTTERFIELD, BENJAMIN, Charlestown 1638, project. sett. at Woburn 1640, with others, was freem. 1643, had Mary, prob. other ch. (perhaps b. in Eng.) and here Nathaniel, 14 Feb. 1643; Samuel, 17 May 1647 ; Joseph, 15 Aug. 1649 ; rem. 1654, to Chelmsford, where his w. Ann d. 19 May 1660. He m. 3 June 1663, Hannah, wid. of Thomas Whittemore of Malden. Prob. he is anc. of the many wh. bear this name in our Co. of Middlesex. JONATHAN, Chelmsford, perhaps s. of the preced. d. 3 Apr. 1673. NATHANIEL, Chelmsford, s. perhaps eldest, of Benjamin, freem. 1682. SAMUEL, Springfield 1636, was k. at Saybrook next yr. prob. by the Pequots, as minute. relat. in Winth. I. 198. Very curious is the coincid. seen in Niles, Ind. and Fr. Wars, as print. 3 Mass. Hist. Coll. VI. 279, that ano. Samuel B. of Groton, a. seventy yrs. later, fell into the hds. of the Ind. but far more strange is the mistake, in the large Hist. of Boston, 203, of the author's note, mak. Niles, with wild anachronism, give "the godly young man" k. by the Pequot, 1636, the name of him, wh. two or three generat. later, was tak. not k. by a differ. tribe: Mr. Drake's devotion to Ind. hist. might excite wonder at such an error, that can mislead no careful reader, wh. will instant. perceive the cause of the hallucinat.

BUTTERWORTH, JOHN, Rehoboth 1643, was one of the found. of first Bapt. ch. 1663, in Swanzey. JOHN, Rehoboth, s. perhaps, of the preced. m. 4 Sept. 1674, Hannah Wheaton, whose f. is not told, had Mary, b. 20 Oct. 1677 ; John, 7 May 1679 ; and Eliz. 15 Jan. 1683 ; perhaps others. NATHANIEL, Groton, perhaps only trans. d. 1682, as Farmer tells. SAMUEL, perhaps of Weymouth, was adm. freem. 13 May 1640, more certain. liv. 1645 at Rehoboth. SAMUEL, Rehoboth, wh. may have been s. of the preced. or of John, of the same, was a soldier of Gallop's comp. in the sad exped. of Sir William Phips against Quebec, 1690 ; but it is not kn. whether he outliv. it.

BUTTOLPH, JOHN, Salem, s. of Thomas, a glover, m. 16 Oct. 1663, Ann, or Hannah, d. of George Gardner, had John, b. 11 Sept. 1664, d. next spring ; Jonathan, 2 Nov. 1665, or (by ano. version of the numerals in rec.) 9 Apr. 1666 ; George, 15 Oct. 1667 ; rem. to Boston, there was freem. 1673 ; rem. to Wethersfield, and m. after 1687, Susanna, wid. of Nathaniel Sandford of Hartford, and d. 14 Jan. 1693. Other ch. he had, as John, again, Abigail, James, perhaps more, and left large est. at W. and Boston. THOMAS, Boston, leather-dresser, or glover, came in the Abigail, from London, 1635, aged 32, with w. Ann, 24, had Thomas, b. 12 Aug. 1637, bapt. 29 Sept. 1639, as he and w. had that mo. unit. with our ch.; John, 28, bapt. 29 Feb. 1640; Abigail, 18, bapt. 19 Feb. 1643 ; and Mehitable, b. 26 Oct. 1651. He was freem. 2 June 1641, constable 1647, and d. 1667. His wid. liv. to 10 Oct. 1680. Abigail m. 15 Aug. 1660, David Saywell, and, next, m. 1673, Thomas Bingley. This name in ch. rec. is Buttall, wh. misled Farmer to count two for one, and is print. Buttels in 2 Mass. Hist. Coll. VIII. 106. THOMAS, Boston, s. of the preced. m. 5 Sept. 1660, Mary, d. of Nicholas Baxter, had Thomas, b. 5 Oct. 1661, d. young ; Thomas, again, 5 Feb. 1663 ; Mary, 21 Jan. 1665 ; Abigail, Jan. 1667 ; and Nicholas, 3 Mar. 1668 ; and d. Jan. 1669. His wid. m. Joseph Swett.

Button, Daniel, perhaps of Haverhill, s. of Matthias, may have had s. Matthias, and was in Lothrop's comp. k. at Bloody brook battle, 18 Sept. 1675. ‖ John, Boston 1633, a miller, freem. 14 May 1634, ar. co. 1643, was a miller in Eng. b. a. 1594, disarm. in 1637, as a favor. of Wheelwright, yet made constable 1640, had w. Grace, wh. d. 9 Mar. 1639. Next yr. he had sec. w. Joan, and a third, in his will of 5 Nov. 1681, is nam. Mary, to wh. he gave most of his prop. exc. £20. to the first ch. "to buy two silver cups." Near 48 yrs. he had been a mem. and his resid. was on Copp's hill, of course near his mill. Matthias, Boston, a Dutchman, by w. Lettice had Mary, bapt. 23 Feb. 1634; and Daniel, 22 Feb. 1635; was of Ipswich 1639, and after at Haverhill, where at gr. age, he d. 1672. Rev. Thomas Cobbet says, he came in 1628, of course with Endicott to Salem. But Mr. Felt perhaps confus. him with Robert. Matthias, Haverhill, perhaps gr.s. of the preced. took o. of alleg. 28 Nov. 1677. Peter, New London, had Peter, b. 1688; Mary, 1689; Matthias, 1692; and d. Eliphal, 1694. Robert, Salem, freem. 1642, m. Abigail, d. of wid. Alice Vermaes, had Samuel, bapt. 27 May of that yr.; Abigail, 7 Jan. 1644; Hannah, 21 Dec. 1645, a. five days old; Sarah, 16 Jan. 1648, a. six days old; and Samuel, again, 24 Feb. 1650, a. nine days old. But the three last were b. and bapt. at Boston, where he was a merch. in large business, constable 1650, and d. next yr. in early manhood. His will of 9 Jan. was pro. 3 weeks after, and his wid. m. in Apr. foll. Edward Hutchinson, jr. Abigail m. Joseph Dudson.

Buttrick, Samuel, Concord, s. of William, was freem. 1679, and perhaps the same wh. serv. in Appleton's comp. as from Cambridge, was wound. in the gr. swamp fight, 19 Dec. 1675, and on the roll wrote his name Bouterick. William, Concord, came, prob. in the Susan and Ellen 1635, aged 18, and he may have come, as Shattuck thot. with Flint, the chief planter of C. as we kn. not what sh. F. came in; yet the est. of F. was so large, that he must have been liable as a subsidy man, so under the Privy council's order not permit. to emb. without special license for the purpose, and to him, as a favorer of puritans, such license might have been refus. B. m. 1646, Sarah Bateman, wh. d. 1664, perhaps mo. of all his ch. Mary; William; John, b. 21 Sept. 1653, wh. was inhab. of Stow; Samuel, 12 Jan. 1655; Edward, 6 Jan. 1657, wh. d. in few days; Joseph, 29 Dec. 1657; and Sarah. I suppose that in Concord rec. when it tells the b. of Mary, 19 Sept. 1648, and d. 1 Nov. foll. and calls her d. of William and Mary, it is a blunder. He was freem. 1647, took sec. w. 1667, Jane Goodenow, possib. wid. of Thomas, wrote his name in three syllab. Butterick, and d. 30 June 1698. William, Cambridge, came in the Planter 1635, aged 20, said to be from Kingston, on Thames, call. ostler ; but it may have been for purpose of deception. He m. I think, Eliz. d. of John Hastings.

BUTTRY, or BUTTERY, JOHN, Reading, perhaps s. of Nicholas, had John, b. 9 May 1660 ; and Eliz. 1 June 1662. NICHOLAS, Cambridge, came, prob. in the James from London 1635, aged 33, with w. Martha, 28, and ch. Grace, 1. This surname is unusual; but when Grace m. 14 Oct. 1653, William Healey, it was spell. Butterice, or Buttress.

BUXTON, ANTHONY, Salem 1637, by w. Eliz. had Anthony, b. 6 Sept. 1653, wh. d. at 22 yrs. ; Samuel, 14 Aug. 1655, wh. d. at 20 yrs. ; James, 8 Aug. 1659, d. young; Thomas, 24 Feb. 1662, d. in few mos. ; Joseph, 17 July 1663 ; and Hannah, 27 Jan. 1666; beside Rachel, that d. on the same day with her br. Samuel; made his will 8 Mar. 1684, and d. soon, leav. wid. and ch. beside the two last nam. Eliz. w. of Isaac Cook; John ; Lydia ; Mary ; and Sarah. CLEMENT, Stamford 1650, d. 2 Aug. 1657, had ds. Sarah and Unity, beside s. Clement. His wid. Unity m. 22 July 1658, Peter Brown of the same, and next, 9 Mar. foll. m. Nicholas Knapp. JOHN, Salem, s. prob. of Anthony, m. 30 Mar. 1668, Mary Small, had Mary, b. 3 Sept. 1669 ; Eliz. 13 Aug. 1672 ; and John, 29 Nov. 1675. His w. d. 27 Jan. foll. and he d. 16 May 1715, aged a. 71 yrs. He had m. sec. w. 7 Oct. 1677, Eliz. Holton, d. perhaps of Joseph of Danvers, then call. Salem vill. and had Joseph, 24 Nov. 1678 ; Sarah, 9 Feb. 1680 ; Anthony, 24 Feb. 1682 ; Hannah, 20 Jan. 1685 ; Rachel, 6 May 1688 ; Ebenezer, 20 June 1690; Lydia, 16 Oct. 1692 ; Benjamin, 10 Mar. 1695 ; James, 28 Sept. 1698 ; Amos, 12 Feb. 1701 ; and Jonathan, 25 July 1706. JOSEPH, Salem, s. prob. of Anthony, by w. Esther had Eliz. b. 17 Nov. 1689 ; Samuel, 2 May 1691 ; James, 2 Mar. 1693 ; John, 25 Feb. 1696; not all at S. however ; and at Ipswich, by w. Eliz. the same man, or his neph. perhaps, had Joseph, 28 May 1709 ; Abigail, 27 Jan. 1712 ; and Rachel, 1 May 1714. THOMAS, Salem 1639, a husbandman, d. June 1654.

BYAM, ABRAHAM, Chelmsford, prob. s. of George, was freem. 1682. GEORGE, Salem, freem. 18 May 1642, had Abraham, bapt. 14 Apr. 1644 ; and Abigail, 7 Jan. preced. was later of Wenham, and from the ch. there dism. to Chelmsford in 1655.

BYFIELD, ‡ * ‖ NATHANIEL, Boston 1674, it is said, was b. 1653, at Long Ditton, Co. Surry, s. of Rev. Richard (wh. bec. a mem. of the famous Westminster Assemb.) and youngest of 21 ch. m. 1675, Deborah, d. of capt. Thomas Clark, wh. d. 1717, had Nathaniel, and four more ch. wh. all, d. young, exc. Deborah, wh. m. 22 Oct. 1696, Edward Lyde. He m. for sec. w. 17 Apr. 1718, Sarah, youngest d. of Gov. Leverett, wh. d. 21 Dec. 1730; was of ar. co. 1679, a propr. and among first sett. of Bristol in Plymouth Col. for wh. he was rep. 1691, and after chart.

of 1692 for the Unit. Prov. speaker of the ho. 1693, a col. judge of
prob. and of com. pleas for the new County of Bristol, after for Suffk.
and judge of the Vice-Admira. as also of his majesty's counc. d. 6 June
1733. See Hutch. II. 211; Baylies, wh. has a valu. note in IV. 53–6;
and Coffin's Newbury, 401, 2. Rev. Richard, ment. as min. of Stratford
on Avon, 1596, by honest Anthony Wood in his Athenæ, was, perhaps,
his gr.f. but he does not tell of his acquaint. with Shakespear.

BYLES, JOSIAH, Boston, a sadler, came from Winchester, Co. Hants,
with w. Sarah, but bef. com. may have had ch. tho. the date is so uncert.
that, I fear, he may hard. be entitl. to room here. Certain. he was in B.
1695, yet not bef. 11 Oct. 1696 did he join with that eh. of whose pastor
in 7 yrs. he m. the d. By w. Sarah, says our rec. he had Samuel, bapt.
11 Oct. 1696, wh. d. young; James, b. 7, bapt. 8 Oct. 1699; Sarah, 24,
bapt. 28 Sept. 1701; and Samuel, again, 30 Jan. bapt. 7 Feb. 1703,
soon after wh. the mo. d. For sec. w. he took, 6 Oct. 1703, Eliz. wid. of
William Greenough, d. of Rev. Increase Mather, had Mather, 15, bapt.
16 Mar. 1707, H. C. 1725, a min. of some note, a wit of remarka.
charact. in Boston.

BYLEY, HENRY, Salisbury, tanner, an orig. sett. 1639, came in the
Bevis from Southampton, 1638, aged 26, with sis. Mary, 22. He had liv.
at Salisbury, O. E. where he left w. Rebecca, to wh. in let. of 11 Oct. 1638
from Newbury, bef. sett. at S. he wrote of the d. of his only br. but adds,
that his sis. and serv. were well. He prays her to come over with Mr.
Dow, and other friends, prepar. to come, or with Mr. Peter Noyes, " wh.
is now a. to take ship," i. e. to go from here to Eng. to bring his fam.
hither; and utters his hope, that she " had been safely deliv. of her ch.
and thus made a joyful mo. of childr." but he d. early. His wid. m. 3 Apr.
1641, Mr. John Hall; and third h. 22 July 1650, Rev. William Worcester; and for fourth h. had dep.-gov. Samuel Symonds, outliv. him,
and d. 21 July 1695. Coffin, in Geneal. Reg. VI. 246, and 341, has
strangely confus. this mo. with her d. Rebecca, wh. m. 15 Dec. 1664,
Rev. John Hale. JOHN, perhaps of Salisbury, and br. of the preced.
came in the same sh. from Eng. 1638, aged 20.

BYNNS, JONAS, Dover 1654. Coffin.

BYRAM, NICHOLAS, Weymouth 1638, a physician, m. a d. of Abraham
Shaw of Dedham; rem. a. 1662 to Bridgewater, was a capt. had sec. w.
a sis. of Rev. James Keith, and d. 1687. His d. Abigail, wh. m. 22 or
27 Nov. 1656, Thomas Whitman of W. and most of the other ch.
Nicholas, Ebenezer, Josiah, Joseph, Mary, beside a d. Bass, are believ.
to have been of first w. Ano. d. Experience, wh. m. sec. deac. John
Willis, was, perhaps, b. by the sec. w. Rev. Eliab, H. C. 1740, min. at
Hopewell, N. J. was descend. of Ebenezer.

CABELL, GEORGE, Boston, among taxab. inhab. 1695. JOHN, Springfield 1636, had come to N. E. 1631, or earlier, had John, b. 12 Jan. 1641; and soon after rem. to Fairfield, where both f. and s. are in the list of freem. 1669, and he m. for sec. w. Ann, wid. of Roger Betts of Branford. The s. wh. wrote his name Cable, d. 1673. SAMUEL, New Haven 1646.

CADMAN, GEORGE, Dartmouth 1685.

CADY, or CADE, AARON, Canterbury, prob. youngest s. of Nicholas, by first w. had James, b. at Watertown, 15 Nov. 1682; and by sec. w. Mercy, d. of Joshua Fuller, at C. had Aaron, 1718. BENJAMIN, Andover, m. 16 Feb. 1664, Mary, d. of Robert Keyes of Newbury; but no more is kn. DANIEL, Groton, s. of Nicholas, by w. Mary had Mary, b. 10 Aug. 1684; Ezekiel, 29 Sept. 1686; Rachel, 18 July 1689; Daniel, 26 Mar. 1692; Jane, 1 Apr. 1696; Ezra, 11 Aug. 1699; Josiah, 7 Feb. 1702; and Eunice; and by sec. w. Abigail had Ephraim, 19 Feb. 1705. JAMES, Hingham 1635, came, it is said from Wales, or the West of Eng. (wh. is very loose), with three s. rem. to Boston with w. Margaret, had Mary, b. 4 Oct. 1640, rem. soon to Yarmouth. JAMES, Watertown, s. of Nicholas, m. 14 June 1678, Hannah, d. of Ellis Barron, rem. to Groton, had there Eliz. b. 10 Apr. 1686; and he d. 2 Dec. 1690. JOHN, Groton, eldest br. of the preced. by w. Joanna had Jonathan, b. 22 Jan. 1694; and Joanna, 14 Oct. 1695; by sec. w. Eliz. had John, 7 Aug. 1699; Eliz. 5 Mar. 1701; rem. to Canterbury, had William, 1704; Eleazer, 1708; and Ebenezer, 1714. JONATHAN, Rowley, m. 12 Nov. 1667, Esther Chandler of Andover. JOSEPH, Groton, s. of Nicholas, by w. Sarah had Joseph, b. 3 Oct. 1690; James, 22 Nov. 1694; Isaac, 17 Jan. 1697; Abigail, 22 June 1699; and Stephen, 16 June 1701; rem. to a planta. in Conn. often call. Killingly, there had more ch. of wh. David, b. Sept. 1703, was gr.f. of Albe C. of Concord, N. H. Esq. NICHOLAS, Watertown 1645, by w. Judith, d. of William Knapp, had John, b. 15 Jan. 1651; Judith, 2 Sept. 1653; James, 28 Aug. 1655; Nicholas, 2 Aug. 1657, wh. d. in few mos.; Daniel, 27 Nov. 1659; Ezekiel, 14 Aug. 1662; Nicholas, again, 20 Feb. 1664; and Joseph, 28 May 1666, perhaps, for the last fig. is lost from the rec. and prob. Aaron. He sold his est. a. 1668, and rem. to Groton, but the last of his W. est. he sold not bef. 29 Apr. 1680. RICHARD, Mass. 1652.

CADOGAN, RICE, or RICHARD, Kittery, adm. freem. 1652.

CADWELL, EDWARD, Hartford, eldest s. of Thomas, by w. Eliz. had Edward, b. 24 Sept. 1681; William, 24 Aug. 1684; Eliz. 5 Dec. 1687; and Rachel, 3 Apr. 1689. MATTHEW, Hartford, br. of the preced. m. 25 Mar. 1695, Abigail, d. of John Beckley, had Matthew, b. 11 June

1696; Abigail, 28 Apr. 1698; Ann, 6 May 1700 ; John, 30 Nov. 1702; and Abel, 27 Nov. 1703. See Hinman, 203. THOMAS, Hartford, m. 1658, Eliz. wid. of Robert Wilson, d. of deac. Edward Stebbing, had Mary, b. 8 Jan. 1659; Edward, 1 Nov. 1660; Thomas, 5 Dec. 1662 ; Edmund, 14 July 1664; Matthew, 5 Oct. 1668; Abigail, 26 Nov. 1670; Eliz. 1 Dec. 1672 ; Samuel, 30 Apr. 1675 ; Hannah, 22 Aug. 1677; and Mehitable, 12 Jan. 1679, or 80; and he d. 9 Oct. 1694. THOMAS, Hartford, s. prob. of the preced. m. 23 Sept. 1687, Hannah Butler ; but whose d. she was is unkn.

CAFFINGE, CAFFINCH, CAFFINS, or CEFFINCH, JOHN, Guilford 1639, an orig. propr. as in Trumbull, I. 107. He was of New Haven 1643, a man of some import. m. perhaps, Mary, d. of the first William Fowler, had Sarah, b. 4, bapt. 9 Mar. 1651 ; Mary, bapt. 9 July 1654 ; and Eliz. bapt. 8 Feb. 1657. SAMUEL, New Haven, perhaps younger br. of the preced. adm. freem. of the Col. 1649. THOMAS, New Haven, br. of the two preced. had good est. d. early in 1647, leav. John, his br. to be excor. of his will.

CAHOON, WILLIAM, Swanzey 1669. Baylies, II. 241.

CAINE, CANE, or CAYNE, CHRISTOPHER, Cambridge, freem. 14 Mar. 1639, d. 9 Dec. 1653 ; by w. Margery, wh. d. 3 Apr. 1687, aged a. 70, had Jonathan, b. 27 Mar. 1640 ; Nathaniel, 5 Aug. 1642; Deborah ; Ruth, 6 Dec. 1647; and Esther, wh. were all bapt. there, and outliv. the f. JONATHAN, Cambridge, s. of the preced. m. 14 May 1674, Deborah Welsh, wh. d. 18 Oct. 1689, aged 56, and he d. 18 Mar. 1695, or 6, the gr.stone being uncert.

CAKEBREAD, ISAAC, Springfield, perhaps, s. of Thomas, had first been of Weymouth, as a soldier serv. in Philip's war on Conn. riv. m. 1677, Hepzibah Jones, was freem. 1678, rem. to Suffield, and after to Hartford, there d. 1698, leav. Isaac, wh. d. soon, and the name ceas. in that region. ‖ THOMAS, Watertown, freem. 14 May 1634, ar. co. 1637, m. Sarah, d. of Nicholas Busby ; rem. for short time to Dedham, after to Sudbury, there d. 4 Jan. 1643. His wid. m. capt. John Grout, and d. Sarah m. 7 Nov. 1649, at S. Philemon Whale. THOMAS, Salem, a capt. had permiss. " by [the] Gen. Ct." says Felt (Ann. of Salem, I. 194, Ed. 2), to take from the fort, two small guns for security against Turk. pirates, prob. in a voyage to Spain, 1644. Yet in Vol. II. 231, the date is giv. 1641, wh. is wrong, as also the name, right at first, but at page 634 corrected *into* error, as Bond, 733, shows.

CALDWELL, JOHN, Ipswich 1654, freem. 1677, m. Sarah, d. of John Dillingham, had Sarah, b. 2 Apr. 1658; John; Ann, 23 Aug. 1661 ; Dillingham, 6 May 1667 ; William, 18 Oct. 1669 ; Mary, 26 Feb. 1672 ; and Eliz. 15 Oct. 1675. All these ch. were liv. when he d. 28 Sept.

1692 ; and Sarah m. an Ayres, and Mary m. a Roper. His wid. d. 26
Jan. 1722, aged 86. JOHN, Ipswich, eldest s. of the preced. m. 1686,
Sarah Foster, had Jacob ; John, b. 19 Aug. 1692, k. by the Ind. on serv.
in Maine, 1724 ; and William. Of this name, six had been gr. in 1828,
at Harv. and six at the other N. E. coll.

CALEF, or CALFE, JAMES, Rowley 1644. JOSEPH, Ipswich, eldest s.
of Robert the first, a physician, by w. Mary had Robert, b. 12 Dec.
1693 ; Joseph, 20 May 1695; Samuel, 25 Jan. 1697 ; Ebenezer ; Peter ;
and Mary ; all liv. when he d. 28 Dec. 1707, aged 36. ROBERT, Roxbury, of wh. we kn. little more, than that he had four s. Joseph, bef.
ment. ; John ; Jeremiah ; and the well-deserv. Robert, beside ds. Martha,
wh. m. 28 Sept. 1700, Solomon Hewes ; and Mary, wh. m. 9 Oct. 1712,
Samuel Stevens ; and that he d. 13 Apr. 1719, and his gr.s. Joseph had
admin. of est. 3 June 1720 ; and his wid. Mary d. 12 Nov. foll. When
the real est. was div. in 1726, names of uncles and aunts of the admor.
to wh. he was bound to pay proportions, are ascertain. ‖ ROBERT, Boston, merch. s. of the preced. perhaps youngest, m. 23 Dec. 1699, Margaret, d. of James Buxton of Newton, had eight ch. if not more, but
most of them d. young, the names of James, Ann, and Margaret alone
being ment. as outliv. the f. perhaps one was Daniel, wh. d. at Roxbury,
13 Aug. 1712. Beside there is rec. of b. by a former w. Mary, of Edward, 30 Jan. 1689, unless this may rather seem to be br. instead of ch.
of the disting. Robert. Of his d. we find not exact date, but it was
betw. Apr. 1722, and 18 Feb. foll. when his will of 2 Jan. 1720 was
pro. Ever honor. will be his name for the small book, call. " More
Wonders of the Invisib. World," print. at London, 1700, giv. hist. of the
baneful superstition of 1692 ; that serv. to prevent renewal of the horrid
tragedies that the patrons of delusion, unsatisfied with their sad experience, would surely have attempt. When Presid. Mather order. the
modest work to be burned in the college yd. he fail. in true policy almost
as deeply as if he had prevail. to obt. similar treatm. of the body of the
author as of his vol. and his own power in the Inst. that had long suffer.
as by nightmare, ceased in few weeks. Once or twice since there have
been partial outcries against witchcraft, but for more than a century no
influence has been exert. to renew crimin. prosecut.

CALL, JOHN, Charlestown 1637, of wh. no more is kn. JOHN,
Charlestown, s. of Thomas, b. in Eng. m. 21 Jan. 1657, Hannah, d. of
Richard Kettell, wh. d. 27 Aug. 1708, aged 71, had John, b. 20 Jan. foll.
perhaps, and Thomas, both bapt. 6 July 1662 ; Jonathan, 27 Sept. 1663 ;
Nathaniel, 1 Apr. 1666 ; Mehitable, 30 Aug. 1668 ; Caleb, 2 Oct. 1670 ;
Hannah, 29 June 1673 ; and Esther, 27 Feb. 1676; d. of smallpox,
1678, all the ch. then liv. But possib. this date of d. may refer, tho. not

prob. to first nam. John. Yet ten yrs. later there were John senr. and John jr. at C. and easi. to be look. at as f. and s. So that I prefer to regard this man as the one adm. of the ch. 29 June 1662, wh. was freem. 1671, deac. and d. 9 Apr. 1697. JOHN, Charlestown, eldest s. of the preced. m. Martha, d. of Richard Lowden, with her join. to the ch. 6 Mar. 1687, had John, bapt. 6 Nov. 1687; and Hannah, 6 Dec. 1691; d. 4 May 1713, aged 55 yrs. 4 mos. 14 days says the scrupul. rec. * JONA- THAN, Charlestown, the rep. of 1689, may have been s. or br. of the sec- John. NATHANIEL, Charlestown, perhaps br. of the preced. by w. Temperance had Hannah, bapt. 20 Oct. 1695. PHILIP, Ipswich, d. Sept. 1662, leav. ch. Philip, b. 17 Jan. 1660; and Mary. THOMAS, Charlestown, on Mistick side, a tilemaker, or husbandman, came in 1636, with w. Bennet, and three ch. from Faversham, in Kent, had Eliz. bapt. 21 Feb. 1641; and Mary, b. 7 Nov. 1643, whose bapt. can hardly be ascert. for the ch. rec. has a gr. gap, and even that of his adm. calls the name John. He was freem. 13 May 1640, perhaps liv. at Concord 1645, but soon went back to Charlestown to m. Joanna, wid. of Daniel Shepard- son, wh. d. 30 Jan. 1661, and he d. May 1676, aged 79. One Mercy C. at Malden m. 4 Nov. 1662, Samuel Lee, but I kn. neither h. nor w. yet venture to conject. that he d. a. mid. age, and that his wid. m. 2 Dec. 1686, Richard Wicks, as this union is sanction. by rec. of M. tho. Rich- ard is as much unkn. as Mercy. THOMAS, s. of the preced. b. in Eng. liv. at Malden, m. 22 July 1657, Lydia Shepardson, d. of his f.'s w. had Joanna, b. Mar. 1660, perhaps no other ch. was freem. 1668, and d. Nov. 1678, aged a. 45. THOMAS, Charlestown, s. of John of the same, m. 22 May 1683, Eliz. d. perhaps of Thomas Croswell, had Jonathan, bapt. 31 Aug. 1684; ano. ch. 21 Nov. 1686; Esther, 19 Nov. 1693; and Jona- than, again, 11 Aug. 1700.

CALLENDER, ELLIS, Boston 1669, a cooper, was one of the found. of that first Bapt. ch. in B. where some time from 1708 he serv. as teach. freem. 1690, had, perhaps, other ch. beside John, and Elisha, H. C. 1710; d. 18 May 1728, aged 87. The excel. John, min. of Newport, b. at Boston 1706, s. of John and H. C. 1723, whose Centu. Sermon is so much valu. was his gr.s. ELISHA, Boston, s. of the preced. ord. 21 May 1718, had Ellis, and perhaps other ch. was of great merit, and d. 31 Mar. 1738. GEORGE, Boston, wh. may have been s. of Ellis, by w. Sarah had Joanna, b. 23 Oct. 1687.

CALLOWAY, or CALLOWE, OLIVER, Watertown 1642, was a mariner, rem. to Boston, m. 29 Feb. 1656, wid. Judith Clock.

CALLUM, JOHN, Haverhill, took o. of fidel. 28 Nov. 1677.

CALVERLY, EDMUND, Warwick 1661, had been in the army at home, and brot. a book in MS. dat. Ely House, London, 1659, contain. the roll of soldiers and their billeting, was chos. town clk. 1664, and in that office serv. till the Ind. destroy. the town in Mar. 1676, when he rem. to Newport, there liv. 1684, but when he d. or whether he had issue, is not kn.

CAMMOCK, THOMAS, Portsmouth 1631 or 2, had two or three yrs. bef. been in Maine, was neph. of the Earl of Warwick, got patent for lds. at Black point, Scarborough, in 1636, sat as one of a Ct. of Commissnrs. at Saco, under power of Sir Ferdinando Gorges, soon after went home, but came back 1638, with John Josselyn, in the Nicholas, and resid. at S. On a voyage to the West Indies he d. 1643, leav. wid. Margaret, wh. m. his fellow-commissnr. Henry Josselyn. No ch. are ment. Sullivan, 128, erron. marks his d. 1663. This name was not rare at Boston, Eng.

CAMP, EDWARD, New Haven 1643, had Edward, b. 1650; Mary, 1652; Sarah, 1655; and perhaps more, but not prob. for he d. 1659. EDWARD, Milford, prob. s. of the preced. m. 1674, Mehitable, d. of John Smith, first of the same. JOHN, Hartford, freem. 1669, m. prob. Mary, d. of Robert Sanford, had Hannah, b. 24 Nov. 1672, John, 13 Feb. 1675; Sarah, 17 Feb. 1677; Joseph, 7 Jan. 1679; Mary, 30 Jan. 1682; James, 23 June 1686; Samuel, 29 Jan. 1691; and Abigail, 30 July 1699. * NICHOLAS, Milford 1639, m. 14 July 1652, as his sec. w. Catharine, wid. of Anthony Thompson, had Joseph, b. 11 Aug. 1653, at New Haven, wh. d. young; but at M. Samuel, 15 Sept. 1655; Joseph, 1658, H. C. 1677; Mary, 1660; John, and Sarah, tw. bapt. 1662; and Abigail, 1662. By first w. no ch. is ment. and he had third w. was rep. 1670, 1, and 2. Lambert says, he d. 1706, and it may be so. SAMUEL, Milford, perhaps s. of the preced. perhaps of the first Edward, m. 13 Nov. 1672, Hannah, d. of Thomas Betts, wh. is not nam. in the will of her f. 1688, and may have d. early. WILLIAM, New London 1683, m. Eliz. d. of Richard Smith, and d. 9 Oct. 1713, leav. s. William, and James. Of this name, in 1829, were eight gr. at Yale, one at Dart. none at Harv.

CAMPBELL, ‖ DUNCAN, Boston 1685, a bookseller from Scotland, ar. co. 1686, by w. Susanna had William, b. 27 May 1687; Archibald, 10 Feb. 1689; Matthew, 14 Feb. 1691; Susanna, 1 Feb. 1696; and Agnes 2 Mar. 1699. Under commis. from home he was made postmaster for our side of the world. Thomas, Hist. of Print. II. 414, cit. Dunton's Life and Errors. JOHN, Boston 1695, perhaps br. but not prob. s. of the preced. (and in doubt, whether he was here bef. May 1692, I have hesitat. to give him place on my page), by w. Mary had Eliz. b. 6 Feb. 1696; and Mary, 23 July 1704; was postmaster, but much more kn. as propr. of the Boston Newsletter, the earliest Gazette on W. side of the ocean, print. by Bartholomew Green, first issu. 17 Apr. 1704; d. 4 Mar. 1728, aged 75. See Thomas, II. 210. Of this name, tho.

Farmer found twenty gr. in 1829, had proceed. from N. J. or Union, or N. E. coll. he could count only three at Harv. two at Dart. none at Yale.

CAMPERWELL, MORDECAI, emb. 1 Apr. 1679 at Barbados for N. E. in the ketch Swallow; but whether he ever reach. our shores, I have not heard.

CAMPFIELD, or CANFIELD, JOHN, Portsmouth, R. I. call. jr. among freem. 1655. * MATTHEW, New Haven 1644, m. Sarah, d. of Richard Treat of Wethersfield, had Samuel, bapt. 19 Oct. 1645; Sarah, 23 (not, 24, as in Geneal. Reg. IX. 358) May 1647; Ebenezer, b. 1649; Matthew, 9 May 1650; Hannah, 21, bapt. 22 June 1651; and Rachel, b. 1652; rem. to Norwalk, and had there Jonathan and Mary, and was rep. 1654 until the union of Conn. and N. H. Cols. in the Royal chart. where this name is insert. and after that union 1665 and 6, then rem. to Newark, N. J. and d. 1673. SAMUEL, Norwalk, freem. 1669, eldest s. of the preced. m. prob. a d. of Francis Willoughby of Charlestown, but nothing more is kn. * THOMAS, Milford 1646, perhaps br. of Matthew, an early but not first sett. rep. 1673 and 4, perhaps rem. For w. Phebe and s. Jeremiah we must trust Cothren, wh. however can tell only, that Jeremiah m. Judith Mallory, had Jeremiah, and other ch. not favor. with names. In the spell. of this name authors vary, even in giv. the chart. of Char. II. Trumbull's Hist. I. 249, may be less accura. than Trumbull, Col. Rec. II. 3. The *p* was drop. and *m* turn. to *n* very early. Farmer found, in 1829, six gr. of this name at Yale, none at Harv. or Dart.

CAMPION, CLEMENT, Portsmouth 1647.

CANADA, JAMES, Rowley 1671.

CANDE, ZACCHEUS, New Haven, a propr. 1685.

CANFIELD. See Campfield.

CANN, JOHN, Boston, m. 30 July 1661, Esther, d. of William Reed.

CANNEY, JOSEPH, Dover, s. of Thomas, m. 25 Dec. 1670, Mary, d. of Job Clements, had Jane, b. 16 Dec. foll.; Joseph, 14 Oct. 1674; and Mary, 25 July 1678. THOMAS, Portsmouth 1631, sent over by Mason, the patentee, was of Dover 1644, had Thomas, b. bef. 1645; Joseph; Mary, wh. m. Jeremy Tibbets; and a d. wh. m. Henry Hobbs. In June 1661, his w. Jane (we may hope not the mo. of those ch.) was indict. for beat. him, his s.-in-law Tibbets, and his w. and he d. 1677, or earlier. THOMAS, Dover, s. of the preced. by w. Sarah had six ch. but tho. their names are not seen, the ages, at his d. early in 1675, were, as Mr. Quint assures us, 11, 9, 8, 6, 4, and 1 yrs. respectiv. His wid. m. bef. May 1677, John Wingate, and had more.

CANNON, JOHN, Plymouth, came in the Fortune 1621; but whether he rem. or went home, is unkn. and his name at the div. of cattle, 1627, is not found. One C. was of Sandwich 1650, wh. may have been that

Robert of New London in 1678, wh. was chos. a town officer in 1680, and prob. rem. soon.

CANTERBURY, CORNELIUS, Hingham 1639, was liv. 1672, but left descend. only thro. female line. Perhaps Ann, wh. m. July 1679, Peter Barnes, was the eldest, b. 14 May 1653; Mary, 29 Oct. 1654; and Cornelius, 11 Jan. 1657; and I hear of no more. JOHN, a soldier in Dec. 1675, of Moseley's comp. was, prob. s. of William. WILLIAM, Lynn 1641, was after of Salem, and d. 1663, leav. wid. Beatrice, and ch. John, Ruth, and Rebecca. The wid. m. 29 Nov. 1665, Francis Plummer of Newbury, and d. Rebecca m. a Woodrow. This name is often Cantelberry, or Cantlebury.

CAPEN, BERNARD, Dorchester, came, perhaps, after his s. for he was adm. freem. not until 16 May 1636, and d. 8 Nov. 1638, aged 70, and his wid. d. of Oliver Purchis, m. on the Monday of Whitsun week, 1596, d. 26 Mar. 1653, aged 75, acc. the gr.stone inscript. thot. to be the earliest in N. E. His will of 9 Oct. preced. his d. was not pro. bef. Nov. 1652. Abstr. of it is in Geneal. Reg. V. 240. Only three ch. are kn. Ruth, b. 7 Aug. 1600; Susanna, 11 Apr. 1602; and John, 26 Jan. 1613. Susanna d. 13 Nov. 1666. He was from Dorchester, in O. E. as appears from nuncup. will of Henry Russell, wh. left him a legacy there. BERNARD, Dorchester, s. of John, m. 2 June 1675, Sarah, d. of Thomas Trott, had Bernard, b. 26 Mar. 1676; John, 18 Feb. 1678, d. in few hours; Sarah, 5 Jan. 1679; Joseph, 28 Nov. 1681, d. at 13 yrs.; James, 8 Apr. 1684, d. in few hours; and John, again, 16 July 1685. The f. d. of smallpox, 3 May 1691, and his wid. d. 2 June 1724, aged 70. CHARLES, Dorchester, a soldier, Dec. 1675, in the comp. of brave capt. Johnson. JAMES, Charlestown, by w. Hannah had James, bapt. 16 Sept. 1683. * ‖ JOHN, Dorchester, only s. of the first Bernard, came bef. his f. as is thot. was freem. 14 May 1634, m. 20 Oct. 1637, Redigon or Radigan Clap, had Joanna, b. 3 Oct. 1638, d. soon; John, 21 Oct. 1639; and his w. d. 10 Dec. 1645. Next, by w. Mary, d. of Samuel Bass of Braintree, m. 20 Sept. 1647, he had Samuel, b. at B. 29 July 1648; Bernard, 24 Mar. 1650; a d. 6 July 1652; ano. ch. 17 Nov. 1654; Preserved, 4 Mar. 1657; Joseph, 20 Dec. 1658, bapt. 2 Jan. foll. H. C. 1677; Hannah, 1 Oct. 1662; and Eliz. 29, bapt. 30 Dec. 1666, wh. d. at 13 yrs. He was of ar. co. 1646, deac. 1656, a capt. rep. 1671, 3–8, and d. 6 Apr. 1692. All of this name in our country, it is said, descend. from him. His wid. d. 29 June 1704, aged 72; and her d. Mary m. 22 Sept. 1674, James Foster. JOHN, Dorchester, s. of the preced. freem. 1666, m. 19 Nov. 1662, Susanna. d. of William Barsham of Watertown, had Susanna, b. 16 Sept. 1664; John, wh. d. 7 Aug. 1681; Samuel, 23 Oct. 1667; Thankful, 22 Apr.

1669; Sarah 9 Dec. 1670; Dorothy, 13 Oct. 1672, d. next mo.;
Dorothy, again, 16 Sept. 1673; Purchase, 14 Nov. 1675; Nathaniel, 1
Oct. 1677, d. at 5 yrs.; Eliz. 17 Apr. 1680; Eliz. again, 21 Mar.
1682; and Hannah, 21, bapt. 26 Oct. 1684. JOSEPH, Topsfield, br. of
the preced. ord. 11 June 1684, m. Priscilla, d. of John Appleton of
Ipswich, had Priscilla, and sev. more ch. and d. 30 June 1725, the w.
and sev. ds. surv. PRESERVED, Dorchester, br. of the preced. m. 16
May 1682, Mary, d. of Edward Payson, had Mary, b. 28 Mar. 1683;
Preserved, 10 Apr. 1686; Eliz. 1 Mar. 1690; Ann, 12 Nov. 1692, d.
soon; John, 16 Oct. 1694; Ebenezer, 6 Sept. 1698, d. soon; Ebenezer,
again, 8 Jan. 1700; and Ann, again, 9 May 1703; and his w. d. 20
Oct. 1708, wh. is the date, also, of his own d. SAMUEL, Dorchester, br.
of the preced. m. 9 Apr. 1673, Susanna, d. of Edward Payson, had
Samuel, b. 1 Feb. 1674, d. at 4 mos.; Samuel, again, 4 Nov. 1675, d. at
2 mos.; Hopestill, 13 Oct. 1677; Mary, 23 Sept. 1679; Ebenezer, 30
Apr. 1682, d. at 6 mos.; Edward, 24 Sept. 1683; Samuel, again,
1 Mar. 1686; Susanna, 10 Nov. 1688; Jabesh, 3 Mar. 1690, d. soon;
Jonathan, 17 Mar. 1691; Susanna, again, 5 Sept. 1693; John, 19 June
1696; and Eliz. 28 Sept. 1698. He was freem. 1674, and d. 19 May
1733, at ripe age (tho. something short of that his gr.stone boasts); and
his wid. d. 3 Feb. 1738, aged 82. Six pages of Thayer's Genealog. are
giv. to this fam. of wh. in 1844, eight had been gr. at Harv. and none at
Yale or Dart.

CAPRON, BENFIELD, Rehoboth, that pt. wh. bec. Attleborough, a. 1680
had w. Eliz. wh. d. 10 Mar. 1735, and ch. Benfield; Joseph; Eliz. b.
22 Oct. 1684; Edward; John; Jonathan, 10 Mar. 1706; and Sarah, 11
Mar. 1709. He is reput. the progenit. of all of the name within gr.
circuit, and d. 25 Aug. 1752, at gr. age. Daggett.

CARD, FRANCIS, a soldier of good serv. in the Ind. war, 1677, at the
E. but Hubbard, 271-5, does not say, whence he came, or where he
resid. RICHARD, Newport, among the freem. in 1655, tho. some suspicion is felt, that his name is only abbreviat. for Carder. WILLIAM,
Newbury 1680, a witness in the prosecut. of Eliz. w. of William Morse,
for witchcr. tho. in the large investigat. bestow. by Coffin on the case in
his delightful Hist. of the town, how his evidence serv. to prove the
charge of the folly, is not seen.

CARDER, JAMES, Warwick, sec. s. of Richard of the same, m. Mary,
eldest d. of the sec. John Whipple of Providence, had only Sarah.
JOHN, Warwick, br. prob. elder, of the preced. m. 1 Dec. 1671, Mary,
d. of Randal Holden, and had John, b. 6 Mar. 1673; William; Richard; Mary; Joseph; and Sarah. At W. descend. are num. But he
had former w. Martha, d. of Gov. Brenton. JOSEPH, Warwick, youngest

br. of the preced. d. 1694, leav. wid. Bethia, and tw. ch. Hannah, and Mary, b. 16 and 17 Apr. 1693. ‡ RICHARD, Roxbury, rem. early to Boston, freem. 25 May 1636, yet was not mem. of the ch. of B. As a support. of the pestilent heresies of Wheelwright and Hutchinson, he was disfranchis. in 1637, and went to R. I. was one of the eighteen orig. purch. of the beautif. isl. of Aquedneck, and partner in the civil compact. In 1643 he was engag. in the purch. of Warwick with Gorton and others, and for sustain. his and their right was made prison. with all the the rest, brot. to Boston, and sentenc. to be incarc. at Roxbury, in irons (when the opin. of the rev. elders, that their offence deserv. death, was overrul.), not to depart on pain of death. See Winth. I. 248, II. 121, 48. Glad eno. was the governm. to disch. him and his fellow-suffer. next yr. with sentence of banishm. on pain of forfeit. life for coming back. He was quiet at W. 1655, had John ; Sarah ; James, b. 2 May 1655 ; Mary ; and Joseph ; perhaps was an Assist. 1665, and d. at Newport in the time of Philip's war 1675 or 6, leav. wid. Mary. His d. Sarah m. 5 Dec. 1672, Benjamin Gorton ; and Mary m. Malachi Rhoades of Providence.

CARLETON, * EDWARD, Rowley, freem. 18 May 1642, rep. 1644 and 7, had Edward, the first b. of the town rec. Perhaps for sec. w. he had Prudence, wid. of the first Anthony Crosby. JOHN, Haverhill, wh. d. 1669, may have had that JOHN, wh. m. 27 Aug. 1688, Hannah Osgood, and JOSEPH, wh. m. 2 Aug. 1694, Abigail Osgood, both, prob. ds. of John of Andover.

CARLILE, BARTHOLOMEW, Sudbury, by w. Hannah had James, b. 1686 ; and Hannah, 1687.

CARMAN, JOHN, Roxbury, came, 1631, prob. with Eliot, in the Lion, by w. Florence had John, b. 8 July 1633 ; Abigail, 1635 ; and Caleb, 6 Aug. 1639, wh. d. young ; rem. to L. I. and was that patentee of Hempstead whose s. Caleb, b. there 9 Jan. 1646, was blind from b. the first ch. there b. of Europ. parents. JOHN, Lynn 1636, rem. next yr. to Sandwich, and d. 1638.

CARNES, ‖ JOHN, Boston, ar. co. 1649, and its capt. THOMAS, New Haven, m. Mary Brown, had Eliz. b. 8 Aug. 1684 ; Alexander, 19 Dec. 1685 ; and Joseph, 4 Aug. 1687.

CARNEY, JAMES, Boston 1686, a surg.

CARPENTER, BENJAMIN, Providence, s. of William of the same, sw. alleg. May 1671. Perhaps he m. Renew, d. of William Weeks of Dorchester, but he was perman. resid. at Rehoboth, had Jotham, b. 1 June 1682, bapt. 1 July 1683 ; John, bapt. 21 June 1691 ; and Submit, 5 Nov. 1693 ; all, I judge, at 'Dorchester, in right of their mo. BENJAMIN, Northampton, s. of the sec. William of Rehoboth, m. 1691, Hannah, d.

of Jedediah Strong, had Freedom, b. 13 July 1692; Amos, 6 Nov. 1693; Benjamin, 3 Oct. 1695; Jedediah, 1 Oct. 1697; Hannah, 15 Aug. 1699; Eliphalet, 16 Oct. 1701, d. in few mos.; Eliphalet, again; Noah, 24 Dec. 1705; Eliz. 15 June 1707; and Ebenezer; rem. to Coventry, there d. 18 Apr. 1738.   His wid. d. 20 Mar. 1762, aged 91. DANIEL, Rehoboth, younger br. of the preced. m. 15 Apr. 1695, Bethia Bliss, d. prob. of Jonathan of the same, wh. d. 27 Feb. 1703; and he m. 30 Mar. 1704, Eliz. Butterworth, d. prob. of John, wh. d. 13 June 1708; and he next m. 19 Mar. 1718, Margaret Hunt, wh. d. in two yrs. and he took fourth w. Mary Hyde, but d. 14 Sept. 1721.   Whether he had issue by any of these ws. is unkn.   An agreeable let. from him to his f. writ. at Weymouth, prob. 27 July 1690, gives acco. of his then engagem. in the doleful exped. of Phips against Quebec in Gallop's comp. of wh. a list is annex. includ. a few Ind. as may be read in Geneal. Reg. IX. 354.   Valuable as is that roll, a better one is furnish. in G. R. XIII. 133, by a writer, who could not have the let. of Carpenter, or he would have avoid. the erron. suppos. that the force was design. for Albany. DAVID, Farmington, d. 22 Jan. 1651, leav. ch. Eliz. b. a. 1644; David, a. 1647; and Mary, Aug. 1650, all bapt. 16 May 1658, some yrs. after their mo. had m. George Orvis, and she next m. Richard Bronson. DAVID, New London, only s. of the preced. m. Sarah, d. of William Hough, had there bapt. Mary, in July 1677; Sarah, Nov. 1679; David, 12 Nov. 1682; and Eliz. and Hannah, 1691; but sold his est. 1688, and d. 1700.   His wid. m. William Stevens.   JOHN, Ipswich 1678. JOHN, Rehoboth, s. of the first William of the same, by w. Hannah had Amos, b. 19 Nov. 1677; Eliphalet, 17 Apr. 1679; and perhaps by w. Dorothy, m. 9 Feb. 1680, had Priscilla, 20 Jan. 1681; and he d. 23 May 1695.   JOHN, Woodstock, eldest s. of the sec. William of Rehoboth, had w. Rebecca, and I see nothing more of him.   JOSEPH, Swanzey, s. of William the first of Rehoboth, b. in Eng. m. 25 Nov. 1655, Margaret Sabin, perhaps eldest d. of William of Rehoboth, had Joseph, b. 15 Aug. 1656; Benjamin, 19 Jan. 1658; Abigail, 15 Mar. 1659; Esther, 6 Mar. 1661; Martha, 1662; John; Hannah, 21 Jan. 1672; Solomon, 27 Apr. 1673, d. next yr. and Margaret, 4 May 1675.   He was one of the found. of the earliest Bapt. ch. in Mass. and was bur. two days after b. of the last nam. ch.   His wid. d. 1700, aged 65.   JOSEPH, Providence, s. perhaps eldest of William the first of the same, rem. to L. I. had s. William, as appears in the will of gr.f. convey. by adv. of his f. in deed of 2 Sept. 1674, his est. at P. to his uncle Stephen Arnold.   JOSIAH, Rehoboth, s. of William the sec. of the same, m. 24 Nov. 1692, Eliz. Read, and d. 28 Feb. 1727; and his wid. d. 18 Oct. 1730.   NATHANIEL, Rehoboth, br. of the preced. had four ws. m. first, 19 [Sept. 1693,

Rachel Cooper, wh. d. 9 July foll. next, 17 Nov. 1695, Mary Preston, wh. d. 25 May 1706; next, 8 July 1707, Mary Cooper, wh. d. 9 Apr. 1712; and, last, 1716, Mary Bacon; but whether he had issue by either, or wh. of the two, h. and w. d. first, is unkn. NOAH, Attleborough, br. of the preced. m. 3 Dec. 1700, Sarah Johnson, had Noah, b. 25 Nov. 1701; Marian, 25 Dec. 1702; Sarah, 24 Sept. 1704; Stephen, 23 July 1706; Asa, 10 Mar. 1708; Mary, 24 Jan. 1710; Margaret, 30 Mar. 1712; Simon, 13 Nov. 1713, d. next mo.; Isaiah, 7 Feb. 1715; Simon, again, 20 Aug. 1716; Martha, 25 May 1719; Elisha, 28 Aug. 1721; Amy, 2 Feb. 1723; and his w. d. 29 Sept. 1726. He m. 22 May 1727, Ruth Follet, had Priscilla, 1 May foll. and this w. d. 10 June 1745. Next, he m. Tabitha Bishop, but d. 7 June 1753. OBADIAH, Rehoboth, br. of the preced. m. 6 Nov. 1703, Deliverance Preston, and he d. 25 Oct. 1749, but his wid. surv. to 12 June 1767. PHILIP, Falmouth or Scarborough 1690, of wh. I kn. no more. SAMUEL, Rehoboth, s. of William the first of the same, perhaps b. in Eng. m. 25 May 1660, Sarah Redoway, or Readaway, had Samuel, b. 15 Sept. 1661; Sarah, 11 Jan. 1664; Abiah, 10 Feb. 1666; James, 12 Apr. 1668; Jacob, 5 Sept. 1670; Jonathan, 11 Dec. 1672; David, 17 Apr. 1675; Solomon, 23 Dec. 1677; Zechariah, 1 July 1680; and Abraham, 20 Sept. 1682; and the f. was bur. 20 Feb. foll. SILAS, Providence, prob. s. of William the first of the same, sw. alleg. 1671. THOMAS, a carpenter, from Amesbury in Wiltsh. came to Boston, 3 June 1635, in the James from Southampton, but nothing more of him is seen. TIMOTHY, Providence, br. of Silas, sw. alleg. at the same time. * WILLIAM, Weymouth, came in the Bevis 1638, from Southampton, aged 62, a carpenter from Horwell, says the clearance at custom ho. with William, 33, prob. his s. and Abigail, w. of the latter, 32, and four gr.ch. " of ten yrs. old or less," not nam. in that docum. was freem. 13 May 1640, rep. 1641, and 3, and d. in the winter of 1659, 60. His will, of 10 Dec. pro. 7 Feb. foll. names s. John and his s. but of this br. nothing is seen after; William, and his s. John; Joseph, and his s. Joseph; Abijah; Samuel; Hannah; and Abigail; and gives to s. of John Titus, wh. had m. testator's d. But I fear some incongr. of time will hardly be reconcil. WILLIAM, Rehoboth 1645, s. of the preced. wh. he accomp. brot. w. Abigail, wh. d. 22 Feb. 1688, and four ch. of wh. we kn. three to be William, Joseph, and Samuel; had b. in this ld. Hannah, 3 Apr. 1640; Abraham, or Abiah, 9 Apr. 1643; and John. After d. of his f. I suppose he went back to Weymouth, where he had first resid. ‡ WILLIAM, Providence 1636, s. of Richard of Amesbury, in Co. Wilts, where the est. to him descend. from his f. was by him, in a deed 4 Dec. 1671, giv. to his sis. Vincent of that borough, describ. as " a ho. in Frog lane in Amesbury, wh. did

belong to her f. R. C." the grantor call. hims. s. and heir of R. C. Perhaps he was br. of that Thomas bef. ment. He m. Eliz. Arnold, prob.
d. but perhaps sis. of the first Benedict Arnold the Gov. had Joseph,
Silas, Benjamin, William, Timothy, and Lydia; was an Assist. 1665,
sw. alleg. 1666, and d. 7 Sept. 1685. In his will of 1674 all the ch. are
ment. as liv. and William, s. of Joseph. Lydia m. Benjamin Smith.
WILLIAM, Rehoboth, s. of the first William of the same, b. in Eng. came
in the Bevis 1638, with f. and gr.f. m. 5 Oct. 1651, Priscilla Bonett, as
tradit. spells the name, had John, b. 19 Oct. 1652; William, 20 June
1659; Priscilla, 24 July 1661, wh. m. Richard Sweet; and Benjamin,
20 Oct. 1663, when the w. d. He m. 10 Dec. foll. Miriam Searle, had
Josiah, b. 18 Dec. 1664; Nathaniel, 12 May 1667; Daniel, 8 Oct.
1669; Noah, 28 Mar. 1672; Miriam, 26, but Col. Rec. says, 16 Oct.
1674, wh. m. 23 June 1691, Jonathan Bliss; Obadiah, 12 Mar. 1678;
Ephraim, 25 Apr. 1681, d. young; Hannah, 10 Apr. 1684, m. 23 Nov.
1703, Jonathan Chase; and Abigail, 15 Apr. 1687, m. 12 Nov. 1706,
Daniel Perrin; was town clk. from 1668 to his d. 26 Jan. 1704, aged
72. His wid. d. 1 or 7 May 1722, aged 76. This stock has been very
prolific. WILLIAM, Providence, s. of the first William of the same, had
Ephraim; Priscilla, wh. m. 31 May 1670, William Vincent; and Susanna, wh. m. 1682, Elisha Arnold; and he was drown. 29 Oct. 1708.
Farmer count. the gr. in 1834 at fourteen, more at Brown than either of
the other N. E. coll. two ea. at Harv. Yale, and Dart.

CARR, § ‡ CALEB, Newport, may be that passeng. in the Elizabeth and
Ann 1635, from London, aged 11, among the freem. 1655, chos. treasr.
of the Col. 1661, an Assist. 1678, and Gov. in May 1695, d. Dec. foll.
by w. Mercy had Nicholas, Caleb, John, Edward, Samuel, and Mercy;
and by w. Sarah had Francis, James, Eliz. and Sarah, as by his will of
8 Mar. 1690 is seen. His w. was then liv. but Samuel was d. leav. s.
Job; and Mercy was w. of Thomas Paine. EDWARD, Newport, s. of
the preced. by w. Hannah, m. 6 Oct. 1686, had Edward, b. 14 Sept.
1689; Hannah, 13 Oct. 1691; Mary, 26 Oct. 1693; Mercy, 24 Feb.
1696; Avis, 29 May 1698; Patience, 14 Feb. 1701; James, 21 Oct.
1703; Phebe, 6 Sept. 1706, d. at 5 yrs.; and Sarah, 28 Dec. 1708.
GEORGE, Ipswich 1633, shipwright, rem. with first sett. to Salisbury,
there was in esteem, by w. Eliz. a sis. of Boston ch. had Eliz. b. at S. 21
Apr. 1642, bapt. at B. 8 Sept. 1650, "a. 8 yrs. old"; George, b. 15
Apr. 1644; Richard, 15 Mar. 1646, d. 25 Apr. 1649; William, 15 Mar.
1648; James, 28 Apr. 1650; Mary, 29 Feb. 1652; Sarah, 17 Dec.
1654; John, 14 Nov. 1656; Richard, again, 2 Apr. 1659; and Ann, 15
June 1661; and he d. 4 Apr. 1682. Eliz. m. 1 May 1662, John Woodmansey of Boston; and Mary m. 17 Sept. 1672, James Bailey of Newbury. JAMES, Newbury, s. of the preced. freem. 1690, m. 14 Nov.

1677, Mary Sears, had Mary, b. 15 Dec. 1678; Hannah, 16 Oct. 1680; Sarah, 8 May 1682; John, 26 Aug. 1684; Catharine, 24 Nov. 1686; James, Apr. 1689; Hepzibah, 24 Apr. 1692; and Eliz. 24 Mar. 1694. JOHN, Stonington 1664, m. Wait, d. of Nicholas Easton the sec. and was liv. there 1688. NICHOLAS, Conanicut, now Jamestown, eldest s. of Gov. Caleb, m. Rebecca, d. of Joseph Nicholson of Portsmouth, R. I. and by his will of 9 Jan. 1710 gives us acquaint. with s. Nicholas, and two minor s. Thomas and Benjamin, ds. Margaret Battey, Jane, Mary, Rebecca, and Ann, prob. nam. in order of b. and br.-in-law Thomas Paine, and br. Edward. RICHARD, Hampton 1640, came in the Abigail, 1635, aged 29, may have resid. in other towns, last at Ipswich 1678, d. 17 May 1689, and his wid. Eliz. d. 6 May 1691. RICHARD, perhaps s. of the preced. may have resid. at Hampton, by w. Eliz. had Eliz. b. 9 June 1691; and by w. Dorothy (as is said), Richard, 3 Jan. 1694. His w. d. 3 Aug. foll. and he perhaps m. third w. 23 Feb. 1702, Sarah Healey. ROBERT, Newport, call. a tailor when he emb. on the Elizabeth and Ann 1635, aged 21, at London, with perhaps his br. Caleb, ten yrs. younger, and was among freem. there 1655. WILLIAM, Salisbury, prob. s. of George, m. 20 Aug. 1672, Eliz. d. of the first Robert Pike, had Sanders, b. 13 May 1674; William, Feb. 1677, wh. d. 8 Mar. of next yr.; a s. 4 Mar. 1679; Sarah, 13 Aug. 1681; Robert, 28 Apr. 1685; and Sylvanus, 1688.

CARRE, *EZEKIEL*, Kingstown, R. I. one of the Huguenot refugees, wh. came a. 1686, to the number of forty-five fams. in that place alone. No acco. of his fam. is seen. See Arnold's Hist. of R. I. I. 497.

CARRIER, RICHARD, Andover, s. of Thomas, and of that victim of horrible delusion, his unhappy w. and, with his sis. of 7 yrs. old. witness, 1692, against the mo. that bore them, as he also was against Rev. George Burrows, wh. was convict. and hang. at the same time with her for the same imagin. crime, m. 18 July 1694, Eliz. Sessions. THOMAS, Billerica, came, perhaps, from Wales, m. 7 May 1664, Martha Allen, when his name in rec. of B. is writ. Morgan, alias Carrier, had sev. ch. of wh. Thomas, the preced. and Sarah, b. a. 1685, were witness. in the unnatur. proceed. that end. in the execut. of their mo. 19 Aug. 1692. He had rem. to Andover short. bef. and in few yrs. after went to Colchester, there live more than 20 yrs. and d. 16 May 1735, said in N. E. Weekly Journ. soon after, to be 109 yrs. old; and exaggera. in this case may not be more than ten or fifteen yrs. The contempo. tells, that he was not gray, nor bald, walk. erect. and short. bef. his d. went six ms. on foot, left 5 ch. 39 gr.ch. and 38 gr. gr.ch. But it was not much less than forty-three yrs. from the judic. murder of his w.

CARRINGTON, * EDWARD, Charlestown 1633, freem. 25 May 1636, by w. Eliz. had Eliz. b. 11, bapt. 17 Mar. 1639; Sarah, 10 Sept. 1643;

and prob. others, liv. on Malden side, for wh. he was rep. 1651, favor. Rev. Mr. Matthews, and was liv. 1678. Frothingham, 84, 128, 183. Mary C. perhaps his d. m. at Malden, 11 Dec. 1661, Phineas Sprague. JOHN, Wethersfield 1644, had w. Joan. JOHN, Farmington, possib. s. of the preced. rem. to Waterbury, there d. 1690, leav. ch. John, Mary, Hannah, Clark, Eliz. and Ebenezer, of wh. I kn. no more, but that John d. 1692, without ch. THOMAS, took o. of alleg. in June 1632 to enable him to emb. from Eng. for N. E. but whether he ever reach. our shore, or at what place he sat down, is unkn. Of this name, in 1822, four had been gr. at Yale.

CARROLL, ANTHONY, Topsfield 1661, oft. writ Carol. Catharine C. perhaps his d. m. 14 Aug. 1685, John Waite of Ipswich.

CARTER, CALEB, Charlestown, m. 14 Dec. 1678, Mary, d. of John Tuttle, wh. surv. him, and d. 27 Feb. 1728. His will was of 1694. HILARY, emb. 1635, aged 27, in the Elizabeth and Ann, at London, but whether he ever reach. N. E. is not kn. JOHN, Charlestown 1640, was among early sett. of Woburn, freem. 1644, by w. Eliz. had Eliz. b. 8 Aug. 1645, wh. d. at 10 yrs.; Mary, 8 Mar. 1647; and Abigail, 24 Apr. 1648; Hannah, 19 Jan. 1651; and John, 6 Feb. 1653. His w. d. 6 May 1691, aged 78. Ano. JOHN of W. freem. 1677, was a capt. and d. 14 Sept. 1692, aged 76. But ano. JOHN wh. may have been s. of the first, and liv. at Ipswich, m. 20 June 1678, Ruth Burnham, perhaps d. of Thomas, had Mary, b. 17 July 1683; John, 8 Aug. 1685; Thomas, 3 July 1687; Abigail, 30 Mar. 1689; Phebe, 11 June 1691; Samuel, 31 Oct. 1694; Esther, 21 Aug. 1696; Josiah, 3 Aug. 1698; Jabez, 17 Sept. 1700; and Nathaniel, and Benjamin, tw. 4 Mar. 1702. JOHN, Salisbury, prob. s. of Thomas of the same, by w. Martha had Mary, b. Apr. 1681, perhaps d. young; Thomas, 9 Mar. 1683; Abigail, 7 Mar. 1686; John, 8 June 1688; Samuel, and Mary, tw. 7 Apr. 1691; and Ephraim, 2 Nov. 1693. JOSEPH, Newbury 1636, rem. perhaps to Woburn bef. 1659, and d. at Charlestown, 30 Dec. 1676. JOSEPH, Woburn, perhaps s. of the preced. by w. Bethia had Bethia, b. 8 June 1671; Susanna, 24 Feb. 1673; Joseph, 28 Nov. 1674; John, 26 Feb. 1677; Abigail, 1 Feb. 1679; Henry, 4 Oct. 1683; and Faith, 28 Apr. 1688. JOSHUA, Dorchester 1633, freem. 14 May 1634, rem. to Windsor, there d. 5 July 1647, leav. Joshua, Elias, and Elisha; the last two were burn. to d. six yrs. after. His wid. Catharine m. 30 Nov. 1647, Arthur Williams of W. JOSHUA, Windsor, s. of the preced. rem. 1660, to Northampton, m. 2 or 4 Oct. 1663, Mary, d. of Zechariah Field, and a. 1673 rem. to Deerfield, there was k. by the Ind. 18 Sept. 1675, with capt. Lothrop, and the flower of Essex, he then aged a. 36, and serv. prob. as a teamster. Of his ch. Samuel, Abigail, and Joshua, are kn.

the former only by name, and the latter, b. 6 June 1668, liv. at Hartford, and had seven ch. LAWRENCE, Hadley 1686. NICHOLAS, Newtown, L. I. 1656. PHILIP, Exeter, took o. of alleg. 30 Nov. 1677. RALPH, Boston 1676. RICHARD, Boston 1640, call. broadweaver, in one place, in ano. carpenter, by w. Ann, wh. surv. him, had Mary, b. 3 July 1641, the only ch. She m. William Hunter, and next, a. 1673, m. Joseph Cowell. RICHARD, York 1680. ROBERT, Plymouth, came in the Mayflower, 1620, as a serv. of William Mullens, and d. the first season after. ROBERT, Malden 1674, had Sarah, b. Sept. 1669; and Eliz. 28 Aug. 1676. ‖ SAMUEL, Charlestown, freem. 1647, ar. co. 1648, had Hannah, b. 28 Oct. bapt. 1 Nov. 1640; Samuel, 8, bapt. 25 Sept. 1642; Zechary, b. 17 June 1644; Mary, 22 Nov. 1645; and perhaps others. Mary m. 2 Sept. 1664, Nathaniel Rand. In his will of 1652 he names gr.s. John Green; but wh. that John was, may not be easy of decis. SAMUEL, Woburn, eldest s. of Rev. Thomas, m. 1672, Eunice, d. of John Brooks, had Mary, b. 24 July 1673; Samuel, 27 Aug. 1675, d. soon; Samuel, again, 7 Jan. 1678; John, 14 Mar. 1680; Thomas, 3 Apr. 1682; Nathaniel, 7 Apr. 1685; Eunice, 29 Mar. 1687; Abigail, May 1689; and Abigail, again, 30 May 1690; liv. most of his days, perhaps, at Charlestown, and d. 1693. His wid. m. John Kendall. SAMUEL, Deerfield, s. of Joshua the first, had at D. eight ch. and in the assault by Fr. and Ind. 29 Feb. 1704, his w. and three ch. were k. three were carr. to Canada, there to contin. and with one or two he went to Norwalk, where in safety the fam. was perpet. A very wild fiction of Samuel being entic. from London by a capt. at twelve yrs. of age, and brot. to Boston, was adm. into so respectab. a work as the Hist. of N. by Hall, p. 234. THOMAS, Charlestown 1636, freem. 9 Mar. 1637, by w. Ann, wh. d. 6 May 1679, in her 72d yr. had Ann, b. 10, bapt. 22 Mar. 1640; Eliz. b. 22 Apr. 1642, d. young; Thomas, 6 July 1644; perhaps others; and d. 30 Dec. 1694, in 88th yr. Ann m. 25 Jan. 1659, John Fowle. THOMAS, Woburn, the first min. there, was bred at St. John's Coll. Cambridge, had his degr. 1629, and 1633, tho. the exemplary careless Mather puts him, with Sherman, into his sec. classis, as if they were younger, instead of elder, than Dunster or Harvard, came 1635, aged 25, in the Planter, as a serv. under George Giddings, to elude detect. no doubt, by the officers under orders of the Privy Counc. to prevent such embark. liv. some yrs. at Watertown, and exert. his faculties first at Dedham, and was ord. at W. 22 Nov. 1642, and there d. 5 Sept. (or by ano. rec. 1 Dec.) 1684, aged 74. His w. Mary, wh. may have been d. of Philemon Dalton, as I infer from the will of his br. Timothy D.'s w. Ruth (hav. no ch.) in wh. she rememb. Mary C. with the ch. of Philemon D. By her prob. his ch. were Samuel, b. 8 Aug. 1640, H. C. 1660; Judith;

Theophilus, 12 June 1645, d. young; Mary, 24 July 1648; Abigail, 10 Aug. 1649; Deborah, 17 Sept. 1651, d. at 16 yrs.; Timothy, 12 June 1653; and Thomas, 8 June 1655. Judith m. 14 Oct. 1660, Samuel Convers, and next, 2 May 1672, Giles Fifield, and d. 1676; Mary m. a. 1671, John Wyman of Charlestown, bore him two ch. and next m. 31 Oct. 1676, Nathaniel Bachiler of Hampton, had eight more ch. and d. 1688; and Abigail, m. 7 May 1674, John Smith. See Johnson's Wondr. w. Prov. 177, 181; Worthington's Dedham, 104; Lamson's Hist. of first ch. in D.; Chickering's Ded. serm.; and 3 Mass. Hist. Coll. VIII. 247. THOMAS, Sudbury, an orig. sett. perhaps was of Ipswich first, freem. 2 May 1638, by w. Mary had Mary, b. 6 Oct. 1641; Thomas, 1643; Martha, Feb. 1645, d. young; Martha, again, Mar. 1647; Eliz. 2 Oct. 1649; John, 18 May 1650; Abigail, Jan. 1653; and Samuel, 25 Oct. 1656; and d. 14 Aug. 1669. THOMAS, Charlestown 1646, call. junr. in the ch. rec. of adm. as mem. and Col. rec. as freem. 1647, but in my opin. was not s. of the first Thomas. THOMAS, York 1663. THOMAS, Charlestown, perhaps, but not prob. s. of the Rev. Thomas of the adj. town, by w. Esther (rec. into the ch. 12 Mar. 1676, " by let. of dism. from the ch. in London, of wh. Mr. Thomas Vincent is pastor"), had Samuel, b. 11, bapt. 16 Sept. 1677; John, b. 8 Jan. 1679, perhaps d. young; Ann, 8, bapt. 15 May 1681; all d. young, as gr.stones tell; Ann, again, bapt. 5 Nov. 1682; Vincent, 1 Mar. 1685; Ebenezer, 31 July 1687; and prob. John, again. His w. d. 11 Dec. 1709, aged 62. THOMAS, Sudbury, m. 1682, Eliz. White. THOMAS, Woburn, prob. youngest s. of Rev. Thomas, m. 1682, Margaret, d. of Francis Whitmore of Cambridge, wh. d. 5 Oct. 1734, had Mary, b. 5 Oct. 1683; Thomas, 13 June 1686; Eleazer, 20 Apr. 1689; Daniel, 10 Aug. 1691; Ebenezer, 24 Sept. 1695; and Ezra, 22 June 1701. TIMOTHY, Woburn, prob. br. of the preced. certain. s. of the Rev. Thomas, m. 3 May 1680, Ann, d. of David Fiske of Cambridge, wh. d. 27 Jan. 1713, had David, b. 17 Oct. 1681; Timothy, 12 July 1683, d. soon; Ann, 17 July 1684; Timothy, again, 19 Oct. 1686; Theophilus, 20 Oct. 1688; Thomas, 17 Aug. 1690; Abigail, 18 Mar. 1692; Sarah, 24 Nov. 1694; Eliz. 27 Aug. 1696; Benjamin, 22 Mar. 1699, d. soon; Mary, 23 June 1700; Martha, 22 July 1702; and Benjamin, again, 8 Nov. 1704; and d. 8 July 1727. WILLIAM, Marblehead 1668. Of this name I find the gr. in 1853 had been 9 at Harv. 8 at Dart. and 5 at Yale.

CARTHEW, JOHN, Boston, a soldier of Turner's comp. Feb. 1676, then disch. was freem. 1690, licens. to sell liquors 1702.

CARTHRICK, or CARTRACK, MICHAEL, Ipswich 1635, a carpenter, freem. 2 June 1641, when it is writ. Katherick in Col. rec. came, perhaps, in the Elizabeth and Ann, 1635; at least we kn. that Sarah, aged 24, and Mildred, 2, then embark. at London for N. E. and if the younger were his d. prob. the elder was his w. Mildred bec. w. of Thomas Brigden, bef. d. of her f. wh. left w. and only s. John.

CARTWRIGHT, ARTHUR, Dorchester 1666. EDWARD, Boston 1662, mariner, m. 1664, Eliz. prob. sis. of Edward Morris of Roxbury, as he and John White of Muddy riv. were made by C. feoffees in tr. for his w. Eliz. and she d. at R. 1673. EDWARD, Nantucket, had Samson, b. 26 Jan. 1678; Susanna, 16 Feb. 1681; Edward, 5 May 1683; and Mary, 29 June 1687; and d. 2 Sept. 1705. NICHOLAS, Nantucket, d. 10 Sept. 1706, of wh. no more is kn. exc. that he had Sarah, b. 13 Oct. 1695; Elinor, 14 Oct. 1697; Hope, 27 Aug. 1699; Lydia, 15 Dec. 1701; and Nicholas, 4 Jan. 1706.

CARVEATH, EZEKIEL, Boston 1674.

CARVER, § JOHN, Plymouth, came in the Mayflower 1620, had been deac. at Leyden, where prob. he liv. ten or a dozen yrs. and much engag. in the negotiat. at London, to wh. he went 1617, and again 1620, to complete the arrangem. for transmigrat. was chos. Gov. in Cape Cod harb. bef. land. and d. in Apr. foll. His wid. Catharine d. early in the first summer. That he ever had ch. is not kn. but certain. he left none. Yet for many yrs. the error was univ. spread, that John Howland, wh. accomp. him, m. his d. Eliz. The orig. Hist. of Gov. Bradford, recent. print. has correct. that, and we now kn. that the f. of Howland's w. was John Tilley. A wild tradit. that a gr.s. of Gov. C. was at work in a field at Marshfield, 1755, with s. gr.s. and gr. gr.s. while an inf. of the 5th genera. was in the ho. overturn. by modern inquiry, had prob. gain. currency, and escap. unquest. bec. it was wonderful. Belkn. got it from Hutch. II. 456, wh. is common. more worthy of trust. In his volum. MS. annals, Pemberton, sub an. 1760, ment. d. of William C. aged 102, "neph. of the Gov." on 2 Oct. of that yr. and the Boston Gazette of 20 of that mo. says, "he was bror.'s s. to the ancient Gov." but that both are wrong is very prob. if not even certain. Mitchell, in Hist. of Bridgewater, 362, writes, that William was gr.s. of Robert, but the relat. of Robert with the Gov. is not clear, and indeed quite improb. See the Memoir in Genealog. Reg. IV. 105, by one equal. assid. in research, and exact in judgm. Seldom is a heavier load laid upon credul. and similar. of name is too oft. rec. for proof. In Eng. it is found, that the fam. name is common. William Penn, on his first visit to his new Prov. 1682, brot. John Carver, with his w. Mary, wh. had Mary soon after land. JOHN, Duxbury, s. of Robert, had gr. of ld. says Winsor, 1640, m. 4 Nov. 1658, Mellicent, d. of William Ford, had William, b. 1659, wh. prob. was the subject of that marvel. story; John; Eliz. 1663; Robert; Eleazer;

David; Mercy, 1672; Ann; and Mehitable, wh. d. 19 Apr. 1679. He was adm. freem. 1660, and d. 23 June 1679, aged 41. His wid. m. 9 Mar. 1681, Thomas Drake. RICHARD, Watertown 1638, of Scratby, a. six ms. from Yarmouth, Co. Norfk. there emb. in 1637, on the Rose, or the John and Dorothy, the two sail. in comp. he then aged 60, with w. Grace, 40, tw. ds. Eliz. and Susanna, 18, and three serv. Isaac Hart, 22; Thomas Flegg, 21; and Marable Underwood, 20. He d. early, his will of 9 Sept. 1641, being pro. 30 Oct. 1643, and nothing is kn. of his fam. exc. that w. and ds. are provid. for, as is seen in the abstr. of Geneal. Reg. II. 262. ROBERT, Marshfield, had gr. of ld. 1638, yet, tho. he sev. times request. the privilege, he was not adm. freem. bef. 1644, had John, bef. ment. and William, perhaps took small est. in Boston 1668, and d. Apr. 1680, aged 85. WILLIAM, Marshfield, s. of the preced. m. 18 Jan. 1682, Eliz. eldest d. of deac. John Foster of the same.

CARWITHEN, CORWITHEN, CURWITHIN, KERWITHY, or CARWITHIE, CALEB, Huntington, L. I. was rec. as freem. of Conn. 1664. DAVID, Salem 1649, or rather 1644, if Mr. Felt's refer. in Ann. I. 168 and 175 mean one person, whose w. Grace unit. with the ch. 1643. Perhaps he is the same, wh. m. at Boston, 22 Sept. 1660, wid. Frances Oldham, but with her former h. it is diffic. to make any acquaint. DICKORY, Boston, shipmaster, d. 6 Sept. 1653, perhaps only trans. and may be the same as two yrs. bef. was here in big sh. ment. by Roger Williams in letters, 3 Mass. Hist. Coll. IX. 252 and 3, and by Davenport in the very mo. preced. the coming in last voyage, Ib. 295. JOSHUA, Boston, mariner, m. 6 Aug. 1657, Eliz. d. of John Farnum, had Eliz. b. 6 June 1659. PHILIP, New London 1650, sold, in 1651, his new-built ho. and rem.

CARY, JAMES, Charlestown 1639, came, as tradit. says, from Bristol, by w. Elinor had John, b. 29 July 1642; James, 7 Mar. 1644, d. soon; Nathaniel, 7 Mar. 1645; Jonathan, 15 Jan. 1647; Eliz. 23 Sept. 1648; and Elinor. Tho. a mem. of the ch. he never was freem. but d. 2 Nov. 1681, aged 81, as gr.stone tells. JOHN, Bridgewater, said to have come from neighb. of Bristol, Eng. at the age of 25, and set down first, 1637, at Duxbury, then hav. gr. of ld. m. June 1644, Eliz. d. of Francis Godfrey, had John, b. 1645; Francis, 1647; Eliz. 1649; and, at Braintree, James, 1652; at Bridgewater, Mary, 1654; Jonathan, 1656; David, 1658; Hannah, 1661; Joseph, 1663; Rebecca, 1665; Sarah, 1667; and Mehitable, 1670. He was the first town clk. and early his name was writ. Carew; but as the Eng. pronounce that name Cary, spell. soon foll. sound. Of his d. 2 Nov. 1681 is the date in report, against wh. suspicion of course aris. that for this the identity of James and John has been confound. Eliz. m. William Brett the sec. and Rebecca m. 1685, Samuel Allen the third. JOHN, Bridgewater, s. of the preced. m. 1670,

Abigail, d. of Samuel Allen the sec. had John, b. 1671, d. soon; Seth, 1672; John, again, 1674; Nathaniel, 1676; Eleazer, 1678; James, 1680; and rem. JONATHAN, Charlestown, s. of James, freem. 1682, by w. Hannah Winsor had two ch. bapt. 14 May 1682, whose names are not giv. on the ch. rec. beside Samuel, 1 Apr. 1683; Ebenezer, 17 Aug. 1684; and Freelove, 26 Feb. 1688; was deac. 1710, and his w. d. 14 Dec. 1715, aged a. 59. He d. 1737, and of his descend. were Rev. Thomas, H. C. 1761; and Rev. Samuel, H. C. 1804. JOSEPH, Norwich, had gr. of ld. 1687 in that pt. now Preston. NATHANIEL, Charlestown, br. of Jonathan, whose w. after barbarous treatm. in the infernal delusion of 1692, was by him secret. convey. to N. Y. there open. protect. by Gov. Fletcher. See Hutch. II. 47 and 8. After the demons were some yrs. gone from C. he return. and with his w. Eliz. was again rec. into the ch. as they had both been bef. when their ch. Eliz. and Martha were bapt. 11 July 1680; Nathaniel, 12 Sept. foll.; John, 28 Jan. 1683; and Mary, 14 Jan. 1690. NICHOLAS, Salem 1637, may have been of Pemaquid 1674. Of this name, in 1838, eight had been gr. at Harv. and two at Yale.

CASE, BARTHOLOMEW, Simsbury, s. of John, m. 7 Dec. 1699, Mary, d. of Samuel Humphrey, had Mary, b. 1701, d. soon; Thomas, 28 June 1702; Mary, again, 8 Nov. 1704; Eliz.; Amos, 1712; Sarah, 1715; Isaac, 23 Oct. 1717; Abraham, 20 Aug. 1720; and Abigail, 1721; and d. 25 Oct. 1725. EBENEZER, Roxbury, m. 13 Mar. 1690, Patience, d. of James Draper, had Mary, b. 20 July 1691; Jonathan, 1 Sept. 1693; and perhaps he rem. * EDWARD, Watertown, rem. soon to Taunton, for wh. he was rep. 1640, and three yrs. more, but again rem. whither is unkn. * JOHN, New London 1656, next yr. rem. to Windsor, and m. Sarah, d. of William Spencer, had Eliz. b. a. 1658; Mary, 22 June 1660; John, 5 Nov. 1662; William, 5 June 1665; Samuel, 1 June 1667; Richard, 27 Aug. 1669; Bartholomew, Oct. 1670; Joseph, 6 Apr. 1674; Sarah, 14 Aug. 1676; and Abigail, 4 May 1682; but the last five were b. after he rem. to Simsbury, of wh. he was constable 1669, and was rep. 1670, and sev. yrs. after. His w. d. 3 Nov. 1691, aged 55; and he m. Eliz. wid. of Nathaniel Loomis, d. of John Moore, and d. 21 Feb. 1704. His wid. d. 23 July 1728, aged 90. All his ch. were liv. in 1700, it is said. Eliz. m. 1674, Joseph Lewis, and, next, 1684, John Tuller, both of S. and d. 9 Oct. 1718; Mary m. 1679, William Alderman, and, next, 30 Mar. 1699, James Hilyer, both of S. and d. a wid. 22 Aug. 1725; Sarah m. 6 Nov. 1699, Joseph Phelps, jr. as his sec. w. and d. 2 May 1704; and Abigail m. 1 Sept. 1701, Joseph Westover, jr. and outliv. him. JOHN, Simsbury, eldest s. of the preced. m. 12 Sept. 1684, Mary, d. of Thomas Olcott the sec. had John, b. 6

Aug. foll. d. soon, as did the mo. and he m. 1693, Sarah, d. of Joshua
Holcomb, had John, b. 22 Aug. 1694; Daniel, 7 Mar. 1696; Mary,
1698; Jonathan, 15 Apr. 1701; Sarah, a. 1703; Hannah, a. 1709; and
he d. 22 May 1733. JOSEPH, Narragansèt in that pt. now Kingstown,
had Joseph, b. 1678; William, 1684; Mary; Hannah; Margaret;
John, 1692; and Emanuel, 1699. JOSEPH, Simsbury, youngest s. of
the first John of the same, m. 6 Apr. 1699, Ann, d. of James Eno the
sec. of Windsor, had Joseph, b. 2 Feb. foll.; Jacob, 19 Mar. 1702;
Aaron, 1705, d. soon; Benajah, a. 1710; Josiah, 1 Feb. 1716; Hezekiah, 26 Apr. 1719; David, a. 1722; and Joel, 30 May 1724; and d.
11 Aug. 1748. His wid. d. 10 June 1760. RICHARD, Hartford 1660,
perhaps br. of the first John, m. Eliz. d. of John Purchase, was propound.
for freem. Oct. 1671, d. 30 Mar. 1694, leav. Richard, John, and Mary.
RICHARD, Simsbury, s. of the first John of the same, m. 1 Sept. 1701,
Amy, d. of Philip Reed of Concord, had Amy, b. a. 1702, d. soon;
Amy, again, a. 1703; Richard, 1710; Timothy, a. 1711; Margaret, a.
1713; Edward, 5 Mar. 1715; Lydia, 15 Mar. 1718; Mary, 30 Jan.
1722; and he d. a. 1746. SAMUEL, Simsbury, br. of the preced. m.
Mary, d. of Josiah Westover of S. wh. d. 27 Sept. 1713, and he m. 8
Nov. 1721, Eliz. d. of Josiah Owen, wid. of Samuel Thrall, and d. 30
July 1725. His ch. by the first w. were Samuel, b. 24 Jan. 1696;
Mary, 15 Nov. 1697; Hannah, 30 Jan. 1699; Mercy, 12 Jan. 1701;
Abigail, 4 Feb. 1702, d. soon; Nathaniel, 26 Apr. 1703; Eunice, July
1704; Josiah, Aug. 1705; Caleb, a. 1707; Azrikam, 16 Feb. 1710;
Benjamin, 1711; and perhaps Pelatiah, wh. d. 1733; and by the sec. w.
Irene, 12 Jan. 1725. THOMAS, Fairfield, rem. to the Dutch a. 1664, and
is by Mather (wh. is always liberal in obloquy against adher. of George
Fox), call. a villain, Magn. VII. 25. We hear not any reason for such
epith. exc. his Quaker. habit. influence among the foll. nam. by the gr.
ecclesiast. histor. " Case's crew," at Southold, L. I. where, he sorrowf.
adds, " to this day (1699), the sect is kn." He was sev. times imprison.
for his cause, and by such treatm. not prob. induc. to reject the inward
light; and d. 1692, perhaps unm. certain. without issue. WILLIAM,
Newport, among the freem. 1655. WILLIAM, Simsbury, br. of Bartholomew, m. 1688, Eliz. d. of Joshua Holcomb, had Eliz. b. Sept.
1689; William, 22 Mar. 1691; James, 12 Mar. 1693; Rachel, 10 Dec.
1694; Mary, 23 Aug. 1696; Joshua, 1 June 1698; Mindwell, 21 Mar.
1700; and he d. ten days after. His wid. m. 10 Mar. 1704, John
Slater; next m. Thomas Marshall; and d. 26 Feb. 1762. This name
was very com. in that region, and I count gr. in 1855, at Yale, ten,
but none in Harv. or Dart. catal.

CASELEY, or CASLEY, EDWARD, Scituate 1638, rem. to Barnstable

1639, says Deane. JOHN, Barnstable 1640–9, may have been br. of the preced. WILLIAM, perhaps a br. of the preced. or even the f. had been freem. of Mass. 2 Nov. 1637, tho. his place of resid. is not found, but soon after he rem. to Sandwich, and this makes it prob. that he was first of Lynn; at S. he m. in Nov. 1639, a sis. of the w. of Rev. Marmaduke Matthews of Yarmouth, may have sett. at Barnstable, where long the name prevail. and spread thence in the last century, to Gorham, Me.

CASEY, JOHN, Boston, serv. to Thomas Gardner of Roxbury, or rather of Muddy riv. in B. was a soldier of Oliver's comp. wound. in the gr. battle of ·Philip's war.

CASH, WILLIAM, Salem, mariner, m. Oct. 1667, Eliz. Lambert, d. perhaps of Richard, had William, b. 23 Feb. 1669 ; John, 10 July 1671, d. in few days; John, again, and Eliz. tw. 10 July 1672, of wh. John d. at 2 yrs.; Mary, and Ann, tw. 29 Apr. 1675 ; Esther, 9 Mar. 1679 ; Eliz. wh. was bapt. adult, Dec. 1693, and m. 7 Mar. 1697, William Tapley; and Mary, wh. m. 28 May 1697, John Meacham. WILLIAM, Salem, s. of the preced. had William, b. 13 Feb. 1694; Eliz. 19 July 1696; John, 7 Sept. 1699 ; Sarah, 5 Aug. 1702 ; and Ruth, 23 Mar. 1706.

CASKIN, WILLIAM, Concord, had Sarah, b. 1642; and perhaps Phebe.

CASMAN, ROGER, Newbury, came in the Confidence 1638, aged 15, serv. to John Saunders.

CASMORE, or CHASMORE, RICHARD, Patuxet 1643, tak. by the marshal of Mass. on a precept in 1657, raising trouble betw. the Cols. of Mass. and R. I. See Geneal. Reg. VIII. 362.

CASS, JAMES, Westerly 1669. JOHN, Hampton 1644, m. Martha, d. of Thomas Philbrick, had John ; Samuel, b. 13 July 1659 ; Joseph; Martha ; Jonathan ; Ebenezer ; Abigail ; Mercy ; and Mary ; of wh. Martha m. John Redman ; and he d. sudden. 7 Apr. 1675. His will was of May 1674. A descend. was maj. Jonathan, wh. d. 14 Aug. 1830, f. of the Hon. Lewis, disting. in our modern polit. hist. JOHN, Windsor, rem. 1670, to Simsbury. JOHN, Hampton, s. of the first John, m. 10 Dec. 1676, Mary, prob. d. of Maurice Hobbs, had John, b. 21 Aug. 1680 ; and Mary, 26 Feb. 1687, perhaps others. His w. d. 23 July 1692; and for sec. w. he took Eliz. wid. of James Chase, wh. had former name Green, perhaps d. of Henry. JOSEPH, Hampton, br. of the preced. had Joseph, wh. d. 22 Jan. 1687 ; and Mary, b. 26 Feb. foll. SAMUEL, Hampton 1678, br. of the preced. m. 7 Dec. 1681, Mary Sanborn. Sometimes this name is distort. to Cash.

CASSELL, or CASSILEY, GEORGE, Mass. 1657. Felt. ROBERT, Hampton 1639, had prob. been of Ipswich 1637, and young. See Belkn. I. 22.

CASTINE, or CAUSTINE, WILLIAM, Boston, had w. Isabel, wh. d. 25

Jan. 1654, but by w. Mary had Lydia, b. 22 Jan. 1655. It may be Costinge.

CASTLE, HENRY, Woodbury 1682, then resid. with Henry, jr. perhaps his s. and d. 2 Feb. 1698, being the first d. on rec. there, but to find wh. was his f. would be more agreea. to us. MATTHEW, Charlestown, m. 4 Aug. 1687, Mary Stowers. WILLIAM, Boston 1673, mariner.

CASWELL, CASEWELL, or CASSELL, STEPHEN, Taunton, eldest s. of Thomas, m. 29 Dec. 1672, Hannah, d. perhaps of Christopher Thrasher, had Stephen, b. 11 Dec. foll.; Joseph, 18 May 1678; and perhaps others. THOMAS, Taunton, had Stephen, b. 15 Feb. 1649; Thomas, 22 Feb. 1651; Peter, 31 Oct. 1652; Mary, 31 Aug. 1654, wh. m. 15 Aug. 1676, Israel Thrasher; John, 31 July 1656; Sarah, 30 Nov. 1658, wh. m. 3 July 1677, William Hoskins; William, 15 Sept. 1660; Samuel, 26 Jan. 1663; Eliz. 10 Jan. 1665, m. 1 June 1685, Uriah Leonard; Abigail, 27 Oct. 1666; and Esther, 4 June 1669.

CATCHAM, or CATCHEM. See Ketcham.

CATE, EDWARD, Portsmouth, was of the gr. jury 1684. JAMES, Portsmouth 1665, d. a. 1677, may have been f. or br. of the preced. JOHN, and WILLIAM, of New Hampsh. 1689, favor. jurisdict. of Mass.

CATER, RICHARD, Dover 1650, had Richard, and d. a. 1690. RICHARD, Dover, s. of the preced. d. 15 June 1703.

CATES, JOHN, Windham, perhaps bef. 1686, but the time or cause of his com. to our country, is equal. unkn. There was a report, that he came from Virg. and possib. he was that passeng. from London in the sh. Safety 1635. Much idle conject. has been expend. on the reason of his withdr. from society, and liv. some time in a cave; and among the most absurd is, that he was a regicide. Perhaps he was only a misanthrop. humorist, perhaps had been a buccanier, and thot. seclusion his safest course. See Hinman. He built, 1689, the first ho. in the town, left ch. in Eng. as his will, 5 May 1696, shows. In it he gave ld. for a sch. more for the poor of W. and money, not (as popul. report was) plate to the ch. and d. 16 July, tho. his inv. appears 11th 1697. See Trumbull's Hist. 408. The name of this stranger is oft. Kates.

CATLIN, or CATLING, JOHN, Hartford, s. of Thomas, m. 27 July 1665, Mary Marshall, had Mary, b. 10 July 1666; Samuel, 4 Nov. 1672; John, 27 Apr. 1676; Thomas, 27 Aug. 1678; and Benjamin, 1 Feb. 1681. Hinman, 123, 203, 58. JOHN, Boston, came from Barbados, was only trans. visit. call. hims. writ.-master, in his will, made on board the Pink Mary, in Cape Cod harb. 21 Dec. 1685, pro. at B. 4 Jan. foll. After small gifts to the capt. of the vessel, and two fellow-passeng. he dispos. the cargo to his only s. Charles, and made Thomas Palmer excor. JOHN, Deerfield, came from Newark, N. J. bef. 1684, with his mo.

Isabel, but they had some yrs. bef. gone thither from Conn. of course. The bapt. name of her first h. is unkn. for sec. she m. James Northam of Wethersfield, wh. d. 1662, and she rem. and had third h. Joseph Baldwin of Hadley. Catlin, the name of whose w. is not kn. had John, Joseph, Jonathan, and four or five ds. of wh. Eliz. m. James Corse. She with her brs. Joseph (wh. left s. John), and Jonathan, and the f. were all k. by the Ind. and Fr. in the assault, 29 Feb. 1704. Yet the name is kept up in the vicin. PHILIP, Lynn, had w. Alice, wh. m. 1659 or 60, Evan Thomas of Boston, was prob. f. of that PHILIP, a soldier at Hadley 7 Apr. 1676. THOMAS, Hartford, had Mary, bapt. 29 Nov. 1646, d. soon; John, bef. ment. and Mary, again, bapt. 6 May 1649; was constable 1662, oft. selectman, and Hinman, 18 and 123, is ready to call him anc. of all of the name in Conn. d. 1690.

CATTELL, JOHN, Hartford 1643, d. next yr. leav. wid.

CAULKINS, CALKINS, CALKIN, or CAWKIN, DAVID, New London, youngest s. of Hugh, m. Mary, d. of Thomas Bliss of Norwich, had David, b. 5 July 1674; Ann, 8 Nov. 1676; Jonathan, 9 Jan. 1679; Peter, 9 Oct. 1681, d. young; beside John, Mary, Joseph, and Lydia, most or all of wh. may have been b. earlier, as neither is seen in the town rec. had the est. of his f. in that pt. of New London, now, nam. Waterford, and d. 25 Nov. 1717. From him descends the modest and dilig. hist. of Norwich and New London. * HUGH, Gloucester, prob. a Welchman, came with Rev. Richard Blinman, and first sat down, 1640, at Marshfield, rem. next yr. to Lynn, perhaps only for short season, was freem. 27 Dec. 1642, when he was of G. selectman 1643-8, rep. 1650-2 but rem. to New London bef. begin. to serve under this last elect. and was selectman and rep. half the yrs. of his resid. there, and town clk. for all, rem. 1662 to Norwich, and was the first deac. on organiz. the ch. rep. also for this town 1663 and 4, and d. 1690, aged 90. From Eng. he brot. w. Ann, and sev. ch. as John, Sarah, and Mary, possib. more, and had b. at G. David; Deborah, 18 Mar. 1645; and Rebecca, wh. d. 14 Mar. 1651; perhaps more at the same. Sarah m. 28 Oct. 1645, William Hough; Mary m. 8 Nov. 1649, Hugh Roberts; and Deborah m. June 1660, Jonathan Royce, or Rice. HUGH, Norwich, eldest s. of John, m. May 1689, Sarah, d. of Thomas Sluman, wh. d. 1703, had Hugh, b. 1690; Ann, 1692; Eliz. 1694; Joshua, 1699; Stephen, 1700; and Daniel, 1702. JOHN, New London 1657, Norwich 1660, eldest s. of the first Hugh, b. in Eng. m. Sarah, d. of Robert Royce of N. L. had Hugh, b. June 1659; John, July 1661, the third male b. in the town; Samuel, Oct. 1663; Sarah, June 1666; Daniel, 1667, d. soon; Mary, May 1669; Eliz. Apr. 1673; and Ann, Aug. 1678; and he d. 8 Jan. 1703; and his wid. d. May 1711. Sarah m. 1684, Thomas Bald-

win, and d. next yr.; Mary m. Samuel Gifford; and Eliz. m. Samuel
Hyde. JOHN, Norwich, s. of the preced. m. 23 Oct. 1690, Abigail, d. of
John Birchard, had Abigail, b. 1691; Sarah, 1694; rem. to Lebanon,
there had Mary, 1697; John, 1699; and James, 1702. SAMUEL, Norwich, br. of the preced. m. Nov. 1691, Hannah, d. of Stephen Gifford,
had John, b. 1693; Hannah, 1694; Ruth, 1695; rem. to Lebanon, there
had Samuel, 1699; Nathaniel, 1703; Stephen, 1706; Nathaniel, again,
1710; and Aquila, 1711, and d. 1720.

CAVE, THOMAS, Salem vill. now Danvers, 1682.

CAWDALL, JOHN, Newport, in Stiles's list of freem. there 1655.

CAWLY, THOMAS, Marblehead 1671, by w. Mary, d. of Benjamin
Parmenter, had Benjamin.

CAYME, ARTHUR, York 1680, took o. of alleg. that yr.

CENTER, JOHN, Boston, by w. Mary had John, b. 8 Aug. 1682; and
Jonathan, 8 Feb. 1685; and by w. Ruth had Elinor, 6 July 1687;
Ruth, bapt. 15 May 1692; Sarah, 20 July 1695; and Jeremiah, 20
June 1697. His wid. m. Josiah Wright, and d. 18 Feb. 1717,
aged 60.

CHADBOURNE, * HUMPHREY, Kittery, sent over 1631, by Mason, the
patentee of Piscataqua, to regul. all the E. side of the riv. liv. at the
falls call. Newichwanuck, now S. Berwick, under jurisdict. of Mass. was
ensign 1653, town clk. 1654, rep. 1657, 9, and till 1663. HUMPHREY,
Kittery, perhaps s. perhaps neph. of the preced. m. Lucy, d. of James
Treworgy, but d. bef. mid. age, prob. betw. 1660 and 1669. His wid. m.
Thomas Wills. JAMES, Kittery 1677. WILLIAM, Kittery 1631, was,
no doubt, br. or other relat. of the first Humphrey, and sent over with him
for interest of the patentee, had sev. ch. of wh. the names and deeds of
all are unkn. except that one d. m. Thomas Spencer. WILLIAM, Kittery
1631, may have been s. of Humphrey or of the preced. for nothing is
kn. but that he was call junr. and rem. to Boston, where by w. Mary he
had Mary, b. Dec. 1644. Well has the name been perpet. and some
descend. of Humphrey, or William, but wh. I kn. not, have part of the
Newichwanuck est. to our day.

CHADDOCK, for this name, Coffin gives an alias Chadwick, that grew
perhaps from the sound.

CHADWELL, BENJAMIN, Dover 1659, may have been s. of Thomas,
and rem. to Lynn, had Eliz. b. 26 Nov. 1667; Benjamin, 5 Mar. 1669;
Joseph, 14 Apr. 1671; Jeremiah, 9 Sept. 1673; Samuel, 26 Feb. 1676;
and Mary, 27 Mar. 1679. His wid. Eliz. m. early in 1681, John Jewett
of Ipswich. MOSES, Lynn, br. of the preced. m. Feb. 1661, Sarah
Ivory, perhaps d. of Thomas, had Thomas, b. 11 Dec. 1662; Sarah, 12
Mar. 1667; Lois, 3 Oct. 1670; Moses, 11 Sept. 1673, d. at 3 yrs.;

Margaret, 30 Sept. 1676 ; and Ann, 17 June 1679. RICHARD, Lynn
1636, rem. next yr. to Sandwich, there m. 22 July 1649, Catharine
Presbury, perhaps wid. of John, may have rem. next to Dover. THOM-
AS, Lynn 1630, had w. Margaret, wh. d. 29 Sept. 1658, had Moses, b.
10 Apr. 1637 ; Benjamin and Thomas. He rem. to Boston, m. Barbara, wid. of John Brimblecom, wh. had been wid. of George Davis,
and, after unit. with ch. of Charlestown, was made freem. 1670. The
sec. w. d. 1665, and he d. Feb. 1683. THOMAS, Lynn, s. of the preced.
was adm. freem. 1691.

CHADWICK, *CHARLES, Watertown, prob. came in Gov. Winth.'s
fleet, req. adm. 19 Oct. 1630, and 18 May foll. was sw. freem. of the
Col. was selectman 1637, and after, rep. 1657 and 9, and d. 10 Apr.
1682, aged 85. In his will of 30 June 1681, the w. Eliz. is ment. wh.
m. Thomas Fox, and d. 22 Feb. 1685. He had John, Thomas, and
prob. more ch. some brot. from Eng. They prob. all d. bef. him, and he
gave his prop. to kinsm. JAMES, Malden, a soldier of Moseley's comp.
wound. in the gr. swamp fight, 19 Dec. 1675, m. Feb. 1677, Hannah
Butler, had Jemima, b. 13 Mar. 1687 ; Benjamin, 9 Apr. 1689 ; and
Abigail, 4 Apr. 1692, perhaps others, and was freem. 1690. JOHN,
Watertown, prob. br. of Charles, b. in Eng. call. serg. by w. Joan, wh. d.
11 July 1674, had Eliz. b. 1 Apr. 1648 ; Sarah, 1 June 1650 ; and
James, 15 Apr. 1653 ; beside John, earlier, perhaps, than either, wh. d.
17 Mar. 1651. He was freem. 1656, rem. early to Malden, and d. soon
after 1680, when he was a witness, aged 79. JOHN, Watertown, prob.
neph. of Charles the first, but wh. was his f. is not seen, yet prob. he was
b. in Mass. by w. Sarah had Hannah ; Eliz. b. 8 May 1673 ; Charles,
19 Nov. 1674; Sarah, 28 Nov. 1676 ; Mary; John, 9 Apr. 1681;
Ebenezer, 3 May 1683 ; Joseph, 28 Nov. 1685 ; and Benjamin, 6 Mar.
1689. His will of Jan. 31, pro. 15 Mar. 1711 ment. w. and the nine ch.
His d. Eliz. m. 11 Nov. 1667, Gershom Hills; and Sarah m. 23 May
1668, the sec. Thomas Grover ; both of Malden. SAMUEL, Reading, m.
22 Jan. 1685, Mary Stocker, had Mary, b. 2 Nov. foll.; Martha, 1687, d.
soon ; Martha, again, 5 June 1689 ; all b. at Woburn, but he was k. at R.
by the fall. of a tree, 27 Feb. 1690. THOMAS, Newbury, br. of John, m.
6 Apr. 1674, Sarah Woolcot, had Sarah, b. 3 Oct. 1675; Thomas, 1677;
rem. to Watertown, there had John, 20 Nov. 1680 ; Eliz. 31 Oct. 1682,
d. at 12 yrs.; Lydia, 22 Mar. 1685, d. at 9 yrs.; Richard, 20 Apr.
1687 ; Daniel, 20 Jan. 1689 ; Jonathan, 4 Apr. 1691 ; and Eliz. again,
14 Oct. 1695.

CHAFFEE, CHAFFY, or CHAFFIN, EBENEZER, Boston, m. bef. 1690,
Eliz. d. of Nathaniel Adams. JOSEPH, Swanzey, s. perhaps of Thomas,
had Mary, wh. d. 7 May 1674 ; John, b. 16 Sept. 1673 ; and Dorothy,

4 Sept. 1682. ‖ MATTHEW, Boston 1636, ship carpenter, freem. 17 May 1637, ar. co. 1642, had w. Sarah, rem. to Newbury, and in Sept. 1649 bot. the large farm of Dr. John Clark. NATHANIEL, Swanzey, s. perhaps of Thomas, by w. Experience had Thomas, b. 19 Oct. 1672; Rachel, 7 Sept. 1673 ; Nathaniel, 8 Feb. 1676 ; Jonathan, 7 Apr. 1678 ; David, 23 Aug. 1680 ; Experience, 24 Mar. of unkn. yr. THOMAS, Hingham 1637, rem. to Swanzey bef. 1660.

CHALCROFT, RICHARD, Salem 1668.

CHALICE, CHALLIS, or CHELLIS, * PHILIP, Salisbury, was at Ipswich 1637, then 20 yrs. old, m. Mary, d. of William Sargent, had John, b. 9 July 1653, d. soon ; John, again, 26 June 1655 ; William, d. soon ; Philip, 19 Dec. 1658 ; William, again, 18 May 1663 ; and Lydia, 31 May 1665 ; beside Thomas ; Eliz. ; Mary, wh. m. Joseph Dow sec. ; Watson ; and Hannah ; was rep. 1662.

CHALKER, ABRAHAM, Saybrook, s. of Alexander, m. 16 Jan. 1680, Hannah, d. of Zechary Sanford, had Hannah, b. 25 Mar. 1682 ; and his w. d. 7 Dec. 1683. He m. 23 Sept. 1686, Sarah Ingham, had Abraham, 1 Sept. foll. and mo. and ch. d. in few days. ALEXANDER, Saybrook, m. 29 Sept. 1649, Catharine Post, prob. d. of Stephen, had Stephen, b. 8 Sept. 1650 ; Samuel ; Mary, 27 Apr. 1653 ; Abraham, 19 Oct. 1655 ; Catharine, 8 Sept. 1657 ; Sarah, 19 Oct. 1659 ; Jane, 25 Mar. 1662 ; and Alexander, 24 Feb. 1666. His wid. m. 23 Sept. 1673, John Hills; and d. Mary m. 7 Mar. 1678, Richard Cozzens. SAMUEL, Saybrook, s. of the preced. m. 31 Oct. or 7 Nov. (the rec. with suspicious impartial. giv. ea. date) 1676, Phebe, d. of Robert Bull, had Stephen, b. 11 Sept. 1677 ; Samuel, 6 Oct. 1679 ; Phebe, 29 Mar. 1682, d. young ; Phebe, again, 9 May 1685 ; beside Alexander, Mehitable, and Ruth ; and d. 1711, when Alexander was 20 yrs. old.

CHALKLEY, or CHAULKLEY, in Col. Rec. ROBERT, Charlestown 1646, freem. 1647, d. 2 Sept. 1672. His will of 27 Aug. preced. gives all his est. to w. Eliz. wh. d. at C. 13 Oct. 1678.

CHALKWELL, EDWARD, Windsor, made his will 17 Oct. 1648, and d. in few wks. as in Trumbull, Col. Rec. I. 492, where we infer, that he had no w. nor ch. nor much est.

CHAMBERLAIN, oft. CHAMBERLIN, ABRAHAM, Newton 1691, was, perhaps, s. of William of Woburn. BENJAMIN, prob. of Roxbury, and s. of Richard, was a soldier at Hadley in 1676. EDMUND, or possib. EDWARD, Woburn, m. 4 Jan. 1647, at Roxbury, Mary Turner, perhaps sis. of John, had Mary, bapt. 16 Apr. 1648 at R. ; Sarah, b. 18 Dec. 1649 ; and ano. d. 11 Mar. 1652 ; both at W. rem. to Chelmsford 1655, there had Edmund, 20 or 30 May 1656, wh. d. young, as he was in Moseley's comp. for the hard campaign of Dec. 1675 ; Jacob, 15 Oct. 1658 ; was freem. 1665; and his w. d. 7 Dec. 1669 at the ho. of Samuel Ruggles in Roxbury. He m. next, Hannah Burden, 22 June 1670, at Malden, there had Susanna, June 1671, wh. d. next yr.; Ebenezer, 1672, d. the same yr.; Susanna, again; and Edmund, again, 31 Jan. 1676; rem. to planta. call. New Roxbury, now Woodstock, there d. leav. wid. Hannah. Susanna m. 14 Nov. 1693, John Tuckerman of Boston. EDMUND, Woodstock, s. of the preced. m. 21 Nov. 1699, Eliz. Bartholomew, prob. d. of William, had Edmund, b. 23 Aug. 1700; Eliz. 6 Mar. 1702; William, 23 Feb. 1704; John; Peter; Mary; and Hannah, 2 Jan. 1721. EDMUND, Billerica, s. of William, m. 26 Aug. 1691, wid. Mercy Abbot. HENRY, Hingham, shoemaker, came in the Diligent 1638, with w. two ch. and his mo. from Hingham in Co. Norfk. was freem. 13 Mar. 1639, and no more with confid. is kn. of him, not even the date of his d. nor names of his ch. tho. strong presumpt. is that they were Henry and William. HENRY, the freem. of 1645, was, I think, of Hingham, and s. of the preced. but no more is heard of him, exc. that he had s. Nathaniel, and possib. Henry. HENRY, Hull, or Hingham, s. perhaps of the preced. was prob. one of Moseley's comp. in Dec. 1675, by w. Jane had Eliz. b. 20 Dec. 1683; Henry, 11 Mar. 1686; John, 29 Jan. 1689; Ursula, 11 Jan. 1691; and Joseph, 10 Apr. 1694. JACOB, whose place of resid. in Mass. is uncert. but Jackson, in Hist. of Newton, says, his w. Experience had brot. him five s. and next m. Jonathan Dyke, and he d. 1712, aged 83. JACOB, Roxbury, s. perhaps of the preced. more prob. of either the first Edmund, or sec. William, m. 24 Jan. 1685, Mary Child, d. of the first Benjamin, as I conject. had Jacob, b. 7 Mar. 1686; John, and ano. s. tw. whose name is not seen, 1 Aug. 1687, was adm. freem. 1690, and next yr. liv. at Newton; but d. 7 Nov. 1721, at Brookline. His will, made four days bef. calls him of Boston, yeoman, names s. Jacob, and John, d. Mary, w. of Samuel Davis, and Eliz. w. of Joseph Weld. JOB, Boston, by w. Joanna had Job, b. 16 May 1685; William, 16 Jan. 1687; Eliz. 11 Jan. 1689; all bapt. 23 Feb. 1690; Susanna, bapt. 26 Nov. 1693; Mary, 8 Dec. 1695; and prob. Jane, 31 Mar. 1706, at Mather's ch. as I think. JOHN, Charlestown, d. at Woburn, 3 Mar. 1652. JOHN, Boston 1651, a currier, m. 19 May 1653, Ann, d. of William Brown, had Ann, b. 6 Feb. 1654; Eliz. 25 Oct. 1656; was imprison. as a Quaker 1659; may have rem. to Newport, where was a John, wh. by w. Catharine had Susanna, b. Aug. 1664; Peleg, Aug. 1666; and Jane, Dec. 1667. JOHN, Charlestown, a soldier at Hadley 1676, by w. Deborah had John, bapt. 14 May 1682, wh. d. 24 July 1684, aged 5; ano. ch. whose name is not found, bapt. at the same time; Mary, 14 Oct. 1683; Deborah, 3 July 1687; and Sarah, 19 Jan. 1690; and he d. 22 Dec. foll. aged 36. JOHN, Malden, freem. 1690, by w. Hannah had

Mary, b. 5 Dec. 1685; Sarah, 25 Nov. 1688, and Sarah, again, 14 Mar. 1706. JOSEPH, Hadley, a soldier there on serv. 1676, perhaps from the E. m. 8 June 1688, Mercy, d. of John Dickinson, first of the same, had Sarah, b. 2 or 9 Nov. 1690, d. soon; Sarah, again, 10 Mar. 1693; and John, 4 Mar. 1700; rem. to Colchester, where his w. d. 30 June 1735, and he d. 7 Aug. 1752, aged 87. NATHANIEL, Hull, s. perhaps of Henry the sec. by w. Abigail had Eliz. b. 8 June 1682; Nathaniel, 23 Aug. 1683; John, 26 Dec. 1684; Mary, 5 Feb. 1686; Joanna, 8 Jan. 1688, and five or six more ds. and last, Thomas, 21 May 1695. But perhaps he rem. to Scituate, and there, Deane thinks, he had more. RICHARD, Braintree, had Richard, b. 19 Dec. 1642, d. in six days; rem. to Roxbury, there had Benjamin, Joseph, Mary, Rebecca, and Ann, all bapt. 4 June 1665; and Mehitable, 28 Jan. 1666. His w. was Sarah, d. of the first Edward Bugbee, but she could only be sec. w. He rem. to Sudbury, and d. bef. 15 Apr. 1673, when his will of 12 Feb. preced. was pro. It names those six ch. as then liv. calls one Mary Smith, and adds to the number Eliz. Daniel, beside gr.ch. John Graves, and perhaps his sis. Mary G. but of such Graves I kn. nothing. ‡ RICHARD, Portsmouth, was the Secr. and a Couns. under the Provinc. gov. 1682. SAMUEL, Chelmsford, br. of Thomas of the same, had Samuel, b. 28 Oct. 1685; and Eliz. and Mary, tw. 29 May 1699. THOMAS, Woburn, freem. 1644, by w. Mary had Thomas, b. elsewhere, possib. in Eng.; Samuel, 7 Oct. 1645; Mary, 30 Jan. or, Shattuck says, 11 June 1649, rem. to Chelmsford; and in old age, m. 19 Apr. 1674, Mary Parker, wh. d. 7 Feb. 1693. Mary m. 1 Dec. 1671, John Graves. THOMAS, Chelmsford, s. of the preced. m. 10 Aug. 1666, Sarah, d. of Robert Proctor, had Thomas, b. 30 May 1667; Sarah, 11 Jan. 1679; Jane, 19 Jan. 1682; Eliz. and perhaps more, and d. 28 May 1727. THOMAS, Newton, m. 18 Apr. 1682, Eliz. d. of the sec. Thomas Hammond of the same, had Thomas, b. 10 Sept. 1683; Eliz. 1 Aug. 1686; Rebecca, 11 Mar. 1689; Mary, 11 Feb. 1693; Sarah, 18 Oct. 1695; and John, 26 Sept. 1698. WILLIAM, Boston 1647, rem. 1649, perhaps to Hingham or Hull, was prob. s. of Henry the first, was liv. there 1657; and in Dec. 1675 one William, his s. or perhaps neph. was one of the Hull soldiers in the Narraganset campaign under Moseley. WILLIAM, Woburn, perhaps br. of Edmund the first, had, at Concord, Timothy, b. 13 Aug. 1649; Isaac, 1 Oct. 1650, d. young; rem. prob. 1654, to Billerica, had Sarah, 18 Jan. 1656; Jacob, 18 Jan. 1658; Thomas, 20 Feb. 1659; Edmund, 15 July 1660; Rebecca, 25 Feb. 1662; Abraham, 6 Jan. 1664; Ann, 3 Mar. 1666; Clement, 30 May 1669; Daniel, 27 Sept. 1671; and Isaac, 20 Jan. 1681. His w. Rebecca, mo. of the four last ch. perhaps of more, d. 26 Sept. 1692, in pris. on the preposter. charge of witchcrf. and he d. 31 May 1706, aged 85. This name, like

Parker, Wheeler, or other designat. of office or employm. was so wide. diffus. in our mo. country, that it must be vain to attempt trac. of relationsh. in various pts. of this contin. In 1834, Farmer found the gr. of this name were three at Dart. one at Harv. one at Yale, and five at other N. E. coll.

CHAMBERS, ROBERT, Marshfield 1643, came in the Hopewell, capt. Babb, late in 1635, from London, aged 13 ; but where he had liv. after coming, or later than 1643, is unkn. THOMAS, Scituate 1640, may have come that yr. from New Haven, and rem. as Deane says, 1658, to Charlestown. If so, he was, perhaps, f. of the Hon. Charles, wh. d. at C. 27 Apr. 1743, in his 83d yr. says the gr.stone. WILLIAM, Ipswich 1649.

CHAMPERNOON, ‡ FRANCIS, Kittery 1639, Portsmouth 1646, York 1665, a neph. of Sir Ferdinando Gorges, was a capt. 1640, maj. and after July 1674 m. Mary, wid. of Robert Cutts, bec. one of the couns. of the Prov. for New Hampsh. 1684, d. at K. early in 1687. His will, of 16 Nov. 1686, pro. 28 Dec. of next yr. shows that he left no ch. In Co. Devon this is an ancient name, and the gent. of the present generat. has fine est. at Dartington. See Hubbard, 584 ; Belkn. I. 83, 102 ; Hutch. Coll. 500, 556 ; Folsom, 66.

CHAMPION, HENRY, Saybrook, m. Aug. 1647, had Sarah, b. 1649 ; Mary, 1651 ; Henry, 1654 ; Thomas, Apr. 1656 ; Stephen, 1658, d. 1660 ; and he m. 21 Mar. 1698, sec. w. Deborah, and d. at gr. age, 17 Feb. 1709. Sarah m. 27 Jan. 1673, Henry Bennett. HENRY, Saybrook, s. of the preced. m. 1 Apr. 1684, Susanna De Wolf, perhaps d. of Balthazar, had Henry, Joshua, Samuel, Stephen, and five ds. and d. July 1704. ROBERT, New Haven 1639. THOMAS, Lyme, s. of Henry the first, m. 23 Aug. 1682, Hannah, d. of Woolstone Brockway, had Thomas, b. 21 Jan. 1691 ; Henry, 2 May 1695 ; and five ds. (of wh. one was Mary, wh. bec. sec. w. of Timothy Fuller of East Haddam) and he d. 1705.

CHAMPLIN, CHRISTOPHER, Westerly 1669, was s. prob. youngest, of Jeffery, had Christopher, b. 26 Sept. 1684, beside Jeffery, William, Joseph, and John. His sec. w. was Eliz. wid. of capt. Joseph Davoll. JEFFERY, Portsmouth and Newport 1639, was adm. freem. 14 Sept. 1640, prob. was of Westerly in 1661, with s. Jeffery, William, and Christopher, d. bef. 1695. ‡ * JEFFERY, Westerly, s. prob. eldest of the preced. rem. early to Kingstown, had s. Jeffery, perhaps William, was rep. 1681, 2, 4, 5, an Assist. from 1696 to 1715. * WILLIAM, Westerly 1669, s. of Jeffery the first, m. Mary, d. of the first James Babcock, wh. in his will, 12 June 1679, names d. Mary C. He had ch. Mary, Ann, and William, was often rep. betw. 1691 and 1713, and d. 1 Dec. 1713, aged 61. This has been a name of celebr. in R. I.

CHAMPNEY, CHRISTOPHER, Cambridge, by w. Margaret had Deborah, b. 17 Jan. 1644. DANIEL, Cambridge, s. of Richard, m. 3 Jan. 1666, Dorcas, d. of Thomas Bridge, had Dorcas, b. 22 Aug. 1667; Daniel, 14 Dec. 1669; Thomas, 12 Sept. 1673; Noah, 27 Sept. 1677; Downing, 31 May 1680; and Abigail, 26 Apr. 1683. His w. d. 7 Feb. 1684, and he m. 4 June foll. Hepzibah, d. of famous sch.master Corlet, then wid. of James Minot, had Hepzibah, 28 June 1687; but bef. this he was of Billerica sev. yrs. freem. 1677; and d. 19 Nov. 1691. JOHN, Cambridge 1635, d. early, leav. wid. Joan, by wh. he had Mary, Sarah, John, and Joseph; but whether all, or wh. of them were b. in Eng. is unkn. His wid. m. Golden Moore. The s. John d. 20 Feb. 1665; and Mary m. 2 May 1654, Theophilus Richardson of Woburn. JOSEPH, Cambridge, freem. 1654, rem. to Billerica, and d. May 1656. His w. was Sarah. RICHARD, Cambridge, br. perhaps of John, came in the Defence 1635, prob. with w. Jane and ch. Esther, six yrs. old, in comp. with Rev. Thomas Shepard, as was in C. believ. but none of this name is that yr. found at the London custom ho. Perhaps he was forbid. to emb. as a subsidy man, yet unwill. to sw. false. and unable to obtain leave without. He bec. freem. 25 May 1636, was a rul. elder, own. est. at Billerica, then belong. to C. had, perhaps, Mary, for the rec. is bad, b. tw. with Samuel, Sept. 1635; Sarah, May 1638; Mary, again, Nov. 1639; John, 28 May 1641; Lydia; and Daniel, 9 Mar. 1645; and d. 26 Nov. 1669. His will of 30 June preced. names w. two s. and four ds. and gives 40 acres near the falls on Charles riv. to Harv. Coll. Esther m. 26 Mar. 1654, Josiah Converse of Woburn; Sarah m. 19 Aug. 1656, William Barrett, and d. 21 Aug. 1661; but John Poole of Reading, in his will of 14 Feb. 1667, calls W. B. his s.-in-law, and speaks of his d. Sarah, as dec. w. of B. wh. seems to me inexplica.; Lydia m. 20 May 1668, John Hastings, as sec. w. and d. 23 Jan. 1691; and Mary m. 26 Sept. 1665, Jacob French, and d. 1 Apr. 1681. *SAMUEL, Cambridge, eldest s. of the preced. m. at Billerica, 13 Oct. 1657, Sarah, d. of James Hubbard, had Samuel, b. 8 Dec. 1658, d. soon; Sarah, 17 Feb. 1660; Mary, 12 May 1662; Esther, 14 May 1664, d. under 3 yrs.; Samuel, again, 9 Mar. 1667; these all at B. but after rem. to C. had Joseph, 1 Sept. 1669; Richard, 20 Aug. 1674; and Daniel. He was rep. for C. 1686, the last yr. of the old chart. again in 1689 after overthrow of Andros, and in 1692 under new chart.

CHANDLER, BENJAMIN, Scituate, s. of Edmund, m. Eliz. d. of John Buck, had Benjamin, b. 1672; Martha, 1673; Samuel, 30 Nov. 1674; John, 1675 or 6; and Mary, 1678. *EDMUND, Duxbury 1633, had Benjamin, Samuel, Joseph, and ds. Sarah, Ann, Mary, and Ruth, of none of wh. is the date of b. kn. He was at Scituate 1650, but d. 1662

at D. after mak. his will of 3 May in that yr. in wh. he gave his est. at
Barbados to three eldest ds. Mary m. Hezekiah Bradford. HENRY,
Andover, s. of Thomas, m. 28 Nov. 1695, Lydia, d. of George Abbot
the sec. of the same, had Henry, b. 3 Sept. 1696 ; Samuel, 11 Oct.
1698 ; Lydia, 27 Nov. 1699 ; Daniel, 1701 ; Nehemiah, a. 1703 ; Abigail ; Sarah, 9 July 1709 ; Deborah ; Hannah, 1712 ; Mary, 14 Mar.
1714 ; Isaac, 1717 ; and Mehitable, 1720 ; and d. at Enfield, 27 Aug.
1737. His wid. d. 11 Mar. 1748. JOHN, Concord, freem. 13 May
1640, had Hannah, b. 28 Feb. 1641 ; and no more of him is kn. JOHN,
Roxbury, s. of William, b. in Eng. was of Boston some yrs. m. 16 Feb.
1659, Eliz. d. of William Douglas, had John, b. 4 Mar. 1660, wh. d. at
9 mos. ; Eliz. 20 Feb. 1662 ; John, again, 16 Apr. 1665 ; Joseph, 3
Apr. 1667, d. next yr. ; Hannah, 18 Sept. 1669 ; Mehitable, 24 Aug.
1673 ; Sarah, 19 Nov. 1676 ; and Joseph, again, 4 June 1683 ; rem.
with others, 1686, to plant Woodstock ; there was deac. made his will 1
June 1702, and d. 15 Apr. 1703, aged a. 68. His wid. d. 23 Sept. 1705
at New London. Eliz. m. 18 Nov. 1682, Robert Mason ; Hannah, m. 7
July 1685, Moses Draper, and d. 9 June 1692 ; Mehitable m. 5 June
1695, John Coit of New London, and Sarah m. 9 June 1697, William
Coit, br. of John, and, next, John Gardiner, propr. of Gardiner's isl. as
his sec. w. JOHN, Portsmouth 1658, a shoemaker. JOHN, Andover,
br. of Henry, m. 20 Dec. 1676, Hannah, d. of George Abbot, the first
of the same, had John, b. Oct. 1677, d. soon ; John, 14 Mar. 1680 ;
Zebediah, 1 Apr. 1683 ; Abiel, 9 Jan. 1686 ; Hannah, 23 May 1690 ; and
Sarah, 19 Oct. 1693 ; was a capt. and d. 19 Sept. 1721. His wid. d. 2
Mar. 1741, aged 90. JOHN, Woodstock, s. of John of the same, m. 10
Nov. 1692, Mary, d. of Joshua Raymond of New London, had John, b.
at N. L. 10 Oct. 1693 ; Joshua, 9 Feb. 1696 ; William, 3 Nov. 1698 ;
Mary, 20 Apr. 1700 ; Eliz. 13 May 1702 ; Samuel, 5 Jan. 1704 ;
Sarah, 11 Oct. 1705 ; Mehitable, 10 Aug. 1707 ; Thomas, 23 July
1709 ; and Hannah, 27 Mar. 1711 ; and he had for sec. w. wid. Esther
Alcock, m. 14 Nov. 1711. His first four ch. were b. at New London,
after wh. most of his days were pass. at Woodstock ; but in 1731 on
organiz. of Worcester Co. he rem. to Worcester, and was appoint. first
judge of the Ct. of C. P. and first judge of Pro. and he d. 10 Aug.
1740. JOSEPH, Andover, s. of William the first of the same, m. 10
June 1708, Mehitable Russell, d. perhaps of Robert, had Mehitable ;
Thomas ; Mary, b. 4 Mar. 1713 ; Phebe, 1714 ; Joseph, 13 Feb. 1716 ;
Bridget, 19 Sept. 1719 ; John, 19 Jan. 1722 ; ano. s. 10 Sept. 1726 ;
and Hannah. JOSEPH, Duxbury, s. of Edmund of the same, of whose
will he was excor. had John, Joseph, and, perhaps, Edmund, and the
Benjamin, wh. d. 26 Mar. 1771, aged 87. JOSEPH, Andover, br. of

Henry, m. 26 Nov. 1691, Sarah, d. of the first Thomas Abbot, had Sarah, b. 10 Mar. 1693; Joseph, 29 June 1694; Isaac, 24 Aug. 1696; Mehitable, 27 Feb. 1699; Jemima, 2 May 1701; Nathaniel, a. 1703; Rhoda, 1705; Phebe; and Jemima, again. JOSEPH, Newbury, s. of William the first of the same, m. 10 Feb. 1700, Mary Hall, had Joseph, and John, tw. b. 23 Apr. 1701; and Samuel, 3 Mar. 1703. JOSEPH, Woodstock, youngest s. of John the first of the same, rem. to Pomfret, m. 29 June 1708, Susanna Perrin, had Joseph, b. 1 Apr. 1709, d. soon; Joseph, again, 16 June 1710; David, 28 May 1712; Susanna, 7 Feb. 1714; Peter, 17 May 1716, d. young; Dorothy, 12 Apr. 1718; Hepzibah, 12 Aug. 1720; Stephen, 25 Aug. 1722; Josiah, 2 Oct. 1724; Eunice, 17 Dec. 1726; Daniel, 21 Mar. 1728; and Peter, again, 23 June 1733; and d. 5 Jan. 1750. His wid. d. 22 Jan. 1755. NATHANIEL, Duxbury 1643. PHILEMON, Andover, s. of William the first of the same, m. Hannah Clary, had Ebenezer, b. 7 June 1703, d. soon; Thomas, 25 Nov. 1705; Philemon, 15 Aug. 1706; Josiah, 4 Oct. 1708; Hannah, 20 Jan. 1713; Mary, 23 Dec. 1714; and Mehitable, 12 Apr. 1719. He had early rem. to Pomfret in Conn. where he was clk. of the proprs. 1713, selectman 1719, and one of the first deac. His w. d. 24 June 1735; and he next m. 2 May 1739, wid. Patience Griggs of Woodstock, and d. 7 May 1752. His wid. d. 4 Oct. 1754. ROGER, Plymouth 1633, may have been br. of Samuel of the same. ROGER, Concord, m. 1671, Mary Simonds, had Mary, b. 7 Jan. 1672; Samuel, 3 Mar. 1673; Joseph, 8 Nov. 1678, d. soon; and Abigail, 31 May 1681. He had rem. bef. 1679, to Billerica, and was freem. 1682. SAMUEL, Plymouth 1633, rem. to Dorchester, there in Dec. 1664 m. Sarah, wid. of Richard Davis, wh. d. Aug. 1665. SAMUEL, Duxbury, prob. s. of Edmund, in 1665 had gr. of 60 acres of ld. d. a. 1683. SAMUEL, Newbury, s. of William the first of the same, m. 12 July 1694, Mercy, d. of Abraham Perkins the sec. had Eliz. b. 5 Aug. 1695. *THOMAS, Andover 1645, brot. from Eng. 1637 by his f. William to Roxbury, m. Hannah Brewer, perhaps d. of Daniel, had Thomas, b. 2 Oct. 1652, wh. d. 6 June 1659; John, b. 14 Mar. 1655; Hannah; William, 28 May 1659; Sarah, 20 Dec. 1661; Thomas, again, 9 Oct. 1664; Henry, 28 May 1667; Joseph, 3 Aug. 1669; was rep. 1678 and 9, and d. 1703, aged a. 73. His wid. d. 25 Oct. 1717, aged 87 perhaps. Hannah m. 2 Dec. 1674, Daniel Bixby of A.; and Sarah m. 29 May 1682, Samuel Phelps of A. THOMAS, Reading, had John, b. 14 Mar. 1655. THOMAS, Andover, s. of Thomas the first, m. 22 May 1686, Mary Peters, d. of Andrew, wh. d. 4 Oct. 1750, had Mary, b. 18 Feb. 1687; Annis, 24 Mar. 1689; Thomas, 4 June 1691; Eliz. 13 Jan. 1693; Timothy, 29 Mar. 1695; Ephraim, 2 Oct. 1696; David, 11 Jan. 1699, d. soon; Hannah, 23 Aug. 1700; and, perhaps, Phebe, Dorcas, Lydia, and Jonathan. He d. 26 Jan. 1737, aged 72. THOMAS, Andover, br. of Philemon, m. a. 1701, Mary Stevens, d. perhaps of Benjamin of the same, but ano. geneal. makes her d. of deac. Joseph of A. had Mary, b. 10 Mar. 1702; William, 14 July 1704; James, 10 June 1706, H. C. 1728; Phebe, 1708; Bridget, a. 1710, d. soon; Bridget, again, 1712; Hannah, 1714; Eliz. 1717; Joseph, 1720; and John, 1723, H. C. 1743. His w. d. 27 Sept. 1751; and he d. 7 Nov. foll. WILLIAM, Roxbury, came in 1637, as the ch. rec. tells, with w. Annis or Hannah, and ch. Hannah, b. a. 1629; Thomas, a. 1630; John; and William, b. 1636; here had Sarah, was freem. 13 May 1640, and d. 19, was bur. 24 Jan. 1642. His wid. m. 2 July 1643, John Dane; Hannah m. 12 Dec. 1646, George Abbot, wh. was the first of Andover; and next, bec. third w. of Rev. Francis Dane; and Sarah m. 4 Nov. 1659, William Cleves. WIL-LIAM, Newbury, had three ws. nam. Mary, and ch. Esther, b. 28 Jan. 1652 by the first, wh. d. 29 Oct. 1666; by the sec. surnam. Lord, m. 26 Feb. 1667, had William, Dec. foll.; Joseph, 19 Nov. 1669; Samuel, 29 Feb. 1672; and Mary, 18 May 1674. This w. d. 3 Oct. 1676, and he m. 16 Apr. foll. a Carter, whether maid or wid. is not kn. and d. 5 Mar. 1701, aged 84. WILLIAM, Andover, s. of William the first, b. in Eng. m. 24 Aug. 1658, Mary, d. of John Dane, of Ipswich, s. of the h. of his mo. had Mary, b. 1659; William, 31 Jan. 1660; Sarah, 29 Jan. 1662, wh. d. soon; Thomas, 1663, d. young; John, 1665, d. at 16 yrs.; Philemon, 24 Aug. 1667, d. soon; Thomas, again, 1668, d. soon; Phile-mon, again, 4 Sept. 1671; Hannah, 5 Feb. 1673; Thomas, again, 5 Dec. 1676; and Joseph, 1679, d. young. His w. d. 10 May 1679, and he m. 8 Oct. foll. Bridget Richardson, prob. wid. of James, and d. of Thomas Henchman of Chelmsford, had Phebe, b. 17 Sept. 1680; Joseph, again, 17 July 1682; and Rhoda, 26 Sept. 1684. He was freem. 1669. Of the ds. Mary m. John Sherwin, wh. is unkn. to me; Hannah m. Nathan-iel Robbins; Phebe m. Jonathan Tyler; both equal. unkn.; and Rhoda m. 19 Apr. 1705, Timothy Holt. WILLIAM, Andover, s. of the first Thomas, m. 21 Apr. 1687, Elinor Phelps, had Elinor, b. 23 Jan. 1688; perhaps William; and Moses. WILLIAM, Andover, s. of William of the same, m. 28 Dec. 1682, Sarah Buckmaster, had Josiah, b. 28 Dec. 1683; Philemon, 15 May 1690; Sarah, 13 Mar. 1693; and Zechariah, 1 May 1695. WILLIAM, Newbury, s. of William of the same, m. 29 Nov. 1692, Hannah Huntington, perhaps d. of John of Salisbury, had John, b. 21 Nov. 1693; Joseph, 19 Oct. 1694; and Mary, 5 Oct. 1696. Twenty of this name had been, as Farmer saw, gr. at Harv. seven at Yale, four at Dart. and five at the other coll. of N. E. in 1828.

CHAPIN, CALEB, Boston, perhaps s. of David, by w. Sarah had Han-nah, b. 4 Jan. 1682; Lydia, 15 Mar. 1683; Caleb, 2 Apr. 1686; and

David, 2 July 1690. DAVID, Springfield, perhaps s. of Samuel, b. in Eng. m. at Boston, 29 Aug. 1654, Lydia Crump, had Lydia, b. 19 June foll.; and Caleb, 2 Apr. 1657, rem. soon, and no more is heard of him. * HENRY, Springfield, s. of Samuel, b. in Eng. m. 15 Dec. 1664, Bethia, d. of Benjamin Cooley, had Henry, Benjamin, and two ds. wh. liv. to adult age, was rep. 1689, and d. 15 Aug. 1718. JAPHET, Springfield, br. of the preced. liv. first at Milford, there m. 22 July 1664, Abilene, d. of Samuel Cooley, had Samuel, b. 4 July foll.; Thomas, 20 May 1671; John; Ebenezer; Daniel; Jonathan; and two ds. of wh. Sarah was b. 15 Mar. 1668. His w. d. 17 Nov. 1710, aged 68, and he m. 31 May foll. Dorothy Root of Enfield, and he d. 20 Feb. foll. aged 70. JOHN, Mass. 1634. Felt. * JOSIAH, Weymouth, s. of Samuel, by w. Mary had Samuel, b. 22 Nov. 1659; perhaps Mary, wh. m. 20 Feb. 1682, Joseph Adams; and other ch. rem. to Braintree 1676, was freem. 1678, rep. for Mendon 1689, where he d. 10 Sept. 1726, aged 92. SAMUEL, Roxbury 1638, brot. from Eng. w. Cicely, call. Sisly on rec. and sev. ch. prob. Henry, Josiah, perhaps David, and two ds. Catharine and Sarah, and at R. had Japhet, b. 15 Oct. 1642; rem. that yr. to Springfield, there had Hannah, 2 Dec. 1644; was freem. 2 June 1641, a propr. of Westfield 1660, a deac. and man of distinct. d. 11 Nov. 1675. Catharine m. 20 Nov. 1646, Nathaniel Bliss; next, 3 or 31 July 1655, Thomas Gilbert; and third, 28 Dec. 1664, Samuel Marshfield, and to ea. bore four ch. Sarah m. 14 Apr. 1667, Rowland Thomas, and d. 5 Aug. 1684; and Hannah m. 27 Sept. 1666, John Hitchcock. * SAMUEL, Mendon, s. prob. of Josiah, was rep. 1692; but no more is kn. to me. SAMUEL, Springfield, s. prob. of Japhet, m. 24 Dec. 1690, Hannah, d. of the first Isaac Sheldon. Of this name, in 1834, gr. were count. by Farmer, 7 at Yale, 4 at Dart. 3 at Harv. and 6 at other N. E. coll.

CHAPLEMAN, MICHAEL, Salem 1668.

CHAPLIN, or CHAPLAIN, * CLEMENT, Cambridge, came in the Elizabeth and Ann from London 1635, was a chandler of Bury St. Edmunds in Co. Suffk. aged 48, and, tho. custom ho. rec. tells no more, he brot. prob. the w. wh. was Sarah Hinds, d. of a goldsmith in that borough, but no ch. is ever ment. freem. 3 Mar. 1636, soon after rem. to Hartford with Hooker and his friends, was one of the orig. purch. of that beautif. city, but sat down at Wethersfield, was next yr. treasr. of the Col. rep. 1643 and 4, and liv. in 1646. He gave all his est. to the w. wh. went home, but date of his d. or her rem. is equal. unkn. See 3 Mass. Hist. Coll. X. 168. HUGH, Rowley, came, prob. with Rev. Ezekiel Rogers, 1638, was freem. 18 May 1642, by w. Eliz. had John, b. 1643; Joseph, 1646; Thomas, 1648; and Jonathan 1651; and d. bef. 31 Mar. 1657, when his will, made two yrs. bef. was pro. He was b. 22 May 1603, it is said, the s. of Ebenezer, wh. was b. 10 May 1572, wh. was s. of Jeremy of Bradford, Co. York, b. 4 Aug. 1541. JOHN, a soldier at Hadley, 1676, was from the E. part of the Col. and may have been s. of the preced. JOSEPH, Rowley, s. of Hugh, by w. Eliz. West had Joseph, b. 1673; John, 1674; Jonathan, 1677; Jeremiah, 1680; and one d.

CHAPMAN, EDWARD, Windsor 1662, m. in Eng. as is said, Eliz. Fox, had Henry, b. 4 July 1663; Mary, 23 Aug. 1664, d. soon; Mary, again, 27 Oct. 1665; Eliz. 15 Jan. 1668; Simon, 30 Apr. 1669; Hannah, 3 May 1671; Margaret, 7 Mar. 1673; and Sarah, 24 May 1675. He was freem. 1667, and k. in the gr. Narraganset fight, 19 Dec. of that yr. and his wid. m. 12 July 1677, Samuel Cross. EDWARD, Ipswich 1642, m. Mary, d. of Mark Symonds, had Symonds, Nathaniel, Mary, Samuel, and John. His w. d. 10 June 1658, and he took sec. w. Dorothy, wid. of Thomas Abbot of Rowley, d. of Richard Swain of R. His will, of 9 Apr. 1678, ment. w. and the first three ch. perhaps the others were dec. Mary m. 24 Jan. 1677, John Barney, as Coffin reads the name, that Mr. Felt calls Barry. HOPE, Westerly, 1680, s. of Richard, had Richard, b. 20 Feb. 1688, Eliz. and Hannah, perhaps more. ISAAC, Barnstable, s. of Ralph the first, m. 2 Sept. 1678, Rebecca, d. of James Leonard, had Lydia, b. 15 Dec. 1679; John, 12 May 1681; Hannah, 26 Dec. 1682, d. under 7 yrs.; James, 5 Aug. 1685; Abigail, 11 July 1687; Hannah, again, 10 Apr. 1690; Isaac, 29 Dec. 1692; Ralph, 19 Jan. 1695; and Rebecca, 10 June 1697. JACOB, Boston 1642. JOHN, the freem. of Mass. 14 May 1634, perhaps of Charlestown, was prob. the same orig. sett. at New Haven 1639, wh. sold his est. there Dec. 1647, and rem. to Fairfield, thence soon to Stamford, where he made his will 1665. His wid. Martha, wh. m. Francis Brown, and two ds. Mary, and Eliz. had all his est. Eliz. m. 12 Mar. 1673, John Judson. * JOHN, Saybrook, eldest s. of Robert, freem. 1667, m. 7 June 1670, Eliz. d. of Joseph Hawley of Stratford, had John, b. 8 Sept. 1671; Joseph, 31 July 1673; Eliz. 10 Feb. 1676, d. at 4 mos. and his w. d. 10 May foll. He m. 26 Mar. 1677, Eliz. d. of William Beamon, had Andrew, 24 Apr. 1678, d. at 5 yrs.; Eliz. 26 Sept. 1679; Thomas, 7 Oct. 1680, d. at 2 mos.; Thomas, again, 23 Jan. 1682, d. at 10 mos.; Ann, 5 Nov. 1684; Andrew, again, 1 Oct. 1686, d. under 4 mos.; and Mehitable, 29 Sept. 1688; rem. to Haddam, there had Jabez, 1690; and Samuel, 1692. His w. d. 30 Oct. 1694. He was capt. and rep. for S. and after for H. JOHN, Ipswich, s. of Edward of the same, perhaps the youngest ch. m. 30 Sept. 1675, Rebecca Smith, had John, b. 7 July 1676; and the f. d. 19 Nov. 1677. * NATHANIEL, Saybrook, youngest s. of Robert, m. 29 June 1681, Mary Collins, perhaps d. of John of Guilford, had Nathaniel, b. 13 May 1682,

d. under five mos.; Nathaniel, again, 19 July 1686; Daniel, 14 Mar. 1690; and John, 18 May 1694. For sec. w. he m. Hannah Bates, prob. sis. of Samuel of S. had Mary, 30 Aug. 1700; Hannah, 29 Aug. 1702; Phineas, 10 Aug. 1704, wh. d. prob. bef. his f. as he is not nam. in the will; Caleb, 6 Oct. 1706; and Ann, 26 Oct. 1709. He was deac. and many yrs. rep. made his will Jan. and d. 5 Apr. 1726, and his wid. d. Dec. 1750. RALPH, Marshfield, came in the Elizabeth 1635, from London, aged 20, a ship-carpenter of Southwark in Surry, close to London, and sat down, first, at Duxbury, m. there, 23 Nov. 1642, the earliest m. in that place, Lydia Wills, or Willis, had Mary, b. 31 Oct. 1643; Sarah, 15 May 1645; Isaac, 4 Aug. 1647; Lydia, b. and d. 26 Nov. 1649; Ralph, 20 June 1653, d. next mo.; and Ralph, again; and d. a. 1671. His will was made 28 Nov. of that yr. Mary m. 14 May 1666, William Troop of Barnstable; and Sarah m. William Norcutt. RALPH, Marshfield, youngest s. of the preced. had John, wh. it is report. liv. more than a hundred yrs. and therefore has sev. stories told of him. RICHARD, Boston, by w. Mary had Richard, wh. d. 17 Nov. 1653. RICHARD, Braintree, by w. Mary had Susan, b. 25 Feb. 1649; Hope, 30 Jan. 1655; Mary, 30 June 1657, d. in few days; Richard, wh. was k. by the Ind. as a soldier in Philip's war; and he d. 1669. His will of 9 Mar. pro. 26 Aug. foll. names w. Joan, and s. Richard. His d. Susan m. an Ellis, it is said, of Stonington, prob. bef. that will. Of this name was ano. also of Braintree, as appears by rec. of Boston ch. adm. on letters of dism. from that ch. of his wid. Florence C. ‡* ROBERT, Saybrook, m. 29 Apr. 1642, Ann, d. of Thomas Bliss of Hartford, had John, b. early in July 1644; Robert, a. mid. Sept. 1646; Ann, a. 12 Sept. 1648, d. at 1 yr.; Hannah, 4 Oct. 1650; Nathaniel, 16 Feb. 1653; Mary, 15 Apr. 1655; and Sarah, 25 Sept. 1657; was a capt. rep. 1652, and most of the yrs. to 1673; an Assist. 1681-5. His w. d. 20 Nov. 1685; and he d. 13 Oct. 1687, aged 70. Tradit. says that he came to Boston, 1635, from Hull, Yorksh. but perhaps this may in part be confus. with deriv. of Ralph, of wh. he may have been br. His d. Hannah m. 27 Feb. 1677, David Bull; Mary m. 2 May 1676, Samuel Bates; and Sarah m. Sept. 1686, Joseph Pratt, as his sec. w. ROBERT, Dover, 1663, by w. Eliz. had Robert, b. 18 Dec. 1664, wh. d. within 3 wks. * ROBERT, Saybrook, s. of the first Robert, freem. 1667, m. 27 July 1671, Sarah, eldest d. of Francis Griswold of Norwich, had Samuel, b. 12 Sept. 1672; Robert, 19 Apr. 1675; Sarah, 12 Sept. 1677, d. next mo.; Francis, 5 Aug. 1678; Dorcas, 26 Aug. 1680, d. soon; Stephen, 24 Nov. 1681, d. young; a s. 6 Mar. 1684, d. in 4 days; Sarah, again, 19 Dec. 1686, d. next mo.; and a s. 6 Nov. 1689, d. in 3 days. His w. d. 7 Apr. 1692; and he m. 29 Oct. 1694, Mary, wid. of Samuel Sheather of Killingworth, had Benjamin, Mar. 1696; Mehitable, 15 May 1697, d. under 10 mos.; Stephen, 5 Mar. 1699; and Abigail, 20 Mar. 1701. He was rep. sev. yrs. and d. in that stat. 10 Nov. 1711. SIMON, Ipswich, freem. 1675, may have had Simon of Windsor wh. d. 12 Oct. 1749, aged 79, and his w. Sarah, aged 60, had d. 21 May 1735, hav. had Simon. * THOMAS, Saybrook 1651, rep. May 1652 and Oct. 1654, unless this be mistak. for Robert, an opin. wh. may be suppos. to have influenc. the mak. of Index to Trumbull's Col. Rec. I. since it does *not* include the pages, where the name of Thomas, in the text, appears at the Gen. Ct. as deput. and *does* include those where Robert's name appears at the Ct. in Sept. 1652 and Sept. 1654. Without much confidence in the conject. I incline to think Thomas entit. to his seat, tho. no more is heard of him. THOMAS, Charlestown, serv. short time in Turner's comp. as a soldier, Mar. 1676, by w. Sarah had Sarah; Eliz. both bapt. 22 Aug. 1680; Mercy, 22 May 1681; Thomas, 22 Apr. 1683; and posthum. d. Abiel, 23 Oct. 1687. WILLIAM, New London 1656, among the freem. 1669, d. 18 Dec. 1699. From his will we get the names of ch. John, William, Samuel, Jeremiah, Joseph, Sarah, and Rebecca; but little can be learn. as to any of the s. and of the ds. nothing. It is said that Jeremiah was b. 1677; and we kn. that he, with William and Samuel, resid. at N. L. that Joseph went to Norwich, and that John, the oldest, was liv. at Colchester in May 1748, when it was affirm. "he will be 95 yrs. old next Nov." so that it would be hazardous to deny, that he was b. 1653. In 1834 Farmer found the gr. at Yale fourteen, at Harv. and Dart. four ea. and two at other N. E. coll.

CHAPPELL, CALEB, Lebanon, was youngest s. of George; and Sedgwick's Hist. of Sharon says, that the name in that town is deriv. from him. GEORGE, Wethersfield, came in the Christian 1635, aged 20, from London, and two yrs. later is found apprent. to learn the trade of carpenter with Francis Stiles of Windsor, wh. had come in the same ship, and, perhaps, paid for his transporta. Fifteen yrs. after he rem. to New London with w. Margery and ch. Mary; Rachel; John; and George, b. 5 Mar. 1654; and there had Eliz. 30 Aug. 1656; Esther, 15 Apr. 1662; Sarah, 14 Feb. 1666; Nathaniel, 21 May 1668; and Caleb, 7 Oct. 1671. He d. 1709, in his will speaks of aged w. Margery, commit. to s. Caleb, and gr.s. Comfort; but wh. was f. of this Comfort is not told. Mary m. 19 Jan. 1665, John Daniels; Rachel m. a. 1667, Thomas Crocker. JOHN, eldest s. of the preced. was, perhaps, a soldier in Turner's comp. 1676, may have been of Lyme 1678, and certain. was of Flushing, L. I. 1704. NATHANIEL, Boston 1634, was in the employm. of Atherton Hough, adm. freem. 22 May 1639. He may have been br. of George. WILLIAM, New London 1659, perhaps br. of George, by w. Christian had Mary, b. Feb. 1669; John, 28 Feb. 1672; two nam. William, d. young; Christian, Feb. 1681, and perhaps more. Mary m. John Wood.

CHARD, HUGH, Boston 1694, s. of William, was not a householder in 1695, perhaps rem. SAMUEL, Weymouth, br. of the preced. by w. Mary had Mary, b. 28 Nov. 1698, and perhaps others. THOMAS, Boston, s. of William, prob. eldest, had serv. as a soldier, in Philip's war, of Turner's comp. at Hadley 1676, but liv. at B. 1678, and was freem. 1680 or 1, enjoy. the advantage of being count. as of the first ch. in the former yr. and of the sec. ch. next yr. See Geneal. Reg. III. 245 and 6. WILLIAM, Weymouth, freem. 1654, had first w. Grace, wh. d. at W. 22 Jan. 1656; and he m. 27 Nov. 1656, Eliz. d. of Matthew Pratt, had Thomas, b. 27 or 29 Sept. 1657; Caleb, 19 Oct. 1660; Mary, 8 Apr. 1663; Samuel, 1 Oct. 1666; Joanna, 17 Aug. 1667; Patience, 21 Apr. 1671; and Hugh, 4 Jan. 1675. Perhaps he rem. to Boston.

CHARLES, JOHN, Charlestown 1636, rem. to New Haven, there had Sarah, b. Oct. 1637, bapt. Oct. 1640; and John, bapt. 20 May 1649; rem. to Branford, was there join. in the compact of sett. 1667, and d. 1673. WILLIAM, Salem 1637, liv. on Marblehead side in 1648, and in 1672 was call. 77 yrs. old. In 1647, Sarah, perhaps his w. perhaps d. unit. with the ch.

CHARLETT, NICHOLAS, Boston 1642, in the employm. of John Mylam, freem. 1645, when the Col. Rec. gives his name Chelett; by w. Catharine had Eliz. b. 15, bapt. 20 July 1645, d. in two mos.; and Mary. In July 1646 he was excom. and prob. d. in few yrs. His wid. m. Richard Haughton of New London, bore him sev. ch. and d. 9 Aug. 1670.

CHASE, AQUILA, Hampton 1640, a mariner from Cornwall, Eng. m. Ann, d. of John Wheeler, had Sarah, and rem. a. 1646, to Newbury, there had Ann, b. 6 July 1647; Priscilla, 14 Mar. 1649; Mary, 3 Feb. 1651; Aquila, 26 Sept. 1652; Thomas, 25 July 1654; John, 2 Nov. 1655; Eliz. 13 Sept. 1657; Ruth, 18 Mar. 1660; Daniel, 9 Dec. 1661; and Moses, 24 Dec. 1663; and d. 29 Aug. 1670, aged 52. His wid. m. 14 June 1672, Daniel Mussiloway, and d. 21 Apr. 1687; Sarah m. 15 May 1666, Charles Annis; Ann m. 27 Apr. 1671, Thomas Barber; Priscilla m. 10 Feb. 1671, Abel Merrill; Mary m. 9 Mar. 1670, John Stevens; Eliz. m. 27 June 1678, at Andover, Zechariah Ayers; and Ruth d. unm. at 17 yrs. AQUILA, Newbury, eldest s. of the preced. m. Esther, d. of John Bond of the same, had Esther, b. 18 Nov. 1674; Joseph, 25 Mar. 1677; Priscilla, 15 Oct. 1681; Jemima; Rebecca; Ann; Hannah; and Abigail. BARTHOLOMEW, Providence 1645. BENJAMIN, Fretown, youngest s. of William the first, had a fam. but details are want. DANIEL, Newbury, s. of the first Aquila, m. 25 Aug. 1683, Martha Kimball, had Martha, b. 18 Aug. 1684; Sarah, 18 July 1686;

Dorothy, 24 Jan. 1689; Isaac, 19 Jan. 1691; Lydia, 19 Jan. 1693; Mehitable, 19 Jan. 1695; Judith, 19 Feb. 1697; Abner, 15 Oct. 1699; Daniel, 15 Oct. 1702; and Enoch; and d. 8 Feb. 1707. ISAAC, Hampton, s. of Thomas of the same, m. Mary Perkins of H. rem. to Edgartown, and had Thomas, b. 9 Nov. 1677; Rachel, 25 Oct. 1679; Isaac, 21 Jan. 1682; Abraham, 10 Jan. 1684; James, 15 Jan. 1686; Joseph, 26 Feb. 1690; Jonathan, 28 Dec. 1691; Hannah, 25 Nov. 1693; Sarah, 15 Oct. 1695; Priscilla, 12 Nov. 1697; and Eliz. 9 Sept. 1703; and he d. 9 May 1727. Descend. of gr. num. are wide. diffus. JOHN, Newbury, s. of the first Aquila, m. 23 May 1677, Eliz. d. prob. of William Bingley, had William, b. 3 Jan. 1679; Philip, 23 Sept. 1688; Charles, 12 Jan. 1690; beside Jacob, Abraham, Phebe, Mary, Lydia, Eliz. and John, of uncert. dates; and by sec. w. Lydia had David, 20 Oct. 1710. JOSEPH, Hampton, br. of Isaac, m. 31 Jan. 1672, Rachel, d. of William Partridge of Salisbury, had Hannah, b. 5 June foll.; Eliz. 11 Mar. 1674, d. next yr.; Jonathan, 14 Mar. 1676; Ann, 11 Jan. 1678; Eliz. again, 14 Feb. 1685; and Rachel, 27 Apr. 1687. He was tak. by the Ind. at Dover, in their assault upon Waldron's ho. 27 June 1689. MOSES, Newbury, youngest s. of the first Aquila, m. 10 Nov. 1684, Ann Follansbee, perhaps d. of the first Thomas, had Moses, and Daniel, tw. b. 20 Sept. foll. of wh. the first d. soon; Moses, again, 20 Jan. 1688; Samuel, 13 May 1690; Eliz. 25 Sept. 1693; Stephen, 29 Aug. 1696; Hannah, 13 Sept. 1699; Joseph, 9 Sept. 1703; and Benoni, 5 Apr. 1708. For sec. w. he m. 1713, Sarah Jacobs of Ipswich. THOMAS, Hampton, perhaps elder br. of the first Aquila, m. Eliz. d. of Thomas Philbrick, had Thomas, b. 1643; Joseph, 1645; Isaac, 1647; James, 1649; and Abraham, 1651; and d. 1652. His wid. m. 26 Oct. 1654, John Garland, and, next, 19 Feb. 1674, Henry Roby, and d. 11 Feb. 1677. Thomas, the eldest s. d. unm. 23 Oct. 1714; and Abraham was k. in Philip's war, 1676, unm. THOMAS, Newbury, sec. s. of the first Aquila, m. 22 Nov. 1677, Rebecca, prob. d. of the first Thomas Follansbee, had Thomas, b. 15 Sept. 1680; Jonathan, 13 Jan. 1683; James, 15 Sept. 1685; Aquila, 15 July 1688; Ruth, 28 Feb. 1691; Mary, 15 Jan. 1695; Josiah, 15 July 1697; Rebecca, 17 Apr. 1700; Nathan, 1702; beside Judith, and Eliz. of unkn. dates. For sec. w. he m. 2 Aug. 1713, Eliz. Mooers. WILLIAM, Roxbury, came in the fleet with Winth. desir. to be freem. 19 Oct. 1630, and was sw. 14 May 1634. He brot. w. Mary, and s. William, had Mary, b. May 1637, wh. d. at 15 yrs. rem. to Scituate, thence to Yarmouth, where he was appoint. constable 1 Mar. 1639, and had Benjamin, b. a. 1640, bapt. 18 Apr. 1652; d. May 1659, and his wid. d. Oct. foll. WILLIAM, Yarmouth, s. of the preced. b. in Eng. had William, John, Eliz. all

b. bef. 1656, and Abraham; and d. 27 Feb. 1685. All the descend. now on Cape Cod, it is thot. are deriv. from sec. s. John. Seventeen of this name had been gr. at Dart. in 1834, as Farmer found, eight at Harv. four at Yale, and four at other N. E. coll.

CHASMORE, or CHASMER, RICHARD, Pawtuxet 1656, has much claim to distinct. only from the arrest by warrant to the marshal-gen. or high sheriff of Mass. in that region usurp. jurisdict. His crime prob. was some crookedness in relig. or concur. with the Gortonists, his neighb. on the opposite side of the riv. but the officer took his prison. to lodge at Providence, on his way to Boston, thus furnish. opportun. for rescue by form of law under civil governm. of Providence. Perhaps this was concerted plan of Gov. Endicott, to affront the adjoin. humble Col. by exercise of this claim, and to render nugatory, at the same time, the effect of his own precept. See perfect statem. of the case in Geneal. Reg. VIII. 293 and 362.

CHATFIELD, FRANCIS, Guilford, one of the first sett. 1639, wh. d. a. 1647, prob. unm. GEORGE, Guilford 1640, br. of the preced. m. Sarah, d. of John Bishop, wh. d. without ch. 20 Sept. 1657; and he next m. 29 Mar. 1659, Isabel, d. of Samuel Nettleton, had John, b. 8 Apr. 1661; George, 18 Aug. 1668; and Mercy, 26 Apr. 1671. He d. on 9 June foll. at Killingworth, whither he had rem. 1663. John, his eldest s. had large fam. at Derby; but I have no details. GEORGE, Killingworth, s. of the preced. m. 10 Feb. 1692, Esther Hall, had Esther, b. 20 Nov. foll. George, 25 Dec. 1693; John, 5 Mar. 1696; Abigail, 9 Aug. 1698; Josiah, 7 Jan. 1700; Alister, 23 Oct. 1703; Cornelius, 3 June 1706; Naomi, 28 July 1709; Philip, 8 Oct. 1711; Mary, 14 Jan. 1716; and his w. d. in few days. He d. a. 1720. THOMAS, Guilford, rem. to New Haven, there m. Ann, d. of Rev. Francis Higginson, rem. to East-hampton, L. I. where he was long a magistr. of Conn. jurisdict. He was br. of Francis and George, and is suppos. to have left no ch.

CHATTERTON, MICHAEL, Portsmouth 1640. Belkn. I. 28. THOMAS, Portsmouth 1631, sent by Mason, the patentee, in Adams's Ann. call. Chatherton. WILLIAM, New Haven 1656, took o. of fidel. 7 Apr. 1657, prob. had w. Mary, and was a propr. 1685.

CHAUNCY, BARNABAS, Cambridge, s. of Presid. C. b. in Eng. short. bef. the migrat. of his f. unit. with ch. 1656, and took his degr. of 1657 and 60, when his name stands last in the class. He was too infirm in body to obt. a livelihood, and depend. after d. of his f. on support of his brs. He d. unm. at mid. age; but the Coll. catal. does not ment. the yr. *CHARLES*, Scituate, a gr. scholar, the ninth ch. fifth s. of George, b. at Yardly, in Co. Herts, a. 30 miles from London, bapt. on Sunday, 5 Nov. 1592, was bred at Westminster sch. and saved on 5 Nov. 1605 by the discov. of Gunpowder plot; at Trinity Coll. Camb. took his degr. A. B.

1613, A. M. 1617 ; B. D. 1624. Much reputa. at the Univ. he gain. by Latin verses of lamenta. on d. 1619, of Queen Ann, and by Greek and Latin on d. of her h. James, and access. of Charles, 1625, as in Cantab. Dolor et Solamen, so that he was chos. profess. for one, if not two chairs. But in cleric. life he was early at Marston St. Lawrence, and had the vicarage of Ware in his native shire, 1627–34, and from that valua. liv. for non-conform. in non-essentials he was forc. by Archbp. Laud. In search of comforta. and secure worship he came to N. E. arr. in Dec. 1637, at Plymouth, there preach. as aid to Reyner, some time, but in 1641 was call. to S. where above twelve yrs. he min. yet with freq. troubles ; and was prepar. to go home for partak. the puritan triumph in Eng. when he was chos. head of the Coll. at Cambridge, on dismiss. in 1654, of Dunster, its first Presid. In this post he d. 19 Feb. 1672, aged 79 yrs. and less prob. than 4 mos. but Mather, mistak. the inscript. on his tomb, under his eye, of 80th for 82d yr. of his age, to make his error consistent, dares to affirm in Magn. III. 134, that he was b. in 1589, instead of 1592, and on p. 140 boldly asserts, that he d. (giv. the right time), " in the eighty-second yr. of his age." Explanat. of his blunder is easi. found. In Roman numerals the day and yr. of his dec. XIX Feb. $\frac{\text{MDCLXXI}}{\text{II}}$ in our Arabic numbers $\frac{1671}{2}$ æt. LXXX. seems plain eno. but the careless author forc. the II out of place, and add. them to the later number. Yet Green's Almanac of 1673 had said, " in his 80th yr." and hardly a min. in the country could have fail. to say, that the first Presid. wh. d. in office, was little over 79 yrs. old. The author (Rev. W. C. Fowler) of the elaborate life of Chauncy, his ancest. and descend. in Geneal. Reg. X. 251, has quot. two paragr. from the Magnalia, suppressing the word " second " after eighty, whereby Mather seems to be compel. to speak the truth. " Fourscore years of age despatched it not," is the sweet commenda. of Mather for his labors ; and contempt for the chronology should not, perhaps, be *so* express. especial. as the earlier author foll. his natural weakness, to show his knowl. of the value of a man, in shekels, above the age of sixty, only 15, but younger, 50 shekels, makes Chauncy's worth " at 80 contin. much what as it was when he was under 60." In his valua. Biogr. Dict. Ed. 1857, Dr. Allen had more scrupulously foll. the error of the Magn. We see, in the Biogr. Britannica, that he descend. from a fam. that came in with the conquest, and he was gr. uncle of Sir Henry C. wh. dignif. the Hist. of Hertfordsh. in two large folios. His w. was Catharine, d. of Robert Eyre, Esq. of Wilts, barrister at law, by his w. Ann, d. of that John Still, Bp. of Bath and Wells, in the latter days of Eliz. a true ch. puritan, wh. desir. more reformat. than her majesty could submit to. She was m. to C. 17 Mar. 1630, and d. 24 Jan. 1668, aged 66, and had Sarah, b. at Ware, 13 Jan. 1631, wh. m. 26 Oct. 1659, Gershom Bulkley ; Isaac, 23 Aug. 1632,

H. C. 1651; Ichabod, 1635, H. C. 1651; Barnabas, H. C. 1657; Nathaniel, and Elnathan, tw. H. C. 1661, as in the same yr. was their
younger br. Israel; and Hannah; the five last b. prob. at S. A celebr.
descend. of the same name, min. of Boston bef. the mid. of the last
centu. had furnish. a Mem. generous in tone, with slight error of detail,
that was preserv. in 1 Mass. Hist. Coll. X. 171. CHARLES, Fairfield,
eldest s. of Israel, the Stratford min. and gr.s. of the Presid. m. 29 June
1692, Sarah, d. of John Burr, and sec. w. m. 16 Mar. 1699, Sarah, d. of
the third Henry Wolcott, wh. d. 5 Jan. 1704. He d. 4 May 1714, and
thro. his sec. w. was gr. gr.f. of Isaac, the celebr. naval officer. CHARLES,
Boston, youngest s. of Isaac, the London min. and gr.s. of the Presid.
b. in Eng. m. Sarah, d. of Hon. John Walley, had Charles, wh. d. inf.;
Charles, again, b. 1 Jan. 1705, H. C. 1721, one of the ablest divines
Boston ever saw; Mary; Walley; and Isaac. He was a merch. and d.
4 May 1711. ELNATHAN, Boston, s. of the Presid. a physician, by w.
Thomasine had Theodore, b. 1 Oct. 1682; and the f. d. beyond sea next
yr. as admin. was gr. to his wid. 29 Apr. 1684. Her d. is ment. in
Sewall's Diary 2 July 1686; and perhaps her s. d. young. ICHABOD,
sec. s. of the Presid. b. in Eng. after gr. at Harv. and study of the sis.
sciences of medicine and theol. went home, was chaplain in the regim. of
Sir Edward Harley at Dunkirk, and had cleric. function in Eng. but
being persecut. for nonconform. bec. a physician, was in Holland 1684,
but soon back to Eng. d. 25 July 1691, at Bristol, where he had good
reput. and prop. He had one s. Charles, b. 14 Mar. 1674, wh. d. in
London, 3 June 1763; and ano. Nathaniel, wh. was min. of the ch. of
Eng. near 50 yrs. at the Devizes in Wilts. ISAAC, eldest br. of the
preced. b. in Eng. went home, and was min. at Woodborough, in Wilts
until eject. in 1662, when he sett. in London as a physician, and after
some yrs. bec. min. to an independ. congrega. in London, where he was
succeed. by the admira. Dr. Watts (who for short time was his collea.)
and d. 28 Feb. 1712. His ch. were Isaac; Uzziel, wh. d. 31 Aug.
1696; Charles, bef. ment.; and Eliz. wh. m. 10 Dec. 1689, Rev. John
Nisbet of London, and d. 1727. ISRAEL, Stratford, youngest br. of the
preced. ord. in aut. of 1666, m. Mary, d. of Isaac Nichols of S. had
Charles, b. 3 Sept. 1668, H. C. 1686, bef. ment.; Isaac, 5 Oct. 1670,
H. C. 1693, the min. of Hadley, 1696 to d. 2 May 1745; and Robert,
15 Oct. 1677, wh. in youth went to Eng. For sec. w. he had m. 11
Nov. 1684, Sarah Hodshon, but had no more ch. Anxiety from many
of his flock wh. prefer. the preach. of Rev. Zechariah Walker, was
dissipat. after long disagreem. by separa. and plant. of a new town.
NATHANIEL, Hatfield, tw. br. of Elnathan, was of Windsor 1667, when
very diverse affections disturb. the declin. yrs. of the first min. Wareham
by means of ris. admira. of Rev. John Woodbridge; of wh. eno. is to be

seen in the Col. Rec. of Trumbull, II. 85, 113. In happier lot, he m. 12 Nov. 1673, Abigail, d. of Elder John Strong, had Isaac, b. 6 Sept. 1674; Catharine, 12 Jan. 1676; Abigail, 14 Oct. 1677; Charles, 3 Sept. 1679, d. in few wks.; rem. 1681, to H. there had Nathaniel, 21 Sept. 1681, Y. C. 1702, first min. at Durham; Ann; and Sarah, 1683; and he d. 4 Nov. 1685. His wid. m. 8 Sept. foll. Medad Pomeroy. In modern times some insert *e* bef. the last let. Of this name, in 1834, gr. at Harv. are twelve, of wh. seven were clerg. and at Yale, eight, of wh. one only was clerg. and all are descend. of the illustr. Presid.

CHEATER, JOHN, Newbury, had Hannah, b. 7 Aug. 1644; Lydia, 12 Jan. 1648; and in 1654, his w. Alice suffer. admonit. of the Ct. for levity of carriage. He rem. to Wells, kept an inn, 1662, and had gr. of the ferry on the way to Cape Porpoise. See Coffin, and Folsom, 108, and especial. Col. Rec.

CHECKETT, JOSEPH, Scituate 1638, prob. rem. with Lothrop to Barnstable.

CHECKLEY, ‖ ANTHONY, Boston, merch. s. of William of a small parish, call. Preston capes, a. 7 ms. from Daventry, in the W. of Northamptonsh. bapt. 31 July 1636, was capt. of ar. co. m. Hannah, d. of Rev. John Wheelwright, had John, b. 30 Dec. 1664; Sarah, 18 June 1668; Eliz. 8 May 1672; Mary, 14 Oct. 1673; and Hannah, 19 Dec. 1674; m. sec. w. 1678, Lydia, wid. of Benjamin Gibbs, d. of Joshua Scottow, by wh. he had no ch. was chos. 1689, atty.-gen. but happi. supersed. bef. the witchcraft infatua. and d. 18 Oct. 1708. His wid. m. 6 Mar. 1712, William Colman; and his d. Hannah m. capt. John Adams. JOHN, Boston 1645, brot. his neph. Anthony bef. ment. m. 5 Mar. 1652, Ann, d. of Simon Eyre, had John, b. 21 Apr. 1653; Ann, 22 Apr. 1659, wh. d. at 2 yrs.; Samuel, 26 Nov. 1661; and Ann, again, 4 Aug. 1669; and he d. 1 Jan. 1685, aged 75. By the inv. render. to Ct. from his w. the est. was only £21, 11, 6. JOHN, Boston 1670, cooper, was from St. Saviour, Southwark, and kept a shop at the Crown and Blue Gate opposite the W. end of the town ho. had John, b. 1680. *JOHN*, Boston, perhaps s. of the preced. m. 28 May 1703, Rebecca Miller, was a min. of gr. capacity for controv. fined for sedition in publish. Leslie's " Short and Easy Method with the Deists," with addit. of a disc. on Episcopacy. Eno. on this portion of Mass. ann. may be seen in Updike's Hist. of Narraganset ch. and perhaps even in the briefer acco. of the candid Biogr. Dict. of Eliot. SAMUEL, Boston, youngest br. of Anthony, bef. ment. and by ano. mo. arr. at B. 3 Aug. 1670, and in the Newsletter of 4 Jan. 1739, obitu. notice, is said to have been b. in Northamptonsh. 14 Oct. 1653. He m. 1680, Mary, d. of Joshua Scottow, had Mary, b. 12 Apr. 1683; Rebecca, 2 Sept. 1684; Samuel, 23 Sept. 1685, d. soon; William, 18 Apr. 1687; Joshua, 8 Feb. 1689; Lydia, 31 Mar. 1690;

Eliz. 3 Sept. 1693, d. within 2 yrs.; Richard, 4 Oct. 1694; Samuel, again, 11 Feb. 1696, H. C. 1715; and Mary, 26 June 1697; and only two of these ten outliv. him, viz. Richard, an apothecary, wh. was deac. and Samuel. SAMUEL, Boston, s. prob. of the first John, by w. Eliz. had Ann, b. 30 May 1687; Rebecca, 4 Feb. 1689; and John, 2 Dec. 1690. *SAMUEL*, Boston, s. of the first Samuel, was ord. the first min. of the New South ch. 15 Apr. 1719, m. 5 Jan. 1721, Eliz. d. of Rev. Benjamin Rolfe of Haverhill, and d. 1 Dec. 1769. He had sev. ch. of wh. one was Samuel, b. 27 Dec. 1723, H. C. 1743, the min. of Old North, successor to three Rev. Doctors nam. Mather.

CHEDSEY, or CHIDSEY, CALEB, New Haven, s. of John, m. 10 May 1688, Ann Thompson, wh. d. 15 Jan. 1692, prob. without ch. and he m. 6 July 1693, Hannah Dickerman, d. prob. of Abraham, had Daniel, b. 25 Mar. 1695; Caleb, 9 May 1697; Abraham, 31 Mar. 1699; and Mary, 30 Oct. 1701; was a deac. and his sec. w. d. 25 Dec. 1703. EBENEZER, New Haven, youngest br. of the preced. m. Priscilla, d. of John Thompson, the farmer, had Sarah, b. 8 Dec. 1689; John, 6 Nov. 1691, d. at 2 yrs.; Eliz. 6 Feb. 1693; John, again, 4 Mar. 1695; Samuel, 6 June 1699; Ebenezer, 6 Dec. 1701; James, 23 Aug. 1704, d. young; Abigail, 1 Apr. 1707; and Isaac, 3 June 1710. JOHN, New Haven 1644, by w. Eliz. had Mary, b. 22 Sept. d. soon; John, 21 Oct. bapt. 10 Nov. 1651; a d. 1653, d. soon; Joseph, b. 5 Dec. 1655; Daniel, 30 July 1657, d. young; Mary, again, 21 Nov. 1659; Caleb, 20, bapt. 24 Nov. 1661; Hannah, 7 Jan. bapt. 28 Feb. 1664; Ebenezer, 10 Feb. bapt. 25 Mar. 1666; Eliz. b. 16 Dec. 1668, d. under 20 yrs. and Sarah (not, as Dodd says, 1670, but many yrs. bef. perhaps 1653, or 4), wh. m. 26 Oct. 1683, Samuel Alling, as his sec. w. Mary m. William Wilmot, and Hannah m. Caleb Mix. He was deac. and d. 31 Dec. 1688, aged 67, his w. hav. d. the same yr. JOHN, New Haven, s. of the preced. d. 1693, unm. JOSEPH, New Haven, s. of John, by w. Sarah had Hannah, b. 28 Jan. 1696; Joseph, 15 Aug. 1698, d. young; Sarah, 13 May 1700; Abigail, 28 Apr. 1702; Rachel, 17 Mar. 1704; Dinah, 14 May 1707; Abel, 7 Mar. 1709; and Joseph, 8 Aug. 1710; and the f. rem. to Guilford.

CHEEVER, BARTHOLOMEW, Boston, cordwainer, came, a. 1637, from Canterbury, Co. Kent, where the name was common. See 3 Mass. Hist. Coll. VIII. 310. He unit. with the ch. 31 May 1646, and was adm. freem. 1647, made constable 1653, and d. 18 Dec. 1693, aged 85, leav. wid. Lydia, sis. of Thomas and William Barrett, but no ch. His est. by will of 21 Oct. bef. was div. to br. David; to six ch. then liv. Lydia, James, Mary, Israel, Eliz. and Sarah; cousin Ezekiel, the pedagogue; cous. Richard, cordwainer, one part in fee, and one to his s. Bartholomew in fee after reach. 21 yrs. Dr. Farmer was misled by tradit. errors in extr. from the fam. bible of W. D. Cheever, as print. in note to a memoir of Mrs. Eleanor Davis, giv. by the Boston Magaz. 4 Apr. 1826, p. 619. Such happy depositories of fam. details often furnish distort. or imperf. materials. DANIEL, Cambridge, br. of the preced. by w. Esther had Mary, b. 14 Feb. 1646; Lydia, 26 Nov. 1647; James; Esther, d. 21 Mar. 1656; Daniel, 1 Jan. 1654, d. soon; Daniel, again, 12 Dec. 1654, d. young; Mary, 6 Oct. 1656; John, bapt. 31 July 1659; Israel, bapt. 26 Jan. 1662; Hannah, and Eliz. tw. d. soon; Eliz. again, bapt. 6 Aug. 1665; all so describ. in the reg. of matchless Mitchell; and Sarah, b. prob. after his pen stop. Eliz. m. Stephen Palmer. * EZEKIEL, New Haven, the famous sch.master, b. in London, 25 Jan. 1616, arr. at Boston 1637, went next yr. with Gov. Eaton to his new planta. there his w. d. wh. he m. 1638, by whom he had Samuel, b. 22 Sept. bapt. 15 Nov. 1639, H. C. 1659 ; Mary, bapt. 29 Nov. 1640; Ezekiel, 12 June 1642, prob. d. young; Eliz. 6 Apr. 1645; Sarah, 20 not (as pr. in Geneal. Reg. IX. 358), 21 Sept. 1646; and Hannah, 25 June 1648; was rep. 1646, rem. 1650 to Ipswich, where his teach. was high. esteem. but in 1660 to Charlestown, and mov. in cycles of 10 yrs. he came last to Boston, where he pass. the residue of his life to 21 Aug. 1708.   For sec. w. he took at I. 18 Nov. 1652, Ellen, d. prob. of Daniel, and sis. of Joshua Rea, as also sis. of the w. of famous capt. Thomas Lothrop, wh. bore him Abigail, 20 Oct. 1653 ; Ezekiel, again, 1 July 1655; Nathaniel, 23 June 1657, d. next mo.; Thomas, 23 Aug. 1658, H. C. 1677; Susanna; and William, bapt. 29 Jan. 1665. His w. d. 10 Sept. 1706, and she had been nam. extrix. in his will of 16 Feb. preced. that he did not alter, tho. he liv. to 21 Aug. 1708. In it he ment. only six ch. (the rest of the twelve, prob. hav. d.) and gr.ch. Ezekiel Russell. Mary had m. 22 Dec. 1671, capt. William Lewis of Farmington, as his sec. w. EZEKIEL, Salem, a tailor, prob. s. of the preced. freem. 1681, liv. in the vill. wh. bec. Danvers. PETER, Salem 1668. RICHARD, Boston, a soldier on serv. at Hadley, 1676, of Turner's comp. a constable in 1693, no doubt, was the man by Bartholomew, in his will, call. cousin, i. e. neph. but wh. of the brothers of B. was his f. is not seen. SAMUEL, eldest ch. of Ezekiel the first, freem. 1669, was the first min. of Marblehead, tho. not the earliest preach. there by thirty-six yrs. m. 28 June 1671, Ruth, d. of Edmund Angier of Cambridge, had prob. other ch. beside Ames, H. C. 1707, min. of Manchester; tho. he preach. from 1677, at Marblehead, he was not ord. bef. 13 Aug. 1684, and d. 29 May 1724. THOMAS, Boston, s. of Ezekiel the first by his sec. w. freem. 1680, was min. at Malden, ord. 27 July 1681, but in Mar. 1686, his ch. " charg. with scandal. immoral." as we learn from Ch. J. Sewall's Diary in Geneal. Reg. VI. 72, caus. his dism. I suppose. He m. 11 Feb. 1702, Mary Bordman of B. wh. liv. not long, and a sec. w. m. 30 July 1707, was Eliz. Warren. Again he was sett. as min. 19 Oct. 1715, at Chelsea, and d. 27 Dec. 1749, old eno. without the exagger. of some parishion. mak. him 93. Of this name, in 1834, gr. at Harv. had been eleven, and three at Bowd.

CHELLIS. See Chalice.

CHELSON, ROBERT, Ipswich 1644. Felt. WILLIAM, Scarborough, d. 1676, leav. one ch. and a wid. wh. gave in, 1 July of that yr. his inv.

CHENERIE. See Genery.

CHENEY, DANIEL, Newbury, s. of John, m. 8 Oct. 1665, Sarah Bayley, prob. d. of John, had Sarah, b. 11 Sept. 1666; Judith, 1668; Daniel, 31 Dec. 1670; Hannah, 3 Sept. 1673; Joseph, 10 July 1676; Elinor, 29 Mar. 1679; and James, 6 Apr. 1685; and d. 10 Sept. 1694. JOHN, Newbury, shoemaker, freem. 17 May 1637, had been the yr. bef. at Roxbury, perhaps br. of William, brot. in 1635 to R. w. Martha, and ch. Mary, Martha, John, and prob. Daniel, b. 1635; had Sarah, Feb. 1637; Peter, 1639; Hannah, 16 Nov. 1642; Nathaniel, 12 Jan. 1645; and Eliz. 14 Jan. 1648; went again to R. there was drown. Dec. 1671. His d. Martha m. a. 1649, Anthony Sadler, and, next, 1652, Nicholas Busby the sec. JOHN, Watertown, an early sett. d. 5 Sept. 1675. Margaret, perhaps his d. m. Apr. 1651, deac. Thomas Hastings, as his sec. w. and John, wh. d. 6 Aug. and Ebenezer, wh. d. 17 Nov. 1689, both at Cambridge, may have been his ch. JOHN, Newbury, eldest s. of the first John, m. 20 May 1660, Mary, d. of Francis Plummer, had Mary, b. 29 Mar. 1661; Martha, 11 Sept. 1663; and John, 29 Jan. 1669; and d. 7 Jan. 1673. Mary m. 24 July 1684, Isaac Kilborne of Rowley, wh. was deaf and dumb. JOHN, New London 1679, had w. Sarah, but prob. soon rem. JOSEPH, Medfield 1678, was, perhaps, s. of William the first of Roxbury. NATHANIEL, Newbury, s. of the first John, took o. of alleg. 25 May 1669. PETER, Newbury, br. of the preced. m. 14 May 1663, Hannah, d. of Nicholas Noyes, had Peter, b. 6 Nov. foll.; John, 10 May 1666; Nicholas, 23 May 1667; perhaps Huldah; Mary, 2 Sept. 1671; perhaps Martha; Nathaniel, 2 Oct. 1675, d. within two yrs.; Jemima, 29 Nov. 1677; Eldad, 24 Oct. 1681; Hannah, 13 Sept. 1683; and Ichabod, 22 Sept. 1685. Huldah m. 20 Jan. 1691, Timothy Worcester; Mary, and Martha m. 29 of same mo. William, and Francis Worcester, respectiv. so that it might seem, that three brs. m. three sis. near the same time, but for the relationsh. I mean not to be responsib.; Jemima m. first, a French, and, next, 1703, Matthew Pettingell. THOMAS, Roxbury, m. 11 Jan. 1656, Jane Atkinson, was of Cambridge, where he had Margaret, b. 26 Nov. foll. and, perhaps Thomas; and William; freem. 1666, at R. had Jane, 5 June 1669; Joseph, 16 Feb. 1671; Hannah, 6 July 1673; Benjamin, 29 Jan. 1676; and Ebenezer, 2 Nov. 1678. Jane m. Thomas Belknap of Woburn. THOMAS, Roxbury, s. prob. of the preced. was press. in Dec. 1675, for Johnson's comp. freem. 1690, m. 24 Sept. 1684, Hannah Woods, had Margaret, b. 8 Apr. 1686; Thomas, and Henry, tw. 16 Sept. 1687, both d. within 10 days; Hannah, 14 Mar. 1689; Melicent, 15 June 1693; Ebenezer, 5 Dec. 1699; and Samuel, 9 Mar. 1701. WILLIAM, Roxbury, had John, b. 29 Sept. 1639, d. soon; John, again, 25 Sept. 1640; Mehitable, 1 June 1643; Joseph, 6 June 1647; and prob. more; was freem. 1666, d. next yr. on 30 June, aged 63. His wid. Margaret m. . . . . . . Burge, and d. July 1686. * WILLIAM, Middletown, freem. of Conn. 1657, rep. 1660, 1, 3, and oft. after, d. 1705, leav. d. Abigail, but no s. WILLIAM, Roxbury, perhaps s. of the first Thomas, or the first William, m. 24 May 1686, Rebecca, d. of Jacob Newell, had Thomas, b. 29 Jan. 1688; Rebecca, 3 Aug. 1690; William, 1 Dec. 1692; and a d. Abiel, 21 May 1696, wh. was posthum. for the f. d. 25 Mar. bef.

CHEREY, DAVID, Wickford 1674.

CHERRALL, WILLIAM, a baker from London, aged 26, was emb. in the Love 1635, with Ursula, 40, if the custom ho. rec. be correct; but where he sat down, or whether she were his mo. aunt, sister, maid, or wid. is like. to be left in the dark.

CHESEBROUGH, CHEESBROUGH, CHESSBRUCK, or CHEESBROOK, * ELISHA, Stonington, s. of William, m. 20 Apr. 1665, Rebecca, d. of Walter Palmer, had only Elihu, b. 3 Dec. 1668, was rep. 1669, and d. 1671. His wid. m. 24 July 1672, John Baldwin of New London. ELISHA, Stonington, s. of the first Samuel of the same, m. Mary, d. of Joseph Minor of the same; but no more is kn. NATHANIEL, Stonington, s. of William, b. in Eng. m. Hannah, eldest d. of the active capt. George Denison, had Ann, b. 12 Oct. 1660; Sarah, 30 Jan. 1662; Nathaniel, 4 Apr. 1666; Bridget, 25 Mar. 1669; Hannah; Samuel, 15 Feb. 1674; Margaret, bapt. 15 Apr. 1677; and Mary, 30 June 1678. He d. 22 Nov. 1678, and his wid. m. 15 July 1680, Joseph Saxton. Bridget m. William Thompson; Hannah m. Joseph Prentice; and Margaret m. 18 Jan. 1696, Joseph Stanton. NATHANIEL, Stonington, s. of the preced. m. Sarah Stanton, perhaps d. of the sec. Thomas of the same. * SAMUEL, Rehoboth, s. of William, b. in Eng. rem. to Stonington with his f. by w. Abigail had Abigail, b. 30 Sept. 1656; Mary, 28 Feb. 1658, d. at 11 yrs.; Samuel, 20 Feb. or Nov. 1660; William, 8 or 30 Apr. 1662; Sarah, 24 Nov. or Dec. 1663; Elisha, 4 Apr. or Aug. 1667; and Eliz. 6 Jan. 1669, all (exc. Mary),

bapt. at New London, of wh. S. was then pt. in 1672; was made freem.
1657, rep. 1665, 6, 70, and later yrs. He d. 31 Jan. 1673, and his wid.
m. 15 June 1675, Joshua Holmes. His d. Abigail m. John Avery; and
Sarah m. 4 Jan. 1689, William Gallup, both of S. SAMUEL, Stonington, eldest s. of the preced. m. Mary, whose surname is not seen, nor the
date of m. had Samuel, b. 16 Sept. 1691; Jeremiah, 7 Aug. 1692, prob.
d. soon; William, 27 Aug. 1693; Jeremiah, again, 25 Aug. 1697; Jonathan, 13 Feb. 1700; Joseph, 12 Apr. 1703; Ann, 9 Oct. 1706; and Mary,
10 Sept. 1710. SAMUEL, Stonington, youngest s. of the first Nathaniel of
the same, m. 4 Jan. 1699, Priscilla Alden, call. gr.d. of Mayflower John,
but wh. was her f. I see not, had Mary, b. 21 Sept. 1702; Priscilla, 6
Nov. 1704; Nathaniel, 19 Aug. 1706, d. young; Amos, 2 Feb. 1709;
Hannah, 16 July 1712; Sarah, 14 Aug. 1714; and Prudence, 28 Feb.
1722. Six of his ch. liv. to be m. * WILLIAM, Boston, came from
Boston, Co. Lincoln (in or near wh. prob. he was b. a. 1594), with w.
Ann, 1630, arr. in the fleet with Winth. He had m. 15 Dec. 1620, Ann
Stevenson, and they had, in Eng. Mary, bapt. 2 May 1622; Martha, 18
Sept. 1623; David, and Jonathan, tw. 9 Sept. 1624; all d. soon; Sam-
uel, 1 Apr. 1627; Andronicus, 6 Feb. 1629 (wh. d. in two days, as did
Junia, a tw. ch. the day bef.) and Nathaniel, 25 Jan. 1630. On this
side of the water they were among earliest mem. of the first ch. of B.
Nos. 44 and 5, on the list, he was adm. freem. 18 May 1631, and the
same day his ho. was burn. Ch. in Boston bapt. were John, 2 Sept. or
11 Nov. 1632, as the numerals for mo. and day are various. read, wh. d.
at Stonington, prob. unm.; Jabez, 3 May 1635, d. young; Elisha, 4
June 1637; and at Braintree b. Joseph, 18 July 1640; and this yr. he
was rep. Soon after he rem. to Rehoboth, where he was active 1643,
and in less than seven yrs. to Pawcatuck, where he was the earliest
perman. sett. in that pt. of New London call. Stonington. This brot. the
Conn. governm. to vindicate their territor. right, and very curious matter
may be read a. the jurisdict. in Trumbull, Coll. Rec. I. 216–17; to the
result, however, the judicious mildness of C. led soon, and he was a rep.
1653, 5, 7, and 64, for New London or Stonington. He d. 9 June 1667,
leav. wid. Ann, wh. d. 29 Aug. 1673. His s. Joseph, under 12 yrs. old,
cut his leg with a scythe, and bled to d. A mo. or sis. I think, may be
found for him in the Boston list of mem. of the ch. Sarah C. No. 78,
and upon the marg. is mark. early d. WILLIAM, Stonington, s. of Samuel of the same, m. 13 Dec. 1698, for sec. w. Mary, d. of Fergus
McDowell, had William, David, Thomas, Abigail, and Mary.

CHESHOLME, CHISHOLM, or CHESEHOLM, ‖ THOMAS, Cambridge
1635, freem. 3 Mar. 1636, ar. co. 1638, had w. Isabel, but prob. no ch.
for none is ment. in that reg. of matchless Mitchell, wh. careful. tells,

how Benoni, s. of the runagate scholar, Nathaniel Eaton, was under his care. He was deac. and d. 18 Aug. 1671, by nuncup. will made that day, gave B. Eaton a field, and left small est. to his friends, Mitchell, and Oakes's childr.

CHESLEY, PHILIP, Dover 1642, by w. Eliz. had Thomas, b. a. 1644; Philip, 1646; Esther; Mary; and Eliz. After 1661 he had sec. w. Sarah, and prob. third, Joanna, in 1673; and was liv. 1685. Esther m. John Hall; and Mary m. Ralph Hall. PHILIP, Dover, s. of the preced. was constable 1695. His will of 18 Dec. in that yr. names w. Sarah, s. Samuel, James, Philip, and Ebenezer. He had also Hannah. A former w. was Eliz. wid. of Philip Cromwell, d. of Thomas Leighton. His eldest s. capt. Samuel, of Durham, had serv. much, as a good soldier, bef. he was k. by the Ind. 17 Sept. 1707. Belkn. I. 168, 74, 6. THOMAS, Dover, s. of Philip the first, m. 22 Aug. 1663, Eliz. Thomas, had Thomas, b. 4 June 1664; John; George; Joseph; Eliz.; Sarah; Susanna; and Mary; and was k. by the Ind. 15 Nov. 1667. Belkn. I. 72.

CHESTER, *JOHN, Wethersfield, s. of Leonard, m. Feb. 1654, Sarah, d. of Gov. Thomas Welles, had Mary, b. 23 Dec. 1654; John, 10 June 1656; Sarah, 11 Nov. 1657; Stephen, 26 May 1659; Thomas, 23 Mar. 1662; Samuel, 23 May 1664; Prudence, 10 Dec. 1666; and Eunice, 17 May 1668; freem. 1658, rep. 1676, and oft. after, was a capt. and d. 23 Feb. 1698; and his wid. d. 16 Dec. foll. LEONARD, Watertown 1633, s. of John of Blaby, Co. Leicester, by Dorothy, sis. of famous Thomas Hooker, had prob. brot. w. Mary, of whose parentage some diversity of opinion aris. Bond, 736, calls her Nevill, but Chester's will that had not been seen by him, speaks of his f. Wade, and yet Goodwin, in his geneal. of the fam. p. 8, quotes an authority that calls her wid. Wade, d. of Nicholas Sharpe, and, in my guess, it may be that she was wid. of Sharpe, and d. of Wade. He had John, b. 3 Aug. 1635 at Watertown, but had left his w. there, while he went to look out for the desira. region, to wh. next yr. his uncle Hooker and Gov. Haynes rem. Wild tradit. makes this s. the first white ch. b. in the town of Wethersfield, where, we may be sure, no Eng. ch. was b. for many mos. later. Other ch. were Dorcas, b. at the new settlem. 1 Nov. 1637, wh. m. 12 Nov. 1656, the sec. Rev. Samuel Whiting; Stephen, 3 Mar. 1639, wh. d. unm. 23 Apr. 1705; Mary, 15 Jan. 1641, d. unm. at 28 yrs.; Prudence, 16 Feb. 1643, m. 30 Dec. 1669, Thomas Russell of Charlestown; Eunice, 15 June 1645, m. 25 Feb. 1673, the sec. Richard Sprague, and d. 27 May 1676; and Mercy, 14 Feb. 1647, d. unm. at 22 yrs. The f. d. 11 Dec. 1648, aged 38 or 9; and his wid. m. not bef. 1655, Hon. Richard Russell of Charlestown, and d. 30 Dec. 1688, near. 80 yrs. old. SAMUEL, New London, 1663, mariner, was also a compet. surveyor, had

first w. Mary, and ch. John ; Susanna ; Samuel ; all bapt. prob. in Oct.
1670 ; and Mercy, 1 June 1673 ; and by w. Hannah, who surv. him,
had Hannah, bapt. Mar. 1695 ; and Jonathan, Mar. 1697. In his will
the first s. nam. is Abraham ; Susanna, Samuel, and Hannah, are not
found ; and Mercy is call. Burrows, perhaps w. of John. SAMUEL,
Boston 1676, a merch. Of this name, in 1831, ten had been gr. at
Yale, and one at Harv.

CHEVALIER, JOHN, New Hampsh. was of the gr. jury 1684.

CHICHESTER, JAMES, Taunton 1643, Salem 1650, when Mary, prob.
his w. unit. with the ch. and on 21 Apr. her ch. John, James, Mary, and
Martha, were bapt. as also Sarah in May 1651 ; James, 9 May 1652 ;
William, 15 May 1653 ; Eliz. 26 Mar. 1654 ; and Susanna, 10 May
1657 ; but perhaps one, two, or more of these were ch. of William ; and
James may have rem. to Huntington, L. I. and was adm. freem. of
Conn. 1664, unless this were s. of the same name, wh. m. a d. of Jonathan Porter of H. wh. is not prob. tho. he may have been 10 yrs. old
when bapt. WILLIAM, Marblehead 1648, perhaps br. of the preced.

CHICK, RICHARD, Roxbury, by w. whose name is not seen, had Richard, b. 26 June 1678 ; and d. 13 Oct. 1686, aged 48, and his wid. d. 19
Mar. 1699. THOMAS, Dover 1671.

CHICKERING, * ‖ FRANCIS, Dedham, freem. 13 May 1640, ar. co.
1643, was ens. rep. 1644 and 53. He came, prob. in 1637, from the N.
part of Co. Suff k. bring. w. Ann, d. of John Fiske of Eng. and sis. of
our John, the first min. of Wenham, with her ch. Ann, and Mary ; here
they had Eliz. b. 26 Sept. 1638, wh. d. young ; Bethia, 23 Dec. 1640 ;
Esther, 4 Nov. 1643 ; John, 19 Apr. 1646, d. perhaps bef. his f. ; and
Mercy, perhaps 10 Apr. 1648 ; m. sec. w. 10 June 1650, Sarah Sibley, wid.
of John, and d. Oct. 1658. His wid. prob. bec. third w. of John Bowles
of Roxbury, and his good est. went chief. to five ds. of wh. Mary m. 22
Mar. 1647, John Metcalf ; Ann m. 3 Nov. 1652, Stephen Paine ;
Bethia m. 6 Dec. 1659, Samuel Newman ; and Esther m. 20 Oct. 1659,
Daniel Smith ; the two last of Rehoboth. * HENRY, Dedham, perhaps
br. of the preced. b. in Eng. had gr. of ld. at Salem, 1640, but prob.
never accept. freem. 2 June 1641, was one of the first deac. at D. and
rep. 1642-4, 7 and 51, had w. Ann, only s. John, perhaps only ch. no
other being ment. in his will, made 23 May 1671, pro. 31 Aug. foll.
Inv. includ. ld. and ho. val. £200, at Henstead, near Wrentham, in the
N. E. part of Suff k. His wid. d. 18 Feb. 1675. JOHN, Dedham, s. of
the preced. was a physician, freem. 1670, by w. Eliz. d. of Samuel
Hagborne of Roxbury, and rem. to Charlestown, had Catharine, b. 16
Feb. 1662, bapt. 15 Feb. 1663 ; Ann, bapt. 7 Feb. 1664 ; Catharine,
again, 21 May 1665 ; Mary, or Mercy, 8 Apr. 1666 ; Eliz. 7 Apr.
1667 ; wh. all d. young ; Mercy, b. 13, bapt. 22 Mar. 1668 ; Eliz. again,

and Catharine third, tw. bapt. 18 Apr. 1669, of wh. Eliz. soon d.; John, 14 Aug. 1670; Ann, again, 3 Dec. 1671; Eliz. third, 30 Mar. 1673, d. soon; and Eliz. fourth, 25 Oct. 1674, d. young; and he d. 28 July 1676, leav. good est. to his wid. Eliz. wh. m. 16 May foll. Thomas Greaves, had one more d. and d. 22 July 1679, aged 44. The third Catharine m. 12 Dec. 1695, Jonathan Ward; the sec. Ann m. Samuel Brackenbury; and Mercy m. 22 Nov. 1699, Jacob Shepard. Of his twelve ch. the only s. liv. at C. and by w. Susanna had sev. ch. of wh. I am not able to furnish details. NATHANIEL, Dedham, call. neph. by the preced. yet wh. was his f. is not kn. m. 30 Dec. 1666, Mary, d. of Samuel Judson, but no issue is ment. On 3 Dec. 1674 he m. Lydia, d. of Daniel Fisher, had Prudence, b. 9 Sept. foll.; Nathaniel, 28 Mar. 1677; Lydia, 1 Dec. 1678; Mary, 15 Dec. 1680; John, 22 Nov. 1682; Abigail, 29 Mar. 1685; Daniel, 1 July 1687; and Samuel, 14 Feb. 1689. He was freem. 1681, and d. early in 1699, when Nathaniel, and his mo. wh. liv. to 17 July 1737, aged 85, had admin. NATHANIEL, Dedham, s. of the preced. m. 14 Aug. 1700, Mary Thorpe, had Nathaniel, b. 15 Apr. foll. and Jeremiah, 20 May 1705. He had sec. w. 26 June 1716, Deborah Wright.

CHILD, or CHILDS, ALWIN, Boston 1673, merch. BENJAMIN, Roxbury, prob. neph. of Ephraim here, s. of Benjamin in Eng. may rather be call. of Boston, as he liv. in Muddy riv. planta. now Brookline, but worship. at R. 1648, by w. Mary, adm. into the ch. of R. 23 Jan. 1659, had Ephraim, wh. was k. by the Ind. at Northfield, 4 Sept. 1675, with capt. Beers; Benjamin; and Joshua; all bapt. 27 Feb. 1659; Mary, 28 Oct. 1660; a ch. d. unbapt. Dec. 1662; Eliz. 21 Feb. 1664; Margaret, 28 Jan. 1666; John, 8 Mar. 1668, d. soon; Mehitable, 29 Aug. 1669; John, again, 1 Oct. 1671; and Joseph, 31 Aug. 1673, d. soon. BENJAMIN, Roxbury, s. of the preced. m. 7 Mar. 1683, Grace, d. of Edward Morris, had Ephraim, b. 18 Dec. foll.; Benjamin, 19 July 1685; Edward, 1 Nov. 1687; Grace, 27 Oct. 1689; Mary, 25 Oct. 1691; Ebenezer, 7 Sept. 1693; Martha, 5 Oct. 1695; William, 14 Oct. 1697; Penuel, 3 Sept. 1699; Richard, 22 Oct. 1701; Thomas, 10 Nov. 1703; and Margaret, 26 May 1706. His w. d. 10 Dec. 1723; and he d. 26 Jan. foll. * EPHRAIM, Watertown, freem. 18 May 1631, may well be thot. to have come in the fleet with Winth. for he had m. at Nayland, Co. Suffk. 8 Feb. 1625, wid. Eliz. Palmer, and req. adm. 19 Oct. 1630, had good est. no ch. was deac. rep. 1635, 46, 9, 50, and often after, d. 13 Feb. 1663, aged 70. His will of 10 Nov. preced. provid. for wid. Eliz. for Richard and John Child, prob. nephs. and Ephraim, ano. neph. s. of his br. Benjamin; beside William Bond, sen. made excor. joint. with his wid. and gave a liberal sum annu. for support of a town sch. forever.

She is conject. by Dr. Bond, pp. 46, 7, and 152, to have been d. of
Jonas Bond of Bury St. Edmunds, gr.f. of our William of Watertown,
for she in her will, 11 June 1667, pro. 1 Oct. foll. made him sole excor.
call. him loving cous. i. e. neph. beside nam. his w. and five of his seven
liv. ch. and Richard, and Benjamin Child, kinsm. of her h. HENRY,
Berwick, k. by the Ind. 28 Sept. 1691. JEREMIAH, Swanzey 1669, by
w. Martha had Jeremiah, b. 2 Sept. 1683. JOHN, Watertown, by Bond
thot. to have been a neph. of Ephraim, by first w. Mary had Mary, b. 8
Jan. 1664; and by sec. w. m. 29 May 1668, Mary Warren, eldest d. of
Daniel, had John, 25 Apr. 1669; Eliz. 24 July 1670; and Daniel,
whose b. is not seen, but his bapt. 5 June 1687, was sev. yrs. after the d.
of his f. and sec. m. of his mo. He d. 15 Oct. 1676, aged 40; and his
wid. m. 13 Apr. foll. Nathaniel Fiske. JOSEPH, Watertown, whose
parentage is unkn. m. 3 July 1654, Sarah Platts, had Joseph, b. 7 Jan.
1659; was freem. 1654, and d. 5 May 1698. JOSEPH, Watertown, s. of
the preced. m. 23 Sept. 1680, Sarah, d. of Richard Norcross the first,
had Sarah, b. 11 Nov. 1681; Joseph, 21 June 1685; Mary, 11 Apr.
1687; John, 29 Mar. 1689; Samuel, 7 Jan. 1695; Isaac, 5 Mar. 1700;
Lydia, 2 June 1706; Abigail, 19 Sept. 1708; and Ebenezer, 19 Jan.
1712; but the last three were by sec. w. m. 25 July 1705, Ruth, wid. of
John Maddock. He d. 3 Nov. 1711, and his wid. says Bond, was innholder 1719. JOSHUA, Roxbury, s. of Benjamin the first, m. 9 Mar.
1686, Eliz. d. of Edward Morris, had Joshua, b. 20 Jan. 1687; Isaac,
18 Dec. 1688; Eliz. 20 July 1691; Mehitable, 27 Oct. 1693; Joseph, 7
Jan. 1696; Abigail, 15 Mar. 1698; Ann, 8 Apr. 1700; Prudence, 22
July 1703; Samuel, 7 Nov. 1705; and Caleb, 16 Sept. 1709. RICH-
ARD, Barnstable, m. 15 Oct. 1649, Mary, d. of Robert Linnell of the
same, but of issue I am ign. RICHARD, Marshfield, m. 24 Jan. 1665,
Mary Truant. Miss Thomas, in Geneal. Reg. XII. 68, makes her d. of
Maurice. RICHARD, Watertown, br. of John of the same, as Bond says,
and he makes him b. 1631, that may seem a yr. or two bef. his time, but
sooner or later, they both, in my opin. were b. on this side of the Atlantic, and prob. neph. of Ephraim, wh. show. them gr. kindness, as their
f. must have d. early, m. 30 Mar. 1662, by Bond, but one rec. says 17
Apr. Mehitable Dimick, d. prob. of Thomas of Barnstable, had Richard,
b. 30 Mar. 1663, wh. d. bef. his f.; Ephraim, 9 Oct. 1664, d. in few
mos.; Shubael, 19 Dec. 1665, wh. perish. with cold in confinem. as
insane, after m. and hav. two ch. bef. the d. of his f.; Mehitable; Experience, 26 Feb. 1670; Abigail, 16 June 1672; Ebenezer, and Hannah, tw. 10 Nov. 1674, of wh. the s. d. soon; and his w. d. 18 Aug.
1676. He m. 16 Jan. 1679, Hannah, youngest d. of the first John
Train, had Joshua, 30 Dec. 1682; Margaret; John, 16 May 1687; and
Rebecca, 4 Feb. 1694. RICHARD, Barnstable, perhaps s. of Richard

the first, m. Eliz. d. of John Crocker, wh. d. 15 Jan. 1716, had Samuel, b. 6 Nov. 1679, d. in few yrs.; Eliz. 23 Jan. 1681, d. soon; Thomas, 10 Jan. 1682, bapt. 6 Apr. 1684, the same day with Samuel, and their f.; Hannah, b. 22 Jan. 1684; Timothy, 22 Sept. 1686; Ebenezer, Mar. 1691; Eliz. again, 6 June 1692; James, 6, bapt. 18 Nov. 1694; Mercy, 7, bapt. 16 May 1697; Joseph, 5 Mar. 1700; and Thankful, 15 Aug. 1702. He was a deac. ROBERT, Boston, a physician, came from Northfleet, Co. Kent, was bred at Corpus Christi Coll. Cambridge, and proceed. A. B. 1631, A. M. 1635, had stud. says Hutch. I. 145, at Padua, and there, perhaps, had his M. D. may have resid. short time at Watertown, unit. with others of that town in petitn. for the gr. of Lancaster; but he was not own. of any ld. at W. In Oct. 1645 he purch. large tract in Maine, kn. as the Vines patent, when the propr. was going to Barbados, but of course he had no purpose to make settlem. See Folsom, 75, 8, and Willis, I. 52. Next yr. he great. alarm. the governm. of Mass. by a petitn. for enlargem. of privileges, wh. by Drake, 292, is oddly ascrib. to Episcopalians, as if that depressed party could gain any thing from the triumph. Presbyterians in Parliam. Our Gen. Ct. in Nov. thereupon issued a Declaration, strange. undignif. against him and his assoc. Part of the denunciat. against C. is that he was a bachelor. Few state papers will afford so much amusement. See Hutch. Coll. 211, also Winslow's N. E. Salamander Discover. and Winth. Hist. II. 291. In 1647 he went home, and did not come back. Of this name, includ. that of Childs (wh. tho. differ. can by no means be disting. in old rec.) Farmer saw the gr. in 1828, were, at Harv. five; Yale, four; and only three at all the other N. E. coll.

CHILLINGWORTH, CHILLINGSWORTH, sometimes SHILLINGSWORTH, THOMAS, Lynn, rem. 1637, to Sandwich, thence to Marshfield, of wh. he was rep. 1648, and 52, d. early next yr. His wid. Jane m. 17 Aug. 1654, Thomas Dagget; d. Sarah was sec. w. of Samuel Sprague; Mary m. John Foster; prob. ano. d. was Mehitable, wh. m. 20 May 1661, Justus Eames; and his only other ch. Eliz. d. 28 Sept. 1655.

CHILSON, or CHILSTONE, JOHN, Lynn, m. 28 July 1667, Sarah, d. of the first Joseph Jenks, had Joseph, b. 31 Aug. 1670; and Sarah, 4 Aug. 1673. WALSINGHAM, Salem 1648, says Felt.

CHILTON, JAMES, a passeng. in the Mayflower, d. at Cape Cod, 8 Dec. 1620, after sign. the immortal compact, and his w. d. soon after land. His d. Mary, wh. accomp. her f. and mo. has by vain tradit. been made the first to leap on Plymouth rock, as that honor is, also, assign. to John Alden, when we kn. it is not due to either, m. John Winslow, and in 1650, Bradford says, she had nine ch. of wh. one was m. and had a ch. She d. 1679, but ano. d. of C. was left by him in Eng. where she m. and came to our country.

CHINN, CHINE, or CHING, GEORGE, Salem 1638, on Marblehead side 1648.

CHIPMAN, * JOHN, Barnstable, had been at Plymouth or Yarmouth a few yrs. bef. 1650, and may have resid. at other towns, since he said, 8 Feb. 1652, it was 21 yrs. ago that he came from Eng. and was now a. 37 yrs. old. So that it seems prob. he came with Allerton in the White Angel, or in the Friendship, that had sail. at the same time, from Barnstaple, in Devon, but had put back, and so reach. here a few days later. He m. Hope, sec. d. of John Howland, had Eliz. b. 24 June 1647, at P. bapt. at B. 18 Aug. 1650, beside one or two more, for he speaks of more than one bef. Hope, 13 Aug. bapt. 5 Sept. 1652; Lydia, b. 25 Dec. 1654; John, 2 Mar. 1657, d. in 3 mos.; Hannah, 14 Jan. 1659; Samuel, 15 Apr. 1662; Ruth, Dec. 1663; Bethia, 1 July 1666; Mercy, 6 Feb. 1668; John, again, 3 Mar. 1670; and Desire, 26 Feb. 1673. His f. Thomas had good est. near Dorchester in Co. Dorset. He was long rul. Elder, and rep. 1663 to 9 every yr. exc. 7, and d. 8 Jan. 1684. Eliz. m. Hosea Joyce of Yarmouth; Hope m. 10 Aug. 1670, John Huckens, and d. 10 Nov. 1678; Lydia m. John Sargent of Malden; Hannah m. 1 May 1680, Thomas Huckens, and d. 4 Nov. 1696. JOHN, Barnstable, s. of the preced. had John, wh. d. young; James, b. 18 Dec. 1694; John, again, 18 Sept. 1697; Mary, and Bethia, tw. 11 Dec. 1699; Perez, 28 Sept. 1702; Deborah, 6 Dec. 1704; Stephen, and Lydia, tw. 9 June 1708; and Ebenezer, 13 Nov. 1709; all by first w. and by sec. w. whose name is unkn. as well as the former's, had Hendley, 31 Aug. 1717; and Rebecca, 10 Nov. 1719. John, Mary, Bethia, Stephen, Lydia, and Ebenezer were bapt. on 18 May 1716, so that other ch. of the first w. may prob. have d. SAMUEL, Barnstable, br. of the preced. m. 27 Dec. 1686, Sarah Cobb, d. of Henry, or James, but of wh. is not told, had Thomas, b. 17 Nov. 1687; Samuel, 6 Aug. 1689; both bapt. 30 Aug. 1691, and, also, at the same time was bapt. John, b. 16 Feb. 1691, H. C. 1711, min. of Beverly, wh. d. 23 Mar. 1775; Joseph, bapt. Mar. 1692, prob. 6, certain. not (as tradit. gives) 4; Mary, 5 June 1692; Jacob, b. 30 Aug. bapt. 6 Oct. 1695; Seth, 24 Feb. bapt. 4 Apr. 1697; Hannah, b. 24 Sept. 1699; Sarah, 1 Nov. 1701; and Barnabas, 24 Mar. bapt. 26 Apr. 1702; and d. 1723. His wid. surv. to 8 Jan. 1742. Three errors are obs. in an affectionate writer's first three lines in Geneal. Reg. VI. 272, where he makes Rev. John to be s. of that John wh. m. Hope Howland; and is here seen to be gr.s. and makes Eliz. her mo. to be d. of Carver, instead of Tilley (but that was the common error ten yrs. ago); and also makes Bethia to be his sis. when she was his aunt. Of this name, in 1834, were five gr. at Harv. one at Yale, and two at Dart.

CHIPPERFIELD, EDMUND, New Haven 1639, in abbrev. form on London custom ho. rec. (as well as that of New Haven often), Chipfield, was passeng. in the Hopewell, capt. Babb, from London in the autumn, 1635, aged 20, a brickmaker, and d. 1648.

CHITTENDEN, HENRY, Scituate 1651, s. of Thomas, b. in Eng. had Joseph, b. 1657, beside Susanna, Eliz. and Ruth, and d. 1713, leav. d. Eliz. extrix. of his will, in wh. he devis. to Nathaniel, s. of Joseph, b. 1694, the lds. at Cohasset, and ment. other gr.ch. Mary Morton, Ruth Stetson, and Alithea, perhaps sis. of Nathaniel. * ISAAC, Scituate, elder br. of the preced. came with his f. m. Apr. 1646, Mary, eldest d. of wid. Ann Vinal, had Sarah, and Rebecca, tw. b. 25 Feb. 1647 ; Mary, 17 Aug. 1648; Israel, 10 Oct. 1651; Stephen, 5 Nov. 1654; Eliz. 9 Sept. 1658; and Isaac, 30 Sept. 1663; beside Benjamin, without date of b. but kn. to have come bef. the last, perhaps even earlier, for he was m. tho. without issue, when he fell, as a soldier under capt. Michael Pierce, 26 Mar. 1676, in that hard Rehoboth fight, when Canonchet took wild compensat. for the cruelty of our N. E. powers to his f. Miantonomi, the saddest example of judicial blindness in our first generat. He was rep. 1658, often after, and was k. 20 May foll. the loss of his s. when the Ind. assault. the town. Sarah m. 1666, capt. Anthony Collamore. ISRAEL, Scituate, s. of the preced. m. 1678, Deborah, d. of Rev. Nicholas Baker, had Nicholas, b. 1678; Isaac, 1681; and Israel, 1690; in wh. yr. he was lieut. in the sad expedit. of Phips, when Sylvester, capt. John Stetson, ens. of his comp. were lost. JOHN, Guilford, youngest s. of William, m. 12 Dec. 1665, Hannah, d. of John Fletcher, had John, b. 19 Oct. 1666; Eliz. 26 Jan. 1669; Joseph, 26 Mar. 1672; Gideon, 23 Sept. 1678, d. young; Abel, 14 May 1681; and Lydia, 30 Mar. 1684; and d. Apr. 1717. NATHANIEL, Guilford, br. of the preced. by w. Sarah had Nathaniel, b. 1 Aug. 1669; Sarah, 2 Mar. 1672; Mary, 16 Feb. 1675; Joseph, 6 Sept. 1677; Hannah, 15 Mar. 1679, or 80; Deborah, 15 Oct. 1682, d. at 2 yrs.; and Cornelius, 1685; and d. June 1690. STEPHEN, Scituate, br. of Isaac, m. 1679, Mehitable, d. of Isaac Bush, had Thomas, b. 1683; and perhaps other ch. THOMAS, Scituate, a linen-weaver from some pt. of Co. Kent, it is said, came from London in the Increase, 1635, aged 51, with w. Rebecca, 40, and those ch. bef. ment. Isaac, 14; and Henry, 6; unit. with his w. 12 Feb. 1637, to Lothrop's ch. had gr. of ho. lot, 1638, on Kent str. He d. 1668, and his will was of 7 Oct. inv. 9 Nov. of that yr. THOMAS, Guilford, eldest s. of William, m. Joanna Jordan, perhaps d. of John, had Samuel, b. 20 Sept. 1664, d. unm. at 30 yrs. ; William, 5 Oct. 1666; Joanna, 13 Dec. 1668, d. young; Abigail, 5 Dec. 1670; Thomas, 12 Jan. 1673; Mehitable, 1675; and Josiah, 1678; and d. Oct. 1683. William and Josiah had progeny, and one (I kn. not wh.) was gr.f. of Thomas, the first Gov. of the State of Vermont, whose s.

Martin, Dart. C. 1789, was also Gov. and d. 1840. * WILLIAM, Guilford, came from E. Guilford, in Co. Sussex, adjoin. Rye, on the British Channel, near the border of Kent, or perhaps from Kent, with w. Joan, d. of Dr. Jacob Sheaffe of Cranbrook in Kent, and sis. of our Jacob Sheaffe, and of the w. of Rev. Henry Whitfield, with wh. they came to Boston 1638. He soon went to New Haven, was of the found. of the ch. at G. 1 June 1639, and trustee of the ld. purch. from the Ind. for the settlem. He had been a soldier in the Netherlands, and reach. the rank of major, here was made lieut. of the force of New Haven Col. and a magistr. for the rest of his days, rep. at 27 sess. betw. 1643 and 61, and d. 1 Feb. of this last yr. His ch. were Thomas, Nathaniel, John, Joanna, Eliz. and Mary, all b. bef. the rec. of town begins ; Hannah, b. 19 Nov. 1649, d. next yr. ; Joseph, and Hannah, tw. 14 Apr. 1652 (of wh. the s. d. in few wks. and the d. unm. d. at 22 yrs.) ; and Deborah, 16 Dec. 1653. His wid. m. 1 May 1665, Abraham Cruttenden, and d. 16 Aug. 1668. Eliz. m. 16 June 1657, Thomas Wright, junr. of Wethersfield, or possib. a differ. Thomas W. ; Mary m. 4 Oct. 1670, John Leete, eldest s. of the Gov.

CHOATE, BENJAMIN, Kingston, an offshoot from Exeter, was prob. youngest s. of the first John, and after leav. coll. was employ. in that new settlem. in preach. sev. yrs. bef. 1725, but was never ord. nor does the catal. give the yr. of his d. No ch. was gather. at K. bef. 1725. JOHN, Ipswich 1648, was then 24 yrs. old, and is first ment. as contrib. for instr. in the milit. art; by w. Ann had John, b. 15 June 1661 ; Samuel ; Mary, 16 June 1666 ; Thomas ; Sarah ; Margaret ; Joseph ; and prob. Benjamin, H. C. 1703. He came, prob. from Sudbury, Co. Suff k. on the border of Essex, not far from the home of our first Gov. Winth. Perhaps he was s. of that goodm. C. wh. in June 1633 sent his regards to the Gov. as convey. by Rev. Henry Jacie in a valua. letter of that date to the younger John. He was serg. and d. 4 Dec. 1695. His wid. d. 16 Feb. 1727. Sarah m. 13 Apr. 1693, John Burnham ; and Margaret m. Abraham Fitts, and d. 28 Feb. 1692. JOHN, Ipswich, s. of the preced. had four ws. m. first, 7 July 1684, Eliz. Graves, sec. Eliz. Giddings, and, third, in 1723, Sarah Perkins, wh. d. 17 Nov. 1728 ; but when the first, or sec. d. or when the sec. was m. or wh. was mo. of the sec. ch. the loss of rec. forbids us to kn. His ch. were Dorothy ; John, b. May 1688 ; Robert, Apr. 1691 ; Ebenezer, Jan. 1695 ; Nehemiah, July 1697 ; Benjamin, a. Nov. 1698, wh. d. Nov. 1716 ; Humphrey, Nov. 1701 ; and Sarah. The fourth w. Prudence Marshall, d. 9 June 1732 ; and he d. 11 July 1733. He was deac. of the new ch. gather. 6 Sept. 1681, when Rev. John Wise, the gr. asserter of congrega. freedom, was ade pastor at the parish call. Chebacco. JOSEPH, Ipswich, br. of

the preced. had in 1702 w. Rebecca, but no more is kn. SAMUEL, Ipswich, br. of the preced. m. 25 Nov. 1688, Mary, d. of Stephen Williams of Roxbury, but of him no more is told in the fam. reg. exc. that he d.
a. 1713. THOMAS, Ipswich, br. of the preced. m. Mary Varney, perhaps
d. of Thomas of the same, had Ann, b. May 1691; Thomas, 7 June
1693; Mary, 18 Mar. 1695; John, July 1697; Abigail, 25 Oct. 1699;
Francis, 13 Sept. 1701; Rachel, 8 Nov. 1703; Ebenezer, Mar. 1706;
and Sarah, 24 July 1708. His w. d. 19 Nov. 1733; and for sec. w. he
had Mary, wid. of Joseph Calef; and he m. 9 Nov. 1743, for third w.
the wid. Hannah Burnham, and made his will next mo. Of this name
in 1829 were five gr. at Harv. and one at Dart. Hon. Rufus, class of
1819, Mass. senator of U. S. the eloquent advocate, wh. d. last summer.
He descends from Francis, s. of Thomas, wh. was s. of John, the first
comer.

CHRISTISON, in Sewel's Hist. of Quakers. See Christopherson.

CHRISTOPHERS, CHRISTOPHER, New London 1667, mariner, of
Devonsh. brot. from Barbados w. Mary, and ch. Richard, John, and
Mary. His w. d. 13 July 1676, aged 54, and he m. Eliz. wid. of Peter
Bradley, d. of Jonathan Brewster, and d. 23 or 25 July 1687, aged 55,
if the gr.stone wh. makes his age ten yrs. less than that of his w. be
correct. Perhaps the best change would be that on the w.'s stone, as
she might well be thot. younger; but the evidence is strong, that the
inequality was real, and she felt her disadvant. ‡ CHRISTOPHER, New
London, s. of Richard of the same, was judge of the Co. Ct. and an
Assist. had Christopher, wh. fill. the same offices after his f. JEFFREY,
New London, br. of Christopher the first, came a. the same time with
him, had ds. Margaret, Joanna, and ano. beside only s. Jeffrey, wh. m.
and d. 1690, of smallpox, with his w. within three wks. leav. no ch. He
was call. 55 yrs. old in 1676, and rem. in old age with the two ds. liv. in
1700 at Southold, L. I. Margaret m. Abraham Coney; Joanna m. 25
Dec. 1676, John Mayhew of New London; and the other d. m. a
Packer of S. JOHN, New London, mariner, younger s. of Christopher
the first, m. 28 July 1696, Eliz. perhaps d. of John Mulford, and d. at
Barbados, 3 Feb. 1703, leav. wid. and four ch. His wid. m. 21 Oct.
1706, John Picket. RICHARD, New London, elder br. of the preced. b.
says a fam. reg. 13 July 1662, at Cherton Ferrers, Torbay, Devonsh. a.
6 ms. from Dartmouth, m. 26 Jan. 1682, Lucretia, d. of Peter Bradlee,
whose mo. m. her f. had Christopher, bef. ment. b. 2 Dec. 1683, H. C.
1702, and other ch. but their names and dates have not been seen. His
w. d. 7 Jan. 1691, and he m. 3 Sept. foll. Grace Turner of Scituate,
perhaps d. of John, by wh. he had more ch. in all fifteen, and d. 9 June
1726. The name bec. extinct at N. L. a dozen yrs. ago, but descend. in

fem. lines are there. RICHARD, Boston, by w. Ann had Deborah, bapt. 30 Aug 1685 ; Lydia, b. 1, bapt. 3 July 1687; and Henry, 6, bapt. 18 Nov. 1688; and was a householder in 1695. That he may have been the same as the preced. is an easy conject. but less prob.

CHUBB, PASCOE, Andover, m. 29 May 1689, Hannah Faulkner, prob. d. of Edmund, was in command of the fort at Pemaquid in July 1696, wh. he basely, it is said, gave up to the Fr. without fir. a gun. Cruelty, beside treachery, to the Ind. on 16 Feb. preced. is ascrib. to him by Niles, wh. would aggravate the infamy of the tragedy by the remark "that it was acted on the Lord's day." With our unchristian natives of the forest the remembr. of injury is near. as strong as their sense of justice, and they totally cut off him, his w. and fam. on Tuesday, 23 Feb. 1698. Hutch. II. 93, 4, 106. THOMAS, Dorchester 1631, was from Crewkerne, Co. Somerset, border. on Devon, rem. 1636, to Salem, prob. that pt. wh. bec. Beverly, and d. 17 Oct. 1688, aged 81. WILLIAM, a soldier from an E. part of the Col. was serv. at Hadley, Apr. 1676.

CHRISTOPHERSON, WENDLOCK, Mass. a. 1660, tried, convict. as a Quaker, and banish. Hutch. I. 201. Sewel writes the name in his Hist. Christison ; and Col. Rec. gives Christianson.

CHUBBUCK, JOHN, Hingham, s. of Thomas, m. Dec. 1668, Martha Beal, had Thomas, John, Jonathan, and Nathaniel, beside ds. Martha, and Alice, all liv. with w. when he d. of smallpox, 26 Nov. 1690, a lieut. in the sad expedit. against Quebec. His wid. Martha had admin. 28 Apr. 1691. NATHANIEL, Hingham, br. of the preced. m. June 1669, wid. of John Garnet of H. and his ho. was burn. by the Ind. 20 Apr. 1676. THOMAS, Charlestown 1634, by w. Alice, wh. was adm. of the ch. 3 Apr. 1635, had Nathaniel, bapt. 4 May 1635 ; rem. prob. next yr. to Hingham, there was made freem. 1672, and d. Dec. 1676, leav. s. Nathaniel, and John, bef. ment. beside ds. Sarah, wh. m. 6 Oct. 1657, Jeremiah Fitch; Rebecca, w. of William Hersey; and Mary, wh. m. 18 Feb. 1663, Thomas Lincoln.

CHURCH, * BENJAMIN, Little Compton, s. of Richard, was a carpenter, but much disting. as capt. in the Ind. wars, m. 26 Dec. 1667, Alice, d. of Constant Southworth of Duxbury, where he liv. sev. yrs. had Thomas, b. 1674 ; Constant, 12 May 1676 ; Benjamin ; Edward ; Charles ; Eliz. 26 Mar. 1684 ; and Nathaniel, 1 July 1686, wh. d. young; was in gr. serv. for the latter part of Philip's war, and liv. some yrs. later at Bristol, of wh. he was the first rep. at Plymouth 1682–4 ; in the E. war, 1689, and 90, had ch. command, and soon after rem. to L. C. there d. 17 Jan. 1718, aged 78, by gr.stone. His wid. d. 5 Mar. 1719, aged 73. Perpet. of the name was by Thomas, Edward, and Charles. Edward was gr.f. of that unhappi. disting. Dr. Benjamin, H. C. 1754, whose

patriotism, that had been promin. was corrupt. in the early day of our
Revo. as is too well kn.   Full acco. of this fam. is giv. by Baylies, IV.
123–181, in wh. some error in detail of geneal. may be seen.   * CALEB,
Watertown, prob. youngest s. of Richard, was a millwright, m. 16 Dec.
1667, Joanna, d. of William Sprague of Hingham, and first sett. at Dedham, had Richard, b. 26 Dec. 1668, d. soon ; Ruth ; Lydia, 4 July 1671;
Caleb, 16 Dec. 1673 ; Joshua, 12 June 1675 ; Deborah, wh. d. young ;
rem. to W. and had there Isaac, and Rebecca, tw. 27 June 1678; and
his w. d. two weeks after.   He was freem. 1690, many yrs. a selectman,
and rep. 1713.   Bond has not mark. his time of d.   CORNELIUS, Groton,
m. 4 June 1670, Mary, whose surname is not kn. was of Charlestown
1680, but went back to G. and d. 2 Dec. 1697.   DAVID, Watertown,
youngest s. of Garrett, by w. Mary had John, bapt. 6 Nov. 1687 ; and
Sarah, 6 Oct. 1689 ; was then an innholder, and prob. rem. soon after to
Marlborough.   EDWARD, Norwalk 1654, s. of Richard of Hartford, b.
in Eng. 1628, had perhaps been some time bef. at New Haven, rem. to
Hatfield, was there deac. had eight ch. or more, of wh. Mary m. 1679,
Philip Russell, as his third w. ; Rebecca m. 1677, Joseph Selden ; and
Hepzibah m. 16 Sept. 1696, Samuel Spencer.   FRANCIS, New Haven
1642–44, of wh. I hear no more.   GARRETT, or JARED, Watertown
1637, was b. 1611, freem. 1649, by w. Sarah had John, b. 10 Mar.
1638 ; Samuel, 12 June 1640 ; Sarah, 10 Mar. 1643 ; Mary, 15 May
1644; Jonathan, 13 Dec. 1646; and David, 1 Sept. 1657.   JOHN, Hartford, s. of Richard of the same, m. 27 Oct. 1657, Sarah, d. of Richard
Beckley, was freem. 1658, and d. 1691, then hav. ten ch. liv. acc. Hinman, 124 with 258 ; viz. Richard ; Sarah Knight, w. perhaps of George ;
John ; Mary Standish ; Ruth ; Samuel ; Ann, aged 18 ; Eliz. 17 ;
Joseph, 15 ; and Deliverance, 12.   JOHN, Dover 1662, at Salisbury m.
29 Nov. 1664, Abigail, d. of John Severance, had Jonathan, b. 12 Apr.
1666 ; John, 12 Apr. 1668 ; Ebenezer, 25 Apr. 1670 ; and Abigail, 12
Aug. 1672 ; was tak. by the Ind. in the war of 1689, and escap. but was
k. 7 May 1696 by them near his own ho.   Belkn. I. 141.   JOHN,
Dover, s. of the preced. by w. Mary had Abigail, b. 5 May 1703 ; John,
1 Apr. 1704 ; Eliz. 2 Apr. 1706 ; Jonathan, 25 July 1708 ; and Mary,
4 Aug. 1710.   He was k. next yr. by the Ind.   JOSEPH, Hingham, br.
prob. of capt. Benjamin, m. Dec. 1660, Mary, d. of John Tucker of the
same, had, says Geneal. Reg. XI. 154, seven ch. but only six, Joseph,
John, Deborah, Mary, Eliz. and Abigail, have been heard of.   He rem. to
Little Compton, there his w. d. 21 Mar. 1710, aged 69, and he d. 5 Mar.
foll. in 73d yr.   NATHANIEL, Scituate, br. of Benjamin, m. Sarah Barstow,
d. of William the first, had Abigail, b. 1666 ; Richard, 1668 ; Nathaniel,
1670 ; Alice, 1679 ; Joseph, 1681 ; Charles, 1683 ; and Sarah, 1686.

In Geneal. Reg. XI. 154, it is said, that he rem. to Virg. but Deane, 233, 4, leads to differ. opin. RICHARD, Plymouth 1633, had, prob. come to Mass. in the fleet with Winth. for he req. adm. as freem. 19 Oct. 1630, yet did not after take the o. but rem. from Weymouth to P. and was rec. as freem. of that Col. 4 Oct. 1632. He m. Eliz. d. of Richard Warren, wh. prob. came with her mo. in the Ann 1623 ; was engag. as a carpenter in build. the earliest ch. edif. at Plymouth, serv. in the Pequot war, sold his est. at P. in 1649, and was at Charlestown 1653, and for final resid. sat down at Hingham. Giv. evid. at Sandwich, 25 Aug. 1664, he call. hims. 56 yrs. old, and he made his will at H. 25 Dec. 1668, and d. at Dedham a few days after. It provides for wid. Eliz. and equal portions to all the ch. without nam. them, exc. that Joseph, on acco. of his lame hd. should have a double one. To name those ch. in order, is not easy, perhaps not all of them with confidence. Beside Joseph, we kn. Benjamin, the gr. soldier, b. 1639 ; Richard, wh. d. young ; Caleb ; Nathaniel ; Hannah, bapt. 8 Aug. 1647 ; Abigail, wh. m. 19 Dec. 1666, Samuel Thaxter, and d. 25 Dec. 1677 ; Charles, k. by casual. 30 Oct. 1659 ; Deborah, b. 27 Jan. 1657, wh. m. John Irish, junr. says Winsor, as his sec. w. (tho. ano. author, wh. gives the date of his m. May 1708, calls her Priscilla) ; and perhaps Mary, wh. d. at Duxbury, 30 Apr. 1662. RICHARD, Hartford 1637, an orig. propr. whose first resid. is unkn. by Cothren, 526, is confus. with the preced. rem. a. 1660, to Hadley, there d. Dec. 1667. His wid. Ann d. 10 Mar. 1684, aged 83, and, in his will, four ch. only are nam. viz. Edward, and John, bef. ment. ; Mary, wh. m. Isaac Graves, and Samuel ; perhaps all b. in Eng. SAMUEL, Hadley, youngest s. of the preced. made freem. of Conn. 1657, rem. to H. after m. with Mary, perhaps eldest d. of Josiah Churchill, and d. 13 Apr. 1684, leav. eight ch. SAMUEL, Watertown, elder br. of David, m. 7 Feb. 1672, Rebecca, d. of William Shattuck, had Rebecca, b. 31 Dec. foll. Of this name in 1830 were eight gr. at Yale, five at Harv. and three at Dart.

CHURCHILL, CHURCHALL, or CHURCHELL, BENJAMIN, Wethersfield, s. of Josiah, by w. Mary, m. 1677, wh. d. 30 Oct. 1712, aged 59, had Prudence, b. 2 July 1678 ; and two other ch. but no more is kn. ELIEZUR, Plymouth, s. of John of the same, m. 8 Feb. 1688, Mary Dotey, wid. I presume, of some gr.s. of the first Edward, and had four or five ch. but by a former w. also Mary, had Hannah, b. 23 Aug. 1676 ; Joanna, 25 Nov. 1678 ; and sev. of the foll. tho. as date of only one is kn. to me, I must not disting. which mo. bore ea. Abigail ; Eleazer ; Stephen, Feb. 1685 ; Jedediah ; Mary ; Elkanah ; Nathaniel ; Josiah ; and Jonathan. His w. d. 11 Dec. 1715 ; and he d. 5 Mar. foll. JOHN, Plymouth 1643, m. 18 Dec. 1644, Hannah, d. of William Pontus,

had Joseph; Hannah, b. 12 Nov. 1649; Eliezur, 20 Apr. 1652; and
Mary, 1 Aug. 1654; and he d. 1 Jan. 1663. Perhaps both ds. were d.
for his nuncup. will names only four ch. all s. to the two bef. ment. giv.
lds. at P. and other prop. to s. John, and William, this last b. 1656.
His wid. m. 25 June 1669, Giles Rickard, and d. 12 Dec. 1690; but by
ano. rept. 1 Apr. 1709. JOHN, Plymouth, s. perhaps youngest, of the
preced. m. 28 Dec. 1686, Rebecca Delano, d. perhaps, of Philip the
first, had Eliz. b. 7 Oct. 1687; Rebecca, 29 Aug. 1689; John, 20 Dec.
1691; Sarah, 10 Feb. 1695; and Hannah, 27 Apr. 1697. His w. d. 6
Apr. 1709; and he d. 1723, aged 67. JOSEPH, Plymouth, s. of the
preced. m. 3 June 1672, Sarah Hicks, had John, b. 3 or 22 July 1678;
Margaret, Oct. 1684; Barnabas, 3 July 1686; and Joseph, Jan. 1692.
JOSEPH, Wethersfield, eldest s. of Josiah of the same, by w. Mary had
there nine ch. when he d. 1 Apr. 1699. JOSIAH, Wethersfield, m. 1638,
Eliz. d. of Nathaniel Foote, had Mary, b. 24 Mar. 1639; Eliz. 15 May
1642; Hannah, 1 Nov. 1644, wh. prob. d. bef. her f. at least is not nam.
in his will; Ann, 1647; Joseph, 2 Dec. 1649; Benjamin, 16 May
1652; and Sarah, 14 Nov. 1657; and he d. 1 Jan. 1686, all these ch.
exc. Hannah, being then liv. His wid. d. 8 Sept. 1700, aged a. 84.
Eliz. m. 31 Oct. 1660, Henry Buck; Sarah m. 11 June 1673, Thomas
Wickham of Wethersfield, and from their f.'s will, we see that Mary m.
a Church, perhaps Samuel; and Ann m. a Rice. WILLIAM, Plymouth,
s. of John, m. 17 Jan. 1684, Lydia Bryant, whose f. is unkn. to me, had
William, b. 2 Aug. 1685; Samuel, 15 Apr. 1688; James, 21 Sept.
1690; Lydia, 17 Apr. 1699; and Josiah, 21 Aug. 1702.

CHURCHMAN, HUGH, Lynn 1640, d. says Lewis, 1644. His will was
prod. 9 July of that yr. Ann, perhaps his d. m. at Weymouth, 16 Apr.
1639, John Rogers. JOHN, took the o. of alleg. 22 June 1632, as qualif.
to come to N. E. in the Lion, arr. 16 Sept.

CHURCHWOOD, HUMPHREY, Kittery 1677. JOSIAH, Wethersfield,
had Hannah, wh. m. 9 Jan. 1667, Samuel Royce of New London.

CHUTE, JAMES, Ipswich, s. of Lionel, b. in Eng. m. (as once was
thot.) a d. of Hon. Samuel Symonds, wh. names s. C. in his will.
But the mean. of the testator may have been s. or s.-in-law of
Martha Epes, or ano. of sev. ws. that S. had; for such seems, also, the
case of Peter Duncan, call. s. of Symonds, because h. of Mary, wh. was
d. of Daniel Epes by that Martha, wh. after was w. of S. By his w.
whatever was her name of bapt. or whoever was her f. he had James,
and rem. 1681, to Rowley. JAMES, Rowley, s. of the preced. m. 10
Nov. 1673, Mary Wood, possib. d. of Isaiah, had Eliz. b. 22 June
1676; Ann, 19 Oct. 1679; Lionel, bapt. 3 Apr. 1681; James, 13 June
1686; Thomas, 31 Jan. 1692; Mary, 12 Sept. 1697; beside Martha;

Ruth; and Hannah; but the three last are less certain. LIONEL, Ipswich 1639, the earliest sch.master there, made his will 4 Sept. 1644, pro. 7 Nov. 1645, leav. by w. Rose, d. of Robert Baker, s. James, and perhaps no other ch. Perhaps he was of a very anc. fam. for I have seen his geneal. trac. back to 1268, bef. the first king Edward.

CLAGHORN, or, as the Col. rec. spells CLEAGUEHORNE, JAMES, Barnstable, an early sett. m. 6 Jan. 1654, Abigail Lombard, prob. d. of Thomas, but may have been his gr.d. had James, b. 29 of the same mo. as the rec. tells; Mary, 28 Oct. 1655; Eliz. Apr. 1658; Sarah, 3 Jan. 1660; Robert, 27 Oct. 1661; and Shubael. Mary m. 28 Mar. 1682, Joseph Davis of B. JAMES, Barnstable, s. of the preced. had Thomas, bapt. 17 June 1694. ROBERT, Barnstable, s. of the first James, m. 6 Nov. 1701, Bethia Lothrop, but whose d. she was is not kn. had Abia, b. 13 Aug. 1702; Joseph, 25 Aug. 1704; Nathaniel, 10 Nov. 1707, and Samuel, 23 June 1711. SHUBAEL, or SHOBAL, br. of the preced. by w. Jane had James, b. Aug. 1689; Thankful, 30 Jan. bapt. 29 Mar. 1701, in right of his w. and d. at 6 yrs.; Thomas, 20 Mar. 1693; Shobal, 20 Sept. 1696; Robert, 18 July, bapt. 13 Aug. 1699; Benjamin, 14 June, bapt. 26 July 1701; Mary, 1707; Jane, 1709; and Ebenezer, 30 July 1712.

CLANFIELD, PETER, Dover 1663.

CLAP, AMBROSE, Dorchester, br. of Nicholas, came, prob. in 1636, if he ever came, that is uncert. for no more is ever heard of him, exc. that he was liv. in Eng. 1655. DESIRE, Dorchester, s. of capt. Roger, freem. 1669, m. Sarah Pond, perhaps d. of Robert the sec. but the Rev. Mr. Danforth had writ. long after, on the paper that ment. bapt. of Sarah, 6 Feb. 1642, that she m. Ezra C. thus mistak. her for her sis. He had William, b. 9 Oct. 1680, d. young; Desire, 6 Mar. 1682, d. young; Experience, 30 Nov. 1683; Sarah, 25 Mar. 1686; Preserved, a d. 8 Aug. 1688; Desire, again, and William, again, tw. 13 Aug. 1694, of wh. Desire d. in few days, but William liv. 49 yrs. was m. and d. without ch. closing the male line of capt. Roger in this branch, beside other tw. Roger, and Daniel, 24 May 1697, wh. both d. soon; and Judith, whose date of b. is not kn. wh. m. Ephraim Payson, prob. as his sec. w. but the date of m. is also unkn. His w. d. 4 Jan. 1716, aged 63; and he m. 27 Dec. foll. wid. Deborah Smith of Boston, and d. Dec. 1717. EBENEZER, Dorchester, s. of Nicholas, freem. 1669, one of the found. of the ch. in Milton 1678. Of his first w. Eliz. we kn. not the surname, but she d. 20 Dec. 1701, aged 57; and for the sec. he m. 11 Nov. 1702, Eliz. Dickerman, and by neither had any ch. He d. 31 July 1712, and his wid. m. Edward Dorr of Roxbury. EDWARD, Dorchester, br. of capt. Roger, came in 1633, and was made freem. 7 Dec. 1636, selectman 1637, deac. 25 or 6 yrs. by first w. Prudence, sis. of Ambrose, John, Nicholas, Richard, and Thomas Clap, had Eliz. b. 1634; Prudence, 28 Dec. 1637; Ezra, 22, bapt. 24 May 1640; Nehemiah, a. Sept. 1646; and Susanna, Nov. 1648; and by sec. w. Susanna had Esther, July 1656; Abigail, 27 Apr. 1659; Joshua, 12 May 1661; and Jonathan, 23 Mar. 1664; but the last three d. young. He d. 8 Jan. 1665; and his wid. d. 16 June 1688. Eliz. m. Jan. 1652 (not 42 yrs. later, as in Geneal. Reg. IX. 177), James Blake; Prudence m. Feb. 1661, Samuel Peck of Rehoboth; and Esther m. 19 June 1684, Samuel Strong of Northampton. ELIJAH, Scituate, was a witness, 1662, to the will of Joseph Wormall. Perhaps, as no more is heard of him, he was only trans. visit. EZRA, Dorchester, eldest s. of Edward, freem. 1666, by first w. Abigail Pond, sis. I suppose, of the w. of his cous. Desire, had Mary, b. 26 Apr. 1667; Edward, Sept. 1672, wh. was lost in Phips's crusade, 1690, against Quebec; Ezra, 29 Jan. 1674, wh. d. 10 Apr. 1691; Abigail, 1675; Sarah, 20 July 1677; Judith, 6 May 1680; and Eliz. 1 Oct. 1682. His w. d. 13 Oct. 1682, and he m. 22 May 1684, Experience, d. of Ralph Houghton of Lancaster, had William, July 1685; Jane, 12 Mar. 1687; Nehemiah; Ezra, again, 18 Mar. 1693; Ebenezer, 3 Feb. 1697; Esther, 10 Feb. 1699; and Susanna, 7 Mar. 1702. He own. much ld. in that part of D. wh. had bec. Milton, and there his w. d. 17 Dec. 1717, and he d. 23 of next mo. * HOPESTILL, Dorchester, s. of Roger, freem. 1678, m. 18 Apr. 1672, Susanna, d. of Thomas Swift, had Susanna, b. 23 Dec. 1673; Eliz. 29 Feb. 1676; Sarah, 13 Jan. 1678; Hopestill, 26 Nov. 1679; Ruth, 10 Oct. 1682; Mary, 22 Sept. 1685, d. soon; Supply, 25 Oct. 1686, d. in few weeks; Jerijah, or Jarizah, 15 Feb. 1689, d. soon; Unite, 2 Oct. 1690, d. soon; was rul. elder, and d. 2 Sept. 1719. Of the eight ch. Hopestill alone could have preserv. the male line in this branch of capt. Roger's descend. but, tho. he liv. to 26 Dec. 1759, and was deac. 36 yrs. he never was m. INCREASE, Barnstable, m. Oct. 1675, Eliz. wid. of Nathaniel Goodspeed, had John, b. Oct. 1676; Charity, Mar. 1678; Benjamin; Thomas, Jan. 1681, d. in two yrs.; and Thomas, again, Dec. 1684, bapt. Mar. foll. JOHN, Dorchester 1636, br. of Nicholas, freem. 1647, had w. Joan, no ch. and d. 14 July 1655. His will explains the fam. much; and the wid. m. next yr. John Ellis of Medfield. NATHANIEL, Dorchester, elder s. of Nicholas, m. 31 Mar. 1668, Eliz. Smith, had Nathaniel, b. 20 Jan. 1669, H. C. 1690; John, 7 Apr. 1671; Jonathan, 31 Aug. 1673; Eliz. 22 May 1676; Ebenezer, 25 Oct. 1678; and Mehitable, wh. d. young. He was freem. 1660, so that we see, as in the case of Cotton Mather, that minors might be adm. if they had stand. in the ch. to the privilege of citizens. He d. 16 May 1707; and his wid. d. 12

33 *

or 19 Sept. 1722, aged 74. NEHEMIAH, Dorchester, s. of Edward, m. 17 Apr. 1678, Sarah, d. of John Leavitt of Hingham, had Edward, b. 20 Dec. foll. d. soon; Edward, again, 9 Dec. 1680; Submit, 2 Aug. 1683, a d.; and perhaps others; was freem. 1683, and d. 2 Apr. 1684. His wid. m. Samuel Howe. NICHOLAS, Dorchester 1636, s. of Richard, b. in Eng. m. his cous. Sarah, sis. of Edward, had Sarah, b. 31 Dec. 1637, perhaps d. young; Nathaniel, 15 Sept. 1640; Ebenezer, July 1643, bapt. 17 Mar. 1644; and Hannah, b. 1646; and by sec. w. Abigail, wid. of Robert Sharp, had Noah, b. 15 July 1667; and Sarah, again, 1670. He was deac. and d. 24 Nov. 1679. Hannah m. 14 Oct. 1668, Ebenezer Strong of Northampton. PRESERVED, Northampton, s. of Roger, m. 1668, Sarah, d. of Benjamin Newberry of Windsor, had Sarah, b. 1668, d. young; Wait, 1670; Mary, 1672, d. at 19 yrs.; Preserved, 1675; Samuel, 1677; Hannah, 1681; Roger, 1684; and Thomas, 1688; was freem. 1690, capt. and rul. elder, and d. Sept. 1720. RICHARD, Dorchester 1636, if he ever came, br. of Nicholas, had Richard, Eliz. and Deborah, as nam. in the will of their uncle John, when f. was in Eng. ROBERT, Boston 1687, may have been short time at Dorchester in 1660, at B. had w. Mary, and three ch. of wh. one was Robert, a sea capt. wh. d. on a voyage. He came, it is said, from Littleham, Co. Devon, a mile and a half E. of Exmouth, but was not, prob. a near relative of the Dorchester tribe. * ‖ ROGER, Dorchester 1630, came in the Mary and John, from Plymouth, 20 Mar. 1630, was b. at Salcomb Regis, on the coast of Devonsh. 6 Apr. 1609, the youngest of five s. and arr. at Nantasket, 30 May, with his rev. friends Maverick and Warham, m. 6 Nov. 1633, Joanna, d. of Thomas Ford, a fellow-passeng. had ten s. and four ds. Samuel, b. 11 Oct. 1634; William, 2 July 1636, d. at 2 yrs.; Eliz. 22 June 1638; Experience, 23 Aug. 1640, d. in few weeks; Waitstill, a s. 22 Oct. 1641, d. under 2 yrs.; Preserved, 23 Nov. 1643; Experience, again, Dec. 1645, d. young; Hopestill, 6 Nov. 1647; Wait, a d. 17 Mar. 1649; Thanks, July 1651, d. young; Desire, 17 Oct. 1652; Thomas, Apr. 1655, d. young; Unite, 13 Oct. 1656; and Supply, a. 1661, wh. d. unm. 5 Mar. 1686, by the burst. of a gun on Castle isl. He was ar. co. 1646, its lieut. 1655, capt. of the castle 1665 on d. of Davenport, in wh. post he contin. until usurp. of Andros, when he relinq. it, rep. many yrs. betw. 1652 and 1673, and d. 2 Feb. 1692, of course in 83d not, as Sewall writes, in 86th yr. His wid. d. 29 June 1695, aged 78. Clap's Memoirs are quite interest. and may be read, as reprint. in Young's Chronicles of Mass. His d. Eliz. m. Joseph Holmes of Roxbury; and Wait m. Jonathan Simpson of Charlestown, and d. 3 May 1717. * SAMUEL, Dorchester, eldest s. of the preced. m. 18 Nov. 1659, Hannah, only d. of Richard Leeds, had Samuel, b. 22

Feb. 1662, d. at six yrs.; John, 16 June 1664, d. at one yr.; Hannah, 28 Sept. 1666, d. at 12 yrs.; Samuel, again, 6 Aug. 1668, a lieut. wh. d. 30 Jan. 1725; Experience, 8 July 1670, d. at one yr.; Unite, 6 Dec. 1672, d. at two yrs.; Return, 11 May 1675, d. next yr.; John, again, 8 May 1677, d. unm. at 24 yrs.; Eliz. 11 Feb. 1680; and Hannah, again, 13 Sept. 1681. He was capt. rul. elder, rep. 1689, 90, 1, 5, 7, 9, and selectman many yrs. and d. 16 Oct. 1708, of grief for loss of his w. aged 68, eight days bef. * SAMUEL, Scituate, s. of Thomas, m. June 1666; Hannah, d. of Thomas Gill, had Samuel, b. 15 May 1667; Joseph, 14 Dec. 1668; Stephen, 4 Mar. 1671; Hannah, 15 Jan. 1673; Bethia, 1675; John, 30 Sept. 1677; Abigail, 1 Oct. 1679; David, Nov. 1684; Deborah, Feb. 1687; and Jane, Nov. 1689; was rep. to Plymouth 8 or 9 yrs. and, after the new chart. five more, to Boston. Deane, wh. has not giv. the time of his d. well commemo. many of his descend. His s. Stephen was a deac. and f. of Rev. Thomas, b. 26 June 1703, H. C. 1722, Presid. of Yale Coll. wh. d. 7 Jan. 1767. * THOMAS, Weymouth, br. of Ambrose, John, Nicholas, and Richard, b. at Dorchester in Dorsetsh. freem. 13 Mar. 1639, had Thomas, b. 15 Mar. 1639, bapt. at Dedham, 17 or 24 May 1640; rem. again to Scituate, there was deac. 1647, rep. 1649, and had Samuel, Eliz. Prudence, Eleazer, wh. fell in Rehoboth fight, 26 Mar. 1676, unm. of all of wh. the dates of b. are unkn. beside John, 1658, and Abigail, 29 Jan. 1660, wh. both d. young; and d. 1684. His will of that yr. calls him 87 yrs. old, provides for w. (prob. a sec. one) Abigail, s. Thomas and Samuel, and d. Eliz. that had m. 1669, Thomas King. THOMAS, Dedham, s. of the preced. m. 10 Nov. 1662, Mary Fisher, d. 1690, leav. wid. Mary, and ch. Thomas, b. 26 Sept. foll.; Joshua, 1667; Mary, 13 Dec. 1669; Eliezer, 4 Nov. 1671; Samuel, 21 Aug. 1682; Abigail; and Hannah, as nam. in his will; beside John, b. Feb. 1665, wh. d. in few days. WILLIAM, Dorchester 1664, with suffix of sen. is one of the patriotic petitioners of D. against compliance with demands of the crown, as print. in Geneal. Reg. V. 394. Yet I can hear nothing of him in other affairs of the town, nor whether he had w. and ch. Some of these productive stocks add a *p* to the common name. Ten of this name had been gr. in 1834, at Harv. and all the other N. E. coll. had made up equal num.

CLAPHAM, ARTHUR, New Hampsh. d. as early as 1676. PETER, Norwalk 1672, had been 2 yrs. bef. at Fairfield, but still at N. 1688; yet it may be some times spell. Clapton, and in the valua. Hist. of N. by Hall, is giv. p. 61, Lupton, by mistake.

CLARK, ADAM, a soldier of Lothrop's comp. the flower of Essex, k. at Bloody brook, 18 Sept. 1675. ANDREW, Boston, s. of Thomas of Plymouth, by w. Mehitable had Thomas, b. 10 July 1672; Susanna, 12 Mar. 1674; and Mehitable, 8 Dec. 1676; rem. to Harwich, there had

Andrew, Scottow, and Nathaniel. ARTHUR, Salem, freem. 13 May 1640, had bef. been at Hampton, rem. 1643 to Boston, by w. Sarah had Sarah, bapt. 17 Mar. 1644, seven days old; and Samuel, 1 Nov. 1646. He d. 1665, prob. for on 31 Oct. of that yr. his wid. took admin. of his small est. in behalf of hers. and s. BENJAMIN, Medfield, freem. 1682. BRAY, or BRIAN, Dorchester 1630, acc. Dr. Harris, but first ment. on town rec. 1634. CAREW, Newport, eldest br. of famous John of the same, was b. 3 Feb. 1603, it is said, in Co. Bedford, had not w. perhaps, certain. no ch. in our country, to wh. he is brot. in comp. with his brs. by tradit. in 1638. CHRISTOPHER, Boston 1646, mariner, by w. Rebecca, wh. join. our ch. 25 Dec. 1647, had Dorothy, b. 6, bapt. 20 Jan. 1650; John, b. 3 Feb. 1652; Peter, 4, bapt. 11 June 1654; Rebecca, b. 4 May 1657; Christopher, 19 Jan. bapt. 19 Feb. 1660; Daniel, b. 10 Feb. as the town rec. tells, wh. may be disbeliev. as he was bapt. 26 Jan. 1662; Eliz. b. 4 Aug. 1663; and Mary, or Mercy, 1 Mar. 1667. He was freem. 1673, a merch. often voyag. betw. Eng. and our country, in one of his pass. was in the Speedwell, emb. at London, 30 May, and land. at B. 27 July 1656. His youngest d. m. 1 Dec. 1686, Stephen Minot. CHRISTOPHER, Salem, mariner, lost at sea a. 1698, as Felt, II. 244, tells, was, perhaps, s. of the preced. DANIEL, Ipswich 1635, Topsfield 1661, had Eliz. wh. m. 24 Oct. 1669, William Perkins of the same. ‡ * DANIEL, Windsor, came, 1639, in comp. with Rev. Ephraim Huet, by wh. he was nam. excor. 1644, of his will, m. 13 June of that yr. Mary, d. of Thomas Newberry, had Mary, b. 4 Apr. 1645, d. young; Josiah, 21 Jan. 1649; Eliz. 28 Oct. 1651; Daniel, 5 Apr. (as Goodwin says), 4 Aug. 1664, as ano. rec. reads; John, 10 Apr. 1656; Mary, again, 22 Sept. 1658; Samuel, 6 July 1661; Sarah, 7 Aug. 1663; Hannah, 25 or 29 Aug. 1665, d. soon; and Nathaniel, 8 Sept. 1666, wh. was k. by the Ind. unm. 1690. His w. d. 29 Aug. 1688, and his sec. w. Martha, sis. of William Pitkin, wid. of Simon Wolcott, and mo. of Roger W. Gov. of the Col. d. 13 Oct. 1719. He was rep. 1657–61, secr. of the Col. 1658–63, Assist. 1662–4, capt. of the cavalry troop 1664, and at his d. 12 Aug. 1710, aged 87, left Josiah, Eliz. Daniel, John, Mary, Samuel, and Sarah. Eliz. m. 25 Nov. 1669, Moses Cooke of Northampton, and, next, 13 Sept. 1677, Job Drake of Windsor; Mary m. 13 Dec. 1683, John Gaylord, jr. (if Goodwin is right), when she would have been 25 yrs. old, and he less than 17; and she next m. a. 1700, Jedediah Watson, and d. 14 Apr. 1738; and Sarah m. a. 1685, Isaac Pinney, and had a sec. h. DANIEL, Hartford, s. of the preced. m. 1678, Hannah, d. of Daniel Pratt, had Daniel, b. 1679; Moses, 1683; John, 1685; perhaps all at Windsor, but at H. had Aaron, bapt. 13 Nov. 1687; Nathaniel, 26 Mar. 1693; Abraham, 10 Nov. 1695; and Noah, 25 Apr. 1697; and after 1710 he rem. to Colchester. ED-

MUND, Lynn 1636, rem. next yr. to Sandwich. EDMUND, Gloucester 1650, was town clk. 1656–65, by w. Agnes had Abigail;
and Joseph, b. 16 Nov. 1650; and d. 26 Feb. 1667. Abigail m.
William Sargent, and d. 8 Mar. 1711, aged 79. EDWARD, Haverhill
1646, perhaps m. a d. of Walter Tibbets of Gloucester, wh. calls him
s.-in-law, was a carpenter, and may have been in 1652 of Kennebunk,
made freem. of Mass. 1653, and prob. in 1663 rem. to New Hampsh.
Ano. EDWARD of Haverhill, perhaps s. of the preced. took o. of alleg.
28 Nov. 1677. EPHRAIM, Medfield, freem. 1673. GEORGE, Plymouth,
m. 22 Jan. 1639, Alice Martin, wh. after his d. m. 5 Dec. 1644, Richard
Bishop, and in 1648, was hang. for murder of Martha, d. of George, wh.
was not his only ch. for in May 1649, the rec. shows provis. for his d.
Abigail.   GEORGE, Milford 1639, husbandman, had George, and six ds.
and d. Aug. 1690, leav. good est. in his will of 25 Apr. preced. nam. d.
Sarah, then wid. of the famous capt. Joseph Sill, but had first been wid.
of Reynold Marvin, as also five ch. of her by ⸢Marvin. GEORGE, Milford, a contempo. of the preced. was call. carpenter for distinct. and this
is all I kn. of him.   * GEORGE, Milford, s. of George, the husbandman,
was deac. often rep. d. soon after, if not even (as is prob.) bef. his f.
leav. no ch.   GEORGE, Roxbury, was a fellmonger, inhab. of Boston bef.
1695, d. 3 Sept. 1696, leav. good est. giv. by his will, pro. 15 Oct. foll.
to w. Ann, eldest s. George, to youngest d. Eliz. £200, eldest d. Mary,
in Eng. £40, s. Richard, d. Martha, w. of William Hannah, £60, and
made her h. excor.   But when, or where these ch. were b. or wh. was
his w. are unkn. matters.   Yet perhaps the Boston rec. ment. him as m.
3 Feb. 1690, Ann Lutterell.   ‡ * HENRY, Windsor 1640, rep. 1641–50;
Assist. 1650–61, rem. to Hadley, there d. 23 Dec. 1675. His w. Jane
had d. 1672, and as he had no ch. he gave most of his est. to relat. but
good proport. to public use, as sch. at H. and to Harv. coll. HENRY,
Newbury, s. of Nathaniel, m. 7 Nov. 1695, Eliz. d. of Stephen Greenleaf, had Stephen, b. 21 Feb. 1697; Henry, 21 Nov. 1698; Judith, 15
Aug. 1700; and Sarah, 7 May 1702. ‖ HUGH, Watertown 1640, by w.
Eliz. had John, b. 13 Oct. 1641; Uriah, 5 June 1644; and Eliz. 31 Jan.
1648; own. est. in Cambridge, but rem. to Roxbury 1657; was freem.
1660, ar. co. 1666. His w. d. 11 Dec. 1692; and he d. 20 July foll. a.
80 yrs. old.   Eliz. m. Joseph Buckminster. ISAAC, Falmouth, s. of
Thaddeus, was tak. by the Fr. and Ind. 1690, carr. to Canada, after
return rem. to Marlborough, m. Sarah Stow, perhaps d. of Samuel, had
Martha, wh. d. at Grafton, 1794, aged, it is said, near 100; Sarah, b. 5
Aug. 1701; Mary, 31 Dec. 1705; Matthias; Jonathan, d. young;
Isaac, 25 Mar. 1709; Jonathan, again, 1712; Rebecca, 30 Sept. 1716.
His w. d. 17 May 1761, in 88th yr. and he d. 26 May 1768, perhaps at
full 100.   JAMES, New Haven 1639, form. with Gov. Eaton and com.

the civil compact 4 June, but rem. bef. 1669 to Stratford, and may have had ch. at both places. JAMES, Plymouth, s. of Thomas, m. 7 Oct. 1657, Abigail, youngest d. of Rev. John Lothrop. JAMES, Boston, but call. sometimes of Roxbury, bec. he attend. ch. there, liv. at Muddy riv. by w. Elinor, in ch. rec. miscall. Eliz. had Eliz. and Mary, wh. we may suppose were bapt. 18 Jan. 1646, if the town rec. were authority instead of the rec. of ch. in wh. no such thing is found; Martha, b. 25 Apr. 1648; Hannah, 23 Dec. 1649; James, bapt. 11 Apr. 1652; Samuel, 9 Apr. 1654; John, 23 Mar. 1656; Abigail, 21 Mar. 1658; Mercy, 2 Sept. 1660; Aaron, 1 Mar. 1663; beside one d. that m. Walter Morse, as we learn from the will of her f. provid. for, but not nam. her. He d. 18 Dec. 1674. JAMES, New Haven, s. of James the first, was adm. freem. 1660. *JAMES*, Newport, youngest s. of the Hon. Jeremiah, m. Hope, d. of Nicholas Power of Providence, had Hope, b. 29 Dec. 1673; and Jonathan, a. 1681. He was a preach. but I kn. no more of him exc. that he d. 7 Dec. 1736, aged 87. JAMES, Roxbury, s. of James bef. ment. m. 27 Apr. 1681, Hannah, d. of Peleg Heath, had James, b. 4 Feb. 1682. His w. d. 30 May 1683, and he rem. to Cambridge, m. 24 Sept. 1685, Sarah, d. of Samuel Champney, had Sarah, b. next yr. wh. d. at 21 yrs.; Ebenezer, d. soon; Mercy, 18 Dec. 1690; Abigail, 31 May 1703; but betw. the last two prob. came Rachel and Benjamin, yet precise dates can hardly be found, as rec. fail in this space of time. ‡ JEREMIAH, Newport 1640, had been at Portsmouth, on the upper end of the isl. 1638, bef. N. was sett. was first constable of the town, treasur. of the Col. 1647, and Assist. 1648, when he was chief officer. He was not, as often said, br. nor even any kn. relat. of John, the well reput. f. of the Col. and d. Jan. 1652, leav. five s. Walter, b. a. 1639; Jeremiah; Latham; Weston, 2 July 1648; James, 1649; beside four ds. of wh. prob. two were older than Walter, Frances, wh. m. Randall Holden; and ano. the first w. of James Barker; Mary, b. 1641, wh. m. Gov. John Cranston, and, next, John Stanton, and d. 7 Apr. 1701; and Sarah, 1651, wh. perhaps was sec. w. of Peter Carr. JEREMIAH, Newport, s. of the preced. m. says the fam. geneal. Ann Audley. She may have been Hannah Odlyn, d. of John of Boston, wh. had much sympathy with the R. I. first sett. as hav. with most of them been ill treat. by the governm. of Mass. in Nov. 1637, for their errors in religious dogmas. To ea. of his ch. Susanna, Henry, James, Samuel, Weston, Frances, Mary, Ann, and Sarah are supplied ws. or hs. respectiv. by the fam. docum. but without names appended. JOHN, Cambridge, freem. 6 Nov. 1632, rem. 1636, to Hartford with Hooker, thence, perhaps, to Milford, where his d. Eliz. m. William Pratt of H. JOHN, Boston, came, perhaps, with John Winthrop jr. in the Lion 1631, join. the ch. early, only seven names on the venera. copy of the roll (some yrs. bef. the first date of orig. rec. of our first ch.)

interven. betw. the s. of the Gov. and this, and with him rem. 1633, from B. to plant the town of Ipswich. JOHN, New Haven 1639, that yr. unit. with first sett. in founda. of governm. He may have come in the Elizabeth to Boston from Ipswich in Co. Suffk. 1634, aged 22; and was made clk. of the milit. comp. Feb. 1648; had John, b. 1637; Samuel, 1639, both bapt. at N. H. 1640, and Esther, 1 Mar. 1646. † ‡ JOHN, Newport, the disting. author of "Ill News from N. E." a physician, came first, he says, to Boston in Nov. 1637, thence driv. the next yr. as a favorer of Mrs. Hutchinson, went to R. I. and is venerat. as f. of the settlem. at N. By fam. rec. he was of Bedfordsh. third s. of Thomas and Rose, b. 8 Oct. 1609; bec. treasr. of the Col. 1649, and was sent to Eng. two yrs. after to prevail on the Council of State to revoke the extra. powers giv. to Coddington, but on his coming to Boston to embark was imprison. 1651. In 1652 he pub. at London his valua. tract, a narrative of the persecut. of his friends here; after long serv. in Eng. he was made dept.-gov. of the unit. col. of R. I. and Providence Planta. in 1669, and 70, again agent to Eng. but d. here 20 Apr. 1676, in his will, made that day, call. hims. a. 66 yrs. old. He names in it two ws. the first a d. of John Harges of Bedfordsh. and the name of the other is unkn. yet he had no ch. says Backus, I. 443. By three of his brs. the name has been hon. perpet. in that prov. and state. Ano. physician was *JOHN of Newbury 1638, wh. bef. com. from Eng. had m. Martha, sis. of Sir Richard Saltonstall, was freem. 22 May 1639, and perhaps rep. the same yr. rem. ten yrs. after to Boston, and was noted in his profess. as also for keep. fine horses. He d. Nov. 1664, in his will of 26 Aug. preced. he ment. wid. Martha, made extrix. s. John, d. Jemima, wh. had m. 6 Nov. 1656, Robert Drew of B. and the ch. of Jemima, names John, and Eliz. His wid. d. 19 Sept. 1680, aged 85. Curious confus. is obs. in Geneal. Reg. XIII. 14 and 15, where are copies, correct. from Prob. Rec. Vols. I. and IV. wherein the wid. is twice call. Martha in the will, yet a few, very few mos. after the inv. purport. to be of her late h. as est. of Mr. John C. is said to be sw. by Eliz. The amt. was large, and part of it was stoves for sav. fire wood, for wh. the Gen. Ct. had giv. him patent, 1652 and 6 for his life. How much it anticip. Dr. Franklin's, of a hundred yrs. later, I suppose can never be learn. but if any one will overcome the above ment. contradict. between will and inv. by find. the orig. papers, he will be more happy than my dilig. search. JOHN, Weymouth 1653. JOHN, Hartford, an orig. propr. rem. to Farmington, there d. 22 Nov. 1712, at gr. age. He had, perhaps, John, wh. d. 1709; Matthew; and nine ds. Mary, b. a. 1667, wh. m. Samuel Huntington; Sarah, w. of Thomas Root; both of Lebanon; Abigail, wh. m. 23 Aug. 1699, Joseph Pixley of Westfield; Rachel, w. of Caleb Jones of Hebron; Eliz. wid. of Thomas Gridley sen.; Rebecca, w. of Samuel Wood; both of Farmington; Martha, w. of Thomas Clark of Milford; Hannah, bapt. 4 Apr. 1680, wh. m. Joseph Woodruff of Farmington, and d. bef. her f.; and Martha, then unm. * JOHN, Saybrook 1640, may have bef. been at Wethersfield, and later at Milford, rep. for S. 1651 to 1664, is nam. in the royal chart. of 1662, and was some yrs. rep. for Milford, had s. John; Joseph, wh. d. bef. his f. and perhaps others, beside sev. ds. tho. only Rebecca is nam. and sec. w. Mary, wid. of John Fletcher; and d. 1674. JOHN, Springfield, m. 1647, Eliz. d. of Rowland Stebbins, and d. 1684, leav. John; Sarah, b. 27 Dec. 1649; and Mary. JOHN, Hampton, d. 18 May 1658. JOHN, Saybrook, perhaps s. of the John of S. bef. ment. m. 16 Oct. 1650, Rebecca Parker, had Rebecca, b. 26 Jan. 1653; John, 17 Nov. 1655; James, 29 Sept. 1657, d. at two yrs. and the f. was k. by a cart 21 Sept. 1677. His wid. m. a Spencer, and d. 9 Jan. 1683. Very difficult it may be at Saybrook to arrange all the Johns, for a gravestone at Lyme, the E. part, formerly, of S. stands over one, wh. d. 1719, aged 82, of wh. I find not b. Possib. the numeral may be wrong. JOHN, New London, rem. 1656, perhaps was a carpenter of Norwich 1680, and d. 1709, leav. John, and five other ch. JOHN, Boston, mariner, and merch. m. Mary, d. of Joshua Atwater, had only ch. Mary, b. May 1681. He d. of smallpox in Barbary, prob. a prisoner, and his wid. m. 8 Oct. 1694, John Coney, and d. 12 Apr. 1726. The d. m. 12 June 1701, Rev. Ebenezer Pemberton, and had two other hs. JOHN, Exeter, call. sen. when he took o. of fidel. 30 Nov. 1677; but perhaps that was only to disting. him from ano. JOHN, call. jun. wh. at the same place, on the same day, went thro. the same formality. * JOHN, Boston, physician, s. of that John, wh. came to B. from Newbury, perhaps b. in Eng. freem. 1673, was rep. 1689, and 90, and d. 17, was bur. 19 Dec. 1690. By w. Martha, d. of John, not of William Whittingham, had, beside Eliz. perhaps the youngest, wh. was w. of Richard Hubbard, mariner, and, next, m. 18 Aug. 1703, Rev. Cotton Mather, as his sec. w. John, b. 27 Jan. 1668, H. C. 1687; William, 19 Dec. 1670; Samuel, 10 Nov. 1673, prob. d. soon; Samuel, again, 10 Nov. 1677. A sec. w. Eliz. whose surname is not heard, unless it were Williams, outliv. him but few days, and in her will of 2 Jan. names Nathaniel Williams excor. call. him br. wh. may mean more than ch. relat. and gives prop. to Eliz. (the d. of her h. by former w.) wh. was then unm. JOHN, New Haven, m. 1661, Sarah, d. of George Smith, but may have had sec. w. Mary, as had one John there 1686. JOHN, Springfield, s. of John of the same, took o. of alleg. 31 Dec. 1678. * JOHN, Northampton, s. of William, was rep. 1699, 1700, 1, and 3, and d. 3 Sept. 1704. He m. 12 July 1677, Rebecca, d. of Thomas Cooper of Springfield, had Sarah, b. 20 Apr. foll. and next mo. his w. d. On 20 Mar. 1679 he m. Mary, d. of the Elder John Strong, had John, 28 Oct. foll.; Nathaniel, 13 May 1681; Ebenezer, 18 Oct. 1682; Increase, 8 Apr. 1684; Mary, 27 Oct. 1685; Rebecca, 22 Nov. 1687; Experience, 30 Oct. 1689; Abigail, Mar. 1692; Noah, 28 Mar. 1694; Thankful, 13 Feb. 1696, d. in few weeks; and Josiah, 11 June 1697. He was deac. and eleven of his ch. m. and had fams. JOHN, Rowley, s. of Richard, m. Mary Poor, perhaps d. of the first John of Newbury, had Richard, b. 1677; John, 1679; Judah, 1682; Ebenezer, 1689; Jonathan, 1691; Joseph, and Benjamin tw. 1693; and four ds. was freem. 1684. JOHN, Newton, s. of Hugh, liv. at Muddy riv. first, had w. Abigail, and s. John. His f. gave him a farm 1681 in N. and his w. d. 2 Jan. 1682. He took sec. w. 1684, Eliz. Norman, had William, b. 20 June 1686; Ann, 18 May 1688; Martha, 11 Jan. 1690; Esther, 1 Mar. 1692; Hannah, 1693, d. young; and Moses, 20 June 1695, posthum. for his will was pro. 25 Mar. preced. JOHN, Roxbury, m. 18 Nov. 1680, Lydia Buckminster, had Eliz. b. 7 Dec. 1681, bapt. 3 Aug. 1684; John, b. 26 Dec. 1683; and Samuel, 14 Feb. 1686. JOHN, Lynn, prob. youngest s. of William of the same, m. 13 July 1681, Susanna Story, wh. may have been wid. of the sec. William, had William, b. 24 Apr. 1682; Mary, 8 Feb. 1685; and perhaps others. JOHN, Simsbury, s. of Hon. Daniel, m. 1685, Mary, eldest d. of Christopher Crow of Windsor, had Hannah, b. 6 Aug. 1686; John; Mary; Jemima; Martha, 19 Mar. 1697; Solomon, 20 May 1699; Eliz. 16 May 1701; Sarah, 28 Oct. 1702, d. young; Daniel, 31 Dec. 1704; Ann, 12 Jan. 1707, d. young; and Benoni, 21 Oct. 1708; and d. Sept. 1715. ‡*JOHN, Boston, s. of John of the same, physician, was a promin. politician, speaker of the House of reps. 1709, and after of the Counc. m. 30 Apr. 1691, Sarah Shrimpton, d. of Jonathan, had Mary, b. 12 Feb. 1692; Sarah, 17 Sept. 1693; both d. young; Martha, 25 Mar. 1695; John, 15 Dec. 1698; Sarah, again, 18 Jan. 1704; Martha, again, 26 June 1706; Sarah, again, 7 May 1708; and Eliz. 27 Feb. 1710; beside sec. Mary, prob. 1700. He d. 6 Dec. 1728. His first w. d. 20 Nov. 1717, and he took sec. w. 10 Apr. foll. Eliz. Hutchinson, and for third w. m. 15 July 1725, Sarah, wid. of Presid. Leverett, wh. had been wid. of William Harris, d. of Richard Crisp, and d. 24 Apr. 1744, as w. of Rev. Benjamin Colman. JOHN, Exeter, s. of Nathaniel, ord. 21 Sept. 1698, m. Eliz. d. of Rev. Benjamin Woodbridge, had Benjamin, Nathaniel, Deborah, and Ward, and d. 25 July 1705. JONAS, Cambridge, by w. Sarah had Thomas, b. 2 Dec. 1642, d. at 6 yrs.; Sarah, 15 Sept. 1644; Jonas, 4 Sept. 1647; and Mary, 15 Nov. 1649, wh. d. young. His w. d. in Feb. foll. and he m. 30 July foll. Eliz. Clark, had Eliz.; Thomas, 2 Mar. 1653, H. C. 1670; John, 30 May 1655, d. young; Timothy; (wh. all, as well as the ch. of former w. were prob.

bapt. but the dates are not kn.) ; Samuel, bapt. 6 Nov. 1659 ; Abigail, 4 May 1662 ; and Mary, 12 Mar. 1665 ; for wh. Mitchell's Reg. is the proof. This w. d. 21 or 25 Mar. 1673, aged 41, and he m. 19 Aug. foll. Eliz. Cook, wh. surv. had John, again, 7 Aug. 1674, d. young ; John, again, 3 Nov. 1675, d. young ; Nathaniel, 27 Oct. 1677 ; Joseph, 5 May 1679 ; Hannah, 16 Dec. 1680, d. very soon ; and Susanna, 20 Oct. 1682. He was rul. elder, and d. 11 Jan. 1700, aged 79. I presume he was that skilful navigator, sent with Andrews by the Mass. governm. in 1653, to ascert. the latit. of a point on the sea shore at the E. as in Belkn. I. 57, is explain. Sarah, d. of his first w. m. 23 Feb. 1662, Samuel Greene, as his sec. w. ; Eliz. d. of his sec. w. m. 23 July 1672, John Woodmansey ; and Mary m. John Bonner, and d. 20 Apr. 1697. JONAS, Boston 1677, s. of the preced. freem. 1678, m. Susanna, only d. of Richard Bennett, d. 14 Jan. 1738, aged 90. JONATHAN, Newbury, m. 15 May 1683, Lydia Titcomb, had Oliver, b. 6 Feb. 1684 ; Samuel, 18 Mar. 1688 ; Jonathan, 24 May 1689 ; Lydia, 17 May 1691 ; and Eliz. 10 May 1694. JONATHAN, Dover, m. 6 Sept. 1686, Mary Magoon, perhaps d. of Henry. JOSEPH, Windsor, br. of Daniel of the same, perhaps had been of Cambridge, and freem. 4 Mar. 1635, was early at W. and d. 1641, leav. Joseph, and Mary, wh. m. 26 Nov. 1656, John Strong. JOSEPH, Dedham, may first have been at Dorchester, by w. Alice, had Joseph, b. 27 July 1642 ; Benjamin, 9 Feb. 1644 ; Ephraim, 4 Feb. 1646 ; Daniel, 29 Sept. 1647 ; Mary, 12 June 1649 ; and Sarah, 20 Feb. 1651 ; rem. to or liv. at Medfield, there had John, 28 Oct. 1652 ; Nathaniel, 6 Oct. 1658 ; and Rebecca, 16 Aug. 1660 ; was freem. 1653 ; took sec. w. 25 June 1663, Mary Allen, had Joseph, 14 June 1664 ; John, again, 31 May 1666 ; and Jonathan, 14 Mar. 1669 ; both of the last two d. bef. mid. life ; and by third w. Mary he had Esther, 12 Mar. 1671 ; and Thomas, 6 Aug. 1672, wh. d. at 18 yrs. and the f. d. 6 Jan. 1684. His will of 24 June 1682, pro. 4 July 1684, ment. w. Alice, s. Joseph, Ephraim, John, and Nathaniel; ds. Rebecca, wh. m. 1 May 1679, John Richardson ; ano. w. of John Adams ; ano. as is conject. was w. of Bowers, bec. it names a gr.ch. John B. ‡JOSEPH, Newport 1639, youngest br. of John of the same, one of the found. of the Bapt. ch. there, was an Assist. 1658, liv. most of his latter yrs. at Westerly, had Joseph, b. 2 Apr. 1643 ; and d. 1 June 1694, aged 75. His w. was Margaret, wh. d. 1694, but her surname is not heard. In the will of his br. Thomas, we find his other ch. liv. 1674, were John, William, Joshua, Thomas, Susanna, Mary, Sarah, Carew, or Carey, and Eliz. JOSEPH, Saybrook, s. of the first John of the same, was, perhaps, that freem. of Conn. 1658, and d. 1663. JOSEPH, Newport, eldest s. of Joseph of the same, m. 16 Nov. 1664, Bethia, d. of Samuel Hubbard of

Westerly, had Judith, b. 12 Oct. 1667; Joseph, 4 Apr. 1670; Samuel, 29 Dec. 1672; John, 25 Aug. 1675; Bethia, 11 Apr. 1678; Mary 27 Dec. 1680; Susanna, 31 Aug. 1683; Thomas, 17 Mar. 1686; and William, 21 Apr. 1688. His w. d. 17 Apr. 1707; and he d. 11 Jan. 1727, many yrs. after rem. to Westerly with his f. JOSEPH, Haverhill, took o. of fidel. 28 Nov. 1677. Perhaps he was s. of Edmund of Gloucester, and m. 27 Mar. 1682, Hannah Davis, possib. d. of Ephraim of H. and d. 29 Nov. 1696. JOSEPH, Haddam, s. of William of the same, m. Ruth, d. of Jared Spencer, had William, Joseph, Daniel, John, Catharine, and Hannah, says Goodwin; but no date of m. b. or d. of any one of these could he give. JOSIAH, Windsor, eldest s. of Hon. Daniel of the same, propound. for freem. 1672, m. Mary, wid. of Christopher Crow, d. of Benjamin Burr (wh. was not a few yrs. older than him, and had brot. many ch. to her first h.) had only Josiah, b. 13 Jan. 1683. LATHAM, Newport, s. of Jeremiah, of wh. it is not easy to learn more. MALACHI, Ipswich 1648. MATTHEW, Boston, m. 4 June 1655, Abigail, d. of Elias Maverick, had Abigail, b. 17 June 1656, was a mariner, and rem. prob. 1661, or earlier, to Marblehead, where certain. he was 1668–74. NATHANIEL, Newbury, freem. 1668, m. 25 Nov. 1663, Eliz. d. of Henry Somerby, had Nathaniel, b. 5 Dec. 1664, d. at 6 mos.; Nathaniel, again, 13 Mar. 1666; Thomas, 9 Feb. 1668; John, 24 June 1670, H. C. 1690, third min. of Exeter; Henry, 5 July 1673; Daniel, 16 Dec. 1675; Sarah, 12 Jan. 1678; Josiah, 7 May 1682; Eliz. 15 May 1684; Judith, Jan. 1687; and Mary, 25 Mar. 1689; d. on board the sh. Six Friends, soon after sail. in the expedit. against Quebec, 25 Aug. 1690, from an injury, aged 46. His wid. m. 8 Aug. 1698, Rev. John Hale. NATHANIEL, Northampton, eldest s. of William of the same, m. 8 May 1663, Mary, d. of Thomas Meakins, had Mary, b. 3 Mar. foll. and Sarah, 25 Aug. 1665; and d. 30 Mar. 1669. His wid. m. 14 Dec. foll. John Allis. ‡NATHANIEL, Plymouth, s. of Thomas, was Secr. of the Col. under the usurpa. and of the Counc. of Andros 1687, d. 31 Jan. 1717, aged 72, leav. no ch. NATHANIEL, Newbury, s. of Nathaniel of the same, m. 15 Dec. 1685, Eliz. Toppan, eldest d. of Peter of the same, had Eliz. b. 27 July 1686; but I kn. nothing more. NICHOLAS, Cambridge 1632, arr. at Boston 16 Sept. in the Lion, rem. to Hartford, where tradit. says, he built, 1635, the first fram. ho. for capt. Talcott, wh. must be one, if not two yrs. anticipat. He d. 2 July 1680, leav. s. Thomas, and one or two ds. PEACEFUL, a soldier, Dec. 1675, in Turner's comp. PIERCY, or PERCIVAL, Boston, freem. 1675, by w. Eliz. had John, b. 1 Nov. 1665; Mary, 18 Oct. 1667; Robert, 20 Apr. 1673; and Ruhama, 4 Apr. 1678; beside Gamaliel, Sarah, and Mercy; d. Apr. 1716. His will, made 17 Nov. 1700, pro. by his wid. Eliz. 30 Apr. after his d.

names s. Gamaliel, ds. Buchanan, Mary Morse, Ruhama Williamson, Sarah, Mary, and gr.s. Percival. RICHARD, Plymouth, a passeng. in the Mayflower, d. soon after land. without w. or ch. RICHARD, Rowley, by w. Alice, said to be the sec. m. in that town, had Judah, b. 1644; and John, 1650, beside three ds. ROBERT, Stratford, among freem. in 1669, had m. some yrs. bef. 1665, Sarah, wid. of Francis Stiles, had by her no ch. but by sec. w. had John, b. a. 1684; and Hannah, a. 1687; both nam. in his will of 13 Nov. 1694. He d. five days after. *ROBERT*, Boston, min. at King's chap. 1686; but when he rem. is not told. Prob. it was on the overthr. of Andros in Apr. 1689. ROWLAND, Dedham, d. 2 Feb. 1639. SAMUEL, Concord, s. of Arthur, m. Rachel Nichols, whose f. is not kn. to me, had Samuel, b. 26 Oct. 1676; William, 30 Dec. 1679; Sarah, 4 July 1681, but this ch. b. at Boston; Rachel, 17 Apr. 1683; Susanna, 26 Apr. 1689; Hannah, 11 Apr. 1691; Benjamin, 13 Oct. 1693; and Arthur, 30 Jan. 1696. His w. d. 1722, and he d. 30 Jan. 1730. SAMUEL, Hatfield, was k. by the Ind. 19 Oct. 1675. SAMUEL, Wethersfield, rem. perhaps to Stamford, at Milford 1669, thence to Hempstead, L. I. m. Hannah, d. of Rev. Robert Fordham, and may in 1685 have been of New Haven. SAMUEL, Boston, by w. Bethia had Samuel, b. 1674. SAMUEL, Northampton, s. of William, m. 1 Mar. 1682, Eliz. d. of Alexander Edwards, had Eliz. b. 22 Jan. 1683; Sarah, 21 Aug. 1686; Samuel, 20 Aug. 1688; Benoni, 12 Mar. 1692, d. young; Joanna, May 1695; Benjamin, 23 Mar. 1697, d. young; Obadiah, 26 Sept. 1698, d. soon; ano. s. Nov. 1699, d. very soon; and Miriam, 21 Sept. 1702; and he d. 5 Aug. 1729; of all his ch. only Samuel and Sarah surv. SAMUEL, Windsor, s. of Daniel, m. 1687, Mehitable, d. of Timothy Thrall, had Samuel, b. 10 Nov. 1688; David, 7 Apr. 1696; Joseph, 13 July 1697; and Nathaniel, 11 Oct. 1699. His w. d. 15 Aug. 1723. More than one other Samuel was of Boston in early days, but I have not learn. any thing of either to convince me, that he was inhab. here bef. 1692. THADDEUS, Falmouth, m. 1663, Eliz. d. of Michael Mitton, was lieut. in the war with the E. Ind. 1689, and was k. 1690 by them at F. His wid. d. at Boston 1736, aged 91. Of his ch. Isaac is above ment. ano. was a wid. Hervey at Boston, 1719, and Eliz. was w. of capt. Edward Tyng. Willis, I. 208. * THOMAS, Plymouth, a carpenter, came in the Ann 1623, m. Susanna, d. of wid. Mary Ring (bef. 1631, when in her mo.'s will he is nam.), had Andrew; James; Susanna, wh. m. 3 Nov. 1658, Barnabas Lothrop; William; John; and Nathaniel. He was rep. 1651 and 5, m. sec. w. 1664, wid. Alice Nichols, d. of Richard Hallet, liv. in 1670 at Harwich, where he had third w. Eliz. Crow, perhaps wid. of John, and d. 24 Mar. 1697, aged, says the gr.stone, 98, or more prob. only 92, since in 1664 he made o. that he was a. 59 yrs. old. But to this suffic. longev. the "Guide to Plymouth," 255, would make alarming addit. in his note, "suppos. mate of the Mayflower." We can hardly doubt, that the oldest surv. of that memo. voyage, within the bounds of the Old Colony, would have been too well known to need a weak tradit. to lean on; and that officer of 1620 must have been older than the oldest liv. in 1697, had he not been d. *many* yrs. bef. In 1627 this Thomas, not the mate, had sh. in the div. of lds. as com. in the Ann, not Mayflower. THOMAS, Newport 1638, elder br. of John of the same, bapt. soon after b. 31 Mar. 1605, one of the found. of the first ch. of Bapt. 1644, and d. 2 Dec. 1674, without ch. leav. est. to childr. of his br. Joseph in his will, where alone we find their names. ‡ * ‖ THOMAS, Boston, merch. had first liv. at Dorchester, 1636, selectman there 1641 and 2, ar. co. 1638, freem. 14 Mar. 1639, a capt. in 1653, and after head of the Boston reg. rep. 1651, and many yrs. more, speaker in 1662, and sev. yrs. later, chos. an Assist. 1673, and d. 28 July 1678. His first w. was Mary, by wh. he had Mehitable, b. 18 Apr. 1640; Eliz. 22 May 1642; and Deborah, bapt. 9 June 1644. Other ch. were Thomas, the only s. and Leah, perhaps, both b. in Eng. but his will, made shortly bef. his d. instr. us that she was w. of Thomas Baker, Deborah, w. of Nathaniel Byfield, and Eliz. Stevens among ds. and sev. gr.ch. with conting. provision for gr. gr.ch. and his wid. was Ann. Surnames of either w. are not kn. High should be our esteem of C. wh. was one of only two mem. of the legislat. the Boston reps. in 1656, that voted against the law for putt. to d. Quakers, wh. ret. after banishm. Dr. Harris, with doubtful propriety, suppos. him to be one of three brs. Bray, Joseph, and Thomas, of D. 1630, commemo. in epit. on a gr.stone:

> Here lie three Clarks, their accounts are even,
> Entered on earth, carried up to heaven.

Ano. THOMAS of Boston, early, adm. of the ch. 18 July 1640, and perhaps the freem. of 2 June 1641, was a blacksmith, and may have liv. on N. side of the harbor, call. Winisemet, now Chelsea, by w. Eliz. had Cornelius, b. Dec. 1639, bapt. 19 July foll.; Jacob, 16, bapt. 22 May 1642; Rachel, 6 July 1646, d. at 7 yrs. and perhaps Benjamin, 4 May 1656. THOMAS, New Haven 1645, prob. d. bef. 1648. THOMAS, Lynn 1640, rem. to Reading, there d. 1693. * ‖ THOMAS, Boston, call. jr. but tho. b. in Eng. he may not be s. of the Hon. Thomas, yet he liv. prob. some time, earlier or later, at Dorchester, was of ar. co. 1644, more than once its capt. rep. 1673–6, and d. 13 Mar. 1683. He was one of the wealthiest merch. of B. and by his will of 15 Aug. 1679, anew declar. 22 May 1680, pro. 22 Mar. 1683, it is judg. that only two ch. were then liv. Mehitable Warren, and Eliz. wh. had m. 28 May 1661, Mr. John

Freak, and was then w. of Elisha Hutchinson. To his wid. Eliz. he
gives £80 a yr. and £50 in plate, to s. Warren £100, and to eldest s. of
his d. Mehitable W. at 21 yrs. of age, or m. with consent of parents,
£1000 ; but if she have no s. this to be equal. div. among ds. if God
give them, also to ea. of said ds. at 21 yrs. or m. with consent £300 ; to
s. Elisha H. £100, and to eldest s. of his d. Eliz. H. at 21 yrs. or m.
with consent £1000 ; then to many relat. in Eng. to sis. Ann Haynes,
Dorothy Muscate, and Joan Smith, sis. Stoughton, cous. i. e. neph.
Thomas Smith ; then to the ch. of wh. he was mem. £50, to ten of his
poor kindr. £5 ea. to the poor of Boston £50, to the poor of Dorchester £20, to the art. comp. to purch. arms for poor mem. £10, with
this striking final provis. " if both my ds. fail of posterity," he gives " for
a good hospital in Boston £1500," and he made overseers his kinsm. Wil-
liam Stoughton, capt. John Richards, Mr. William Tailer, and Mr. Thom-
as Smith, and £10 to ea. of them. It is not easy to discrimin. betw. this
Thomas and the first of the name, wh. was the speaker. Perhaps in
Geneal. Reg. V. 398, the two in some particul. are confus. THOMAS,
Reading, had first w. Else, wh. d. 28 June 1658, and he m. 31 Aug. foll.
Mary, had Eliz. b. 3 Nov. 1659 ; and Thomas, 13 Oct. 1661. THOMAS,
Hartford, s. of Nicholas, made freem. 1658, had (says Hinman, 203)
Thomas, Daniel, and Joseph. THOMAS, Boston, early liv. on Noddle's
isl. had d. Sarah, that m. 11 June 1662, George Hiskett. THOMAS,
New Haven, master of the iron works there 1669. THOMAS, Ipswich,
freem. 1674. THOMAS, Scituate 1674, by Deane lightly conject. to be
s. or gr.s. of the mate of the Mayflower, because he came from Plymouth,
m. 1676, Martha, d. of Richard Curtis, had Thomas, Joseph, Daniel,
Samuel, Nathaniel, Mercy, Deborah, Rachel, Ann, Charity, and Mary.
Bef. that m. he serv. in Philip's war. THOMAS, Chelmsford, s. of Jonas,
ord. 1677, by w. Mary had Lucy ; Eliz. both liv. to m. beside sev. wh.
d. young ; Jonas, b. 20 Dec. 1684 ; and Thomas, 28 Sept. 1694. His
w. d. 2 Dec. 1700, and he m. 2 Oct. 1702, Eliz. d. of Rev. Samuel
Whiting, and d. 7 Dec. 1704. He was an able man, and by the exercise
of strong common sense, that (in so early a day) too many of the clergy
were afraid to show, saved one woman, accus. as a witch. THOMAS,
Yarmouth, m. 15 Feb. 1682, Rebecca, d. of the sec. John Miller of the
same, had Susanna, b. 21 Feb. 1684 ; and Thomas, 25 Dec. 1685.
THOMAS, Charlestown, m. 15 Oct. 1684, Sarah, d. of Joseph Lynde of
the same, had Thomas, b. 22 June foll. He liv. on Malden side, I presume, d. early, and his wid. m. 12 Jan. 1692, Seth Sweetser. THOMAS,
Newbury, s. of Nathaniel, by w. Sarah had Sarah, b. 25 Dec. 1690 ;
Thomas, 2 Sept. 1692 ; Nathaniel, 23 Oct. 1694 ; Martha, 12 Apr.
1696; Mary, 16 Aug. 1698; and Daniel, 26 Jan. 1701. * TIMOTHY,

Boston, an import. man, was constable 1693 ; rep. 1700, capt. and some
yrs. selectman. He was s. of the first Jonas by sec. w. d. 15 June 1737,
aged 80. TRISTRAM, or THURSTON, Plymouth, came from Ipswich, Co.
Suffk. in the Francis 1634, aged 44, prob. with w. Faith, tho. not nam.
in the list of the custom ho. certain. with d. Faith, 15, wh. m. 6 Jan.
1635, Edward Dotey, and next m. 14 Mar. 1667, John Phillips, and
surv. him. He had rem. to Duxbury, and d. 6 Dec. 1661 ; had s. Thurston, and Henry, both imbec. put under guardians. URIAH, Roxbury, s.
of Hugh, by w. Joanna, in Boston, had Uriah, b. 5 Oct. 1677 ; but by w.
Mary had at R. Thomas, 29, bapt. 30 Nov. 1679 ; John, 10, bapt. 12 Feb.
1682 ; Mary, bapt. 26 Aug. 1683, at the same time with her br. Uriah ;
and a ch. b. in Apr. 1685, that d. soon ; Hannah ; Richard ; rem. 1693 to
Watertown, and had Peter, 12 Mar. 1694, H. C. 1712, a celebr. min. of
Danvers, progenit. of a num. line ; Benjamin, 6 Nov. 1696 ; Nathaniel,
20 June 1698 ; and Samuel, 15 July 1700. Soon after his w. d. and he
m. 21 Nov. of that yr. third w. Martha Pease, had Susanna, 13 Nov.
1701, d. young ; and Pease, bapt. 2 Aug. 1703. He was selectman
1699 and 1700 ; and d. 26 July 1721, in his will of 27 May preced. of
wh. s. Richard was excor. names w. liv. ch. Peter, Richard, Benjamin,
Uriah, Nathaniel, Samuel, Mary Kimball, and Hannah Clark, and for
the wid. and ch. of his s. John, as well as for Eliz. Hastings on acco. of
dec. s. Thomas, has tender remembr. yet it is not seen in Bond, that s.
Pease was ment. in it. The name is pervert. to Uzijah in Geneal. Reg.
V. 394. § † ‡ WALTER, Newport, eldest s. of Jeremiah (an absurd tradit.
that he was b. a. 1637, on the ocean, prob. had its origin from the sound
of his name, Water), by first w. Content, bur. 27 Mar. 1666, had, perhaps, near half of his ch. but one was a s. whose name is not told, and
only Mary, b. 11 Jan. 1662, is ment. By sec. w. m. 1666, Hannah, d.
of Richard Scott sec. of N. wh. d. 24 July 1681, he had Hannah, 28
Oct. 1667 ; beside other ds. Catharine, Content, and Deliverance, of wh.
it is not kn. whether the sec. w. or a third was mo. of the youngest.
His s. Jeremiah, b. 21 Feb. 1674, wh. d. young, was prob. his only one,
if Francis, b. 17 Jan. 1673, were a d. as is supposed. The third w. was
Freeborn, d. of famous Roger Williams, wid. of Thomas Hart, wh. he
m. 6 Mar. 1683, and wh. d. 10 Dec. 1709. Late in life he m. 1711
fourth w. Sarah, d. of Matthew Prior of L. I. wid. of John Gould. He
was a Quaker, and emin. for attract. confidence of his brethr. had been
dept.-gov. bef. 1676, in wh. yr. of trial he was chos. gov. again in 1686,
made one of Andros' Counc. by K. James II. when he unit. the N. E.
cols. and gov. again after the separat. 1696, 7 and last in 1700, and d. 22
May 1714, aged 74. WESTON, Newport, br. of the preced. m. 25 Dec.
1668, Mary, eldest d. of Peter, not Nicholas (as sometimes said) Easton,

had Mary, b. 11 Jan. 1670; John, 15 July 1672; Weston, 18 Feb. 1675, d. soon; Weston, again, 15 Apr. 1677; and Jeremiah, 29 Nov. 1685. Yet this last may have been ch. of his sec. w. Rebecca, d. of Edward Thurston. WILLIAM, Ipswich, came, prob. in the fleet with Winth. desir. in Oct. 1630, adm. as freem. and was sw. 18 May foll. went with the earliest sett. 1633, to I. and may have rem. to other town bef. his d. for we kn. nothing more of him. WILLIAM, Watertown 1631, freem. 22 May 1639, by w. Margery had Mary, b. 10 Dec. 1640; Eliz. 26 Nov. 1642; Lydia; and rem. to Woburn, there had Hannah, 3 Feb. 1646. He d. 15 Mar. 1682, aged 87, and his wid. d. 11 Oct. 1694, aged 95. Mary m. 27 Dec. 1655 (rather young) William Locke; Eliz. m. 20 Dec. 1659, George Brush, both of Woburn; Hannah m. 1667, William Frissell of Concord; and Lydia had two ds. and was a wid. when in his will of 10 Dec. 1681, her f. provid. for them. A careful writer in Geneal. Reg. V. 248, 9, conject. that this man emb. at London in the Plain Joan, and his w. in the Primrose, in May and July respectiv. 1635, both for Virg. but he next yr. own. to me, that he was satisf. of the contra. WILLIAM, Salem, was suppos. by Mr. Felt to be the man wh. wish. adm. as freem. 1630, tho. in my opin. he came first in 1634, by the Mary and John. He kept an ordinary, and was censur. by the governm. 1645, for offence in petitn. to Eng. See Winth. II. 301. By a former w. he had a s. and d. and by w. Catharine (wh. surv. him, and in May 1647 was licens. to cont. the tavern) had four more ch. Est. was good acc. inv. giv. by the wid. July 1647, up to £587, 3, 2. * WILLIAM, Dorchester, a. 1636, by w. Sarah had Sarah b. 21 June 1638, d. soon; Jonathan, 1 Oct. 1639; Nathaniel, 27 Jan. 1642; Experience, 30 Mar. 1643; Increase, 1 Mar. 1646, wh. d. at 16 yrs.; Rebecca, a. 1648; John, 1651; Samuel, bapt. 23 Oct. 1653; William, b. 3 July 1656; and Sarah, again, Mar. 1659. He was selectman 1646 and 7, rem. 1659 to Northampton, for wh. he was rep. 1663, and 13 yrs. more, but not consecut. and lieut. in Philip's war. His w. d. 6 Sept. 1675, and he m. 15 Nov. 1676, Sarah, wid. of Thomas Cooper of Springfield, wh. d. 8 May 1688; and he d. 18 July 1690, aged 81. Rebecca m. 9 Dec. 1669, Israel Rust; and Sarah m. 3 Dec. 1675, John Parsons. WILLIAM, Lynn 1640, had Lydia, b. 31 Oct. 1642; Hannah, 11 Jan. 1644; Sarah; Mary; prob. William; Eliz. 6 Oct. 1652; Martha, 15 Apr. 1655, d. under 7 yrs.; and John, 2 Jan. 1659, wh. d. the yr. after his f. that d. 5 Mar. 1683. His will was made 1679, and his wid. Mary d. 19 Aug. 1693; and his d. Hannah d. 26 Oct. foll. WILLIAM, Hartford 1639, serv. of John Crow, rem. to Haddam, d. 1681, leav. William, John, Joseph, Thomas, and sev. ds. WILLIAM, Yarmouth, d. 7 Dec. 1668, prob. unm. giv. his little prop. by nuncup. will to Joseph Benjamin.

WILLIAM, Duxbury, s. of Thomas of Plymouth, m. Martha, d. of Samuel Nash, was surveyor of highways 1659, rem. prob. to Bridgewater, and may have m. 1 Mar. 1660, at P. Sarah Woolcot, whose f. is unkn. to me. He made his will 3 Jan. 1687, and soon after d. leav. as is thot. neither w. nor ch. WILLIAM, Boston, by w. Ann had Joseph, b. 10 Sept. 1659. Ano. WILLIAM of Boston m. 18 Sept. 1661, Martha, d. of George Farr of Lynn, had Samuel, b. 28 June 1663; John, 3 Apr. 1666; and Mary, 22 Mar. 1668. WILLIAM, Lynn, perhaps s. of William of the same, m. 23 Aug. 1669, Elinor Dearnford, as Felt gives the name in Geneal. Reg. V. 95, rem. I conject. to Boston (where his w. on rec. is Ellen), and had Joanna, b. 22 Aug. 1670. WILLIAM, Northampton, s. of the first William of the same, m. 15 July 1680, Hannah, d. of Elder John Strong, had Hannah, b. 5 May 1681; Abigail, 25 Jan. 1683, d. at 4 yrs.; William; Jonathan, 13 May 1688; Thomas, 14 Apr. 1690; Joseph, 1691; Benoni, 1 Feb. 1693; and his w. d. 10 days after. By sec. w. Mary he had Timothy, 9 Oct. 1695; and Gershom, 18 Nov. 1697. He was freem. 1690, and rem. to Lebanon a. 1700, and was a promin. man; but whether he had more ch. or when he d. is uncert. WILLIAM, Saybrook, m. 7 Mar. 1678, Hannah, d. of the sec. Francis Griswold. WILLIAM, Boston, by w. Rachel had William, b. 30 Dec. 1679, was a capt. and the same, or more prob. ano. by w. Rebecca had William, b. 31 Mar. 1681; and either was, or even a third, perhaps, the freem. of 1690. * WILLIAM, Boston, br. of the Hon. John, was rep. 1720-2 & 5. See Hutch. II. On this copious name, in some fam. using e instead of a, and in more end. with e, it seem. best to have uniform. spell. as there exists nothing but confus. in the variety, I have bestow. gr. labor, but feel sure, that many omiss. may be detect. and ought to rejoice if graver failure be not found. Grad. at Harv. count 29, at Yale 27, at Dart. 10 in 1829, prob. 30 more at the other N. E. coll. of wh. at Harv. twelve were clerg. and above twenty as the aggreg. of the other Inst.

CLARY, JOHN, Watertown, m. 5 Feb. 1644, Sarah Cady, perhaps sis. of Nicholas, but Bond, 162, calls the w. Mary Cassell, had Sarah, b. 4 Oct. 1647; perhaps John; and Gershom, 7 Sept. 1650, wh. prob. d. young; rem. to Hadley, and d. 1690, leav. no ch. but giv. his est. to ch. of John and of Sarah his ch. This d. m. 13 Dec. 1667, John Perry of W. Bond's acco. makes the sec. w. of Clary to be Sarah, and that she d. 23 Dec. 1681; but perhaps p. 742 explains some former part of his narr. JOHN, Hatfield, s. of the preced. m. 1670, Ann Dickinson, at Northfield d. 1688, perhaps shot by Ind. He left John, Joseph, and Mary.

CLAUKLIN, THOMAS, Providence 1645.

CLAWSON, JOHN, Providence 1646. STEPHEN, Stamford 1670, then propound. for freem.

CLAY, HUMPHREY, New London 1651, innholder, had w. Catharine, d. Sarah, and rem. a. 1666. JONAS, Salem 1668. JOSEPH, Guilford, m. 18 Apr. 1670, Mary Law, had Mary, b. 10 Jan. 1671; Sarah, 5 Mar. 1674; Hannah, and Eliz. tw. 3 Aug. 1677, both d. young. His w. d. Dec. 1692; and he d. 30 Nov. 1695. THOMAS, Scituate 1643, had been seen in Mass. 1640, by Mr. Felt.

CLAYDON, BARNABAS, Salem 1629, came in June, aged 23, from London. RICHARD, Salem, br. of the preced. came the same yr. aged 34, with w. a d. and a sis. aged 14, accomp. Higginson. He was a wheelwright, but as neither of their party is again heard of, they perhaps went home.

CLAYS, JOHN, Casco 1665. See Hutch. Coll. 398.

CLAYTON, THOMAS, Dover 1650, perhaps rem. to R. I. may have been f. of Ann, sec. w. of Gov. Nicholas Easton, and next, Gov. Henry Bull; and of Sarah, wh. m. 4 Mar. 1674, Matthew Borden.

CLEAR, GEORGE, Newport 1639. JOHN, Boston 1674, a shoemaker. JOHN, Boston, call. 1677, jun. shoemaker, perhaps was s. of the preced.

CLEAVELAND, AARON, Woburn, sec. s. of Moses the first, m. 26 Sept. 1675, Dorcas Wilson, whose f. is unkn. to me, had Dorcas, b. 29 Oct. 1676; Hannah, 18 Nov. 1678, d. next yr.; Aaron, 9 July 1680; Hannah, again, 2 June 1687; Moses, 24 Feb. 1690; Sarah, 5 Mar. 1692; Miriam, 9 Júly 1694; Isabel, 6 Apr. 1697, d. at 17 yrs.; and Benjamin, 16 May 1701. His w. d. at Cambridge, 29 Nov. 1714, and he had, it is said, sec. w. Prudence, but d. 14 Sept. 1716. Prob. that Rev. Aaron, H. C. 1735, wh. d. 18 Aug. 1757, at Philadelphia, in the ho. of Dr. Franklin, was his gr.s. EDWARD, and ISAAC, brs. of the preced. acc. fam. tradit. had fams. but neither the dates of m. nor of b. of ch. nor names of mos. nor residence of fs. can be found. ENOCH, youngest s. of the first Moses, was a tailor, and liv. in var. places, had w. Eliz. and eldest s. Jonathan, ano. s. and a d. whose names are not heard. He d. at Concord 1729, and his wid. d. soon after. JOSIAH, Chelmsford 1691, br. of the preced. had serv. in Ind. war, by w. Mary had Josiah, b. 7 Oct. 1690; and Joseph, 13 June 1695; rem. to Canterbury, Conn. there had Henry, perhaps 1697; Mary, prob. 1699; John; Rachel; Lydia, 7 Dec. 1704; d. Deliverance, 13 July 1707, and d. Abiel, posthum. 9 Oct. 1709; the f. d. 26 Apr. preced. MOSES, Woburn, came, says fam. tradit. (with his master, a joiner, of wh. he was apprent.) from Ipswich, Co. Suffk. m. 26 Sept. 1648, Ann, d. of Edward Winn, had Moses, b. 1 Sept. 1651; Hannah, 4 Aug. 1653; Aaron, 10 Jan. 1655; Samuel, 9 June 1657; Miriam, 10 July 1659; Joanna, 19 Sept. 1661, d. soon; Edward, 20 May 1663; Josiah, 26 Feb. 1667; Isaac, 11 May 1669; Joanna, again, 5 Apr. 1670; and Enoch, 1 Aug.

1671 ; and d. 9 Jan. 1702. Hannah m. 24 Sept. 1677, Thomas Hensher
of W.; Miriam m. a Fosdick of Charlestown; and Joanna m. a Keyes.
MOSES, Woburn, eldest s. of the preced. m. 4 Oct. 1676, Ruth Norton,
had Ann, b. 7 Nov. 1677; and Joseph, 31 Mar. 1686. SAMUEL,
Canterbury, br. of the preced. m. 17 May 1680, Jane, d. of Solomon
Keyes of Chelmsford, wh. d. 4 Nov. 1681. He m. 23 May foll. Persis,
d. of Richard Hildreth, wh. d. 22 Feb. 1698; and he prob. d. 1736.
His ch. b. at Chelmsford were Persis, 21 Apr. 1683; Samuel, 12 Jan.
1685; and Joseph, 18 July 1689; but after his rem. to Canterbury
in 1693, he had Mary, 14 June 1696; and by a third w. m. 25 July
1699, wid. Margaret Fish, he had Abigail, 23 Apr. 1700; and Timothy,
Aug. 1702. It is suppos. that all of this name, sometimes writ. Cleve-
land, derive from Moses the first; and in 1834 seven had been gr. at
Yale, five at Harv. and eleven at other N. E. coll. beside the honora.
M. D. to eight more.

CLEMENT, CLEMENS, CLEMENTS, or CLEMENCE, ABRAHAM, Newbury,
m. 10 Mar. 1683, Hannah Gove, prob. d. of Edward of Hampton, had
Edmund, b. 3 Mar. 1684, rem. to Hampton, and there, Coffin says, had
seven more. Perhaps he was s. of the first Robert of Haverhill, and
took o. of alleg. 28 Nov. 1677. AUSTIN or AUGUSTINE, Dorchester, a
painter, came from Southampton in the James of London, Apr. 1635,
but may have been on this side of the water in 1632; yet greater is the
prob. that he went home in 1636, and came again in May 1637, by the
Mary Ann of Yarmouth, tho. against either conject. strong suggest. arise.
By w. Eliz. he had Eliz. prob. b. in Eng. certain. the eldest ch.; Samuel, b. 29 Sept. 1635; Joanna, 19 Nov. 1638, d. soon; John, 21 Oct.
1639, wh. prob. d. young; and was freem. 25 May 1636, rem. to Boston
1652, but after some yrs. went back to D. there d. 1 Oct. 1674. He
had good est. and in his will of 30 Jan. 1672 ment. w. Eliz. s. Samuel,
and d. Eliz. with her seven ch. DANIEL, Haverhill, s. of Robert, sw.
alleg. Nov. 1677. JAMES, Marshfield, m. 28 Dec. 1674, Martha Deane,
whose mo. was a wid. that came in the Planter 1635; but his parentage
is unkn. and he d. in few weeks after m. His wid. m. next yr. James
Powell, and wh. he was, I ask in vain. JASPER, Middletown 1660, had
a w. in Eng. but desir. one here, d. 1677, leav. w. but no ch. ‡JOB,
Haverhill 1646, eldest s. of Robert, b. in Eng. a tanner, was freem.
1647, m. 25 Dec. 1644, Margaret Dummer, wh. must have been a d. of
one of the three brs. Richard, Stephen, or Thomas, rem. to Dover, there
serv. 1655 on gr. jury, had sec. w. Lydia, and took for the third, 16
July 1673, Joanna, wid. of Thomas Leighton, was made couns. of the
Prov. 1683, and d. 1683. His wid. d. 15 Jan. 1704. Of ch. only Job
is ment. wh. liv. to 1717, but wh. of the three ws. was his mo. I do not

learn from Belkn. I. 410, or Pike's Journ. or Mirick, 25, 6, 30, or Kelly's MS. * JOHN, Haverhill 1645, m. 1649, perhaps as sec. w. Sarah, d. of John Osgood of Andover, had Rebecca, I suppose to be meant by the name (call. in the will of gr.f. O. next yr. Bakah), perhaps others, may have been 1651 at Marblehead, was rep. 1654, and d. by shipwreck on voyage to Eng. not long after. JOHN, Haverhill, s. of Robert, sw. alleg. 28 Nov. 1677, m. 28 Sept. 1688, Eliz. Richardson, perhaps d. of Joseph of Woburn, and rem. to Lynn. RICHARD, Providence, perhaps s. of Thomas, by w. Sarah had Sarah, b. 11 Nov. 1687; Mary, 24 May 1689; Ann, 11 Dec. 1690; Thomas, 6 Aug. 1693; Abigail, 4 Dec. 1695; and Richard, 19 July 1698. * ROBERT, Haverhill, br. of John, came, it is said, from London 1642, bring. many ch. was rep. 1647–53, had admin. on est. of br. John, and d. 27 Sept. 1658, in his will names oldest s. Job; Robert; John; Abraham; Daniel; Moses Pingree, h. of his d. Abigail; John Osgood, wh. m. 15 Nov. 1653, his d. Mary; and Abraham Morrill, wh. had m. 10 June 1645, his d. Sarah. ROBERT, Haverhill, s. of the preced. m. 2 Apr. 1667, Joanna Carr, perhaps d. of George, and had sec. w. a d. of John Fawne, and d. 1712. He took o. of fidel. at the same time with Abraham, Daniel, and John, his brs. SALMON, Boston, m. 13 June 1660, Joanna Riland. SAMUEL, Boston, s. prob. eldest of Austin, m. 7 July 1657, Hannah, d. of Maudit Ings or Inglis, wh. d 9 Apr. foll. By sec. w. Deborah he had Augustine, b. 20 Apr. 1669; Samuel, 18 July 1670; both bapt. 2 May 1675; Hannah, b. 5 Nov. 1673; and Rebecca, 7 July 1678. THOMAS, Providence 1645, is among the freem. 1655, and was too brave, or too old, to leave the place in Philip's war. By w. Eliz. he had Eliz. and perhaps Richard, certain. s. Content. WILLIAM, Cambridge 1636, was unhappy with his w. separat. from her, and desir. div. 1656. But if her name was Martha, as is prob. he bec. free, by her d. 10 Dec. 1659, to m. 3 Apr. foll. Ann Taylor, and in 1672 gave to Daniel Hudson all his est. on condit. of support for hims. and w. Ann for the resid. of their lives. Even with Jackson's aid, as he ment. no ch. I am not able to disting. him from ano. WILLIAM of Cambridge, call. jun. wh. d. 16 July 1669. ‖ WILLIAM, Boston, ar. co. 1662, m. Mary, d. of Joseph Rock, and of him I hear no more. With or without final s, and without t in some fams. the name may be the same.

CLESSON, MATTHEW, Northampton, an Irish serv. of one of the early inhabs. m. 1670, Mary, d. of Nathaniel Phelps, had nine ch. of wh. Mary, prob. eldest, d. 11 Dec. 1671, and ano. Mary, d. 15 Apr. 1687; was freem. 1690, rem. to Deerfield, where live descend.

CLEVERLY, JOHN, Braintree 1669, a blacksmith, freem. 1671, when he was mem. of the first ch. of Boston, and his name is pervert. to

Cleanesby on the rec. as transcr. by Paige in Geneal. Reg. III. 241, or
Cleavesby by Pulsifer in Mass. Col. Rec. IV. pt. 2, p. 585, yet prob. the
first wrong to his good name was the fault of Mr. Secr. Rawson, or of
his careless sub-official. But the strangeness of the surname might have
stimulat. a doubt. By w. Sarah, wh. d. 25 Oct. 1692, aged 54, he had
Stephen, wh. d. 10 Mar. 1692, aged 19, perhaps other ch. was a lieut.
and d. 1703.

CLEVERTON, THOMAS, Newport, is among the freem. 1655.

CLEVES, or CLEAVES, BENJAMIN, Beverly, youngest s. of William of
the same, b. little more than a yr. after the extra-judic. murder of his
gr.f. Giles Corey, m. 2 June 1719, Rebecca Conant, d. of John, had
Bethia, b. 25 July 1720; Benjamin, 4 Jan. 1722; Joshua, 2 Feb. 1724;
Deborah, 2 Feb. 1725; Rebecca, 29 Feb. 1728; Lydia, 29 Aug. 1731;
and Andrew, 1 Oct. 1735. His w. d. 13 Sept. 1770, aged 74; and he
d. 14 Sept. 1775. EBENEZER, Beverly, br. of the preced. m. 15 Jan.
1713, Sarah, d. of John Stone, had Ambrose, b. Dec. 1718; Margaret,
17 Nov. 1720; Sarah, 4 Feb. 1722, d. young; Sarah again, 6 June
1728; Robert, 18 Sept. 1730; Martha, 24 May 1733; and Ebenezer.
* GEORGE, Falmouth, came in 1630, I think, from Plymouth, in
Devonsh. and sat down, first, at Spurwink, or Scarborough, and in two
yrs. rem. a little further E. to be the earliest inhab. of F. no doubt,
drawn thither by its superior harbor, was of the gr. jury 1640, unit. with
Richard Tucker of Saco, both in trade, and ld. speculat. thereby promot.
gr. discord a. patents. He had Eliz. wh. m. first, Michael Mitton, next,
a Harvey, and d. 1681; but whether bless. with other ch. is not told.
Adm. freem. 1658, of Mass. he was rep. 1663, and d. a. 1667, prob. a
very old man, for he testif. in 1663, that his w. Joan was of 87 yrs.
Copious details of him are in Willis and Folsom. See also Winth. I.
237; II. 256; and Sullivan, 312-6. JOHN, Beverly, s. of the first William, m. 26 June 1699, Mercy Eaton, d. of Joseph, had Martha, b. 20
Oct. 1703; Robert, 26 Apr. 1707; Elinor, 8 June 1709; John, 1713;
John, again, 1715; and William, 27 Mar. 1720. Sec. w. he took 22
Aug. 1723, Rebecca Corning; and 21 Aug. 1725, a third w. and he d.
14 Sept. 1753. WILLIAM, Roxbury, m. 4 Nov. 1659, Sarah, d. of
William Chandler, had Sarah, b. 12 Aug. 1660. As no more appears
on the rec. exc. censure of his w. by the ch. 1670, it might be infer. that
he rem. but he was k. at Sudbury fight, 21 Apr. 1676. His wid. m. it
is said, three other hs. WILLIAM, Beverly, m. Martha, d. of Giles
Corey, that sufferer of the horrible punishm. of press. to d. never inflict.
on any other in N. E. had John, b. 11 Oct. 1676; Elinor, 1678; Martha,
1681; and for sec. w. had Margaret, sis. of the first w. and by her, William, 23 July 1686; Hannah, 31 Mar. 1688; Robert, 21 July 1689;

Ebenezer, 13 Oct. 1691 ; and Benjamin, 23 Oct. 1693. When he d. is not told; but his wid. m. 3 May 1716, Jonathan Byles. WILLIAM, Beverly, s. of the preced. m. 11 Jan. 1711, Rebecca, d. of Thomas Whittredge of Ipswich, had Thomas, and Joseph, tw. b. 14 Feb. 1715 ; and William, 15 Sept. 1720.

CLIFFORD, ‖ GEORGE, Boston, was of ar. co. 1644, had John, bapt. 10 May 1646. ISRAEL, Hampton, perhaps s. of John of the same, took o. of alleg. Dec. 1678, by w. Ann had Mehitable, b. 9 July 1686. JOHN, Hampton 1658, m. 18 Aug. 1670, Sarah, d. of deac. William Godfrey prob. for sec. w. as he seems to have sev. ch. at that time, certain. Hannah, wh. m. 20 Nov. 1677, Luke Malone ; and prob. two or three s. was freem. 1676, prob. for third w. had Bridget, wid. of John Huggins, and d. 1694, aged 80. JOHN, Lynn, freem. 1678, next yr. was of Salem, d. 17 June 1698, aged 68. JOHN, Hampton, s. of John of the same, took o. of alleg. 25 Apr. 1678, had John, b. 6 Feb. 1687.

CLIFT, WILLIAM, Marshfield, m. 1691, says Deane, Lydia, d. of Samuel Willis of Scituate, and d. 17 Oct. 1722.

CLIFTON, THOMAS, was freem. of Mass. 2 June 1641, yet of what town a resid. is unkn. his name wh. in the print. list is giv. Clipton, stands between an inhab. of Dorchester and one of Concord, but rem. with early sett. 1643 to Rehoboth, and at last sett. in R. I. there by w. Mary had Patience, b. 2 July 1646, wh. m. 4 Sept. 1664, John Beere. Ano. ch. prob. elder, with the soft name of Hope, was banish. under pain of d. for return. from Mass. as a Quaker, 1658.

CLISBY, CLEESBY, or CLESBY, EZEKIEL, Boston, brot. by his uncle John in 1670, aged 7, by w. Sarah had Ezekiel, b. 25 Nov. 1689, and was sw. freem. 1690. EZEKIEL, Charlestown, s. of the preced. m. 21 Feb. 1715, Abigail, d. of Nathaniel Frothingham. JOHN, Charlestown, went home 1669 to bring here, next yr. four ch. of a br. dec. whose wid. was Eliz. of wh. we have names only of Mary, 11 yrs. old, and John and Ezekiel, ea. 7, but the youngest, a. 5 yrs. d. soon after arr. His w. was Hannah, and he d. Dec. 1695. She d. 26 July 1724, aged 86 by gr.stone, 88 by rec.

CLOADE, ANDREW, Boston, wine-cooper, m. 29 Sept. 1653, Eliz. Bugby, had Eliz. b. 13 Sept. foll. wh. d. at one yr. ; Mary, 22 July 1656 and he d. early in 1664, his inv. of £40 being brot. in by his wid. in Apr. of that yr.

CLOATHER, JEREMIAH, Weymouth, was a soldier, 1676, on Conn. riv.

CLOSE, THOMAS, Greenwich 1672-97.

CLOUGH, EBENEZER, Boston 1690, by w. Martha had John, bapt. 4 Mar. 1694 ; Martha, 26 May 1695 ; Mary, 19 July 1697 ; Ebenezer, 19 Mar. 1699, d. soon, as did his mo. and by w. Thankful had Ebenezer, again, 27 Jan. 1702, d. young; John, 18 May 1704; William, 21 Feb. 1707; Susanna, 23 Aug. 1709; Mary, 25 June 1711; Eliz. 23 Sept. 1714; Ebenezer, again, 29 Nov. 1716; and John, 9 Feb. 1720. Under his will of 3 Jan. 1724, pro. 27 of same, the wid. and her ch. alone have portions of est. to the exclus. of ch. by first w. exc. that to Elias Parkman, s. of his d. Martha £40. are giv. with an apology, "bec. he will have considerable, wh. I ought to have had with my first w. wh. was his gr.mo." JOHN, Watertown, tailor, came in the Elizabeth 1635, aged 22, was freem. 18 May 1642, by w. Jane had Eliz. b. 16 Dec. 1642; Mary, 30 July 1644; Sarah, 28 June 1646; John, 9 Mar. 1648. But he had sec. w. Susanna, tho. neither the d. of former w. nor m. of this is heard of, when he convey. his messuage to William Shattuck of W. and he rem. to Salisbury. Other ch. too he had, as Thomas, 29 May 1651; Martha, 21 Mar. 1654; and Samuel, 26 Feb. 1657, yet we may hardly be right to give the sec. w. more than the two last, or to deny her half a doz. His w. d. 16 Jan. 1680, and he d. 26 July 1691. JOHN, Charlestown 1652, was of Boston soon after, by w. Eliz. had Priscilla, b. 28 Jan. 1655. JOHN, Hartford, freem. of Conn. 1654, may have been f. of that JOHN, wh. little over ten yrs. later was petitnr. for the planta. of Killingworth. JOHN, Boston, feltmaker, was call. jun. in 1674, and may have been s. of the former Boston John, or not. JOHN, Salisbury, s. of the first John, freem. 1690, m. 13 Nov. 1674, Mercy Page, had Benoni, b. 23 May 1675; Mary, 8 Apr. 1677; John, 30 June 1678; Cornelius, 7 May 1680; Caleb, 26 Oct. 1682; Joseph, 14 Oct. 1684; Sarah, 5 Apr. 1686; Jonathan, 11 Apr. 1688; Martha, 17 Mar. 1691; Moses, 26 Mar. 1693; Aaron, 16 Dec. 1695; and Tabitha, 12 Feb. 1698. One JOHN, of New Hampsh. m. 15 Jan. 1686, but the fam. name of his w. Martha, is not clear. RICHARD. See Cluff. WILLIAM, Charlestown, by w. Mary had Mary, b. 21 Nov. 1657; Joseph, 18 Sept. 1659; Benjamin, bapt. 30 Mar. 1662, the f. join. the ch. 25 Aug. 1661; Samuel, 10 Dec. 1665; and Nathaniel, 22 Mar. 1668; perhaps liv. at Boston, 1690, when adm. freem. One WILLIAM, a soldier, perhaps s. of the preced. was k. in Hatfield, 27 Aug. 1675.

CLOUTMAN, THOMAS, Salem, by w. Eliz. had Mary, b. 12 Aug. 1681, d. soon; Thomas, 23 Jan. 1683; John, 14 June 1685; Mary, again, 13 May 1691; and Joseph, 19 Sept. 1693.

CLOYES, or CLOYCE, JOHN, Watertown, 1637, mariner, Charlestown 1658, Falmouth 1660, by w. Abigail had John, b. 26 Aug. 1638; Peter, 27 May 1640; Nathaniel, 6 Mar. 1643; Abigail, wh. m. Jenkin Williams; and Sarah, wh. m. Peter Housing; and by a sec. w. Jane, said to be wid. Spurwell, had Thomas; perhaps Mary, 1 July 1657; and Martha, 13, bapt. 16 Oct. 1659. He was prob. k. by the Ind. 1676.

JOHN, Charlestown, s. prob. of the preced. m. 1664, Mary Long, perhaps d. of Robert, rem. to Wells, there m. 1681, a d. of Thomas Mills. NATHANIEL, Wells, br. of the preced. m. a d. of Thomas Mills. PETER, Wells, br. of the preced. by w. Hannah had Mary, and Hannah, rem. to Salem, where his sec. w. Sarah, by wh. he had three or four ch. was sad. torment. with charge of witchcraft in the reign of superstition, 1692, being long imprison. at Boston bef. trial, and at Ipswich hardly escap. the doom desir. by the preposter. indictm. He last rem. to that pt. of Sudbury wh. soon bec. Framingham, there m. 2 or 21 Jan. 1704, third w. Susanna, wid. of Eliezer Beers of Watertown, was town treasr. and selectman, and d. 18 July 1708. THOMAS, Saco 1671, br. of the preced. rem. soon to Falmouth, m. Susanna, d. of George Lewis, had Thomas, George, and Hannah; was k. by the Fr. and Ind. 1690, at the sec. destruct. of F. WALTER, Salem, of wh. no more is kn. but that he was freem. 1678. In the Watertown rec. his name slides into Clayse, and even Clarse; but at other places other transmut. occur.

CLUFF, JOHN. See Clough. RICHARD, Plymouth 1634, after 1637 rem. to Mass. Prob. this fam. name was the same as Clough.

CLUGSTONE, MICHAEL, Fairfield, m. a d. of Rev. Samuel Wakeman, and d. 1697; by his inv. seem. to have good est.

CLUTTERBUCK, WILLIAM, Boston 1678, then perhaps a shipmaster, had w. Eliz. at Charlestown 1686, and was a lieut. 1689.

COACHMAN, is the misspell. of Cushman at Plymouth.

COALBORNE, NATHANIEL, Dedham, freem. 2 June 1641, by w. Priscilla had Sarah, b. 5 Apr. 1640; Rebecca, 17 Feb. 1643; Nathaniel, 3 Mar. 1645; perhaps John; certain. Hannah, 30 Jan. 1653, wh. m. 16 Jan. 1678, Thomas Aldridge. He was freem. 1684.

COATES, JOHN, Lynn, s. of Thomas, m. 14 Apr. 1681, Mary Witherdin, had Mary, and John, tw. b. 14 Jan. 1682, and his w. d. 18 June foll. ROBERT, Lynn, had Abigail, b. 10 Apr. 1663, he then aged 36, so that he may have had other ch. bef. her. She m. 16 Jan. 1684, Samuel Rhoades. ROBERT, Boston 1673, perhaps s. of the preced. was a soldier on Conn. riv. in 1676, under capt. Turner, prob. after liv. at Lynn, there had Robert, b. 17 Oct. 1683. THOMAS, Lynn 1658, had John, bef. ment. James, and Thomas. Lewis. One Eleazer C. was k. 1677, careless. by John Flint, and £40. fine was impos. on F. one half to the f. of C. as Felt, in Col. Rec. II. 459, found; and in Col. Rec. V. 142, may be seen that one half of the £20. was remit. by the governm. on petitn. of Edward F. perhaps the f. of John.

COBB, AUGUSTINE, Taunton 1670, had Eliz. b. 10 Feb. 1671; Morgan, 29 Dec. 1673; Samuel, 9 Nov. 1675; Bethia, 5 Apr. 1678; Mercy, 12 Aug. 1680; and Abigail, 1684. Of him descend. David, one of the aids of Washington in the army of the revol. EDWARD, Taunton, br. perhaps of the preced. sw. fidel. 1657, m. 28 Nov. 1660, Mary Haskins, prob. d. of William, and d. 1675, leav. Edward. GERSHOM, Swanzey, perhaps s. of Henry, was bur. 24 June 1675, I suppose he resid. at Barnstable, but was k. with eight others that day, being the earliest hostile act of Philip's forces in the gr. war. * HENRY, Barnstable, one of the first set. had been of Plymouth a. 1629, and of Scituate in 1633, there one of the found. of the ch. 8 Jan. 1635, of wh. he was that yr. chos. deac. was, prob. from Kent, by w. Patience, d. I presume, of deac. James Hurst, wh. was bur. 4 May 1648, had John, b. 7 June 1632; James, 14 Jan. 1635, both at P.; Mary, 24, bapt. 26 Mar. 1637; Hannah, bapt. 6 Oct. 1639; both at S. whence he rem. that yr. with Rev. John Lothrop; Patience, 15 Mar. 1642; Gershom, 10, bapt. 12 Jan. 1645; and Eleazer, 30 Mar. bapt. 2 Apr. 1648. As sec. w. he took, 12 Dec. 1649, Sarah, d. of Samuel Hinckley, had Mehitable, 1, bapt. 7 Sept. 1651, d. at 6 mos.; Samuel, b. 12 Oct. 1654; Sarah, 15 Jan. 1658, d. in few days; Jonathan, 10 Apr. 1660; Sarah, again, 10 Mar. 1663; Henry, 3 Sept. 1665; Mehitable, again, 15 Feb. 1667; and Experience, 11 Sept. 1671. He was rep. 1645, and six yrs. more, and d. 1679. Mary m. 15 Oct. 1657, Jonathan Dunham, as sec. w.; Hannah m. 9 May 1661, Edward Lewis; Patience m. Aug. 1667, Robert Parker; Sarah m. 27 Dec. 1686, Samuel Chipman, or Benjamin Hinkley, but wh. is uncert. for two Sarahs, cous. were contempo. and one liv. to 8 Jan. 1742. HENRY, Barnstable, s. of the preced. m. 10 Apr. 1690, Lois Hallett, had Gideon, b. 11 Apr. 1691; Eunice, 18 Sept. 1693; Lois, 2 Mar. 1696; and Nathan. JAMES, Barnstable, br. of the preced. m. 26 Dec. 1663, Sarah, d. of George Lewis, had Mary, b. 26 Nov. 1664; Sarah, 26 Jan. 1666; Patience, 12 Jan. 1668; Hannah, 28 Mar. 1671; James, bapt. with the last, 8 July 1673; Gershom, 31 Aug. 1675; John, 20 Dec. 1677; Eliz. 6 Oct. 1680; Martha, 6 Feb. bapt. 16 Sept. 1683; Mercy, 9 Apr. 1685; and Thankful, 10 June 1687. When he d. is not told; but his wid. m. 23 Nov. 1698, Jonathan Sparrow. JOHN, Taunton 1659, thot. to be br. of Augustine, took o. of fidel. 1657, m. 13 June 1676, Jane Woodward, had John, b. 31 Mar. 1678; and no more is seen. JOHN, Plymouth, m. 28 Aug. 1658, Martha Nelson, had John, b. 24 Aug. 1662, d. young; Samuel; Israel; and Eliz. whose dates are not giv. and Elisha, 3 Apr. 1678; and James, 20 July 1682. JONATHAN, Barnstable, s. of Henry the first, m. 1 Mar. 1683, Hope Huckins, perhaps d. of the first Thomas of the same, had Samuel, b. 23 Feb. bapt. 6 Apr. 1684; Jonathan, b. 26 Apr. 1686; Ebenezer, 10 Apr. 1688; Joseph, 24 Aug. bapt. 21 Sept. 1690; and Lydia, 7 Jan. bapt. 5 Mar. 1693. SAMUEL, Barnstable, br. of the preced. by w. Eliz.

d. of Richard Taylor, m. 20 Dec. 1680, had Sarah, b. 20 Aug. 1681;
Thomas, 1 June 1683; Eliz. Nov. 1685; Henry, 17 Feb. 1687; Samuel, and Mehitable, tw. 10 Sept. 1691; Experience, 8 Jan. 1693; Jonathan, 25 Dec. 1694; Eleazer, 14 Jan. 1696; and Lydia, 8 Dec. 1699;
and he d. 7 Dec. 1727. Descend. are very num. of wh. Ebenezer, that
d. at Kingston, 8 Dec. 1801, at the age, as was said, of more than
107 and ½ yrs. was, perhaps, the oldest man wh. ever was b. and liv. on
the soil of Mass. Of this name, gr. at Harv. in 1828, were by Farmer
found six; at Yale, and Dart. two ea. and nine at the other N. E. coll.

COBBETT, JAMES, came in the Elizabeth and Ann 1635, aged 23,
from London, but no more is found of him. JOHN, Ipswich, s. of the
Rev. Thomas, was made freem. 1683. JOSIAH, Cambridge, as he came
in the Elizabeth and Ann 1635, aged 21, may be well thot. br. of James
rem. to Hingham 1637, but was a propr. of Salisbury 1640, may have
been a resid. but, if so, soon rem. was freem. 7 Oct. 1640, and no more
is kn. but that at Boston, by w. Mary, he had Ruth, b. 6 Aug. 1657.
SAMUEL, Ipswich, eldest s. of the Rev. Thomas, freem. 1674, rem. to
Lynn, perhaps there had Margaret, b. 17 Aug. 1676, wh. d. next mo.
No more is heard of him, yet in the coll. catal. 1698, every one of his
class, exc. hims. is mark with * as d. THOMAS, Lynn, a man of high
esteem, b. 1608 at Newbury, in Co. Bucks, was bred at Oxford, but could
not take his degr. being driv. away by the plague, at his native town stud.
under famous Dr. Twisse, and first preach. in Lincolnsh. unless Mather
be wrong. This brot. him acquaint. with Whiting of Boston; and both,
by the intolerance of the High ch. party, were forc. to leave their places.
In his wonted looseness the author of the Magn. makes him come in
the same ship with Davenport, and says that his parents came after to
our shore. Of them we never hear a word; and if we may not infer
from silence of Winth. wh. notes that ano. min. wh. was passeng. in the
Hector with D. arr. 26 June 1637, was not C. or the Gov. would have
nam. him, yet the New Haven tradit. as if the brother of their Gov.
Eaton were that min. bears high probabil. C. was adm. freem. 2 May
1638, tho. the prefix of respect is want. in the rec. Unm. on his arr. I am
not able to tell even what w. he found here, but her bapt. name was Eliz.
and their ch. Samuel, H. C. 1663; Thomas; Eliz.; John; and Eliezer,
wh. d. of consumpt. After long serv. at L. he rem. to Ipswich to fill the
place of Nathaniel Rogers in 1656, and there was min. to his d. 5 Nov.
1685, tho. with his usual license Mather says " a. the beginning of the yr.
1686." Magn. III. 166. Lewis, Hist. of Lynn, 140–3, and the dilig.
of Kimball, Eccl. Hist. Ipswich, 19–21, leave us ign. of many details
that should be desir. of so famous a divine. THOMAS, Ipswich, s. of the
preced. tak. by the Ind. in Philip's war, as in Hubbard may be read;

and slight acco. of his redempt. may be gather. from the Magn. and most abundant from the narrat. by the f. in Geneal. Reg. VII. 215–7.

COBBLE, EDWARD, Salisbury, by w. Judith had Edward, b. 17 Jan. 1652, d. young; Mary, 1 Nov. 1653; Benjamin, 3 Mar. 1655; Sarah, Mar. 1657; Judith, 5 May 1659; Eliz. 19 Apr. 1663; and Edward, again, 28 Sept. 1666.

COBHAM, JOSIAH, Salisbury, by w. Mary had Mary, b. 25 Aug. 1640; Joseph, 12 Apr. 1642; Martha, 3 July 1643; Moses, 3 Nov. 1645; Sarah, 25 Nov. 1646; Joshua, 15 Mar. 1648; and Marah, 21 May 1652; was a webster, and rem. 1659 to Boston. JOSIAH, Boston, clothier, call. junr. 1666, was, perhaps, s. of the preced.

COBLEICH, JOHN, Swanzey, by w. Mary had John, b. 5 Jan. 1673. This name, if not an impossib. one, must be very rare. In his large acco. of the early settlem. at S. Baylies has not giv. it. Perhaps the Ind. war exting. within three yrs. our means of verificat. or amendm.

COBURN. See Colbron.

COCHRAN, WILLIAM, Boston 1684.

COCKERILL, WILLIAM, Hingham 1635, rem. to Salem, there d. 1661.

COCKERUM, WILLIAM, Hingham 1635, went home, and came again, 1637 in the Mary Ann of Yarmouth, when he call. hims. of Southold, in Suff k. mercer, aged 28, with Christian, his w. 26, two ch. and two serv. was freem. 13 Mar. 1639, sail. for home, again, 3 Oct. 1642. By deed of 25 Mar. 1657 he convey. his est. to s. William, wh. on 25 Sept. foll. transfer. it to John Tower of H. as in our Reg. III. 62, 3, appears.

COCKSHOTT, JAMES, Haddam, d. 1693, leav. wid. Eliz. wh. d. 20 Mar. 1700, at Durham.

CODDINGTON, HENRY, Boston 1670, perhaps s. of the foll. JOHN, Boston 1650, by w. Emma had Sarah, b. 4 Oct. 1651, d. young; John, 9 Feb. 1654; perhaps Henry, older than either. He d. 18 Aug. 1655 and his wid. m. 7 May foll. John Jepson or Jephson. JOHN, Boston, s. of the preced. m. Hannah, d. of Richard Gardner of Charlestown; and his half br. John Jepson m. Ruth, ano. d. of Gardner. In rec. of deeds this name is Cuddington. JOHN, Newport, s. of William the first, d. 1 June 1680, prob. without issue. JOSEPH, of Block isl. 1684, I fear, can have nothing more told of him. ‡ NATHANIEL, Newport, s. of the first William, m. Susanna, d. of the sec. Edward Hutchinson, had Ann, b. 26 Dec. 1677; Catharine, 8 Feb. 1779; William, 15 July 1680; Edward, 28 July 1687; John, 23 Mar. 1690; and Nathaniel, 18 Jan. 1692. To his s. William, prob. Callender dedicat. his invalua. Century Sermon. STOCKDALE, Roxbury, where his w. Hannah was bur. 20 July 1644, in advanc. age, hav. d. of apoplexy, as the ch. rec. tells, may have been f. or gr.f. of John the first, rem. and d. a. 1650. THOMAS, Newport, s. of

the first William, by w. Priscilla had William, b. 1684, d. 19 Feb. 1689;
Thomas, 17 Apr. 1687; and by a sec. w. Mary Howard of New York,
m. 22 Jan. 1690, had William, again, 1 Feb. 1691; and Mary, 15 Jan.
1693; and he d. 4 or 6 Mar. foll.   His wid. m. 18 Jan. 1694, Anthony
Morris.   § ‡ * WILLIAM, Boston, an Assist. of the comp. chos. in Eng.
1630, bef. the embark. of Winth. with wh. he came, had liv. at Boston,
Co. Lincoln, where the rec. of St. Botolph's ch. shows he had Michael,
bapt. 8 Mar. 1627, wh. d. in two wks.; and Samuel, 17 Apr. 1628, bur.
21 Aug. 1629.   His w. was Mary, d. of Richard Moseley of Ouseden,
in Co. Suff k. and she d. here in few wks. after arr.   On 1 Apr. 1631
he left Boston, in the Lion, with his friends, Rev. John Wilson, and Sir
Richard Saltonstall, soon found new w. Mary, and had a ch. in Eng.
1632, and in May 1633 came again to Boston, here had Mary, bapt. 2
Mar. 1634; and Benajah, 1 May 1636.   He was treasr. of the Col.
1634, 5, and 6, and as one of the antinom. party left out of office next
yr. but chos. rep. for B. and early in the foll. yr. went to R. I. wh. he
purch. with other heretics, wh. made him Gov.   Perhaps he had other
ch. in R. I. by the sec. w. wh. was bur. at Newport 30 Sept. 1647; and
in Jan. foll. or perhaps 1649, he went again to Eng. carr. his d. and there
resid. some yrs. got ano. w. Ann, by wh. he had William, b. there 18
Jan. 1651, unless this means 1652, and came back to N. July 1651, arr.
in Nov. bring. new chart. of 3 Apr. 1651, as sign. by the Lord Presid.
Bradshaw.   Other ch. by this third w. were Nathaniel, b. 23 May 1653;
Mary, again, 16 May 1654; Thomas, 5 Nov. 1655; John, 24 Nov.
1656; Noah, 12 Dec. 1658; Ann, 6 June 1660, prob. d. young; and
Ann, again, 20 July 1663.   He was Gov. again late in his days, having
been many yrs. withdrawn from public affairs, embrac. relig. views of
the Quakers, by the persecut. of wh. at Boston he was so much disturb.
in spirit, as to write to his old friend Gov. Bellingham and some of the
counc. a letter of admonit. 12 Aug. 1672, wh. by B. without communicat.
to the others was burn. as C. says, wherefore he wrote again 20 Oct.
foll. by the hands of Leverett.   See " Demonstration of True Love,"
writ. by C. print. 1674, a very rare tract.   He d. in office 1 Nov. 1678,
aged 77, and his wid. d. 9 May 1708, aged 80.   § ‡ WILLIAM, Newport,
s. of the preced. perhaps b. in Eng. was an Assist. 1680, Gov. 1683 and
4, and d. unm. 5 Feb. 1689.

  CODMAN, RICHARD, York 1653, s.-in-law of Richard Bonython. ROB-
ERT, Salem 1637, had gr. of ld. (and his fam. then count. four) and s.
Benjamin, bapt. 14 Nov. 1641, and in this yr. had gr. of ld. at Salisbury
whither he rem. and there had James, b. 15 Apr. 1644; and in 1650
rem. to Hartford, leav. Samuel Hall of S. his agent, and came not
back to Mass. but rem. to Saybrook 1654, and after to Edgartown, where

he d. 1678. He left two s. Joseph, a mariner, wh. d. the same yr. with his f. and Stephen. STEPHEN, Charlestown, a. 1680, possib. s. of the preced. by w. Eliz. had Stephen (perhaps the ch. bapt. 11 Feb. 1683, when ch. rec. omits the name) wh. d. at the age of 30 yrs. and 8 mos. after his f.; Benjamin, 12 Oct. 1684, wh. d. at 4 yrs.; Hepzibah, 5 Dec. 1686; Susanna, 2 Mar. 1690; both d. young; Benjamin, again, 28 Jan. 1694; and John, 4 Oct. 1696; and d. 5 Apr. 1706, aged 56. His wid. d. 1 Apr. 1708, aged 54. Their s. John m. Parnell, d. of Richard Foster, but I kn. no more, exc. that he was a capt. and d. 1755, his w. hav. d. 15 Sept. 1752, aged 56. ‡ * WILLIAM, Portsmouth, R. I. sev. yrs. bef. 1661, rep. 1672, and Assist. 1676. Of this name, the gr. in 1834 at Harv. had been four, and as many at the other N. E. coll.

CODMORE. See Codner.

CODNER, CHRISTOPHER, perhaps of Marblehead, d. 1660, or, at least, Coffin found his inv. of that yr. See Geneal. Reg. VI. 248. EDWARD, New London 1651, had w. Priscilla, rem. 1669 to Saybrook, there d. 1670; but his s. Lawrence cont. at N. L. 1666. GEORGE, New London 1664, may have been s. of the preced. GREGORY, HENRY, JOHN, and JOSIAH, with JOSIAH, jr. unit. in petitn. to our Gen. Ct. from Marblehead, 1668; and perhaps the elder Josiah was f. of the other four; but of neither of them is any thing further kn. exc. that John was of Manchester in 1686. LAWRENCE, New London, s. of Edward, was enga. in lawsuit 1682. PETER, Boston, a mariner, had, in 1674, w. Rachel, d. of James Neighbors, d. Mary, b. 3 Sept. bapt. with Rachel, 29 July 1677; Martha, 7, bapt. 11 Sept. 1681. RICHARD, Swanzey, m. 23 May 1671, Phebe, d. of Rufus Barton of Warwick, had Richard, b. 11 Aug. 1676; Eliz. bapt. at Boston 3 Feb. 1678; and Savory, 2 Mar. 1679.

COE, BENJAMIN, s. of Robert, b. in Eng. came with his f. to Watertown, thence to Stamford, and after with him to Hempstead, L. I. where he was among the earliest sett. m. Abigail Carman, and was at Jamaica 1660, where are still descend. ISAAC, s. of Matthew, may have liv. at Falmouth, but of him I kn. only that he m. at Roxbury, 11 Sept. 1706, Martha Ramsey. * JOHN, eldest br. of Benjamin, b. in Eng. went with his f. to L. I. and was of Newtown 1655, of Greenwich 1660, and that yr. was one of the purch. of Rye, but soon went back to the isl. was a capt. and appoint. a magistr. by Conn. in 1664, chos. rep. perhaps soon after, and was of Stratford 1685. There his s. John m. His other ch. were Robert, Jonathan, Samuel, and David. JOHN, Duxbury, eldest s. of Matthew, m. 10 Nov. 1681, Sarah, d. of William Peabody, had Lydia, b. 26 Feb. 1683; Sarah, 25 Feb. 1686; rem. to Little Compton, and had Samuel, 12 Dec. 1692; Eliz. 28 Mar. 1694; Hannah, 29 Dec. 1696; John, 1 Feb. 1699; and Joseph, 24 Mar. 1700; perhaps some earlier. JOHN, Stratford, only s. perhaps of the sec. Robert, m. 20 Dec. 1682, Mary, d. of Joseph Hawley of the same, had Robert, b. 21 Sept. 1684; Joseph, 2 Feb. 1686; Hannah, 14 Apr. 1689 ; Mary, 11 Aug. 1691; John, 5 Dec. 1693 ; Sarah, 26 Mar. 1696 ; Ephraim, 18 Dec. 1698; Catharine, 23 Sept. 1700; Abigail, 11 Nov. 1702 ; and Ebenezer, 18 Aug. 1704; and d. 19 Apr. 1741. MATTHEW, Portsmouth 1645, a fisherman, rem. to Gloucester, m. 15 June 1647, Eliz. d. of Thomas Wakley, had John, b. 30 June 1649; Sarah, 14 Mar. 1651; Abigail, 5 June 1658; Matthew, 3 June 1661, wh. d. at 8 mos. and others, among wh. some were b. at Casco, as Isaac, bef. ment. ; Martha, wh. m. Farnum of Boston, and Eliz. wh. m. Benjamin Tucker of Roxbury; beside ano. d. wh. m. Joseph Ingersoll of Falmouth, whither he rem. 1661, with his f.-in-law and two other Wakleys, and d. bef. Philip's war. ROBERT, Watertown 1634, came that yr. in the Francis from Ipswich, aged 38, with w. Ann, 43, by the rec. at custom ho. and ch. John, 8 ; Robert, 7 ; and Benjamin, 5 ; freem. 3 Sept. 1634, rem. to Wethersfield, 1635 or 6, after some yrs. to Stamford, or Stratford 1650, and last to Hempstead, or Jamaica, on L. I. perhaps both, 1662 ; in 1664 he was betrust. with some power by Coun. and in N. Y. jurisdict. made Sheriff 1669–72. ROBERT, Stratford 1651, s. of the preced. by w. Hannah had a d. b. there that yr. perhaps Susanna, wh. m. a. 1672, John Alling, jr. of New Haven ; and John, 10 May 1658 ; and d. 1659. This early d. was lament. by Rev. Abraham Pierson in verses less disting. for elegance than simplicity. His wid. m. Nicholas Elsey. SAMUEL, Newtown, L. I. s. of the first John, m. Margaret Van Zandt, had Samuel; John, b. 7 Dec. 1719 ; Benjamin ; William ; Isaac ; Matthew ; Daniel; Margaret ; Sarah ; and Abigail; and d. 1742. Jane C. was a passeng. in the Susan and Ellen from London 1635, aged 30 ; but whether maid, w. or wid. is unkn.

COFFIN, JAMES, Newbury, s. of the first Tristram b. in Eng. 1 or 12 Aug. 1640, liv. some yrs. at Dover, perhaps bef. m. 3 Dec. 1663, Mary, d. of John Severance of Salisbury, had Mary, bapt. 18 Apr. 1665, rem. to Nantucket, there had Ebenezer, b. 30 Mar. 1678; Joseph, 4 Feb. 1680; Benjamin, 28 Aug. 1683; and Jonathan, 28 Aug. 1692 ; beside sev. others, prob. earlier, by fam. tradit. in all fourteen ch. and d. 28 July 1720. He was twelve yrs. judge of Pro. progenit. of the late admiral, Sir Isaac, and d. 28 July 1720. JAMES, Newbury, s. of the sec. Tristram, m. 16 Nov. 1685, Florence Hooke, had Judith, b. 7 Oct. 1686 ; Eliz.; Sarah, 20 Aug. 1689 ; Mary, 18 Jan. 1691; Lydia, 1692 ; Tristram, 19 Oct. 1694 ; Daniel, 10 May 1696 ; Elinor, 16 May 1698 ; Joanna, 2 May 1701 ; and James, and Florence, tw. 1 Jan. 1705. JAMES, Nantucket, s. prob. of the first James, m. 19 May 1692, Ruth Gardner, d. of John of the same, had George, b. 22 Apr. 1693 ; Sarah,

9 Mar. 1695; Nathan, 13 Nov. 1696; Elisha, 10 Aug. 1699; Joshua,
16 Sept. 1701; Eliz. 27 Oct. 1703; Priscilla, 3 June 1708; Mary, 29
July 1710; and James, 10 June 1713. JOHN, Nantucket, s. of the
first Tristram, m. Deborah Austin, had Lydia, b. 1 June 1669; Peter,
5 Aug. 1671; John, 10 Feb. 1674; Love, 23 Apr. 1676; and three
other ch. and d. 1711. NATHANIEL, Newbury, s. of the sec. Tristram,
m. 29 Mar. 1693, Sarah Dole, had John, b. 29 Jan. 1694; Enoch, 7
Feb. 1696, H. C. 1714; Apphia, 9 June 1698; Samuel, 24 Aug. 1700,
H. C. 1718; Joseph, 30 Dec. 1702; Jane, 5 Aug. 1705; Edmund, 19
Mar. 1708; and Moses, 11 June 1711; and d. 20 Feb. 1748. ‡* PETER,
Dover, merch. eldest s. of the first Tristram, b. in Eng. 1631, m. Abigail, d. of Edward Starbuck, had Abigail, b. 20 Oct. 1657; Peter, 20
Aug. 1660; Jethro, 16 Sept. 1663; Tristram, 18 Jan. 1665; Edward,
20 Feb. 1669; Judith, 4 Feb. 1672; Eliz. 27 Jan. 1680; and Robert;
was freem. 1666, a lieut. 1675 on serv. in Philip's war, rep. 1672, 3, and
9, couns. 1692–1714, judge of the Sup. Ct. of N. H. d. at Exeter, 21
Mar. 1715. PETER, Nantucket, prob. s. of the preced. m. 15 Aug.
1682, Eliz. d. of Nathaniel Starbuck, had Abigail, b. 9 July 1683;
Nathaniel, 26 Mar. 1687; Lemuel, 26 Feb. 1689; Barnabas, 12 Feb.
1690; and prob. Eunice, 23 Sept. 1693. PETER, Newbury, s. of the
sec. Tristram, m. Apphia, d. of Richard Dole, had Hannah, b. 3 Mar.
1688; Judith, 9 Oct. 1693; Tristram, 10 Aug. 1696; Richard; Sarah,
24 Aug. 1701; Apphia, d. young; and Apphia, again; rem. to Gloucester. ROBERT, Dover, s. of the first Peter, was a capt. in the E.
Ind. war of 1708, and d. without ch. STEPHEN, Newbury, s. of the
first Tristram, m. Mary Bunker, had at Nantucket, Dinah, b. 21 Sept.
1671; Peter, 14 Nov. 1673; Stephen, 20 Feb. 1676; and sev. more,
perhaps, among them Paul, 15 Apr. 1695. STEPHEN, Newbury, s. of
the sec. Tristram, m. 1685, Sarah, d. of John Atkinson, had Sarah, b.
16 May 1686; Tristram, 14 Jan. 1688, d. soon; Tristram, again, 6
Mar. 1689; Lydia, 21 July 1691; Judith, 23 Feb. 1693; and John,
20 Jan. 1695. TRISTRAM, Nantucket, b. it is said, at Brixton, near
Plymouth, Co. Devon, a. 1605, or by ano. rept. 1609, s. of Peter and
Joanna, m. Dionis Stevens, had Peter, b. 1631; Tristram, 1632; Eliz.;
James, 12 Aug. 1640; and John; after d. of his f. came, 1642, to N. E.
bring. beside the bef. ment. childr. his mo. (wh. d. May 1661, aged 77),
two sis. Eunice, wh. m. William Butler, and Mary, wh. m. Alexander
Adams of Boston; sat down, first, at Salisbury, soon rem. to Haverhill,
where his youngest ch. d. had Mary, b. 20 Feb. 1645; and John, again,
13 Dec. 1647; rem. a. 1648, to Newbury, where Stephen was b. 10
May 1652; again rem. to Salisbury, there was a county magistr. and
finally rem. 1660, to Nantucket with his aged mo. w. and four ch. and d.

2 or 3 Oct. 1681. His d. Eliz. m. 13 Nov. 1651, and d. 19 Nov. 1678;
and Mary m. at Nantucket Nathaniel Starbuck, had six ch. and d. 1717.
TRISTRAM, Newbury, sec. s. of the preced. b. in Eng. m. 2 Mar. 1653,
Judith, d. of capt. Edmund Greenleaf, wid. of Henry Somerby, had
Judith, b. 4 Dec. 1653; Deborah, 10 Nov. 1655; Mary, 12 Nov. 1657;
James, 22 Apr. 1659; John, 8 Sept. 1660; Lydia, 22 Apr. 1662;
Enoch, 21 Jan. 1663, d. at 12 yrs.; Stephen, 18 Aug. 1664; Peter, 27
July 1667; and Nathaniel, 22 Mar. 1669. He was freem. 1668, deac.
for 20 yrs. and a magistr. for the Co. d. 4 Feb. 1704, aged 72; and his
wid. d. 15 Dec. 1705, aged 80 by one story or 77 by more prob. acco.
leav. 177 descend. WILLIAM, Salem, perhaps was a soldier, when k. 29
Aug. 1708, in the assault by the Fr. and Ind. on Haverhill. Of this
name, twenty-six descend. of the first Tristram, gr. in 1828 of the sev.
N. E. coll. fifteen were at Harv. alone, seven of wh. as Farmer learn.
from Joshua C. were b. in one ho. three at Dart. and none at Yale.

COGGAN, COGAN, or COGGIN, spell. with var. other shapes in dif. rec.
HENRY, Barnstable 1639, by w. Abigail had Abigail, b. prob. bef. sett. at
B.; Thomas, bapt. 1 Mar. 1640, wh. d. 26 Jan. 1659; John, 12 Feb.
1643; Mary, 20 Apr. 1645, d. in few days; and Henry, 11 Oct. 1646;
went home for a vis. and d. there June 1649. His wid. m. 10 June
1650, John Phinney, and d. 6 May 1653; d. Abigail m. 21 June 1659,
John French of Billerica, and d. early. JOHN, Boston, had first been
of Dorchester 1632, was freem. 5 Nov. 1633, in July foll. his w. Ann
join. the ch. at B. had Ann, bapt. 6 Nov. 1636; and Lydia, 14 July
1639, as from ch. rec. is kn. We may see here how heedless. the town
rec. was kept, as our municip. assurance for the former is — b. 7 (9)
1636, i. e. the day after she was bapt. and may doubt, whether that for
the latter — 14 (5) 1639, i. e. the same day as the bapt. be wholly trustworthy. Possib. this may be true, as we kn. that in the case of Dr.
Franklin he had the benefit of so early sprinkl. yet prob. the distance
from C.'s house to the ch. was much longer than that of the f. of F. but
in the earlier case, we see its blunder, and can readily account for it.
Ano. w. Mary, d. 14 Jan. 1652, but he soon found consol. in m. 10 Mar.
foll. with Martha, wid. of Gov. Winth. wh. bef. had been wid. of Thomas
Coytemore, and by her had Caleb, b. 15, bapt. 26 Dec. 1652. But he
had brot. from Eng. d. Mary, and perhaps Eliz. unless this last were b.
at Dorchester. He d. 1658, hav. made his will 16 Dec. 1657 preced. in
wh. w. Martha is provid. for; also s. Caleb, wh. d. young; d. Mary, that
had been w. of John Woody of Roxbury, and was now w. of Thomas
Robinson of Scituate, and had three ch. and for d. Eliz. w. of Joseph
Rock; beside a gold ring for John, s. of his br. Humphrey; and £20. to
the ch. of Windsor. Of his wid. a letter of Rev. John Davenport, pr.

in 3 Mass. Hist. Coll. X. 45, contains story of unusual interest. JOHN, Boston, call. jr. s. of Humphrey (wh. never came to our shore, I think), was adm. freem. 18 May 1642, had Sarah, b. 25 Dec. 1657; and d. 1674. JOHN, Charlestown, m. 22 Dec. 1664, Mary Long, perhaps d. of the sec. Robert, was a householder 1678, may have had w. Mary, wh. d. at C. 7 May 1679, and ch. Henry and John to live at Woburn. THOMAS, Taunton 1643, d. 4 Mar. 1653.

COGGESHALL, or COXSALL, JAMES, Newport, s. prob. of John the first, m. Mary, d. of the first Henry Bull. §‡ * JOHN, Roxbury, a mercer from Co. Essex, came in the Lion 16 Sept. 1632, and was adm. freem. 6 Nov. foll. rem. with w. Mary to Boston, had Hananeel, bapt. there 3 May 1635; d. Wait, 11 Sept. 1636; and Bedaiah, 30 July 1637, whether s. or d. is not kn. He was rep. in the first Gen. Ct. of 1634, and sev. sess. in after yrs. but in 1637 sympathiz. with Wheelwright, he was expel. from his seat, disarm. and next yr. banish. then went to R. I. was chos. Assist. 1641, and in 1647 Presid. of the Col. and one of the chief men at Newport after, treasr. of the Col. He d. after fill. other hon. places, in Nov. of the yr. 1689, perhaps, but it may be diffic. sometimes to tell what office was giv. to him, what to his s. of the same name. His d. Ann, b. in Eng. m. 15 Nov. 1643, Peter Easton; Wait m. 18 Dec. 1651, Daniel Gould; and I presume that it was the f. wh. was made by the crown one of the Counc. of Andros, and on the overthrow of A. reassum. his place as dept.-gov. Winth. Hist. I. 130. JOHN, Newport, s. of the preced. b. in Eng. m. a. 1647, Eliz. youngest d. of William Balstone, had William; and John, b. 12 Feb. 1650; beside one or more ds. of wh. Eliz. m. John Warner. He and w. by mut. cons. separat. in 1654, and he gain. leave of Ct. to m. again, she obtain. the same license next mo. and m. Thomas Gould of Narraganset next yr.; C. m. Dec. 1655, Patience Throgmorton, prob. d. of John, had Freegift, 1 Mar. 1658; James, 17 Feb. 1660; Mary, 10 Mar. 1662; Joseph, 30 May 1664 or 5, but which, is uncert.; Rebecca, 20 June 1667; Patience, 13 Aug. 1669; Benjamin, 27 July 1672; Content, 28 Mar. 1674; and Content, again, 10 May 1676; and his w. d. 7 Sept. foll. Descend. are still in repute. JOHN, Newport, s. of the preced. m. 24 Dec. 1670, Eliz. d. of Henry Timberlake of the same, had Eliz. b. 27 Nov. 1670, unless we may presume the rec. of parent's m. or ch.'s b. is wrong, and that *this* should be 1671, or *that* 1669; Balstone, 29 Sept. 1672, wh. d. soon, as did the former; John, 23 Sept. 1673, perhaps d. young; Mary, 18 Sept. 1675; William, 7 Sept. 1677; Patience, 1 Jan. 1680; Constant, 14 Mar. 1682; Peter, 18 June 1684; James, 29 May 1686; Rebecca, 9 Oct. 1688; Balstone, again, 8 Oct. 1690, Daniel, 25 Oct. 1693; and John, again, 10 Nov. 1694. ‡ JOSHUA, Newport, s. I suppose, of the first John, perhaps b. in Eng. m. 22 Dec. 1652, Joan West, had Mary, b. Feb. 1655; Joshua, May 1656; John, Dec. 1659; Josiah, Nov. 1662; Daniel, Apr. 1665; Humilis, Jan. 1670; and Caleb, 17 Dec. 1672. His w. d. 24 Apr. 1676, aged 41, and he m. 21 June 1677, Rebecca Russell, and d. 1 Mar. 1689. WILLIAM, Boston 1686. He was surety in a bond with Nathaniel Peck, for sav. harmless, E. Randolph, the Secr. of the royal governm. in giv. a license for P. to be m. a very curious docum. to be read in 3 Mass. Hist. Coll. VII. 170.

COGSWELL, EDWARD, perhaps of Ipswich, s. of John, b. in Eng. d. a. 1700, leav. William, Jonathan, John, Adam, and four ds. JOHN, Ipswich, came from Bristol, 1635, in the Angel Gabriel, wreck. 15 Aug. at Pemaquid, freem. 3 Mar. 1636, and d. 29 Nov. 1669. His wid. d. 2 June 1676. He brot. William, b. a. 1619; John, 1623; and Edward, 1629; had also ds. Mary, perhaps that maid serv. of Gov. Bellingham, that join. the Boston ch. 29 Aug. 1647; Hannah; Abigail; and Sarah, b. a. 1647, wh. m. Simon Tuttle. The other ds. m. but of details I am ign. and prob. sev. of these ch. were not by w. Eliz. JOHN, perhaps of Ipswich, s. of the preced. d. 1653, leav. three ch. JOHN, Ipswich, s. of William, by w. Eliz. had John, and William, perhaps, also, a d. that m. Cornelius Waldo, unless this w. of W. were d. of the first John, as seems more likely. JONATHAN, Ipswich, s. of Edward or of William, m. 14 May 1686, Eliz. d. of Francis Wainwright. ROBERT, New Haven 1643, rem. soon. SAMUEL, Saybrook, m. 27 Oct. 1668, Susanna Hearn, had Hannah, b. 4 June 1670; Susanna, 23 Nov. 1672; Wastall (or some happier name), 17 Feb. 1674; Samuel, 3 Aug. 1677; Robert, 7 July 1679; Joseph, 10 Apr. 1682; Nathaniel, 16 Dec. 1684; and John, 7 Aug. 1688. WILLIAM, Ipswich 1646, s. of the first John, b. in Eng. had, beside others, Jonathan; and John, a. 1650, gr.-gr.f. of the late Rev. Dr. William C. (wh. began the publicat. of the Geneal. Reg.) and d. a. 1701. Ano. William, perhaps his gr.s. m. Martha, d. of Rev. John Emerson of Gloucester.

COIT, or COYTE, JOHN, Salem 1638, was a shipwright, had w. Mary, rem. 1644, to Gloucester, there was selectman 1648, and to New London 1651, there d. 25 Aug. 1659, leav. John, Joseph, Mary, wh. m. John Stevens, and Martha, wh. m. first, Hugh Mould, and next, Nathaniel White of Middletown, beside ano. s. and two ds. refer. to in his will. His wid. d. 2 Jan. 1676, aged 80. JOHN, Gloucester, s. of the preced. perhaps b. in Eng. m. 21 May 1652, Mary, d. of William Stevens, had Abigail, b. 3 Apr. 1657; and Nathaniel, 13 Apr. 1659; and d. 15 Apr. 1675. Abigail m. 13 Nov. 1677, Isaac Eveleth. JOHN, New London, prob. eldest s. of Joseph of the same, m. 5 or 25 June 1695, Mehitable, d. of John Chandler, had John, b. 25 May 1696; Joseph, 15 Nov. 1698;

Samuel, 18 Feb. 1700; Thomas, 1 June 1702; and Eliz. 1 Apr. 1706. JOSEPH, New London, s. of the first John, b. prob. in Eng. m. 13 July 1667, Martha, d. of William Harris of Middletown, had John, b. 1 Dec. 1670; Joseph, 14 Apr. 1673, H. C. 1697, first min. of Plainfield; William, 5 Jan. 1676; Daniel, Dec. 1677; Solomon, 29 Nov. 1679; and Samuel; was deac. and is anc. of most of the name in this country, as is said, and d. 27 Mar. 1704. SOLOMON, Gloucester, perhaps br. of the preced. by Mr. Felt was seen there 1651. WILLIAM, New London, prob. s. of Joseph, m. 9 June 1697, Sarah, youngest d. of John Chandler of the same, had only Daniel, b. 25 Oct. 1698; and his wid. m. John Gardiner of Gardiner's isl.

COKER, BENJAMIN, Newbury, s. of Robert, m. 31 May 1678, Martha Perley, had Benjamin, b. 13 Sept. 1680; Hannah, 10 Mar. 1683; Moses, 4 Aug. 1686; Sarah, 13 Apr. 1688; Mary, 18 Sept. 1691; Mercy, 22 Oct. 1693; John, 9 June 1698; and Judith, 9 June 1701. JOSEPH, Newbury, br. of the preced. m. 13 Apr. 1665, Sarah, d. of John Hathorne of Salem, had Sarah, wh. d. young; Benjamin, 11 Mar. 1671; Sarah, again, 11 Nov. 1676; and Hathorne, 25 Apr. 1679; was freem. 1690. His w. d. 8 Feb. 1688, and he m. Mary, wid. of Thomas Woodbridge of N. RICHARD, perhaps of Hartford, had a lawsuit, 1640. ROBERT, Newbury, came in the Mary and John 1634, d. 19 May 1680, aged 74. By w. Catharine, wh. d. 2 May 1678, had Joseph, b. 6 Oct. 1640; Sarah, 24 Nov. 1643; Hannah, 15 Jan. 1645; and Benjamin, 30 June 1650; and he d. 19 Nov. 1680, hav. made his will 28 Sept. 1678. Sarah m. 26 July 1667, James Smith.

COLBRON, COLBORNE, or COLBURN, EDWARD, Chelmsford, came, perhaps, in the Defence, 1635, aged 17, was liv. 1692. EDWARD, a soldier, that may have been s. of the preced. was k. by the Ind. at Brookfield, 2 Aug. 1675. JOHN, Dedham, m. 1672, Experience, only d. of Henry Leland of Sherborn, had John, b. 1675; Ebenezer, 1677; Deborah, 1680; Hannah, 1683; Bethia, 1686; Daniel, 1689; and Experience, 1692. NATHANIEL. See Coalborne. RICHARD, Dorchester 1641. ROBERT, Ipswich, came in the Defence, 1635, aged 28, perhaps br. of Edward, had Robert. SAMUEL, Salem, kn. only as hav. gr. of ld. 1637. SAMUEL, Dedham, perhaps s. of Nathaniel, was a soldier in Moseley's comp. Dec. 1675. * WILLIAM, Boston, came in the fleet, 1630, with Winth. hav. been active in the engagem. to emb. 1629, in the list of ch. mem. stands No. 9, was chos. the first yr. a deac. on the d. of Gager, and after rul. Elder, ask. adm. as freem. 19 Oct. 1630, and 18 May foll. was sw. his identi. being pro. by prefix of respect, tho. Mr. Secr. chang. his spell. rep. 1635, but in 1637, tho. he was guilty of support. opinions of Wheelwright, was neither disarm. nor disfranchis.

and even permit. to cont. selectman very oft. He d. 1 Aug. 1662, the date of his will, that is cop. into Geneal. Reg. XI. 174. His ch. surv. were Sarah Pierce, w. of William ; Mary Turin, Turand, or Turell, wh. had been w. of John Barrell ; and Eliz. Paine. WILLIAM, Boston, perhaps s. of the preced. left at home at sch. came in the James, 1635, aged 16, from London, and if so, prob. d. bef. his f.

COLBY, ANTHONY, Boston 1630, prob. came with Winth. No. 93 on list of ch. mem. may have been, 1632, at Cambridge, freem. 14 May 1634, rem. to Salisbury, there, by w. Susanna, had Isaac, b. 6 July 1640 ; Rebecca, 11 Mar. 1643 ; Mary, 19 Sept. 1647; and Thomas, 8 Mar. 1651 ; but he had four other ch. earlier, of wh. two only are kn. by name, John, bapt. 8 Sept. 1633, the same day with Seaborn Cotton, and Sarah, wh. m. 6 Mar. 1654, Orlando Bagley. He d. 1 Feb. 1661 ; and his wid. m. 1664, William Whitteridge of Amesbury, was again wid. liv. in Sept. 1682, infirm with age. Rebecca m. 9 Sept. 1661, John Williams ; and Mary m. 23 Sept. 1668, William Sargent. ARTHUR, Ipswich 1637, may have been br. of the preced. ISAAC, Salisbury 1663, s. of Anthony, by w. Martha had Anthony, b. 24 Jan. 1670 ; rem. to Rowley, and prob. d. bef. 1691, when his wid. was tax. for the est. JOHN, Salisbury, eldest ch. of Anthony, m. 14 Jan. 1656, Frances, d. of John Hoyt, had John, b. 19 Nov. 1656; Sarah, 17 July 1658 ; Frances, 10 Dec. 1662 ; and Anthony, and Susanna, tw. 10 May 1665. * SAMUEL, Amesbury, perhaps s. of Anthony, took o. of alleg. with John and Thomas, 20 Dec. 1677, by w. Eliz. d. of William Sargent, had Dorothy; Eliz. b. 1 June 1670 ; and was rep. 1689. THOMAS, Amesbury, youngest s. of Anthony, sw. alleg. 20 Dec. 1677. Of this name, in 1834, gr. at N. E. coll. were eleven, says Farmer.

COLCORD, EDWARD, Exeter 1638, but as a ch. his first com. is reckon. 1631, rem. 1640, to Dover, and Hampton 1644, perhaps to Saco 1668, but back to H. there, in 1673, call. hims. 56 yrs. old, of course b. a. 1617, and d. 10 Feb. 1682. Perhaps his wid. d. 24 June 1689, for Pike's Diary, on that day, ment. d. of a Mrs. C. He had seven ds. of wh. Hannah m. 28 Dec. 1665, Thomas Dearborn; Sarah m. 30 Dec. 1668, John Hobbs; Mary m. 28 Dec. 1670, Benjamin Fifield; Mehitable m. 20 Dec. 1677, Nathaniel Stevens; and prob. the others, Shuah, b. 12 June 1660 ; Deborah, 21 May 1664; and Abigail, 23 July 1667 ; all d. young, or certain. unm. Of three s. the eldest, Jonathan, d. 31 Aug. 1661, in his 21st yr. the sec. was Edward, k. by the Ind. 13 June 1677 ; and the other was Samuel. To support the reputa. of the famous forged deed of Ind. Sachems, that gr. to John Wheelwright, and others, all the E. and centr. region of N. H. 17 May 1629, more than seven yrs. bef. W. came over the ocean, it was pro. by o. of W. tak. 13 Oct. 1663, that he employ. Colcord to purchase from some Ind. the lds. upon or near wh. he design. to found the new town of Exeter, a refuge from the intolerance of Mass. in 1638. It must be evid. that tho. C. were competent to such dealing in 1638, he was less than fourteen yrs. of age in May 1629, when W. was 20 yrs. older, as he had tak. his A. B. at Cambridge Univ. 1614; and both would surely have been jeer. by the lords of the forest for such attempt at a treaty. * SAMUEL, Hampton, youngest s. of the preced. by w. Mary had Jonathan, b. 4 Mar. 1684; and Eliz. 6 Dec. 1686; was rep. 1682. Descend. are num. in N. H. of wh. one, Ebenezer, d. at Brentwood, 1824, in his 99th yr.

COLDAM, or COLDHAM, ‖ CLEMENT, Lynn 1630, a miller, was of ar. co. 1645, of wh. I kn. no more but that he had Clement, and prob. others, and sw. 26 May 1661, that he had kn. William Longley at L. 23 yrs. CLEMENT, Lynn, s. of the preced. b. in Eng. rem. to Gloucester, had Judith, wh. d. 28 Feb. 1650, testif. 28 May 1678, that he was in his 55th yr. and d. 18 Dec. 1703, so aged 80. Eliz. prob. his d. m. at G. 15 Oct. 1663, Francis Norwood, and Mary, perhaps his wid. d. 26 Jan. 1705. JOHN, Gloucester, freem. 1664, was, perhaps, br. or s. of the preced. THOMAS, Lynn 1630, was, perhaps, br. of Clement the first, kept Mr. Humfrey's mill, freem. 14 May 1634, d. 8 Apr. 1675, aged 73. Thomas jr. of Lynn, perhaps his s. perhaps his neph. d. 18 Mar. or May 1673.

COLE, COALE, or COALES, ABRAHAM, Salem, perhaps s. of Isaac, was a tailor, wh. may first have liv. at Hampton, where he took o. of fidel. Dec. 1678, and in evil hour rem. to S. and there his w. in 1692 was charg. with witchcraft. Felt, II. 481. Yet if the charge imply, as usual. it does, old age, she was very fortunate not to have been tried, were her h. the same man, call. as witness so early as 1645; and in Jan. 1693 she was liberat. on bail by her h. ALEXANDER, Salem 1685, a Scot from Dunbarton, m. Bethia, wid. of Henry Silsbee, had only ch. Alexander, and d. 1687, in his will of 24 June, pro. 24 Aug. of that yr. ment. two maid. sis. Ann, and Jeannett at D. ARTHUR, Cambridge, d. 4 Sept. 1676, leav. young wid. Lydia, wh. m. 13 Apr. 1680, William Eager, or Eger. He had m. her 27 Nov. 1673, had Arthur, b. 10 Dec. 1674, wh. d. 30 Oct. 1702; and Daniel, 7 Mar. 1676. CLEMENT, Boston, came in the Susan and Ellen, 1635, from London, aged 30, as serv. with capt. Keayne, prob. with w. and ch. for in 1639 he had a lot for seven heads gr. at Braintree. DANIEL, Yarmouth, rem. to Eastham 1643, was br. of Job, first town clk. rep. 1652, and six yrs. more, by w. Ruth had John, b. 15 July 1644, Timothy, 4 Sept. 1646; Hepzibah, 15 Apr. 1649; Ruth, 15 Apr. 1651; Israel, 8 Jan. 1653; James, 30 Nov. 1655; Mary, 10 Mar. 1659; and William, 15 Sept. 1663. He d. 21 Dec. 1694, aged

80; and his w. Ruth d. six days bef. aged only 67. Hamblen gives him
other ch. Thomas, and Esther, and says, Mary m. 26 May 1681, Joshua
Hopkins, and Ruth m. John Young. EDWARD, Pemaquid 1674.
ELISHA, Kingstown, R. I. prob. s. of John, by w. Eliz. had Thomas, wh.
d. 1722; but others, earlier, or later, or both, he had, for in 1725,
Dr. McSparran, missiona. of the London Soc. for Prop. Gosp. bapt. his
w. and ch. John, Edward, Susanna, Ann, Eliz. and Abigail. He d. early
in 1729 at London, whither he had gone on a lawsuit. EPHRAIM,
Plymouth, a. 1690, blacksmith, m. Rebecca Gray, wh. has been thot. d.
of Edward, and he was suppos. s. of James; but neither of h. nor w. is
the f. ascert. FRANCIS, Boston, by w. Sarah had Sarah, b. 29 Apr.
1689. GEORGE, Lynn 1637, rem. to Sandwich, d. a. 1653, but perhaps
had gone back to L. at least inv. of 28 June in that yr. of a Lynn man
is seen. GEORGE, perhaps of Lynn, was one of Lothrop's comp. kn. as
the flower of Essex, k. at Bloody brook, 18 Sept. 1675. GERSHOM,
Swanzey, k. by the Ind. on the first day of hostil. 24 June 1675.
GILBERT, Boston, freem. 1677, by w. Frances had Samuel, b. 30 Nov.
1678; but this was thot. to stand for Colesworthy, among the frequent
blunders of our Secr. of the Col. or his dep. yet it is pr. Cole in the list
of mem. of O. S. ch. in Boston, adm. 30 Mar. 1677, being the same day,
when Samuel Sewall, afterward ch. just. was rec. and S. follows next
after C. See the note of Mr. Colesworthy in Geneal. Reg. VI. 389.
In the O. S. rec. Gilbert had Thomas (wh. by town rec. was b. 14),
bapt. 20 June 1680. GREGORY, Portsmouth, R. I. 1655. HENRY,
Sandwich 1643, perhaps went to Middletown, there m. 10 Dec. 1646,
Sarah Rusco (prob. d. of William b. by his first w. in Eng.) had Henry,
b. 20 Sept. 1647; James, 8 Feb. 1650; John, 14 Feb. 1652; William,
25 Apr. 1653; Sarah, 22 Oct. 1654; Samuel, 10 Sept. 1656; Mary, 11
June 1658; Joanna, 1 Aug. 1661; Abigail, 28 Oct. 1664; and Rebecca,
8 Apr. 1667; rem. to Wallingford, there d. 1676. The wid. d. at Saybrook, Jan. 1688, and nine of those ten ch. (Sarah not ment.) div. the
est. in the same yr. Henry, eldest s. with Samuel, the youngest, then
liv. at Wethersfield; James, and William, at Wallingford; John, at Boston; Mary, w. of Richard Goodale, at Middletown; Joanna, or Hannah,
w. of Samuel Taylor, at Wethersfield; Abigail, w. of John Stephens, at
Killingworth; and Rebecca, then unm. HENRY, Boston, by w. Mary
had Ann, b. 9, bapt. 13 Nov. 1687; Henry, 2, bapt. 6 Jan. 1689; Mary,
bapt. 14 Dec. 1690; and perhaps more. Henry, s. of one Henry, appears on rec. as b. 27 July 1676; but there it is spell. Coole. * HUGH,
Plymouth 1653, shipwright, perhaps s. of James the first, rem. to
Swanzey, m. 8 Jan. 1655, Mary, d. of Richard Foxwell of Scituate, had
James, b. 3, or (by ano. page on the same Col. Rec.) 8, Nov. 1655;

Hugh, 8, or 15, Mar. 1658; John, 15 May 1660; Martha, 16 Apr. 1662; Ann, 14 Oct. 1664; Ruth, 8, or 17, Jan. 1666; and Joseph, 15 May 1668, was rep. 1673, 80, 3-6. He had sec. w. Eliz. wid. of Jacob Cook, m. 1 Jan. 1689, of wh. he was third h. and in 1698 took third w. the wid. Mary Morton. ISAAC, Charlestown, came from Sandwich, Co. Kent, 1635, in the Hercules, with w. Joanna, and two ch. and h. and w. join. the ch. in Sept. 1638, had, here, Abraham, b. 3 Oct. 1636, bapt. Sept. 1638; Isaac, 1637; Mary, bapt. 20 Jan. 1639; Jacob, 16, bapt. 18 July 1641; and Eliz. b. 26 Sept. 1643. He was adm. freem. 14 Mar. 1639, and d. 10 June 1674. ISAAC, Woburn, s. of the preced. m. 1 Feb. 1659, Jane Britton, wh. d. 10 Mar. 1687, was constable 1662. ISÁAC, Hull, was a soldier in Johnson's comp. Dec. 1675. ISRAEL, Eastham, s. of Daniel, m. 24 Apr. 1679, Mary Rogers, perhaps d. of John of Duxbury, had Hannah, b. 28 June 1681; Israel, 28 June 1685; and was liv. there in 1695. JACOB, Charlestown, by w. Sarah, d. of John Train of Watertown, m. 12 Oct. 1679, says Bond, 606, where the date should be, I think, ten yrs. earlier, had Sarah, Abigail, and Hannah, all bapt. 23 Apr. 1676; and Jacob, 18 Feb. 1677. He had been a soldier in Moseley's comp. in the gr. Narraganset fight, 19 Dec. 1675. JAMES, Plymouth 1633, first occup. of the little hill, where the early pilgrims had been bur. was that yr. at Saco, perhaps, as in Haz. Coll. I. 326, or Folsom, 33, 125; by w. Mary, had James; Hugh, b. a. 1632, bef. ment.; John; Mary, wh. m. John Almy. He kept an inn from 1638 to 1660, and he was liv. in 1688, very aged. JAMES, Hartford 1639, by first w. had John, wh. perhaps d. young; and Abigail, wh. m. Daniel Sillivant; and he m. in Eng. says fam. tradit. wid. Ann, mo. of William Edwards, progenit. of famous Jonathan, by her had, prob. no ch. and d. 1652. JAMES, Plymouth, call. junr. 1643, when he was enrol. among the able to bear arms, s. prob. of James the first, m. 23 Dec. 1652, at Scituate, Mary Tilson, had Mary, b. 3 Dec. 1653, and Deane says he soon rem. from S. to York, and, perhaps, in 1654 to Kennebeck. * JAMES, Swanzey, was a lieut. and Baylies says rep. 1690. He may have been the same as the foregoing. JOB, Duxbury, br. of Daniel, m. 15 May 1634, Rebecca, d. of William Collier, had John; Job; Daniel; and Rebecca, b. 26 Aug. 1654; seems to have been much giv. to migrat. was at Yarmouth, among the fencibles, 1643, again at D. 1646, at Eastham 1652; and his d. is not ment. but the w. or wid. Rebecca d. Dec. 1698, aged 88. JOHN, Boston, by w. Joan had Sarah, b. 15 Jan. 1642; and John, 17 Nov. 1643; and may have rem. soon, or d. JOHN, Salisbury 1640-50, perhaps came in the Confidence, 1638, and d. 1682. JOHN, Lewis finds at Lynn 1642, and says he d. 8 Oct. 1703; but of w. or fam. nothing. JOHN, Boston, s. of Samuel of the same, was, prob. b. in Eng. m. 30 Dec. 1651, Susanna, youngest ch. of William Hutchinson, wh. had been tak. by the Ind. 1643, when they k. her wid. mo. had Samuel, b. 24 Mar. 1656; Mary, 6 Oct. 1658; John, 23 Jan. 1660, prob. d. soon; Ann, 7 Mar. 1661; John, again, 17 Jan. 1666; Hannah, 17 Dec. 1668; and William, 13 July 1671; perhaps Elisha, and other ch. whose names are not heard, rem. bef. 1664 to look after lds. of Hutchinson, to the Narraganset, when the jurisdict. of Conn. appoint. him and others to be magistr. there, and d. early in 1707. His w. Susanna and s. William had admin. JOHN, Eastham, s. prob. of Daniel, m. says Hamblen (in Geneal. Reg. VI. 44), 12, but Col. Rec. has 10, Dec. 1666, Ruth Snow, perhaps d. of Nicholas, had Ruth, b. 11 Mar. 1668; John, 6 Mar. 1670; Hepzibah, June 1672; Hannah, 27 Mar. 1675; Joseph, 11 June 1677; Mary, 22 Oct. 1679; and Sarah, 10 June 1682. His w. d. 27 Jan. 1717; and he d. 6 Jan. 1725. JOHN, Hartford, had Sarah, bapt. 7 Feb. 1647; and Mary, b. a. 27 June 1654, was constable 1657, and adm. freem. the same yr. d. 1685, in his will of 4 Aug. 1683 names ch. John, of Farmington, Samuel, and Nathaniel, of Hartford, Job, in Eng. Ann, w. of Andrew Benton, and Lydia, w. of John Wilson. JOHN, Wells 1653, perhaps s. of Thomas, d. 1661, or his inv, is produc. of 20 Apr. of that yr. JOHN, Boston, m. 10 Nov. 1659, Susanna, d. of Nicholas Upshur; but this rec. is more prob. of Joseph Cox, yet John and Susanna Cole by rec. had John, b. 22 Jan. 1661. JOHN, Hadley 1666, freem. that yr. is the same as Cowles. He was call. farmer, to disting. him from the other John, the carpenter, when both liv. at Hartford; and the object of change in surname was to prevent confus. but it has increas. the evil. As well as the carpenter John, this farmer had ch. John, Samuel, and perhaps others. JOHN, Duxbury, s. of Job, m. 21 Nov. 1667, Eliz. Rider; but this man is very indistinct. seen in Winsor, 247. JOHN, Swanzey 1669. JOHN, Farmington, s. of John, the Hartford carpenter, may be the man, wh. by w. Rachel had John, aged 24; Rachel, perhaps wid. of Joseph Smith, 21; Samuel, 13; and Nathaniel, 11, when his will of Sept. 1689, and his inv. of Nov. foll. were brot. in. But no slight uncertain. attends this inquiry. Ano. JOHN of Farmington, perhaps s. of the Cowles farmer, had Dorothy, bapt. 3 July 1681; and Lydia, 22 Mar. 1685. Under Cowles the cloud may be scattered or increas. JOHN, Gloucester, by w. Mehitable had Daniel, b. 14 May 1669. JOHN, Pemaquid 1674. JOHN, Groton, had a d. perhaps Hepzibah, b. 20 Feb. 1672. JOHN, Boston, m. Mary, d. of the brave John Gallop, k. in the decis. battle of Philip's war, had Samuel, b. 16, bapt. 21 Sept. 1684; Thomas, 23, bapt. 25 Apr. 1686; Mary, 9 May 1688, bapt. 9 Mar. 1690. JOSEPH, York 1680, spell. with double *o* and final *e*. MATTHEW, Northampton

1663, m. Susanna, only ch. of Henry Cunliffe, was k. by lightning, 28 Apr. 1665. NATHANIEL, Hempstead, L. I. s. of Robert of Providence or Warwick, from wh. prob. on m. of his mo. he rem. m. 30 Aug. 1667, Martha Jackson. NATHANIEL, Hartford, s. of John, the carpenter of the same, m. Nov. 1676, Lydia Davis, had Nathaniel, b. 6 Nov. 1682. His w. d. 25 Jan. 1684, and he m. 23 Oct. foll. Mary Benton, had no other ch. and d. 20 Apr. 1708, leav. good est. to his s. NICHOLAS, Wells, was constable 1658, had Jane, wh. m. Joseph Litchfield, and next, 2 July 1698, John Heard of Dover. Perhaps he had, also, NICHOLAS, of Wells, a soldier, k. by the Ind. 11 May 1704. His name on Maine rec. appears Coole. RICE, or RISE, Charlestown 1630, among mem. of the ch. of Boston precedes Rev. John Eliot, and he is of those dism. Oct. 1632, to form the new ch. at C. with his w. of the odd name of Arrold, wh. does not, however, stand in the Boston list, was adm. freem. 1 Apr. 1633, and d. 15 May 1646. From the will of his wid. call. Harrold Colles, made 20 Dec. 1661, pro. six days after, we learn, that he had s. John, and also it names gr.ch. John and Mary C. beside s. Lowden, and Pierce, wh. had, of course, m. ds. and gr.ch. John, Mary, and James L. ROBERT, Roxbury, came in the fleet with Winth. req. to be made freem. 19 Oct. 1630, and was adm. 18 May foll. rem. perhaps to Salem, and to Ipswich, was oft. punish. for drunken. yet in 1638 seems to be reform. if remis. of fines may just. be thus understood, tho. it may only have been act of policy to ensure his rem. from our jurisdict. But at last he went to Providence, was reform. in earnest, and bec. one of the found. of the first Bapt. ch. there. By w. Mary he had John, beside Daniel, Nathaniel, Robert, and ds. Sarah, perhaps youngest; Ann, wh. m. Henry Townsend; Eliz. wh. m. John Townsend; both from L. I. where Quakers were persecut. by the Dutch. He d. bef. 18 Oct. 1654, when the town counc. exercis. their duty of mak. distrib. of his prop. in the way he should have made his will. The wid. m. Matthias Harvey, and rem. to Oyster Bay, L. I. with her s. Nathaniel and Daniel, and the two ds. that m. Townsend foll. ROBERT, Boston, by w. Ann had d. Staines, b. 19 Jan. 1681; s. Staines, 10 Dec. 1682; and Richard, 21 Jan. 1685. SAMPSON, Boston 1673, m. Eliz. d. of Edward Weeden, had Eliz. b. 7 June 1674, d. young; Eliz. again, 19 Nov. 1679; David, 21 Dec. 1683; and Jonathan, 2 Sept. 1686. ‖ SAMUEL, Boston, came in the fleet with Winth. and with his w. Ann join. the ch. as Nos. 40 and 41 of the mem. desir. adm. as freem. 19 Oct. 1630, and was sw. 18 May foll. and of ar. co. 1637, being one of its found. The first ho. of entertain. in B. was open. by him 1633. His w. d. early, and how many ch. she had is not cert. but prob. the sec. w. wh. was wid. Margaret Green, and his third, m. 16 Oct. 1660, Ann, wid. of Robert Keayne, gave him none. The will, of 21 Dec. 1666, pro. 13 Feb. foll. speaks of s. John ; d. Eliz. w. of Edward Weeden ; Mary, w. of Edmund Jackson, and his ch. by her, Elisha, and Eliz. gr.ch. Sarah, w. of John Senter ; gr.s. Samuel, eldest s. of his s. John ; and gr.ch. Samuel Royal, ch. of Phebe Green, d. of his sec. w. that was w. of William Royal ; so that we may well infer, that most of his own ch. if not all, were b. in Eng. SAMUEL, Farmington, s. of farmer John of the same, call. Cowles, m. 1661, Abigail, d. of Timothy Stanley, had Samuel, b. 17 Mar. 1662; Abigail, Jan. 1664; Hannah, Dec. 1664; Timothy, 4 Nov. 1666; Sarah, bapt. 27 Dec. 1668 ; John, b. 28 Jan. 1671 ; Nathaniel, 11 Feb. 1673 ; Isaac, 28 Mar. 1675 ; Joseph, 18 June 1677 ; Eliz. 17, bapt. 21 Mar. 1680 ; and Caleb, bapt. 25 June 1682, all the eleven liv. when the f. d. 17 Apr. 1691. SAMUEL, Hartford, s. of John, the carpenter, d. 16 Mar. 1694, in his will, made the day bef. names w. Mary, ch. Samuel, Ichabod, John, Jonathan, Eliz. Dorothy, and Hannah. THOMAS, Hampton 1638, prob. came in the Mary and John 1634, with w. Eunice, was an orig. propr. there, but found at Salem 1649. WILLIAM, Exeter 1639, was the yr. bef. witness to the deed (true, not spurious), from the Ind. to Wheelwright, with wh. he rem. to Wells, 1640, was constable 1645, submit. with John and Nicholas, perhaps his s. perhaps brs. 1653, to the Mass. jurisdict. may have rem. to Hampton, there d. 26 May 1662, in his 82d yr. WILLIAM, Boston, by w. Ann had Mary, b. 6, and d. 23 Dec. 1653. Of him I hear no more. WILLIAM, Boston, by w. Martha had William, b. 14 Apr. bapt. at O. S. ch. in her right 24 July 1687, as was Martha, again, with tw. William, b. 7, bapt. 10 Feb. 1689 ; and Martha, again, with tw. Mary, bapt. 16 Nov. 1690. WILLIAM, Eastham, s. of Daniel of the same, m. 2 Dec. 1686, Hannah Snow, prob. d. of Stephen of the same, had Elisha, b. 26 Jan. 1689 ; Daniel, 4 Oct. 1691 ; Hannah, 15 Dec. 1693 ; and Jane, 4 Jan. 1696 ; and his w. d. 23 June 1737. WILLIAM, Kingstown, s. of John, in his will names ch. John, Samuel, Joseph, Benjamin, Wignal, Mary Dickinson, Ann, Hannah, and Susanna. It was made 22 Sept. 1727, and pro. 18 Sept. 1734. Three of this name were in the list of gr. at Harv. 1834, and six at other N. E. coll. some hav. *a* aft. *o*, and some final *s*, wh. it is beyond my power to discrim.

COLEMAN, ISAAC, Nantucket, s. of Thomas, was drown. 6 June 1669, unm. JOHN, Nantucket, br. of the preced. m. Joanna, eldest d. of Peter Folger, had John, b. 2 Aug. 1667 ; Thomas, 17 Oct. 1669 ; Isaac, 6 Feb. 1672 ; Phebe, 15 June 1674 ; Benjamin, and Abigail, tw. 17 Jan. 1677 ; Solomon ; and Jeremiah ; and d. 1716. His wid. d. 18 July 1719. JOHN, Hatfield, s. of Thomas of Wethersfield, freem. 1672, had been freem. of Conn. 1658, prob. rem. 1659, had Thomas, b. 1664 ;

Hannah, 1667 ; John, 1669 ; Noah, 1671 ; Sarah, 1673 ; Bethia, 1676, k. with her mo. 1677 ; Ebenezer, 1680 ; and Nathaniel, 1684 ; was deac. His sec. w. is unkn. as also the first, but third was Mary, d. of Robert Day wh. was wid. of Thomas Stebbins, and bef. wid. of Samuel Ely, and d. 1725. Of the s. three or four went to Conn. JOSEPH, Nantucket, s. of Thomas, m. Ann, d. of George Bunker, had Joseph, b. 17 Nov. 1673, drown. in youth ; and Ann, 10 Nov. 1675 ; d. 1690. NOAH, Hadley, br. of John of Hatfield, freem. 1671, m. Mary, d. of John Crow, had seven ch. of wh. six d. young, and he d. 1676. His d. Sarah m. 1692, Westwood Cook. THOMAS, Newbury, from Marl-borough, in Wilts, arr. at Boston 3 June 1635 in the James from South-ampton, came out under contr. with Sir Richard Saltonstall and others, to keep their cattle, in wh. he was neglig. and unfaithf. as the Ct. rul. yet was adm. freem. 17 May 1637, by w. Susanna, wh. d. 17 Nov. 1650, had Tobias, b. 1638 ; Benjamin, 1 May 1640 ; Joseph, 2 Dec. 1642 ; John, 1644 ; Isaac, 20 Feb. 1647, bef. ment. ; and Joanna ; rem. to Hampton, m. 11 July 1651, Mary, wid. of Edmund Johnson, wh. d. 30 Jan. 1663 ; and he took for third w. Margery, d. of Philip Fowler (wid. of Thomas Rowell of Andover, wh. had been wid. of first Christopher Osgood of A.) He rem. to Nantucket bef. 1663, there d. 1682, aged 83. Perhaps Susanna, wh. d. 2 Jan. 1643, was his d. Coffin says he spell. his name " Coultman," but in my opin. it was Coaleman, or Coulman, as in old writ. e is freq. tak. for t, and u for a is common eno. error in mod. * THOMAS, Wethersfield 1639, rep. 1652 and 6, rem. to Hadley, freem. 1661, there d. 1674, leav. good est. to two s. bef. ment. and three ds. of wh. Sarah m. the sec. Richard Treat, one m. Philip Davis of Hartford ; and Deborah m. Daniel Gunn of Milford. Part of the prop. was at Evesham, Worcestersh. Eng. His sec. w. was wid. Frances Welles, by wh. he had only Deborah. Mrs. Welles had Thomas, John, Mary, wh. m. Jonathan Gilbert, bef. her m. with Coleman. TOBIAS, Rowley, eldest s. of Thomas of Newbury, had Jabez, b. 27 May 1668 ; Sarah, 17 June 1670 ; Thomas, 26 Mar. 1672 ; Lydia ; Deborah, 25 May 1676 ; Eleazer ; Ephraim ; and Judah. The eldest was k. by the Ind. at Kingston.

COLEY, PETER, Milford, eldest s. of Samuel, rem. to Fairfield, there d. 1690. With his inv. of 31 Mar. in that yr. the names of five ds. and one s. are ret. Sarah, aged 22 ; Ann, 16 ; Mary, 13 ; Eliz. 8 ; Han-nah, 6 ; and Peter, whose yrs. are not told. SAMUEL, Milford 1639, one of the first sett. join. the ch. 1640, m. Ann, d. of James Prudden, had Peter, bapt. 1641 ; Abilene, 1643 ; Samuel, 1646 ; Sarah, 1648 ; Mary, 1651 ; Hannah, 1654 ; and Thomas, 1657 ; and d. in 1684. In his will of 1678, and in the will of his wid. 1689, the same 7 ch. are nam.

Abilene m. Japhet Chapin; Sarah m. a Baldwin; Mary m. first, Peter Simpson, and sec. John Stream; and Hannah m. Joseph Garnsey. THOMAS, Milford, s. of the preced. m. Martha, d. of John Stream.

COLFAX, or COLEFOX, RICHARD, Newtown, L. I. 1656, perhaps s. of William of Wethersfield. WILLIAM, Wethersfield 1645, had sev. ch. b. there, and d. bef. 1661. WILLIAM, Gloucester 1654, possib. s. of the preced. freem. 1673, m. 14 Nov. 1662, wid. Bridget Roe; d. 18 Apr. 1680, and his wid. d. 2 May foll.

COLLAMORE, COLLEMORE, or CULLIMORE, ANTHONY, Scituate, neph. of Peter, b. in Eng. m. 1666, Sarah, d. of Isaac Chittenden, had Mary, b. 1667; Peter, 1671; Sarah, 1673; Martha, 1677; and Eliz. 1679; was capt. of militia, master of a vessel, and perish. by wreck, 16 Dec. 1693, on a ledge, still call. Collamer's, near his home. Mary m. Robert Stetson. ISAAC, Boston 1636, shipwright, writ. Cullimer, in our old book of poss'sns. and Colimer, in Col. Rec. in 1638 had gr. of lot at Braintree for 4 heads, freem. 1643, had w. Margaret, wh. d. 13 Dec. 1651; and he m. 22 Jan. 1652, Margery Page. JAMES, Salem 1668. PETER, Scituate 1643, had no ch. and went home to find relat. brot. br's. s. Anthony, bef. ment. and sis's. s. William Blackmore, and in his will, 1684, provides for ch. of both, as also his w. Mary. PETER, Scituate, s. of Anthony, m. 1695, Abigail, d. of Tobias Davis of Roxbury, had Abigail, b. 1695; Sarah, 1697; Anthony, 1699; Peter, 1701; Mary, 1703; John, 1704; Isaac, 1707; Thomas, 1709; and Samuel, 1712.

COLLANE, MATTHEW, of Isle of Shoals, d. a. 25 Dec. 1650; and the Court at Kittery appoint. 11 Mar. foll. Teague Mohonas admor.

COLLAR, or COLLER, JOHN, Cambridge, by w. Hannah, d. prob. of James Cutler, had John, b. 6 Mar. 1661; and Thomas, 14 Dec. 1663; perhaps others; as prob. in Boston, Jane, 20 July 1681. Hannah, prob. his d. m. 16 June 1679, James Cutting. JOHN, Sudbury, s. of the preced. by w. Eliz. had Thomas, John, Phineas, Uriah, Joseph, Hezekiah, Susanna, Priscilla, and Sybilla.

COLLICOTT, or COLLACOT, * EDWARD, Hampton 1642. Hist. Coll. N. H. II. 214. * ‖ RICHARD, Dorchester, freem. 4 Mar. 1633, was serg. in the Pequot war; ar. co. 1637, selectman 1636, rep. 1637, rem. bef. 1656 to Boston, was rep. for Falmouth 1669, and Saco 1672, d. 7 July 1686, aged 83, as his gr.stone on Copp's hill reports. His will of 23 Apr. preced. is good for names of gr.ch. wh. might be lost for want of it. His first w. Joanna d. 5 Aug. 1640, and by ano. w. Thomasin, wh. surv. him, he had d. Experience, b. 29 Sept. 1641; s. Dependence, 5 July 1643, wh. d. bef. his f.; and Preserved, bapt. 28 Jan. 1649; Eliz. and Bethia. Experience m. Richard Miles; Eliz. m. Richard Hall; and Bethia m. 21 July 1692, Rev. Daniel Gookin, as his sec. w. Winth. II. 336. Hutch. II. 515. The rec. gives the name Colcott sometimes.

Collier, Ambrose, emb. at Barbados, for Boston, 11 Mar. 1679, in the Society. Joseph, Salisbury, had Mary, b. 9 Apr. 1662, wh. prob. d. young, and he rem. to Hartford, a. 1666, d. 16 Nov. 1691, leav. Joseph, aged 23 ; Mary (Phelps), 22 ; Sarah, 18 ; Eliz. 16 ; Abel, 14 ; John, 12 ; Abigail, 9 ; Susanna, 7 ; and Ann, 4½. His w. was, I presume, Eliz. d. of Robert Sanford of H. Moses, Hingham, s. of Thomas, m. 29 Mar. 1655, Eliz. Jones, had Benoni, b. 5 Apr. 1657. She d. five days after, and he m. 17 Dec. 1657, Eliz. Bullard ; freem. 1652. Thomas, Hingham 1635, freem. 1646, d. 6 Apr. 1647, the date of his will, as in Geneal. Reg. VII. 173, 4, appears (tho. IX. 172, the abstr. of rec. of d. is one yr. earlier), aged 71, leav. w. and d. Susanna, s. Moses and Thomas. Thomas, Hingham, s. of the preced. a propr. at Hull 1657, freem. 1663, was lieut. d. 1691, betw. 25 June, date of his will, and 9 July, when it was pro. leav. w. Jane and five ch. ‡ William, Duxbury, a merch. of London, came 1633, hav. for sev. yrs. act. as one of the adventurers, and had so generous a spirit, as not to be content with mak. profit by the enterprise of the pilgrims, unless he shar. their hardships. Whether he brot. w. from home, or had any here, is doubtful ; but four ds. came, of excellent character, Sarah, wh. m. 15 Mar. or May 1634, Love Brewster ; Rebecca, m. 15 Mar. or May 1634, Job Cole ; Mary m. 1 Apr. 1635, Thomas Prence, afterwards the gov. and surv. to 1676, being his sec. w. but tradit. makes her wid. of Samuel Freeman ; and Eliz. m. 2 Nov. 1637, Constant Southworth. He was assist. 28 yrs. betw. 1634 and 1665, and one of the two plenipo. at the first meet. of the Congr. of Unit. Col. 1643, among the first purch. of Dartmouth 1652, and d. 1670.

Collins, Abraham, Dover 1666. Alexander, emb. at Barbados for N. E. 15 Sept. 1679. Anthony, New Hampsh. of the gr. jury 1684. The d. 22 Mar. 1700 of aged wid. C. is ment. in Pike's MS. Journ. Benjamin, Salisbury, m. 5 Nov. 1668, Martha, d. of John Eaton, had Mary, b. 8 Jan. 1670 ; John, 1673 ; Samuel, Jan. 1676 ; Ann, 1 Apr. 1679 ; Benjamin, 29 May 1681 ; and Ephraim, 30 Sept. 1683 ; and the f. d. 10 Dec. foll. Benjamin, Lynn, freem. 1691, m. 25 Sept. 1673, Priscilla Kirtland, had Susanna, b. 9 July 1674 ; William, 14 Oct. 1676, d. at 12 days ; the mo. d. soon after, and he m. 5 Sept. 1677, wid. Eliz. Putnam, had Priscilla, 2 May 1679 ; Eliz. 3 Jan. 1682 ; and Benjamin, 5 Dec. 1684. Bernard, New London, drown. 1660. Christopher, Boston, had, in 1640, gr. of lot for 2 heads at Braintree ; Saco 1660, was constable of Scarborough 1664, there d. 1666, aged 58, under some suspic. of murder by a neighb. wh. on tr. was acquit. and the jury say, "the said C. was slain by misadv. and culpable of his own d." He left good est. and s. Christopher and Moses. See the valua.

Hist. of Scarborough by Wm. S. Southgate in Maine Hist. Coll. III.
His wid. Jane ret. good inv. of £422, 14, 0, includ. 23 cows. DANIEL,
Enfield 1683, d. 3 May 1690, aged a. 42, leav. wid. Sarah, d. of Thomas
Tibbals, wh. next yr. m. Joseph Warriner, and ch. Daniel; Patience;
Nathan, b. 1683; and Sarah, 1686. DANIEL, Boston, s. of John of
Lynn, m. 13 Dec. 1693, Rebecca, d. of Samuel Clement, had Clement.
EBENEZER, New Haven, m. a. 1683, Ann, wid. of John Trowbridge, d.
of Gov. Leete, had Mehitable, and a posthum. ch. * EDWARD, Cambridge 1638, freem. 13 May 1640, was deac. rep. 1654–70, exc. 61, liv.
many yrs. on planta. of Gov. Cradock at Medford, and at last purch. it,
sold to Richard Russell 1600 acres, and other parts to others. Mather,
Magn. IV. 8, in his whole chap. on the tw. s. John and Nathaniel, does
not equal in value the few lines of Mitchell, from wh. we learn, his w.
was Martha, and ch. Daniel, a. 9 yrs. old when his parents unit. with his
ch. possib. f. of Phebe, wh. d. at C. 5 Jan. 1654; liv. at Koningsburg, in
Prussia; John, H. C. 1649; Samuel, liv. in Scotland for some yrs.;
and Sibyl, w. of Rev. John Whiting, all b. in Eng.; beside these,
Martha, b. Sept. 1639; Nathaniel, 7 Mar. 1643, H. C. 1660; Abigail,
20 Sept. 1644; and Edward, 1646, all bapt. here. Abigail m. prob. in
1663, John Willet, s. of capt. Thomas, wh. d. 2 Feb. 1664; and Martha,
it is thot. m. Rev. Joshua Moody. The patriarch d. at Charlestown, 9
Apr. 1689, aged a. 86. ELIZUR, Warwick 1644, s. of that wid. Ann C.
wh. m. John Smyth, Presid. of the Col. of R. I. 1649. On the d. of his
mo.'s h. she and her s. had the est. of Smyth. Of him I learn, that, in
1667, his age was 45; had m. Sarah Wright, wh. brot. him Thomas, b.
26 Oct. 1664; Elizur, 11 June 1666; William, 8 Mar. 1668; Ann, 4
Mar. 1670, wh. m. 7 Jan. 1686, the sec. John Potter; and Eliz. 1 Nov.
1672. FRANCIS, Salem 1637, had Hannah, wh. m. 30 June, tho. ano.
acco. says 27 Jan. 1669, John Brown of Salem; ask. permis. in 1687,
on the strength of his half century's resid. to keep a house of entertainm.
and ten yrs. lat. a wid. C. prob. his, of the same town, had the same
leave. HENRY, Lynn, came in the Abigail, 1635, aged 29, with w. Ann,
30; and ch. Henry, 5; John, 3; Margery, 2; and four serv. says the
London custom ho. rec.; freem. 9 Mar. 1637, d. Feb. 1687, leav. Henry,
John, and Joseph. HENRY, Lynn, s. of the preced. had Henry, b. 2
Oct. 1651; Hannah, 1 Feb. 1660; John, 19 Aug. 1662; Sarah, 9 Jan.
1666; Rebecca, 9 June 1668; and Eliezer, 9 Oct. 1673. HENRY,
Lynn, s. of the preced. m. 3 Jan. 1682, Hannah Lamson; and, 24 June
1685, a sec. w. Sarah. HUGH, Norwich, or perhaps Lyme, a devisee
in the will of young Joshua Uncas, the Moheagan sachem, for wh. see
Geneal. Reg. XIII. 236; but I find nothing more. JAMES, Salem, a
shipmaster, lost at sea 1685. JOHN, Gloucester, may have had gr. of

ld. at Salem 1643 ; had w. Joan, s. John, b. perhaps in Eng. ; James, b.
16 Sept. 1643 ; Mary, 8 Mar. 1646 ; selectman 1646 and 70, beside oft.
intermed. yrs. freem. 1646, d. 25 Mar. 1675 ; and his w. d. 25 May
1695. Joan, prob. his d. m. 25 Dec. 1661, Robert Scamp, and d. 9 Nov.
1663 ; Mary, prob. ano. d. m. 15 June 1665, Josiah Elwell. ‖ JOHN,
Boston, br. of Edward, ar. co. 1644, had, beside eldest s. John, by w.
Susanna, Thomas, bapt. 5 Apr. 1646, 7 mos. old, and at same time, Susanna, a. 3 yrs. and 12 days old ; and Eliz. 16 Apr. 1648, a. 8 days old ;
was a shoemaker, and d. 29 Mar. 1670. In 1640 he had gr. of lot at
Braintree for 3 heads. His d. Susanna m. 25 Mar. 1662, Thomas Walker.
JOHN, Boston, shoemaker, s. of the preced. rem. 1663, with w. to
Middletown, thence, soon to Saybrook, thence, in 1668, to Branford,
where he unit. in form. the ch. that yr. ; was propound. for freem. Oct.
1669, and by Hinman is nam. dept. in Oct. 1672, wh. is a mistake,
thence, 1671, to Guilford, where he d. 1704. By first w. wh. d. 1668,
he had John, b. 1665, and Robert, 1667. His sec. w. was Mary, wid.
of Henry Kingsnoth, m. 2 June 1669, had Mary ; and he m. 6 Mar.
1700, third w. Dorcas, wid. of John Taintor, d. of Samuel Swain. JOHN,
Lynn, perhaps s. of Henry, had Mary, b. 26 Nov. 1656, d. at 3 mos. ;
John, 17 Dec. 1657, d. soon ; Samuel, 19 May 1659 ; Abigail, 23 Mar.
1661 ; John, again, 10 Sept. 1662 ; Joseph, 6 June 1664 ; Eliz. 8 Apr.
1666 ; Benjamin, 19 Sept. 1667 ; Mary, again, 20 Feb. 1670 ; Daniel, 3
Mar. 1671 ; Nathaniel, 1 Apr. 1672 ; Hannah, 26 Apr. 1674 ; Sarah,
28 Dec. 1675, d. within 6 mos. ; Lois, 12 May 1677 ; Alce, or Alice, 30
Apr. 1678 ; and William, 28 June 1679. JOHN, Cambridge, s. of deac.
Edward, b. in Eng. after study. at Cambridge, went to Edinburgh, was
chaplain to Monk, bef. he mov. into Eng. for the restorat. of Charles II. ;
afterwards a min. at E. and last in London, where he d. 3 Dec. 1687.
In Hutch. Coll. are preserv. four very valua. letters from him to Gov.
Leverett. JOHN, Gloucester, s. of John of the same, b. prob. in Eng.
by w. Mehitable had John, b. 12 Dec. 1659, d. soon ; John, 1662 ;
Ezekiel, 23 Feb. 1665 ; Ebenezer, 5 Feb. 1667 ; Samuel, 3 Apr. 1671,
d. soon ; Amos, 14 Apr. 1672 ; and Benjamin, 24 Jan. 1675. His w.
was d. of Edward Giles of Salem. JOHN, New London 1680-3. JOHN,
Salisbury, s. of Benjamin of the same, by w. Eliz. had Jonathan, b. 11
Oct. 1695 ; and a d. Oct. 1697. JOSEPH, Lynn, perhaps s. of first
Henry, had Sarah, b. 18 Oct. 1669, d. next mo. ; Joseph, 16 Sept. 1671 ;
Henry, 23 Nov. 1672 ; Ann, 13 Feb. 1674 ; Dorcas, or Dorothy, 6 Mar.
1676 ; Sarah, again, 10 Aug. 1678 ; and Esther, 2 Jan. 1680. JOSEPH,
Eastham, m. 20 Mar. 1672, Duty Knowles, had Sarah, b. 2 Jan. 1673 ;
John, 18 Dec. 1674 ; Lydia, July 1676 ; Joseph, June 1678 ; Hannah,
Feb. 1680 ; Jonathan, 20 Aug. 1682 ; Jane, 3 Mar. 1684 ; Benjamin, 6

Feb. 1687; and James, 10 Mar. 1689, d. at 3 wks. Moses, Scarborough, s. of Christopher, was, in 1671, whip. as a Quaker. NATHANIEL, Middletown, s. of deac. Edward, ord. 4 Nov. 1668, m. 3 Aug. 1664, Mary, d. of William Whiting of Hartford, d. 28 Dec. 1684, had Mary, b. 11 May 1666; John, 31 Jan. 1668; Susanna, 26 Nov. 1669; Sibyl, 20 Aug. 1672, d. young; Martha, 26 Dec. 1674; Nathaniel, 13 June 1677, H. C. 1697; Abigail, 31 July 1681; and Daniel, or Samuel, 16 Apr. 1683, d. in 1 wk. His wid. d. 25 Oct. 1709. Mary m. Jan. 1685, John Hamlin; Susanna m. 26 May 1692, William Hamlin; and Abigail m. 1702, William Ward; but she may have been d. of Samuel. NATHANIEL, Hatfield, k. by the Ind. 19 Oct. 1675. PETER, New London 1650, is not thot. to be s. of any in our country, nor to have had w. or ch. at his d. May or June 1655, div. his prop. among John Gager and other neighb. PETER, Pemaquid, in 1674 sw. fidel. to Mass. ROBERT, came in the Arabella, from London, 1671, but I kn. no more of him, unless he were f.-in-law of that Daniel Rolfe in 1672, wh. was k. in Philip's war. * SAMUEL, Middletown, br. of Rev. Nathaniel, b. in Eng. aft. com. with his f. to Cambridge, there m. bef. 1664, and had Edward, b. 8 Jan. 1664, went to Scotland, perhaps a. 1658 or 9, came back soon, and was, perhaps, casually at Cambridge 1675, and Charlestown 1678, but sat down at M. there was rep. 1672, and d. 1696, leav. Edward; Martha, b. 3 Mar. 1666; Samuel, 21 Oct. 1668; Sibyl, 25 Feb. 1671; Mary, 16 June 1672; Abigail, 2 June 1673; and Daniel, 5 Oct. 1675. His w. d. 5 Mar. 1714. See Hutch. Coll. 475. SAMUEL, New London 1680–3; perhaps rem. to Lyme, m. 6 Aug. 1695, Rebecca, wid. of Joseph Hunt of Duxbury, wh. d. 15 June preced. SAMUEL, Salisbury, s. of Benjamin of the same, m. 16 Mar. 1699, Sarah White, had Benjamin, b. 5 Dec. 1699; and Joseph, 27 June 1702. THOMAS, Boston 1677, merch. THOMAS, Warwick, eldest s. of Elizur of the same, m. Abigail House, had Elizur, b. 17 Nov. 1693; William, 8 Feb. 1695; Thomas, 3 Jan. 1697; Sarah, 31 Oct. 1698; Thankful, 27 Aug. 1700; and by sec. w. Ann had Ann, 16 July 1707; Samuel, 30 May 1709; and Abigail, 20 Nov. 1711. WILLIAM, New London 1664, tax. in 1667, but is not kn. to have had fam. perhaps rem. to New Haven, and that yr. m. Sarah, d. of Blanch Marett; and was a propr. 1685. Gov. Winth. in II. 8, 38, and 136, ment. a scholar, of this name, wh. came 1640, from Barbados, was a preacher, m. a d. of William Hutchinson, and was cut off by the Ind. when the fam. of the prophetess was brok. up; but he does not give the bapt. prefix which in Backus is found to be William. Of this name, in 1834, four had been gr. at Harv. and fourteen at other N. E. coll.

COLLISHAW, or COWLISHAWE, as ch. rec. has it, WILLIAM, Boston

1633, came, possib. at the same time as Cotton, with w. Ann, and Sarah Morrice her d. for the three were rec. into our ch. the mo. foll. the adm. of our teacher; freem. 4 Mar. 1634. No more is kn.

COLLOHANE, HUGH, a strange name, seen nowhere but in the list of Moseley's comp. Dec. 1675.

COLMAN, *BENJAMIN*, Boston, s. of William, first min. of Brattle str. ch. by Increase and Cotton Mather stigmatiz. as the "Manifesto" ch. preach. first at Bath, Ipswich, and other places in Eng. but was ord. for the society in Boston, 4 Aug. 1699, at London, m. 8 June 1700, Jane, d. of Thomas Clark, had Benjamin, b. 1 Sept. 1704, d. in few days; Jane, 25 Feb. 1708; and Abigail, 14 Jan. 1715. He had sec. w. Sarah, d. of Richard Crisp, wh. had been wid. of William Harris, Hon. John Leverett, and Hon. John Clark, in succession, m. 6 May 1731, and d. 24 Apr. 1744; and his third w. m. 12 Aug. 1745, was Mary, d. of William Pepperell, and sis. of Sir William, wid. of Hon. John Frost, wh. surv. him, and m. Benjamin Prescott. He was emin. for serv. to Harv. Coll. beyond all others of the age; and d. 29 Aug. 1747. In Eliot's Biogr. Dict. a valua. acco. of him is found. EDWARD, Boston, m. 27 Oct. 1648, Margaret, d. of Thomas Lumbard of Barnstable, had Eliz. 28 Jan. 1652; Mary, 12 Sept. 1653, d. under four yrs.; Martha, 8 Aug. 1655; James, 31 Jan. 1657; and other ch. certain. Abigail, nam. in will of gr.f. L. JOHN, Dover 1661. JOHN, Hatfield, freem. 1672. See Coleman. JOHN, Boston, s. of William, one of the found. of the ch. in Brattle str. JOSEPH, Scituate, shoemaker, came in 1635 or 6, from Sandwich, in Kent, with w. Sarah, and four ch. was first at Charlestown, but went, 1638, to S. thence rem. perhaps to Norwich bef. 1690; had at S. Joseph, Zechariah, Thomas, and sev. ds. Deane. WILLIAM, Boston, came with w. Eliz. in the Arabella, 1671, from London, had Mary, b. 3 Dec. 1671, and Benjamin, 19 Oct. 1673, H. C. 1692, bef. ment. They were from Satterly, in Norfolk, and perhaps brot. John. Five of this name, in 1834, had been gr. at Harv. and nine at other N. E. coll.

COLSON, ADAM, Reading, an early sett. m. 7 Sept. 1668, Mary, had Josiah, b. 6 Mar. 1673, d. in few mos.; Eliz. 9 Oct. 1676; Lydia, 31 Mar. 1680; and David, 26 Apr. 1682; and d. 1 Mar. 1687. NATHANIEL, Newport, by w. Susanna, had Ann, b. 8 June 1678.

COLT, or COULT, JOHN, Windsor 1668, liv. to old age, had Sarah, bapt. at Hartford, says Hinman, 7 Feb. 1647, and sev. s. of wh. one or more sett. at Lyme. In his sec. Ed. 672–8, Hinman gives many names of descend. yet with no precis. of line. But the orig. is quite mythical. The sett. was b. in Colchester, Co. Essex, a. 50 ms. from London, came to Dorchester when a. 11 yrs. old, rem. to Hartford a. 1638, as says the book, with no inherent improb. but it is sure to encourage distrust of such tale, that he is made gr. gr. gr. gr.s. of a peer of Eng. wh. was dispossess. of his est. &c. Such examples may, I hope, be shun. and not imitat. Mr. Hinman had too respectab. a name to encourage the relat. of such old wives' invent.

COLTMAN, or COULTMAN, JOHN, Wethersfield 1645, a sch.master, wh. had been a serv. with Leonard Chester, or his wid. Mary, wh. in her will of 20 Nov. 1688, then wid. of Hon. Richard Russell, remem. his serv. near fifty yrs. bef. His d. Mary m. 1 May 1684, John Nash of Norwalk, and d. 1698; and he d. a. 1688, or 9, leav. wid. and three ds.

COLTON, EPHRAIM, Springfield, s. of George, m. 17 Nov. 1670, Mary, d. of Job Drake, had four s. of wh. Samuel, the youngest, was b. 17 Jan. 1680 ; and his w. d. 19 Oct. 1681. He next m. 26 Mar. 1685, Esther Mansfield, perhaps d. of Samuel, and had seven s. and six ds. by her, of wh. only Esther, b. 23 Oct. 1687 is kn. to me; but the last, his seventeenth ch. was b. aft. his d. 14 May 1713. His name is misprint. Cotton in Geneal. Reg. XII. 176, and repeat. of course, in Index. * GEORGE, Springfield 1644, came from Sutton Coldfield, as is said, Co. Warwick, a. 8 ms. from Birmingham, m. Deborah Gardner, had Isaac, b. 1646; Ephraim, 1648 ; Mary, or Mercy, 22 Sept. 1649 ; Thomas, 1651 ; Sarah, 1653 ; Deborah, 1655 ; Hepzibah, 1657 ; John, 1659 ; and Benjamin, 1661, d. young; was freem. 1665, a grantee of Suffield 1670, call. "quartermaster" in the rec. rep. 1669, 71, and 7. His w. d. 5 Sept. 1689, and he m. 1692, Lydia, d. of deac. Samuel Wright, wid. of John Lamb, wh. had been wid. of John Norton, and bef. him of Lawrence Bliss ; d. 17 Dec. 1699. ISAAC, Springfield, eldest s. of the preced. with brs. Ephraim, and Thomas, took o. of alleg. the last day of Dec. 1678, or the foll. was made freem. with br. John, 1690, and had Rebecca. THOMAS, Springfield, br. of the preced. m. Sarah, d. of Matthew Griswold, had only Sarah, b. 25 Sept. 1678, was a capt. freem. with Ephraim, 1681, perhaps liv. at Lyme, a short time, where this b. is on rec. Eleven in fifteen of this name, gr. at Yale, have been clerg.

COLVER, or CULVER, EDWARD, Dedham 1640, by w. Ann had John, b. 15 Apr. 1640 ; Joshua, 12 Jan. 1642 ; and Samuel, 9 Jan. 1645.

COLWELL, or COLEWAY, ROBERT, Providence, adm. freem. 1658, took o. of alleg. May 1666. SAMUEL, emb. at Barbados, 21 Mar. 1679.

COLY, COLIE, or COLEY, sometimes COLE, PETER, Fairfield 1668–81. SAMUEL, Milford 1639–69.

COMBERBACH, THOMAS, came from Norwich 1637, aged 16, in the employ. of Michael Metcalf.

COMBS, COMBE, COOMES, COOMBE, or COOMBS, FRANCIS, Plymouth 1666, s. of John. GEORGE, Charlestown, d. 27 July 1659, was, perhaps only a transient man. JOHN, Plymouth, freem. 1633, is call. gent. next yr. had w. Sarah, and s. Francis, seems to have d. bef. 1645, when William Spooner, wh. was his serv. in 1642, was by the Ct. order. to have charge of the childr. of Combs, and in 1666, the s. Francis got gr. of ld. in his f.'s right. JOHN, Boston, cooper, m. 24 Feb. 1662, Eliz. wid. of Thomas Barlow, had Eliz. b. 30 Nov. 1662 ; John, 20 July 1664, prob. the freem. 1690; and Mary, 28 Nov. 1666; and he d. May 1668. He spent much of Barlow's est. and the Ct. order. provis. for B.'s only ch. and his wid. wh. m. John Warren as his sec. w. and d. early in 1672. JOHN, Northampton, had there twelve ch. rem. to Springfield, and had one more, b. 1714. Sometimes this name has e final, instead of s ; and other var.

COMBY, or COMBEE, ROBERT, Boston 1681.

COMEE, or COMY, DAVID, Woburn, had Mary, b. 30 Jan. 1663 ; rem. to Concord 1664, d. 31 Mar. 1676. His d. Mary m. 24 May 1688, Joshua Kibby. This may be the same name as the next.

COMER, ISAAC, Weymouth 1662. JOHN, Weymouth, perhaps the same as the preced. by w. Sarah had Sarah, b. 10 July 1662. JOHN, Newport, a Bapt. preacher 1656. JOHN, Boston, by w. Elinor had John, b. 12 Aug. 1674 ; William, 28 Nov. 1678 ; Thomas, 6 Sept. 1680 ; and Mary, 15 Dec. 1685. RICHARD, perhaps of Ipswich 1651, m. a d. of Humphrey Gilbert.

COMPTON, JOHN, Roxbury, freem. 3 Sept. 1634, had w. Susanna, in R. ch. rec. spell. Cumpton, as also in list of freem. ; rem. to Boston, was disarm. with the majority in 1637. Winth. I. 248. Snow's Hist. 108. His d. Abigail m. 30 Jan. 1652, Joseph Brisco, but the f. was prob. d. tho. his wid. liv. to Nov. 1664. WILLIAM, Ipswich, bot. ld. in 1662 of Daniel Ladd.

COMSTOCK, CHRISTOPHER, Fairfield 1661, m. 6 Oct. 1663, Hannah, d. of Richard Platt of Milford, had Daniel, b. 21 July 1664; Hannah, 15 July 1666; Abigail, 27 Jan. 1669, d. at 20 yrs.; Mary, 19 Feb. 1671 ; Eliz. 7 Oct. 1674; Mercy, 12 Nov. 1676 ; and Samuel, 6 Feb. 1680; had good est. kept a tavern, and d. 28 Dec. 1702. DANIEL, New London 1652, s. of William, was, perhaps, six yrs. bef. at Providence, m. a d. of John Elderkin, d. 1683, aged a. 53, leav. wid. Pelatiah ; ch. Daniel, and eight ds. all bapt. as Caulkins says, in Apr. and Nov. 1671 ; Kingsland, b. 1673; and Samuel, 1677. His d. Bethia m. Daniel Stebbings. DANIEL, Norwalk, s. of Christopher, m. 13 June 1692, Eliz. d. of John Wheeler of Fairfield. JOHN, Weymouth 1639, indent. serv. of Henry Russell, sat down at Saybrook, E. part, now Lyme, had Abigail, b. 12 Apr. 1662; Eliz. 9 June 1665 ; William, 9 Jan. 1669 ; Christian, 11 Dec. 1671; Hannah, 22 Feb. 1673 ; John, 30 Sept. 1676 ; and Samuel, 6 July 1678. Abigail m. 24 June 1679, William Peake. SAMUEL, Wethersfield 1648. SAMUEL, Norwalk, s. of Christopher, m. 27 Dec. 1705, Sarah, d. of Rev. Thomas Hanford, had Sarah, b. 25 Mar. 1707; Samuel, 12 Nov. 1708; and Mary, 5 Aug. 1710. WILLIAM, Wethersfield, came from Eng. and there liv. sev. yrs. with w. Eliz. and prob. s. William, and Daniel, rem. 1649 to New London. His s. William had William, left wid. Abigail, wh. m. a Huntley of Lyme.

CONANT, CHRISTOPHER, Plymouth 1623, came in the Ann, had sh. in div. of ld. next yr. but was gone in 1627, perhaps to Cape Ann, for he had not sh. in the div. of cattle that yr. But if he had gone home, he must have come back to our country, for he was on the first jury for crim. trial here, impan. for the case of Walter Palmer for manslaught. Nov. 1630. * EXERCISE, Salem, s. of Roger, freem. 1663, one of the found. of the ch. in Beverly, on wh. side he liv. 1667, rep. 1682–4; had w. Sarah, s. Josiah, and Caleb, rem. in latter days to Windham, there, in part now Mansfield, d. and his gr.stone remains. Caleb had seven ch.; Josiah had only one, wh. was deac. col. judge at M. JOSHUA, Salem, br. of the preced. d. 1659. LOT, Salem, br. of the preced. b. 1624, perhaps at Cape Ann, had Nathaniel, John, Lot, Eliz. all bapt. 26 May 1662; Martha, bapt. 12 Oct. 1664; and William and Sarah, 3 July 1667; one of the found. of ch. at Beverly, 1667, but in 1674 was of Marblehead, had ten ch. provid. for in his f.'s will, 1678, wh. may render just conclus. of his prior d. * ROGER, Salem, was one of the earliest sett. of Mass. hav. been in 1623 at Plymouth, next at Nantasket, thence rem. to Cape Ann, there resid. betw. one and two yrs. and rem. to Naumkeag, a. 1627. He was s. of Richard and Agnes, br. it is said of Dr. John of the gr. Assemb. of Divines at Westminster, b. in the hundred of E. Budleigh, bapt. at the parish ch. of the same, in Devon, 9 Apr. 1593; appoint. 1625, gov., agent, or superintend. for the Dorchester project. of the planta. as Endicott, wh. supersed. him, was, 1629, for the Gov. and Comp. of Mass. bef. the com. of Winth. the first chart. Gov. in the country. [Felt, I. 106. Hubbard, 109, 10.] Gibbs says his gr.f. John was of French, i. e. Norman, extract. his ancest. for many generat. hav. been at Gittisham, betw. Honiton and Ottery St. Mary's. He req. to be freem. 19 Oct. 1630, was adm. 18 May foll. was rep. at the first gen. Ct. of Mass. 1634, d. 19 Nov. 1679, in 87th yr. at Beverly (wh. he earnestly desir. to be name Budleigh). Young, Chron. 24, gives him four s. I think he had five; but even the assiduous fondness of Felt, in a Mem. of gr. dilig. filling fourteen pages of Geneal. Reg. II. has not furnish. complete fam. acco. His abstr. of the will, made 1 Mar. 1678, refers to s. Exercise and childr.; s. Lot's ten ch.; gr.ch. John, s. of Roger; gr.ch. Joshua C. whose f. may have been John, or Roger;

ds. Eliz. C. prob. never m. ; Mary, w. of the sec. William Dodge, and her five ch. ; Sarah, and her ch. John and four ds. ; a gr.ch. Rebecca C. whose f. may have been either of the s. John, or Roger ; beside cous. Mary, w. of Hilliard Verin, but whose d. is unkn. ; Adoniram Veren, and his sis. Hannah, with her two ch. and three ds. of his cous. James Mason, dec. and it is equally unkn. wh. she was. Of Exercise, perhaps the third s. b. at Cape Ann, a. 1636, bapt. 24 Dec. 1637 ; Joshua ; and Lot, above, is all that is kn. to me ; John was of Beverly ch. 1671, prob. d. bef. his f. ; Roger, the first b. ch. at Salem is spok. of next. His w. was Sarah, but neither h. nor w. unit. early with the ch. ROGER, Salem, s. of the preced. the first ch. (said the rec. as early as 1640) b. in Salem (tho. the claim has been by a recent tradit. put in for John Massey), and had a gr. of ld. on that score, says Felt ; had John, bapt. 26 May 1662, was of Marblehead, there d. Saturday 15 June 1672, as his w. wrote in her Bible, still to be seen. His youngest s. Samuel d. not 9 May preced. as oft. said, but Saturday 4 May, as his mo. wrote. 3 Mass. Hist. Coll. VII. 255. At Charlestown the fam. was cont. Four of the name had, 1834, been gr. at Harv. five at Yale, and five at the other N. E. coll.

CONCKLIN, ANANIAS, Salem 1638, freem. 18 May 1642, had Lewis, bapt. 30 Apr. 1643 ; Jacob, and Eliz. 18 Mar. 1649 ; rem. to Long Isl. JEREMIAH, L. I. m. Mary, d. of Lyon Gardiner, d. 1712, in 78th yr. JOHN, Salem, perhaps, at least he is in Felt's list, as hav. gr. of ld. 1640, and he, and Ananias, prob. his s. were there in 1645 ; was of Southold, L. I. adm. freem. of Conn. 1662, as was John jr. perhaps his s.

CONDY, COUNDY, or CANDY, SAMUEL, Marblehead 1668–74. THOM- AS, a soldier in Turner's comp. Feb. 1676, prob. of Boston. WILLIAM, New London, had a lot gr. 1664, was master of a vessel in the West Ind. trade, m. Mary, d. of Ralph Parker, had Richard, William, Eben- ezer, and Ralph, all bapt. 23 Mar. 1673 ; rem. to Boston, was master of a vessel going to London, in 1679, tak. by the Algerines ; d. 26 Aug. 1685. WILLIAM, Boston, prob. s. of the preced. by w. Eliz. had Jere- miah, b. 2 Jan. 1683, wh. by w. Susanna had beside sev. others, first William, b. 15, bapt. 17 Aug. 1707 ; and Jeremiah, 9, bapt. 20 Feb. 1709, H. C. 1726, a disting. min. of Boston in the first Bapt. ch. He was, I presume, a capt. and his wid. m. 3 Nov. 1696, Nathaniel Thomas, Esq. as sec. w. and d. 11 Oct. 1713, aged 60.

CONE, CALEB, Haddam, s. of the first Daniel, by first w. Eliz. m. 16 Dec. 1701, wh. d. 14 Nov. 1714, had Caleb, b. 12 Jan. bapt. 16 July 1704 ; Joseph, 26 Jan. bapt. 3 June 1705 ; Noah, 14 July, bapt. 21 Sept. 1707 ; Elisha, 11 Sept. bapt. 23 Oct. 1709, wh. d. 6 Mar. 1809, hav. been deac. 67 yrs. ; Eliz. 22 Jan. bapt. 4 May 1712 ; and Joshua, b.

14 July 1714. He m. sec. w. 6 Sept. 1723, Eliz. Cunningham, had Simon, b. 11 June 1724; Daniel, 22 Dec. 1725; Beriah, 12 Feb. 1728; Abigail, 2 July 1730; Mary, 20 Mar. 1732; and Lydia, 29 Jan. 1736; and he d. 22 Sept. 1743. DANIEL, Haddam, by w. Mehitable, d. of Jared Spencer, had Ruth, b. 7 Jan. 1663; Hannah, 6 or 8 Apr. 1664; Daniel, 21 Jan. 1666; Jared, 7 Jan. 1668; Rebecca, 6 Feb. 1670; Ebenezer; Jared, again, 1674; Nathaniel; Stephen; Caleb, a. 1680; and d. 24 Oct. 1706, aged 80. DANIEL, Haddam, eldest s. of the preced. m. 14 Feb. 1694, Mary, d. of George Gates of the same, had Daniel, b. 26 Dec. foll.; Sarah, 27 June 1697; Mehitable, 27 June 1699; Mary, 6 Jan. 1701; Dorothy, 29 Apr. bapt. 21 May 1704; Abigail, 27, bapt. 30 June 1706; George, 16, bapt. 18 July 1708; Deborah, bapt. 4 Mar. 1711; Joseph, 20, bapt. 30 Mar. 1714; and Jared, 12, bapt. 23 Jan. 1715; was deac. and d. 15 or 25 June 1725. His wid. d. 12 May 1742. EBENEZER, Haddam, br. of the preced. had Ebenezer, and David, both bapt. 18 June 1704; Phebe, 23 May 1708; Sarah, 26 Sept. 1714; Ann, 7 June 1719; John, 27 Nov. 1720; and Samuel, 3 Sept. 1721. JARED, Haddam, br. of the preced. had Ruth, bapt. 16 July 1704; Hannah, 18 Nov. 1705; Stephen; Thomas; and Eliz.; and d. 1719. NATHANIEL, Haddam, br. of the preced. by w. Sarah, d. of Thomas Hungerford the sec. wh. d. 25 Sept. 1753, had James, b. 24 Aug. 1698, perhaps d. soon; Nathan; Daniel, 9 May 1701, prob. d. soon; Sarah, 11 Feb. 1703, with Nathan bapt. 18 June 1704; Esther, 27 Apr. bapt. 17 June 1705; Lucy, 24 May, bapt. 27 July 1707; Mehitable, bapt. 21 May 1710; Nathaniel, 19 Jan. bapt. 10 Feb. 1712; Jemima, 19, bapt. 21 Mar. 1714; and Jonathan, 11, bapt. 22 Jan. 1716. STEPHEN, Haddam, br. of the preced. m. 5 Feb. 1702 Mary Hungerford, had Mary, b. 5 Nov. 1702; Rebecca, 6 Mar. bapt. 21 May 1704; Stephen, 11 Mar. bapt. 28 Apr. 1706; Susanna, 15 July, bapt. prob. 29 Aug. 1708; Elenor, or Helena, 25 Dec. 1710, bapt. 28 Jan. foll. d. under 20 yrs.; Jared, 10 Mar. bapt. 19 Apr. 1713, d. next yr.; Mehitable, 14 July, bapt. 21 Aug. 1715; Deborah, 2 Apr. bapt. 4 May 1718; John, 25 Oct. bapt. 27 Nov. 1720; and Reuben, 30 May, bapt. 30 June 1723.

CONEY, JAMES, Braintree, had Joshua, b. Apr. 1640, d. Dec. 1642; Patience, and Experience, tw. ds. Aug. 1642; and James, d. Dec. 1642. JEREMY, Exeter, took o. of alleg. 30 Nov. 1677. ‖ JOHN, Boston, cooper, m. 20 June 1654, Eliz. d. of Robert Nash, had John, b. 5 Jan. 1656; Sarah, 22 May 1660; Joseph, 27 Apr. 1662; Eliz. 2 Apr. 1664; William, 5 July 1665; Thomas, 26 Sept. 1667; Mary, 10 Mar. 1669; Rebecca 18 June 1670; Eliz. again, 24 Feb. 1672; and Benjamin, 16 Oct. 1673; was of ar. co. 1662, freem. 1669, and Sewall says, he was bur.

Thursday, 25 Dec. 1690. JOHN, Boston, perhaps s. of the preced. by
w. Sarah had John, b. 17 Sept. 1678; Robert, 12 Dec. 1679; James,
12 Oct. 1685; and, perhaps, others; took for sec. w. Mary, wid. of John
Clark, d. of Joshua Atwater; d. 29 Aug. 1722. His wid. d. 12 Apr.
1726. Oft. the name has doub. *n*, and sometimes in rec. is Cunney.

CONIGRAVE, WALTER, Warwick, was on the freem.'s list 1655, and
soon aft. at Newport; but no more can be heard of him, exc. that he
was capt. 1661; and so strange a name would be obs. if perpet. in any
rec. as it is when made worse in Col. Rec. R. I., I. 455, where it is
distort. to Cemigrave.

CONLEY, or CONNELLY, ABRAHAM, Kittery 1640, took the o. of fidel.
1652, constable 1647–59; by Sullivan, 343, writ. Cunley.

CONNEBALL, JOHN, Boston, a soldier of Turner's comp. in the Falls
fight, Mar. 1676, was of O. S. ch. and freem. 1690, d. 10 Apr. 1724,
aged 75. His s. Samuel had his sh. of ld. in Bernardston, gr. 1736 for
those in that bloody field. The name now is Cunnable.

CONNELL, THOMAS. See Cornhill.

CONNER, CORNELIUS, Exeter, quite early; rem. to Salisbury, there,
by w. Sarah had Sarah, b. 23 Aug. 1659; John, 8 Dec. 1660; Samuel,
12 Feb. 1662; Mary, 27 Dec. 1663; Eliz. 26 Feb. 1665; Rebecca, 10
Apr. 1668; Ruth, 16 May 1670; Jeremiah, 6 Nov. 1672; a d. prob.
Ursula, in rec. Husly, 10 Aug. 1673; Cornelius, 12 Aug. 1675; and
Dorothy, 1 Nov. 1676. Ruth m. 1687, Thomas Clough of S. as his
sec. w. JEREMIAH, Exeter, s. of the preced. m. 3 July 1696, Ann, d.
of Edward Gove. JOHN, Salisbury, br. of the preced. by w. Eliz. had
Joseph, b. 1 Sept. 1691; Cornelius, 25 July 1693; Dorothy, 25 May
1696; and George, 16 Oct. 1699. WILLIAM, Plymouth, came in the
Fortune 1621, but d. or more prob. rem. bef. 1627, as he has no pt. of
div. of cattle.

CONNOWAY, JEREMIAH, Charlestown 1678. Ann, perhaps his w. d.
21 July 1692, aged 58.

CONSTABLE, THOMAS, Boston, d. a. 1650, and his wid. Ann m. Philip
Long, wh. came from Ipswich. At New Haven 1643 was a Mrs. C.

CONVERS, or CONVERSE, ALLEN, Woburn, freem. 1644, wh. Felt
says, had gr. of ld. at Salem 1639, had Zechary, b. 11 Oct. 1642; Eliz.
7 Mar. 1645, d. young; Sarah, 11 July 1647; Joseph, 31 May 1649;
Mary, 26 Sept. 1651, d. soon; Theophilus, 21 Sept. 1652, d. soon;
Samuel, 20 Sept. 1653; Mary, again, 26 Nov. 1655; Hannah, 13 Mar.
1660. He d. 19 Apr. 1679, and his w. d. three days aft. prob. of smallpox. * EDWARD, Charlestown, came in the fleet with Winth. 1630,
with w. Sarah, and childr. req. 19 Oct. to be, and, 18 May foll. was adm.
freem. They were dism. from our ch. to be among first of that in C.
where he was selectman 1634–40, had gr. of first ferry to Boston in

1631, rem. 1643 to Woburn, was rep. 1660, and deac. His w. Sarah, d.
14 Jan. 1662. He may have been f. of all in this region, exc. Allen,
and, perhaps, was his br.; d. 10 Aug. 1663. His d. Mary m. 19 Dec.
1643, Simon Thompson, wh. d. 1658; she m. a Sheldon next yr. His
will, of Aug. 1659, names w. Sarah, s. Josiah, James, and Samuel, Edward,
s. of James, as well as alludes to others, childr. of d. Mary Thompson,
wh. was then w. of Sheldon, kinsm. Allen C. and John Parker, kinswom.
Sarah Smith. EDWARD, Woburn, s. of the preced. b. in Eng. m. 9
Sept. 1662, may be sec. or third w. Joanna Sprague, perhaps wid. of
Ralph, and prob. rem. EDWARD, Woburn, gr.s. of the first Edward, by
s. James; freem. 1685, d. 26 or 28 July 1692, aged 37, m. 5 Nov. 1684,
Sarah, d. of Samuel Stone, had Samuel, b. 9 Oct. 1685 ; Ann, 3 Oct.
1687 ; Sarah, 14 Sept. 1689 ; and Edward, 26 Oct. 1691, d. in two days.
JAMES, Woburn, s. of first Edward, b. in Eng. m. 24 Oct. 1643, Ann, d.
of Robert Long of Charlestown, wh. d. 10 Aug. 1691, aged 69, had Ann,
b. 15 July 1644, d. in 6 mos.; James, 16 Nov. 1645; Deborah, 25 July
1647, wh. m. 1 July 1663, John Pierce; Sarah, 21 Apr. 1649; Re-
becca, 15 May 1651; Lydia, 8 Mar. 1653, d. at two yrs.; Edward, 27
Feb. 1655; Mary, 29 Dec. 1656; Abigail, 13 Oct. 1658; and Ruth, 12
Feb. 1661; was a lieut. and d. 10 May 1715, aged 95. Abigail m.
Jonathan Kettle of Charlestown ; Ruth m. 25 Dec. 1698, Philemon
Dean of Ipswich. * JAMES, s. of the preced. was of Woburn, m. 1
Jan. 1669, Hannah Carter, had James, b. 5 Sept. 1670 ; John, 22
Aug. 1673; Eliz. 20 Apr. 1675; Robert, 29 Dec. 1677; Hannah,
12 June 1680 ; Josiah, 24 May 1683, d. soon; Josiah, again, 12 Sept.
1684; Patience, 6 Nov. 1686; and Ebenezer, 16 Dec. 1688, d. under
5 yrs.; and his w. d. 10 Aug. 1691; freem. 1671, rep. 1679, 84-6, 9, and
92, and speaker in 1699, 1702 and 3; was disting. as capt. and major in
the Ind. war, d. 8 July 1706, aged 61. Mather, VII. Appx. art. 16. Niles.
Hutch. II. 67. 73. 88. Short. bef. his d. a petty agitat. against him led to
some ecclesiast. trouble in the ch. of W. for wh. see Geneal. Reg. XIII. 31.
JOSIAH, Woburn, s. of first Edward, b. in Eng. freem. 1651, was deac.
m. 26 Mar. 1651, Esther, d. of Richard Champney, and had Josiah, b.
15 Mar. 1660; d. 3 or 8 Feb. 1690, aged 72. JOSIAH, Woburn, s.
prob. of the preced. m. 8 Oct. 1685, Ruth Marshall, had Ruth, b. 28
May 1686; Esther, 3 Oct. 1688; Josiah, 8 Feb. 1691; Timothy, 6
July 1693, d. in few wks.; Rebecca, 2 Nov. 1694; Josiah, again, 14
Apr. 1697; Kezia, 27 Mar. 1699; Mary, 12 Jan. 1702; Josiah, again,
25 Apr. 1704; and Hannah, by sec. w. Hannah, 25 Oct. 1707; Josiah,
again, 2 Mar. 1710; and Patience, 21 July 1712; Ruth, again, 28 July
1714; and Dorothy, 20 Jan. 1717. SAMUEL, Woburn, br. of the first
Josiah, freem. 1666, m. 14 Oct. 1660, Judith, d. of Rev. Thomas Carter,
had Samuel, b. 4 Apr. 1662, perhaps he rem. but his s. SAMUEL liv. at

W. had w. Sarah, and Joseph, b. 4 May 1691; Hannah, 28 Dec.
1693; Josiah, 10 May 1699; and, perhaps, d. 1699. ZECHARIAH,
Woburn, m. 12 June 1667, Hannah Bateman, d. of John of Boston, wh.
d. 1 Jan. 1679, had Zechariah, b. 4 Nov. 1670; Eliz. 29 Oct. 1672;
Ruth, 3 Oct. 1674, d. at 3 mos.; and he d. 22 Jan. 1679. Of this
name, spell. sometimes with *i* for *e* and oft. with final *e*, tho. the soldier
wrote it, as I have, two had, in 1834, been gr. at Harv. and eight at
other N. E. coll.

COOK, or COOKE, * AARON, Dorchester, freem. 6 May 1635, rem.
1636, with the gr. body of others, to Windsor, m. there a d. of Thomas
Ford, had Joanna, bapt. 5 Aug. 1638; Aaron, 21 Feb. 1641; Miriam,
12 Mar. 1643; Moses, 16 Nov. 1645; Samuel, 21 Nov. 1650; Eliz. 7
Aug. 1653; and Noah, 14 June 1657; the last three by sec. w. Joan, d.
of Nicholas Denslow, wh. d. Apr. 1676. He had gr. at Mussaco, now
Simsbury, but was discourag. prob. by a controversy and rem. to Northampton 1661, was a propr. 1667 at Westfield, rep. 1668; by a third
w. Eliz. m. 2 Dec. 1676, d. of John Nash of New Haven, had no ch.;
m. fourth w. 1688, Rebecca, wid. of Philip Smith, d. of Nathaniel
Foote; was capt. and major; and d. 5 Sept. 1690, aged 80. Miriam
·m. 8 Nov. 1661, Joseph Leeds, and Eliz. m. prob. Samuel Parsons.
* AARON, Hadley, s. of the preced. m. 30 May 1661, Sarah, only ch. of
William Westwood, wh. d. 24 Mar. 1730, aged 86, had Sarah, b. 31
Jan. 1662; Aaron, 1663; Joanna, 10 July 1665; Westwood, 29 Mar.
1670; Samuel, 16 Nov. 1672; Moses, 5 May 1675; Eliz. 1677; and
Bridget, 1683; rep. 1689, 91, 3, and 7, and d. 1716. His gr.stone tells,
that he was "a justice near 30 yrs. and a capt. 35." William, H. C.
1716, min. of East Sudbury, and Samuel, H. C. 1735, min. were his
gr.s. CALEB, Watertown, m. 31 July 1685, Mary Parmenter, had
Caleb, b. 1 Apr. 1686. ‡ * ELISHA, Boston, s. of Richard, a physician,
of good esteem, better kn. as politician; freem. 1673; by w. Eliz. d. of
Gov. Leverett, m. June 1668, had Elisha, b. 18 Aug. 1670, d. young;
John, 11 July 1673; Sarah, 31 July 1677; and Elisha, 20 Dec. 1678;
rep. 1681-3, and speaker, an Assist. 1684-6, of the counc. of safety in
the revo. 1689, agent in 1690 and 1691 for Mass. in Eng. to negotiate
for the col. with Oakes and Mather, and differ. on points of policy with
the latter; judge of Pro. 1701, on d. of Stoughton, but supersed. by
Addington, Nov. 1702, aft. Dudley bec. Gov. wh. also negativ. him as
counsel. wh. he had long been, d. 31 Oct. 1715. His w. Eliz. d. 21 July
preced. The s. Elisha, H. C. 1697, a very busy politician, rep. for
Boston, chos. speaker, and counsel.; negativ. in both, m. 7 Jan. 1703,
Jane, d. of Hon. Richard Middlecot, had Middlecot, H. C. 1723, and d.
Aug. 1737. ELKANAH, Boston 1658. FRANCIS, Plymouth, came in

the Mayflower 1620, with one ch. John; his w. Esther, and other ch.
Jacob, Jane, and Esther, com. in the Ann, 1623, so that he count. six sh.
in div. of lds. 1624; and in 1626 was b. Mary, and he had seven sh. at
div. of cattle. He was call. by Bradford, ".a very old man," in 1650,
wh. saw his "children's childr. hav. childr." and had m. in Holland a
nat. of the Netherlands, of the Walloon ch. was one of the first purch.
of Dartmouth 1652, and of Middleborough 1662; d. 7 Apr. 1663. His
will, of 7 Dec. 1659, made w. Esther, and s. John excors. Jane m. a.
1628, Experience Mitchell; Esther m. Nov. 1644, Richard Wright;
and Mary m. 26 Dec. 1645, John Thomson, wh. d. 16 June 1696, aged
80, and she d. 21 Mar. 1715. * ‖ GEORGE, Cambridge, came in the
Defence 1635, aged 25, with elder br. Joseph, in Harlakenden's comp.
in the ship's clearance at the London custom ho. call. with others, ser-
vants of H. for decept. of the gov. no doubt, for in the yr. foll. our rec.
gives both the prefix of resp.; freem. 3 Mar. 1636; rep. 1636, 42–5,
and speaker 1645, ar. co. 1643, capt. by w. Alice had Eliz. b. 27 Mar.
1640, wh. d. Aug. foll.; Thomas, b. 19 June 1642, d. at 2 mos.; Joseph,
27 Dec. 1643; Eliz. again, 21 Aug. 1644; and Mary, 15 Aug. 1646.
He went home, and was a col. on serv. in Ireland, there d. or was k.
1652. His d. Mary m. it is said, Samuel Annesley, Esq. of Westminster, call. "her mo.'s younger br." with wh. she was liv. 1691; and
Eliz. m. Rev. John Quick of St. Giles, Cripplegate, London. Admin.
on his est. here was gr. 1653, to Presid. Dunster and Joseph Cooke.
GREGORY, Cambridge, shoemak. by w. Mary, wh. d. 17 Aug. 1681, had
Stephen, b. a. 1647; and Susanna, wh. d. 13 Nov. 1674; liv. in that pt.
now Newton in 1672; next yr. was of Watertown, yet had some yrs.
been at Mendon, was there selectman 1669; of Watertown again, 1684,
and at C. was selectman 1678, and aft.; m. 1 Nov. 1681, wid. Susanna
Goodwin, and d. 1 Jan. 1691, and his wid. m. 15 Sept. foll. Henry
Spring. HENRY, Salem 1638, m. June 1639, Judith Burdsall, d. 25
Dec. 1661, when his inv. is produc. and his ch. nam. with their ages,
Isaac, 22; Samuel, 20; John, 14; Judith, 18; Rachel, 16; Mary, and
Martha, 12; Henry, 8; and Hannah, 4. ISAAC, Salem, m. 3 May
1664, Eliz. d. of Anthony Buxton, had Eliz. b. 23 Sept. 1665; Isaac, 9
Jan. 1667; and Mary, 12 Nov. 1668. JACOB, Plymouth, younger s. of
Francis, b. in Holland, came with his mo. in the Ann, 1623, m. 1646,
Damaris, d. of Stephen Hopkins, had Eliz. b. 18 Jan. 1648, wh. m. a. 1667,
John Dotey; Caleb, 29 Mar. 1651; Jacob, 26 Mar. 1653, and liv. to 1748;
Mary, 12 Jan. 1658; Martha, 16 Mar. 1660; Francis, 5 Jan. 1663, d.
soon, and Ruth, 17 Jan. 1666. He m. sec. w. 18 Nov. 1669, Eliz. wid.
of William Shurtleff. He d. 1676, and his wid. m. 1 Jan. 1689, her third
h. Hugh Cole, wh. outliv. her. Martha m. Elkanah Cushman, and d. 17

Sept. 1722. JACOB, Plymouth, s. of the preced. m. 29 Dec. 1681, Lydia, d. of the sec. John Miller of the same, had William, b. 5 Oct. 1683; Lydia, 18 May 1685; Rebecca, 19 Nov. 1688; Jacob, 18 June 1690; Margaret, 3 Nov. 1695; and Josiah, 14 May 1699. JAMES, Boston, d. 15 Dec. 1690. JOHN, Plymouth 1633, call. senr. prob. rem. 1643 to Rehoboth, is not kn. to have been relat. of the succeed. Perhaps he rem. to Warwick, was town serj. 1651, freem. there 1655, and prob. d. that yr. for his wid. Mary m. 1656, Thomas Relph. He left s. John, and d. Eliz. wh. m. 24 Dec. 1666, John Harrod. *JOHN, Plymouth, call. junr. s. of Francis, came with his f. in the Mayflower, was old eno. to be tax. in 1634 as high as either his f. or John senr. m. 28 Mar. 1634, Sarah, d. of Richard Warren, had four ch. liv. in 1650, says Bradford, 453; of wh. perhaps Esther, b. 16 Aug. 1650, was one; Mercy, 25 July 1654, ano. was Mary, 1657; at least one must have been m. and had more than one ch. to justify the extr. boast for old Francis to the letter, that in 1650 he "hath seen his children's childr. have childr." Jane, the sis. of John, had done her part for the blessing, I presume; and his d. Sarah m. 20 Nov. 1652, Arthur Hathaway; and Eliz. m. 28 Nov. 1661, Daniel Wilcox. But in this branch the exult. phrase of Bradford fails of truth. He was deac. but disagreed with Reyner; rem. and was min. of Dartmouth 1676, of wh. he was one of the first purch. and rep. 1673; and was liv. 1694, the oldest surv. perhaps, of the male passeng. in the Mayflower. JOHN, Salem 1637, came, perhaps, in the Abigail, 1635, aged 27, freem. 18 May 1642, had Sarah, bapt. 19 Sept. 1640; Eliz. 16 May 1641; and Mary, 22 Oct. 1643. He d. I suppose, in 1650, when his inv. was brot. in. JOHN, Ipswich 1664. JOHN, Portsmouth, R. I. 1655, of wh. I learn no more, unless that he had w. Ruth in 1682, then was 51 yrs. old, and John jr. prob. his s. was 26, and other s. Joseph and Thomas, beside sev. ds. and his will was record. 1691. As early as 1647 he was made one of two "water bailies" of the Col. if there be no mistake. One JOHN, a young man, Winth. II. 97, says, was k. by accid. at Boston, 23 June 1643; and a JOHN was at Windsor 1644. JOHN, Portsmouth, R. I. s. of Thomas of the same, freem. 1678, was "licensed" 1688, tho. for what purpose I see not. He may have been one of the chief men at Tiverton or Dartmouth 1686; then having a fam. there. JOHN, of Boston, was of the vestry of King's Chapel 1689; and a JOHN, a soldier in the comp. of Moseley, Dec. 1675, and again in Philip's war, 1676, at Hadley; may have been of Gloucester, m. 2 Feb. 1680, Mary Elwell, had John, b. 20 Nov. 1680. JOHN, Middletown, at his d. 16 Jan. 1705, left ch. John, and Mary of full age; Daniel, 14 yrs.; Sarah, 12; Ebenezer, 7. His w. Hannah, d. of capt. Daniel Harris, could not have been the first. His will was made 15 Aug. 1698. JOHN,

Warwick, perhaps s. of that John, whose wid. m. 1656, Thomas Relph, went to New Providence, and there had childr. as his w. Phebe alleg. when in 1684 she obt. divorce from him. JOHN, Hampton, m. 26 Nov. 1686, Mary Downs. JOHN, Windsor, s. perhaps of Nathaniel of the same, m. 1688, Sarah Fiske of Wenham, had John, b. 1692 ; and no more is seen of him. * ‖ JOSEPH, Cambridge, elder br. of George, came in the Defence, 1635, aged 27. They were of Earl's Colne in Essex, and there had enjoy. the spiritual guidance of Shepard, wh. came in the same sh. freem. 3 Mar. 1636, rep. 1636–40, ar. co. 1640, had w. Eliz. and ch. Eliz. 16 Mar. or Aug. 1645 ; Mary, 30 Jan. 1647 ; Grace, 9 Dec. 1648, d. soon ; Grace, again, 1 May 1650 ; and Ruth ; all bapt. at C. I think it not unlikely, that after admin. on his br.'s est. he went home. JOSEPH, Cambridge, s. of George of the same, H. C. 1660 or 61, remarkab. as it seems that so early in the exist. of the coll. ea. yr. should be entit. to one of this name, perhaps it may seem that the other was s. of Richard. But it is more strange that of neither is the date of death mark. in our catal. although both were gone in 1698. He m. 4 Dec. 1665, Martha, d. of John Stedman, had John, bapt. 26 Jan. 1668 ; and Joseph, a. 1671 ; beside Alice, prob. youngest ch. wh. m. a. 1694, Rev. John Whiting, and next, 19 May 1701, Rev. Timothy Stevens and bore childr. to both. JOSEPH, Wells, sw. alleg. 1680. * JOSEPH, Portsmouth, R. I. perhaps s. of John of the same, was rep. 1704. JOSIAH, Plymouth, m. 16 Sept. 1635, Eliz. wid. of Stephen Deane, d. of wid. Mary King, adm. freem. 1637, rem. with Gov. Prence to Eastham, had Josiah, and Ann, wh. m. 18 Jan. 1655, Mark Snow, and d. 7 July 1656 ; Bethia, wh. m. 4 Apr. 1660, Joseph Harding ; and d. 17 Oct. 1673 ; and his wid. d. a. 1687. JOSIAH, Eastham, perhaps s. of the preced. m. 27 July 1668, Deborah Hopkins, had Eliz. b. 12 Oct. 1669, d. in 6 mos. ; Josiah, 12 Nov. 1670 ; Richard, 1 Sept. 1672 ; Eliz. again, June 1674 ; Caleb, 15 Nov. 1676 ; Deborah, 15 Feb. 1679 ; Joshua, 4 Feb. 1683 ; and Benjamin, 28 Apr. 1687. JOSIAH, Windsor, youngest ch. of Nathaniel of the same, by w. Ruth had Josiah, b. 1690 ; Ruth, 1692 ; and William, 1695. His w. d. 1697, and he m. 1703, Sarah, but, perhaps, had no more ch. MOSES, Westfield, s. of first Aaron, m. 25 Nov. 1669, Eliz. d. of Hon. Daniel Clark, had Eliz. b. 25 Aug. 1673, and Moses, 17 Apr. 1675. He was k. in Philip's war 1676. The wid. m. 13 Sept. 1677, lieut. Job Drake ; and the d. Eliz. m. 1693, Benjamin Griswold. NATHANIEL, Windsor, m. 29 June 1649, Lydia, d. of Richard Vore, had Sarah, b. 28 June 1650 ; Lydia, 9 Jan. 1653 ; Hannah, 21 Sept. 1655 ; Nathaniel, 13 May 1658 ; Abigail, 1 Mar. 1660 ; John, 3 Aug. 1662 ; and Josiah, 22 Dec. 1664. He was adm. freem. of Conn. 1650, and d. 19 May 1688. The wid. d. 14 June 1698. Sarah m. 30 June 1670, Samuel Baker ; Lydia d. unm. bef.

24 yrs.; Hannah m. Thomas Buckland the younger, wh. d. 28 May 1676; and she next m. Joseph Baker, wh. d. 11 Dec. 1691; and she m. third h. John Loomis; and Abigail m. Joshua Pomeroy, and next, David Hoyt, and next, Nathaniel Royce. NOAH, Northampton, s. of first Aaron, liv. at Hartford first, there m. Sarah, prob. d. of Joseph Nash, had Joseph, b. a. 1680; Sarah, a. 1682; Eliz. a. 1685; and at N. had Mary, 12 Mar. 1686; Noah, 1688; Miriam, 30 Sept. 1690; Eliakim, 6 May 1693; Esther, 21 May 1695; and Aaron, 3 Oct. 1697; and d. 1 June 1699. PEYTON, Saco 1635, call. gent. was clk. of the assemb. of Lygonia 1648. Folsom, 32. PHILIP, Cambridge, freem. 1647, d. 10 Feb. 1667, by w. Mary, d. of Barnabas Lamson, had Mary, b. 26 July 1652; Philip, 19 Aug. 1654; Samuel; Hannah, 4 July 1657; and Sarah; all, exc. Philip, wh. prob. d. young, bapt. at C.; also Philip, again, bapt. 5 May 1661; John, 30 Aug. 1663; and Barnabas, 4 June 1665; as in matchless Mitchell's reg. appears. But it must be, that he had two ds. nam. Hannah, for town rec. shows d. of Hannah, 13 July 1654, and b. of Samuel, 1655. Sarah d. 12 May 1661. His will, of 18 July bef. his d. dispos. of ch. John, 3 yrs. old; Philip, 5; and Hannah, 9; leav. wid. Mary, to bring up others to trades. A discrepance betw. Mitchell and the inscript. on gr.stone of sec. Philip may be obs. if Harris, 57, has correctly giv. it, that he d. 25 Mar. 1718, aged 55 yrs. 10 mos. 25 days, so that by such comput. he was born 30 Apr. 1662. Prob. the gr.stone is false, Mitchell may be foll. and we may suppose he was bapt. at 5 days old. RALPH, Charlestown 1640, may have had w. Sarah, adm. of the ch. 30 Nov. 1643. RICHARD, Charlestown, came in the Jonathan, 1639, aged 31, join. with the ch. 30 May 1641, liv. on Malden side, had w. Frances, and d. Mary, b. May 1649; was of friends of M. Matthew's preaching, and d. 14 Oct. 1658. His will names ch. of his w. by former h. Isaac, Thomas, Eliz. and Sarah, Wheeler; but I think the s. were b. in Eng. Eliz. m. 12 Sept. 1659, William Greene; and Sarah m. 18 Dec. 1660, John Greene. His wid. m. 5 Sept. 1659, Thomas Green; and his only d. Mary m. 1666, Samuel Green. * ‖ RICHARD, Boston, tailor, came, it is said, from Gloucestersh. freem. 4 Mar. 1635, ar. co. 1643, lieut. 1656, rep. for Dover 1670; by w. Eliz. had Elhanan, b. 30 June, bapt. 17 July 1636, d. Nov. foll.; Elisha, bef. ment. 16 Sept. bapt. 5 Nov. 1637, H. C. 1657; Elkanah, bapt. 12 Apr. 1640, but the town rec. gives a false date of b.; Joseph, b. 2, bapt. 8 May 1642, wh. may have been H. C. 1660, or 61; and Benjamin, bapt. 4 Aug. 1644, a. 5 days old, d. May foll. His will, made 18 Dec. 1671, pro. 25 Dec. 1673, names w. Eliz. and only ch. Elisha, beside brs. William and Walter in Eng. His wid. d. 7 Oct. 1690, in 75th yr. RICHARD, Norwich, had gr. of lot 1680, in the part now Preston, and s. Obed,

b. 1 Feb. 1681. ROBERT, Charlestown, freem. 2 June 1641, by w. Sarah had Samuel, b. 10 Aug. 1644. I feel some hesitat. in this case, whether he and Richard were not one, for Richard is not in the Col. rec. as freem. which would not, however, be very surpris. tho. rather observ.; but how Robert, whose name is not found in the ch. was adm. freem. is strange. ROBERT, Portsmouth, R. I. m. 5 Dec. 1678, Tamar, d. of John Tyler of Bristol, had Mary, b. 27 June 1682; Miriam, 9 Dec. 1689; and Samuel, 19 Dec. 1695. ROGER, Marshfield 1643. SAMSON, Gloucester, d. 26 Jan. 1674. SAMUEL, Dedham 1640, call. gent. late of Dublin, in Ireland, when his excors. convey. his est. 1652. SAMUEL, Cambridge, s. of Philip, m. 14 Nov. 1681, Abigail, d. of Joseph Griggs, wh. d. 28 Jan. 1714, had Samuel, wh. d. at 17 yrs.; John; perhaps others; and d. 22 Aug. 1731, aged 76. SAMUEL, New Haven, m. 2 May 1667, Hope, d. of Edward Parker, had Samuel, b. 3 Mar. 1668; John, 3 Dec. 1669; and a d. without name; rem. to Wallingford 1673, where the residue of his ch. nam. in his will, twelve in all, were b. Mary Ives, Judith, Isaac, Joseph, Hope, Israel, Mabel, Benjamin, Ephraim, and Eliz. A sec. w. Mary, he had, but we kn. not, wh. of these ch. if any, were hers. He made his will Mar. 1703, and soon d. STEPHEN, Mendon, freem. 1673, perhaps br. of Gregory, rem. to Watertown, was one of the found. of the sec. ch. a deac. and d. 24 Apr. 1714. STEPHEN, Watertown or Newton, s. of Gregory, m. 19 Nov. 1679, Rebecca, d. of Thomas Flagg, had Mary, b. 2 Dec. 1681; Stephen, 9 Jan. 1683; Isaac, 28 Apr. 1685; John, 15 Mar. 1687; James, 23 Jan. 1689; Samuel, 3 Dec. 1690; Peter, 10 Aug. 1692; and Daniel; freem. 1690, deac. and d. 1738. His w. d. 20 June 1721. THOMAS, Salem, was d. Sept. 1650, when inv. of £40 was ret. Perhaps he was unm. THOMAS, Taunton 1639, propr. with Thomas jr. in 1643, prob. both rem. to Portsmouth, R. I. early, was call. capt. and in 1659, honor. with commiss. to run the W. line of the Col. THOMAS, Watertown, had d. bef. 1647, and may be that mariner wh. d. at Boston, Feb. 1646. THOMAS, Guilford, of whose early yrs. I kn. not the resid. brot. two ch. Thomas jr. and Sarah, wh. m. Thomas Hall. There he m. 30 Mar. 1668, sec. w. Hannah Lindon, wh. d. 7 July 1676, and he d. 1 Dec. 1692. THOMAS, Guilford, s. of the preced. m. 15 Apr. 1677, Sarah Mason of Saybrook, wh. d. 6 July 1701, had Eliasaph, b. 2 June 1678, d. at 7 mos.; Thomas, 24 Dec. 1679, d. young; Alice, 3 June 1681; Samuel, 1683, d. young; Sarah, 2 Aug. 1685, d. at 6 yrs.; Samuel, again, 23 Nov. 1687, prob. Y. C. 1705; Eliz. 22 Feb. 1689; Sarah, again, 17 Mar. 1692, d. young; Mehitable, 7 Mar. 1694; and Deliverance, 12 Jan. 1696; and he d. 1701. His inv. is of 29 Dec. in that yr. THOMAS, Windsor, of wh. no connex. with any other of the name is kn. had w. and d. Martha, wh. d. 8 Nov. 1683; and Mary, ano.

d. d. 10 Mar. 1689; and he d. 18 Nov. 1697. He had good est. and prob. left childr. to enjoy it. THOMAS, Braintree, one of a milita. watch 1689. WALTER, Weymouth 1643, freem. 1653, had Ebenezer, b. 30 May 1656; Walter, 10 Sept. 1657; and Nicholas, the last b. 9 Feb. 1660. WILLIAM, Maine 1665. Eleven of this name, a few includ. without final e, had been gr. at Harv. in 1834, nineteen at Yale, and twenty-two at other N. E. coll. among wh. were twelve clerg.

COOKERY, HENRY (an odd name), m. at Charlestown, 22 Oct. 1657, Hannah Long, d. of the first Robert.

COOLEDGE, or COOLIDGE, * JOHN, Watertown, may be youngest s. of William, gent. of Cottenham, Co. Cambridge, bapt. 16 Sept. 1604, so of good lineage; freem. 25 May 1636, selectman 1639, and oft. aft. rep. 1658, d. 7 May 1691, left wid. Mary, by her had John; Nathaniel; Simon; all, perhaps, b. in Eng.; Mary, b. 14 Oct. 1637; Stephen, 28 Oct. 1639; Obadiah, 15 Apr. 1642; and Jonathan, 10 Mar. 1647. In his will, made 19 Nov. 1681, pro. 16 June 1691, he names all the ch. but O. wh. d. 1663, unm.; and Mary, wh. m. 19 Sept. 1655, Isaac Mixer, and d. 2 Nov. 1660, but her ch. Sarah and Mary are ment. JOHN, Watertown, s. of the preced. prob. b. in Eng. m. 14 May 1655, Hannah, d. of John Livermore, had Hannah, b. 29 Jan. 1657; Mary, 12 Sept. 1658, d. in few days; Sarah, 15 Sept. 1659, d. at 5 mos.; John, and Jonathan, tw. 22 Sept. 1660, d. Nov. and Dec. foll.; John, 19 Feb. 1662; Grace, 25 Feb. 1664; Richard, 13 Apr. 1666; Abigail, 3 Feb. 1669; Eliz. 26 May 1671, d. young; Eliz. again, 1 Nov. 1673; Daniel, 24 Apr. 1676, d. at 8 yrs.; and Sarah. His w. d. 23 Dec. 1678, aged 45; and he m. 13 Sept. 1679, Mary, wid. of Henry Mattocks, had Mary, 27 June 1680; and he d. 8 Feb. 1691. Hannah m. 6 Aug. 1679, John Bond; Grace m. 29 Jan. 1689, Jonas Bond, and d. 11 Apr. 1699; Sarah m. 14 Oct. 1696, Nathan Fiske; and Mary m. 28 May 1697, Daniel Livermore. JOHN, Sherborn, s. of the preced. was a soldier, perhaps the youngest, in Philip's war, by w. Mary had Isaac, b. 21 Apr. 1685; Daniel, 6 Jan. 1687, d. at 20 yrs.; John, 31 Aug. 1689, d. at 22 yrs.; Hannah, 8 Jan. 1692; Sarah, 13 Oct. 1694; James, 17 Oct. 1696; perhaps Peter; Mary, 13 May 1701; and Amos, 16 May 1705. His wid. in her will of 5 Sept. pro. 12 Oct. 1724, names four s. three ds. JOHN, Watertown, s. of Nathaniel, m. 16 Jan. 1700, Margaret, d. of William Bond, had John, b. and d. 1702; Huldah, 10 Jan. 1705; Ann, 23 July 1706; Melicent, 12 Sept. 1708; Deborah, and William, tw. 13 Mar. 1713; Mindwell, 17 Jan. 1716; Henry, 3 Nov. 1717; Elisha, 9 July 1720; and Hepzibah, 1722. He was town clk. selectman, deac. and d. 2 Apr. 1755. JONATHAN, Watertown, s. of first John, m. 3 Dec. 1679, Martha, d. of Joseph Rice of Sudbury, wh. d. 25 Dec. 1695. He was deac. had Martha, b. 6 June 1683; Rebecca, 20 Apr. 1685; Mary,

16 Apr. 1687; Jonathan, 19 Jan. 1689; John, 4 Feb. 1691, the found.
of the Boston fam.; Josiah, 11 Aug. 1695, d. in 4 yrs.; and Joseph;
tho. in his will of 12 Feb. pro. 16 Mar. 1726, he ment. only d. Martha,
s. Jonathan and John, and gr.d. Martha Spooner. JOSEPH, Cambridge,
s. of Simon, was a deac. d. 17 Dec. 1737, by w. Rebecca Frost, d. of
John, had Rebecca, b. 1699; Mary, 14 Apr. 1706; Stephen, 18 Apr.
1708, H. C. 1724; and Mary, again, 15 Jan. 1711. JOSEPH, Watertown, s. of Nathaniel, m. 9 May 1717, Eliz. d. of John Bond, had Susanna, b. 17 Apr. 1718; Eliz. 5 Jan. 1720; Samuel, 18 Feb. 1722;
Benoni, 1723; Mercy, 3 May 1725; and Mary, 5 Mar. 1727. His w.
d. 1736, and he m. 10 Nov. 1737, Esther, d. of Joseph Mason. He was
capt. and deac. and d. 17 Apr. 1749; and his wid. m. 13 Dec. 1750,
Edward Johnson. NATHANIEL, Watertown, s. of first John, perhaps b.
in Eng. freem. 1668, m. 15 Oct. 1657, Mary, d. of Henry Bright, had
Abigail, b. 21 Sept. 1658, d. at 4 mos.; Nathaniel, 9 May 1660; Samuel, 14 Feb. 1662; Henry, 16 May 1664, d. soon; Henry, again, 6
Aug. 1665; Mary, 16 June 1667; Eliz. 1669, d. soon; Thomas, 24
Apr. 1670; Jonathan, 1672; John, a. 1674; Joseph; Hepzibah, 27
Feb. 1681; and Ann, wh. m. Benjamin Lawrence of Charlestown. He
was selectman 1677, and d. 1711. NATHANIEL, Weston, s. of the
preced. m. 2 Jan. 1688, Lydia, d. of Josiah Jones, had Samuel, b. 30
Sept. 1688; Lydia, 1690; Josiah; Mary, 6 Jan. 1695; Abigail, bapt.
22 Sept. 1700; and Thankful; and d. 29 Jan. 1733. OBADIAH, Sher-
born, s. of Simon, m. 28 Feb. 1687, Eliz. Rouse of Hartford, had seven
ch. rem. to Watertown, and d. 16 May 1707. * RICHARD, Watertown,
s. of John the sec. m. 21 June 1693, Mary, d. of William Bond, had
William, b. Mar. 1694; John, 22 Oct. 1697; and Richard, bapt. 30
Apr. 1699; and by sec. w. Susanna, had Nathaniel, Mar. 1702; Sam-
uel, 16 Aug. 1703; John, Oct. 1704; Daniel, Dec. 1707; Thaddeus, 6
Oct. 1710; and Eliz. 20 July 1712; was rep. 1722, and d. 23 or 25
Oct. 1732, both dates being seen in Bond. Of his fifth s. Samuel, H. C.
1724, librarian at the coll. and chapl. at Castle William in Boston harb.
many tales are relat. as a very eccentric, if not insane subject. SIMON,
Watertown, s. of first John, prob. b. in Eng. m. 17 Nov. 1657,
Hannah, d. prob. of Ellis Barron, first of the same, had Mary, b. 11
Dec. 1660; Obadiah, July 1663, d. soon; Obadiah, again, a. 1664;
Joseph, 31 May 1666, both bef. ment.; Sarah, wh. m. 10 July 1701,
Samuel Hastings, as sec. w.; Hannah, 7 Dec. 1671, wh. m. 3 Nov.
1693, Daniel Smith, and next, 22 May 1729, deac. Nathan Fiske;
Stephen, 1 June 1674, d. young; and Lydia, 1677, d. soon. His w. d.
24 July 1680, and he m. 19 Jan. 1682, Priscilla Rogers, and d. 27 Dec.
1693, aged 71. His wid. d. next yr. STEPHEN, Watertown, br. of the
preced. had w. Rebecca, wh. d. 1702, and he d. 1711, without ch. His

br. Jonathan had admin. THOMAS, Watertown, s. of first Nathaniel, m. 16 Nov. 1699, Sarah, d. of Samuel Eddy, had Sarah, b. 8 Sept. 1700; Tabitha, 2 Nov. 1702; and David, 25 Jan. 1705. The w. d. Nov. 1711, and he m. 15 Jan. 1713, Mary Smith of Boston; and d. 15 May 1737. Eliz. wh. m. 17 June 1656, Gilbert Crackbone of Cambridge, prob. his sec. w. was, perhaps, sis. of first John. Seven of this name, all descend. it is thot. of John, had been gr. in 1834 at Harv. and three at some of the other N. E. coll.

COOLEY, sometimes COLEY, BENJAMIN, Springfield 1646, d. 17 Aug. 1684; by w. Sarah wh. d. 6 days after, had Bethia, b. 16 Jan. 1644; Obadiah, 27 Jan. 1647; Eliakim, 8 Jan. 1649; Daniel, 2 May 1651; Sarah, 27 Feb. 1654; Benjamin, 1 Sept. 1656; Mary, 22 June 1659; and Joseph, 6 Mar. 1662; all liv. at his d. Bethia m. 15 Dec. 1664, Henry Chapin. BENJAMIN, Springfield, s. of the preced. with his four brs. took o. of alleg. on the last day of Dec. 1678, and he was freem. 1690. DANIEL, Springfield, s. of the first Benjamin, m. Eliz. d. of the first Simon Wolcott of Windsor, was freem. 1684. DENNIS, Stonington, writ. Coolie, d. 1683. ELIAKIM, Springfield, s. of Benjamin, m. Hannah, d. of Thomas Tibbals, was freem. 1690. HENRY, Boston 1670, cooper, had w. Rebecca, wh. surv. He d. bef. Nov. 1677. JOHN, Ipswich 1638, rem. to Salem, d. Mar. 1654. JOSEPH, Springfield, youngest s. of the first Benjamin, and freem. 1690. PETER, Fairfield, freem. of Conn. 1664. WILLIAM, Mass. 1634. Felt. He was a mariner, of New London, 1652, and call. hims. in 1664, a. 60. Eight of this name had been gr. in 1834 at some of the N. E. coll.

COOMBS, ALISTER, Maine 1665. FRANCIS, Middleborough 1676, perhaps s. of John, had w. Mary. HENRY, Marblehead 1647. HUMPHREY, Salem 1668, m. 29 July 1659, Bathshua, d. of Richard Raymond; had Hannah, b. 26 May 1660. JOHN, Plymouth 1630, m. that yr. Sarah, d. of Cuthbert Cuthbertson, was tax. 1633 and 4. JOHN, Boston, m. 24 Feb. 1662, Eliz. wid. of Thomas Barlow, diminish. her prop. but liv. not long. JOHN, Sherborn 1676. Bigelow, 38. THOMAS, Maine 1665. Often this name appears Combs.

COOPER, ANTHONY, Hingham 1635, came with w. four s. four ds. and four serv. (any one of whose names I would gladly learn) from old Hingham, d. very early, for his inv. was tak. 26 Feb. 1636. BENJAMIN, Salem, was of Brampton in the E. part of Suffolk, came from Yarmouth, in the Mary Ann, 1637, aged 50, with w. Eliz. 48, and five ch. Lawrence, Mercy, Rebecca, Benjamin, and Francis Fillingham, his s.-in-law, aged 32, his sis. aged 48, and two serv. John Filin and Philemon Dickerson. Of the f. or ch. we kn. no more, but the s.-in-law, and Dickerson are ment. shortly after at Salem; he d. soon, and his inv. tak. 27 Sept.

of that yr. shows good est. JOHN, Watertown, d. 1637, in his 80th yr. it is said. But this may be tradit. error, for Thomas. JOHN, Lynn, came, 1635, in the Hopewell, capt. Bundock, aged 41, with w. and ch. Mary, 13 ; John, 10 ; Thomas, 7 ; and Martha, 5. He was from Olney, Co. Bucks; freem. 8 Dec. 1636; was one of the purch. from the Ind. for the projectors of the col. at Southampton, L. I. and there was liv. 1664. JOHN,. Cambridge, came, with sis. Lydia, after their f.'s d. in comp. of Gregory Stone, wh. m. their mo. Lydia. His sis. m. David Fiske. He was freem. 18 May 1642, constable, selectman, very many yrs., deac. town clk. from 1669 to his d. 22 Aug. 1691 ; by w. Ann, d. of Nathaniel Sparhawk, had Ann, b. 16 Nov. 1643, wh. m. Edward Pinson; Mary, 11 Sept. 1645 ; Samuel, 3 Jan. 1654; John, 1656; Nathaniel, bapt. 8 May 1659, d. 19 Dec. 1661; Lydia, 13 Apr. 1663 ; and Hannah, 29 Dec. 1667. JOHN, Scituate, m. 1634, Priscilla, wid. of William Wright, wh. was sis. of Gov. Bradford's w. Alice ; rem. 1639 to Barnstable, there d. without ch. His will was made 1676. * JOHN, New Haven 1639, was agent for iron works, rep. 1664–7, had Mary, b. 1631, prob. in Eng. bapt. 15 Aug. 1641 ; Hannah, 1638, wh. was bapt. at same time with Mary, and m. 1661, John Potter ; and Sarah, bapt. 21 Sept. 1645, wh. m. 1662, Samuel Hemenway, and he d. 23 Nov. 1689. JOHN, Weymouth, whose will in Geneal. Reg. V. 303, seems to show that he was only trans. visit. in aut. of 1653. JOHN, New Haven, s. of John, m. 27 Dec. 1666, Mary, d. of John Thompson the first, had Rebecca, wh. d. 1668, at 2 yrs.; ano. d. 1668; Mary, d. soon ; John, b. 23 Feb. 1671 ; Samuel, 3 June 1675 ; and Abigail, 3 Oct. 1679. JOHN, Duxbury 1666. JOHN, Cambridge, s. of John, perhaps was soldier, Dec. 1675, in Moseley's comp. m. 28 Apr. 1686, Eliz. Bordman, wh. d. 15 Nov. 1714, aged 56 ; and he d. 12 Feb. 1736. JOSIAH, Boston, cordwainer, prob. from Hingham, perhaps s. of Anthony, m. 13 Sept. 1661, Wait a while, d. of Thomas Makepeace, had Eliz. b. 5 May 1663; Thomas, 5 Apr. 1665 ; Josiah, 4 Apr. 1667 ; and Anthony, call. in the rec. *daughter*, 23 June 1669. NATHANIEL, Rehoboth, had Thomas, b. 12 July 1676; Abijah, 1 May 1677, d. soon. PETER, Rowley 1643, came, 1635, in the Susan and Ellen, aged 28, may have rem. to Rehoboth, there bur. 28 Feb. 1678. SAMUEL, Rowley 1691. was, perhaps, s. of the preced. SAMUEL, Cambridge, s. of John, m. 4 Dec. 1682, Hannah, d. of Walter Hastings, was a deac. d. 8 Jan. 1718. She d. 9 Oct. 1732, aged 67. SIMON, Newport 1663, a physician, m. 20 Jan. 1664, Mary Tucker, call. in the Friend's rec. of Shelter Island, wh. may have been d. of that John of Watertown and Hingham, had Robert, b. 10 Oct. 1664; Joseph, 4 Feb. 1667; Mary, 20 July 1669 ; and Simon, 1 Apr. 1672. THOMAS, Watertown, bur. 20 June 1637, aged 80, as the rec. says. *THOMAS, Hingham, came in the Diligent, 1638, with w. two ch. and two serv. from old Hingham, rem. perhaps 1643, to Rehoboth, was rep. 1652 and 3; m. 17 Oct. 1656 for sec. w. Ann, wid. of Zaccheus Bosworth. He was deac. and bur. third w. Eliz. 1 Feb. 1681. Davis, in Morton's Mem. 442. Baylies, II. 198. THOMAS, Boston, came, perhaps, in the Christian, 1635, aged 18, was prob. early at Windsor, rem. 1641, to Springfield, freem. 1649, a lieut. k. by the Ind. 5 Oct. 1675. His d. Rebecca m. 12 July 1677, John Clark of Northampton. Ano. THOMAS of Boston had prob. m. a wid. Smith of Watertown, for Matthew S. is call. on the rec. of his d. s.-in-law of Thomas C. in May 1658. THOMAS, Springfield, s. perhaps, of Thomas of the same, m. 1659, Desire, d. it may be, of that capt. George Lamberton of New Haven, lost 13 yrs. bef. in the N. H. built sh. going to London. THOMAS, Rehoboth, perhaps s. of Thomas of the same, had Judith, b. 11 Sept. 1673. THOMAS, Southampton, L. I. 1673, s. of John. THOMAS, Boston, a merch. perhaps s. of Josiah, m. Mehitable, d. of James Minot, and niece of Lieut. Gov. Stoughton, had William, H. C. 1712, collea. with Dr. Colman at Brattle st. ch. of wh. this Thomas was one of the found. His wid. m. 19 Dec. 1706, Peter Sargent, Esq. and next, 12 May 1715, Hon. Simeon Stoddard, not Solomon S. as Shattuck, in Geneal. Reg. I. 172, says. William was f. of Rev. Samuel, H. C. 1743, D. D. a disting. politician, call. " silver-tongued," and of William, the celebr. town clk. of Boston for 50 yrs. TIMOTHY, Lynn 1637, d. Mar. 1659, had John, b. 1647; Timothy, 1651; and four ds. TIMOTHY, Springfield 1668. TIMOTHY, Groton, m. 2 June 1669, Sarah Morse, d. of Joseph of Watertown, had Timothy, b. 24 Mar. 1670; John, 5 Mar. 1672, d. next mo.; Sarah, 20 Mar. 1673; and John, 5 May 1675. WILLIAM, Piscataqua, one of the men sent over, 1631, or earlier, by Mason for sett. of his planta. Belkn. I. 425; and prob. Winth. I. 120, ment. the loss of same man in a storm. Six of this name had been gr. 1834, at Harv. and two at other N. E. coll.

COPE, EDWARD, Providence 1640, or prob. earlier by 2 or 3 yrs. Sometimes this spell. is used for the fam. name of Copp, wh. see.

COPELAND, JOHN, Boston, came in July 1656, in the Speedwell, aged 28, from London, a Quaker. He was next yr. banish. from Plymouth col. and whip. in Mass. JOHN, Braintree, s. of Lawrence, by w. Ruth had John, b. Sept. 1683; Samuel, 20 Sept. 1686; William, and Ruth, tw. 5 Apr. 1689; Lydia, 24 Apr. 1692; Bethia, 19 Mar. 1694; Seth, 22 Jan. 1698; and Mercy, 10 Dec. 1700. LAWRENCE, Braintree, m. 12 Dec. 1651, Lydia Townsend, sad. pervert. to 16 Feb. 1654, in Geneal. Reg. XII. 110, had Thomas, b. 10 May 1652 [Geneal. Reg. XI. 334.] d. next mo.; Thomas, again, 12 Aug. 1654, or 6 or 8 Feb.

1655; William, 15 Nov. 1656; John, 10 Feb. 1659; Lydia, 31 May
1661; Ephraim, 17 Jan. 1665; Hannah, 25 Feb. 1668; Richard, 11
July 1672; and Abigail, 1674. This last m. 23 Nov. 1715, says
Thayer, but the name of her h. is, I think, an impossib. one. Ephraim,
his s. d. unm. of smallpox on board a ship of his fleet, bef. the sail. of
the disastrous exped. of Sir William Phips, 1690; he d. 30 Dec. 1699,
b. says the rec. " in the reign of our gracious sov. Queen Eliz. of blessed
mem." Farmer, wh. was much indebt. to Ch. Just. Sewall's fondness
for instances of unusual longevity, refers to his diary, as saying he was
110. Perhaps this is mistake. In the diary of Marshall, call. Fairfield's by Dr. Harris, when he present. it to the Hist. Soc. I read, under
date 1 Jan. 1700 (so that it seems he was wise enough to be half a
century ahead of the law in reckoning the beginning of a yr.) " old
Lawrence C. bur. aged 100 yrs. wh. d. last Saturday." M. was a towns-
man, and his authority may be sufficient; but the gr.st. also says 30 Dec.
1699, 100 yrs. old. His w. Lydia, d. 8 Jan. 1688. THOMAS, Braintree,
s. of the preced. was one of brave capt. Johnson's soldiers in Dec. 1675,
m. 3 Feb. 1692, wid. Mehitable Atwood, had Mary, b. 24 Nov. foll. and
his w. d. 2 Nov. 1695, aged a. 30 yrs. His sec. w. Mercy d. perhaps
without ch. 20 Feb. 1699; and he m. 17 May foll. Mary, d. of John
Arnold, had Thomas, 10 Apr. 1700; Sarah, 23 Dec. 1701; Nathaniel,
30 Apr. 1704, d. at 2 yrs.; and Eliz. 18 June 1706; and he d. 6 June
preced. WILLIAM, Braintree, br. of the preced. m. 13 Apr. 1694,
Mary, wid. of Christopher Webb, jr. d. of John Bass, had William, b. 7
Mar. 1695; Ephraim, 1 Feb. 1697; Ebenezer, 16 Feb. 1698; Jonathan, 31 Aug. 1701; David, 15 Apr. 1704; Joseph, 18 May 1706;
Benjamin, 5 Oct. 1708; Moses, 28 May 1710; and Mary, 28 May 1713.
Nine pages of Thayer's Genealogy are fill. with descend.

COPIE, JAMES, prob. of Braintree, freem. 13 May 1640.

COPLEY, THOMAS, Springfield, s. of a wid. Eliz. wh. m. 1650, Nathaniel Phelps of Windsor, and with her h. rem. to Northampton, where
her d. Eliz. m. 1665, Praisever Turner, and sec. Samuel Langton in
1676, and for third h. had David Alexander. But the s. was of Springfield 1672, m. at Westfield, 13 Nov. 1672, and had Thomas, b. 28 July
1678; rem. to Suffield 1679, there d. 29 Nov. 1712, leav. Thomas,
Matthew, and Samuel.

COPP, DAVID, Boston, s. of William, freem. 1670, by w. Obedience,
d. of Clement Topliff of Dorchester, wh. he m. 20 Feb. 1660, had
David, b. 8 Dec. 1661, d. soon; David, again, 2 Mar. 1663; Jonathan,
23 Feb. 1665; William, 14 Mar. 1667; Sarah, 1 Mar. 1669; and
Samuel, 15 Apr. 1671; was rul. Elder of sec. ch. and d. Nov. 1713,
aged 78. JONATHAN, Boston, br. of the preced. by w. Margaret had

Jonathan, b. 6 Apr. 1670; Moses, 19 June 1672; but the rec. also ment. perhaps erron. Jonathan, 6 Apr. 1672. The former ch. of 1670 may have soon d. and Moses be a false entry. Yet it is doubtful. He was a soldier in Philip's war, 1676, prob. impress.; represent. in a petit. that his wages will not maintain w. and two ch. Many ch. he had, of wh. descend. are spread. A Jonathan, prob. his s. was of New London aft. 1700, had been at Stonington, m. 18 Aug. 1690, but he may have been s. of the rul. Elder. RICHARD, perhaps br. of William, came in the Blessing, 1635, aged 24, but no more is kn. of him. WILLIAM, Boston, came, prob. in the Blessing, 1635, a shoemaker, from London, aged 26, freem. 2 June 1641; by w. Judith had Joanna, prob. Ann and David, perhaps b. in Eng.; Naomi, bapt. 5 July 1640 (the day aft. his join. with the ch.) wh. d. 8 Oct. 1653; Jonathan, 23 Aug. 1640; Rebecca, b. 6 May 1641; Ruth, 24, bapt. 26 Nov. 1643; and Lydia, July 1646. Ann m. 11 Aug. 1646, Herman Atwood. His est. was in part of that beautif. hill wh. bore his name; and he d. Mar. 1670. On 27 of the mo. foll. his will was pro. wh. had been made 31 Oct. 1662, and David was excor.

CORBEE, or CORBY, SAMUEL, East Haddam, s. of William, m. 28 Jan. 1690, Mary Crippin, had Mary, b. 13 Nov. 1691; and Samuel, posthum. 10 Dec. 1692; the f. dying 10 Apr. preced. WILLIAM, Haddam, an early sett. in 1640 was indent. serv. of James Olmstead at Hartford; d. 1674, leav. William, 18 yrs. old; John, 16; Mary, 12; Samuel, 9; and Hannah, 6. Hinman, 20. The name has been writ. Corbey, and Corbe.

CORBESSON, SAMUEL, Maine 1665.

CORBETT, ABRAHAM, Portsmouth, disaffect. to Mass. in 1665, when the royal commissnrs. came to N. E. occasion. much trouble. Belkn. I. 60–2. CLEMENT, Boston, m. 7 Mar. 1655, Dorcas, d. of Thomas Buckmaster. See Corbin. ROBERT, Weymouth, a soldier in Philip's war, 1675 and 6, in serv. on Conn. riv.

CORBIN, or CORBYN, CLEMENT, Boston, in Muddy riv. grants, worship. at Roxbury, where he had bapt. Jabez, 23 Feb. 1668; Dorcas, 13 Nov. 1670; Joanna, 9 Feb. 1672; and Margaret, 21 Mar. 1673. Prob. he had others earlier, as JOHN, a soldier in Johnson's comp. Dec. 1675. ROBERT, Casco 1663, a man of conseq. there many yrs. m. Lydia, d. of Richard Martin, had no issue, was k. by the Ind. Aug. 1676, and his w. tak. Hubbard, Wars, 33. Willis, I. 129. 143. Perhaps he was at Boston, Aug. 1637, master of the Speedwell. Winth. II. 348.

CORLESS, or CORLISS, GEORGE, Haverhill 1645, had w. Joane. His d. Mary m. 23 Jan. 1665, William Neff, wh. d. 1689, and eight yrs. aft. she was tak. prison. by the Ind. and partook in the heroic act of Mrs. Duston, and d. 22 Oct. 1722. Ano. d. m. Thomas Eastman; and ano.

m. Samuel Ladd; and Huldah C. prob. a d. m. 5 Nov. 1679, Samuel Kingsbury. Descend. of sixth generat. still liv. on his farm. JOHN, Haverhill, prob. s. of the preced. took o. of alleg. 28 Nov. 1677, and perpet. the fam. I suppose.

CORLET, ELIJAH, Cambridge, s. of Henry of London, bred at Lincoln Coll. Oxford, where he was matric. 16 Mar. 1627, was sch.master from 1641, when N. E. First Fruits, writ. 1642, takes notice of his merit in that serv. until he d. 24 Feb. 1687, aged 76, as one acco. tells, or by ano. in 78th yr. He was freem. 1645; by w. Barbara, d. prob. of William Cutter, had Rebecca, b. 14 Aug. 1644; Hepzibah; and Ammi Ruhamah, H. C. 1670. This s. taught the gr. sch. at Plymouth 1672, and d. at Cambridge in office of tutor, 1 Feb. 1679. Hepzibah m. 21 May 1673, James Minot, and, 4 June 1684, Daniel Champney.

CORNELL, GEORGE, Portsmouth, R. I. prob. s. of the first Thomas of the same, m. Deliverance, d. of Gov. Walter Clarke. SAMUEL, Dartmouth, took o. of fidel. 1684. THOMAS, Boston 1639, rem. to Portsmouth, R. I. 1654, or earlier, was freem. there 1655, perhaps had Thomas jr. of wh. perhaps that he was hang. for murder of his mo. is all that is now wish. to be kn.

CORNELLY, WILLIAM, Duxbury 1637. Winsor, 248, 306, with strange spell. at the first.

CORNEY, or CURNEY, JOHN, Falmouth, had Elisha, b. 1668; rem. to Salem or Gloucester. Willis, I. 209. At G. he m. 18 Nov. 1670, Abigail Skilling, had Elisha, b. 25 Sept. 1672; Abigail, 8 Feb. 1676; and John, 27 Sept. 1678, d. at 2 wks.

CORNHILL, or CORNING, RICHARD, Newtown, L. I. 1666. SAMUEL, Salem 1638, b. a. 1616, freem. 2 June 1641, was one of the found. of the ch. in Beverly 1667, had Samuel, wh. was of B. 1657; and Sarah, bapt. 4 June 1643. THOMAS, Boston 1638, then allow. to keep an ordinary; had ld. at Mt. Wollaston, now Braintree, prob. accomp. Mrs. Hutchinson to R. I. thence to Long Island, and there, in 1643, was cut off by the Ind. Perhaps the spell. is sometimes Connell.

CORNISH, EDWARD, serv. of John Harris, emb. at Barbados, 28 May 1679, for Boston, in the William and John. GABRIEL, perhaps of Norwalk, s. of James, m. 1686, Eliz. d. of George Wolcott. JAMES, Saybrook 1662, sch.master at Northampton 1664, where his w. d. 28 Dec. of that yr. rem. to Westfield, freem. 1669; in 1678 was desir. at Norwalk for some serv. and in Andros's time was clk. of the County Ct. had Gabriel, wh. was under age in 1667; James, wh. went to Simsbury; and perhaps other ch. RICHARD, Plymouth, of wh. no more is heard, than that he was there 1637, and descend. are still. RICHARD, Mass. 1634, surety for his w.'s behavior [Hutch. I. 436,] may be the same wh.

Winth. II. 210, tells of, as rem. from Weymouth to York, there murder. 1644. SAMUEL, Salem 1637, had d. Remember, bapt. 3 May 1640; and Samuel, 14 Mar. 1641. Possib. in Felt, I. 174, or Col. Rec. or ch. rec. of bapt. Corning and Cornish may be confus. THOMAS, Gloucester, m. 4 Sept. 1641, Mary, d. of John Stone, had John, b. 1 Sept. 1642; was of Exeter 1652. THOMAS, Boston, possib. s. of the preced. d. 5 Jan. 1724, aged a. 75 yrs. His w. Martha d. 8 Jan. 1725, aged 66.

CORNWELL, JACOB, Middletown, s. of William of the same, m. 16 Jan. 1678, Mary, d. of capt. Nathaniel White of the same, had Mary, b. 2 Nov. 1679; Jacob, 9 Aug. 1681, d. soon; Jacob, again, Oct. 1682; Nathaniel, 30 Aug. 1684; Giles, 14 Aug. 1686, d. young; Daniel, 19 Apr. 1688; Isaac, 22 Sept. 1690; Wait, a s. 18 Sept. 1692; Eliz. 21 July 1697; and Timothy, 23 Aug. 1700; and d. 18 Apr. 1708. JOHN, Middletown, eldest br. of the preced. m. 8 June 1665, Martha, d. of deac. Paul Peck of Hartford, had Mary, b. 20 Nov. 1666; Martha, 13 Aug. 1669; John, 13 Aug. 1671; William, 17 May 1673; Paul, 6 June 1675; Hannah, 5 Sept. 1677; Joseph, 5 Oct. 1679; Thankful, 1 Mar. 1683, d. young; Thankful, again, 26 July 1685; and Benjamin, 23 Dec. 1688; and d. 1707. The wid. d. 1708. SAMUEL, Middletown, br. of the preced. m. 15 Jan. 1667, Rebecca Bull, had Mary, b. 21 Oct. 1667, d. early; Rebecca, 26 Dec. 1670; William, 22 Jan. 1673; and d. 6 Dec. 1728. Perhaps he was of Dartmouth 1686. THOMAS, Portsmouth, R. I. d. bef. 1673. THOMAS, Middletown, s. of William of the same, m. Nov. 1672, Sarah Clark, had Thomas, b. 27 Dec. 1673; Hannah, 27 Feb. 1676; Daniel, 8 Aug. 1677; Jonathan, 19 Dec. 1679; Abraham, 4 Sept. 1682; Stephen, 6 July 1683; and David, Sept. 1687; and d. Nov. 1702. * WILLIAM, Roxbury 1634, when his w. was Joan, rem. to Hartford 1639, thence to Middletown, was rep. 1654, 64, and 5, d. 21 Feb. 1678, leav. wid. Mary, s. John, b. Apr. 1640; William, 24 June 1641; Samuel, Sept. 1642; Jacob, Sept. 1646; Thomas, Sept. 1648; beside Sarah, Oct. 1647, wh. m. 16 Oct. 1675, Daniel Hubbard; Esther m. 1671, John Wilcox of the same, and next, 1678, John Stow of the same; and Eliz. wh. m. John Hall. WILLIAM, Middletown, s. of the preced. m. 30 Nov. 1670, Mary Bell, had William, b. 13 Sept. 1671; Jacob, 3 Oct. 1673; Experience, a d. 14 Apr. 1682; Ebenezer, 13 Jan. 1689, d. young; Eliezur, 1692, posthum. d. soon; and d. 18 June 1691. The wid. d. 25 Nov. 1717.

CORRINGTON, JOHN, came in the Susan and Ellen, 1635, aged 33, with w. Mary, 33.

CORSE, JAMES, Deerfield bef. 1690, m. Eliz. d. of John Catlin of the same, d. 15 May 1696, leav. Ebenezer, James, and Eliz.

CORWIN. See Curwin.

CORY, COREE, COUREE, or COREY, ABRAHAM, Southold, L. I. 1662, was made freem. of Conn. that yr. m. Margaret, d. of Jeffrey Christophers, had Margaret, wh. m. Willoughby Lynde of Saybrook. GILES, Salem 1649, had d. Deliverance, b, 5 Aug. 1658, by w. Margaret ; and m. sec. w. 11 Apr. 1664, Mary Britz, wh. d. 27 Aug. 1684, aged 63. . He had third w. Martha, wh. was adm. of the ch. at the vill. now Danvers, 27 Apr. 1690, impris. in Mar. 1692, convict. and hang. for witchcraft on the Thursday foll. the suffer. of her h. At the age of almost 77, he was the victim of that execrable fanaticism of 1692. When the preposterous indictment was read, he stood mute, tho. he had bef. said he was not guilty; and was, by force of sentence under the cruel old common law, pressed to death, Felt says, on 19th (other acco. 16th, wh. must be wrong) Sept. being the only person wh. ever endur. that barbarous process in Mass. On 25 July he confirm. the will made in prison 24 Apr. preced. giv. est. to his s.-in-law William Cleves of Beverly, and John Moulton of Salem. He was a mem. of the first ch. by wh. of course he was excommunicat. 18 Sept. the day bef. his dreadful fate; and so long did the infernal delus. last, that this sentence was eras. by vote only at the end of 20 yrs. tho. in case of his w. mem. of ano. ch. the malignity last. but eleven yrs. Felt, II. 475–85. Hutch. II. 59. Calef, More Wonders of Invis. World, 217. 18. The late Hon. Daniel P. King of Danvers occup. the homestead of poor Cory. In Essex Hist. Coll. I. 56, is petitn. of his d. Eliz. for self and other ch. His d. Martha m. Cleves. JOHN, and THOMAS, were of Chelmsford 1691; but I kn. no more of either. WILLIAM, Portsmouth, R. I. had Michael, b. 21 Apr. 1688 ; and no more is heard of him.

COSIN, COZENS, or COUSINS, ABRAHAM, Sherborn, m. at Woburn, 19 Nov. 1684, Mary Eames, had Abraham, b. 22 Aug. 1685 ; Isaac, 2 June 1688 ; Jacob, and Joseph, tw. 13 Aug. 1692 ; and Mary, 10 May 1695. Morse thinks him s. of Isaac of Rowley, and that he had serv. in the war against Philip. Tho. the two points are not utterly inconsist. I look on their concur. as improb. EDMUND, Boston, liv. at Pulling point, m. 1656 or 7, Margaret Bird, serv. to John Grover of Rumney marsh. ‖ FRANCIS, was of ar. co. 1640. GEORGE, whose name is Coussens in the custom ho. rec. came in the James from Southampton to Boston, arr. 3 June 1635. ISAAC, Rowley, a. 1650, was from Marlborough, in Wilts, went to New London, where he had a gr. of lot, 1651, but did not take it, and went back to R. ; had w. Ann in 1658, on the Boston rec. of m. (when the date is omit. tho. we may be sure it was 1657), call. Hunt, formerly w. of John Edwards ; but on the same rec. it appears, that by former w. Eliz. wh. d. 14 Dec. 1656, he had Sarah, b. 31 Aug. preced. JOHN, Casco, in that pt. now North Yarmouth 1645, b. a. 1596, d. at York 1689. Willis, I. 44. 55. 65. 231. MATTHEW, Boston 1656. RICHARD, Saybrook, m. 7 Mar. 1678, Mary, d. of

Alexander Chalker, had Hannah, b. 17 Mar. 1679; Sarah, 10 May 1683 ; and Bethia, 4 Nov. 1685. Sarah was b. at Block Isl. WILLIAM, Boston 1649.

COSMORE, ‡ JOHN, Southampton, L. I. an Assist. of Conn. 1647–58, exc. 51, 2, 3, and 4, when, perhaps, he was gone from this country. Strange is it, that we kn. no more.

COSSER, HERCULES, Boston 1659. WILLIAM, Boston 1657. Two Scots, of whose names I see not any other ment. exc. that they were early mem. of the Charit. Soc. preserv. in Drake's Hist. of Boston, 455. Yet the name may be Courser, to wh. one of the references in the Index points.

COSTIN, or COSTING, WILLIAM, Concord, had Sarah, and Phebe, a. 1642, perhaps was of Boston in 1654, call. Castine, and at Wickford 1674.

COTHILL, JOHN, a person nam. in Hutch. I. 354, as one of Sir E. Andros's counc. but as no such name is heard of, we may fear this a typogr. error, for H. could not be wrong, on such a point.

COTTA, COTTY, or COTTEY, ‖ JOHN, Boston, freem. 1671, m. 1668, Mary, d. of Jeremiah Moore, ar. co. 1679, d. 20 Nov. 1723, aged 77. JOHN, Boston, perhaps s. of the preced. m. a. 1699, Sarah, d. of Richard Wharton. ROBERT, Salem, freem. 6 May 1635, prob. had w. Joan and a s. whose name is not giv. bapt. 28 Jan. 1638; Bathshua, 24 Mar. 1639; Mary, 20 Sept. 1640 ; Peter, 1 May 1642; Obadiah, 10 Sept. 1643; and John, 11 May 1645.

COTTER, WILLIAM, New London 1660–8, had w. Elinor.

COTTERILL, COTTEREL, or COTTRELL, FRANCIS, Wells 1668. GERSHOM, Westerly 1679, prob. s. of Nicholas. NICHOLAS, Newport 1639, freem. 1655, rem. to Westerly 1669, and d. 1715. His ch. were Nicholas; Gershom; Mary, wh. m. Edward Larkin of Newport; Eliz.; John; Samuel; Nathaniel; and Dorothy. ROBERT, Providence 1645.

COTTLE, EDWARD, Nantucket, had Judith, b. 13 Apr. 1670 ; Lydia, 17 May 1672; Ann, 3 Mar. 1674; and John, 7 Sept. 1675. Dorothy, perhaps his w. d. 1 Oct. 1681. But he had first liv. at Salisbury, there, by w. Judith, had Edward, b. 17 Jan. 1652, d. in few mos.; Mary, 1 Nov. 1653 ; Benjamin, 2 Mar. 1655 ; Sarah, Mar. 1657; Judith, 5 Mar. 1659, prob. d. young; Eliz. 19 Apr. 1663 ; and Edward, again, 28 Sept. 1666. EZRA, Newbury, only s. of William, m. 6 July 1695, Mary, d. of Thomas Woodbridge, had William, b. 2 July 1696; Mary, 31 Mar. 1698; and Edmund, 15 Feb. 1700. WILLIAM, Newbury, came in the Confidence 1638, from Southampton, aged 12, as serv. of John Saunders. He was s. of Edward of the city of Salisbury, Wilts, wh. d. 15 June 1653; had Ezra, b. 5 May 1662; Ann, 12 July 1663; and Susanna, 16 Aug. 1665, and d. 30 Apr. 1668.

COTTON, *JOHN*, Boston, the most disting. divine that came from Eng. in the first age, b. at Derby, 4 Dec. 1585, s. of Rowland Cotton, Esq. was ent. at the Univ. of Cambridge, when 14 yrs. old, bred at Trinity Coll. where he took his A. M. 1606, bec. fellow of Emanuel, after spend. as he says, fourteen yrs. at Cambridge, preach. at Boston, Lincolnsh. twenty-one yrs. from 1612, being by the choice of the corpor. made vicar; came with sev. of his parish in the Griffin, arr. 4 Sept. 1633, with w. Sarah and their first ch. nam. at bapt. Seaborn (from the circumstance of his b.), rec. at the ch. on Sunday foll. 8 Sept., on 10 Oct. was ord. teacher of that ch. freem. 4 May 1634, d. 23 Dec. (yet the old copy of town rec. of wh. I presume no orig. has been kn. for 150 yrs. has it 15), 1652. His d. ensu. on tak. cold in cross. the ferry as he went to preach a few days bef. at Cambridge. His will of 30 Nov. of that yr. with codic. of 12 Dec. ment. the four ch. Seaborn, John, Eliz. and Mary, w. Sarah, and "ho. and garden in the market-place of Boston, in Lincolnsh." as well as the "small part of my house, wh. Sir Henry Vane built, whilst he sojourn. with me," and at his departure, gave by deed, to s. Seaborn; and also ment. cous. Henry Smith, and cous. John Angier, with his w. and ch. all liv. at his ho. and kinswom. Martha Mellowes, wh. I judge to be wid. of Abraham. But the name of gr.ch. Betty Day, in the codic. can only be explain. by suppos. that his w. had by former h. a d. wh. had m. a Day and had this ch. We kn. she was not gr.ch. in nat. descent. He liv. 18 yrs. with w. Eliz. Horrocks, and had no ch.; by sec. w. wid. Sarah Story, wh. outliv. him, and m. 26 Aug. 1656, Richard Mather, outliv. him, and d. 27 May 1676, had the s. bef. ment. b. on the ocean, 12 Aug. 1633, bapt. 4 days aft. reach. port; Sarah, b. 12, bapt. 20 Sept. 1635, betroth. to Jonathan Mitchell, but d. of smallpox, 20 Jan. 1650; Eliz. 9, bapt. 10 Dec. 1637; John, 15, bapt. 22 Mar. 1640, H. C. 1657; Mary or Maria, 16, bapt. 20 Feb. 1642; and Rowland, a. 6 days old, bapt. 24 Dec. 1643, d. of smallpox, 29 Jan. 1650. Eliz. m. 12 Oct. 1655, Jeremiah Eggington, d. 31 Aug. foll. hav. Eliz. b. 15 Aug. wh. d. soon; Maria m. 6 Mar. 1663, Rev. Increase Mather, and d. 4 Apr. 1714. Twenty-one of his descend. in the male line (beside the many thro. male or fem. of the Mather blood, and many gr.ds. and other females), had been, in 1818, gr. at Harv. of wh. two thirds were clerg. *JOHN*, Plymouth, s. of the preced. after being some yrs. at Wethersfield, where he was excor. of the will of Gov. Wells, m. 7 Nov. 1660, Joanna, d. of Dr. Bray Rossiter, wh. outliv. him, and d. 12 Oct. 1702, aged 60; was preacher at W. and freem. of Conn. 1661; but rem. without sett. back to his nat. town, had unhappiness of being excom. by his father's ch. for three aggrav. offences, May 1664, I presume without public prosecut. and happily long aft. d. of his pious f.;

but aft. open confess. was restor. next mo. went soon and preach. at
Guilford 1664 ; ord. at P. 30 June 1669, but when he had serv. near 28
yrs. was dism. (Judge Sewall marks in his Almanac 29 Sept.) 5 Oct.
1697, under very unpleasant circumstances, went to Charleston, S. C.
in Nov. 1698, there was min. to his d. of the yellow fever, 18 Sept. foll.
A letter to his wid. at Plymouth by his neph. Cotton Mather, of 23 Oct.
foll. ment. arr. of news that "the horrible plague of Barbados was brot.
into " C. " by an infected vessel," that a. the end of Sept. it had been there
little above a fortnight, yet in this little time "had made an incredible
destruct." " many above an hundred were dead," and that his friends
wrote "that all the ministers in C. were dead." Whether in this
incredible loss, all the ministers were one, or two, beside Cotton, is not
told ; but in so small a city, I judge the smaller number most worthy of
belief. Mather never cultivat. precision or sobriety of narrat. and his
word must seldom be tak. as *exact* truth. No exagger. of the suffer.
in the gr. mart of Mediterranean commerce, by the terrible plague of
1720, was attempt. when history told how M. de Belsance stood in his
post of duty, and outliv. the peril more than thirty-five yrs. tho. our
great ethical poet immortaliz. the deed, without nam. the prelate :

> Why drew Marseilles' good bishop purer breath,
> When Nature sickened, and each gale was death ?

His ch. were John, b. 3 Aug. 1661, H. C. 1681 ; Eliz. ; Sarah, 17 June
1665, d. young ; Rowland, 27 Dec. 1667, H. C. 1685 ; Sarah, again, 5
Apr. 1670 ; Maria, 14 Jan. 1672 ; a s. 28 Sept. 1674, wh. d. soon ;
Josiah, 10 Sept. 1675, d. young ; Samuel, 10 Feb. 1678, d. young ;
Josiah, again, 8 Jan. 1680, H. C. 1698, well kn. in public offices of
Plymouth Co. where he d. 19 Aug. 1756 ; and Theophilus, 5 May 1682,
H. C. 1701. Of these ch. John was min. of Yarmouth, and by w.
Sarah, d. of Richard Hubbard of Ipswich, had seven ds. and d. 21 Feb.
1706 ; Eliz. m. Rev. James Alling, and 2d his successor, Rev. Caleb
Cushing of Salisbury, as was confidently said, yet she wh. m. these min.
is also call. d. of Rev. Seaborn with more prob. ; Rowland, min. of Sand-
wich, ord. 2 Nov. 1694, by w. Eliz. only d. of Nathaniel Saltonstall, and
wid. of Rev. John Denison, had, beside four ds. and s. Rowland, H. C.
1719, four other s. John, Nathaniel, Josiah, and Ward, all mins. and d.
22 Mar. 1722, and his wid. d. 8 July 1726, at Boston ; Josiah, by s. Rev.
John of Halifax, was head of an excel. line, includ. Rev. Ward and
Rev. Josiah ; and Theophilus, min. of Hampton Falls, ord. 2 Jan. 1712,
d. 18 Aug. 1726, had two ws. but no ch. *JOHN*, Hampton, s. of Rev.
Seaborn, succeed. his f. aft. long interval, ord. 19 Nov. 1696, d. 27 Mar.
1710, by w. Ann, d. of capt. Thomas Lake of Boston, m. 17 Aug. 1686,
had John, b. 5 Sept. 1687, d. young ; Mary, 5 Nov. 1689, Dorothy, 16

July 1693 ; Thomas, 28 Oct. 1695, bapt. 26 Apr. 1696, when his f. was of Boston; Ann, 13 Nov. 1697 ; Simon, 21 Dec. 1701; and Samuel, and Lydia, tw. of wh. the last three d. young. SEABORN, Hampton, eldest s. of first John, b. 12 Aug. as is said, by me, without proof, by the author. of dilig. Mr. Thornton, in the pedigree, Geneal. Reg. I. 164, on the passage, but bapt. in Boston, 8 Sept. 1633, H. C. 1651, freem. 1655, m. 14 June 1654, Dorothy, eldest d. of Gov. Bradstreet, wh. d. 26 Feb. 1672, had Dorothy, b. 11 Nov. 1656 ; John, 8 May 1658, H. C. 1678, bef. ment. ; Sarah, 22 Feb. 1660, d. soon; Ann, 22 Aug. 1661 ; Sarah, 2 July 1663 ; Eliz. 13 Aug. 1665; Mercy, 3 Nov. 1666; Abiah, 5 Apr. 1669, d. soon; and Mary, 22 Apr. 1670. He for sec. w. m. 9 July 1673, Prudence, d. of Jonathan Wade of Ipswich, and wid. of Dr. Anthony Crosby of Rowley, had Rowland, b. 29 Aug. 1674, H. C. 1696; and Wade, 6 Oct. 1676, d. young. He had prob. preach. at Windsor, and other places, but was ord. at H. aft. long trial, 1660, and he d. 19, was bur. 23 Apr. 1686. Of these ch. Dorothy m. Joseph Smith; Ann m. a Carr, and, next, a Johnson, and d. 7 Dec. 1702 at Boston ; Sarah m. 27 Aug. 1680, Richard Pierce of Boston, and d. 2 Aug. 1690; Eliz. m. Rev. William Williams of Hatfield, as was once said, but erron. for she m. Rev. James Alling of Salisbury, and his successor, Rev. Caleb Cushing; Mercy m. Peter Tufts, f. of Rev. John, H. C. 1708 ; Mary m. first, John Atwater of Salem, and, next, Samuel Partridge of Hadley ; and Rowland, wh. had ent. Coll. in 1692, left for ill health, went to Eng. and Holland to acq. skill in medicine, had a degr. in it, and was a physician at the Isle of Wight. But in the Diary of his neph. the dilig. Reg. of Plymouth, he is said to have been a min. sett. at Warminster, in Wilts, and d. 1753. In the copious progeny of famous Cotton, of the sec. and third generat. it is quite observ. how small is the proportion of those wh. pass. mid. age. THOMAS, Roxbury, had Thomas, b. 21 Apr. 1664, may be he wh. d. at Chelmsford, 30 Sept. 1687. ‖ WILLIAM, Boston, a butcher, may have been bef. join. our ch. in May 1647, first at Gloucester, for one William, either this or the next, own. ld. in 1642, at that place, where no more is told of him, b. a. 1610, freem. 1647, ar. co. 1650, by w. Ann had Mary, b. Dec. 1641 ; John, Dec. 1643 ; William, 31 May 1646, d. young; the three bapt. 16 May 1647 ; Sarah, 19 Mar. 1649 ; William, again, 23 Feb. 1651, wh. d. at 6 mos.; Rebecca, 2 Jan. 1653 ; William, again, 4 Feb. 1655; Thomas, 18 Jan. 1657 ; Hannah, 1660 ; and Benjamin, bapt. 25 Mar. 1666. John, his s. may have been of Concord 1665, and 1679, perhaps the freem. of 1680, belong. to sec. ch. of Boston. Mary, his d. m. 7 Mar. 1660, John Matson. WILLIAM, a witness, 12 Dec. 1653, at Weymouth, to will of Joseph Shaw, is not kn. for any thing else. WILLIAM, Portsmouth

1640, of the gr. jury 1669, d. a. 1677. WILLIAM, Boston, possib. the same as first, by w. Mary had John, b. 1666; and Jeremiah, 1670.

COTTRELL. See Cotterill.

COUCH, JOHN, York, freem. 1652. ROBERT, New Hampsh. 1656–69. SIMON, Fairfield, freem. 1664. In the Col. rec. his name has an r. THOMAS, Wethersfield 1666, and d. there 1687; had Susanna, then 20 yrs. old; Simon, 18; Rebecca, 15; Hannah, 13; Thomas, 12; Mary, 11; Sarah, 8; Abigail, 6; and Martha, 3. Hinman, I. 27.

COUNTER, EDWARD, Salem 1668.

COUNTS, EDWARD, Charlestown, m. 25 Feb. 1663, Sarah, d. of Richard Adams of Malden, had Samuel, b. July 1671; Sarah; and Eliz. all bapt. 10 June 1677. He liv. some time at Malden.

COURSER, ARCHELAUS, Lancaster, had est. in Boston, and, I think, was of Charlestown 1658, where the rec. has the name Hercules, rem. to L. 1664, or earlier. WILLIAM, Boston, shoemak. came in the Elizabeth and Ann, 1635, aged 26, join. with the ch. a wk. aft. Vane, but was not of his side two yrs. later; freem. 25 May 1636, was allow. to be innholder, had Deliverance, b. 4 Mar. 1638; Joanna, 9 Feb. 1640; and John, bapt. 8 May 1642, a. 4 days old, but the dates of b. suspiciously *concur* with the ch. rec. of bapt. and the originality of one or the other may well be doubted.

COURTEOUS, THOMAS, York, freem. of Mass. 1652; and in 1680 sw. alleg. to the k. WILLIAM, Newbury, d. 31 Dec. 1654.

COUSSENS. See Cosin.

COVE, FRANCIS, Salisbury 1650.

COVELL, JOHN, Marblehead 1668. PHILIP, Malden, m. 26 Nov. 1688, Eliz. d. of Philip Atwood of the same, had Sarah, b. 13 Apr. 1689; but in Geneal. Reg. VI. 338, his name is print. Fowle, as it had been p. 336.

COVENTRY, JONATHAN, Marshfield 1651. Thacher's Hist. of Plymouth, 106.

COVEY, JAMES, Boston, had gr. of lot at Braintree for four heads, in 1640.

COVINGTON, JOHN, Ipswich 1635. Felt, 11.

COWDALL, JOHN, Boston 1644, m. 1655, Mary, wid. of William Davis, was that yr. freem. of Newport, and at New London 1659 and 60, but rem.

COWDRY, NATHANIEL, Reading, s. of William, by w. Eliz. m. 21 Nov. 1654, had Samuel, b. 16 May 1657; Eliz. 13 Aug. 1659, d. at 2 mos.; and his w. d. a few days aft. By ano. w. had Nathaniel, 18 Aug. 1661; was deac. left wid. Mary, wh. d. 27 Feb. 1729, aged 94, as is said. * WILLIAM, Lynn 1630, was b. a. 1602, perhaps was of Weymouth 1640, rem. to Reading 1642; there was selectman, town clk. and rep. 1651, yet I find no adm. as freem.; d. 1687; had Nathaniel, Matthias, and Bethia, perhaps others.

COWELL, EDWARD, Boston 1645, cordwainer, by w. Margaret had John; Joseph; Eliz. b. 17 Aug. 1653, d. next yr.; and William, perhaps the youngest, b. 28 June 1655; was capt. some time in Philip's war; d. 12 Sept. 1691. Perhaps he took sec. w. Sarah Hobart, m. at Hingham, June 1668. EZRA, Plymouth 1643, able to bear arms. JOHN, Boston 1670, blacksmith, s. of Edward, d. Dec. 1693. JOSEPH, Boston, cooper, br. of the preced. m. a. 1673, Mary, d. of Richard Carter, wid. of William Hunter. JOSEPH, Woburn, m. 27 Feb. 1685, Alice Palmer, had Eliz. b. 25 Nov. 1686; Alice, 6 Apr. 1689; Philip, 12 Feb. 1692, d. very soon; Joseph, 9 Dec. 1694; Sarah, Aug. 1698; and perhaps rem.

COWEN, ISRAEL, Scituate, s. of John, had Mary, b. 1691; Hannah, 1694; Eliz. 1697; Israel, 1699; Jonah, 1704, d. young; Gethelus (?) 1708; Job, 1713; Joseph, 1715; and Sarah, 1717. JOHN, Scituate, a Scotchman, purch. est. there and m. 1656, Rebecca, wid. of Richard Man, had Joseph, b. 1657; Mary, 1659; John, 1662; Israel, 1664; and Rebecca, 1666. Joseph was k. in Philip's war, at Rehoboth fight, 1676. Rebecca m. 19 Dec. 1693, Obadiah Hawes of Dorchester. JOHN, Scituate, s. of the preced. m. 1687, Deborah Litchfield, had Sarah, b. 1688; Joseph, 1690; John, 1692; Joshua, 1694; Caleb, 1696; Israel, 1701; and Mary, 1705. Deane.

COWLAND, RALPH, Portsmouth, R. I. in Dr. Stiles's list of freem. 1655, had m. Alice, wid. of Sampson Shotten, and by sec. w. Sarah had Mary, wh. bec. w. of John Greene of Newport, and Sarah, d. by the former h. of his sec. w. m. Henry Greene.

COWLES, JOHN, Farmington 1652, rem. a. 1664, to Hatfield, d. Sept. 1677, leav. wid. Hannah, wh. d. at Hartford 1684; JOHN, of Hatfield, freem. 1690, wh. m. Deborah, d. of Robert Bartlett of Hartford; Samuel of Farmington; beside four ds. One had m. Nathaniel Goodwin of Hartford; Esther, ano. d. m. Thomas Bull. This person was thot. to be br. of James Cole, and so was his own name; but the rec. vary. to Coale, Cowle, Coales, Colles, Cowles, Coule, or Coules, the descend. have gen. adopt. the w. sometimes without the e. JOHN, sen. and JOHN jr. were at Hadley 1668. ROBERT, Plymouth 1633.

COWLEY, ABRAHAM, Maine 1656. Maine Hist. Coll. I. 298. AMBROSE, Boston 1660. HENRY, Marblehead 1660, br. of the preced. JOHN, Ipswich 1641. Felt, 11. WILLIAM, Newport 1639.

COWPER. See Cooper.

COWLISHAW. See Collishaw.

COX, COCK, or COXE, EDWARD, Boston 1672, mariner, had w. Margaret, and d. June 1675. FRANCIS, emb. at Barbados, 25 Aug. 1679, for N. E. but he may only have been trans. visit. GEORGE, Salem, m. 10 Sept. 1671, Mary, eldest ch. of John Ingersoll. JOHN, Boston, by w. Mary had Philip, b. 9 Feb. 1674; d. 1690. JOHN, Pemaquid, took the o. of fidel. to Mass. 1674. JOSEPH, Boston, freem. 1673, m. 10 Nov. 1659, Susanna, d. of Nicholas Upshall, had Nicholas; Susanna; Eliz.; Ann, b. 10 June 1676; Joseph, 15 Sept. 1679, posthum. and Mary, and d. 15 Jan. 1679. MOSES, Hampton 1639, then a young man, unm. In 1657, his w. Alice, s. John, and six other persons, going in a boat from H. 20 Oct. were all drown. He d. 28 May 1687, " aged a. 93 yrs." is the add. in the report, Geneal. Reg. VII. 117, the latitude of wh. phrase may justify a subtract. if not of twenty, certain. of ten yrs. Alice, perhaps his d. m. 24 May 1662, Matthew Abdy; ano. d. m. Francis Jenness; and his d. Leah m. 13 Dec. 1681, James Perkins of the same, and d. 19 Feb. 1749, aged 88. NICHOLAS, Boston, s. of Joseph, by w. Sarah had Susanna, b. 23, bapt. 26 Mar. 1693. RICHARD, Salem 1645. Felt. ROBERT, Boston, mariner, freem. 1666, by w. Martha had Eliz. b. 15 Apr. 1677. THOMAS, Pemaquid, with two others, nam. Thomas, took o. of fidel. 1674. Perhaps he had been driv. by the Ind. hostil. to Boston, there, by w. Martha, had Jacob, b. 4 Jan. 1678.

COY, MATTHEW, Boston 1653, came, it is said, in 1638, aged 15, m. 29 Aug. 1654, Eliz. Roberts, had Matthew, b. 5 Sept. 1656; Richard, 6 Sept. 1658; John, 2 Sept. 1666; and Samuel, 19 Feb. 1668. MAT-THEW, perhaps s. of the preced. had gr. of a lot at Norwich 1685, that pt. now Preston. RICHARD, Salisbury, br. of Matthew, came with him, it is said, in 1638, aged 13, liv. some yrs. at Boston bef. and aft. 1650, when he was at S.; there, by w. Martha, had Caleb, b. 15 Aug. 1666; was of Brookfield 1673, there k. by the Ind. 2 Aug. 1675. Perhaps he and his br. were brot. by sis. Mary, wh. m. John Lake of B. WILLIAM, was one of the first sett. 1637, at Taunton.

COYTEMORE, * ‖ THOMAS, Charlestown 1636, s. of wid. Catharine C. whose fam. name was Myles, and her sec. h. Rowland C. but by former h. a Gray, she had Parnell, w. of Increase Nowell, and Catharine, w. of Thomas Graves; and by Coytemore, Eliz. wh. was first w. of William Tyng; all m. in Eng. bef. she came. Mr. Frothingham, 86, gives her ano. d. Sarah, wh. m. a Williams. She made her will 28 Apr. 1658, and d. 28 Nov. 1659. He was of ar. co. 1639, freem. 13 May 1640, selectman and rep. that yr. and once or twice aft. was master of good est. an enterpriz. merch. went in sev. voyages to distant lds. and was lost on a voyage to Malaga by shipwr. 27 Dec. 1645, on the coast of Spain; by w. Martha, d. of Capt. Rainsborough, m. doubtless in Eng. had Thomas, b. 25 Feb. 1642, bapt. next day; and William, 6 Feb. 1643,

d. in six days. His inv. shows £1266, 9, 7. His wid. m. Dec. 1647, Gov. Winthrop, brot. him s. Joshua, wh. d. within two yrs. and m. next, 10 Mar. 1651, John Coggan, bore him Joshua, Caleb, and Sarah; and after his d. in 1658, wish. to be m. again, as relat. by Rev. John Davenport; and, it is said, poison. hers. for ill success. The will of his mo. aids our research for genealogy. Its date is 30 Apr. 1658, and names the four ch. of William Tyng, wh. had m. her eldest d. Eliz.; five of Increase Nowell; five of Thomas Graves; wh. were all the liv. gr.ch.; besides the ds. Sarah Williams, to wh. she gave ld. at Woburn; Parnell Nowell; and Catharine Graves, as also, Martha, the wid. of Coggan, wh. had bef. been wid. of her s. Thomas, and of Gov. Winthrop.

CRABB, HENRY, Boston, m. 1 Jan. 1658, Hannah, d. of Thomas Emmons, had Samuel, nam. in the will of his gr.f. E. 20 Jan. 1661. JOHN, Dorchester 1630, came, I presume, in the Mary and John, req. 19 Oct. to be made freem. but prob. went home soon, at least never took the o.; tho. Dr. Harris, wh. finds him in town rec. 1632, says he rem. to Conn. As this could not be bef. 1635, it is liable to doubt. * RICHARD, Wethersfield, was rep. 1639, 40, and 1; sold est. 1643, and rem. prob. to Stamford, and in 1655 was of Greenwich. See Hinman, 127.

CRABTREE, JOHN, Boston 1639, a joiner, by w. Alice had John, b. 25 Oct. 1639; and Deliverance, 3 Sept. 1641, d. within two yrs. He d. late in 1656, and his wid. m. 11 Feb. 1657, Joshua Hewes. JOHN, Swanzey 1683, perhaps s. of the preced. m. Mary, 1 Nov. of that yr. had Mary, b. 25 May of that yr. wh. d. in six days, if the Col. Rec. be proof; but she prob. was sec. or third w. for the same Col. Rec. shows he had Benjamin, b. 12 Oct. 1673.

CRACKBONE, GILBERT, Dorchester, freem. 7 Dec. 1636, rem. soon to Cambridge, had, perhaps, the four, whose d. is on rec. Mary, 30 May; Judith, 1 July, both of 1655; Hannah, 24 Sept. 1658; and Benjamin, 27 Apr. 1661; yet we kn. not, wh. was mo. of either. But as he m. 17 June 1656, Eliz. Cooledge, it is clear the first two were by former w.; and of the last nam. we may doubt for two reasons, that in his reg. matchless Mitchell says: "his s. Benjamin was a. 5 or 6 yrs. old, when his f. join. here," tho. he leaves it uncert. how old he was when that was writ. still we might infer, that he was contin. in life. Next, we kn. that one Benjamin C. was k. by the Ind. 4 Sept. 1675 at Northfield, under capt. Beers, and prob. was this man's s. He d. 9 Jan. 1672. His will, of 28 Dec. with codic. of 2 Jan. preced. names s. Benjamin, and his ch. Joseph and Sarah. His wid. was Eliz.

CRACKSTONE, or CRAXTON, JOHN, Plymouth, came in the Mayflower 1620, with s. of the same name, d. bef. end of Mar. foll. JOHN, Plymouth, s. of the preced. had his sh. in div. of ld. as a comer in the

Mayflower, 1624, and in 1627 in the div. of cattle with the comp. of Allerton; but d. in the foll. yr. from a fever brot. on by freez. his feet, when lost in the woods, as Bradford tells.

CRADDING, WILLIAM, Taunton 1638.

CRAFORD, or CRAFFORD, JOHN, Dover 1671. MORDECAI, Salem, in 1663 had w. Judith. MUNGO, Boston 1686, a Scotchm. had been some yrs. here, apprent. or a serv. of John Smith, the mason, and this yr. was allow. to be an inhab. By w. Mary he had Eliz. b. 19 May 1681, wh. d. young; was, I believe, among the adher. of Andros, imprison. Apr. 1689, but did not go home, and is among the tax. 1695; by sec. w. Susanna had only ch. Mary, wh. m. Stephen Paine; and d. 1712. The inv. of £109, 9, 10, had drugs and medicines for two fifths. His wid. Susanna made her will 27 Aug. 1713, pro. 15 Sept. aft. mak. d. Mary and her h. Stephen excors. giv. all to Mary, exc. £20 to ea. of the gr.ch. An early sett. Mr. Craford, prob. of Watertown, had been drown. [See Winth. I. 138], and lieut. Feake, and three other gent. of that town, by order of 6 Oct. 1634, were to take inv. of his est. for the Court. STEPHEN, Kittery 1640, d. at Isle of Shoals 1647, leav. w. and one ch.

CRAFTS, * ‖ GRIFFIN, Roxbury 1630, came, prob. with w. Alice and d. Hannah, in the fleet with Winth. freem. 18 May 1631; had John, b. 10 July 1630, the earliest b. in town rec.; Mary, 10 Oct. 1632; Abigail, 28 Mar. 1634; Samuel, 12 Dec. 1637; and Moses, 28 Apr. 1641; was lieut. selectman, rep. 1663–7, ar. co. 1668, and d. 1690, leav. wid. Dorcas, his third or fourth w. wh. d. 30 Dec. 1697; but he had former w. for he m. 15 July 1673, Ursula, wid. of William Robinson of Dorchester, being her fourth h.; and in the rec. is Alice C. d. 26 Mar. 1673, aged 73. In his will, made 18 May 1689, pro. 9 Nov. 1690, of wh. Samuel was excor. he names Abigail, wh. had first m. 24 Jan. 1651, John Ruggles, as w. of Edward Adams; Hannah, as w. of Nathaniel Wilson; and gr.ch. Ephraim, s. of John. Apostle Eliot spells his name Crofts; in some other rec. e is used for s final; and often the first five letters made the name. JOHN, Roxbury, eldest s. of the preced. m. 7 June 1654, Rebecca Wheelock, prob. d. of Ralph, had John, b. 5 Aug. 1658, wh. was drown. 5 May 1684, I think, unm.; Rebecca, 28 Aug. 1660; Mary, 16 Oct. 1662; wh. three were bapt. 17 May 1663; and Joseph, 5 May 1666, d. at two mos. His w. d. Nov. 1667, and he m. 30 Mar. 1669, Mary Hudson of Lynn, wh. d. 3 Jan. 1724; had Abigail, 6 Mar. 1670; Mehitable, 31 Aug. 1673; Sarah, 17 Feb. 1675; Ephraim, 9 Aug. 1677; and Lydia, 8 Apr. 1681; and he d. 3 Sept. 1685. MOSES, Roxbury, br. of the preced. m. 24 Jan. 1667, Rebecca, d. of Peter Gardner, had Rebecca, b. 22 Apr. 1668, d. next yr.; Moses, 8 Aug. 1669, d. young; Rebecca, again, 2 Mar. 1671; and Abigail, 1677. He rem. to Deerfield among the early sett. a. 1673, but aft. the destruct. of that town by the Ind. in Philip's war, he was a short time at Roxbury again, and soon rem. to Hatfield, thence to Wethersfield, where he was in 1702. SAMUEL, Roxbury, br. of the preced. freem. 1671, m. 16 Oct. 1661, Eliz. Seaver, had Hannah, b. 14 Dec. 1662 ; Samuel, 24 May 1664, d. soon ; Eliz. 2 Oct. 1665 ; Samuel, again, 16 June 1667 ; Joseph, 13 July 1669 ; Mary, 15 Oct. 1671 ; Abigail, 1 Dec. 1673 ; Nathaniel, 4 Jan. 1677 ; and Benjamin, 23 Oct. 1683 ; and d. 9 Dec. 1709. THOMAS, Hadley 1678, d. 1692, leav. six ch. of wh. only John, wh. was of Hatfield, had issue. Five of this name had, in 1833, been gr. at Harv. and four at the other N. E. coll.

CRAGG, JOHN, emb. at Barbados for N. E. 31 Jan. 1679, perhaps only trans. visit.

CRAGGAN, JOHN, Woburn, m. 4 Nov. 1661, Sarah Dawes, had Abigail, b. 4 Aug. 1662 ; Sarah, 10 Aug. 1664 ; Eliz. 3 Aug. 1666 ; Mercy, 25 Mar. 1669 ; Ann, 6 Aug. 1673 ; John, 19 Sept. 1677 ; and Rachel, and Leah, tw. 14 Mar. 1680, both d. in 4 days.

CRAM, BENJAMIN, Hampton, perhaps s. of John, m. 25 Nov. 1662, Argentine, d. of Giles Cromwell of Newbury, took o. of fidel. 25 Apr. 1678. JOHN, Boston 1637, Exeter 1639, Hampton 1658, d. 5 Mar. 1682. In 1665 he had w. Esther, ch. Benjamin, Thomas, Lydia, and Mary. THOMAS, Hampton, perhaps br. of Benjamin, took o. of alleg. 1678. Descend. continue. in that vicin.

CRAMPTON, DENNIS, Guilford 1656, m. 16 Sept. 1660, Mary, d. of John Parmelee, had Hannah, Eliz. and Nathaniel, this last b. Mar. 1667, and she d. 16 of the same mo. By sec. w. Sarah, wid. of Nicholas Munger, had Sarah, b. 17 Dec. 1669 ; Thomas, 25 Nov. 1672 ; and John, 16 June 1675 ; liv. some yrs. at Killingworth, but went back to G. bef. m. of third w. Frances, was liv. there 1685 ; and d. 31 Jan. 1690, leav. good est. He is the man, call. by Kellond and Kirk (to wh. Gov. Endicot had issu. warrant for arrest of Whalley and Goffe, the regicides), Dennis Scranton, when they made report of their unsuccessful errand. Of this docum. not exceed. in curious detail by any in N. E. hist. see Hutch. Coll. 334. Eliz. m. 1686, John Lee of Westfield, as his sec. w. and Sarah m. John Evarts as his sec. w. JOHN, Norwalk 1672, was a soldier in Philip's war, had liv. 1661 at Fairfield, there m. Hannah, d. of Francis Andrews, and by her had Hannah, b. 1662, wh. m. 5 Mar. 1680, Benjamin Scribner, or Skrivener ; and for sec. w. m. 8 Oct. 1676, Sarah, d. of John Rockwell of Stamford, had Sarah, b. 10 Sept. 1679 ; Abigail, 9 Aug. 1681 ; and John, 7 Jan. 1683. NATHANIEL, Guilford, s. of John, by first w. I presume, sold est. and rem. to Wethersfield. Hinman, 232, says he d. 13 Mar. 1693, and gave his est. to William Goodrich. SAMUEL, a soldier of Lothrop's comp. k. at Bloody brook, 18 Sept. 1675.

CRAMWELL, JOHN, Boston, d. 1639. Ano. JOHN, Boston, by w. Rebecca had Rebecca, b. 20 July 1654. But this is more prob. Cromwell.

CRANBERRY, NATHANIEL, k. by the Ind. at Deerfield, Sept. 1675, was, prob. a soldier.

CRANCH, ANDREW, New Hampsh. b. a. 1646, was of gr. jury 1684 and 5.

CRANDALL, EBER, Westerly, s. of the first John, had three ws. as from his will of 22 Aug. 1727 may be presum. for aft. nam. w. Mary, he adds ch. John, Eber, Samuel, and Joseph, "that I had by my sec. w." he gives to Mary, Nathaniel, Jonathan, Ebenezer, and Jeremiah, "that my now w. hath liv." and he also calls Nathaniel Cottrell of N. Kingston br. JAMES, Westerly 1675, or bef. JEREMIAH, Westerly, s. of John of the same, by w. Priscilla had Jeremiah, John, James, Ann, Hannah, Sarah, Experience, Patience, Susanna, and Mary. JOHN, Providence 1637, m. Eliz. d. of Samuel Gorton; and adopt. his opin. I suppose, for in Aug. 1651, he was imprison. at Boston for a Bapt. freem. at Newport 1655, rem. to Westerly, preach. as 7th day Bapt. and d. 1676. He had two ds. of wh. one m. Job Babcock; the other, Josiah Witter. Other ch. were John, Jeremiah, Peter, Joseph, and Eber. JOHN, Westerly, s. of the preced. had, as we learn from his will of 25 Jan. 1704, w. Eliz. s. John, Peter, and Samuel, ds. Eliz. w. of Stephen Wilcox, and Mary Phillips. JOSEPH, Westerly, s. of the first John, m. Deborah, d. of Robert Burdick, was ord. 8 May 1715, and d. 12 Sept. 1737. PETER, Westerly 1675, perhaps earlier, was br. of the preced.

CRANE, BENJAMIN, Medfield 1649, m. 12 Sept. 1656, Elinor Breck, prob. d. of Edward of Dorchester, rem. to Wethersfield, freem. of Conn. 1658, d. 31 May 1691, leav. Benjamin, Jonathan, Joseph, John, Abraham, Jacob, Israel, Eliz. and Mary. Perhaps he liv. some yrs. late in life at Taunton, for his s. John there took his w. and (wh. is better ground for the infer.) there Samuel Hackett m. 28 Mar. 1690, his d. Mary. BENJAMIN, Milton, perhaps s. of the preced. was a soldier in the comp. of brave capt. Johnson, and wound. in the desperate battle of 19 Dec. 1675 at the Narraganset swamp. CHRISTIAN, Cambridge 1647. But I doubt, that Farmer was delud. into deriv. this name from Christopher Cane, wh. see. HENRY, Dorchester 1658 in Milton 1667–77, m. a d. of Stephen Kingsley. HENRY, Guilford 1664, was, perhaps, f. of that Mercy, wh. m. 30 Oct. 1701, John Hoadley the sec. ‡ * JASPER, New Haven 1639, had, beside Hannah, wh. m. Thomas Huntington, Deliverance, bapt. 12 June 1642; Mercy, 1 Mar. 1645; Micah, 3 Nov. 1647; and Jasper, b. 1651; rem. to Branford in 1668, had been rep. of N. H.

1650, an Assist. of New Haven col. ten yrs. bef. and of the unit. col. of Conn. three yrs. JOHN, a youth, came to Boston in the Speedwell 1656, aged 11, from London, of wh. I hear no more. JOHN, of Braintree or Dorchester, m. 13 Dec. 1686, Hannah, d. of the sec. James Leonard, and no more is kn. JONATHAN, Norwich 1680, m. 19 Dec. 1678, Deborah, eldest d. of Francis Griswold, had Sarah, Jonathan, John, and Mary. Perhaps he had been first of Killingworth. JOSEPH, Wethersfield, prob. s. of Benjamin of the same, m. 16 Dec. 1684, Sarah, d. of the first John Kilborne, had Sarah, Hannah, Benjamin, Joseph, Esther, and David. NATHANIEL, Newton, by w. Mary had Thomas, b. 27 Feb. 1687. WILLIAM, a soldier in Philip's war, from some E. part of the Col. was at Northampton, Apr. 1676.

CRANFIELD, † EDWARD, New Hampsh. came in Oct. 1682, as lieut.-gov. sway. tyrannic. till he went home 1685, d. bef. 1704. Belkn. I. 91–115. Chalmers, 493–7.

CRANIVER, RICHARD, Salem, m. 7 Apr. 1665, Eliz. Woolland, as giv. for the name of w. had William, b. 27 Dec. foll.; Eliz. 13 Sept. 1668 ; Richard, 12 July 1671 ; and Edward, 28 Mar. 1674.

CRANSTON, § JOHN, Newport 1651, among freem. 1655, m. Mary, d. of Jeremiah Clark, was a physician, chos. Gov. 1679 ; by fond tradit. call. descend. thro. his gr.f. John of Poole, from Lord William C.; d. 12 Mar. 1680, aged 54. His wid. m. John Stanton, d. 7 Apr. 1711. § SAMUEL, Newport, s. of the preced. m. Mary, d. of Thomas Hart and Freeborn Williams, wh. d. 17 Sept. 1710 ; Gov. 1698, and 25 yrs. more by success. elect. d. 26 Apr. 1727, aged 68. WALTER, Woburn, m. 4 June 1683, Mary, d. of George Brush of the same.

CRANWELL, JOHN, Boston 1630, prob. came in the fleet with Winth. req. adm. as freem. 19 Oct. 1630 ; took the o. 4 Mar. 1634, had lot at Muddy riv. 1638; and as he is no more ment. I suppose him the same person above, call. Cramwell in the town rec. of his d.

CRARY, PETER, New London 1676, m. Dec. 1677, Christobel, d. of John Gallup the sec. had Peter, John, William, Robert, Christobel, Margaret, and Ann, all liv. at his d. 1708.

CRAW, ROBERT, Newport 1651.

CRAWLEY, THOMAS, Exeter 1639, had sev. ch. of wh. the name of Phebe only is kn. He prob. went to Maine, where, in 1677, the Ind. tenderness to one of the name is relat. Belkn. I. 20. 147.

CRAYFOOT, Mr. perhaps CRAWFORD, with whose prefix of resp. we would gladly purchase a Christian name, came in 1634 by the same sh. with Simon Willard. Possib. the name was, at Springfield, Crowfoot. See that.

CREHORE, TEAGUE, Milton 1670, had w. Mary, d. of Robert Spurr, perhaps had Timothy. TIMOTHY, Milton, perhaps s. of the preced. may have had Timothy, and other ch. and his gr.stone says, he d. 15 Aug. 1739, aged 72.

CRESEY, or CRESSEY, MICHAEL, Ipswich, d. 1670, as Coffin says. Perhaps he had Michael, and William, wh. were tax. at Rowley 1691.

CRIBB, JOHN, came in the Christian, 1635, aged 30.

CRITCHLEY, CRUTCHLEY, or CROYCHLEY, RICHARD, Boston, blacksmith, freem. 18 May 1642, m. Aug. 1639, Alice, wid. of William Dinely, had Samuel, b. 25 Dec. 1640; Joseph, 3, bapt. 7 May 1643, and d. Aug. 1645. But by ano. w. for Alice d. 26 Mar. 1645, and his w. Jane was adm. of our ch. 27 Nov. 1647, had Jane, 1647; Eliz. 28 Nov. bapt. 11 Dec. 1653; Mary, 18 Jan. bapt. 2 Mar. 1656; and John, 1657. He liv. at Rumney marsh, now Chelsea.

CRICK, or CREEK, ANDREW, Topsfield, d. 1658. ‖ EDWARD, Boston, ar. co. 1674, ens. in Philip's war, of Turner's comp. on Conn. riv. lieut. with a comm. of 34 men at Wells, 7 Sept. 1676, and a capt. aft. d. 6 May 1702.

CRIPS, GEORGE, Plymouth 1643, able to bear arms. Perhaps this should be Crisp or Crispe.

CRISP, or CRISPE, BENJAMIN, Watertown 1630, freem. 1646, had, by .w. Bridget, Eliz. b. 8 Jan. 1637; Mary, 20 May 1638; Jonathan, 29 Jan. 1640; Eleazer, 14 Jan. 1642; Mehitable, 21 Jan. 1646; and Zechariah. From Bond we learn, that in 1630, he was serv. of Maj. Gibbons, and, perhaps, came as early as 1629; late in life rem. to Groton, but was ret. bef. 1682 to W. and had m. Joanna, wid. of William Longley. Eliz. m. 27 or 29 Sept. 1657, George Lawrence. RICHARD, Boston, merch. came from Jamaica, m. 1666, Hannah, wid. of Benjamin Richards, d. of William Hudson, jr.; and in 1671, m. Sarah, youngest d. of Rev. John Wheelwright, and liv. not long aft. I presume; had Sarah, b. 15 Sept. 1672, wh. m. 11 Apr. 1695, William Harris, and, next, 5 Apr. 1722, Presid. Leverett, and next, 15 July 1725, Hon. John Clark, and, for fourth h. 6 May 1731, Rev. Benjamin Colman, and she d. 24 Apr. 1744. RICHARD, Boston, permit. to teach fencing, 1686. 3 Mass. Hist. Coll. VIII. 157. A Joanna C. d. at Charlestown 18 Apr. 1698, aged 78. Perhaps she was wid. of Benjamin, driv. from Groton by the Ind.

CRITCHET, HENRY, Boston 1678, was of sec. ch.

CROADE, JOHN, Salem, m. 17 Mar. 1659, Eliz. d. of Walter Price, had Eliz. b. 21 Oct. 1661, bapt. 27 Apr. 1662; John, 14, bapt. 21 June 1663; Hannah, 14, bapt. 23 July 1665; and Jonathan, b. 14 Jan. 1668; was freem. 1663, and d. 1670. His wid. m. John Ruck. JOHN, Marshfield, perhaps s. of the preced. m. 1 Dec. 1692, Deborah, d. of Nathaniel

Thomas. RICHARD, Boston 1664, merch. s. of Richard of Frampton, Co. Dorset, Eng. came from Bristol, had liv. first at Hingham, there m. Frances, d. of William Hersey, 29 May 1656, and had John, b. 26 Nov. 1657 ; and others; but rem. to Salem, there had Sarah, 3, bapt. 18 Feb. 1666; William, b. 9 Feb. 1668; Hannah, 14 Nov. 1671; and John, again, 25 Feb. 1673. He was licensed, 1678, to keep an inn, d. 1689, aged 61, leav. w. Frances, and ch. Hannah, Richard, William, John, Judith, and Sarah. His d. Judith m. Joseph Neal, and d. bef. her f.

CROAKHAM, CROWKHAM, or CROCUM, FRANCIS, Boston 1665, m. wid. Joan Waller, to whose s. Thomas he gave his est. d. a. 1669. By Joan he had Hannah, b. 15 Feb. 1657, prob. d. young. JOHN, Boston, m. Rebecca, d. of Abraham Josselyn, d. Dec. 1678, without issue. His wid. m. Thomas Harris next yr.

CROCKER, DANIEL, Boston, m. 30 Nov. 1660, Sarah Baldwin, d. at Marshfield, 5 Feb. 1692. EDWARD, Boston, was the publ. executioner 1684. In July 1690 Edward of Salem, perhaps his s. was k. by the Ind. at Casco or Falmouth. ELEAZER, Barnstable, s. of William, m. 7 Apr. 1682 (if the rec. is correct), Ruth, d. of John Chipman, wh. d. 8 Apr. 1698, had Benoni, b. 13 May 1682, d. at 19 yrs.; Bethia, 23 Sept. 1683 ; Nathan, 27 Apr. 1685 ; Daniel, 23 Mar. 1687 ; Sarah, 23 Mar. 1689 ; Theophilus, 11 Mar. 1691 ; Eleazer ; and Ruth, tw. 3 Aug. 1693; Abel, 15 June 1695; and Rebecca, 10 Dec. 1697. FRANCIS, Barnstable 1643, of age to bear arms. His w. d. Mar. 1693 at Marshfield. JOB, Barnstable, s. of William, was deac. and d. Mar. 1719, says Hamblin, m. Nov. 1668, Mary Walley, perhaps d. of Rev. Thomas, had a s. b. 18 Oct. 1669, d. soon ; Samuel, 15 May 1671; Thomas, 19 Jan. 1674. By sec. w. m. 19 July 1680, Hannah, d. of Richard Taylor, wh. d. 14 May 1743, aged 85, had Mary, 29 June 1681 ; John, 24 Feb. 1683 ; both bapt. 16 (not 17, as print.) Sept. of this yr.; Hannah, 2 Feb. 1685 ; Eliz. 15 May 1688 ; Sarah, 19 Jan. 1690, bapt. 22 Mar. 1691 ; Job, 4, bapt. 29 Apr. 1694 ; David, 5 Sept. bapt. 10 Oct. 1697 ; and Thankful, 16 June 1700. JOHN, Scituate 1636, had William, b. 1637 ; Eliz. 1639 ; Samuel, 1642 ; Job, 1644; Josiah, 1647; Eleazer, 1650; and Joseph, 1654; rem. prob. to Barnstable. Deane. But one of necessity distrusts the names and dates of all these ch. exc. the first, bec. they so wonderfully concur with those of his br. William's ch. and in his will of 10 Feb. 1669, I find good reason, for he gives to his w. Joan, and to six ch. of his br. William, viz. John, Job, Samuel, Josiah, Elisha, and Joseph ; made Job, excor. and names no ch. of his own. JOHN, Barnstable, s. of William, m. Nov. 1659, Mary Bodfish, perhaps d. of Robert, had Eliz. b. 7 Oct. 1660 ; Jonathan, 15 July 1662, and his w. d. Dec. foll. He m. next, 25 Apr. Mary Bursley, d. of the first John, had John, b. 17 Feb.

1664; Hannah, 10 Oct. 1665; Joseph, 1 Mar. 1668; Benjamin; Nathaniel; Experience; Jabez; Mary; Abigail; and Bathshua; and he d. May 1711. Hannah m. 1 July 1686, Samuel Lothrop. JOSEPH, Barnstable, youngest s. of William, m. Dec. 1677, Temperance Bursley, prob. d. of the first John, had William, b. 25 Aug. 1679; Timothy, 30 Apr. 1680, prob. d. soon; Noah, 8 Dec. 1683; Joanna, 18 July 1687, bapt. with brs. William, and Noah, 21 Sept. 1688; Martha, 22 Feb. 1689, bapt. 3 Aug. 1690; Temperance, 26 Aug. 1694; and Remember, 26 Aug. bapt. 15 Oct. 1699. JOSIAH, Barnstable, br. of the preced. m. 22 Oct. 1668, Meletiah, d. of Gov. Thomas Hinckley, had a s. b. 20 Aug. 1669, d. next mo.; Thomas, 28 May 1671; Mercy, 12 Feb. 1674; Mary, 14 Sept. 1677; Alice, 25 Dec. 1679; Meletiah, 20 Nov. 1681; Josiah, 8 Feb. 1684; Ebenezer, 30 May 1687; Seth, 23 Sept. 1689; these eight bapt. together, 5 June 1692; Benjamin, 26 Sept. 1692. The f. wh. had been a soldier in the Narraganset fight, 1675, of Gorham's comp. d. 2 Feb. 1698; and the wid. d. 2 Feb. 1714. RICHARD, Marblehead 1674. THOMAS, New London 1660, by w. Rachel had Mary, b. 4 Mar. 1669; Thomas, 1 Sept. 1670; John, 1672; William, 1675, d. young; Samuel, 27 July 1676; William, again, 1680; and Andrew, bapt. 1 Apr. 1683; was constable 1684, call. in 1693, a. 60 yrs. old, d. 18 Jan. 1716. * WILLIAM, Barnstable, br. of first John, and tradit. makes their arr. 1634, was first at Scituate, unit. with the ch. 25 Dec. 1636, by w. Alice had John, b. 3 May, bapt. 11 June 1637; and at B. Eliz. 22 Sept. bapt. 22 Dec. 1639, d. at 18 yrs.; Samuel, b. 3 July 1642; Job, 9 Mar. 1645; Josiah, 19 Sept. 1647; Eleazer, 21 July 1650; and Joseph, 1654; was rep. 1670, 1, and 4. Twelve of this name had, in 1834, been gr. at Harv. and five at Yale.

CROCKETT, THOMAS, Kittery 1648, York 1652. Haz. I. 575. Belkn. I. 425, shows him here in 1633.

CROFOOT. See Crowfoot.

CROFT, GEORGE, Wickford 1674. THOMAS, Hadley, m. 6 Dec. 1683, Abigail, d. of John Dickinson, first of the same, had John, b. 8 Nov. 1684; Mary, 2 Feb. 1686; Abigail, 29 Sept. 1688; Thomas, 27 Feb. 1690, d. at 24 yrs.; Eliz. 17 Apr. 1691; and Benoni, 22 Oct. 1692. He d. 27 Feb. 1693, and his wid. m. 30 Nov. 1704, Samuel Crofoot. WILLIAM, Lynn 1650 to 75, had m. Ann, wid. of Thomas Ivory the first, wh. made her will 25 June 1675, in wh. she names her s. Thomas Ivory, d. Sarah Chadwell, s. Theophilus Bailey and s. John Burrill. Yet that will was not pro. bef. 26 Nov. 1689, the same time with his will of 5 Mar. preced. in wh. also are nam. the Ivory, Chadwell, Bailey, and Burrill connex. with addit. gift to "cous. the eldest childr. ea. of Peter, Nathaniel, Samuel, and William Frothingham;" but the relat. is less easily discov.

CROMWELL, DAVID, Dover 1662, prob. s. of Philip, but may have been br. GILES, Newbury, an early sett. whose w. d. 14 June 1648. She was prob. mo. of all his ch. but he m. 10 Sept. 1648, Alice Wiseman, wh. d. 6 June 1669. He had Argentine, wh. m. 25 Nov. 1662, Benjamin Cram; Dorothy, and Philip, prob. older, as well as Thomas; and, perhaps, John; and d. 25 Feb. 1673. Dorothy d. at Salem 27 Sept. 1673, aged 67, as the gr.stone has it. JOHN, Newbury, b. a. 1636, may have been s. of the preced. m. 2 Nov. 1662, Joan Butler. JOHN, Boston, by w. Rebecca had Rebecca, b. 20 July 1654. JOHN, Salem, s. of Philip of the same, had w. Hannah, but no ch. prob. His will, pro. 27 Sept. 1700, names none, but gives £30 to establ. sch. for poor ch. JOHN, Dover, prob. s. of Philip of the same, m. 13 Jan. 1692, Eliz. Thomas. PHILIP, Salem 1647, s. of Giles, b. in Eng. a. 1614, wheelwright, says Felt; butcher, says Coffin; was freem. 1665; selectman 1671-5; had John, bef. ment. by w. Dorothy, wh. d. 28 Sept. 1673; by w. Mary, wid. Lemon, m. 19 Nov. 1674, wh. d. 14 Nov. 1683, aged 72; and also third w. Margaret, nam. in his will, no ch. is kn. and he d. 30 Mar. 1693, aged 83. PHILIP, Dover 1657-74, m. Eliz. d. of Thomas Laighton, had Ann, b. 19 Aug. 1674; and was, prob. too old to have more, call. 74 in 1686. By former w. or ws. he, perhaps, had eno. ch. of wh. Sarah that m. Timothy Wentworth may have been one. SAMUEL, Mass. freem. 3 Sept. 1634. THOMAS, Newbury 1637, then 20 yrs. old, s. of Giles, rem. to Hampton 1639, was a physician, rem. to Salem; had w. Ann, s. Thomas, wh. d. 16 Mar. 1663; and ds. Jane, wh. m. 19 Mar. 1666, Jonathan Pickering; and Ann, m. Benjamin Ager or Auger; next, 26 June 1672, m. David Phippen, and was liv. as his wid. Jan. 1714. THOMAS, Boston, mariner, styl. hims. of London, made a large fortune by privateering, came hither to enjoy it, 1646, had w. Ann, d. Eliz. and d. bef. 10 Oct. 1649. His will of 29 Aug. was pro. 26 Oct. of that yr. Winth. II. 264, says he was brot. into the world by the Cæsarian operat. and never saw f. or mo. His wid. soon m. Robert Knight of Boston, and shortly aft. his d. 1655, m. John Joyliffe. His d. Eliz. m. 18 Aug. 1659, Richard Price. Sometimes the name in our rec. appears, as it sound. Crumwell.

CROOKER, DANIEL, Marshfield, perhaps s. of Francis, m. 20 Jan. 1682, Mary Bumpas. FRANCIS, Scituate, m. 1647, Mary Gaunt of Barnstable, perhaps d. of Peter, rem. soon after 1648, it is thot. to Marshfield. See Deane for curious note about his health.

CROSBY, ANTHONY, Rowley 1643, surgeon, had Anthony, wh. was 23 yrs. old in 1659; Joseph, 25 in 1665; and prob. Hannah, wh. m. 1 Dec. 1655, John Johnson. Perhaps his wid. Prudence was sec. w. of Edward Carlton. ANTHONY, Rowley, surgeon, s. of the preced. perhaps b. in

Eng. m. 29 Dec. 1659, or, as ano. acco. says, 1666, Prudence, d. of Jonathan Wade of Ipswich, had Nathaniel, b. 1667 ; Nathan, 1669 ; and, perhaps, others, earlier or later. His wid. m. 9 July 1673, Rev. Seaborn Cotton, as sec. w. ELEAZUR, Eastham, s. of the first Thomas, m. 24 Oct. 1706, Patience Freeman, had Rebecca, b. 12 May 1709 ; Sylvanus, 1712 ; Isaac ; and seven others. * JOSEPH, Braintree, youngest s. of Simon, m. 1 June 1675, Sarah, d. of Bichard Brackett, had Sarah, b. 29 Oct. 1677 ; Thomas and Simon, tw. 16 Jan. 1689 ; Ebenezer ; and other ch.; rep. 1689, d. 26 Nov. 1695. JOSEPH, Eastham, s. of Thomas of the same, had Theophilus, b. 31 Dec. 1694. NATHANIEL, Rowley 1691, s. of Anthony. SIMON, Cambridge, came in the Susan and Ellen, 1635, aged 26 ; with w. Ann, 25 ; and s. Thomas, 8 wks. ; freem. 3 Mar. 1636 ; had Simon, b. Aug. 1637 ; and Joseph, Feb. 1639 ; selectman 1636 and 8, d. Sept. 1639. His young wid. m. Rev. William Tompson of Braintree. His est. by sev. mesne conveyances pass. 1707, to Rev. William Brattle, being that partly occup. now by the Brattle ho. * SIMON, Billerica, s. of the preced. freem. 1668 ; rep. 1692, 7, and 8 ; m. 15 July 1659, Rachel, d. of Richard Bracket, had Rachel, b. 20 Aug. 1660 ; Simon ; Thomas, 10 Mar. 1666 ; Joseph, 5 Mar. 1669 ; Hannah, 30 Mar. 1672; Nathan, 9 Feb. 1675 ; Josiah, 11 Nov. 1677 ; Mary, 23 Nov. 1680 ; and Sarah, 27 July 1684. Descend. are spread thro. Maine, Mass. and New Hampsh. SIMON, Eastham, s. of Thomas, m. 27 Aug. 1691, Mary Nickerson, had Samuel, b. 11 July 1692 ; and Eliz. 15 Sept. 1693. THOMAS, Cambridge 1640, perhaps rem. to Rowley. THOMAS, Eastham, eldest s. of first Simon, b. in Eng. an inf. brot. by his f. ; H. C. 1653, preach. yet not ord. at E. d. 1721 acc. the Catal. but by the later rept. of a very careful searcher, 13 June 1702, at Boston; had Thomas, b. 7 Apr. 1663 ; Simon, 5 July 1665 ; Sarah, 24 Mar. 1667 ; Joseph, 27 Jan. 1669 ; John, and Thomas, tw. 4 Dec. 1670, of wh. Thomas d. in 10 wks. ; William, Mar. 1673 ; Ebenezer, 28 Mar. 1675 ; Ann, Mercy, and Increase, at one b. 15 Apr. 1678, d. all soon; and Eleazer, 30 Mar. 1689. THOMAS, Eastham, s. of the preced. by w. Hannah, wh. d. 8 Jan. 1729, had John, wh. d. 25 May 1714; and the f. d. 12 Apr. 1731. Twelve of this name had been gr. in 1834 at Harv. and twelve at the other N. E. coll.

CROSCUM, GEORGE, Marblehead 1653, a fisherman.

CROSS, GEORGE, Ipswich, perhaps s. of the first Robert, had Thomas, b. 10 Mar. 1689. HENRY, came in the Increase, 1635, a carpenter, aged 20. JOHN, Watertown, came in the Elizabeth from Ipswich, 1634, aged 50, with w. Ann, 38 ; but sec. w. Mary had Mary, b. 10 May 1641 ; he d. 15 Sept. 1640. His wid. m. 1642, Robert Saunderson, the silversmith, d. 13 Nov. 1669. * JOHN, Ipswich 1635, by w. Ann had Ann, bapt. 9 Oct. 1638 ; rem. to Hampton, freem. 6 Sept. 1639, rep. 1640, perhaps in 1642 at Dover, and back again to I. d. 1652. His inv. of Sept. was of £382, 5, 2 ; and the only ch. Susanna m. Thomas Hammond. JOHN, Windsor 1645, had, perhaps, been at Stamford. JOHN, Wells, was constable there 1647, d. a. 1676, leav. wid. Frances, and s. John, and Joseph, of wh. John d. soon aft. his f. JOHN, Boston 1663, a brewer. JOHN, a soldier of Moseley's comp. Dec. 1675. JOSEPH, Plymouth 1638, rem. perhaps, to Maine, was constable of Wells 1670. NATHANIEL, br. of John of Windsor. PETER, Ipswich 1673. PETER, Norwich, had gr. of lot 1680. RALPH, Ipswich, s. of Robert the first, d. 1711, leav. wid. Mary. ROBERT, Ipswich 1639, had serv. in the Pequot war ; by w. wh. d. 29 Oct. 1677, had sev. ch. but names of only Robert, perhaps eldest, Martha, wh. m. William Durgin or Durkee, Stephen, and Ralph, b. 15 Feb. 1659, prob. youngest, have reach. me. ROBERT, Ipswich, s. of the preced. m. 19 Feb. 1665, Martha, youngest d. of Thomas Treadwell, had Robert, b. 21 Jan. foll. ; and Thomas, 29 Nov. 1667. SAMUEL, was, perhaps, first at Stamford, went to Windsor, m. 12 July 1677, Eliz. wid. of Edward Chapman, had Hannah, b. 11 June 1678, d. at 2 yrs. ; and Samuel, b. and d. 10 Dec. 1679 ; d. 1707, without ch. STEPHEN, Ipswich 1664, perhaps s. of the first Robert, by w. Eliz. had one s. b. 1686, wh. d. soon ; and John, a. 1687 ; and the f. was d. in Jan. 1705. STEPHEN, Boston, m. 1690, Mary, wid. of Robert Lawrence, d. of John Phillips of Dorchester, wh. had been wid. of George Munjoy of Falmouth. WILLIAM, Hartford 1645, says Hinman, 19, was of Fairfield 1649.

CROSSING, WILLIAM, emb. at Barbados, for Boston, 1 Apr. 1679 in the ship Blessing, but was not prob. an inhab.

CROSSMAN, JOHN, Taunton, one of the first purch. a. 1639, had Robert. JOHN, Taunton, perhaps eldest s. of the first Robert, m. 7 Jan. 1690, Joanna Thayer. JOSEPH, Taunton, s. of the first Robert, m. 24 Nov. 1685, Sarah Alden. ROBERT, Taunton, s. of John, perhaps b. in Eng. by w. Sarah had John, b. 16 Mar. 1654 ; Mary, 16 July 1655, wh. m. 24 Aug. 1673, John Gould ; Robert, 3 Aug. 1657 ; Joseph, 25 Apr. 1659 ; Nathaniel, 7 Aug. 1660 ; Eleazer, 16 Mar. 1663, d. young ; Eliz. 2 May 1665 ; Samuel, 25 July 1667 ; Mercy, 20 Mar. 1669 or 70 ; Thomas, 6 Oct. 1671 ; Susanna, 14 Feb. 1673. Nathaniel was k. by the Ind. 8 Mar. 1676, at Wrentham. ROBERT, Taunton, s. of the preced. m. 21 July 1679, Hannah Brooks, had Nathaniel, b. 10 Mar. 1680. SAMUEL, Taunton, br. of the preced. m. 19 Dec. 1689, Eliz. Bell ; and 22 Dec. 1696, he m. Mary Sawyer. THOMAS, youngest br. of the preced. was a soldier of Gallop's comp. in the Canada exped. 1690.

CROSSTHWAYTE, or CROSWAIT, CHARLES, Boston, by w. Judith had

George, b. 16 June 1671; George, again, 3 Mar. 1676; Charles, 3 Feb. 1678; and John, 7 May 1680; but of him I see no more.

CROSWELL, THOMAS, Charlestown, had w. Priscilla, d. of deac. John Upham, wh. d. 8 Dec. 1717, aged 75.

CROUTCH, CROWCH, or CROUCH, SIMON. See Couch. WILLIAM, Charlestown 1654, by w. Sarah, m. 21 Feb. 1657, had David, 16 Jan. 1659; Mary, bapt. 22 Dec. 1661; Eliz. 4 Sept. 1664; Richard, and Hannah, tw. 17 Mar. 1667; Joseph, 22 Aug. 1669; and William, b. 16 Nov. 1678. A wid. C. was liv. there in 1678; and, in a diff. ho. a William, perhaps her s. The name was contin. in C. for I find the gr.stone of Jonathan there, wh. d. 25 Nov. 1714, aged 58.

CROW, CHRISTOPHER, Windsor, freem. of Conn. 1658, m. 15 Jan. 1657, Mary, d. of Benjamin Burr; d. 1680, leav. Samuel, Benoni, Thomas, and four ds. Hinman, 127, says he d. 1681, and gives the ages of the ch. Samuel, 21 yrs.; Mary, 18; Hannah, 15; Martha, 14; Benoni, 12; Margaret, 11; and Thomas, 5. His wid. m. Josiah Clark of W. and Mary m. John Clark, br. of Josiah. ELI, a soldier from some E. part of the Col. was at Northampton, Apr. 1676. * JOHN, Charlestown 1635, whose w. Elishua came, says Frothingham, 84, in the preced. yr. and we see in Budington she was rec. of the ch. 4 Jan. of this yr. had Moses, bapt. 24 June 1637, wh. prob. d. young; John, perhaps 1638, in wh. yr. he rem. to the new planta. of Yarmouth, in Plymouth Col. bec. freem. 1640, rep. 1641–3, and d. Jan. 1673; had, I presume, b. at Y. Samuel and Thomas, perhaps more ch. JOHN, Hartford, an orig. propr. was, perhaps, there in 1637, or 8, m. Eliz. only ch. of William Goodwin, the famous rul. Elder, had s. John, Samuel, Daniel, and Nathaniel, ds. Esther, wh. m. Giles Hamlin of Middletown; Sarah, b. 1 Mar. 1647; Ann, or Hannah, 13 July 1649, wh. m. Thomas Dickinson of Hadley; Mehitable, m. Samuel Partridge of Hadley; Eliz. 1650, m. William Warren, and not, next, Phineas Wilson, as sometimes said; Mary m. Noah Coleman of Hadley, and, next, 16 Sept. 1680, Peter Montague; Sarah m. Daniel White of Hatfield; and Ruth m. William Gaylord, and next, John Haley, both of Hadley. Here are one s. and one d. more than Porter ment. beside that the intermarriages in sev. cases of the ds. are diff. from his. He tells us, that Warren, the h. of Eliz. d. 1689, and she m. Phineas Wilson, wh. d. 1691, and she d. 1727. He sided with his f.-in-law in the relig. controv. and with him went to plant Hadley, bec. freem. of Mass. 1666, but many yrs. aft. rem. back to Hartford, there d. 16 Jan. 1686. His s. Daniel d. 1693, leav. wid. but no ch. JOHN, Fairfield, s. of the preced. a merch. in the W. I. trade, d. 1667, on the ocean, leav. good est. but no w. nor ch. JOHN, Yarmouth, s. of first John, m. Mehitable, d. of Rev. John Miller, had John,

b. 1662; Samuel; Mehitable ; Lydia; Jeremiah; Eliz.; Susanna; and Hannah ; prob. in differ. order of success. and d. 28 Jan. 1689 ; and his wid. d. 23 Feb. 1715. The name bec. Crowell in the third generat. JOHN, Billerica, a propr. 1655. NATHANIEL, Hartford, s. of John, by w. Deborah had Eliz. b. 1685; John, 1687 ; and Deborah, 1694; and he d. 1695. His wid. m. Andrew Warner, and d. 1697. SAMUEL, Hadley, br. of the preced. m. Sarah, d. of William Lewis of Farmington, had Samuel, and Mary, was k. May 1676 in the Falls fight. His wid. m. the same yr. Daniel Marsh. THOMAS, Yarmouth. His est. is still enjoy. by descend. See Crowell. WILLIAM, Plymouth 1643, able to bear arms, m. 1 Apr. 1664, Hannah, d. of first Josiah Winslow, had no ch. d. Jan. 1684, aged a. 55, says her gr.stone, in his will ment. brs. Samuel, Robert, and Thomas, all of Coventry, Eng. * YELVERTON, or ELVERTON, Plymouth, had, in 1643, been of Yarmouth, there had Thomas and Eliz. tw. b. 9 May 1649 ; rep. 1663. Baylies, II. 55.

CROWELL, JOHN, Yarmouth. See Crow. THOMAS, Yarmouth, perhaps br. of John, by w. Agnes had (beside, perhaps, others), John, Thomas, and Lydia; d. 9 Mar. 1690, leav. wid. and those ch. Lydia m. Feb. 1677, Ebenezer Goodspeed.

CROWFOOT, JOSEPH, Springfield 1658, freem. 1672, d. 8 Apr. 1678, leav. Joseph, Mary, John, Samuel, James, Daniel, Matthew, and David. SAMUEL, Hadley, s. of Joseph, m. Mary, d. of Isaac Warner, wh. d. 9 Apr. 1702, had six ch. by her, and m. 30 Nov. 1704, Abigail, d. of John Dickinson, first of the same, wid. of Thomas Croft, had Sarah, b. 25 May 1706 ; his w. d. 1714, and he d. 10 Oct. 1733, aged 71, as his gr.stone tells. In Conn. some descend. write their name Crowfut or Crofut.

CROWNE, HENRY, Newcastle 1676, perhaps s. of William, m. 1 May of that yr. Alice Rogers, had John, b. 10 Nov. 1679; Eliz. 27 May 1684; Agnes, 19 July 1686; Rebecca, 23 Jan. 1690 ; and William, 1 Jan. 1692; kept an alehouse 1683. WILLIAM, Boston 1657, came with a patent of 8 Sept. 1656 from his Highness, Oliver, Lord Protector, &c. in conjunct. with the Sieur de La Tour, and Col. Thomas Temple. He was to have, in div. of this grand province of Acadia, all W. of Machias for 30 lea. includ. Penobscot, and up Machias riv. 130 lea. on its W. bank; was freem. 1660, and had more productive, tho. narrower, est. by gr. of the Col. 500 acres near Sudbury in 1662, and by purchase of 1674 at Mendham. See a valua. paper in Geneal. Reg. VI. 46, a. his serv. as friend of N. E. But I do not concur with the writer in claim. his s. John, the poet, "as an American by b." wh. in my opin. preced. the first com. of his f. hither.

CROWTHER, JOHN, Portsmouth 1631, sent by Mason the patentee, was there 1640.

CRUFTS, WILLIAM, Kittery 1687.

CRUMB, or CROMB, DANIEL, Westerly 1669, m. Alice, wid. of Richard Haughton; but by a former w. I suppose, had William, and a d. wh. m. Edward Austin. He d. 1713, and his wid. d. 29 Jan. 1716. WILLIAM, Westerly, s. of the preced. by w. Hannah had Joseph, William, Rachel, Mercy, Jemima, and Eliz. but not a single date is attach. to any.

CRUTTENDEN, ABRAHAM, Guilford 1639, brot. w. Mary, and one or more ch. from Eng. d. Jan. 1683; had, prob. Abraham, Isaac, Mary, Eliz. Hannah, Deborah, and Thomas, wh. d. unm. 8 Feb. 1698. Mary m. George Bartlett, and d. 11 Sept. 1669; Eliz. m. John Graves; Hannah m. George Highland; and Deborah d. 24 Apr. 1658, prob. unm. His sec. w. m. 31 May 1665, was Joanna, wid. of William Chittenden, wh. d. 16 Aug. 1668. ABRAHAM, Guilford, s. of the preced. perhaps b. in Eng. m. 13 May 1661, Susanna, d. of Thomas Grigson of New Haven, had Abraham, b. 6 Mar. 1662; Sarah, 21 Aug. 1665; Thomas, 31 Jan. 1667; John, 15 Aug. 1671; and Joseph, 9 Apr. 1674; and d. 25 Sept. 1694. ABRAHAM, Guilford, s. of the preced. m. 6 May 1686, Susanna, d. of John Kirby of Middletown, had Abraham, b. 1 Apr. 1687; Mary, 16 Dec. 1690; John, 15 Dec. 1693; Daniel, 27 May 1696; Ann, 10 May 1701; and Ebenezer, 1 Sept. 1705. ISAAC, Guilford, s. of first Abraham, m. 20 Sept. 1665, Lydia, d. of John, or (more prob.) of his br. Anthony, Thompson of New Haven, had Isaac, b. 9 Aug. 1666, d. young; Lydia, 17 July 1668; Eliz. 22 Sept. 1670; Deborah, 23 Oct. 1673; Samuel, 1 Nov. 1675; Hannah, 27 Mar. 1678; Jabez, 25 Feb. 1680, d. young; Mehitable, 11 Apr. 1682; Naomi, 23 June 1685, d. soon; and Naomi, again, 1687, d. young. JOHN, Guilford, s. of sec. Abraham, m. 6 May 1702, Bathsheba, d. of Isaac Johnson, had Eliz. b. 3 Feb. 1704; Bathsheba, 8 Oct. 1705; Rachel, 24 Oct. 1707; John, 2 May 1710; Mary, 30 Mar. 1713; David, 3 Dec. 1716; and Isaac, 3 Apr. 1720; and d. 16 May 1751. JOSEPH, Guilford, youngest br. of the preced. m. 2 May 1700, Mary, d. of Jonathan Hoyt, wh. d. 3 Jan. 1750, had Hannah, b. 6 Apr. 1703; Deborah, 3 June 1705; Joseph, 17 Aug. 1708; Mercy, 4 Feb. 1711; Seth, 14 Oct. 1718; and Jane, 23 Feb. 1721; and he d. 5 Feb. 1753. THOMAS, Guilford, br. of the preced. m. 11 Sept. 1690, Abigail, d. of John Hull of Killingworth, had Abigail, b. 23 Dec. 1691; Eliz. 1693; Sarah, 6 Feb. 1694; Thomas, 1696; Esther, 1698; Lydia; Hull, 1706; Susanna, 1708; and Josiah, 1710; d. 14 Sept. 1754.

CUDDINGTON. See Coddington.

CUDWORTH, ISRAEL, Scituate, s. of James, had Mary, b. 1678. † ‡ * JAMES, Scituate 1634, by Deane is suppos. to have come in the Charles with Hatherly 1632, a very valua. man, join. the ch. 18 Jan.

1635, with his w. wh. bore him James, bapt. 3 May 1635, under his own roof, prob. the place where the congr. then worship.; Mary, 23 July 1637; Jonathan, 16 Sept. 1638, d. in few days; Israel, 18 Apr. 1641; Joanna, 26 Mar. 1643; beside a s. bur. very young, 24 June 1644; and others, certain. Hannah, and ano. Jonathan, of wh. we find not the bapt. rep. 1649–56, and again in 1659, when for his tenderness to the Quakers he was reject.; an Assist. 1656–8, capt. of the militia, and in the early part of Philip's war comm. of the whole force of Plymouth col. in 1681 dep.-gov. d. 1682. He was in London, as Col. agent, where he d. of smallpox soon aft. arr. and he had serv. as Commiss. of the Un. Col. in 1657. Baylies, I. 280. IV. 13–15. Mary m. 1660, Robert Whitcomb of Scituate. He had rem. with Lothrop to Barnstable, but aft. few yrs. went back to S. In his will, early in 1682, he gives to James, Israel, Jonathan, and ds. Hannah Jones, and four ch. of d. Mary Whitcomb. JAMES, Scituate, s. of the preced. had Mary, b. 1667; Sarah, 1669; James, 1670; Joanna, 1671; Eliz. 1672; Abigail, 1674; and John, 1677; all liv. at his d. His wid. Mary d. 1699. JONATHAN, Scituate, br. of the preced. m. Sarah, d. of Jonathan Jackson, had Nathaniel, b. 1667; Bethia, 1671; Hannah, 8 May 1674; Sarah, 1676; Jonathan, 1679; James, 1682; Israel, 1683; and Rachel, 1689.

CULLEN, JAMES, a soldier in Turner's comp. 1676, for Philip's war.

CULLICK, ‡ * JOHN, Hartford 1639, a capt. rep. 1644, 6, and 7, Assist. and Secr. 1648 and sev. yrs. aft. m. 20 May 1648, Eliz. sis. not d. (as I had said in note upon Winth. Hist. I. 228, of Ed. 1853, hav. been misled by some Conn. author.) of George Fenwick, Esq. of Saybrook, prob. as sec. w. had John, b. 4 May 1649, H. C. 1668; and Eliz. 15 July 1652; rem. to Boston, where he was receiv. into the ch. 27 Nov. 1659 with his w. and two elder ch. John and Mary. I suppose it was an elder d. Hannah, wh. m. 20 May 1660, Pelatiah Glover. He was from Felstead, Essex, serv. as Commiss. of the Un. Col. for Conn. and d. at B. 23 Jan. 1663. His wid. m. Richard Ely, and much contention foll. a. the est. His d. Eliz. m. Oct. 1671, Benjamin Batten of Boston. JOHN, Boston, s. of the preced. d. bef. 1698, prob. many yrs.

CULLIMORE. See Collamore.

CULLIVER, JOHN, Boston 1655, mariner.

CULVER, EDWARD, Dedham, wheelwright, had John, b. 15 Apr. 1640; Joshua, 12 Jan. 1643; Samuel, 9 Jan. 1645; Gershom, bapt. 3 Dec. 1648; and Hannah, 11 Apr. 1652, both at Roxbury, whither he had rem. but next yr. went to New London, where he had Joseph, and, perhaps, Edward. His w. was Ann; and he d. 1685, near the head of Mistick, on Groton side of the town. EDWARD, Norwich 1680, perhaps s. of the preced. m. 15 Jan. 1682, Sarah, had Ephraim, b. 1683;

John, 1685 ; Sarah, 1688, d. soon ; Edward, 1689 ; Samuel, 1690 ;
Hezekiah, 1692 ; and Sarah, again, 1694. JOHN, New Haven, s. of
first Edward, had Abigail, b. 1676 ; and James, 1679 ; rem. to New
London, Groton side, where he had been in 1667 ; in 1703, with w.
Mary, gave s. James, est. JOSEPH, New London 1676, br. of the
preced. JOSHUA, New London, br. of the preced. went, aft. 1667, to
New Haven, m. 23 Dec. 1672, Eliz. d. of Timothy Ford, there had ch.
but rem. last to Wallingford. SAMUEL, New London, br. of the preced.
for some misdemean. withdrew a. 1674, and is not again kn.

CUMBY, or CUMBEE, HUMPHREY. Boston, mariner, by w. Sarah had
John, b. 23 Jan. 1651 ; Robert, 14 Feb. 1655 ; and Esther, 1 Mar.
1657 ; was liv. 1673.

CUMMINGS, COMINGS, CUMMENS, or with single *m*, with, or without
s, and COMYNS, ABRAHAM, Dunstable, s. of John, had, at Woburn, by
w. Sarah, Abraham, b. 7 Oct. 1690 ; Sarah, 10 Feb. 1694 ; Jacob, 3
Jan. 1696 ; and at D. Josiah, 12 July 1698. DAVID, Dorchester 1664,
d. 12 Dec. 1690. Eliz. prob. his w. d. 13 Nov. 1689. ISAAC, Ipswich,
freem. 18 May 1642, may have been at Watertown bef. and aft. at
Topsfield, for in 1661 Isaac sen. a deac. and Isaac jun. (wh. by w. Mary
had a s. b. 3 Nov. in that yr. and was liv. in 1686) were there. In his
will of 1676 he names s. Isaac, s.-in-law John Jewett, h. of Eliz. and
John Pease, h. of Ann. ISAAC, Topsfield, perhaps s. of the preced.
freem. 1673. JOHN, Rowley 1667, possib. but not prob. s. of Isaac,
Topsfield, where, by w. Sarah, d. of Thomas Howlett, I think, he had
Sarah, b. 28 Jan. 1662 ; freem. 1673, rem. to Dunstable 1684, and next
yr. was one of the found. of the ch. selectman, and town clk. He had
w. Sarah, and ch. John ; Nathaniel ; Sarah ; Thomas, b. 1659 ; Abra-
ham ; Isaac ; and Ebenezer ; the last two d. 2 Nov. 1688 ; and he d. 1
Dec. 1700, and his w. d. six days aft. His d. Sarah m. 24 Dec. 1682,
Samuel French. JOHN, Dunstable, s. of the preced. m. 13 Sept. 1680,
Eliz. had John, b. 7 July 1682 ; Samuel, 6 Oct. 1684 ; Eliz. 5 Jan.
1687 ; Ann, 14 Sept. 1698 ; Lydia, 24 Mar. 1701 ; and William, 24
Apr. 1702. His w. was k. by the Ind. 3 July 1706. Belkn. I. 173.
NATHANIEL, Dunstable, br. of the preced. had John, b. 14 Jan. 1698 ;
Nathaniel, 8 Sept. 1699 ; Eliezer, 19 Oct. 1701 ; and Joseph, 26 May
1704. RICHARD, of Isle of Shóals, join. with Thomas Turpin in purch.
of all est. of Francis Williams of Portsmouth, in Dec. 1645, and in
short time rem. to Mass. freem. 1669, but went back, I presume, to
Maine, and d. at Scarborough 1676, where his prop. was not small.
THOMAS, Dunstable, s. of first John, m. 19 Dec. 1688, Priscilla Warner,
had Priscilla, b. 1 Oct. 1689 ; Mary, 25 Apr. 1692 ; Ann, 6 Feb. 1699 ;
Thomas, 10 Apr. 1701 ; Jonathan, 3 July 1703 ; Ephraim, 10 Mar.

1706; and Samuel, 12 Apr. 1708; and d. 20 Jan. 1723. WILLIAM, Salem 1637, prob. the support. of Wheelwright, disarm. that yr. Ann, possib. his d. m. 8 Oct. 1669, at S. John Pease. Seven of this name, with its various spell. had been gr. at Harv. in 1820, and eleven at other N. E. coll.

CUNDY, SAMUEL, Marblehead 1674.

CUNLIFF, CUNLITH, or CUNDLIEF, HENRY, Dorchester, freem. 1644, when the rec. has Cunlithe or Gunlithe as Mr. Paige reads it; by w. Susanna had Susanna, b. 15 Mar. 1645; rem. with early sett. 1659, to Northampton, was one of the found. of the ch. 18 June 1661, there d. 14 Sept. 1673. His wid. d. 19 Nov. 1675. His only ch. Susanna had been betroth. to Eldad Pomeroy, wh. d. 1662, and she m. 1663, Matthew Cole; and, 12 Dec. 1665, John Webb, jr.

CUNNINGHAM, ANDREW, Boston 1684. PATRICK, Springfield, d. 12 Sept. 1685. Sprague. Four of this name had been gr. at Harv. and one at Yale in 1834.

CURNEY, or CORNEY, JOHN, Gloucester, m. 18 Nov. 1670, Abigail Skilling, perhaps d. of Thomas, had Elisha, b. 25 Sept. 1672; Abigail, 8 Feb. 1676; John, 27 Sept. 1678, d. in few days, and he d. 1722. My suspic. is strong, that this name is mistak. for Carney or Gurney.

CURRIER, RICHARD, Salisbury 1640, by w. Ann' had Hannah, b. 8 July 1643; Thomas, 8 Mar. 1646; and, earlier, prob. Sarah, wh. m. 23 June 1659, Samuel Fogg of Hampton; and he d. 17 May 1689. Hannah m. 23 June 1659, Samuel Foote. SAMUEL, Haverhill, m. 1670, Mary, d. of Thomas Hardy. He may have been s. of the preced. Martha, of Andover, was one of the victims of the baneful superstit. a. witchcraft, execut. 19 Aug. 1692, at the same time with Rev. George Burrows, suffer. by the same horrid delus. Yet her punishm. was, to some extent, less than his, as the greater culprit met the maledict. of Cotton Mather, the ch. inquisit. THOMAS, Amesbury, perhaps s. of Richard, freem. 1690.

CURTIS, CURTICE, CURTISE, or CURTIZE, BENJAMIN, Portsmouth, s. of Thomas of York, bought of Mason ld. at Newcastle 1681. BENJAMIN, Stratford 1685, was s. of John of the same. BENJAMIN, Scituate, s. of William, m. 1689, Mary, d. of Capt. Joseph Sylvester, had Mary, b. 1691; Benjamin, 1692; Ebenezer, 1694; Lydia, 1695; Sarah, 1697; Ruth, 1700; Susanna, 1702; Deborah, 1704; William, 1706; David, 1708; and Peleg, 1710. Descend. are still on ancestr. est. DANIEL, Stratford 1685, was s. of William of the same. DEODATE, Braintree, a. 1643, had Solomon; and by w. Rebecca had Ruth, b. 8 Jan. 1648. EBENEZER, Stratford 1685, was br. of Daniel of the same. EPHRAIM, Topsfield, prob. s. of Henry, freem. 1686. He had liv. at Sudbury bef.

the gr. Ind. war, in wh. he was very active, at Brookfield. FRANCIS, Plymouth, m. 28 Dec. 1671, Hannah Smith, had John, b. 26 July 1673; Benjamin, 11 Aug. 1675; Francis, mid. Apr. 1679; Eliz. 15 June 1681; and Elisha, Mar. 1683. GEORGE, Boston, freem. 13 May 1640, join. our ch. 4 Aug. preced. call. "serv. to our teacher Mr. John Cotton." He had gr. of a lot for two heads, 30 Dec. 1640, when, prob. he was recent. m. at Muddy riv. HENRY, Watertown 1636, an orig. propr. of Sudbury, m. Mary, d. of Nicholas Guy, had Ephraim, b. 31 Mar. 1642; John, 1644; and Joseph, 1647; nam. in their gr.mo.'s will, 1666; and d. 8 May 1678. HENRY, Windsor, m. 13 May 1645, Eliz. Abell; had Samuel, b. 26 Apr. 1649; Nathaniel, 15 July 1651; rem. to North-ampton, and d. 30 Nov. 1661, leav. wid. Eliz. (wh. m. 22 June 1662, Richard Weller, from Windsor), and these s. of wh. Samuel d. 11 Sept. 1680. HENRY, Boston, by w. Jane had John, b. 2 July 1657. HENRY, Marblehead, perhaps went to Pemaquid bef. 1674, where he and Henry jr. in that yr. took the o. of fidel. ISAAC, Roxbury, youngest ch. of William, m. 10 May 1670, Hannah, d. of John Polley, had Isaac, b. 25 Jan. 1671, d. young; Hannah, 9 Dec. 1672; Samuel, d. young; Su-sanna, 2 Feb. 1680; Mehitable, 11 Mar. 1684; Isaac, again, 10 Nov. 1685; Samuel, again, 2 Sept. 1688; and d. 31 May 1695. His wid. d. 6 Feb. 1720. Samuel, wh. m. 6 June 1711, Hannah Gore, and d. 19 Feb. 1772, had eleven ch. of wh. are num. descend. in Boston and Rox-bury. The sixth Isaac in regular success. now enjoys his inherit. of the same est. giv. to first Isaac by his f. for maintain. f. and mo. ISRAEL, Stratford·1669, s. of that lubricous John of the same (suppos. to have been found as s. of William of Roxbury), by w. Rebecca had Israel, b. 20 May 1668; John, Oct. 1670; Stephen, 24 Aug. 1673; Peter; Han-nah; and Rebecca; and he d. Oct. 1704, as in Cothren is set forth. JOHN, Dover, adm. an inhab. 24 Apr. 1656, but, perhaps, as no more is heard of him there, he rem. to Roxbury. JOHN, Stratford 1650-85. Trumbull, I. 105, says he came from Roxbury; and he had John, b. Oct. 1642. But all of it seems erron. He was really s. of the wid. C.; had, says the preposter. tradit. d. Eliz. old eno. to m. John, the eldest s. of Gov. Thomas Welles, bear. to him sev. ch. and, next, m. 19 Mar. 1663, John Wilcockson. Almost every word of Trumbull, and of Cothren, borro. from T. in relat. to the Roxbury deriv. of John, and William, is wrong; and must have been a tradit. of the mid. of the eighteenth century. Yet a true John of S. by w. Eliz. wh. d. as Cothren tells, 1682, beside that John of 1642, had Israel, Apr. 1644; Eliz. May 1647 (wh. by the tradit. bec. w. of John Welles, eldest s. of the Gov. bore him one s. in 1648, the yr. aft. her own b. and tw. 1651); Thomas, Jan. 1649; Joseph, Nov. 1650; Benjamin, Sept. 1652; and

Hannah, Feb. 1654 or 5. None of this must be reject. but perhaps when Cothren adds, that he d. 6 Dec. 1707, aged 96 yrs. and that his wid. Margaret d. 1714, acquiesc. of our judgm. may not be so easy. JOHN, Roxbury 1660, s. of William, m. 26 Dec. 1661, Rebecca, d. of late Thomas Wheeler. He may have been of Dover 1656. JOHN, Scituate, s. of Richard, m. 1678, Miriam, d. of William Brooks, had Mercy, b. 1679; Hannah, 1681; and William, 15 Sept. 1683. JOHN, Topsfield, m. 4 Dec. 1672, Sarah Locke, freem. 1690. JOHN, Scituate, s. of William, m. 1707, Experience, d. of John Palmer, had John, b. 1709; and Bezaleel, 1711. JONATHAN, Stratford 1668, eldest s. of William of the same, m. Abigail, d. of John Thompson of the same, and tho. we kn. not their names, her childr. are rememb. in the will of her br. John. JOSEPH, Wethersfield, s. of Thomas, by w. Mercy had Joseph, b. 1674; Henry, 1676; Sarah, 1678; Thomas, 1680; and David, 1682; and d. 1683. JOSEPH, Kittery, s. of Thomas of York, m. 1678, Sarah, d. prob. youngest, of Richard Foxwell, had Eunice, and prob. others, was sheriff of Yorksh. wh. was almost all the Province. JOSEPH, Scituate, s. of William of the same, by w. Rebecca, m. 1692, had Joseph, b. 1693; Josiah, 1696; Rebecca, 1699; Martha, 1701; Richard, 1702; Elisha, 1704; Thankful, 1707; and Jesse, 1709. NATHANIEL, Northampton 1668, was a soldier, k. 2 Sept. 1675 at Northfield by the Ind. but wh. was his f. is not kn. ‖ PHILIP, Roxbury, s. of William, b. in Eng. ar. co. 1666, by w. Obedience, d. of John Holland of Dorchester, had Sarah, b. 24 Aug. 1659, d. young; Philip, 8 Sept. 1660; Abigail, 14 Nov. 1662, d. young; Joseph, 14 Mar. 1665; Abigail, again, 10 Apr. 1667; Josiah, 11 Mar. 1669; Holland, 1671; William, 2 Feb. 1675; and Abiel, posthum. 2 Mar. 1676. He was a lieut. k. by the Ind. in Philip's war, 9 Nov. 1675, near Mendham. See Hubbard, 45. His wid. pray. next yr. for assist. to her and seven ch. but m. 11 Feb. 1678, Benjamin Gamlin of R. and had more ch. RICHARD, Dorchester 1642, freem. 1647, by w. Eliz. had Eliz. b. 17 July 1643. His w. d. 28 May 1657; and he m. 25 Sept. foll. Sarah, had Isaac, 17 June 1658; and Joseph, 4 Sept. 1661. RICHARD, Salem, there had, by w. Sarah, Caleb, b. 24 Sept. 1646; and Sarah, 19 Mar. 1650; both bapt. 21 Apr. 1650; Samuel, 1 Apr. bapt. 18 May 1651; Richard, 14, bapt. 20 Feb. 1653; Sarah, again, bapt. 15 Apr. 1655; Hannah, b. 16 Sept. 1656, bapt. 25 Jan. foll.; John, b. 2 Feb. 1659, d. soon; John, again, b. 4 June 1660, d. soon; and Mary, b. 11 Feb. 1663. RICHARD, Boston 1657, had w. Sarah, prob. wid. of John Strange. RICHARD, Marblehead 1648, rem. to Scituate, m. 1649, Ann, d. of John Hallet, had Ann, b. 1649; Eliz. 1651; John, 1 Dec. 1653; Mary, 1655; Martha, 1657; Thomas, 18 Mar. 1659; Deborah, 1661, and Sarah, 1663; and he d.

1693. His will, of 1692, provides for sec. w. Lydia, the two s. and ds. Ann; Eliz. Brooks, w. of Nathaniel; Mary Badcocke; and Martha Clark, w. of Thomas. So it is to be infer. that the youngest two ds. d. bef. their f. SAMUEL, Northampton 1668. SAMUEL, Scituate, s. of Thomas, by w. Eliz. had Eliz. b. 1694; Samuel, 1695; Benjamin, 1699; and Abigail, 1703. SAMUEL, Scituate, youngest s. of William, m. 1707, Ann Barstow, had Samuel, b. 1708; Ann, 1711; Martha, 1713; Miriam, 1715; Deborah, 1717; Simeon, 1 June 1720; Amos, 1722; and Mehitable, 1726. THEOPHILUS, Woburn, freem. 1684. THOMAS, Wethersfield, an early sett. had John, b. 1639; James, 1641; Joseph, 1644; Samuel, 1646; Isaac, 1647; Eliz. and Ruth; all liv. 13 Nov. 1681, at his d. in Wallingford, whither he rem. 1670. Eliz. m. 26 May 1674, John Stoddard; Ruth m. Eleazur Kimberly the Secr. of the Col. THOMAS, York, rem. to Scituate, there had Eliz. bapt. 1649; and Samuel, 1659, bef. ment.; went back to York, 1663; had Benjamin, bef. rem. first, prob. there was in 1684. With spell. of Courteous he is seen sw. alleg. to Mass. 1652 in Col. Rec. IV. pt. I. 129. THOMAS, Scituate, s. of Richard, m. 1694, Mary, d. of William Cook, had Deborah, b. 1697; Ruth, 1699; Mary, 1701; Thomas, 5 Mar. 1704; and Ruth, 1711. WILLIAM, Roxbury 1632, came in the Lion, arr. at Boston 16 Sept. with w. Sarah, and ch. Thomas, Mary, John, and Philip; freem. 4 Mar. 1633, first nam. in the list of that day; had here, says Ellis, Hannah; Eliz.; and Isaac, b. 22 July 1641. His eldest s. William, wh. came in 1631, perhaps with Eliot in the Lion, was "a hopeful scholar, but God took him in 1634," says the ch. rec. Thomas, d. 26 June 1650, of "long and tedious consumpt." says the ch. rec. unm. it is presum. His d. Hannah m. 25 Aug. 1651, William Geary; and Eliz. m. 14 Dec. 1659, John Newell. He d. 8 Dec. 1672, aged 80; and his wid. d. 20 or 26 Mar. foll. aged 73. WILLIAM, Stratford 1642–1702, s. of a wid. C. that came so (I presume), from Eng. with John and this s. by Trumbull, I. 105, said to have come from Roxbury, erron. as must be thot. for his obs. on John. But Cothren shows, that he of S. (wh. may never have seen R.), was one of the grantees of Woodbury in 1672, tho. he rem. not from S. but there d. 21 Dec. 1702, in his will of six days preced. nam. his ch. Sarah, wh. was b. Oct. 1642; Jonathan, Feb. 1644; Joshua, Oct. 1646; Daniel, Nov. 1652; Eliz. Feb. 1654; Ebenezer, July 1657; Zechariah, Nov. 1659; and Josiah, Aug. 1662. Wh. was his f. is uncert. His sec. w. was Sarah, wid. of William Goodrich, but all the ch. were by first w. whose name is not seen. Both h. and w. d. 1702, as is said. WILLIAM, Scituate 1643, br. of Richard, had Joseph, b. 1664; Benjamin, 1666; William, 1668; John, 1670; Miriam, 1673; Mehitable, 1675; Stephen, 1677; Sarah,

s. of first Matthew, b. at old Hingham, 1627, came with his f. 1638, and m. at Hingham, 1657, Sarah, d. of Matthew Hawks, and in few yrs. mov. to S. had John, b. 28 Apr. 1662; Thomas, 26 Dec. 1663; Matthew, 23 Feb. 1665; Jeremiah, 13 July 1666, bef. ment.; James, 27 Jan. 1668, bef. ment.; Joshua, 27 Aug. 1670; Sarah, 26 Aug. 1671; Caleb, 6 Jan. 1673, bef. ment. H. C. 1692; Deborah, 14 Sept. 1674; Mary, tw. with last, d. 1698, unm.; Joseph, 23 Sept. 1677; and his w. d. 1679, prob. at b. of Benjamin, 4 Feb.; was selectman, rep. 1674, 6, 9, 82–6, an Assist. of Plymouth col. 1689–91; and first rep. under new Chart. of Mass. 1692, and 7, and d. 31 Mar. 1708. Sarah m. 20 Dec. 1689, David Jacob; and Deborah m. 19 Apr. 1699, Thomas Loring. Of Joshua, tho. he liv. to 1750, we kn. not whether he was m. and Deane says, he left no fam. The youngest s. Benjamin, was of Boston, a merch. ar. co. 1700, trad. to Barbados, perhaps never m. and is thot. not to have left fam. ‡ * JOHN, Scituate, eldest s. of the preced. m. 20 May 1687, Deborah, d. of Thomas Loring, had Sarah, b. 8 Jan. 1689; a s. d. soon; Deborah, 4 Apr. 1693; John, 17 July 1695; Elijah, 7 Mar. 1698; Mary, 24 Nov. 1700; Nazareth, 11 Sept. 1703; Benjamin, 17 Apr. 1706; and Nathaniel, 9 July 1709, H. C. 1728; and she d. 1713. By sec. w. m. 1714, wid. Sarah Holmes, had Josiah, b. 29 Jan. 1715; and Mary, 24 Oct. 1716; was rep. 1701, couns. 1710–28, and Judge of Sup. Ct. from 1728 to his d. 19 Jan. 1738. His s. John, also Judge of the Sup. Ct. was f. of William, H. C. 1751, one of the Justices of the Sup. Ct. of the U. S. appoint. by Washington, wh. d. 13 Sept. 1810. JOSEPH, Scituate, br. of the preced. m. 1 Jan. 1710, Mary, or Mercy, d. of Nathan Pickels (Deane, 259, and 324, is responsib. for both names), was a deac. had only s. Joseph, H. C. 1721, wh. was f. of Nathan, H. C. 1763, one of the Judges of the Sup. Ct. MATTHEW, Hingham 1638, from Hingham in Co. Norfk. s. of Peter, b. in 1588, the yr. of the Spanish Armada, m. 5 Aug. 1613, Nazareth Pitcher, had, as by reg. of old Hingham appears, Daniel, bapt. 20 Apr. 1619; Jeremiah, 1 Jan. 1621; Matthew, 5 Apr. 1623; Deborah, 17 Feb. 1625; and John, whose bapt. is, I believe, omit. and I have heard, that it was in a neighbour. parish; came in the Diligent, emb. at Gravesend, 26 Apr. and land. at Boston 10 Aug. 1638, with that w. and those ch. He is the ancest. of all the myriads of this name in New Eng. and thence indefinitely spread; and d. 30 Dec. 1660. His wid. d. 1681, aged 95, as is said. Her sis. wid. Frances Ricroft came in the same voyage, but d. in few wks. aft. arr. In his will all the ch. exc. Deborah, wh. m. May 1648, Matthew Briggs, are nam. as liv.; and the share to this s.-in-law was large. MATTHEW, Hingham, s. of the preced. b. in Eng. m. 25 Jan. 1653, Sarah, d. of Nicholas Jacob, had Matthew, the freem. of 1679,

and other ch. MATTHEW, Hingham, s. of Daniel the first, m. 31 Dec.
1684, Jael, d. of John Jacob, had, beside four ch. wh. d. very early,
Solomon, b. 29 Jan. 1692; Job, 19 July 1694, H. C. 1714, min. of
Shrewsbury; Samuel, 14 Feb. 1699; Isaac, 28 Apr. 1701; and Jael, 14
Feb. 1706. His w. d. Dec. 1708; and he d. 23 June 1715. MATTHEW,
Hingham, s. of first John, m. 1689, Deborah, d. of John Jacob. PETER,
Hingham, s. of Daniel the first, m. June 1685, Hannah, d. of Matthew
Hawke, wh. d. 4 Apr. 1737, had Peter, b. 1686; Jonathan, 1689, H. C.
1712, min. cf Dover; and Stephen. THEOPHILUS, Hingham, came in
the Griffin, 1633, with Gov. Haynes, at whose farm he liv. some yrs.
He was from old Hingham, and d. in March 1679, aged a. 100 yrs. of
wh. he was blind for 25, had, it is thot. no ch. THEOPHILUS, Hingham,
s. of the first Daniel, m. 1688, Mary, d. of John Thaxter, and this led,
as in the early days was oft. found, to the union of the surv. parents of
the young couple. ‡ ‖ THOMAS, Boston, s. of first John, m. 17 Oct.
1687, Deborah, d. of John Thaxter, had John, b. 6 Sept. 1688; Eliz.
bapt. 8 Nov. 1691; Thomas, 4 Feb. 1694, H. C. 1711; Margaret, 19
July 1696; Deborah, 18 June 1699; Jonathan, 16 Mar. 1701; Hannah, 17 Jan. 1703; and Samuel, 14 Jan. 1705; was of ar. co. 1709,
and mem. of the Counc. His w. d. 16 Feb. 1712, and he m. 8 Dec.
foll. Mercy, wid. of Joseph Bridgham, d. of John Wensley, outliv. him,
and d. 3 Oct. 1740, aged 72. Thomas, his s. was speaker, as rep. for
Boston 1742–6, in wh. yr. he d. and f. of the disting. patriot Thomas,
H. C. 1744, speaker 1766, mem. of the Philadelphia Congress 1774,
Lieut. Gov. of Mass. 1780–8, when he d. In 1838 thirty-three male
descend. it is believ. of first Matthew had been gr. at Harv. of wh. nine
were clerg. and an unusual proport. serv. in highly import. public office.

CUSHMAN, ELEAZER, Plymouth, s. of Elder Thomas, m. 12 Jan. 1687,
Eliz. Combes, perhaps d. of Francis, had Lydia, b. 13 Dec. foll.;
John, 13 Aug. 1690; Moses, a. 1693; James; and William, 27 Oct.
1710. ELKANAH, Plymouth, br. of the preced. m. 16 Feb. 1677, Eliz.
Cole, had Elkanah, b. 15 Sept. 1678; James, 20 Oct. 1679; and Jabez,
28 Dec. 1681, d. in May foll. The mo. d. 4 Jan. 1682, and he m.
Martha, d. of Jacob Cooke, had Allerton, 21 Nov. 1683; Eliz. 17 Jan.
1686; Josiah, 21 Mar. 1688; Martha, bapt. 1691; and Mehitable, b. 8
Oct. 1693. * ISAAC, Plymouth, s. of Thomas, rep. 1689–91, for P.; but
bec. a min. of Plympton, ord. 1698, d. 21 Oct. 1732, aged 83 by exagger.
By w. Rebecca Rickard, whose f. is not told, he had Isaac, b. 15 Nov.
1676; Rebecca, 30 Nov. 1678; Mary, 12 Oct. 1682; Sarah, 17 Apr.
1684; Ichabod, 30 Oct. 1686; and Fear, 10 Mar. 1689. JAMES, Scituate,
from 1639 to 48, says Deane. His will, 25 Apr. 1648, pro. 24 May foll.
names only cous. It is not easy to offer a reasona. conject. wh. he was.

ROBERT, Plymouth, one of the most active promot. of the migrat. from Holland in 1620 of the pilgr. in the Mayflower, of wh. he was one, but when adverse circumstances compel. that ship to put back, he gave up his place for the good of other companions in the Speedwell, wh. was abandon.; came next yr. in the Fortune, arr. 10 Nov. the first ship after the Mayflower, with s. Thomas, yet staid here only one month, went home in the same little bark, and came again no more. He had m. at Leyden, 3 June 1617, Mary Singleton (on the Dutch rec. spell. Chingelton), of Sandwich, he being designat. a woolcarder of Canterbury, both in Co. Kent. The first sermon preach. in N. E. was by him, on the highly appropr. subject of self-denial. He was constant in serv. at London for the emigr. and in Dec. 1624 spoke of his hope of com. in the next season; but Gov. Bradford notes, that he was d. bef. receipt of his answer from Plymouth of June 1625; and his fam. came soon aft. to partake in the fortunes of the planta. By gen. consent, he was assign. a sh. in the div. of ld. with the comers of the Mayflower. Davis, in Morton's Memo. 128. Young's Chron. of the Pilgr. 99. 249. THOMAS, Plymouth, s. of the preced. was brot. by him, in the Fortune, 1621, aged 14 only, and on ret. of his f. next mo. giv. to Gov. Bradford, wh. brot. him up, was chos. Rul. Elder 1649, after Brewster, and ord. 6 Apr. This " precious servant of God " d. 10 Dec. 1691, aged 83; by w. Mary, d. of Isaac Allerton, the latest surviv. of the blessed comp. of the Mayflower, wh. d. 1699, aged 89, had Thomas, b. 16 Sept. 1637; Isaac, 8 Feb. 1648, bef. ment.; Elkanah, 1 June 1651; Fear, 20 June 1653; Eleazer, 20 Feb. 1657; Sarah, wh. m. 11 Apr. 1661, John Hawks of Lynn, as his sec. w.; Mary, m. . . . . . . a Hutchinson of Lynn, and was d. bef. 1690; and Lydia, wh. m. William Harlow jr. THOMAS, Plymouth, s. of the preced. m. 17 Nov. 1664, Ruth, d. of John Howland, wh. d. soon after, but had first brot. him Robert, b. 4 Oct. 1664; and he m. 16 Oct. 1679, Abigail Fuller, and had Job, a. 1680; Bartholomew; Samuel, b. 16 July 1687; and Benjamin, bapt. 1 Mar. 1691. Twelve of this name had been gr. at the N. E. coll. in 1834.

CUTHBERTSON, CUTHBERT, Plymouth, came in the Ann, 1623, and in the div. of lds. next season, was count. for six heads, if the rec. be right, yet at div. of cattle, 1627, he, and w. Sarah, wh. I presume, had been wid. of Digory Priest (that d. at Plymouth 1 Jan. 1621), and m. 21 Nov. foll. at Leyden, and s. Samuel are all; but we may suppose, that some ds. had been m. in the interval, and at this div. are count. by other names. Sarah, his d. m. 1630, John Coombs, it is said, and ano. m. Phineas Pratt. He was a Dutchman, unit. with the fathers at Leyden, and Winslow gives his name, as, perhaps, in earlier life, the man wrote it, Godbert Godbertson. He d. bef. 23 Oct. 1633, the date of inv. of

CUTLER. 493

both hims. and w. so that she was prob. d. a short time bef. By descend.
the last syllable of the surname is now reject. Davis, in Morton, 379.
SAMUEL, Plymouth 1643, s. of the preced. was one of the orig. purch.
of Dartmouth in 1652, and most prob. had fam. beyond my knowl.

CUTLER, JAMES, Watertown, by w. Ann had James, b. 6 Nov. 1635;
Hannah, 26 July 1638; Eliz. 28 Jan. 1640, d. soon; and Mary, 29 Mar.
1643. His w. d. Sept. in the foll. yr. and he m. 9 Mar. 1645, Mary,
wid. of Thomas King, had Eliz. 29 July 1646; Thomas, a. 1648;
Sarah; Joanna; Jemima; John, 19 Mar. 1663; Samuel, 18 Nov. 1664;
Phebe; and, perhaps, one or more of the latest were by third w. Phebe,
d. of John Page. He had rem. 1648 to an outlying planta. call.
Cambridge Farms, now Lexington, and there his will of 24 Nov. 1684,
call. hims. 78 yrs. old, was made, and yet not pro. bef. 20 Aug. 1694.
Ann m. prob. John Coller; Eliz. m. John Parmenter of Sudbury;
Sarah m. Thomas Waite; and Joanna m. Philip Russell. JAMES,
Cambridge, s. of the preced. m. 15 June 1665, Lydia, wid. of Samuel
Wright, d. of John Moore of Sudbury, had James, b. 12 May 1666;
Ann, 20 Apr. 1669; Samuel, and Joseph, tw. 2 May 1672; John, 14
Apr. 1675; Thomas, 15 Dec. 1677; and Eliz. 14 Mar. 1681; and he d.
31 July 1685. His will was made 3 days bef. In some circumstances
this name has been read Cutter, from the easy confus. of the clk. writ.
indifferently, single or double t bef. the l. JOHN, Hingham, came in
1637, with w. seven ch. and one serv. from some part of Norfolk, Eng.
and d. I suppose, a. 1671, for next yr. his wid. Mary, then bec. Hewet,
join. with s. Nathaniel of Reading, Samuel of Topsfield, and Thomas of
Charlestown, in sale of the est. at H. JOHN, Woburn, m. 3 Sept. 1650,
Olive Thompson, had Mary, b. 7 Aug. 1651, d. young; Susanna, 22
Mar. 1653; and Mary, again, 5 May 1663. He d. of the smallpox,
1678 or 9. Mary m. 20 June 1684, Matthew Smith. Ano. JOHN of
Woburn, perhaps, m. 12 May 1682, Susanna Baker, prob. d. of John,
but may have rem. aft. hav. John, b. 7 Dec. 1684, d. soon. * ‖ JOHN,
Charlestown, s. of Robert, b. prob. in Eng. by w. Ann had John, b. a.
1650; Sarah, 20 Oct. 1655; Samuel, 1 Aug. 1658; Robert, bapt. 22
Nov. 1663; Rebecca, 11 Nov. 1666; and Mary, 21 Nov. 1669; was
deac. 1673, ar. co. 1681, rep. 1680 and 2. His w. Ann d. 24 July 1681,
and he m. again, 29 Oct. 1684, Mehitable, wid. of William Hilton, d. of
Increase Nowell, d. 26 Mar. 1694. He serv. as capt. in some exped. in
Philip's war, and was gr.f. of Rev. Timothy, H. C. 1701, D. D. and
head of Yale Coll. afterwards rector of Christ's church, Boston, wh. d.
17 Aug. 1765, aged 81. His w. Ann, d. of Robert Woodmansey, in
ano. rec. is report. to have d. 30 Aug. 1683, a. 56. Mather, VI. 78, tells,
of course, a wonderful story of the d. of her s. Robert at same hour in

VOL. I. 42

Barbados. JOHN, Charlestown, s. of the preced. by w. Martha had John, bapt. 18 July 1680; Margaret, 19 Dec. 1680; Timothy, 1 June 1684, H. C. 1701; Margaret, 9 Jan. 1691; Ruth, 21 May 1693; and Sarah, 8 Sept. 1695. He was major, and d. 12 Aug. 1708. JOHN, Cambridge Farms, or Lexington, s. of the first James, m. 1 Jan. 1694, Mary, d. of Isaac Stearns, had Samuel, b. 20 Dec. 1694; John, 1 June 1696; Ebenezer, 24 July 1700; Mary, 1 Apr. 1702; and Sarah, 20 Apr. 1704. NATHANIEL, Reading, s. of the first John, had Mary, b. 15 July 1656; Nathaniel, 12 Mar. 1659; Hannah, 9 June 1662; and perhaps more, aft. or bef. or both. NATHANIEL, Charlestown, s. of Robert, by w. Eliz. had Nathaniel, bapt. 3 Apr. 1670; Joseph, 2 Apr. 1671; Eliz. 3 Aug. 1673; Timothy, 19 Sept. 1675; and Rebecca, 14 Oct. 1677; was freem. 1674, and d. 13 Aug. 1678. NATHANIEL, Reading, s. of Nathaniel the first, d. says the gr.stone, 7 June 1714. ROBERT, Charlestown 1637, freem. 2 May 1638, deac. 1659, d. 7 Mar. 1665, leav. w. Rebecca and ch. beside John, bef. ment.; Rebecca, m. 1649, Abraham Errington; Hannah, m. 29 Aug. 1654, Matthew Griffin; and Nathaniel, bapt. 8 Nov. 1640, H. C. 1663. He had good est. by his will, made 1 May preced. his d. distrib. to w. four ch. and to gr.childr. beside beq. to officers of the church. SAMUEL, Marblehead 1654, was 71 yrs. old in 1700. SAMUEL, Topsfield, br. of the first Nathaniel, may be the man at Gloucester, whose w. Eliz. hav. brot. him, at Salem, Samuel in 1661, and Ebenezer in 1664, d. 17 Mar. 1693, at T. SAMUEL, Charlestown, by w. Dorothy, had Samuel, bapt. 9 Dec. 1683. THOMAS, Reading, br. of Nathaniel of the same, m. 9 Mar. 1660, Mary, d. of Bridget Very, had Thomas, b. 24 Feb. 1661; and, perhaps, rem. to Charlestown, there d. 7 Dec. 1683. THOMAS, Lexington, or Cambridge Farms, s. of the first James, by w. Abigail had Abigail, b. 31 Oct. 1674; Thomas, 19 Jan. 1678; Mary, 15 Mar. 1681; Hannah, 7 Mar. 1683; James, bapt. 9 Jan. 1687; Jonathan, 17 June 1688; and Benjamin, b. 4 July, bapt. 3 Oct. 1697, at Watertown, as were the two preced. THOMAS, Reading, s. of Thomas of the same, m. 30 Dec. 1686, Eliz. Felch or Fitch. TIMOTHY, Charlestown, perhaps s. of deac. John, by w. Eliz. d. of William Hilton, m. 22 Dec. 1673, had Eliz. bapt. 10 Oct. 1675; William, 9 May 1680; Ann, b. 2, bapt. 8 Jan. 1682; Robert, 30 Dec. 1683; Mary, 19 Feb. 1688, Rebecca, 16 Feb. 1690, and Mary, again, 16 May 1693. His wid. Eliz. in her will, pro. 10 Nov. 1694, names no ch. but Joseph.

CUTT (or CUTTS in modern days), § JOHN, Portsmouth (s. of that Richard, a mem. of Oliver's parliam. 1654, in wh. yr. he d.) was a merch. from Wales, m. 30 July 1662, Hannah Star, had John, b. 30 June 1663; Eliz. 30 Nov. 1664, d. next yr.; Hannah, 29 July 1666; Mary, 17 Nov. 1669; and Samuel; was appoint. by the crown, 1679,

presid. of the prov. undertook the office next yr. and d. 27 Mar. 1681,
leav. large est. A sec. w. Ursula surv. but was k. by the Ind. 1694, on
a Saturday, as Mather tells, VII. 86 ; and from Belkn. we may guess it
was on 21 July. Hannah m. 16 Feb. 1681, Richard Waldron, d. 14
Feb. 1683; and Mary m. 1 July 1687, Samuel Penhallow. Belkn. I.
90. 91. 141. Chalmers, 490. JOHN, Portsmouth, prob. s. of the preced.
join. with the gr. body of his neighb. in that addr. 20 Feb. 1690, for
jurisdict. of Mass. * RICHARD, Portsmouth, mariner, br. of the preced.
was, I find, engag. here bef. 1647 ; freem. of Mass. 1665, and rep. same
yr. as also 1669–70, 72–76, in wh. yr. he d. He had prosecut. the
trade of fishing much at Isle of Shoals and P. ; left Margaret, wh. m. 8
Dec. 1668, William Vaughan, d. 22 Jan. 1693, aged 40 ; and Bridget,
w. of Thomas Daniel, and aft. of Thomas Graffort, but d. a wid. 29 May
1701. RICHARD, Portsmouth, s. of Robert, by w. Joanna, d. of Thomas
Wills of Kittery, had Richard, b. 5 Apr. 1698, wh. d. 30 Mar. 1795.
ROBERT, Portsmouth, br. of John, went to Barbados, from N. E. came
back, liv. at Kittery, a. 1663, built many vessels ; by sec. w. Mary had
Richard, bef. ment. ; Eliz. wh. m. Humphrey Eliot ; Robert ; Bridget,
wh. m. Rev. William Scriven ; Mary ; and Sarah. His will, of 18 June
1674, pro. 6 July foll. names s. Richard, also, so that we may assume he
was b. by the former w. In the inv. of £890, large for that neighb. are
includ. eight negro slaves, but their aggreg. value is only £111. His
wid. m. Francis Champernoon. ROBERT, Portsmouth, s. of the preced.
m. Dorcas, d. of Joseph Hammond of Kittery. Of this fam. five had
been, in 1823, gr. at Harv. and two of them were memb. of Congr.
    CUTTER, EPHRAIM, Charlestown, s. of Richard, m. 11 Feb. 1679,
Bethia Wood, had Ephraim ; Jonathan, b. 5 May 1685 ; Bethia, 2 Dec.
1686 ; both these at Cambridge ; Mary, d. young ; Hannah, 22 July
1690 ; and John, 23 July 1700. GERSHOM, Cambridge, br. of the
preced. m. 6 Mar. 1678, Lydia Hall, d. of wid. Mary, had Gershom, b.
1 June 1679 ; Lydia, 14 Sept. 1682 ; Hannah, 26 Nov. 1684 ; and
Isabel, 9 May 1687 ; and he d. 1738. NATHANIEL, Cambridge, youngest
s. of Richard, m. 8 Oct. 1688, Mary, d. of Thomas Fillebrown, wh. d.
14 Mar. 1714, had Nathaniel, Jacob, Mary, Ebenezer, John, Richard,
and Eliz. but the two last by sec. w. Eliz. ‖ RICHARD, Cambridge,
freem. 2 June 1641, ar. co. 1643, by first w. Eliz. had Eliz. b. 15 July
1645, d. at 18 yrs. ; Samuel, 3 Jan. 1647 ; Thomas, 19 July 1648, d.
soon ; William, 22 Feb. 1650 ; Ephraim ; Gershom ; and Mary ; all,
says Mitchell, b. and bapt. in this ch. exc. Thomas. His w. d. 5 Mar.
1662, not 1663, as Harris, Epit. I. has it, aged a. 42, and he m. 14 Feb.
1663, Harris, 23 (wh. was bef. the d. of Eliz. as by him giv.) Frances,
wid. of Isaac Amsden, had Nathaniel, 11 Dec. 1663. bapt. 24 Jan. 1664 ;

Rebecca, 5 Sept. bapt. 8 Oct. 1665; Hepzibah, 11 Nov. bapt. 1 Dec. 1667, d. at 3 mos.; Eliz. b. 1 Mar. 1669; Hepzibah, again, 15 Aug. 1671; Sarah, 31 Aug. 1673; and Ruhamah; and he d. 16 June 1693, aged a. 72. Frances, his w. outliv. him; and his d. Mary m. Nathaniel Sanger; Rebecca m. 19 Dec. 1688, Thomas Fillebrown; Eliz. m. a Hall; and Sarah m. 5 Dec. 1700, James Locke of Woburn. ‖ WILLIAM, Cambridge 1636, freem. 18 Apr. 1637, ar. co. 1638, br. of the preced. was liv. some yrs. later; had gr. 1648, of ld. in C. and in short time aft. went home, and sent power of Atty. in 1653 to his br. Corlet from Newcastle on Tyne. Eliz. I think his mo. wh. d. 10 Jan. 1664, in her will of 16 Feb. preced. calls hers. a. 87 yrs. says she has liv. now a. 20 yrs. with Mr. Elijah Corlet, wh. m. her d. Barbara, and gives them all her little prop. mak. the d. extrix. WILLIAM, Cambridge, s. of Richard, had, by w. Rebecca Rolfe, Eliz. b. 5 Mar. 1681; Richard, 13 Nov. 1682; Mary, wh. d. 6 Apr. 1685, 2 mos. old; Hannah, 20 May 1688; John, 15 Oct. 1690; Rebecca, 18 Jan. 1693; William, a. 1697; Samuel, 14 June 1700; Sarah, bapt. 18 Oct. 1702; and Ammi Ruhamah, 6 May 1705, H. C. 1725, min. of North Yarmouth; and d. 1 Apr. 1723. Four of this name had been gr. at Harv. in 1834, and six at other N. E. coll.

CUTTING, JAMES, Watertown, s. of Richard, m. 16 June 1679, Hannah, perhaps d. of John Collar, had James, b. 20 Mar. 1680; Richard, 10 Dec. 1683; Thomas, 10 Nov. 1685; Jonathan, and David, tw. 12 Jan. 1688; and Hezekiah, 17 Feb. 1689. JOHN, Watertown 1636, aft. at Charlestown, thence rem. was a. 1642 at Newbury; had Sarah, m. James Brown; and Mary, m. 9 Nov. 1657, Samuel Moody. He made many voyages, and brot. very many passeng. from Eng. and d. 20 Nov. 1650. His wid. Mary m. a Miller, and d. 6 Mar. 1664. JOHN, Boston 1655. JOHN, Watertown, s. of Richard, m. 9 Feb. 1672, Susan, eldest ch. of Robert Harrington, had Susanna, b. 4 June 1673; Sarah, 1675; Mary, d. 29 Nov. 1677; Eliz. b. 10 May 1678; John, 10 Mar. 1680; Robert, 15 Oct. 1683; and George, 26 Apr. 1686. He d. 1689, as also did, prob. all the ch. exc. John, bef. his f. wh. nam. this gr.ch. in his will. His wid. m. 21 Apr. 1690, Eleazer Beers; and next, 2 Jan. 1705, Peter Cloyse. RICHARD, Watertown, came in the Elizabeth from Ipswich, 1634, a youth of 11 yrs. under care of Henry Kimball; by w. Sarah, wh. d. 4 Nov. 1685, aged 60, had James, b. 26 Jan. 1648; John, bef. ment.; Susanna; Sarah, 2 Sept. 1661; and Lydia, 1 Sept. 1666, beside Zechariah, wh. may have been the eldest. He made his will 24 June 1694, in wh. he ment. the four ch. alive, and ch. of John, nam. John, and ch. of Sarah nam. Eliz. Susanna m. 2 June 1672, Peter Newcomb of Braintree; Sarah m. 5 Mar. 1683, John Barnard, jr. and d. 6 May

1694; and Lydia m. Henry Spring. WILLIAM, a passeng. in the Elizabeth from Ipswich, 1634, aged 26. It may be ask. if he were relat. to the youth Richard, wh. came in the same ship with him, or of John, wh. was master of the Francis, wh. sail. on the same day from the same port, and both reach. Boston the same day, without loss of any passeng. Yet where the answer will come from, or what it will be, is beyond conject.

CUTTRISS, HENRY. See Curtis.

ADDITIONS AND CORRECTIONS.

PAGE 7, l. 16 from bot. aft. July, strike out all that follows to THOMAS, and ins. bapt. 17 Aug. 1707; Nicholas, 17 Dec. 1708, bapt. 6 Mar. foll.; Nathaniel, bapt. 30 Dec. 1711, but the town rec. gives him b. 7 Nov. foll.; Gideon, 14 Apr. bapt. 20 May 1716; Desire, 24 Feb. bapt. 30 Mar. 1718; Eliz. 16 Jan. bapt. 18 Feb. 1722; and Benajah, b. 10 July 1729. JOHN, Haddam, br. of the preced. m. 23 May 1699, Rebecca, eldest d. of John Spencer, was serg. and d. 25 Aug. 1736, leav. s. John to admin. his est. NICHOLAS, Hartford 1655, rem. as early sett. to Haddam, and d. 29 Apr. 1695, leav. wid. Miriam, and ch. John; Thomas; Nathaniel, wh. d. 27 Feb. 1710, perhaps unm.; Samuel; James; Hannah; Eliz.; Mary; Sarah, wh. m. William Spencer; and Lydia; but it is believ. all the ch. were by a former w. SAMUEL, Haddam, s. of the preced. by w. Bethia had Samuel, b. 8 Dec. 1703, bapt. with f. and mo. 6 Oct. 1706; Jerusha, 29 Mar. bapt. 4 May 1707; Deborah, 11 July, bapt. 14 Aug. 1709; Lydia, 14 Aug. bapt. 30 Sept. 1711 ; Simeon, 10 Jan. bapt. 21 Feb. 1714; Stephen, 25 July, bapt. 26 Aug. 1716; Elijah, 28 Mar. bapt. 3 May 1719 ; Isaac, 6, bapt. 8 Oct. 1721; Bezaleel, 4 Feb. bapt. 8 Mar. 1724; and Nathaniel, 14 June, bapt. 17 July 1726. He d. 27 Apr. 1745, and his wid. d. 12 Mar. 1764.

Page 9, l. 11 from bot. aft. 103. ins. Again he went home, and, in Oct. 1651, by his atty. sold est. at D.

Page 12, l. 12, bef. 1677, ins. 6 Dec.

"   " l. 13, bef. 1681 ; ins. 8 July — also, for " early in," read 15 Mar.

"   14, l. 17 and 16 from bot. strike out, " was s. of N. of Weymouth, and "

"   " l. 15 from bot. aft. 1684. add, He had Nathaniel, b. 12 Jan. 1681 ; Daniel, or David, 19 Nov. 1682 ; Nicholas, 8 Oct. 1684, d. soon ; Hannah, 3 Oct. 1686, bapt. 6 Mar. 1687 ; Ann, 15, bapt. 19 Aug. 1688, d. next mo.; Ann, again, bapt. 2 Aug. 1691, d. under 16 yrs.; Wilmot, 21 Aug. 1692; Mary, 29 Aug. 1702, d. under 13 yrs.; Abigail, b. 17, bapt. 21 Apr. 1706, d. under 2 yrs.; Ann, again, 31 Mar. 1708, d. soon ; and Ann, again, 2, bapt. 15 Jan. 1710.

Page 14, l. 11 from bot. aft. Bond, add 747.

Page 14, l. 9 from bot. aft. Hannah, for 1658, r. 16 Jan. 1657;

" 18, l. 3, aft. Wainwright, add, d. of William Norton of Ipswich,

" 20, l. 10, aft. 1653 ; add, as is said ; certain. Sarah, 11 Mar. 1654;

" " l. 12, aft. 434. add, Lydia, m. 30 Oct. 1658, Alexander Lovell ; and

" 25, l. 17, bef. JOHN, ins. JAMES, Medfield 1664.

" 27, l. 11, aft. Eliz. add, but his w. brot. to Boston ch. for bapt. 5 Dec. 1647, s. Jonathan, a. six days old, wh. d. under 16 yrs.

Page 28, l. 12 from bot. bef. 1693, ins. 21 Sept. — also, bef. 1695, ins. 9 Sept.

" " l. 11 from bot. bef. 1697, ins. 25 July — also, aft. 1697 ; ins. William, 9 Apr. 1701, d. soon ; — also, aft. Mary, ins. 7 June — also, aft. 1702, add, d. soon ;

Page 28, l. 10 from bot. aft. John, add, 12 Oct. 1705

" " l. 7 from bot. bef. ANDREW, ins. ALEXANDER, Windsor, eldest s. of the preced. m. 17 May 1716, Hannah, prob. d. of John Marshall of W. wh. d. 30 Nov. 1772, aged 77, had Abigail, b. 4 Feb. 1717, d. at 2 yrs. ; Alexander, 25 Dec. 1718; Abigail, again, 28 Aug. 1721 ; Mary ; and Hannah; and d. 2 Apr. 1742.

Page 29, l. 9, aft. him ins. John, Ann, Isaac, and

" " l. 11, strike out 4 — also, bef. Martha, ins. Ann m. 2 Apr. 1661, Abraham Jewett ; and

Page 31, l. 16, aft. Mary, ins. and Martha, tw. 15 June 1659 ;

" 32, l. 12 from bot. aft. certain. ins. Eliz. and

" " l. 9 from bot. strike out "Jonathan," and ins. perhaps Nathan

" " l. 8 from bot. aft. bart. ; add, Eliz. m. 11 Mar. 1674, Nathan Hayman, and Rebecca m. 28 Mar. 1678, John Goodrich of Wethersfield.

Page 33, l. 9, bef. m. ins. s. of Samuel,

" " l. 17, bef. d. ins. m. 25 Oct. 1677, Mercy, wid. of Samuel Lee, d. of Thomas Call,

Page 33, l. 18, strike out Mary

" 35, l. 9, aft. 1678. add, Ruth, wid. of one Richard A. m. 5 Oct. 1660, Philip Knell of Charlestown.

Page 35, l. 10, aft. 1641, ins. was soon aft. of Salem, had there gr. of ld. 1643, as he had in Feb. 1639.

Page 36, l. 11 from bot. for 13 r. prob. 23

" 37, l. 11 from bot. bef. the *fourth* WILLIAM, add, He had m. the wid. of Thomas Atkinson of C. but prob. had no ch. and admin. on his est. was giv. to John Hayward, wh. had m. the eldest d. of Atkinson

Page 38, l. 11, aft. Mary, add, wh. was call. Collins, from Newbury, Co. Berks, m. at Leyden, 4 Nov. 1611, the same day that his wid. sis. m. there Digory Priest ;

Page 43, l. 1, aft. ALLY, ins. JACOB, Charlestown, by w. Ann had five ch. whose names are not seen, 1687, and onwards. ROGER, Charlestown, with w. Jane, were rec. into the ch. at C. from Weymouth 20 Nov. 1659.

Page 43, l. 13 from bot. bef. 1671, ins. 1 Feb.

" " l. 8 from bot. bef. OBADIAH, ins. MATTHEW, Windsor, s. of Thomas and gr.s. of the preced. m. 5 Jan. 1686, Eliz. eldest d. of the third Henry Wolcott, had Matthew, b. 9 Aug. 1687 ; Pelatiah, 3 May 1689 ; Josiah, 9 Mar. 1693 ; Thomas ; Henry, 16 Dec. 1699, and Theophilus, 26 Aug. 1702.

Page 44, l. 12 from bot. bef. Oct. ins. 21

" " l. 10 from bot. bef. 1665 ; ins. 24 June

" " l. 6 from bot. bef. 1686, ins. 6 Jan.

" " l. 5 from bot. aft. wh. ins. had Martha, b. 1 Sept. liv. only two days, and the mo. liv. only four days more, for she

Page 47, l. 8, bef. 1688; ins. 27 Apr. — also, bef. 1690; ins. 24 Mar. — also, bef. 1692; ins. 8 May

Page 47, l. 9, bef. 1699; ins. 14 Jan. — also, bef. 1702; ins. 1 Mar. — also, bef. 1703, ins. 22 Nov.

Page 47, l. 9 and 10, strike out, "and perhaps more," and ins. beside Eliz. again, 27 Apr. 1706; and Job, 26 Aug. 1708.

Page 50, l. 4 from bot. aft. Catharine add Richardson, m. 12 Sept. 1672,

" " last l. aft. London. ins. His first w. m. 5 June 1667, was Hannah Nichols, wh. d. 18 July 1671.

Page 52, l. 15 from bot. bef. ABRAHAM, ins. often ANDROS,

" 53, l. 11, aft. Mather. add, He d. 3 Dec. 1702, aged 59, and s. Thomas, 24, with Samuel, 19, d. next mo. all of the smallpox.

Page 55, l. 18, aft. and add, in his will of 16 May 1668, pro. 1 July foll. he names s. Thomas, Robert, Joseph, and John, ds. Eliz. m. 14 Apr. 1662, Samuel Symonds; Hannah, w. of John Peabody; Rebecca; Sarah; and Ruth. Prob. his s. Thomas was

Page 55, l. 2 from bot. aft. 16 add, or 23

" 56, l. 22, aft. same, add, had Joseph, b. 22 Sept. 1656.

" " last l. aft. 1645. add, His d. Abigail d. May 1653.

" 57, l. 13 from bot. aft. Dexter, add, had John, b. 4 Oct. 1691; perhaps more

" 58, l. 11, aft. Eliz. add, bapt. 2 May

" 59, l. 15, aft. Hannah, add, prob. d. of Christopher Osgood,

" 60, l. 13, aft. sea, ins. 1664,

" " l. 18, at the end, add, Perhaps Hannah A. wh. m. 8 Nov. 1658, Isaac Burnap, was d. of Thomas.

Page 74, l. 15, strike out, "by w." and ins. m. for sec. 11 Aug. 1687, wid. — also, aft. Abigail add, Jones,

Page 75, l. 20, aft. 1669. ins. But he had an elder d. Rebecca, that m. John Hayward; and the wid. of Atkinson m. William Allen.

Page 79, l. 11 from bot. aft. abroad. add, In Hist. Coll. of Essex Inst. I. 11, Mr. Patch finds the date of his will to be 3 Mar. and of pro. June of that yr.

Page 80, l. 11, bef. 1666; ins. 22 Sept.

" " l. 12, bef. 1668; ins. 7 Dec. — also, bef. 1672; ins. 22 Oct. — also, bef. 1678; ins. 20 May

Page 80, l. 13, bef. 1684; ins. 20 Apr. — also, bef. 1686; ins. 11 Jan. — also, bef. 1708, ins. 29 Aug.

Page 80, l. 16 from bot. for 1702, r. 1802

" 81, l. 14, aft. us. ins. His d. Mary m. 17 May 1674, Richard Gardner, jr. of Nantucket; but she was by sec. w.

Page 81, l. 17, aft. more, ins. exc. by his will of 1736, pro. 18 June 1739, in wh. w. Eliz. is nam. beside ch. Joseph, Richard, Abigail, w. of Samuel Webb, and Eliz. w. of Eleazer Johnson.

Page 81, l. 17 from bot. aft. 7, add, bapt. 28

" " l. 12 from bot. bef. *SAMUEL, ins. His wid. Mehitable m. 4 Jan. 1700, Benjamin Gibson. RICHARD, Suffield, eldest s. of Anthony, m. 18 Jan. 1699, Dorothy Adams, had Richard, b. 4 Oct. foll.; Dorothy, 26 July 1701; Jacob, 1 June 1704; Ebenezer, 22 Apr. 1706; Ann, 16 Jan. 1709; Joseph, 26 Jan. 1711; Rebecca, 16 Apr. 1713; Moses, 25 Apr. 1716; and Elias, 14 Apr. 1718.

Page 83, l. 9, bef. ROBERT, ins. MATTHEW, Charlestown, mariner, had w. Ann, and s. John, to wh. by his will of 20 Apr. 1642, being then at London, pro. 13 of next Apr. he devis. his 400 acres of ld. at C.

Page 84, l. 13 from bot. aft. and ins. had

"   86, l. 4, at the end; add, Christopher, 11 Nov. 1678; Richard, 1 Oct. 1680, wh. d. in 5 mos. Richard, again, 14 July 1682; and Nehemiah, 25 Mar. 1684,

Page 86, l. 8, aft. JAMES, ins. Portsmouth, R. I. 1642,

"   "   l. 17, aft. 1679, ins. the day he d.

"   "   l. 20, strike out "1685," and ins. a. 1698

"   "   l. 3 from bot. bef. RETURN, ins. JOSEPH, Westerly, s. prob. youngest, of the first James, m. 13 Apr. 1696, Dorothy Key, had Eliz. b. 29 Jan. 1698; and his w. d. 14 Dec. 1727. By sec. w. Hannah Coats, he had Authority, 2 Feb. 1730; Abigail, 30 Apr. 1731; Joseph, 14 Oct. 1733; and John, 26 Jan. 1736.

Page 88, l. 16, aft. 1678; add, beside Josiah, 6 Mar. 1680; and he d. 6 Aug. 1684, and the wid. d. within two wks. aft. Ano. JOHN, at Salem 1692,

Page 88, l. 19 from bot. bef. JOSHUA, ins. JOSEPH, Charlestown, s. of William, m. 22 Dec. 1670, Agnes, wid. of William Gillingham. JOSEPH, Salem, youngest s. of the first John of the same, m. 8 Oct. 1677, Miriam Moulton, had Joseph, b. 18 July foll.

Page 88, l. 7 from bot. aft. Eliz. add, She was wid. of John Knill of Charlestown, m. 23 Oct. 1689.

Page 90, l. 10, aft. 1665, strike out all to the end of the sentence, and ins. Alice, 28 Oct. 1669, d. soon; Susanna, 18 July 1670; Mary, 8 June 1673; Michael, 23 Oct. 1676; Lydia, 23 Feb. 1679, d. young; and John, 24 Jan. 1681.

Page 90, at the end of the l. at the bot. ins. By Mr. Wyman I am inform. that he m. 2 Sept. 1668, Susanna, d. of James Draper, had John, b. 27 Aug. 1670; Susanna, 3 Jan. 1672; and Ephraim, 17 Nov. 1675. The day bef. his d. he made his will in favor of the two s. of wh. John was liv. sev. yrs. aft.

Page 92, l. 17, aft. 1640, add, br. of Michael,

"   "   l. 18, bef. 1653, ins. Nov.

"   "   l. 19, at the end of the sentence, add, His will ment. w. and s. also Ann Potter.

Page 92, l. 22, aft. massacre. ins. Her will of 23 Mar. 1655, pro. 29 Nov. foll. names cous. i. e. niece, Ann Potter, and John Bacon, beside sis. Judith in O. E.

Page 92, l. 11 from bot. bef. GEORGE, ins. ENOCH, Dorchester, br. of Robert, d. 1711, leav. William, Susan, Mary, Eliz. and Sarah.

Page 92, last l. bef. Ebenezer, ins. Caleb, 1660;

"   93, l. 1, aft. 1663, ins. Hopestill, 8 Nov. 1663; Hannah, 28 May 1665;

"   "   l. 14 from bot. aft. there. add, One John, perhaps a s. was a soldier, and James was ano. of Gallop's comp. to Quebec, 1690.

Page 93, l. 13 from bot. strike out "prob." and aft. Orlando, ins. b. at Boston, 18 Feb. 1659;

Page 94, l. 3, at the end, ins. or Salisbury, see Bayley and strike out the rest of the five l. to JOHN

Page 96, l. 9, strike out "in wh. yr." and ins. and 7 July foll.

"   "   l. 18 from bot. aft. me. ins. To this Ipswich John and his w. Eliz. the wid. Alice Ward gave, on her deathbed, Mar. 1655, her d. Sarah and her prop. to bring up the said ch.

Page 97, l. 18 from bot. aft. ch. add, His w. d. 16 May 1700.

"   "   l. 4 from bot. aft. Samuel, ins. 17 Oct. 1684,

"   "   l. 3 from bot. aft. Loomis. add, Yet the recent hist. of W. p. 526, gives two more ch. Hannah, 19 Dec. 1686, wh. d. next yr.; and Ebenezer, 17 July 1689, wh. may be correct. But great is my doubt of the accura. of his add. of sec. w. 8 July 1702, Hannah Pomeroy of Northampton, and ten more ch. the latest, 14 May

1722. Hinman, in his Catal. of 1852, p. 110, says, his will was made 1691, and he d. that yr. refer. to Windsor rec. Prob. Stiles confus. two persons.

Page 98, l. 16 from bot. bef. All ins. The wid. Grace d. 22 Jan. 1697.

" 98, l. 2 from bot. aft. James add White, m. 22 Feb. 1665, tho. the Hist. of D. makes her b. three yrs. later than this m. p. 106 ; — also, for oné r. Mary

Page 99, l. 17, aft. 1669, ins. then among freem.

" " l. 10 from bot. bef.. Thomas, ins. Thomas, Boston, by w. Leah had Rachel, b. 7 Feb. 1659.

Page 100, l. 20 from bot. aft. Sarah, ins. (Mr. Wyman calls her Mary)

" 101, l. 12, aft. Balch. add, From Benjamin, it is thot. all of this name in N. E. descend.

Page 101, l. 18 from bot. aft. issue, add, exc. d. Mary, again,

" " l. 7 from bot. strike out 1674 — also, at the end, add, had Sarah, wh. d. 8 Dec. 1665, prob. very young ; Hannah, 16 Mar. 1668 ; John, 15 Oct. 1669 ; Eliz. 14 Aug. 1672 ; and Joseph, 17 Dec. 1674. The s. had est. at Sudbury, giv. by their gr.f.

Page 104, l. 22, for Dell. r. Dellaclose. — also, aft. Felt, add, II. 589, shows, that Mrs. B. a French lady, from the Isle of Jersey, join. the ch. of S. 4 Aug. 1678. In a MS. he had reduc. her name, when wid. to the first syl.

Page 106, l. 10, aft. multitude. ins. One of this name, in 1684, was liv. at Block Isl.

" 108, l. 14, aft. Ballard, ins. oft. writ. as sound. Ballatt,

" " l. 9 from bot. aft. John, ins. 23 Nov. 1672 ;

" " l. 7 from bot. aft. first, add, wh. d. 14 May 1691 ; and 4 Sept. foll. he m. third w. Lydia Hale ;

Page 110, l. 12, aft. Sarah, ins. 26 Feb. — also, aft. John, ins. again, 19 Dec. — also, bef. 1694, ins. 10 May

Page 110, l. 13, aft. Thomas, ins. 14 Dec.

" " l. 14 from bot. aft. d. ins. 6 Aug.

" 111, l. 16, bef. d. ins. m. 2 June 1670, Eliz. Long, had one s. and — also, at the end, add, His wid. d. 16 Aug. 1689.

Page 111, l. 14 from bot. for Herrick r. Merrick

" 112, l. 7 from bot. bef. Thomas, ins. Nathan, Charlestown, by w. Mary had Nathan, wh. d. 29 Mar. 1669, prob. young ; and Mary, b. 24 Jan. foll.

Page 113, l. 20 from bot. bef. 1672, ins. 29 May — also, bef. and ins. Thomas, 4 Feb. 1675 ;

Page 113, l. 19 from bot. aft. Mary, ins. 13 Feb.

" " l. 17 from bot. aft. prove ; ins. or whether the name of only one person was writ. twice.

Page 113, l. 14 from bot. aft. Simsbury, add, s. of the first Thomas,

" " l. 13 from bot. aft. 1679 ; add, and prob. sev. others.

" " l. 6 from bot. for " a " r. Ruth, — also, strike out, " prob. Hannah "

" " l. 5 from bot. aft. 1681 ; add, Ruth, 24 July 1683 ; Eliz. 9 Feb. 1685 ; and, perhaps, others ; but I dare not copy the list of Stiles, 528.

Page 114, l. 1, aft. 5 ins. (not 15, as print. in Hist. of W. 528)

" " l. 2 strike out, Josiah had, &c. to the end of the l.

" 114, l. 5, bef. Thomas, ins. Thomas, Charlestown, s. of William of Marblehead, m. 25 June 1667, Hannah Roper, wh. d. 27 Mar. 1691. He took sec. w. 12 Jan. 1693, Hannah Stedman, and d. 14 July 1725. His ch. were Thomas, Hannah, wh. m. a Newman, and Rebecca ; but by wh. w. ea. was b. is not kn.

502ADDITIONS AND CORRECTIONS.

Page 115, l. 14, aft. more, add, but that he m. 6 Dec. 1666, Ann, eldest ch. of
Maximilian Jewett.

Page 115, l. 17, aft. 95. add, His w. was, Oct. 1692, in gaol under charge of witchcr.
" " l. 12 from bot. aft. 1651, ins. b. a. 1617, brot. by his f. James in 1634 on
board the Mary and John, with prob. no other ch. and his f. d. on the passage. To
the protect. of his sis. Christian, w. of Thomas Beecher of Charlestown, was this
youth of seventeen yrs. commit. and she, soon aft. the d. of her h. m. Nicholas Easton
as his sec. w. and it is thot. E. had come over in the same sh. with Barber. At least
he rec. friend. care of E. until reach. full age. He came from Harwich, Co. Essex,
m. 1644, Barbara Dungan, or Dungin, d. of Thomas of Newport, bec.

Page 115, l. 10 from bot. aft. 1678, strike out all to the end of l. 8 from bot. and
ins. aft. d. of Gov. Coddington. His ch. were Eliz. wh. m. 30 Nov. 1666, the sec.
Nicholas Easton; James; Mary, wh. m. Elisha Smith, and, next, 16 Apr. 1677,
Israel Arnold of Warwick; William; Joseph; Peter; Christian, wh. m. William
Phillips; and Sarah, unm. at d. of her f.

Page 115, l. 6 from bot. bef. JOHN, ins. JAMES, Newport, s. of James of the same,
m. bef. Dec. 1674, Sarah, d. of William Jeffery of the same, but I hear no more.

Page 116, l. 9, aft. King. ins. JOSEPH, Newport, s. of the first James of the same,
m. Sarah Read.

Page 116, l. 13, bef. RICHARD, ins. PETER, Newport, s. of James the first of the
same, m. a d. perhaps of John Bliss, at least my corresp. says Major Bliss.

Page 116, l. 5 from bot. at the end, add, WILLIAM, Newport, br. of Peter of the
same, m. Eliz. Easton, prob. d. of Peter of the same.

Page 117, l. 4, aft. heard. add, But I think his bapt. name may have been EDMUND,
for Mr. Wyman gives me such a one, with w. Mary, who in his will, pro. 1697,
names ch. James; Mary; Sarah Grover, perhaps w. of Simon; Eliz. Whiting; and
Deborah Hovey; beside gr.ch. Edmund, and Eliz. Chadwick.

Page 117, l. 16 from bot. aft. Sarah. ins. THOMAS, Charlestown, m. 29 Oct. 1681,
Eliz. Mellins, had ds. Eliz. Hurd and Mary Moore.

Page 117, bef. l. 5 from bot. ins. paragr. In Duyckinck's Cycloped. I. 391, large
extr. in more than twelve pages are giv. from the poetry of B. with impartial
election from pleasant, indiffer. or dull pieces, and even his detesta. homage to the
guillotine; but much gratitude is due for publica. of the last notes of the dying
swan, a few days bef. he d. in Advice to a Raven in Russia, being far the most forcible
lines ever composed by him. They seem to be a holy cry of vengeance for the
degrading serv. to wh. he was call.

Page 118, l. 6, bef. Oct. ins. 25
" 119, l. 9, aft. man, ins. Phebe, m. capt. Joseph Bowman,
" 120, l. 17 from bot. bef. THOMAS, ins. STEPHEN, Nantucket, s. of Nathaniel,
m. Damaris, d. of Joseph Gardner.

Page 123, l. 7 from bot. at the end, add, JOHN, Salem, with alias, Barbart, m. 14
Oct. 1661, Mary Bishop, had Mary, b. 30 Oct. 1662; Familiar (if a possib. name),
26 Sept. 1664; and Eliz. 5 July 1666.

Page 124, bef. l. 15, ins. BARR, CHRISTOPHER, Charlestown, a young man, wh. d.
of fever, 17 Oct. 1694. JOHN, Ipswich 1667,

Page 127, l. 18, at the end, add, Perhaps he had s. John to be a soldier of Gallop's
comp. 1690.

Page 129, l. 13 from bot. aft. 1657; ins. beside Sarah, b. 29 Jan. 1659;
" " l. 5 from bot. aft. 1646, ins. on voyage from Boston to London, prob.
unm. certain. leav. no w. or ch. as is infer. from his will of 6 Jan. pro. 4 Aug. foll.

Page 130, l. 2, aft. His ins. wid. d. 29 Jan. 1683 ; and
"   "   l. 3, aft. Ipswich, add, and, next, the first Jacob Green of Charlestown.
"   "   l. 6, bef. and, ins. to Hatfield, where one of his ch. was tak. by the Ind. 19 Sept. 1677 ;
Page 130, l. 13, aft. Rebecca, ins. beside Sarah,
"   "   l. 5 from bot. bef. GEORGE, ins. EDWARD, Windsor, a young man prob. but certain. had no w. or ch. when, 24 Feb. 1676, he was call. to serve in the Ind. war, and made his will ; nor does Stiles give him any relat.
Page 131, l. 8, aft. 1674 ; add, Sarah, 30 May 1677 ; James, 7 Dec. 1681 ; Joseph ; Samuel, 4 Apr. 1688 ; and Isaac, 22 May 1696 ; and d. 14 June 1718.
Page 131, l. 12, aft. Isaiah, ins. whose name is wild. spell. on rec. Stiles, 532,
"   "   l. 19 from bot. bef. JOSEPH, ins. JONATHAN, Marblehead 1656.
"   133, l. 10 from bot. aft. 1680 ; add, and William, again, b. 4 Oct. 1682.
"   134, l. 11, at begin. ins. 7 or
"   "   l. 19, aft. Salem, ins. 58 yrs. old in 1709, — also, aft. had add, Susanna, b. 10 May 1680 ;
Page 134, l. 20, bef. 1682 ; ins. 6 Nov. — also, aft. 1682 ; ins. Sarah, 1 Apr. 1685 ; and Eliz. 20 Apr. 1687.
Page 134, l. 11 from bot. aft. 1675. ins. THOMAS, Charlestown, by w. Eliz. wh. d. 21 Jan. 1673, had Eliz. b. five days bef. wh. d. in July foll.
Page 134, l. 5 from bot. strike out b. 27 and ins. bapt. 7
"   135, l. 10 from bot. aft. Medfield, ins. where he liv. sev. yrs.
"   136, l. 4, aft. BASSETT, ins. DAVID, Boston, had Mary, bapt. at O. S. ch. 13 Apr. 1684 ; and David, 25 Sept. 1687. The rec. marks him, as French, so that, I presume, he was a Huguenot.
Page 136, l. 18, aft. Eliz. add, m. at Leyden, as his sec. w. 13 Aug. 1611, being the earliest m. of any of our pilgrims in that foreign ld.
Page 136, l. 20 from bot. for Burgess r. Burge
"   "   l. 17 from bot. aft. 1666. add, His w. was, I suppose, a d. of Hugh Burt of L. wh. in his will, of 7 Oct. 1661, calls B. his s.
Page 138, l. 19, aft. Elder. add, His d. Susanna, m. 16 Dec. 1658, Nathaniel Blanchard.
Page 138, l. 5 from bot. aft. had ins. Joseph, bapt. 20 Nov. 1653 ;
"   "   l. 4 from bot. aft. 1655 ; ins. Solomon, 23 Aug. 1657 ; and
"   139, l. 17, aft. m. ins. 28
"   "   l. 18, for 1659 r. 1658
Page 141, l. 3 from bot. aft. 1703. add, Of ch. Mr. Wyman gives me the list, Hannah, b. 11 Oct. 1663 ; Sarah, 2 July 1665 ; John, 14 Aug. 1667 ; William, 5 July 1670 ; Mary, 3 Dec. 1672 ; all bapt. 10 June 1677, when their mo. was adm. of the ch. ; Abigail, 17 May 1675, d. soon ; Abigail, again, 14 June 1676, d. soon ; Abigail, again, 5 Nov. 1677, d. soon ; and Isaac, and Rebecca, tw. 8, bapt. (both) 12 Sept. 1680. Hannah m. 30 Apr. 1685, George Luke ; and, next, John Price ; and Sarah m. 10 Sept. 1685, Samuel Wilson.
Page 141, l. 2 from bot. aft. f. ins. and Essex Inst. Hist. Coll. I. 35, makes her name Whiterig, but to her it may be equal. hard to find f.
Page 142, l. 1, aft. mos. ins. beside William, 14 Oct. 1676. His w. d. 22 Nov. foll. and he m. 4 Nov. 1679, wid. Eliz. Macmallen, had Sarah, b. 15 Aug. 1680 ; and Samuel, 10 June 1683.
Page 142, l. 14 from bot. aft. 1673 ; ins. James, 12 Apr. 1675 ; John, 29 Sept. 1676, d. next yr. ; John, again, 10 May 1678 ; Samuel, 2 Mar. 1680 ;

Page 142, l. 13 from bot. at the begin. ins. all exc. the first aft.

" 143, l. 15, bef. JONAS, ins. JOHN, Salem, had John, b. May 1681; Thomas, 16 May 1682; Eliz. 16 July 1684; and Nicholas, 26 Sept. 1686.

Page 144, l. 17, aft. JOHN, ins. New Haven 1644, — also, aft. 1660, ins. not.

"   " l. 19, aft. 1670. add, His ch. were Eliz. b. 1652, wh. m. Eliasaph Preston; John, 1654; Mary, 1656; Thomas, 1659; Nathaniel, 1662; Hannah, 1665; Sarah, 1667; Isaac, 1669; Joseph, 1671; and Benjamin, 1674; and d. very sudden. 1677.

Page 144, l. 6 from bot. aft. Salem, ins. s. of Samuel,

"   " l. 2 from bot. aft. had ins. Dorothy, b. 8 Mar. 1660;

"   " last l. for "foll." r. 1663; — also, aft. 1664. ins. His will ment. ch. Nathaniel, Dorothy, Samuel, Thomas, and Eliz.

Page 145, l. 4, aft. inn. add, His w. bore him other ch. Mary, 21 May 1678; Lemon, 30 July 1680; Hannah, 18 Dec. 1682; Robert, 14 Nov. 1684; Jonathan, 24 July 1687, wh. d. within 10 mos. and Caleb, 24 Feb. 1689.

Page 145, l. 7, for 1685 r. 1686, — also, for "young" r. soon

"   " l. 21 from bot. bef. Nov. ins. Oct. or

"   " l. 20 from bot. bef. Sarah, ins. John, 28 Nov. 1655;

" 146, l. 13 from bot. bef. ROGER, ins. ROBERT, by Morse call. an orig. prop. of Sudbury 1640.

Page 147, l. 13, aft. 1678. ins. Mary m. 23 Jan. 1690, Henry Cookery, as sec. w. and Thankful had m. 27 Sept. 1683, Nathaniel Wilson. . But this last is unkn. to me.

Page 147, l. 19 from bot. bef. SIMON, ins. SAMUEL, Windsor, prob. s. of William, m. 18 May 1693, Margaret Chapman, had Hannah, b. 2 Apr. 1698; Samuel, 6 June 1704; and his w. d. 12 Aug. 1715, unless this Margaret were a d. not mark. on rec.

On pp. 148 and 9, the articles, BEARDSLEY and BEARSLEY are sad. confus. part of the one belong. to the other. Yet the extra. involut. of the statem. from orig. author. in Conn. could not but mislead any wh. did not wish to reject, and could not reconcile.

Page 149, l. 9 from bot. aft. BEAUCHAMP, ins. or BEACHUM,

"   " l. 5 from bot. bef. "in" ins. Mar. 1668,

" 151, l. 14 from bot. aft. BECKLEY, ins. JOHN, Hartford, prob. s. of Richard, had Hannah, wh. m. 10 Sept. 1689, Robert Webster.

Page 156, at the top, for BEL. r. BELCHER.

"   " l. 19 from bot. aft. 1658; add, and Mary, 4 Apr. 1659.

"   " l. 2 from bot. aft. 1656; ins. John, wh. d. 9 Feb. 1659; — also, bef. 11 Mar. ins. again,

Page 157, l. 14, aft. 1696. ins. Two other ch. by that w. he had, and five more by sec. w. m. 11 Oct. 1705, by name of Ruth Knight.

Page 158, l. 9, aft. k. ins. with one of the ch.

"   " l. 19, aft. yr. add, His inv. was tak. 16 Feb. foll. sign. by Mary B. prob. his wid.

Page 158, l. 21 from bot. aft. m. ins. 6 Dec. 1663,

"   " l. 13 from bot. aft. d. add, Ruth, 27 Nov. 1668;

"   " l. 11 from bot. aft. Hannah, ins. 8 June 1673;

"   " l. 10 from bot. aft. Ruth, add, 17 Mar. 1677; — also, aft. Abigail, add; 27 June 1679; — also, aft. 1682; add, beside Samuel, wh. with the eldest s. Joseph, was made excor. by the will of 29 Nov. 1710, pro. 5 Dec. 1712. Of these dates of b. three or four are tak. from a careful paper in Geneal. Reg. XIII. 15, tho. the writer inadvert. refers for rec. of the will to the wrong departm. of our County offices, and most curious. fail to discov. the earliest ancest. on our side of the ocean.

Page 159, l. 18, aft. 1663. add, It was on 31 Dec. 1662, that he, with ano. man, was wreck. near home, and both drown. Very oft. this surname is confus. with Beal, but, perhaps, only for Abraham. See Beal.

Page 160, l. 19, aft. B. add of Salem

"   "   l. 20, aft. 1681. add, He m. 10 Dec. 1680, Rebecca, d. of Samuel Ebborne, had Thomas, b. 26 Aug. 1681; and George, 10 June 1684.

Page 161, l. 7, strike out, "or as ano. rep. is 1670," and ins. and next mo. inv. of small amt. was render.

Page 161, aft. l. 9, ins. BELLAMONT, RICHARD, the Earl of, Gov. of Mass. appoint. by the crown, as success. to Sir William Phips, was the only peer ever thus deput. came to Mass. from New York, 26 May 1699, and went back next yr.

Page 162, aft. l. 16, ins. BELLINGTON, JOSEPH, Block Isl. 1684.

Page 167, at the top, for BEN r. BENNETT

"   "   l. 9 from bot. bef. JOHN, ins. JAMES, Charlestown, perhaps s. of John of the same, m. 4 Feb. 1681, Eliz. d. perhaps, of Thomas Tarbell the first of Watertown.

Page 167, l. 7 from bot. bef. JOHN, ins. There he liv. not long, for inv. of his wid. was produc. in June 1663.

Page 167, l. 6 from bot. aft. m. add, He was drown. 15 Apr. preced. then aged 42, had Josiah, James, and perhaps others.

Page 168, l. 6, bef. JOHN, ins. JOHN, Charlestown, m. 3 Jan. 1684, Ruth Bradshaw, d. of Humphrey of Cambridge.

Page 168, l. 15 from bot. bef. WILLIAM, ins. THOMAS, Charlestown, m. 9 Dec. 1686, Eliz. Gillingham, perhaps d. of William; liv. not long, for his wid. it is said, bec. fourth w. of Benjamin Lawrence. — also, aft. 1637, ins. there m. Mar. 1674, Eliz. Smith, had Grace, b. Feb. 1677, wh. d. soon;

Page 169, l. 9 from bot. aft. Margaret, add and ch. Richard, b. 5 Jan. 1688, bapt. 22 June 1690; John, and Mary, tw. 20, bapt. 21 Sept. 1690, both d. soon; Sarah, bapt. 27 Mar. 1692, d. soon; John, again, 9, bapt. 15 Sept. 1695; Joseph, 29 Dec. 1696, bapt. 3 Jan. foll.; Anthony, bapt. 5 Mar. 1699; and Margaret, bapt. 19 Jan. 1701; but at his d. 1709, only three s. and d. Margaret partake his est. Margaret m. a Callum.

Page 169, last l. aft. Ann, add, d. of John Cole of H.

"   170, l. 10, aft. 1676, add, had a ch. at Charlestown next yr.

"   172, l. 20, aft. 1671, add, or 2

"   "   last l. aft. w. ins. 17 June foll. — also, aft. Eliz. add, had Mary, b. 8 Mar. 1680; Richard, 21 Oct. 1681; and Margaret, 5 Jan. 1683; — also, at the end, add, and d. 27 Sept. 1716, aged 60.

Page 174, aft. l. 12, ins. BEXTER, GREGORY, is the false official copy, print. in Geneal. Reg. V. 334, and truly means Baxter. I wish no worse perversions perplex. some of our rec.

Page 174, l. 11 from bot. aft. preced. ins. He m. 2 Dec. 1669, Hannah Bell.

"   "   l. 8 from bot. aft. 1658. add, Elder ch. were Samuel, aged 13; John, 11; Sarah, 10; ano. d. 8.

Page 174, l. 5 from bot. aft. Waddams, ins. b. 2 Oct. 1644,

"   175, l. 17, aft. he ins. liv. aft. 1652, and

"   177, l. 6 from bot. for James r. Jacob,

"   178, l. 20 from bot. aft. again, add, bapt. 23 Nov. 1645; — also, aft. Ebenezer; add, Samuel; both bapt. 26 Oct. 1651; also, aft. Roger, ins. b.

Page 178, l. 18 from bot. aft. 1662 add or 3

Page 178, l. 17 from bot. for young r. 14 Jan. 1678

"   "   l. 7 from bot. aft. 1703, ins. H. C. 1724.

"   183, l. 16, aft. preced. add, d. Feb. 1698, leav. wid. Phebe, and ch. Hannah, aged 26; Abel, 19; Joseph, 16; and Dinah, 9 yrs.

Page 183, l. 20 from bot. aft. John, ins. 19 Sept. — also, bef. July ins. 30

"   "   l. 16 from bot. aft. 1681; ins. but Stiles says, 17 June 1682; — also, for 1685, he has 22 Sept. 1686; — also, for 1687, 9 Sept. 1688.

Page 183, l. 11 from bot. bef. d. ins. only

"   "   l. 7, at the end, add, But the valua. Hist. of W. 538, strange. makes this Richard to be Daniel.

Page 184, l. 1, aft. Beverly. ins. Those ch. were, prob. all by w. Hannah, and her d. Hannah m. William Raymond. His sec. w. was Bridget Oliver. — also, aft. Sarah add Wild, d. of William of Ipswich,

Page 184, l. 4, aft. redeem. add, He went to Rehoboth, where no witcher. was thot. of.

Page 184, l. 5, aft. B. ins. w. of his f. no doubt,

"   185, l. 15 from bot. bef. JOHN, ins. Perhaps he was s. of the sec. Edward, or his br.

Page 185, l. 14 from bot. aft. more. ins. JOSEPH, Stamford, assum. to be one of the early sett. with Denton; but as the name is never found, exc. once, and this is recent date, I doubt, that the Rev. John is meant in that place.

Page 186, l. 5, bef. Alice ins. to

"   "   l. 4 from bot. aft. 1639, ins. the progenit. of many disting. men,

"   "   l. 2 from bot. bef. bapt. ins. b. 24,

"   187, l. 8, aft. entry, add, and d. 1693.

"   "   l. 17, aft. David, ins. 18 Nov.

"   "   l. 19, bef. 1686, ins. 27 Dec. — also, strike out, "is not kn." and ins. Stiles makes 12 Mar. 1714.

Page 187, l. 18 from bot. bef. 1682. ins. 18 Sept.

"   "   l. 13 from bot. aft. 2 add, or 22

"   "   l. 4 from bot. at the end, add, Fourteen pages of Stiles's Hist. are fill. by this honora. fam.

Page 188, l. 18, at the end, add, b. respectiv. 18 Sept. 1675; 18 Dec. 1681; 15 Feb. 1688; and 5 Mar. 1696; beside the ds. Hannah, 13 Dec. 1679; Sarah, 19 Jan. 1683; Mehitable, 3 Apr. 1690; and Mary, 10 Apr. 1693;

Page 188, l. 19 from bot. bef. of ins. then — also, strike out 1649

"   "   l. 13 from bot. aft. rec. ins. Bigsby or

"   189, l. 17 from bot. aft. had ins. Eliz. b. 25 May 1659;

"   190, l. 17, at the end, add, whose d. Mary he m. 25 Aug. 1663. But the man's name was Blackmore,

Page 193, l, 8, aft. heard, add, but that he was gr. of Harv. 1711, and d. within four yrs.

Page 194, l. 16, for ADAM, r. *ADAM*,

"   195, l. 7, aft. Wheeler, ins. (tho. it may be doubt. for she was b. 28 Mar. 1647)

Page 195, l. 19 from bot. for 30 r. 12. — also, aft. Abigail, ins. 12 Aug. 1680

"   "   l. 15 from bot. for 4 Dec. r. 14 Sept.

"   "   l. 4 from bot. aft. Concord. add, He had two ws. and by the first were b. Joseph, and Eliz. wh. m. 15 Apr. 1675, George Grimes; and by the sec. w. was George; but of the dates of any, or of the mo. of the first nam. ch. I am ign.

Page 196, l. 11, strike out, "prob."—also, aft. Stephen, add, 23 Aug. 1694.

"   " l. 17, bef. Bates, ins. d. of Edward

'   " l. 16 from bot. aft. May, ins. or 4 Oct.

" 197, l. 11 from bot. aft. 13, add, bapt. 15—also, aft. 1673; add, Sarah, 17, bapt. 18 July 1675; Ann, 25, bapt. 27 May 1677; Mary, b. 29 Mar. 1679; Rebecca, 13, bapt. 20 Feb. 1681; Catharine, 15, bapt. 18 Feb. 1683; and John, 3, bapt. 4 Jan. 1685.

Page 197, l. 10 from bot. at the end, add, His will was pro. 1706.

" 198, l. 9, aft. Willey, ins. wh. had been sec. w. of Thomas Hungerford,

" 199, bef. l. 11 from bot. ins. BLETHIN, JOHN, Salem, m. 10 May 1674, Jane Marks, had John, b. 14 Mar. 1677.

Page 199, l. 7 from bot. aft. 1658, add, m. 10 Sept. 1691, Sarah, wid. of William Everton. THOMAS, Boston, s. of the preced. m. Sarah Reynolds.

Page 202, l. 9, for 20 r. 26

" 204, l. 19 from bot. at the end, r. 1640

" 205, l. 13, bef. His ins. In comp. with a br. he sold, 1 May 1649, small est. at Ruddington, in Nottinghamsh.

Page 205, l. 16, aft. 1692, add, but one acco. has the yr. 1701.

" 206, l. 17 from bot. strike out, "had w." and ins. m. 9 June 1680,—also, aft. Ann, add, d. of John Fosdick,

Page 206, l. 16 from bot. aft. 62, add, had Samuel, b. 24 June, bapt. 3 July 1681, d. soon; Ann, 27 May 1683, bapt. the same day; Mary, 7, bapt. 12 Apr. 1685, d. young; Abigail, 16, bapt. 22 Sept. 1689; Samuel, again, 14, bapt. 17 Jan. 1692; and John, 23 Feb. bapt. 1 Mar. 1696.

Page 206, l. 6 from bot. for 1671 r. 1670

" 211, l. 3, aft. Mary, add, d. of Jonas Clark of Cambridge,

" 212, last l. aft. SIMEON, ins. or SIMON,

" 213, l. 3, bef. He ins. Stiles, in Hist. of Windsor, 557, makes him a Welshman, and his w. Scotch, neither of wh. seems prob. to me.

Page 213, l. 12, at the end, ins. Matthew or

" 215, l. 5 for 1 r. 10

"   " l. 9, aft. 315; ins. but the com. spell. is Bowman. His s. Samuel was k. 26 Mar. 1676, in the hard fight under capt. Pierce, at Rehoboth.

Page 218, l. 5, at the end, add, Mr. Wyman tells me, the name was Burt.

" 223, l. 7, at the end, for 3 r. 28

"   " l. 8, for 1655 r. 1654;—also, add, Barbara, 4 Jan. 1656; Eliz. 8 Dec. 1657; Mary, 16 Sept. 1660; Henry, 20 June 1665; Ann, 14 Oct. 1668; Bathsheba, 4 June 1671; and Jonathan, 11 Aug. 1673; and by ano. w. Eliz. had Mary, again, 20 May 1679, d. in few mos.

Page 225, l. 19 from bot. at the end, add, He liv. some yrs. at Charlestown, where was b. his s. Benjamin, 29 May 1683, and his w. d. 18 Mar. 1687.

Page 226, l. 5, at the end, add, The name is, by Mr. Patch, Hist. Coll. of Essex Inst. pp. 50 and 51, read by mistake, Boyle.

Page 226, l. 18 from bot. strike out, "perhaps"

" 228, l. 5, strike out, "where his w." and ins. m. 10 Aug. 1681,—also, aft. Dorcas add, Green, perhaps d. of Thomas, wh. had d. Dorcas, and—also, strike out, "He" and ins. The s.

Page 228, l. 7, aft. His ins. f's

" 235, l. 1, aft. 1694. ins. Ruth m. 3 Jan. 1684, John Bennett of Charlestown.

" 236, last l. at the end, add, HENRY, Salem, m. 17 Dec. 1677, Eliz. McMullen, had Eliz. b. 7 Sept. 1678; Mary, 24 Mar. 1680; Henry, 12 Apr. 1682; William, 17 Oct. 1684; Sarah, 26 Mar. 1687; and Alexander, 6 Mar. 1689.

Page 239, l. 3 from bot. bef. THOMAS, ins. ROBERT, Salem, perhaps s. of the preced. m. 5 Nov. 1685, but in the Hist. Coll. of Essex Inst. I. 114, the name of w. is omit. had John, b. 4 Sept. 1686; Robert, 22 Dec. 1688; Priscilla, 11 Mar. 1690; Benjamin, 27 Sept. 1692; and Christian, 19 Mar. 1694.

Page 240, l. 22, aft. 354, ins. and compare with the more correct list in XIII. 13, espec. as to the coincid. of the christian names of Philip in the two.

Page 240, l. 21 from bot. aft. had ins. w. Magdalen,

"   "   l. 13 from bot. for bapt. r. b. perhaps, — also, aft. 6 ins. not (as the Hist. of D. says) bapt. 18

Page 249, l. 19 from bot. aft. 1688. ins. On the sad mistake a. witcher. in 1692, his w. and ch. were imprison.

Page 250, l. 18, aft. 1655, add, and I find, his will was pro. in Nov.

"   254, l. 22, bef. DANIEL, ins. ALEXANDER, Charlestown 1650, s. of William, of wh. I hear nothing aft. 1654.

Page 254, l. 21 from bot. aft. Nicholls, add, by one acco. — also, for "ano. acco. erron." r. better

Page 254, l. 17 from bot. aft. the *first* Mary, ins. perhaps sis. of the first Thomas, or the first John,

Page 260, l. 9 from bot. bef. ISAAC, ins. HUGH, Concord, s. of Joshua, m. 9 Apr. 1701, Abigail Barker, as Bond says, had Abigail, b. 15 May 1703; Jonathan, 8 Jan. 1705; Sarah, 23 July 1711, and Mary, 11 July 1714.

Page 261, l. 13, aft. ds. add, JOHN, Watertown, s. of Joshua, m. 8 Nov. 1682, Deborah, d. of Samuel Garfield, and d. 18 May 1697. Bond names no ch.

Page 261, l. 14 from bot. aft. 1668; ins. Eliz. 16 Dec. 1672; — also, aft. 1675, ins. d. young.

Page 263, l. 14 from bot. aft. JOHN, ins. Windsor, rem. to

"   "   l. 13 from bot. aft. m. add, 15 Nov. 1650,

"   265, l. 15 from bot. bef. DANIEL, ins. CORNELIUS, Windsor, youngest s. of Peter of the same, m. 4 Dec. 1701, Abigail Barber, had Abigail, b. 6 Sept. 1702; Rachel, and Mabel, tw. 21 Nov. 1704, of wh. Mabel d. soon; Cornelius, 1 May 1707; Hildah, 17 Nov. 1709; Hepzibah, 19 Jan. 1712; Titus, 11 Nov. 1714; Eliz. 1 Oct. 1717; and Aaron, 31 May 1725; was deac. and d. 26 Jan. 1747.

Page 267, l. 2, bef. HENRY, ins. * GEORGE, Billerica, only s. of William, m. 30 Jan. 1690, Sarah, d. of James Kidder of B. had Joseph, b. 3 Nov. foll. Sarah, 8 Mar. 1692; Eliz. 12 Jan. 1694; Josiah, 19 Apr. 1695; William, 21 Oct. 1696; Mary, and James, tw. 27 Sept. 1698; John, and Thomas, tw. 27 Nov. 1699; Samuel, 27 Jan. 1701; Ephraim, and Isaac, tw. 23 Jan. 1702; Dorothy, 1 Jan. 1704; and Sarah, 21 Dec. 1707. He was a man of gr. public spirit, capt. and rep. 1716 and for six yrs. more, d. in honora. age. See William Brown.

Page 268, l. 17 from bot. aft. d. add, 13 Nov.

"   "   last l. for Huse r. House

Page 269, l. 1, aft. and add, d. in Apr. 1676, a few wks. bef. his f. JAMES, Salem and — also, aft. Ipswich, ins. had

Page 269, l. 4, aft. 1687; add, perhaps John, wh. d. Dec. 1690.

"   "   l. 18, aft. Hugh. ins. He had wish. to live at Charlestown, but was denied the privilege, went abroad, and not being heard of for some yrs. his br. infer. that he was d.

Page 271, l. 6 from bot. for 1680 r. 1692

Page 272, l. 18, aft. 1725. add, JOHN, Windsor, eldest s. of Peter, m. 4 Feb. 1692, Eliz. d. of John Loomis, had Eliz. b. 11 Feb. 1693 ; Mary, 11 Sept. 1694 ; Ann, 1 Sept. 1696, d. soon ; Hannah, 24 Aug. 1697 ; John, 11 Mar. 1700 ; Ann, again, 11 Aug. 1702 ; Sarah, 11 Jan. 1704 ; Isaac, 17 Mar. 1707 ; Daniel, 20 Mar. 1709 ; Margaret, 11 Mar. 1711 ; and Esther, 17 Mar. 1712 ; and his w. d. 11 Dec. 1723. He d. 4 Feb. 1728.

Page 272, l. 12 from bot. bef. 1696, ins. 1 Oct.

" " l. 11 from bot. aft. b. add, 8 Jan. — also, aft. 1699 ; add, Ruth, 11 Jan. 1702 ; Martha, 7 Sept. 1704 ; Jonathan, 20 June 1707 ; David, 8 Mar. 1709 ; Ephraim, 25 Aug. 1712 ; Eunice, 16 May 1715 ; Jonathan, again, 10 May 1718 ; and Benjamin, 14 July 1721.

Page 274, l. 9, at the end, add, Stiles, in Hist. of Windsor, 558, confus. gr. of lds. at Plymouth and Salem. He also adopts a tradit. that I do not respect, mak. this Plymouth pilgr. f. of Windsor Peter.

Page 274, l. 15 from bot. aft. the *first* same, add, had Peter, b. 28 Jan. 1700 ; Dinah, 4 Jan. 1702 ; Samuel, 28 Aug. 1705 ; Mary, 28 Aug. 1708 ; Benjamin, 11 Aug. 1711 ; Ebenezer, 26 Aug. 1713 ; and Mindwell, next day.

Page 275, l. 7, aft. 1660. add, His will was pro. 24 June next yr.

" 276, l. 10, bef. THOMAS, ins. This last nam. s. was k. by the Ind. at Scarborough prob. in the fight under capt. Swett, 28 June 1677, as admin. on his est. was giv. to his br.-in-law 28 Sept. foll.

Page 278, l. 15, for 1657 ; r. 1658 ; and add, beside Eliz. 5 May 1659 ; and George, 5 Apr. 1668. But my confidence does not reach to all the statem. in a genealog. table, publ. in 1852, by a descend. that makes this last ch. b. "soon after his parents landed." Prob. the compiler paid too much regard to an untrustworthy tradit. that they, " William and Eliz. emigra. from Scotland a. that time, i. e. 1667 — that he was a seafar. man, and that he d. soon aft. land. in Mass. that Eliz. his wid. m. a man by the name of Baldwin, and sett. in Woburn." The only William in Boston, wh. had near those days w. Eliz. had been here, I think, at least thirteen yrs. and to me it seems very improb. that he came from Scotland bef. 1655. I may not disbelieve, that he d. soon aft. b. of the only s. but fourth ch. yet much do I doubt the story of wid.'s m. to a Baldwin of Woburn, for the only man at W. of that surname wh. had w. Eliz. was Timothy, and she bore him sev. ch. down to 1692, wh. is quite inconsist. with her being wid. of Boston William Brown.

Page 278, l. 19 from bot. strike out, " very soon," and ins. next yr.

" " l. 8 from bot. aft. Downs, ins. had Eliz. b. and d. that yr. James, 3 Aug. 1666, and William, 6 Aug. 1668.

Page 278, l. 3 from bot. aft. Charlestown, add, perhaps br. of Job,

" " last l. aft. 54. add, Other ch. he had, most, perhaps not all, by this w. as in his will of 1721 are nam. William, John, Sarah, w. of Richard Randall, Mary, w. of Samuel Whitehead, Martha, w. of Elias Kingsley, and Abigail, then unm.

Page 285, l. 19 from bot. aft. 1681 ; add, beside Ebenezer, wh. d. as did the preced. young. His w. d. 28 Oct. 1684 ; and by sec. Eliz. Drake, d. prob. of the sec. John, m. 3 Mar. 1686, he had a third John, 10 Dec. foll. ; Nicholas, 8 Jan. 1688 ; both d. soon ; and Eliz. 19 July 1692. This w. d. 20 Feb. 1698, and he had third w. Hannah Strong, wh. d. 27 Mar. 1719 ; and he d. 24 Aug. 1728. In Stiles some confus. of this fam. is seen.

Page 285, l. 11 from bot. aft. 1654 ; ins. beside John, 26 Jan. 1661 ; and — also, bef. 1681. ins. 26 July

Page 285, l. 6 from bot. for s. r. eldest br.

Page 285, l. 3 from bot. aft. 1679. add, He d. 31 May 1689, and his wid. d. 20 Dec. 1727.

Page 286, l. 5, aft. 1688, add, had Joseph, bapt. 5 Apr. 1691 ; and Richard, b. 5 Oct. 1695, both bapt. at Charlestown ;

Page 287, l. 13 from bot. strike out, " and she," and ins. wh. — also, at the end, add, Nathaniel, 1 June 1659,

Page 290, l. 16, bef. but ins. aft. 1644,

" " aft. l. 18, ins. BULLFLOWER. See Bellflower.

Page 295, l. 7, aft. w. ins. A fourth w. he found, 2 May 1672, in Jane Else, wid. of Roger.

Page 297, l. 19, aft. crippled. add, He m. 3 Aug. 1681, Mary Maverick, had Eliz. b. 22 June 1683 ; and John, 5 Apr. 1686.

Page 297, l. 22, aft. 1667. add, One Richard was of the comp. of Gallup in the wild expedit. of Phips, 1690.

Page 299, l. 16 from bot. aft. Howard, add, perhaps wid. of Nathaniel Hayward or Howard, d. of the Rev. Thomas Gould,

Page 299, l. 15 from bot. bef. rec. ins. town

" 300, l. 12 from bot. at the end, add, Twice in Hist. Coll. of the Essex Inst. I. pp. 5 and 10, this name is giv. Burthum, and this error is more observa. on account of the gen. accura. of Mr. Patch. Often the letter c in the old engross. hand resembles our modern t. Suspicion aris. also, that the same man may be passing under the name of Beacham, wh. see.

Page 301, l. 9, aft. 245, add, or Hist. Coll. of Essex Inst. I. 95 ;

" " l. 5 from bot. at the end, add, d. 1651. Perhaps the name is Burchal in the Essex Inst. Hist. Coll. I. 39 ; and prob. he was f. of that Judith B. wh. m. Henry Cooke of S. June 1639.

Page 303, l. 1, aft. 1664 ; add, but bore him James, b. 24 Apr. 1659.

" " l. 5, aft. 1660, add, had liv. at Charlestown. His will, of 9 Aug. 1662, was not brot. to pro. by his w. for near twenty yrs.

Page 303, l. 14 from bot. aft. Fearnot, ins. b. 18 Dec. 1679,

" " l. 13 from bot. at the end, add, FEARNOT, Windsor, s. of the preced. m. 8 Feb. 1705, Eliz. Buckland, perhaps d. of Timothy, had Esther, b. 15 Feb. 1706 ; Daniel, 30 Dec. 1707 ; Eliz. 2 July 1709 ; Ebenezer, 8 May 1711 ; Job, 7 Aug. 1714 ; Daniel, again, 7 Mar. 1718 ; and Mary, 3 Mar. 1721. The name appears with varied spell. sometimes losing the last syl.

Page 303, l. 6 from bot. aft. Thomas, add, had Isaac, wh. is ment. in the will of his gr.f. A.

Page 304, l. 7, aft. same, add, m. 9 Oct. 1674, Ann Moore.

" " l. 17 from bot. bef. 1683 ; ins. 11 July — also, bef. 1685 ; ins. 20 Sept. — also, aft. Mercy, ins. 14 Apr.

Page 304, l. 16 from bot. aft. Richard, ins. b. 6

" " l. 15 from bot. aft. Charles, ins. b. 23, bapt.

" " l. 14 from bot. aft. Michael, ins. b. 30 May

" 305, l. 16, aft. 1696 ; add, perhaps two or three more. He d. 12 May 1726,

" 308, l. 21 from bot. aft. 1659 ; strike out the rest of the sentence, and ins. John, wh. perhaps, was sev. yrs. old, bapt. 27 May 1660 ; Bethia, 26 May 1661 ; and Ruth, b. 28 Feb. bapt. 5 Mar. 1665. He d. 19 Oct. 1685, in his 68th yr. Perhaps he had also, d. Joanna, wh. m. William Mitchell ; certain. Mary m. John Marshall ;

Page 308, l. 19 from bot. aft. Poor ; add Sarah m. 5 Apr. 1682, William Johnson ; and Ruth m. 4 June 1683, Ignatius White.

Page 308, l. 16 and 15 from bot. strike out "had Bethia," &c. to the end of the sentence, and ins. m. 15 June 1675, Susanna Cutler, perhaps d. of John of Woburn, and d. 1 Jan. 1678. His wid. m. 15 Jan. 1680, Alexander Logan.

Page 310, l. 5 and 4 from bot. strike out "may have for" &c. to vill. inclus. and ins. was arrest. in Apr. at W. and brot. to Salem, where the gaol was soon too full of these harmless victims;

Page 311, l. 18, aft. heirs. ins. That valua. paper may be read in Hist. Coll. of Essex Inst. I. 57.

Page 314, l. 4, aft. 1647; add, and made his will 7 Oct. 1661, d. 21 of next mo. But the s. d. bef. his f. wh. ment. ch. of his s. Hugh dec. as Mary and Sarah.

Page 323, l. 15 from bot. aft. Hartford, ins. (unless this was ano. man)
"   " l. 14 from bot. aft. had, ins. by w. Sarah, at Salem, — also, aft. again, add, 1 July 1688; Hannah, 9 Dec. 1689;

Page 324, l. 14, aft. Robert. ins. Perhaps his d. Sarah m. 6 Jan. 1674, James Kingsbury.

Page 327, aft. l. 6, ins. CAD, or CADD, BARTHOLOMEW, Boston, merch. d. 1665, leav. wid. Mary to admin. upon his est. as in Prob. rec. IV. 227 and 8 appears to be good, compris. one third of a vessel, ho. and ld. near the new meeting ho. and ld. at Casco, apprais. 14 June. By the exquis. dilig. of Mr. Trask, in Geneal. Reg. XIII. 156, I was led to scrutinize the hopes of his origin; but among m. or b. I find nothing, nor does the labor of Willis, in Hist. of Portland, enlighten us. Even for any surname, begin. with C. I find no Bartholomew.

Page 329, l. 13, aft. 1719, add, aged 71, as his gr.stone at Roxbury tells;
"   " l. 7 from bot. aft. kn. add, but that he join. the ch. 24 Oct. 1639, and, perhaps, d. 1678.

Page 329, last l. at the end, strike out "tho. not" and ins. more
" 330, l. 10, aft. Temperance add Hurry, d. of William, m. 1690,
"   " l. 13, aft. ch. ins. of wh. one was Mary,
"   " l. 14, Mr. Wyman instructs me, for Mary should be r. Mercy
"   " l. 18, bef. Mercy strike out "One," — also, aft. strike out C.
"   " l. 19, strike out "but I kn. neither" &c. to the end of the sentence, and ins. and, next, 25 Oct. 1677, John Allen; and Eliz. m. Samuel Tingley, and, next, the sec. Daniel Shepardson.

Page 330, l. 20 from bot. at the end ins. Lydia; and
" 332, bef. l. 18 from bot. ins. CAMPLIN, RICHARD, Salem, d. 23 Apr. 1662.
" 333, l. 8, bef. 1663, ins. 1 June
"   " l. 9, aft. Rebecca, add, all, with the childr. of the latter, ment. in his will of 2 Apr. 1661.

Page 333, l. 10, bef. m. ins. had
"   " l. 16 from bot. aft. Hannah, add, prob. d. of John Lawrence of C.
"   " l. 15 from bot. aft. 1683; add, and Hannah, b. 13 Oct. 1686.
" 335, l. 21 from bot. aft. had ins. for w. Hannah, eldest d. of the first Joseph Jewett, m. 15 June 1640. Perhaps by her had

Page 335, l. 19 from bot. at the end, add, tho. the dates appear to make the hs. to be gr.ch. of him. But the wid. of John the first m. 5 Oct. 1674, as I judge, Christopher Babbage, and had more ch.

Page 340, l. 12, at the end, add, NATHANIEL, Salem, by w. Mary had Mary, b. 20 July 1662.

Page 340, l. 16, aft. 1640, ins. s. of the first Thomas,
"   " l. 18, for 1645, r. 1643
"   " l. 20, aft. 78. add, JOHN, Charlestown, s. of the sec. Thomas, mariner,

m. 21 Apr. 1680, Sarah Stowers, d. prob. of Richard of the same, in his will of 1689 refers to no issue, but names wid. Sarah, wh. m. Rev. John Emerson.

Page 340, l. 12 from bot. aft. 1676. add, He was br. prob. elder, of the first Thomas, and may have had ch.

Page 340, l. 7 from bot. aft. Joshua, ins. bapt. Mar. 1638 ; — also, aft. Elias, ins. 13 Aug. 1643;

Page 340, l. 6 from bot. strike out "six yrs. aft." and ins. May 1653.

"   341, l. 6, at the end, add, One Richard, and he may be the same as the preced. had Isaac, bapt. at Dorchester, 20 June 1658.

Page 341, l. 10, aft. Charlestown, ins. s. of the first Thomas,

"   "   l. 14, aft. decis. add, SAMUEL, Charlestown, s. of the preced. m. Bethia, d. of William Cowdry, wh. d. 17 Nov. 1663, and he m. 18 Sept. 1667, Abigail Damon, d. perhaps, of John of Reading, had Samuel, b. 8 Aug. 1668 ; and d. of smallpox, 4 July 1678.

Page 341, l. 20, aft. 1693. ins. But he had former w. Winifred.

"   "   l. 16 from bot. aft. 1636, add, s. perhaps, of a wid. of Thomas, that was call. old in 1656 (and she prob. brot. also, Joseph, and Samuel, wh. seem too old to be ch. of this Thomas, and may well be thot. his brs.) was

Page 341, l. 14 from bot. aft. others ; strike out "and" and ins. may have tak. 24 Oct. 1679, ano. w. Eliz. Johnson, wh. d. 6 Oct. 1684, and he

Page 341, l. 2 from bot. aft. D. ins. d. 6 Mar. 1665.

"   342, l. 5, for Charlestown r. Woburn

"   "   l. 17, strike out, "perhaps, but" also, "prob."

"   "   l. 18, aft. town, ins. but s. of Thomas of C. the first nam.

"   344, l. 18 from bot. at the end, add, His wid. m. 1663, Edmund Mumford.

"   "   l. 16 from bot. aft. CARY, add FRANCIS, Roxbury, d. 3 Sept. 1672, aged 71, says gr.stone, in Geneal. Reg. XIV. 52, but I entertain strong suspicion of error.

Page 344, l. 13, strike out "and Elinor. Tho. a mem. of the ch. he"

"   345, l. 5, strike out "beside" and ins. but by town rec. as Mr. Wyman assures me, were James, b. 7 Dec. 1679; and Abigail, 13 Jan. 1682. An earlier ch. Eleanor, b. 10 Dec. 1677, d. in few days. Also he had bapt.

Page 345, l. 12, aft. 8. add, but the gr. historian of Mass. mistook the name of the br. wh. had this afflict. as in the charm. Lectures on Witcher. from p. 71 to 78, is shown by Upham.

Page 346, l. 9 from bot. aft. 1655. ins. WILLIAM, Charlestown, m. 28 Jan. 1686, Mary Starkey,

Page 348, l. 7, bef. STEPHEN, ins. JOHN, Taunton, prob. s. of Thomas, m. 26 Nov. 1689, Eliz. Hall.

Page 349, l. 10, bef. THOMAS, ins. SAMUEL, Hartford, s. of John, m. 5 Jan. 1703, Eliz. Norton of Farmington.

Page 350, l. 6 from bot. aft. Lynn, ins. m. 20 Dec. 1666, Eliz. Hawes,

"   351, l. 8, aft. he add m. Abigail, wid. of Thomas Jones of C. and

"   352, l. 12, at the end, ins. He was a weaver from London.

"   353, l. 8 from bot. aft. 1656; add, and Henry, 3 Feb. 1659 ;

"   "   l. 4 from bot. aft. Deborah add Templar

"   "   last l. aft. 36. ins. Mr. Wyman ascert. him to be s. of William of Hull, and that his wid. m. a Miller.

Page 354, l. 1, at the begin. ins. perhaps Hannah, b. at Charlestown, 15 Aug. 1681 ;

Page 356, l. 14, bef. RICHARD, ins. MAURICE, or MORRIS, Marblehead, sw. in 1721, then aged 79, that fifty yrs. bef. Richard Fullford had liv. at Muscongus.

Page 359, bef. l. 2 from bot. ins. paragr. CHANTEREL, or CANTREL, JOHN, Boston, by w. Mary had John, b. last of Feb. 1671 ; Mary, 24 May 1672; Joseph, 9 June 1673 ; Emma, 15 Apr. 1678 ; and Dean, 1 Nov. 1686.

Page 361, l. 5, at the end, add, WILLIAM, Dorchester 1664, then had w. Mary, s. Moses, and Peter.

Page 361, l. 17, bef. HOPE, ins. HENRY, Windsor, s. of the first Edward, m. 11 May 1692, Hannah, d. of Tahan Grant, had Mary, b. 15 Feb. 1693 ; Edward, 8 Apr. 1695 ; Hannah, 2 Mar. 1699; Betty, 12 Apr. 1702 ; and Sarah, 10 Nov. 1706 ; and he d. 22 Dec. 1713.

Page 361, l. 18, aft. Hannah, add, and d. 3 May 1698.

"   363, l. 3, strike out, "may have had Simon of " and ins. SIMON,

"   "   l. 5, aft. 1735. ins. He was s. of Edward the first, had Samuel, b. 2 Mar. 1696 ; and — also, aft. Simon, ins. 14 Nov. 1700,

Page 363, l. 12, bef. serv. ins. m. 8 Sept. 1675, Sarah Mirick,

"   "   l. 13, strike out " by w. Sarah "

"   "   l. 15, aft. 1687 ; add, for her f. was drown. 22 Aug. preced.

"   368, l. 2, aft. tw. add, b. at Plymouth, a. 1639, bapt. at Scituate 1641, both

"   "   l. 7, aft. Israel, ins. (not of Nathaniel, as Stiles, 567, in Hist. of Windsor, has it)

Page 368, l. 9, aft. He add, by first w. had Israel, b. 29 June 1693; and John, 7 Nov. 1695; and by the next w. had Abiah, 22 Jan. 1700; Robert, 20 Nov. 1701 ; and Ichabod, b. 4 days bef. d. of his mo. and bapt. as many days aft. it ; but he took third w. Eliz. nam. in his will, and

Page 369, l. 2, aft. b. ins. 5, bapt.

"   "   l. 3, aft. Jan. ins. bapt. 16 Apr. — also, aft. Abigail, ins. bapt. — also, bef. Sept. ins. bapt. 7

Page 369, l. 4, aft. Nathaniel, ins. b.

"   371, l. 12 from bot. aft. 1668, add, m. 19 Apr. 1669, Lydia Haley, perhaps d. of William, had Peter, and Samuel, tw. b. 29 Dec. 1678.

Page 373, l. 16 from bot. at the end, add, Her name is wrong, I think, in Geneal. Reg. XIII. 25.

Page 375, l. 22, bef. LEONARD, ins. JOHN, Charlestown, m. 30 June 1663, Eliz. Pitman.

Page 367, l. 6, for Ward r. Wardwell

"   "   l. 8, aft. Susanna add, Symmes, — also, for sev. ch. r. three s. and three ds.

Page 380, bef. l. 1, ins. paragr. CHINERY. See GENERY, and obs. that the name of his w. there giv. correct. is misprint. in Geneal. Reg. XIII. 217.

Page 386, l. 15, bef. Richard, ins. Eliz. wh. m. 20 Jan. 1658, Caleb Hobart;

"   387, l. 17 from bot. aft. will ins. names wid. Ambrose, wh. is unkn. to me, his own s. Josiah, and d. Hannah, both minors, and

Page 389, l. 8, aft. 177, add, when she d.

"   390, l. 12, bef. 1668, ins. 4 June

"   392, l. 19 and 18 from bot. strike out " 4 Aug. 1664, " and ins. 14 Apr. 1654,

"   393, l. 6, aft. law, add, names John and Joseph, prob. s.

"   "   l. 7, at the end, add, But the true bapt. name, as by Hist. Coll. of Essex Inst. I. 9, is prov. was Edmund, the same person as the preced.

Page 399, l. 15, aft. more ; ins. but that by w. Hope he had Latham, wh. d. 25 Feb. 1690 ; and Hope, b. 10 Mar. 1690; and his w. d. 13 Oct. foll.

Page 401, l. 7 from bot. aft. 1693. ins. THOMAS, Ipswich 1663.

" 403, l. 17, aft. 1703. add, But the gr.stone inscript. makes w. Hannah, aged 25, d. 28 Feb. 1682, as in Geneal. Reg. XIV. 52, and this, or Bond, 160, must be wrong.

Page 403, l. 15 from bot. aft. Jan. ins. or Feb.

"   " l. 13 from bot. aft. Catharine, add, 1 May 1669 ; — also, aft. Content, add, 1 Aug. 1671 ; and, aft. Deliverance, add, 16 June 1678. and strike out all the resid. of the sentence.

Page 403, l. 11 from bot. aft. Feb. ins. or Mar.

"   " l. 10 from bot. aft. Jan. ins. or Feb.

" 404, l. 20, at the end, add, when he was lieut.

" 407, l. 2, strike out "a Fosdick" and ins. 13 Dec. 1683, Thomas Fosket

"   " l. 13 from bot. aft. Eliz. add, w. of the sec. William Sumner,

" 408, l. 17, aft. Sarah. add, He is strang. call. Rev. in Geneal. Reg. XIII. 118. — also, aft. preced. ins. went to Eng. aft. d. of his br. John to look aft. his prop.

Page 411, l. 10 from bot. bef. s. ins. not — also, aft. 1675 ; add, but William, s. of William, d. 8 Feb. 1664.

Page 412, l. 3, aft. Mills. add, His w. Sarah was adm. of the ch. as in Budington's list appears, 1 Jan. 1699.

Page 414, l. 17, aft. Thomas, add, rememb. in the will of Francis Lightfoot, then being a small ch. Dec. 1646,

Page 417, l. 3, strike out, "by w." and ins. m. 19 Nov. 1674, — also, aft. Eliz. add, Randall, — also, aft. Stephen, strike out what follows down to name) inclus. and ins. b. 16 Aug. foll.

Page 417, l. 5, at the begin. ins. soon — also, aft. f. ins. Eliz. 24 Dec. 1677 ; Robert, 19 May 1680, d. at 17 yrs. ; Joseph, 22 Sept. 1682 ;

Page 417, l. 15, aft. 248. add, The Hist. Coll. of Essex Inst. I. 94, names his ch. Mary, 5 yrs. old, and Christopher, 3.

Page 419, l. 17, aft. 1715. add, Abigail m. 16 Dec. 1673, Daniel Davison.

" 421, l. 4, aft. Mary ins. d. of Michael — also, aft. Long, strike out, in that and the next l. to Mary inclus.

Page 421, l. 6, for 1679, r. 1681, — also, aft. strik. out "Henry and John" ins. John, b. 27 Aug. 1666 ; Henry, 13 Apr. 1669 ; also, Abigail, 1671, wh. m. 1702, John Teal, sch.master, all

Page 425, l. 19 from bot. strike out, "wh. may first have liv. at" and ins. m. 11 June 1670, Sarah Davis, had Samuel, b. 11 May foll. wh. d. next mo. ; Sarah, 29 Aug. 1672 ; Abraham, 6 Jan. 1674 ; and he rem. to

Page 427, l. 15, aft. Charlestown, ins. s. prob. of Isaac of the same,

"   " l. 20, aft. 1675. add, He d. oᶠ smallpox, as did, prob. all his ch. 1678.

" 428, l. 16 from bot. bef. JOHN, ins. JOHN, Salem, m. 28 May 1667, Mary Knight, had John, b. 18 Nov. foll. ; Thomas, Nov. 1669, d. soon ; Mary, 1 Sept. 1671 ; and Hannah, 12 Dec. 1674.

Page 429, l. 11, aft. RISE, ins. abbrev. for RICHARD,

"   " l. 15, aft. 1646. ins. He was s. of Isaac, and brot. from Eng. prob. by his f.

Page 431, l. 2, bef. 1677 ; ins. 19 Sept.

" 432, l. 5, bef. WILLIAM, ins. VENUS (wh. seems an odd name for a man), Salem, m. 20 Aug. 1666, Mary Day, perhaps d. of John, had Eliz. b. 14 June foll. ; Mary, 24 Jan. 1671 ; Hannah, 7 May 1672, wh. d. soon ; and John, 18 Sept. 1674.

Page 432, l. 3 from bot. aft. Bethia ; add, beside Ebenezer, 6 Sept. 1659 ; and Ebenezer, again, 2 June 1661.

Page 434, l. 15 from bot. bef. had ins. by w. Hannah

"   "   l. 14 from bot. aft. Salem; add, William, 9 Sept. 1669, d. soon; Abigail, Oct. 1671 ; and Benjamin, 14 May 1674. Whether these ch. were all by one w. may be doubt. as also what Hannah C. m. Nathaniel Ingersoll; both these points hav. worried my conject.

Page 435, l. 12 from bot. aft. Mehitable, add, d. of Edward Giles, m. 9 Mar. preced.

"   439, l. 10, aft. 1714. add, MICHAEL, Salem, by w. Joan had Michael, b. 22 Mar. 1669 ; and Joshua, 23 Feb. 1671.

Page 440, l. 18, aft. preced. add, by w. Seeth had Joshua, b. 15 June 1657 ; and — also, aft. 1659. add, His w. gave inv. to Ct. 28 May.

Page 440, l. 16 from bot. aft. Westminster, add, tho. ano. acco. makes his f. William,

Page 441, l. 1, aft. Mary, add, wh. had been wid. in 1662, of the sec. John Balch, now

Page 441, l. 21 from bot. bef. JEREMIAH, ins. CORNELIUS, Salem, d. 21 Mar. 1668.

"   443, l. 14 from bot. aft. 1678, ins. m. 3 Apr. 1671, — also, aft. Ann strike out, "perhaps his w." and ins. Wilson, wh.

Page 443, l. 4 from bot. aft. pox. add, In his will, five days bef. he rememb. the young ch. of his d. Hannah Pierce.

Page 445, l. 3, aft. Woburn, ins. s. of Allen,

"   "   l. 5, aft. 1679, add, prob. of smallpox.

"   "   l. 19, aft. 80. add, This last w. is by Stiles, in Hist. of W. 572, mistak. for a d. of Henry Smith, gr.d. of William Pynchon.

Page 449, l. 4, bef. NOAH, ins. NATHANIEL, Windsor, s. of the preced. had Nathaniel, b. 6 Apr. 1689; Sarah, 10 Feb. 1691 ; Ebenezer, June 1692; Daniel, 9 Jan. 1694 ; Lydia, 13 Mar. 1696 or 7 ; Mary, 16 Jan. 1701 ; Richard, 30 Aug. 1703 ; Abigail, 12 Jan. 1706 ; Eliz. 3 Oct. 1707 ; Jemima, 23 Sept. 1709 ; Benjamin, 26 Mar. 1711 ; Joseph, 1 Apr. 1713 ; and Aaron, 22 Apr. 1715. Stiles has not nam. the w. or ws. that bore these; but ment. the d. of the f. 28 Feb. 1725.

Page 451, l. 9, at the end, add, He had sec. w. Mary, d. of Gamaliel Beaman.

"   457, l. 20, aft. preced. add, But some discord betw. var. rec. appears ; and the date of m. in Geneal. Reg. IV. 137, must be wrong.

Page 464, l. 3, bef. SEABORN, ins. LEBRON is the strange reading in the valua. Hist. of Windsor, 574, by Stiles, for the ensuing.

Page 467, l. 2, at the end, add, 23 Feb. 1668, Mary Mason, had George, b. 24 Nov. foll. ; James, 3 Dec. 1670; and Mary, 20 June 1672.

Page 467, l. 3, at the begin. strike out "10 Sept. 1671," and ins. GEORGE, Salem, eldest s. of the preced. m.

"   472, l. 6, for eldest r. fourth

"   473, bef. l. 18, ins. paragr. CRIPPIN, JABEZ, Haddam, youngest ch. of Thomas the first, m. 9 July 1707, Thankful, d. of that John Fuller, wh. had rem. to H. from Barnstable, had Susanna, b. 21 May foll.; Frances, 26 June 1710; both bapt. 1 July 1711; Lydia, 17 Mar. 1713 ; Thomas, 15 May, bapt. 19 June 1715 ; Jabez, 14 July, bapt. 18 Aug. 1717 ; John, 20 Mar. bapt. 17 Apr. 1720 ; Mehitable, 6 July, bapt. 19 Aug. 1722 ; Samuel, 7 July, bapt. 9 Aug. 1724 ; Joseph, 7 June, bapt. 10 July 1726 ; and Thankful, 2 Apr. bapt. 26 May 1728. THOMAS, Haddam, had been there many yrs. bef. Apr. 1689, when he gives deed of ld. to Shubael Rowley, wh. had m. his eldest d. Catharine. He had, also, Mary, wh. m. 28 Jan. 1690, Samuel Corbee ; beside Mercy, Experience, Thomas, and Jabez ; but no dates can be heard of, exc. as to the bapt. when the subjects were adult. THOMAS, Haddam, eldest s. of the preced. m. Mary, d. of Nicholas Ackley of the same, wh. d. 25 Oct. 1732, had Thomas, b. 3 Dec. 1696; Eliz. 14 June 1699; Hannah, 25 May 1703; all, with their f. bapt. 27 Aug. 1704; and Lydia, bapt. 26 Jan. 1707.

Page 476, l. 15, aft. Dorothy, add, that had been wid. of Allen Kingston,

"   478, l. 7, bef. JOSEPH, ins. JOHN, Windsor, perhaps s. of William, m. 3 Nov. 1686, Mary Grant, wh. d. 29 June 1720, had Hannah, b. 10 Apr. 1694, d. under 3 yrs. Other ch. are nam. in his will, Nathaniel, Mary Picket, Hannah Jagger, and Mary Bates. He d. 23 July 1721.

Page 478, l. 18, at the end, add, There he d. a. 1655, leav. wid. and, perhaps, ch.

"   479, l. 17, bef. ELI, ins. CHRISTOPHER, Salem, m. 8 Oct. 1657, Deliverance Bennett, had Hannah, b. perhaps, 10 Sept. foll.

Page 480, l. 9, bef. THOMAS, ins. SAMUEL, Windsor, s. prob. of the first Christopher, m. 30 Jan. 1690, Martha, d. of John Moses of the same, had Martha, b. 13 Nov. foll.

Page 480, l. 20, bef. d. ins. m. 14 Apr. 1658, Mary Hillier,

"   488, l. 17, aft. Robert, add, d. of Gov. Edward Winslow,

"   493, l. 14 from bot. aft. m. ins. 2 Mar. 1682, tho. ano. rec. says

"   "   l. 10 from bot. aft. 1650, ins. Timothy ;

"   "   l. 6 from bot. aft. 1694. add, Most of his ch. d. under mid. age ; but Sarah m. 29 Oct. 1688, William Eustis ; and Rebecca had two hs. yet d. 25 Jan. 1714; Samuel liv. few days over 30 yrs.; and Mary, d. 1 Sept. 1703.

Page 494, l. 1, aft. Martha, ins. d. of John Wiswall of Boston, m. 23 Apr. 1674, — also, aft. had, add, Margaret, wh. d. 8 Mar. 1678 ;

Page 494, l. 2, aft. John, add, b. 27 Sept. 1678, — also, aft. Margaret, ins. again, 14, bapt. — also, aft. 1680, add, prob. d. young — also, aft. Timothy, add, bapt.

Page 494, l. 3, aft. Margaret, ins. again, b. — also, aft. Ruth, ins. bapt.

"   "   l. 4, aft. Sarah, add, 3, bapt.

"   "   l. 11, aft. Eliz. add Carter, m. 2 Sept. 1668, wh. d. 3 Nov. 1694,

"   "   l. 19 from bot. aft. Dorothy, add, d. of Abraham Bell, m. 30 June 1681, — also, bef. bapt. ins. b. 4 May, — also, aft. 1683 ; add, Abraham, b. 6 July 1685, bapt. in Boston at O. S. ch. 3 Jan. foll. His wid. m. 3 Dec. 1698, Josiah Treadway.

Page 494, l. 10 from bot. strike out, "perhaps"

"   "   l. 7 from bot. at the end, add, He went, with his f. as a blacksmith, in some part of Philip's war.

Page 496, l. 15, for a r. John

END OF VOL. I.